PHILIP'S

LOCAL EXPLORER

NORFOLK

www.philips-maps.co.uk

Published by Philip's, a division of
Octopus Publishing Group Ltd
www.octopusbooks.co.uk
Carmelite House, 50 Victoria Embankment,
London EC4Y 0DZ
An Hachette UK Company
www.hachette.co.uk

First edition 2024
First impression 2024
NOREA

ISBN 978-1-84907-644-9

© Philip's 2024

Ordnance Survey
Licensed Data
This product
includes mapping
data licensed from
Ordnance Survey®
with the permission
of the Controller of His Majesty's Stationery
Office. © Crown copyright 2024. All rights
reserved. Licence number 100011710.

Photographic acknowledgements:
Alamy Stock Photo: /R. Hughes III top right;
/Geraint Tellem/robertharding II;
/travellinglight III top left; /Ivan Vdovin III
bottom. *Shutterstock:* /Helen Hotson
front cover.

Printed in China

CONTENTS

II **Best places to visit**

IV **Key to map pages**

VI **Route planning**

X **Key to map symbols**

1 **Street maps** at 1¾ inches to 1 mile

132 **Street maps** at 3½ inches to 1 mile

178 **Street map** of Norwich city centre at
7 inches to 1 mile

179 **Index** of towns, villages, streets, hospitals, industrial
estates, railway stations, schools, shopping centres,
universities and places of interest

T0329506

Best places to visit

▲ *Thurne Mill, Norfolk Broads*

Outdoors

Binham Priory Remains of a Benedictine monastery founded in 1091. The nave of the priory church has been preserved as the local parish church and is particularly noted for its 13th-century west front and Norman arches. Substantial ruins surround the church, giving a clear impression of the layout and scale of the original monastery. *Holt*
🖥 www.english-heritage.org.uk **6 E2**

Broads National Park More than 125 miles of navigable lakes (or Broads) and rivers fringed by marshes and meadows. The Broads formed in the 14th century when shallow pits from medieval peat digging became flooded, and have been popular for pleasure boating since Victorian times. There are many nature reserves within the park, including **Hickling Broad** and How Hill, which support a wide variety of rare wetland plant and animal species. Among the many picturesque villages are Horning and Ranworth; the latter is dominated by a 14th-century church known as the 'Cathedral of the Broads'. Also of historical interest is **St Benet's Abbey**, a ruined Anglo-Saxon monastery. The **Museum of the Broads** tells the story of the area through its wide-ranging collections and hands-on activities. The **Bure Valley Railway**, a narrow-gauge heritage steam railway, runs through the Broads between Aylsham and Wroxham. Boats can be hired at various locations within the Broads. *Stalham*
🖥 www.museumofthebroads.org.uk
🖥 www.visitthebroads.co.uk **39 B3**

Castle Acre Priory Well-preserved ruins of a late 11th-century Cluniac monastery in the medieval village of Castle Acre. The imposing west front church gable dominates the site, and there are substantial remains of the buildings round the cloister. There is an exhibition inside the former prior's lodgings and a recreated herb garden. Also in the village are the remains of **Castle Acre Castle**, a Norman motte-and-bailey castle, and its earthwork ramparts.
🖥 www.english-heritage.org.uk **46 F1**

Castle Rising Well-preserved 12th-century castle keep surrounded by a large area of massive protective earthworks. The castle's interesting history includes a period as a royal residence, when Queen Isabella, widow of Edward II, lived here. Visitors can see the remains of the royal apartments, as well as those of the Great Hall. Also on site are the remains of an 11th-century church. *King's Lynn*
🖥 www.english-heritage.org.uk **27 C3**

East Ruston Old Vicarage Garden Modern gardens, a series of garden 'rooms' of all kinds, imaginatively designed and planted with a wide and unusual variety of species. The gardens include sunken, woodland, desert, exotic and Mediterranean gardens, as well as many more. There are regular guided tours. *Stalham* 🖥 https://eastruston oldvicarage.co.uk **24 A3**

Fairhaven Woodland and Water Garden 130 acres of woodland, criss-crossed with creeks and paths, beside the South Walsham Inner Broad. It is a haven for local wildlife, and there are bird hides and an area for den-building. Visitors can take boat trips on the Broad in the summer. *South Walsham*
🖥 www.fairhavengarden.co.uk **74 A8**

Holt Country Park Large area of mixed woodland, with waymarked trails, including an easy access route. There is a visitor centre, sensory garden, orienteering course and play area. It is a good place to spot birds, butterflies and other wildlife. It is just outside the attractive Georgian market town of Holt. **137 C4**

Norfolk Lavender Lavender farm and distillery. The main lavender fields are not open to the public, but visitors can see the national collection of lavenders and the lavender distillery, and explore gardens planted with various lavenders among other plants. There is an animal garden, with small mammals, birds, insects and reptiles, and outdoor play area. *Hunstanton*
🖥 https://norfolk-lavender.co.uk **133 E6**

Sheringham Park More than 1,000 acres of parkland and woodland, designed in the early 19th century by renowned landscape designer Humphry Repton, surrounding Sheringham Hall (private). The grounds were laid out to make the most of the coastal views. The Wild Garden has an extensive collection of rhododendrons. There are walking trails and children's activities. *Sheringham*
🖥 www.nationaltrust.org.uk **9 B4**

Thetford Forest Nearly 20,000 hectares of manmade forest in south Norfolk, a mixture of broadleaved trees, pines and heathland. Peaceful walking trails can be found at Lynford Arboretum and Great Hockham, whereas High Lodge is a recreational area with woodland play areas, adventure golf, archery and mountain biking trails. *Brandon*
🖥 www.forestryengland.uk/ thetford-forest **115 C3**

Whitlingham Country Park Waterfront woodlands and meadows beside the Great and Little Broads and the River Yare. There are woodland trails, an accessible path round the Great Broad and a conservation area. *Norwich* 🖥 www. whitlinghamcountrypark.com **163 E4**

Towns & villages

Cromer Seaside town on the north Norfolk coast with sandy beaches and a traditional pier. It was an important fishing town in the Middle Ages, when its imposing 15th-century parish church was built, but then declined before developing as a fashionable resort in the late 19th century. The **Cromer Museum** is housed in several fishermen's cottages and has an extensive collection of artefacts relating the history of Cromer and Norfolk. The nearby **RNLI Henry Blogg Museum** tells the story of Cromer's lifeboats and crew. Just outside the centre, **Amazona Zoo** is home to birds and animals from South America. There are play areas and an aquarium. 🖥 https://amazonazoo.co.uk
🖥 www.museums.norfolk.gov.uk/ cromer-museum **139 C7**

Great Yarmouth Seaside town centred on a strip of land between the River Yare and the North Sea. It is known for its **Pleasure Beach theme park**, **aquarium**, **Merrivale Model Village**, Victorian Winter Gardens glasshouse and other amusements that line the seafront. A wealthy trading centre in the Middle Ages, it has an impressively large 13th-century market place, and its parish church, **Great Yarmouth Minster**, dating from the 12th century, is one of the largest in the country. It has an unusually complete medieval city wall, and historic houses lining narrow streets. Particularly well preserved are the **Row Houses** and **Old Merchant's House**, which are open to the public. The **Time and Tide** museum of Norfolk life is housed in a converted Victorian herring curing works. It relates the history of Great Yarmouth, and its herring industry in particular, with interactive displays and hands-on activities. On the quayside, the **Elizabethan House Museum**, a 16th-century merchant's house, has period rooms that range from Tudor to Victorian. Nearby, the **Tollhouse Gaol** dates from the 12th centuryand now houses a museum of crime and punishment. The **Venetian Waterways** is an unusual park, consisting of a network of winding canals, bridges and islands, enhanced with colourful planting and a boating lake. 🖥 https://pleasure-beach. co.uk 🖥 www.visitsealife.com/ great-yarmouth **169 C5**

King's Lynn Historic port town on the Great Ouse, just inland from The Wash. It flourished in the Middle Ages through trade with the Hanseatic League. There are two unusually large market squares. On the Saturday Market Square is **King's Lynn Minster**, which was founded in 1101 as St Margaret's. Major refurbishments over the centuries mean that very little of the 12th-century church remains. Within the Town Hall is the **Stories of Lynn museum**. As well as artefacts and hands-on activities illustrating the long history of the town, there are medieval prison cells and access to some of the town hall's grand reception rooms. The **Lynn Museum** is housed in the Union Baptist Chapel. It is particularly known for its archaeological displays, which include 'Seahenge', a Bronze Age henge discovered under the sea. **True's Yard Fisherfolk Museum** is devoted to the social history of the working class area of North End. It occupies original fishermen's cottages and a restored smokehouse. There are many other interesting historic buildings in the town, notably the 17th-century Custom House overlooking Purfleet Harbour; Marriott's Warehouse, a restored 17th-century warehouse; Hanse House, built in the 15th century; and the medieval St George's Guildhall.
🖥 https://kingslynnminster.org
🖥 www.storiesoflynn.co.uk **147 A5**

Norwich Cathedral city on the River Wensum, founded by the Anglo-Saxons. It grew after the Norman Conquest to become one of medieval England's most important cities. Its skyline is dominated by the tall spire of the **cathedral**, which was founded as a Benedictine monastery in the 11th century. Built in Romanesque style, the cathedral is particularly admired for its large cloisters and carved stone roof bosses. The area around the cathedral and its grounds is filled with well-preserved Tudor buildings. **Norwich Castle** was founded in the 11th-century. The medieval stone keep, with battlements and dungeons, was designed to be a Royal Palace. The Victorian prison block now contains galleries, which cover the history of the city, including Boudica and the Romans, as well as fine art. The Museum of Norwich occupies the old Bridewell prison. Very little of the original 14th-century building remains apart from the vaulted undercroft where the prisoners were held. The museum explores the industrial heritage of the city, from textiles and shoes to mustard and aircraft, with a working Jacquard loom a highlight. The Tudor **Strangers' Hall** was lived in by various prominent citizens over the centuries. Its rooms are furnished according to different periods and together tell the story of the house and its occupants. Other buildings of historic interest include the medieval Guildhall and Dragon Hall, and the Georgian Assembly House. The **Plantation Garden** occupies an old chalk quarry and was built in the late 19th century to resemble the garden of a Victorian country house, complete with terraces, follies, and medieval-style fountain and walls. On the outskirts of the city, the University of East Anglia is well known for its 1960s architecture. Its campus is the location of the **Sainsbury Centre**, an international art gallery, museum and sculpture park. 🖥 www.museums.norfolk.gov. uk/norwich-castle 🖥 www.museums. norfolk.gov.uk/museum-of-norwich 🖥 www.sainsburycentre.ac.uk **178 A3**

Thetford Historic market town east of Thetford Forest. It was the capital of the Iceni tribe, who flourished in the later Iron Age and early Roman period. **Thetford Priory**, founded in 1107, was one of the most important and richest monasteries in East Anglia. Nearby is the ruined nave of the **Church of the Holy Sepulchre**, which is all that remains of another medieval monastery. A large grassy mound surrounded by ditches marks the location of Thetford Castle, a Norman motte-and-bailey castle. Visitors can climb the steps

◄ King's Lynn Custom House

Horsey Windpump
Fully restored windpump – a windmill used to pump water. Visitors can climb to the top for views over the surrounding Broads landscape, with its shallow lakes and grazing marshes, and to learn about the windpump's history. There is a wildlife garden, children's activities and opportunities to take boat trips. *Great Yarmouth* 🖥 www.nationaltrust.org.uk **40 D1**

▲ North Norfolk Railway

for far-reaching views. The **Ancient House** museum occupies an early Tudor building. Its period rooms and galleries focus on local history and famous former Thetford residents, including the political writer Thomas Paine. Small museums include the **Charles Burrell Museum**, which has working steam engines, and the **Dad's Army Museum**, which has memorabilia associated with the sitcom *Dad's Army*, which was filmed in the town. 🖥 www.english-heritage.org 🖥 www.museums.norfolk.gov.uk/ancient-house 🖥 https://dadsarmythetford.org.uk **176 B4**

Buildings

Blickling Estate Elegant Jacobean mansion with colourful formal gardens surrounded by a large area of historic parkland. The house was built in the early 17th century and is noted for its elaborate plasterwork, portraits and the Long Gallery. The garden has lots of interesting features, including a parterre, orangery, walled garden and wilderness garden. Also on the estate is RAF Oulton Museum, which relates the story of the airfield built on the estate in World War 2. *Aylsham* 🖥 www.nationaltrust.org.uk **35 F7**

Felbrigg Hall Elegant country house dating from the 17th century. It is particularly known for its contents, notably paintings, wallpaper and furniture, which were acquired from all over the world, mainly in the 18th century. Outside is a large walled garden and woodland, known as the Great Wood, which contains a wide variety of species. There are walking trails within the wood and surrounding parkland. *Cromer* 🖥 www.nationaltrust.org.uk **10 B2**

Holkham Hall Impressive Palladian-style country house, within a large estate encompassing a walled garden, parkland and a National Nature Reserve leading down to the coast. The house dates from the mid-18th century and has ornate state rooms, with an impressive collection of Old Master paintings. Within the parkland are nature trails, a woodland play area and a lake with boating. The long beach is backed by the increasingly rare habitats of saltmarsh and sand dunes. *Wells-next-the-Sea* 🖥 www.holkham.co.uk **5 A5**

Houghton Hall Grand Palladian mansion set within spacious parkland, built in the 1720s for Sir Robert Walpole, Britain's first prime minister. The state rooms are lavishly decorated, with painted ceilings and elaborate carvings. The large walled garden contains colourful ornamental areas as well as fruit and vegetable gardens. Within the grounds are a large number of contemporary sculptures. Houghton is also home to the Soldier Museum, the largest private collection of model soldiers in the world. *Fakenham* 🖥 www.houghtonhall.com **29 D7**

Oxburgh Hall Moated manor house dating from the late 15th century, with Victorian Gothic Revival interiors. The Catholicism of the owners impacted the history of the house, and there is a priest hole in the turreted gatehouse. The garden is a mixture of formal and wilderness and woodland areas. There are walking routes within the surrounding parkland and meadows. *Swaffham* 🖥 www.nationaltrust.org.uk **81 E4**

Sandringham Estate Country home of the British royal family since 1862, surrounded by landscaped gardens and parkland. The house was largely rebuilt in the 1870s by the future Edward VII, and the ground floor rooms open to the public remain much as they were in Edwardian times. The gardens comprise formal areas of planting, alongside lawns, rare trees and ornamental lakes. *King's Lynn* 🖥 https://sandringhamestate.co.uk **27 F7**

Museums & galleries

City of Norwich Aviation Museum
Collection of about 30 aircraft and cockpits, ranging from military bombers to large airliners, exhibited on an airfield on the outskirts of Norwich Airport. There is an exhibition hall with displays on Norfolk's aviation history and other related memorabilia, and guided tours of some of the aircraft. *Norwich* 🖥 www.cnam.org.uk **53 D1**

Gressenhall Farm and Workhouse
Historic workhouse, farm and museum. Within the old workhouse building, which dates from 1777, visitors can learn about the lives of the real people who lived and worked here, and see the rooms that were used as the school room and laundry. Also within the workhouse building is the **Museum of Norfolk Life**, with galleries relating the history of rural life, including the Women's Land Army. Neighbouring Gressenhall Farm is a traditional working farm, long associated with the workhouse. *Dereham* 🖥 www.museums.norfolk.gov.uk **49 D4**

Muckleburgh Military Collection
Museum of military memorabilia and vehicles, with a large collection of tanks, armoured cars and weaponry on display. Based at an old military training camp, it also houses the collection of the Suffolk and Norfolk Yeomanry. There are occasional tank demonstrations. *Sheringham* 🖥 www.muckleburgh.co.uk **8 E6**

RAF Air Defence Radar Museum
Museum dedicated to the role of radar in World War 2 and the Cold War. It is housed in old RAF buildings, including a radar operations building from 1942. The displays give an insight into air defence and the threat of nuclear war at that time. *Horning* 🖥 www.radarmuseum.co.uk **55 E5**

Sheringham Museum Museum dedicated to the social history and fishing industry of Sheringham. The collection includes several lifeboats and fishing boats, as well as stories and crafts associated with fishing. There are galleries devoted to the history of the town. There is an information centre for the Sheringham Shoal Offshore Windfarm and a viewing tower offering views over the town and out to sea. 🖥 www.sheringhammuseum.co.uk **138 D7**

Family activities

Banham Zoological Gardens
Zoo with a wide range of animals and activities. Popular are the big cats, which include tigers, cheetahs and leopards, the many different monkey species, giraffes, penguins, sea lions and many more. Among the activities are talks, a birds of the world display, adventure playgrounds and a mini train. *Diss* www.zsea.org/banham **119 C6**

BeWILDerwood Outdoor family activity park set within a large wood full of adventure play activities, including zip wires, mazes, giant swings and slides, den-building and more. There is also a boating lake, and there are storytelling sessions and craft workshops. *Horning* 🖥 https://norfolk.bewilderwood.co.uk **55 D5**

Bressingham Steam & Gardens
Colourful gardens and steam museum, where visitors can travel on several different narrow-gauge steam trains around the site and ride on a Victorian steam 'Gallopers' or carousel. The linked gardens are stocked with a huge number of different species, providing year round interest. There is a museum devoted to the Norfolk-based sitcom Dad's Army, with a recreation of the set. *Diss* 🖥 www.thebressinghamgardens.com **129 C7**

Church Farm Stow Bardolph Farm park and rare breeds centre, with a focus on rare breeds of farmyard animals, in particular sheep and pigs. There is a wide range of hands-on activities, ranging from holding chicks to feeding lambs or grooming goats. There are indoor and outdoor play areas, tractor rides and nature walks. *Downham Market* 🖥 www.churchfarmstowbardolph.co.uk **79 F8**

Mid-Norfolk Railway Heritage railway running between Dereham and Thuxton, with plans to restore more of the original line, which first opened in 1846. Heritage steam and diesel locomotives pull 1950s and 60s carriages along the 12-mile route. There is a railway museum at Dereham station and frequent special events. 🖥 www.midnorfolkrailway.co.uk **154 E5**

North Norfolk Railway Heritage railway, also known as the Poppy Line, formerly part of the Midland and Great Northern Joint Railway. Steam and diesel trains run through 5 miles of attractive countryside between Sheringham and Holt. The William Marriott Museum at Holt station is packed with railway memorabilia. 🖥 www.nnrailway.co.uk **9 B6**

Pettitts Animal Adventure Park
Family amusement park aimed at younger children, alongside a small zoo with interactive activities. There is a reptile house with snakes and lizards, an aviary, and small mammals. Within the amusement park are rides and play areas, crazy golf and a mini train. *Reedham* 🖥 www.pettittsadventurepark.co.uk **93 A5**

Thrigby Hall Wildlife Gardens
Wildlife park with walkways leading through and above the enclosures and viewing platforms allowing close-up views of the gibbons and tigers among others. Highlights include Amur leopards and Sumatran tigers, and there are crocodiles and alligators in the swamp house, as well as a reptile house and aviary. *Great Yarmouth* 🖥 www.thrigbyhall.com **75 E7**

Watatunga Wildlife Safari Wildlife reserve, a large area of wetland, grassland and forest, home to rare species of deer, antelope and birds. The animals roam freely, with visitors exploring the reserve by electric buggy or trailers, on guided tours. *King's Lynn* 🖥 www.watatunga.co.uk **61 F7**

▼ Holkham Hall

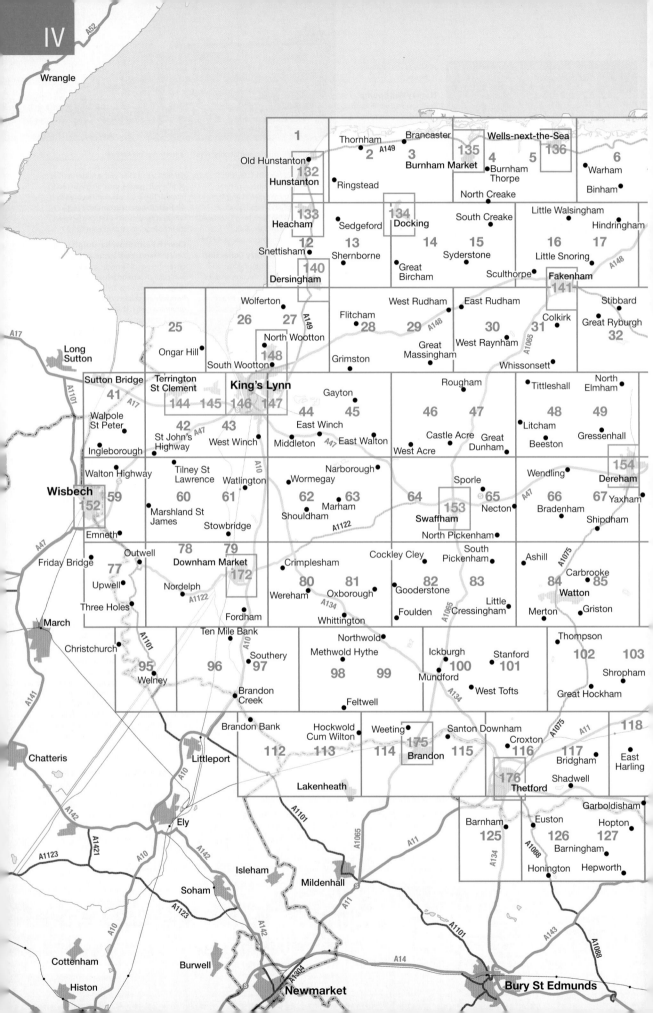

Wrangle

A52
A17

Long Sutton

Sutton Bridge

Walpole St Peter

Ingleborough

Walton Highway

Wisbech
152
59

Emneth

Friday Bridge

Upwell

Three Holes

March

Christchurch

Chatteris

Welney

95

Cottenham

Histon

Burwell

Soham

Isleham

Ely

Littleport

Mildenhall

Newmarket

1

Thornham
2 A149
Old Hunstanton
132
Hunstanton

Ringstead

133
Heacham

Snettisham

12

13

140
Dersingham

Sedgeford

Shernborne

Wolferton

26   27

25

Ongar Hill

North Wootton

South Wootton

Terrington
St Clement

144 145

146 147
King's Lynn

42

43

St John's
Highway

West Winch

Tilney St
Lawrence

60

Watlington

61

Marshland St
James

Stowbridge

Outwell

77

78
Downham Market

79

172

Nordelph

Fordham

Ten Mile Bank

Southery

96

97

Brandon
Creek

Brandon Bank

112

113

Lakenheath

Feltwell

Hockwold
Cum Wilton

Brancaster

Burnham Market
3   135
4
Burnham
Thorpe
North Creake

Docking
134

14

Great
Bircham

West Rudham

Flitcham

28
Grimston

Gayton

44   45

East Winch

Middleton

West Winch

East Walton

Wormegay

62

Marham

Shouldham

Crimplesham

80

Wereham

Whittington

Northwold

Methwold Hythe

98   99

Wells-next-the-Sea

5   136
Warham

Binham

South Creake

Little Walsingham

Hindringham

6

16
Little Snoring

Little Walsingham

Sculthorpe

Fakenham
141

Colkirk

East Rudham

29   A148

30
West Raynham

Great
Massingham

West Acre

Castle Acre

Narborough

63

A1122

64

153
Swaffham

North Pickenham

Oxborough

81

Foulden

Weeting

Great
Dunham

Sporle

65
Necton

Stibbard

17

Great Ryburgh

32

31   A1065

Whissonsett

Rougham

46   47

Litcham

Beeston

Wendling

66

Bradenham

Cockley Cley

South
Pickenham

82   83

Gooderstone

Little
Cressingham

Tittleshall

48

North
Elmham

49

Gressenhall

154
Dereham

67 Yaxham

Shipdham

Ashill

84

Watton

85

Merton   Griston

Carbrooke

A1075

Ickburgh

Mundford

100

West Tofts

A134

Santon Downham

Croxton

114   175
Brandon

115

116

Stanford

101

Thompson

102   103

Shropham

Great Hockham

Thetford
176

A11

118

Bridgham   117

Shadwell

East
Harling

Garboldisham

Hopton

Barnham

125

126
Barningham

Honington Hepworth

127

Euston

A143

Bury St Edmunds

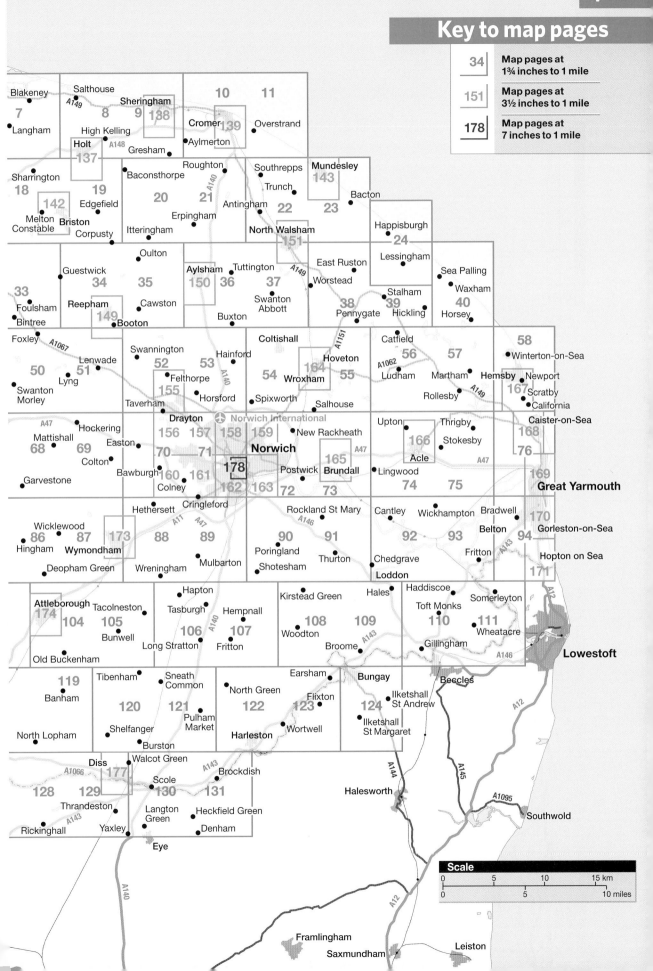

Key to map pages

34	Map pages at 1¾ inches to 1 mile
151	Map pages at 3½ inches to 1 mile
178	Map pages at 7 inches to 1 mile

Blakeney
Salthouse
Sheringham
7
Langham
A149
8
9
138
10
11
High Kelling
Cromer
139
Overstrand
Holt
Aylmerton
137
A148
Gresham
Roughton
Southrepps
Mundesley
Sharrington
Baconsthorpe
Trunch
143
18
142
19
20
21
Antingham
22
Bacton
23
Edgefield
Melton
Constable
Briston
Erpingham
North Walsham
Happisburgh
Corpusty
Itteringham
151
24
Oulton
East Ruston
Lessingham
33
Guestwick
34
35
Aylsham
36
Tuttington
37
Worstead
Sea Palling
Waxham
Foulsham
Reepham
150
Swanton
Abbott
38
Stalham
39
40
Bintree
149
Booton
Cawston
Buxton
Pennygate
Hickling
Horsey
Foxley
A1067
Swannington
Coltishall
Catfield
56
57
58
Winterton-on-Sea
Lenwade
52
53
Hainford
164
Hoveton
A1062
50
51
54
55
Ludham
Martham
Hemsby
Newport
Scratby
Swanton
Morley
Lyng
Felthorpe
155
Horsford
Wroxham
Rollesby
A149
167
California
Taverham
Spixworth
Salhouse
168
Drayton
Norwich International
Upton
Thrigby
Caister-on-Sea
Hockering
156
157
158
159
New Rackheath
166
Stokesby
68
69
Easton
70
71
Norwich
Acle
A47
76
Colton
Postwick
165
Brundall
Lingwood
169
Garvestone
Bawburgh
160
161
178
72
73
74
75
Great Yarmouth
Colney
162
163
Rockland St Mary
Cantley
Wickhampton
Bradwell
170
Hethersett
Cringleford
A146
Belton
Gorleston-on-Sea
Wicklewood
173
88
89
90
91
92
93
94
86
87
Wymondham
Poringland
Chedgrave
Fritton
A143
Hopton on Sea
Hingham
Mulbarton
Thurton
Deopham Green
Wreningham
Shotesham
Loddon
171
Hapton
Kirstead Green
Hales
Haddiscoe
Somerleyton
Attleborough
Tacolneston
Tasburgh
Hempnall
108
109
Toft Monks
110
111
174
104
105
106
107
Woodton
Broome
A143
Gillingham
Wheatacre
Bunwell
Long Stratton
Fritton
Lowestoft
Old Buckenham
Tibenham
Sneath
Common
North Green
Earsham
Bungay
Beccles
119
Banham
120
121
122
Flixton
123
124
Ilketshall
St Andrew
A12
Shelfanger
Pulham
Market
Harleston
Wortwell
Ilketshall
St Margaret
North Lopham
Burston
A144
A145
Diss
Walcot Green
Brockdish
A1066
177
Scole
130
131
A1095
128
129
Halesworth
Thrandeston
Langton
Green
Heckfield Green
Southwold
Rickinghall
A143
Yaxley
Denham
Eye
A140
A12

Framlingham
Leiston
Saxmundham

Route planning

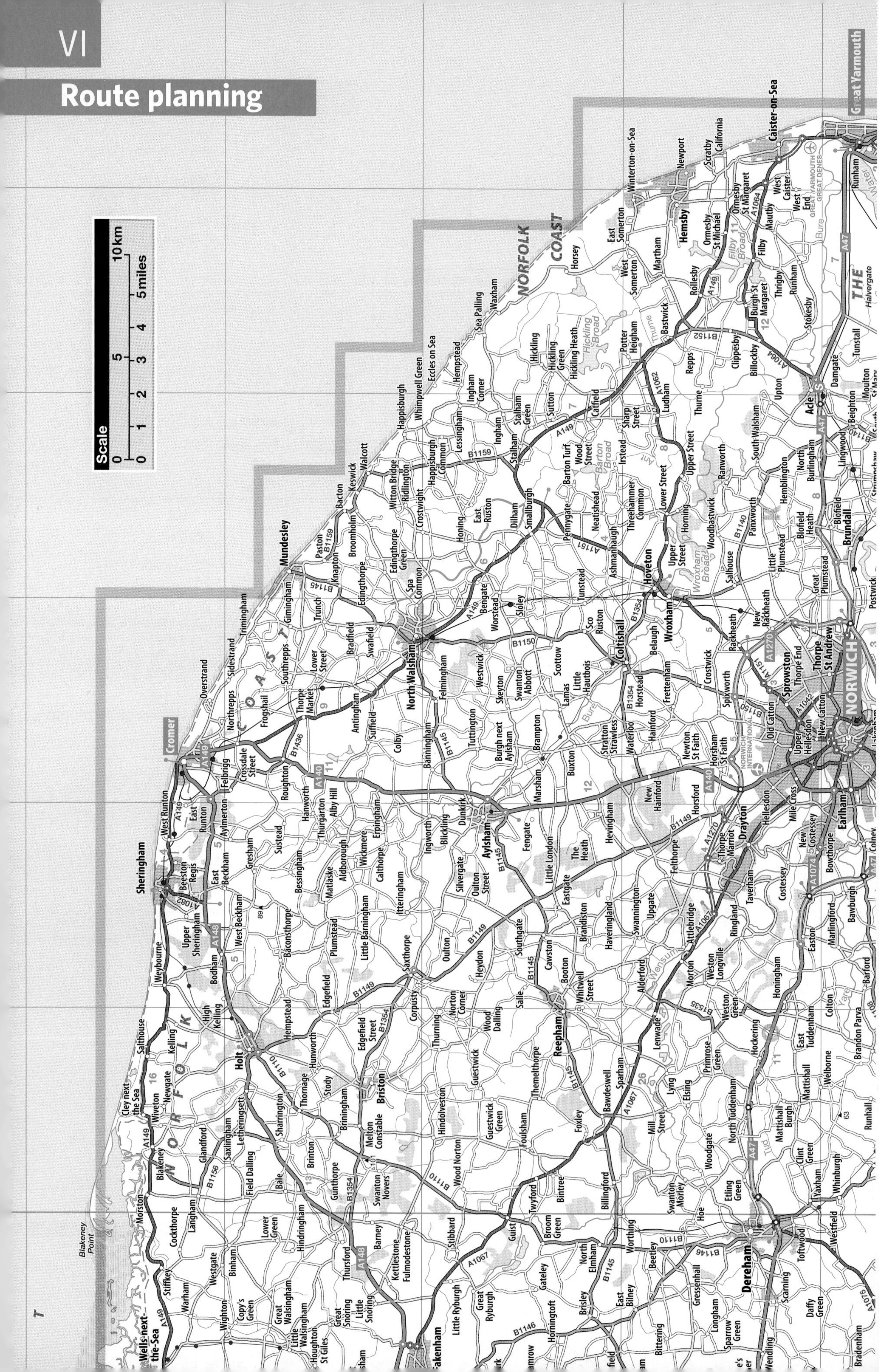

Scale

10 km

5 miles

0 1 2 3 4 5

0 5

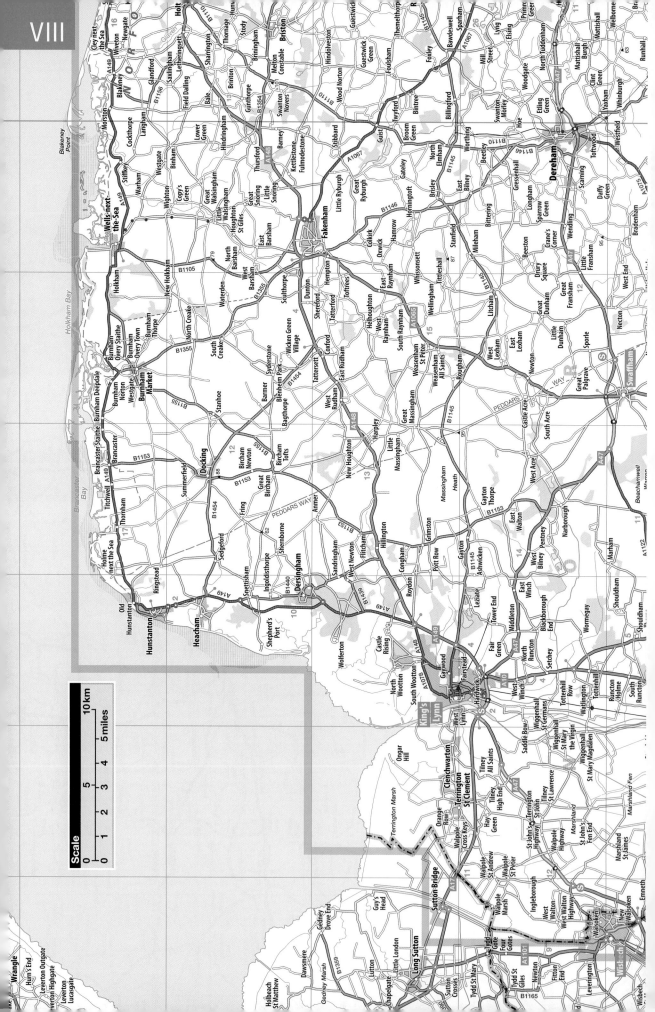

Key to map symbols

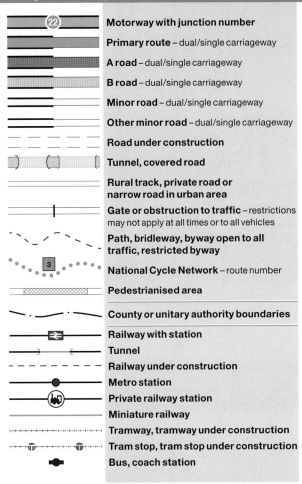

Motorway with junction number

Primary route – dual/single carriageway

A road – dual/single carriageway

B road – dual/single carriageway

Minor road – dual/single carriageway

Other minor road – dual/single carriageway

Road under construction

Tunnel, covered road

Rural track, private road or narrow road in urban area

Gate or obstruction to traffic – restrictions may not apply at all times or to all vehicles

Path, bridleway, byway open to all traffic, restricted byway

National Cycle Network – route number

Pedestrianised area

County or unitary authority boundaries

Railway with station

Tunnel

Railway under construction

Metro station

Private railway station

Miniature railway

Tramway, tramway under construction

Tram stop, tram stop under construction

Bus, coach station

Ambulance station

Coastguard station

Fire station

Police station

Accident and Emergency entrance to hospital

H Hospital

+ Place of worship

i Information centre

Shopping centre, parking

P&R PO Park and Ride, Post Office

Camping site, caravan site

Golf course, picnic site

Church ROMAN FORT Non-Roman antiquity, Roman antiquity

Univ Important buildings, schools, colleges, universities and hospitals

Woods, built-up area

River Medway Water name

River, weir

Stream

Canal, lock, tunnel

Water

Tidal water

58 87

246

Adjoining page indicators and overlap bands – the colour of the arrow and band indicates the scale of the adjoining or overlapping page (see scales below)

The dark grey border on the inside edge of some pages indicates that the mapping does not continue onto the adjacent page

The small numbers around the edges of the maps identify the 1-kilometre National Grid lines

Abbreviations

Acad	Academy	Meml	Memorial
Allot Gdns	Allotments	Mon	Monument
Cemy	Cemetery	Mus	Museum
C Ctr	Civic centre	Obsy	Observatory
CH	Club house	Pal	Royal palace
Coll	College	PH	Public house
Crem	Crematorium	Recn Gd	Recreation ground
Ent	Enterprise		
Ex H	Exhibition hall	Resr	Reservoir
Ind Est	Industrial Estate	Ret Pk	Retail park
IRB Sta	Inshore rescue boat station	Sch	School
		Sh Ctr	Shopping centre
Inst	Institute	TH	Town hall / house
Ct	Law court	Trad Est	Trading estate
L Ctr	Leisure centre	Univ	University
LC	Level crossing	W Twr	Water tower
Liby	Library	Wks	Works
Mkt	Market	YH	Youth hostel

Enlarged maps only

Railway or bus station building

Place of interest

Parkland

The map scale on the pages numbered in green is 1¾ inches to 1 mile
2.76 cm to 1 km • 1:36 206

0	½ mile	1 mile	1½ miles	2 miles
0	500m	1 km	1½ km	2km

The map scale on the pages numbered in blue is 3½ inches to 1 mile
5.52 cm to 1 km • 1:18 103

0	¼ mile	½ mile	¾ mile	1 mile
0	250m	500m	750m	1km

The map scale on the pages numbered in red is 7 inches to 1 mile
11.04 cm to 1 km • 1:9051

0	220yds	440yds	660yds	½ mile
0	125m	250m	375m	500m

A   B   C   D   E   F

8

45

7

44

BROADWATER RD

P
BEACH

6

Peddars Way & Norfolk Coast Path   WESTGATE RD

BEACH ROAD

A149

43

132

CH Hotel

Old Hunstanton

P   P

WATSON RD

PARK RD

Motel

St Edmund's Point

P

GOLF COURSE ROAD

WODEHOUSE RD

HAMILTON RD

HUNSTANTON RD

Chalkpit Wood

Birthday Wood

5

P

OLD HUNSTANTON RD

PO

CHURCH RD

Hunstanton Hall

42

LIGHTHOUSE CL

St Edmund's Chapel

B1161

BERNARD CRESCENT

PEDDARS DR

Chapel Bank

Deodara Wood

CLIFF PARADE

BELGRAVE AVE

CLAREN CE RD

POPPY CREST

Kimberley Plantation

Ilex Wood

4

VICTORIA AVE

Ada Grove

Heart Plantation

Sensory Park

CROMER ROAD

Glebe House Sch

NORTHGATE

HUNSTANTON

Hunstanton Park Earthwork

132

132

41

Cross

i   PO

GREVEGATE

Hartley Cl

Hunstanton Inf Sch

Oak Grove

Half Moon Plantation

WESTGATE

NURSERY LDR

KING'S LYNN RD

Liby

P

CRESCENT LA

SANDRINGHAM RD

DOWNS RD

Lodge Farm

3

SOUTHEND ROAD

SEAGATE RD

MELTON DR

Smithdon High Sch

Old Bank Wood

Hunstanton Sea Life Sanctuary

Cemy

WA

South Hill Wood

Larch Plantation

SOUTH BEACH RD

MANOR RD

WINDSOR RISE

Hunstanton Prim Sch

40

BISHOP'S RD

B1161 OASIS WAY

PRINCESS DR

St Andrew's Chapel (remains of)

Downs Farm

Hill Wood

Ringstead Downs Nature Reserve

2

REDGATE HILL

The Firs

Redgate Hill

Ringstead Downs

CHALK RIVER RD

CH

39

SOUTH BEACH ROAD

Searles Golf Course

KINGFISHER LA

Pit

RINGSTEAD ROAD

NORTH BEACH

Manor Farm

MANOR RD

Long Wood

Little Wood

Whin Covert

133

1

ROBIN HILL

HALL CL

GARDENERS CT

Ind Est

Heacham Park

A149

CHURCH FARM RD

Church Farm

38

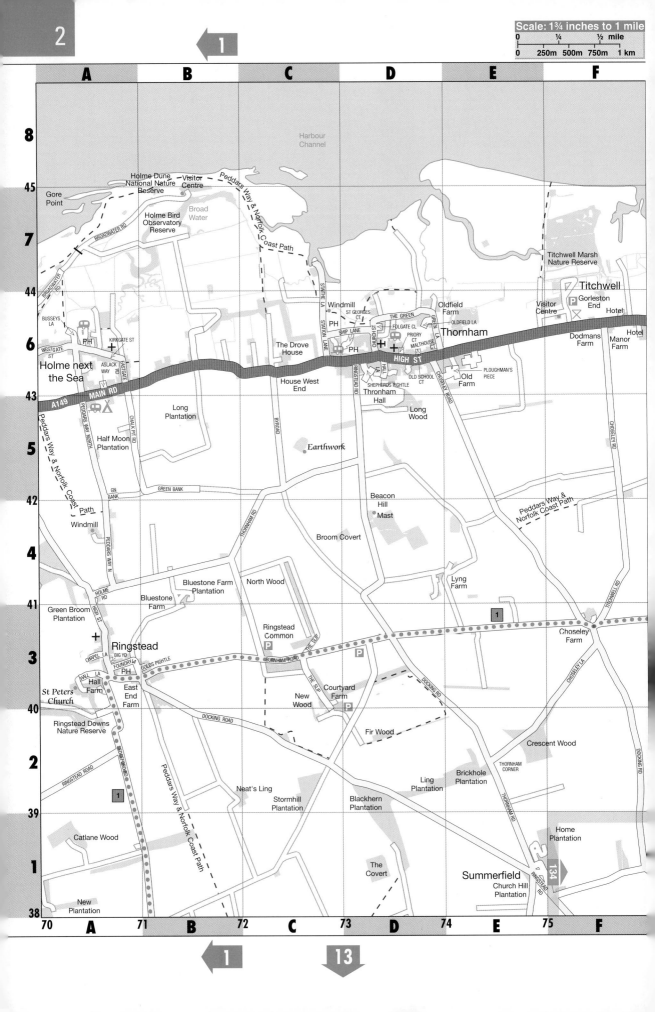

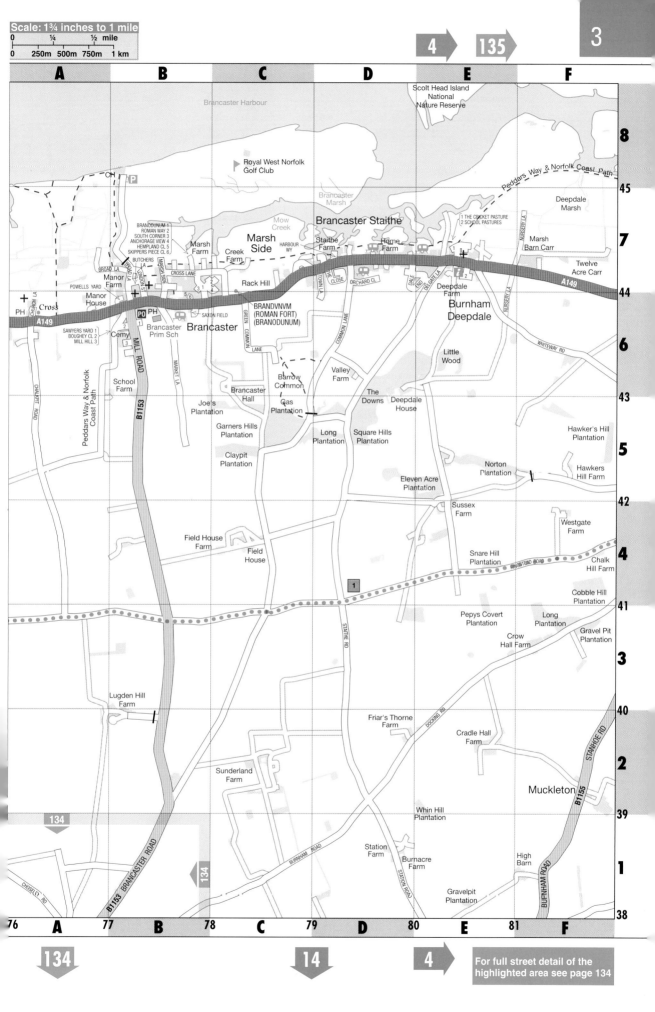

A   B   C   D   E   F

Norton Creek

Scolt Head Island
National Nature Reserve

Gun Hill

8

Trowland Creek

Burrow Gap

Meals House

Peddars Way & Norfolk Coast Walk

45

135

Fort

Overy Marsh

Decoy Wood

7

Burnham Overy Staithe

Overy Marshes

Bone's Drive

Marsh Farm

Gun Hill Farm

Marsh House Farm

Dale Hole

Hotel

44

WELLS ROAD

A149

A149

Dairy Farm

Burnham Overy Mill

Burnham Norton

NEW ROAD

TOWER ROAD

LUCAS LANE

MILL ROAD

GONG LA

GLEBE LA

GONG LANE

Church Wood

Bone's Belt

MODEL FARM RD B1155

6

135

River Burn

MARSH LA

Burnham Overy Town

B1155

Model Farm

Howe Hill

Peterstone Farm

BURNHAM RD

Sandpit Plantation

Garden Cottage

43

135

B1355

Cross (remains of)

Church Farm

BELLAMY'S LA

HERRING'S LA

Cemy

Sch

Friary

FRIAR'S LA

Leath House

Mill Farm

Tumulus

Osier Carr

Lucas Hill Wood

5

Mill Wood

Hall Farm

OVERY RD

MILL RD

Sewage Works

Whiteway Farm

WHITEWAY ROAD

PH

THE GN

Westgate

NORTH ST

FRONT ST

Manor House Moat

42

Mound

STATION RD

PO

Chalk Hill

RINGSTEAD ROAD

CHURCH WK

Church

Burnham Market

Burnham Thorpe

CHURCH LA

LOWE'S LA

MILL LA

BACK LA

East End Farm

Pagets Farm

Cottage End

CAMBERS LA

BEACON HILL RD

CREAKE RD

Gravelpit Hill

PH

Ivy House Farm

WALSINGHAM RD

Whitehall Farm

4

Croft's Wood

Gallow Hill Farm

Beacon Hill

135

Hillock Wood

Herongound Plantation

RECTORY LA

GREEN LANE

Scarboro' Wood

41

Gallow Hill

B1155

Rectory Wood

1

Longlands Farm

3

Gallow Hill Wood

Mast

B1355

Cottage Glebe

CREAKE ROAD

Coldham's Cross Wood

40

Open Meadow Plantation

BURNHAM THORPE RD

Field Barn

Neil's Plantation

2

MUCKLETON LA

St Mary's Abbey

Fox Covert

Deepdale Wood

Crossways Farm

BURNHAM RD B1355

Abbey Farm

Crowdale Wood

39

GREEN LA

Glebe Farm

WELLS ROAD

FIELD BARN LA

Chantry Hills

Mill Hill Plantation

NORMANS LA

Larch Wood

1

Long Plantation

DUNNS LA

North Creake

BAKERS BELT

STANHOE RD

Plateau Plantation

Ringate Wood

WEST STREET

PH

SHAMMER LA

38

82   A   83   B   84   C   85   D   86   E   87   F

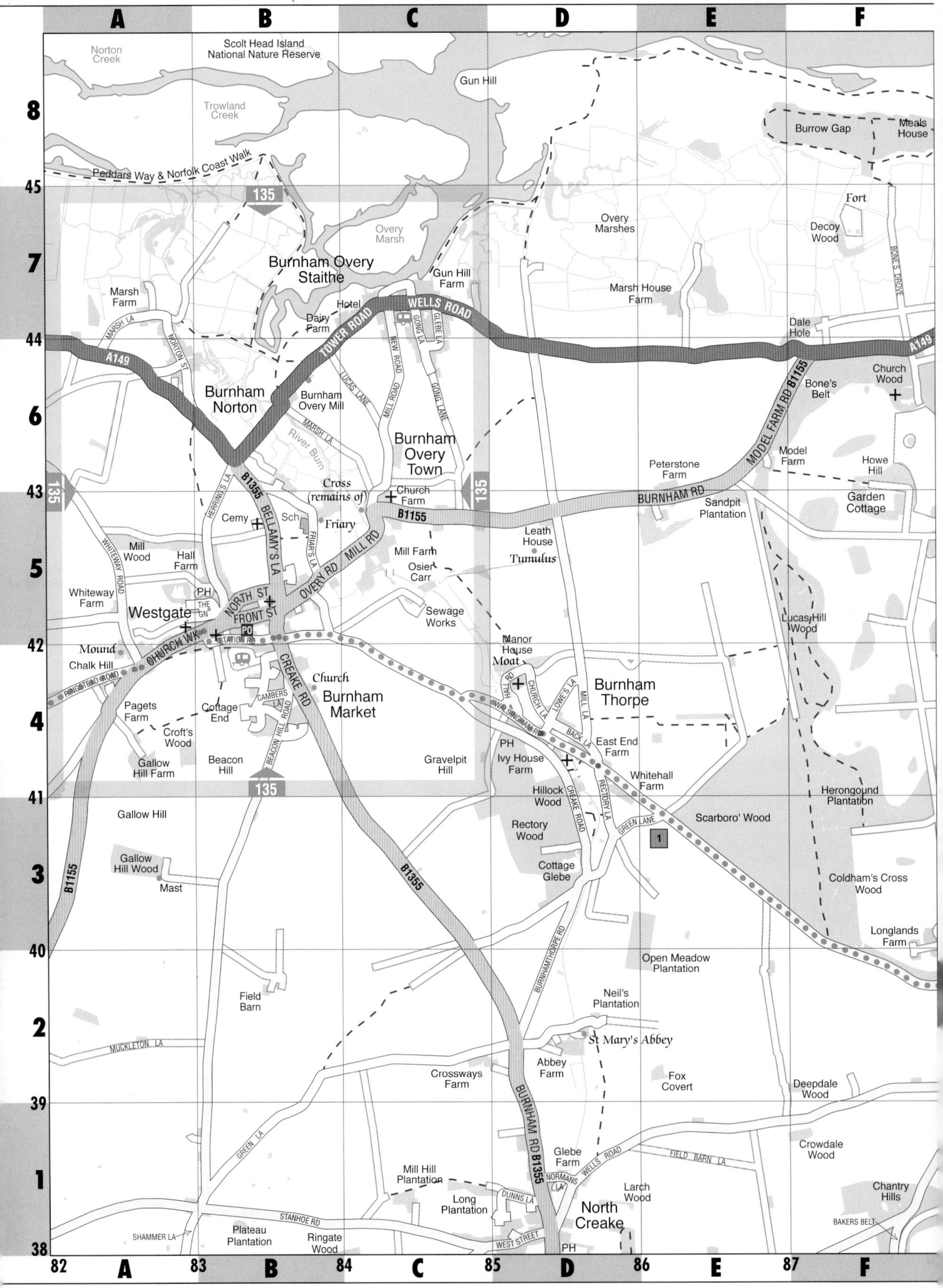

For full street detail of the highlighted area see page 135

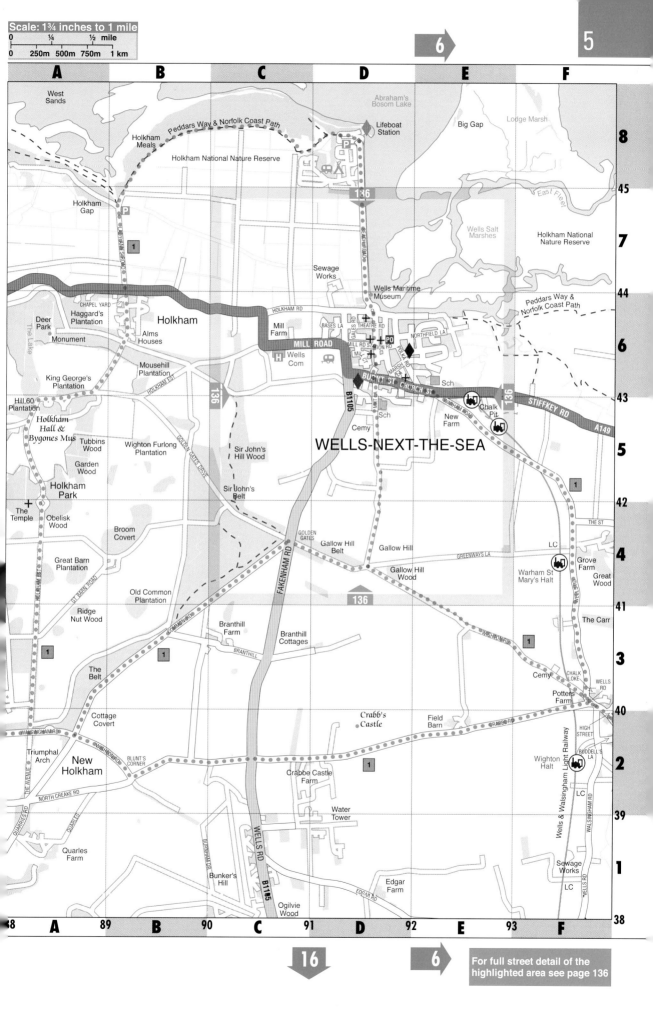

West Sands

Abraham's Bosom Lake

Big Gap

Lodge Marsh

Holkham Meals

Peddars Way & Norfolk Coast Path

Lifeboat Station

8

Holkham National Nature Reserve

P

45

East Fleet

Holkham Gap

P

136

Wells Salt Marshes

Holkham National Nature Reserve

7

1

CHAPEL YARD

Haggard's Plantation

HOLKHAM RD

Sewage Works

Wells Maritime Museum

Peddars Way & Norfolk Coast Path

44

Deer Park

Monument

Holkham

Alms Houses

Mill Farm

MILL ROAD

BASES LA

GALES RD

THEATRE RD

NORTHFIELD LA

MILL RD STATION RD

PO

6

The Lake

Mousehill Plantation

Wells Com

MARSH

POLKA RD

BURNT ST

CHURCH ST

Sch

136

STIFFKEY RD

43

King George's Plantation

HOLKHAM EST

B1105

WARHAM RD

Chalk Pit

A149

Hill 60 Plantation

Holkham Hall & Bygones Mus

Tubbins Wood

Wighton Furlong Plantation

Sir John's Hill Wood

Sch

Cemy

WELLS-NEXT-THE-SEA

New Farm

5

Garden Wood

GOLDEN GATES DRIVE

Sir John's Belt

1

42

The Temple

Obelisk Wood

Broom Covert

Gallow Hill Belt

GOLDEN GATES

Gallow Hill

Gallow Hill Wood

GREENWAYS LA

Warham St Mary's Halt

LC

Grove Farm

Great Wood

4

Holkham Park

Great Barn Plantation

FAKENHAM RD

136

The Carr

41

GT BARN ROAD

Ridge Nut Wood

Old Common Plantation

COMMON RD

Branthill Farm

Branthill Cottages

BRANTHILL

WIGHTON RD

1

Cemy

CHALK LOKE

WELLS RD

3

HOLKHAM EST

1

1

The Belt

Cottage Covert

WALSINGHAM RD

WIGHTON RD

BLUNT'S CORNER

Crabb's Castle

Field Barn

CRABB RD

Potters Farm

40

Triumphal Arch

New Holkham

Crabbe Castle Farm

1

Water Tower

HIGH STREET

BUDDELL'S LA

Wighton Halt

LC

2

QUARLES RD

NORTH CREAKE RD

Wells & Walsingham Light Railway

39

QUARLES RD

Quarles Farm

BURNHAM RD

WELLS RD

Bunker's Hill

B1105

Ogilvie Wood

EDGAR RD

Edgar Farm

Sewage Works

LC

WELLS RD

1

For full street detail of the highlighted area see page 136

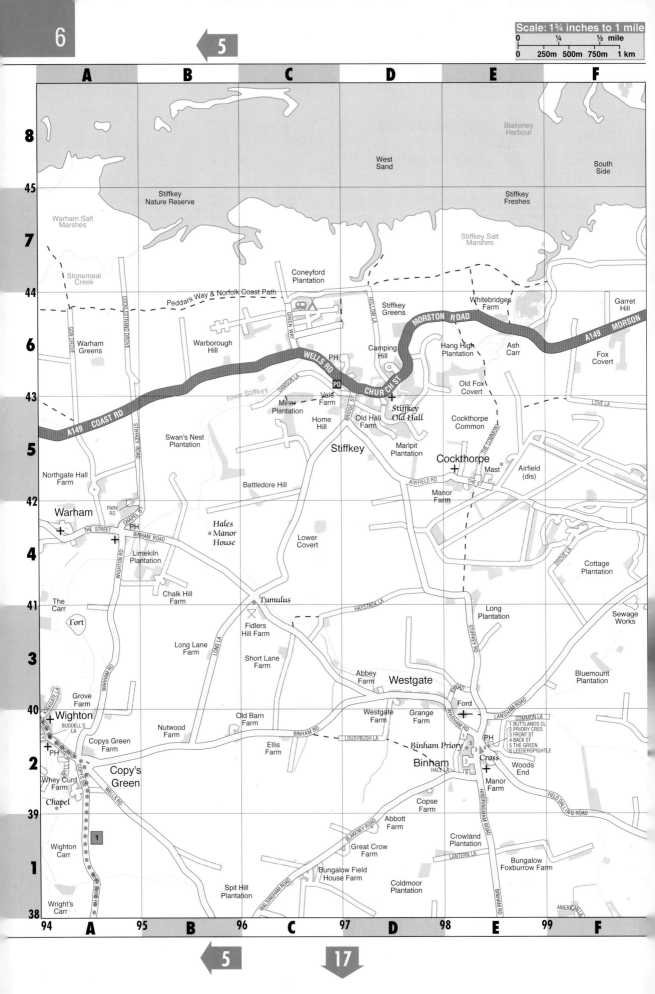

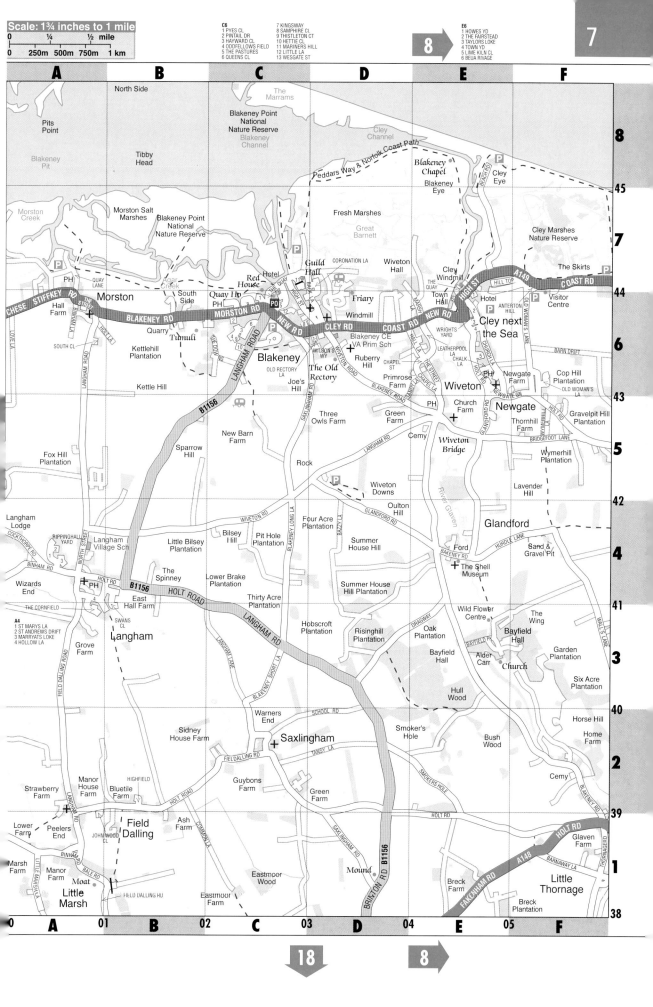

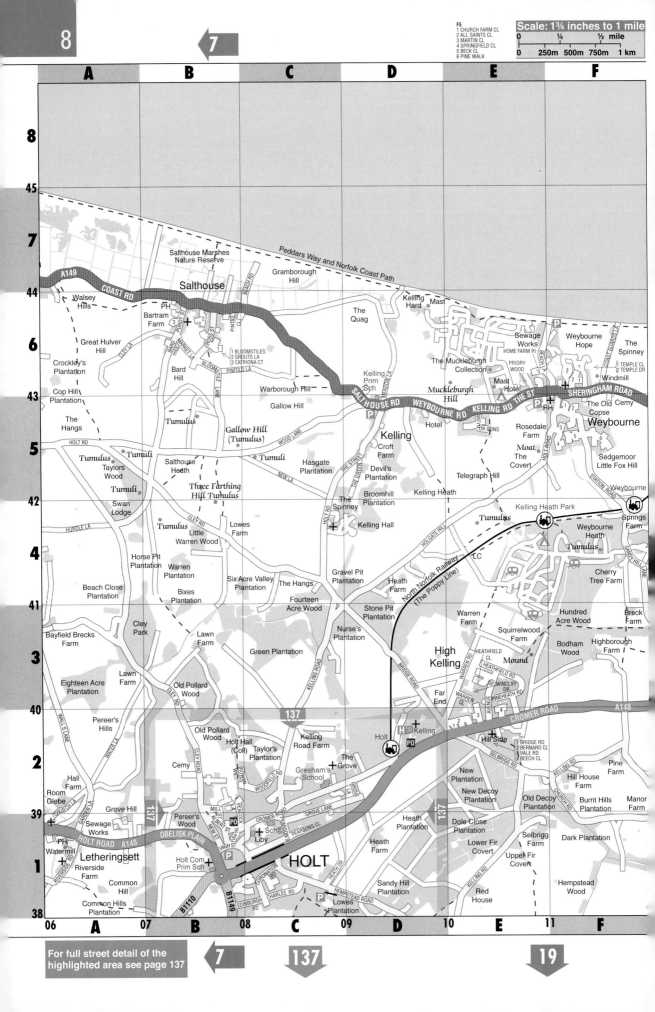

8

7

F5
1 CHURCH FARM CL
2 ALL SAINTS CL
3 MARTIN CL
4 SPRINGFIELD CL
5 BECK CL
6 PINE WALK

Scale: 1¾ inches to 1 mile
0   ¼   ½ mile
0 250m 500m 750m 1 km

A B C D E F

8

45

7

Peddars Way and Norfolk Coast Path

Salthouse Marshes
Nature Reserve

Gramborough
Hill

Kelling
Hard   Mast

44

A149   COAST RD   Salthouse

Walsey
Hills

PH
Bartram
Farm

The
Quag

Kelling
Prim
Sch

Sewage
Works

Weybourne
Hope

The
Spinney

1 TEMPLE CL
2 TEMPLE DR

6

Great Hulver
Hill

CLEY LA

BARD RD
MARKET LA

ST JOSS
PURDY ST

PINTAIL CL
BEACH RD

1 BLOOMSTILES
2 GROUTS LA
3 CATRIONA CT

HOME FARM RI

The Muckleburgh
Collection

PRIORY
WOOD

Windmill

Crockley's
Plantation

Bard
Hill

BLOOMSTILE
LANE

PINFOLD LA

Warborough Hill

Kelling
Sch

Muckleburgh
Hill

Mast
Hotel

Mast

WEYBOURNE RD

KELLING RD THE ST

SHERINGHAM ROAD

The Old
Copse

Cemy

43

Cop Hill
Plantation

SALT HOUSE RD

WEYBOURNE RD

Hotel

PH

Weybourne

The
Hangs

HOLT RD

Gallow Hill

Gallow Hill
(Tumulus)

WOOD LANE

Kelling

Croft
Farm

MOOR GDNS

Rosedale
Farm

HOLT ROAD

Moat
The
Covert

Sedgemoor
Little Fox Hill

5

Tumulus

Tumuli

Taylors
Wood

Salthouse
Heath

NEW LA

Tumuli

THE STREET

Devil's
Plantation

Hasgate
Plantation

Kelling Heath

Telegraph Hill

STATION ROAD

Weybourne

Tumuli

Swan
Lodge

Three Farthing
Hill Tumulus

THE GREEN

Broomhill
Plantation

Tumulus

Kelling Heath Park

Weybourne
Heath

Springs
Farm

42

HURDLE LA

Tumulus

CLEY RD

Lowes
Farm

HOLT RD

The
Spinney

HOLGATE HILL

North Norfolk Railway
(The Poppy Line)

LC

Tumulus

SANDY HILL LANE

Cherry
Tree Farm

4

Horse Pit
Plantation

Little
Warren Wood

Kelling Hall

Heath
Farm

Warren
Farm

Squirrelwood
Farm

Hundred
Acre Wood

Breck
Farm

Beach Close
Plantation

Warren
Plantation

Six Acre Valley
Plantation

The Hangs

Gravel Pit
Plantation

Stone Pit
Plantation

HEATHFIELD
CL

Mound

Bodham
Wood

Highborough
Farm

41

Bixes
Plantation

Fourteen
Acre Wood

WARREN RD

HEATHFIELD RD

WINCLIFF
DR

PINEHEATH RD

Cley
Park

Nurse's
Plantation

High
Kelling

3

Bayfield Brecks
Farm

KELLING ROAD

Green Plantation

BRIDGE ROAD

Far
End

WARREN
CL

AVENUE

Eighteen Acre
Plantation

Lawn
Farm

CLEY RD

Old Pollard
Wood

40

WALL'S LANE

Pereer's
Hills

Old Pollard
Wood

137

Holt

H

Kelling

CROMER ROAD

A148

WATER LA

Holt Hall
(Coll)

Taylor's
Plantation

Kelling
Road Farm

PO

Hill Side

1 BRIDGE RD
2 BERNARD CL
3 VALE RD
4 BEECH CL

KELLING RD

Pine
Farm

2

Hall
Farm

Cemy

RUNTON RD

WOODFIELD RD

Gresham's
School

The
Grove

GROVE LA

GROVE LANE

New
Plantation

SELBRIGG RD

Hill House
Farm

CHURCH RD

Manor
Farm

Room
Glebe

GARDEN LA

137

Pereer's
Wood

MILL ST

PEACOCK

ALBERT ST

PEARSON ST

PEARSONS CL

New Decoy
Plantation

Old Decoy
Plantation

Burnt Hills
Plantation

39

PH

Sewage
Works

HIGH ST

Sch

Liby

Heath
Plantation

Dole Close
Plantation

Selbrigg
Farm

Dark Plantation

Watermill

HOLT ROAD

A148

OBELISK PLAIN

Holt Com
Prim Sch

CROMER ROAD

HEATH DR

Lower Fir
Covert

KELLING RD

Letheringsett

RIVERSIDE LA

Riverside
Farm

B1149

Heath
Farm

Upper Fir
Covert

Hempstead
Wood

1

Common
Hill

CROMATION RD

EDINBURGH RD

CHARLES RD

P

HEMPSTEAD ROAD

HOLT

Sandy Hill
Plantation

Red
House

38

Common Hills
Plantation

B1110

B1149

Lowes
Plantation

06   A   07   B   08   C   09   D   10   E   11   F

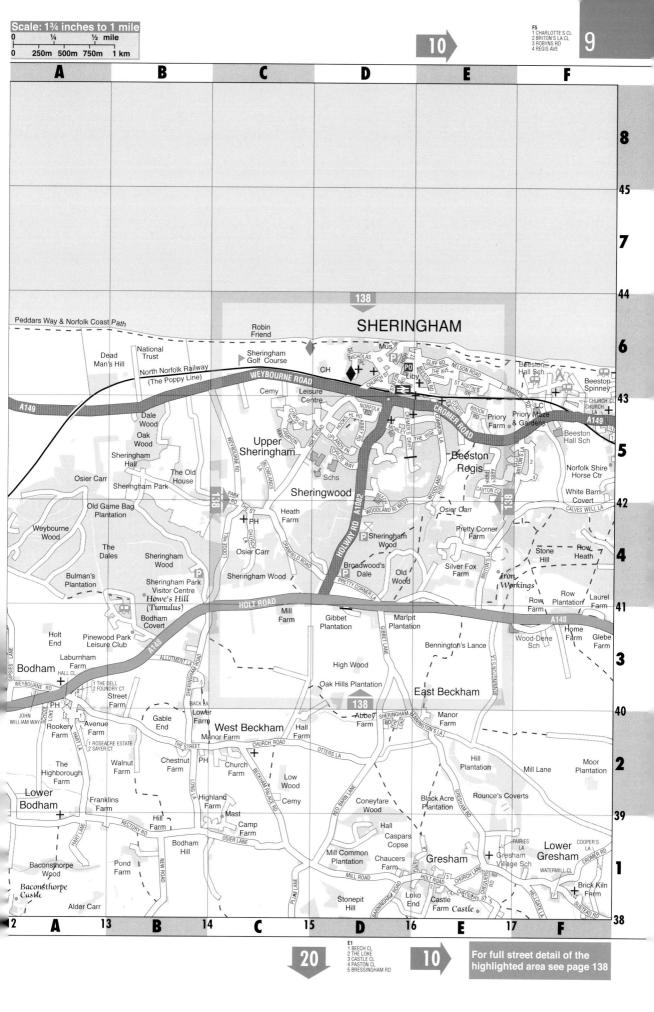

Scale: 1¾ inches to 1 mile

0   ¼   ½ mile
0 250m 500m 750m 1 km

10 ▶

9

F5
1 CHARLOTTE'S CL
2 BRITON'S LA CL
3 ROBYNS RD
4 REGIS AVE

A   B   C   D   E   F

8

45

7

44

SHERINGHAM

Peddars Way & Norfolk Coast Path

138

6

Robin
Friend

St
Nicholas
PL   Mus

Dead
Man's Hill

National
Trust

Sheringham
Golf Course

Beeston
Hall Sch

Beestop
Spinney

North Norfolk Railway
(The Poppy Line)

CH

PO
Liby

CLIFF RD
NELSON ROAD
THE AVE

43

WEYBOURNE ROAD

Cemy

Leisure
Centre

CHURCH ST
STATION RD
NELSON RD
ST AUSTIN'S
GR

NELSON

CHURCH CL
CHURCH

A149

Dale
Wood

Norfolk
RD

ABBEY RD

HOOK'S HL RD
UPLANDS PK

CREMER'S DRIFT

MORLEY RD

THE RISE

CROMER ROAD

COMMON LA

BROOK
RD

Priory
Farm

Priory Maze
& Gardens

LC

A149

Oak
Wood

Upper
Sheringham

CAMPION WAY

CHURCH

CHOS. WAY

HOLT ROAD

CAXTON CT

BRITON'S LA

Beeston
Hall Sch

5

Sheringham
Hall

The Old
House

Schs

Beeston
Regis

Norfolk Shire
Horse Ctr

Osier Carr

Sheringham Park

BLOWLANDS

Sheringwood

BEECH AVE

ABBEY RD

White Barn
Covert

Old Game Bag
Plantation

PARK RD

THE ST

CHURCH LA

Heath
Farm

HOLWAY RD   A1082

WOODLAND RI WEST

Osier Carr

WOODLAND RISE

Osier Carr

138

CALVES WELL LA

42

Weybourne
Wood

138

Pretty Corner
Farm

Stone
Hill

Row
Heath

4

The
Dales

Sheringham
Wood

Osier Carr

Sheringham Wood

CRANFIELD ROAD

PRETTY CORNER LA

P

Sheringham
Wood

Broadwood's
Dale

Old
Wood

Silver Fox
Farm

BRITON'S LA

Iron
Workings

Row
Plantation

Laurel
Wood

Bulman's
Plantation

Sheringham Park
Visitor Centre
Howe's Hill
(Tumulus)

Bodham
Covert

HOLT ROAD

A148

Mill
Farm

Gibbet
Plantation

Marlpit
Plantation

Row
Farm

A1148

Home
Farm

Glebe
Farm

41

Holt
End

Pinewood Park
Leisure Club

Bennington's Lance

Wood-Dene
Sch

3

GIPSIES' LANE

Laburnham
Farm

HALL CL

ALLOTMENT LA

SHERINGHAM ROAD

High Wood

Oak Hills Plantation

BENNINGTON'S LA

East Beckham

Bodham

WEYBOURNE RD

PH

BACK LA

138

Manor
Farm

40

JOHN
WILLIAM WAY

SCHOOL RD

PH

Avenue
Farm

Gable
End

Lower
Farm

Abbey
Farm

THE LOKE

SHERINGHAM RD
BENNINGTON'S LA

Rookery
Farm

HART LA

1 THE DELL
2 FOUNDRY CT

Street
Farm

1 ROSEACRE ESTATE
2 SAYER CT

THE STREET

West Beckham

Hall
Farm

OTTERS LA

Hill
Plantation

Mill Lane

Moor
Plantation

2

The
Highborough
Farm

Walnut
Farm

Chestnut
Farm

PH

Church
Farm

CHURCH ROAD

Low
Wood

BECKHAM PALACE RD

RED BARN LANE

GRESHAM RD

Rounce's Coverts

Lower
Bodham

Franklins
Farm

LONG LA

Highland
Farm

Cemy

Coneyfare
Wood

Black Acre
Plantation

FAIRIES
LA

COOPER'S
LA

Lower
Gresham

39

HART LANE

RECTORY RD

Hill Farm

NEW ROAD

Mast

Camp
Farm

OSIER LANE

Hall
Caspars
Copse

DAIRY

Gresham
Village Sch

WATERMILL CL

CROMER RD

Baconsthorpe
Wood

Pond
Farm

Bodham
Hill

Mill Common
Plantation

Chaucers
Farm

Gresham

Gresham
Castle

CHENVERS LA

CHEQUERS RD

HELGATE LA

Brick Kiln
Farm

1

Baconsthorpe
Castle

PLUM LANE

MILL ROAD

Stonepit
Hill

BARRINGTON RD

Loko
End

Castle
Farm   Castle

HOLT ROAD

CHURCH LANE

SUSTEAD RD

Alder Carr

2   A   13   B   14   C   15   D   16   E   17   F   38

20

10

E1
1 BEECH CL
2 THE LOKE
3 CASTLE CL
4 PASTON CL
5 BRESSINGHAM RD

For full street detail of the
highlighted area see page 138

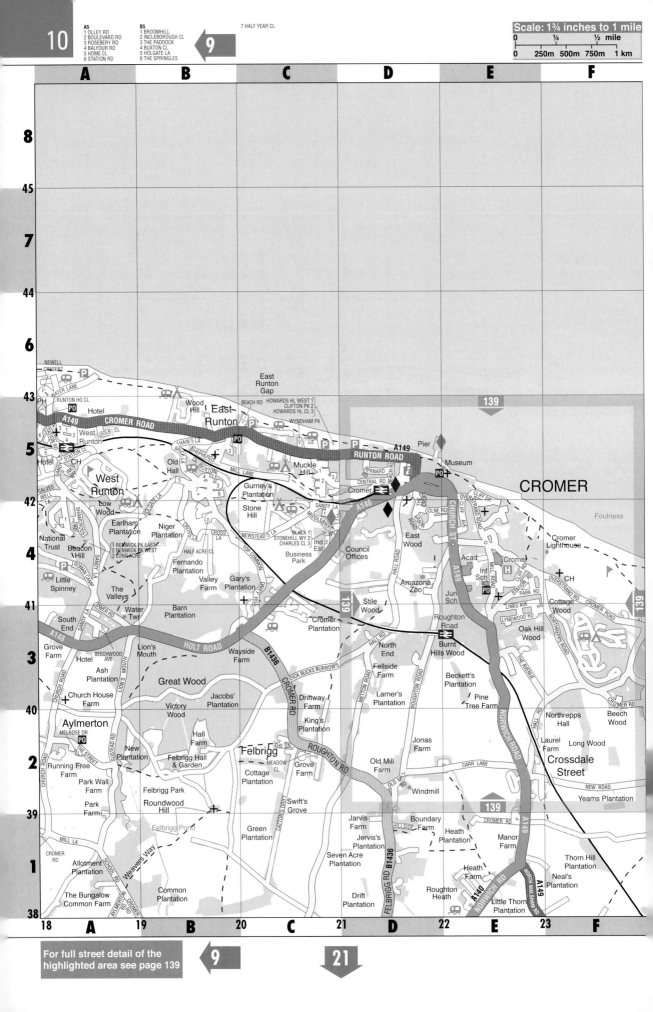

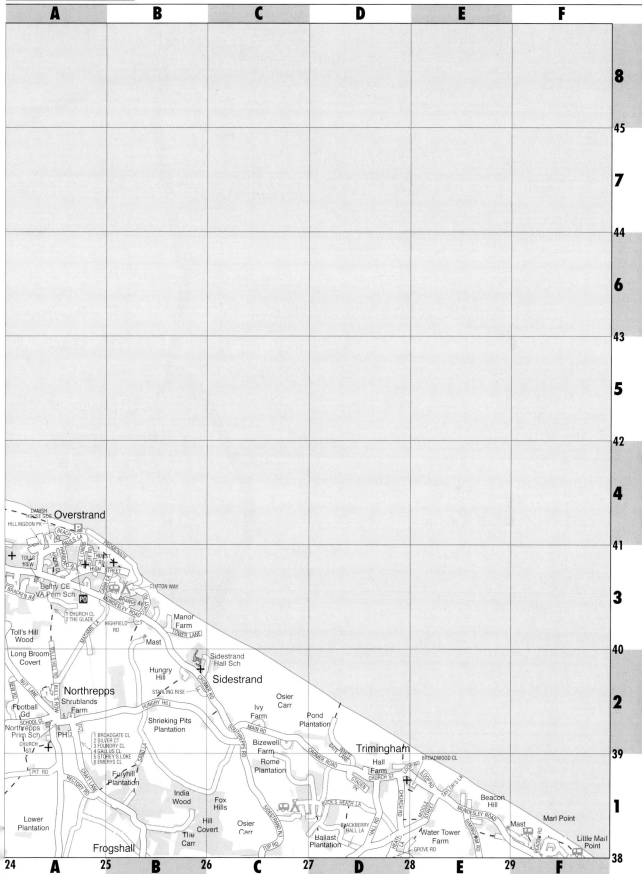

Scale: 1¾ inches to 1 mile

0   ¼   ½   mile
0   250m 500m 750m 1 km

A **B** **C** **D** **E** **F**

8
45
7
44
6
43
5
42
4
41
3
40
2
39
1
38

24 **A** 25 **B** 26 **C** 27 **D** 28 **E** 29 **F** 38

Overstrand

DANISH HOUSE GDS
HILLINGDON PK
TOLL'S VIEW
BEACH
PAULS LA
PROMENADE
THE LONDS
CLIFT RD
THURST RD
HIGH STREET
Belfry CE VA Prim Sch
GRANGE AV
CLIFTON WAY
BRACKEN AV
MUNDESLEY ROAD
PO
1 CHURCH CL
2 THE GLADE
HIGHFIELD RD
Manor Farm
TOWER LANE
Mast

Toll's Hill Wood
Long Broom Covert
NUT LANE
TOLL'S HILL RD
BUTL'S ROW
MADMS LA
Hungry Hill
CROMER RD
STARLING RISE
Sidestrand Hall Sch
Sidestrand

Northrepps
Shrublands Farm
Football Gd
SCHOOL CL
Northrepps Prim Sch
CHURCH ST
PH
Shrieking Pits Plantation
HUNGRY HILL
SAND LA
1 BROADGATE CL
2 SILVER CT
3 FOUNDRY CL
4 GALLUS CL
5 STOREY'S LOKE
6 EMERYS CL
SOUTHREPPS RD
Ivy Farm
Osier Carr
MAIN RD
Bizewell Farm
Rome Plantation
Pond Plantation
CROMER ROAD
WHITE GATE LANE
Trimingham
Hall Farm
CHURCH ST
STADEN PK
BROADWOOD CL
LOOP RD
TAYLOR'S LA
Beacon Hill

PIT RD
RECTORY RD
CRAFT LANE
Furyhill Plantation
India Wood
Hill Covert
Fox Hills
Osier Carr
SIDESTRAND RD
TOP RD
BUCK'S HEATH LA
BLACKBERRY HALL LA
HALL RD
KEATE LA
CHURCH RD
MIDDLE STREET
GROVE RD
Water Tower Farm
GIMINGHAM RD
MUNDESLEY ROAD
Mast
BEACON RD
Marl Point
Little Marl Point

Lower Plantation
The Carr
Frogshall
Ballast Plantation

Scale: 1¾ inches to 1 mile

0   ¼   ½   mile
0   250m   500m   750m   1 km

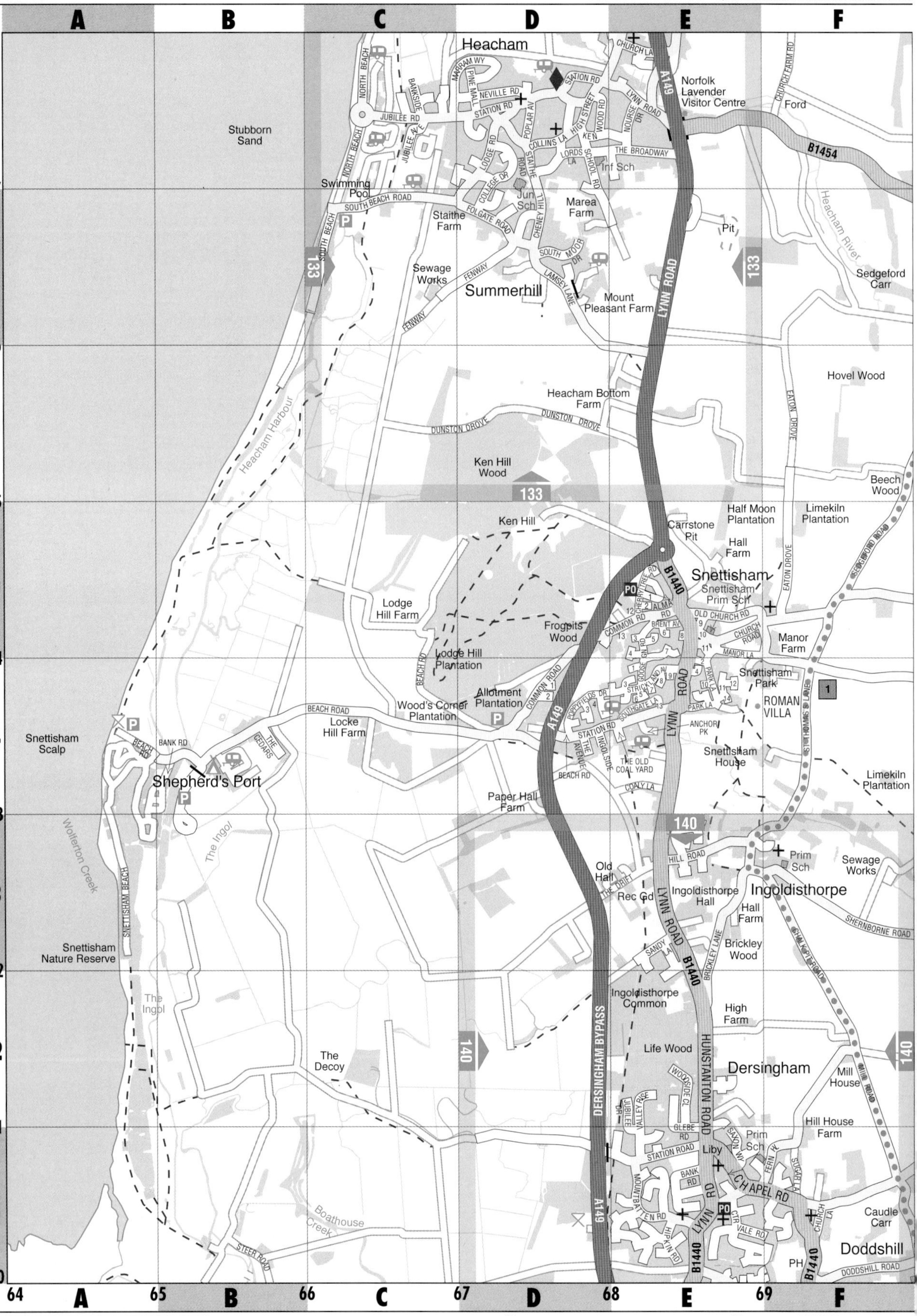

A   B   C   D   E   F

Heacham

Church La

Norfolk Lavender Visitor Centre

Ford

B1454

Stubborn Sand

Morgan Wy

Pine Mall

Neville Rd

Station Rd

Poplar Av

Collins La

High Street

Lords La

Wood Rd

The Broadway

Inf Sch

Heacham River

North Beach

Jubilee Rd

Bankside

Marsh Rd

Jun Sch

College Dr

Lodge Rd

Cheney Hill

Folgate Road

Marea Farm

Pit

Swimming Pool

South Beach Road

Staithe Farm

South Moor Dr

Sedgeford Carr

South Beach Road

Fenway

Summerhill

Lamsey Lane

Mount Pleasant Farm

Lynn Road

Sewage Works

Fenway

Heacham Bottom Farm

Dunston Drove

Dunston Drove

Hovel Wood

Heacham Harbour

Ken Hill Wood

B1440

Eaton Drove

Beech Wood

Ken Hill

Carrstone Pit

Half Moon Plantation

Hall Farm

Limekiln Plantation

Snettisham

Snettisham Prim Sch

Old Church Rd

Church Road

Manor Farm

Lodge Hill Farm

Frogpits Wood

Common Rd

Brent Av

Alma

Lodge Hill Plantation

Beach Rd

Common Road

Manor La

Snettisham Park

ROMAN VILLA

Beach Road

Wood's Corner Plantation

Allotment Plantation

Chiffields Dr

Station Rd

Park La

Snettisham House

Limekiln Plantation

Snettisham Scalp

The Cedars

Bank Rd

Locke Hill Farm

Beach Rd

A149

The Old Coal Yard

Coaly La

Anchor Pk

Park La

St John Holmes Rd

Beach Rd

Shepherd's Port

Paper Hall Farm

Old Hall

The Drift

Rec Gd

Hill Road

Prim Sch

Sewage Works

Ingoldisthorpe Hall

Hall Farm

Ingoldisthorpe

Walterton Creek

The Ingol

Snettisham Beach

Snettisham Nature Reserve

The Ingol

Sandy La

B1440

Brickley Lane

Brickley Wood

Shernborne Road

Dersingham Bypass

Ingoldisthorpe Common

Life Wood

High Farm

The Decoy

Lynn Road

Hunstanton Road

Dersingham

Mill House

A149

Woodside Cl

Valley Rise

Jubilee Drive

Glebe Rd

Station Road

Bank Rd

Liby

Chapel Rd

Prim Sch

Fern La

Hill House Farm

Boathouse Creek

Steer Road

Moorend

Lynn Rd

Hipkin Rd

B1440

Vale Rd

Church

PH

B1440

Caudle Carr

Doddshill

Doddshill Rd

For full street detail of the highlighted areas see pages 133 and 140

27

140

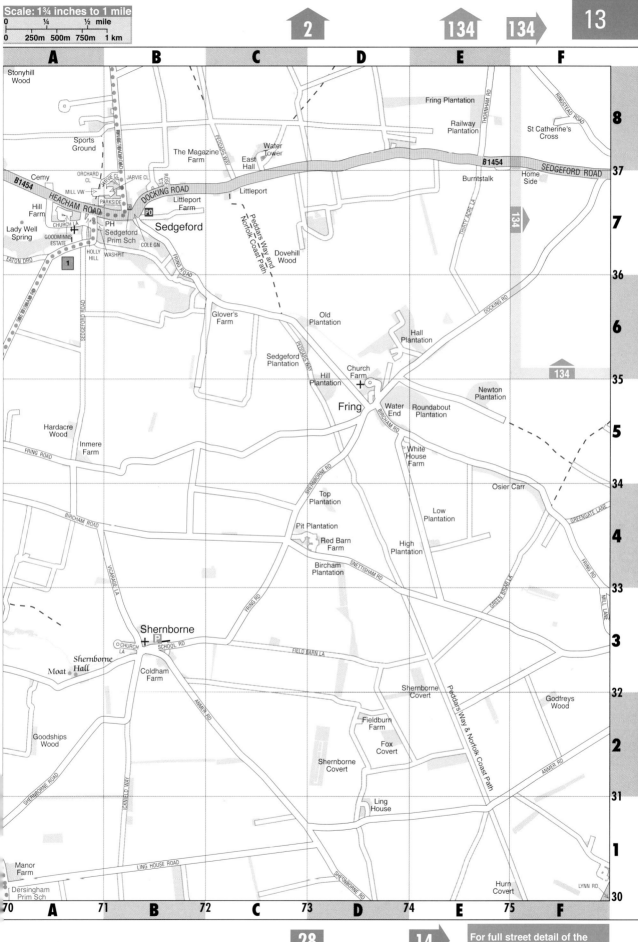

A B C D E F

Stonyhill Wood

Sports Ground

Cemy

Hill Farm

B1454 HEACHAM ROAD

Lady Well Spring

ORCHARD CL

JARVIE CL

JARVIE CL

PARKSIDE

MILL VW

ROSE CT

DOCKING ROAD

PO

CHURCH LA

PH

GOODMINNS ESTATE

Sedgeford Prim Sch

COLE GN

WASHPIT

HOLLY HILL

Sedgeford

1

EATON DRO

SEDGEFORD ROAD

FRING ROAD

PEDDARS WAY

The Magazine Farm

East Hall

Water Tower

Littleport

Littleport Farm

Peddars Way and Norfolk Coast Path

Dovehill Wood

Glover's Farm

Old Plantation

Sedgeford Plantation

Hill Plantation

Church Farm

Fring

Fring Plantation

Railway Plantation

THORNHAM RD

B1454

SEDGEFORD ROAD

Burntstalk

Home Side

THIRTY ACRE LA

134

DOCKING RD

Hall Plantation

Newton Plantation

Water End

Roundabout Plantation

St Catherine's Cross

RINGSTEAD ROAD

134

Hardacre Wood

FRING ROAD

Inmere Farm

BIRCHAM ROAD

VICARAGE LA

Shernborne

CHURCH LA

Moat

Shernborne Hall

Coldham Farm

Goodships Wood

SHERNBORNE ROAD

ICKNIELD WAY

AMMER RD

Manor Farm

Dersingham Prim Sch

LING HOUSE ROAD

FRING RD

SHERNBORNE RD

Top Plantation

Pit Plantation

Red Barn Farm

Bircham Plantation

SNETTISHAM RD

SCHOOL RD

FIELD BARN LA

Fieldburn Farm

Fox Covert

Shernborne Covert

Ling House

SHERNBORNE RD

BIRCHAM RD

White House Farm

Low Plantation

High Plantation

Osier Carr

GREEN BANK LA

Shernborne Covert

Peddars Way & Norfolk Coast Path

Godfreys Wood

GREENGATE LANE

FRING RD

MILL LANE

ANMER RD

Hurn Covert

LYNN RD

8
37
7
36
6
35
5
34
4
33
3
32
2
31
1
30

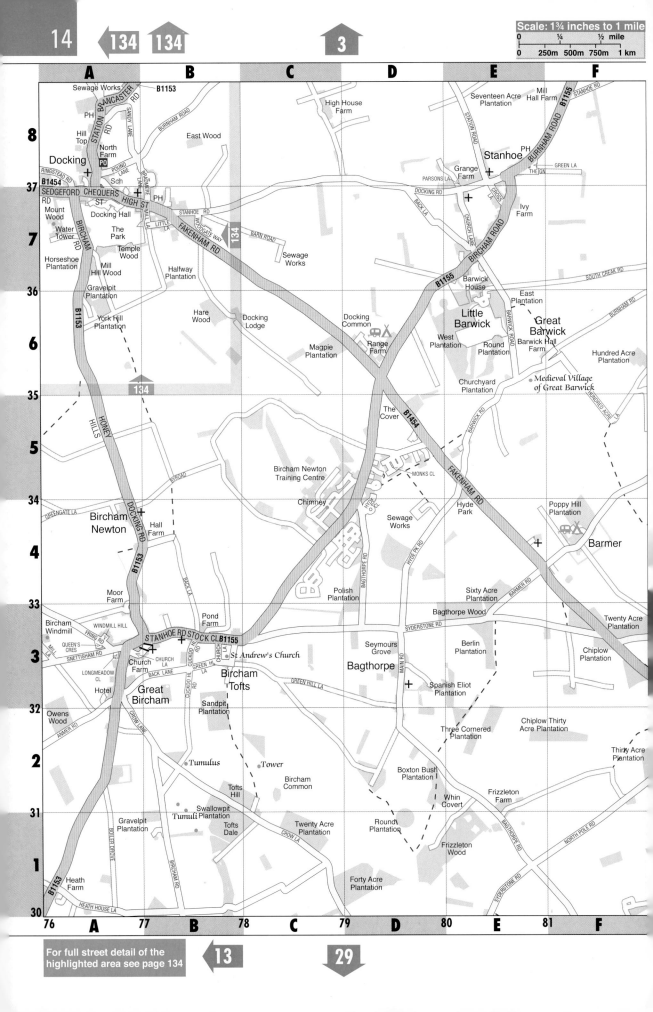

Scale: 1¾ inches to 1 mile
0   ¼   ½ mile
0   250m   500m   750m   1 km

Sewage Works
B1153
PH
STATION RD
BRANCASTER RD
SANDY LANE
BURNHAM ROAD
East Wood
High House Farm
Seventeen Acre Plantation
Mill Hall Farm
B1155
STANHOE RD

Hill Top
North Farm
PO
Docking
PH
Stanhoe
Grange Farm
PARSONS LA
BACK LA
DOCKING RD
CROSS LA
THE GN
GREEN LA

Sch
POUND LANE
BRAEMERE LANE
STATION ROAD
CHURCH LANE
B1454
SEDGEFORD RD
CHEQUERS ST
HIGH ST
Docking Hall
PH
MILL LA
LITTLE LA
STANHOE RD
WOODGATE WAY
FAKENHAM RD
134
BARN ROAD
Ivy Farm

Mount Wood
Water Tower
BIRCHAM RD
The Park
Temple Wood
Sewage Works
B1155
Barwick House
BIRCHAM ROAD
SOUTH CREEK RD
East Plantation

Horseshoe Plantation
Mill Hill Wood
Halfway Plantation
Hare Wood
Docking Lodge
Docking Common
West Plantation
Little Barwick
Round Plantation
Great Barwick
Barwick Hall Farm
Hundred Acre Plantation

B1153
Gravelpit Plantation
York Hill Plantation
Magpie Plantation
Range Farm
Churchyard Plantation
BARWICK RD
Medieval Village of Great Barwick
HUNDRED ACRE

134
HONEY HILLS
The Cover
B1454
FAKENHAM RD

BYROAD
Bircham Newton Training Centre
Chimney
MONKS CL
HYDE CL
Hyde Park
Poppy Hill Plantation
Barmer

GREENGATE LA
DOCKING RD
Bircham Newton
Hall Farm
BACK LA
Sewage Works
HYDE PK RD
BAGTHORPE RD
BARMER RD

B1153
Moor Farm
Polish Plantation
Sixty Acre Plantation
Bagthorpe Wood
SYDERSTONE RD
Twenty Acre Plantation

Bircham Windmill
WINDMILL HILL
FRING RD
Pond Farm
STANHOE RD
STOCK CL
B1155
Seymours Grove
Berlin Plantation
Chiplow Plantation

QUEEN'S CRES
MILL
SNETTISHAM RD
Church Farm
CHURCH LA
BACK LANE
CUCKOO HL RD
GREEN HL RD
CHURCH LA
St Andrew's Church
Bircham Tofts
Bagthorpe
MAIN RD
Spanish Eliot Plantation

LONGMEADOW CL
Hotel
Great Bircham
Sandpit Plantation
GREEN HILL LA
Three Cornered Plantation
Chiplow Thirty Acre Plantation

Owens Wood
ANMER RD
CROW LANE
BIRCHAM RD
Tumulus
Tower
Bircham Common
Boxton Bush Plantation
Whin Covert
Frizzleton Farm
Thirty Acre Plantation

Gravelpit Plantation
BOILER DROVE
Tumuli
Swallowpit Plantation
Tofts Hill
Tofts Dale
CROW LA
Twenty Acre Plantation
Round Plantation
Frizzleton Wood
STYDERSTONE RD
BAGTHORPE RD
NORTH POLE RD

B1153
Heath Farm
HEATH HOUSE LA
Forty Acre Plantation

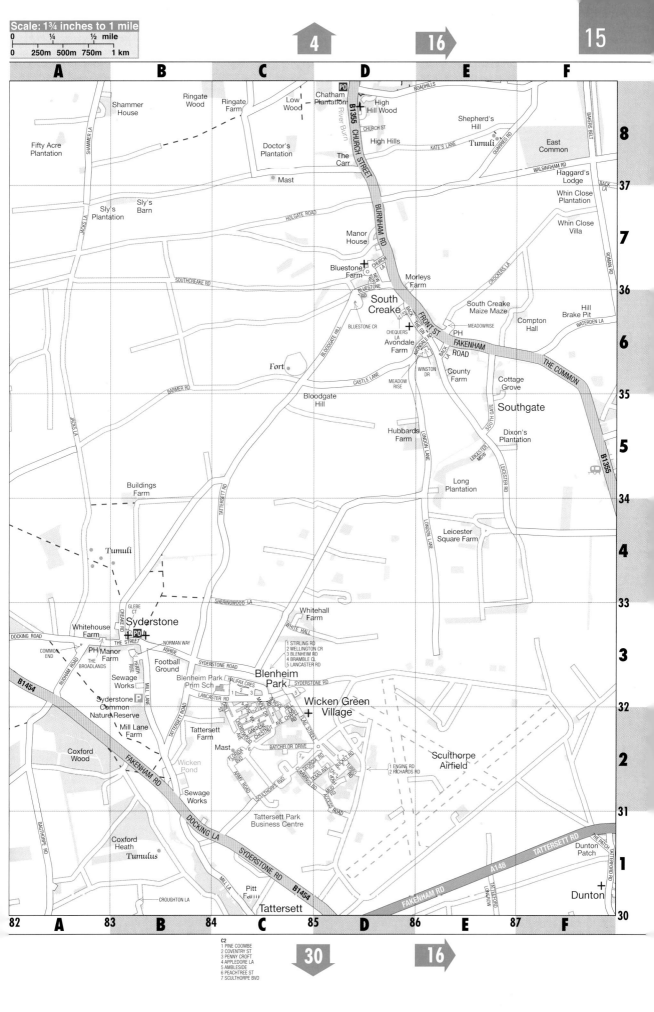

A   B   C   D   E   F

8

Fifty Acre
Plantation

Shammer
House

Ringate
Wood

Ringate
Farm

Low
Wood

Chatham
Plantation

High
Hill Wood

ROADHILLS

Shepherd's
Hill

East
Common

SHAMMER LA

Doctor's
Plantation

CHURCH ST

High Hills

KATE'S LANE

Tumuli

QUARRIES RD

WALSINGHAM RD

Haggard's
Lodge

BACK LA

37

Mast

The
Carr

Sly's
Plantation

Sly's
Barn

JACK'S LA

SOUTHCREAKE RD

HOLGATE ROAD

Manor
House

BURNHAM RD

CHURCH ST

Bluestone
Farm

Whin Close
Plantation

Whin Close
Villa

ROMAN RD

7

36

Morleys
Farm

CROCKERS LA

South Creake
Maize Maze

Hill
Brake Pit

BLOODGATE HILL

BLUESTONE RD

South
Creake

FRONT ST

BACK THE RD LN

Bluestone CR

Chequers
Avondale LA
Farm

PH

MEADOWRISE

FAKENHAM
ROAD

Compton
Hall

WATERDEN LA

THE COMMON

6

Fort

BARMER RD

CASTLE LANE

MEADOW
RISE

WINSTON
DR

BACK LA

County
Farm

Cottage
Grove

SOUTH GATE

Southgate

35

B1355

Bloodgate
Hill

Hubbards
Farm

LONDON LANE

LEICESTER MDW

Dixon's
Plantation

LEICESTER RD

5

TATTERSETT RD

Buildings
Farm

Long
Plantation

34

Tumuli

SHERINGWOOD LA

Whitehall
Farm

LONDON LANE

Leicester
Square Farm

4

33

CREAKE RD

GLEBE
CT

Syderstone

WHITE HALL

1 STIRLING RD
2 WELLINGTON CR
3 BLENHEIM RD
4 BRAMBLE CL
5 LANCASTER RD

3

DOCKING ROAD

Whitehouse
Farm

PO

THE STREET

NORMAN WAY

ASHIDE

SYDERSTONE ROAD

SYDERSTONE RD

B1454

COMMON
END

PH Manor
Farm
THE
BROADLANDS

HEARN
RISE

Football
Ground

MILL LANE

Blenheim Park
Prim Sch

HALIFAX CRES

Blenheim
Park

SYDERSTONE RD

32

Sewage
Works

P

Syderstone
Common
Nature Reserve

Mill Lane
Farm

LANCASTER RD

Wicken Green
Village

Coxford
Wood

FAKENHAM ROAD

Wicken
Pond

Tattersett
Farm

Mast

BATCHELOR DRIVE

1 ENGINE RD
2 RICHARDS RD

Sculthorpe
Airfield

2

BAGTHORPE RD

Sewage
Works

ARMY ROAD

SCULTHORPE BVD

ACCESS ROAD

Tattersett Park
Business Centre

31

Coxford
Heath

Tumulus

DOCKING LA

SYDERSTONE RD

B1454

MILL LA

Pitt
Farm

A148

FAKENHAM RD

TATTERSETT RD

LONGHAM

TATTERFORD RD

THE PATCH

Dunton
Patch

1

CROUGHTON LA

Tattersett

Dunton

30

82   A   83   B   84   C   85   D   86   E   87   F   30

C2
1 PINE COOMBE
2 COVENTRY ST
3 PENNY CROFT
4 APPLEDORE LA
5 AMBLESIDE
6 PEACHTREE ST
7 SCULTHORPE BVD

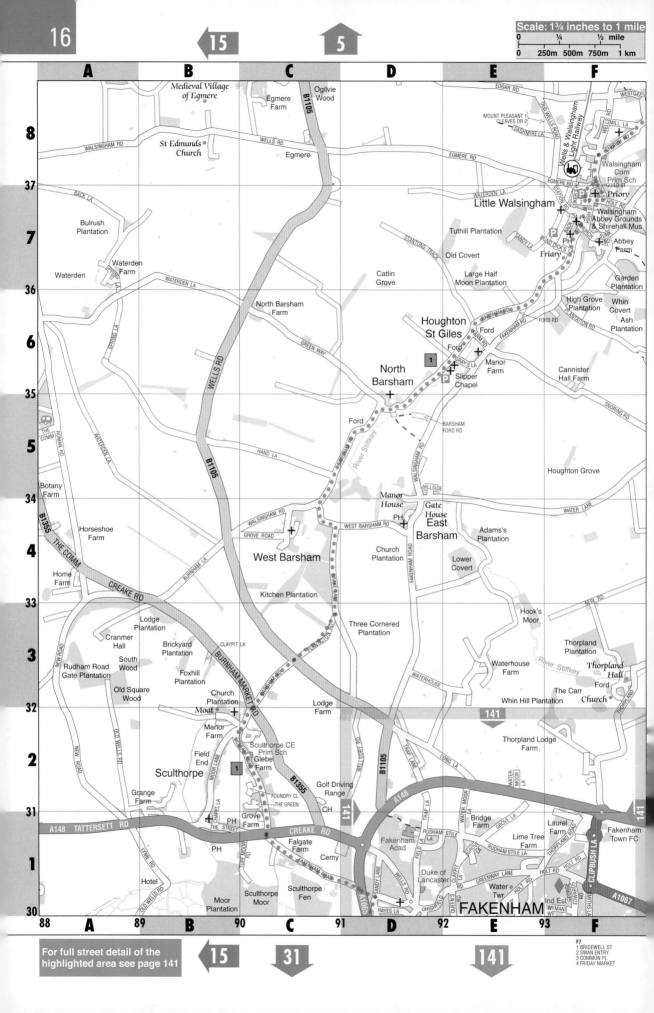

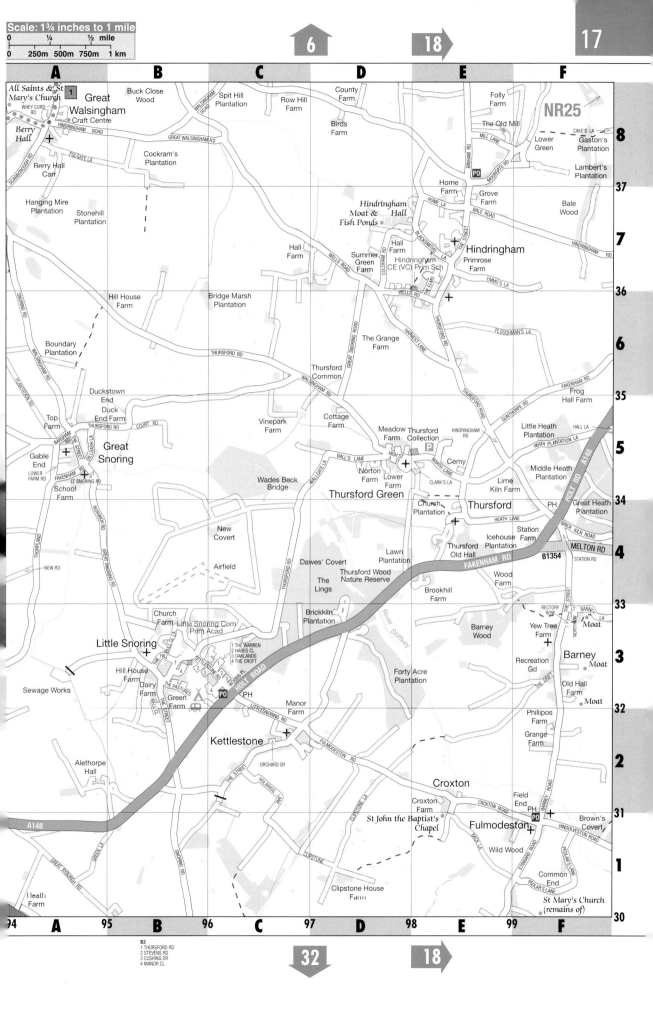

A **B** **C** **D** **E** **F**

NR25

All Saints & St Mary's Church
Great Walsingham
Buck Close Wood
Spit Hill Plantation
Row Hill Farm
County Farm
Folly Farm
WHEY CURD RD
Craft Centre
Birds Farm
The Old Mill
Lower Green
Gaston's Plantation
Berry Hall
HINDRINGHAM ROAD
GREAT WALSINGHAM RD
MILL LANE
MOORGATE RD
CAKE'S LA
Lambert's Plantation
8
FOLGATE LA
Cockram's Plantation
Home Farm
Grove Farm
BINHAM RD
PO
37
Hanging Mire Plantation
Stonehill Plantation
Hindringham Moat & Fish Ponds
Hindringham Hall
HOME LA
BALE ROAD
Bale Wood
SCARBOROUGH RD
Berry Hall Carr
Hall Farm
Summer Green Farm
Hindringham CE (VC) Prim Sch
Hindringham
THE STREET
HINDRINGHAM RD
7
Hill House Farm
Hall Farm
Bridge Marsh Plantation
Hall Farm
BLACKSMITHS LA
Primrose Farm
EMMS'S LA
36
WELLS ROAD
WELLS RD
THE ELMS
THURSFORD RD
PLOUGHMAN'S LA
6
SNORING RD
Boundary Plantation
THURSFORD RD
GREAT SNORING ROAD
The Grange Farm
HARVEST LANE
WALSINGHAM RD
Thursford Common
Thursford Common
FAKENHAM RD
Frog Hall Farm
35
WALSINGHAM RD
PLANTATION RD
Duckstown End
Duck End Farm
Vinepark Farm
Cottage Farm
Meadow Farm
Thursford Collection
HINDRINGHAM RD
GUNTHORPE RD
Little Heath Plantation
HEATH PLANTATION LA
Middle Heath Plantation
HOLT RD
A148
Top Farm
THURSFORD RD
COURT RD
BALL'S LANE
HIGH ST
P
Cemy
5
BARSHAM RD
Great Snoring
Gable End
FAKENHAM RD
LT SNORING RD
Wades Beck Bridge
WALGATE LA
Norton Farm
Lower Farm
NORTH LANE
CLARK'S LA
Lime Kiln Farm
Great Heath Plantation
34
LOWER FARM RD
School Farm
New Covert
Thursford Green
Church Plantation
Thursford
HEATH LANE
PH
BRICK KILN ROAD
4
THE STREET
NORWICH RD
GREAT SNORING RD
THORPLAND RD
Dawes' Covert
Lawn Plantation
Thursford Old Hall
Station Farm
Icehouse Plantation
Station Plantation
MELTON RD
B1354
STATION RD
FAKENHAM RD
NEW RD
Airfield
The Lings
Thursford Wood Nature Reserve
Brookhill Farm
Wood Farm
RECTORY ROW
BARNEY LA
Moat
33
River Stiffkey
Brickkiln Plantation
Barney Wood
Yew Tree Farm
NORTH ROW
THE STREET
Barney
Moat
3
Little Snoring
Church Farm
Little Snoring Com Prim Acad
1 THE WARREN
2 HARES CL
3 OAKLANDS
4 THE CROFT
Forty Acre Plantation
Recreation Gd
Old Hall Farm
Moat
THE HILL
THE BULL CL LA
KETTLESTONE RD
DIXONS PL
THE STREET
BARNEY ROAD
Phillipos Farm
Hill House Farm
Dairy Farm
THE PASTURES
HOLT ROAD
Green Farm
PO
PH
Manor Farm
Grange Farm
32
Sewage Works
THE STREET
BELL CL
LITTLESNORING RD
Kettlestone
FULMODESTON RD
Alethorpe Hall
ORCHARD GR
Croxton
Phillipos Farm
2
A148
THE STREET
HOLBROOK LANE
Croxton Farm
CROXTON ROAD
Field End
PO
PH
Brown's Covert
31
GREEN LA
GREAT RYBURGH RD
SNORING RD
CLIPSTONE LA
St John the Baptist's Chapel
BACK LA
Fulmodeston
HINDOLVESTON ROAD
Wild Wood
STIBBARD ROAD
BARNEY ROAD
PEDLAR'S LANE
Common End
1
Heath Farm
CLIPSTONE
Clipstone House Farm
St Mary's Church (remains of)
PEDLAR'S LANE
30

94 **A** 95 **B** 96 **C** 97 **D** 98 **E** 99 **F**

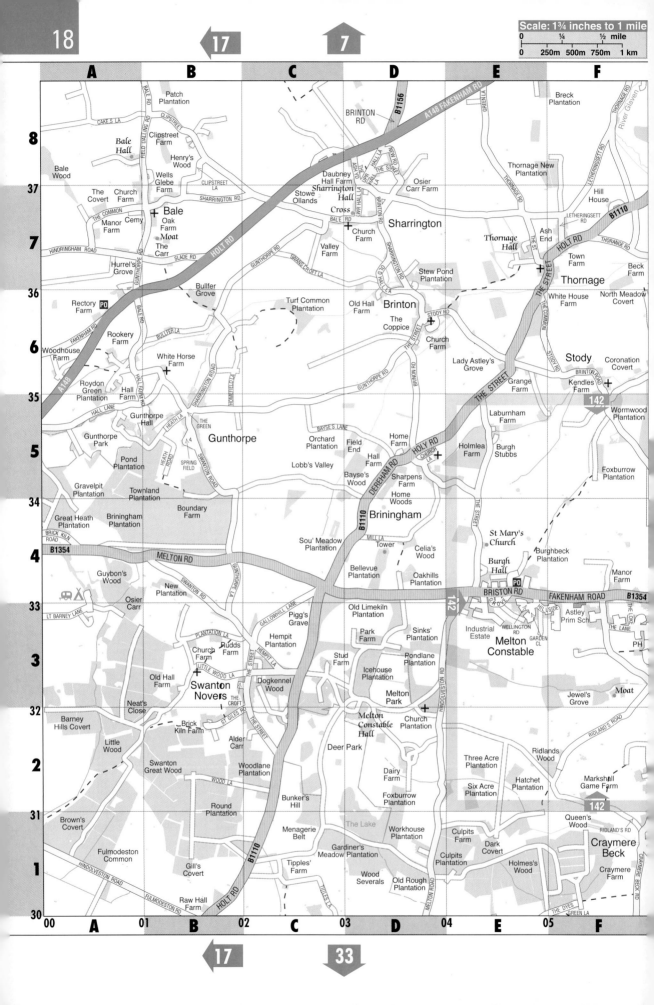

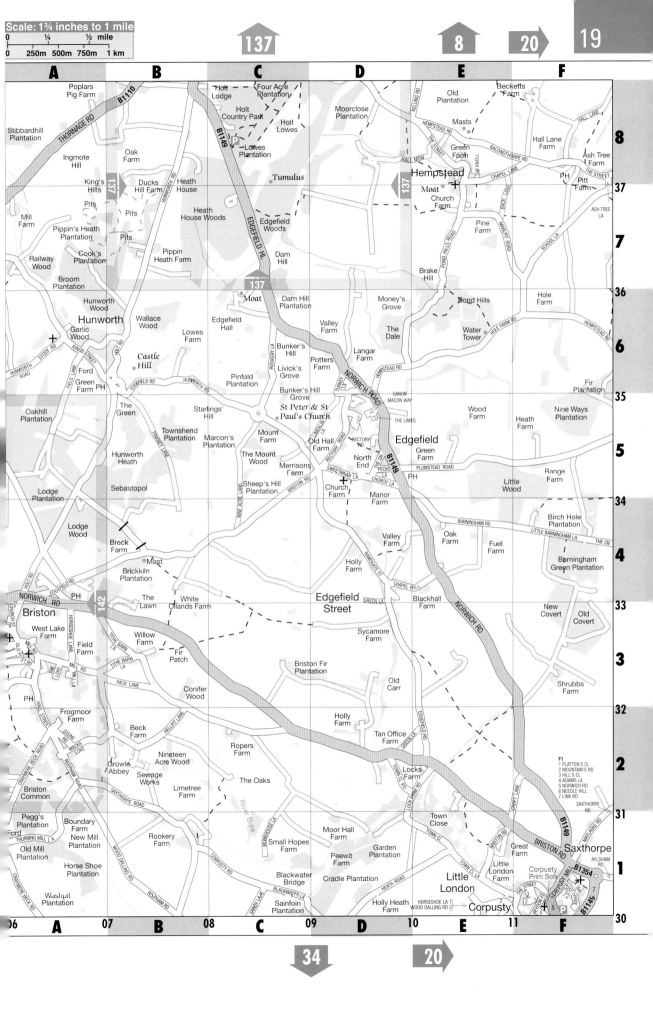

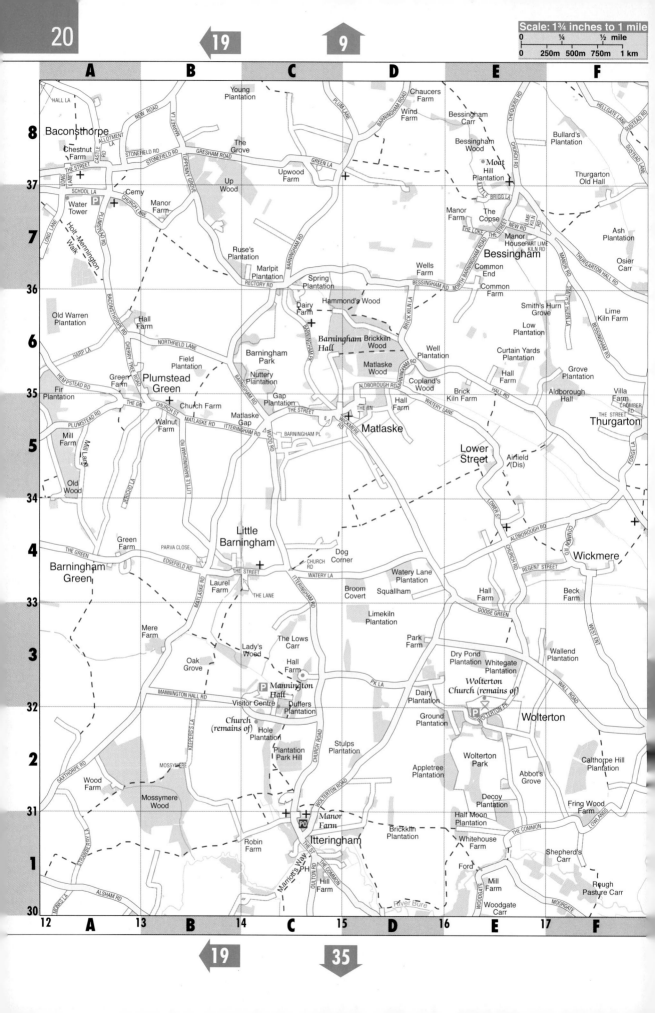

A   B   C   D   E   F

HALL LA

Baconsthorpe
8

New Road
Chestnut Farm
Stonefield Rd
Gresham Road
THE STREET
CASTLE RD
ALLOTMENT
MARKET LA
TUPPENNY GROVE

Young Plantation
The Grove
Upwood Farm
Up Wood
Green La

Chaucers Farm
Wind Farm
BARNINGHAM ROAD
PLUM LANE

Bessingham Carr
Bessingham Wood
CHEQUERS RD
HELLGATE LANE
SUSTEAD RD

Bullard's Plantation

37

Long Lane
SCHOOL LA
Water Tower
P
Cemy
CHURCH LANE
PLUMSTEAD RD

Manor Farm

Moat
Hill Plantation
LITTLE BRIGG LA
CHURCH RD

Thurgarton Old Hall

7

Holt–Mannington Walk
BACONSTHORPE RD

Ruse's Plantation
Marlpit Plantation
RECTORY RD
BARNINGHAM RD

Spring Plantation

Manor Farm
The Copse
NEW RD
LIME KILN
THE STREET
PART LIME KILN RD
THE LOKE

Bessingham
Manor House
MANOR RD
THURGARTON HALL RD

Ash Plantation
Osier Carr

36

Old Warren Plantation
HARP LA
Hall Farm
CHERRY TREE ROAD
Northfield Lane

Dairy Farm
Hammond's Wood
Barningham Hall
Brickkiln Wood
Matlaske Wood
BRICK KILN LA
BESSINGHAM RD
NORTH BARNINGHAM RD

Wells Farm
Common End
Common Farm

Smith's Hurn Grove
Low Plantation
SMITH'S HURN LA

Lime Kiln Farm
BESSINGHAM RD

6

HEMPSTEAD RD
Fir Plantation
Green Farm
Plumstead Green
Field Plantation
Nuttery Plantation
BARNINGHAM RD

Barningham Park
Gap Plantation
Well Plantation
N.LDBOROUGH RD
Copland's Wood

Hall Farm

Curtain Yards Plantation
Grove Plantation

35

PLUMSTEAD RD
Mill Farm
THE GN
Walnut Farm
CHURCH ST
LITTLE BARNINGHAM RD
Matlaske Road
Matlaske Gap
ITTERINGHAM RD
WOOD RD
THE STREET
BARNINGHAM PL

Hall Farm
THE BN
WICKMERE
Matlaske
WATERY LANE

Brick Kiln Farm
HALL RD
Aldborough Hall
CROMBER RD
THE STREET

Villa Farm

Thurgarton

5

Mill Lane
JERICHO LA
Old Wood
Church Farm

Lower Street
Airfield (Dis)
LOWER ST
FORGE LA

34

THE GREEN
Green Farm
PARVA CLOSE
EDGEFIELD RD
MATLASKE RD
LITTLE BARNINGHAM RD

Little Barningham
CHURCH RD
Dog Corner
ITTERINGHAM RD
ALDBOROUGH RD
CHURCH RD

4

Barningham Green
THE STREET
Laurel Farm
THE LANE
WATERY LA

Broom Covert
Squallham
Watery Lane Plantation
REGENT STREET

Hall Farm
GOOSE GREEN

Wickmere
Beck Farm
WEST END

33

Mere Farm
Oak Grove
Lady's Wood
The Lows Carr
Hall Farm
Limekiln Plantation
Park Farm

Dry Pond Plantation
Whitegate Plantation

Wallend Plantation

3

MANNINGTON HALL RD
KEEPERS LA
Mannington Hall
P
Visitor Centre
Duffers Plantation
PK LA

Dairy Plantation
Wolterton Church (remains of)
Ground Plantation
P
WOLTERTON PK

Wolterton
WALL ROAD

32

SAXTHORPE RD
Church (remains of)
Hole Plantation
Plantation Park Hill
Stulps Plantation
MOSSYMERE
CHURCH ROAD
WOLTERTON ROAD

Wolterton Park
Appletree Plantation
Abbot's Grove

Calthorpe Hill Plantation

2

Wood Farm
Mossymere Wood
Robin Farm
MARRIOTT'S WAY
THE ST
OULTON RD
PO
PH
Manor Farm
Itteringham
Hill Farm
WOLTERTON ROAD
THE COMMON
River Bure

Brickkiln Plantation
Half Moon Plantation
Whitehouse Farm
Ford
Decoy Plantation
Half Moon Plantation
WOODGATE
MOORGATE

Fring Wood Farm
Shepherd's Carr
LOWLANDS
THE COMMON

1

STRAWBERRY LA
MONKS LA
ALSHAM RD

Mill Farm
Woodgate Carr

Rough Pasture Carr

30

12   A   13   B   14   C   15   D   16   E   17   F

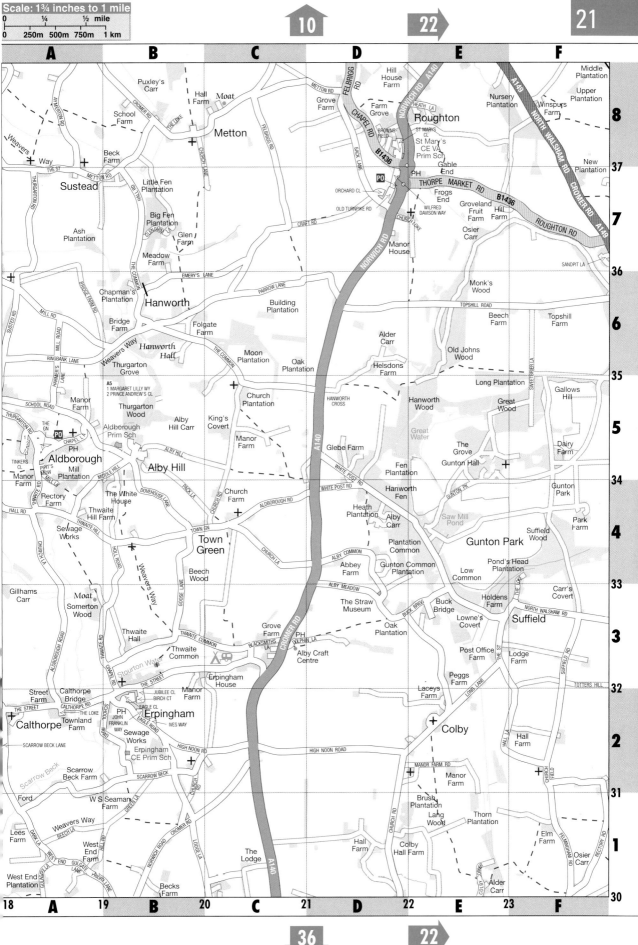

Scale: 1¾ inches to 1 mile

0   ¼   ½   mile
0   250m   500m   750m   1 km

| A | B | C | D | E | F |

8
37
7
36
6
35
5
34
4
33
3
32
2
31
30

Middle Plantation
Upper Plantation
Winspurs Farm
New Plantation

Puxley's Carr
Hall Farm
Moat
Hill House Farm
Grove Farm
Farm Grove
Nursery Plantation

School Farm
Metton
Roughton
St Marys CL
St Mary's CE VA Prim Sch
Gable End
PH

Weavers Way
Beck Farm
Little Fen Plantation
PO
THORPE MARKET RD
B1436
Frogs End
Groveland Fruit Farm
Hill Farm

Sustead
Big Fen Plantation
Glen Farm
ORCHARD CL
OLD TURNPIKE RD
WILFRED DAVISON WAY
Osier Carr
SANDPIT LA

Ash Plantation
Meadow Farm
CRAFT RD
Manor House
Monk's Wood

Chapman's Plantation
EMERY'S LANE
PARROW LANE
Topshill Road
Beech Farm
Topshill Farm

Hanworth
Bridge Farm
Folgate Farm
Building Plantation
Alder Carr
Old Johns Wood

Weavers Way
Hanworth Hall
Moon Plantation
Oak Plantation
Helsdons Farm
Long Plantation
Gallows Hill

Thurgarton Grove
THE COMMON
Hanworth CROSS
Hanworth Wood
Great Wood
SWETBRIER LA

Manor Farm
A5 1 MARGARET LILLY WY 2 PRINCE ANDREW'S CL
Church Plantation
Great Water
The Grove
Dairy Farm

SCHOOL ROAD
Thurgarton Wood
Alby Hill Carr
King's Covert
Glebe Farm
Gunton Hall
Gunton Park

Aldborough Prim Sch
Manor Farm
Fen Plantation
Great Water
Park Farm

Aldborough
Mill Plantation
Alby Hill
Church Farm
WHITE POST RD
Hanworth Fen
Saw Mill Pond
Suffield Wood

Manor Farm
Rectory Farm
The White House
ALDBOROUGH RD
Heath Plantation
Alby Carr
Gunton Park

Sewage Works
Thwaite Hill Farm
TOWN GN
Town Green
Plantation Common
Gunton Common Plantation
Low Common
Pond's Head Plantation
Carr's Covert

Gillhams Carr
Moat
Somerton Wood
Beech Wood
ALBY MEADOW
Abbey Farm
The Straw Museum
Buck Bridge
Holdens Farm
NORTH WALSHAM RD
Suffield

Thwaite Hall
THWAITE COMMON
Thwaite Common
Grove Farm
PH DOLPHIN LA
Oak Plantation
BUCK BRIGG
Lowne's Covert
Post Office Farm
Lodge Farm

Stourton Water
Erpingham House
BLACKSMITHS LA
Alby Craft Centre
Peggs Farm
TOTTERS HILL

Street Farm
Calthorpe Bridge
JUBILEE CL BIRCH CT
Manor Farm
Laceys Farm
Hall Farm

Calthorpe
Townland Farm
PH JOHN FRANKLIN WAY
EAGLE CL
IVES WAY
Erpingham
HIGH NOON RD
HIGH NOON ROAD
Colby

SCARROW BECK LANE
Sewage Works
Erpingham CE Prim Sch
MANOR FARM RD
Manor Farm
CHURCH FIELD

Scarrow Beck Farm
SCARROW BECK
Brush Plantation
Lang Wood
Thorn Plantation
Elm Farm

Ford
W S Seaman Farm
Hall Farm
Colby Hall Farm
Osier Carr

Lees Farm
Weavers Way
West End Farm
The Lodge
Alder Carr

West End Plantation
Becks Farm

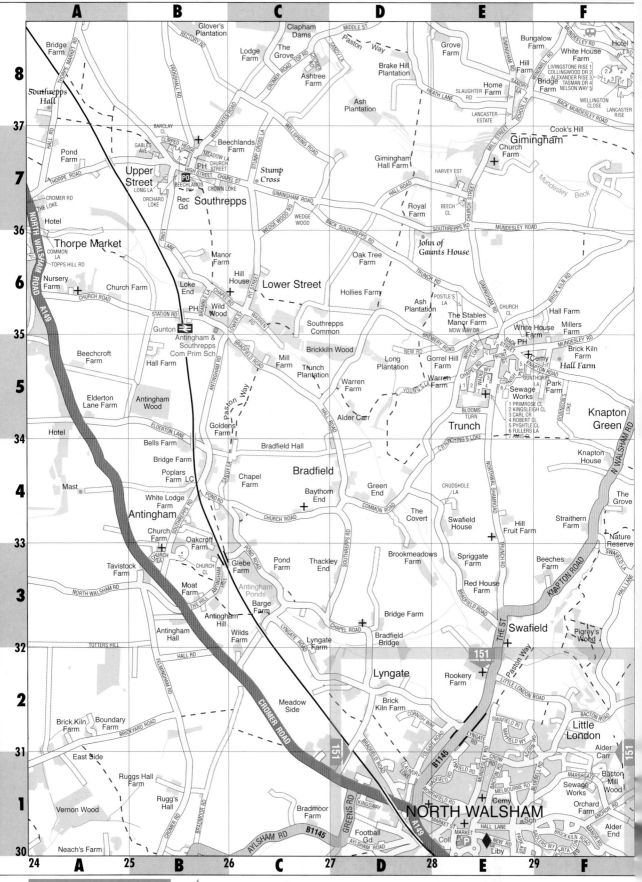

A B C D E F

8

37

7

36

6

35

5

34

4

33

3

32

2

31

1

30

24   A   25   B   26   C   27   D   28   E   29   F

Southrepps Hall

Bridge Farm

THORPE MARKET RD

HALL RD

Pond Farm

CROMER RD

THE LOKE

Hotel

Thorpe Market

COMMON LA

TOPPS HILL RD

Nursery Farm

Church Farm

CHURCH ROAD

NORTH WALSHAM ROAD

A149

Beechcroft Farm

Hall Farm

Elderton Lane Farm

Antingham Wood

ELDERTON LANE

Hotel

Mast

Bells Farm

Bridge Farm

Poplars Farm LC

White Lodge Farm

Antingham

Church Farm

CHURCH LA

Oakcroft Farm

CHURCH CL

THE HILL

ANTINGHAM HILL

Moat Farm

Antingham Hall

Wilds Farm

Barge Farm

Antingham Ponds

Glebe Farm

Tavistock Farm

NORTH WALSHAM RD

FELMINGHAM RD

HALL RD

TOTTERS HILL

Brick Kiln Farm

Boundary Farm

BRICKYARD ROAD

East Side

Ruggs Hall Farm

Rugg's Hall

BRADMOOR RD

CROMER ROAD

Vernon Wood

Neach's Farm

Glover's Plantation

RECTORY RD

FROGSHALL RD

Lodge Farm

CROMER ROAD

TOP RD

The Grove

DENMER RD

Ashtree Farm

BARCLAY CL

CLIPPED HEDGE

WHITEGATES ROAD

Beechlands Farm

GABLES AVE

MEADOW LA

HIGH STREET

CHURCH STREET

PH

CHAPEL ST

Upper Street

LONG LA

PO

BEECHLANDS PK

ORCHARD LOKE

Rec Gd

CROWN LOKE

Southrepps

Manor Farm

Loke End

BRAMBLE LA

CHAPEL RD

PIT STREET

Hill House

PH

Wild Wood

LOVERS RD

WARREN RD

STATION RD

Gunton

Antingham & Southrepps Com Prim Sch

ANTINGHAM RD

BRADFIELD ROAD

SANDY LA

Goldens Farm

Paston Way

Chapel Farm

POND RD

Pond Farm

Clapham Dams

MIDDLE ST

SANDY LA

Paston Way

Brake Hill Plantation

HEATH LANE

Ash Plantation

STUMP CROSS LA

WELLSPRING ROAD

Stump Cross

GIMINGHAM ROAD

Gimingham Hall Farm

BACK SOUTHREPPS RD

WEDGE WOOD RD

Lower Street

Southrepps Common

Mill Farm

Trunch Plantation

Brickkiln Wood

HALL ROAD

Warren Farm

Alder Carr

Bradfield Hall

Bradfield

Pond Farm

Baythorn End

Green End

COMMON ROAD

CHURCH ROAD

Thackley End

SOUTHREPPS RD

Oak Tree Farm

Hollies Farm

Ash Plantation

POSTLE'S LA

Long Plantation

The Covert

CRUDSHOLE LA

Brookmeadows Farm

Bridge Farm

CHAPEL ROAD

Bradfield Bridge

LYNGATE ROAD

Meadow Side

AYLSHAM RD

B1145

151

GREENS RD

KINGSWAY

Football Gd

AYLSHAM ROAD

B1145

Bradmoor Farm

Grove Farm

MUNDESLEY RD

Bungalow Farm

White House Farm

Hotel

HILL RD

WILL RD

Hill Farm

SCHOOL LA

LIVINGSTONE RISE 1
COLLINGWOOD DR 2
ALEXANDER RISE 3
TASMAN DR 4
NELSON WAY 5

Bridge Farm

WELLINGTON CLOSE

BACK MUNDESLEY ROAD

Lancaster Rise

Cook's Hill

Gimingham

Church Farm

MILL STREET

HARVEY EST

Slaughter Farm

LANCASTER RD

Home Farm

LANCASTER ESTATE

HALL ROAD

Royal Farm

BEECH CL

Mundesley Beck

SOUTHREPPS RD

John of Gaunts House

TRUNCH RD

The Stables Manor Farm

MDW WAY DR

GIMINGHAM RD

CHURCH CL

CHURCH STREET

White House Farm

PH

Hall Farm

Millers Farm

Brick Kiln Farm

Hall Farm

BRICK KILN RD

BACK STREET

FRONT STREET

Cemy

KNAPTON ROAD

Gorrel Hill Farm

Warren Farm

BREWERY ROAD

NEW RD

WRIGHT'S RD

CHAPEL RD

WADS WY

GUNTHORPE RD

YOUNG'S LA

BLOOMS TURN

Sewage Works

1 PRIMROSE CL
2 KINGSLEIGH CL
3 CARL CR
4 ROBERT CL
5 PYGHTLE CL
6 FULLERS LA
7 AMIS CL

Trunch

CRUTCHING'S LOKE

NORTHWAL SHAM ROAD

Spriggate Farm

Swafield House

Hill Fruit Farm

Red House Farm

BRADFIELD ROAD

TRUNCH RD

Park Farm

ROBINSON'S LOKE

Knapton Green

Knapton House

N WALSHAM ROAD

The Grove

Straithern Farm

Nature Reserve

SWAFIELD LA

Beeches Farm

HALL LANE

KNAPTON ROAD

THE ST

Swafield

Pigrey's Wood

151

Paston Way

LITTLE LONDON ROAD

Rookery Farm

Lyngate

Brick Kiln Farm

CORNISH WAY

BRADFIELD ROAD

FOLGATE ROAD

LANDED LOKE

B1145

SWAFIELD RI

LYNGATE RD

CROW RD

MUNDESLEY RD

MELBOURNE RD

MAYFIELD WY

ACORN RD

BLUEBELL RD

Little London

MARSHGATE

Sewage Works

BACTON ROAD

Alder Carr

Bacton Mill Wood

151

N WALSHAM ROAD

ANCHOR RD

Orchard Farm

BRICK KILN ROAD

Alder End

MANOR RD

PARK AVE

MILLERS WY

NORTH WALSHAM

A149

MARKET ST

Cemy

HALL LANE

NEW RD

Coll

Liby

Sch

Scale: 1¾ inches to 1 mile

0 ¼ ½ mile
0 250m 500m 750m 1 km

A B C D E F

8
37
7
36
6
35
5
34
4
33
3
32
2
31
1
30

Cliftonville
SEA VW RD
CROMER ROAD
LINKS ROAD
Liby
Mundesley Maritime Museum
Mundesley
Water Tower
Hotel
HEATH LANE
WARREN DR
HEATH RD
CHURCH LA
HIGH ST
BEACH RD
PO
MEADOW CL
BECKMEAD WY
PASTON RD
Schs
WATER LANE
Stow Mill
Stow Hill Farm
Stow Hill
Holiday Centre
Paston Way
143
B1145
KNAPTON RD
TRUNCH ROAD
MUNDESLEY ROAD
POND LANE
Paston
The Spinney
Knapton
Water Tower
Sewage Works
Church Farm
THE ST
BEARS CHAPEL RD
VICARAGE RD
Great Barn
Hall Farm
BACTON RD
Rookery Plantation
Gas Distribution Station
Mast
Mast
BACTON ROAD
B1159
PASTON RD
PASTON ROAD
COAST ROAD
Beach Rd
Bacton Green
Bacton
CLIFF TOP
PH
Watch House Gap
WODEHOUSE RD
NEWLANDS EST
Bromholm Field End
Lowlands Farm
Church Farm
CHURCH RD
Hall Farm
THE PADDOCKS
GOOCH CL
WATCH HO LA
BROMHOLME
Keswick
ANNE STANNARD WAY
KESWICK RD
BEACH RD
Old Hall Street
Paston Green
Paston Way
Parrs Farm
Church Farm
Croft Farm
CHURCH LANE
Church Farm
RECTORY ROAD
Pollard Street
Grange Farm
SANDY LANE
NORTH WALSHAM RD
Bacton Prim Sch
ST GEORGES CL
Abbey Farm
ABBEY'S STREET
Broomholm
BACK LA
PRIORY RD
WALCOTT RD (COAST RD)
PH
Rudram's Gap
Gap End
ST HELENS RD
HELENA RD
THE CEDARS
B1159
PO
POPLAR DR
COAST RD
Hill Farm
STABLE LA
The Grove
HALL RD
Edingthorpe
WELL STREET
Stories Farm
The Grange
Mill Common
Rookery Farm
Barrington Farm
REED WAY
PH
Dead Man's Grave
Barchams Farm
Heath Farm
Honeytop Farm
Clay Lane Farm
CLAY LANE
THE GREEN
HENNESSEY'S LOKE
BOUNDARY LANE
THE STREET
SCHOOL ROAD
BACTON RD
North Plantation
BRIARY LANE
Ash Tree Farm
Park Farm
OFF BACTON RD
Odessa Farm
Common Farm
Stonebridge Cottage
Selfs Carr
MILL COMMON ROAD
ROOKERY FARM ROAD
Rookery Farm
Edingthorpe Green
Green Farm
Cooper's Covert
WITTON WOODS
Witton Hall
Church Plantation
STONEBRIDGE ROAD
Witton Bridge
BACHELOR'S LANE
HAPPISBURGH ROAD
NORTH WALSHAM RD
Edingthorpe Heath
MILL ROAD
THATCHED COTTAGE RD
Manor Farm
THE GREEN
CHAPEL RD
Church Farm
Ridlington
THE STREET
Bacton Wood
Road Plantation
BACTON ROAD
CROSS WAYS LA
Ivy Farm
HODDLEHOUSE RD
MARSH LOKE
South Side
Spa Common
Muckle Hill Farm
Witton Heath
Philip's Grove
Verona Plantation
Hoole House
Primrose Farm
HALL RD
Ridlington Street
NASH'S LANE
Nashs Farm
OLD LANE
MUNN'S RD
Heath Farm
Ridlington Plantation
Old Hall
OLD RD
NORTH WALSHAM ROAD
Bransmeadow Carr
Tumulus

38 24

For full street detail of the highlighted area see page 143

Scale: 1¾ inches to 1 mile
0   ¼   ½   mile
0   250m 500m 750m 1 km

A   B   C   D   E   F

8

33

Walcott
1 ARCHIBALD RD
2 THE CRESCENT
3 LYNTON RD
4 THE WALKWAY
5 OSTEND PL

7

SEEVIEW CL
Dane End
OSTEND GAP
Ostend
HORIZON VIEWS
OSTEND RD

32

COAST RD

The Chimneys

6

NORTH WALSHAM ROAD
OSTEND ROAD
Church Farm
THE ST
BLACKSMITHS LA
CHURCH ISP
THE HILL
IRB Station
Happisburgh

31

Walcott House
The Spinney
PO
PH
P
BEACH RD
BEACH RD

WALCOTT GW
Walcott Hall
Happisburgh Prim Sch
LIGHTHOUSE LA
LANTERN LANE
Barron Lodge Farm
Littlewood Farm
Seacroft Farm
PH
Happisburgh Lighthouse
LIGHTHOUSE CL

5

MILL LA
HILL SIXTY
GRUB STREET
WHIMPWELL ST

B1159
Old

Summers Farm
PH
Hill Farm
UPTON WAY
WHIMPWELL
WROXHAM WAY
DOGGETTS LA
P

30

HALL LANE
Water Tower
Hall Farm
Holly Farm
39
Cart Gap
CROWDEN RD

East Ruston Hall
GRUB STREET
Manor Farm
Whimpwell Green
CART GAP RD
Green Farm
CART GAP ROAD
CART GAP ROAD
Bush Estate
Eccles on Sea
BUSH DR
ABBOTS WY

4

MILL ROAD
Windmill
SHORT LANE
CORONATION CL
Lower Farm
Mill Farm
SEASIDE LANE
CROSS LANE
SUNSET WK 1
HEDGEHOG WK 2
BEACH

29

POUND RD
VICARAGE ROAD
Happisburgh Common
SCHOOL COMMON RD
College Farm
HAPPISBURGH ROAD
Hempstead End
BEACH ROAD
North Gap

East Ruston Old Vicarage Garden
Barney Farm
Moat Moat Farm
Church Farm
Church Farm
CHURCH LANEO
Castle Farm

3

Whittletons Farm
HAPPISBURGH ROAD
Thirsts Farm
Willow Farm
PH
All Saints Sch
SCHOOL RD
HEMPSTEAD ROAD
Hempstead
Beach Farm

BACK LANE
Moat Farm
HIGH ROAD
STAR HILL
Pear Tree Farm
THE STREET
Lessingham
HEATH ROAD

28

Church Farm
Lessingham Manor farm
Grange Farm
Hempstead Heath

Manor Farm
Brunstead Grange
CHAPEL LOKE
INGHAM ROAD
Stone House Farm
COMMON RD
Heath Farm

2

Manor House
INGHAM RD
BRUMSTEAD ROAD
Stonebridge Farm
Ingham Fen
WATER LANE
Ingham Corner
Hempstead Marshes

BACK RD
LONG COMMON
B1159
THE LOKE
Lodge Farm
Orchard Farm
The Carr
White Horse Farm
Manor Farm
Marshlands Farm
Windmill
STALHAM RD

27

OLD RECTORY ROAD
Brunstead Hall
Dairy Plantation
Moat
New Hall
GRUB'S LA
PALLING ROAD
Manor House
Causeway Farm
Boundary Farm
HICKLING RD

Brumstead Common
THE AVENUE
Moat Hill Plantation
The Grove
GROVE ROAD
INGHAM CORNER
Junction Farm
SIDNEY ROAD
Bluebell Wood
Randall's Mill
PALLING ROAD
Lound Bridge

1

Home Farm
BRUMSTEAD ROAD
Old Barn Farm
GROVE ROAD
Church Farm
Old Hall

COMMON ROAD

26

36   A   37   B   38   C   39   D   40   E   41   F   4

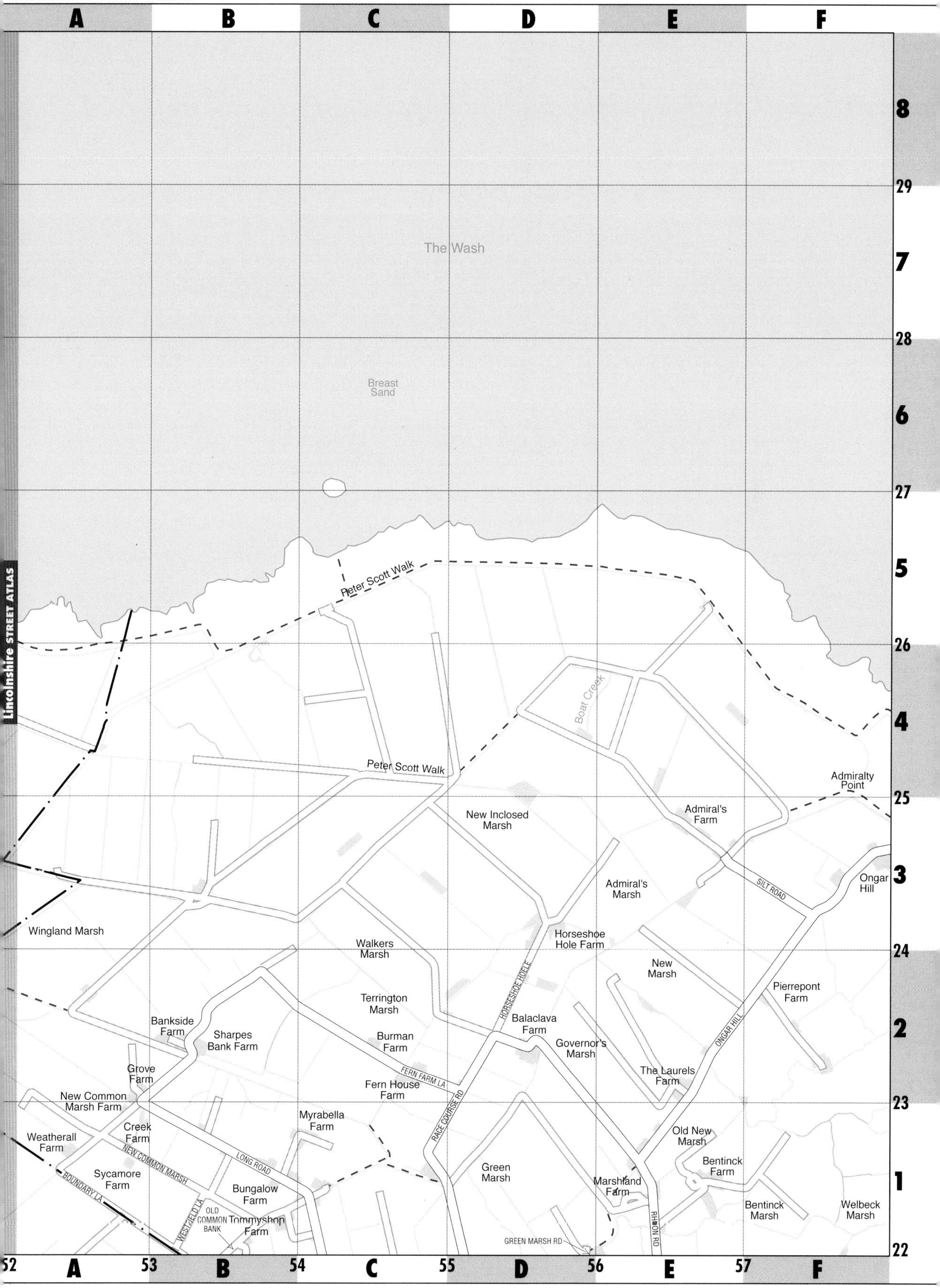

A   B   C   D   E   F

8

29

7

28

The Wash

6

Breast
Sand

27

5

Peter Scott Walk

26

4

Boat Creek

Peter Scott Walk

Admiralty
Point

25

New Inclosed
Marsh

Admiral's
Farm

Admiral's
Marsh

SILT ROAD

Ongar
Hill

3

Wingland Marsh

Walkers
Marsh

Horseshoe
Hole Farm

New
Marsh

24

Pierrepont
Farm

Terrington
Marsh

HORSESHOE HOLE

Balaclava
Farm

Governor's
Marsh

ONGAR HILL

2

Bankside
Farm

Sharpes
Bank Farm

Burman
Farm

The Laurels
Farm

Grove
Farm

FERN FARM LA

Fern House
Farm

RACE COURSE RD

New Common
Marsh Farm

Myrabella
Farm

Old New
Marsh

23

Creek
Farm

Bentinck
Farm

Weatherall
Farm

Green
Marsh

Marshland
Farm

NEW COMMON MARSH

Sycamore
Farm

LONG ROAD

RHON RD

Bentinck
Marsh

Welbeck
Marsh

1

BOUNDARY LA

Bungalow
Farm

WESTFIELD LA

OLD
COMMON
BANK

Tommyshop
Farm

GREEN MARSH RD

22

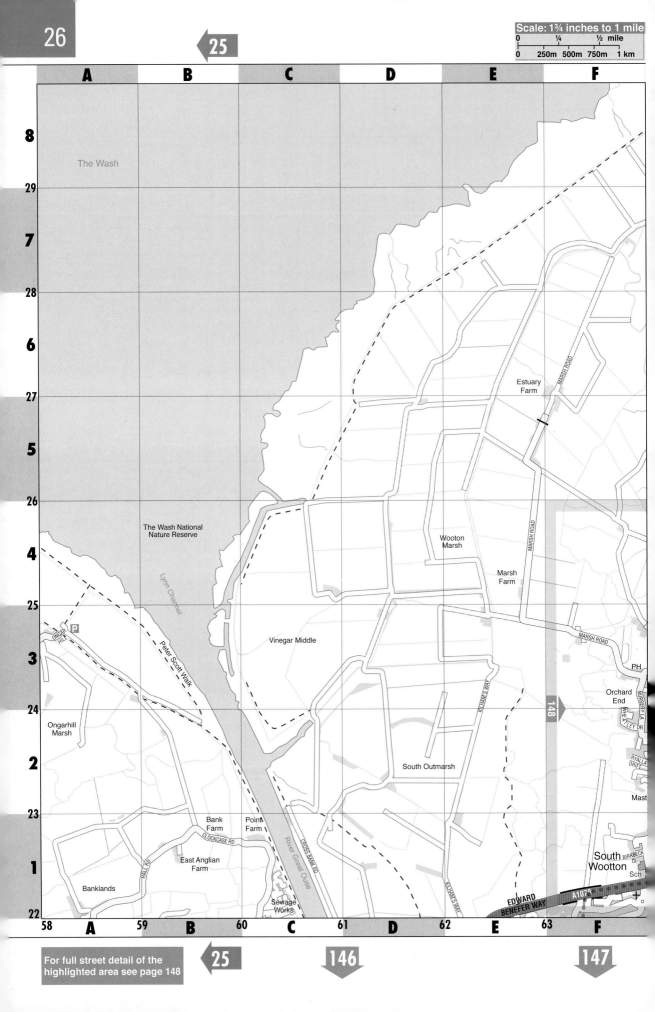

A   B   C   D   E   F

8

29

7

28

6

27

5

26

4

25

3

24

2

23

1

22

The Wash

The Wash National
Nature Reserve

Lynn Channel

Estuary
Farm

MARSH ROAD

Wooton
Marsh

Marsh
Farm

MARSH ROAD

MARSH ROAD

ONGAR HILL

P

Peter Scott Walk

Vinegar Middle

KILHAM'S WAY

148

Orchard
End

PH

NURSERY LA

WHEATLEY DR

RYALLA
DRIFT

Ongarhill
Marsh

South Outmarsh

Mast

Bank
Farm

Point
Farm

CLOCKCASE RD

HALL RD

East Anglian
Farm

Banklands

Sewage
Works

CROSS BANK RD

River Great Ouse

KILHAM'S WAY

South
Wootton

BIRKBECK
CL

Sch

EDWARD BENEFER WAY

A1075

58   A   59   B   60   C   61   D   62   E   63   F

For full street detail of the
highlighted area see page 148

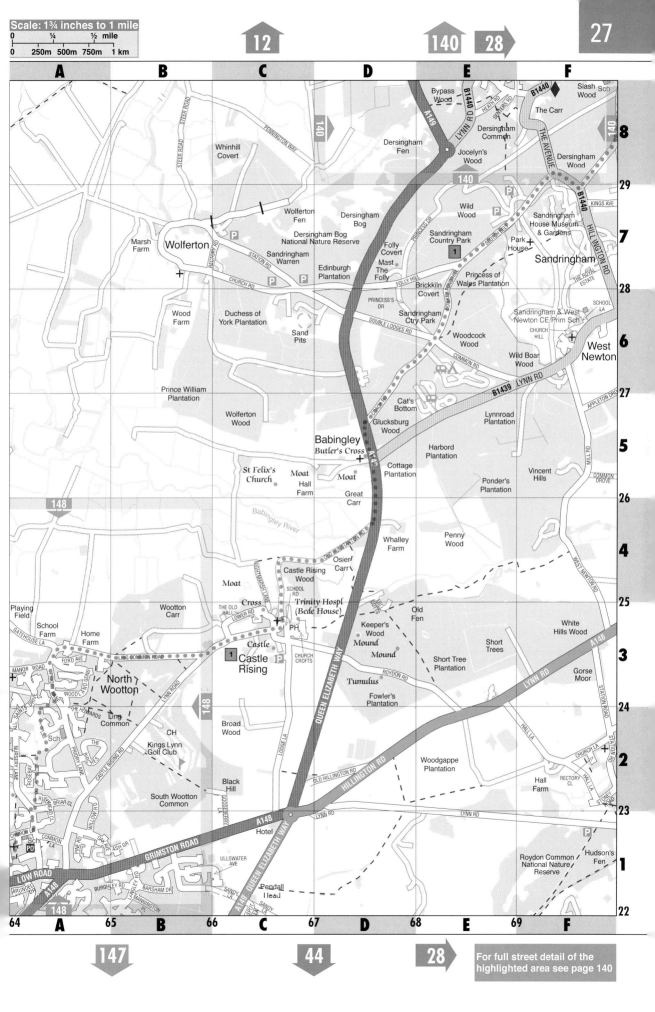

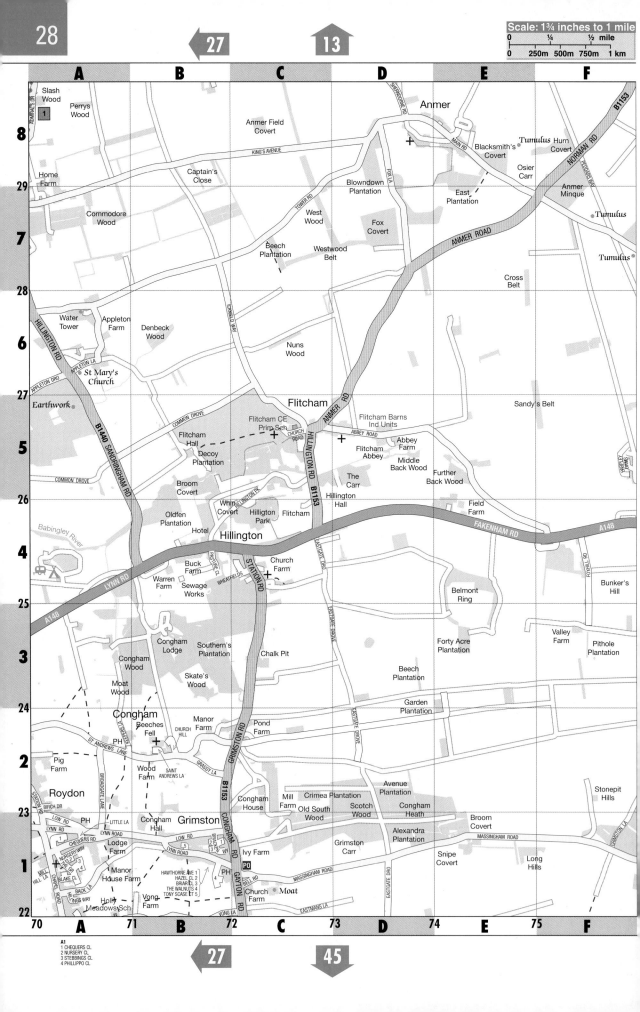

A B C D E F

8

Slash Wood
1

Perrys Wood

Anmer

Anmer Field Covert

King's Avenue

Blacksmith's Covert

Tumulus Hurn Covert

B1153

NORMAN RD

29

Home Farm

Captain's Close

Blowndown Plantation

East Plantation

Osier Carr

Anmer Minque

7

Commodore Wood

West Wood

Fox Covert

Anmer Road

Tumulus

TOWER RD

FOX LA

MAIN RD

SHERNBORNE RD

PEDDARS WAY

Beech Plantation

Westwood Belt

Cross Belt

Tumulus

28

Water Tower

Appleton Farm

Denbeck Wood

Nuns Wood

HILLINGTON RD

IDONALD WAY

6

St Mary's Church

Flitcham

Flitcham Barns Ind Units

Sandy's Belt

27

Earthwork

COMMON DROVE

Flitcham CE Prim Sch

Abbey Road

WARPLEY DMMS

B1440 SANDRINGHAM RD

APPLETON DRO

APPLETON LA

Flitcham Hall

Decoy Plantation

CHURCH ROAD

Flitcham Abbey

Abbey Farm

Middle Back Wood

Further Back Wood

ANMER RD

5

COMMON DROVE

Broom Covert

The Carr

26

Babingley River

Oldfen Plantation

Whin Covert

Hilligton Park

Flitcham

Hillington Hall

Field Farm

HILLINGTON PK

Hotel

B1153

Hillington

FAKENHAM RD

A148

4

LYNN RD

Buck Farm

Warren Farm

Sewage Works

PASTURE CL

WHEATFIELDS

STATION RD

Church Farm

EASTGATE DRO

Belmont Ring

Bunker's Hill

A148

25

Congham Lodge

Southern's Plantation

Chalk Pit

Forty Acre Plantation

Valley Farm

Pithole Plantation

3

Congham Wood

Skate's Wood

Beech Plantation

EASTGATE DRIVE

Moat Wood

Garden Plantation

24

Congham

Manor Farm

Pond Farm

EASTGATE DRIVE

IVY SHEEPS

ST ANDREWS LANE

Beeches Fell

CHURCH HILL

GRIMSTON RD

Stonepit Hills

2

Pig Farm

Wood Farm

SAINT ANDREWS LA

GRASSY LA

Avenue Plantation

BROADGATE LANE

Roydon

Congham House

Mill Farm

Crimea Plantation

Old South Wood

Scotch Wood

Congham Heath

CONGHAM RD

B1153

23

BIRCH DR

STATION RD

PH

LITTLE LA

Congham Hall

Grimston

LOW RD

LOW RD

Broom Covert

LOW RD

LYNN RD

CHEQUERS RD

LYNN ROAD

Lodge Farm

LYNN ROAD

BRACK CL

Grimston Carr

Alexandra Plantation

MASSINGHAM ROAD

GRIMSTON LA

1

NURSERY WAY

Manor House Farm

HAWTHORNE AVE 1
HAZEL CL 2
BRIAR CL 3
THE WALNUTS 4
TONY SCASE CT 5

PH

Ivy Farm

PO

GATTON RD

Snipe Covert

Long Hills

BLAKE CL

HILL LA

CHAPEL RD

BACK RD

KINGS WAY

Holly Meadows Sch

Vong Farm

Church Farm

Moat

MASSINGHAM ROAD

GELL RD

EASTGATE DRO

22

VONG LA

EASTMANS LA

70 A 71 B 72 C 73 D 74 E 75 F

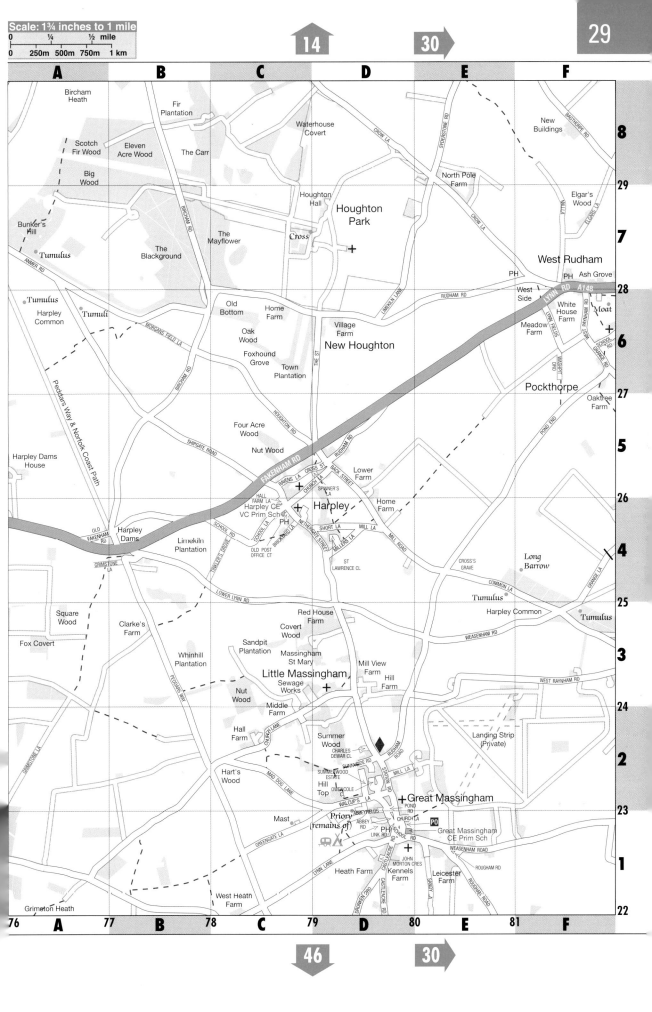

Scale: 1¾ inches to 1 mile

0   ¼   ½ mile
0   250m   500m   750m   1 km

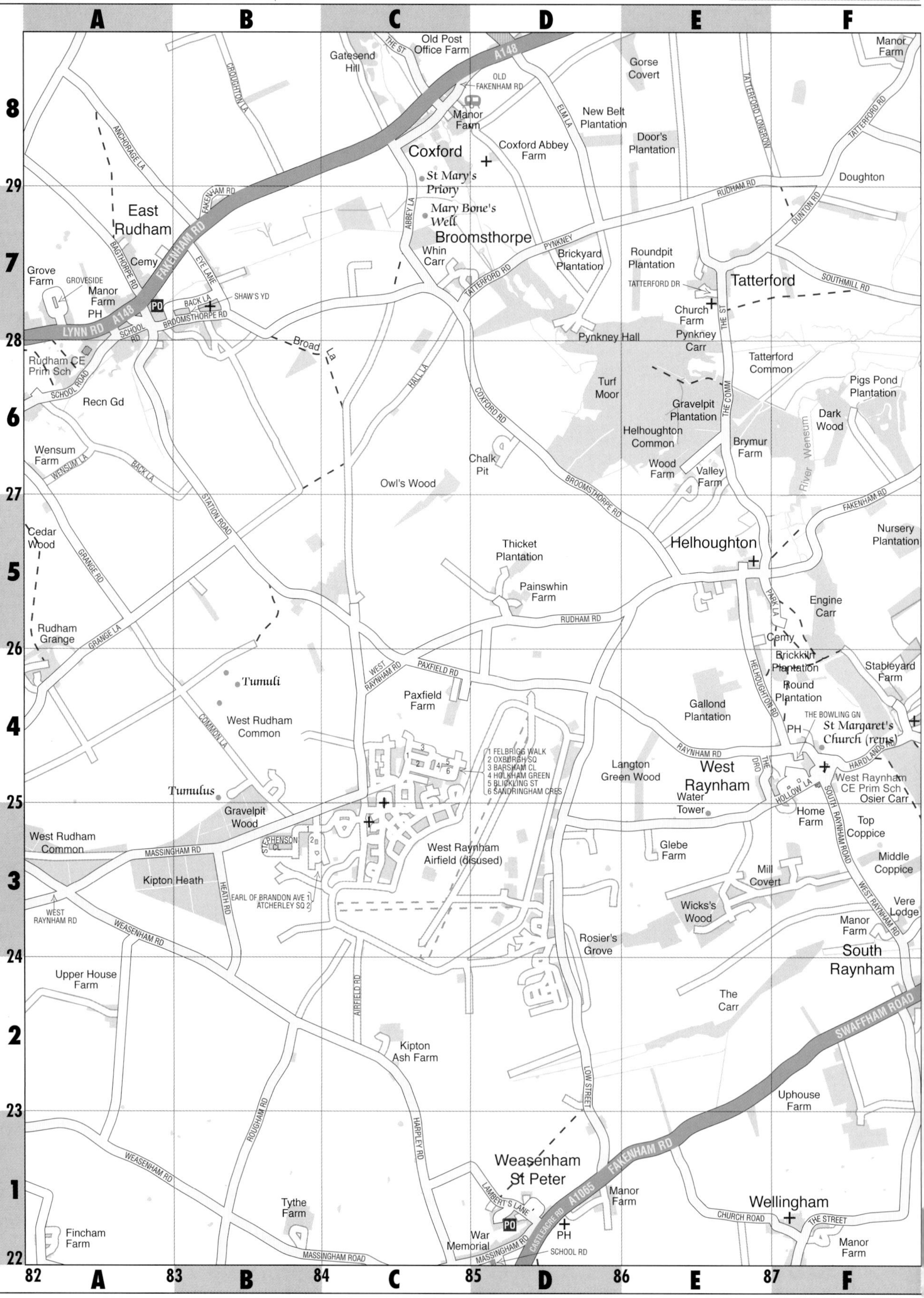

A B C D E F

8

29

7

28

6

27

5

26

4

25

3

24

2

23

1

22

Old Post Office Farm
Gatesend Hill
THE ST
CROUGHTON LA
A148
OLD FAKENHAM RD
Manor Farm
Coxford
St Mary's Priory
Mary Bone's Well
Broomsthorpe
Whin Carr
ELM LA
Coxford Abbey Farm
New Belt Plantation
Gorse Covert
Door's Plantation
Manor Farm
Doughton
TATTERFORD LONG ROW
TUNTON RD

East Rudham
ANCHORAGE LA
Cemy
FAKENHAM RD
EYE LANE
SHAW'S YD
Grove Farm
GROVESIDE
Manor Farm PH
P0
BACK LA
BROOMSTHORPE RD
LYNN RD
A148
SCHOOL RD
Rudham CE Prim Sch
Recn Gd
BROAD LA
HALL LA
Broad La
TATTERFORD RD
COXFORD RD
Brickyard Plantation
PYNKNEY
Pynkney Hall
Turf Moor
Gravelpit Plantation
Helhoughton Common
Wood Farm
Valley Farm
Roundpit Plantation
TATTERFORD DR
Church Farm
Pynkney Carr
Tatterford
SOUTHMILL RD
Tatterford Common
Pigs Pond Plantation
Dark Wood
Brymur Farm
THE ST
THE COMM
RUDHAM RD
River Wensum
FAKENHAM RD
Nursery Plantation

Wensum Farm
WENSUM LA
BACK LA
STATION ROAD
GRANGE RD
Cedar Wood
Rudham Grange
GRANGE LA
COMMON LA
Owl's Wood
Chalk Pit
Thicket Plantation
Painswhin Farm
RUDHAM RD
Helhoughton
Engine Carr
Cemy
PACK LA
Brickkiln Plantation
Stableyard Farm

Tumuli
West Rudham Common
Tumulus
Gravelpit Wood
WEST RAYNHAM RD
Paxfield Farm
PAXFIELD RD
1 FELBRIGG WALK
2 OXBURGH SQ
3 BARSHAM CL
4 HOLKHAM GREEN
5 BLICKLING ST
6 SANDRINGHAM CRES
Langton Green Wood
Gallond Plantation
Round Plantation
RAYNHAM RD
West Raynham
Water Tower
THE BOWLING GN
PH
St Margaret's Church (rems)
West Raynham CE Prim Sch
Osier Carr
HELHOUGHTON RD
HARDLANDS RD
Top Coppice
Middle Coppice
Vere Lodge
Manor Farm
South Raynham

West Rudham Common
MASSINGHAM RD
Kipton Heath
HEATH RD
STEPHENSON CL
EARL OF BRANDON AVE 1
ATCHERLEY SQ 2
West Raynham Airfield (disused)
Glebe Farm
Wicks's Wood
Mill Covert
Home Farm
THE HOLLOW LA
SOUTH RAYNHAM ROAD
WEST RAYNHAM RD
WEASENHAM RD
Upper House Farm
Rosier's Grove
The Carr
Manor Farm

ROUGHAM RD
AIRFIELD RD
HARPLEY RD
Kipton Ash Farm
LOW STREET
SWAFFHAM ROAD
Uphouse Farm
FAKENHAM RD

WEASENHAM RD
Tythe Farm
War Memorial
P0
Weasenham St Peter
LAMBERT'S LANE
CASTLEACRE RD
A1065
Manor Farm
PH
SCHOOL RD
CHURCH ROAD
Wellingham
THE STREET
Fincham Farm
MASSINGHAM ROAD
Manor Farm

82 83 84 85 86 87

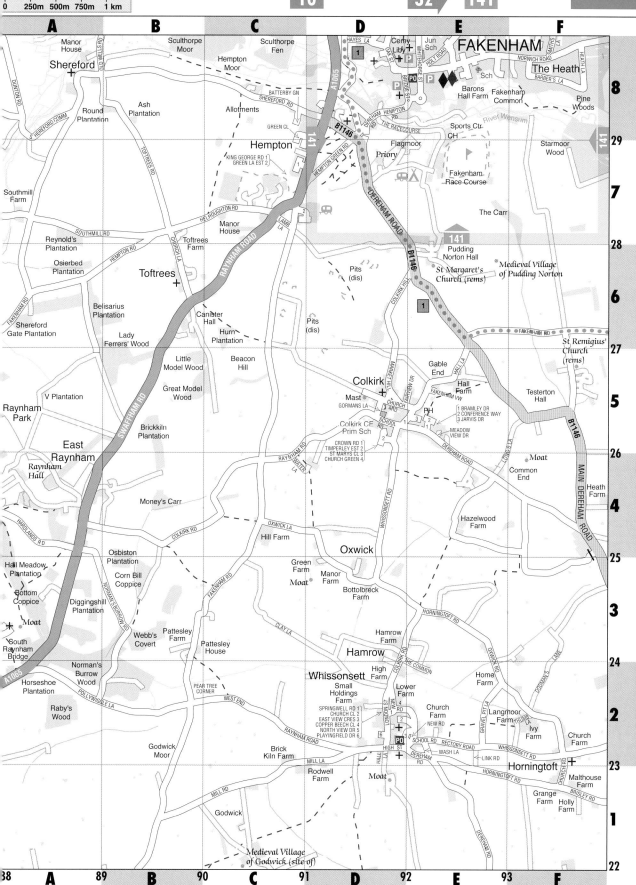

A B C D E F

Manor House
Shereford
Sculthorpe Moor
Sculthorpe Fen
Hempton Moor
HAYES LA
Cemy
Liby
Jun Sch
FAKENHAM
NORWICH ROAD
The Heath

8

Round Plantation
Ash Plantation
Allotments
SHEREFORD RD
GREEN CL
BATTERBY GN
Barons Hall Farm
Fakenham Common
Pine Woods
Sch
BARBER'S LA

Southmill Farm
Reynold's Plantation
King George Rd 1
Green La Est 2
Hempton
Flagmoor
Priory
Sports Ctr
CH
River Wensum
Starmoor Wood

29

141

7

Osierbed Plantation
Hempton Rd
Toftrees Farm
Manor House
Helhoughton Road
Lamb La
DEREHAM ROAD
Fakenham Race Course
The Carr

28

Shereford Gate Plantation
Belisarius Plantation
Toftrees
Canister Hall
Hurn Plantation
Pits (dis)
B1146
Pudding Norton Hall
Medieval Village of Pudding Norton

St Margaret's Church (rems)

6

V Plantation
Lady Ferrers' Wood
Little Model Wood
Great Model Wood
Beacon Hill
Pits (dis)
FAKENHAM RD
St Remigius' Church (rems)

27

Raynham Park
Brickkiln Plantation
Colkirk
Mast
GORMANS LA
Gable End
Hall Farm
HALL LA
FAKENHAM VW
Testerton Hall

5

East Raynham
Raynham Hall
SWAFFHAM RD
Colkirk CF Prim Sch
SCHOOL RD
PH
3
1 BRAMLEY DR
2 CONFERENCE WAY
3 JARVIS DR
MEADOW VIEW DR
Moat
B1146

26

Hall Meadow Plantation
Osbiston Plantation
Money's Carr
CROWN RD 1
TIMPERLEY EST 2
ST MARYS CL 3
CHURCH GREEN 4
WHISSONSETT RD
Common End
Heath Farm
MAIN DEREHAM ROAD

4

Bottom Coppice
Moat
Corn Bill Coppice
COLKIRK RD
OXWICK LA
Hill Farm
Oxwick
Hazelwood Farm

25

Diggingshill Plantation
NORMAN'S BURROW RD
Green Farm
Moat
Manor Farm
Bottolbreck Farm
HORNINGTOFT RD

3

South Raynham Bridge
Webb's Covert
Pattesley Farm
Pattesley House
CLAY LA
Hamrow Farm
Hamrow
High Farm
Home Farm

24

A1065
Norman's Burrow Wood
PEAR TREE CORNER
WEST END
Whissonsett
Small Holdings Farm
Lower Farm
Langmoor Farm
Ivy Farm

Horseshoe Plantation
Raby's Wood
POLLYWIGGLE LA
RAYNHAM ROAD
SPRINGWELL RD 1
CHURCH CL 2
EAST VIEW CRES 3
COPPER BEECH CL 4
NORTH VIEW DR 5
PLAYINGFIELD DR 6
NEW RD
Church Farm
RECTORY ROAD
WHISSONSETT RD
Church Farm

2

Godwick Moor
Brick Kiln Farm
MILL LA
Rodwell Farm
Moat
HIGH ST
DEREHAM RD
SCHOOL RD
WASH LA
LINK RD
Horningtoft
Malthouse Farm
BRISLEY RD

23

MILL RD
Godwick
Medieval Village of Godwick (site of)
HORNINGTOFT RD
DEREHAM RD
Grange Farm
Holly Farm

1

22

A B C D E F
38 89 90 91 92 93

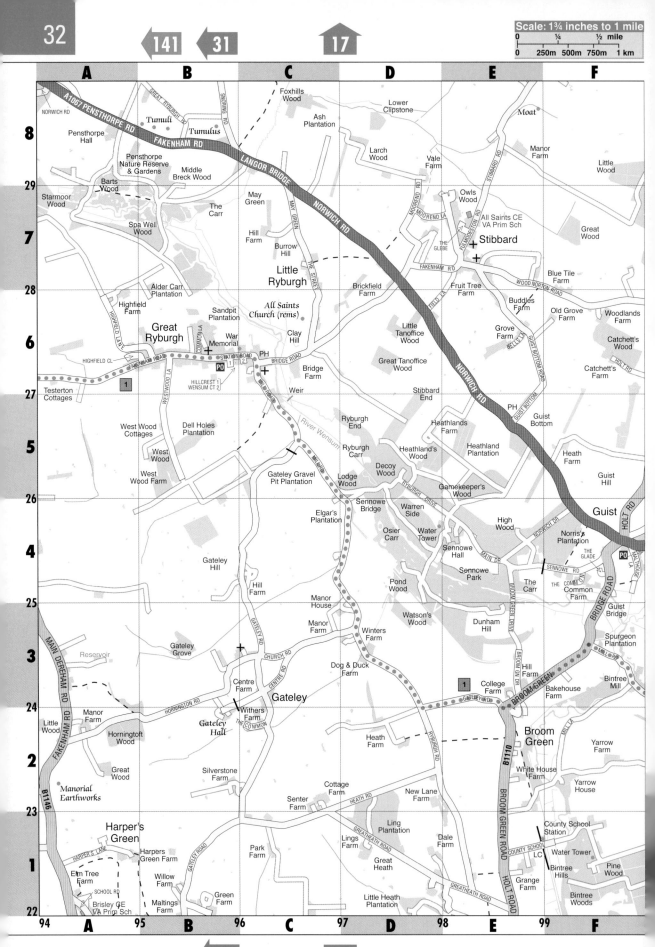

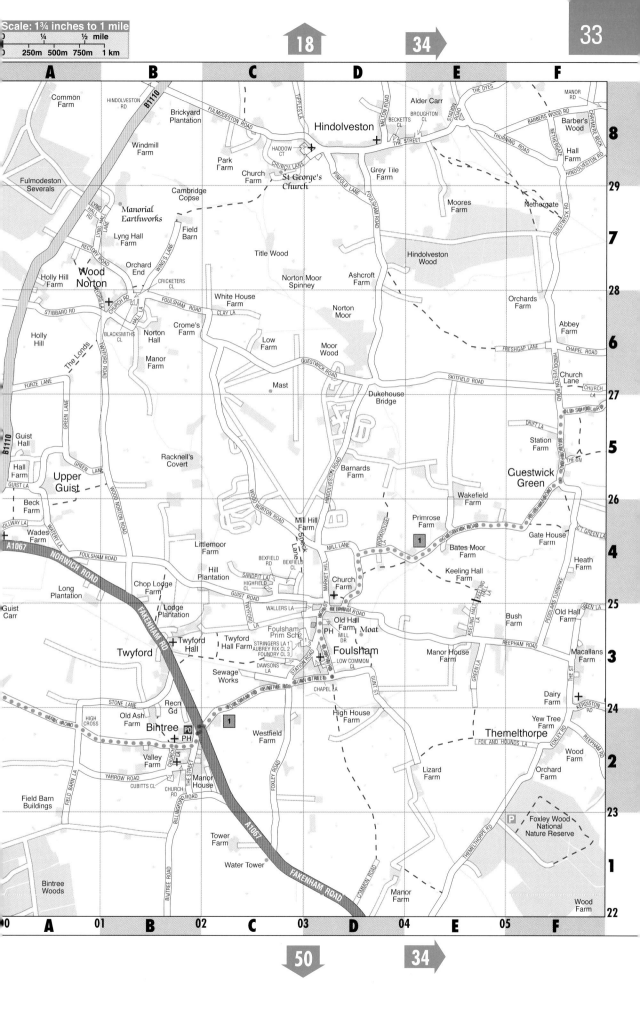

A B C D E F

8
MANOR RD
CRAYMERE BECK RD
Burnt House Farm
Roundabout Farm
Thurning Wood
HEPHAM ROAD
WOOD DALLING RD
SANDY LANE
Conifer Plantation
Blackwater Plantation
Black Water
HEATH
BLACKWATER LANE
Coconut Grove
WOOD DALLING RD
Leechpit Plantation
Valley Farm
HORSESHOE LA
ADAMS LA
IRMINGLAND RD
POST OFFICE
Ivy Farm
MONK'S RD
B1149
NORWICH RD
HOLT RD

29
HINDOLVESTON ROAD
Icehouse Plantation
Gravelpit Plantation
Hall Farm
Ash Carr
Low Carr
Thurning
Victoria Farm
CORPUSTY ROAD
Bell's Grove
Corpusty Hill
VALLEY RD
HEYDON RD

7
BRAY'S LANE
Manor Farm
Wade's Carr
Foundry Hill
Wiggets Farm
TEN ACRE LA
WIGGETS LA
RED PITS
Moat Farm
NORTON CORNER
CRABGATE LANE NORTH
Red Pits
Oak Grove
Grove Farm
BLACKWATER LA
Dairy Farm
Cropton Hall
Massingham's Grove
Bullock Shed Plantation
HOLT RD

28
James Wood
Page's Farm
Tyby
CROW HILL
BSTON ROAD
Glebe Farm
Norton Corner
BACK ROAD
Moat
Palm Farm
Woodhouse Farm
FRONT ROAD
PROSPECT LA
Grove End
HEYDON LANE
Holly Grove
GROVE LA
Cross
Icehouse Plantation
Heydon Hall
The Grove

6
Moat
CHURCH RD
CHURCH LA
Old Hall
WOOD DALLING ROAD
GUESTWICK RD
Tyby Farm
Blue Tile Farm
TYBY LA
CHURCH HILL
HEYDON ROAD
Wood Dalling
Crabgate Farm
Crabtree Farm
Crabgate
HEYDON RD
HEYDON RD
Heydon
THE STREET
PH
American Plantation

27
Guestwick
Church Farm
OLD SCHOOL RD
Wood Dalling Hall
HALL ROAD
School Farm
REEPHAM ROAD
Low Farm
HOLLY LANE
CRABGATE LA SOUTH
Hill Farm
WATER LA
Cottages
Harold's Grove
Fieldhouse Farm
Brookdish Plantation

5
Seaman's Farm
Odessa Farm
CHURCH LANE
Church Plantation
BURNTHOUSE LA
Home Farm
Hempskey Wood

26
Palgrave Farm
Palgrave Wood
CT GN LA
GREEN LA
BUSTY MILL LANE
George Farm
Newlands Farm
Forest Farm
Potash Wood
Swahhills Plantation
Stinton Hall Farm

4
Thorney Farm
Primrose Farm
NEWLANDS LA
KERDY GREEN LA
KERDYGREEN LA
MERRISON'S LA
Gatehouse Farm
THE STREET
Manor Farm
HEYDON RD
BLUESTONE LA
Manor House

25
OLD HALL LA
LINK RD
Kerdiston
Manor Farm
Salle Moor Hall
Bottom Wood
149
Salle
Water Tower
Salle Park

3
GATEHOUSE LA
Carr Farm
FORWATER ROAD
Blue Tile Farm
Moat
Moat
Upper Barn Farm
WOOD DALLING ROAD
B1145
Bath Plantation

24
KERDISTON ROAD
Old Hall Farm
Marriot's Way
New Plantation
Renpark Farm
HONEY LANE
CAWSTON ROAD
ORCHARD LA
Manor Farm
THE MOOR
Moor Farm

2
FIR LANE
OLD LANE
Wood Farm
BRICK KILN LA
Brick Kiln Farm
The Grove
Pettywell
Grange Farm
149
Reepham
STATION ROAD
NEW ROAD
NORWICH RD
Reepham Moor
Beck Farm
Booton Common Nature Reserve
Booton
149

23
Oaks Farm
Model Cottage Farm
BAWDESWELL RD
Vale Farm
Marriot's Way
MARKET PL
DEREHAM RD
Park Farm
PARK LA
PO
SMUGGLERS LA
Rookery Farm
Reepham Moor
Town Farm
Booton Hall

1
B1145
Hackford Hall
Cemy
Prim Sch
Sch & Coll
MILL ROAD
Whitwell Street
THE STREET
FURZE LANE
Dairy Farm

22
06 A 07 B 08 C 09 D 10 E 11 F

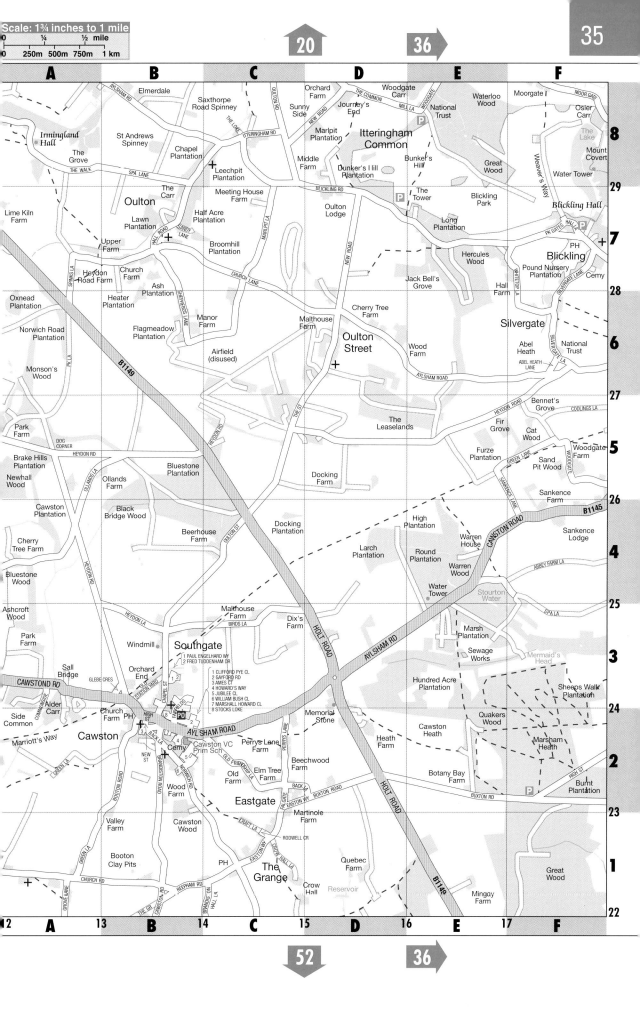

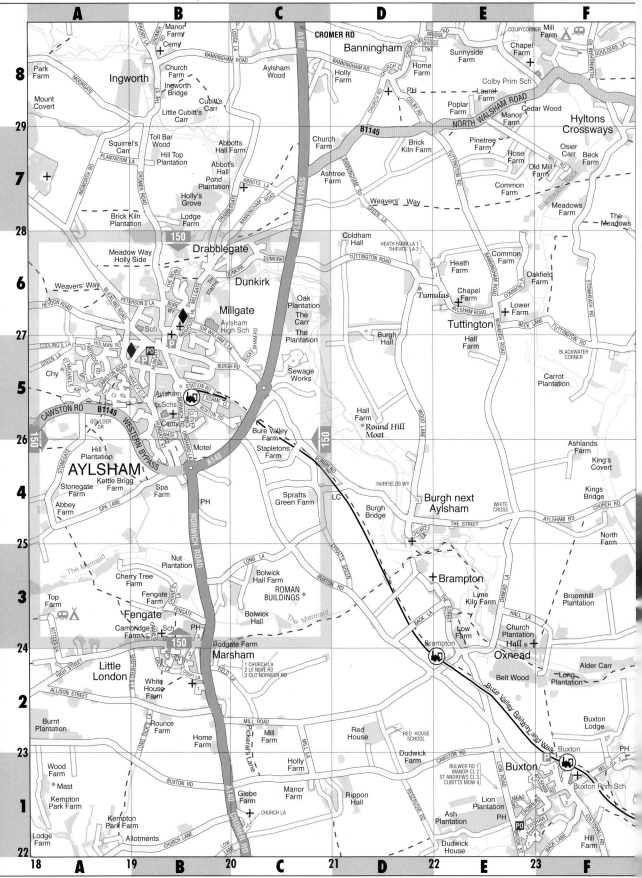

Scale: 1¾ inches to 1 mile

0 ¼ ½ mile
0 250m 500m 750m 1 km

A B C D E F

8
Park Farm
Mount Covert
MOORGATE
Ingworth
PRIORY LA
CROMER LA
Manor Farm
Cemy
Church Farm
Ingworth Bridge
BANNINGHAM ROAD
Cubitt's Carr
Little Cubitt's Carr
Aylsham Wood
LODGE LA
A140
CROMER RD
Banningham
BANNINGHAM RD
Holly Farm
CHURCH RD
CHURCH CL
BRIGGS LOKE
BRIDGE
PH
Home Farm
Sunnyside Farm
COLBYCORNER
Chapel Farm
Mill Farm
GOULDERS LA
FELMINGHAM RD

29
Squirrel's Carr
PLANTATION LA
Toll Bar Wood
Hill Top Plantation
Abbotts Hall Farm
ABBOTS LA
Church Farm
B1145
Ashtree Farm
Brick Kiln Farm
COLBY RD
Poplar Farm
Pinetree Farm
Manor Farm
NORTH WALSHAM ROAD
Laurel Farm
Colby Prim Sch
Cedar Wood
Rose Farm
Old Mill Farm
MILL RD
Osier Carr
Beck Farm
Hyltons Crossways

7
INGWORTH RD
CROMER ROAD
Abbot's Hall Pond Plantation
Holly's Grove
GRABBLEGATE
BANNINGHAM ROAD
AYLSHAM BYPASS
GREEN LA
Weavers' Way
TUTTINGTON RD
Common Farm
BANNINGHAM ROAD
Meadows Farm
Blackwater Beck
The Meadows

28
Brick Kiln Plantation
Lodge Farm
Drabblegate
DUNKIRK
Coldham Hall
HEATH FARM LA 1
THIEVES LA 2
TUTTINGTON ROAD
Heath Farm
Chapel Farm
Common Farm
Oakfield Farm
STOWHEATH RD

6
Meadow Way
Holly Side
THE MEWS
DUNKIRK
THE STAITHE
Dunkirk
Millgate
Aylsham High Sch
Oak Plantation
The Carr
The Plantation
Tumulus
AYLSHAM ROAD
Lower Farm
COMMON LA
BECK LANE
TUTTINGTON RD

27
Weavers' Way
HEYDON ROAD
PETERSON'S LA
BUCKLING ROAD
GASHOUSE HL
MILLGATE
BURE WY
Sch
SIR WILLIAM'S LA
Tuttington
Hall Farm
BLACKWATER CORNER
BECK LANE

5
CODLING'S LA
GREEN LA
ST MICHAELS AVE
HOLMAN RD
PARTRIDGE RD
P
P
BURGH RD
Aylsham Schs
STATION RD
SOAME CL
BUXTON RD
CLOVER
Sewage Works
Burgh Hall
WOOD LANE
Hall Farm
Round Hill Moat
Carrot Plantation

26
CAWSTON RD
B1145
GOULDER DR
WESTERN BYPASS
A140
Cemy
WADE
HUNGATE LA
ORCHARD LA
NORWICH RD
Bure Valley Farm
Stapletons Farm
Motel
150
BURGH RD
FAIRFIELDS WY
Ashlands Farm
King's Covert

4
AYLSHAM
Stonegate Farm
Kettle Brigg Farm
Hill Plantation
Abbey Farm
SPA LANE
Spa Farm
PH
NORWICH ROAD
Spratts Green Farm
LC
Burgh Bridge
Burgh next Aylsham
THE STREET
WHITE CROSS
Kings Bridge
CHURCH RD
AYLSHAM ROAD
North Farm

25
The Mermaid
Nut Plantation
CRANE'S LA
LONG LA
SPRATTS GREEN
BUXTON RD
BACK LA
CHURCH LA
OXNEAD LA
HALL LA
Broomhill Plantation

3
Top Farm
KITTLES LA
Cherry Tree Farm
Fengate Farm
FENGATE
CRANE'S LA
Fengate
ROMAN BUILDINGS
Bolwick Hall Farm
Bolwick Hall
The Mermaid
Brampton
Lime Kiln Farm
Low Farm
Church Plantation
Hall
Oxnead
Alder Carr
Long Plantation

24
HIGH STREET
SHEPHERDS LA
Cambridge Farm
Sch
PH
3
150
NETHER WY
Rodgate Farm
Marsham
1 CHURCH LA
2 LE NEVE RD
3 OLD NORWICH RD
Brampton
Belt Wood
BACK LANE
Buxton Lodge

2
Little London
ALLISON STREET
DUCK RD
White House Farm
CROST LA
FIELD LA
1
MILL ROAD
Mill Farm
Red House
RED HOUSE SCHOOL
CAWSTON RD
Bure Valley Railway and Walk
Buxton
PH

23
Burnt Plantation
Rounce Farm
Home Farm
Pickeral's Lane
MILL LA
Holly Farm
Dudwick Farm
BULWER RD 1
MANOR CL 2
ST ANDREWS CL 3
CUBITTS MDW 4
LION ROAD
P
Buxton
Buxton Prim Sch
MILL ST
5

1
Wood Farm
Mast
Kempton Park Farm
BUXTON RD
Glebe Farm
CHURCH LA
Manor Farm
Rippon Hall
RESERVOIR RD
Ash Plantation
Lion Plantation
PH
MEAD CL
CROMWELL RD
LEVISHAW
PO
BACK LANE
Hill Farm
COLTISHALL RD

22
Lodge Farm
Kempton Park Farm
Allotments
CHURCH LANE
LOW LANE
A140
CROMER RD
Dudwick House
BROOK ST

18 A 19 B 20 C 21 D 22 E 23 F

F1
1 STRACEY RD
2 SEWELL RD
3 DRAKES LOKE
4 CHURCH CL
5 MILL REACH
6 BULWER CL

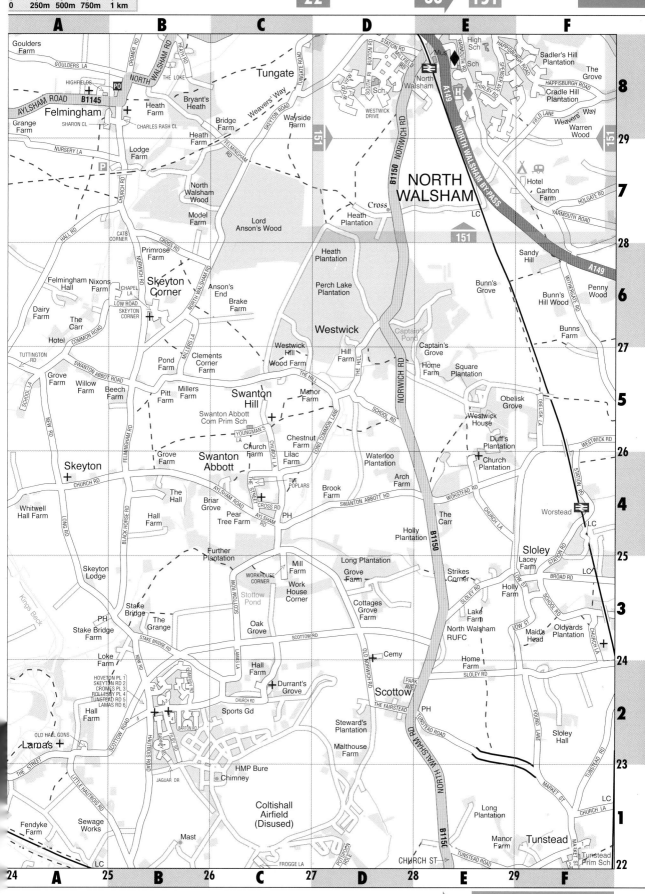

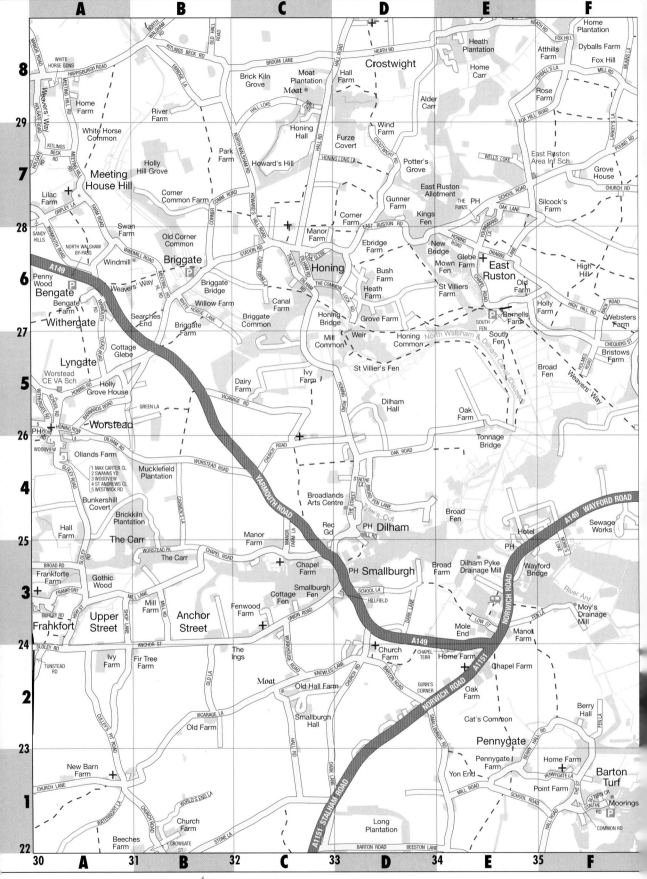

151 37 23

Scale: 1¾ inches to 1 mile
0   ¼   ½ mile
0 250m 500m 750m 1 km

A B C D E F

8
Home Plantation
White Horse Gdns
Home Farm
Heath Plantation
Atthills Farm
Dyballs Farm
Fox Hill
Brick Kiln Grove
Moat Plantation
Moat
Hall Farm
Crostwight
Home Carr
Rose Farm

29
River Farm
White Horse Common
Honing Hall
Wind Farm
Alder Carr
East Ruston Area Inf Sch
Grove House

7
Meeting House Hill
Holly Hill Grove
Park Farm
Howard's Hill
Furze Covert
Potter's Grove
East Ruston Allotment
Wells Loke
Silcock's Farm

Corner Common Farm
Corner Farm
Gunner Farm
Kings Fen
East Ruston
Glebe Farm
High Hill

28
Lilac Farm
Swan Farm
Old Corner Common
Briggate
Manor Farm
Honing
Ebridge Farm
New Bridge
Old Farm
Holly Farm
Websters Farm

Sandy Hills
Windmill
Briggate Bridge
Willow Farm
Bush Farm
Heath Farm
St Villiers Farm
Bornells Farm
Bristows Farm

6
Penny Wood
Bengate
Bengate Farm
Withergate
Searches End
Briggate Farm
Briggate Common
Canal Farm
Honing Bridge
Grove Farm
Honing Common
South Fen
Broad Fen

27
Lyngate
Cottage Glebe
Mill Common
Weir
Honing Common
North Walsham & Dilham Canal (Disused)
Weavers' Way

Worstead CE VA Sch
Holly Grove House
Dairy Farm
Ivy Farm
St Villier's Fen
Dilham Hall
Oak Farm

5
Green La
Vicarage Rd
Tonnage Bridge

26
Worstead
Woodview
Ollands Farm
Mucklefield Plantation
Worstead Road
Church Road
Oak Road

1 MAX CARTER CL
2 SWANNS YD
3 WOODVIEW
4 ST ANDREWS CL
5 WESTWICK RD
Bunkershill Covert
Brickkiln Plantation
Broadlands Arts Centre
Rec Gd
Tyler's Cut
Broad Fen

4
Hall Farm
The Carr
Manor Farm
Dilham
Hotel

25
The Carr
Worstead Pk
Chapel Road
Chapel Farm
Smallburgh
Broad Farm
Dilham Pyke Drainage Mill
Wayford Bridge
Sewage Works

3
Frankforte Farm
Gothic Wood
Mill Farm
Smallburgh Fen
School La
Hillfield
Mole End
Manor Farm
Moy's Drainage Mill

Frankfort
Cottage Fen
Fenwood Farm
Union Road
Dark Lane
Wayford Bridge
River Ant

Upper Street
Anchor Street

24
Ivy Farm
Fir Tree Farm
The Ings
Church Farm
Chapel Terr
Home Farm
Chapel Farm
Manor Farm

New Barn Farm
Moat
Old Hall Farm
Gunn's Corner
Oak Farm
Cat's Common
Berry Hall

2
Vicarage La
Smallburgh Hall
Pennygate
Home Farm
Barton Turf

23
Old Farm
Pennygate Farm
Yon End
Point Farm
Moorings

1
Church Lane
Church Farm
Long Plantation
School Road
Common Rd

22
Beeches Farm
Crowgate St
Stone La
Barton Road
Beeston Lane

30 A 31 B 32 C 33 D 34 E 35 F

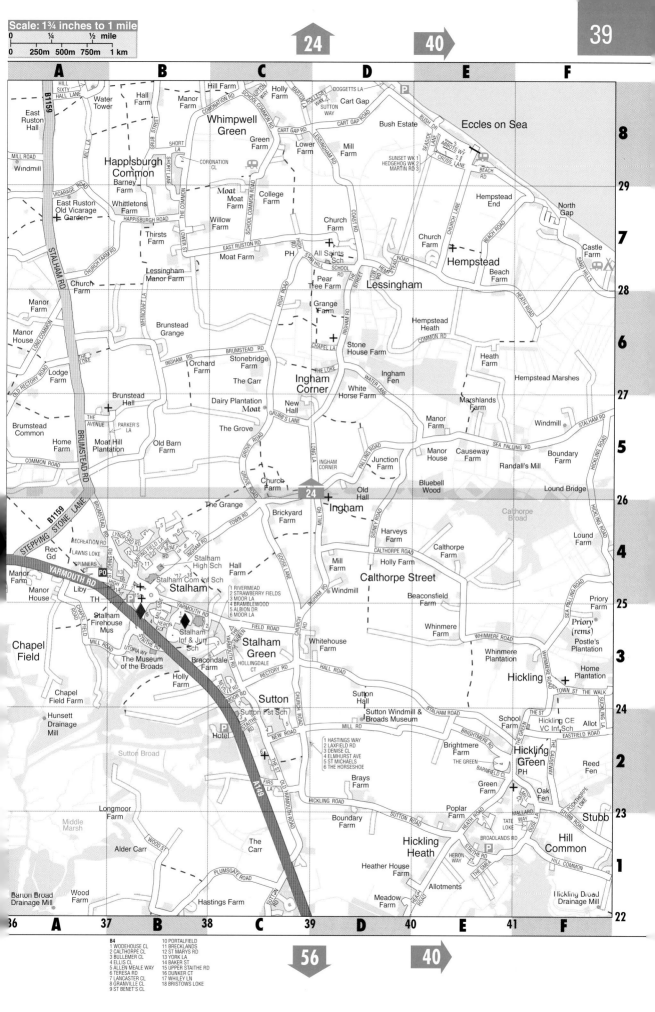

East Ruston Hall

Windmill

HILL SIXTY
HALL LANE

Water Tower

Hall Farm

Manor Farm

Hill Farm

Happisburgh Common

Barney Farm

Whittletons Farm

East Ruston Old Vicarage Garden

Thirsts Farm

Church Farm

Manor Farm

Manor House

Lodge Farm

Brunstead Hall

Brumstead Common

Home Farm

Moat Hill Plantation

Church Farm

Whimpwell Green

Coronation CL

Green Farm

Moat Moat Farm

Willow Farm

College Farm

Lessingham Manor Farm

Moat Farm

Brunstead Grange

Orchard Farm

Stonebridge Farm

The Carr

Dairy Plantation Moat

The Grove

Old Barn Farm

Parker's La

The Avenue

Lower Farm

Mill Farm

Church Farm

All Saints Sch

PH

Pear Tree Farm

Grange Farm

Ingham Corner

White Horse Farm

New Hall

Doggetts La

Cart Gap

Sutton Way

Mill Farm

Bush Estate

Church Farm

Church Farm

Eccles on Sea

Hempstead End

North Gap

Castle Farm

Hempstead

Beach Farm

Lessingham

Hempstead Heath

Heath Farm

Hempstead Marshes

Stone House Farm

Ingham Fen

Marshlands Farm

Windmill

Manor Farm

Manor House

Causeway Farm

Randall's Mill

Boundary Farm

Water Lane

Junction Farm

Bluebell Wood

Lound Bridge

Old Hall

Ingham

Harveys Farm

Calthorpe Broad

Calthorpe Farm

Lound Farm

The Grange

Brickyard Farm

Mill Farm

Holly Farm

Calthorpe Street

Beaconsfield Farm

Priory (rems)

Postle's Plantation

Stalham High Sch

Hall Farm

RIVERMEAD
STRAWBERRY FIELDS
MOOR LA
BRAMBLEWOOD
ALBION DR
MOOR LA

Windmill

Whinmere Farm

Whinmere Road

Priory

Home Plantation

Hickling

Stalham

Stalham Firehouse Mus

Chapel Field

Chapel Field Farm

Hunsett Drainage Mill

The Museum of the Broads

Holly Farm

Stalham Inf & Jun Sch

Bracondale Farm

Stalham Green

Sutton

Sutton Fst Sch

Hotel

Sutton Broad

Whitehouse Farm

Sutton Hall

Sutton Windmill & Broads Museum

Whinmere Plantation

Hickling Green

School Farm

Hickling CE VC Inf Sch

Allot

Reed Fen

Brightmere Farm

HASTINGS WAY
LAXFIELD RD
DENISE CL
ELMHURST AVE
ST MICHAELS
THE HORSESHOE

Brightmere Rd

Barnfield Cl

Green Farm

Oak Fen

Stubb

Hill Common

Middle Marsh

Longmoor Farm

Alder Carr

The Carr

Brays Farm

Boundary Farm

Poplar Farm

Hickling Heath

Heather House Farm

Meadow Farm

Allotments

Hill Common

Barton Broad Drainage Mill

Wood Farm

Hastings Farm

Hickling Broad Drainage Mill

B4
1 WODEHOUSE CL
2 CALTHORPE CL
3 BULLEMER CL
4 ELLIS CL
5 ALLEN MEALE WAY
6 TERESA RD
7 LANCASTER CL
8 GRANVILLE CL
9 ST BENET'S CL
10 PORTALFIELD
11 BRECKLANDS
12 ST MARYS RD
13 YORK LA
14 BAKER ST
15 UPPER STAITHE RD
16 DUNKER CT
17 WHILEY LN
18 BRISTOWS LOKE

Scale: 1¾ inches to 1 mile

0   ¼   ½   mile
0   250m 500m 750m 1 km

A   B   C   D   E   F

8

29

7

28

SAND HILLS

THE MARRAMS

Keith
Farm

CLINK RD

P ✕ Inshore Rescue
Boat Station

6

Sea
Palling

PH

BEACH RD

☩

Northend
Farm

CHAPEL RD

PO

27

STALHAM RD

THE STREET

CHURCH CL

The
Hall

PH

CHURCH RD

WILLOW
CT

Rec
Gnd

WAXHAM ROAD

☩

Sewage
Works

The
Hall

WAXHAM CT 1
ST MARGARETS PL 2

BLACK WALL

☩

Waxham

5

Lambridge
Covert

CHURCH RD

Old Alder
Carr

26

Frenchs
Farm

Marram
Hills

Great Moss
Fen

New Cut

Decoy
Covert

4

Lambrigg
Mill

Brograve
Farm

Poplar
Farm

Long Gore
Marsh

25

COAST RD

North Hills
Marsh

Hickling
Wall

Walnut
Farm

Warren
Farm

3

P

Brograve
Level

WAXHAM NEW CUT

Fir Tree
Farm

P

Home
Plantation

Bells
Marsh

Horsey
Corner

HORSEY GAP

24

NORTH HILL RD

EASTFIELD ROAD

Mill
Marsh

Delph
Farm

PALLING RD

Eastfield
Farm

Brograve
Drainage Mill

2

Reed
Fen

Horsey

Commissioners' Drain

The
Hall

ALL SAINTS BINSLEY CL

Willow
Copse

Eye
Farm

Hall
Farm

☩

☩

23

STUBB MILL LA

Brayden
Marshes

Street
Farm

PH

THE STREET

1

Stubb
Farm

Willow
Farm

STUBB ROAD

Moorings

P

SOMERTON RD

CRINKLE HILL

Fords
Farm

Bramble
Hill

North
Wood

Hickling Broad
Visitor Centre

Stubb
Mill

Horsey
Mere

Horsey
Windpump

22

42   A   43   B   44   C   45   D   46   E   47   F   48

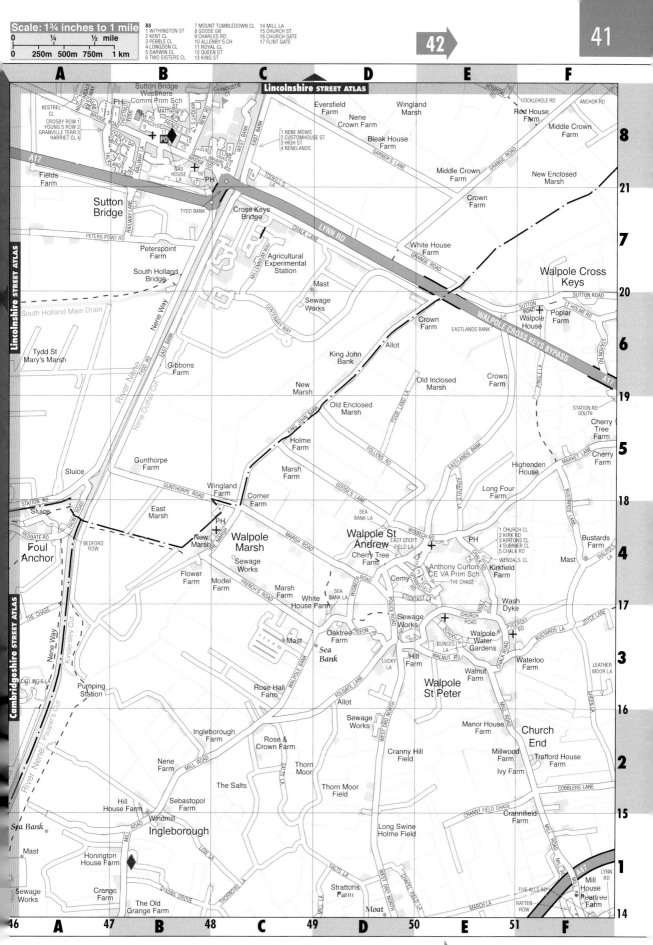

Scale: 1¾ inches to 1 mile

0   ¼   ½ mile

0   250m 500m 750m 1 km

B8
1 WITHINGTON ST
2 KENT CL
3 PEBBLE CL
4 LONGDON CL
5 DARWIN CL
6 TWO SISTERS CL
7 MOUNT TUMBLEDOWN CL
8 GOOSE GN
9 CHARLES RD
10 ALLENBY'S CH
11 ROYAL CL
12 QUEEN ST
13 KING ST
14 MILL LA
15 CHURCH ST
16 CHURCH GATE
17 FLINT GATE

Lincolnshire STREET ATLAS

Lincolnshire STREET ATLAS

Cambridgeshire STREET ATLAS

Labels on map (A–F, 14–8):

KESTREL CL
CROSBY ROW 1
YOUNG'S ROW 2
GRANVILLE TERR 3
HARRIET CL 4

Sutton Bridge Westmere Comm Prim Sch

CARNOUSTIE CT

Fields Farm

Sutton Bridge

A17

PETERS POINT RD

Peterspoint Farm

South Holland Bridge

South Holland Main Drain

TYDD BANK

Tydd St Mary's Marsh

River Nene

Nene Way

Gibbons Farm

Gunthorpe Farm

EAST BANK

TYDD RD

Nene Outfall Cut

Sluice

STATION RD

Sluice

REDGATE RD

Foul Anchor

BEDFORD ROW

GUNTHORPE ROAD

East Marsh

THE MARSH

New Marsh

Walpole Marsh

Flower Farm

Model Farm

FRENCH'S ROAD

MARSH ROAD

Marsh Farm

White House Farm

Sea Bank

Mast

Oaktree Farm

PIGEON ST

Sea Bank

THE CHASE

Nene Way

Kindersley Cut

Pauper's Cut

Pumping Station

CATLING'S LA

River Nene

Ingleborough Farm

Nene Farm

MILL ROAD

The Salts

SALTS LA

Hill House Farm

Sebastopol Farm

Windmill

Ingleborough

LOW LA

DIXON'S DROVE

THORNUM LA

Honington House Farm

Grange Farm

The Old Grange Farm

Sewage Works

Mast

Sea Bank

Mast

Cross Keys Bridge

CHALK LANE

Agricultural Experimental Station

MILLENNIUM WAY

CENTENARY WAY

Mast

Sewage Works

New Marsh

King John Bank

KING JOHN BANK

Holme Farm

Marsh Farm

Wingland Farm

Corner Farm

PH

New Marsh

Sewage Works

WISBECH ROAD

WALPOLE BANK

Rose Hall Farm

Rose & Crown Farm

THORN MOOR

Thorn Moor

Thorn Moor Field

SNITH ST

Moat

Strattons Farm

SALTS LA

WEST DRO NORTH

CHAPEL FIELD LA

Eversfield Farm

Nene Crown Farm

Bleak House Farm

1 NENE MDWS
2 CUSTOMHOUSE ST
3 HIGH ST
4 NENELANDS

East Bank

TOOKILL'S LA

LYNN RD

White House Farm

GRANGE ROAD

Crown Farm

EASTLANDS BANK

Old Inclosed Marsh

Old Enclosed Marsh

POOLE LAND LA

FOLLENS RD

GOOSE'S LANE

SEA BANK LA

EAST CROFT FIELD LA

Walpole St Andrew

Cherry Tree Farm

SPRINGFIELD

Cemy

STICKFAST LA

POLICE ROAD

Sewage Works

Hill Farm

WALNUT RD

LUCKY LA

FOLGATE LANE

Allot

WEST DRO NORTH

Sewage Works

Cranny Hill Field

Long Swine Holme Field

WEST DRO NORTH

FIVE ALLS RD

RATTEN ROW

MARCH LA

Wingland Marsh

Middle Crown Farm

Crown Farm

White House Farm

GRANGE ROAD

WALPOLE CROSS KEYS BYPASS

Crown Farm

EASTLANDS BANK

KIRKFIELD LA

Long Four Farm

Highenden House

SEA BANK LA

Anthony Curton CE VA Prim Sch

THE CHASE

1 CHURCH CL
2 KIRK RD
3 KIRTONS CL
4 SUMMER CL
5 CHALK RD
WENDALS CL

Kirkfield Farm

PH

CHALK LA

MOLT

Wash Dyke

CHURCH ROAD

Walpole Water Gardens

DUNCES LA

SCHOOL RD

PYECROFT

Walnut Farm

Walpole St Peter

Manor House Farm

Millwood Farm

Ivy Farm

Trafford House Farm

Church End

CRANNY FIELD CHASE

Crannifield Farm

COBBLERS LANE

MILL ROAD

GREEN LA

LEATHER MOOR LA

Waterloo Farm

BUSTARDS LA

JOYCE LANE

A17

LYNN RD

Mill House Farm

Peartree Farm

HOSPITAL RD

COCKLEHOLE RD

ANCHOR RD

Red House Farm

Middle Crown Farm

New Enclosed Marsh

Walpole Cross Keys

SUTTON ROAD

LT HOLME RD

Walpole House

Poplar Farm

SAXON RD

A17

PINGLE LA

BUSTARDS LANE

STATION RD SOUTH

Cherry Tree Farm

MARKET LANE

Cherry Farm

Bustards Farm

Mast

WALPOLE LA

41 25

Scale: 1¾ inches to 1 mile

0 ¼ ½ mile
0 250m 500m 750m 1 km

144

Home Farm
BOUNDARY LA
ANCHOR ROAD
OLD COMM. BANK
MIDDLE ROAD
FLEET RD
Old Common Marsh
Sea Bank (course)
Bellmount
Sewage Works
LONG ROAD
NEW ROMAN BANK
GREEN MARSH RD
Green Marsh Farm
Harts Marsh
TOWER ROAD
BEINS LANE
Rhoon Farm
Rhoon Marsh
Gallow Marsh
Orange Row
Church Farm
NORTHGATE WAY
ALMA AV
Brown Farm
DUN COW GDNS
RHOON ROAD
Emorsgate
GREEN LA
OLD ROMAN BANK
BRUSH MEADOW LANE
CRASKE LANE
BEACON HILL LA
HARGATE LANE
EMORSGATE
High Sch
Sch
PO
Alma Lodge
ALMA AV
Church Bank
HUNTERS CL
MARSH RD
OXFORD PL
SANDGATE LA
SPELLOW CL
Poplar Tree Farm
Walpole Cross Keys Com Prim Sch
Spencer Farm
PH
Dovecote Farm
LYNN ROAD
ORANGE ROW RD
LOW LANE
CHAPEL ROAD
THE SALTINGS
HILLGATE ST
WESLEY RD
PH
CHURCHGATE WAY
BEINS LANE
LYNN ROAD
SANDYGATE LANE
Kenfield Farm
MAIN ROAD
144
SUTTON RD
Plumbs Farm
GERMAN'S LANE
POPE'S LANE
WANTON LA
Terrington St Clement
WHITECROSS LANE
STATION ROAD
Spellowgrove Farm
STATION ROAD
STATION RD N
South Green
SUTTON ROAD
Carters Farm
MARKET LANE
Lovell's Hall
STATION RD
Kenwick Hall
A17 CLENCHWARTON BYPASS
A17 WALPOLE CROSS KEYS BYPASS
TERRINGTON ST CLEMENT BYPASS
Kenwick Farm
HANKINSON'S EST
STATION RD S
MARKET LANE
WRONG LA
HAY GN RD
HAY GN RD
Ivy Farm
Experimental Husbandry Farm
GREENS LA
Balsamfield House
WHITECROSS LANE
Primrose Farm
Old Hall
CHURCH ROAD
STATION ROAD
DIDDLE'S DAM
Sea Bank
Tuxhill Farm
ELVERS LA
Feale Abbey
Hay Green
MOAT ROAD
BULLOCK ROAD
STATION ROAD
Grove Farm
Sewage Works
GLEBE EST
TUXHILL RD
BRITCH
TUXHILL CH
JANKIN LA
Shepherd's Gate
144
Tilney All Saints
SHEPHERDSGATE RD
CHURCH RD
Tilney All Saints CE VC Prim Sch
Allot
Jankinsfield Farm
WATERLOW ROAD
Harwood Farm
FIVE MILE BANK
Tilney High End
CHURCH LA
CHURCH RD
Eagles Golf Course
CH
WILLOW DR
MAIN ROAD
Shore Boat Farm
A47
WALPOLE LANE
FENCE BANK
JOYCE LA
Broken Cross
FENDITCH LA
Whitehouse Farm
LYNN ROAD
Ivy Farm
Scrimshaw Farm
The Limes
Sea Bank
Islington Hall Farm
FENCE BANK
ST JOHN'S WEST GATES
Duncans Farm
ISLINGTON RD
St Peter's Lodge
MIDDLE GATES DRO
Bentinck Farm
VICTORIA ROAD
Church Farm
White House Farm
PH
MILL LANE
MOORDITCH LANE
Salgate Farm
CHURCH LANE
Terrington St John
LYNN RD
MOORDITCH LANE
COBBLERS LANE
FENCE BANK
Antioch Farm
NEW RD
CHURCH RD
Wynds Bridge
Stud Farm
CHURCH RD
LYNN RD
Aylmer Hall
CRABB LANE
White Hall Farm
Bank Farm
A47
Buttermans Farm
CHERRY TREE DR
OLD CHURCH RD
St John's Highway
NEW ROAD
Orchard Farm
Church Farm
Cott End
WORKHOUSE LA
CHURCH ROAD
HIGH ROAD
LYNN RD
MAIN ROAD
FENCE BANK
MIDDLE RD
DRO
NEWCOMBE CL 1
ELY ROW 2
ORCHARD WAY 3
MANOR DR 4
SCHOOL RD
MILL RD
PH
ST JOHN'S RD
MILL FIELD CL
WESTFIELDS CL
Airstrip

52 A 53 B 54 C 55 D 56 E 57 F

For full street detail of the highlighted area see page 144

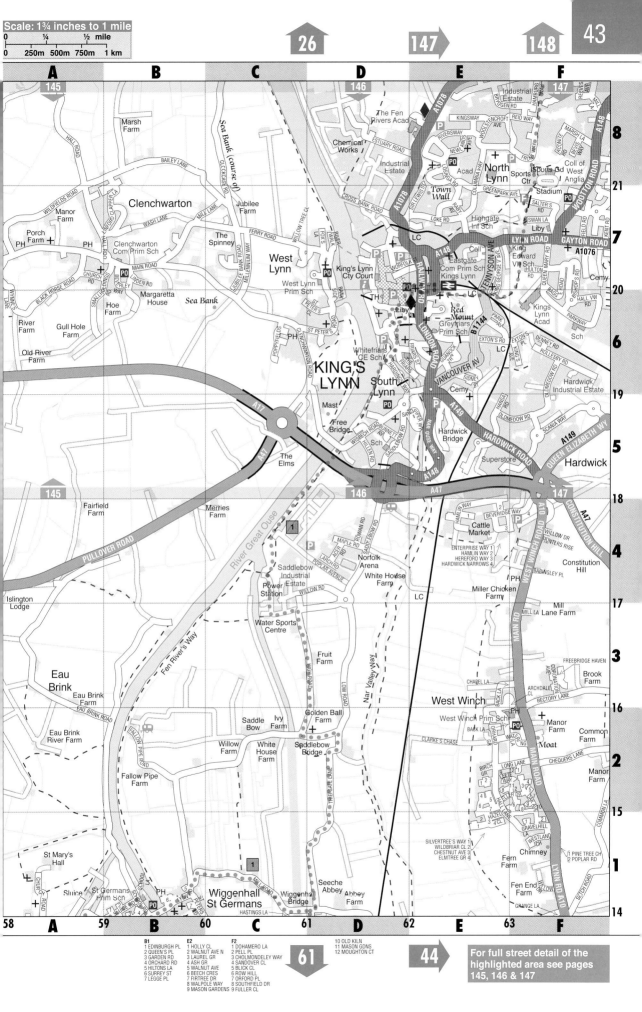

26
147
148
61
44

A B C D E F

145
146
147
145
146
147

KING'S LYNN

Clenchwarton

West Lynn

North Lynn

Hardwick

Eau Brink

West Winch

Wiggenhall St Germans

For full street detail of the highlighted area see pages 145, 146 & 147

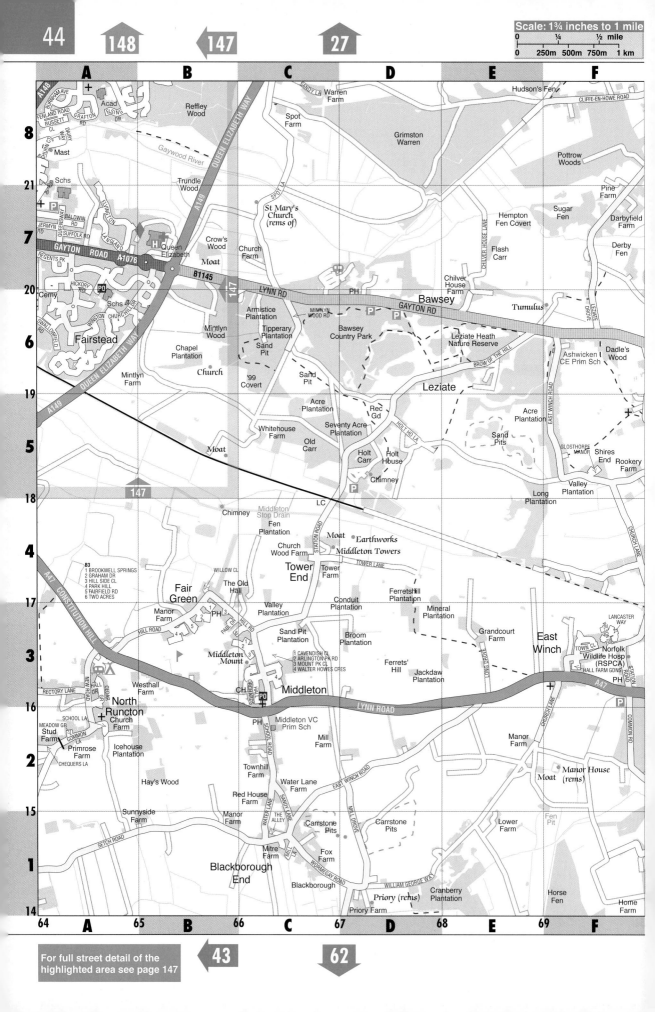

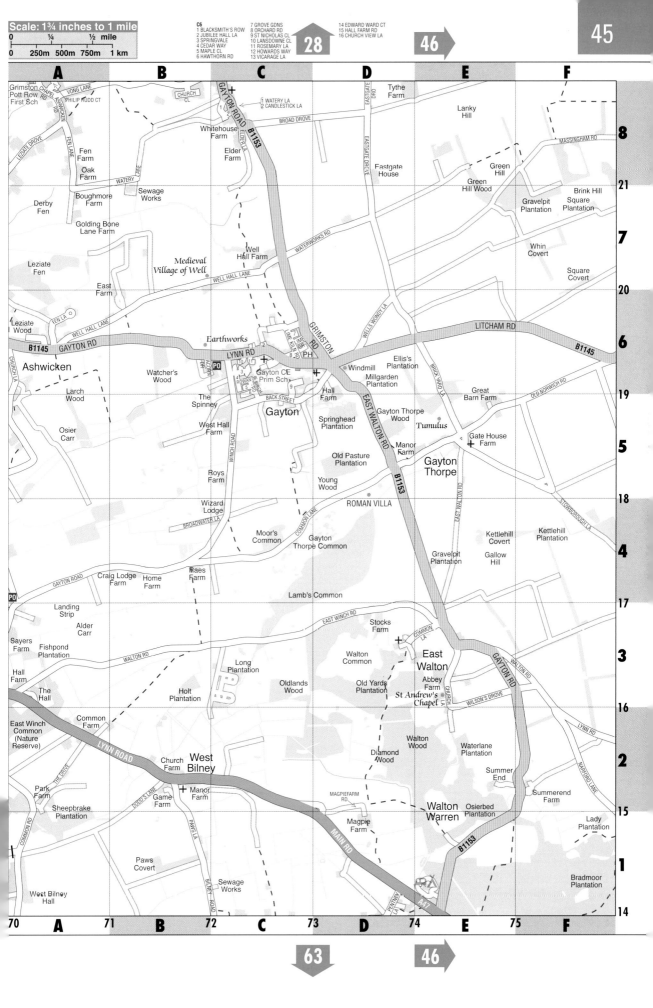

C6
1 BLACKSMITH'S ROW
2 JUBILEE HALL LA
3 SPRINGVALE
4 CEDAR WAY
5 MAPLE CL
6 HAWTHORN RD

7 GROVE GDNS
8 ORCHARD RD
9 ST NICHOLAS CL
10 LANSDOWNE CL
11 ROSEMARY LA
12 HOWARDS WAY
13 VICARAGE LA

14 EDWARD WARD CT
15 HALL FARM RD
16 CHURCH VIEW LA

28

46

Grid columns (top): A B C D E F

Grid rows (right): 8 21 7 20 6 19 5 18 4 17 3 16 2 15 1 14

Grid columns (bottom): A B C D E F

Grid coordinates (bottom): 70 71 72 73 74 75

63

46

Grimston
Pott Row
First Sch
Chapel Rd
Vong Lane
Philip Rudd Ct
Ashwicken Rd
Leziate Drove
Fen Lane
Church Cl

Whitehouse Farm
Broad Drove
1 Watery La
2 Candlestick La
Eastgate Dro
Tythe Farm

Lanky Hill

Elder Farm
Gayton Road
B1153
Eastgate Drove

Fen Farm
Oak Farm
Watery

Fastgate House
Green Hill
Green Hill Wood

Derby Fen
Boughmore Farm
Sewage Works

Massingham Rd

Golding Bone Lane Farm
Well Hall Farm
Waterworks Rd

Gravelpit Plantation
Brink Hill Square Plantation

Leziate Fen
East Farm
Well Hall Lane
Medieval Village of Well

Whin Covert

Leziate Wood
Fen La
Well Hall Lane
Earthworks
Lynn Rd
Grimston Rd

Square Covert

B1145
Gayton Rd
Ashwicken
Watcher's Wood
PO
PH
Windmill
Ellis's Plantation
Wells Wendy La
Litcham Rd
B1145

Larch Wood
The Spinney
Gayton CE Prim Sch
Back Street
Hall Farm
Millgarden Plantation
Great Barn Farm
Old Norwich Rd

Osier Carr
West Hall Farm
Gayton
Springhead Plantation
Gayton Thorpe Wood
Tumulus
Brick Yard La
Gate House Farm

Winch Road
Roys Farm
Old Pasture Plantation
Manor Farm
Gayton Thorpe
East Walton Rd

Wizard Lodge
Broadwater La
Young Wood
ROMAN VILLA

Moor's Common
Gayton Thorpe Common
Gravelpit Plantation
Kettlehill Covert
Kettlehill Plantation
Stowbrough La

Gayton Road
Craig Lodge Farm
Home Farm
Raes Farm
Common Lane
Gallow Hill

PO
Landing Strip
Lamb's Common
East Winch Rd
Stocks Farm
Common La
Gayton Rd

Sayers Farm
Fishpond Plantation
Alder Carr
Walton Rd
Walton Common
East Walton
Walton Rd

Hall Farm
The Hall
Long Plantation
Oldlands Wood
Old Yards Plantation
Abbey Farm
St Andrew's Chapel
Church La
Wilson's Drove
Lynn Rd

East Winch Common (Nature Reserve)
Common Farm
Lynn Road
Holt Plantation
Walton Wood
Waterlane Plantation
Marford Lane

Park Farm
Church Farm
West Bilney
Manor Farm
Diamond Wood
Summer End
Summerend Farm

Sheepbrake Plantation
Game Farm
Dodd's Lane
Paws La
Magpiefarm Rd
Walton Warren
Osierbed Plantation
B1153
Lady Plantation

Paws Covert
Bilney Road
Magpie Farm
Main Rd
Fritmas La
A47
Bradmoor Plantation

West Bilney Hall
Sewage Works
Common Rd
The Drove

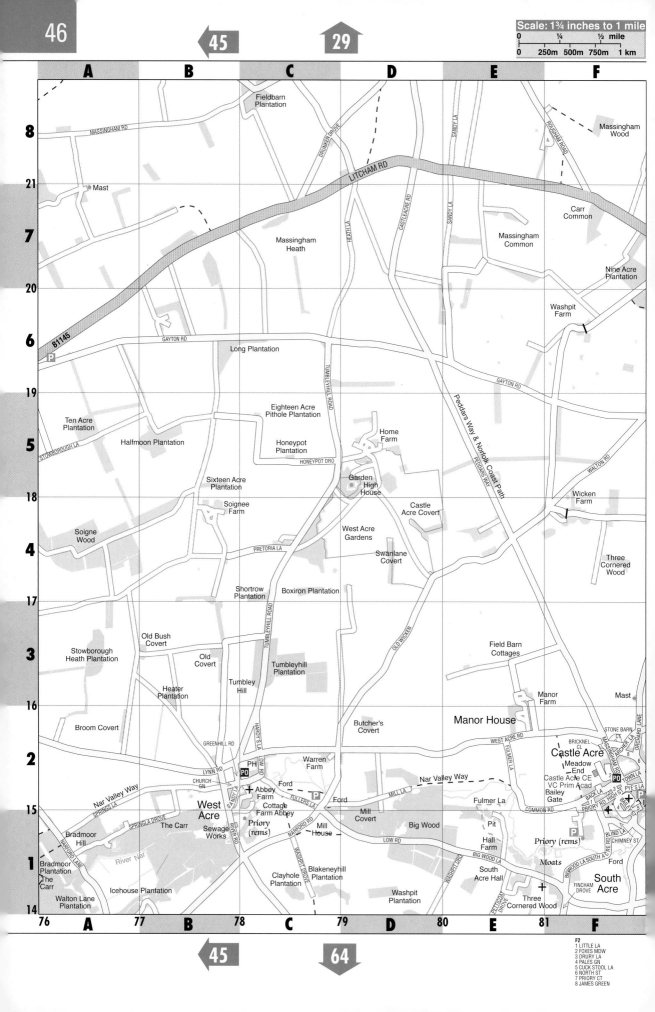

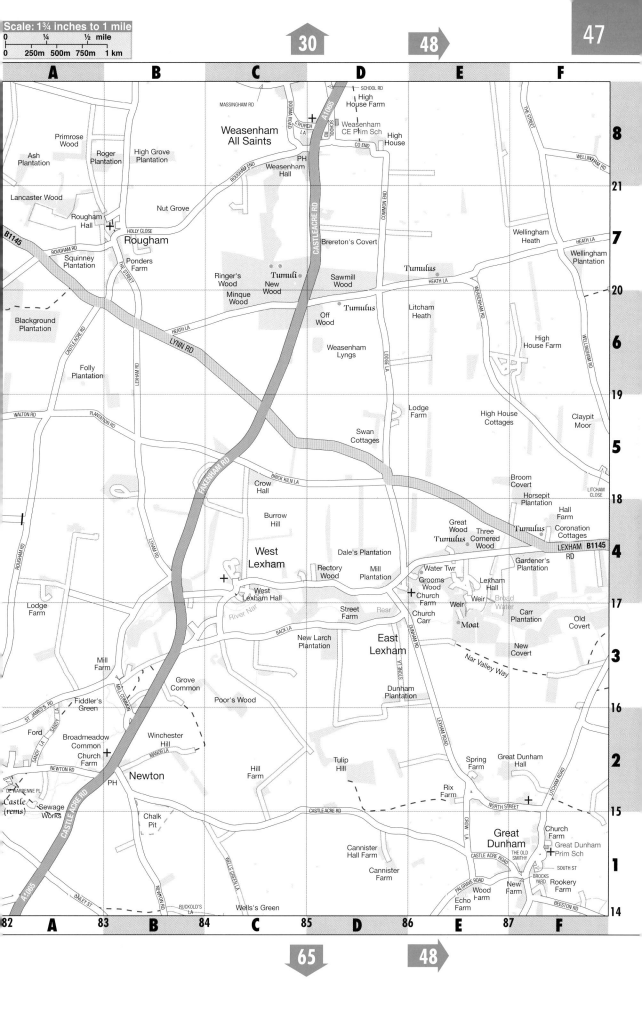

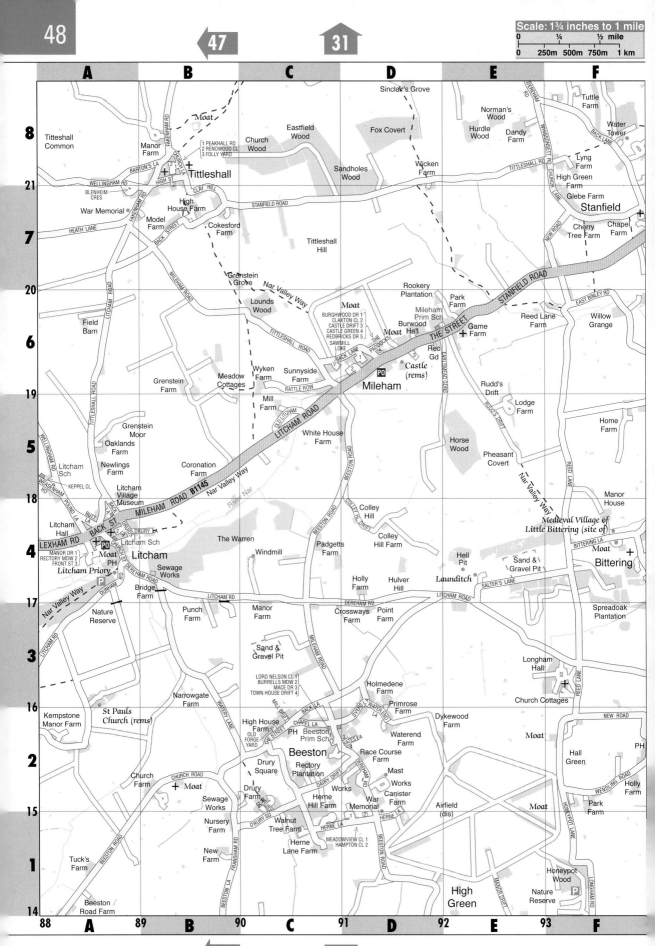

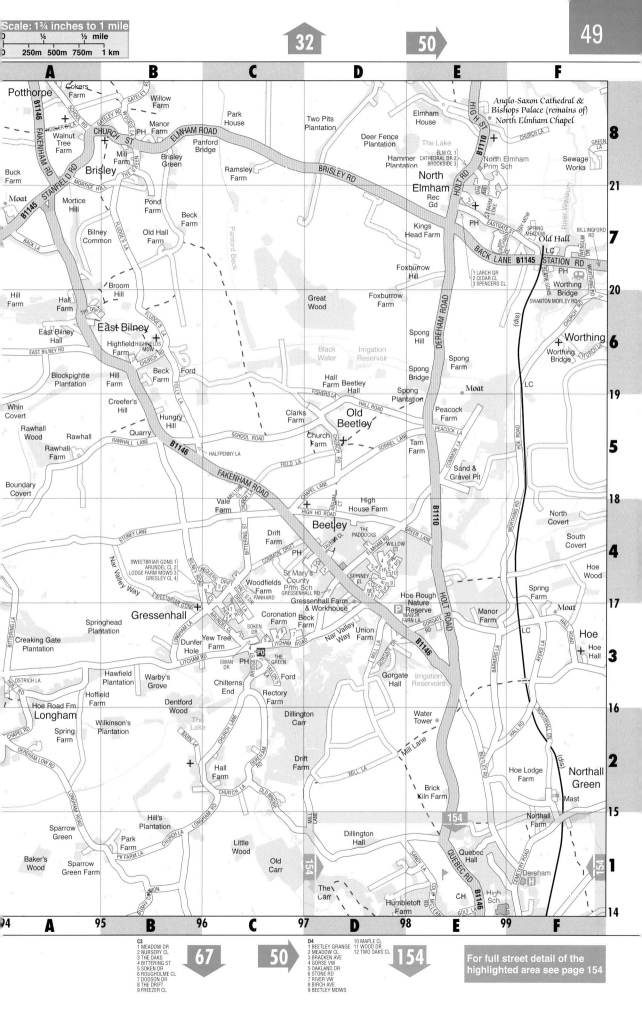

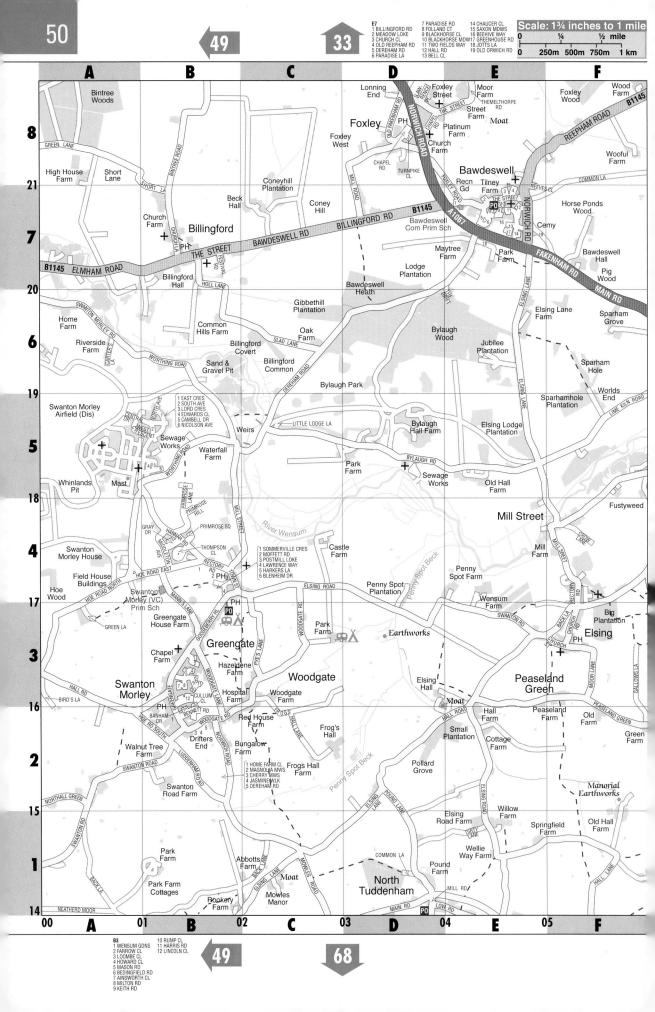

49
33

49
68

E7
1 BILLINGFORD RD
2 MEADOW LOKE
3 CHURCH CL
4 OLD REEPHAM RD
5 DEREHAM RD
6 PARADISE LA

7 PARADISE RD
8 FOLLAND CT
9 BLACKHORSE CL
10 BLACKHORSE MDW
11 TWO FIELDS WAY
12 HALL RD
13 BELL CL

14 CHAUCER CL
15 SAXON MDWS
16 BEEHIVE WAY
17 GREENHOUSE RD
18 JOTTS LA
19 OLD ORWICH RD

Scale: 1¾ inches to 1 mile

0   ¼   ½   mile
0   250m   500m   750m   1 km

B3
1 WENSUM GDNS
2 FARROW CL
3 LOOMBE CL
4 HOWARD CL
5 MASON RD
6 BEDINGFIELD RD
7 AINSWORTH CL
8 MILTON RD
9 KEITH RD

10 RUMP CL
11 HARRIS RD
12 LINCOLN CL

Bintree Woods

High House Farm

Short Lane

GREEN LANE

Church Farm

Billingford

SHORT LA

BINTREE ROAD

CHURCH LA

Beck Hall

Coneyhill Plantation

Coney Hill

Lonning End

Foxley West

Foxley

Foxley Street

CHAPEL RD

Moor Farm

Street Farm

THEMELTHORPE RD

Moat

Foxley Wood

Wood Farm

B1145

OLD FAKENHAM RD

NORWICH RD

Platinum Farm

Church Farm

REEPHAM ROAD

Wooful Farm

Bawdeswell

Tilney Farm

PO

Horse Ponds Wood

Cemy

COMMON LA

PH

THE STREET

BAWDESWELL RD

FESTIVAL RD

BILLINGFORD RD

A1067

Bawdeswell Com Prim Sch

FOLEY ROAD

Recn Gd

NORWICH RD

FAKENHAM RD

Bawdeswell Hall

Pig Wood

B1145

ELMHAM ROAD

Billingford Hall

HOLL LANE

Bawdeswell Heath

Lodge Plantation

Maytree Farm

Park Farm

MAIN RD

Home Farm

SWANTON MORLEY RD

CARTERS LA

Riverside Farm

Common Hills Farm

WORTHING ROAD

Billingford Covert

Sand & Gravel Pit

Billingford Common

SLAD LANE

Oak Farm

DEREHAM ROAD

Gibbethill Plantation

Bylaugh Wood

Jubilee Plantation

Elsing Lane Farm

Sparham Grove

Sparham Hole

THE DRIFT

ELSING LANE

Sparhamhole Plantation

Worlds End

LIME KILN ROAD

Swanton Morley Airfield (Dis)

1 EAST CRES
2 SOUTH AVE
3 LORD CRES
4 EDWARDS CL
5 CAMBELL DR
6 NICOLSON AVE

NORTH AVE

CENTRAL DR

WEST CRESCENT

Weirs

LITTLE LODGE LA

Bylaugh Park

Bylaugh Hall Farm

BYLAUGH RD

Elsing Lodge Plantation

Sewage Works

Waterfall Farm

WORTHING ROAD

Park Farm

Sewage Works

Old Hall Farm

Whinlands Pit

Mast

PRIMROSE LANE

PRIMROSE HILL

MILL STREET

Mill Street

Fustyweed

River Wensum

Swanton Morley House

GRAY DR

HANNAH RD

MIDDLETON AVE

PRIMROSE SQ

THOMPSON CL

1 SOMMERVILLE CRES
2 MOFFETT RD
3 POSTMILL LOKE
4 LAWRENCE WAY
5 HARKERS LA
6 BLENHEIM DR

Castle Farm

PENNY SPOT BECK

Penny Spot Farm

Mill Farm

MILL STREET

PROW LANE

Field House Buildings

HOE ROAD EAST

RECTORY RD

PH ST

Elsing Road

Penny Spot Plantation

Wensum Farm

SWANTON RD

BACK LA

CHURCH LA

RECTORY LA

Big Plantation

Hoe Wood

HOE ROAD NORTH

Swanton Morley (VC) Prim Sch

MANN'S LANE

PO

Greengate House Farm

GOOSEBERRY RD

PH

Park Farm

WOODGATE RD

Earthworks

Elsing

MOOR LANE

CHURCH RD

GALLOWS LA

GREEN LA

Chapel Farm

Greengate

Hazeldene Farm

PYE'S LANE

Woodgate

Elsing Hall

Moat

Peaseland Green

Swanton Morley

BIRD'S LA

HALL RD

PH

BANHAM DR

GREENGATE

WOODGATE LANE

CULLUM CL

BENNETT RD

Hospital Farm

Woodgate Farm

FROG'S HALL LANE

Frog's Hall

HALL RD

Moat

Hall Farm

Peaseland Farm

Old Farm

PEASELAND GREEN

Green Farm

Walnut Tree Farm

NORDELPH RD

Drifters End

Red House Farm

Small Plantation

Cottage Farm

SWANTON ROAD

LUDDENHAM RD

Bungalow Farm

1 HOME FARM CL
2 MAGNOLIA MWS
3 CHERRY MWS
4 JASMINE WLK
5 DEREHAM RD

Frogs Hall Farm

Pollard Grove

Manorial Earthworks

Swanton Road Farm

NORTHALL GREEN

SWANTON RD

PENNY SPOT BECK

POUND LANE

ELSING LANE

Elsing Road Farm

Willow Farm

Springfield Farm

Old Hall Farm

DIRTY LANE

ELSING ROAD

Park Farm

Abbotts Farm

BACK LANE

ELSING LANE

Moat

Mowles Manor

MOWLES ROAD

COMMON LA

North Tuddenham

MAIN RD

MILL RD

LOW RD

Wellie Way Farm

Pound Farm

Park Farm Cottages

Rookery Farm

NEATHERD MOOR

HALL LANE

PO

00   A   01   B   02   C   03   D   04   E   05   F

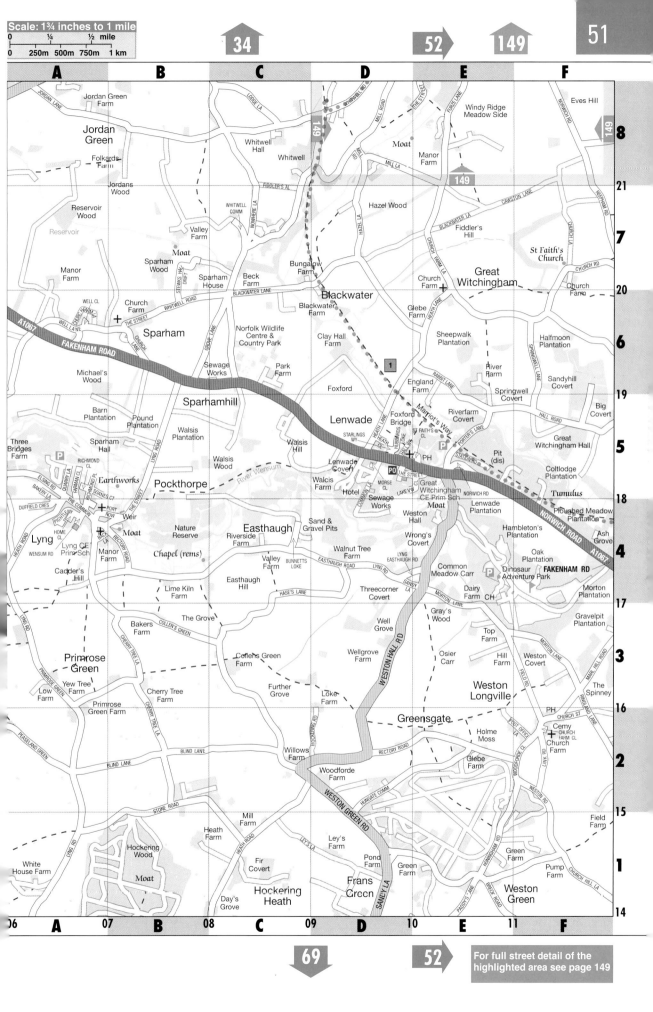

51
35

Scale: 1¾ inches to 1 mile

0   ¼   ½ mile
0   250m   500m   750m   1 km

A   **B**   **C**   **D**   **E**   **F**

The Grove
GROVE LA
Brandiston
CAWSTON RD
NORWICH RD
DUCK ROW
Hall Farm
Moat
Great Wood
Haveringland Hall Park
B1149
Buxton Heath
P Nature Reserve

8

Church Farm
Oaklands Farm
WOODLANDS PK
CHARMBECK PK
Haveringland Hall (rems of)
Haveringland Lake
Beck Farm
THE HEATH
Common Farm

21

Goton Hall
Stump Cross (rems)
Stump Cross Farm
Newstead Farm
SCHOOL ROAD
GREEN LANE
Cherry Tree Farm

7

Little Witchingham Hall
CRABBS LA
MARK'S CLOSE LA
REEPHAM ROAD
KETT'S LANE
Old Duckpond Plantation
Furtherpit Plantation
CLAY LANE
Moegoe's Plantation
Quakers Farm
QUAKER CT
Valley Farm
Grange Farm
Pye's Plantation
HOLT ROAD

20

CHURCH FARM LA
Hengrave Farm
WELTONS LOKE
MANOR DR
Swannington Hall
HAVERINGLAND ROAD
Long Covert
The Old King's Head
THE GN
Carter Farm
Beck Farm

6

Hengrave
Gardens
CHURCH LANE
Moat
Swannington
THE STREET
PH
Six Acre Plantation
ABBEY LANE
BLACKSMITHS LA
Little Plantation
SHORT THORN RD

19

H Road Farm
Alderford
Church Farm
Bell Farm
SCHOOL ROAD
BROAD LANE
SWAN CL
Nut Pit Farm
SWIFFERS LA
Abbey Farm
Cushion's Common Plantation
HALL LANE
Felthorpe Hall
SAWMILL LA
THE STREET
Recreation Gd
Hollygate Farm

5

HALL ROAD
ALDERFORD COMMON
Alderford Common
Upgate
Millhill Plantation
MILL LANE
CHAPL LA
PH

Tumulus
Black Breck Farm
Broom Plantation
Swannington Bottom Plantation
155
PH
Felthorpe
Houghen Farm

18

Bush Meadow Plantation
STATION ROAD
REEPHAM ROAD
WENSUM VALLEY VIEW
Bottom Plantation
Swannington Bottom Plantation
THE STREET
Mill Farm
Church Farm
BILNEY LANE

Slade Plantation
RIVER WENSUM
Marriot's Way
Bungalow Farm
Upgate House
SANDY LA
Gilham's Heath Plantation
FELTHORPE RD
Yew Tree Farm
CHURCH LANE
Houghen Plantation

4

Morton
A1067
White House Farm
CHURCH FIELD
Pet Farm
1
Big Plantation
TAVERHAM ROAD
BRAND'S LANE
Dole Plantation

17

THE STREET
Ashtree Farm
FELTHORPE RD
Attlebridge
OLD FAKENHAM RD
Mileplain Plantation
Nursery Plantation
Steward's Plantation
Wood Farm

Orchard End
Triumph Plantation
Foxburrow Plantation
KING WILLIAM'S DR
Foxburrow Plantation
FIR COVERT RD
P
Spring Farm
Fir Covert Farm
Home Plantation
Drayton Drewray

3

Ivy Cottages
Potato Plantation
Fir Covert
FURZE LA

Attlebridge Hills
155
Deighton Hills
DOG LANE
155

16

Morton Hall
THETFORD HALL EST
Attlebridge Hall
FAKENHAM ROAD
Old Hall Farm
River Wensum
Walsingham Plantation
FIR COVERT ROAD
Wits End
Breck Farm
BRECK FARM LANE
Marrior's Way
REEPHAM ROAD
Thorpe Marriott
DREWRAY DRIVE
Nature Farm
LONG DALE
FEESHAM WAY
SCHOOL ROAD

2

Oak Grove
Broom Hills
Rose Carr
Low Farm
KINGSWOOD AVENUE
PO

Long Plantation
Primrose Grove
RINGLAND LANE
Long Plantation
Wensum Valley Golf Course
CH
BEECH AVE
OLD WARREN
GARDENIA
PO
LITTLEWOOD

15

BLACKBRECK LA
Gravelpit Plantation
Primrose Grove
Royal Hill
Taverham High Sch
MAPLE DR
CEDAR CT
LLOYD
SANDY LA
ST EDMUND'S RD
Taverham Sch
ROSSONS RD
OLD WARREN
BALDRIC
WINDSOR CH
A1067
Drayton Com Inf Sch

1

Church Hill Plantation
THE STREET
WESTON RD
BACK LA
Glebe Farm
Round Wood
RINGLAND ROAD
Snake Wood
Taverham
NIGHTINGALE DR
LABURNUM AVE
Liby
PO
SETON RD
CATOP

14

12   **A**   13   **B**   14   **C**   15   **D**   16   **E**   17   **F**

For full street detail of the highlighted area see page 155

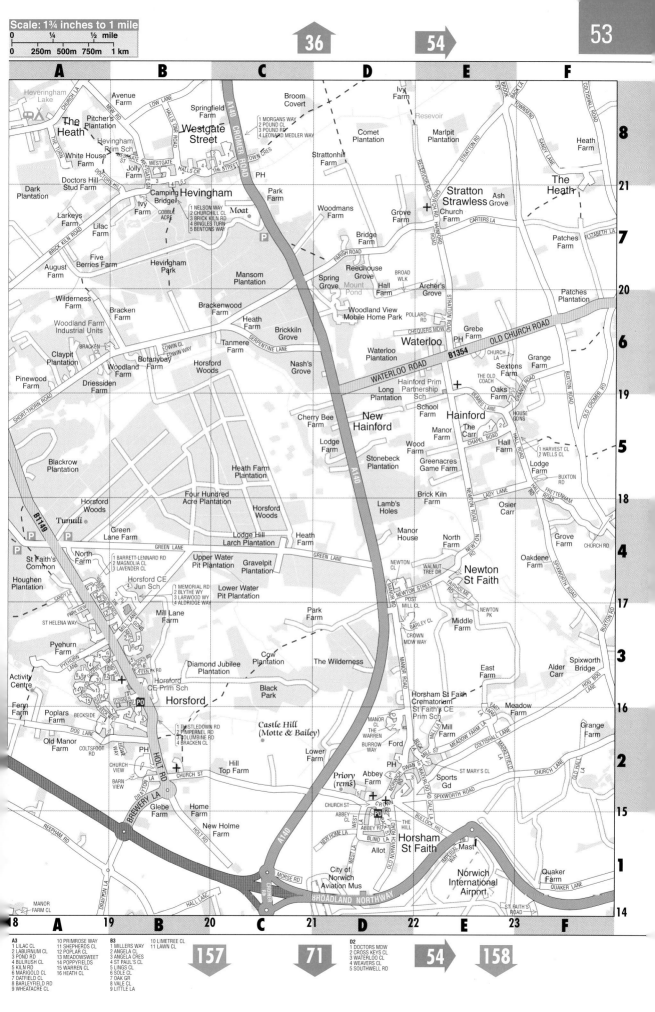

C6
1 CHURCH CL
2 RECTORY RD
3 ST MARGARET'S CL
4 CAUSEWAY DR
5 GLEBE WAY
6 TUNGATE WAY

7 HAVERGATE
8 PATRICIA AVE
9 CHURCH CL

53

C7
1 LING CL
2 ADDISON CL
3 HANCOCK CL
4 HIGHFIELD WAY

37

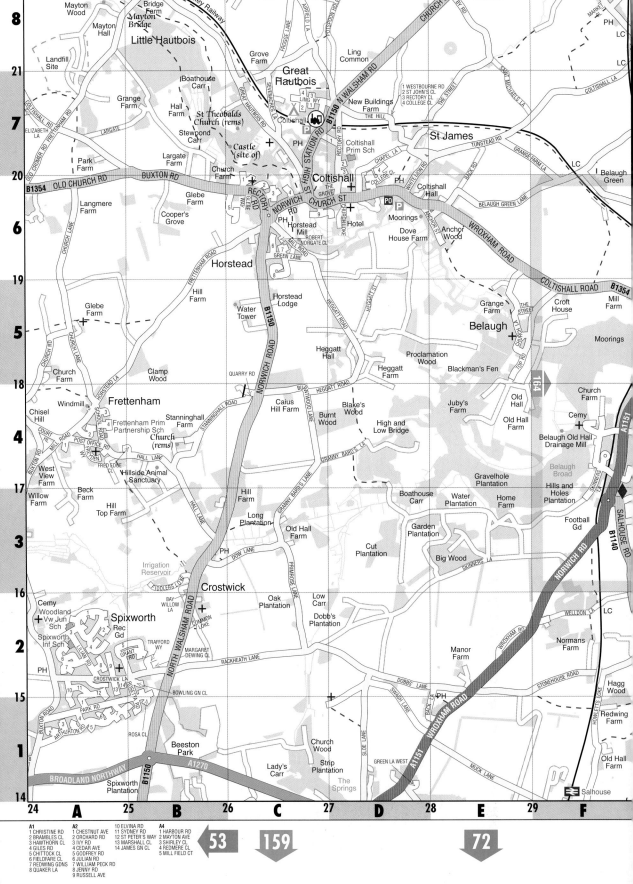

A1
1 CHRISTINE RD
2 BRAMBLES CL
3 HAWTHORN CL
4 GILES RD
5 CHITTOCK CL
6 FIELDFARE CL
7 REDWING GDNS
8 QUAKER LA

A2
1 CHESTNUT AVE
2 ORCHARD RD
3 IVY RD
4 CEDAR AVE
5 GODFREY RD
6 JULIAN RD
7 WILLIAM PECK RD
8 JENNY RD
9 RUSSELL AVE

10 ELVINA RD
11 SYDNEY RD
12 ST PETER'S WAY
13 MARSHALL CL
14 JAMES GN CL

A4
1 HARBOUR RD
2 MAYTON AVE
3 SHIRLEY CL
4 REDMERE CL
5 MILL FIELD CT

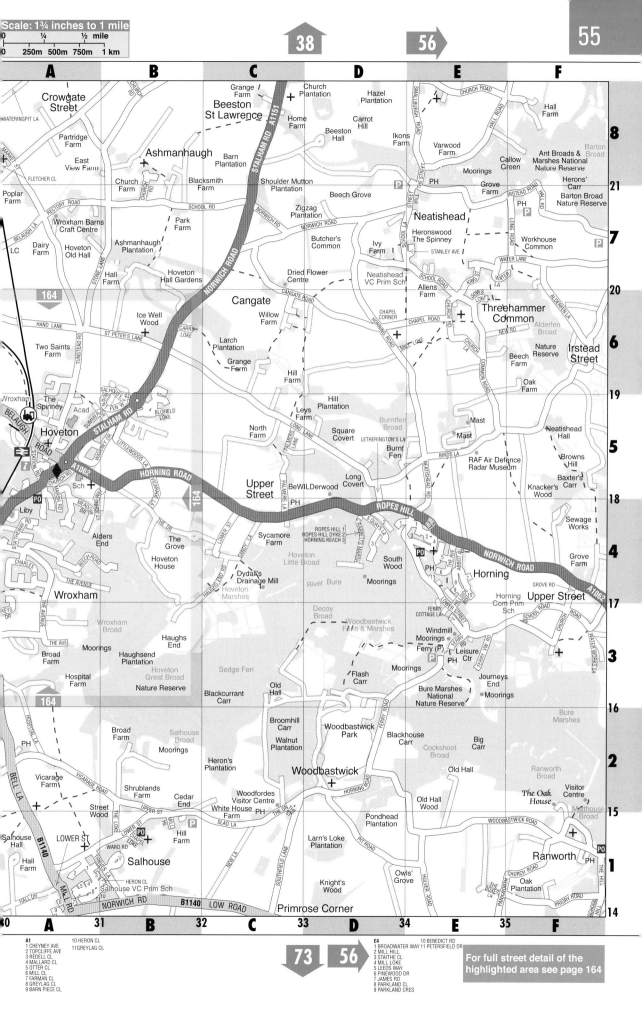

C5
1 LAURELS CRES
2 WILLOW WAY
3 SCHOOL CL
4 PIKES NURSERY

C8
1 CHAPELFIELD CL
2 LEA RD
3 LIMES RD
4 CANON WAKE CT
5 ST CATHERINE'S AVE

F6
1 VICARAGE CL
2 GLEBE CL
3 ORCHARD DR
4 DOVE HOUSE LA
5 STATION RD

Scale: 1¾ inches to 1 mile

0   ¼   ½   mile
0   250m   500m   750m   1 km

A   B   C   D   E   F

Barton Broad
Nature Reserve

Fenside

Catfield

Alder
Carr

Catfield Common

Hickling Broad

8

Barton
Broad

WOOD STREET ROAD
LODGE RD
DALE LANE
BACK LA
NEW RD
NEW ROAD
PH
A149
STAITHE ROAD
WEAVERS' WAY
POTTER HEIGHAM ROAD

Staithe
Farm

Middle Marsh
Drainage Mill

Catfield
Hall

Catfield VC
CE Prim Sch

Heath
Farm

Oak
Farm

Swim Cootts
Drainage Mill

21

CHURCH ROAD
HALL RD
SCHOOL ROAD
THORN RD
THE STREET
LUDHAM RD
MILL LANE
BY PASS
LONG LANE

Little Fen

Church
Wood

Hurst
Wood

Laurels
Farm

DECOY ROAD
Swim Coots

Irstead

Deek
Side
Little
Fen

Catfield Broad

Sharp
Street

ELDERBUSH LANE
LAURELS RD

High
House Farm

BACK LANE

Rose
Farm

Coll's
Plantation

WOODBINE CL

7

VESTEAD RD
WATER LA
SHOALS RD
MILES LOKE
SHARP ST

Summer
House
Farm

Furrows
End

REYNOLDS LANE

Rookery
Farm

CHAPEL LA
Old
Carr
CHURCH LANE

Moorings

Cobbs
Farm

YARMOUTH RD

20

Falgate
Carr
HALL FEN

How Hill
Nature Reserve

Jock's
Wood

Broad
Fen

Cottage
Grove
Farm

MALTHOUSE LANE

Water
Tower

Walton
Hall

Allot
GREEN LANE

Potter
Heigham

6

Clay Rack
Drainage Mill

HOW HILL ROAD
HOWFIELD LOKE
WATERING PIECE LANE
GOOSES LANE
LUDHAM ROAD
NUN'S LOKE
GRIGGS LANE
CATFIELD ROAD
MARKET ROAD

Pigeon
Wood

Gromes
Farm

Summer House
Wood

Sewage
Works

Ludham
Airstrip

SCHOOL RD
STATION RD

St Nicholas
WAY

Boardman's
Drainage Mill

Toad Hole
Wood

How
Hill

CRINGLES LA
BOWER RD

Post Office
Farm

19

Toad Hole Cottage Mus
Reedham
Marsh

How Hill
Farm

Pages
Farm

WILGRESS LOKE

Ludham
Prim Sch

GRANGE RD

Fritton

A1062   LUDHAM RD

PH   PO

5

Turf Fen Drainage Mill
Turf Fen

Moorings

SCHOOL ROAD
TURF FEN LANE
WHITEGATES
POUND ROAD
MALTHOUSE LA
FRITTON ROAD
FRITTON LANE

High
Mill Hill

High
House Farm

Red Roofs
Farm

Lower
Farm

Potter Heigham
New Bridge

18

Broad Mead
Farm

The Limes
Farm

BLIND LA

CLINT'S LA

Rec
Gd

BROAD
REACHES

NORWICH ROAD
YARMOUTH ROAD
Ludham
1 GRANGE CL
2 LATCHMOOR PK
3 LATCHMOOR LA
STAITHE ROAD
OLDMILL LA
HORSEFEN ROAD

Green
Farm

Horse
Fen

Journey's
End

WEAVERS WAY

Repps Level

4

Neaves Mill
White House
Farm

Moorings

Willow
Fen

Fen
Hill

Ludham
Hall

PH

Hall Common

THE WILK
LOVERS' LA

Manor
Farm

Moorings

MARSH WALL

Horse
Fen

Womack Water
Drainage Mill

River Thurne

Repps

Elm Tree
Farm

17

Johnson
Street

Ludham Bridge
Drainage Mill

Bridge
Farm

HALL LANE
HALL COMM ROAD
ST BENET'S RD
COLD HARBOUR ROAD
Womack Water

STAITHE ROAD
MARSH RD

Hall
Farm

3

A1062

Ludham
Bridge

Wind
Farm

River Ant

Cold
Harbour Farm

Hundred Dike

Shallam Dike

COMMON RD
REPPS ROAD

Woodside
Farm

Lilac
Farm

Abbey
Farm

16

Horning
Hall

St Benet's Abbey
Drainage Mill

St Benet's
Abbey

St Benet's Level
Drainage Mill

Thurne Dyke
Drainage Mill

Thurne

THE STREET
THE STAITHE
PH
CHURCH ROAD

Home
Farm

School
Farm

Ashby
Hall

2

Ward Marsh

River Bure

Thurne Mouth

Manor
Farm

BOUNDARY RD

Glebe
Farm

15

Ranworth
Marshes

Fleet Dike

Boundary
House

CROSS ROAD

New House
Farm

Harrisons
Farm

1

Dairy
Farm
FARM LA

Reed
Side
COMMON LA

Moorings

FLEET LA
MARSH LA
MARCH RD

Tall Mill
Drainage Mill

Manor
Farm

Dovehouse
Plantation

14

South Walsham
Broad

36   A   37   B   38   C   39   D   40   E   41   F

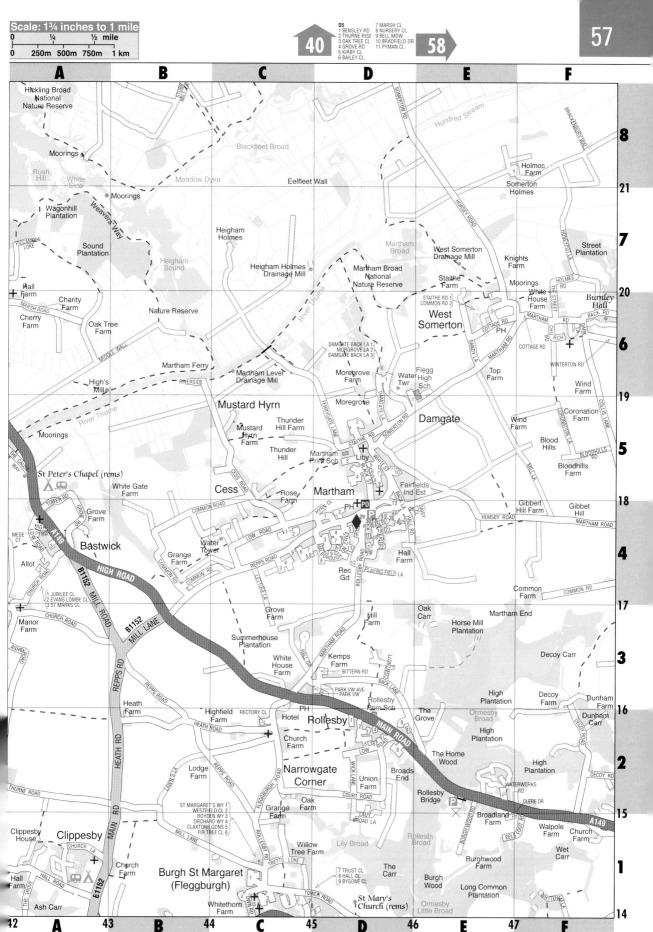

Scale: 1¾ inches to 1 mile

0   ¼   ½ mile
0 250m 500m 750m 1 km

D5
1 BENSLEY RD
2 THURNE RISE
3 OAK TREE CL
4 GROVE RD
5 KIRBY CL
6 BAILEY CL

7 MARSH CL
8 NURSERY CL
9 BELL MDW
10 BRADFIELD DR
11 PYMAN CL

40   58

57

Hickling Broad National Nature Reserve

Blackfleet Broad

Hundred Stream

Brackenbury Wall

Moorings

Rush Hill

White Slea

Meadow Dyke

Eelfleet Wall

Holmoc Farm

Somerton Holmes

Wagonhill Plantation

Weavers' Way

Heigham Holmes

Martham Broad

West Somerton Drainage Mill

Knights Farm

Street Plantation

PICCAMORE LOKE

Hall Farm

Charity Farm

Sound Plantation

Heigham Sound

Heigham Holmes Drainage Mill

Martham Broad National Nature Reserve

Staithe Farm

Moorings

White House Farm

Burnley Hall

MARSH ROAD

Cherry Farm

Oak Tree Farm

Nature Reserve

River Thurne

DAMGATE BACK LA 1
MORGROVE LA 2
DAMGATE BACK LA 3

STAITHE RD 1
COMMON RD 2

West Somerton

COTTAGE RD

PH

COTTAGE RD

WINTERTON RD

MIDDLE WALL

Martham Ferry

Martham Level Drainage Mill

Moregrove Farm

Water Twr

Flegg High Sch

Top Farm

Wind Farm

High's Mill

RIVERSIDE

River Thurne

Mustard Hyrn

FERRYGATE LANE

STAITHE RD

SOMERTON RD

Moregrove

Damgate

Wind Farm

Coronation Farm

COLLIS LANE

Moorings

Mustard Hyrn Farm

Thunder Hill Farm

Thunder Hill

Martham Prim Sch

Liby

Wind Farm

Blood Hills

BLOODHILLS RD

St Peter's Chapel (rems)

White Gate Farm

Cess

Rose Farm

Martham

Fairfields Ind Est

Gibbert Hill Farm

Bloodhills Farm

Gibbet Hill

THE CAUSEWAY

Grove Farm

COMMON ROAD

PH

PO

HEMSBY ROAD

MARTHAM ROAD

MEDE CT

A149

Bastwick

Grange Farm

Water Tower

LOW ROAD

REPPS ROAD

Hall Farm

Common Farm

COMMON RD

Allot

1 JUBILEE CL
2 EVANS LOMBE CL
3 ST MARKS CL

CHURCH ROAD

COMMON RD

Rec Gd

ROLLESBY ROAD

PLAYING FIELD LA

HIGH ROAD

B1152

Grove Farm

Hall Farm

Oak Carr

Horse Mill Plantation

Martham End

Manor Farm

CHURCH ROAD

MILL LANE

B1152

Summerhouse Plantation

White House Farm

Kemps Farm

BITTERN RD

Martham Road

BACK LANE

Decoy Carr

ASHBY RD

REPPS RD

Heath Farm

Highfield Farm

RECTORY CL

PARK VW AVE
PARK VW

Rollesby Prim Sch

High Plantation

Decoy Farm

Dunham Farm

HEATH RD

HEATH ROAD

Hotel

PH

Rollesby

The Grove

Ormesby Broad

High Plantation

Dunham Carr

DECOY RD

Lodge Farm

Church Farm

LOW

Narrowgate Corner

WICK LANE

Union Farm

MAIN ROAD

The Home Wood

High Plantation

LAWN'S LN

COURT ROAD

WATERWORKS RD

Rollesby Bridge

P

Broadland Farm

CLERE DR

A149

Walpole Farm

Church Farm

Clippesby House

Clippesby

CHURCH LA

Grange Farm

ST MARGARET'S WY 1
WESTFIELD CL 2
ROYDEN WY 3
ORCHARD WY 4
CLAXTONS GDNS 5
FIR TREE CL 6

Oak Farm

LADY BROAD LA

Lily Broad

Rollesby Broad

Burghwood Farm

Wet Carr

MAIN RD

THE GROVE

HALL ROAD

Hall Farm

B1152

Church Farm

Willow Tree Farm

7 TRUST CL
8 HALL CL
9 BYGONE CL

The Carr

Burgh Wood

Long Common Plantation

EELS FOOT RD

WHITEHALL

Ash Carr

Burgh St Margaret (Fleggburgh)

Whitethorn Farm

TWIN RD

TOWER ROAD

St Mary's Church (rems)

Ormesby Little Broad

C4
1 DEEPDALE AVE
2 PEARTREE AVE
3 RISING WAY
4 ROCHFORD RD
5 MERRIMAN RD
6 BOSGATE RISE
7 HELEN AVE
8 SIDNEY CL
9 RISING WY

D2
1 CORONATION AVE
2 KING GEORGE'S AVE
3 KING GEORGE CL
4 SCHOOL CL
5 MEADOW LA
6 COURT CL
7 GREBE CL
8 ROMANY CL
9 ROLLESBY GDNS

10 BARLEY VW CL

D4
1 REPPS RD
2 CORONATION AVE
3 PLAYING FIELD LA
4 BLENHEIM AVE
5 TRELAWNY RD
6 STATION CL
7 CROMWELL CL
8 WELBECK AVE
9 HAMILTON WLK

10 CLARENDON DR
11 OXFORD WAY
12 PLAYING FIELD LA
13 HEMSBY RD
14 HOLLY CL
15 BROOM CL
16 WILLOWS CT
17 PINE CL
18 WILLOW WAY
19 CEDAR CL

20 MAPLE CL
21 ALMOND CL
22 ACACIA AVE
23 SYCAMORE AVE
24 WALNUT TREE AVE
25 CHERRY TREE AVE
26 JUNIPER DR
27 HAZEL DR
28 ASPEN CLOSE
29 SAXON CLOSE

30 JUBILEE WALK

B6
1 BACK PATH
2 OLD CHAPEL RD
3 BACK RD
4 THE LOKE
5 MARINE CRES
6 WINMER AVE
7 ACKLAND CL
8 GEORGE BECK RD
9 THE COBBLEWAYS
10 GREENCOURTS
11 SPINDRIFT CL
12 LAVENDER CT
13 SANDPIPER CT
14 MARKET PL

57

Scale: 1¾ inches to 1 mile
0 ¼ ½ mile
0 250m 500m 750m 1 km

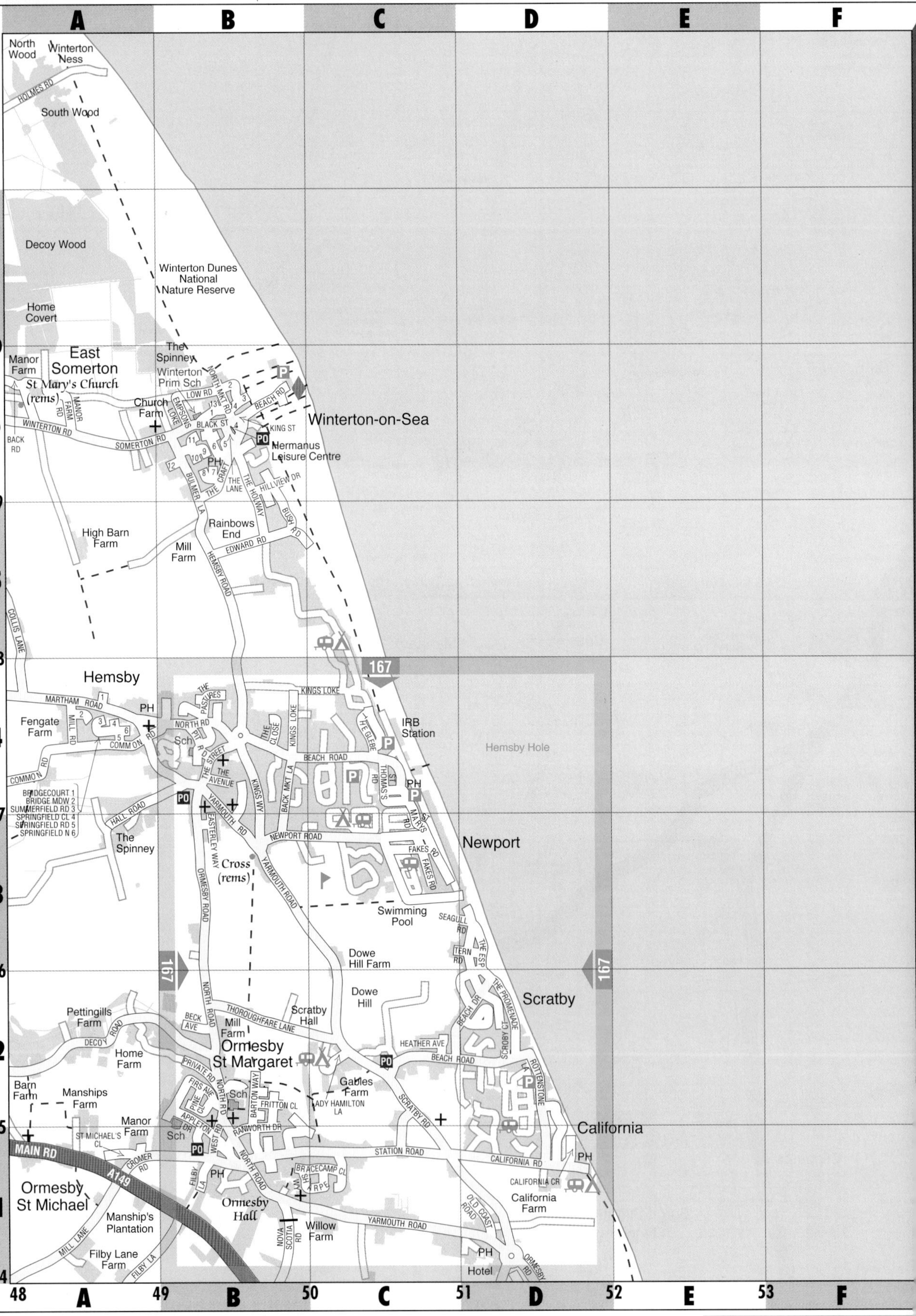

A B C D E F
8
21
7
20
6
19
5
18
4
17
3
16
2
15
1
14
48 49 50 51 52 53
North Wood
Winterton Ness
HOLMES RD
South Wood
Decoy Wood
Winterton Dunes National Nature Reserve
Home Covert
Manor Farm
East Somerton
St Mary's Church (rems)
MANOR FARM RD
The Spinney
Winterton Prim Sch
Church Farm
LOW RD
NORTH MKT RD
BEACH RD
Winterton-on-Sea
EMPSONS LOKE
BLACK ST
KING ST
WINTERTON RD
BACK RD
SOMERTON RD
Hermanus Leisure Centre
PH
BULMER LA
THE CRAFT
THE LANE
THE HOLWAY
HILLVIEW DR
BUSH RD
Rainbows End
EDWARD RD
High Barn Farm
Mill Farm
HEMSBY ROAD
COLLIS LANE
167
Hemsby
MARTHAM ROAD
PH
THE PASTURES
KINGS LOKE
Fengate Farm
MILL RD
COMMON RD
NORTH RD
Sch
PIT RD
THE STREET
THE CLOSE
KINGS LOKE
THE GLEBE
IRB Station
Hemsby Hole
BEACH ROAD
THE AVENUE
KINGS WAY
BACK MKT LA
ST THOMAS'S RD
ST MARYS RD
PH
BRIDGECOURT 1
BRIDGE MDW 2
SUMMERFIELD RD 3
SPRINGFIELD CL 4
SPRINGFIELD RD 5
SPRINGFIELD N 6
HALL ROAD
PO
YARMOUTH RD
EASTERLEY WAY
NEWPORT ROAD
FAKES RD
Newport
The Spinney
Cross (rems)
ORMESBY ROAD
YARMOUTH ROAD
Swimming Pool
SEAGULL RD
TERN RD
THE ESP
167
Dowe Hill Farm
Dowe Hill
THE PROMENADE
Scratby
NORTH ROAD
Pettingills Farm
BECK AVE
THOROUGHFARE LANE
Scratby Hall
BEACH DR
SCROBY CT
DECOY ROAD
Mill Farm
Ormesby St Margaret
HEATHER AVE
BEACH ROAD
Home Farm
PRIVATE RD
PO
ROTTENSTONE LA
Barn Farm
Manships Farm
FIRS AVE
PINE CL
Sch
BARTON WAY
FRITTON CL
Gables Farm
LADY HAMILTON LA
SCRATBY RD
Manor Farm
APPLETON DR
RANWORTH DR
California
ST MICHAEL'S CL
Sch
WEST RD
MAIN RD
CROMER RD
STATION ROAD
CALIFORNIA RD
PH
BRACECAMP CL
SHARPE WAY
A149
FILBY LA
CALIFORNIA CR
Ormesby St Michael
Ormesby Hall
California Farm
OLD COAST ROAD
Manship's Plantation
NOVA SCOTIA RD
Willow Farm
YARMOUTH ROAD
MILL LANE
Filby Lane Farm
FILBY LA
PH
Hotel
ORMESBY RD

76
57
168

For full street detail of the highlighted area see page 167

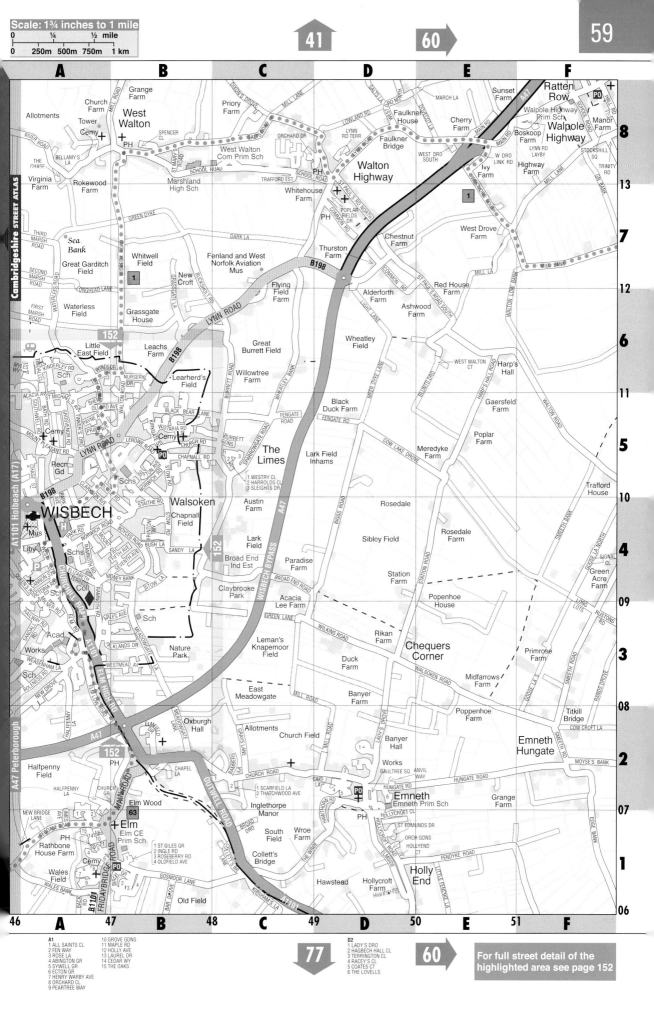

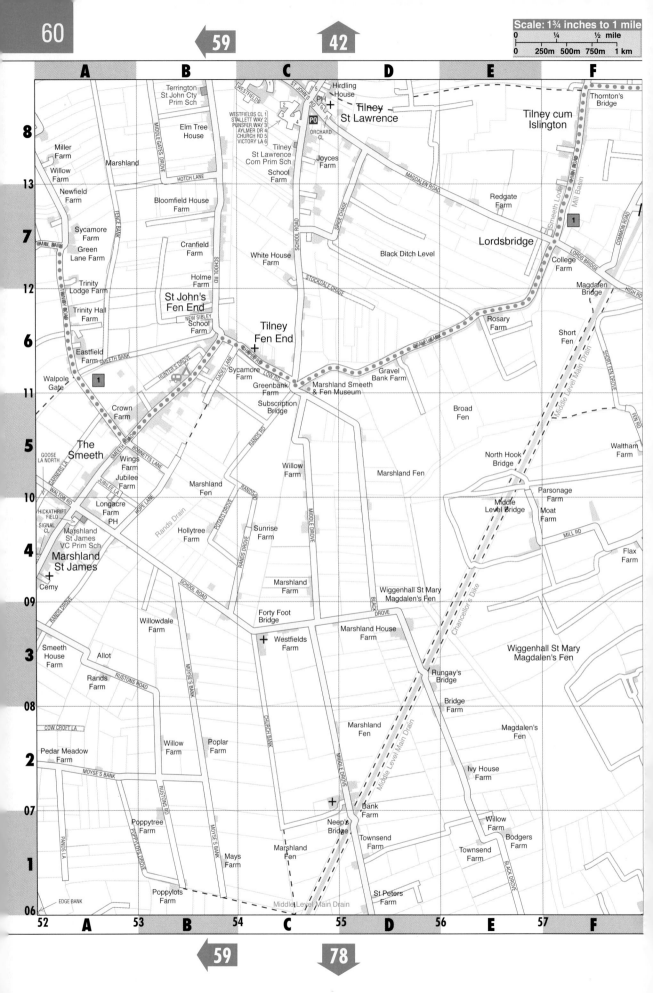

A   B   C   D   E   F

8

Miller Farm

Terrington St John Cty Prim Sch

Elm Tree House

WESTFIELDS

WESTFIELDS CL 1
STALLETT WAY 2
PUNSFER WAY 3
AYLMER DR 4
CHURCH RD 5
VICTORY LA 6

ST JOHN'S RD

Hirdling House

PH

Tilney St Lawrence

Tilney cum Islington

Thornton's Bridge

Marshland

13

Willow Farm

Newfield Farm

Bloomfield House Farm

Tilney St Lawrence Com Prim Sch

School Farm

PO
ORCHARD CL

Joyces Farm

Magdalen Road

Redgate Farm

Smeeth Lode

Mill Basin

HIGH ROAD

COMMON ROAD

7

Sycamore Farm

Green Lane Farm

HOTCH LANE

Cranfield Farm

MIDDLE GATES DROVE

SCHOOL RD

White House Farm

SPICE CHASE

Black Ditch Level

Lordsbridge

1

College Farm

LORDS BRIDGE

HIGH RD

Trinity Lodge Farm

FENCE BANK

Holme Farm

SCHOOL RD

St John's Fen End

STOCKDALE CHASE

Magdalen Bridge

12

Trinity Hall Farm

NEW SIBLEY

School Farm

Tilney Fen End

Short Fen

MIDDLE LEVEL MAIN DRAIN

SHORT FEN DROVE

FEN RD

6

Eastfield Farm

SMEETH BANK

HUNTER'S DROVE

DADES LANE

GLEBE RD

LOW RD

Sycamore Farm

Greenbank Farm

Marshland Smeeth & Fen Museum

GRAVEL BANK

Gravel Bank Farm

Rosary Farm

Walpole Gate

1

TRINITY ROAD

Crown Farm

SMEETH ROAD

RANDS RD

Subscription Bridge

Broad Fen

North Hook Bridge

Waltham Farm

11

The Smeeth

GOOSE LA NORTH

CARThERS LA

WALTON RD

BONNETTS LANE

JUBILEE LA

HOPE LANE

Wings Farm

Jubilee Farm

Marshland Fen

RANDS DROVE

RANDS RD

Willow Farm

Marshland Fen

Parsonage Farm

Middle Level Bridge

Moat Farm

5

10

Longacre Farm PH

HICKATHRIFT FIELD

SIGNAL CL

Marshland St James VC Prim Sch

Rands Drain

POTATO DROVE

Hollytree Farm

Sunrise Farm

MIDDLE DROVE

Marshland Fen

Chancellor's Dike

MILL RD

Flax Farm

4

Marshland St James

Cemy

RANDS DROVE

SCHOOL ROAD

Marshland Farm

BLACK DROVE

Wiggenhall St Mary Magdalen's Fen

Wiggenhall St Mary Magdalen's Fen

09

Smeeth House Farm

Allot

RUSTONS ROAD

Willowdale Farm

Forty Foot Bridge

Westfields Farm

Marshland House Farm

Middle Level Main Drain

Rungay's Bridge

3

Rands Farm

MOYSE'S BANK

CHURCH BANK

Bridge Farm

08

COW CROFT LA

Pedar Meadow Farm

MOYSE'S BANK

Willow Farm

Poplar Farm

MIDDLE DROVE

Marshland Fen

Magdalen's Fen

2

RUSTONS RD

RANDS LA

Ivy House Farm

07

Poppytree Farm

POPPYLOTS DROVE

MOYSE'S BANK

Mays Farm

Marshland Fen

Neep's Bridge

Bank Farm

Townsend Farm

Willow Farm

Townsend Farm

Bodgers Farm

BLACK DROVE

1

EDGE BANK

Poppylots Farm

Middle Level Main Drain

St Peters Farm

06

52   A   53   B   54   C   55   D   56   E   57   F

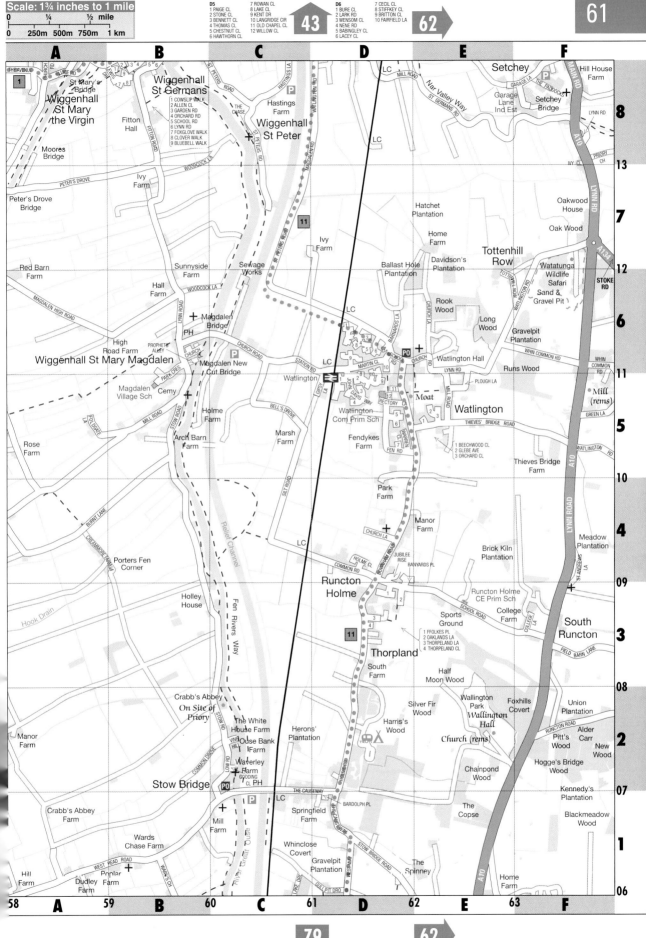

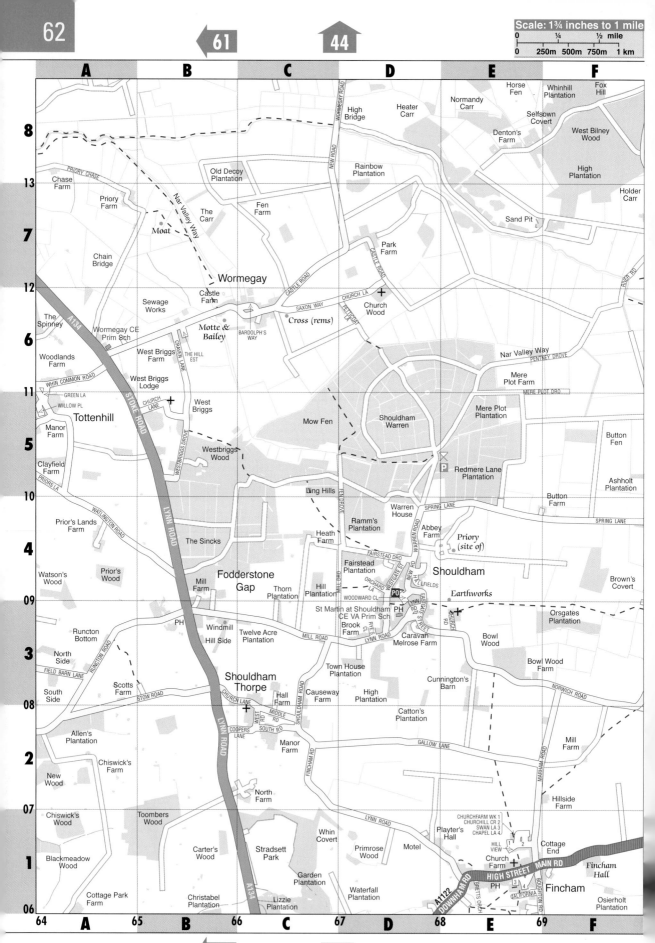

A   B   C   D   E   F

Horse
Fen
Whinhill
Plantation
Fox
Hill

Normandy
Carr
Selfsown
Covert
West Bilney
Wood

8

Denton's
Farm

High
Bridge
Heater
Carr

New Road

Warmegay Road

Old Decoy
Plantation
Rainbow
Plantation
High
Plantation

13
Chase
Farm
Holder
Carr

Priory
Farm
Fen
Farm
Sand Pit

Priory Chase

The
Carr

Nar Valley Way

7
Moat
Park
Farm

Castle Road

Church La

River Rd

Chain
Bridge
Wormegay
Cross (rems)
Church
Wood

12
Castle
Farm
Saxon Way

Sewage
Works

A134

The
Spinney
Wormegay CE
Prim Sch
Motte &
Bailey
Petticoat

6
Bardolph's
Way

Nar Valley Way
Pentley Drove

Woodlands
Farm
West Briggs
Farm
The Hill
Est
Mere
Plot Farm

Craven Lane

Whin Common Road

West Briggs
Lodge
Mere Plot Dro

11
Green La
Church
Lane
Mere Plot
Plantation
Button
Fen

Willow Pl
West
Briggs
Shouldham
Warren

Stone Road

Tottenhill
Mow Fen

5
Manor
Farm
Westbriggs
Wood
Ashholt
Plantation

Westbriggs Drove

Clayfield
Farm
P
Redmere Lane
Plantation
Button
Farm

10
Priors La
Ling Hills
Warren
House
Spring Lane
Spring Lane

Lynn Road

Prior's Lands
Farm
Ramm's
Plantation
Abbey
Farm
Priory
(site of)

Watlington Road

Heath
Farm
Feldrove

4
The Sincks
Fairstead Dro

Watson's
Wood
Prior's
Wood
Mill Dro
Fairstead
Plantation
Shouldham
Brown's
Covert

Mill
Farm
Orchard La
Earthworks
Orsgates
Plantation

Foddestone
Gap
Thorn
Plantation
Hill
Plantation
Woodward Cl
Westgate St
PO
New

St Martin at Shouldham
CE VA Prim Sch
PH

09
PH
Hill
Plantation
Brook
Farm
Pres Rd
Eastgate Street
Church Rd
Bowl
Wood

Windmill
Hill Side
Twelve Acre
Plantation
Caravan
Melrose Farm

3
Runcton
Bottom
Cunnington's
Barn
Bowl Wood
Farm

Runcton Road

North
Side
Mill Road
Town House
Plantation

Field Barn Lane

Norwich Road

Scotts
Farm
Shouldham
Thorpe
Causeway
Farm

08
South
Side
Hall
Farm
High
Plantation
Catton's
Plantation

Church Lane
Middle
Rd

Stow Road
Coopers
Lane
West
Rd

Allen's
Plantation
South Rd
Gallow Lane
Mill
Farm

2
Manor
Farm

Fincham Rd

Lynn Road

Shouldham Road

Marham Road

New
Wood
Chiswick's
Farm

Hillside
Farm

North
Farm

07
Churchfarm Wk 1
Churchill Cr 2
Swan La 3
Chapel La 4

Chiswick's
Wood
Toombers
Wood
Whin
Covert
Lynn Road
Player's
Hall
Cottage
End

Motel
Hill
View
1 2

Stradsett
Park
Primrose
Wood
Church
Farm
PH

1
Blackmeadow
Wood
Carter's
Wood
High Street
Main Rd
Fincham
Hall

A134
Garden
Plantation
Waterfall
Plantation
A1122
Downham Rd
Bretts Orch
California
Fincham

Cottage Park
Farm
Christabel
Plantation
Lizzie
Plantation
Osierholt
Plantation

Boughton Rd

06
A   B   C   D   E   F

64   65   66   67   68   69

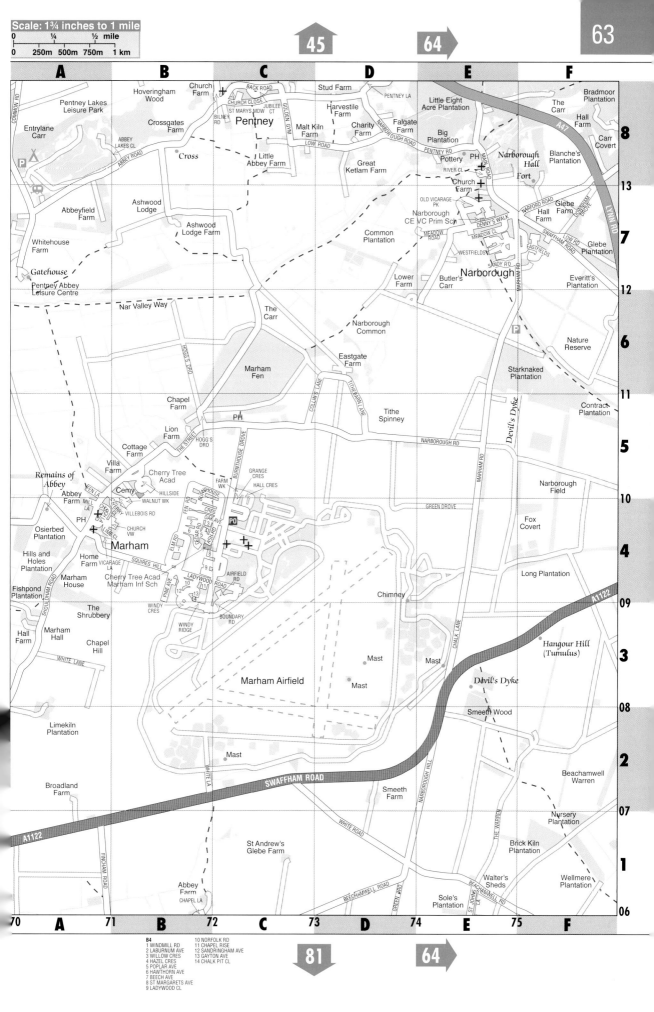

63
46

Scale: 1¾ inches to 1 mile

0   ¼   ½   mile
0   250m   500m   750m   1 km

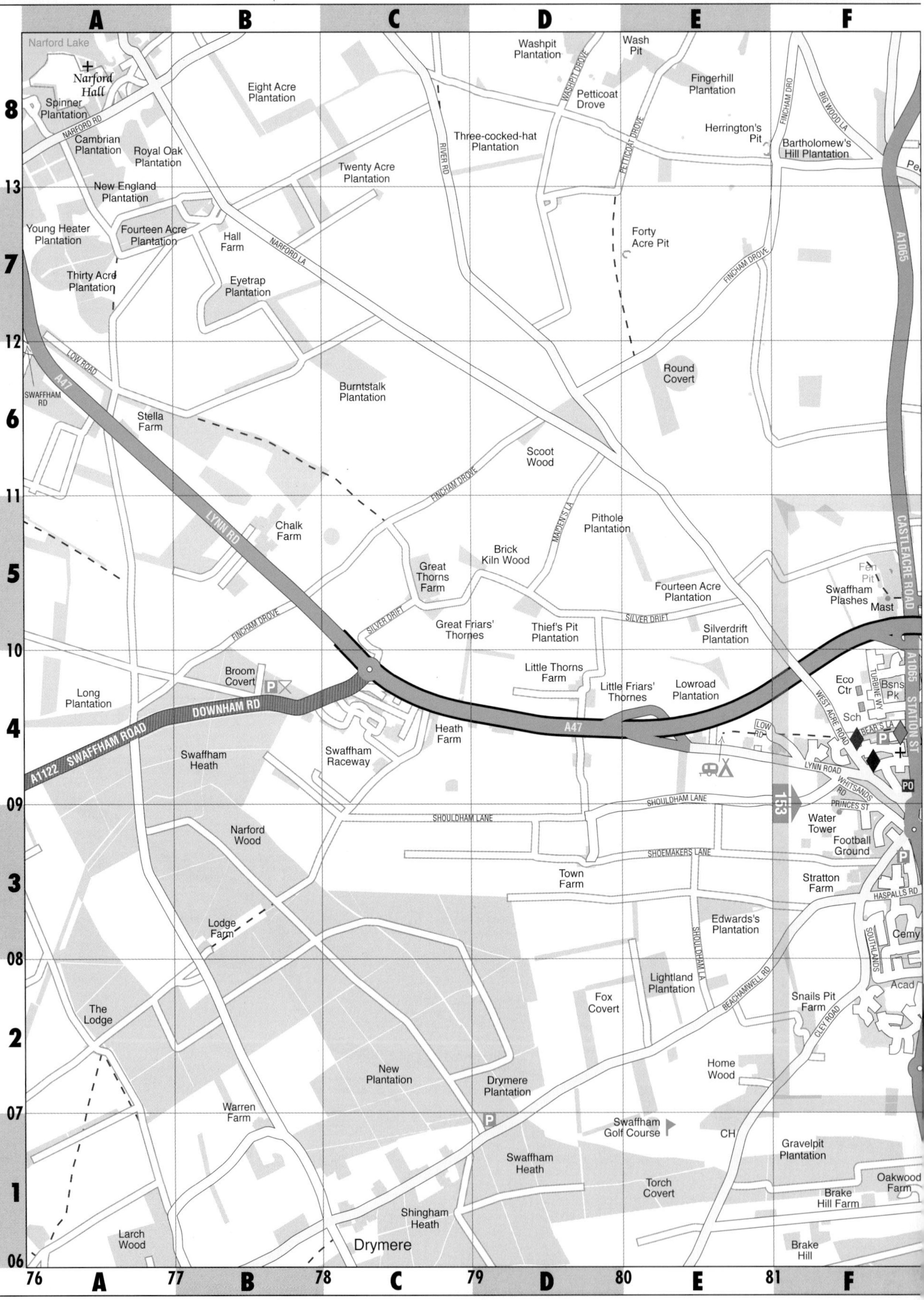

A B C D E F

8

Narford Lake
Narford Hall
Spinner Plantation
Cambrian Plantation
Royal Oak Plantation
New England Plantation
Eight Acre Plantation
Twenty Acre Plantation
Three-cocked-hat Plantation
Washpit Plantation
Washpit Drove
Wash Pit
Petticoat Drove
Fingerhill Plantation
Herrington's Pit
Bartholomew's Hill Plantation

NARFORD RD
RIVER RD
PETTICOAT DROVE
FINCHAM DRO
BIG WOOD LA
A1065

13

Young Heater Plantation
Fourteen Acre Plantation
Hall Farm
NARFORD LA
Forty Acre Pit

7

Thirty Acre Plantation
Eyetrap Plantation
FINCHAM DROVE

12

LOW ROAD
SWAFFHAM RD
A47
Stella Farm
Burntstalk Plantation
Round Covert

6

LYNN RD
Chalk Farm
Scoot Wood
MACEN'S LA
Pithole Plantation
Fen Pit
Swaffham Plashes
Mast

11

FINCHAM DROVE
Great Thorns Farm
Brick Kiln Wood
Fourteen Acre Plantation

5

FINCHAM DROVE
SILVER DRIFT
Great Friars' Thornes
Thief's Pit Plantation
SILVER DRIFT
Silverdrift Plantation
Eco Ctr
Bsns Pk
Sch
TURBINE VW
A1065

10

Long Plantation
Broom Covert
Little Thorns Farm
Little Friars' Thornes
Lowroad Plantation
LOW RD
WEST ACRE ROAD
BEAR'S LA

4

A1122 SWAFFHAM ROAD
DOWNHAM RD
Swaffham Heath
Swaffham Raceway
Heath Farm
A47
LYNN ROAD
STATION ST
WHITSANDS RD
PRINCES ST
Water Tower
Football Ground
Stratton Farm
HASPALLS RD
153

09

SHOULDHAM LANE
SHOULDHAM LANE
SHOEMAKERS LANE
SHOULDHAM LA
Edwards's Plantation
SOUTHLANDS
Cemy
Acad

3

Narford Wood
Town Farm
BEACHAMWELL RD
CLEY ROAD

08

Lodge Farm
Fox Covert
Lightland Plantation
Snails Pit Farm

2

The Lodge
New Plantation
Drymere Plantation
Home Wood
Gravelpit Plantation
Oakwood Farm

07

Warren Farm
Swaffham Golf Course
CH
Brake Hill Farm

1

Larch Wood
Shingham Heath
Swaffham Heath
Torch Covert
Brake Hill

06

Drymere

76 A 77 B 78 C 79 D 80 E 81 F

63
82

For full street detail of the highlighted area see page 153

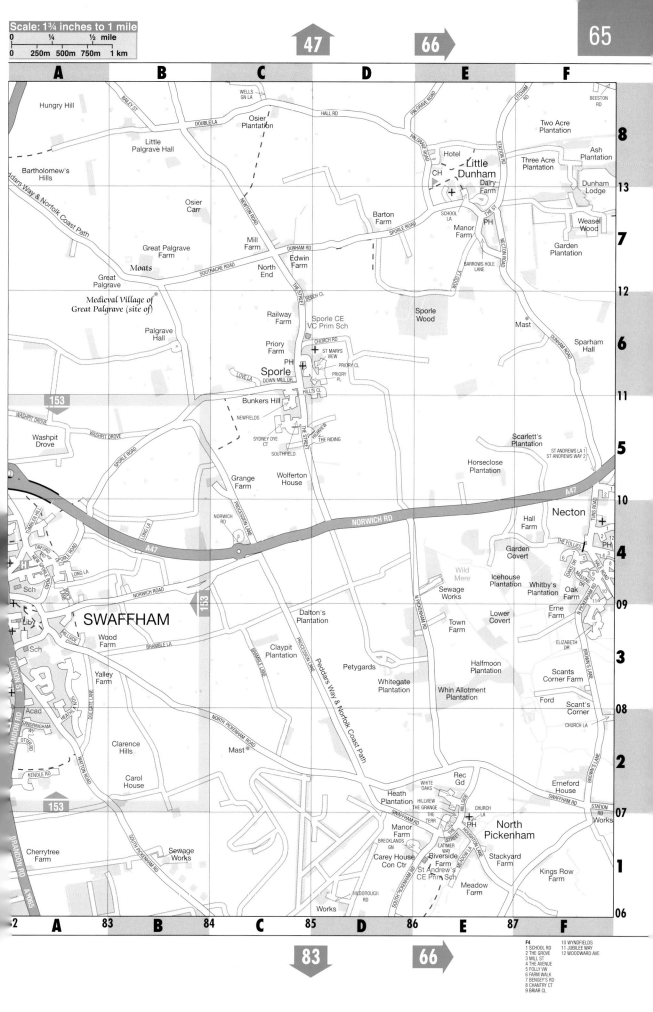

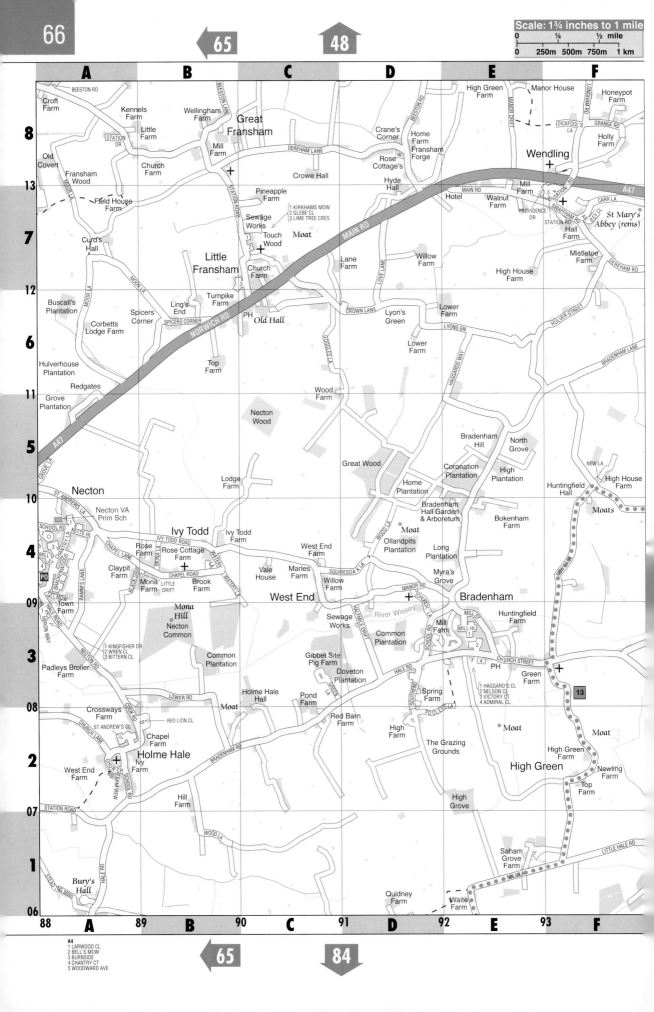

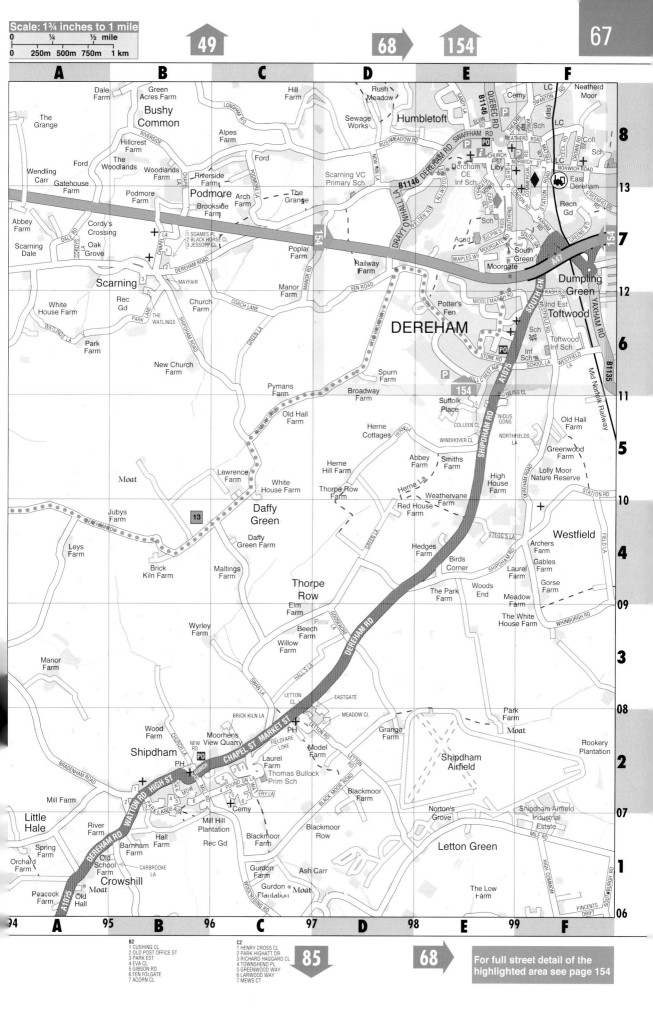

B2
1 CUSHING CL
2 OLD POST OFFICE ST
3 PARK EST
4 EVA CL
5 GIBSON RD
6 FEN FOLGATE
7 ACORN CL

C2
1 HENRY CROSS CL
2 PARK HIGHATT DR
3 RICHARD HAGGARD CL
4 TOWNSHEND PL
5 GREENWOOD WAY
6 LARWOOD WAY
7 MEWS CT

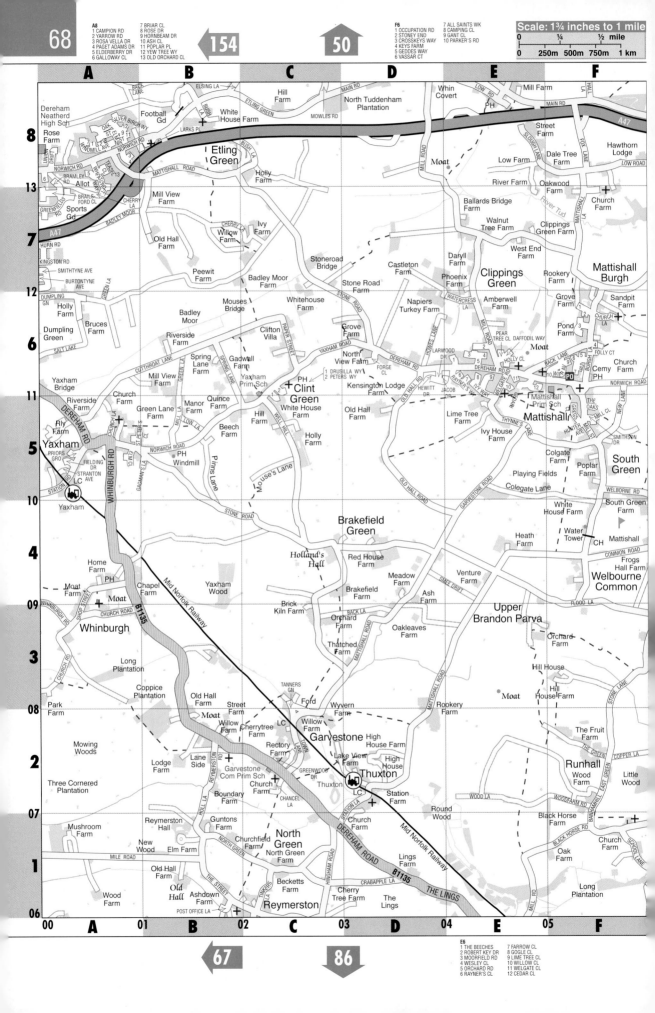

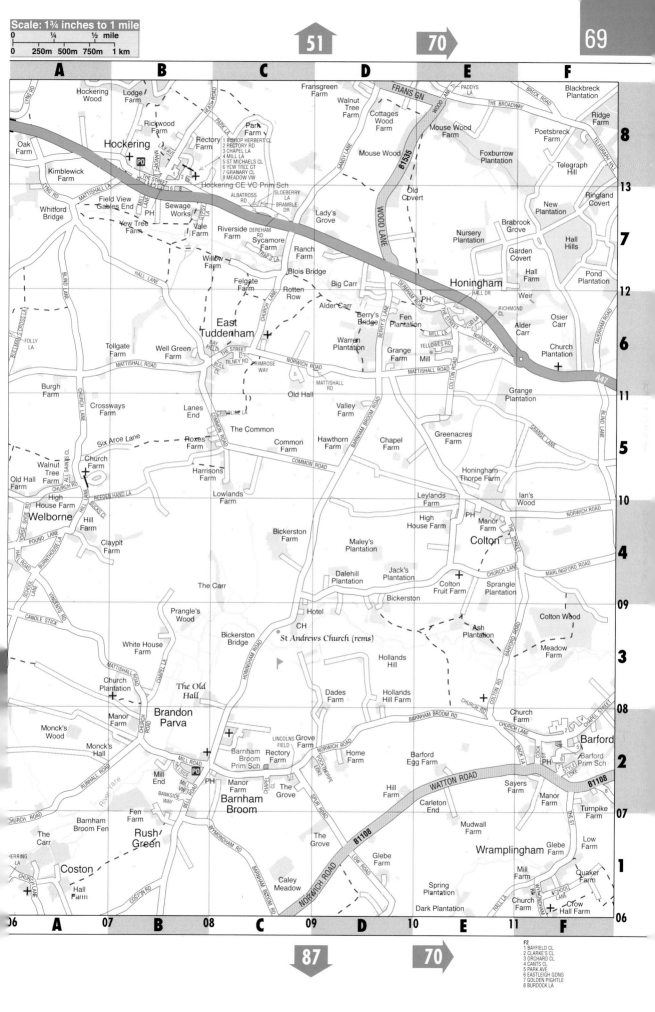

Map labels

A   B   C   D   E   F

FRANS GN

Fransgreen Farm

Blackbreck Plantation

Hockering Wood

Lodge Farm

PADDYS LA

BRECK ROAD

THE BROADWAY

Ridge Farm

Walnut Tree Farm

Cottages Wood Farm

Mouse Wood Farm

Poetsbreck Farm

WOOD LANE

Rickwood Farm

Park Farm

1 BISHOP HERBERT CL
2 RECTORY RD
3 CHAPEL LA
4 MILL LA
5 ST MICHAELS CL
6 YEW TREE CT
7 GRANARY CL
8 MEADOW VW

Mouse Wood

Foxburrow Plantation

Telegraph Hill

Oak Farm

Hockering

Rectory Farm

PO

Mouse Wood

B1535

Hall Fm

8

Kimblewick Farm

Hockering CE VC Prim Sch

ALBATROSS RD

SLOEBERRY LA

Old Covert

Honingham

New Plantation

Ringland Covert

13

MATTISHALL LA

Field View Gables End

Sewage Works

DEREHAM RD

BRAMBLE DR

Lady's Grove

Nursery Plantation

Brabrook Grove

Whitford Bridge

Yew Tree Farm

PH

Vale Farm

Riverside Farm

Sycamore Farm

TRAP'S LA

Ranch Farm

DEREHAM ROAD

HALL DR

PH

Hall Farm

Garden Covert

Hall Hills

7

BLIND LANE

HALL LANE

Willow Farm

Felgate Farm

Blois Bridge

Big Carr

Berry's Bridge

Fen Plantation

RICHMOND CL

Weir

Pond Plantation

12

Rotten Row

Alder Carr

NORWICH RD

Alder Carr

Osier Carr

BUCKLAM STROSS LA

FOLLY LA

East Tuddenham

CHURCH LANE

Warren Plantation

MILL LA

FELLOWES RD

Church Plantation

6

Tollgate Farm

Well Green Farm

BAY FIELD

THE STREET

TILNEY RD

Grange Farm

Mill

Burgh Farm

CHURCH LANE

BULL CL

PRIMROSE WAY

NORWICH ROAD

MATTISHALL RD

MATTISHALL ROAD

COLTON ROAD

Grange Plantation

A47

11

Crossways Farm

Lanes End

CRINGLINE LA

Old Hall

Valley Farm

BLIND LANE

Six Arce Lane

COMMON ROAD

The Common

Common Farm

Hawthorn Farm

Chapel Farm

Greenacres Farm

GRANGE LANE

5

Church Farm

Foxes Farm

COMMON ROAD

Honingham Thorpe Farm

Ian's Wood

NORWICH ROAD

10

Walnut Tree Farm

Harrisons Farm

Lowlands Farm

Bickerston Farm

Maley's Plantation

Leylands Farm

PH

Manor Farm

Old Hall Farm

High House Farm

REEDEN HAND LA

High House Farm

THE STREET

Welborne

ALL SAINTS CL

Hill Farm

Claypit Farm

The Carr

Dalehill Plantation

Jack's Plantation

Colton

4

HORSE SHOE LA

POUND LANE

BUCKS CL

Bickerston

Colton Fruit Farm

Sprangle Plantation

MARLINGFORD ROAD

HALL ROAD

BURNTHOUSE LA

VINCENTS RD

MATTISHALL ROAD

Prangle's Wood

HONINGHAM ROAD

Hotel

CH

BARFORD ROAD

Colton Wood

09

SCHOOL LANE

CANDLE STICK

White House Farm

Bickerston Bridge

St Andrews Church (rems)

Hollands Hill

Ash Plantation

Meadow Farm

3

CHAPEL LA

The Old Hall

Dades Farm

Hollands Hill Farm

08

Church Plantation

Manor Farm

Brandon Parva

BARNHAM BROOM RD

Church Farm

CHAPEL STREET

Barford

Monck's Wood

CHURCH ROAD

LINCOLNS FIELD

Grove Farm

NORWICH ROAD

Home Farm

PH

Barford Prim Sch

STYLE LO

Monck's Hall

Barnham Broom Prim Sch

Rectory Farm

WOODTHORPE LOKE

Barford Egg Farm

BACK LA

COCK ST

PH

Manor Farm

2

RUNHALL ROAD

MILL ROAD

PO

CHAPEL LA

The Grove

Hill Farm

WATTON ROAD

Sayers Farm

B1108

Mill End

PH

Manor Farm

SPUR ROAD

Carleton End

Turnpike Farm

07

CHURCH ROAD

Fen Farm

BANKSIDE WAY

BELL RD

MILL SIDE

Barnham Broom

Barnham Broom Fen

Rush Green

WYMONDHAM RD

The Grove

B1108

Mudwall Farm

Manor Farm

Glebe Farm

Low Farm

Wramplingham

1

HERRING LA

The Carr

Coston

COSTON RD

BARNHAM BROOM RD

Caley Meadow

NORWICH ROAD

LOW ROAD

Glebe Farm

Spring Plantation

Mill Farm

THE ST

Quaker Farm

CHURCH LANE

Hall Farm

Dark Plantation

Church Farm

WYMONDHAM RD

SCHOOL LANE

Crow Hall Farm

River Yare

06

A   07   B   08   C   09   D   10   E   11   F   06

F2
1 BAYFIELD CL
2 CLARKE'S CL
3 ORCHARD CL
4 CANTS CL
5 PARK AVE
6 EASTLEIGH GDNS
7 GOLDEN PIGHTLE
8 BURDOCK LA

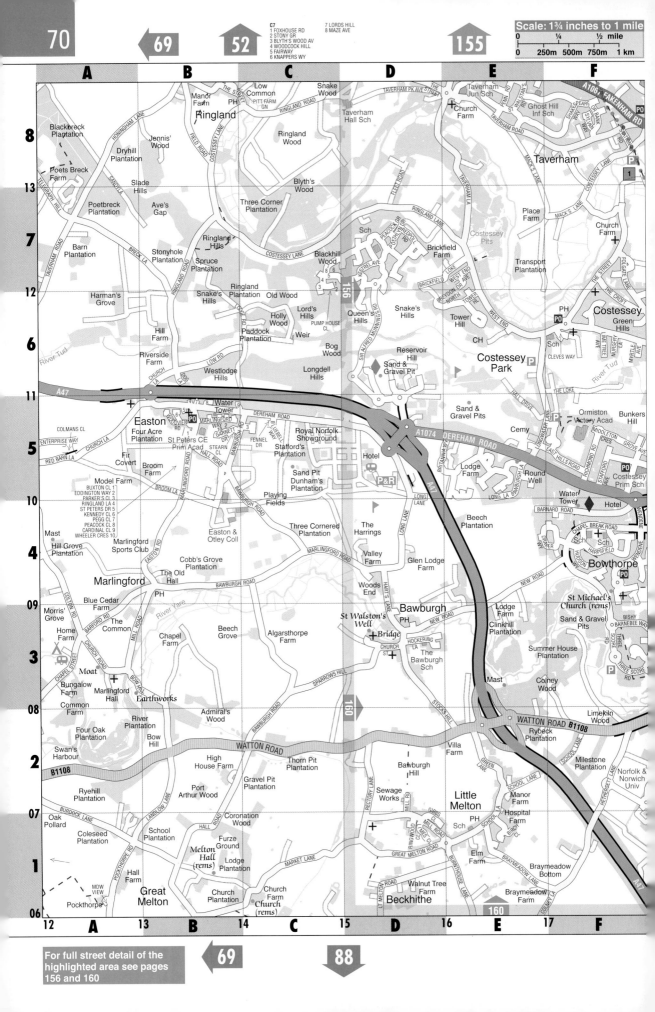

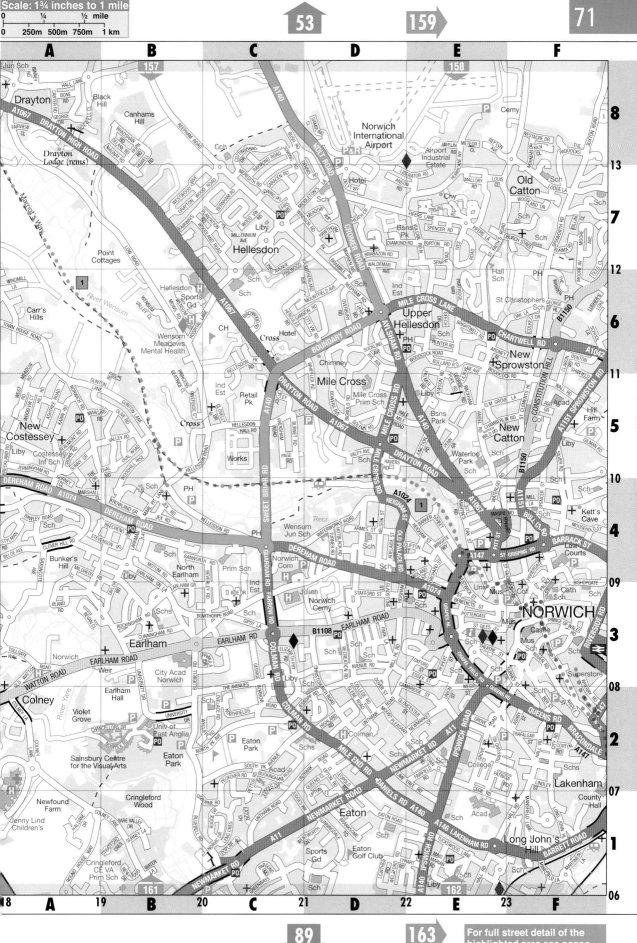

Scale: 1¾ inches to 1 mile

89
163

For full street detail of the
highlighted area see pages
157, 158, 161 and 162

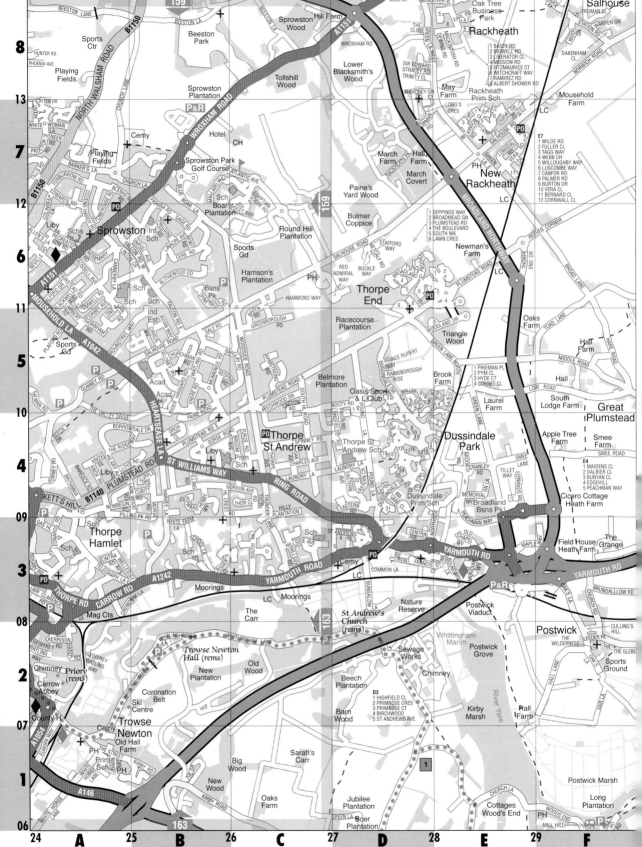

158
54

D6
1 ALTONGATE
2 HALLGATE
3 NORTHGATE
4 BROAD VW
5 BARKER WAY
6 BEECHBANK DR

7 HEATHERWOOD CL
8 ST DAVIDS DR
9 HEATH RD
10 PERCY HOWES CL

D5
1 WOODLANDS CRES
2 LUCAS CT
3 GUNNER CL
4 FIENNES RD
5 DOWSING CT
6 FAIRFAX DR

7 LYNN CL
8 LEVEN CL
9 JOYCE WAY
10 MARVELL GN

Scale: 1¾ inches to 1 mile

0   ¼   ½   mile
0   250m 500m 750m 1 km

E7
1 WILDE RD
2 FULLER CL
3 TAGG WAY
4 WEBB DR
5 WILLOUGHBY WAY
6 LUSCOMBE WAY
7 CANFOR RD
8 PALMER RD
9 BURTON CL
10 VERA CL
11 BERNARD CL
12 CORNWALL CL

E4
1 MAIDENS CL
2 DALBIER CL
3 BUNYAN CL
4 EDGEHILL
5 PEACHMAN WAY

D3
1 HIGHFIELD CL
2 PRIMROSE CRES
3 PRIMROSE CL
4 BIRCHWOOD
5 ST ANDREWS AVE

For full street detail of the
highlighted area see pages
159 and 163

162
90

D4
1 MONTROSE CT
2 ASSOCIATION WAY
3 NEWCASTLE CL
4 FLEETWOOD DR
5 PARLIAMENT CT
6 HOPTON CL
7 MARSTON MOOR
8 MINION CL
9 CULVERIN CL

10 TURNHAM GN
11 SAKER CL
12 COMMONWEALTH WAY
13 DUSSINDALE DR
14 INDEPENDENT WAY
15 WINCESEY CL
16 ROWTON HEATH
17 ROUNDWAY DOWN
18 LENTHALL CL
19 HAMPDEN DR

20 NEWBURY WAY
21 WINSTANLEY RD
22 NEWARK CL
23 NASEBY WAY
24 LAUD CL
25 IRETON CL
26 ROUNDHEAD CT
27 DRAGOON CL
28 ROYALIST DR
29 MUSKETEER WAY

30 CAVALIER CL
31 MARY CHAPMAN CL
32 EASTERN CL
33 CHALGROVE FIELD

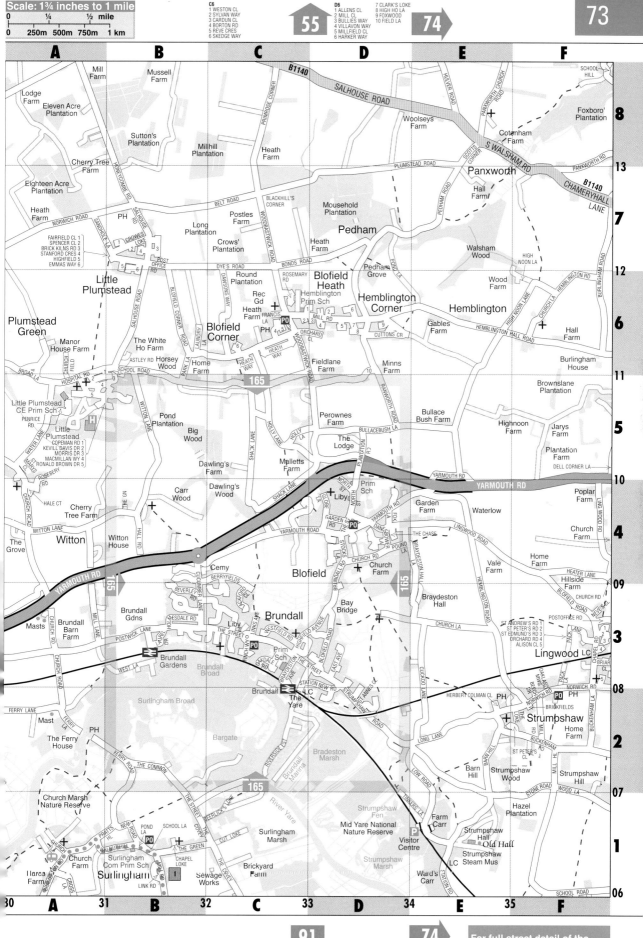

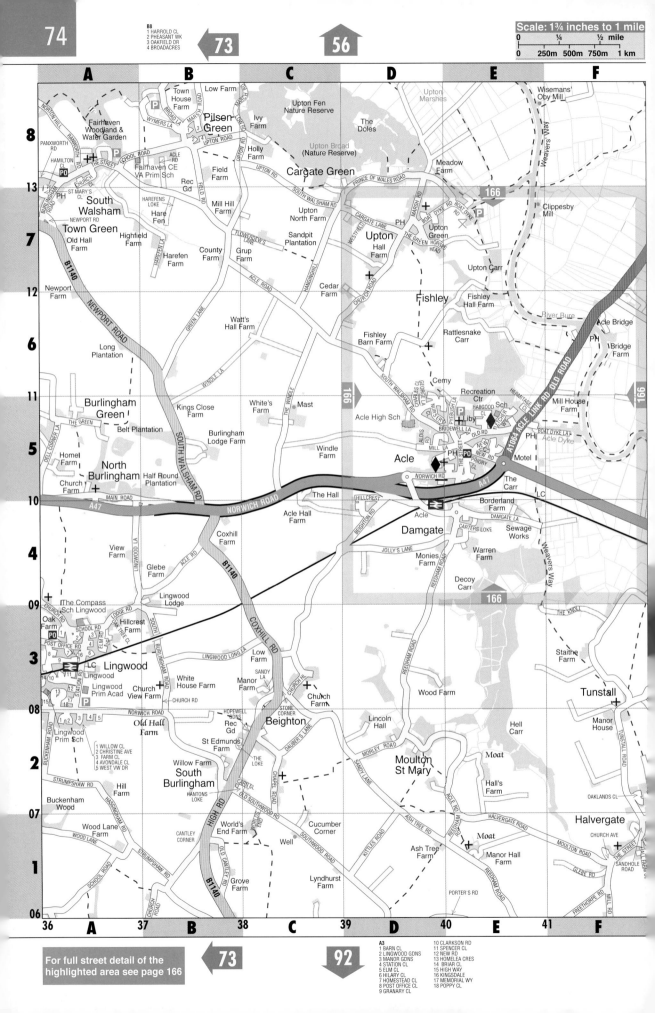

B8
1 HARROLD CL
2 PHEASANT WK
3 OAKFIELD DR
4 BROADACRES

73   56

A3
1 BARN CL
2 LINGWOOD GDNS
3 MANOR GDNS
4 STATION CL
5 ELM CL
6 HILARY CL
7 HOMESTEAD CL
8 POST OFFICE CL
9 GRANARY CL
10 CLARKSON RD
11 SPENCER CL
12 NEW RD
13 HOMELEA CRES
14 BRIAR CL
15 HIGH WAY
16 KINGSDALE
17 MEMORIAL WY
18 POPPY CL

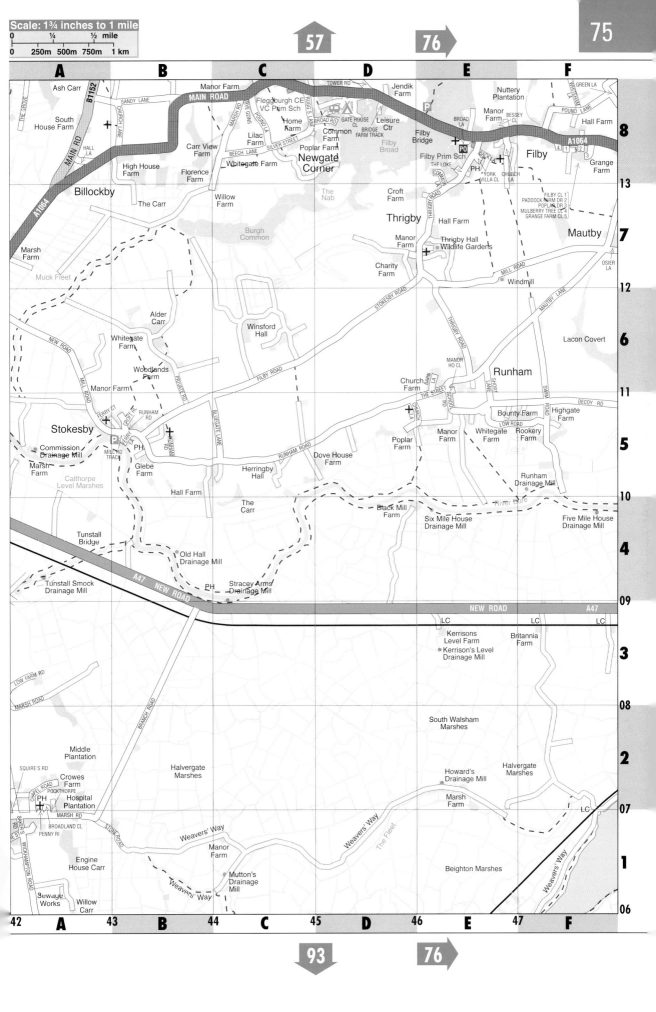

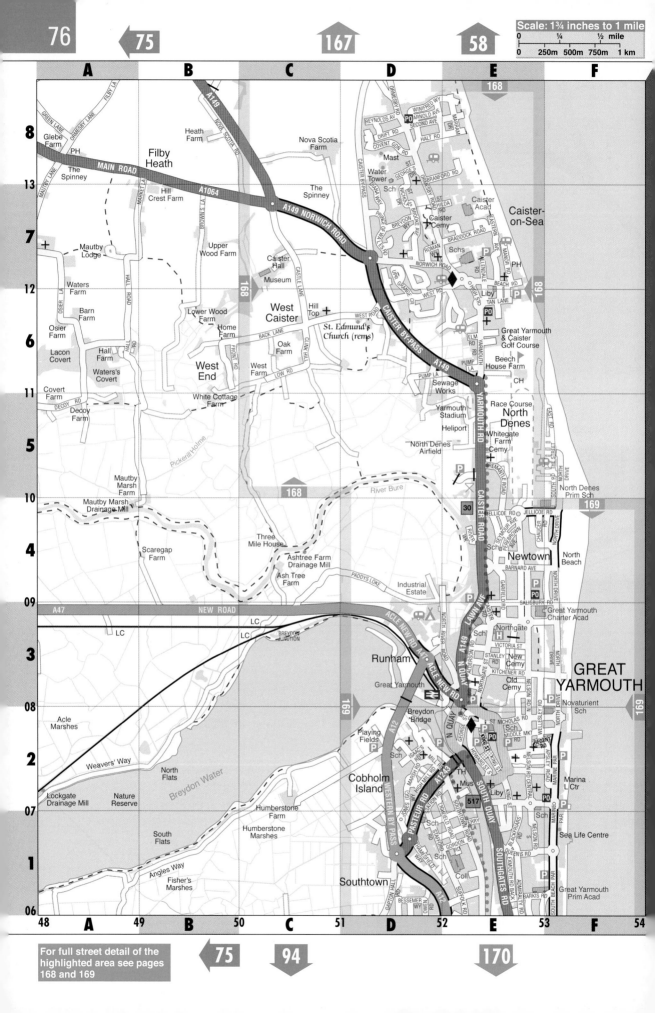

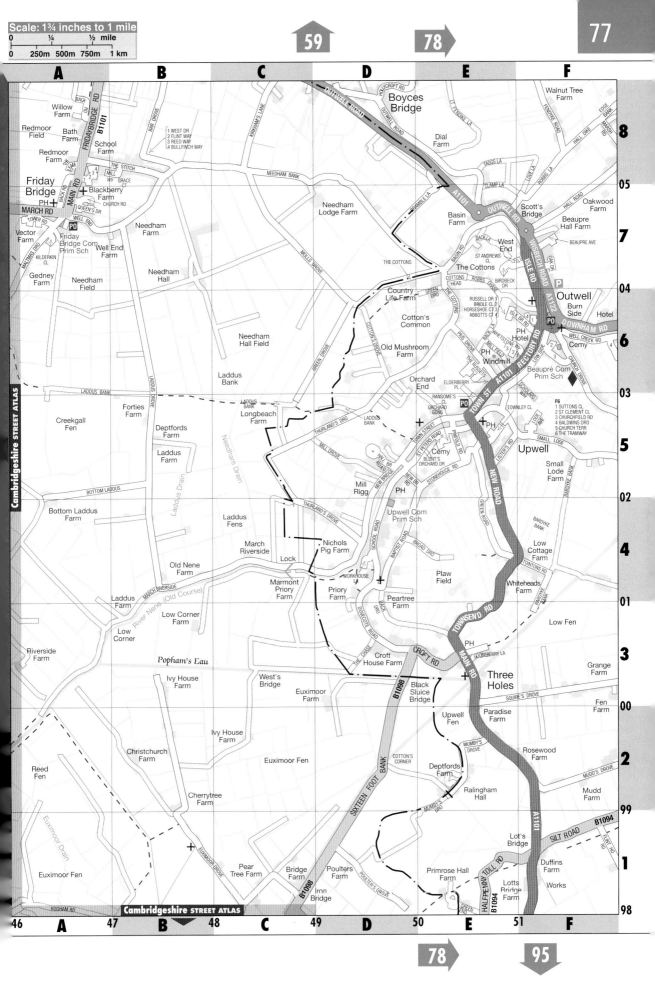

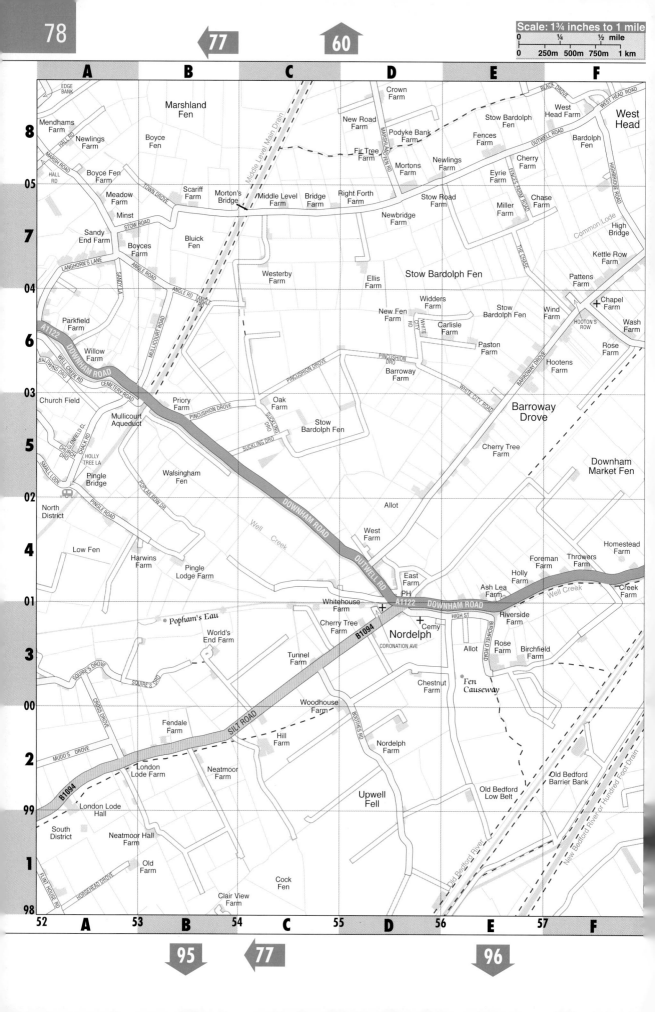

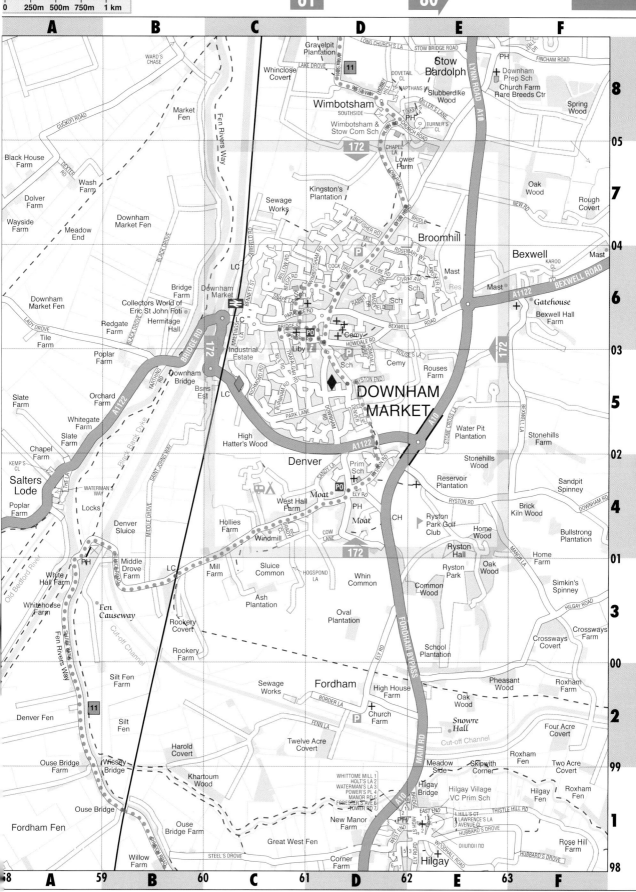

Scale: 1¾ inches to 1 mile

| 0 | ¼ | ½ mile |
| 0 | 250m 500m 750m | 1 km |

61

80

A B C D E F

8
05
7
04
6
03
5
02
4
01
3
00
2
99
1
98

WARD'S CHASE

Gravelpit Plantation

LONG CHURCH'S LA

STOW BRIDGE ROAD

Stow Bardolph

PH

FINCHAM ROAD

Downham Prep Sch
Church Farm Rare Breeds Ctr

Whinclose Covert

LAKE DROVE

11

DOVETAIL CL

NAPTHANS LA

Slubberdike Wood

Spring Wood

Wimbotsham

SOUTHSIDE

MILLER'S LANE

TURNER'S CL

PH

CHURCH ROAD

Oak Wood

Rough Covert

Bexwell

Mast

Market Fen

CUCKOO ROAD

Black House Farm

Dolver Farm

Wayside Farm

Wash Farm

Meadow End

Downham Market Fen

Sewage Works

Kingston's Plantation

KINGFISHER RD

172

Lower Farm

CHAPEL LA

BRIDLE LA

Broomhill

Mast

Mast

KAROO CL

Gatehouse

Bexwell Hall Farm

BEXWELL ROAD

A1122

Downham Market Fen

Redgate Farm

Bridge Farm

Hermitage Hall

Collectors World of Eric St John Foti

BENNETT ST

Downham Market

LC

LC

WILLOW RD

BEECH RD

SNAPE RD

ROSEMARY WY

GLEBE RD

COCK DRO

RABBIT

MASSEY

CIVRAY AVE

Sch

Sch

Cemy

Cemy

BEXWELL

HOWDALE RD

ROUSE'S LA

Rouses Farm

Res

172

BEXWELL LA

Stonehills Farm

Tile Farm

Poplar Farm

LADY DROVE

Orchard Farm

BLACK DROVE

Slate Farm

Whitegate Farm

Slate Farm

Chapel Farm

KEMP'S CL

Salters Lode

Poplar Farm

THE LA

A1122

WATERMAN'S WAY

Locks

Farthing RD

Downham Bridge

Bsns Est

LC

BRIDGE RD

172

SAINT JOHN'S WAY

Industrial Estate

RICHMOND RD

BURNHAM RD

Liby

PO

BRIDGE ST

TRAFALGAR RD

PARADISE RD

Sch

DOWNHAM

MARKET

RYSTON END

High Hatter's Wood

High Wood

Denver

SANDY LA

PO

Moat

ELY RD

Prim Sch

MAIN RD

A1122

A10

STONE CROSS LA

Water Pit Plantation

Stonehills Wood

Sandpit Spinney

Brick Kiln Wood

DOWNHAM RD

Bullstrong Plantation

Home Farm

MANOR LA

Home Wood

Simkin's Spinney

HILGAY ROAD

Crossways Covert

Crossways Farm

Slate Farm

White Hall Farm

Whitehouse Farm

PH

SLUICE BANK

FEN RIVERS WAY

SILICE RD

Middle Drove Farm

Denver Sluice

MIDDLE DROVE

Fen Causeway

Cut-off Channel

LC

Hollies Farm

West Hall Farm

BRADY

Windmill

COW LANE

Moat

PH

CH

Ryston Park Golf Club

Ryston Hall

Ryston Park

Oak Wood

Common Wood

Reservoir Plantation

RYSTON RD

Mill Farm

Sluice Common

Ash Plantation

Rookery Covert

Rookery Farm

HOGSPOND LA

Whin Common

Oval Plantation

172

School Plantation

Old Bedford River

Silt Fen Farm

11

Silt Fen

Denver Fen

Harold Covert

Sewage Works

Fordham

BORDER LA

High House Farm

Church Farm

FENN LA

Oak Wood

Pheasant Wood

Roxham Farm

FORDHAM BYPASS

ELY RD

Ouse Bridge Farm

Wissey Bridge

Khartoum Wood

Twelve Acre Covert

Snowre Hall

Four Acre Covert

MAIN RD

A10

Roxham Fen

Two Acre Covert

Ouse Bridge

Fordham Fen

Willow Farm

Ouse Bridge Farm

STEEL'S DROVE

Great West Fen

Corner Farm

WHITTOME MILL 1
HOLT'S LA 2
WATERMAN'S LA 3
POWER'S PL 4
MANOR RD 5
FORESTER'S AVE 6
TOWER RD 7

New Manor Farm

Meadow Side

Skipwith Corner

Hilgay Bridge

WEST END

Hilgay Village VC Prim Sch

PH

HIGH ST

EAST END

ST LAWRENCE'S LA
HILL'S CT
AVENUE CL

HUBBARD'S DROVE

THISTLE HILL RD

Hilgay Fen

Roxham Fen

Rose Hill Farm

Hilgay

GEORGE RD

W CHISHALL ROAD

HUBBARD'S DROVE

96

A B C D E F

80 **97**

For full street detail of the highlighted area see page 172

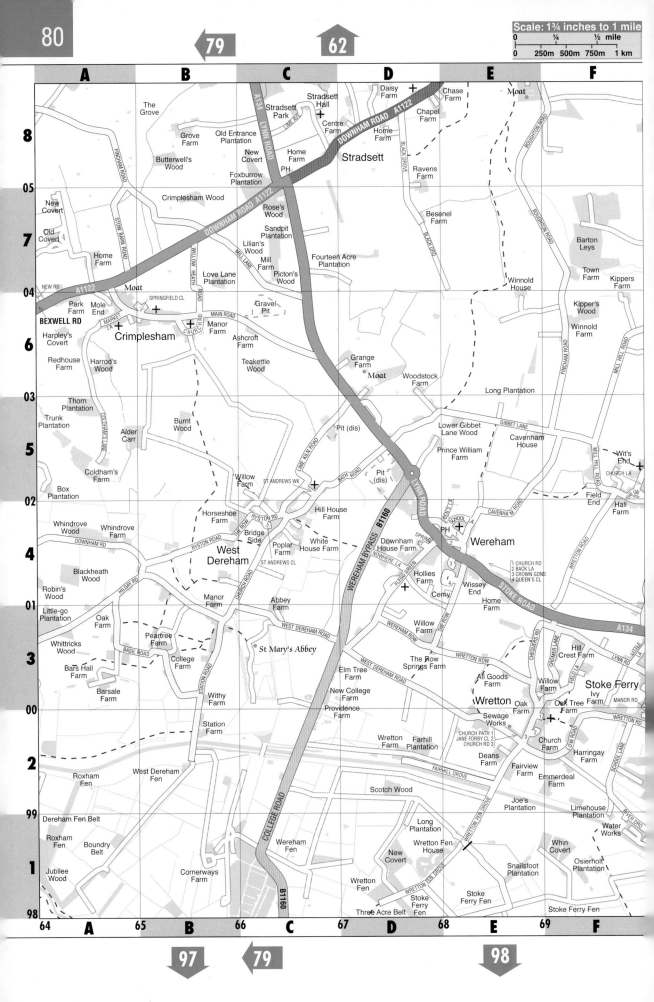

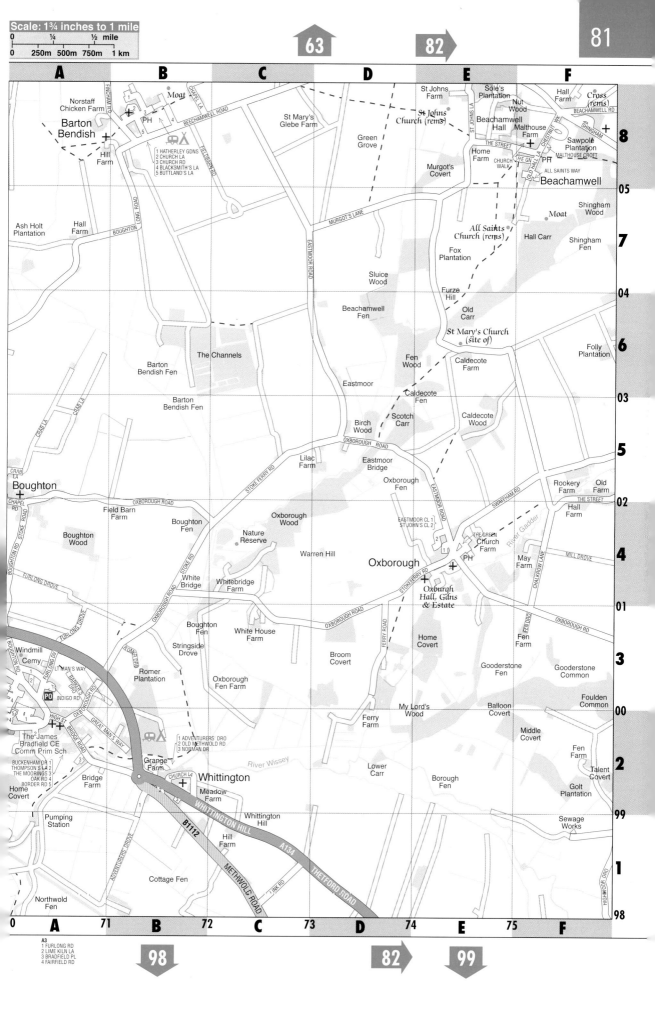
A B C D E F

Norstaff
Chicken Farm

Moat

Barton
Bendish

Hill
Farm

St Mary's
Glebe Farm

Green
Grove

St Johns
Farm

Sole's
Plantation

Nut
Wood

Hall
Farm

Cross
(rems)

BEACHAMWELL RD

St Johns
Church (rems)

Beachamwell
Hall

Malthouse
Farm

SHINGHAM WK

Sawpole
Plantation

MALTHOUSE CROFT

8

1 HATHERLEY GDNS
2 CHURCH LA
3 CHURCH RD
4 BLACKSMITH'S LA
5 BUTTLAND'S LA

Murgot's
Covert

Home
Farm

CHURCH
WALK

YE GN

PH

Beachamwell

ALL SAINTS WAY

05

Ash Holt
Plantation

Hall
Farm

BOUGHTON

MURGOT'S LANE

EASTMOOR ROAD

All Saints
Church (rems)

Fox
Plantation

Hall Carr

Shingham
Wood

Moat

Shingham
Fen

7

Sluice
Wood

Furze
Hill

Old
Carr

04

Beachamwell
Fen

St Mary's Church
(site of)

Folly
Plantation

6

The Channels

Fen
Wood

Caldecote
Farm

03

Barton
Bendish Fen

Eastmoor

Caldecote
Fen

Caldecote
Wood

Barton
Bendish Fen

Birch
Wood

Scotch
Carr

OXBOROUGH ROAD

Lilac
Farm

Eastmoor
Bridge

5

CRAB
LA

Boughton

STOKE FERRY RD

Oxborough
Fen

SWAFFHAM RD

Rookery
Farm

Old
Farm

THE STREET

02

CHAPEL
RD

STOKE ROAD

Field Barn
Farm

OXBOROUGH ROAD

Boughton
Fen

Oxborough
Wood

EASTMOOR ROAD

EASTMOOR CL 1
ST JOHN'S CL 2

River Gadder

Hall
Farm

CRAB LA

CRAB LA

Boughton
Wood

Nature
Reserve

Warren Hill

Oxborough

The Green
Church
Farm

PH

May
Farm

MILL DROVE

FEN DRO

4

FURLONG DROVE

STOKE RD

White
Bridge

Whitebridge
Farm

Oxburgh
Hall, Gdns
& Estate

CHALKROW LANE

01

OXBOROUGH ROAD

BOUGHTON RD

Boughton
Fen

White House
Farm

OXBOROUGH ROAD

FERRY ROAD

Home
Covert

Fen
Farm

FEN DRO

Windmill
Cemy

LT MAN'S WAY

ROMER DRO

Stringside
Drove

Broom
Covert

Home
Covert

Gooderstone
Fen

Gooderstone
Common

3

FURLONG DV

BARKERS

INDIGO RD

Romer
Plantation

Oxborough
Fen Farm

My Lord's
Wood

Balloon
Covert

Foulden
Common

00

PO

GREAT MAN'S WAY

BRIDGE ROAD

1 ADVENTURERS' DRO
2 OLD METHWOLD RD
3 NORMAN DR

Ferry
Farm

Middle
Covert

Fen
Farm

HIGH ST

The James
Bradfield CE
Comm Prim Sch

Grange
Farm

Whittington

River Wissey

Lower
Carr

Talent
Covert

2

BUCKENHAM DR 1
THOMPSON S LA 2
THE MOORINGS 3
OAK RD 4
BORDER RD 5

Bridge
Farm

CHURCH LA

Meadow
Farm

Borough
Fen

Golt
Plantation

Home
Covert

Pumping
Station

WHITTINGTON HILL

Whittington
Hill

Sewage
Works

99

ADVENTURERS' DROVE

B1112

METHWOLD ROAD

Hill
Farm

A134

THETFORD ROAD

LINK RD

HIGHMOOR DRO

1

Northwold
Fen

Cottage Fen

98

A3
1 FURLONG RD
2 LIME KILN LA
3 BRADFIELD PL
4 FAIRFIELD RD

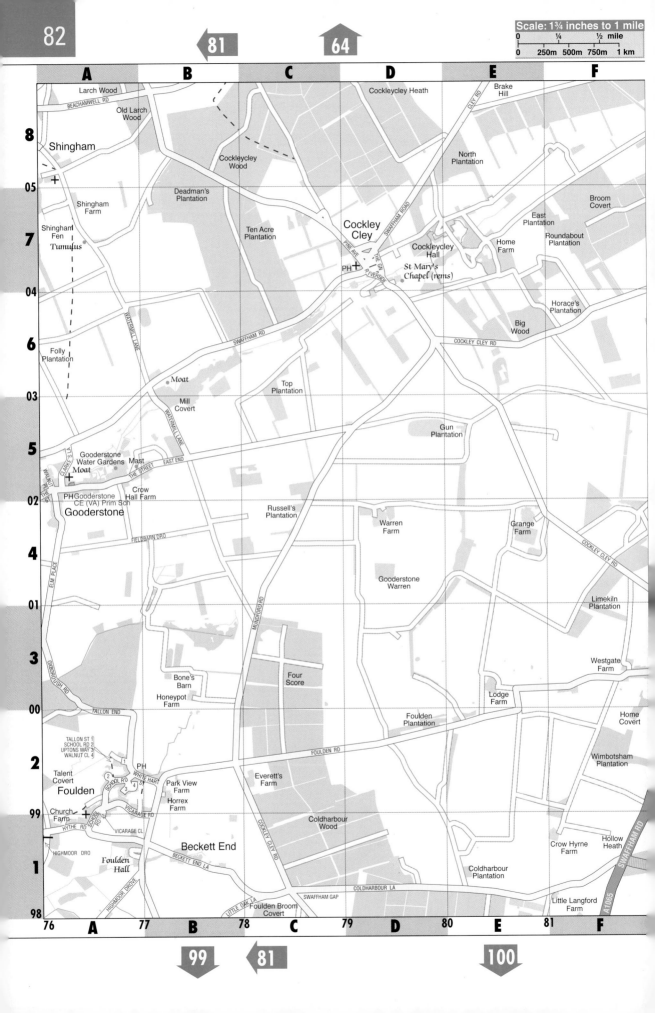

Scale: 1¾ inches to 1 mile
0   ¼   ½   mile
0 250m 500m 750m 1 km

81   64

A   B   C   D   E   F

Larch Wood
BEACHAMWELL RD
Old Larch Wood
Cockleycley Heath
CLEY RD
Brake Hill

8

Shingham
Cockleycley Wood
North Plantation

05

Shingham Farm
Deadman's Plantation
Broom Covert
East Plantation

7

Shingham Fen
Tumulus
Ten Acre Plantation
Cockley Cley
SWAFFHAM ROAD
Cockleycley Hall
Home Farm
Roundabout Plantation

04

PINE AVE
THE GN
PH
St Mary's Chapel (rems)
R VERSEN

6

Folly Plantation
WATERMILL LANE
SWAFFHAM RD
COCKLEY CLEY RD
Horace's Plantation
Big Wood

03

Moat
Top Plantation
Mill Covert
Gun Plantation

5

Gooderstone Water Gardens   Mast
Moat
EAST END   THE STREET
CLARK'S LA

02

PH
Gooderstone CE (VA) Prim Sch
Crow Hall Farm
Russell's Plantation
Warren Farm
Grange Farm
COCKLEY CLEY RD

Gooderstone
FIELDBARN DRO
Gooderstone Warren
Limekiln Plantation

4

ELM PLACE
WALNUT PL
MUNDFORD RD

01

3

OXBOROUGH RD
Bone's Barn
Four Score
Westgate Farm

00

Honeypot Farm
TALLON END
Foulden Plantation
Lodge Farm
Home Covert

TALLON ST 1
SCHOOL RD 2
UPTONS WAY 3
WALNUT CL 4
FOULDEN RD

2

Talent Covert
Foulden
PH
WHITE HART ST
SCHOOL RD
Park View Farm
Everett's Farm
Wimbotsham Plantation

Horrex Farm

99

Church Farm
VICARAGE RD
Coldharbour Wood
COCKLEY CLEY RD
Crow Hyrne Farm
Hollow Heath

HYTHE RD
BECSO RD
VICARAGE CL
Beckett End

HIGHMOOR DRO
Foulden Hall
BECKETT END LA
Coldharbour Plantation
Little Langford Farm
SWAFFHAM RD
A1065

1

HIGHMOOR DROVE
LITTLE OAK LA
Foulden Broom Covert
SWAFFHAM GAP
COLDHARBOUR LA

98

76   A   77   B   78   C   79   D   80   E   81   F

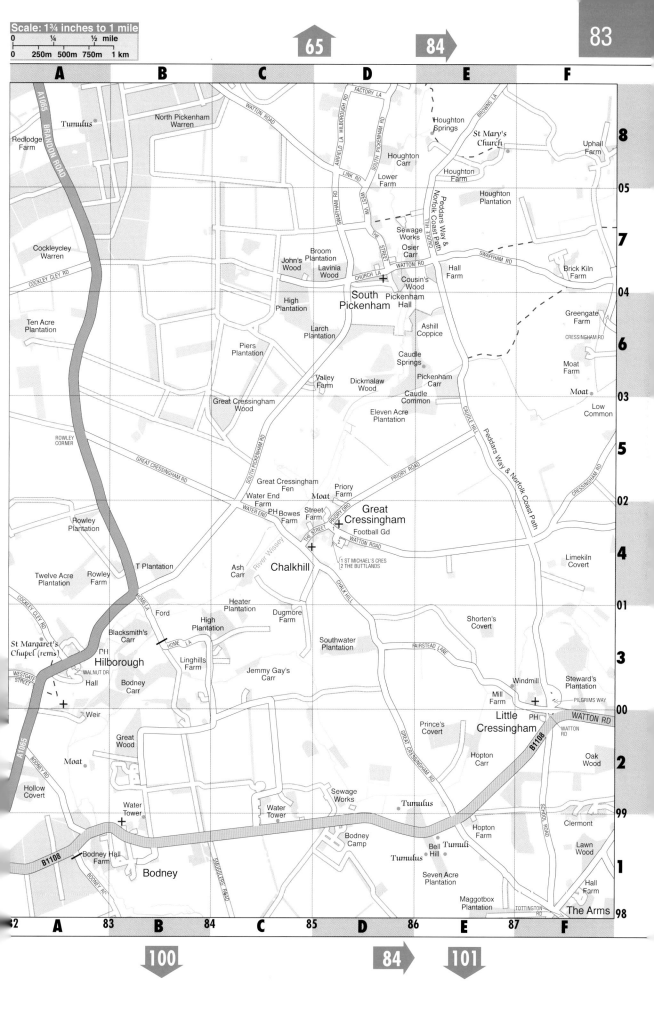

83
66

F3
1 HENRY'S CT
2 SLESSOR CL
3 DOWDING RD
4 TRENCHARD CRES
5 CHANGI RD
6 HASTINGS RD
7 COMET RD
8 HALTON RD
9 FARNBOROUGH RD
10 CRANWELL RD
11 SALMOND RD
12 HARRIS RD
13 HENDON AVE
14 PADDOCK CL
15 SHIRE HORSE WY
16 THE GALLOPS
17 HORSE SHOE CL
18 FARRIER RD
19 SADDLERS DR
20 MOSQUITO CL

C3
1 LANGMERE RD
2 RINGMERE RD
3 RINGMERE RD
4 WAYLAND AVE
5 THREE POST RD
6 WEST END CT
7 CURLEW CL
8 WOODPECKER DR
9 TERN CL
10 MALLARD RD
11 KINGFISHER WAY
12 HERON WAY
13 GOLDFINCH WAY
14 PEDDARS CR
15 SAFFRON CL
16 AIRCRAFT DR
17 PINGO RD
18 PLOVER RD

THE OVAL 1
NEVILLE CL 2
OLD HALL CL 3
ST GEORGE'S CL 4

BELLMERE WAY 1
MERE CL 2
WOODVIEW CL 3
AMYS CL 4
SHEPHERDS DR 5

SOUTHVIEW 1
WHITEBEAM CRES 1
MITCHELL CL 2
FIELD MAPLE RD 3
GOAT WILLOW CL 4

Map place names:
Hannover Farm, Granary Fields, Reeves Farm, Uphall Grange, Mill Farm, Ashill, Ashill VC Prim Sch, The Woodlands, Old Hall Farm, Ashill Fruit Farm, Crossways Farm, The Limes, Water End Farm, Lodge Farm, Low Common Farm, Saham Hall, Hall Farm, The Grove, Sandpit Plantation, Church Farm, Sewage Works, Threxton Hill, Threxton House, Oak Wood, The Arms, Blackhill Plantation, Deal Wood

Cutbush Farm, Ashill Common, Devils Dyke, Homestead Farm, Green Farm, Panworth Farm, Panworth Hall, Lower Homestead Farm, Field Farm, Hunts Farm, Page's Place, Grange Farm, Stanway Farm, Parker's CE Prim Sch, Saham Mere, The Grove, Slate Plantation

ROMAN EARTHWORK (SITE OF), Bungalow Farm, White House Farm, Saham Hills, High House Farm, The Lodge, Saham Toney, Brick Kiln Farm, Windmill, Sanctuary Mdw, Richmond Park Golf Course, Martins Cl, Ladybird La, Fairway Rd, Brandon Rd, Watton Junior Sch, Westfield Inf Sch, Watton Rd Ind Est, Watton Plantation, Merton Common, Wick Farm, New Plantation, Grove Farm, Hawthorne Farm, Home Farm, Moat, Merton, Old Farm, North West Covert

Park Farm, Woodbottom Farm, Saham Wood, Saham Park, Wood Farm, Dairy Farm, Dorrs Farm, Neaton, Sports Centre, Walnut Gr, Lime Tree Wk, WATTON, Wayland Com High Sch, Rabbit Plantation, Milestone Grove, Broom Hill Farm, Broadflash Farm, Victoria Plantation

Fisher's Plantation, Peter's Plantation, Corner Farm, Coe Farm, Dye Farm, Pear Tree Farm, Willow Bushes Plantation, Otterwood Farm, Highfield Farm, College Farm, Earthworks, Alston Farm, Rose Farm, Daisy Farm, Waterend Farm, Ovington, Church Farm, Bleak House Farm, Grape Farm, Bush Farm, Redhill, Moat, Watton Green, Redhill Farm, Rokeles Hall, Breckland Business Park, Water Twrs, Norwich Road, Fairhead Way, Wayland Wood Nature Reserve, Hall Farm House, HMP Wayland, Cottage Farm, Wood Farm

Roads: HALE ROAD, SWAFFHAM RD, WATTON ROAD, B1108, BRANDON ROAD, THETFORD ROAD, DEREHAM ROAD, NORWICH ROAD, B1108, A1075, LONG ROAD, SAHAM RD, OVINGTON ROAD, THE STREET, CARBROOKE RD, GRISTON ROAD, SLEIGH LANE, LOW COMMON LA, BROOMHILL LA

101
83
102

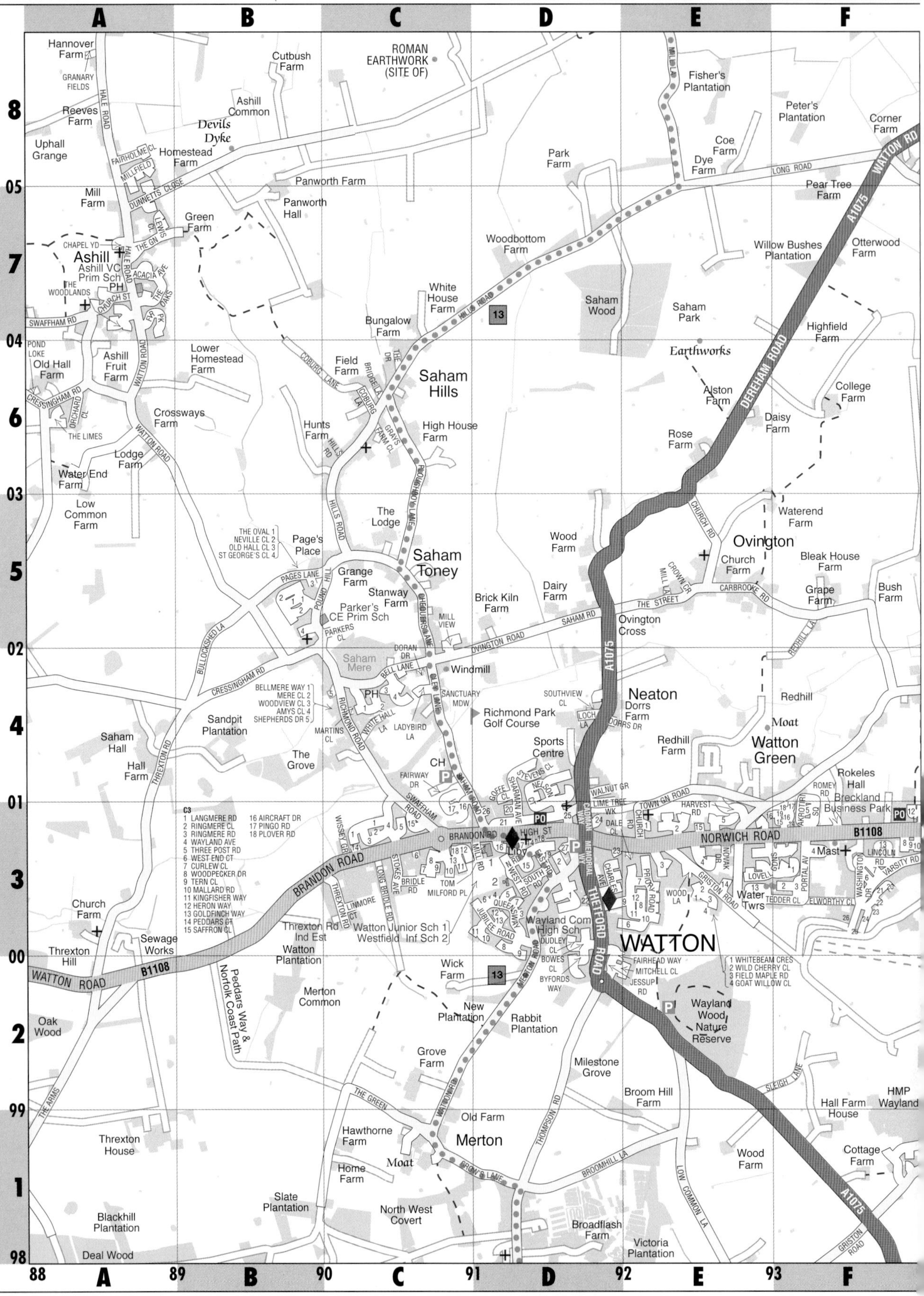

D3
1 CHURCHILL CL
2 GREEN OAK RD
3 WICK FARM CL
4 WINDSOR CT
5 WILLIAM CL
6 SANDRINGHAM CT
7 PRINCESS CL
8 FLEMING CT
9 MALTHOUSE
10 COBURG CL
11 WODEHOUSE CT
12 SPENCER CT
13 EDINBURGH CL
14 GODDARDS CT
15 GEORGE TROLLOPE RD
16 VINCENT PL
17 CLARENCE CT
18 BEECHWOOD AVE
19 ORCHARD CL

D3
19 ORCHARD CL
20 FROST ST
21 HARVEY ST
22 VICTORIA CT
23 REGAL CT
24 KITTEL CL
25 DEREHAM RD
26 MEADOW GR
27 GREGOR SHANKS WAY

E3
1 ST MARY'S CL
2 HUNTERS OAK
3 LINMORE CRES
4 GARDEN CL
5 BLENHEIM WAY
6 CANON CL
7 GLEBE RD
8 CHESTNUT RD
9 MONKHAMS DR
10 ABBEY RD
11 VICARAGE WK
12 ASHTREE RD
13 TEDDER CL
14 BURR CL
15 FORMAN CL
16 THE STABLES

F3
21 FORTRESS RD
22 HURRICANE CL
23 LIBERATOR RD
24 MARAUDER RD
25 ADLAND RD
26 SPITFIRE DR
27 ANSON WY

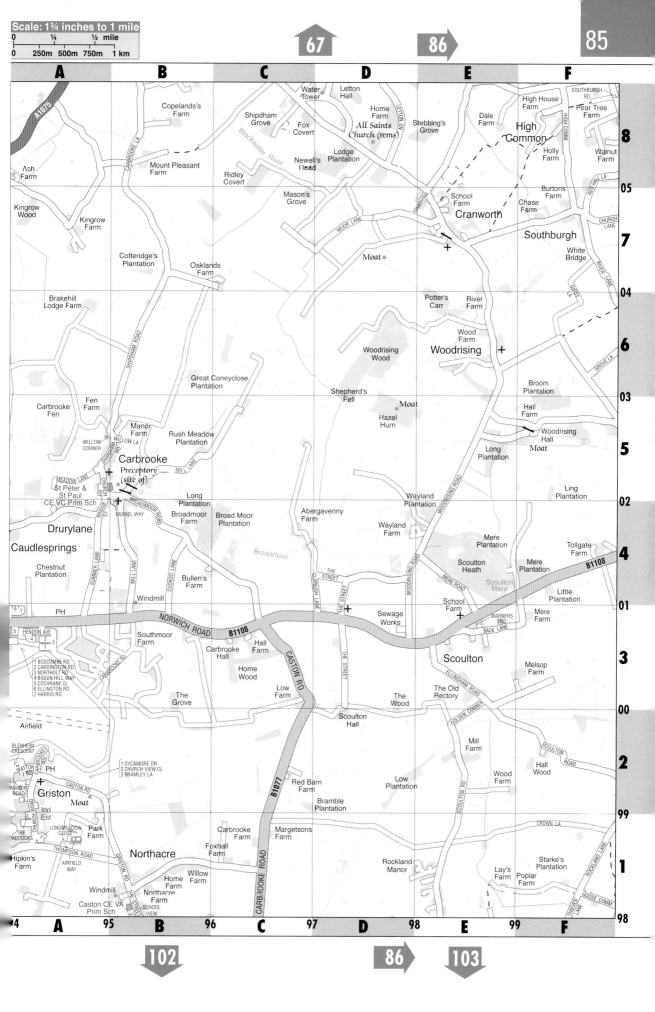

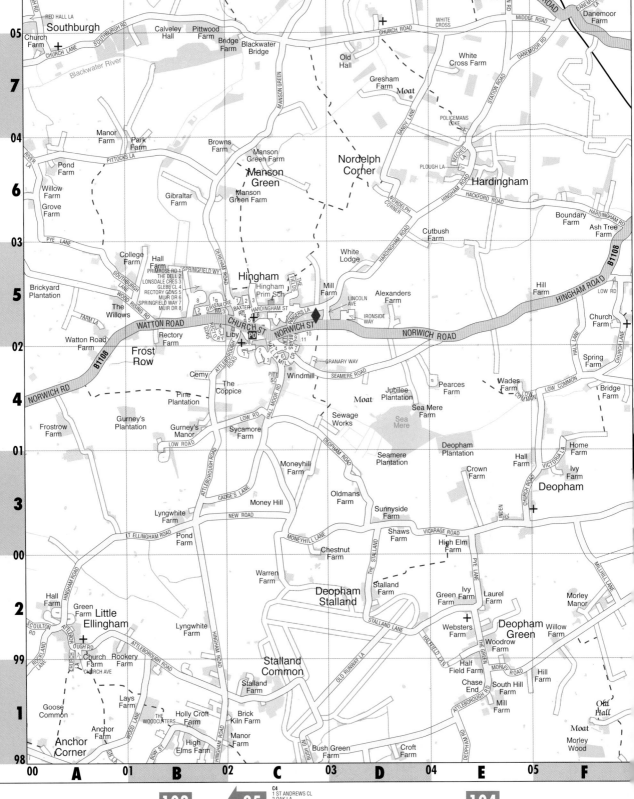

85 68

C5
1 BELL MDW
2 BAXTER CL
3 FOLLY LA
4 POTTLES ALLEY
5 BOND ST
6 CHAPEL ST
7 ADMIRALS WK
8 COPPER LA
9 DRINKWATER CL
10 MALTSTERS DR
11 HOPSACK RD

Scale: 1¾ inches to 1 mile

0 ¼ ½ mile
0 250m 500m 750m 1 km

Moat

THE LINGS
Long Plantation

Station Farm

Danemoor Green

Southburgh

Red Hall La
Church Farm
Church Lane
Southburgh Rd

Blackwater River

Calveley Hall
Pittwood Farm
Bridge Farm
Blackwater Bridge

The Grove

Low Street Farm

Low Street

Danemoor Farm

Mid Norfolk Railway

NORWICH ROAD

LOW ST
B1135

STATION RD
MIDDLE ROAD
DANEMOOR RD

Church Road

WHITE CROSS

White Cross Farm

White Cross

Old Hall

Gresham Farm
Moat

Manor Farm
Park Farm
PITTOCKS LA

Pond Farm

Browns Farm

Manson Green

Manson Green Farm

Nordelph Corner

Hardingham

STATION RD

Willow Farm
Grove Farm

RIVER LA

Gibraltar Farm

Manson Green Farm

NORDELPH CORNER

PLOUGH LA
POLICEMANS LOKE

BEECHES LA

HINGHAM RD

Boundary Farm

Ash Tree Farm

HARDINGHAM RD

PYE LANE

College Farm
Hall Farm

Brickyard Plantation

DEREHAM ROAD

Hingham

White Lodge

Cutbush Farm

HARDINGHAM ROAD

HACKFORD ROAD

B1108

Hill Farm

LOW RD

HINGHAM ROAD

The Willows
FARM LA

SOUTHBURGH LANE
WOOD RISING RD

SPRINGFIELD WY
PRIMROSE RD 1
THE DELL 2
LONSDALE CRES 3
GLEBE CL 4
RECTORY GDNS 5
SPRINGFIELD WAY 7
MUIR DR 8
MUIR DR 6

THE FIELDS
Hingham Prim Sch

Mill Farm

Lincoln AVE
Alexanders Farm
IRONSIDE WAY

Church Farm

Watton Road Farm
WATTON ROAD

Rectory Farm

Frost Row

CHURCH ST
RECTORY GDNS

B1108

NORWICH RD

Liby
PO

HARDINGHAM ST
GREENACRE
BAXTER CL
KINGERS LA

NORWICH ST

NORWICH ROAD

Spring Farm

HALL LANE

CHURCH ROAD

Cemy

The Coppice

Pine Plantation

Windmill

PITT SQ
MILL LA
BEARS CL

GRANARY WAY

SEAMERE ROAD

Moat

Jubilee Plantation

Pearces Farm

Wades Farm

LOW COMMON

Bridge Farm

Frostrow Farm

Gurney's Plantation

Gurney's Manor

LOW ROAD

Sycamore Farm

ATTLEBOROUGH ROAD

Sewage Works

Sea Mere

Seamere Plantation

Deopham Plantation

Crown Farm

Hall Farm

VICTORIA LA

Home Farm

Ivy Farm

Deopham

Lyngwhite Farm

CADGE'S LANE
NEW ROAD

Money Hill

Moneyhill Farm

Oldmans Farm

Sunnyside Farm

VICARAGE ROAD

High Elm Farm

LINDEN CL

CHURCH ROAD

LT ELLINGHAM ROAD

Pond Farm

MONEYHILL LANE

Chestnut Farm

Shaws Farm

THE STALLAND

PYE LANE

MILLHILL LANE

Warren Farm

Deopham Stalland

Stalland Farm

Green Farm

Ivy Farm

Laurel Farm

Morley Manor

Hall Farm

Green Farm
Little Ellingham

HINGHAM ROAD

Lyngwhite Farm

STALLAND LANE

Websters Farm

Deopham Green

Woodrow Farm

Willow Farm

SCOULTON RD
ATTLEBOROUGH RD
ROCKLAND LA

CHURCH LA

 Church Farm
Rookery Farm
CHURCH AVE

ATTLEBOROUGH ROAD

OLD RUNWAY LA

HALFIELD LA

THE GREEN

Half Field Farm

MORLEY ROAD

Hill Farm

Goose Common

Lays Farm

THE WOODCUTTERS

BOW ST

Holly Croft Farm

Brick Kiln Farm

Stalland Common

Stalland Farm

NO HSTH RD

Chase End

South Hill Farm

Mill Farm

Oat Hall

Anchor Corner

Anchor Farm

WOOD LANE

High Elms Farm

HINGHAM ROAD

Manor Farm

Bush Green Farm

Croft Farm

DEOPHAM RD

ATTLEBOROUGH RD

Moat

Morley Wood

103 85 104

C4
1 ST ANDREWS CL
2 OAK LA
3 HALL CL
4 FLEETERS HILL
5 STONE LA
6 THE MEADOWS
7 BEARS CL

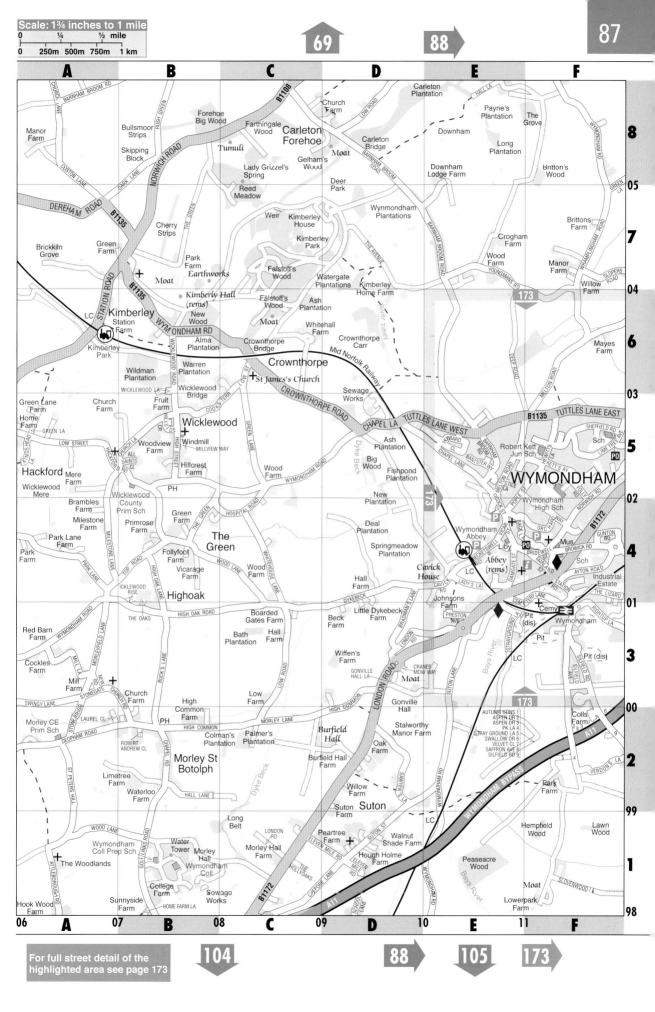

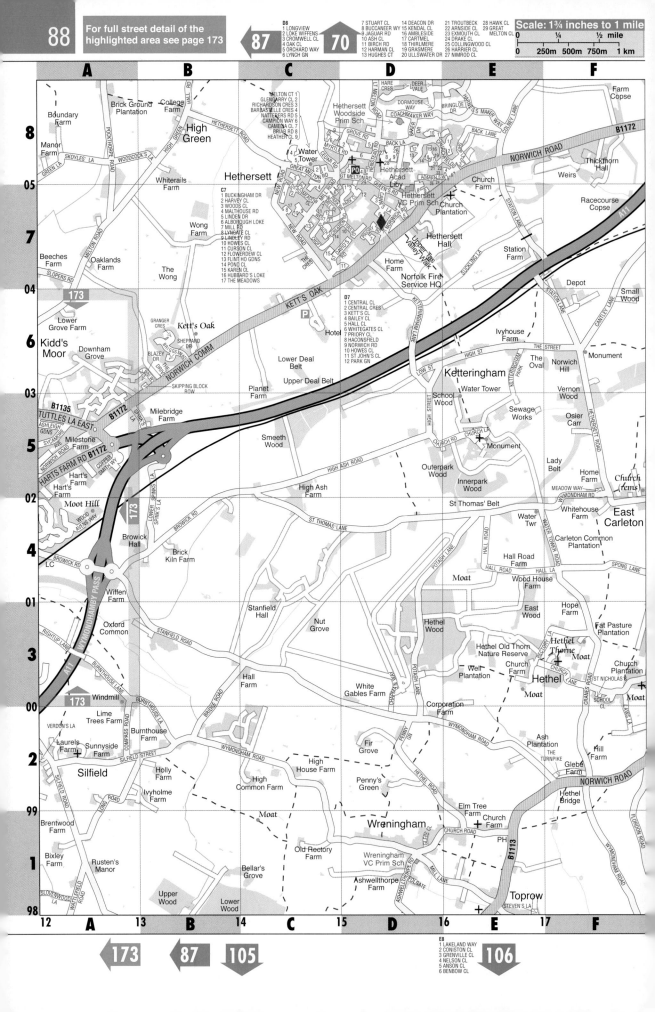

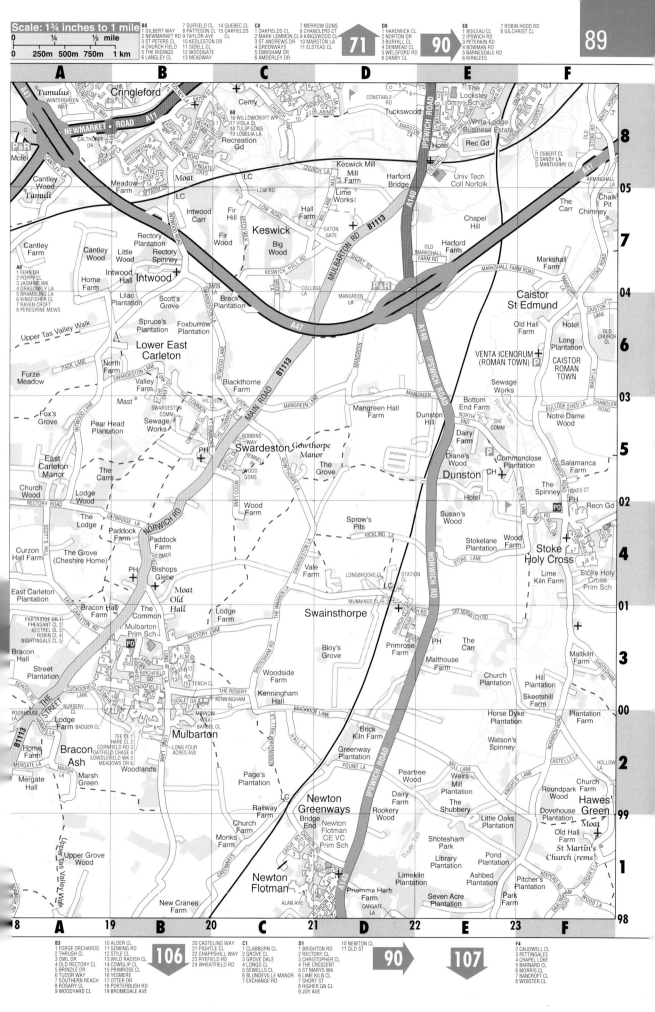

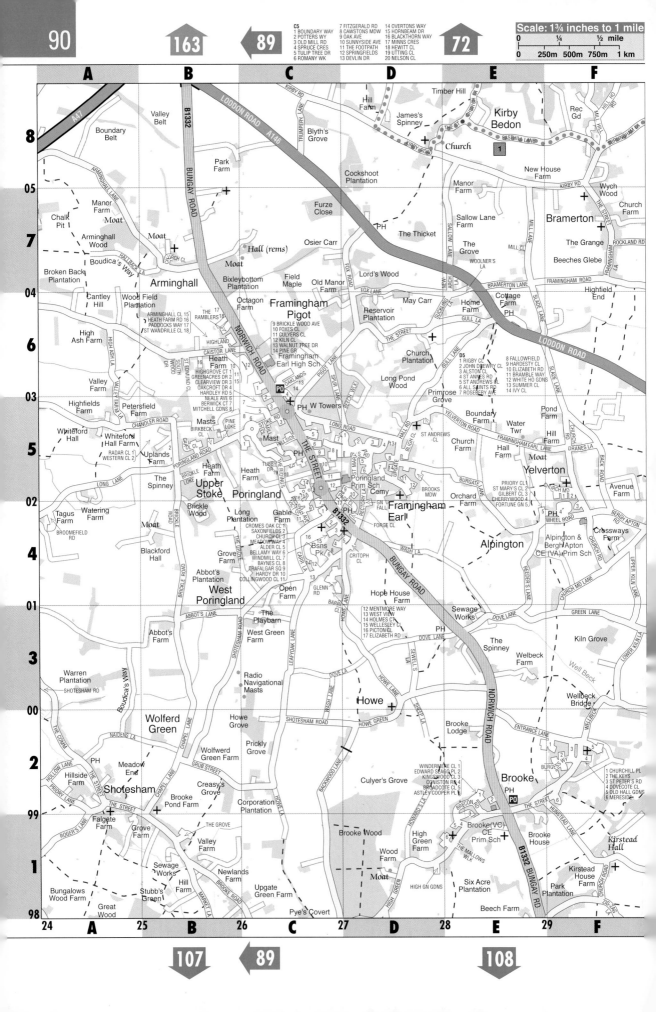

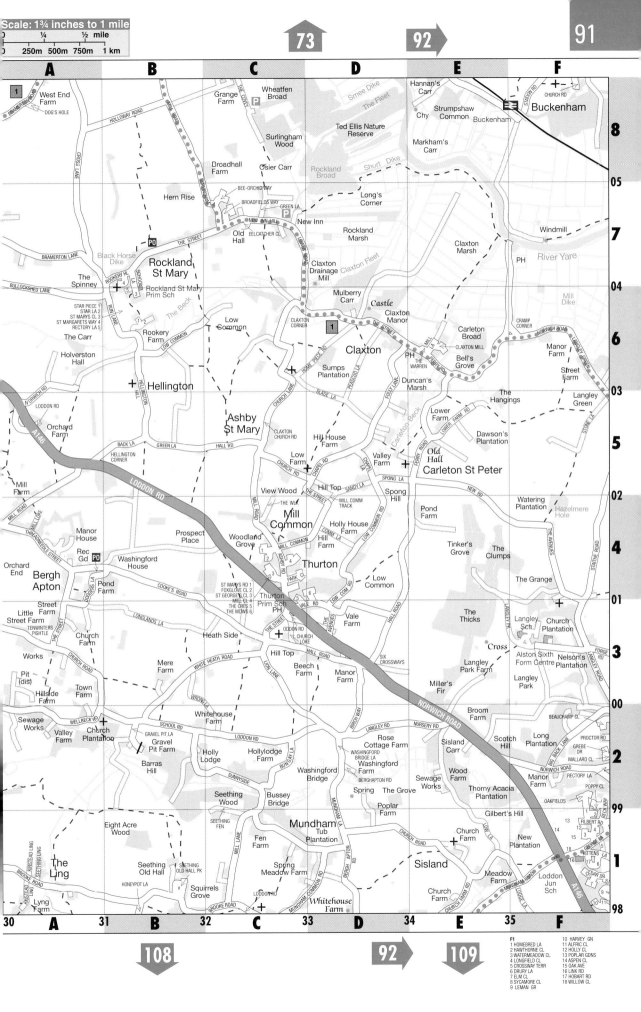

A B C D E F

Buckenham Carrs
Fleet Dike
Broad Farm
Hassingham
Cottage Carr
CARRS ROAD
CHURCH ROAD
HASSINGHAM RD
Earth Wall Carr
Goldie's Carr
Swill's Meadow
STRUMPSHAW RD
Thatch Farm
HIGH RD
MANOR RD
PH
Primrose Grove
SOUTHWOOD RD
Hall Farm
GROVE ROAD
Grove Farm
Southwood
PORTER'S ROAD
LOWER RD
Windmill
Reedham Farm
Lower Green Farm
Lower Green
CHURCH RD
MILL ROAD
LOW ROAD
SCHOOL RD
Church
Oaks Farm
THE LOKE
Manor House
White House Farm
Freethorpe
Wheelwrights CL
PO
Sutton Cres
PALMER'S LA
THE GREEN
CHURCH RD

8
05
Manor Farm
COW MDW ROAD
Church
Barn End
GRIMMER LANE
SCHOOL LANE
Cantley Prim Sch
B1140
Cantley
LC
Sports Gd
GRANGE LA
LIMPENHOE RD
CANTLEY ROAD
Spong Carr
Wood Farm
Cantley Grange
Cantley View Farm
NORWICH ROAD
SOUTHWOOD RD
CH RD
Limpenhoe
GRANARY CL 1
PEARSONS CL 2
YOUNG'S CRES 3
BOWLERS CL 4
PRESTON CL 5
CRICKETER'S WLK 6
WALPOLE WY 7
PROSPECT CL 8
CHAPELFIELD
PH
Freethorpe Com Prim Sch
THE COMMON
OLD CHAPEL RD
Mast

7
04
CHURCH CL
PEREGRINE CL
MARIE CL 1
STANLEY CL 2
MALTHOUSE LA 3
Cantley
STATION RD
BURNT RD
CHURCH RD
Marsh Farm
Red House
Factory
Chimney
Chimney
Chimney
Chimney
Marsh Farm
MARSH ROAD
WELL RD
FREETHORPE RD
Low Farm
Hill Farm
SANDY LANE
REEDHAM ROAD

6
03
Monks Plantation
River Yare
Moat
Langley Abbey
PH
The Wherry
LANGLEY GN
Abbey Carr
LANGLEY DIKE
Sewage Works
1 LANGLEY RD
2 HIGHLAND CL
3 WINDSOR RD
4 STATION RD
Reservoir
Settling Basins
Round House
Limpenhoe Marshes
LC
Limpenhoe Hill
John's Carr
Sprowston Wood
Gurney Wood
Wood Farm
LOW FARM RD
POTTLE'S LA
1 STATION DR
2 WITTON CL
3 THE HAVAKER
Reedham

5
02
STAITHE ROAD
Staithe Farm
Poplars Farm
Langley Marshes
Hardley Drainage Mill
Limpenhoe Drainage Mill
Reedham Ferry (V)
PH
Reedham Drainage Mill
STATION ROAD
BARN OWL CL 1
THE HILLS
PO

4
01
Willow Farm
LANGLEY STREET
Langley Street
Chestnut Farm
Great Yard Farm
White House Farm
Westgate Farm
Rustygate Farm
HARDLEY DIKE
Hardley Street
Church Farm
Hardley Marshes
Hardley Cross
Norton Staithe
Norton Drainage Mill
YARE VIEW CL 1
CLIFF CL 2
NEW RD 3
MIDDLE HILL 4
RIVERSIDE 5

3
00
Ash Plantation
WHERRYMANS WALK
Boundary Farm
FORGE ROAD
COCK ROAD
CROSS STONE ROAD
Avenue Farm
LOWER HARDLEY ROAD
HARDLEY ROAD
HARDLEY STREET
HARDLEY HALL LANE
River Chet
Norton Marshes
Marshlands Farm
Nogdam End
Leys Farm
FARM ROAD
MILL DYKE
Mill Dyke
BOYCE'S DYKE
Norton Marshes
NEW DAM

Broom Hill
Hardley Hall
Hall Carr
Moat
31
Hill House
Old Hall Carr
Firs Farm
LOW ROAD
Ash Carr
Thatched House Farm
Carr Farm
Walnut Tree Farm

2
Chedgrave Hills
Chedgrave
HILLSIDE
RECTORY LA
PITS LA
Chedgrave Carr
LOWER HARDLEY ROAD
COMM LOKE
Hardley Wood
Hardley Flood Nature Reserve
Loddon Common
Riverside Farm
Valley Farm
Little Church Farm
Church Farm
Beacon Hill
Highfield Farm
Norton Subcourse
Church Farm
Elm Farm
Willow Farm
Low Farm
Soc Dyke
THE BECK
Church Farm
NEW ROAD
LOW ROAD
Thurlton Prim Sch

99
LODDON QUAY
WHERRY CL
Liby
Bsns Ctr
Hobart PH
High Sch
PO
Loddon Inf Sch
PES MILL ROAD
MILTON DR
Beechgrove Farm
Hall Green Farm
HECKINGHAM HOLES
NORTON ROAD
Heckingham
Hall
Avocet House
High House Farm
Hill Farm
SCHOOL LANE
BRIAR LANE
FARM RD
Reservoir
BUTTER LA
Norton Plantation
BOUNDARY RD
Loddon Road
Thurlton
PH
BOYCES RD
THE STREET
CROFT RD
CHURCH ROAD
MILL RD

1
98
Loddon
Ind Est
LOW BUNGAY RD
KITTENS LA
SANDY LANE
BECCLES RD
KETTLE'S RD

36 A 37 B 38 C 39 D 40 E 41 F

A1
1 GARDEN CT
2 GEORGE LA
3 OLD MARKET GN
4 MARKET PL
5 SALE CT
6 BEECH CL
7 DAVY PL
8 LEMAN CL
9 LEMAN GR
10 CEDAR DR
11 CANNELL RD
12 FOXES LOKE
13 REEDS WAY
14 BROWNES GR
15 Loddon Inf Sch

A2
1 BIG BACK LA
2 BEAUCHAMP RD
3 PROCTOR AVE
4 PROCTOR CL
5 PROCTOR RD
6 SNOW'S HILL
7 HILLCREST
8 HURST RD
9 MALLARD CL
10 THE RISE
11 FARM CL
12 NORWICH RD
13 CHURCH CL

F1
1 LOW RD
2 TITHEBARN LA
3 HAMPTON AVE
4 LINKS WAY
5 MEADOW CL
6 LINKS CL
7 QUEENS HEAD CL

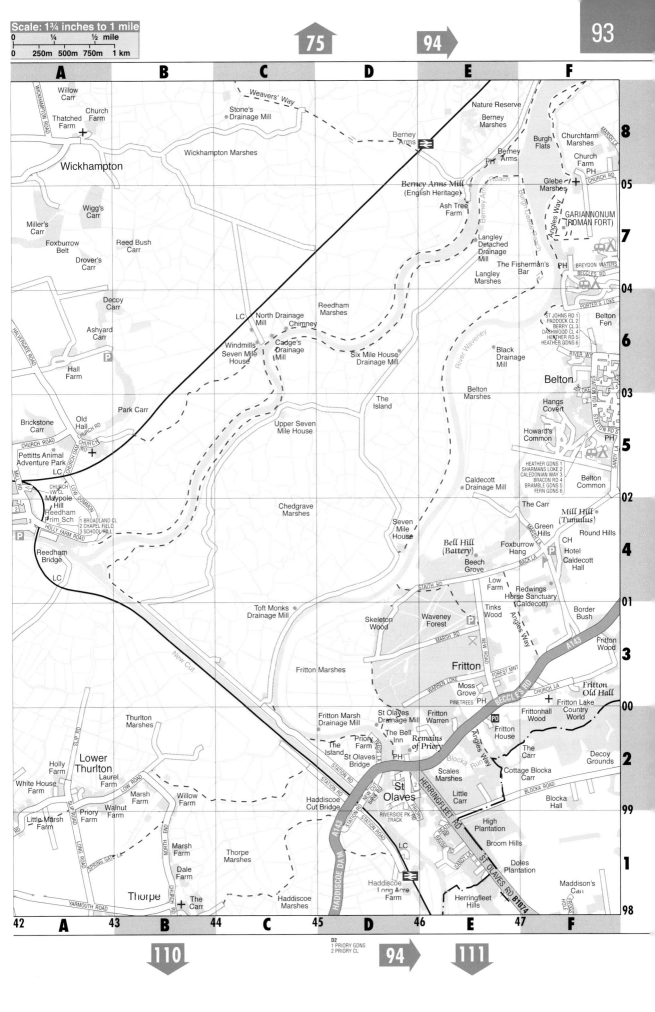

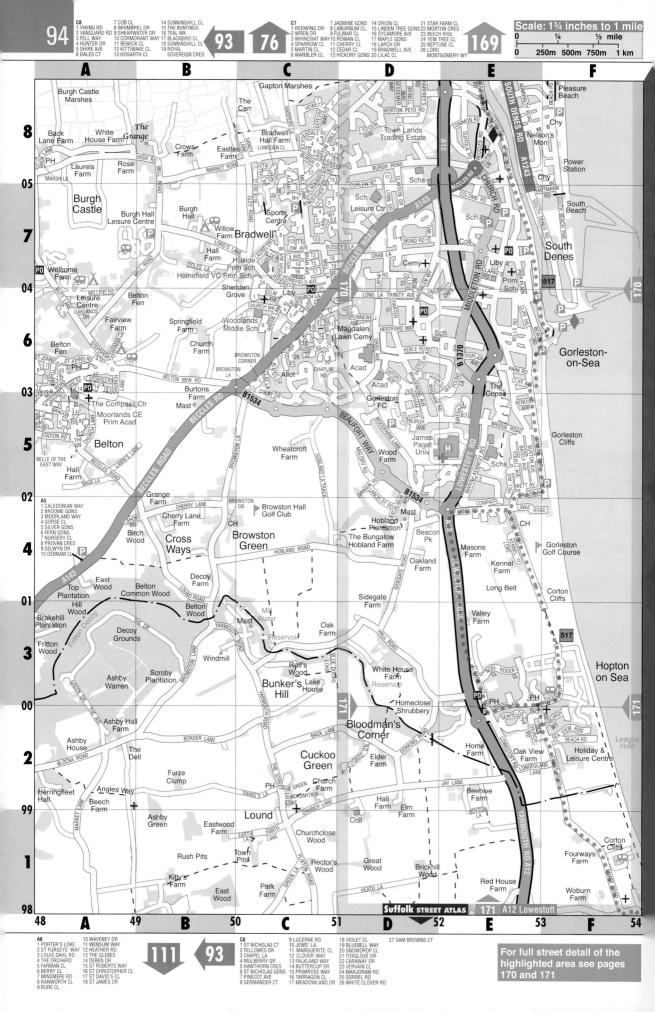

94

C8
1 VIKING RD
2 VANGUARD RD
3 FELL WAY
4 HUNTER DR
5 SHIRE AVE
6 DALES CT
7 COB CL
8 WHIMBREL DR
9 SHEARWATER DR
10 CORMORANT WAY
11 BEWICK CL
12 KITTIWAKE CL
13 HOGARTH CL
14 SUNNINGHILL CL
15 THE BUNTINGS
16 TEAL WK
17 BLACKBIRD CL
18 SUNNINGHILL CL
19 ROYAL
   SOVEREIGN CRES

93   76

C7
1 REDWING DR
2 WREN DR
3 WHINCHAT WAY
4 SPARROW CL
5 MARTIN CL
6 WARBLER CL
7 JASMINE GDNS
8 LABURNUM CL
9 FULMAR CL
10 ROWAN CL
11 CHERRY CL
12 CEDAR CL
13 HICKORY GDNS
14 ORION CL
15 LINDEN TREE GDNS
16 SYCAMORE CL
17 MAPLE GDNS
18 LARCH DR
19 BRADWELL AVE
20 LILAC CL
21 STAR FARM CL
22 MORTON CRES
23 BEECH RISE
24 YEW TREE CL
25 NEPTUNE CL
26 LORD
   MONTGOMERY WY

169

Scale: 1¾ inches to 1 mile
0   ¼   ½   mile
0 250m 500m 750m 1 km

For full street detail of the highlighted area see pages 170 and 171

Suffolk STREET ATLAS   171 A12 Lowestoft

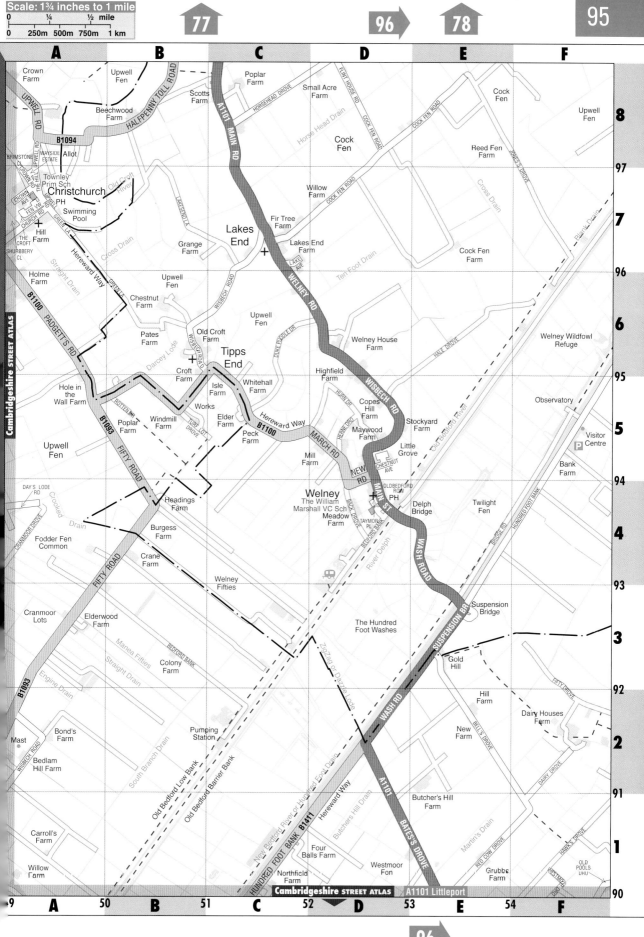

Scale: 1¾ inches to 1 mile

Cambridgeshire STREET ATLAS

Crown Farm
Upwell Fen
Beechwood Farm
HALFPENNY TOLL ROAD
UPWELL RD
B1094
Allot
WAYSIDE ESTATE
BRIMSTONE LA
Townley Prim Sch
Christchurch
PH
Swimming Pool
CHURCH RD
THE CROFT
SHURBBERY CL
Hill Farm
Holme Farm
B1100
PADGETT'S RD
Hereward Way
GREEN LA
Cross Drain
Straight Drain
Chestnut Farm
Pates Farm
Upwell Fen
Darcey Lode
ROTTEN DRO
B1093
Poplar Farm
FIFTY ROAD
Hole in the Wall Farm
Windmill Farm
TUBE LOTT DROVE
Upwell Fen
Croft Farm
Isle Farm
Elder Farm
Peck Farm
Works
Headings Farm
Burgess Farm
Crane Farm
Fodder Fen Common
CRANMOOR DROVE
Cooked Drain
DAY'S LODE RD
Cranmoor Lots
Elderwood Farm
Manea Fifties
BEDFORD BANK
Colony Farm
Straight Drain
Engine Drain
WISBECH ROAD
Mast
Bond's Farm
Bedlam Hill Farm
South Branch Drain
Old Bedford Low Bank
Old Bedford Barrier Bank
Pumping Station
Carroll's Farm
Willow Farm

Scotts Farm
Poplar Farm
Small Acre Farm
HORSEHEAD DROVE
FLINT HOUSE RD
COCK FEN ROAD
A1101 MAIN RD
Horse Head Drain
Cock Fen
Willow Farm
COCK FEN ROAD
Fir Tree Farm
Lakes End
Lakes End Farm
Ten Foot Drain
WELNEY RD
LAKE AVE
Grange Farm
WISBECH ROAD
LAKESNUT LA
Upwell Fen
Old Croft Farm
Tipps End
Whitehall Farm
Highfield Farm
DUKE PUDDLE DR
Welney House Farm
WISBECH RD
Hereward Way
B1100
MARCH RD
HURN DRO
Copes Hill Farm
Maywood Farm
HEINE DRO
Mill Farm
Stockyard Farm
Little Grove
CHESTNUT AVE
Welney
The William Marshall VC Sch
Meadow Farm
NEW RD
MAIN ST
OLDBEDFORD ROW
PH
Delph Bridge
BACK DROVE
BEDFORD BANK
River Delph
TAYMOR PL
The Hundred Foot Washes
WASH ROAD
Zig Zag or Dazzle Long
New Bedford River or Hundred Foot Drain
HUNDRED FOOT BANK
Hereward Way
B1411
Four Balls Farm
Northfield Farm
Butchers Hill Drain
Westmoor Fen
A1101
BATES'S DROVE

Cock Fen
Upwell Fen
Reed Fen Farm
JONES'S DROVE
Cross Drain
Cock Fen Farm
Plank Drain
Welney Wildfowl Refuge
Observatory
HALF DROVE
Old Bedford River
Visitor Centre
P
Bank Farm
Twilight Fen
Delph Bridge
HUNGERFOOT FOOT BANK
BRIDGE RD
Suspension Bridge
SUSPENSION BR
Gold Hill
FIFTY DROVE
Hill Farm
Dairy Houses Farm
New Farm
BELL'S DROVE
DAIRY DROVE
Butcher's Hill Farm
Martin's Drain
RED COW DROVE
HAWK'S DROVE
Grubbs Farm
OLD POOLS DRO
CHRISTMAS DRO

Welney Fifties

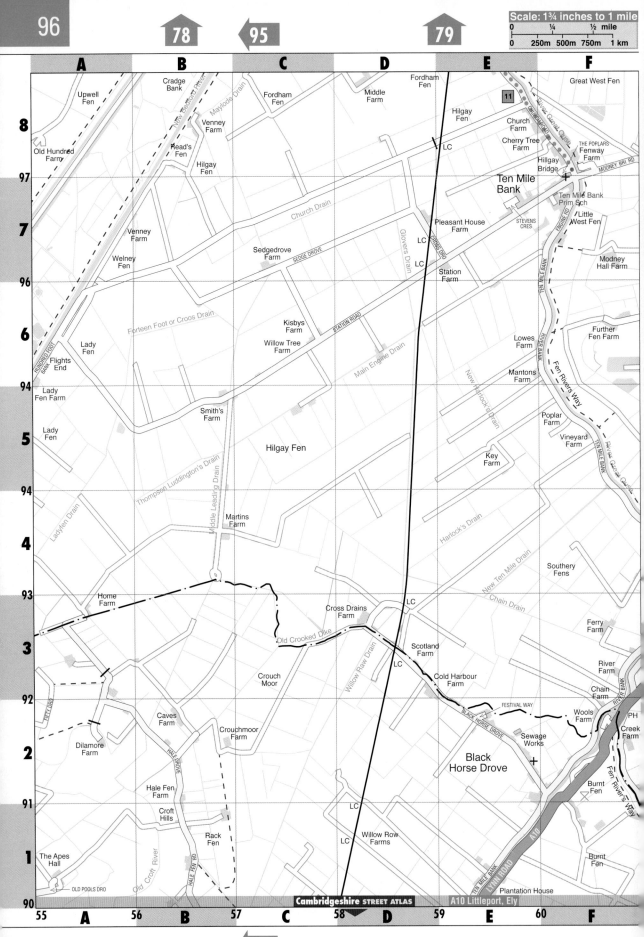

Scale: 1¾ inches to 1 mile
0 ¼ ½ mile
0 250m 500m 750m 1 km

A **B** **C** **D** **E** **F**

Upwell Fen

Cradge Bank

Fordham Fen

Middle Farm

Fordham Fen

Great West Fen

Hilgay Fen

Church Farm

Cherry Tree Farm

THE POPLARS
Fenway Farm

MODNEY BRI RD

Old Hundred Farm

Read's Fen

Venney Farm

Hilgay Fen

Ten Mile Bank

Hillgay Bridge

Ten Mile Bank Prim Sch

STEVENS CRES

Little West Fen

Modney Hall Farm

Venney Farm

Church Drain

Sedgedrove Farm

SEDGE DROVE

Pleasant House Farm

Glovers Drain

CROSS DRO

LC

LC

Station Farm

Welney Fen

Fourteen Foot or Croos Drain

Kisbys Farm

STATION ROAD

Willow Tree Farm

Main Engine Drain

Lowes Farm

Further Fen Farm

Lady Fen

Flights End

HUNDRED FOOT BANK

Lady Fen Farm

Smith's Farm

New Harlock's Drain

Mantons Farm

Poplar Farm

Vineyard Farm

Lady Fen

Ladyfen Drain

Thompson Luddington's Drain

Middle Leading Drain

Hilgay Fen

Key Farm

Harlock's Drain

Southery Fens

New Ten Mile Drain

Chain Drain

Martins Farm

Home Farm

Cross Drains Farm

LC

Ferry Farm

Old Crooked Dike

Scotland Farm

LC

River Farm

Crouch Moor

Willow Raw Drain

Cold Harbour Farm

Chain Farm

Caves Farm

Crouchmoor Farm

FESTIVAL WAY

Wools Farm

PH

Creek Farm

Dilamore Farm

FEN RIVER

Black Horse Drove

BLACK HORSE DROVE

Sewage Works

Black Horse Drove

Hale Fen Farm

HALE DROVE

Croft Hills

LC

Burnt Fen

The Apes Hall

Rack Fen

HALE FEN RD

Old Croft River

LC

LC

Willow Row Farms

A10

LYNN ROAD

TEN MILE BANK

Burnt Fen

OLD POOLS DRO

A10 Littleport, Ely

Plantation House

A **B** **C** **D** **E** **F**

55 56 57 58 59 60

8 97 7 96 6 94 5 94 4 93 3 92 2 91 1 90

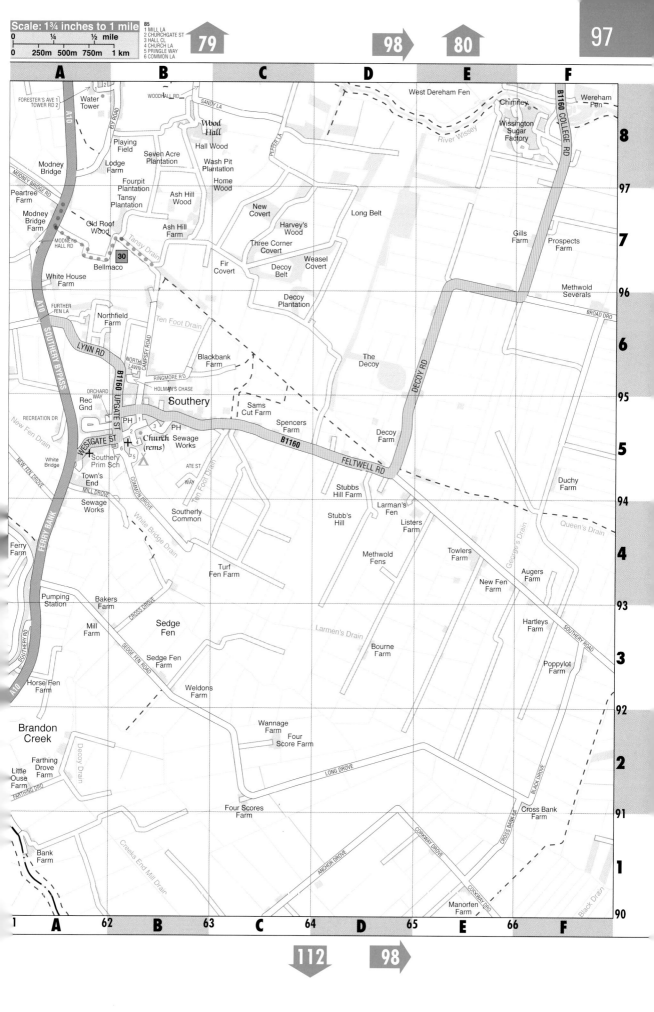

80
97
81

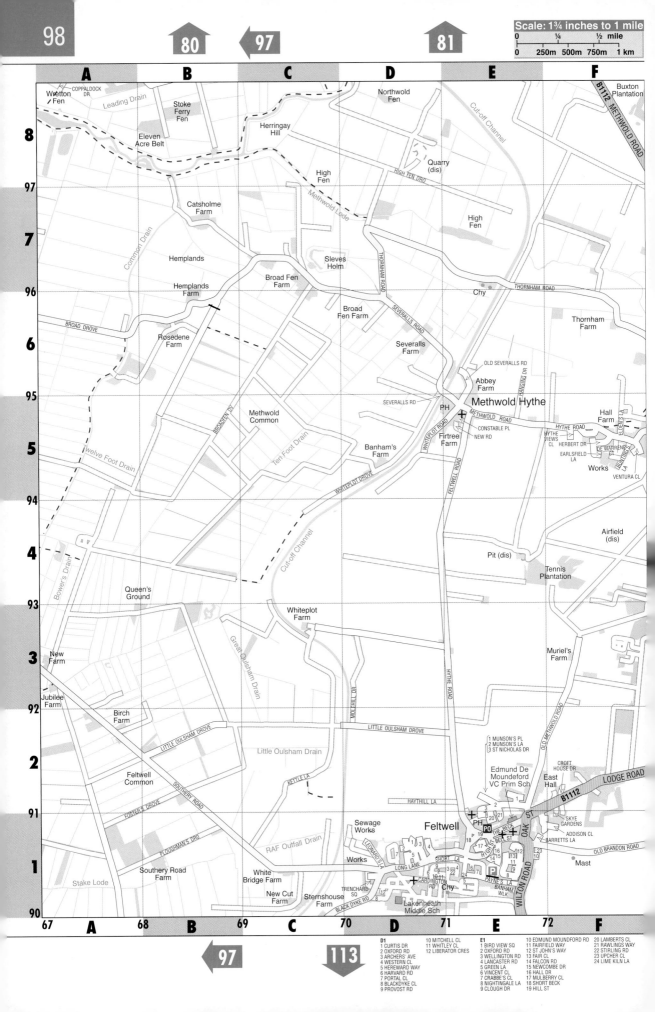

A **B** **C** **D** **E** **F**

Wretton Fen
COPPALDOCK DR
Leading Drain
Stoke Ferry Fen
Northwold Fen
Buxton Plantation
B1112, METHWOLD ROAD

Eleven Acre Belt
Herringay Hill
High Fen
Cut-off Channel

Catsholme Farm
HIGH FEN DRO
Quarry (dis)
High Fen

Common Drain
Hemplands
Methwold Lode
Sleves Holm
High Fen

Hemplands Farm
Broad Fen Farm
THORNHAM ROAD
Chy
THORNHAM ROAD
Thornham Farm

Broad Drove
Rosedene Farm
Broad Fen Farm
SEVERALLS ROAD
Severalls Farm
OLD SEVERALLS RD
Abbey Farm
HANGING DR

BROADFEN DV
Twelve Foot Drain
Methwold Common
SEVERALLS RD
PH
Methwold Hythe
METHWOLD ROAD
CONSTABLE PL
NEW RD
Hall Farm
ELDEN'S LA
HYTHE ROAD
HYTHE VIEWS CL
HERBERT DR
EARLSFIELD LA
DE WARRENE
Works
BULWINGS LA
VENTURA CL

WHITEPLOT ROAD
Firtree Farm
Ten Foot Drain
Banham's Farm

FELTWELL ROAD
WHITEPLOT DROVE
Cut-off Channel
Airfield (dis)

Bower's Drain
Queen's Ground
Pit (dis)
Tennis Plantation

New Farm
MOLEHILL DR
Whiteplot Farm
HYTHE ROAD
Muriel's Farm

Jubilee Farm
Great Oulsham Drain
LITTLE OULSHAM DROVE
Little Oulsham Drove
OLD METHWOLD ROAD

Birch Farm
Little Oulsham Drain
KETTLE LA
1 MUNSON'S PL
2 MUNSON'S LA
3 ST NICHOLAS DR
CROFT HOUSE DR
LODGE ROAD

Feltwell Common
SOUTHERY ROAD
Edmund De Moundeford VC Prim Sch
East Hall
B1112

FOSTER'S DROVE
HAYTHILL LA
PH
P
SKYE GARDENS
ADDISON CL
BARRETTS LA

PLOUGHMAN'S DRO
RAF Outfall Drain
Sewage Works
Feltwell
OAK ST
OLD BRANDON ROAD

Southery Road Farm
Works
LEONARD'S LA
LONG LANE
SHORT LA
HIGH ST
Mast

Stake Lode
White Bridge Farm
New Cut Farm
Sternshouse Farm
TRENCHARD SQ
CARDINGTON RD
BANHAM WLK
Chy
WILTON ROAD

BLACK DYKE RD
Lakenheath Middle Sch

A **B** **C** **D** **E** **F**

67 68 69 70 71 72

D1
1 CURTIS DR
2 OXFORD RD
3 ARCHERS' AVE
4 WESTERN CL
5 HEREWARD WAY
6 HARVARD RD
7 PORTAL CL
8 BLACKDYKE CL
9 PROVOST RD
10 MITCHELL CL
11 WHITLEY CL
12 LIBERATOR CRES

E1
1 BIRD VIEW SQ
2 OXFORD RD
3 WELLINGTON RD
4 LANCASTER RD
5 GREEN LA
6 VINCENT CL
7 CRABBE'S CL
8 NIGHTINGALE LA
9 CLOUGH DR
10 EDMUND MOUNDFORD RD
11 FAIRFIELD WAY
12 ST JOHN'S WAY
13 FAIR CL
14 FALCON RD
15 NEWCOMBE DR
16 HALL DR
17 MULBERRY CL
18 SHORT BECK
19 HILL ST
20 LAMBERTS CL
21 RAWLINGS WAY
22 STIRLING RD
23 UPCHER CL
24 LIME KILN LA

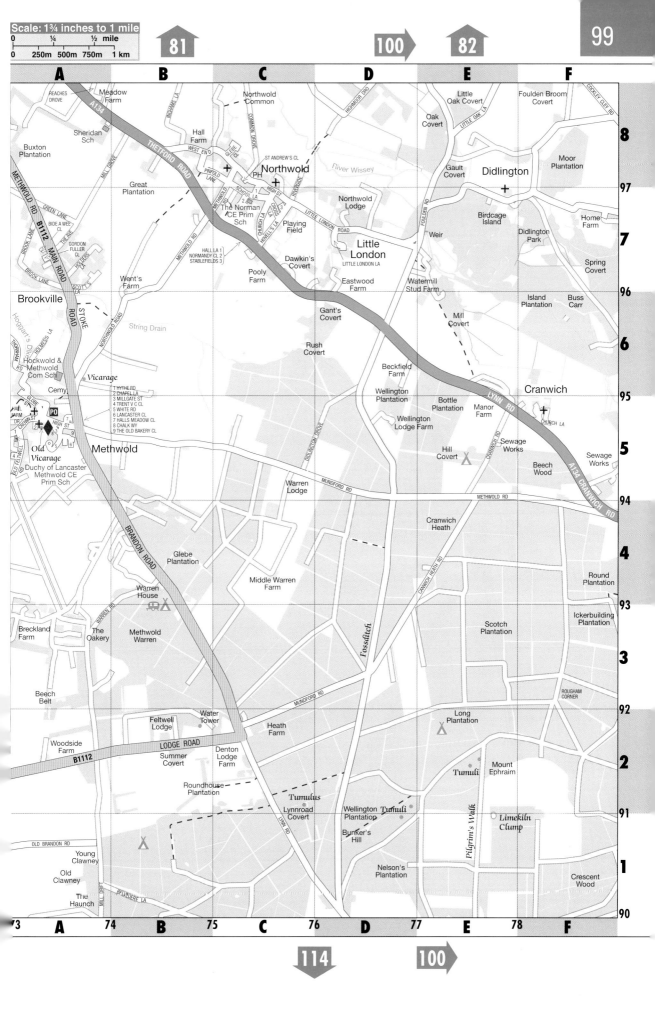

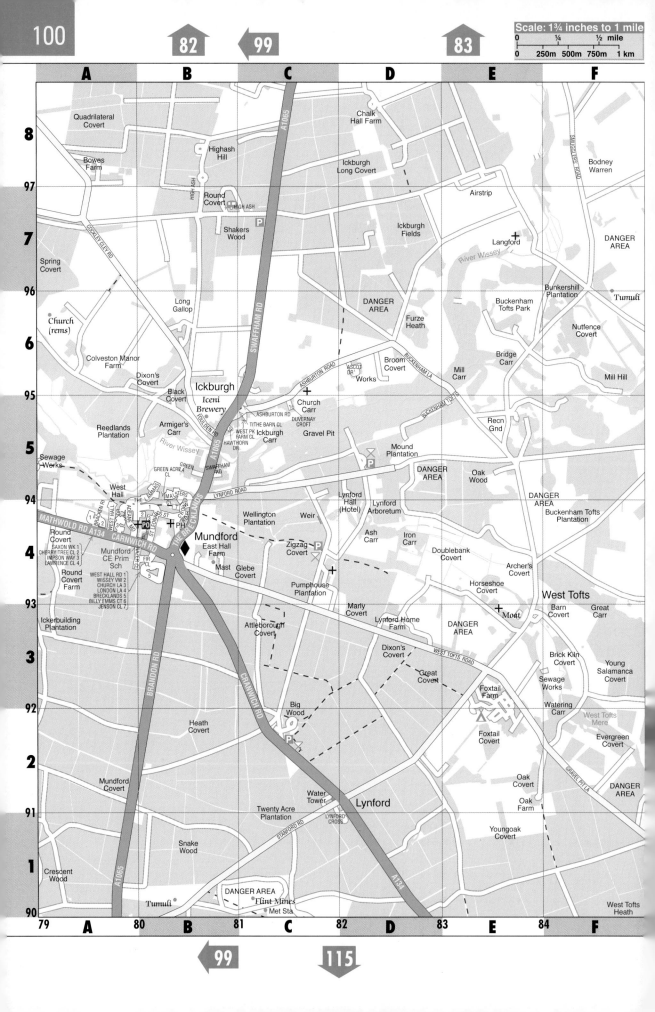

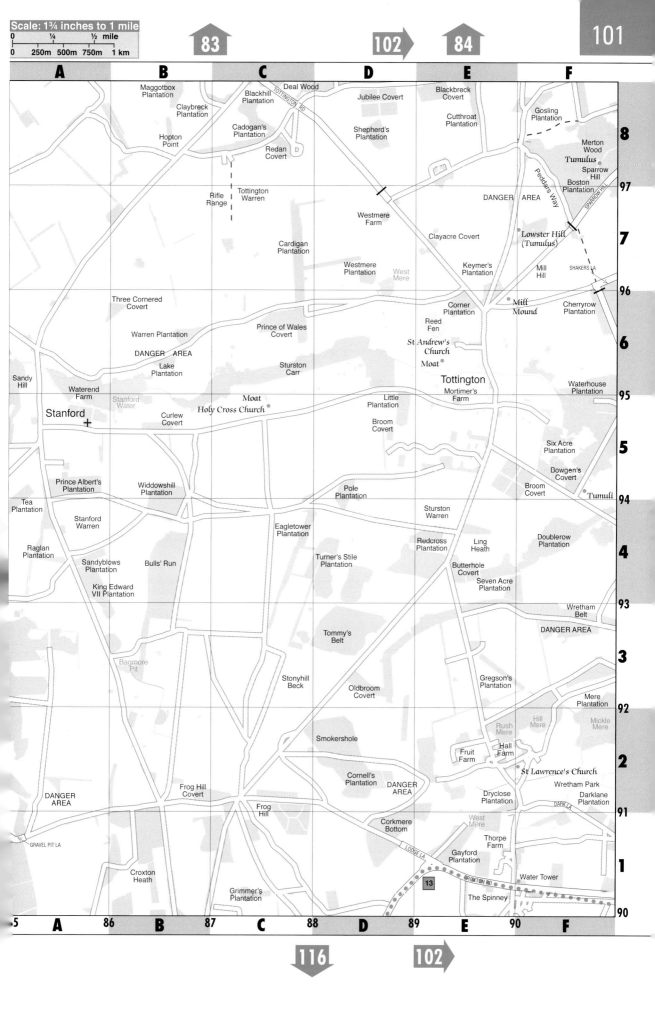

Scale: 1¾ inches to 1 mile

0   ¼   ½   mile
0   250m 500m 750m 1 km

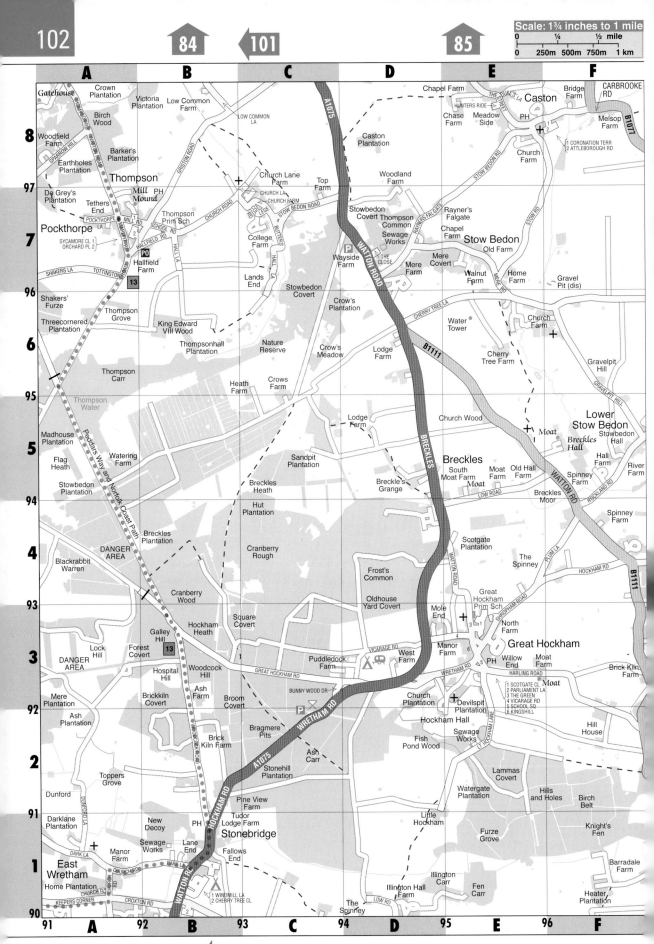

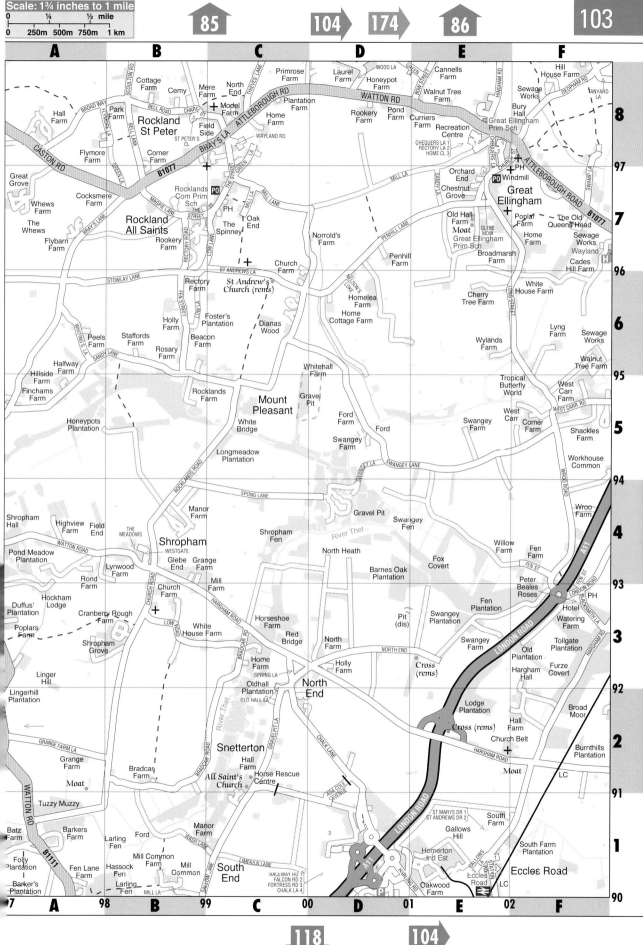

Scale: 1¾ inches to 1 mile

0   ¼   ½   mile
0   250m   500m   750m   1 km

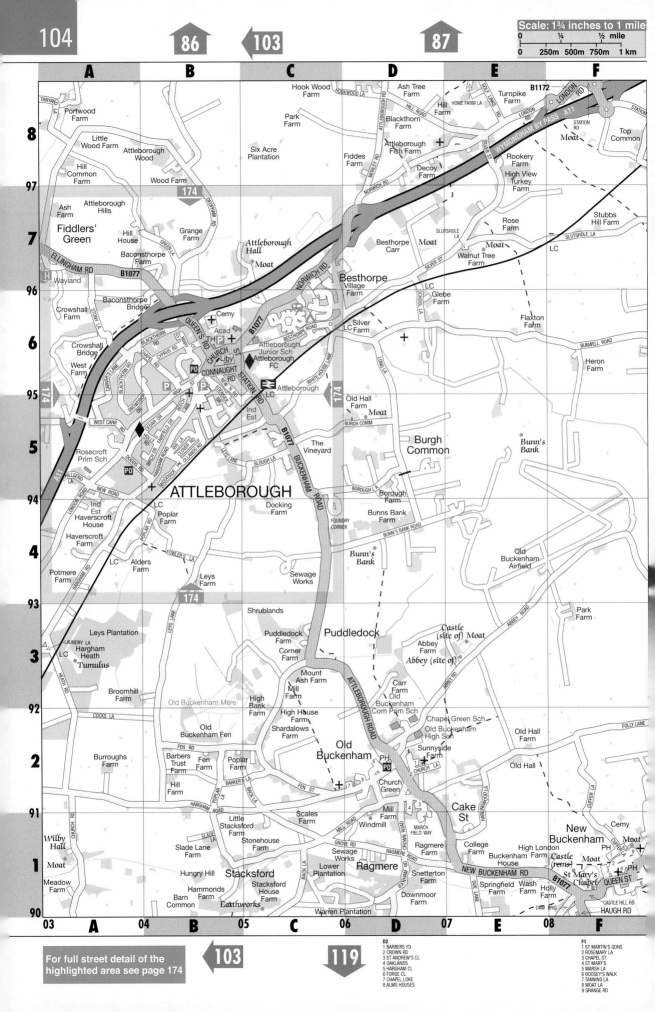

A B C D E F

8

97

7

96

6

95

5

94

4

93

3

92

2

91

1

90

03 A 04 B 05 C 06 D 07 E 08 F

Fiddlers' Green

ATTLEBOROUGH

Besthorpe

Puddledock

Old Buckenham

Stacksford

Ragmere

Cake St

New Buckenham

Burgh Common

Portwood Farm
Little Wood Farm
Attleborough Wood
Hill Common Farm
Wood Farm
Ash Farm
Attleborough Hills
Hill House
Grange Farm
Baconsthorpe Farm
Wayland
Baconsthorpe Bridge
Crowshall Farm
Crowshall Bridge
West Farm
Rosecroft Prim Sch
West Carr
Haverscroft House
Haverscroft Farm
Potmere Farm
Alders Farm
Poplar Farm
Leys Farm
Leys Plantation
Hargham Heath
Tumulus
Broomhill Farm
Burroughs Farm
Hill Farm
Wilby Hall
Moat
Meadow Farm
Hungry Hill
Barn Common
Hammonds Farm
Stacksford House Farm
Earthworks
Slade Lane Farm
Little Stacksford Farm
Stonehouse Farm
Barbers Trust Farm
Fen Farm
Poplar Farm
Old Buckenham Fen
Old Buckenham Mere
High Bank Farm
Mount Ash Farm
Mill Farm
High House Farm
Shardalows Farm
Shrublands
Puddledock Farm
Corner Farm
Scales Farm
Windmill
Lower Plantation
Sewage Works
Warren Plantation
Downmoor Farm
Snetterton Farm
Springfield Farm
Wash Farm
Holly Farm
Ragmere Farm
College Farm
Buckenham House
London Castle (rems)
St Mary's Chapel
Castle Hill Rd
Haugh Rd
New Buckenham
Moat
Cemy
Church Green
Sunnyside Farm
Old Hall
Old Hall Farm
Chapel Green Sch
Old Buckenham High Sch
Old Buckenham Com Prim Sch
Carr Farm
Castle (site of) Moat
Abbey Farm
Abbey (site of)
Park Farm
Old Buckenham Airfield
Bunn's Bank
Bunn's Bank
Bunns Bank Farm
Borough Farm
Foundry Corner
The Vineyard
Docking Farm
Old Hall Farm
Moat
Heron Farm
Flaxton Farm
Glebe Farm
Besthorpe Village Farm
Silver LC Farm
Besthorpe Carr
Moat
Walnut Tree Farm
Moat
Rose Farm
Stubbs Hill Farm
High View Turkey Farm
Rookery Farm
Turnpike Farm
Home Farm La
Hill Farm
Ash Tree Farm
Blackthorn Farm
Attleborough Fish Farm
Decoy Farm
Fiddes Farm
Park Farm
Six Acre Plantation
Hook Wood Farm
Attleborough Hall
Moat
Top Common
Moat
Poplar Farm
Ind Est
Foundry Corner

Norwich Rd
Besthorpe Road
London Rd
B1172
B1077
Station Rd
Buckenham Road
Attleborough Road
New Buckenham Rd
B1077
Ellingham Rd
Hargham Rd
Bunwell Road
Slutshole La
Abbey Road
Folly Lane
174

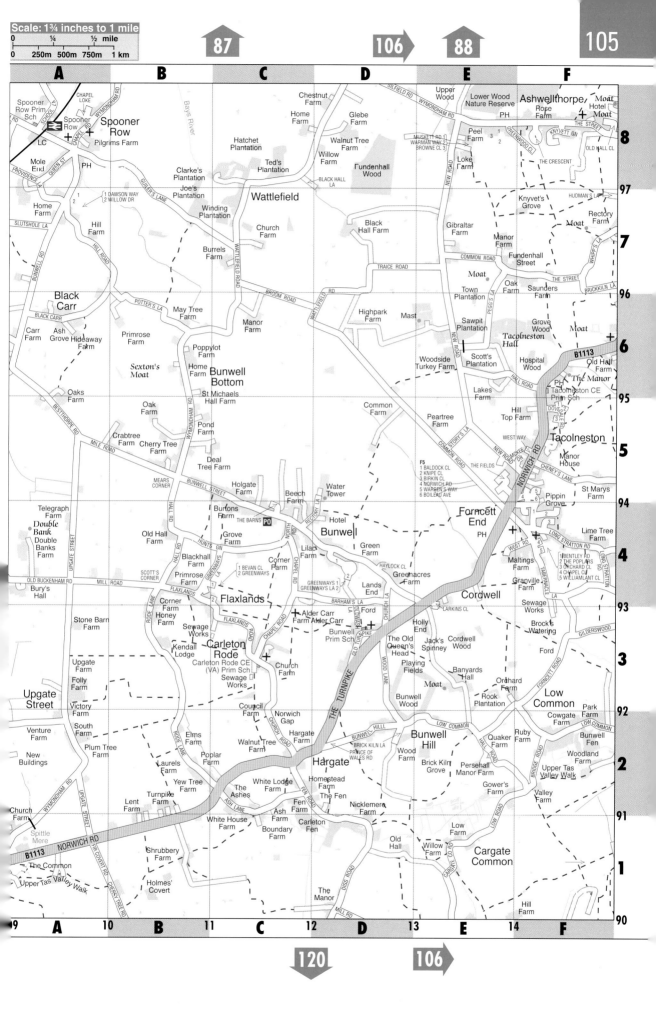

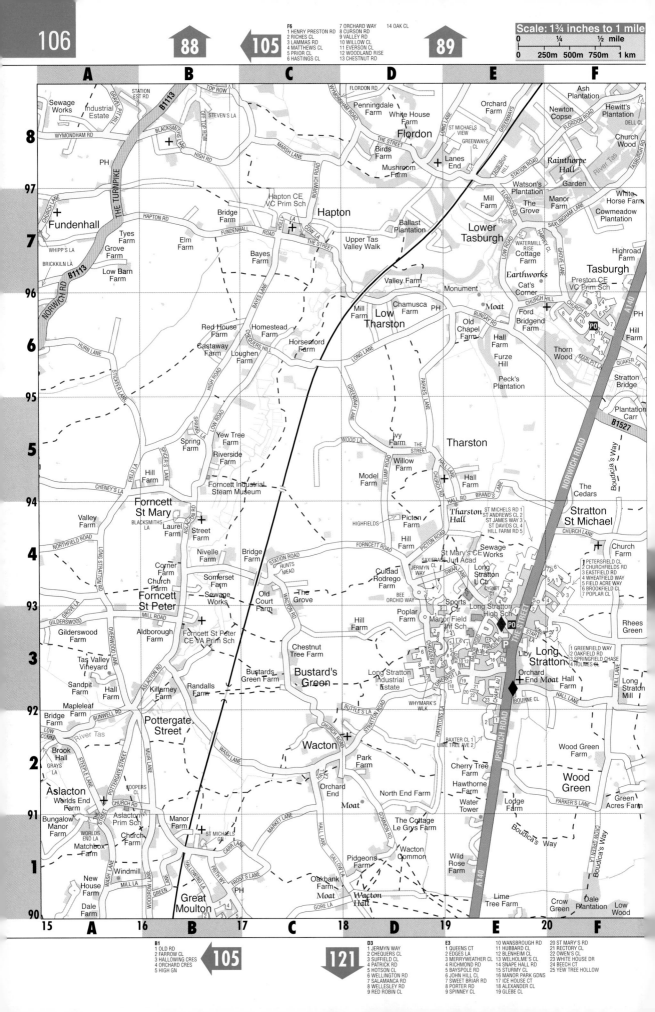

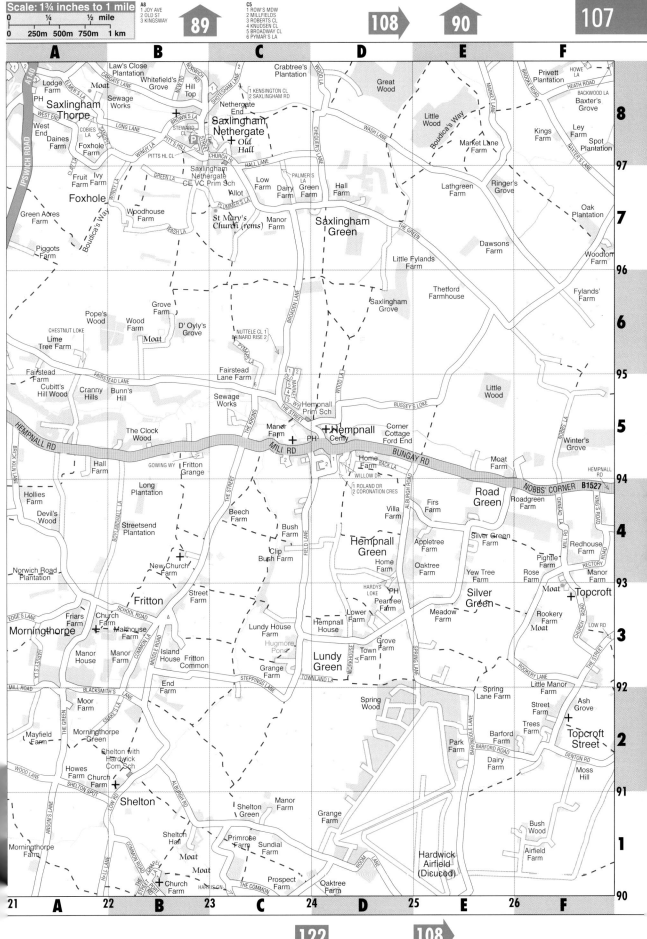

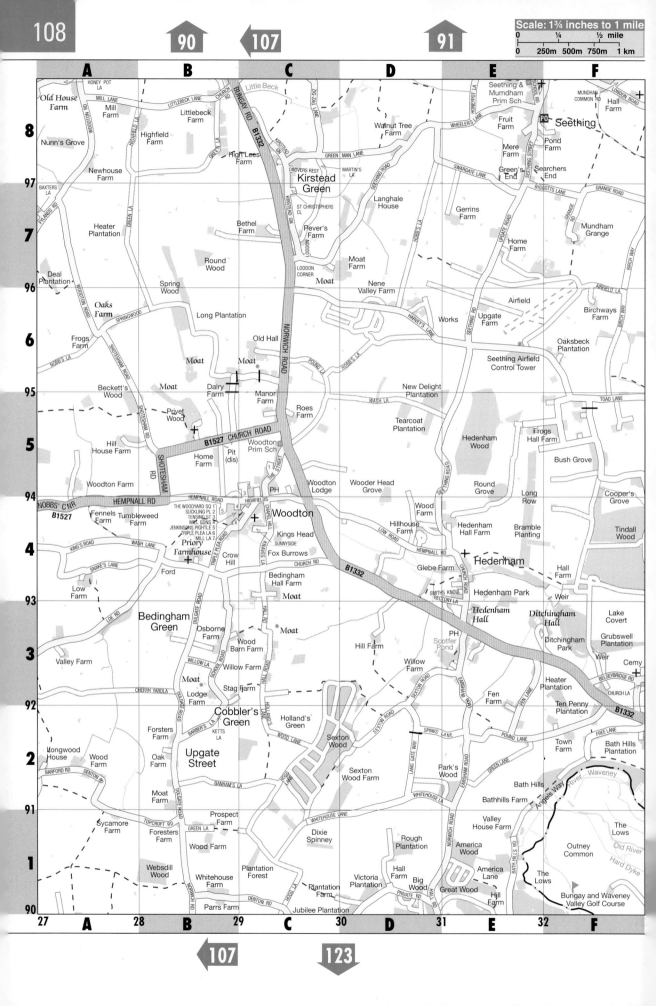

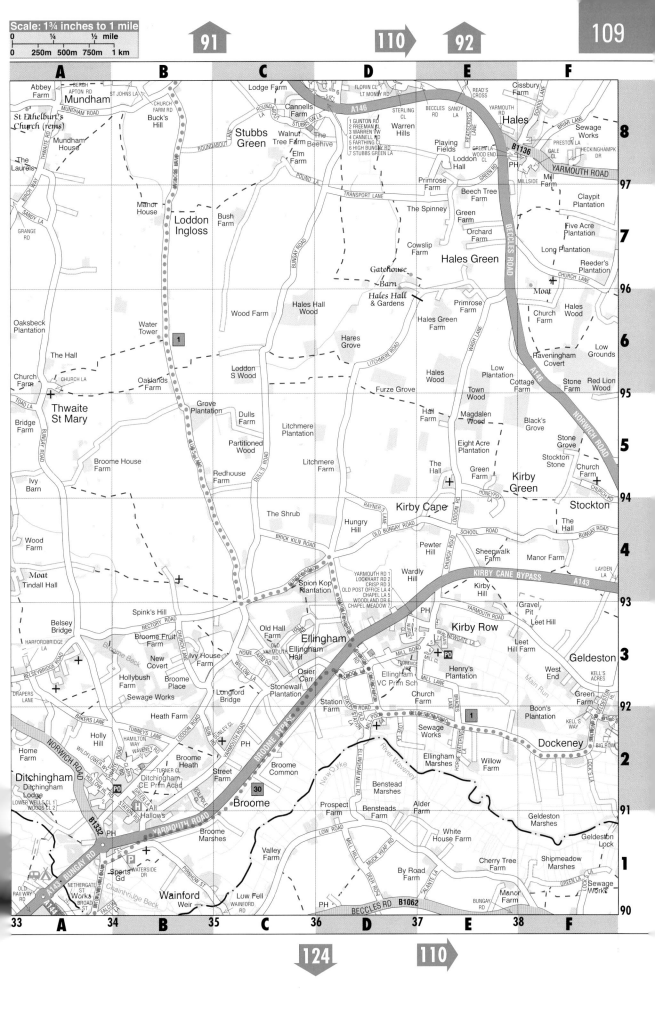

Scale: 1¾ inches to 1 mile

0   ¼   ½ mile
0   250m   500m   750m   1 km

A   B   C   D   E   F

8

Craft Plantation

BOUNDARY RD

North Farm

North Belt

Redhouse Farm

COLLEGE RD

Hall Farm

Hill Farm

The Carr

White House Farm

Haddiscoe

Manor Farm

GRAVEL PIT LANE

THE ST.

PH

97

B1136   YARMOUTH ROAD

LODDON ROAD

B1136   A143

Sycamore Farm

Castell Wood

Crossway Farm

Downings Farm

Hall Farm

CHURCH LA

CHURCH HILL

Church Hill

7

Raveningham

Hall Farm

+ Hall

Lock Plantation

Pockthorpe

Orchard Farm

Three Cocked Hat

Glebeland Com Prim Sch

The Chestnuts

Hill Top

96

Reservoir

Raveningham Moat Gardens

31

STONY LA

BILBYS

PEDDARS LA

GREEN LANE

LODDON ROAD

Clinks Farm

NEW ROAD

FIELDS ROAD

Long Row Wood

Grange Farm

HADDISCOE ROAD

6

Dam Plantation

Brundish Wood

Brundish

The Raveningham Ctr

Tiled House Farm

Priory Farm

Church Farm

Pond Farm

Eaton Farm

Maypole Green

Toft Monks House

Middle Row Wood

Wood Farm

Blyth Wood

The Grove

Brundish Farm

BRUNDISH RD

Three Corner Plantation

Daw's Wood

Moat

Moat

+

Toft Monks

Moat

Great Wood

Thumpers End

Church Farm

95

Mill Mount

Stockton Old Hall

Grove Farm

Water Tower

College Farm

Bulls Green Farm

Hill House Farm

FULLER'S CL

PH

MARDLE RD

Moat

Woodstock Farm

Waterheath Farm

Waterheath

STATION ROAD

5

Calfpightle Clump

High Grove

Bull's Green

ST BENEDICTS CL

Windle Hills

Virginia Farm

POST OFFICE RD

Moat

George's Wood

Grove Farm

Long Plantation

BRICK KILN LANE

BULLS GREEN LANE

BECCLES ROAD

WATERHEATH RD

WOOD LANE

The Elms

ELMS RD

Waterloo

CHURCH LANE

BURROWS GN

94

A146   NORWICH ROAD

Forge End

Lodge Farm

Old Grove

Lodge Wood

Black's Grove

Boundary Farm

Waterloo

CRABTREE LA

THE STREET

Aldeby

4

BUNGAY RD

STOCKTON RD

Upland Farm

Primrose Grove

Hobb's Hill Wood

Ivy House Farm

Round Wood

Gillingham Wood

Cottages Woods

Thrower's Grove

Freelands Plantation

HOLLOW WAY HILL

Stanley Hills

BECCLES RD

THE STREET

93

A143   YARMOUTH RD

Hall Farm

Kell's Heath

Winston Game Farm

Winston Hall Farm

Rose Farm

William's Wood

RECTORY RD

Town Wood

DOGS LA

YARMOUTH ROAD

A143

Dogs Lane Plantation

Boathouse Hill

Hill Farm

Angles Way

Stanley Carrs

Round Hill

Remains of Priory

Moat

3

STOCKTON ROAD

HEATH ROAD

NORWICH ROAD

OLD YARMOUTH RD

Brick Kiln Plantation

War Memorial Plantation

Church Plantation

Hall

HEMMANT WAY
TODHUNTER AVE
ASHFORD CL
KENYON ROW
FORGE GR

Beech Wood

Hill Farm

Gillingham Marshes

Alder Carrs

River Waveney

92

Dunburgh Farm

Bigod's Hill

GELDESTON RD

Gillingham CE Prim Acad

Church Plantation

+

+

Our Lady's Grove

Little Carr

Beccles Marshes

Worlingham Wall

2

Geldeston

GELDESTON DYKE

THE BOUNDARIES 1
DAISY WAY 2
TULIP CL 3

Dunburgh Wood

Dunburgh Hill

1

Hillside Farm

Manor House Farm

Gillingham

KINGS DAM

PH Motel

THE STREET

Gillingham Marshes

NORWICH ROAD

BECCLES

Beccles New Bridge

Beccles Marshes

LC

Worlingham Wall

East Fen Carr

91

PH

Reservoir

1

BECCLESGATE

River Waveney

NEW RD

Beccles Old Bridge

Ravensmere Inf Sch

Hotel

FEN LA

P

A145

GEORGE WESTWOOD WY

Boney's Island

LC

LC

Lotman's Carr

Wild Carr

Marsh Farm

MARSH LANE

1

Moat

Barsham Hall (rems)

Barsham Marshes

P

CAXTON RD

Printing Mus

STATION RD

PO

Liby

Football Gd Beccles

P

CH

Beccles Common

Woodview Farm

Westhill Covert

Wolsey's Woods

Horseshoe Covert

Worlingham Hall

Firhill Covert

Sewage Works

A146

90

Suffolk STREET ATLAS

Beccles Mus

A145 Saxmundham (A12)

Beccles Carr

Lowestoft A146

39   A   40   B   41   C   42   D   43   E   44   F

D1
1 CLOWES CT
2 COMMON LA NTH
3 DOBSON WAY
4 OLD MILL TERRACE
5 ST BENEDICT'S RD
6 ROOK'S LA
7 MIDMEADOW
8 GOOSE GREEN WEST
9 KINGSTON DR
10 MAPLE WAY
11 POUND RD
12 QUEENS RD
13 NOELS WLK
14 NEWGATE
15 SMALL GATE
16 THE WLK
17 HUNGATE

For full street detail of Beccles see Philip's STREET ATLAS of Suffolk

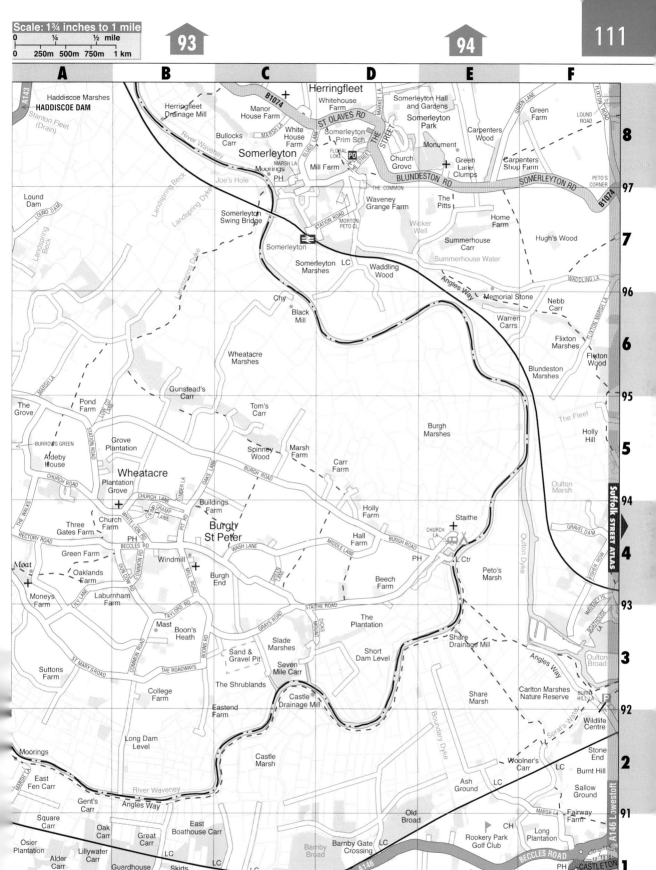

Haddiscoe Marshes
HADDISCOE DAM

Herringfleet

Whitehouse Farm

Somerleyton Hall and Gardens

Somerleyton Park

Green Farm

Green Lane

LOUND ROAD

Manor House Farm

White House Farm

Herringfleet Drainage Mill

Somerleyton Prim Sch

Carpenters Wood

Carpenters Shop Farm

Bullocks Carr

Somerleyton

Mill Farm

Monument

Green Lane Clumps

ST OLAVES RD

Stanton Fleet (Drain)

Lound Dam

Landspring Beck

Landspring Dyke

Joe's Hole

Moorings
PH

FLORAL LOKE

PO

Church Grove

BLUNDESTON RD

THE STREET

THE COMMON

SOMERLEYTON RD

PETO'S CORNER

B1074

Lound Dam

Landspring Beck

Landspring Dyke

Somerleyton Swing Bridge

Somerleyton

STATION ROAD

Waveney Grange Farm

The Pitts

Home Farm

Hugh's Wood

MORTON PETO CL

Wicker Well

Summerhouse Carr

Summerhouse Water

Angles Way

Memorial Stone

Nebb Carr

WADDLING LA

Somerleyton Marshes

LC

Waddling Wood

Chy

Black Mill

Warren Carrs

Flixton Marshes

Flixton Wood

Wheatacre Marshes

Gunstead's Carr

Tom's Carr

Burgh Marshes

Blundeston Marshes

The Fleet

The Grove

Pond Farm

LOW ROAD

STATION ROAD

Grove Plantation

Spinney Wood

Marsh Farm

Carr Farm

Holly Hill

BURROWS GREEN

Aldeby House

CHURCH ROAD

Wheatacre

Plantation Grove

CHURCH LANE

CINDER LA

OAKS LANE

BURGH ROAD

Holly Farm

Staithe

Oulton Marsh

Three Gates Farm

RECTORY ROAD

WHITE LION RD

CRT

CHURCH LANE

CRAMP LANE

Church Farm

PIT RD

Buildings Farm

Burgh St Peter

MIDDLE LANE

Hall Farm

BURGH ROAD

CHURCH LA

LC Ctr

PH

Peto's Marsh

GRAVEL DAM

Oulton Dyke

FISHER ROW

Moat

Green Farm

Oaklands Farm

PH

BECCLES RD

Windmill

DUN DAM RD

COMMON RD

MILL ROAD

Burgh End

GREEN LANE

PH

Beech Farm

FISHER ROW

WAVENEY HE

Moneys Farm

Laburnham Farm

LILY LANE

TAYLORS RD

BOONS RD

Mast

Boon's Heath

Sand & Gravel Pit

WASH LANE

STAITHE ROAD

GRAYS ROAD

DICKS MOUNT

The Plantation

Short Dam Level

Share Drainage Mill

Angles Way

Oulton Broad

BOATHOUSE LA

Suttons Farm

ST MARYS ROAD

COMMON ROAD

THE ROADWAYS

Slade Marshes

Seven Mile Carr

Share Marsh

Carlton Marshes Nature Reserve

BURGH HILL LA

P

College Farm

The Shrublands

Eastend Farm

Castle Drainage Mill

Share Marsh

Wildlife Centre

Long Dam Level

Castle Marsh

BOUNDARY DYKE

Woolner's Carr

LC

Stone End

Burnt Hill

SPRAT'S WATER

Moorings

East Fen Carr

Gent's Carr

Angles Way

River Waveney

Old Broad

Ash Ground

LC

MARSH LA

Sallow Ground

Fairway Farm

Square Carr

Oak Carr

Great Carr

LC

East Boathouse Carr

Bamby Broad

Barnby Gate Crossing

LC

Rookery Park Golf Club

CH

Long Plantation

BECCLES ROAD

Osier Plantation

Alder Carr

Lillywater Carr

Guardhouse Plantation

Skirts Plantation

LC

MARSH LA

EWAL LANE

WA

Moat

Wade Hall

Ned Oak Farm

A146

Candy Hill

Eade's Farm

EADES FARM RD

A1145

PH

CASTLETON

AVE

East Anglia Transport Mus

HEDLEY RD

CHAPEL RD

Three Acre Plantation

Dole's Covert

Low Farm

Suffolk STREET ATLAS

A143

A146 Lowestoft

A1145

517

F1
1 THORNYCROFT GDNS
2 BURLINGHAM DR
3 MILNES WAY
4 WILLOWBROOK CL
5 MONARCH WAY
6 AVELING WAY
7 ANCHOR WAY
8 GALLEY CL
9 CAPSTAN WAY
10 PORTHOLE CL
11 CABIN CL
12 KEEL CL
13 MAST CL
14 APPLEWOOD CL

Scale: 1¾ inches to 1 mile

0   ¼   ½   mile

0   250m   500m   750m   1 km

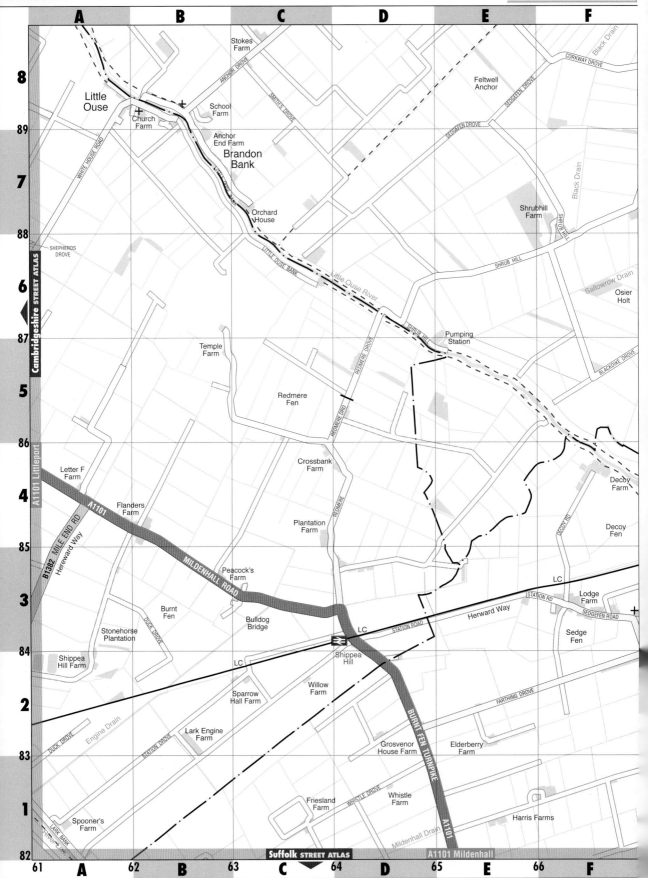

Cambridgeshire STREET ATLAS

A1101 Littleport

Little Ouse

Stokes Farm

School Farm

Church Farm

Anchor End Farm

Brandon Bank

Feltwell Anchor

Corkway Drove

Black Drain

Sedgefen Drove

Sedgefen Drove

Shrubhill Farm

Black Drain

Shrub Hill

Orchard House

Little Ouse Bank

Little Ouse River

Sallowrow Drain

Osier Holt

Shepherds Drove

White House Road

Smiths Drove

Anchor Drove

Temple Farm

Redmere Fen

Pumping Station

Shrub Hill

Blackdike Drove

Redmere Dro

Redmere Dro

Crossbank Farm

Decoy Farm

Letter F Farm

Redmere

Decoy Fen

Flanders Farm

Plantation Farm

Decoy Rd

Mildenhall Road

Peacock's Farm

LC

Lodge Farm

Station Rd

Hereward Way

A1101

B1382 Mile End Rd

Hereward Way

Burnt Fen

Duck Drove

Bulldog Bridge

LC

Station Road

Herward Way

Sedgefen Road

Sedge Fen

Stonehorse Plantation

Shippea Hill

LC

Shippea Hill Farm

Farthing Drove

Sparrow Hall Farm

Willow Farm

Lark Engine Farm

Duck Drove

Engine Drain

Station Drove

Burnt Fen Turnpike

Grosvenor House Farm

Elderberry Farm

Friesland Farm

Whistle Drove

Whistle Farm

Harris Farms

Spooner's Farm

Lark Bank

A1101

Mildenhall Drain

A1101 Mildenhall

| 61 | A | 62 | B | 63 | C | 64 | D | 65 | E | 66 | F |

| A | B | C | D | E | F |

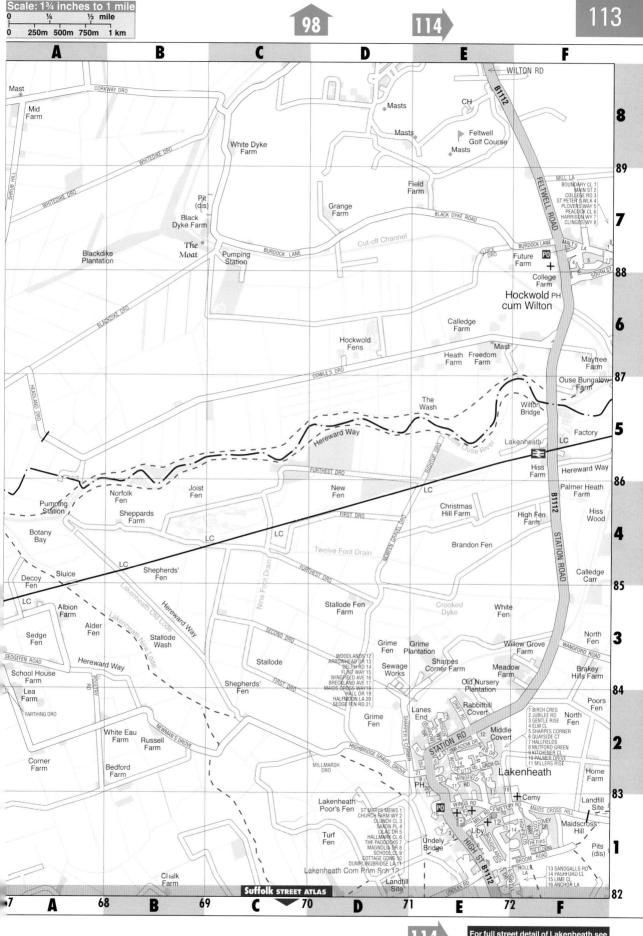

A   B   C   D   E   F

WILTON RD

B1112

Mast

Mid Farm

CORKWAY DRO

Masts

CH

Masts

Feltwell Golf Course

Masts

FELTWELL ROAD

MILL LA

1 BOUNDARY CL 1
MAIN ST 2
COLLEGE RD 3
ST PETER'S WLK 4
PLOVERS WAY 5
PEACOCK CL 6
HARRISON WY 7
CLINGOS WY 8

SHRUB HILL

WHITEDIKE DRO

White Dyke Farm

Field Farm

BLACK DYKE ROAD

WHITEDIKE DRO

Grange Farm

Cut-off Channel

BURDOCK LANE

MALT'S LA

Pit (dis)

Black Dyke Farm

SLUICE DRO

Future Farm

PO

SOUTH ST

Blackdike Plantation

The Moat

Pumping Station

BURDOCK LANE

College Farm

Hockwold PH cum Wilton

BLACKDIKE DRO

Calledge Farm

Hockwold Fens

Mast

Heath Farm

Freedom Farm

Maytree Farm

COWLES DRO

Ouse Bungalow Farm

HEADLAND DRO

The Wash

Wilton Bridge

Factory

Lakenheath

LC

Hereward Way

Little Ouse River

Hiss Farm

Hereward Way

FURTHEST DRO

LC

Palmer Heath Farm

B1112

Norfolk Fen

Joist Fen

New Fen

LC

Christmas Hill Farm

Hiss Wood

Pumping Station

Sheppards Farm

FIRST DRO

High Fen Farm

STATION ROAD

Botany Bay

LC

LC

Twelve Foot Drain

Brandon Fen

Calledge Carr

Decoy Fen

Sluice

SHEPHERDS' FEN

FURTHEST DRO

Crooked Dyke

White Fen

LC

Hereward Way

Nine Foot Drain

Stallode Fen Farm

Willow Grove Farm

North Fen

WANGFORD ROAD

Albion Farm

Alder Fen

Lakenheath Old Lode

SECOND DRO

Grime Fen

Grime Plantation

Brakey Hills Farm

Sedge Fen

Lakenheath New Lode

Stallode Wash

Stallode

WOODLANDS 12
ARROWHEAD DR 13
DELPH RD 14
FLINT WAY 15
WINGFIELD AVE 16
BRECKLAND AVE 17
MAIDS CROSS WAY 18
HALL DR 19
HALFMOON LA 20
SEDGE FEN RD 21

Sewage Works

Sharpes Corner Farm

Meadow Farm

Old Nursery Plantation

Poors Fen

SEDGEFEN ROAD

Hereward Way

Shepherds' Fen

FIRST DRO

Grime Fen

1 BIRCH CRES
2 JUBILEE RD
3 GENTLE RISE
4 ELM CL
5 SHARPES CORNER
6 QUAYSIDE CT
7 HALLFIELDS
8 MUTFORD GREEN
9 KITCHENER CL
10 PALMER DRIVE
11 MILLERS RISE

North Fen

School House Farm

POULTRY RD

Lea Farm

Lanes End

Rabbithill Covert

FARTHING DRO

STATION RD

Middle Covert

Home Farm

White Eau Farm

NEWMAN'S DROVE

Russell Farm

HIGHBRIDGE GRAVEL DROVE

SHARPER'S CORNER

WINGFIELD RD

Lakenheath

Corner Farm

Bedford Farm

MILLMARSH DRO

PH

Cemy

Landfill Site

Lakenheath Poor's Fen

ST MARYS MEWS 1
CHURCH FARM WY 2
CLUNCH CL 3
SAXON PL 4
LILAC DR 5
HALLMARK CL 6
THE PADDOCKS 7
MAGNOLIA DR 8
SCHOOL CL 9
COTTAGE GDNS 10
DUMPLINGBRIDGE LA 11

WINGS RD

PO

P

MILL RD

CEMETERY RD

MAIDS CROSS HILL

Maidscross Hill

Turf Fen

HIGHFIELDS

COVEY DR

THE FIRS

Pits (dis)

Undely Bridge

Liby

HIGH ST

B1112

BROOM RD

HOLLY LA

ANCHOR LA

13 SANDGALLS RD
14 PASHFORD CL
15 LIME CL
16 ANCHOR LA

Chalk Farm

Lakenheath Com Prim Sch 12

Landfill Site

UNDELEY RD

A 68 B 69 C 70 D 71 E 72 F

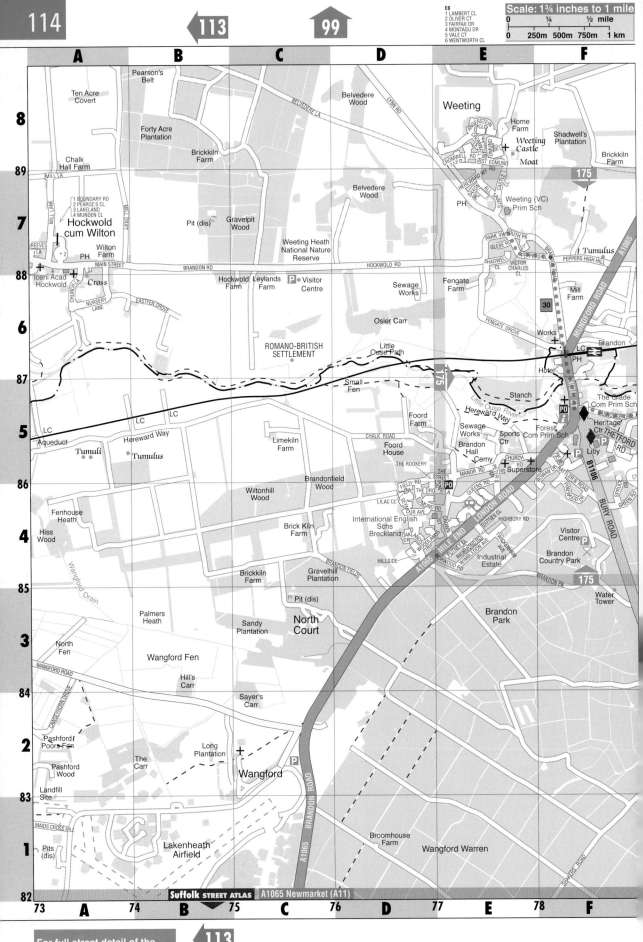

E8
1 LAMBERT CL
2 OLIVER CT
3 FAIRFAX DR
4 MONTAGU DR
5 VALE CT
6 WENTWORTH CL

Scale: 1¾ inches to 1 mile

0   ¼   ½   mile

0   250m   500m   750m   1 km

Ten Acre Covert

Pearson's Belt

Belvedere Wood

Weeting

Home Farm

Weeting Castle

Shadwell's Plantation

Brickkiln Farm

Forty Acre Plantation

Brickkiln Farm

Chalk Hall Farm

MILL LA

175

MILL LANE

Belvedere Wood

Weeting (VC) Prim Sch

1 BOUNDARY RD
2 PEARCE'S CL
3 LAKELAND
4 MUNDEN CL

Pit (dis)

Gravelpit Wood

Weeting Heath National Nature Reserve

PARK VW

SOUTH PK

Tumulus

Hockwold cum Wilton

GLEBE RD

PEPPERS HIGH HILL

MILL DRIFT

Wilton Farm

PH

REEVES LA

SHADWELL CL

VICTOR CHARLES CL

Mill Farm

30

Iceni Acad Hockwold

Main Street

BRANDON RD

Cross

Hockwold Farm

Leylands Farm

Visitor Centre

HOCKWOLD RD

Fengate Farm

Works

Brandon

NURSERY LANE

EASTFEN DROVE

Sewage Works

FENGATE DROVE

LC

PH

Osier Carr

ROMANO-BRITISH SETTLEMENT

Little Ouse Path

175

Hotel

Stanch

The Glade Com Prim Sch

Small Fen

Little Ouse River

Hereward Way

PO

Heritage Ctr

THETFORD RD

LC

LC

Aqueduct

LC

Hereward Way

Foord Farm

CHALK ROAD

Sewage Works

Brandon Hall Cemy

Forest Com Prim Sch

P

Liby

B1106

Tumuli

Tumulus

Limekiln Farm

Foord House

THE ROOKERY

Sports Ctr

CHURCH RD

Superstore

Brandonfield Wood

THE STREET

MANOR RD

PO

PETER'S

Fenhouse Heath

Wiltonhill Wood

FIELD RD

EDMUND RD

QUEENS RD

HIGHBURY RD

Hiss Wood

Brick Kiln Farm

International English Schs Breckland

CROWN

BARTLES CL

MILE END

LONDON ROAD

Visitor Centre

Brickkiln Farm

Gravelhill Plantation

BRANDON FIELDS

HILLSIDE

WORWOOD RD

A1065

Industrial Estate

Brandon Country Park

BURY ROAD

Palmers Heath

Pit (dis)

Sandy Plantation

North Court

Brandon Park

175

North Fen

Wangford Fen

WANGFORD ROAD

Hill's Carr

Water Tower

Pashford Poors Fen

Sayer's Carr

Long Plantation

BRANDON ROAD

Pashford Wood

The Carr

P

Wangford

Landfill Site

MAIDS CROSS HILL

Broomhouse Farm

Wangford Warren

SKAKERS ROAD

Pits (dis)

Lakenheath Airfield

A1065

For full street detail of the highlighted area see page 175

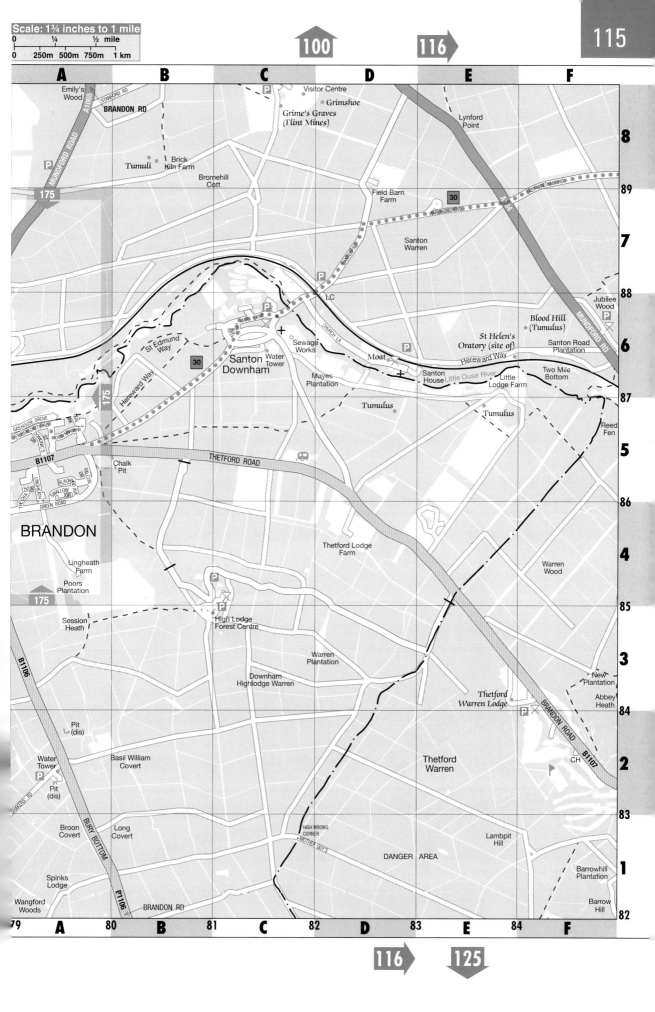

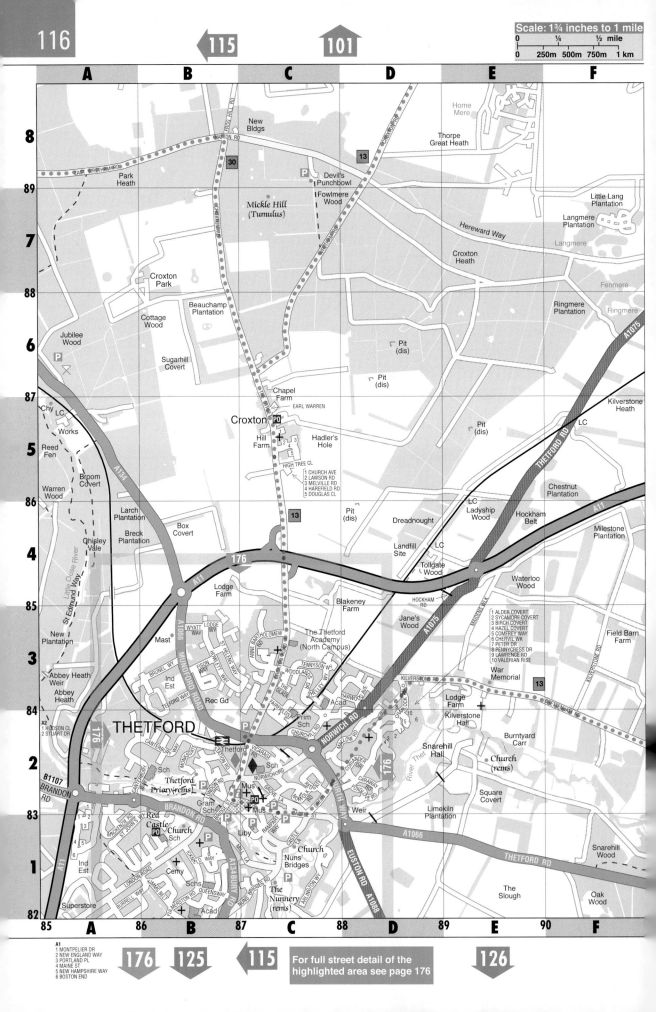

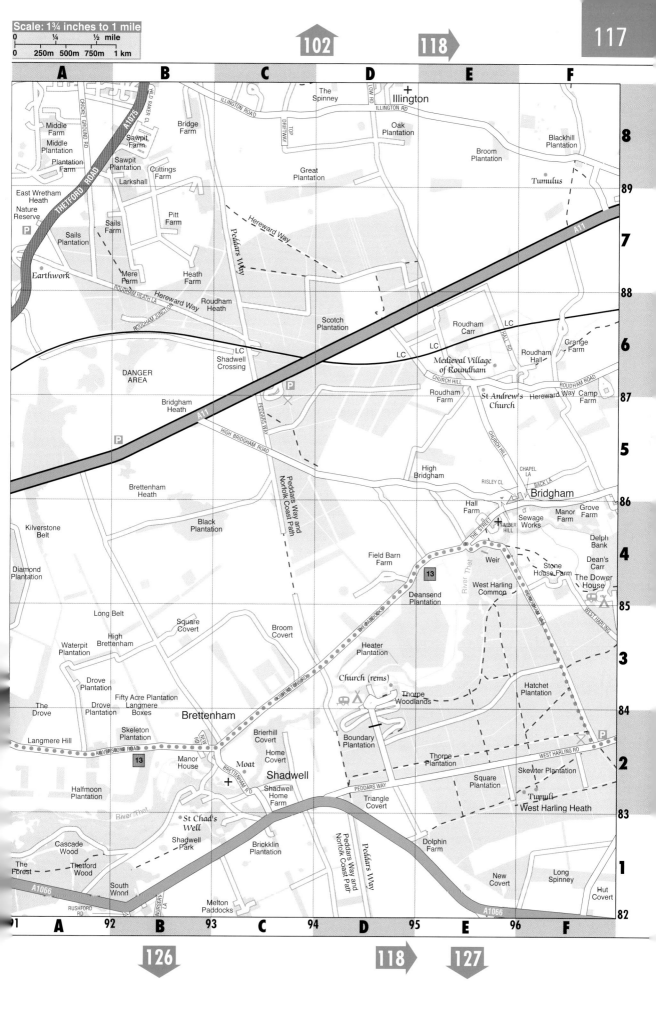

A | **B** | **C** | **D** | **E** | **F**

CRICKET GROUND RD

Middle Farm
Middle Plantation
Plantation Farm

A1075
THETFORD ROAD
WILD RAKER CL

Sawpit Farm
Sawpit Plantation
Cuttings Farm
Larkshall

Bridge Farm

ILLINGTON ROAD
The Spinney
LOW RD
ILLINGTON RD
Illington

TOP DRIFTWAY
Oak Plantation

Broom Plantation

Blackhill Plantation

8

East Wretham Nature Reserve
P

Sails Farm
Pitt Farm
Heath Farm

Great Plantation

Tumulus

89

Sails Plantation

PEDDARS WAY
Hereward Way

A11

7

Earthwork

Mere Farm
Heath Farm

ROUDHAM HEATH LA
Hereward Way
Roudham Heath

Scotch Plantation

Roudham Carr

LC

Grange Farm

88

ROUDHAM JUNCTION
LC
Shadwell Crossing

LC

LC
LC

Roudham Hall
HALL RD
ROUDHAM ROAD

6

DANGER AREA

A11

Bridgham Heath

PEDDARS WAY

P

X

HIGH BRIDGHAM ROAD

Medieval Village of Roundham
CHURCH HILL
Roudham Farm
St Andrew's Church
Hereward Way
Camp Farm

87

P

Brettenham Heath

High Bridgham

CHURCH HILL

CHAPEL LA
BACK LA
Bridgham

5

Black Plantation

Peddars Way and Norfolk Coast Path

RISLEY CL

Hall Farm
THE STREET
TIMBER HILL
Sewage Works
Manor Farm
Grove Farm

86

Kilverstone Belt

Field Barn Farm

Weir
West Harling Common

Delph Bank
Dean's Carr
The Dower House

4

Diamond Plantation

Long Belt

Square Covert

Broom Covert

RIVER Thet
13
Deansend Plantation
Heater Plantation

RIVER Thet

Stone House Farm

WEST HARLING

85

Waterpit Plantation
High Brettenham

ROUDHAM ROAD

Hatchet Plantation

3

The Drove
Drove Plantation
Fifty Acre Plantation
Langmere Boxes
Drove Plantation

KILVERSTONE ROAD

Church (rems)
Thorpe Woodlands

84

Langmere Hill

KILVERSTONE ROAD
13

Skeleton Plantation
Brettenham
VIEW RD

Brierhill Covert
Home Covert
Moat
Shadwell
Boundary Plantation
Thorpe Plantation
WEST HARLING RD
Square Plantation
Skewter Plantation
P
X

2

Halfmoon Plantation

BRETTENHAM RD
Manor House
St Chad's Well

Shadwell Home Farm
PEDDARS WAY
Triangle Covert
Tumuli
West Harling Heath

83

River Thet
Cascade Wood
Thetford Wood

Shadwell Park
Brickklin Plantation

Peddars Way and Norfolk Coast Path
Peddars Way
Dolphin Farm

New Covert
Long Spinney

1

The Forest
South Wood

A1066
RUSHFORD RD
NURSERY LA
Melton Paddocks
Peddars Way
A1066
Hut Covert

82

117
103

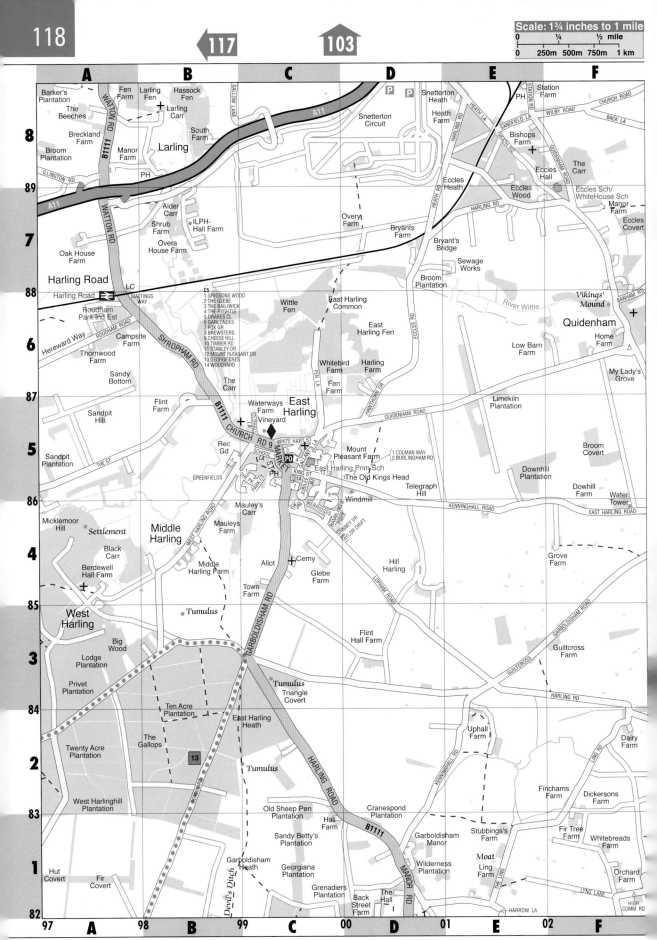

A   B   C   D   E   F

8

Barker's Plantation
The Beeches
Breckland Farm
Broom Plantation
Fen Farm
Larling Fen
Hassock Fen
Larling Carr
South Farm
Larling
Manor Farm
PH
WATTON RD
ILLINGTON RD
B1119

Snetterton Heath
Heath Farm
Snetterton Circuit
P   P
Station Farm
PH
WILBY ROAD
CHURCH ROAD
BACK LA
HEATH LA
SANDFIELD LA
STATION RD
HARLING RD
Bishops Farm
Eccles Hall
The Carr
Eccles Wood
QUIDENHAM ROAD

89

A11

Eccles Sch/ WhiteHouse Sch
Manor Farm
Eccles Covert

7

Oak House Farm
Alder Carr
Shrub Farm
Overa House Farm
ILPH- Hall Farm
Overy Farm
Bryants Farm
Bryant's Bridge
Sewage Works
Broom Plantation
Eccles Heath
Eccles Wood
HARLING RD
HARLING ROAD
WATTON RD

Harling Road
Harling Road
LC
MALTINGS WAY
Roudham Park Ind Est
ROUDHAM ROAD
SHROPHAM RD

88

River Wittle
Vikings' Mound
Quidenham
Home Farm
BANHAM RD

6

Hereward Way
Thornwood Farm
Campsite Farm
Sandy Bottom
C5
1 GRIGSONS WOOD
2 THE GLEBE
3 THE BAILIWICK
4 THE PYGHTLE
5 DRAKES CL
6 GARLONDES
7 FOX GR
8 BREWSTERS
9 CHEESE HILL
10 TIMBER RD
11 STANLEY DR
12 MOUNT PLEASANT DR
13 GEORGE CRES
14 WOODYARD
Wittle Fen
East Harling Common
East Harling Fen
Whitebird Farm
Harling Farm
Fen Farm
FEN LA
Low Barn Farm
My Lady's Grove
ECCLES RD

87

Sandpit Hill
Flint Farm
The Carr
B1111 CHURCH RD 9
Waterways Farm Vineyard
East Harling
Mount Pleasant Farm
QUIDENHAM ROAD
HAWTHORN DR
Limekiln Plantation
Broom Covert
THE ST

5

Sandpit Plantation
Rec Gd
SCHOOL LA
WHITE HART ST
GALLANTS LA
1 COLMAN WAY
2 BURLINGHAM RD
East Harling Prim Sch
The Old Kings Head
Telegraph Hill
Downhill Plantation
Dowhill Farm
Water Tower

86

GREENFIELDS
THE PL
PO
PH
KING ST
JUBILEE AV
Windmill
KENNINGHALL ROAD
EAST HARLING ROAD
Mauley's Carr
Mauleys Farm
IKERRIDGES
RAMBLER PIECE

4

Micklemoor Hill
Settlement
Middle Harling
Black Carr
Berdewell Hall Farm
WEST HARLING ROAD
Middle Harling Parm
Allot
Cemy
Glebe Farm
Hill Harling
SPRINGLEY DR
TAYLOR DRIFT
Grove Farm
LOPHAM ROAD

85

West Harling
Tumulus
Town Farm
GARBOLDISHAM RD

3

Lodge Plantation
Privet Plantation
Big Wood
Ten Acre Plantation
Tumulus
Triangle Covert
East Harling Heath
Flint Hall Farm
GUILTCROSS
Guiltcross Farm
HARLING RD

2

Twenty Acre Plantation
The Gallops
13
Tumulus
HARLING ROAD
Old Sheep Pen Plantation
Cranespond Plantation
B1111
Uphall Farm
Dairy Farm
Finchams Farm
Dickersons Farm
KENNINGHALL RD
THE LING
LING RD

1

Hut Covert
Fir Covert
West Harlinghill Plantation
Garboldisham Heath
Sandy Betty's Plantation
Georgiana Plantation
Grenadiers Plantation
Hall Farm
MANOR RD
Garboldisham Manor
Wilderness Plantation
Stubbings's Farm
Moat
Ling Farm
Fir Tree Farm
Whitebreads Farm
Orchard Farm
LYNG LANE
HIGH COMM RD

82

Devil's Ditch
Back Street Farm
The Hall
HARROW LA

97   98   99   00   01   02

A   B   C   D   E   F

127
117
128

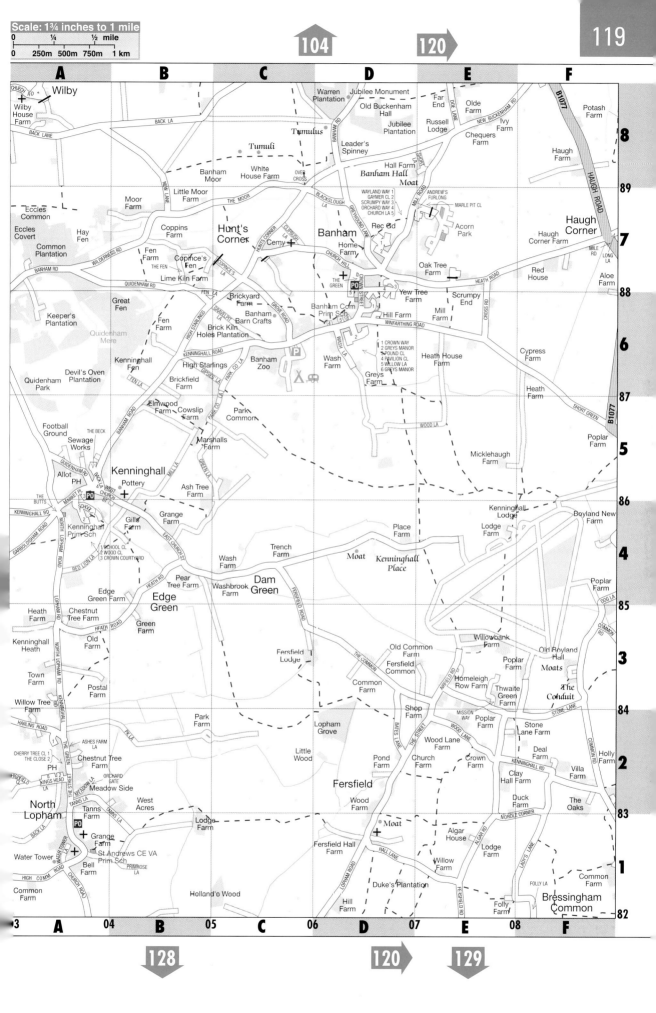

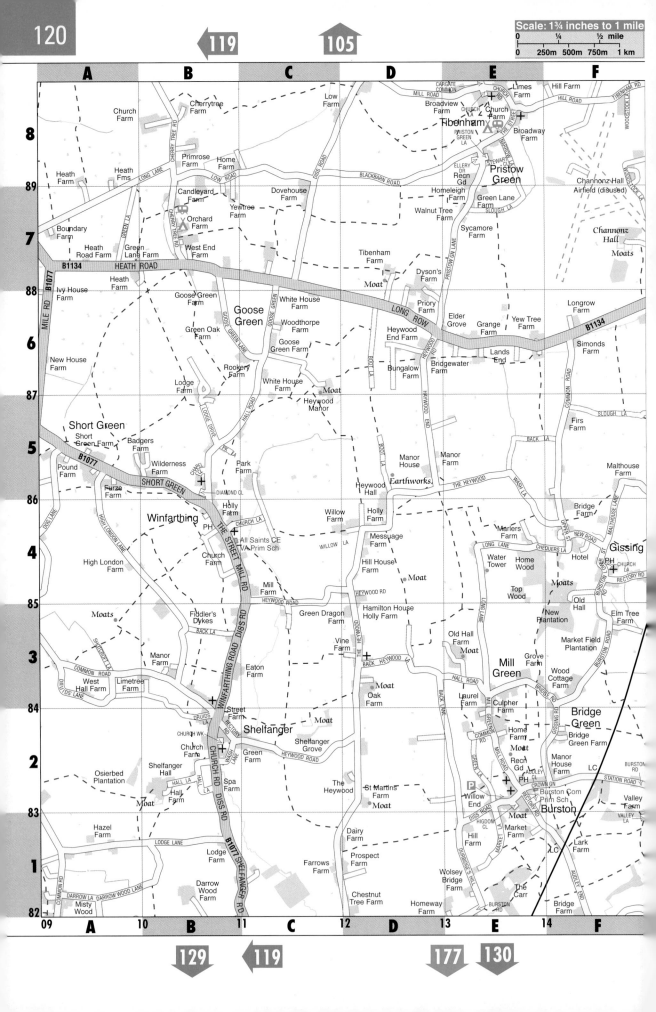

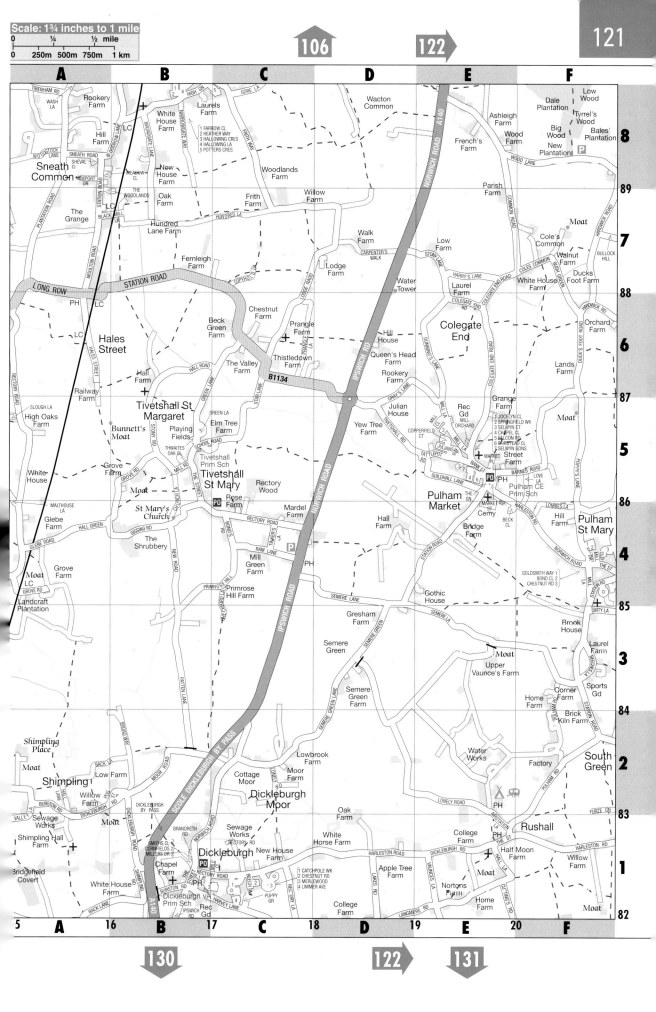

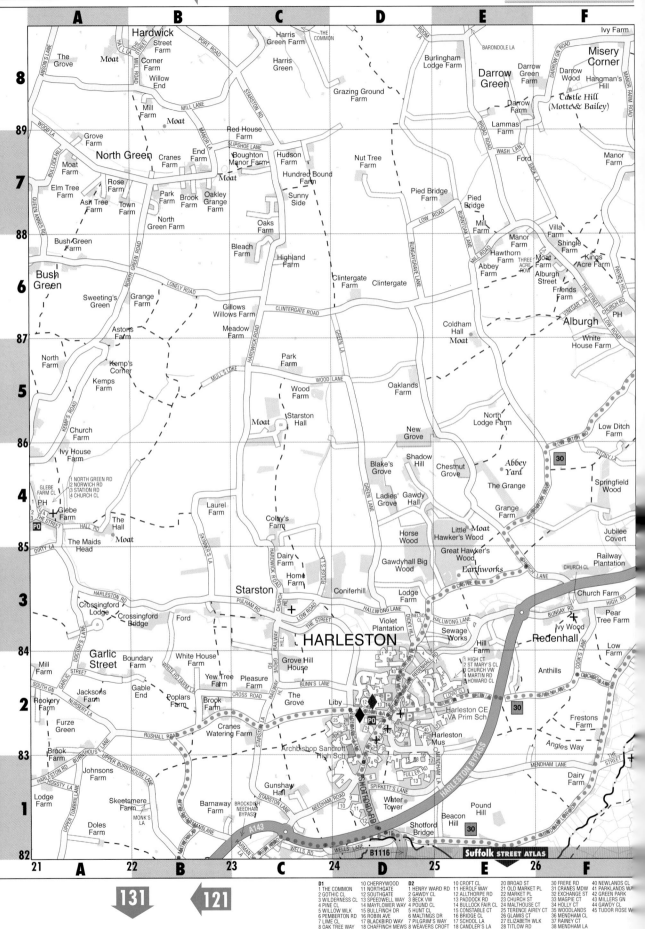

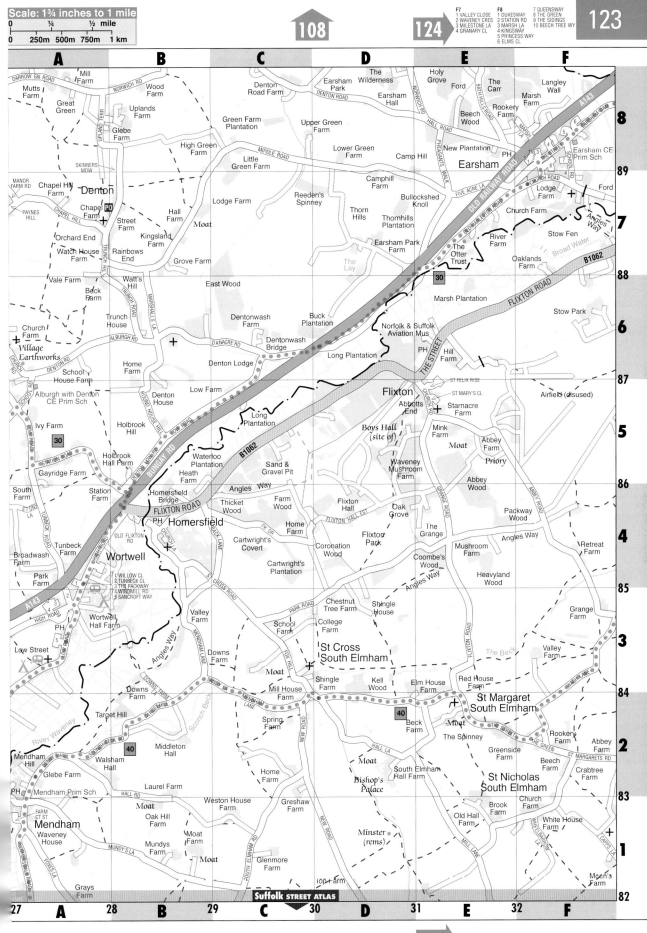

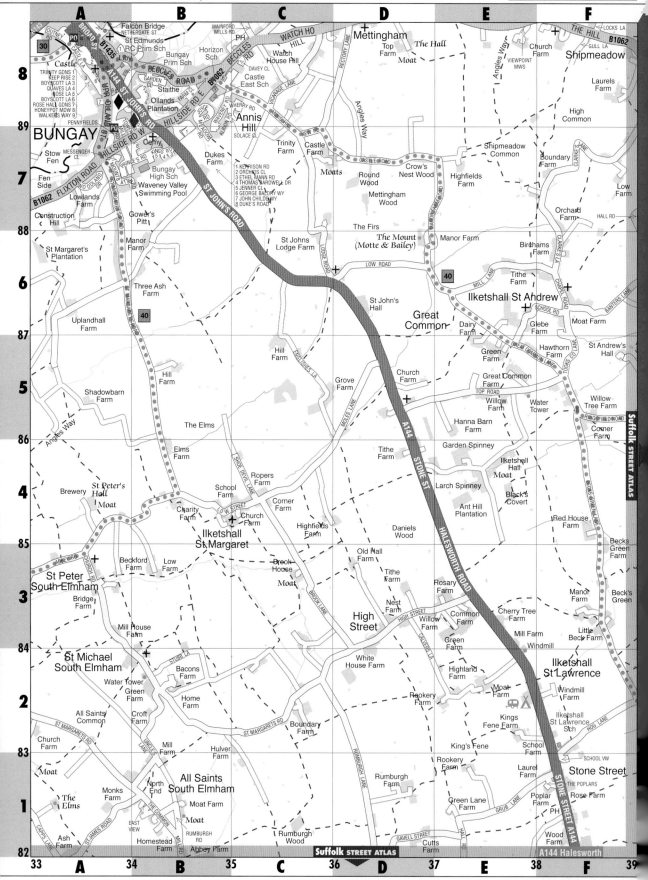

B8
1 ANNIS HILL LA
2 YEOMAN'S CL
3 REEVE'S CL
4 MILLERS CL
5 OLD GRAMMAR LA
6 BIGOD RD

Mettingham
Top Farm
The Hall
Moat
Shipmeadow
Church Farm
Angles Way
VIEWPOINT
MWS
THE HILL
B1062
LOCKS LA
GULL LA
Laurels Farm
High Common

St Edmunds
RC Prim Sch
Bungay Prim Sch
Horizon Sch
WATCH HO
HILL
PH
Watch House Hill
DAVEY CL
Castle East Sch
Falcon Bridge
NETHERGATE ST
WAINFORD MILLS RD
BECCLES RD
VICARAGE LANE
RECTORY LANE

Castle
TRINITY GDNS 1
KEEP RISE 2
BOYSCOTT LA 3
QUAVES LA 4
ROSE LA 5
BOYSCOTT LA 6
ROSE HALL GDNS 7
HONEYPOT MDW 8
WALKERS WAY 9

30
PO
OUTNEY RD
CASTLE LA
LILY
B1435
BROAD ST
GARDEN STAITHE
Ollands Plantation
FARM DL
BECCLES ROAD
HILLSIDE RD E
ALBAN RD
JOYCE RD
WHERRY RD
NINNS RD
Annis Hill
SOLACE CL
Trinity Farm
New RD
Castle Farm
Crow's Nest Wood
Shipmeadow Common
Boundary Farm
CLARKE'S LANE
Low Farm

BUNGAY
PENNYFIELDS
MESSENGER CL
Stow Fen
Fen Side
Construction Hill
B1062
FLIXTON ROAD
LOWLANDS FARM RD
Lowlands Farm
UPR OLLAND ST
ST JOHNS RD
HILLSIDE RD W
PO
PRINCES RD
KINGS RD
Cemy
Bungay High Sch
Waveney Valley Swimming Pool
Gower's Pitt
ST JOHN'S ROAD
Dukes Farm
1 KENRISON RD
2 ORCHIDS CL
3 ETHEL MANN RD
4 THOMAS HARDWELL DR
5 JENNER CL
6 GEORGE BALDRY WY
7 JOHN CHILDS WY
8 DUKE'S ROAD
Moats
Round Wood
Mettingham Wood
The Firs
St Johns Lodge Farm
LODGE ROAD
WANGFORD RD
The Mount
(Motte & Bailey)
Manor Farm
Highfields Farm
Orchard Farm
HALL RD
Birchams Farm
CLARKE'S LA
89

St Margaret's Plantation
Manor Farm
MANGREEN ROAD
Three Ash Farm
40
Uplandhall Farm
Hill Farm
Shadowbarn Farm
Angles Way
Hill Farm
ENGLISHES LA
Grove Farm
Low Road
40
St John's Hall
Great Common
Dairy Farm
Tithe Farm
MILL LANE
Ilketshall St Andrew
SCHOOL RD
Glebe Farm
Moat Farm
St Andrew's Hall
BANTERS LANE
CHARLES LA
TOOKS CO LANE
GREAT COMMON LANE
Green Farm
Hawthorn Farm
Great Common Farm
TOP ROAD
Willow Farm
Water Tower
Willow Tree Farm
RINGSFIELD ROAD
Corner Farm
BECKS GREEN LA
88

7

6

5

86

The Elms
Elms Farm
SHOE DEVIL LANE
School Farm
LOW ST
Ropers Farm
Corner Farm
Highfields Farm
MOLES LANE
A144
STONE ST
HALESWORTH ROAD
Tithe Farm
Garden Spinney
Hanna Barn Farm
Larch Spinney
Ilketshall Hall Moat
Black's Covert
Ant Hill Plantation
Red House Farm
Becks Green Farm

4

Brewery
St Peter's Hall
Moat
Charity Farm
Church Farm
Ilketshall St Margaret

85

St Peter South Elmham
ABBEY RD
CHURCH RD
Beckford Farm
Low Farm
Brook House
Moat
BROOK LANE
Daniels Wood
Old Hall Farm
Tithe Farm
Nest Farm
Rosary Farm
Manor Farm
Beck's Green

Bridge Farm
Mill House Farm
ST MARGARETS RD
High Street
High Street
CALVERS LN
Willow Farm
Common Farm
Cherry Tree Farm
Mill Farm
Windmill
Little Beck Farm

84

St Michael South Elmham
Water Tower
Green Farm
STUBBS LA
Bacons Farm
Home Farm
White House Farm
Green Farm
Highland Farm
Ilketshall St Lawrence
Windmill
Moat Farm
Rookery Farm
Ilketshall St Lawrence Sch
HOG LANE

2

All Saints Common
Church Farm
Croft Farm
Mill Farm
LINGLES LA
Hulver Farm
RUMBURGH RD
MILL RD
Boundary Farm
RUMBURGH LANE
Rookery Farm
King's Fene
Kings Fene Farm
Highland Farm
Green Lane Farm
GRUB LANE
School Farm
SCHOOL VW
Stone Street
THE POPLARS
Poplar Farm
Rose Farm
PH
STONE STREET A144

Moat
The Elms
Monks Farm
North End
All Saints South Elmham
Moat Farm
Moat
EAST VIEW
THE COMMON
ST JAMES ROAD
CAPPS LANE
Ash Farm
Homestead Farm
Abbey Farm
Rumburgh Wood
GAVELL STREET
Cutts Farm
HALL RD
Laurel Farm
Wood Farm
A144 Halesworth

83

1

82

Suffolk STREET ATLAS

A 33 34 B 35 C 36 D 37 E 38 F 39

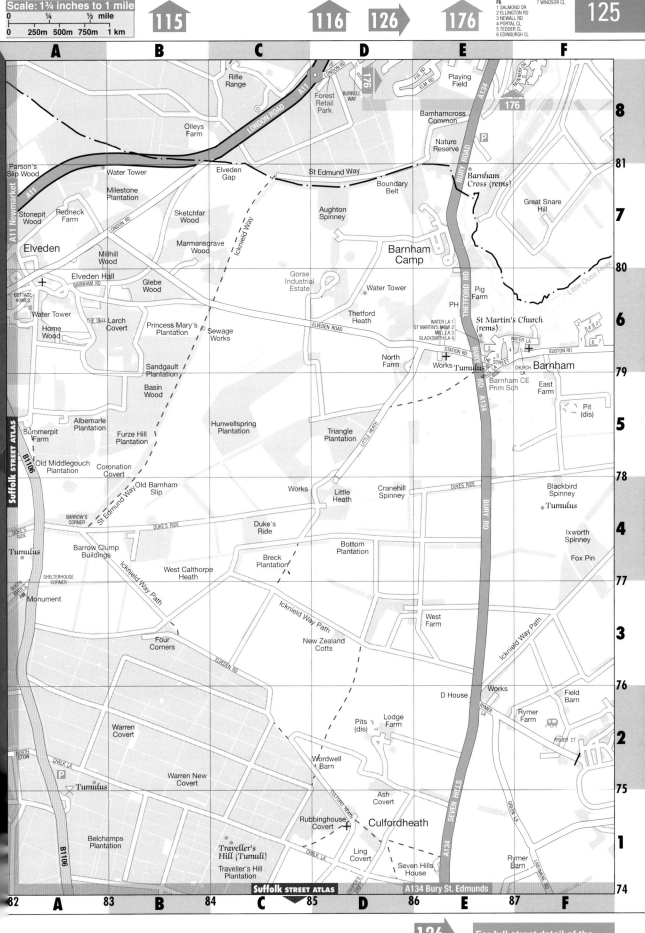

126

176 116

125 176

117

Scale: 1¾ inches to 1 mile

0   ¼   ½ mile
0   250m 500m 750m 1 km

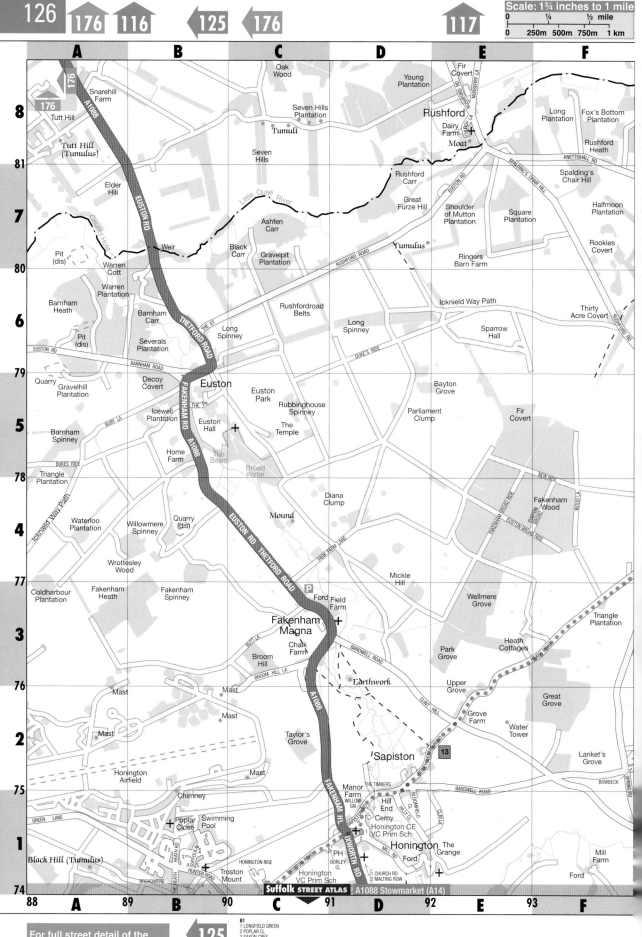

For full street detail of the
highlighted area see page 176

125

B1
1 LONGFIELD GREEN
2 POPLAR CL
3 SAXON CRES
4 NORFOLK RD
5 ST EDMUNDS GATE
6 TUDOR WLK
7 ST EDMUNDS SQ

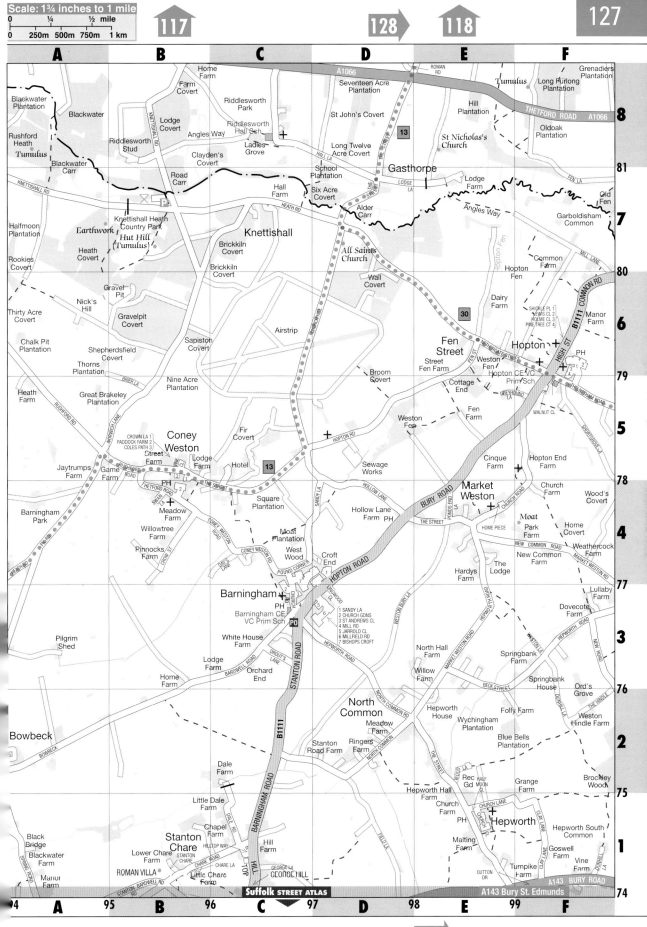

Scale: 1¾ inches to 1 mile

0   ¼   ½   mile
0   250m 500m 750m 1 km

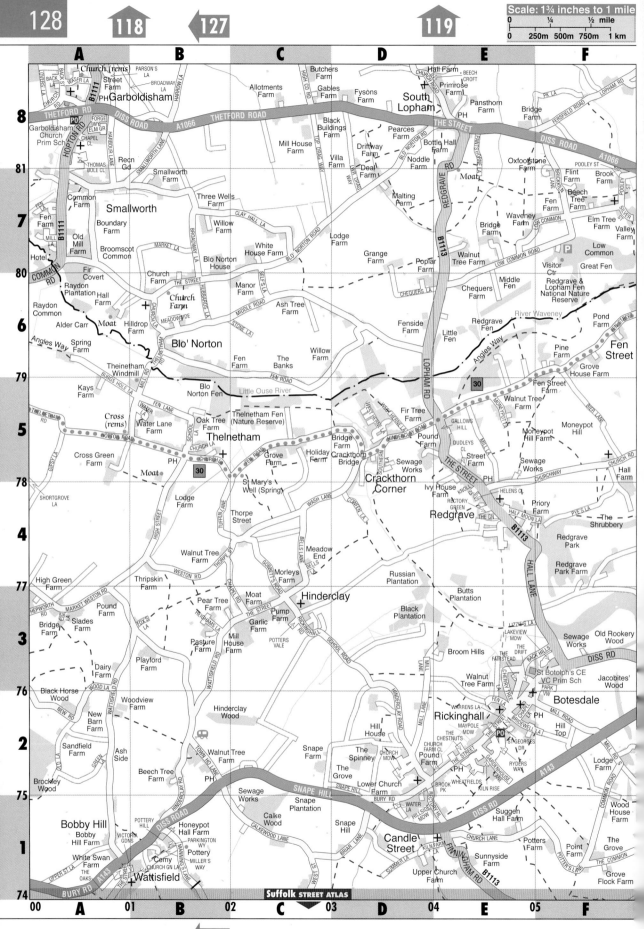

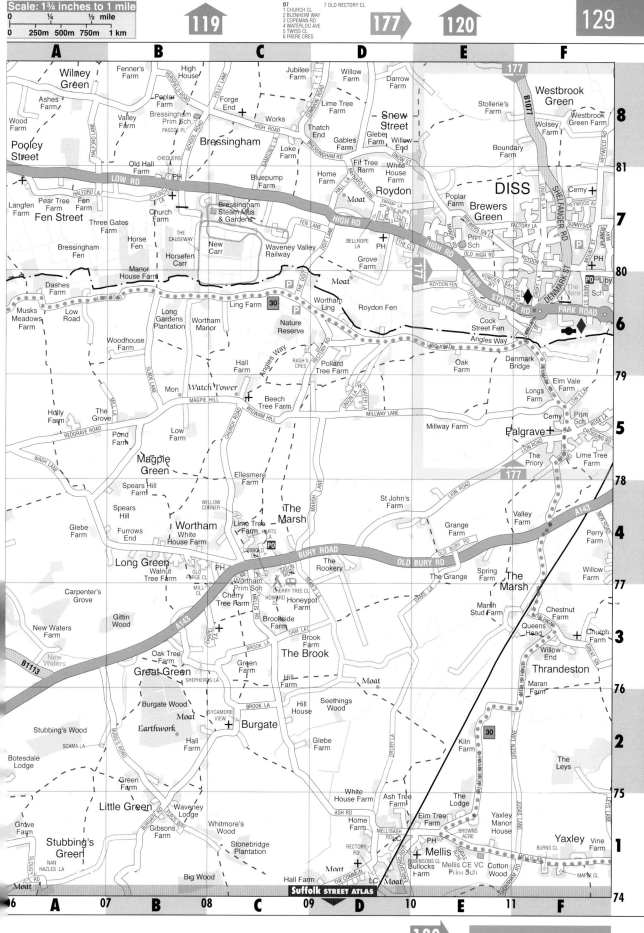

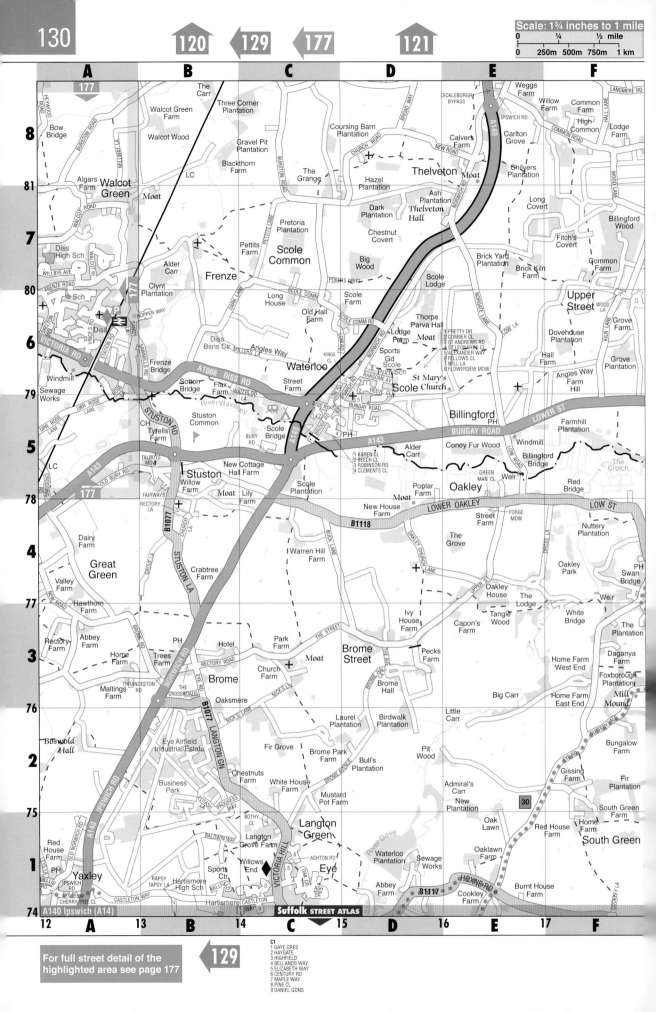

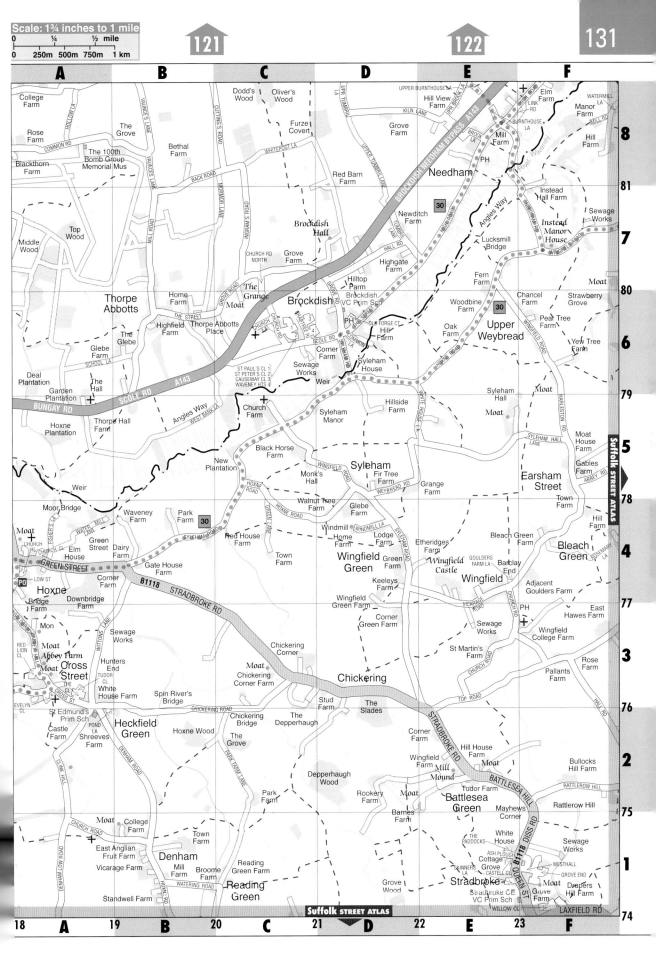

A B C D E F

8

7

42

6

5

41

4

3

40

2

1

39

Old Hunstanton

Hotel

Smugglers CL

SMUGGLERS LA

IRB Station

Motel

GOLF COURSE RD

SANDY LANE

ASHDALE

WODEHOUSE RD

HAMILTON RD WEST

HAMILTON ROAD

WATERWORKS ROAD

CHURCH ROAD

St Edmund's Point

KELSEY CL

THE BIG YARD

OLD HUNSTANTON RD

A149

SEA LANE

HAMILTON LANE

ERPINGHAM CT

PO

SALTHINGHAM GR

HOWARDS CL

Lighthouse (dis)

LIGHTHOUSE LANE

CHAPEL BANK

LIGHTHOUSE CL

St Edmund's Chapel

BERNARD CRESCENT

KINGS CRESCENT

PEDDARS DR

OLD TOWN WY

B1161

CROMER ROAD

Bernard Crescent

LASTLEY CRESCENT

BELGRATE AVE

PEDDARS

QUEENS DRIVE

KINGS RD

HASTINGS

QUEENS GDNS

CLARENCE RD

CLIFF PARADE

CLARENCE CT

BUCKINGHAM CT

Glebe House Sch

VICTORIA AVE

ST EDMUND'S AV

YORK AVE

1 LOWER LINCOLN ST
2 AUSTIN ST
3 NORTHGATE PREC
4 THE GREEN

LINCOLN SQ N

GLEBE AVE

LINCOLN SQUARE S

NORTHGATE

LINCOLN STREET

Boston Sq Sensory Park

BOSTON SQ

CHURCH STREET

HUNSTANTON

CLIFF CT

CLIFF TR

A149

VALENTINE COURT

Hunstanton Inf Sch

NORTH PROM

TH

GREEVEGATE

CHURCH ST

HIGH ST

Cross

Princess Theatre

ST EDMUND'S TERR

ST JAMES ST

PO

WESTGATE

Rec Gd

CYPRESS

CAM

HARTLEY CL

PL

LEMING CRES

Beech Wood

SIR DOUGLAS BADER ESPLANADE

LESTRANGE

BEACH TERR RD

Liby

VALENTINE RD

ALFRED GDNS

NURSERY DR

GOWER

DOWNS CL

SYLEMAN ST

DOWNS ROAD

Lodge Farm

The Coal Shed Gall

AVENUE RD

CHAPEL LA

HOMEFIELDS RD

DOWNS

Oasis Sports & Leisure Centre

YH

Smithdon High Sch

Chimney

Coach Park

CR

HILL STREET

PARK RD

NENE

SANDRINGHAM ROAD

Hunstanton Commercial Park

Hunstanton Sea Life Sanctuary

SEAGATE

SOUTHEND RD

CRESCENT

MELTON DR

WILLOW

LYNDHURST CT

HANOVER GDNS

FROBISHER

KING'S LYNN ROAD

CHILTERN CR
PRINCE WILLIAM CL 2
GEORGE RAINES CL 3

ALEXANDRA RD

CHATSWORTH RD

RAMSAY GDNS

NELSON CL

EVANS

COLLINGWOOD RD

Superstore

Cerny

BISHOP'S RD

ELIZABETH CL

JUBILEE CL

WAVENEY RD

St Andrew's Chapel (remains of)

MERCEDES AVE

Cottages Downs Farm

B1161

MANOR RD

OASIS WAY

1 TUDOR CRES
2 MARGARETS CL

Hill Wood

SOUTH BEACH RD

WINDSOR RI

RENNEY CL

Downs Farm

SOUTH PROMENADE

CHARLES

PRINCESS DR

SARAHS DR

ANDREWS PL

PHILLIPS

REDGATE HILL

1 KINGFISHER LA
2 HERON VALE
3 CURLEW CL
4 LAPWING LA
5 SANDPIPER ST
6 AVOCET AVE
7 FULMAR GDNS
8 BUTTERFIELD RISE

SOUTH BEACH ROAD

DIANAS DRO

HARRY WAY

A149

Redgate Hill

NORTH BEACH

CH

CHALK RIVER RD

Searles Golf Course

HUNSTANTON RD

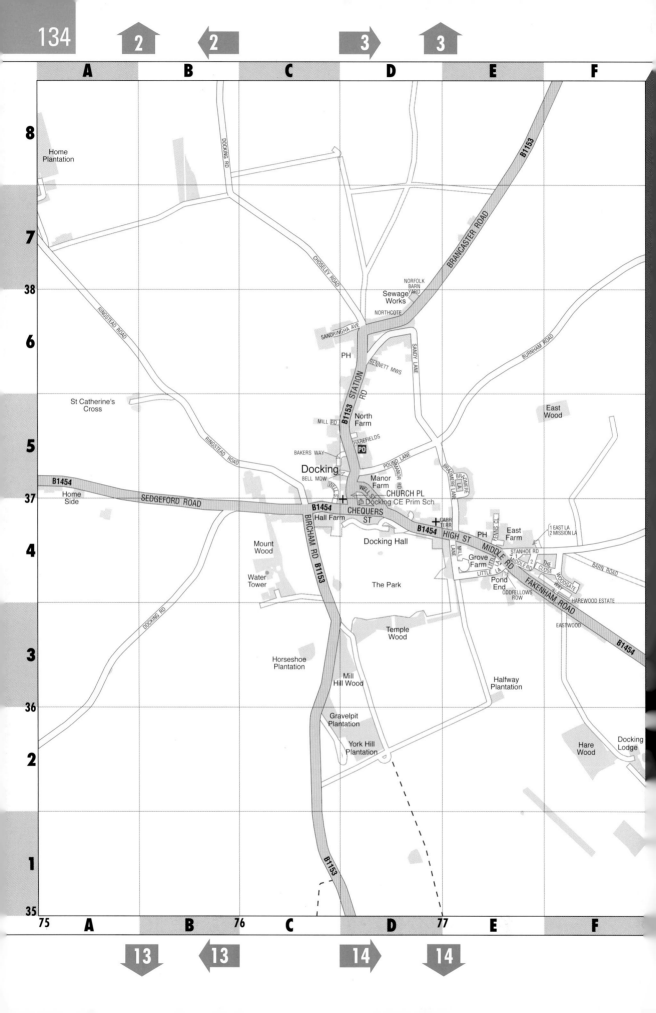

Home Plantation

St Catherine's Cross

RINGSTEAD ROAD

DOCKING RD

B1454

Home Side

SEDGEFORD ROAD

Mount Wood

Water Tower

DOCKING RD

Horseshoe Plantation

Gravelpit Plantation

York Hill Plantation

B1153

Mill Hill Wood

Hall Farm

BIRCHAM RD B1153

Docking Hall

The Park

Temple Wood

CHOSELEY ROAD

Sewage Works

NORFOLK BARN YARD

NORTHCOTE

SANDRINGHA AVE

PH

B1153 STATION RD

BENNETT MWS

MILL RD

North Farm

HAREFIELDS

PO

BAKERS WAY

Docking

BELL MDW

WELLS CL

CHEQUERS ST

Manor Farm

CHURCH PL

Docking CE Prim Sch

B1454

B1454

CARR TERR

HIGH ST

Grove Farm

LITTLE LA

Pond End

ODDFELLOWS ROW

SANDY LANE

POUND LANE

MANOR RD

BRANMERE LANE

BRANMERE

BURNHAM ROAD

East Wood

BRANCASTER ROAD

B1153

PH

East Farm

FENNS CL

MIDDLE RD

STANHOE RD

MIDDLE RD

THE CLOSE

WOODGATE WAY

1 EAST LA
2 MISSION LA

BARN ROAD

FAKENHAM ROAD

HAREWOOD ESTATE

EASTWOOD

B1454

Halfway Plantation

Hare Wood

Docking Lodge

2 2 3 3

13 13 14 14

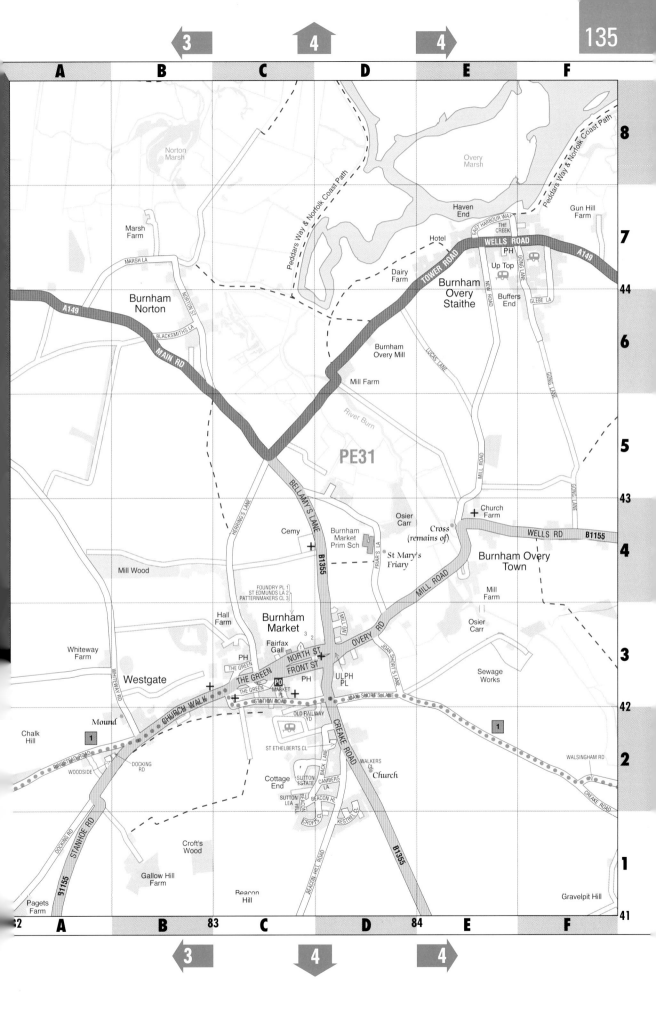

WELLS-NEXT-THE-SEA

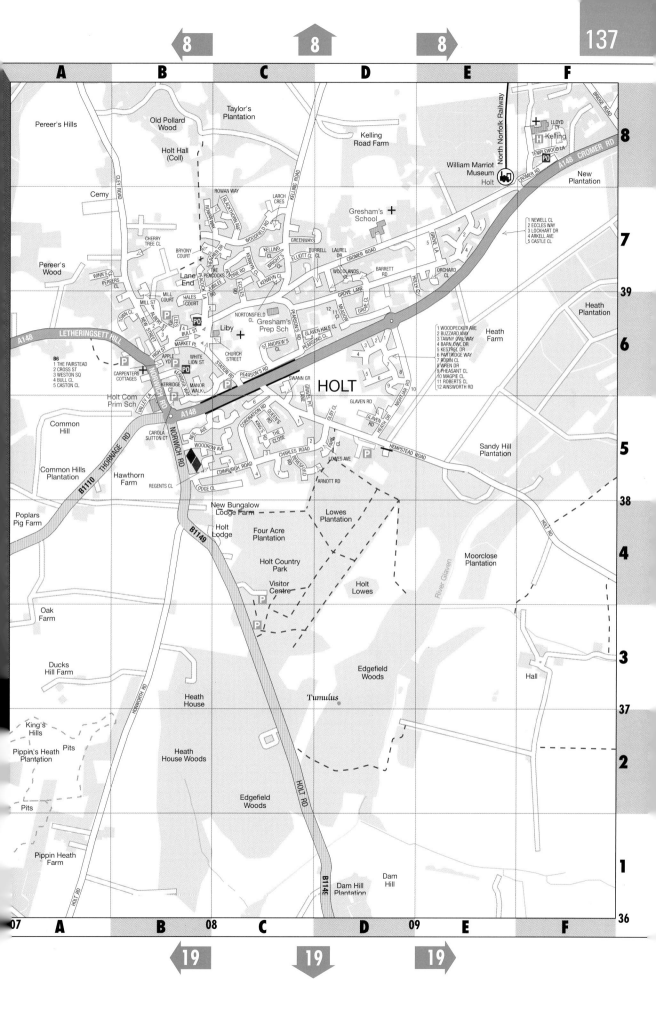

HOLT

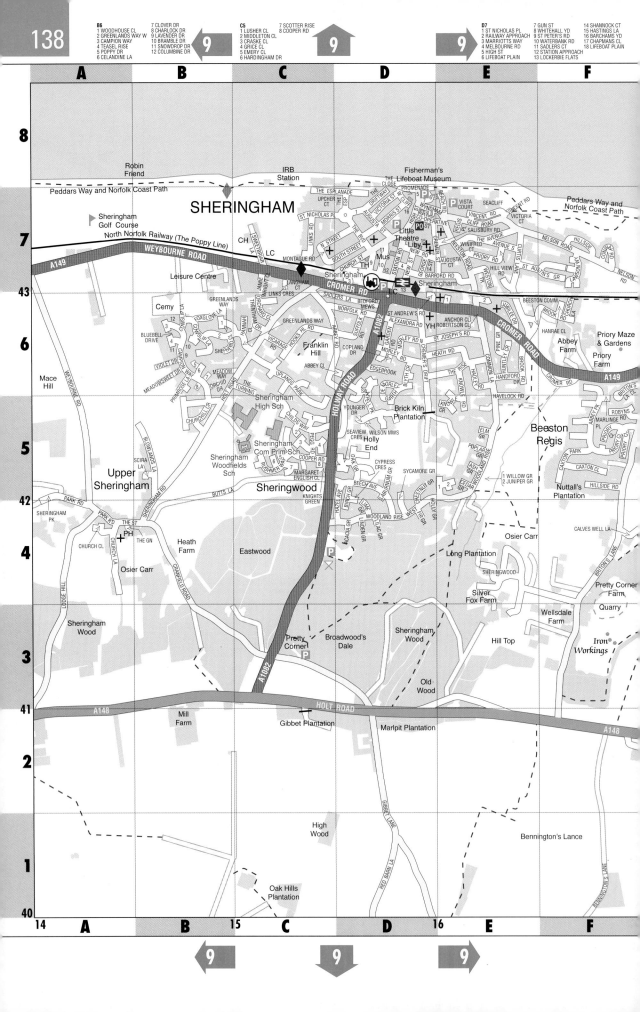

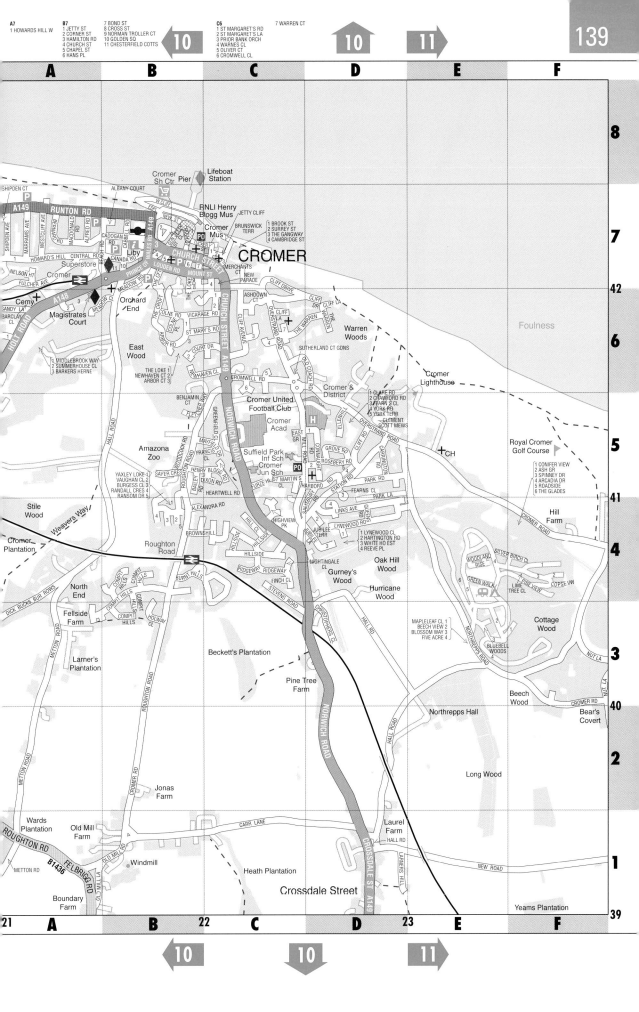

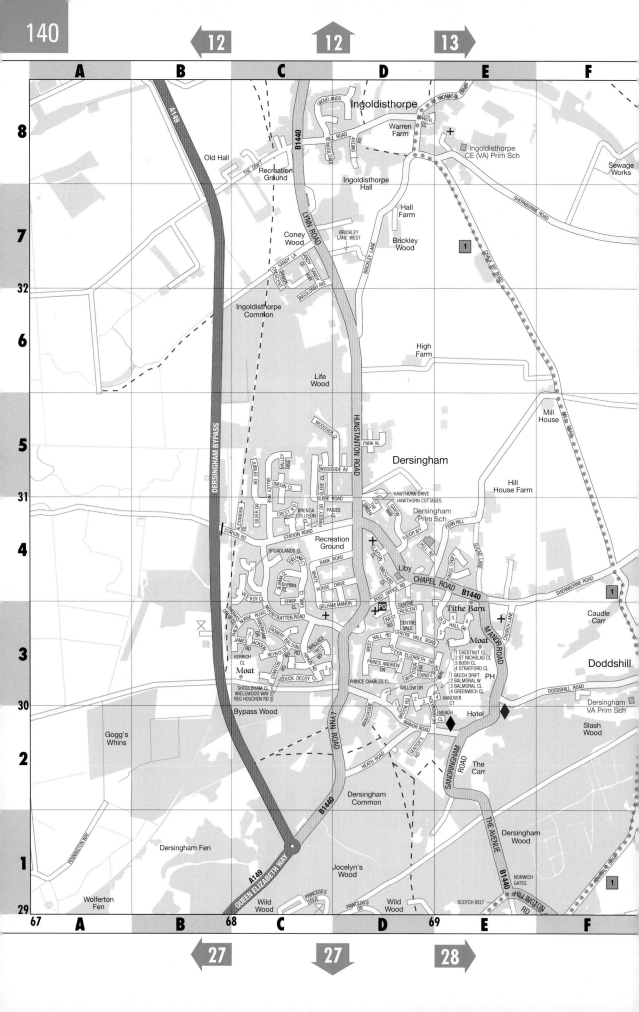

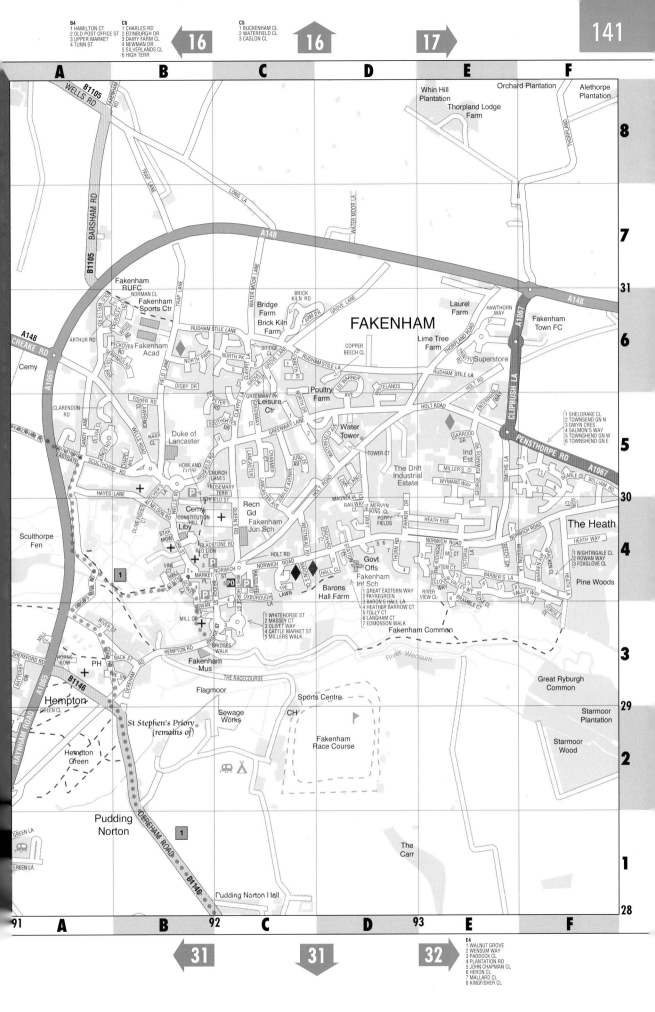

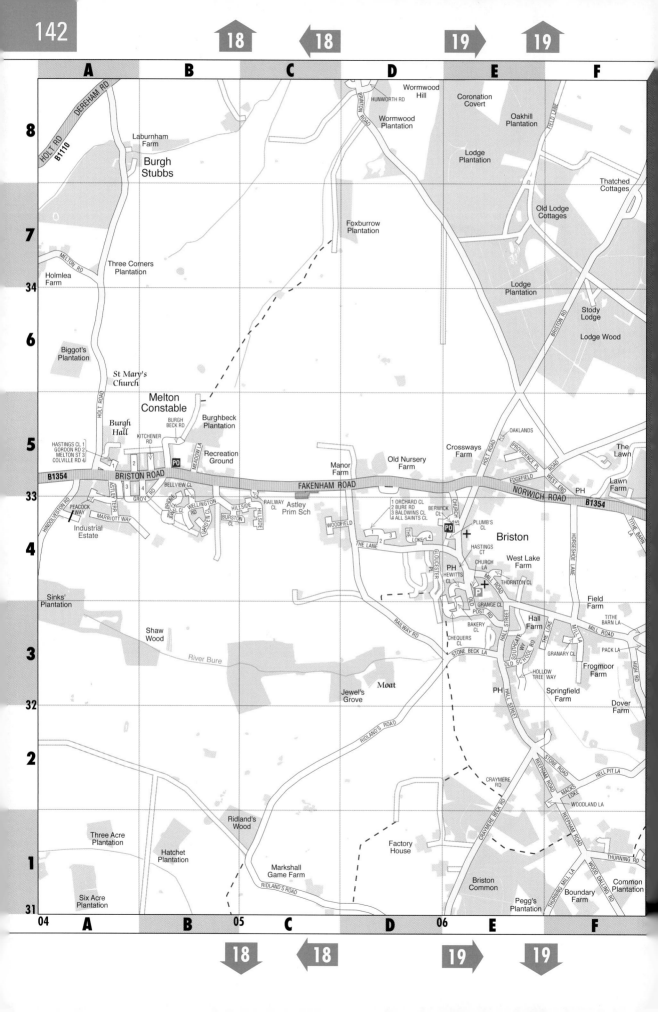

A B C D E F

8

Wormwood Hill
HUNWORTH RD
Wormwood Plantation
Coronation Covert
Oakhill Plantation
FIELD LANE
HOLT RD
B1110
DEREHAM RD
Laburnham Farm
Burgh Stubbs
Lodge Plantation
Thatched Cottages

7

Foxburrow Plantation
Old Lodge Cottages
MELTON RD
Three Corners Plantation
Holmlea Farm

34

Lodge Plantation
BRISTON RD
Stody Lodge

6

Biggot's Plantation
St Mary's Church
Lodge Wood

5

Melton Constable
Burgh Hall
Burghbeck Plantation
BURGH BECK RD
KITCHENER RD
PO
Recreation Ground
MEADOW LA
Manor Farm
Old Nursery Farm
Crossways Farm
OAKLANDS
HOLT RD
PROVIDENCE PL
BRISTON RD
The Lawn
HASTINGS CL 1
GORDON RD 2
MELTON ST 3
COLVILLE RD 4

B1354
BRISTON ROAD
FAKENHAM ROAD
EDGEFIELD RD
WEST END
NORWICH ROAD
B1354
PH
Lawn Farm

33

HINDOLVESTON RD
PEACOCK WAY
ASTLEY TERR
MARRIOTT WAY
GROV
BRIDGE
JEWEL CL
BELLVIEW CL
GARDEN CL
WELLINGTON RD
BURSTON CL
HILLSIDE
HILLSIDE
RAILWAY
Astley Prim Sch
Woodfield
THE LANE
1 ORCHARD CL
2 BURE RD
3 BALDWINS CL
4 ALL SAINTS CL
BERWICK CL
CHURCH ST
PO
PLUMB'S CL
Briston
HASTINGS CT
CHURCH LA
West Lake Farm
HORSESHOE LANE
THE BARN LA
Industrial Estate

4

Sinks' Plantation
THE LOKE
GLOUCESTER PL
PH
HEWITTS CL
P
THORNTON CL
Field Farm
TITHE BARN LA
MILL ROAD
OLD POST RD
GRANGE CL
BAKERY CL
CHEQUERS CL
HALL STREET
Hall Farm
THE LOKE
MILL LA
GRANARY CL
PACK LA
Frogmoor Farm
MILL ROAD
HIGH RD

3

Shaw Wood
River Bure
RAILWAY RD
STONE BECK LA
OLD SOUTHGATE WY
OLD SCHOOL RD
HOLLOW TREE WAY
Springfield Farm
Dover Farm

32

Jewel's Grove
Moat
PH
HALL STREET
STONE ROAD
REEPHAM ROAD
MACKS LOKE
HELL PIT LA
WOODLAND LA

2

RIDLAND'S ROAD
CRAYMERE RD
CRAYMERE BECK RD

Ridland's Wood
Three Acre Plantation
Hatchet Plantation
Markshall Game Farm
Factory House
Briston Common
Pegg's Plantation
THURNING MILL LA
WOOD DALLING RD
REEPHAM ROAD
THURNING RD
Boundary Farm
Common Plantation

1

Six Acre Plantation
RIDLAND'S ROAD

31

04 A B 05 C D 06 E F

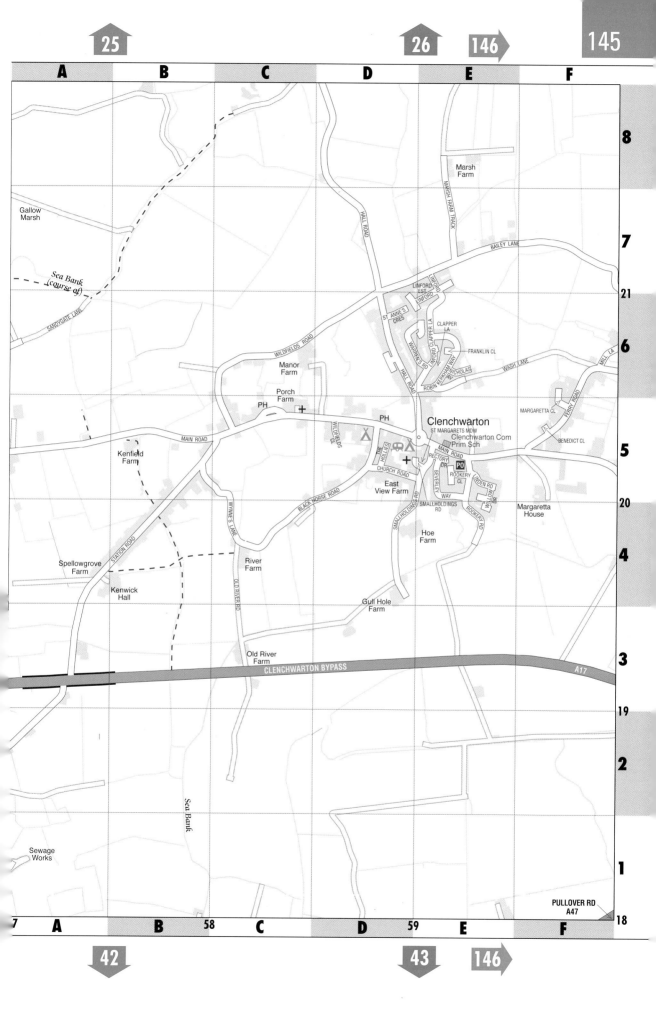

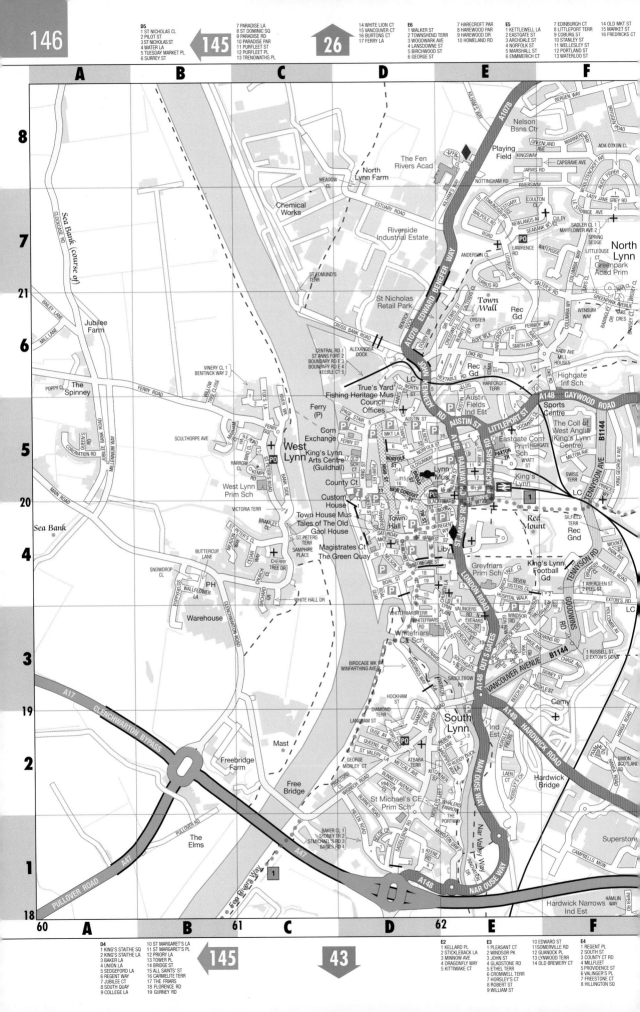

A8
1 WHISSON CL
2 SOMERSBY CL
3 WESTHORPE CL
4 EVELYN WAY
5 WATERDEN CL
6 SEGRAVE RD
7 BRAEBURN CL

B6
1 SOUTHFIELDS
2 DENMARK RD
3 BUTTERWICK
4 LEONARD CL
5 LAVENDER CT

C5
1 BRUMMEL CL
2 FREISTON
3 BUTTERWICK
4 COPPERFIELD
5 GENERALS WLK
6 THREE OAKS
7 WINDMILL CT

D5
1 RODINGHEAD
2 SHEPLEY CRES
3 WALSHAM CL
4 ORMESBY
5 RANWORTH
6 CENTRE POINT

C4
1 PANDORA
2 MIDDLEWOOD
3 HIGHAM GN
4 FIVE ELMS
5 WOODSIDE
6 KINGS GN
7 BROCKLEY GN

148 44 43 44 44

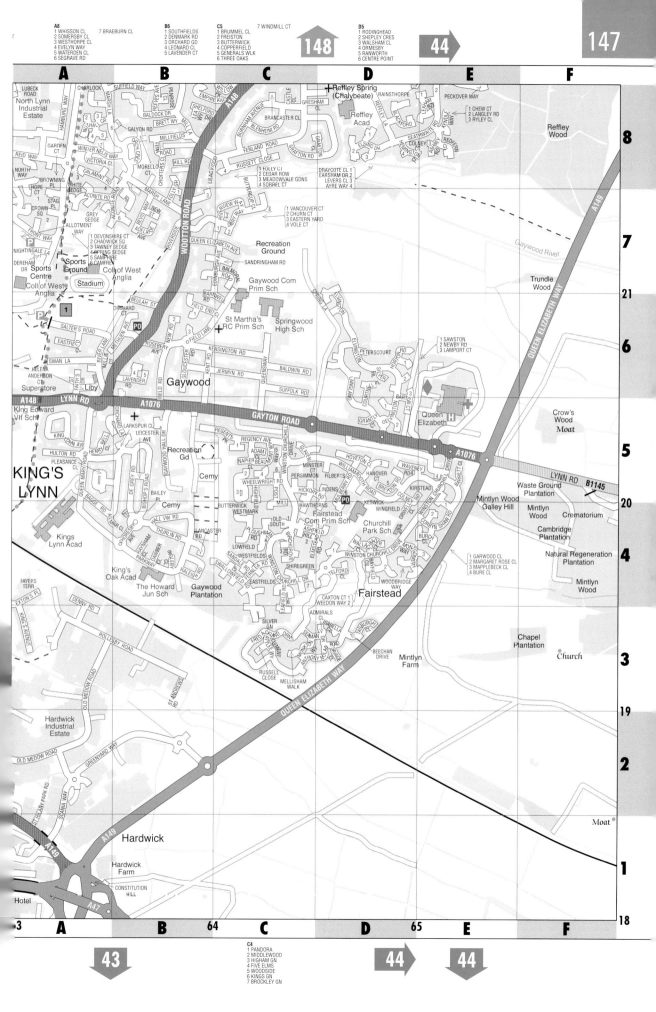

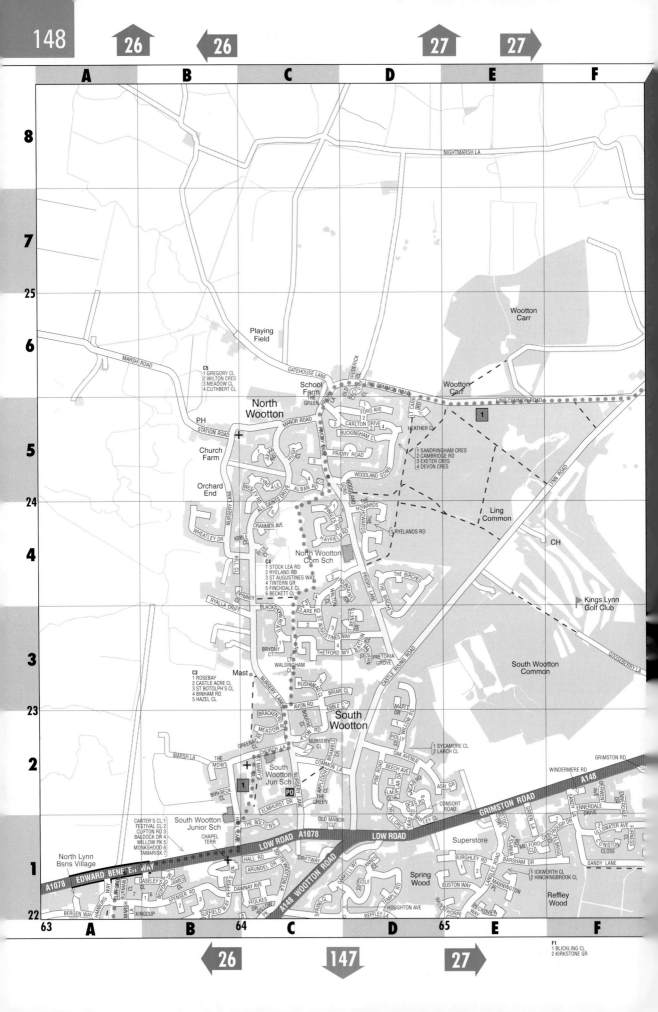

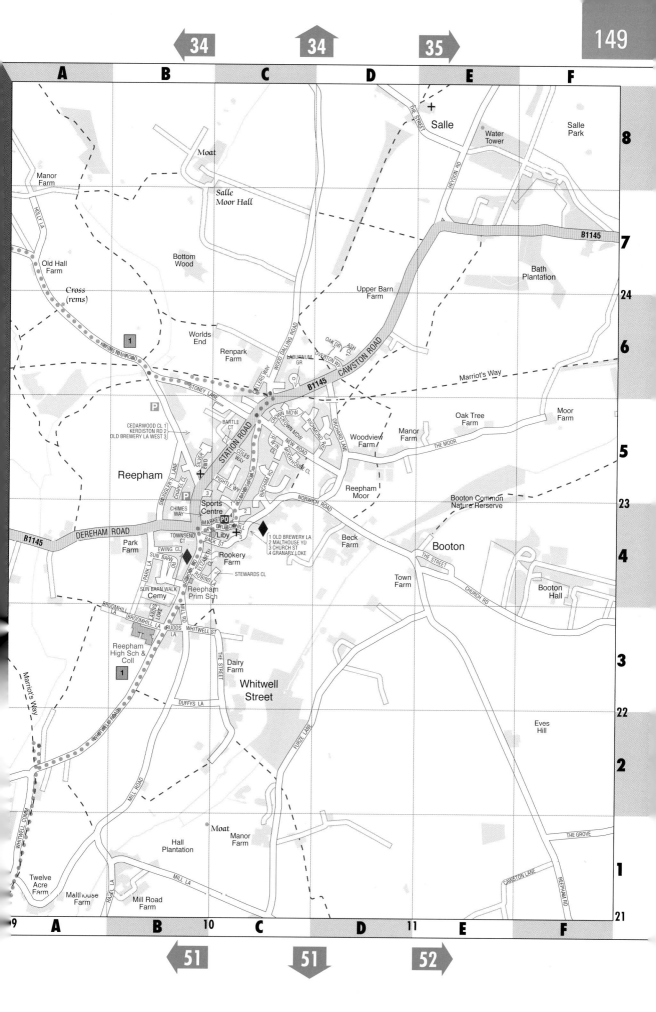

A   B   C   D   E   F

8

Salle

Salle
Park

Water
Tower

Manor
Farm

HOLLY LA

Moat

Salle
Moor Hall

THE STREET

HEYDON RD

B1145   7

24

Old Hall
Farm

Bottom
Wood

Bath
Plantation

Cross
(rems)

Upper Barn
Farm

WOOD DALLING ROAD

1

KERDISTON ROAD

STONEY LANE

Worlds
End

Renpark
Farm

LABURNUM
GR

OAK DRY
ASH CL

OVERTON WY

CAWSTON ROAD

Marriot's Way

6

MILLER'S WAY

B1145

Moor
Farm

24

P

CEDARWOOD CL 1
KERDISTON RD 2
OLD BREWERY LA WEST 3

BARTLE
CT

CROWN MDW

CROWN MDW

RICHMOND RIS

ORCHARD LANE

Woodview
Farm

Oak Tree
Farm

Manor
Farm

THE MOOR

5

STATION ROAD

SILVER END

COLES
WAY

NEW ROAD

IRWIN
CL

WOODHOUSE CL

BIRCHAM RD

Reepham

SMUGGLER'S LANE

CHAPEL CL

PIGHTLE WY

ALBANS CL

Reepham
Moor

NORWICH ROAD

Booton Common
Nature Reserve

23

CHIMES
WAY

Sports
Centre

P

MARKET PL
CHURCH HILL

PO

2
3

4

1 OLD BREWERY LA
2 MALTHOUSE YD
3 CHURCH ST
4 GRANARY LOKE

Beck
Farm

Booton

B1145

DEREHAM ROAD

TOWNSEND
CT

BACK ST

Liby

Booton
Hall

23

Park
Farm

SUN BARN RD

EWING CL

ELIZABETH DR

ROBINS LA

Rookery
Farm

STEWARDS CL

THE STREET

Town
Farm

CHURCH RD

4

PARK LA

SUN BARN WALK

Cemy

Reepham
Prim Sch

MILL RD

BROOMHILL LA

EWING LANE

RUDDS
LA

WHITWELL ST

Dairy
Farm

Eves
Hill

3

Reepham
High Sch &
Coll

1

WHITWELL ROAD

THE STREET

Whitwell
Street

22

Marriot's Way

DUFFYS LA

22

WHITWELL COMM

2

MILL ROAD

Moat

Manor
Farm

FURZE LANE

THE GROVE

1

Twelve
Acre
Farm

Malthouse
Farm

HAGEL LA

Mill Road
Farm

MILL LA

Hall
Plantation

CAWSTON LANE

REEPHAM RD

21

9   A   B   10   C   D   11   E   F

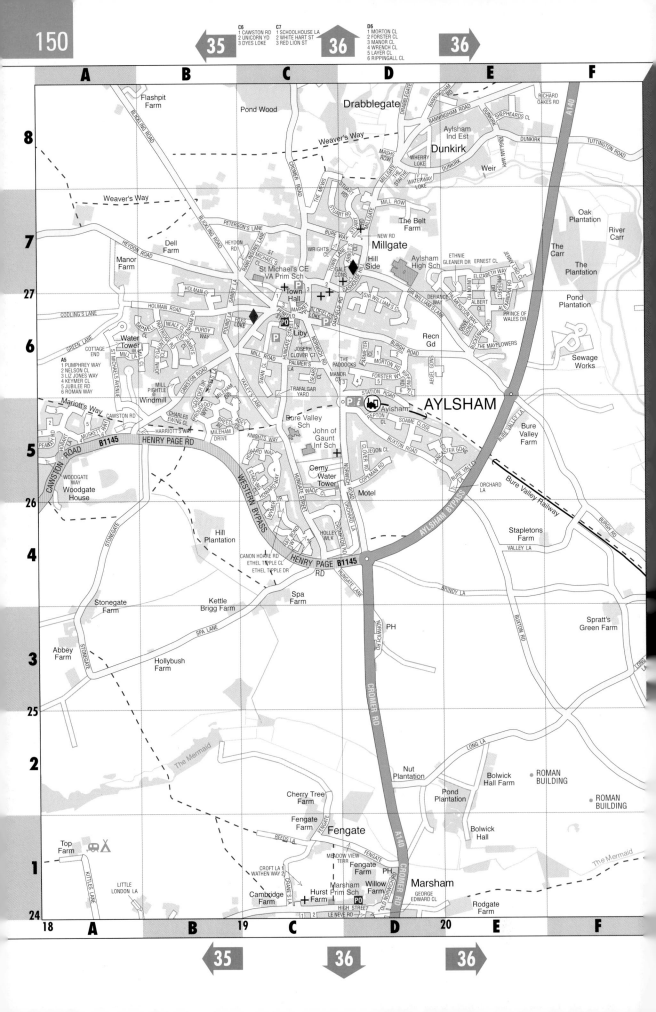

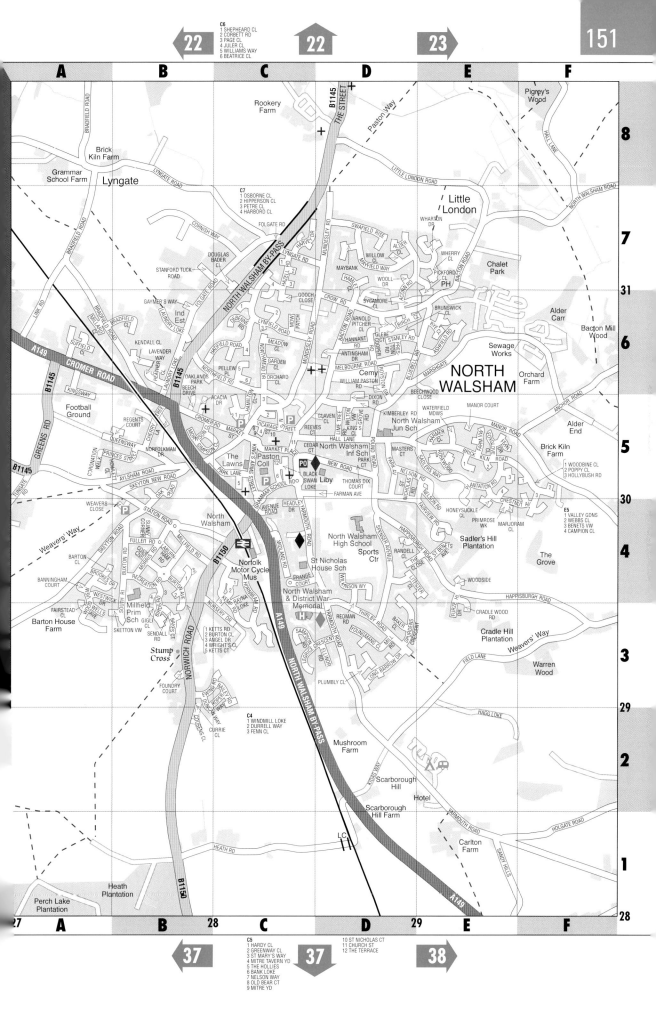

C6
1 SHEPHEARD CL
2 CORBETT RD
3 PAGE CL
4 JULER CL
5 WILLIAMS WAY
6 BEATRICE CL

C7
1 OSBORNE CL
2 HIPPERSON CL
3 PETRE CL
4 HARBORD CL

E5
1 WOODBINE CL
2 POPPY CL
3 HOLLYBUSH RD

E5
1 VALLEY GDNS
2 WEBBS CL
3 BENETS VW
4 CAMPION CL

C4
1 WINDMILL LOKE
2 DURRELL WAY
3 FENN CL

C5
1 HARDY CL
2 GREENWAY CL
3 ST MARY'S WAY
4 MITRE TAVERN YD
5 THE HOLLIES
6 BANK LOKE
7 NELSON WAY
8 OLD BEAR CT
9 MITRE YD
10 ST NICHOLAS CT
11 CHURCH ST
12 THE TERRACE

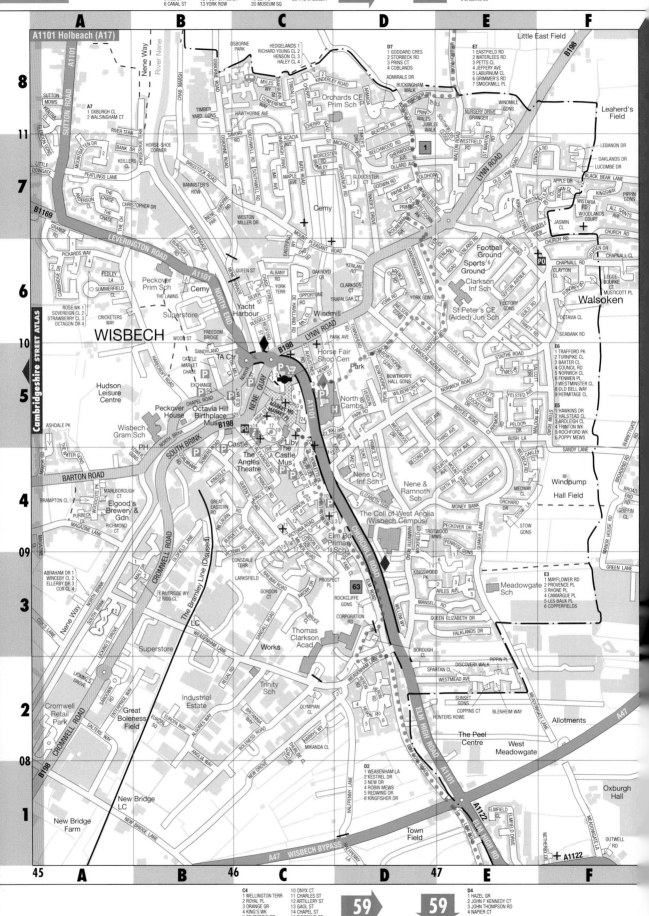

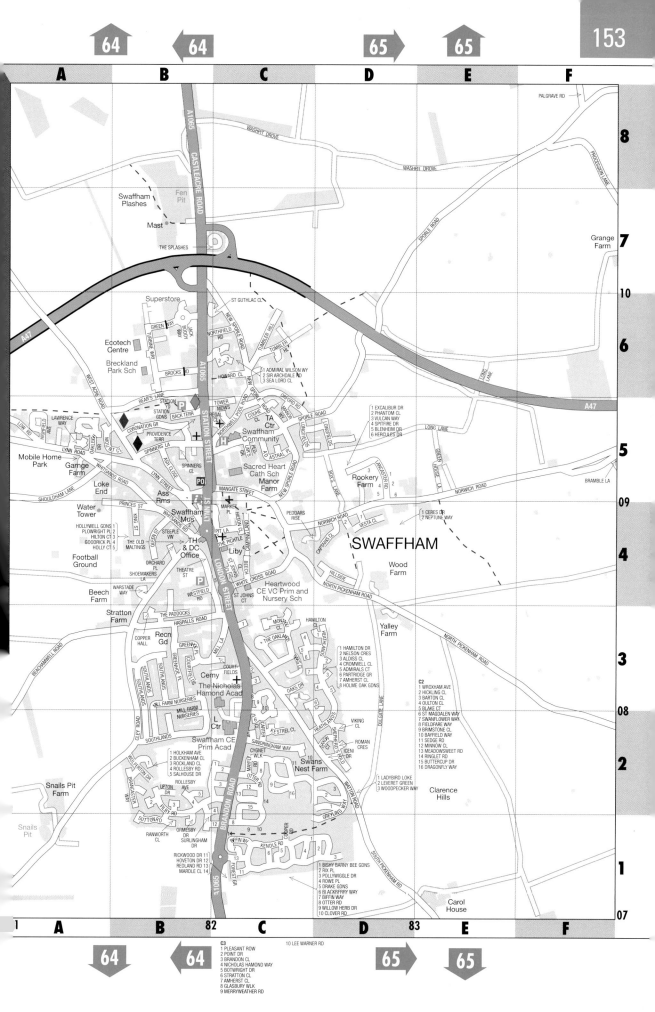

SWAFFHAM

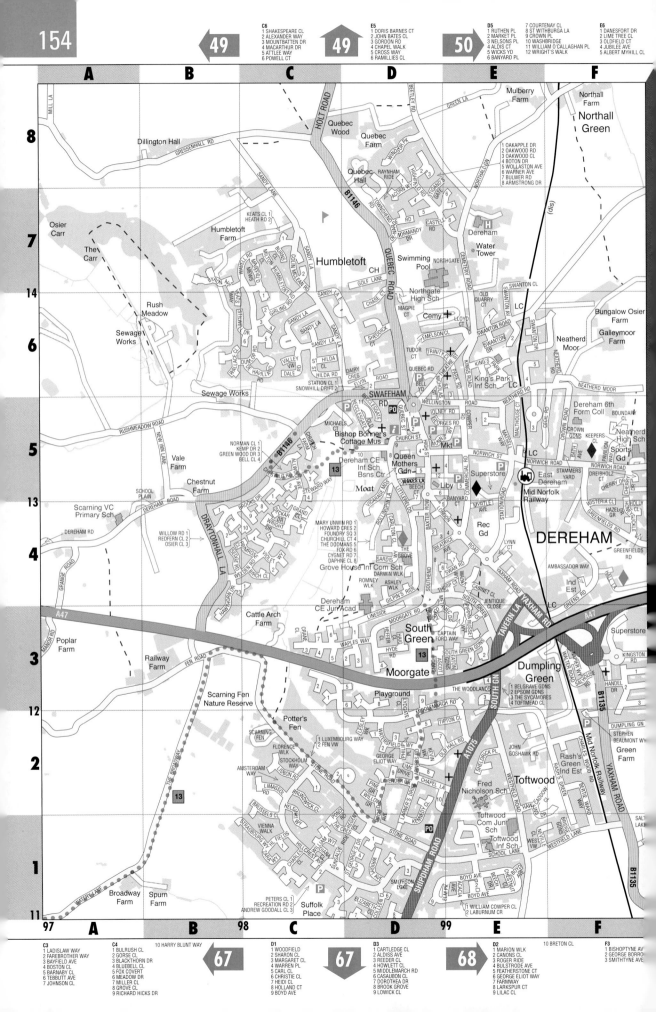

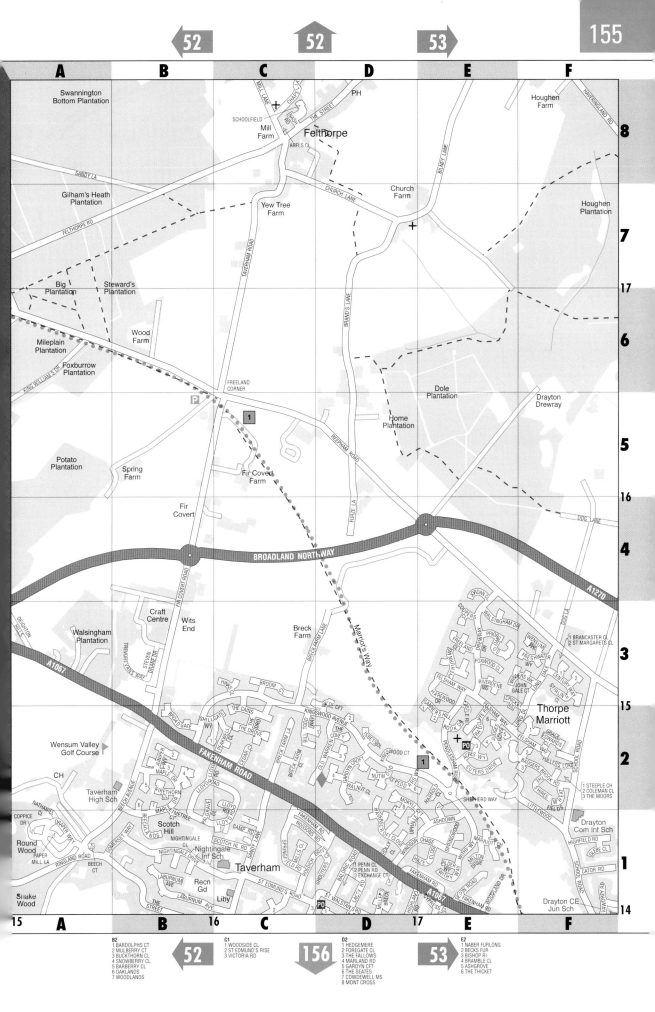

B2
1 BARDOLPHS CT
2 MULBERRY CT
3 BUCKTHORN CL
4 SNOWBERRY CL
5 BARBERRY CL
6 OAKLANDS
7 WOODLANDS

C1
1 WOODSIDE CL
2 ST EDMUND'S RISE
3 VICTORIA RD

D2
1 HEDGEMERE
2 FOREGATE CL
3 THE FALLOWS
4 MARLAND RD
5 GARDYN CFT
6 THE SEATES
7 COWDEWELL MS
8 MONT CROSS

E2
1 NABER FURLONG
2 BECKS FUR
3 BISHOP RI
4 BRAMBLE CL
5 ASHGROVE
6 THE THICKET

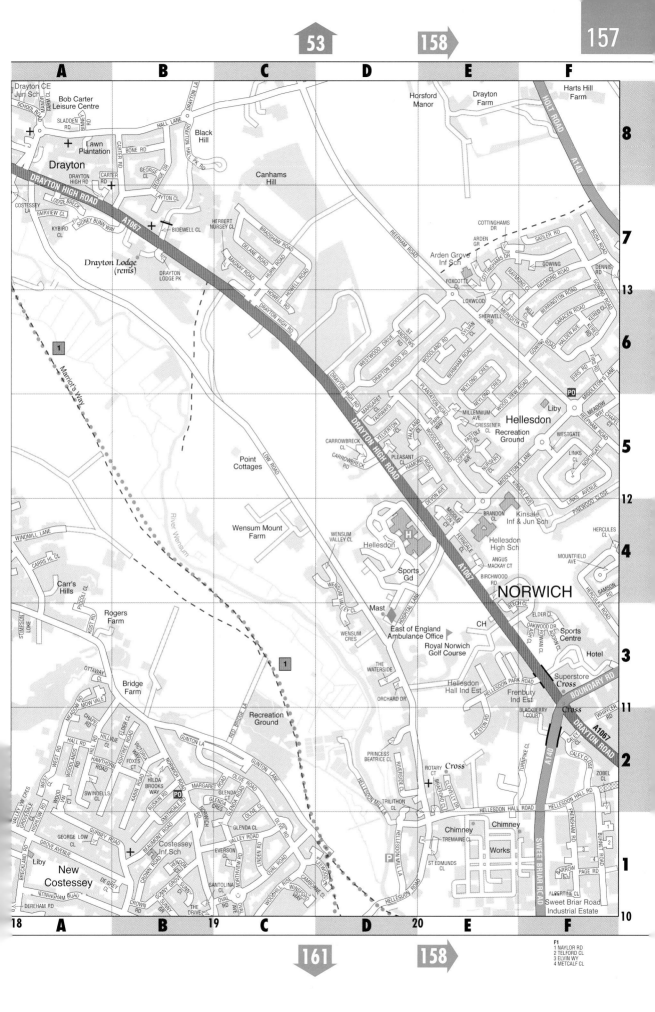

158

157 53

D5
1 PENNYROYAL
2 BRYONY CL
3 WOODRUFF CL
4 SOUTHERWOOD
5 ROSEBAY CL
6 WHITETHORN CL

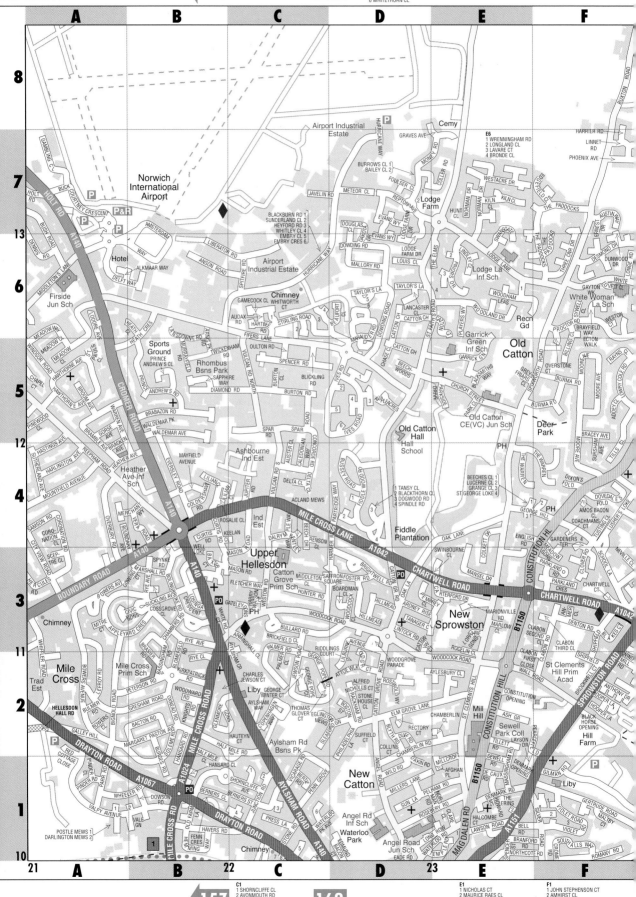

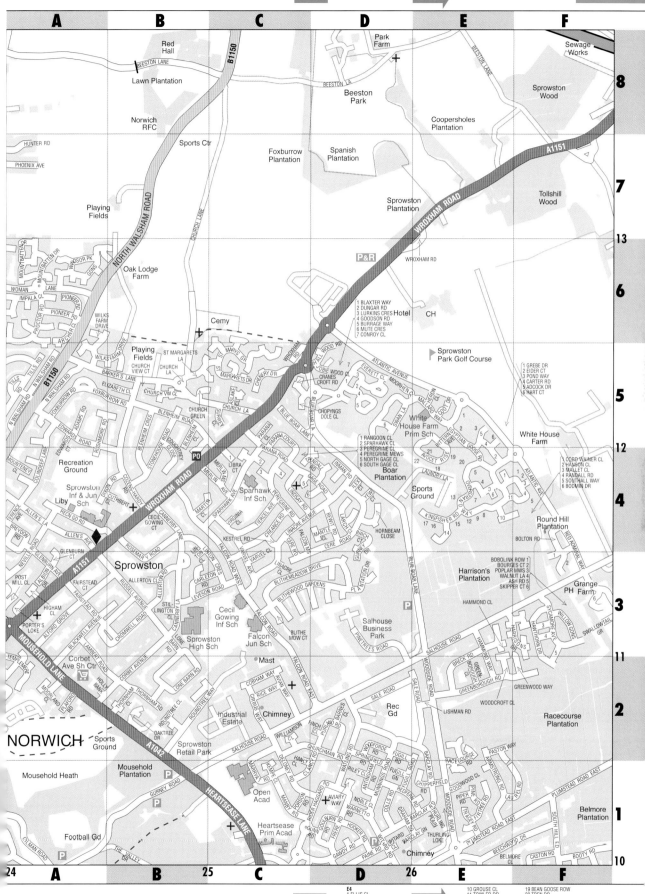

E4
1 ELLIS CL
2 SCOTT CL
3 FLYCATCHER WAY
4 PETER CL
5 OYSTERCATCHER CL
6 CORMORANT DR
7 SANDPIPER WAY
8 SHEARWATER DR
9 STARLING AVE

10 GROUSE CL
11 TOWLER DR
12 PARTRIDGE CL
13 WAXWING WAY
14 NUTHATCH RD
15 NIGHTJAR WAY
16 WARBLER CL
17 PHEASANT LOKE
18 GREYLAG CL

19 BEAN GOOSE ROW
20 TREN DR
21 CANADA GOOSE CT
22 SHELDUCK WAY

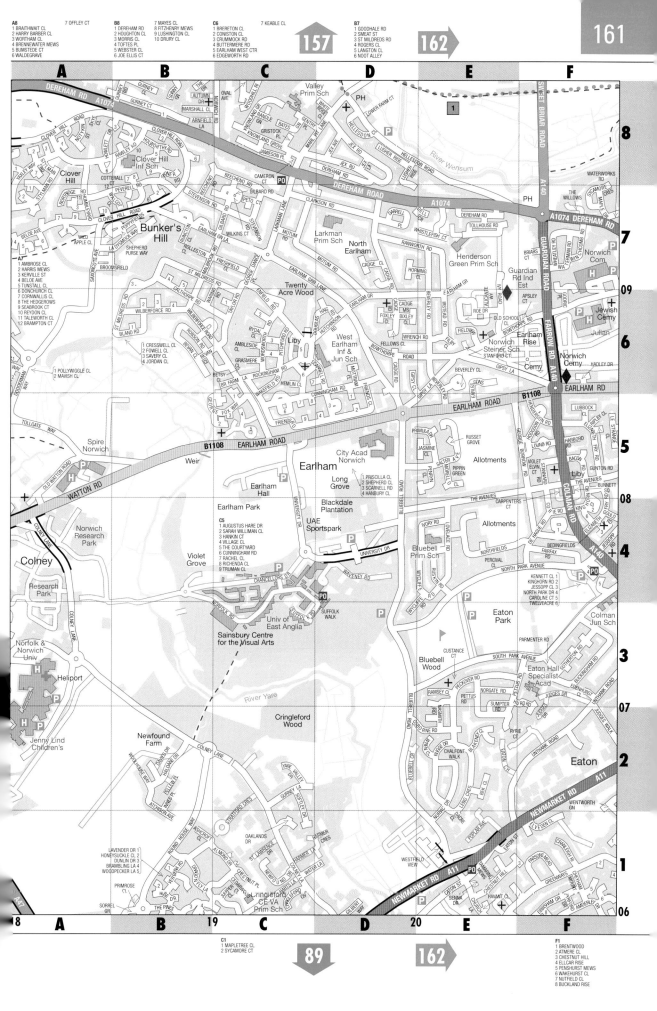

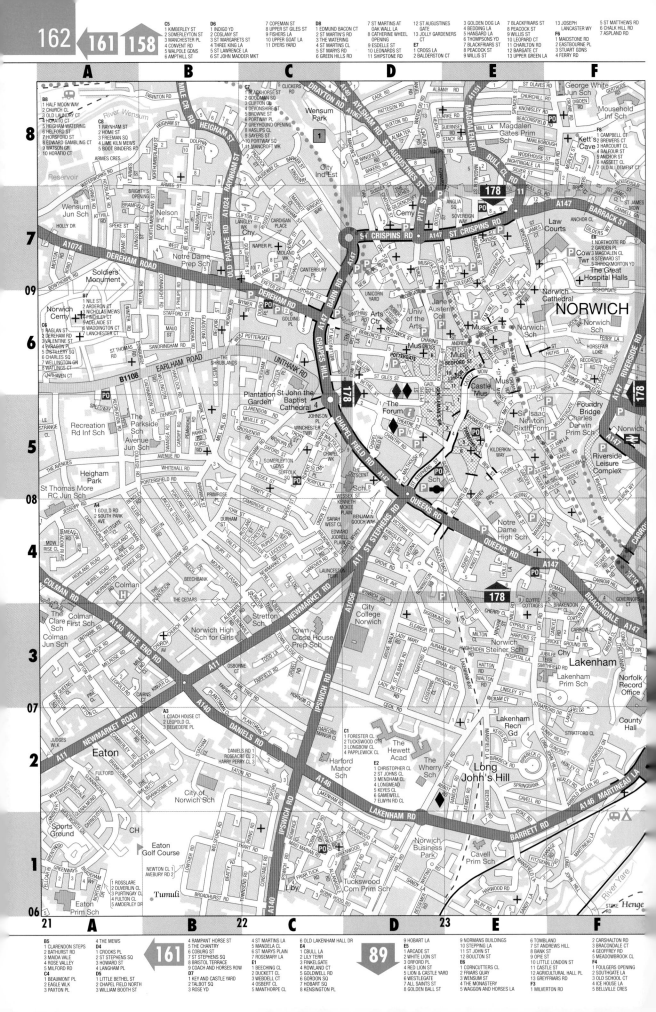

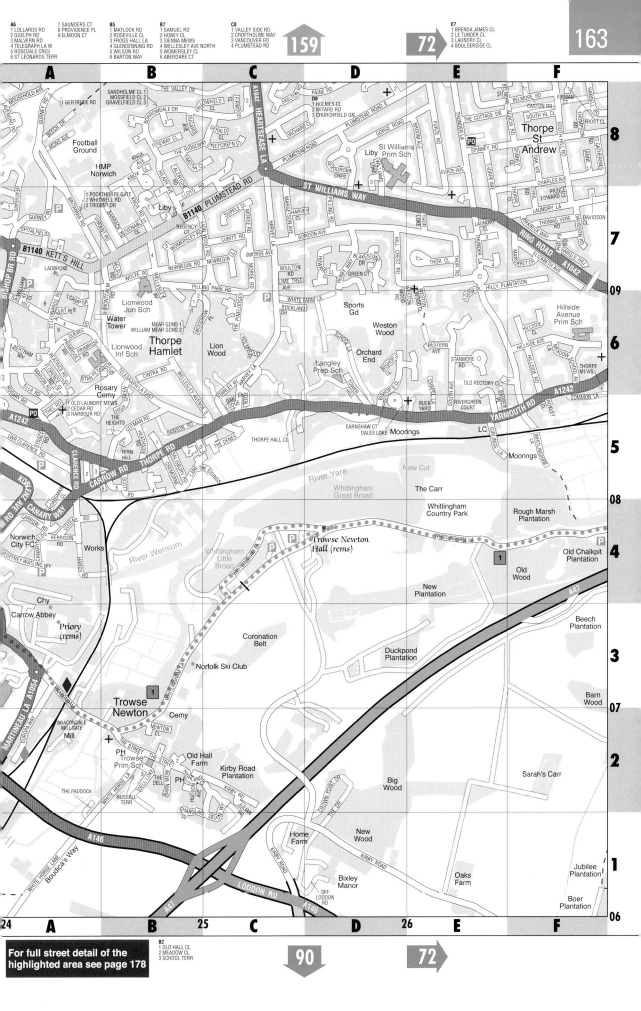

159
72
90
72
For full street detail of the highlighted area see page 178

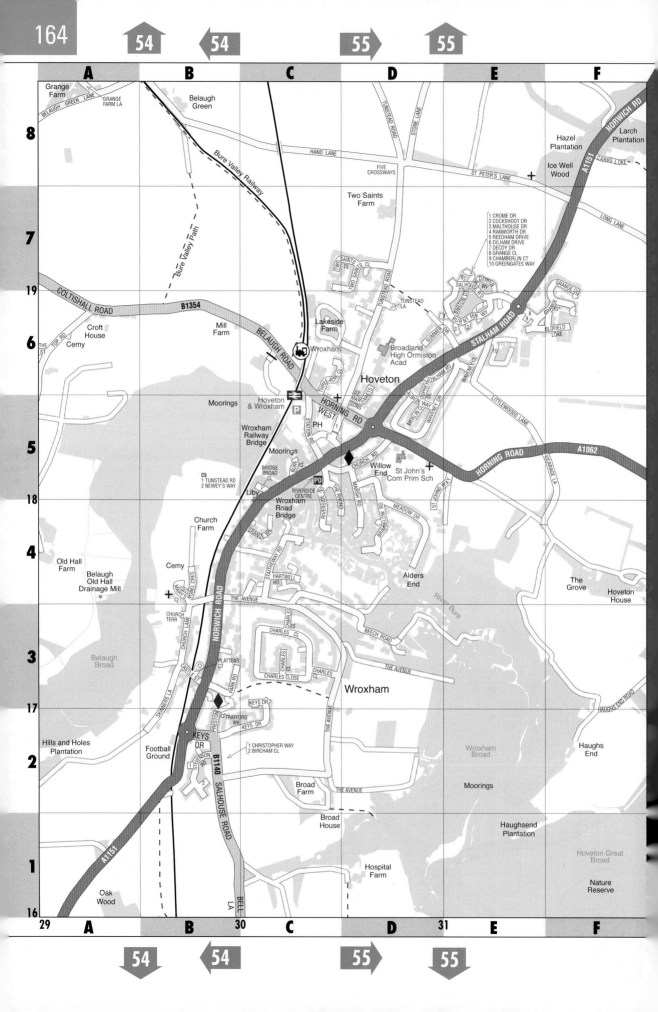

A B C D E F

8

Grange Farm

GRANGE FARM LA

BELAUGH GREEN LANE

Belaugh Green

Bure Valley Railway

HAND LANE

TUNSTEAD ROAD

STONE LANE

FIVE CROSSWAYS

St PETER'S LANE

NORWICH RD

Hazel Plantation

Larch Plantation

Ice Well Wood

CARRS LOKE

A1151

LONG LANE

7

Bure Valley Path

Two Saints Farm

TWO SAINTS CL

TWO SAINTS CL

TUNSTEAD ROAD

TUNSTEAD LA

SUMMER DR

1 CROME DR
2 COCKSHOOT DR
3 MALTHOUSE DR
4 RANWORTH DR
5 REEDHAM DRIVE
6 DILHAM DRIVE
7 DECOY DR
8 GRANGE CL
9 CHAMBERLIN CT
10 GREENGATES WAY

TERESA CL

SALHOUSE WY

BARTON DR

BURNT FEN WY

GRANGE CH

GRANGE CL

BLOFIELD LOKE

19

COLTISHALL ROAD

THE TOP RD

THE ST

Croft House

Cemy

B1354

Mill Farm

BELAUGH ROAD

THREE ACRE CL

Lakeside Farm

Wroxham

Broadland High Ormiston Acad

Hoveton

STALHAM RD

ST MARGRETS

ALBION WAY

MERLIN CL

OSPREY CL

WAVENEY DR

STALHAM ROAD

WAVENEY CL

LITTLEWOODS LANE

6

Moorings

Hoveton & Wroxham

P

Station Rd

HORNING RD WEST

PH

St MARGRETS GDNS

Willow End

St John's Com Prim Sch

HORNING ROAD

A1062

VICARAGE LA

5

Wroxham Railway Bridge

Moorings

BRIDGE BROAD CL

BURE CL

PO

RIVERSIDE RD

MARSH RD

CHURCH RD

St JOHNS WAY

18

C5
1 TUNSTEAD RD
2 NEWEY'S WAY

Liby

Riverside Centre

Wroxham Road Bridge

GRANGE VW

THE AVENUE

STALHAM RD

MEADOW DR

BRIMBELOW RD

4

Old Hall Farm

Belaugh Old Hall Drainage Mill

Church Farm

Cemy

STAITHEWAY RD

HARTWELL RD

CHURCH LANE

ASBEL CRES

MARY'S LA

Alders End

River Bure

The Grove

Hoveton House

3

Belaugh Broad

CHURCH TERR

CASTLE ST

SKINNERS LA

PLATTENS CT

PARK RD

NORWICH ROAD

CHARLES CL

CHARLES CL

CHARLES CLOSE

CHARLES CL

Wroxham

BEECH ROAD

THE AVENUE

17

KEYS DR

PRESTON RD

TRAFFORD WK

KEYS DR

THE AVENUE

HAUGHS END ROAD

2

Hills and Holes Plantation

Football Ground

KEYS DR

STEVENSON RD

B1140

SALHOUSE ROAD

1 CHRISTOPHER WAY
2 BIRCHAM CL

Broad Farm

THE AVENUE

Wroxham Broad

Moorings

Haughs End

1

A1151

Broad House

Hospital Farm

Haughsend Plantation

Hoveton Great Broad

Nature Reserve

16

Oak Wood

BELL LA

29 A B 30 C D 31 E F

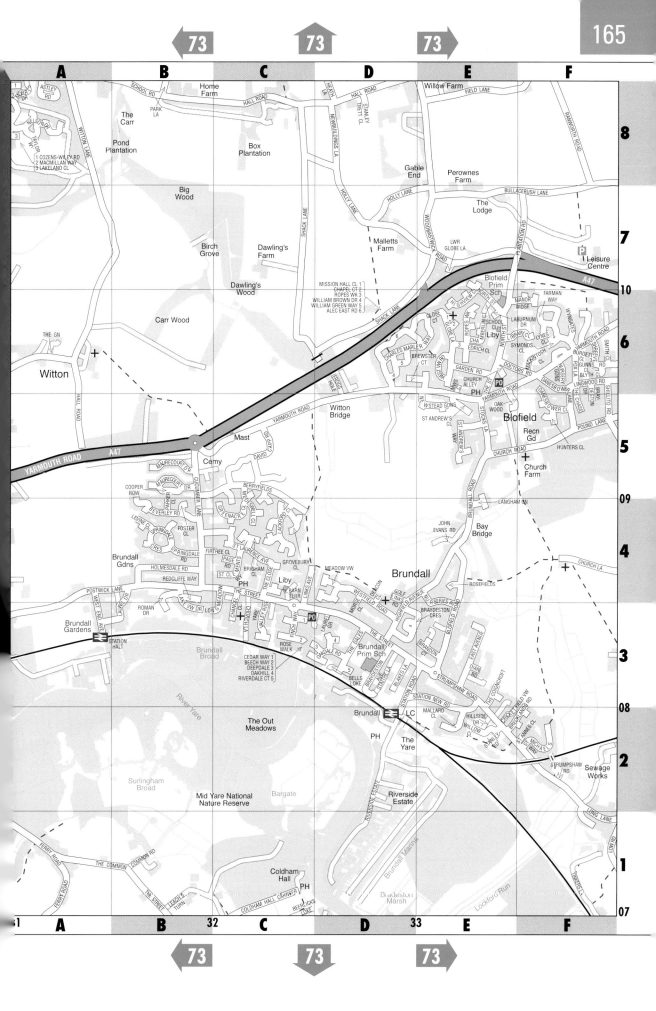

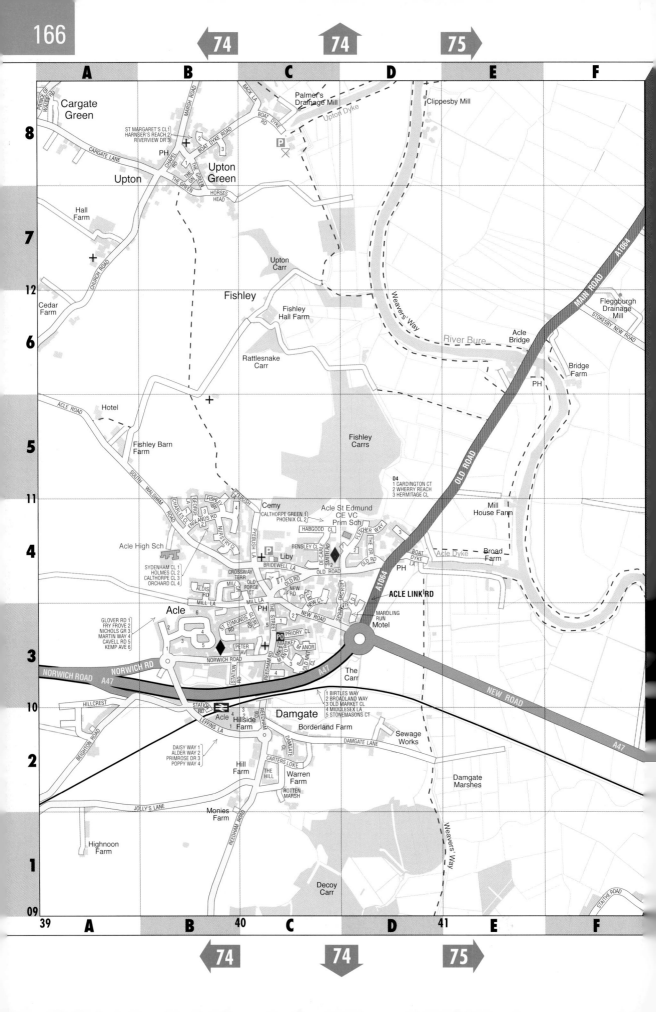

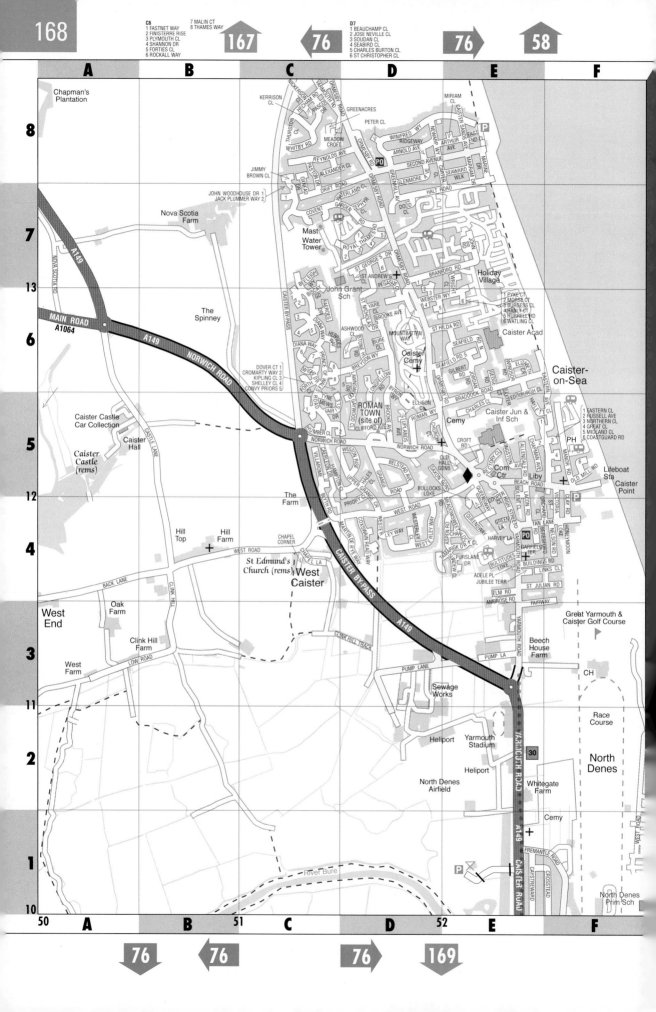

C6
1 FASTNET WAY
2 FINISTERRE RISE
3 PLYMOUTH CL
4 SHANNON DR
5 FORTIES CL
6 ROCKALL WAY

7 MALIN CT
8 THAMES WAY

D7
1 BEAUCHAMP CL
2 JOSE NEVILLE CL
3 SOUDAN CL
4 SEABIRD CL
5 CHARLES BURTON CL
6 ST CHRISTOPHER CL

167
76
76
58

Chapman's Plantation

Nova Scotia Farm

The Spinney

KERRISON CL
JIMMY BROWN CL
JOHN WOODHOUSE DR 1
JACK PLUMMER WAY 2

GREENACRES
PETER CL
MIRIAM CL

Mast Water Tower
MEADOW CROFT
WHITBY RD
REYNOLDS AVE
DRIFT ROAD

WINIFRED WY
RIDGEWAY
ARNOLD AVE
SECOND AVENUE
HALT ROAD

John Grant Sch
St Andrew's
ST GEORGE'S DR
PEGASUS
Royal Thames
BRANFORD RD
WEBSTER WY

Holiday Village

Caister Acad
1 PYKE CT
2 MORSE CT
3 BURGESS CL
4 HANLY CT
5 HUBBELL RD
6 WATLING CL

Caister Cemy
Mountbatten WY

SEAFIELD
SEAFIELD RD N
SEAFIELD RD S
GILBERT RD

Caister-on-Sea

ROMAN TOWN (site of)
CLIFFORD AVE

Caister Jun & Inf Sch
Cemy
CROFT RD

1 EASTERN CL
2 RUSSELL AVE
3 NORTHERN CL
4 GREAT CL
5 MIDLAND CL
6 COASTGUARD RD

PH
Corn Ctr
Liby
Lifeboat Sta
Caister Point

DOVER CT 1
CROMARTY WAY 2
KIPLING CL 3
SHELLEY CL 4
CONVY PRIORS 5

The Farm
NORWICH ROAD

West Road
CHAPEL CORNER
St Edmund's Church (rems)
West Caister

Hill Top
Hill Farm

BACK LANE
Oak Farm
Clink Hill Farm
LOW ROAD
West Farm
West End

CLINK HILL TRACK

PUMP LA
PUMP LANE

Sewage Works

Beech House Farm

Great Yarmouth & Caister Golf Course

CH

Race Course

Heliport
Yarmouth Stadium
Heliport

30

North Denes

North Denes Airfield
Whitegate Farm

Cemy

River Bure

FREMANTLE ROAD
CAISTER ROAD
CROSSTEAD

North Denes Prim Sch

A1064 MAIN ROAD
A149 NORWICH ROAD
A149 CAISTER BY-PASS
A149 YARMOUTH ROAD

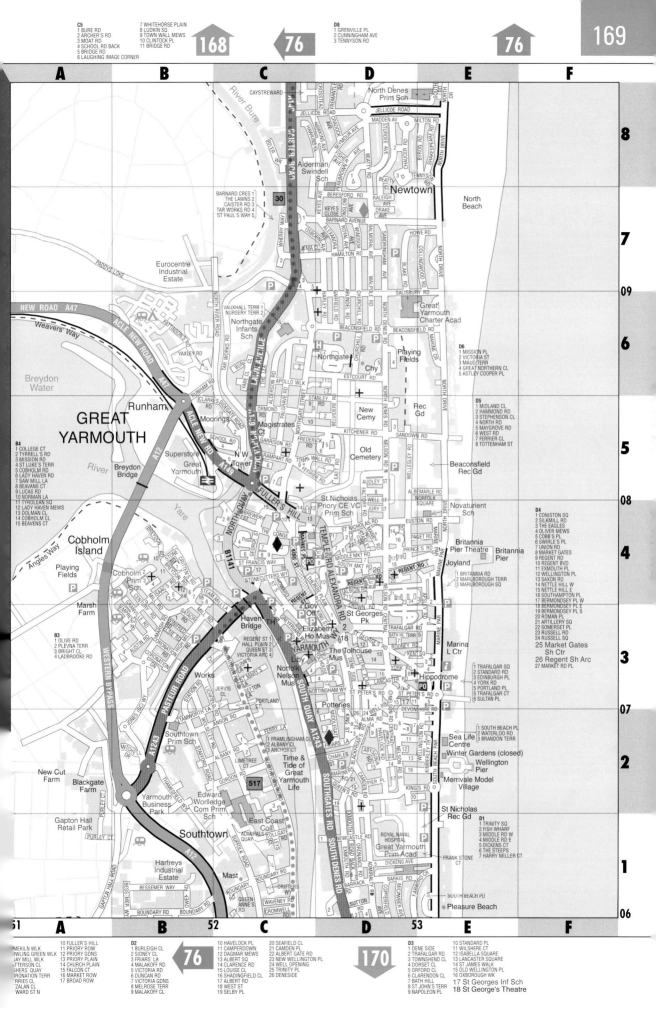

168
76
76

C5
1 BURE RD
2 ARCHER'S RD
3 MOAT RD
4 SCHOOL RD BACK
5 BRIDGE RD
6 LAUGHING IMAGE CORNER
7 WHITEHORSE PLAIN
8 LUDKIN SQ
9 TOWN WALL MEWS
10 CLINTOCK PL
11 BRIDGE RD

D8
1 GRENVILLE PL
2 CUNNINGHAM AVE
3 TENNYSON RD

North Denes Prim Sch

Newtown

North Beach

B4
1 COLLEGE CT
2 TYRRELL'S RD
3 MISSION RD
4 ST LUKE'S TERR
5 COBHOLM RD
6 LADY HAVEN RD
7 SAW MILL LA
8 BEAVANS CT
9 LUCAS RD
10 NORMAN LA
11 TYROLEAN SQ
12 LADY HAVEN MEWS
13 DOLMAN CL
14 COBHOLM CL
15 BEAVANS CT

B3
1 OLIVE RD
2 PLEVNA TERR
3 BRIGHT CL
4 LADBROOKE RD

GREAT YARMOUTH

Runham

Breydon Water

Cobholm Island

D6
1 MISSION PL
2 VICTORIA RD
3 MAUD TERR
4 GREAT NORTHERN CL
5 ASTLEY COOPER PL

D5
1 MIDLAND CL
2 HAMMOND RD
3 STEPHENSON CL
4 NORTH RD
5 MAYGROVE RD
6 WEST RD
7 FERRIER CL
8 TOTTENHAM ST

D4
1 CONISTON SQ
2 SILKMILL RD
3 THE EAGLES
4 OLIVER MEWS
5 COBB'S PL
6 SWIRLE'S PL
7 UNION RD
8 MARKET GATES
9 REGENT RD
10 REGENT BVD
11 EXMOUTH PL
12 WELLINGTON PL
13 SAXON RD
14 NETTLE HILL W
15 NETTLE HILL E
16 SOUTHAMPTON PL
17 BERMONDSEY PL W
18 BERMONDSEY PL E
19 BERMONDSEY PL S
20 ROMAN PL
21 ARTILLERY SQ
22 SOMERSET PL
23 RUSSELL RD
24 RUSSELL SQ
25 Market Gates Sh Ctr
26 Regent Sh Arc
27 MARKET RD PL

D2
1 TRAFALGAR CL
2 STANDARD RD
3 EDINBURGH PL
4 YORK RD
5 PORTLAND PL
6 SULTAN PL

1 SOUTH BEACH PL
2 WATERLOO RD
3 BRANDON TERR

D1
1 TRINITY SQ
2 FISH WHARF
3 MIDDLE RD E
4 MIDDLE RD
5 DICKENS CT
6 THE STEEPS
7 HARRY MILLER CT

Southtown

76
170

D2
1 BURLEIGH CL
2 SIDNEY CL
3 FRIARS' LA
4 MALAKOFF RD
5 VICTORIA RD
6 DUNCAN RD
7 VICTORIA GDNS
8 MELROSE TERR
9 MALAKOFF CL
10 HAVELOCK PL
11 CAMPERDOWN
12 DAGMAR MEWS
13 ALBERT SQ
14 CLARENCE RD
15 SHADINGFIELD CL
16 DENESIDE
17 ALBERT RD
18 WEST ST
19 SELBY PL
20 SEAFIELD CL
21 CAMDEN CL
22 ALBERT GATE RD
23 NEW WELLINGTON CL
24 WELL OPENING
25 TRINITY PL
26 DENESIDE

D3
1 DENE SIDE
2 TRAFALGAR RD
3 TOWNSHEND CL
4 DORSET CL
5 ORFORD CL
6 CLARENDON CL
7 BATH HILL
8 ST JOHN'S TERR
9 NAPOLEON PL
10 STANDARD PL
11 WILSHERE CT
12 ISABELLA SQUARE
13 LANCASTER SQUARE
14 ST JAMES WALK
15 OLD WELLINGTON CL
16 OXBOROUGH WK
17 St Georges Inf Sch
18 St George's Theatre

10 FULLER'S HILL
11 PRIORY ROW
12 PRIORY GDNS
13 PRIORY RD
14 CHURCH PLAIN
15 FALCON CT
16 MARKET ROW
17 BROAD ROW

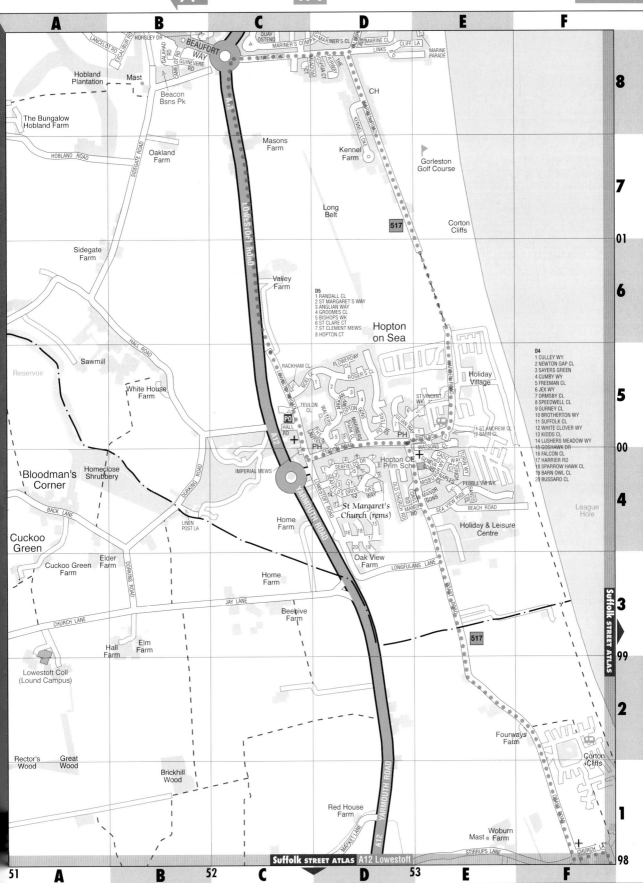

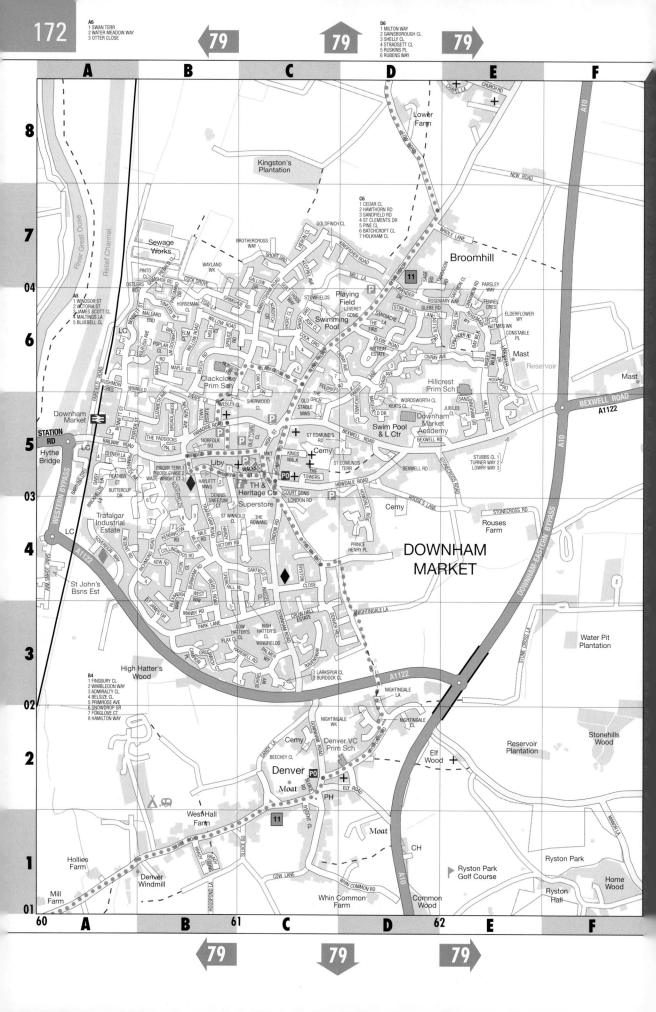

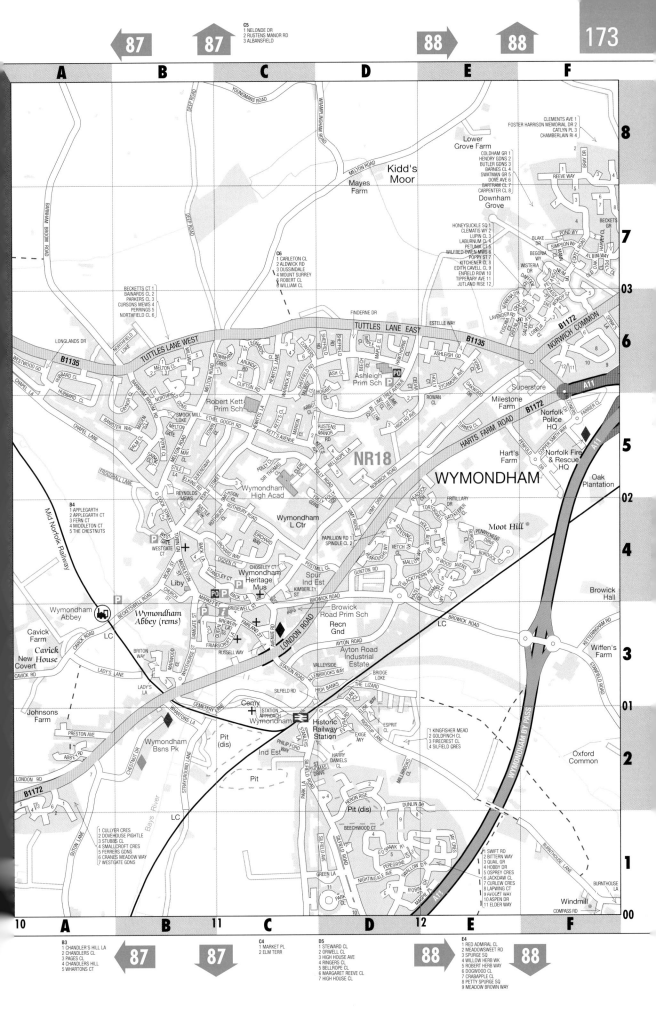

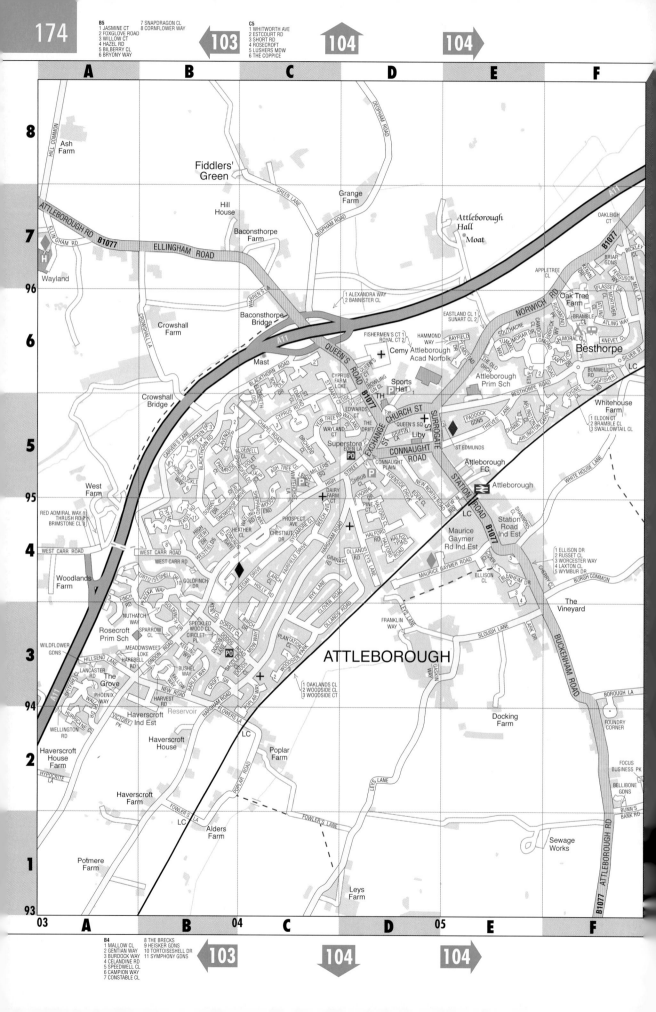

103
104
104

B5
1 JASMINE CT
2 FOXGLOVE ROAD
3 WILLOW CT
4 HAZEL RD
5 BILBERRY CL
6 BRYONY WAY
7 SNAPDRAGON CL
8 CORNFLOWER WAY

C5
1 WHITWORTH AVE
2 ESTCOURT RD
3 SHORT RD
4 ROSECROFT
5 LUSHERS MDW
6 THE COPPICE

A   B   C   D   E   F

Ash
Farm

Fiddlers'
Green

Hill
House

Grange
Farm

Attleborough
Hall
Moat

OAKLEIGH
CT

ATTLEBOROUGH RD
B1077
ELLINGHAM RD
ELLINGHAM ROAD

Baconsthorpe
Farm

B1077

Wayland

Crowshall
Farm

Baconsthorpe
Bridge

1 ALEXANDRA WAY
2 BANNISTER CL

NORWICH RD

BRIAR
GDNS

BICKLEY
CL

Oak Tree
Farm

Besthorpe

Crowshall
Bridge

Mast

A11

1 EASTLAND CL
2 SUNART CL

FISHERMEN'S CT 1
ROYAL CT 2

HAMMOND
WAY

Cemy Attleborough
Acad Norfolk

Attleborough
Prim Sch

West
Farm

QUEEN'S ROAD

B1077

Sports
Hall
TH

Attleborough
FC

Whitehouse
Farm

1 ELDON CT
2 BRAMBLE CL
3 SWALLOWTAIL CL

RED ADMIRAL WAY 1
THRUSH RD 2
BRIMSTONE CL 3

EXCHANGE CHURCH ST
ST
SURROGATE
ST
CONNAUGHT
ROAD

Superstore
EDEN LA
PO

St Edmunds

STATION ROAD

Attleborough
LC

Station
Road
Ind Est

WEST CARR ROAD
WEST CARR RD

Maurice
Gaymer
Rd Ind Est

1 ELLISON DR
2 RUSSET CL
3 WORCESTER WAY
4 LAXTON CL
5 WYMBUR DR

Woodlands
Farm

MAURICE GAYMER ROAD

The
Vineyard

Rosecroft
Prim Sch

ATTLEBOROUGH ROAD

BUCKENHAM ROAD

BOROUGH LA

WILDFLOWER
GDNS

ATTLEBOROUGH

1 OAKLANDS CL
2 WOODSIDE CL
3 WOODSIDE CT

Franklin
Way

Docking
Farm

FOUNDRY
CORNER

The
Grove

Haverscroft
Ind Est

Reservoir

LC

FOCUS
BUSINESS PK

HYPOCRITE
LA

Haverscroft
House
Farm

Haverscroft
House

Poplar
Farm

BELLIBONE
GDNS

A11

POPLAR ROAD

FOWLER'S LANE

Sewage
Works

BUNN'S
BANK RD

B1077

Haverscroft
Farm

LC

Alders
Farm

FOWLER'S LANE

Potmere
Farm

Leys
Farm

03   A   B   04   C   D   05   E   F

B4
1 MALLOW CL
2 GENTIAN WAY
3 BURDOCK WAY
4 CELANDINE RD
5 SPEEDWELL CL
6 CAMPION WAY
7 CONSTABLE CL
8 THE BRECKS
9 HEISKER GDNS
10 TORTOISESHELL DR
11 SYMPHONY GDNS

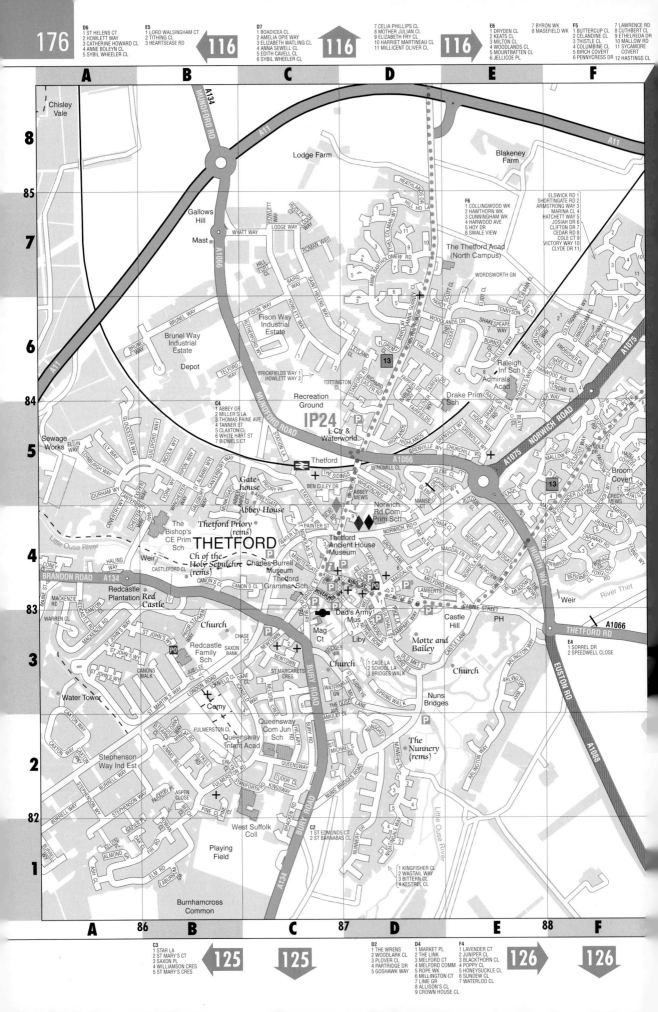

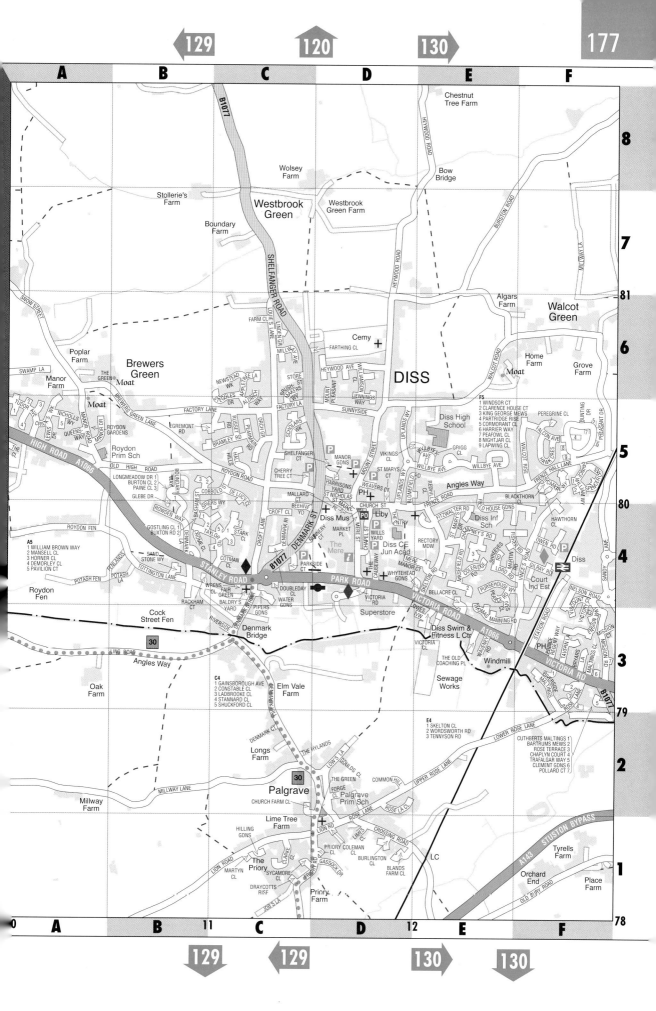

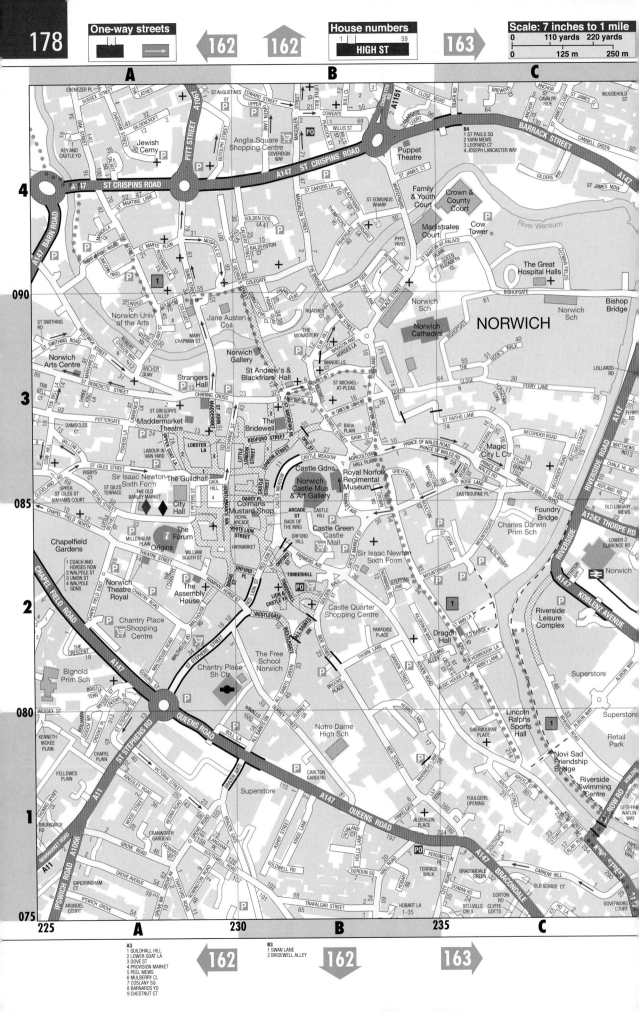

Index

Place name May be abbreviated on the map

Location number Present when a number indicates the place's position in a crowded area of mapping

Locality, town or village Shown when more than one place has the same name

Postcode district District for the indexed place

Page and grid square Page number and grid reference for the standard mapping

Church Rd **6** Beckenham BR2.........**53** C6

Cities, towns and villages are listed in CAPITAL LETTERS

Public and commercial buildings are highlighted in magenta   **Places of interest** are highlighted in blue with a star *

Abbreviations used in the index

Acad	**Academy**	Comm	**Common**	Gd	**Ground**	L	**Leisure**	Prom	**Promenade**
App	**Approach**	Cott	**Cottage**	Gdn	**Garden**	La	**Lane**	Rd	**Road**
Arc	**Arcade**	Cres	**Crescent**	Gn	**Green**	Liby	**Library**	Recn	**Recreation**
Ave	**Avenue**	Cswy	**Causeway**	Gr	**Grove**	Mdw	**Meadow**	Ret	**Retail**
Bglw	**Bungalow**	Ct	**Court**	H	**Hall**	Meml	**Memorial**	Sh	**Shopping**
Bldg	**Building**	Ctr	**Centre**	Ho	**House**	Mkt	**Market**	Sq	**Square**
Bsns, Bus	**Business**	Ctry	**Country**	Hospl	**Hospital**	Mus	**Museum**	St	**Street**
Bvd	**Boulevard**	Cty	**County**	HQ	**Headquarters**	Orch	**Orchard**	Sta	**Station**
Cath	**Cathedral**	Dr	**Drive**	Hts	**Heights**	Pal	**Palace**	Terr	**Terrace**
Cir	**Circus**	Dro	**Drove**	Ind	**Industrial**	Par	**Parade**	TH	**Town Hall**
Cl	**Close**	Ed	**Education**	Inst	**Institute**	Pas	**Passage**	Univ	**University**
Cnr	**Corner**	Emb	**Embankment**	Int	**International**	Pk	**Park**	Wk, Wlk	**Walk**
Coll	**College**	Est	**Estate**	Intc	**Interchange**	Pl	**Place**	Wr	**Water**
Com	**Community**	Ex	**Exhibition**	Junc	**Junction**	Prec	**Precinct**	Yd	**Yard**

Index of towns, villages, streets, hospitals, industrial estates, railway stations, schools, shopping centres, universities and places of interest

100th Bomb Group Memorial Mus,The *
IP21 . . . . .131 A8

A

Abbey Barns Ct IP24 . . . . .176 B5
Abbey Cl
 Horsham St Faith & Newton St
 Faith NR10. . . . . .53 D1
 Sheringham NR26 . . . . . . 138 D6
 Wendling NR19 . . . . .66 F7
Abbey Farm La NR11. . . . 35 F4
Abbeyfields PE32 . . . . .29 D1
Abbeygate IP24 . . . . .176 C5
Abbey Gn **1** IP24. . . . . . .176 C4
Abbey Hill IP21. . . . . .131 A3
Abbey La
 Broomsthorpe PE31 . . . . . .30 C7
 Haveringland NR10 . . . . . .52 D6
 Norwich NR1 . . . . .178 C2
Abbey Lakes Cl PE32. . . . 63 B8
Abbey Mews IP24. . . . . . .176 D5
Abbey Pk NR26 . . . . .138 F5
ABBEY RD NR16 . . . . . . .124 A3
Abbey Rd
 Flitcham with Appleton
  PE31 . . . . .28 D5
 Flixton NR35 . . . . .123 F4
 Great Massingham PE32. .29 D1
 Horsham St Faith NR10 . . .53 D1
 Old Buckenham NR17 . . . 104 D3
 Pentney PE32. . . . . .63 B8
 Sheringham NR26 . . . . . .138 C6
 10 Watton IP25. . . . . . . .84 E3
 Wingfield IP21. . . . . .131 B5
 Wymondham NR18 . . . . . 173 A2
Abbey St NR12. . . . . .23 E4
Abbot Cl NR18 . . . . .173 C5
Abbot Rd Horning NR12 . . 55 E4
 Norwich NR1 . . . . .162 D2
Abbot's Cl NR11 . . . . .150 D7
Abbots La NR11. . . . . .36 C7
Abbot's La NR14. . . . . .90 B3
Abbots Way NR12. . . . . . . 24 E4
Abbotts Ct PE14 . . . . .77 C6
Abel Heath La NR11. . . . . .35 F6
Abels Cl NR11. . . . . .155 C8
Abels Ct NR29 . . . . .167 D3
Aberdeen St PE30. . . . . . .146 F4
Abinger Way NR4. . . . . . . .89 D8
Abington Gr **4** PE14 . . . . 59 A1
Abraham Dr PE14. . . . . . .152 A3
Abram Ct NR20 . . . . .49 D4

Abyssinia Rd NR30 . . . . . .169 D2
Acacia Ave Ashill IP25 . . . .84 A7
 East Dereham NR19 . . . . .154 E1
 22 Martham NR29. . . . . . . .57 D4
 Wisbech PE13 . . . . .152 C8
Acacia Cl NR28 . . . . .151 B5
Acacia Gr NR26 . . . . .138 C4
Acacia Rd NR7. . . . . .163 E8
Access Rd NR21 . . . . .15 D2
Acer Rd PE34. . . . . .43 D4
Achilles Dr NR5. . . . . .156 B1
Ackland Cl **7** NR29 . . . . . .58 B6
Acland Mews NR6 . . . . . .158 C4
ACLE NR13. . . . . .166 B3
Acle High Sch NR13. . . . .166 B4
Acle Link Rd Acle NR13 . . 74 E5
 Acle NR13 . . . . .166 D4
Acle New Rd NR30 . . . . . .169 B5
Acle Rd Beighton NR13 . . . 74 E2
 Beighton, Lingwood &
  Burlingham NR13 . . . . . .74 B4
 South Walsham NR13 . . . . 74 C7
 Upton with Fishley NR13. .166 A5
Acle St Edmund CE VC Prim
  Sch NR13 . . . . .166 D4
Acle Sta NR13 . . . . .166 B2
Aconite Rd PE30 . . . . . . .147 B7
Acorn Cl Hellesdon NR6 . .157 F3
 7 Shipdham IP25. . . . . . . .67 B2
Acorn Dr PE32. . . . . .45 B6
Acorn Park NR16 . . . . . . .119 E2
Acorn Rd NR28 . . . . .151 D6
Acorn Way NR19. . . . . . . .154 D7
Acres Way NR8 . . . . .155 E2
Ada Coxon Cl PE30. . . . . .146 F8
Adam Cl PE30 . . . . .147 C5
Adams La **4** NR11 . . . . . . .19 F1
Adams Rd NR7. . . . . .159 A5
Adastral Pl PE37. . . . . . . .153 C5
Adcock Dr NR7 . . . . .159 E5
Addey Cl NR6. . . . . .158 F5
Addison Cl
 2 Coltishall NR12 . . . . . .54 C7
 Feltwell IP26 . . . . .98 F1
Addison Rd **2** NR31 . . . . .170 C7
Adeane Mdw IP26 . . . . . .100 A4
Adelaide Ave PE30. . . . . .147 D7
Adelaide St **5** NR2 . . . . . .162 B7
Adele Pl NR30. . . . . .168 E4
Adey Cl NR11. . . . . .150 B5
Adland Rd **25** IP25 . . . . . . 84 F3
Admiral Cl **4** IP25. . . . . . . .66 E3
Admirals Acad IP24 . . . . .176 E6
Admirals Ct PE37. . . . . . .153 D3
Admirals Dr PE13 . . . . . .152 D8

Admiral's Dr PE35 . . . . . .140 F1
Admirals Quay NR31 . . . .169 C1
Admirals Way
 Hethersett NR9 . . . . .88 D8
 Thetford IP24 . . . . .176 E5
Admirals Wlk **7** NR9. . . . . .86 C5
Admiralty Cl **3** PE38. . . . .172 B4
Admiralty Rd NR30. . . . . .169 D1
Admiral Wilson Wy
  PE37. . . . . .153 C6
Adventurers' Dro PE33. . . .81 B1
Aegel Gdns NR11 . . . . . .150 D6
Aerodrome Cres NR7 . . . .163 D8
Afghan Pl NR3. . . . . .158 E1
Aggas Acre IP23 . . . . . . .129 E1
Agricultural Hall Plain
  NR1 . . . . .178 B3
Ailmar Cl PE30. . . . . .147 A4
Ainsworth Cl **7** NR20. . . . .50 B3
Ainsworth Rd NR25 . . . . .137 D6
Aircraft Dr **16** IP25. . . . . . .84 C3
Airedale Cl **4** NR3 . . . . . .158 C1
Airfield La Coltishall NR12 . 54 C8
 Mundham NR14 . . . . . . .108 F7
 South Pickenham PE37 . . .83 D8
Airfield Rd
 Cockthorpe NR25. . . . . .6 C1
 Fersfield Common IP22. . .119 E3
 Marham PE33 . . . . .63 C4
 Weasenham St Peter PE32 30 C2
Airport Ind Est NR6 . . . . .158 C6
Airstation La IP21 . . . . . .121 E2
Akrotiri Sq IP25 . . . . .84 F3
Alan Ave NR15. . . . . .89 D1
Alan Jarvis Way PE34 . . .144 D6
Alan Rd NR1. . . . . .178 C1
Alban Rd PE30. . . . . .148 C5
Albansfield **3** NR18 . . . . .173 C5
Albany Cl NR31 . . . . .169 C2
Albany Ct NR27 . . . . .139 B7
Albany Rd
 Great Yarmouth NR31 . . .169 C2
 Norwich NR3 . . . . .162 D8
 Wisbech PE13 . . . . .152 C6
Albatross Rd NR20 . . . . . .69 C7
Albemarle Rd
 Great Yarmouth NR30 . . .169 D5
 Norwich NR2. . . . . .162 B3
Albert Cl NR11. . . . . .150 E6
Albert Ct **18** PE13 . . . . . . .152 C4
Albert Gate Rd **22** NR30 .169 D2
Albert Myhill Cl **5**
  NR20 . . . . .154 E6
Albert Pl NR1. . . . . .163 A6

Albert Rd **17** NR30 . . . . . .169 D2
Albert Shower Rd NR13 . . 72 E8
Albert Sq **13** NR30. . . . . .169 D2
Albert St Holt NR25 . . . . .137 B6
 King's Lynn PE30 . . . . . .146 D5
Albert Terr NR2. . . . . .162 C4
Albini Wy
 Kidd's Moor NR18 . . . . . .88 B6
 Wymondham NR18 . . . . .173 F7
Albion Dr Norwich NR7. . .159 A3
 Stalham NR12 . . . . .39 B3
Albion Rd Bungay NR35 . .124 B8
 Great Yarmouth NR30 . . .169 D4
 Mundesley NR11 . . . . . . .143 A7
Albion St PE30. . . . . .146 E5
Albion Way Norwich NR1 .178 C1
 Wroxham/Hoveton NR12 .164 D6
Alborough Loke **6**
  NR9 . . . . .88 C7
ALBURGH IP20 . . . . .122 F6
Alburgh Rd Denton IP20. .123 B6
 Hempnall NR15 . . . . . . .107 D4
 Shelton & Hardwick NR15 107 B1
Alburgh with Denton CE
  Prim Sch IP20. . . . . . . .123 A5
ALBY HILL NR11 . . . . .21 B5
Alby Hill NR11 . . . . .21 B5
Alby Meadow NR11 . . . . .21 D3
ALDBOROUGH NR11 . . . . .21 A5
Aldborough Prim Sch
  NR11 . . . . .21 B5
Aldborough Rd
 Alby Hill NR11 . . . . .21 C4
 Erpingham NR11 . . . . . . .21 A3
 Matlaske NR11 . . . . .20 D6
 Matlaske NR11 . . . . .20 E4
ALDEBY NR34. . . . . .110 F4
Aldeby Rd NR34. . . . . . . .110 F6
Alder Cl
 Great Yarmouth NR31 . . . .94 C7
 10 Mulbarton NR14. . . . . .89 B3
 North Walsham NR28 . . .151 D7
 Poringland NR14 . . . . . . .90 D4
Alder Covert IP24. . . . . . .116 D2
Alderfen La NR12 . . . . . . .55 F6
Alderfen Wy NR12 . . . . . .164 E7
ALDERFORD NR9 . . . . . . .52 A5
Alderford Common NR9. . .52 A5
Alderman Peel High Sch
  NR23 . . . . .136 D4
Alderman Swindell Sch
  NR30. . . . . .169 D8
Alderson Pl NR1 . . . . .178 B1
Alderson Rd NR30 . . . . . .169 C5

Alder Way
 Damgate NR13. . . . . .166 B2
 Taverham NR8 . . . . .155 E1
Aldis Ct NR19 . . . . .154 D5
Aldis Ave NR19 . . . . .154 D3
Aldiss Cl PE37 . . . . .153 D3
Aldiss Ct PE13 . . . . .154 D6
Aldrich Way IP22 . . . . . . .177 C5
Aldridge Way NR10 . . . . . .53 B4
Aldryche Rd NR1. . . . . . . .163 B8
Aldwick Rd **2** NR18. . . . . .173 C6
Alec East Rd **6** NR13. . . . .165 D6
Alexander Cl
 Caister-on-Sea NR30. . . .168 C8
 18 Long Stratton NR15. .106 E3
Alexander Rise NR11. . . . . 22 F8
Alexander Way **1** NR19 154 C6
Alexander Wy IP21 . . . . .130 D5
Alexandra Ave NR30 . . . .169 D7
Alexandra Cl PE31 . . . . . .140 C4
Alexandra Rd
 Aylsham NR11 . . . . .150 E6
 Cromer NR27. . . . . .139 B4
 Great Yarmouth NR30 . . .169 D4
 Hunstanton PE36. . . . . . .132 C3
 Mundesley NR11 . . . . . . .143 A8
 Norwich NR2 . . . . .162 B6
 Sheringham NR26 . . . . . .138 D6
 Wisbech PE13 . . . . .152 C5
Alexandra Way
 Attleborough NR17 . . . . .174 C6
Alex Moorhouse Way
  NR5 . . . . .156 A3
Alford Gr Norwich NR7. . . .72 A6
 Norwich NR7 . . . . .159 A3
Alfred Nicholls Ct NR3 . . .158 D2
Alfred Rd NR27 . . . . .139 A7
Alfric Cl **11** NR14. . . . . . . .91 F1
Algar Rd IP22 . . . . .119 E1
Algores Way PE13 . . . . . .152 B2
Alicante Wy NR5. . . . . . . .161 E6
Alice Fisher Cres PE30 . .146 F7
Alison Cl NR13. . . . . .73 F3
Alkmaar Way NR6 . . . . . .158 A6
Allanadale Rd NR4. . . . . .162 C1
Allenbrooks Way NR18. . .173 C3
Allenby's Chase **10** PE12 . 41 B8
Allen Cl PE34 . . . . .61 B8
Allendale Rd
 Caister-on-Sea NR30. . . .168 E5
 Great Yarmouth NR30 . . . .76 C2
Allen Meale Way **5**
  NR12 . . . . .39 B4
Allen's Ave NR7. . . . . . . .159 A4

Allens Cl **1** NR13 . . . . . . .73 D6
Allens La NR2. . . . . .162 C4
Allen's La NR7. . . . . .159 A4
Allerton Cl NR7. . . . . .159 B3
Allerton Rd NR7 . . . . .159 B3
Alley The PE32. . . . . .44 C1
All Hallows' Hospl NR35 .109 B2
Allison's Cl **8** IP24 . . . . . .176 C4
Allison St NR10 . . . . .36 A2
Allotment La
 Baconsthorpe NR25. . . . . .20 A8
 Bodham NR25 . . . . .9 B3
Allotment Way PE30 . . . .147 A2
All Saints IP27. . . . . .175 B8
All Saints Ave PE13 . . . . .152 F2
All Saints CE VA Prim Sch
 Stibbard NR21. . . . . .32 E7
 Winfarthing IP22. . . . . . .120 B4
All Saints Cl
 Briston NR24 . . . . .142 D4
 Little Melton NR9. . . . . . .160 B3
 Runhall NR20. . . . . .69 A5
 2 Weybourne NR25 . . . . .8 F5
 Wicklewood NR18 . . . . . .87 B5
 1 Wisbech PE14 . . . . . . .59 A1
All Saints Dr PE30. . . . . .148 C4
All Saints Gn NR1 . . . . . .178 B1
ALL SAINTS SOUTH
  ELMHAM IP19. . . . . . . .124 B1
All Saints' St **15** PE30. . . .146 D4
All Saints Way
 Beachamwell PE37 . . . . . .81 F8
 Mundesley NR11 . . . . . . .143 C6
All Saints Wlk **7** NR20 . . . 68 F6
Allthorpe Rd **12** IP20. . . .122 D2
Allwood Ave
 Dereham NR19 . . . . .67 E3
 East Dereham NR19 . . . .154 C5
Alma Ave PE34. . . . . .144 D6
Alma Chase PE34 . . . . . .144 D6
Alma Rd
 Great Yarmouth NR30 . . . 169 D2
 Snettisham PE31 . . . . . . .12 E5
Alma Terr NR3. . . . . .162 D8
Almond Cl **3** NR29 . . . . . .57 D4
Almond Dr NR4. . . . . .161 C1
Almond Gr IP24 . . . . .176 A1
Almond Rd NR31. . . . . . . .170 B6
Alms Houses **8** NR17 . . .104 D2
Alpha Rd NR31. . . . . .170 C8

ALPINGTON NR14........90 E4
Alpington & Bergh Apton
  CE Prim Sch NR14....90 F4
Alsham Rd NR11.........20 A1
Alston Cl 3 NR14.......90 D5
Alston Rd NR6.........157 E2
Alston Sixth Form Centre
  NR14................91 F3
Althaea Gn 2 NR31....170 B5
Altongate 1 NR13......72 D6
Amazona Zoo* NR27...139 B5
Ambassador Way NR20 .154 F4
Ambleside
  16 Hethersett NR9.....88 D8
  5 Sculthorpe Airfield
  NR21................15 C2
Ambleside Cl NR5.....161 C6
Ambrose Cl 1 NR5....161 A7
Ambrose Rd NR30.....168 E3
Amderley Dr 6 NR4....89 C8
Amelia Opie Way 2
  IP24...............176 D7
American La NR21........6 F1
Ames Ct NR10..........35 B2
Amethyst Cl NR1......170 D2
Amherst Cl 7 PE37....153 C3
Amhirst Cl 2 NR6.....158 F1
Amhurst Gdns NR31....94 A5
Amis Cl 7 NR8.........22 E5
Amos Bacon Cl NR6...158 F4
Ampthill St 6 NR2....162 C5
Amsterdam NR6........158 B6
Amsterdam Way PE13..154 C2
Amulet Cl IP24.......176 C2
Amys Cl IP25..........84 C4
Ancar Rd PE30........148 D2
Anchorage La PE31.....30 A8
Anchorage View PE31....3 B6
Anchor Cl Norwich NR3..178 C4
  Sheringham NR26....138 E6
ANCHOR CORNER NR17 ..86 A1
Anchor Ct NR31.......169 C2
Anchor Dro PE38......112 B8
Anchor La IP27.......113 F1
Anchor Pk PE31........12 E4
Anchor Quay NR2......178 A3
Anchor Rd
  North Walsham NR28..151 F5
  Sutton Bridge PE34...41 F8
Anchor St Coltishall NR12..54 D6
  5 Norwich NR3.....162 F8
  Norwich NR3........178 C4
  Tunstead NR12.......38 B2
ANCHOR STREET NR3....38 B3
Anchor Way 7 NR33...111 F1
Anderson Cl
  King's Lynn PE30....146 E7
  Wisbech PE13.......152 A7
Andrew Goodall Cl
  NR19...............154 C1
Andrew's Furlong
  NR16...............119 C7
Andrews Pl PE36......132 D2
Angela Cl 1 NR10......53 B3
Angela Cres 3 NR10....53 B3
Angela Rd NR10........53 B3
Angel Dr NR28........151 B4
Angel Rd NR3.........158 C1
Angel Road Inf Sch
  NR3................158 D1
Angel Road Jun Sch
  NR3................158 D1
Angerstein Cl IP27...114 E8
Angle Rd PE14.........78 A7
Anglian Way
  Aylsham NR11.......150 E8
  3 Hopton on Sea NR31..171 D5
Anglia Sq NR3........178 B4
Anglia Way PE14......158 B8
Anglo-Saxon Cath & Bishops
  Pal (remains of)* NR20..49 F8
Angus Mackay Rd NR6..157 E4
ANMER PE31............28 E8
Anmer Cl NR3.........158 F3
Anmer Rd Bircham PE31..13 F2
  Flitcham with Appleton
  PE31...............28 C5
  Flitcham with Appleton
  PE31...............28 E7
  Great Bircham PE31...14 A2
  Harpley PE31........29 A7
  Shernborne PE31.....13 B2
Anna Gurney Cl NR11..170 D6
Anna Sewell Cl 4 IP24..176 D7
Anne Bartholomew Rd
  IP24...............176 D7
Anne Boleyn Cl 4 IP24..176 D7
Anne Cl NR7..........163 F8
Anne Rd PE12..........41 B8
Annes Cl NR30........148 D1
Annes Dr PE36........132 D1
Anne Stannard Way
  NR12...............23 F4
ANNIS HILL NR35......124 C8
Annis Hill NR35......124 C8
Annis Hill La 1 NR35..124 B8
Anson Cl
  5 Hethersett NR9.....88 E8
  Mundesley NR11......143 A7
Anson Rd
  Great Yarmouth NR31..169 C2
  Norwich NR6........158 B6
Anson's La PE31......122 A8
Anson Wy 27 IP25......84 F3
Ant Broads & Marshes
  National Nature Reserve*
  NR12................55 F8
Anterton Hill NR25.....7 F7

Anthony Curton CE VA Prim
  Sch PE14............41 E4
Anthony Nolan Rd PE30.147 D3
ANTINGHAM NR28........22 B4
Antingham Dr NR28....151 D6
Antingham Hill NR28...22 B3
Antingham Rd
  Lower Street NR11....22 B5
  Norwich NR7........159 D1
Antingham & Southrepps
  Com Prim Sch NR11...22 B5
Anvil Way PE14........59 D2
Apeldoorn Wlk PE13...152 D7
Apollo Cres NR5......156 B1
Apollo Wlk NR30......169 C6
Appleacres NR6.......158 F4
Appledore La 4 NR21...15 C2
Apple Dr PE13........152 F7
Applegarth 1 NR18....173 B4
Applegarth 2 NR18....173 B4
Appleton Dr NR29......67 A8
Appleton Dro PE31.....27 F5
Appleton La PE35......28 A6
Appletree Cl
  Besthorpe NR17.....174 F7
  Heacham PE31.......133 C6
Appletree La IP22....177 C5
Applewood Cl NR33....111 F1
Appleyard Cres NR3...158 A3
Apple Yd NR25........137 B6
Apsley Ct NR5........161 F6
Apsley Rd NR30.......169 E3
Arbor Cl NR27........139 B6
Arbor Rd NR27........139 B6
Arcade St NR1........178 B2
Archbishop Sancroft High
  Sch IP20............122 D2
Archdale Cl PE33......43 F3
Archdale St 3 PE30...146 E5
Archer Cl NR6........159 A5
Archer La PE32........46 F2
Archer's Ave 3 IP26...98 D1
Archer's Rd 2 NR30...169 C5
Arches Ct NR31.......170 A5
Archibald Rd NR12.....24 A7
Arden Cl NR27.........11 A3
Arden Gr NR10........157 E7
Arden Grove Inf Sch
  NR10...............157 E7
Arderon Ct 2 NR2.....162 B7
Ardleigh Cl 3 PE13...152 E5
Ardney Rise NR3......158 D3
Argyle St
  King's Lynn PE30....146 E3
Argyll Cres NR8......156 E8
Arkell Ave NR25......137 E7
Arles Ave PE13.......152 E3
Arlington Cl NR17....174 E5
Arlington Gdns NR17..174 E5
Arlington La NR2.....162 C4
Arlington Pk Rd PE32..44 C3
Arlington Way IP24...176 E3
Armada Cl PE13.......152 D8
Armes Cres NR2.......162 A8
Armes St NR2.........162 B7
ARMINGHALL NR14......90 B7
Arminghall Cl
  Norwich NR3........158 C3
  Poringland NR14.....90 B6
Arminghall La NR14....89 B8
Armitage Cl NR4.......89 B8
Arms Pk Rd NR6.......158 B6
ARMS THE IP25.........83 F1
Arms The IP25.........84 A2
Armstrong Dr NR19....154 E7
Armstrong Rd NR7.....159 E2
Armstrong Way IP24...176 F7
Army Rd NR21..........15 C2
Arnfield La NR5......161 B8
Arnold Ave NR30......168 D8
Arnold Miller Rd NR1..162 F2
Arnold Pitcher Cl NR28..151 D6
Arnott Ave NR31......170 D1
Arnott Rd NR25.......137 D5
Arnside Cl 22 NR9.....88 D8
Arrowhead Dr IP27....113 E2
Arthur Ave NR30......168 E8
Arthur Rd NR21......141 A6
Arthurton Rd NR10.....54 A1
Artillery Sq 21 NR30..169 D4
Artillery St PE13.....152 C4
Arundel Cl
  Gressenhall NR19.....49 C3
  Gressenhall NR20.....49 C4
Arundel Ct NR2.......178 A1
Arundel Dr PE30......148 C1
Arundel Rd
  Great Yarmouth NR30..169 D6
  Wymondham NR18....173 C6
Ascension Ave
  Costessey NR5......156 C1
  Costessey NR5......160 C8
Ascot Dr IP26........100 D6
Ascot Gdns NR19......154 D3
Ashbey Rd PE30.......147 E8
Ashbourne Ind Est NR6..158 C4
Ashburton Cl NR23....136 C4
Ashburton Rd IP26....100 C5
Ashby Rd NR29.........57 A3
ASHBY ST MARY NR14...91 C5
Ash Cl Brandon IP27..175 E3
  Downham Market PE33..172 C6
  10 Etling Green NR20..68 A8
  Hellesdon NR6......157 F3
  10 Hethersett NR9....88 D8
  Reepham NR10.......149 D6
  Swaffham PE37......153 B5

Ash Cl continued
  Thetford IP24.......176 A1
  Wymondham NR18....173 D6
Ashcroft Cl NR4......161 B1
Ashdale Pk
  Old Hunstanton PE36..132 F8
  Wisbech PE13.......152 A5
Ashdown NR8..........155 E1
Ashdown Ct NR17.....139 C6
Ash Dr IP23..........130 C1
Ashes Farm La IP22...119 A2
Ashfield Cl PE34.....144 D6
Ashfield Hill PE30...147 C4
Ashfield Rd NR28.....151 E6
Ashford Cl NR34......110 C2
Ash Gn 11 NR31.......170 B6
Ash Gr King's Lynn PE30..148 D2
  Norwich NR3........158 E2
  Sheringham NR26....138 E5
  4 West Winch PE33...43 E2
Ashgrove 5 NR8.......155 E2
Ashide PE31...........15 B3
ASHILL IP25...........84 A7
Ashill VC Prim Sch IP25..84 A7
Ash La NR16..........105 C2
Ashleigh Gdns NR18...173 E6
Ashleigh Prim Sch
  NR18...............173 D6
Ashley Rd NR20........49 D4
Ashley Wlk PE33......154 D4
ASHMANHAUGH NR12....55 B8
Ash Plough IP21......131 E1
Ash Rd Marham PE33....63 B4
  Mellis IP23.........129 D1
  Sprowston NR7......159 F3
Ash Tree Cl NR17.....174 C5
Ash Tree La NR11......19 E8
Ash Tree Rd NR13......74 D1
Ashwell Ct NR5.......160 F7
ASHWELLTHORPE
  NR16...............105 F8
Ashwellthorpe Rd NR16..88 D1
  Sheringham NR26....138 E7
  Snettisham PE31......12 D3
ASHWICKEN PE32........45 A6
Ashwicken CE Prim Sch
  PE32...............44 F6
Ashwicken Rd PE32.....45 A8
Ashwood Cl NR30.....168 D6
Ash Yd NR4............18 D8
Aslack Way PE36........2 A6
ASLACTON NR15........106 A2
Aslacton Prim Sch
  NR15...............106 A1
Aslacton Rd NR16.....106 B3
Aslake Cl NR7........159 C5
Aspen Cl 14 Loddon NR14..91 F1
  28 Thetford IP24....176 B2
Aspen Dr
  Wymondham NR18.....87 F2
  Wymondham NR18....173 D1
Aspen Rd NR30........168 E4
Aspen Way NR41........89 B8
Aspland Rd NR1.......178 C3
Assembly House The
  NR2................178 A2
Association Way 2 NR7..72 D4
Astell Rd NR1.........89 F8
Astley Cooper Pl
  5 Brooke NR15........90 E1
  5 Great Yarmouth NR31..169 D6
Astley Cres PE36......132 D6
Astley Prim Sch NR24..142 C4
Astley Rd
  Great & Little Plumstead
  NR13................73 B6
  Little Plumpstead NR13..165 A8
  Norwich NR5........160 F8
Astley Terr NR14.....142 A4
Astor Ct IP27........175 D4
Atbara Terr NR30.....146 E2
Atcherley Sq PE31.....30 B3
Atchison Ave NR4.....161 B1
Atkinson Cl NR5......160 E8
Atlantic Ave
  Sprowston NR7......159 D5
  Sprowston NR7......159 F4
Atling Cl NR17.......174 F6
Atling Way NR17......174 F6
Atmere Cl 2 NR4......161 F1
Attlesey Way NR5.....160 E8
Atthill Rd NR2.......162 A7
ATTLEBOROUGH NR17...174 D3
Attleborough Acad Norfolk
  NR17...............174 D6
Attleborough Jun Sch
  NR17...............174 E6
Attleborough Prim Sch
  NR17...............174 E6
Attleborough Rd
  Attleborough NR17...174 A7
  Attleborough NR17...174 F1
  Caston NR17........102 F8
  Deopham NR18........86 E1
  Great Ellingham NR17..103 F8
  Little Ellingham NR17..86 A2
  Morley NR18.........87 A1
  Rockland St Peter NR17..103 C8
  Attleborough NR17...174 E5
ATTLEBRIDGE NR9......52 B3
Attlee Way 4 NR19....154 C6
Attoe Wlk NR3........158 D2
Aubrey Rix Ct NR20....33 C3
Audax Rd NR6........158 C6
Audley Cl IP22.......120 C2
Audley Ct IP24.......176 C7
Audley End IP21......120 F1
Audrey St NR30.......169 D5
Augusta Ct NR26......138 E7
Augusta St NR26......138 D7

Augustus Hare Dr 1
  NR4................161 C5
Aurania Ave NR1......162 D3
Auster Cl NR6........158 C4
Austin Fields PE30...146 E5
Austin Fields Ind Est
  PE30...............146 E5
Austin Rd NR31.......169 B3
Austin St
  Hunstanton PE36....132 C5
  King's Lynn PE30....146 D5
Austin Wy NR6........158 F7
Autumn Cl IP24.......176 E4
Autumn Dr NR5.......161 B8
Autumn Gdns NR18.....87 F2
Avebury Rd NR4......162 B1
Aveling Way 6 NR33..111 F1
Avenue Cl PE38........79 E1
Avenue Jun Sch NR2...162 B5
Avenue Rd
  Great Yarmouth NR31..170 D6
  High Kelling NR25.....8 E2
  Hunstanton PE36....132 C4
  King's Lynn PE30....146 F4
  North Walsham NR28..151 C4
  Norwich NR2........162 B5
  Wymondham NR18....173 C3
Avenue S NR26........138 E7
Avenues The
  Langley with Hardley
  NR14................91 F4
  Norwich NR4........161 E4
  Thurton NR14........91 D3
Avenue The
  Brome & Oakley IP23..130 D3
  Brookville IP26......99 A7
  Brumstead NR12......24 A1
  Dersingham PE35....140 E1
  Hemsby NR29........167 A7
  Horning NR12........55 E4
  Mundesley NR11.....143 C5
  4 Necton PE37.......65 F4
  Northrepps NR27....139 D3
  Sheringham NR26....138 E7
  Snettisham PE31......12 D3
Avian Way NR7........159 C2
Aviary Wy NR7........159 D1
Avocet Ave PE36......132 D1
Avocet House NR14.....92 C1
Avocet Rise NR7......159 E4
Avocet Way NR18......173 D1
Avondale Cl NR13......74 A2
Avondale Rd
  Great Yarmouth NR31..170 D5
  South Creake NR21....15 E6
Avonmouth Rd 2 NR3..158 C1
Avon Rd PE30.........148 C2
Awdry Dr PE13........152 C3
Ayers La NR20.........49 F3
Aylesbury Cl NR3.....158 D2
Aylmer Dr PE34.......60 C8
AYLMERTON NR11.......10 A2
Aylmerton Rd NR11....10 A1
AYLSHAM NR11.........150 B5
Aylsham Bypass
  Aylsham NR11.......150 E4
  Drabblegate NR11....36 C7
Aylsham Cres NR3.....158 C3
Aylsham High Sch
  NR11...............150 D7
Aylsham Ind Est NR11..150 E8
Aylsham Rd
  Brampton NR11.......37 F4
  Burgh & Tuttington NR11..36 E8
  Cawston NR10........35 B2
  Cawston NR10........35 D3
  Felmingham NR28.....37 A8
  North Walsham NR28...22 C1
  Norwich NR3........158 C1
  Oulton NR11.........35 B8
  Oulton NR11.........35 C6
  Saxthorpe NR11......19 F1
  Swanton Abbott NR10..37 C4
Aylsham Sta NR11.....150 D5
Aylsham Rd Bsns Pk
  NR6................158 C2
Aymerton Rd NR11.....21 A8
Ayre Way PE30........147 D8
Ayton Rd NR18........173 D3
Ayton Rd Ind Est NR18..173 D3

B

BABINGLEY PE31........27 D5
Babingley Cl 5 NR31...61 D6
Babingley Dr PE30....146 F6
Babingley Pl PE33.....43 F4
Babylon Dr 5 NR5.....156 C1
Bachelor's La NR28....23 E2
Back Chapel La NR11..170 D6
Back Dro Upwell PE14..77 D4
  Welney PE14.........95 D8
Back Heywood La IP22..120 D3
Back Hills IP21......128 E3
Back La Alburgh IP20..122 F7
  Barford NR9.........69 F2
  Beeston with Bittering
  PE32................48 C2
  Belton NR31.........94 A5
  Bircham PE31........14 B3
  Blakeney NR25.........7 C6
  Brampton NR10.......36 D3
  Bridgham NR16......117 F5
  Broomholm NR28......23 E4

Back La continued
  Burgh Castle NR31....94 A8
  Burnham Market PE31..135 D2
  Burnham Thorpe PE31....4 D4
  Buxton with Lammas NR10..53 E8
  Castle Acre PE32.....46 F2
  Catfield NR29........56 C8
  Cawston NR10........35 B2
  Dereham NR20........50 A1
  Dereham NR20........68 A8
  Diss IP22...........120 D3
  East Rudham PE31.....30 A6
  East Rudham PE31.....30 B7
  East Rudham PE31.....24 A3
  East Ruston NR12.....38 F7
  Elsing NR20..........50 F3
  Filby NR29...........75 E8
  Fritton and St Olaves NR31..93 F4
  Fulmodeston PE31.....17 E1
  Garboldisham IP22...128 A8
  Garvestone, Reymerston &
  Thuxton NR9.........68 D3
  Gissing IP22........120 E5
  Great Bircham PE31...14 B4
  Happisburgh PE12.....23 F2
  Hellington NR14.......91 B5
  Hempnall NR15......107 D5
  4 Hethersett NR9.....88 E8
  Hethersett NR9.......88 E8
  Kenninghall NR16...119 A5
  Litcham PE32.........48 A4
  Lound NR32..........94 C2
  Lyng NR9............51 A4
  Marthan NR29........57 D5
  Mattishall NR20......68 E6
  North Elmham NR20...49 E7
  North Lopham IP22...119 A1
  Old Buckenham NR17..104 C2
  Potter Heigham NR29..56 E7
  Quidenham NR16.....118 F8
  Quidenham NR16.....119 A8
  Rackheath NR13......54 D1
  Ringland NR8........52 C1
  Rollesby NR29.......57 D3
  Roughton NR11.......21 D8
  Roydon PE32.........28 A1
  St Mary, South Elmham
  otherwise Homersfield
  IP20...............123 B4
  Scole IP22..........121 C3
  Scoulton NR9.........85 E3
  Shelfanger IP22.....120 B3
  Shimpling IP21......121 A2
  South Creake NR21....15 E6
  Stacksford NR16.....119 B8
  Stacksford NR17.....104 C1
  Stanfield NR20.......48 F8
  Stanhoe PE31........14 D7
  Upton with Fishley NR13..166 C8
  Walsingham NR22.....16 F7
  Wereham PE33........80 E4
  West Beckham NR25....9 B3
  West Caister NR30...168 A4
  West Winch PE33.....43 E2
  Wymondham NR18....173 C4
Back Mkt La NR29.....167 B7
Back Mundesley Rd
  NR11...............22 F8
Back of the Inns NR1..178 B2
Back Path 1 NR29.....58 B6
Back Pier Plain NR31..170 D4
Back Rd Brockdish IP21..131 B8
  Coltishall NR12......54 E7
  East Ruston NR12.....38 F6
  Elm PE14............77 A8
  Pentney PE32........63 D8
  Somerton NR29.......57 F6
  Wisbech PE14........77 A7
  Wood Dalling NR11....34 D6
  Yelverton NR14......90 F5
Back Southrepps Rd
  NR11...............22 D6
Back St Binham NR21....6 E2
  Fakenham NR21......141 B3
  Gayton PE32.........45 C5
  Harpley PE31........29 A6
  Horsham St Faith NR10..53 D1
  Lakenheath IP27.....113 E1
  Litcham PE32........48 A4
  Mundesley NR11.....143 C5
  Reepham NR10.......149 B4
  South Creake NR21....15 D6
  Tittleshall PE32......48 B7
  Trunch NR28.........22 E5
Back Terr PE37.......153 B5
Backwood La Howe NR15..90 C2
  Shotesham NR15.....107 F8
Bacon Rd NR4........161 D5
BACONSTHORPE NR25....20 A8
Baconsthorpe Castle*
  NR25................9 A1
Baconsthorpe Rd
  Hempstead NR11......19 E8
  Plumstead NR11......20 A6
BACTON NR12..........23 E5
Bacton Cl PE30.......148 D3
BACTON GREEN NR12....23 D5
Bacton Prim Sch NR12..23 E5
Bacton Rd Bacton NR28..23 C3
  Happisburgh NR12.....23 F2
  North Walsham NR28..151 D6
  Norwich NR3........158 B2
  Paston NR28.........143 E2
Bader Cl PE30........147 D4
Bader Ct NR14.........89 A2
Badger Rd NR5........156 D1
Badgers Brook Rd NR8..155 F2
Badley Moor NR19......68 A7

Bagge Rd
  King's Lynn PE30....147 A5
  King's Lynn PE30....147 B5
BAGTHORPE PE31........14 D3
Bagthorpe Rd
  Bagthorpe PE31......14 D4
  East Rudham PE31....14 E1
  East Rudham PE31....15 A1
  East Rudham PE31....30 A7
  West Rudham PE31....29 F8
Bahram Rd NR8.......156 A4
Bailey Cl
  1 Hethersett NR9.....88 D7
  6 Marham NR29.......57 D5
  Old Catton NR6.....158 D7
Bailey La PE34.......145 E7
Bailey Pl PE30.......147 B4
Bailey Rd Cromer NR27..139 B5
  North Walsham NR28..151 C3
Bailey St Castle Acre PE32..46 F2
  Newton PE32..........47 A2
  Sporle with Palgrave PE32..65 B8
Bailiwick The 3 NR16..118 C5
Baillie Cl 3 NR31....170 B1
Bainard Rise NR5.....107 C6
Bainards Cl NR18.....173 B6
Baines Rd 4 PE30....146 D1
Baines Way 2 NR5....160 E8
Baird Way IP24......176 C7
Bakeney Rd NR25.......7 E4
Baker Cl
  King's Lynn PE30....146 D1
  North Walsham NR28..151 D3
Baker Dr NR9.........88 D8
Baker La 3 PE30......146 D4
Bakers Belt
  North Creake NR21....4 F1
  South Creake NR21....15 F8
Bakers La NR35.......109 A2
Bakers Rd NR3.......162 D8
Baker's Rd NR13......75 A1
Baker St
  Great Yarmouth NR31..170 D5
  14 Stalham NR12......39 B4
Bakers Way PE31......134 D5
Bakers Yd NR23......136 C6
Bakery Cl NR24.......142 E3
Bakery La NR9........51 A5
Balderston Ct NR3....178 B4
Baldock Cl 1 NR16...105 F5
Baldock Dr PE30......147 B8
Baldric Rd NR8......155 D1
Baldry's Yard IP22...177 C4
Baldwin Cl 5 PE13...152 D5
Baldwin Rd PE30.....147 C6
Baldwins Cl NR24.....142 D4
Baldwins Dro 4 PE14...77 F6
Baldwin Way NR18....173 D1
BALE NR21............18 B7
Bale Rd Brinton NR24..18 C7
  Field Dalling NR25....7 A1
  Field Dalling NR25...18 A8
  Gunthorpe NR24......18 A6
  Hindringham NR21....17 E7
Balfour Rd 4 NR27....10 A5
Balfour St 4 NR1....162 F8
Baliol Rd NR31......170 C5
Ball's La NR21........15 D1
Ballygate NR34.......110 C1
Balmoral Ave NR30...169 D7
Balmoral Cl
  Attleborough NR17...174 F6
  Dersingham PE33.....140 D3
Balmoral Cres PE31...133 C5
Balmoral Rd PE30.....147 C7
Balmoral W NR1......140 D3
Baltic Wharf NR1.....178 C2
Bambers La PE14......59 C2
Bancroft 7 NR14......89 F4
BANHAM NR16.........119 D7
Banham Dr NR20.......50 B2
Banham Hill NR9......68 F2
Banham Rd
  Banham NR16.......119 D8
  Kenninghall NR16...119 B5
  Quidenham NR16.....118 F6
  Banham NR16.......104 D1
Banham's La NR35....108 B2
Banham Wlk IP26......98 E1
Banham Zoo* NR16....119 C6
Banister Way NR18....173 A5
Bank Dr PE13........152 A7
Bank Loke 6 NR28....151 C5
Bank Plain NR1......178 B3
Bank Rd
  Dersingham PE31....140 C4
  Shepherd's Port PE31..12 B4
Bankside PE31.......133 B6
Bank Side PE34......146 C5
Bankside Way NR9.....69 B2
Bank St Norwich NR2..178 B3
  Pulham Market IP21..121 E5
BANNINGHAM NR11.....36 D8
Banningham Ct NR28..151 A4
Banningham Rd
  Aylsham NR11.......150 D8
  Banningham NR11.....36 D7
  Drabblegate NR11....36 D7
Bannister Cl NR17...174 C6
Bannister's Row PE13..152 A7
Banters La NR34.....124 F6
Banyard Ct PE13.....154 E5
Banyard Rd 1 NR19...154 C5
Banyards Pl PE33......61 D4
Baptist Rd PE14......77 D4
Barbastelle Cres NR9..88 C8

Barbel Cl NR14 . . . . .89 B2
Barber Pl NR7 . . . . .163 E5
Barberry Cl 5 NR8 . . . .155 B2
Barber's La
 Bedingham NR35. . . . . .108 B2
 Fakenham NR21. . . . . .141 E4
Barbers Wood Rd NR21 . .33 F8
Barbers Yd 1 NR17. . . .104 D2
Barchams Yd 16 NR26. . .138 D7
Barclay Cl Cromer NR27 . .139 A6
 Southrepps NR11. . . . . .22 B7
Barclay Gn NR7 . . . . .159 D1
Barclay Rd NR7 . . . . .159 E1
Bard Hill NR25 . . . . .8 B6
Bardolph Pl PE34 . . . . . . .61 D1
Bardolphs Ct 1 NR8 . . .155 B2
Bardolph's Way PE33 . . .62 C6
Bar Dro PE14 . . . . .77 B8
Bardwell Rd
 Barningham IP31. . . . . .127 C3
 Fakenham Magna IP24 . . .126 D3
 Stanton IP31. . . . . .127 B1
Bardyke Bank PE14 . . . . .77 F4
BARFORD NR9. . . . . .69 F2
Barford Prim Sch NR9 . . .69 F2
Barford Rd
 Marlingford NR9. . . . . .69 E3
 Sheringham NR26 . . . . . . .138 D7
Bargate Ct NR3 . . . . .178 B4
Barham Ct NR31. . . . . . . .170 D5
Barham's La NR16 . . . . . .105 D4
Barker's Dro PE33 . . . . . .81 A3
Barkers La NR21 . . . . .49 E3
Barker's La Norwich NR7 .159 A5
 Old Buckenham NR17. . . . .104 B2
Barker St NR2 . . . . .162 C8
Barker Way 5 NR13 . . . .72 C6
Barkis Rd NR30. . . . . . . .169 D1
Barley Cl
 Newton St Faith NR10. . . . .53 D3
 South Wootton PE30 . . . . .148 D1
Barleycroft NR29 . . . . . .167 B7
Barleyfield Rd 8 NR10. . .53 A3
Barleyview 10 NR29 . . . .57 D2
Barley Way
 Attleborough NR17 . . . . . .174 B3
 Thetford IP24 . . . . .176 D6
BARMER PE31 . . . . .14 F4
Barmer Rd Barmer PE31. . .14 E4
 South Creake PE31. . . . . . . .15 B6
Barnaby Cl 5 NR9 . . . . .154 C3
Barnard Ave NR30 . . . . .169 D7
Barnard Cl
 Great Yarmouth NR31 . . . .170 C1
 5 Stoke Holy Cross NR14 .89 F4
Barnard Cres NR30 . . . . .169 C7
Barnard Rd Norwich NR5 .160 E8
 Norwich NR5 . . . . .160 F8
Barnards La PE33 . . . . . . .61 D6
Barnards Rd NR28 . . . . . .38 A5
Barnards Yd 8 NR3. . . .178 A3
Barnaway La NR25. . . . . . . .7 F1
Barnby Rd NR10 . . . . .37 B2
Barn Cl
 2 Hopton on Sea NR31. .171 E5
 1 Lingwood NR13 . . . . . .74 A3
Barn Drift NR25. . . . . .7 F6
Barnes Cl Brandon IP27 . .175 A2
 Norwich NR7 . . . . .159 D2
 Wymondham NR18 . . . . . .173 F7
Barnesdale Rd 5 NR4 . . .89 E8
Barnes' Rd IP21 . . . . .121 E5
BARNEY NR21 . . . . .17 F3
Barney Rd NR21 . . . . .17 F2
Barnfield Cl NR12. . . . . . .39 E2
BARNHAM IP24. . . . . . . .125 F6
Barnham Broom Prim Sch
 NR9. . . . . .69 C2
BARNHAM BROOM NR9 . .69 C2
Barnham Broom Rd
 Barford NR9. . . . . .69 C2
 Carleton Forehoe NR9. . . . .69 C1
 Coston NR9 . . . . .87 A8
 East Tuddenham NR20. . . . .69 D5
 Wymondham NR18 . . . . . .173 A7
Barnham CE Prim Sch
 IP24 . . . . .125 E5
Barnham Rd
 Barnham IP24 . . . . .126 B6
 Elveden IP27 . . . . .125 A6
Barn Hill NR13. . . . . .73 E2
Barnigham Rd NR11 . . . .20 B5
BARNINGHAM IP31. . . . .127 C3
Barningham CE VC Prim Sch
 IP31. . . . . .127 C3
BARNINGHAM GREEN
 NR11. . . . . .20 A4
Barningham Pk NR11. . . .20 C6
Barningham Pl NR11. . . . .20 C5
Barningham Rd
 Edgefield NR24 . . . . .19 E4
 Gresham NR11. . . . . .20 D8
 Matlask NR11 . . . . .20 C7
 Matlaske NR11 . . . . .20 D6
 Stanton IP31. . . . . .127 C1
Barn La Gressenhall NR19 . .49 B2
 Intwood NR4 . . . . .89 C7
 Mautby NR29 . . . . .75 E6
Barn Mdw NR14 . . . . . . .163 B2
Barn Owl Cl
 Hopton on Sea NR31. . . . .171 D4
 Reedham NR13 . . . . .92 F4
Barn Owl Dr NR25. . . . . .137 D6
Barn Piece Cl 9 NR13. . .55 A1
Barn Rd Docking PE31. . . .134 F4
 Norwich NR2 . . . . .178 A4
Barns The NR16. . . . . . . .105 C4
Barn Terr NR13 . . . . .165 C4
Barn View NR10 . . . . .53 B2
Barnwell Rd PE30. . . . . .147 B6

Barondole La
 Alburgh IP20. . . . . .122 E8
 Topcroft NR35 . . . . .107 C2
Baron's Cl NR21 . . . . . . .141 C4
Baron's Hall La NR21 . . .141 D4
Barrack Rd
 Great Yarmouth NR30 . . . .169 D1
 Norwich NR1 . . . . .72 A4
 Norwich NR1 . . . . .163 B7
Barrack St NR3 . . . . .178 C4
Barr Dr IP27. . . . . .113 E2
Barrett Cl PE30 . . . . .147 E5
Barrett-Lennard Rd
 NR10. . . . . .53 A4
Barrett Rd Holt NR25 . . . .137 D7
 Norwich NR1 . . . . .162 E1
Barretts La IP26 . . . . .98 E1
Barri Cl NR14. . . . . .90 C3
Barroway Dro PE38 . . . . .78 E6
Barrow Cl NR3. . . . . .157 F1
Barrow's Cnr IP24 . . . . . .125 A4
Barrows Hole La PE32. . . .65 E7
Barsham Cl NR21 . . . . . . .30 C4
Barsham Dr PE30 . . . . . .148 E1
Barsham Ford Rd NR22. . .16 D5
Barsham Rd
 Great Snoring NR21 . . . . . .17 A5
 Houghton St Giles NR22 . . .16 E6
 North Barsham NR22 . . . . .16 D5
 Sculthorpe NR21 . . . . .141 A7
 West Barsham NR21. . . . . .16 C3
Bartle La NR10 . . . . .149 C5
BARTON BENDISH PE33. . .81 A8
Barton Broad Nature
 Reserve* NR12 . . . . .55 F7
Barton Cl
 North Walsham NR28 . . . .151 A4
 Swaffham PE37 . . . . .153 C2
Barton Ct PE30 . . . . .147 D5
Barton Dr NR12. . . . . . . .164 E6
Barton La NR12. . . . . .39 C8
Barton Rd
 Ashmanhaugh NR12 . . . . . .38 D1
 Coltishall NR10 . . . . .37 B2
 Wisbech PE13 . . . . .152 A4
Bartons Dro PE38. . . . . .172 A5
Barton's La PE32. . . . . . . .48 A8
BARTON TURF NR12 . . . . .38 F1
Barton Way
 6 Norwich NR1 . . . . .163 B5
 Ormesby St Margaret
 NR29 . . . . .167 B3
Bartram Cl NR18. . . . . . .173 F7
Bartrums Mews IP22. . . .177 F3
Barwick Rd Barwick PE31. . .14 E5
 Barwick PE31. . . . . .14 E6
Bases La NR23 . . . . .136 C6
Basey Rd NR13 . . . . .72 E8
Basham St IP22. . . . . . . .177 B4
Basil Dr PE38 . . . . .172 E6
Basil Rd PE33. . . . . .80 A3
Basin Rd PE14 . . . . .77 E7
Bassingham Rd NR3 . . . .158 B2
BASTWICK NR29. . . . . . . .57 A4
Batchcroft Cl 6 PE38. . .172 C6
Batchelor Dr NR21 . . . . . .15 C2
Bately Ave NR31. . . . . . .170 D1
Bateman Cl 3 NR5 . . . .160 F7
Bates Gn NR5. . . . . .161 C8
Bates La Beeston PE32. . . .48 D2
 Bressingham IP22 . . . . . . .119 D2
Bath Ave NR20 . . . . .154 F5
Bath Hill 7 NR30 . . . . . .169 D3
Bath Hills Rd
 Earsham NR35. . . . . .108 A3
 Earsham NR35. . . . . .123 E8
Bath Rd
 West Dereham PE33. . . . . . .80 D5
 Wisbech PE13 . . . . .152 C7
Bathurst Rd 2 NR22. . . .162 B5
Batley Gn
 Fakenham NR21. . . . . .141 A3
 Hempton NR21. . . . . .31 C8
Battery Rd NR30. . . . . . .170 D8
BATTLESEA GREEN
 IP21. . . . . .131 E2
Battlesea Hill IP21. . . . .131 E2
BAWBURGH NR9 . . . . . . .160 B6
Bawburgh Cl NR5. . . . . .156 D1
Bawburgh La NR5. . . . . .156 D1
Bawburgh Rd NR9 . . . . . .70 B5
Bawburgh Sch The NR9 .160 B6
BAWDESWELL NR20 . . . . .50 E7
Bawdeswell Com Prim Sch
 NR20. . . . . .50 E7
Bawdeswell Rd
 Billingford NR20. . . . . .50 C7
 Reepham NR20 . . . . .34 B1
BAWSEY PE32. . . . . .44 D6
Bawsey Cl PE30. . . . . . . .146 F6
Bawsey Ctry Pk* PE32. . .44 D6
Baxter Cl 2 Hingham NR9 .86 C5
 Long Stratton NR15. . . . . .106 E2
 3 Wisbech PE13 . . . . . . .152 E6
Baxter Ct
 Caister-On-Sea NR30. . . . .168 E6
 Norwich NR3 . . . . .158 B3
Baxter Rd NR9 . . . . .86 C5
Baxter Row NR19 . . . . . .154 D4
Baxter's La NR15. . . . . . .107 F8
Baxter's Lane NR15 . . . .108 A7
Bayes La NR28 . . . . .151 B3
Bayes Rd NR16 . . . . .106 C6
Bayfield Rd NR17 . . . . . .174 E6
Bay Field NR20 . . . . .69 C6
Bayfield Ave 3 NR19. . .154 C3
Bayfield Cl
 1 Ixworth NR9 . . . . .69 F2
 King's Lynn PE30 . . . . . . .147 D4

Bayfield Pk NR25 . . . . .7 E3
Bayfield Way PE37 . . . . .153 C2
Baynard's La IP22 . . . . . .129 D7
Baynes La NR14. . . . . . . .90 C4
Bays Cl PE30. . . . . .146 F7
Bayspole Rd 5 NR15. . . .106 E3
Bay Willow La NR12. . . . .54 B2
Bay Wlk PE38. . . . . .172 E6
Bazzy La NR14 . . . . .7 D4
BEACHAMWELL PE37. . . . .81 F8
Beachamwell Rd
 Beachamwell PE37. . . . . . . .63 E1
 Beachamwell PE37. . . . . . . .81 F8
 Shingham PE37. . . . . .82 A8
 Swaffham PE37 . . . . .153 C1
Beach Cl Hemsby NR29. . .167 E3
 Mundesley NR11 . . . . .143 C6
 Overstrand NR27. . . . . .11 A4
Beach Dr NR29 . . . . .167 E4
Beach La NR25 . . . . .8 E3
Beach Rd Bacton NR12. . . .23 E5
 Caister-on-Sea NR30. . . . .168 E5
 Cley next the Sea NR25. . . . .7 E8
 Cromer NR27 . . . . .139 B7
 Eccles on Sea NR12. . . . . . .24 E4
 3 Great Yarmouth NR31 .170 D4
 Happisburgh NR12 . . . . . . .24 C5
 Hemsby NR29 . . . . .167 C7
 Holme next the Sea PE36 . . .1 F6
 Hopton on Sea NR31 . . . . .171 E4
 Mundesley NR11 . . . . .24 E3
 Mundesley NR11 . . . . .143 C6
 Runton NR27 . . . . .10 C5
 Salthouse NR25. . . . . .8 C6
 Sea Palling NR12 . . . . .40 A6
 Sheringham NR26 . . . . . . .138 E7
 Snettisham PE31. . . . . .12 A4
 Wells-next-the-Sea NR23 . .136 C7
 Winterton-on-Sea NR29 . . .58 B6
Beach Terr 8 NR1 . . . . .163 B5
Beacon Bsns Pk NR31. . .171 B8
Beacon Hill PE31 . . . . . .135 C2
Beacon Hill Rd PE34. . . .144 A6
Beacon Hill PE31 . . . . . .135 C1
Beacon Rd NR11 . . . . .11 F1
Beaconsfield Rd
 Great Yarmouth NR30 . . . .169 D6
 Norwich NR3 . . . . .162 E8
Bean Goose Row 19
 NR7 . . . . .159 E4
Bean's La IP22. . . . . .129 D3
Bears Cl 7 NR9. . . . . . . .86 C4
Bears La NR9 . . . . .86 C5
Bear's La PE37. . . . . .153 B5
Bears Rd NR28. . . . . .143 D2
Beatie Gdns NR20. . . . . . .49 F7
Beatrice Ave NR19 . . . . .154 D4
Beatrice Cl 8 NR28. . . . .151 C6
Beatrice Rd
 Norwich NR1 . . . . .163 A6
 Wisbech PE13 . . . . .152 D7
Beatty Cl
 Great Yarmouth NR30 . . . .169 D8
 Thetford IP24 . . . . .176 E5
Beatty Rd
 Great Yarmouth NR30 . . . .169 D8
 Norwich NR4 . . . . .162 B1
Beauchamp Cl
 1 Caister-on-Sea NR30. .168 D7
 Chedgrave NR14 . . . . .91 F2
Beauchamp Rd 2 NR14. .92 A2
Beaufort Cl NR6 . . . . . . .158 D6
Beaufort Way
 Great Yarmouth NR31 . . . .170 B1
 Hopton on Sea NR31. . . . .171 B8
Beaumont Pl 1 NR2 . . .162 C4
Beaumont Rd NR5 . . . . . .157 B1
Beaumont Way NR5. . . . .147 C5
Beaupre Ave PE14 . . . . . .77 F7
Beaupré Com Prim Sch
 PE14. . . . . .77 F6
Beavans Ct 8 NR31. . . . .169 B4
Beavens Ct 15 NR31 . . . .169 B4
Beavor La IP27 . . . . .175 C4
Beccles Rd Aldeby NR34. .110 F4
 Aldeby, Wheatacre, Burgh St
 Peter NR34 . . . . .111 A3
 Belton with Browston NR31 .94 A5
 Bungay NR35. . . . . .124 B8
 Burgh Castle NR31 . . . . . . .93 F7
 Carlton Colville NR33. . . . .111 F1
 Fritton & St Olaves NR31 . . .93 E3
 Great Yarmouth NR31 . . . .170 A5
 Haddiscoe NR14 . . . . .110 E7
 Hales NR14 . . . . .109 E7
 Loddon NR14 . . . . .92 A1
 Loddon NR14 . . . . .109 E8
 Mettingham NR35 . . . . . . .109 D1
 Raveningham NR14 . . . . . .110 A7
 Thurlton NR14 . . . . .92 F1
Beccles Sta NR34. . . . . .110 D1
Beccles The NR14 . . . . . .109 D8
Dickleburgh IP21. . . . . . . .121 C1
Beech Wlk
 Framingham Earl NR14. . . . .90 D5
 Keswick NR4 . . . . .89 C7
Beechwood Ave
 Aylmerton NR11. . . . . .10 A3
 18 Watton IP25. . . . . .84 D7
Beechwood Cl
 North Walsham NR28 . . . .151 D6
 Watlington PE33 . . . . .61 E5
Beechwood Ct NR18 . . . .173 D1
Beechwood Dr NR7. . . . .159 E1
Beechwood Rd
 Hemsby NR29 . . . . .167 A8
 Wisbech PE13 . . . . .152 D7
Beechwoods NR6. . . . . . .158 D5
Beehive The NR14 . . . . . .109 D8
Beehive Yd IP27 . . . . . . .177 C4
Beeleigh Way NR30 . . . .168 C7
Bee Orchid Way NR13. . . .91 C7
Beerlicks La NR14 . . . . . .165 C1
Beerlick's Loke NR14 . . .73 B1
BEESTON PE32 . . . . .48 C2
Beeston Comm NR26 . . .138 E6
Beeston Hall Sch
 Beeston Regis NR27 . . . . . .9 F5
 West Runton NR27 . . . . .9 F5
Beeston La
 Barton Turf NR12. . . . . . . .38 D1

Beck La
 Burgh & Tuttington NR11. . .36 E6
 Horsham St Faith & Newton St
 Faith NR10. . . . . .53 D2
Beckmeadow Way
 NR11. . . . . .143 C5
Becks Fur 2 NR8 . . . . . .155 E2
Becks Gn La NR34. . . . . .124 F4
Beckside NR10 . . . . .53 A2
Beck St IP22. . . . . .127 E3
Beck The Feltwell IP26 . . . .98 E1
 Kenninghall NR16. . . . . . . .119 A5
Beck View 3 IP20. . . . . .122 D2
Beck Way NR14 . . . . .91 F1
Bedding La NR3. . . . . . . .178 B4
Bede Cl PE30 . . . . .148 C4
Bedford Bank
 Manea PE15. . . . . .95 B3
 Welney PE14 . . . . .95 D4
Bedford Dr PE30 . . . . . . .148 B1
Bedford Mews NR26 . . . .138 D6
Bedford Row PE14 . . . . . .41 A4
Bedford St Norwich NR2. .178 B3
 Wisbech PE13 . . . . .152 C6
Bedingfield 6 NR20 . . . .50 B3
Bedingfields
 Earlham NR2 . . . . .161 F4
 Norwich NR1 . . . . .161 F4
 Norwich NR4 . . . . .161 F4
BEDINGHAM GREEN
 NR35. . . . . .108 B3
Beechamwell Rd PE33 . . .81 B8
Beechan Dr PE30 . . . . . .147 D3
Beech Ave
 Attleborough NR17 . . . . . .174 C4
 King's Lynn PE30 . . . . . . .148 D2
 7 Marham PE33. . . . . . . .63 B4
 Sheringham NR26 . . . . . . .138 D5
 Taverham NR8 . . . . .155 B1
Beechbank NR2 . . . . .162 B4
Beechbank Dr 6 NR13. . .72 D6
Beech Cl Gimingham NR11 . .22 E7
 1 Gresham NR11. . . . . .9 E1
 Hellesdon NR6. . . . . .157 E3
 High Kelling NR25 . . . . .8 E2
 Loddon NR14 . . . . .92 A1
 Scole IP21. . . . . .130 C5
 Sporle PE32. . . . . .65 C6
 Swaffham PE37 . . . . .153 C4
 Thetford IP24 . . . . .176 B2
 Wymondham NR18 . . . . . .173 D6
Beech Cres 6 PE33 . . . . .43 E2
Beechcroft NR5. . . . . . . .156 F1
Beech Croft IP22 . . . . . . .128 E8
Beech Ct
 24 Long Stratton NR15. . .106 E3
 Swaffham PE33 . . . . .154 D5
 Taverham NR8 . . . . .155 A1
Beech Dr
 East Dereham NR19 . . . . . .154 C4
 North Walsham NR28 . . . .151 B6
 Norwich NR1 . . . . .163 A8
 Norwich NR1 . . . . .162 B4
 Norwich NR6 . . . . .71 E6
 Norwich NR6 . . . . .158 C4
 Strumpshaw NR13 . . . . . . .73 F3
Beech Drift PE31. . . . . . .140 D3
Beecheno Rd NR5 . . . . . .157 B4
Beeches Cl NR6. . . . . . . .158 E4
Beeches La
 Hardingham NR9. . . . . .86 E6
 Pulham St Mary IP21. . . . .121 F3
Beeches The 1 NR20 . . . .68 E6
Beechey Cl PE38 . . . . . . .172 C5
Beechfields IP27 . . . . . . .175 F4
Beech Gr NR21 . . . . .141 E4
Beeching Cl 1 NR1 . . . . .162 E1
Beeching Rd NR1 . . . . . .162 E2
Beech La Erpingham NR11 . .21 A1
 Fleggborough NR29. . . . . . .75 C8
Beechlands NR8 . . . . . . .155 B1
Beechlands Pk NR11. . . . .22 E7
Beech Rd Beetley NR20. . . .49 D4
 Downham Market PE38. . .172 B6
 King's Lynn PE30 . . . . . . .146 E3
 Wroxham/Hoveton NR12 .164 D3
Beech Rise 23 NR31 . . . .94 C7
Beech Tree Wy 10 NR35. .123 F8
Beech Way
 Brundall NR13 . . . . .165 C3

Beeston La continued
 Beeston St Andrew NR12 .159 B8
 Fransham NR19 . . . . .66 B8
Beeston Prim Sch NR26. .48 C2
Beeston Rd
 Beeston with Bittering
 PE32. . . . . .48 D1
 Great Dunham PE32 . . . . . .47 F1
 Great Dunham PE32 . . . . . .65 F8
 Great Dunham PE32 . . . . . .66 A8
 Mileham PE32 . . . . .48 D5
 Sheringham NR26 . . . . . . .138 E7
BEESTON REGIS NR26. . .138 F5
BEESTON ST LAWRENCE
 NR12 . . . . .55 C8
BEETLEY NR20. . . . . .49 D4
Beetley Grange 1 NR20. .49 D4
Beetley Mdws 9 NR20. . .49 D4
Beetley Rd
 Dereham NR19 . . . . .154 D8
 Northall Green NR19. . . . . .49 F2
Beevor Rd NR30 . . . . . . .170 E7
Begdale Rd PE14 . . . . . . .59 A1
Begonia Wy NR18 . . . . . .173 F7
BEIGHTON NR13 . . . . .74 C2
Beighton Rd NR13 . . . . .166 A2
Bek Cl NR4 . . . . .161 E2
BELAUGH NR12 . . . . .54 E5
Belaugh Gn La NR12 . . .164 A8
Belaugh La NR12 . . . . . . .55 A7
Belaugh Rd NR12 . . . . . .136 D5
Belfry CE VA Prim Sch
 NR27 . . . . .11 A3
Belgrave Ave NR36. . . . .132 C6
Belgrave Gdns NR19 . . . .154 E3
Bellacre Cl IP22 . . . . . . .177 E4
Bellamy Cl NR31. . . . . . .170 A3
Bellamy's La
 Burnham Norton PE31. . . .135 C5
 West Walton PE14. . . . . . . .59 A8
Bellamy Way NR14 . . . . .90 C4
Bellands Way 4 IP23 . . .130 C1
Bell Cl
 13 Bawdeswell NR20. . . . .50 E7
 East Dereham NR19 . . . . . .154 C5
 Little Snoring NR21. . . . . . .17 B3
 Norwich NR6 . . . . .157 E5
 Taverham NR8 . . . . .156 E8
Belle of the East Way
 NR31. . . . . .94 A5
Bellibone Gdns NR17. . . .174 F2
Bell La Rocklands NR17 . . .103 B8
 Saham Toney IP25. . . . . . . .84 C4
 Salhouse NR13 . . . . .148 A1
Bellmere Way IP25 . . . . . .84 C4
 9 Marthan NR29 . . . . . . .57 D5
BELLMOUNT PE34 . . . . . .144 A7
Bellomonte Cres NR8 . . .156 F8
Bell Rd
 Barnham Broom NR9. . . . . .69 B2
 Grimston PE32. . . . . .28 C1
 Norwich NR3 . . . . .158 E1
 Rocklands NR17 . . . . .103 B8
Bellrope Cl 5 NR18. . . . .173 D5
Bellrope La Roydon IP22 .129 D7
 Wymondham NR18 . . . . . .173 D5
Bell's Dro Littleport CB6. . .95 E2
 Runton Holme PE33. . . . . . .61 C5
 9 Marthan NR29 . . . . . . .57 D5
Bells La Hinderclay IP22 . .128 C4
 Norwich NR31. . . . . .32 E6
Bells Loke NR13 . . . . . . .165 D3
Bell's Marsh Rd NR31 . . .170 D5
Bell's Mdw 2 PE37. . . . . .66 A4
Bells Rd NR31 . . . . .170 D4
Bell St PE26. . . . . .98 E1
Bellview Cl NR24. . . . . . .142 B4
Bellville Cres NR1. . . . . .178 C1
Belmore Rd NR7 . . . . . . .159 E1
Belmore Rd NR7 . . . . . . .163 F8
Beloe Av 4 NR5. . . . . . . .161 A7
Beloe Cres PE30 . . . . . . .146 D1
Belseybridge Rd NR35. . .108 F3
Belsize Cl 4 PE38 . . . . . .172 B4
Belsize Rd NR31 . . . . . . .163 B7
Belstead Ave NR30. . . . .168 D5
BELTON NR31 . . . . .94 A6
Belton New Rd NR31. . . .94 A5
Belt Rd NR13 . . . . .73 C7
Belvedere La
 Hockwold cum Wilton
 IP26. . . . . .99 B1
 Weeting IP27. . . . . .114 C8
Belvedere Pl 3 NR4 . . . .162 A3
Belvidere Rd NR30. . . . . .169 D5
Belvoir St NR2 . . . . .162 A3
Benbow Cl 6 NR9 . . . . . .88 E8
Benbow Rd PE34 . . . . . . .146 F8
Ben Culey Dr IP24 . . . . . .176 C5
Bendish Ave NR31 . . . . . .170 D2
Bendish Way NR5. . . . . . .160 E7
Benedict Cl 3 NR28 . . . .145 F5
Benedict Rd 10 NR1. . . . .55 E4
Benets View 3 NR28. . . .151 E5
BENGATE NR28 . . . . .38 A6
Bengey's Rd 7 PE37. . . . .65 F4
Benjamin Ct NR27 . . . . . .139 B5
Benjamin Gooch Wy
 NR2 . . . . .178 A1
Bennett Cl
 Hunstanton PE36 . . . . .132 D2
 3 Watlington PE33. . . . . . .61 D5
Bennett Cres NR9 . . . . . .160 C5
Bennett Mws PE13. . . . . .152 C6
Bennett Rd NR20 . . . . . . .50 B2
Bennett St NR28 . . . . . . .172 A5
Bennington's La
 Aylmerton NR11. . . . . .138 F1
 East Beckham NR11 . . . . . .9 D2

Benn's La PE34 . . . . .144 C5
Ben's La PE33 . . . . .80 E4
Bensley Cl NR13 . . . . . . .166 C4
Bensley Rd
 1 Marthan NR29 . . . . . . .57 D5
 Norwich NR29 . . . . .162 A4
Benstead Cl PE21 . . . . . .133 D5
Bentick Dock PE30. . . . . .146 D6
Bentinck Way 2 PE34 . . .146 C5
Bentley Cl NR16. . . . . . . .105 F4
Bentley Way NR1. . . . . . .158 C4
Bentons Way NR10. . . . . .53 B8
Berberis Gn 3 NR31. . . .170 B5
Beresford Rd
 Caister-on-Sea NR30. . . . .168 E4
 Great Yarmouth NR30 . . . .169 D7
 Holt NR25. . . . . .137 C5
Bergamot Cl IP24. . . . . . .176 F4
Bergen Way PE30 . . . . . .146 F8
BERGH APTON NR15. . . . .91 A4
Berghapton Rd NR15. . . .91 D2
Berkeley Cl NR13 . . . . . . .90 F4
Berkley Way PE30 . . . . . .162 A4
Bermondsey Pl E 19
 NR30 . . . . .169 D4
Bermondsey Pl S 18
 NR30 . . . . .169 D4
Bermondsey Pl W 17
 NR30 . . . . .169 D4
Bernard Cl
 High Kelling NR25 . . . . .8 E2
 11 New Rackheath NR13 . .72 E7
Bernard Cres PE36. . . . . .132 C6
Bernard Rd
 Cromer NR27 . . . . .139 A7
 Great Yarmouth NR31 . . . .170 D2
Berners St NR3 . . . . .158 B1
Berners St NR3 . . . . .158 B1
Berney Arms Sta NR3 . . .93 D8
Berney Arms Windmill*
 NR30 . . . . .93 E7
Bernham Rd NR6 . . . . . . .157 E6
Berrington Rd NR6. . . . . .157 F6
Berry Cl NR31. . . . . .93 F6
Berryfields NR13 . . . . . . .165 C5
Berry Hall Rd NR12. . . . . .38 E1
Berry's La NR9. . . . . .69 C3
Ber St NR1 . . . . .178 B1
Bertie Rd NR3 . . . . .158 C1
Bertie Ward Way NR19. . .154 F2
Bertram Wy NR1. . . . . . .163 A6
Berwick Cl NR24 . . . . . . .142 E4
Berwick Ct NR14. . . . . . . .90 C5
Bessemer Rd NR4. . . . . . .162 D1
Bessemer Way NR31 . . . .169 B1
Bessey Cl NR29 . . . . .75 C8
BESSINGHAM NR11. . . . . .20 E7
Bessingham Rd
 Bessingham NR11. . . . . . . .20 D5
 Bessingham NR11. . . . . . . .20 F6
BESTHORPE NR17 . . . . . .174 F6
Besthorpe Rd NR17 . . . . .174 E5
Besthorpe Rd NR16 . . . . .105 A5
Bethel St NR2 . . . . .178 A3
Betjeman Cl IP24 . . . . . .176 E6
Betsy Cl NR5. . . . . .161 C6
Beulah St PE30 . . . . .147 B6
Bevan Cl
 Carleton Rode NR16 . . . . .105 C4
 Norwich NR5 . . . . .71 A3
 Norwich NR5 . . . . .161 B6
Beveridge Way PE33 . . . .43 E4
Beverley Cl NR5 . . . . . . .161 E6
Beverley Rd
 Brundall NR13 . . . . .165 B4
 Norwich NR5 . . . . .161 E6
Beverley Way
 Clenchwarton PE34. . . . . .145 E5
 Taverham NR8 . . . . .156 F8
Beverly Ct NR31. . . . . . . .170 A7
Bevis Way PE30. . . . . . . .147 B7
Bewfield Rd 4 NR5 . . . . .160 E8
Bewick Cl
 11 Great Yarmouth NR31 .94 C8
 5 Snettisham PE31. . . . . .12 C5
Bewit Rd NR7. . . . . .159 D4
Bexfield Cl NR20. . . . . . . .33 C4
Bexfield Rd NR20 . . . . . . .33 C4
BEXWELL PE38 . . . . .79 F5
Bexwell La PE38. . . . . . . .79 F5
Bexwell Rd Bexwell PE38. . .79 F6
 Crimplesham PE33 . . . . . . .80 A6
 Downham Market PE38. . .172 D5
Bickley Cl NR17. . . . . . . .174 F7
Bide A Wee Cl IP29 . . . . .99 A7
Bidewell Cl Drayton NR8. .71 A8
 Taverham NR8 . . . . .157 B7
Bidwell Rd NR13 . . . . . . .72 E8
Bidwels ct IP24. . . . . . . .176 C4
Bier La IP22 . . . . .128 F5
Biffin Way PE37 . . . . . . .153 C2
Biffin Wy PE37. . . . . .153 C1
Big Back La 1 NR14 . . . .92 A2
Biggin Hill Way IP25 . . . .85 A3
Biggotts La NR15 . . . . . .108 E7
Biggs Rd PE14 . . . . .59 D4
Bignold Prim Sch NR2 . .178 A2
Bignold Rd NR3. . . . . . . .158 A2
Bigod Rd 8 NR35 . . . . . . .124 B8
Big Row NR34 . . . . .109 F2
Bigods La PE32 . . . . .46 F1
Big Wood La
 South Acre PE32 . . . . .64 E3
 South Acre PE32 . . . . .64 F3
Big Yard PE36. . . . . .2 A3
Big Yard The PE36. . . . . .132 E7

Bilberry Cl **5** NR17 . . . . . 174 B5
Bilbys NR14 . . . . 110 B6
Billing Cl NR6 . . . . 158 F5
BILLINGFORD
  Billingford NR20 . . . . 50 B7
  Dickleburgh and Rushall
  IP21 . . . . 130 E5
Billingford Rd
  1 Bawdeswell NR20 . . . . . 50 E7
  Bintree NR20 . . . . 33 B1
  North Elmham NR20 . . . . . 49 F7
BILLOCKBY NR29 . . . . . . 75 A7
Bill Todd Way NR8 . . . . . 155 C2
Billy Emms Ct IP26 . . . . . 100 B4
Bilney La NR10 . . . . 155 E8
Bilney Rd Beetley NR20 . . . 49 B4
  East Winch PE32 . . . . . . 45 B1
  Pentney PE32 . . . . 63 C8
Bingles Turn NR10 . . . . . 53 B7
BINHAM NR21 . . . . 6 E2
Binham La NR25 . . . . 7 A6
Binham Priory ★ NR21 . . . . 6 E2
Binham Rd
  Binham NR21 . . . . 6 E1
  Field Dalling NR25 . . . . . 7 A1
  Hindringham NR21 . . . . . 17 E8
  4 King's Lynn PE30 . . . . 148 C3
  Langham NR25 . . . . 7 A4
  Warham NR22 . . . . 6 B3
  Warham NR23 . . . . 6 A4
Binney Rd Drayton NR8 . . . 71 A8
  Drayton NR8 . . . . 157 A8
Binsley Cl NR29 . . . . 40 D2
BINTREE NR20 . . . . 33 B2
Bintree Rd
  Billingford NR20 . . . . . . 50 B8
  Foulsham NR20 . . . . 33 D3
Binyon Gdns NR8 . . . . . . 156 D8
Birbeck Rd NR1 . . . . 162 E2
Bircham Cl NR12 . . . . . . 164 B2
BIRCHAM NEWTON PE31 . 14 A4
Bircham Rd
  Docking PE31 . . . . 134 C4
  Fring PE31 . . . . 13 D5
  Great Bircham PE31 . . . . 14 B1
  Harpley PE31 . . . . 29 B6
  Houghton PE31 . . . . 29 B7
  Reepham NR10 . . . . . . 149 C5
  Snettisham PE31 . . . . . . 13 A4
  Stanhoe PE31 . . . . 14 E7
BIRCHAM TOFTS PE31 . . 14 B3
Bircham Windmill ★
  PE31 . . . . 14 A3
Birch Ave **8** NR20 . . . . . . 49 D4
Birch Cl
  East Dereham NR19 . . . . 154 C4
  Little Melton NR9 . . . . . . 70 E1
  Little Melton NR9 . . . . . 160 D2
  North Walsham NR28 . . . 151 D6
  6 Snettisham PE31 . . . . 12 E4
Birch Covert **5** IP24 . . . . 176 F5
Birch Cres IP27 . . . . 113 E2
Birch Ct Erpingham NR11 . . 21 B2
  Norwich NR7 . . . . 159 D4
Birch Dr
  Attleborough NR17 . . . . 174 C3
  Roydon PE32 . . . . 28 A2
Birches The PE30 . . . . . . 148 D4
Birchfield Gdns NR14 . . . . 89 B3
Birchfield La NR14 . . . . . . 89 B3
Birchfield Rd PE38 . . . . . . 78 E3
Birch Gr
  Sheringham NR26 . . . . . 138 D4
  West Winch PE33 . . . . . . 43 E2
  Wisbech PE14 . . . . 59 B1
Birchgrove Rd PE30 . . . . 147 C4
Birch Rd Gayton PE32 . . . . 45 C6
  11 Hethersett NR9 . . . . . 88 D8
Birch Tree Cl PE30 . . . . . 146 E4
Birch Way
  4 Great Yarmouth
  NR31 . . . . 170 B3
  Mundham NR14 . . . . . . 108 F6
  Thurton NR15 . . . . 91 D2
Birchwood **4** NR7 . . . . . 72 D3
Birchwood Rd
  Helleston NR6 . . . . 157 E4
  Norwich NR6 . . . . 71 C6
Birchwood St **5** NR6 . . . 146 E6
Birchwood Way PE38 . . . 172 B6
Birdbeck Dr PE14 . . . . . . 77 E7
Birdcage Wlk PE30 . . . . . 146 D3
Bird Cl IP24 . . . . 176 A4
Bird Cl **4** NR6 . . . . 146 C5
Birds Cnr IP25 . . . . 67 E4
Birds La Cawston NR11 . . . 35 B3
  Horning NR12 . . . . 55 E5
Bird's La NR20 . . . . 50 A3
Birds Rd NR28 . . . . 151 B3
Bird View Sq **1** IP26 . . . . 98 E1
Birkbeck Cl
  King's Lynn PE30 . . . . . 148 B2
  Norwich NR18 . . . . 162 E2
  Stoke Holy Cross NR14 . . . 90 B5
Birkbeck Way NR7 . . . . . 163 F7
Birkdale NR4 . . . . 162 A2
Birkin Cl **3** NR16 . . . . . 105 F5
Birtles Way NR13 . . . . . . 166 C3
Biscay Gdns NR30 . . . . . 168 C6
Bishop Bonner's Cottage
  Mus ★ NR19 . . . . 154 D5
Bishop Bridge Rd NR1 . . . 163 A6
Bishopgate NR1 . . . . 178 C3
Bishop Herbert Cl NR20 . . 50 C3
Bishop Rise **3** NR8 . . . . 155 E2
Bishop's CE Prim Sch The
  IP24 . . . . 176 B4
Bishop's Cl NR7 . . . . 163 D5
Bishops Croft IP31 . . . . . 127 C4

Bishop's Rd
  Hunstanton PE36 . . . . . 132 C2
Bishops Wlk **5** NR3 . . . . 171 D5
Bishoptyne Ave **1**
  NR19 . . . . 154 F3
Bishy Barnebee Way
  NR5 . . . . 160 F6
Bishy Barny Bee Gdns
  PE37 . . . . 153 C1
BITTERING NR19 . . . . . . 48 F4
Bittering La
  Bittering NR19 . . . . 48 F4
  Longham NR19 . . . . 49 A3
Bittering St
  4 Beetley NR20 . . . . . . 49 C4
  4 Gressenhall NR20 . . . . 49 C3
  Necton PE37 . . . . 66 A3
  Thetford IP24 . . . . 176 D1
Bittern Cres NR12 . . . . . . 38 F1
Bittern Rd NR29 . . . . 57 D3
Bittern St NR8 . . . . 156 B5
Bittern Way NR18 . . . . . 173 D1
Bixley Cl NR5 . . . . 161 D6
Blackbarn Rd NR16 . . . . 120 D8
Black Bear La PE13 . . . . 152 F7
Blackberry Cl NR6 . . . . . 157 F2
Blackberry Gr NR27 . . . . . 10 C4
Blackberry Hall La NR11 . . 11 D1
Blackberry Way PE37 . . . 153 C1
Blackbird Ave IP27 . . . . . 175 F3
Blackbird Cl **17** NR31 . . . . 94 C8
Blackbird Wy **17** IP20 . . . 122 D1
BLACKBOROUGH END
  PE33 . . . . 44 C1
Blackbreck La NR9 . . . . . 52 A1
Blackburn Rd NR6 . . . . . 158 C6
BLACK CARR NR17 . . . . 105 A6
Black Carr NR17 . . . . . . 105 A6
Blackdike Dro IP27 . . . . . 112 F5
Black Drif PE37 . . . . 66 A4
Black Dro
  Downham West PE38 . . . . 79 B6
  Feltwell PE38 . . . . 97 F2
  Fincham PE33 . . . . 80 D7
  Marshland St James PE14 . 60 D4
  Stow Bardolph PE34 . . . . 78 E8
Blackdyke Cl **8** IP26 . . . . 98 D1
Black Dyke Rd
  Feltwell IP26 . . . . 98 D1
  Hockwold cum Wilton
  IP26 . . . . 113 E7
Blackford PE30 . . . . 147 D8
Blackfriars Rd
  King's Lynn PE30 . . . . . 146 E5
  8 Wisbech PE13 . . . . . 152 C5
Blackfriars' Rd NR30 . . . . 169 D2
Blackfriars St
  King's Lynn PE30 . . . . . 146 D4
  Norwich NR3 . . . . 178 B4
Black Hall La NR16 . . . . 105 C8
Blackhill Wood Ln NR8 . . 156 A5
Blackhorse Cl **9** NR20 . . . 50 E7
Black Horse Cl NR19 . . . . 67 B7
Black Horse Dro CB6 . . . . 96 E2
Blackhorse Mdw **10**
  NR20 . . . . 50 E7
Black Horse Opening
  NR6 . . . . 158 F2
Black Horse Rd
  Clenchwarton PE34 . . . . 145 C4
  Runhall NR9 . . . . 68 F1
  Skeyton NR10 . . . . 37 B4
Blackhorse St **1** NR2 . . . 162 C7
Blackhorse Yd NR23 . . . . 136 C6
Black Mill La NR15 . . . . . 121 A7
Black Moor Rd IP25 . . . . . 67 D2
Blackmoor Row IP25 . . . . 67 D1
Blackslough La NR16 . . . 119 D7
Blacksmith La
  Barnham IP24 . . . . 125 E6
  Quidenham NR16 . . . . . 103 F3
Blacksmiths Cl NR20 . . . . 33 B6
Blacksmiths La
  Ashwellthorpe NR16 . . . 106 B8
  Burnham Norton PE31 . . 135 B6
  Erpingham NR11 . . . . . . 21 C3
  Forncett St Mary NR16 . . 106 B4
  Happisburgh NR12 . . . . . 24 B6
  Haveringland NR10 . . . . . 52 E6
  Hindringham NR21 . . . . . 17 E7
Blacksmith's La
  Barton Bendish PE33 . . . . 81 B8
  Morning Thorpe NR15 . . 107 A3
Blacksmith's Row **1**
  PE32 . . . . 45 C6
Blacksmiths Way NR6 . . . 158 E5
Black St Hemsby NR29 . . . 58 B6
  Marthan NR29 . . . . 57 D5
Blackthorn Ave NR25 . . . 137 C7
Blackthorn Cl Diss IP22 . . 177 F5
  Norwich NR6 . . . . 158 D4
  3 Thetford IP24 . . . . . 176 F4
Blackthorn Dr **3** NR19 . . 154 C4
Blackthorn Rd
  Attleborough NR17 . . . . 174 B5
  King's Lynn PE30 . . . . . 148 C3
  Wymondham NR18 . . . . 173 D4
Blackthorn Way **16** NR4 . . 90 C5
Black Wall NR12 . . . . 40 B5
Blackwall Reach NR31 . . . 170 D5
BLACKWATER NR9 . . . . . 51 D6
Blackwater Cnr NR11 . . . . 36 F5
Blackwater La
  Great Witchingham NR9 . . 51 C6
  Great Witchingham NR9 . . 51 E7
  Heydon NR11 . . . . 34 D8

Blackwater La continued
  Heydon NR24 . . . . 34 E7
  Thurning NR20 . . . . 19 C1
Blackwell Ave NR7 . . . . . 159 A3
Bladewater Rd NR5 . . . . . 160 F5
Blake Cl PE32 . . . . 28 A1
Blake Ct PE13 . . . . 153 C2
Blake Dr
  Great Yarmouth NR31 . . . 170 A7
  Wymondham NR18 . . . . 173 F7
BLAKENEY NR25 . . . . . . 7 C6
Blakeney CE VA Prim Sch
  NR25 . . . . 7 D6
Blakeney Cl NR4 . . . . . . 161 E2
Blakeney Long La NR25 . . . 7 C4
Blakeney Point National
  Nature Reserve ★ NR25 . 7 C8
Blakeney Rd Binham NR21 . 6 C1
  Binham NR21 . . . . 6 D1
  Letheringsett with Glandford
  NR25 . . . . 7 F2
  Morston NR25 . . . . 7 B6
Blakeney Short La NR25 . . 7 C3
Blake Rd 169 D7
Blakes Ct NR3 . . . . 158 F3
Blakes Ct NR13 . . . . 165 C3
Blakestone Dr NR7 . . . . . 163 D7
Bland Rd NR5 . . . . 161 B6
Blands Farm Cl IP22 . . . . 177 D1
Blatchford Way PE31 . . . 133 B5
Blaxter Way NR7 . . . . . . 159 D5
Blazey Dr NR18 . . . . 88 B6
Blenco Terr **28** PE13 . . . . 152 C5
Blenheim Ave **4** NR29 . . . 57 D4
Blenheim Cl
  12 Long Stratton NR15 . . 106 E3
  Norwich NR7 . . . . 159 B5
Blenheim Cres
  Beeston with Bittering
  PE32 . . . . 48 D2
  Griston IP25 . . . . 85 A2
  Norwich NR7 . . . . 159 B5
  Tittleshall PE32 . . . . 48 A7
Blenheim Dr
  Attleborough NR17 . . . . 174 E4
  Swaffham PE37 . . . . . . 153 D5
  Swanton Morley NR20 . . . 50 B4
Blenheim Rd
  King's Lynn PE30 . . . . . 147 C8
  Norwich NR7 . . . . 159 B5
  Sculthorpe Airfield NR21 . 15 C3
Blenheim Way
  Emneth PE14 . . . . 152 E2
  2 Roydon IP22 . . . . . . 129 D7
  5 Watton IP25 . . . . . . 84 E3
Blick Cl **5** PE33 . . . . . . 43 F2
BLICKLING NR11 . . . . . . 35 F7
Blickling Cl **1** NR10 . . . 148 F1
Blickling Hall ★ NR11 . . . 35 F7
Blickling Rd
  Blickling NR11 . . . . 150 A8
  Norwich NR6 . . . . 158 C5
  Oulton NR11 . . . . 35 D7
Blickling St NR1 . . . . 90 D5
Bligh Cl NR14 . . . . 90 D5
Blind Dick's La NR22 . . . . 16 E7
Blind La
  Castle Acre PE32 . . . . . . 46 F1
  Hockering NR9 . . . . 51 A2
  Honingham NR9 . . . . . . 69 F5
  Horsham St Faith NR10 . . 53 D1
  Ludham NR29 . . . . 56 A5
  Mattishall NR20 . . . . . . 69 A7
Blithe Mdw Ct NR7 . . . . . 159 C3
Blithemeadow Dr NR7 . . . 159 C3
Blithewood Gdns NR7 . . . 159 C3
Blocka Rd NR32 . . . . 93 F2
BLOFIELD NR13 . . . . . . 165 F5
Blofield Cnr Rd NR13 . . . . 73 B4
BLOFIELD CORNER NR13 . 73 C6
BLOFIELD HEATH NR13 . . 73 D6
Blofield Loke NR12 . . . . . 164 E6
Blofield Prim Sch NR13 . . 165 E7
Blofield Rd
  Brundall NR13 . . . . 165 E3
  Lingwood & Burlingham
  NR13 . . . . 73 F3
Blomefield Rd Diss IP22 . . 177 D4
  Norwich NR3 . . . . 158 B2
BLO' NORTON IP22 . . . . 128 B6
Blo' Norton Rd IP22 . . . . 128 C7
Bloodgate Hill NR21 . . . . 15 D6
Bloodhills Rd NR29 . . . . . 57 F5
BLOODMAN'S CORNER
  NR32 . . . . 171 A4
Bloomfield Cl IP31 . . . . . 126 D1
Bloomfield Rd NR30 . . . . 170 E7
Bloomstile La NR25 . . . . . 8 B6
Bloomstiles NR25 . . . . . . 8 B6
Blooms Turn NR26 . . . . . 22 E5
Blowlands La NR26 . . . . . 138 B5
Bluebell Cl
  Attleborough NR17 . . . . 174 B5
  5 Downham Market
  PE38 . . . . 172 A5
  4 East Dereham NR19 . . 154 C4
  Thetford IP24 . . . . 176 F4
Bluebell Cres NR4 . . . . . 161 D2
Bluebell Dr NR26 . . . . . . 138 B6
Bluebell Gdns NR23 . . . . 136 E5
Bluebell Prim Sch NR4 . . 161 E4
Bluebell Rd
  Mulbarton NR14 . . . . . . 89 B3
  North Walsham NR28 . . . 151 D6
  Norwich NR4 . . . . 161 D3
Bluebell Way **19** NR31 . . . 94 C6

Bluebell Wlk
  Brandon IP27 . . . . 175 A2
  Wiggenhall St Germans
  PE34 . . . . 61 B8
Blue Boar La NR7 . . . . . . 159 D3
Blue Doors NR31 . . . . . . 94 C3
Blue Sky NR31 . . . . 94 C7
Bluestone Cres NR21 . . . . 15 D6
Bluestone La Salle NR21 . . 34 F4
  South Creake NR21 . . . . 15 D7
Bluestone Rd NR21 . . . . . 15 D6
Blundeston Rd NR32 . . . . 111 F8
Blundeville Manor **6**
  NR15 . . . . 89 C1
Blunt's Cnr NR23 . . . . . . 5 B2
Blunts Dro PE14 . . . . 59 E6
Blunt's Orchard Dr PE14 . . 77 E5
Blyth Cl NR13 . . . . 165 F6
Blyth Cres NR26 . . . . . . 138 D6
Blythe Wy NR10 . . . . 53 B4
Blyth Rd
  Caister-on-Sea NR30 . . . 168 C4
  Norwich NR3 . . . . 158 D2
Blyth's Wood Av **3** NR8 . . 70 C7
Boadicea Cl **1** IP24 . . . . 176 D7
Boal Quay PE30 . . . . 146 D4
Boal St PE30 . . . . 146 D4
Boardman Cl NR6 . . . . . 158 D3
Boat Dyke La NR13 . . . . . 166 D4
Boat Dyke Rd NR13 . . . . 166 B8
Boathouse La NR32 . . . . 111 F3
Boatmans Row NR13 . . . 136 C6
Bobbins Way NR14 . . . . . 89 C5
BOBBY HILL IP22 . . . . . 128 A1
Bob Carter Leisure Ctr
  NR8 . . . . 157 A8
Bobolink Row NR7 . . . . . 159 F3
BODHAM NR25 . . . . 9 A3
Bodleian Cl NR31 . . . . . 170 B2
Bodmin Dr NR7 . . . . 159 F4
BODNEY IP26 . . . . 83 B1
Bodney Rd
  Bodney IP26 . . . . 83 A1
  Bodney IP26 . . . . 83 A2
Boileau Ave **6** NR16 . . . . 105 F5
Boileau Cl **1** NR4 . . . . . 89 E8
Boiler Drove PE31 . . . . . . 14 A1
Boleness Rd PE13 . . . . . 152 C2
Bolingbroke Rd NR3 . . . . 158 B3
Boltons The PE30 . . . . . 148 C1
Bolts Cl NR13 . . . . 136 D6
Bond Cl IP21 . . . . 121 F4
Bonds Rd NR13 . . . . 73 C7
Bond's Rd NR15 . . . . . . 121 C4
Bond St **3** Cromer NR27 . 139 B7
  5 Hingham NR9 . . . . . . 86 C5
  Norwich NR2 . . . . 162 A7
Bone Rd NR8 . . . . 157 B8
Bone's Dro NR23 . . . . 4 F7
Boniface Cl NR4 . . . . . . 162 C1
Bonnetts La PE14 . . . . . . 60 B5
Boons Rd NR34 . . . . 111 B3
Boosey's Wlk **6** NR6 . . . 104 F1
Boot Binders Rd
  7 New Catton NR6 . . . . 158 C1
  5 Norwich NR6 . . . . . 162 C8
Boothes Rd PE38 . . . . . . 78 D2
Boot La Diss IP22 . . . . . . 120 D6
Boot La NR19 . . . . 120 D5
Heywood IP22 . . . . 120 D5
BOOTON NR10 . . . . 149 E4
Booton Comm Nature
  Reserve ★ NR10 . . . . . 149 E5
Booton Rd NR10 . . . . 35 B2
Booty Rd NR7 . . . . 159 F1
Borage Cl IP24 . . . . 176 F4
Border La Fordham PE38 . . 79 D2
  Somerleyton, Ashby &
  Herringfleet NR32 . . . . 94 B2
Border Rd PE33 . . . . 81 A2
Borley Cl IP31 . . . . 126 D1
Borough Cl PE13 . . . . . . 152 D3
Borough La NR17 . . . . . 174 F3
Borough's La NR17 . . . . . 104 D5
Borrowdale Dr NR1 . . . . 163 B8
Borton Rd NR13 . . . . 73 C6
Boscombe Rd IP25 . . . . . 85 A3
Bosgate Rise **6** NR29 . . . 57 C4
Boston Cl **4** NR31 . . . . . 94 A3
Boston End **6** IP24 . . . . 116 A1
Boston Sq PE36 . . . . . . 132 C5
Boston Sq Sensory Pk
  PE36 . . . . 132 C5
Boston St NR3 . . . . 158 D2
BOTESDALE IP22 . . . . . 128 F2
Bothy Cl IP23 . . . . 130 C1
Botolph St NR3 . . . . 178 A4
Boton Dr NR15 . . . . 154 D7
Bottom Breck Cl NR5 . . . 156 F2
Bottom Laddus PE14 . . . . 77 A5
Botwright Dr **5** PE37 . . . 153 C3
Boudica's Way NR14 . . . . 163 A1
Boughey Cl PE31 . . . . . . 3 B6
BOUGHTON PE33 . . . . . 81 A5
Boughton Long Rd PE33 . 81 B7
Boughton Rd
  Fincham PE33 . . . . 62 E1
  Stoke Ferry PE33 . . . . . 81 A3
Boulderside Cl **4** NR7 . . 163 E7
Boulevard Rd **2** NR27 . . . 10 A5
Boulevard The
  Sheringham NR26 . . . . . 138 D7
  Thorpe End NR13 . . . . . 72 E6
Boulters The NR31 . . . . . 170 C1
Boulton Rd NR7 . . . . . . 163 C7
Boulton St NR1 . . . . 178 C2
Boundaries The NR34 . . . 110 B2
Boundary Ave NR6 . . . . . 158 A4
Boundary Cl
  Brandon IP27 . . . . 175 C5
  Dereham NR20 . . . . . . 154 F5

Boundary Cl continued
  Hockwold cum Wilton
  IP26 . . . . 113 F7
Boundary La Norwich NR7 . 72 E3
  Paston NR28 . . . . 23 B3
  Terrington St Clement PE34 25 A1
  Terrington St Clement PE34 42 B8
Boundary Rd
  Ashby with Oby NR29 . . . 56 E2
  Great Yarmouth NR31 . . . 169 B1
  1 Hockwold cum Wilton
  IP26 . . . . 114 A7
  Marham PE33 . . . . 63 C3
  Norton Subcourse NR14 . . 92 D1
  Norwich NR6 . . . . 157 F5
  Raveningham NR14 . . . . 110 B8
Boundary Road East
  PE30 . . . . 146 D6
Boundary Road West
  PE30 . . . . 146 D6
Boundary Way **1** NR14 . . 90 C5
Boundary Wy IP22 . . . . . 177 B5
Bourges Ct NR7 . . . . . . 159 F3
Bourne Cl
  King's Lynn PE30 . . . . . 148 C2
  Long Stratton NR15 . . . . 106 E3
BOWBECK IP31 . . . . . . 127 A2
Bower Cl NR29 . . . . 56 F6
Bowers Ave NR3 . . . . . . 158 A2
Bowers Cl NR3 . . . . 158 A2
Bowes Cl IP25 . . . . 84 D3
Bow Hill NR9 . . . . 70 A3
Bowlers Cl NR13 . . . . . . 92 E7
Bowling Gn Cl
  Attleborough NR17 . . . . 174 D6
  Crostwick NR12 . . . . . . 54 B2
Bowling Gn The
  Raynham NR21 . . . . 30 F4
  Wells-next-the-Sea NR23 136 D5
Bowling Gn Wlk **2**
  NR30 . . . . 169 C4
Bowman Rd **4** NR4 . . . . 89 E8
Bow St NR9 . . . . 86 B1
BOWTHORPE NR5 . . . . . 160 F7
Bowthorpe Hall Gdns ★
  PE13 . . . . 152 D5
Bowthorpe Hall Rd NR5 . . 160 F7
Bowthorpe Rd
  Norwich NR5 . . . . 161 D6
  Wisbech PE13 . . . . 152 D5
Boxes La The NR13 . . . . . 55 E1
Box's La PE13 . . . . 153 D5
Boyces Rd PE13 . . . . . . 152 E5
Boyd Ave **9** NR19 . . . . . 154 D1
Boylandhall La NR15 . . . . 107 B4
Boyscott La NR35 . . . . . 124 B8
Boyton La NR31 . . . . 94 E2
Brabazon Rd NR6 . . . . . 158 B5
Bracecamp Cl NR29 . . . . 167 C2
Braces La NR35 . . . . 109 E3
Bracey Ave NR6 . . . . . . 158 F5
Bracken Ave
  3 Beetley NR20 . . . . . . 49 D4
  Norwich NR6 . . . . 158 A4
  Overstrand NR27 . . . . . . 11 A3
Brackenbury Wall NR29 . . 57 F8
Bracken Cl
  Fakenham NR21 . . . . . . 141 F4
  Horsford NR10 . . . . 53 B2
  Stratton Strawless NR10 . . 53 A6
Bracken Dr NR17 . . . . . . 174 B5
Bracken Rd
  King's Lynn PE30 . . . . . 148 C2
  Thetford IP24 . . . . 176 C1
Bracken Rise
  Brandon IP27 . . . . 175 E3
  Mundford IP26 . . . . . . 100 A4
Bracken Way PE32 . . . . . 28 B1
Brackenwoods NR7 . . . . 66 A4
BRACON ASH NR14 . . . . 89 A2
Bracondale NR1 . . . . . . 178 C1
Bracondale Ct **3** NR1 . . 162 F3
Bracondale Gn NR1 . . . . 178 C1
Bracondale Millgate
  NR14 . . . . 163 A2
Bracon Rd NR31 . . . . . . 93 F5
Bradcar Rd NR17 . . . . . . 103 B2
Braddock Rd NR30 . . . . 168 E5
Bradeham Way NR4 . . . . 162 A1
BRADENHAM IP25 . . . . . 66 E4
Bradenham Hall Gdn &
  Arboretum ★ IP25 . . . . 66 E4
Bradenham La NR19 . . . . 66 F6
Bradenham Rd
  Holme Hale IP25 . . . . . . 66 B2
  Shipdham IP25 . . . . 67 A2
BRADFIELD NR28 . . . . . 22 C4
Bradfield Cl NR28 . . . . . 151 A6
Bradfield Dr **10** NR29 . . . 57 D5
Bradfield Pl **3** PE33 . . . . 81 A3
Bradfield Rd
  Antingham NR28 . . . . . . 22 C5
  North Walsham NR28 . . . 151 A6
  Swafield NR28 . . . . 22 E3
Bradman's La NR18 . . . . . 87 D3
Bradmere La PE31 . . . . . 134 E5
Bradmoor Rd NR28 . . . . . 22 B1
Bradshaw Rd NR8 . . . . . 157 C7
BRADWELL Bradwell NR31 . 94 C7
  Great Yarmouth NR31 . . . 170 A4
Bradwell Ave **3** NR31 . . . 170 A4
Brady Cl PE38 . . . . 172 B1
Brady Gdns PE38 . . . . . 172 B1
Braeburn Ave PE13 . . . . 152 C8
Braeburn Cl **7** PE30 . . . 147 A8
Braeford Cl NR6 . . . . . . 158 A2
Brailsford Cl NR20 . . . . . 68 A7
Braithwait Cl **1** NR5 . . . 161 A8
BRAKEFIELD GREEN
  NR19 . . . . 68 D4
Brake La NR21 . . . . 16 C4

Bramble Ave NR6 . . . . . 158 A5
Bramble Cl
  Attleborough NR17 . . . . 174 F6
  Besthorpe NR17 . . . . . 174 F6
  Mundesley NR11 . . . . . 143 D5
  Sculthorpe Airfield NR21 . 15 C3
  4 Taverham NR8 . . . . 155 E2
Bramble Ct NR21 . . . . . . 141 E4
Bramble Dr
  Hockering NR20 . . . . . . 69 C7
  King's Lynn PE30 . . . . . 148 C2
  10 Sheringham NR26 . . . 138 B6
Bramble Gdns NR31 . . . . 93 F5
Bramble La
  Lower Street NR11 . . . . . 22 B6
  Outwell PE14 . . . . 77 D7
  Swaffham PE37 . . . . . . 65 B3
  Swaffham PE37 . . . . . . 153 F5
Brambles Cl **2** NR10 . . . . 54 A1
Bramble Way
  1 Poringland NR14 . . . . 90 D5
  Wymondham NR18 . . . . 173 E4
Bramblewood NR12 . . . . 39 B3
Brambling La
  5 Cringleford NR4 . . . . 89 A8
  Cringleford NR4 . . . . . . 161 B1
BRAMERTON NR14 . . . . . 90 F7
Bramerton La
  Framingham Pigot NR14 . . 90 E7
  Rockland St Mary NR14 . . 91 A7
Bramerton Rd NR14 . . . . 91 A8
Bramfield Cl NR2 . . . . . . 162 A7
Bramley Cl
  Wells-next-the-Sea
  NR23 . . . . 136 D6
  West Lynn PE34 . . . . . . 146 C4
Bramley Dr NR21 . . . . . . 31 E5
Bramley La **3** IP25 . . . . . 85 A2
Bramley Rd
  Dereham NR20 . . . . 68 A8
  Diss IP22 . . . . 177 C5
  Wisbech PE13 . . . . 152 C7
BRAMPTON NR10 . . . . . 36 E3
Brampton Cl PE13 . . . . . 152 A4
Brampton Ct **12** NR5 . . . 161 A7
Brampton Sta NR10 . . . . . 36 E3
BRANCASTER PE31 . . . . . 3 B6
Brancaster Cl
  King's Lynn PE30 . . . . . 147 C8
  Taverham NR8 . . . . 155 B2
Brancaster Prim Sch PE31 3 B6
Brancaster Rd PE31 . . . . 134 E7
BRANCASTER STAITHE
  PE31 . . . . 3 D7
Brancaster Way PE37 . . . 153 B2
Branch Rd NR13 . . . . . . 75 B2
BRANDISTON NR10 . . . . . 35 C2
Brandiston Hall La NR10 . 35 C1
Brandiston Rd NR10 . . . . 35 B2
BRANDON IP27 . . . . . . 175 D3
BRANDON BANK PE38 . . 112 B7
Brandon Cl Norwich NR6 . 157 E4
  3 Swaffham PE37 . . . . 153 C3
BRANDON CREEK PE38 . . 97 A2
Brandon Ct NR13 . . . . . 165 C3
Brandon Fields IP27 . . . . 114 D4
Brandon Her Ctr ★ IP27 . 175 D4
BRANDON PARVA NR9 . . . 69 E2
Brandon Pk IP27 . . . . . . 114 F4
Brandon Rd
  Cockley Cley PE37 . . . . . 83 A8
  Culfordheath IP28 . . . . . 125 A1
  Elveden IP27 . . . . 115 B1
  Hockwold cum Wilton
  IP26 . . . . 114 B7
  Methwold IP26 . . . . 99 B4
  Mundford IP26 . . . . . . 100 B3
  Saham Toney IP25 . . . . . 84 B3
  Swaffham PE37 . . . . . . 65 A1
  Thetford IP24 . . . . 176 A4
  Wangford IP27 . . . . . . 114 C4
  Watton IP25 . . . . 84 C3
  Weeting-with-Broomhill
  IP27 . . . . 115 A8
  Weeting-with-Broomhill
  IP27 . . . . 175 C5
Brandon Sports Ctr
  IP27 . . . . 175 B3
Brandon Sta IP27 . . . . . 175 C5
Brandon Terr NR30 . . . . 169 E2
Brandreth Rd IP21 . . . . . 121 B1
Brand's La
  Felthorpe NR10 . . . . . . 155 D6
  Tharston & Hapton NR15 . 106 E5
Brandvnvm (Roman Fort)
  (Branodunum) ★ PE31 . 3 C6
Branford Rd
  Caister-on-Sea NR30 . . . 168 D7
  Norwich NR3 . . . . 158 E1
Branksome Cl NR4 . . . . . 162 B2
Branksome Rd NR4 . . . . 162 A2
Branodunum PE31 . . . . . 3 B7
Bransby Cl PE30 . . . . . . 146 F4
Branthill NR23 . . . . 5 C2
Brasenose Ave NR31 . . . 170 B3
Brasier Rd NR3 . . . . 158 B2
Braydeston Ave NR13 . . . 165 D3
Braydeston Cres NR13 . . 165 D3
Braydeston Dr NR13 . . . . 165 F6
Braydeston Hall La NR13 . 73 E4
Bray Dr NR3 . . . . 173 F8
Brayfield Way NR6 . . . . . 158 F6
Braymeadow NR9 . . . . . 160 D2
Braymeadow La NR9 . . . . 160 D2
Bray's La Guestwick NR20 . 34 A6
  Rocklands NR17 . . . . . 103 A7
Brazen Gate NR1 . . . . . . 178 A1
Breck Farm Cl NR8 . . . . 155 C2
Breck Farm La NR8 . . . . 155 C2
Breck La NR8 . . . . 70 A7
Breckland Ave IP27 . . . . 113 E2

Breckland Bsns Ctr
NR19 . . . . .154 D5
Breckland Bsns Pk IP25 . .84 F3
Breckland Leisure Ctr &
Waterworld IP24 . . . . . .176 D5
Breckland Park Sch
PE37 . . . . .153 B6
Breckland Rd NR5 . . . . . .157 A1
Brecklands
Mundford IP26 . . . . .100 B4
11 Stalham NR12 . . . . . . .39 B4
Breckland Sch
Brandon IP27 . . . . .114 D4
Brandon IP27 . . . . .175 A2
Brecklands Gn PE37 . . . .65 D1
Brecklands Rd NR13 . . . .165 E2
Brecklands The IP26 . . . .100 B4
BRECKLES NR17 . . . . . . .102 E5
Breck Rd Norwich NR7 . . .159 E2
Weston Longville NR9 . . . .51 E1
Brecks The **8** NR17 . . . .174 B4
Brecon Rd NR15 . . . . . . .90 E2
Breeze Ave NR11 . . . . . .150 B5
Brellows Hill PE34 . . . . . .144 A5
Brenda Collison Cl
PE31 . . . . .140 C4
Brenda James Cl **11**
NR7 . . . . .163 E7
Brennewater Mews **4**
NR5 . . . . .161 A8
Brent Ave PE31 . . . . .12 E5
Brentwood Eaton NR4 . . .162 A1
1 Norwich NR4 . . . . . . .161 F1
Brereton Cl **1** NR5 . . . .161 C6
BRESSINGHAM IP22 . . . .129 C8
BRESSINGHAM COMMON
IP22 . . . . .119 F1
Bressingham Prim Sch
IP22 . . . . .129 B8
Bressingham Rd
5 Gresham NR11 . . . . . .9 E1
Roydon IP22 . . . . .129 C8
Bressingham Steam Mus &
Gdns* IP22 . . . . .129 C7
Breton Cl **10** NR19 . . . .154 D2
Brett Ave NR31 . . . . .170 D1
BRETTENHAM IP24 . . . . .117 B2
Brettenham Rd
Kilverstone IP24 . . . . . . .116 F3
Shadwell IP24 . . . . .117 C2
Brettingham Ave NR4 . . .89 B8
Bretts Orch PE33 . . . . . . .62 E1
Brett Way PE30 . . . . .147 B8
Brewers Ct NR3 . . . . .178 C4
Brewers Gn La IP22 . . . . .177 B6
BREWERS GREEN IP22 . . .177 B6
Brewery La Horsford NR10 .53 B2
Wymondham NR10 . . . . . .173 C3
Brewery Rd NR28 . . . . . .22 D5
Brewery St NR30 . . . . . . .169 C4
Brewster Ct NR15 . . . . . .165 D6
Brewsters **8** NR16 . . . .118 C5
Breydon Dr NR8 . . . . . . .156 C4
Breydon Dr N NR8 . . . . . .156 C5
Breydon Junc NR30 . . . . .76 C3
Breydon Rd
Great Yarmouth NR31 . . . .169 B4
King's Lynn PE30 . . . . . . .147 D5
Norwich NR7 . . . . .159 A4
Breydon Waters NR31 . . . .93 F7
Breydon Way NR30 . . . . .168 D6
Brian Ave NR1 . . . . .162 D3
Briar Ave NR3 . . . . .94 C7
Briar Cl **7** Dereham NR20 .68 A8
Grimston PE32 . . . . .28 B1
King's Lynn PE30 . . . . . . .148 C3
14 Lingwood NR13 . . . . .74 A3
9 Necton PE37 . . . . . . .65 F4
Briar Gdns NR17 . . . . . . .174 F7
Briar La Edinthorpe NR28 . .23 B2
Heckingham NR14 . . . . . .109 F8
Rickinghall Inferior IP22 . .128 D1
Swainsthorpe NR14 . . . . . .89 D3
Briar Rd
39 Harleston IP20 . . . . .122 D2
Hethersett NR9 . . . . .88 C8
Briars Ct NR5 . . . . .161 F7
Brickfield Cl NR3 . . . . . . .158 C3
Brickfield Loke NR8 . . . . .156 C5
Brickfields NR13 . . . . . . .73 F2
Brickfields La PE38 . . . . .172 A5
Brickfields Way IP24 . . . .176 C6
Brickkiln La
Ashwellthorpe NR16 . . . . .105 F7
Mulbarton NR14 . . . . .89 C2
South Lopham IP22 . . . . . .128 F7
Brick Kiln La
Bunwell NR16 . . . . .105 D2
Gillingham NR34 . . . . . . .110 C5
Lexham PE32 . . . . .47 B5
Long Stratton NR15 . . . . .107 A5
Matlask NR11 . . . . .20 D6
Shipdham IP25 . . . . .67 C2
Brick Kiln Rd
Ellingham NR35 . . . . .109 C4
Fakenham NR21 . . . . .141 C6
Hevingham NR10 . . . . . . .53 A7
North Walsham NR28 . . . .151 E5
Thursford NR21 . . . . .17 F4
Trunch NR28 . . . . .22 F6
Brick Kilns Rd NR13 . . . . .73 B7
Brick Klin Lka NR20 . . . . .34 B2
Brick La NR27 . . . . .10 B5
Brickle Loke NR14 . . . . . .90 B5
Brickle Rd NR14 . . . . .90 B4
Brickle Wood Ave NR14 . .90 C6
Brickley La PE31 . . . . . . .140 D7
Brickley La West PE31 . . .140 D7
Bricknel Cl PE32 . . . . . . .46 F2
Brickyard La PE31 . . . . . .29 C4
Brick Yard La PE32 . . . . . .45 E6

Brickyard Rd NR28 . . . . . .22 A2
Bridewell Alley **2** NR2 . .178 B3
Bridewell La Acle NR13 . .166 C4
Botesdale IP22 . . . . .128 C2
Bridewell Mus The★
NR2 . . . . .178 B3
Bridewell St
1 Little Walsingham
NR22 . . . . .16 F7
Wymondham NR18 . . . . . .173 C3
Bridge Broad Cl NR12 . . .164 C5
Bridge Cl
Fakenham NR21 . . . . .141 C6
16 Harleston IP20 . . . . .122 D2
Heacham PE31 . . . . .133 C5
Melton Constable NR24 . . .142 B4
Bridgecourt NR29 . . . . . .58 A4
Bridge Farm La NR4 . . . .161 C6
Bridge Farm Rd NR11 . . . .21 A4
Bridge Farm Track NR29 . .75 D8
Bridgefoot La NR25 . . . . . .7 F5
Bridge Gdns NR19 . . . . . .154 E1
BRIDGE GREEN IP22 . . . .120 F2
Bridge Ind Est NR18 . . . .173 C2
Bridge La IP25 . . . . .84 C6
Bridge Loke NR18 . . . . . .173 D3
Bridge Mdw NR29 . . . . . .58 A4
Bridge Rd
Brome & Oakley IP21 . . . .130 C5
Bunwell NR16 . . . . .105 E8
Burston & Shimpling IP22 .120 E3
Colby NR11 . . . . .36 D8
Downham West PE38 . . . . .79 B5
Great Ryburgh NR21 . . . . .32 C6
5 Great Yarmouth NR30 .169 C5
11 Great Yarmouth NR31 .169 C5
High Kelling NR25 . . . . . .137 F8
North Elmham NR20 . . . . .32 F3
Potter Heigham NR29 . . . .56 F5
Stoke Ferry PE33 . . . . . . .81 A2
Sutton Bridge PE12 . . . . . .41 A8
Welney PE14 . . . . .95 E4
Wighton NR22 . . . . .6 A2
Wymondham NR18 . . . . . .88 B2
Bridge St Brandon IP27 . .175 C4
Carbrooke IP25 . . . . .85 A4
Downham Market PE38 . . .172 B5
Fakenham NR21 . . . . .141 B3
Gressenhall NR20 . . . . . . .49 C3
Hilgay PE38 . . . . .79 E1
14 King's Lynn PE30 . . .146 D4
Loddon NR14 . . . . .92 A2
Stiffkey NR23 . . . . .6 C1
Thetford IP24 . . . . .176 C4
14 Wisbech PE13 . . . . .152 C5
Bridges Wlk
Fakenham NR21 . . . . .141 A3
Thetford IP24 . . . . .176 C2
Thetford IP24 . . . . .176 D3
Bridgford Cl NR31 . . . . . .170 C2
BRIDGHAM NR16 . . . . . . .117 F5
Bridgham La NR16 . . . . . .117 F4
Bridle Cl PE14 . . . . .77 E6
Bridle La
Downham Market PE38 . . .172 D7
Keswick NR4 . . . . .89 C7
Bridle Rd IP25 . . . . .84 C3
Brier La IP31 . . . . .127 B5
Briggs Loke NR11 . . . . . .36 D8
Briggs Mead NR18 . . . . . .88 B6
Brigg St NR1 . . . . .178 A2
Brigham Cl NR13 . . . . . . .165 C4
Bright Cl **3** NR31 . . . . .169 B3
Brightmere Rd NR12 . . . .39 E2
Brighton Rd **1** NR15 . . .89 C1
Brightwell Rd
Norwich NR3 . . . . .71 C6
Norwich NR3 . . . . .158 D3
Brighty's Opening NR2 . . .162 B7
Brig Sq NR23 . . . . .136 C5
Brigstock Rd PE13 . . . . . .152 B7
Brimbelow Rd NR12 . . . .164 D4
Brimstone Cl
Christchurch PE14 . . . . . . .95 A4
Swaffham PE37 . . . . .153 C2
Brindle Dr **5** NR14 . . . . .89 B3
Brindy La NR11 . . . . .150 D4
Brinell Way NR31 . . . . . . .170 B8
Bringloe Dr NR9 . . . . .88 E8
BRININGHAM NR24 . . . . .18 D4
Brinon Rd NR24 . . . . .18 D6
BRINTON NR24 . . . . .18 D6
Brinton Rd
Saxlingham NR25 . . . . .7 D1
Sharrington NR25 . . . . . . .18 D7
Sharrington NR25 . . . . . . .18 D8
Stody NR24 . . . . .142 D8
Briscoe Way IP27 . . . . . .113 E2
BRISLEY NR20 . . . . .49 A8
Brisley CE VA Prim Sch
NR20 . . . . .32 A1
Brisley Rd
Horningtoft NR20 . . . . . . .31 F1
North Elmham NR20 . . . . .49 D8
Bristol Rd NR5 . . . . .156 C1
Bristol Terr NR2 . . . . .178 A2
BRISTON NR24 . . . . .142 E4
Briston Rd Briston NR24 . .142 A5
Briston NR24 . . . . .142 F6
Corpusty NR11 . . . . .19 F1
Edgefield NR24 . . . . .19 C5
Saxthorpe NR11 . . . . .19 E1
Wood Dalling NR11 . . . . . .34 C6
Bristows Loke **18** NR12 . .39 B4
Britannia Pier Theatre
NR30 . . . . .169 E4
Britannia Rd
Great Yarmouth NR30 . . . .169 E4
Norwich NR1 . . . . .163 A7
Britannia Way PE13 . . . . .152 C2

Britannia Wy NR5 . . . . . .156 C1
Britch La PE34 . . . . .42 B4
Briton's La
Beeston Regis NR26 . . . . .138 C4
Sheringham NR26 . . . . . . .9 F5
Briton's La Cl
2 Beeston Regis NR27 . . .9 F5
Sheringham NR26 . . . . . .138 F5
Briton Way NR18 . . . . . . .173 B3
Britton Cl **9** PE33 . . . . . .61 D6
Broadacres **4** NR13 . . . .74 B8
Broadside NR12 . . . . .20 E8
Broad Dro Emneth PE14 . .59 C1
Grimston PE32 . . . . .45 C8
Methwold IP26 . . . . .97 F6
Upwell PE14 . . . . .77 D4
Broad End Ind Est PE14 . .59 C4
Broad End Rd
Walsoken PE13 . . . . .152 F4
Walsoken PE14 . . . . .152 F4
Broaden La NR15 . . . . . . .107 C6
Broad Fen La NR28 . . . . . .38 D4
Broadfields Way NR14 . . . .91 C7
Broadgate NR8 . . . . .155 B2
Broadgate CI NR27 . . . . . .11 A2
Broadgate La
Great Moulton NR15 . . . . .121 B8
Roydon PE32 . . . . .28 A2
Broadhurst Rd NR1 . . . . . .162 F1
Broad La Brancaster PE31 . .3 A7
Filby NR29 . . . . .75 E8
Great & Little Plumstead
NR13 . . . . .72 F6
Plumstead Green NR13 . . .73 A6
South Walsham NR13 . . . .74 B8
Swannington NR9 . . . . . . .52 B5
Broadland
Gorleston-On-Sea NR31 . .170 C7
Reedham NR13 . . . . .93 A4
Broadland Dr NR13 . . . . .72 D6
Broadland High Ormiston
Acad NR12 . . . . .164 D6
Broadland Northway
Horsham St Faith NR10 . . .53 D1
Spixworth NR12 . . . . .54 A1
Taverham NR10 . . . . .155 C4
Thorpe Marriott NR8 . . . . .52 E2
Broadlands Cl PE31 . . . . .140 C4
Broadlands The PE31 . . . .15 A3
Broadland Way
Acle NR13 . . . . .166 C3
Postwick with Witton NR7 . .72 E3
Broadmead Gn NR13 . . . .72 E6
Broadmere IP31 . . . . .126 B1
Broad Rd Alburgh IP20 . . .122 E8
Fleggburgh NR29 . . . . . . .75 C8
Sloley NR10 . . . . .37 F3
Sloley NR12 . . . . .38 A3
Broad Reaches NR29 . . . .56 C5
Broad Row **17** NR30 . . .169 C4
Broad St Bungay NR35 . . .124 A8
Ditchingham NR35 . . . . . .109 A1
20 Harleston IP20 . . . . .122 D2
King's Lynn PE30 . . . . . . .146 D5
Broad View **4** NR13 . . . .72 D6
Broadwater La PE32 . . . . .45 B4
Broadwater Rd PE36 . . . . .1 F7
Broadwater Way **1**
NR12 . . . . .55 C4
Broad Way
Dickleburgh & Rushall
IP21 . . . . .130 D8
Rocklands NR17 . . . . .103 A8
Shimpling IP21 . . . . .121 B2
Broadway Cl **5** NR15 . . .107 C5
Broadway La
Blo' Norton IP22 . . . . .128 B7
Garboldisham IP22 . . . . . .128 B8
Broadway The
Heacham PE31 . . . . .133 D5
Honingham NR9 . . . . .69 E8
Scarning NR19 . . . . .154 B2
Broad Wlk NR10 . . . . .53 D6
Broadwood Cl NR11 . . . . .11 E1
Brockdish Needham Bypass
Needham IP20 . . . . .122 C1
Needham IP20 . . . . .131 E8
Brockdish VC Prim Sch
IP21 . . . . .131 D6
Brockley Gn **7** PE30 . . . .147 C4
Brocks Rd PE37 . . . . .153 B6
Brockwell Ct NR3 . . . . . . .158 F2
BROME IP23 . . . . .130 B3
Brome Ave IP23 . . . . .130 D2
Bromedale Ave **19** NR14 . .89 B3
Brome Hall La IP23 . . . . .130 D3
Brome Rd IP21 . . . . .130 A3
BROME STREET IP23 . . . .130 D2
Bromholme Cl NR12 . . . . .23 E4
Bronde Cl NR6 . . . . .158 E6
BROOKE NR15 . . . . .90 E2
Brooke Ave NR30 . . . . . . .168 D5
Brooke CE Prim Sch
NR15 . . . . .90 E1
Brooke Rd Kirstead NR15 . .91 A1
Seething NR15 . . . . .91 C1
Shotesham NR15 . . . . . . .107 F8
Brookes Dr NR28 . . . . . . .151 A4
Brookfield Cl NR15 . . . . . .106 F4
Brook Gr **8** NR15 . . . . .107 A7
Brook La Brookville IP26 . .99 A7
Burgate IP22 . . . . .129 C2
Burgate IP22 . . . . .129 C2

Brook La *continued*
Needham IP20 . . . . .131 E8
St Margaret, Ilketshall
NR35 . . . . .124 C3
Brook Pk IP22 . . . . .128 D2
Brook Pl NR1 . . . . .178 B2
Brook Rd
Dersingham PE31 . . . . . . .140 D2
Norwich NR7 . . . . .72 C4
Sheringham NR26 . . . . . . .138 E6
Brooks Dr NR19 . . . . .154 B4
Brookside NR20 . . . . .49 E8
Brooks Mdw NR14 . . . . . .90 D5
Brooks Rd NR10 . . . . .53 B3
Brook St
Buxton with Lammas
NR10 . . . . .36 E1
Cromer NR27 . . . . .139 C7
Lamas NR10 . . . . .53 E8
BROOK THE IP22 . . . . . . .129 C3
BROOKVILLE IP26 . . . . . .99 A6
Brookwell Springs **1**
PE32 . . . . .84 A3
Broom Ave Norwich NR6 . .158 A5
Norwich NR7 . . . . .163 B8
Broom Cl
15 Marthan NR29 . . . . .57 D4
Norwich NR1 . . . . .162 F3
Taverham NR8 . . . . .155 C3
BROOME NR35 . . . . .109 C2
Broome Bypass NR35 . . . .109 C2
Broomefield Rd NR14 . . . .90 A4
Broome Gdns **2** NR14 . . .94 A5
Broom Gn Dr NR20 . . . . . .32 E2
Broom Gn Rd NR20 . . . . . .32 E2
BROOM GREEN NR20 . . . .32 E2
BROOMHILL PE38 . . . . . .172 E7
Broomhill **1** NR27 . . . . . .10 B5
Broomholm NR12 . . . . . . .23 E4
Broom La Easton NR9 . . . .70 B5
Witton NR28 . . . . .38 C8
Broom Rd
Lakenheath IP27 . . . . . . .113 F1
Wymondham NR18 . . . . . .105 C6
Broomsfield NR5 . . . . . . .161 A7
BROOMSTHORPE PE31 . . .30 C7
Broomsthorpe Rd
East Rudham PE31 . . . . . . .30 A7
Helhoughton NR21 . . . . . .30 D6
Brothercross Way PE38 . .172 C7
Brotherton Wy **10** NR31 .171 D4
Browick Rd
Wymondham NR18 . . . . . .173 C4
Wymondham NR8 . . . . . . .88 B4
Browick Road Prim Sch
NR18 . . . . .173 C3
Browne Cl NR16 . . . . . . .105 D4
Brownes Gr **14** NR14 . . .92 A1
Brownes La NR14 . . . . . . .89 B6
Browne St **5** NR2 . . . . .162 C7
Browning Pl PE30 . . . . . .147 A8
Browns Acre IP23 . . . . . .129 E1
Brownsfield NR11 . . . . . . .21 D8
Brownshill NR27 . . . . . . .139 B4
Browns La PE37 . . . . .83 E8
Brown's La
Holme Hale IP25 . . . . .65 C1
Mautby NR29 . . . . .76 B7
Necton PE37 . . . . .65 F3
Saxlingham Nethergate
NR15 . . . . .107 B8
Brow of the Hill PE32 . . . .44 E6
Browston Corner NR31 . . .94 C6
Browston Gn NR31 . . . . . .94 C4
BROWSTON GREEN
NR31 . . . . .94 C4
Browston Hall Leisure Ctr
NR31 . . . . .94 C4
Browston La
Belton with Browston
NR31 . . . . .94 B5
Somerleyton, Ashby &
Herringfleet NR32 . . . . . .94 B3
Bruce Cl PE13 . . . . .152 C3
Brummel Cl **1** PE30 . . . .147 C5
Brumstead Rd
Brumstead NR12 . . . . .24 A1
Stalham NR12 . . . . .39 A4
BRUNDALL NR13 . . . . . . .165 D4
Brundall Gdns Sta
NR13 . . . . .165 A3
Brundall Low Rd NR13 . . .72 F3
Brundall Prim Sch
NR13 . . . . .165 D3
Brundall Rd NR13 . . . . . .165 E4
Brundall Sta NR13 . . . . . .165 D2
BRUNDISH NR14 . . . . . . .110 A6
Brundish Rd NR14 . . . . . .110 A6
Brunel Way IP24 . . . . . . .176 B6
Brunel Way Ind Est
IP24 . . . . .176 B6
Brunswick Cl
Dereham NR19 . . . . .154 C2
North Walsham NR28 . . . .151 D6
Brunswick Rd NR2 . . . . . .162 C4
Brunswick Terr NR27 . . . .139 C7
Brushmakers Way IP22 . .177 C6
Brussels Cl NR19 . . . . . . .154 C2
Bryans La IP22 . . . . .177 F3
Bryggen Rd PE30 . . . . . .146 E8
Bryony Cl **2** NR8 . . . . . .155 D1
Bryony Cour NR25 . . . . . .137 B7
Bryony Ct PE30 . . . . .148 C3
Bryony Way **6** NR17 . . . .174 B5
Buccaneer Way **8** NR9 . .88 D8
Buck Brigg NR11 . . . . .21 D3

Buck Courtney Cres
NR6 . . . . .158 A7
BUCKENHAM NR13 . . . . .91 F8
Buckenham Cl
1 Fakenham NR21 . . . . .141 C5
Swaffham PE13 . . . . .153 B2
Buckenham Dr PE33 . . . . .81 A2
Buckenham La
Ickburgh IP26 . . . . .100 D6
Lingwood & Burlingham
NR13 . . . . .73 F2
Buckenham St Nicholas
CE Prim Sch NR13 . . . . . .91 F8
Buckenham Sta NR13 . . . .91 F8
Buckenham Tofts IP26 . . .100 D5
Bucket Rd NR21 . . . . .15 D2
Buckingham Cl PE36 . . . .132 C5
Buckingham Dr **1** NR9 . . .88 C7
Buckingham Rd NR4 . . . . .161 F3
Buckingham Wlk PE13 . . .152 D8
Buckland Rise **8** NR4 . . .161 F1
Buckle Way NR15 . . . . . . .72 B6
Bucks Cl NR20 . . . . .69 A4
Buck's Heath La NR11 . . . .11 D1
Buck's La NR18 . . . . .87 B3
Buckthorn Cl **3** NR8 . . . .155 B2
Buck Yd NR7 . . . . .163 E5
Buddell's La NR23 . . . . . . .5 F2
Buggs Hole La IP22 . . . . .128 A6
Bugg's Rd IP22 . . . . .129 B2
Buildings Rd NR30 . . . . . .168 E4
Bullace Bush La NR13 . . .165 E7
Bullace Rd NR5 . . . . .156 F2
Bullard Rd Norwich NR3 . .71 E6
Norwich NR3 . . . . .158 C3
Bull Cl
East Tuddenham NR20 . . . .69 C6
4 Holt NR25 . . . . .137 B6
Norwich NR3 . . . . .178 B4
Bull Cl La NR21 . . . . .17 B3
Bull Cl Rd NR3 . . . . .178 B4
Bullemer Cl **3** NR12 . . . .39 B4
Bullen La NR14 . . . . .18 B6
Bullfinch Dr **15** IP20 . . .122 D1
Bullfinch Way **4** PE14 . . .77 A8
Bullies Way **8** NR13 . . . .73 D6
Bull La NR11 . . . . .178 A1
Bullman's Cross La NR20 . .69 A6
Bullock Fair Cl **14** IP20 . .122 D2
Bullock Hill
Bush Green IP21 . . . . . . .121 F7
Horsham St Faith & Newton St
Faith NR10 . . . . .53 E1
North Green IP21 . . . . . . .122 A7
Bullock Rd PE34 . . . . . . .144 B1
Bullockshed La
Bramerton NR14 . . . . .91 A7
Saham Toney IP25 . . . . . . .84 B5
Bullock Shed La NR14 . . . .89 F5
Bullocks Loke NR30 . . . . .168 E4
Bulls Gn La NR34 . . . . . .110 C6
Bulls Gn Rd NR34 . . . . . .110 C6
BULL'S GREEN NR14 . . . .110 C5
Bull's Cl NR3 . . . . .170 D6
Bull's Row NR27 . . . . .11 A2
Bull St NR25 . . . . .137 B6
Bulmer Rd NR3 . . . . .158 A2
Bulrush Ave PE38 . . . . . .172 A6
Bulrush Cl
East Dereham NR19 . . . . .154 C4
4 Horsford NR10 . . . . . .53 A3
Bulstrode Ave **4** NR19 . .154 D2
Bultitudes Loke NR30 . . . .168 E4
Bulwer Cl **6** NR10 . . . . . .36 F1
Bulwer Rd
East Dereham NR19 . . . . .154 E1
Lamas NR10 . . . . .36 E1
Bumstede Ct **5** NR5 . . . .161 A8
BUMWELL HILL NR16 . . . .105 E2
Bungalow La NR7 . . . . . . .72 D3
BUNGAY NR35 . . . . .124 A8
Bungay High Sch NR35 . .124 A7
Bungay La NR15 . . . . .91 C2
Bungay Rd NR35 . . . . . . .124 A8
Bungay Rd
Alburgh IP20 . . . . .123 B5
Bixley NR14 . . . . .90 B8
Brockdish IP21 . . . . .131 A5
Brooke NR15 . . . . .90 E1
Brooke NR15 . . . . .108 B8
Dickleburgh & Rushall
IP21 . . . . .130 E5
Ditchingham NR35 . . . . . .109 A1
Ellingham NR35 . . . . .109 C4
Hempnall NR15 . . . . .108 C4
Loddon NR14 . . . . .109 C2
Low Tharston NR15 . . . . .106 C6
Poringland NR14 . . . . .90 D4
Redenhall IP20 . . . . .122 F3
Scole IP21 . . . . .130 D5
Shipmeadow NR35 . . . . . .109 E1
Stockton NR34 . . . . .109 F4
Stockton NR34 . . . . .110 A4
Thwaite NR35 . . . . .109 C4
Bunkel Rd NR13 . . . . .72 E8
BUNKER'S HILL
Lound NR32 . . . . .94 C3
Norwich NR5 . . . . .161 B7
Bunnett Ave NR31 . . . . . .170 A4
Bunnetts Loke NR9 . . . . . .51 C4
Bunnett Sq NR4 . . . . .161 F5
Bunnewell Ave NR31 . . . .170 A4

Bunn's Bank Rd
Attleborough NR17 . . . . . .174 F2
Old Buckenham NR17 . . . .104 D4
Bunn's La
Great Yarmouth NR31 . . . .169 C3
Starston IP20 . . . . .122 C2
Bunny Wood Dr IP24 . . . .102 C3
Bunting Dr IP22 . . . . .177 F5
Bunting's La PE21 . . . . . . .98 F5
Buntings The **15** NR31 . . .94 C8
BUNWELL NR16 . . . . .105 D4
Bunwell Bottom
NR16 . . . . .105 C6
Bunwell Hill NR16 . . . . . .105 D3
Bunwell Prim Sch NR16 . .105 D3
Bunwell Rd
Aslacton NR16 . . . . .106 A2
Attleborough NR17 . . . . . .174 F6
Besthorpe NR17 . . . . .104 A3
Black Carr NR17 . . . . .105 A7
Bunwell St NR16 . . . . . . .105 B8
Bunyan Cl **3** NR13 . . . . .72 E4
Burch Cl PE30 . . . . .147 A4
Burcroft Rd PE13 . . . . . . .152 B6
Burdett Cl NR13 . . . . .165 E6
Burdett Rd PE13 . . . . . . .152 B4
Burdock Cl
Downham Market PE38 . . .172 C3
Wymondham NR18 . . . . . .173 E4
Burdock La
Hockwold cum Wilton
IP26 . . . . .113 C7
8 Wramplingham NR9 . . .69 F2
Burdock Way **3** NR17 . . .174 B4
Bure Cl **9** Belton NR31 . . .94 A6
Caister-on-Sea NR30 . . . .168 D6
Great Yarmouth NR30 . . . .169 C6
4 King's Lynn PE30 . . . .147 C5
8 Watlington PE33 . . . . .61 D6
Wroxham/Hoveton NR12 . .164 C5
Bure Marshes National
Nature Reserve★ NR13 . .55 C3
Bure Rd Briston NR24 . . . .142 D4
1 Great Yarmouth NR30 .169 C5
Bure Valley La NR11 . . . .150 E5
Bure Valley Sch NR11 . . .150 C5
Bure Way NR11 . . . . .150 C7
BURGATE IP22 . . . . .129 C2
Burgate La NR14 . . . . . . .90 E5
Burgate Rd IP22 . . . . . . .129 B1
Burgess Cl
Caister-on-Sea NR30 . . . .168 D4
Cromer NR27 . . . . .139 B4
Burgess Rd NR3 . . . . . . .158 B2
Burgess Way NR15 . . . . . .90 E2
Burgh Beck Rd NR24 . . . .142 B5
BURGH CASTLE NR31 . . . .94 A7
Burgh Comm NR17 . . . . .104 D5
BURGH COMMON
NR31 . . . . .94 B7
Burgh Common NR17 . . . .174 F4
Burgh Hall Leisure Ctr
NR31 . . . . .94 B7
Burgh La NR20 . . . . .68 F6
Burghley Rd PE30 . . . . . .148 E1
BURGH NEXT AYLSHAM
NR11 . . . . .36 D4
Burgh Rd Aylsham NR11 . .36 C4
Aylsham NR11 . . . . .150 D4
Aylsham NR11 . . . . .150 E6
Burgh St Peter NR34 . . . .111 C5
Great Yarmouth NR31 . . . .170 B7
BURGH ST MARGARET
(FLEGGBURGH) NR29 . . . .57 C2
BURGH ST PETER NR34 . .111 C4
BURGH STUBBS NR24 . . .142 B8
Burghwood Dr PE32 . . . . .48 D6
Burgh Wood Rd NR29 . . . .57 E1
Burhill Cl **3** NR4 . . . . . . .89 D8
Burkitt St PE30 . . . . .146 E6
Burleigh Cl **1** NR30 . . . .169 C4
Burley Rd NR21 . . . . .38 A3
Burlingham Dr **2** NR33 . .111 F1
BURLINGHAM GREEN
NR13 . . . . .74 A5
Burlingham Rd
East Harling NR16 . . . . . .118 D5
South Walsham NR13 . . . .73 F6
Burlington Cl IP22 . . . . . .177 D1
Burma Rd PE31 . . . . .140 C4
Burma Rd NR6 . . . . .158 C5
Burnet Rd
Great Yarmouth NR31 . . . .94 C6
Norwich NR3 . . . . .157 F1
Burney Rd PE30 . . . . .146 D2
Burnham Ave PE30 . . . . .147 C6
BURNHAM DEEPDALE
PE31 . . . . .3 E6
Burnham Dr NR22 . . . . . . .5 C1
Burnham Green La PE31 . .15 A4
Burnham La NR22 . . . . . . .16 B4
BURNHAM MARKET
PE31 . . . . .135 C3
Burnham Market Rd
NR21 . . . . .16 B3
Burnham Mkt Prim Sch
PE31 . . . . .135 D4
BURNHAM NORTON
PE31 . . . . .135 B6
BURNHAM OVERY STAITHE
PE31 . . . . .135 E4
BURNHAM OVERY TOWN
PE31 . . . . .135 E4
Burnham Rd
Burnham Overy Town NR23 . .4 E5
Docking PE31 . . . . .134 C7
Downham Market PE38 . . .172 B4
Great Barwick PE31 . . . . . .14 F6
North Creake NR21 . . . . . . .4 D2

Burnham Rd continued
Ringstead PE36 . . . . 2 C3
South Creake NR21 . . . . 15 D7
Burnhams The PE34 . . . . . 144 E7
BURNHAM THORPE PE31 . . 4 D4
Burnham Thorpe Rd NR21 . 4 D2
Burns Cl
East Dereham NR19 . . . . 154 C7
Thetford IP24 . . . . 176 E6
Yaxley IP23 . . . . 129 F1
Burnside 3 PE37 . . . . 66 A4
Burnt Fen Turnpike
IP28 . . . . 112 D2
Burnt Fen Wy NR12 . . . . . . 164 E6
Burnt Hill La NR33 . . . . 111 F3
Burnt Hills NR27 . . . . 139 B4
Burnthouse Cres PE33 . . . . 63 B4
Burnthouse Dro PE33 . . . . 63 C5
Burnthouse La
Hethersett NR9 . . . . 160 C1
Needham NR20 . . . . 131 E8
Runhall NR20 . . . . 69 A4
Scole IP20 . . . . 122 A1
Toft Monks NR34 . . . . 110 D5
Wood Dalling NR11 . . . . 34 D5
Wymondham NR18 . . . . . . 173 F1
Burnt House Rd NR18 . . . . 92 B6
Burnt La
Great Yarmouth NR31 . . . . 170 C7
Wiggenhall St Mary Magdalen
PE34 . . . . 61 A4
Burntoak La IP20 . . . . 122 E4
Burnt St NR23 . . . . 136 D5
Burntwood La NR12 . . . . . . 54 C4
Burrage Way NR7 . . . . 159 D5
Burr Cl 14 IP25 . . . . 84 E3
Burrell Cl NR25 . . . . 137 D7
Burrell Way NR7 . . . . 176 A1
Burrettgate Rd PE13 . . . . 152 F5
Burrett Gdns PE13 . . . . 59 C5
Burrett Rd PE13 . . . . 59 C5
Burroughs Way NR18 . . . . 173 D4
Burrow Dr IP27 . . . . 113 E2
Burrows Cl NR6 . . . . 158 D7
Burrows Gn NR26 . . . . 110 F5
Burrows Green NR34 . . . . 111 A5
Burrow Way NR10 . . . . 53 D2
BURSTON IP22 . . . . 120 F2
Burston Cl NR24 . . . . 142 B4
Burston Com Prim Sch
IP22 . . . . 120 E2
Burston Rd Burston IP22 . . 120 E1
Dickleburgh & Rushall
IP21 . . . . 130 C8
Diss IP22 . . . . 177 E2
Gissing IP22 . . . . 120 F3
Scole IP21 . . . . 121 B1
Shimpling IP21 . . . . 120 F2
Shimpling IP21 . . . . 121 A2
Burton Ave NR28 . . . . 151 B4
Burton Cl
North Walsham NR28 . . . . 151 B4
Norwich NR6 . . . . 158 C5
Roydon IP22 . . . . 177 B5
Burton Dr 9 NR13 . . . . 72 E7
Burton Rd NR6 . . . . 158 C5
Burtons Cl 16 PE30 . . . . . . 146 D5
Burtontyne Ave NR19 . . . . 68 A7
Bury Bottom
Brandon IP27 . . . . 115 A1
Brandon IP27 . . . . 175 D2
Bury La IP24 . . . . 126 A5
Bury Rd Barnham IP24 . . . 125 A4
Barnham IP24 . . . . 125 E4
Barnham IP24 . . . . 125 E6
Brandon IP27 . . . . 175 C3
Brandon IP27 . . . . 175 D2
Hepworth IP22 . . . . 127 F4
Market Weston IP22 . . . . . 127 E4
Stuston IP23 . . . . 130 C5
Thetford IP24 . . . . 176 C1
Wattisfield IP22 . . . . 128 A1
Wortham IP22 . . . . 129 C4
Bury St NR2 . . . . 162 B4
Bush Cl PE31 . . . . 140 E3
Bush Dr NR12 . . . . 24 E4
Bushel Way NR17 . . . . . . 174 B3
Bush Est NR12 . . . . 24 D4
Bush Gn NR17 . . . . 86 C1
BUSH GREEN IP21 . . . . . . 122 A6
Bush Green IP21 . . . . 121 F7
Bush La Dereham NR20 . . . 68 B8
Wisbech PE13 . . . . 152 E5
Bush Rd Hemsby NR29 . . . 58 B5
Norwich NR6 . . . . 157 F7
BUSHY COMMON NR19 . . 67 B8
Bussard Cl NR31 . . . . 171 D4
Bussey Rd NR6 . . . . 158 D4
Busseys La PE36 . . . . 2 A6
Bussey's La NR31 . . . . . . 170 D5
Bussey's Loke
Great Yarmouth NR31 . . . . 170 A4
Hempnall NR15 . . . . 107 D5
BUSTARD'S GREEN
NR16 . . . . 106 C3
Bustards' La PE14 . . . . 41 F3
Butchers La PE31 . . . . 3 B7
Butcher's La NR21 . . . . . . 141 B4
Butler Gdns NR18 . . . . . . 173 F7
Buttercup Cl
North Lynn PE30 . . . . 147 C2
1 Thetford IP24 . . . . . . 176 F5
Buttercup Dr
Downham Market PE38 . . 172 A5
Downham Market PE38 . . 172 B5
14 Great Yarmouth NR31 . . 94 C6
Swaffham PE37 . . . . 153 C2
Buttercup La PE34 . . . . . 146 B4

Buttercup Way NR5 . . . . . 160 F6
Butterfield Rise PE36 . . . 132 D1
Butter La NR14 . . . . 92 D1
Buttermere 1 NR29 . . . . . 167 B2
Buttermere Rd 4 NR5 . . . 161 C6
Butter's Hall La NR12 . . . . 102 C7
Butterwick 3 PE30 . . . . . 147 C5
Butt La Belton NR31 . . . . . . 94 A6
Fakenham Magna IP24 . . 126 C3
Litcham PE32 . . . . 48 A4
Buttlands Cl NR21 . . . . 6 E2
Buttland's La PE33 . . . . 81 B8
Buttlands The
Great Cressingham IP25 . . 83 D4
Wells-next-the-Sea NR23 . 136 D5
Buttle's La NR15 . . . . 106 D3
Butts La NR26 . . . . 138 B5
Butts The
Kenninghall NR16 . . . . . . 119 A4
Norwich NR5 . . . . 160 F8
BUXTON NR10 . . . . 36 E1
Buxton Ave NR31 . . . . . . 170 D1
Buxton Cl 4 Cromer NR27 . 10 B5
Easton NR9 . . . . 70 B5
Buxton Prim Sch NR10 . . . 36 C3
Buxton Rd Aylsham NR11 . . 36 C3
Aylsham NR11 . . . . 150 D5
Aylsham NR11 . . . . 150 E3
Cawston NR10 . . . . 35 D2
Diss IP22 . . . . 177 B4
Frettenham NR12 . . . . 53 F3
Hainford NR10 . . . . 53 F5
Horstead with Stanninghall
NR12 . . . . 54 B6
Marsham NR10 . . . . 35 E2
Marsham NR10 . . . . 36 B1
North Walsham NR28 . . . 151 B4
Norwich NR3 . . . . 162 D8
Spixworth NR10 . . . . 158 F8
Buxton Sta NR10 . . . . 36 F2
Buzzard Way NR25 . . . . . 137 D6
Byfield Ct 3 NR3 . . . . 158 C1
Byfords Way IP25 . . . . 84 D2
Bygone Ct NR29 . . . . 57 C1
Bylaugh Rd NR20 . . . . 50 D5
Byroad IP21 . . . . 6 E3
Byron Ave PE13 . . . . 154 B7
Byron Rd
Great Yarmouth NR30 . . . 169 E8
Taverham NR8 . . . . 156 D8
Byron Way NR30 . . . . 168 D6
Byron Wlk 7 IP24 . . . . . . 176 E6

Cabbell Rd NR27 . . . . 139 B7
Cabin Cl 11 NR33 . . . . . . 111 F1
Cabinet Cl NR19 . . . . 154 E4
Cadamys Yd NR23 . . . . . . 136 D5
Caddow Cl NR19 . . . . 154 E2
Cadge Cl NR5 . . . . 161 D7
Norwich NR5 . . . . 161 D6
Cadge's La NR9 . . . . 86 B3
Cadiz Way NR31 . . . . 171 E4
Cadman Way IP25 . . . . 84 D3
Cadogan Rd NR27 . . . . . . 139 B7
Caerleon Dr NR30 . . . . . . 168 C5
Caernarvon Rd NR2 . . . . . 162 B6
Cage La IP24 . . . . 176 D3
Cains The NR8 . . . . 155 C2
Cairns Ct NR4 . . . . 162 A3
Caister Acad NR30 . . . . . . 168 E6
Caister By-pass NR30 . . . 168 C4
Caister Castle Car
Collection ★
Caister Jun & Inf Sch
NR30 . . . . 168 A5
CAISTER-ON-SEA NR30 . . 168 F6
Caister Rd NR30 . . . . 169 C7
Caister Sands Ave NR29 . . 168 E8
Caistor La
Caistor St Edmund NR14 . . 89 F6
Poringland NR14 . . . . 90 B6
Caistor Roman Town ★
NR14 . . . . 89 F6
CAISTOR ST EDMUND
NR14 . . . . 89 F6
Caius Cl PE31 . . . . 133 C5
Cake La PE14 . . . . 59 D2
Cake's La
Field Dalling NR21 . . . . . . 17 F8
Little Marsh NR25 . . . . . . 18 A8
CAKE ST NR17 . . . . 104 D1
Calamint Rd PE30 . . . . . . 147 A8
Caledonian Way
1 Belton NR31 . . . . 94 A5
Upper Hellesdon NR6 . . . 158 C4
Caley Cl NR3 . . . . 157 F2
Caley St PE31 . . . . 133 D5
Calf La NR10 . . . . 53 E2
CALIFORNIA NR29 . . . . . . 167 E3
California PE33 . . . . 62 E1
California Ave NR29 . . . . . 167 E4
California Cotts IP23 . . . . 136 E5
California Cres NR29 . . . . 167 F2
California Rd NR29 . . . . . . 167 E2
Calkewood La IP22 . . . . . 128 C1
CALTHORPE NR11 . . . . 21 A2
Calthorpe Cl Acle NR13 . . 166 B4
2 Stalham NR12 . . . . . . 39 B4
Calthorpe Dr NR4 . . . . 89 A8
Calthorpe Green NR13 . . 166 C4
Calthorpe Rd
Calthorpe NR11 . . . . 21 C1
Ingham NR12 . . . . 39 D4
Norwich NR5 . . . . 161 B6
CALTHORPE STREET
NR12 . . . . 39 D4

Calvers La NR35 . . . . 124 D3
Calvert St NR3 . . . . 178 B4
Calves Well La
Beeston Regis NR26 . . . . 138 F4
Sheringham NR27 . . . . . . 10 A5
Camargue Pl 4 PE13 . . . . 152 E3
Cambell Dr NR20 . . . . 50 B5
Camberley Rd NR4 . . . . . . 162 A2
Cambers La PE31 . . . . 135 D2
Cambridge Ave NR31 . . . . 170 A3
Cambridge Dr PE13 . . . . . 152 A6
Cambridge Rd PE30 . . . . . 148 D5
Cambridge St
Cromer NR27 . . . . 139 C7
Norwich NR2 . . . . 162 C4
Cambridge Way NR31 . . . 170 B3
Camden Pl 21 NR30 . . . . . 169 D2
Camden Rd NR30 . . . . 169 D2
Camelia Cl NR9 . . . . 88 C8
Camelot Rd NR31 . . . . . . 171 B8
Cameron Cl PE31 . . . . 133 C4
Cameron Cres 4 PE31 . . . 12 E4
Cameron Cl NR5 . . . . 161 C8
Cameron Gn NR8 . . . . 156 E8
Camfrey 6 PE30 . . . . 147 B7
Campbell Cl PE36 . . . . . . 132 D4
Campbell Ct 1 NR3 . . . . . 162 F8
Campbells Mdw PE30 . . . 146 F1
Camperdown 11 NR30 . . . 169 D2
Camp Gr NR1 . . . . 163 A6
Camping Cl 8 NR20 . . . . . 68 E6
Camping Field La NR12 . . 39 B4
Campingland IP25 . . . . . . 153 C4
Campion Ave NR31 . . . . . . 170 B3
Campion Cl 4 NR28 . . . . . 151 E5
Campion Pl PE38 . . . . 172 B3
Campion Rd
1 Dereham NR20 . . . . . . 68 A8
Thetford IP24 . . . . 176 F4
Campion Way
6 Attleborough NR17 . . 174 B4
3 Sheringham NR26 . . . 138 B6
Campion Wy NR9 . . . . 88 C8
Camp La NR7 . . . . 10 A4
Camp Rd NR8 . . . . 155 C1
Campsey Rd PE38 . . . . . . 97 B6
Canada Cl 6 PE31 . . . . . . 12 E5
Canada Goose Ct 21
NR7 . . . . 159 E4
Canada Rd NR27 . . . . 139 B7
Canal Farm La NR28 . . . . 38 C6
Canal St 6 PE13 . . . . 152 C5
Canaryfields NR1 . . . . 163 A4
Canary Way NR1 . . . . 163 A4
Canberra Rd PE25 . . . . 84 F3
Candler's La 18 IP20 . . . . 122 D2
Candle Stick NR9 . . . . 69 A3
Candlestick La PE32 . . . . . 45 C8
CANDLE STREET IP22 . . . 128 D1
Canfor Rd 7 NR13 . . . . . . 72 E7
CANGATE NR12 . . . . 55 C6
Cangate Rd NR12 . . . . . . 55 C6
Cannell Gn NR3 . . . . 178 C4
Cannell Rd 11 NR14 . . . . . 92 A1
Norwich NR7 . . . . 159 B3
Cannon St PE13 . . . . 152 C4
Cannon Terr 9 PE13 . . . . 152 C4
Cann's La NR9 . . . . 88 D7
Canon Cl 6 IP25 . . . . 84 E3
Canon Hoare Rd NR11 . . 150 C4
Canon Macon Way NR4 . 19 D5
Canon Pickering VC Jun Sch
IP20 . . . . 122 D2
Canon Pott Cl PE31 . . . . 133 D6
Canons Cl 2 NR19 . . . . . . 154 D2
Canon's Cl IP24 . . . . 176 B4
Canons Wlk IP24 . . . . 176 B3
Canon Wake Ct 4 NR29 . . 56 C8
Canterbury Pl NR2 . . . . . . 162 C7
Canterbury Way IP24 . . . 176 B5
CANTLEY NR13 . . . . 92 B7
Cantley Cnr NR13 . . . . 74 B1
Cantley La Cringleford NR4 . 89 A5
Ketteringham NR18 . . . . . 88 F6
Cantley Primary Sch
NR13 . . . . 92 B7
Cantley Rd NR13 . . . . 92 D7
Cantley Sta NR13 . . . . 92 B6
Cants Cl 4 NR9 . . . . 69 F2
Canwich Heath Rd IP26 . . 99 E4
Capgrave Rd PE30 . . . . . . 146 F8
Capps La IP20 . . . . 123 F1
Capstan Way 9 NR33 . . . . 111 F1
Captain Ford Wy NR19 . . 154 E3
Caraway Cl IP25 . . . . 153 D4
Caraway Dr 22 NR31 . . . . 94 C6
Caraway Rd PE14 . . . . . . 176 F4
CARBROOKE IP25 . . . . 85 B5
Carbrooke La
Crowshill IP25 . . . . 67 B1
Shipdham IP25 . . . . 85 B8
Carbrooke Rd
Carbrooke IP25 . . . . 85 B3
Caston NR17 . . . . 85 C1
Griston IP25 . . . . 85 A2
Ovington IP25 . . . . 84 E5
Cardiff Rd NR2 . . . . 162 B5
Cardigan Pl NR2 . . . . 162 C7
Cardinal Cl NR9 . . . . 70 B5
Cardington Cl 1 NR13 . . 166 D4
Cardington Rd
Feltwell IP26 . . . . 98 D1
Watton IP25 . . . . 85 A3
Cardun Cl 3 NR13 . . . . . . 73 C6

Cargate Common NR16 . 120 E8
Cargate Comm Rd
NR16 . . . . 105 E1
CARGATE GREEN NR13 . . 166 A8
Cargate La
Saxlingham Nethergate
NR15 . . . . 107 A8
Saxlingham Thorpe NR15 . 89 D7
Upton with Fishley NR13 . 166 A8
Carl Cl 9 NR14 . . . . 154 D1
Carl Cres NR28 . . . . 22 E5
Carleton Cl 4 NR8 . . . . . . 173 C6
CARLETON FOREHOE
NR9 . . . . 87 C8
CARLETON RODE NR16 . . 105 C3
Carleton Rode CE Prim Sch
NR16 . . . . 105 C3
CARLETON ST PETER
NR14 . . . . 91 E5
Carlton Cl NR19 . . . . 154 D4
Carlton Dr NR30 . . . . 148 D5
Carlton Gdns NR1 . . . . . . 178 B1
Carlton Marshes Nature
Reserve ★ NR33 . . . . . . 111 F3
Carlyle Rd NR1 . . . . 162 F3
Carmelite Terr 16 PE30 . 146 D4
Carmen's La NR28 . . . . . . 38 B3
Carnation Way NR31 . . . . 170 B7
Carn Cl NR13 . . . . 74 B2
Carnoustie 5 NR4 . . . . . . 162 A1
Carnoustie Ct PE31 . . . . . 41 C8
Carnwich Rd IP26 . . . . . . 100 A4
Carola Sutton Ct NR25 . . 137 B5
Carol Cl NR14 . . . . 90 B5
Caroline Ct NR4 . . . . 161 F4
Carpenter Cl NR18 . . . . . 173 F7
Carpenters Cotts NR25 . . 137 B6
Carpenter's Wlk NR15 . . . 121 D7
Carrell Rd NR1 . . . . 170 B1
Carrington Rd NR21 . . . . . 139 D5
Carr La
Great Moulton NR15 . . . . 106 A3
Northrepps NR27 . . . . . . 139 C1
Overstrand NR27 . . . . . . 11 A3
Poringland NR14 . . . . 90 C4
Wendling NR19 . . . . 66 F4
Carrow Abbey NR1 . . . . . . 163 A3
Carrowbreck Cl NR8 . . . . 157 D5
Carrowbreck Rd NR6 . . . . 157 D5
Carrow Cl NR1 . . . . 162 F3
Carrow Hill NR1 . . . . 178 C1
Carrow Rd NR1 . . . . 178 C1
Carrs Hill Cl NR8 . . . . 157 A4
Carrs Loke NR12 . . . . 164 F8
Carrs Rd NR13 . . . . 92 A8
Carr Terr PE31 . . . . 134 E5
Carshalton Rd 2 NR1 . . . 162 F3
Carter Cl
Caister-on-Sea NR30 . . . 168 D8
Swaffham PE37 . . . . 153 C2
Carterford Dr NR6 . . . . . . 158 E3
Carter Rd Drayton NR8 . . 71 A8
Sprowston NR7 . . . . 159 E5
Taverham NR8 . . . . 157 A8
Carter's Cl PE30 . . . . 148 B1
Carters La NR10 . . . . 53 E7
Carter's La NR20 . . . . 50 A6
Carters Loke NR13 . . . . . 166 C2
Cart Gap Rd NR12 . . . . . . 24 C4
Cartledge Cl 1 NR19 . . . 154 D1
Cartmel 17 NR9 . . . . 88 D8
Carver's La PE31 . . . . . . 174 B5
Casaubon Cl 8 NR19 . . . 154 D3
Caslon Cl 9 NR21 . . . . . . 141 C5
Castelins Way 20 NR14 . . 89 B3
Castell Cl IP21 . . . . 131 E1
Castell Rd NR19 . . . . 154 D7
CASTLE ACRE PE32 . . . . . 46 F2
Castle Acre Castle ★
PE32 . . . . 47 A2
Castle Acre CE VC Prim
Acad PE32 . . . . 46 F1
Castle Acre Cl 2 PE30 . . 148 C3
Castle Acre Priory ★
PE32 . . . . 46 F1
Castleacre Rd
Great Massingham PE32 . . 29 D1
Great Massingham PE32 . . 46 D8
Newton PE32 . . . . 47 A1
Swaffham PE37 . . . . 153 B8
Castle Acre Rd
Great Dunham PE32 . . . . 47 E1
Rougham PE32 . . . . 47 A6
Castle Cl 3 Gresham NR11 . 9 E1
Holt NR25 . . . . 137 C5
King's Lynn PE30 . . . . . . 147 C8
Weeting IP27 . . . . 175 D8
Castle Dr PE31 . . . . 140 E4
Castle East Sch NR35 . . . 124 B8
Castlefold Cl IP24 . . . . . . 176 B4
Castle Gn NR31 . . . . 170 B4
Castle Green PE32 . . . . . . 48 C6
Castle La Bungay NR35 . . 124 A8
Harleston IP20 . . . . 122 E3
Thetford IP24 . . . . 176 E3
West Caister NR30 . . . . . 168 B5
Castle Lane NR21 . . . . . . 15 D6
Castle Mdw NR1 . . . . 178 B2
Castle Mkt St NR1 . . . . . 178 B2
Castle Rd
Baconsthorpe NR25 . . . . . 20 A8
Mettingham NR35 . . . . . . 124 E5
Wormegay PE33 . . . . 62 C6
Castle Rise NR8 . . . . 155 C2
CASTLE RISING PE31 . . . . 27 C3
Castle Rising Castle ★
PE31 . . . . 27 C3

Castle Rising Rd PE30 . . . 148 D3
Castle Sq 18 PE13 . . . . . 152 C5
Castle St Norwich NR2 . . . 178 B3
Thetford IP24 . . . . 176 D4
Wroxham/Hoveton NR12 . 164 B3
Castleton Ave NR33 . . . . . 111 F1
Castleton Cl 1 NR5 . . . . . 160 F8
Castleton Way NR13 . . . . 130 A1
CASTON NR17 . . . . 102 C8
Caston CE VA Prim Sch
NR17 . . . . 85 B1
Caston Cl 9 NR25 . . . . . . 137 B6
Caston Rd Carbrooke PE25 . 85 B4
Griston IP25 . . . . 85 A2
Norwich NR7 . . . . 163 F8
Catalpa Way 5 NR31 . . . 170 B5
Catbridge La NR14 . . . . . . 89 A4
Catchpole Wlk IP21 . . . . 121 C1
CATFIELD NR29 . . . . 56 C8
Catfield Rd NR29 . . . . 56 D6
Catfield VC CE Prim Sch
NR29 . . . . 56 C8
Cathedral Dr NR20 . . . . . 49 E8
Cathedral St NR1 . . . . . . 178 C3
Catherine Howard Cl 3
IP24 . . . . 176 D6
Catherine Wheel Opening 8
NR3 . . . . 162 D8
Catling's La PE13 . . . . . . 41 A3
Catlyn Pl NR18 . . . . 173 F8
Catmere Herne NR14 . . . . 89 F2
Cator Rd NR8 . . . . 155 F1
Catriona Ct NR25 . . . . 8 B6
Cats Cnr NR10 . . . . 37 B7
Cattle Market Chase
NR13 . . . . 152 A7
Cattle Mkt St 4 NR21 . . 141 C4
Catton Chase NR6 . . . . . 158 E6
Catton Ct NR6 . . . . 158 E6
Catton Grove Prim Sch
NR3 . . . . 158 C3
Catton Gr Rd NR3 . . . . . 158 D2
Catton's Drift NR11 . . . . . 10 C2
Catton View Ct NR3 . . . . 158 D3
Caudle Hill
Great Cressingham IP25 . . 83 E5
South Pickenham PE37 . . 83 E7
CAUDLESPRINGS IP25 . . . 85 A4
Caudwell Cl 2 NR14 . . . . 89 F4
Causeway Cl
Brockdish IP21 . . . . 131 C6
Norwich NR2 . . . . 162 C8
Causeway Dr 4 NR12 . . . 54 C6
Causeway The
Bressingham IP22 . . . . . 129 B7
Heigham Bridge NR29 . . . 57 A5
Hickling NR12 . . . . 39 F2
Stow Bedon PE34 . . . . . . 61 D1
Stow Bridge PE34 . . . . . . 61 C2
Cavalier Cl 30 NR7 . . . . . 72 D4
Cavell Cl NR14 . . . . 89 C5
Cavell Prim Sch NR1 . . . . 162 E1
Cavell Rd Acle NR13 . . . . 166 B3
Norwich NR1 . . . . 162 E2
Cavendish Cl PE32 . . . . . . 44 C3
Cavenham Rd PE33 . . . . . . 80 E4
Cave's Cl PE34 . . . . 144 B5
Cavick Rd NR18 . . . . 173 A3
Cawdor Cl NR17 . . . . 174 E6
Cawseyhorn Drove
IP27 . . . . 114 A2
CAWSTON NR10 . . . . 35 B2
Cawston La
Great Witchingham NR9 . . 51 E7
Little Witchingham NR9 . . 149 E1
Cawston Rd
Aylsham NR11 . . . . 150 A5
Brandiston NR10 . . . . 35 B1
Brandiston NR10 . . . . 52 B8
Buxton NR10 . . . . 36 E1
Reepham NR10 . . . . 149 D6
Swannington NR9 . . . . . . 52 B6
Cawston VC Prim Sch
NR10 . . . . 35 B2
Caxton Cl NR26 . . . . 138 F5
Caxton Ct PE30 . . . . 147 D4
Caxton Pk NR26 . . . . 138 F5
Caxton Rd NR34 . . . . 110 D1
Caxton Way 2 NR12 . . . . 176 A2
Caystreward NR30 . . . . . 168 E1
Cecil Cl 7 PE33 . . . . 61 D6
Cecil Gowing Ct NR7 . . . 159 B4
Cecil Gowing Inf Sch
NR7 . . . . 159 C3
Cecil Rd
East Dereham NR20 . . . . 154 F5
Norwich NR1 . . . . 162 D3
Cedar Ave 4 NR10 . . . . . . 54 A2
Cedar Cl
1 Downham Market
PE38 . . . . 172 C6
12 Great Yarmouth NR31 . 94 C2
19 Martham NR29 . . . . . . 57 D4
12 Martham NR29 . . . . . . 68 E6
North Elmham NR20 . . . . 49 E7
Cedar Dr
Attleborough NR17 . . . . . 174 C4
10 Loddon NR14 . . . . . . 92 A1
Cedar Gr
North Runcton PE33 . . . . 44 A3
Sheringham NR26 . . . . . . 138 E5
Cedar Rd Hethersett NR9 . 88 C8
Marham PE33 . . . . 63 B4
Norwich NR1 . . . . 163 A5

Cedar Rd continued
Thetford IP24 . . . . 176 F7
Cedar Rise NR20 . . . . 68 E6
Cedar Row PE30 . . . . 147 B7
Cedar Springs PE31 . . . . 138 C6
Cedars The Keswick N12 . . 23 F3
Norwich NR2 . . . . 162 B4
Shepherd's Port PE31 . . . 12 B4
Cedar Way Brandon IP27 . 175 D2
Brundall NR13 . . . . 165 C3
4 Gayton PE32 . . . . 45 C6
King's Lynn PE34 . . . . . . 146 C4
Cedarwood Cl
Cringleford NR4 . . . . 161 C1
Reepham NR10 . . . . 149 B5
Cedar Wy 14 NR7 . . . . . . 59 A1
Celandine Cl 2 IP24 . . . . 176 F5
Celandine La 6 NR26 . . . 138 B6
Celandine Rd 4 NR17 . . . 174 B4
Celia Phillips Cl 7
IP24 . . . . 176 D7
Cemetery La NR18 . . . . . 173 B3
Cemetery Rd
East Dereham NR19 . . . . 154 F4
Lakenheath IP27 . . . . . . 113 E1
Outwell PE14 . . . . 78 A4
Centenary Way PE12 . . . . 41 C6
Central Ave NR7 . . . . 72 C3
Central Cl 1 NR9 . . . . 88 D7
Central Cres 2 NR9 . . . . . 88 D7
Central Dr NR20 . . . . 50 A5
Central Rd Cromer NR27 . 139 A7
King's Lynn PE30 . . . . . . 146 D6
Centre Cres PE31 . . . . . . 140 D3
Centre Point 6 PE30 . . . . 147 D5
Centre Rd NR20 . . . . 32 C3
Centre Vale PE31 . . . . . . 140 D3
Centre Vale Rd PE31 . . . . 140 D3
Century Rd 8 Eye IP23 . . 130 C1
Great Yarmouth NR31 . . . 169 B3
Century Way NR8 . . . . . . 155 F3
Cere Rd NR7 . . . . 159 C4
Ceres Dr PE37 . . . . 153 D4
Cess Rd NR29 . . . . 57 C5
CESS NR29 . . . . 57 C5
Chadwick Sq 2 PE30 . . . 147 A7
Chaffinch Mews 18
IP20 . . . . 122 D1
Chalfont Wlk NR4 . . . . . . 161 E2
ChalGr Field 33 NR7 . . . . 72 D4
Chalk Cl IP24 . . . . 176 D4
CHALKHILL IP25 . . . . 83 C4
Chalk Hill IP25 . . . . 83 C4
Chalk Hill Rd NR1 . . . . . . 178 C3
Chalk La
Cley next the Sea NR25 . . . 7 E6
Culford IP31 . . . . 125 C1
Narborough PE32 . . . . . . 63 E5
North End NR16 . . . . 106 D2
Snetterton NR16 . . . . . . 103 D1
Sutton Bridge PE12 . . . . . 41 C7
West Stow IP28 . . . . 125 A2
Chalk Loke NR23 . . . . 5 F3
Chalk Pit Cl 14 PE33 . . . . 63 B4
Chalkpit Rd PE31 . . . . 3 A2
Chalk Pit Rd
Heacham PE31 . . . . 133 F3
Holme next the Sea PE36 . 2 E4
Ingoldisthorpe PE31 . . . . 140 E7
Chalk Rd Brandon IP27 . . 114 D5
Brandon IP27 . . . . 175 A3
Outwell PE14 . . . . 78 A4
5 Walpole St Andrew
PE14 . . . . 41 E4
Chalk River Rd
Hunstanton PE36 . . . . 1 D2
Hunstanton PE36 . . . . . . 132 D1
Chalkrow La PE33 . . . . . . 81 F4
Chalk Wy IP26 . . . . 99 A5
Chamberlin Ri NR18 . . . . 173 F8
Chamberlin Cl NR3 . . . . . 158 E2
Chamberlin Ct
Brundall NR13 . . . . 165 E6
Hoveton NR12 . . . . 164 E6
Chamberlin Rd NR3 . . . . 158 E1
Chambers Rd NR3 . . . . . 158 B3
Chameryhall La NR13 . . . . 73 F3
Champney's Rd IP22 . . . . 177 E4
Chancel Cl NR13 . . . . 165 C3
Chancel La NR9 . . . . 68 C2
Chancellors Dr
Norwich NR4 . . . . 71 B2
Norwich NR4 . . . . 161 C4
Chandler Rd NR14 . . . . . . 89 F5
Chandlers Cl 2 NR13 . . . 173 B3
Chandlers Ct 8 NR4 . . . . 89 C8
Chandlers Hill 4 NR18 . . 173 B3
Chandler's Hill La 1
NR18 . . . . 173 B3
Changi Rd 5 PE75 . . . . . . 84 F3
Chantry Cl 9 PE37 . . . . . . 65 F4
Chantry La PE37 . . . . 66 A4
Chantry Rd NR2 . . . . 178 A2
Chantry The NR1 . . . . . . 178 A2
Chapel Ave NR15 . . . . . . 106 E3
Chapel Bank PE36 . . . . . 132 E6
Chapel Break Inf Sch
NR5 . . . . 160 F8
Chapel Break Rd NR5 . . 160 E7
Chapel Cl
Barnham Broom NR9 . . . 69 C2
Garboldisham IP22 . . . . . 128 A8
Pulham Market IP21 . . . . 121 E5
Reepham NR10 . . . . 149 B5
Tacolneston NR16 . . . . . 105 F4
Winfarthing IP22 . . . . . . 120 B5
Chapel Cnr NR12 . . . . 55 D6
Chapel Corner NR30 . . . 168 C4
Chapel Ct
2 Blofield NR13 . . . . . . 165 D6
Blofield NR13 . . . . 165 E6

Chapel Ct continued
Brundall NR13 . . . . .165 E6
Hellesdon NR6 . . . . .158 A5
Norwich NR6 . . . . .157 F5
Chapelfield NR13 . . . . . .92 E7
CHAPEL FIELD NR12 . . . .39 A3
Chapel Field NR13 . . . . .93 A4
Chapelfield Cl 1 NR29 . . .56 C8
Chapel Field E NR2 . . . .178 A2
Chapel Field La PE14 . . .41 D1
Chapel Field N NR2 . . . .178 A2
Chapel Field Rd
Norwich NR2 . . . . .178 A2
Stalham NR12 . . . . .39 A3
Chapel Green Sch
NR17 . . . . .104 D2
Chapel Hill Denton IP20 .123 A7
Edgefield NR24 . . . . .19 D5
Fakenham NR21 . . . . .141 B5
Woodton NR35 . . . . .108 C4
Chapel La
Aldborough NR11 . . . . .21 A5
Ashby St Mary NR14 . . . . . .91 D5
Barton Bendish PE33 . . . . .81 B8
Beeston with Bittering
PE32 . . . . .48 C2
Beetley NR20 . . . . .49 C4
Botesdale IP22 . . . . .128 E2
Brandon Parva NR9 . . . . . . .69 B3
Bridgham NR16 . . . . .117 F5
Burgate IP22 . . . . .129 C3
Coltishall NR12 . . . . .54 D7
East Dereham NR19 . . . . .154 D2
Emneth PE14 . . . . .59 B2
Felthorpe NR10 . . . . .155 C8
Fincham PE33 . . . . .62 E1
Foulsham NR20 . . . . .33 D3
3 Great Yarmouth NR31 . .94 C6
Hempstead NR25 . . . . .19 E8
Hockering NR20 . . . . .69 B8
Hunstanton PE36 . . . . . . .132 C4
Ingham Corner NR12 . . . . .39 D6
Kirby Row NR35 . . . . .109 E3
Methwold IP26 . . . . .99 A5
Necton PE37 . . . . .66 A4
Norwich NR7 . . . . .163 E6
Potter Heigham NR29 . . . . .56 F7
Ringstead PE36 . . . . .2 A3
Scarning NR19 . . . . .67 B7
Sculthorpe NR21 . . . . .16 B1
Shelton NR15 . . . . .107 B1
Shotesham NR15 . . . . .90 B2
Skeyton NR10 . . . . .37 B6
West Caister NR30 . . . . . .168 C4
West Winch PE33 . . . . .43 E3
Wimbotsham PE34 . . . . . .172 E8
Wiveton NR25 . . . . .7 E6
Wymondham NR18 . . . . . .173 A5
Chapel Loke
Lessingham NR12 . . . . .24 C2
7 Old Buckenham NR17 104 D2
Salhouse NR13 . . . . .55 B1
4 Stoke Holy Cross NR14 . .89 F4
Surlingham NR14 . . . . .73 B1
Wymondham NR18 . . . . . .105 A8
Chapel Mdw NR35 . . . . .109 E3
Chapel Rd
Alby with Thwaite NR11 . . . .21 B3
Ashby St Mary NR14 . . . . . .91 D5
Attleborough NR17 . . . . . .174 C5
Beighton NR13 . . . . .74 C2
Boughton PE33 . . . . .81 A4
Carleton Rode NR16 . . . . .105 C3
Dersingham PE31 . . . . . . .140 D4
Dilham NR20 . . . . .38 B3
East Ruston NR12 . . . . .38 E6
Foxley NR20 . . . . .50 D8
Grimston PE32 . . . . .28 A1
Guestwick NR20 . . . . .33 H6
Hainford NR10 . . . . .53 E5
Halvergate NR13 . . . . .75 A2
Hinderclay IP22 . . . . .128 C3
Lingwood NR13 . . . . .73 F3
Longham NR19 . . . . .49 A2
Lowestoft NR33 . . . . .111 F1
Morley NR18 . . . . .87 B2
Neatishead NR12 . . . . .55 E6
Necton PE37 . . . . .66 B4
Norwich NR5 . . . . .157 A2
Paston NR28 . . . . .143 D1
Roughton NR11 . . . . .21 D8
Roydon PE32 . . . . .45 A8
St Andrew, Ilketshall
NR34 . . . . .124 F6
St John's Fen End PE14 . . . .60 C6
Sea Palling NR12 . . . . .40 A6
Southrepps NR11 . . . . .22 B6
Swafield NR28 . . . . .22 D3
Terrington St Clement
PE34 . . . . .144 B5
Trunch NR28 . . . . .22 E5
Upton with Fishley NR13 . .166 B8
Wicken Green Village NR21 15 C2
Wisbech PE13 . . . . .152 B5
Witton NR28 . . . . .23 E2
Wymondham NR18 . . . . . .105 A8
Chapel Rise 11 PE33 . . . .63 B4
Chapel St Barford NR9 . . .70 A3
Cawston NR10 . . . . .35 B3
3 Cromer NR27 . . . . .139 B7
Diss IP22 . . . . .177 D4
6 Hingham NR9 . . . . .86 C5
Ixworth NR9 . . . . .69 F2
King's Lynn PE30 . . . . . . .146 D5
8 Old Buckenham NR16 .104 F1
Rocklands NR17 . . . . .103 B8
Shipdham IP25 . . . . .67 C2
Southrepps NR11 . . . . .22 C7
Warham NR23 . . . . .6 A4
14 Wisbech PE13 . . . . . .152 C4
Wiveton NR25 . . . . .7 E6

Chapel Terr
Smallburgh NR12 . . . . .38 E2
South Wootton PE30 . . . .148 B1
Chapel Wlk 4 NR19 . . . .154 E5
Chapel Yard NR23 . . . . . . .5 B6
Chapel Yd Ashill IP25 . . . . .84 A7
Wells-next-the-Sea NR23 .136 C6
Chaplin Rd NR31 . . . . .94 B6
Chaplyn Ct IP22 . . . . . . .177 F3
Chapman Ave NR30 . . . .168 E5
Chapmans Cl 17 NR26 . .138 D7
Chapman Way NR14 . . . .88 D3
Chapnall Cl PE13 . . . . . . .152 F6
Chapnall Rd PE13 . . . . . .152 F6
Chappshill Way 22 NR14. .89 B3
Chare La IP31 . . . . .127 B1
Chare Rd IP31 . . . . .127 B1
Charing Cross NR2. . . . . .178 A3
Charles Ave
Norwich NR7 . . . . .163 F6
Watton NR25 . . . . .84 D3
Charles Burrell Mus ★
IP24 . . . . .176 C4
Charles Burton Cl 5
NR30 . . . . .168 D7
Charles Cl Acle NR13 . . . .166 B4
Caister-on-Sea NR30 . . . . .168 E5
Cromer NR27 . . . . .10 C4
Dereham NR19 . . . . .154 C1
Wroxham/Hoveton NR12 .164 C3
Charles Darwin Prim Sch
NR1 . . . . .162 C8
Charles Dewar Cl PE32. . .29 D2
Charles Ewing Cl NR11 . .150 B5
Charles Jewson Ct NR6 .158 B2
Charles Marler Way
NR13 . . . . .165 D6
Charles Rash Cl NR28 . . .37 B8
Charles Rd
Fakenham NR21 . . . . .141 C4
Holt NR25 . . . . .137 C5
Hunstanton PE36 . . . . . . .132 C2
9 Sutton Bridge PE12 . . .41 B8
Charles Sq 6 NR2 . . . . . .162 C6
Charles St
Great Yarmouth NR30 . . . .169 D2
King's Lynn PE30 . . . . . . .146 E3
11 Wisbech PE13 . . . . . .152 C4
Charles Watling Way 1
NR5 . . . . .72 B7
Charles Wood Rd NR19. .154 F2
Charlock PE30 . . . . .147 A8
Charlock Cl NR30 . . . . . .168 E4
Charlock Dr 8 NR26 . . . .138 B6
Charlotte's Cl 1 NR27 . . .9 F5
Charlton Rd NR3. . . . . . .178 B4
Charmbeck Pk NR10 . . . . .52 D8
Charolais Cl NR14 . . . . . .163 B2
Charter Cl NR31 . . . . . . .170 B4
Chartwell Ct NR7 . . . . . .158 F3
Chartwell Rd NR6 . . . . . .158 D3
Chase Ave PE30 . . . . .146 E3
Chase Cl NR6 . . . . .158 D5
Chase Ct
East Dereham NR19 . . . .154 D6
Thetford IP24 . . . . .176 B3
Chase St PE13 . . . . .152 C6
Chase The Brandon IP27 .175 F2
Brundall NR13 . . . . .165 F6
Foul Anchor PE13 . . . . . . .41 A3
Stow Bardolph PE34 . . . . . .78 E7
Upwell PE14. . . . . .77 D3
Walpole St Andrew PE14 . . .41 D2
West Walton PE14. . . . . . . .59 A8
Wiggenhall St Peter PE34. . .61 C8
Chatham St NR3 . . . . . . .178 A4
Chatsworth Rd NR36 . . . .132 C3
Chaucer Cl 14 NR20 . . . . .50 E7
Chaucer Rd NR30 . . . . . .169 D8
Checker St PE30 . . . . . . .146 E3
CHEDGRAVE NR14 . . . . . .92 A2
Cheese Hill 9 NR16. . . . . .118 C5
Chenery Dr NR7 . . . . . . .159 C5
Cheney Cres PE31 . . . . . .133 D4
Cheney Hill PE31 . . . . . . .133 D4
Cheney's La NR16. . . . . . .105 F5
Chepore La NR18 . . . . .87 C1
Chequers Cl
Briston NR24 . . . . .142 E3
2 Long Stratton NR15. . .106 D3
1 Roydon PE32 . . . . .28 A1
Chequers Hill NR16 . . . .106 C6
Chequers La
Bressingham IP22. . . . . . .129 B7
Burston & Shimpling IP22 120 E4
Great Ellingham NR17 . . . .103 E8
Gressenhall NR20 . . . . .49 B4
North Runcton PE33 . . . . . .44 A2
Saham Toney IP25 . . . . . . .84 C5
South Creake NR21 . . . . . .15 D6
South Lopham IP22 . . . . . .128 D6
West Winch PE33 . . . . .43 F2
Chequer's La NR15. . . . . .107 E8
Chequers Mdw NR10. . . . .53 E6
Chequers Rd
Gresham NR11. . . . . .9 E1
Gresham NR25. . . . . .20 E8
Roydon PE32 . . . . .28 A1
Tharston & Hapton NR15 106 D3
Wretton PE33 . . . . .80 E3
Chequers St
Docking PE31. . . . . .134 D4
East Ruston NR12 . . . . . . .38 F5
Gresham NR11. . . . . .9 E1
Cherry Cl
Attleborough NR17 . . . . . .174 F4
11 Great Yarmouth NR31 . .94 C7
Marham PE33 . . . . .63 A4
Norwich NR1 . . . . .162 E2
Cherry Dr NR19 . . . . .154 F5
Cherry Drift NR19 . . . . . .154 E6

Cherry La
Belton with Browston
NR31 . . . . .94 B4
Dereham NR20 . . . . .68 A7
Dereham NR20 . . . . .68 B7
Cherry Mws NR20 . . . . . .50 B2
Cherry Orch NR20. . . . . .154 F5
Cherry Rd
Great Yarmouth NR31 . . . .170 B6
Wisbech PE13 . . . . .152 C8
Cherry Tree Acad PE33 . . .63 B5
Cherry Tree Acad Marham
Inf Sch PE33 . . . . .63 B4
Cherry Tree Ave 25 NR7 .158 E7
Cherrytree Cl PE31. . . . . .133 D6
Cherry Tree Cl
Brandon IP27 . . . . .175 D2
Holt NR25. . . . . .137 B7
Mundford IP26 . . . . .100 A4
North Lopham IP22 . . . . . .119 A2
Wortham IP22 . . . . .129 C4
Wretham IP24 . . . . .102 B1
Cherry Tree Ct IP22 . . . . .177 C5
Cherry Tree Dr
King's Lynn PE34 . . . . . . .146 C4
Terrington St John PE14 . . .42 B1
Cherry Tree La
Botesdale IP22 . . . . .128 E3
North Walsham NR28 . . . .151 B5
Primrose Green NR9 . . . . . .51 B3
Stow Bedon NR17 . . . . . . .102 D6
Cherry Tree Rd
Banham NE16 . . . . .120 B8
Carleton Rode NR16 . . . . .105 A1
Plumstead NR11 . . . . .20 A6
Snettisham PE31 . . . . .12 E5
Tibenham NR16 . . . . .120 B7
Cherrywood
Alpington NR14 . . . . .90 F4
10 Redenhall with Harleston
IP20. . . . . .122 D7
Cherrywood Ave NR21 . . .15 C2
Cherry Yard la NR35 . . . .108 A3
Chervil Wlk IP24. . . . . . . .176 B2
Cherwell Way 2 NR31 . . .170 B2
Chesterfield Cotts 11
NR27 . . . . .139 B7
Chester Pl NR2 . . . . .162 C6
Chester St NR2 . . . . .162 C4
Chester Way IP24. . . . . . .176 A4
Chestnut Ave
Great Yarmouth NR31 . . . .170 A5
North Walsham NR28 . . . .151 E4
Sculthorpe Airfield NR21. . .15 C2
1 Spixworth NR10. . . . . .54 A2
Welney PE14 . . . . .95 D5
West Winch PE33 . . . . .43 E1
Chestnut Cl
Brandon IP27. . . . . .175 C2
Dersingham PE31 . . . . . . .140 E3
East Dereham NR19 . . . . .154 E1
Norwich NR5 . . . . .156 E2
Swardeston NR14 . . . . .89 B5
5 Watlington PE33 . . . . . .61 D5
Chestnut Ct 9 NR2 . . . . .178 A3
Chestnut Dr
Attleborough NR17 . . . . . .174 B4
Wymondham NR18 . . . . . .173 B2
Chestnut Gr NR26. . . . . . .138 D4
Chestnut Hill 8 NR4 . . . .161 F1
Chestnut Loke NR15 . . . .107 A6
Chestnut Pl NR4 . . . . .161 C1
Chestnut Rd
Dickleburgh IP21. . . . . . . .121 C1
East Dereham NR19 . . . . .154 C5
Pulham St Mary IP21 . . . .121 F4
1 Snettisham PE31 . . . . . .12 E4
13 Tasburgh NR15. . . . . .106 F6
8 Watton IP25. . . . . .84 E3
8 Wisbech PE13 . . . . . . .152 C4
Chestnuts The
Rickinghall Inferior IP22. . .128 E2
Wymondham NR18 . . . . . .173 B4
Chestnut Terr PE12 . . . . . .41 B8
Chestnut Wlk PE37. . . . . . .81 F8
Chew Ct NR20. . . . . .147 E8
Cheyham Mount NR4 . . .161 F1
Cheyney Ave 1 NR13 . . . .55 A1
CHICKERING IP21 . . . . . .131 D3
Chickering Rd IP21 . . . . . .131 B2
Childs Rd NR9 . . . . .88 C8
Childs Way NR26. . . . . . . .138 C5
Chiltern Cres PE36. . . . . .132 C6
Chilver House La PE32 . . .44 E7
Chilvers Pl PE31 . . . . .133 D5
Chimes Way NR10 . . . . . .149 B8
Chimney Springs NR29. .167 A3
Chimney St PE32 . . . . .46 F1
Chipperfield Rd NR7 . . . .159 E1
Chittock Cl 5 NR11 . . . . . .54 A1
Cholmondeley Way 3
PE33. . . . . .43 F2
Chopyngs Dole Cl NR7 . .159 C5
Choseley Ct NR18. . . . . . .173 C4
Choseley La PE31 . . . . .2 D2
Choseley Rd
Docking PE31. . . . . .134 C7
Thornham PE36. . . . . .2 D6
Titchwell PE31. . . . . .2 D7
CHRISTCHURCH PE14. . . .95 A7
Christchurch Rd NR2 . . . .162 B6
Christ Church Rd NR31. .170 A4
Christie Cl 6 NR19 . . . . .154 D1
Christine Ave NR13 . . . . . .74 A2
Christine Rd 1 NR10. . . . .54 A1
Christopher Cl
1 Newton Flotman NR15 .89 D1
1 Norwich NR1 . . . . . . .162 E2
Christopher Dr PE13 . . . .152 A7
Christophers Cl NR27 . . .139 D3
Christopher Way NR12. .164 B2

Church Alley NR13 . . . . .165 E6
Church Ave Croxton IP24 116 C5
Halvergate NR13 . . . . .74 F1
Little Ellingham NR17 . . . . .86 A1
Norwich NR4 . . . . .162 B3
Church Ave E NR2 . . . . . .162 B3
Church Bank
Marshland St James PE14 .60 C2
Terrington St Clement
PE34 . . . . .144 B6
Church Cl Antingham NR28. .22 B3
3 Bawdeswell NR20 . . . . .50 E7
Beeston Regis NR27 . . . . . .9 F5
Bixley NR14 . . . . .90 B7
Brandon IP27. . . . . .175 B3
Caister-on-Sea NR30 . . . .168 D5
Cantley NR13. . . . . .92 C7
Colby NR11 . . . . .36 D8
6 Coltishall NR12. . . . . . .54 C6
Grimston PE32. . . . . .45 B8
Hepworth IP22 . . . . .127 E1
1 Horstead with Stanninghall
NR12. . . . . .54 C6
Hoxne IP21 . . . . .131 A4
King's Lynn PE34 . . . . . . .146 C4
Lamas NR10. . . . . .36 F1
13 Loddon NR14 . . . . .92 A2
2 Norwich NR2. . . . . . . .162 B8
Overstrand NR27. . . . . . . .11 A3
Pentney PE32. . . . . .63 C8
Poringland NR14 . . . . .90 C4
Pulham St Mary IP21 . . . .122 A4
Sea Palling NR12 . . . . .40 B5
South Walsham NR13 . . . . .74 A8
Swainsthorpe NR14. . . . . . .89 D3
Trunch NR28 . . . . .22 E5
Upper Sheringham NR26. .138 A4
Walpole St Andrew PE14 . . .41 E4
Whissonsett NR20. . . . . . . .31 D2
Wiggenhall St Mary Magdalen
PE34 . . . . .61 B6
Wortwell IP20 . . . . .122 F3
Church Cotts NR19. . . . . . .48 E3
Church Crofts PE31. . . . . .27 C3
Church Dam NR13 . . . . . .93 A5
Church Dro PE14 . . . . .77 F6
CHURCH END PE14 . . . . . .41 F2
Church End IP27. . . . . . . .175 B3
Church Farm IP24 . . . . . .102 C7
Church Farm Cl
Palgrave IP22 . . . . .177 C2
Rickinghall Superior IP22 .128 E2
Weston Longville NR9 . . . . .51 F2
1 Weybourne NR25. . . . . .8 F5
Church Farm Cres
NR29 . . . . .167 B6
Church Farm La
Alderford NR9 . . . . .52 A6
Bircham Newton PE31. . . . .14 A4
East Dereham NR19 . . . . .154 C5
Sparham NR9 . . . . .51 A6
Church Farm Rare Breeds
Ctr ★ PE34 . . . . .79 F8
Church Farm Rd
Happisburgh Common
NR12 . . . . .39 A7
Heacham PE31. . . . . .12 F8
Heacham PE31. . . . . .133 F7
Heckingham NR14. . . . . . . .92 C1
Hemblington NR13. . . . . . .73 F6
Hepworth IP22 . . . . .127 E1
Hevingham NR10 . . . . .36 B1
Hevingham NR10 . . . . .53 A8
Hindolveston NR20 . . . . . .33 C8
Hockwold cum Wilton
IP26. . . . . .114 A6
Holme Hale PE37 . . . . .65 F2
Ixworth NR9 . . . . .69 E2
Kettringham NR18 . . . . . . .88 E5
King's Bedon NR14 . . . . . . .92 B1
Langley with Hardley NR14 92 C3
Lessingham NR12 . . . . .24 E3
Letheringsett NR25 . . . . . . .8 A2
Leziate PE32 . . . . .44 F4
Little Ellingham NR17 . . . . .86 A1
Little Massingham PE32 . . .29 C2
Little Withingham NR9. . . . .51 F7
Long Stratton NR15. . . . . .106 F4
Lound NR32 . . . . .171 A3
Lynford IP27 . . . . .115 D6
Marham PE33 . . . . .63 A4
Marlingford NR9 . . . . .69 E4
Marsham NR10 . . . . .36 B2
Mattishall NR20 . . . . .68 F6
Mautby NR29 . . . . .75 D5
Mundesley NR11 . . . . .143 C6
Mundford IP26 . . . . .100 A4
Neatishead NR12. . . . . .55 E6
North Elmham NR20 . . . . . .49 E8
North Pickenham PE37 . . . .65 E1
Northwold PE33. . . . . .81 B2
Norwich NR14 . . . . .72 E1
Norwich NR4 . . . . .161 E1
Norwich NR7 . . . . .159 C5
Old Buckenham NR17 . . . .104 D2
Oulton NR11. . . . . .35 C7
Potter Heigham NR29 . . . . .56 F7
Ravenningham NR14 . . . . .110 A7
Redenhall with Harleston
IP20. . . . . .122 D3
Rickinghall Superior IP22 .128 E1
Roydon PE32 . . . . .28 A1
Runcton Holme PE33. . . . . .61 D4
Runhall NR20 . . . . .69 A6
Rushford IP24 . . . . .126 E8
St Mary, South Elmham
otherwise Homersfield
IP20. . . . . .123 B4
Sedgeford PE36 . . . . .13 A7

Churchill Rd continued
Norwich NR3 . . . . .162 E6
Thetford IP24 . . . . .176 E5
Wisbech PE13 . . . . .152 D4
Churchill Way PE38. . . . . .172 B4
Church La Alby Hill NR11. . .21 C3
Aldeby NR34 . . . . .110 F5
Aldeby, Wheatacre, Burgh St
Peter NR34 . . . . .111 B5
Antingham NR28 . . . . .22 B3
Ashwellthorpe NR16 . . . . .106 A4
Baconsthorpe NR25. . . . . . .19 F7
Baconsthorpe NR25. . . . . . .20 A7
Bacton NR28 . . . . .23 C3
Banham NR16 . . . . .119 D7
Barton Bendish PE33. . . . . .81 B8
Beetley NR20. . . . . .49 C5
Belaugh NR12 . . . . .54 E5
Belton with Browston NR31 94 A5
Billingford NR20 . . . . .50 B7
Bintree NR20 . . . . .33 B2
Bircham PE31 . . . . .14 B3
Blo' Norton IP22 . . . . .128 B6
Boughton PE33 . . . . .80 F5
Bracon Ash NR14. . . . . . . .88 F3
Bradenham IP25 . . . . .66 D4
Bressingham IP22. . . . . . .129 B7
Briningham NR24. . . . . . . .18 D5
Briston NR24 . . . . .142 E4
Brockdish IP21 . . . . .131 C6
Broome NR35 . . . . .109 B3
Brundall NR13 . . . . .73 E3
Brundall NR13 . . . . .165 F4
Bunwell NR16 . . . . .105 D3
Burgh St Peter NR34. . . . .111 E4
Burgh & Tuttington NR11. . .36 D4
Burnham Thorpe PE31. . . . . .4 D4
Claxton NR14 . . . . .91 C5
Cley next the Sea NR25. . . . .7 E6
Corton NR32 . . . . .171 F1
Cranwich PE26 . . . . .99 F5
Cranworth IP25 . . . . .85 F7
Deopham NR18 . . . . .86 F4
Dersingham PE31 . . . . . . .140 E3
Ditchingham NR35. . . . . . .108 F3
Easton NR9 . . . . .70 A5
Easton NR9 . . . . .70 B6
East Tuddenham NR20. . . . .69 C6
East Walton PE32 . . . . .45 E3
East Winch PE32 . . . . .44 F2
Edgefield NR24 . . . . .19 D5
Felthorpe NR10 . . . . .155 D7
Filby NR29 . . . . .75 E8
Fleggburgh NR29. . . . . . . .57 A1
Frettenham NR12 . . . . .54 A5
Fritton & St Olaves NR31 . .93 F3
Gissing IP22 . . . . .120 F4
Great Bircham PE31 . . . . . .14 A3
Great Massingham PE32. . .29 D1
Great Yarmouth NR31 . . . .170 C5
Gresham NR11. . . . . .9 E1
Gressenhall NR19 . . . . .49 C2
Guestwick NR20 . . . . .33 F6
Guestwick NR20 . . . . .34 A6
Haddiscoe NR14 . . . . .110 E7
Hales NR14 . . . . .109 F7
Harpley PE31 . . . . .29 C5
Heacham PE31. . . . . .133 E6
Heckingham NR14. . . . . . . .92 C1
Hemblington NR13. . . . . . .73 F6
Hepworth IP22 . . . . .127 E1
Hevingham NR10 . . . . .36 B1
Hevingham NR10 . . . . .53 A8
Hindolveston NR20 . . . . . .33 C8

Church La continued
Sheringham NR26 . . . . . . .138 F6
Shernborne PE31 . . . . .13 B3
Shipdham IP25 . . . . .67 B2
Shouldham Thorpe PE33 . . .62 B3
Sloley NR10 . . . . .37 E4
Sloley NR10 . . . . .37 F3
South Creake NR21 . . . . . .14 D7
4 Southery PE38 . . . . . . .97 B5
South Pickenham PE37 . . . .83 D7
Sparham NR9. . . . . .51 B6
Sparrow Green NR19 . . . . . .49 B1
Spixworth NR10 . . . . .53 F2
Sprowston NR7 . . . . .159 B5
Stanfield NR20 . . . . .48 F8
Stanhoe PE31 . . . . .14 E7
Stuston IP21 . . . . .130 B4
Surlingham NR14. . . . . .73 A1
Sustead NR11 . . . . .21 B8
Swannington NR9 . . . . .52 B6
Swanton Abbott NR10. . . . .37 C5
Terrington St John PE14 . . .42 B2
Thelnetham IP22 . . . . . . .128 B5
Thompson IP24 . . . . .102 C7
Thwaite NR35 . . . . .109 A6
Tibenham NR16 . . . . .120 E8
Tilney All Saints PE34 . . . . .42 E4
Tittleshall PE32 . . . . .48 B8
Tivetshall St Mary NR15 . .121 B4
Toftrees NR21 . . . . .31 B6
Tunstead NR12. . . . . .37 F1
Upper Sheringham NR26. . . .9 C4
Upper Sheringham NR26. .138 A4
Waterloo NR10 . . . . .53 E6
Watlington PE33 . . . . .61 E6
Weasenham All Saints
PE32 . . . . .47 C8
West Runton NR26 . . . . . . .9 F5
Winfarthing IP22 . . . . .120 B4
Wood Dalling NR11 . . . . . .34 B5
Wormegay PE33 . . . . .62 D6
Worthing NR20 . . . . .49 F6
Wroxham/Hoveton NR12 .164 B3
Yaxham NR19 . . . . .68 A5
Church Lanes NR21 . . . .141 B5
Church Loke
Coltishall NR12 . . . . .54 D6
Roughton NR11 . . . . .21 D7
Thurton NR14. . . . . .91 C3
Churchman Rd NR7 . . . .159 C4
Church Marsh Nature
Reserve ★ NR14 . . . . . . .73 A1
Church Mdw
Rickinghall Inferior IP22. . .128 D2
Yelverton NR14 . . . . .90 E5
Church Mdw La NR14 . . .90 F4
Church Mews NR15 . . . .152 C5
Church of the Holy
Sepulchre (rems) ★
IP24 . . . . .176 B4
Church Path PE33 . . . . . . .80 E2
Church Pl PE31 . . . . .134 D5
Church Plain
14 Great Yarmouth
NR30 . . . . .169 C4
Wells-next-the-Sea NR23 136 D5
Church Rd Alburgh IP20. .122 F6
Alby with Thwaite NR11. . .21 C4
Alpington NR4 . . . . .90 F4
Aslacton NR15. . . . . .106 A2
Aylmerton NR11. . . . . .10 A3
Bacton NR28 . . . . .23 D4
Badersfield NR10. . . . . . . .37 C2
Banham NR16 . . . . .119 A8
Banningham NR11 . . . . . . .36 D8
Barford NR9. . . . . .69 E3
Barningham IP31 . . . . .127 C3
Barton Bendish PE33. . . . . .81 B8
Barton Turf NR12 . . . . .55 E8
Beeston with Bittering
PE32 . . . . .48 B2
Beetley NR20. . . . . .49 B6
Bergh Apton NR15. . . . . . . .91 A3
Bessingham NR25 . . . . . . .20 E8
Bintree NR20 . . . . .33 B2
Booton NR10 . . . . .149 E4
Brampton NR11. . . . . .36 F4
Brandon IP27. . . . . .175 B3
Bridgham NR16 . . . . .118 B5
Brockdish IP21 . . . . .131 C6
Brooke NR15 . . . . .108 B8
Burgh Castle NR31 . . . . . . .93 F8
Cantley NR13. . . . . .92 D7
Carleton Rode NR16 . . . . .105 C2
Catfield NR29. . . . . .56 C8
Cawston NR10. . . . . .35 A1
Christchurch PE14. . . . . . . .95 A7
Clenchwarton PE34 . . . . . .145 D5
Colby NR11 . . . . .21 D1
Colby NR11 . . . . .36 D8
Colkirk NR21 . . . . .31 D5
Crimplesham PE33 . . . . . . .80 B6
Denham IP21. . . . . .131 A1
Deopham NR18 . . . . .86 E3
Dickleburgh & Rushall
IP21. . . . . .130 D8
Dilham NR28 . . . . .38 C4
Downham Market PE38. . . .172 C5
Earsham NR35. . . . . .123 F7
East Ruston NR12 . . . . . . .38 F7
Ellingham NR35 . . . . .109 D3
Elm PE14 . . . . .77 B7
Elsing NR20 . . . . .50 F3
Erpingham NR11 . . . . .21 B1
Felmingham NR28 . . . . . . .37 B7
Flitcahm PE31 . . . . .28 C5
Flixton NR35 . . . . .123 E5

Church Rd continued
Fordham PE38 . . . .**79** B1
Freethorpe NR13 . . . .**92** F8
Frettenham NR10 . . . .**53** F4
Garboldisham IP22 . . . . . .**128** A8
Gateley NR20 . . . .**32** C3
Gillingham NR34 . . . .**110** C3
Great & Little Plumstead
NR13 . . . .**73** A4
Great Yarmouth NR31 . . .**170** C7
Griston IP25 . . . .**85** A1
Haddiscoe NR14 . . . .**110** E8
Hardingham NR9 . . . .**86** D7
Hedenham NR35 . . . .**108** E4
Hilgay PE38 . . . .**79** E1
Hoe NR20 . . . .**49** F6
Holme Hale IP25 . . . .**66** A2
Honing NR28 . . . .**38** D8
Honington IP31 . . . .**126** D1
Horning NR12 . . . .**55** F3
Horningtoft PE20 . . . .**31** F1
Hunstanton PE36 . . . .**132** F7
Itteringham NR11 . . . .**20** C2
Ketteringham NR18 . . . .**88** D5
Kirby Cane NR35 . . . .**109** E4
Kirstead NR15 . . . .**90** F1
Leverington PE13 . . . .**152** F7
Lingwood & Burlingham
NR13 . . . .**73** F3
Little Barningham NR11 . . .**20** C4
Little Witchingham NR9 . . .**51** F7
Lower Bodham NR25 . . . .**8** F2
Market Weston IP22 . . . . . .**127** C4
Marlingford NR9 . . . .**70** A3
Morley NR18 . . . .**87** A3
Neatishead NR12 . . . .**55** E6
Newton Flotman NR15 . . . .**89** C1
North Lopham IP22 . . . . . .**119** A1
Norton Subcourse NR14 . . .**92** E1
Ovington IP25 . . . .**84** E5
Postwick with Witton NR13.**72** F3
Potter Heigham NR29 . . . . .**56** F6
Quidenham NR16 . . . .**118** F8
Redgrave IP22 . . . .**128** F5
Reedham NR13 . . . .**92** E1
Repps with Bastwick NR29 **57** A4
Runhall NR9 . . . .**69** A1
Runhall NR9 . . . .**87** A8
St Peter South Elmham
NR35 . . . .**124** A3
Sea Palling NR12 . . . .**40** A5
Shelfanger IP22 . . . .**120** B2
Shouldham PE33 . . . .**62** E3
Shropham NR17 . . . .**103** B3
Sisland NR14 . . . .**91** D1
Skeyton NR10 . . . .**37** A4
Smallburgh NR12 . . . .**38** D2
Snettisham PE31 . . . .**12** E5
Somerton NR29 . . . .**57** F6
South Lopham IP22 . . . . . .**128** D8
Sporle PE32 . . . .**65** D6
Stockton NR34 . . . .**109** F5
Stoke Ferry PE33 . . . .**80** E2
Stratton Strawless NR10 . . .**53** F7
Strumpshaw NR13 . . . .**91** F8
Sutton NR12 . . . .**39** C3
Swafield NR28 . . . .**22** C4
Swainsthorpe NR14 . . . .**89** D4
Tasburgh NR15 . . . .**106** F6
Tharston & Hapton NR15 **106** D5
Thompson IP24 . . . .**102** B7
Thurlton NR14 . . . .**92** F1
Thurne NR29 . . . .**56** E2
Thurton NR14. . . . .**91** C5
Tibenham NR16 . . . .**120** E8
Tilney All Saints PE34 . . . .**144** F1
Toft Monks NR34 . . . .**110** D6
Topcroft NR35 . . . .**107** F3
Tunstead NR12 . . . .**55** B8
Upton with Fishley NR13 . .**166** A6
Wacton NR15 . . . .**106** C2
Walpole St Andrew PE14 . . .**41** E3
Walsingham NR22 . . . .**16** F8
Watlington PE34 . . . .**61** C6
Watton IP25 . . . .**84** E3
Wellingham PE32. . . . .**30** E1
Wereham PE33 . . . .**80** E4
West Beckham NR25 . . . .**9** C2
West Dereham PE33 . . . .**80** B4
Wheatacre NR34 . . . .**111** A5
Whinburgh & Westfield
NR19 . . . .**68** A3
Wicklewood NR18 . . . .**87** B5
Wiggenhall St Germans
PE34 . . . .**61** A8
Wilby NR16 . . . .**104** A1
Wimbotsham PE34 . . . .**172** E8
Wingfield IP21 . . . .**131** E3
Wolferton PE31 . . . .**27** C7
Wood Norton NR21 . . . .**33** B6
Woodton NR35 . . . .**108** B5
Woodton NR35 . . . .**108** C4
Wortham IP22 . . . .**129** C5
Wreningham NR16 . . . .**88** E1
Wroxham/Hoveton NR12 **164** D5
Yelverton NR14 . . . .**90** F5
Church Rd N IP21 . . . .**131** C7
Church St Ashill IP25 . . . .**84** A7
Attleborough NR17 . . . . . .**174** D5
Bawburgh NR9 . . . .**160** A6
Bradenham IP25 . . . .**66** E3
Brisley NR20 . . . .**49** A8
Briston NR24 . . . .**142** E4
Carbrooke IP25 . . . .**85** A5
Coltishall NR12 . . . .**54** C6
Cromer NR27 . . . .**139** C6
Diss IP22 . . . .**177** D4
East Dereham NR19 . . . .**154** D5

Church St continued
Elsing NR20 . . . .**50** F3
Gimingham NR11 . . . .**22** E7
Great Ellingham NR17 . . . .**103** E7
23 Harleston IP20 . . . .**122** D2
Hingham NR9 . . . .**86** C5
Holt NR25 . . . .**137** C6
Horsford NR10 . . . .**53** B2
Hunstanton PE36 . . . .**132** C4
Kenninghall NR16 . . . .**119** B4
King's Lynn PE30 . . . .**146** D4
Litcham PE32 . . . .**48** A4
Little Walsingham NR22 . . .**16** F7
North Creake NR21 . . . .**15** D8
Northrepps NR27 . . . .**11** A1
11 North Walsham NR28 **151** D5
Norwich NR6 . . . .**158** E5
Plumstead NR11 . . . .**20** A5
Reepham NR10 . . . .**149** C4
Sco Ruston NR12 . . . .**54** E8
Sheringham NR26 . . . .**138** D7
Southrepps NR11 . . . .**22** B7
Stiffkey NR23 . . . .**6** D6
15 Sutton Bridge PE12 . . . .**41** B8
Thornham PE36 . . . .**2** D6
Trimingham NR11 . . . .**11** D1
Wells-next-the-Sea NR23 **136** D5
Weston Longville NR9 . . . . .**51** F2
Wymondham NR18 . . . . . .**173** B4
Church Terr
5 Outwell PE14 . . . .**77** F6
21 Wisbech PE13 . . . .**152** C5
Wroxham NR12 . . . .**164** B3
Church View
Freethorpe NR13 . . . .**92** E8
Harleston IP20 . . . .**122** E2
Horsford NR10 . . . .**53** B2
Marham PE33 . . . .**63** B4
Ormesby St Margaret
NR29 . . . .**167** B2
Church View Cl
2 Griston IP25 . . . .**85** A2
Norwich NR7 . . . .**159** B5
Reedham NR13 . . . .**93** A5
Church View Ct NR7 . . . .**159** B5
Church View La 16 PE32. .**45** F6
Churchway IP22 . . . .**128** F5
Church Wlk
Beachamwell PE37 . . . .**81** E8
Burnham Market PE31 . . . .**135** B2
Great Yarmouth NR31 . . . . .**94** C6
Shelfanger IP22. . . . .**120** B2
Churn Ct PE30 . . . .**147** C7
Cider Cl NR17. . . . .**174** E4
Cinder La NR34 . . . .**111** B4
Cinnamon Rd PE38 . . . . .**172** E6
Cintra Rd NR11 . . . .**163** B6
Circlet Pl NR17 . . . .**174** B3
Cirrus Way NR7 . . . .**159** C2
City Acad Norwich NR4 .**161** D5
City Coll Norwich NR2 .**162** D3
City Ind Est NR7 . . . .**162** C4
City of Norwich Aviation
Mus ★ NR6 . . . .**53** D1
City of Norwich Sch
NR4 . . . .**162** B2
City Rd NR1 . . . .**178** C1
City View Rd NR6 . . . . . .**158** A4
Civic Gdns NR3 . . . .**158** B3
Civray Ave PE38 . . . .**172** C6
Clabburn Cl 1 NR15 . . . . .**89** C2
Clabon Fst Cl NR3 . . . . . .**158** F2
Clabon Rd NR3 . . . .**158** F2
Clabon Second Cl NR3 . .**158** F2
Clabon Third Cl NR3 . . . .**158** F3
Clackclose Prim Sch
PE38. . . . .**172** B6
Clackclose Rd PE38 . . . .**172** C6
Clamp La PE14. . . . .**77** E7
Clancy Rd NR7. . . . .**159** C1
Clapper La PE34 . . . .**145** E5
Clare Rd Cromer NR27 . . .**139** D5
King's Lynn PE30 . . . .**148** C3
Clare Sch The NR4 . . . . .**162** A3
Clarke Cl IP22 . . . .**177** C1
Clarke Rd NR3 . . . .**162** D8
Clarke's Chase PE33 . . . . .**43** E2
Clarke's Cl 2 NR9 . . . .**69** F2
Clarke's La
Barsham NR34. . . . .**124** F7
Gooderstone PE33. . . . .**82** A5
Clarkes Rd NR30 . . . .**169** B5
Clarke's Rd NR21 . . . .**141** E5
Clark Rd NR35 . . . .**109** B2
Clark's La NR15 . . . .**17** E5
Clark's Loke 7 NR13 . . . . .**73** D6
Clarkson Ave PE13 . . . . .**152** D5
Clarkson Ct PE13 . . . . . .**152** D6
Clarkson Inf Sch PE13 . .**152** E6

Clarkson Rd
10 Lingwood NR13 . . . . . .**74** A3
Norwich NR5 . . . .**161** C7
CLAXTON NR14 . . . .**91** D6
Claxton Church Rd
Ashby St Mary NR14 . . . . . .**91** C5
Thurton NR14. . . . .**91** C4
Claxton Cl Mileham PE32 . .**48** D6
5 Thetford IP24 . . . .**176** C4
Claxton Cnr NR14 . . . .**91** C6
Claxton Gr NR35 . . . .**91** E6
Claxton Mill NR14. . . . . . .**91** E6
Claxtons Gdns NR29 . . . . .**57** C1
Claydon Gr NR35 . . . .**170** B7
Clay Hall La IP22. . . . .**128** C7
Clay Hill PE32. . . . .**48** B7
Clay La Bacton NR28 . . . . .**23** B3
Bradwell NR31 . . . .**94** C5
Hamrow NR20 . . . .**31** C3
Hepworth IP22 . . . .**127** F1
Sapiston IP31 . . . .**126** E1
Saxlingham Nethergate
NR15 . . . .**107** A7
Swannington NR9 . . . .**52** C7
Wood Norton NR21 . . . .**33** C6
Claypit La
Fakenham NR21. . . . .**141** C5
Sculthorpe NR21 . . . .**16** B3
Claypit Rd NR20 . . . .**33** D3
Clay Rd NR30 . . . .**168** F5
Clayton Cl
Dersingham PE31 . . . .**140** D4
Wisbech PE13 . . . .**152** F6
Clearview Dr NR14 . . . .**90** C5
Cleaves Dr NR22 . . . .**16** F8
Clematis Way NR18 . . . . .**173** F6
Clement Attlee Wy
PE30. . . . .**147** C3
Clement Gdns IP22 . . . . .**177** F3
Clements Ave NR18 . . . . .**173** F8
Clements Cl IP21 . . . .**130** C5
Clement Scott Mews
NR27 . . . .**139** D5
Clements Ct PE34. . . . . . .**144** B5
CLENCHWARTON PE34. .**145** E5
Clenchwarton Bypass
Tilney All Saints PE34 . . . . .**42** F6
Tilney All Saints PE34 . . . .**144** D3
Tilney All Saints PE34 . . . .**145** C3
Tilney All Saints PE34 . . . .**146** A2
Clenchwarton Com Prim Sch
PE34. . . . .**145** E5
Clenchwarton Rd PE34. .**146** B4
Clere Cl NR18. . . . .**173** C5
Cleveland Rd NR2 . . . . . .**178** A3
Cleves Way NR18 . . . .**173** C5
Cley La Saham Toney IP25. .**84** C4
Salthouse NR25. . . . .**8** A6
Cley Marshes Nature
Reserve ★ NR25 . . . .**7** F7
CLEY NEXT THE SEA NR25. **7** E6
Cley Rd Blakeney NR25 . . . .**7** D6
Bradwell NR31. . . . .**94** C7
Cockley Cley PE37 . . . .**82** E8
Holt NR25. . . . .**137** B8
Salthouse NR25. . . . .**8** B4
Swaffham PE37 . . . .**153** B2
Clickers Rd NR3 . . . .**162** C8
Cliff Ave Cromer NR27 . . .**139** C6
Great Yarmouth NR31 . . . .**170** D3
Cliff Cl NR13 . . . .**92** F4
Cliff Ct PE36 . . . .**132** C6
Cliff Dr NR27 . . . .**139** C7
Cliffe-en-Howe Rd PE32 . .**44** F8
Cliff Hill
Gorleston-on-Sea NR31 . . . .**94** E6
4 Great Yarmouth NR31 **170** D4
Cliff La Cromer NR27 . . . . .**139** C6
Great Yarmouth NR31 . . . .**171** D8
Clifford Ave NR30 . . . . . .**168** D5
Clifford Burman Cl
PE30. . . . .**148** A1
Clifford Pye Cl NR10 . . . . .**35** B2
Cliff Par PE30 . . . .**132** C5
Cliff Pk Ormiston Acad
NR31 . . . .**170** D1
Cliff Rd Cromer NR27 . . . .**139** D5
Overstrand NR27 . . . .**11** A3
Sheringham NR26 . . . .**138** E7
Cliff Terr PE36 . . . .**132** C5
Cliff Top NR12 . . . .**23** E5
Clifton Cl 3 NR2 . . . .**162** C7
Clifton Dr IP24 . . . .**176** F7
Clifton Pk NR27 . . . .**10** C5
Clifton Rd
King's Lynn PE30 . . . .**148** B1
Wymondham NR18 . . . . . .**173** C6
Clifton St NR2 . . . .**162** B7
CLIFTONVILLE NR11 . . . .**143** B7
Clifton Way NR27 . . . .**11** B3
Clingos Wy IP26 . . . .**113** F7
Clink Hill
Heckfield Green IP21 . . . .**131** A2
West Caister NR30 . . . .**168** E4
Clink Hill Track NR30 . . .**168** D3
Clink Rd NR12 . . . .**40** A8
Clintergate Rd IP20. . . . .**122** C6
CLINT GREEN NR19 . . . . .**68** E2
Clint Hill IP31 . . . .**126** D2
Clintock Pl 10 NR30 . . . .**169** C5
Clint St NR29 . . . .**56** B5
Clipbush La
Banham NR16 . . . .**119** C7
Fakenham NR21. . . . .**141** E5
Scoulton NR9 . . . .**85** C4
Clipped Hedge La NR11 . .**22** B7
CLIPPESBY NR29 . . . .**57** A6
CLIPPINGS GREEN NR20 . .**68** E7
Clipstone La NR21 . . . .**17** D1
Clipstreet NR25. . . . .**18** B8

Clipstreet La NR21 . . . .**18** B8
Clockcase Rd
Clenchwarton PE34 . . . .**26** B1
Clenchwarton PE34 . . . .**43** C7
Clenchwarton PE34 . . . . . .**146** A7
Close The Brancaster PE31. . **3** D7
Brundall NR13 . . . .**165** C4
Docking PE31. . . . .**134** E4
Great Yarmouth NR31 . . . .**170** A5
Hemsby NR29 . . . .**167** B7
Holt NR25. . . . .**137** C5
Hoxne IP21 . . . .**131** A3
Little Melton NR9. . . . .**160** D2
North Lopham IP22 . . . . . .**119** A2
North Walsham NR28 . . . .**151** B4
Norwich NR1 . . . .**178** C3
Rackheath NR13 . . . .**72** D8
Roydon IP22 . . . .**177** A5
Sheringham NR26 . . . .**138** D8
Stow Bedon NR17 . . . .**102** D7
Clough Dr 9 IP26 . . . .**98** E1
Clough La PE30 . . . .**146** D4
Clovelly Dr NR6. . . . .**157** E2
Clover Dr 7 NR29 . . . . . .**167** B8
Clover Hill Rd NR5 . . . . . .**160** F8
Clover Hill VA Inf & Nursery
Sch. NR5. . . . .**161** B8
Clover La PE38. . . . .**172** A5
Cloverland Dr 6 NR29 . . .**167** B7
Clover Rd
Attleborough NR17 . . . . . .**174** C3
Aylsham NR11 . . . .**150** D5
Norwich NR7 . . . .**158** F3
Swaffham PE37 . . . .**153** C1
Clover Way
Fakenham NR21. . . . .**141** E4
Great Yarmouth NR31 . . . .**170** A4
Thetford IP24 . . . .**176** D5
Clover Wlk PE34 . . . .**61** B8
Clowes Ct 1 NR34 . . . . . .**110** D1
Clubbs La NR21 . . . .**136** D6
Clunch Cl IP27 . . . .**113** E1
Clyde Dr IP24 . . . .**176** F7
Clydesdale Dr NR29 . . . . .**167** A7
Clydesdale Rise NR31 . . . .**94** C8
Clyffe Cotts NR1 . . . .**162** F3
Coach & Horses Row
NR2 . . . .**178** A2
Coach House Ct 1 NR4 .**162** A3
Coach La NR19 . . . .**67** C6
Coachmaker Way NR9 . . . .**88** D8
Coachmans Ct NR7 . . . . .**158** F4
Coach Rd PE31 . . . .**27** D5
Coal Shed Gall, The ★
PE36. . . . .**132** C4
Coalwharf Rd PE13 . . . . .**152** B4
Coaly La PE13 . . . .**12** E4
Coastguard Rd NR30 . . . .**168** F5
Coast Guards La PE35. . . . . .**8** F6
Coast Rd Bacton NR12. . . .**23** E4
Cley next the Sea NR25. . . . . **7** F7
Corton NR32 . . . .**171** F1
Happisburgh NR12 . . . .**23** F3
Hopton on Sea NR31. . . . .**171** C4
Lessingham NR12 . . . .**39** D7
Overstrand NR27 . . . .**11** B3
Salthouse NR25. . . . .**8** A7
Sea Palling NR12. . . . .**40** C3
Warham NR23 . . . .**6** A5
Warham NR23 . . . .**136** F5
Wiveton NR25 . . . .**7** D7
Coates Ct 5 PE14. . . . .**59** D2
Cobble Acre NR16 . . . .**53** B7
COBBLER'S GREEN
NR35 . . . .**108** B2
Cobblers La PE14 . . . .**41** F2
Cobbleways The 9 NR29. **58** B6
Cobbold Cl IP22 . . . .**129** C4
Cobbold St IP22 . . . .**177** B5
Cobbs Hill PE34 . . . .**146** A4
Cob's Pl 5 NR30 . . . .**169** B4
Cob Cl 7 NR31 . . . .**169** B4
Cobham Way NR7 . . . . . .**159** C2
Cobholm Cl 1 NR31 . . . .**169** B4
COBHOLM ISLAND
NR31 . . . .**169** A4
Cobholm Prim Sch
NR31 . . . .**169** B4
Cobholm Rd 8 NR31. . . .**169** B4
Cobies La NR15. . . . .**107** A8
Coblands 4 PE13. . . . .**152** D7
Coburg Cl 10 PE25 . . . . . .**84** D3
Coburg La IP25 . . . .**84** B6
Coburg St
9 King's Lynn PE30 . . . . .**146** E5
Norwich NR2 . . . .**178** A2
Cochrane Cl IP25. . . . .**85** A3
Cock Dro PE38 . . . .**172** B7
Cocketts Dr PE13 . . . .**152** E5
Cock Fen Rd PE14. . . . . . .**95** D7
Cockehole Rd PE34 . . . . . .**41** F8
Cocklestrand Drove NR23 . **6** A6
COCKLEY CLEY PE37 . . . . .**82** D7
Cockley Cley Rd
Cockley Cley PE37 . . . .**82** E6
Cockley Cley PE37 . . . .**83** A7
Didlington IP26 . . . .**99** F8
Didlington IP26 . . . .**100** A7
Foulden IP26 . . . .**82** C1
Hilborough IP26 . . . .**82** F4
Hilborough IP26 . . . .**83** A3
Cock Rd NR14 . . . .**92** A3
Cockshoot Dr NR12 . . . . .**164** E6
Cocks La NR17 . . . .**104** A2
Cock St Ixworth IP31 . . . .**126** F3
Wymondham NR18 . . . . . .**173** B5
COCKTHORPE NR23. . . . . . .**6** E5
Cockthorpe Rd NR25. . . . . .**7** A4
Codlings La NR11. . . . .**35** F5
Codling's La NR11 . . . . . .**150** A6
Coigncroft NR13. . . . .**165** E3

Coke Rd NR1 . . . .**162** E1
Coker's Hill NR22 . . . .**16** F7
COLBY NR11. . . . .**21** E2
Colby Corner
Banningham NR11 . . . .**36** E8
Colby NR11 . . . .**21** E1
Colby Dr NR31 . . . .**94** C5
Colby Prim Sch NR11 . . . .**36** E8
Colby Rd NR11 . . . .**36** D8
Coldershaw Rd NR6. . . . .**158** B4
Coldham Cl IP24 . . . .**167** B3
Coldham Gr NR28 . . . .**173** F7
Coldham Hall Carnser
NR14 . . . .**165** C1
Coldham Rd NR21 . . . .**17** D7
Coldham's La PE33 . . . . . .**80** A5
Coldharbour La PE26. . . . .**82** D1
Cold Harbour Rd NR29 . . .**56** D4
Coldhorn Cres PE13. . . . . .**152** D7
Coleburn Rd NR11 . . . .**89** E8
Cole Cl IP24 . . . .**176** F7
Colegate NR3. . . . .**178** A3
COLEGATE END IP21 . . . .**121** E6
Colegate End Rd IP21. . . .**121** E6
Cole Gn PE36 . . . .**13** B7
Coleman Cl
Palgrave IP22 . . . .**177** D1
Taverham NR8 . . . .**155** F2
Coleridge Cl NR8 . . . .**156** D8
Coleridge Rd IP22 . . . . . .**177** E4
Coles Common IP21 . . . .**121** F7
Coles Path IP31 . . . .**127** B5
Coles Way NR10 . . . .**149** C5
Colindeep La NR7. . . . . . .**159** A4
Colin Mclean Rd NR19 . .**154** C7
Colkett Dr NR6. . . . .**158** E3
COLKIRK NR21 . . . .**31** D5
Colkirk CE Prim Sch
NR21 . . . .**31** D5
Colkirk Hill NR21 . . . .**31** D6
Colkirk Rd
East Raynham NR21 . . . .**31** B4
Hamrow NR20 . . . .**31** D2
Collectors World of Eric St
John Foti PE38 . . . .**79** B6
Colleen Cl Dereham NR19 .**67** E5
East Dereham NR19 . . . . . .**154** D1
College Cl NR12 . . . .**54** D7
College La 1 NR31 . . . . . .**169** B4
College Dr NR31 . . . .**133** C4
College La Keswick NR4 . . .**89** C7
9 King's Lynn PE30 . . . . .**146** D4
Runcton Holme PE33. . . . . .**61** F3
College Rd
Hockwold cum Wilton
IP26. . . . .**113** F7
Norwich NR2 . . . .**162** A5
Thompson IP24 . . . .**102** C7
Thurlton NR14 . . . .**110** C8
Wereham PE33 . . . .**97** F8
Collen's Gn NR9 . . . .**51** B3
Coller Rd NR6 . . . .**158** D7
Collers Way NR10 . . . .**149** C6
Collett's Bridge La PE14. .**59** C1
Colley Hill Drift PE32. . . . .**48** D4
Collingwood Cl
Heacham NR29 . . . .**133** D3
25 Hethersett NR9 . . . . . .**88** D7
Poringland NR14 . . . .**90** C4
Collingwood Dr NR11. . . .**22** F8
Collingwood Rd
Downham Market PE38. . . .**172** B4
Great Yarmouth NR30 . . . .**169** E7
Hunstanton PE36. . . . .**132** D3
Collingwood Way IP24. . .**176** F6
Collingwood Wlk 1
IP24 . . . .**176** F6
Collins Ct NR6 . . . .**158** D2
Collins La PE31 . . . .**133** D5
Collin's Le PE33 . . . .**63** C5
Collis La NR29 . . . .**57** F5
Coll of W Anglia (King's Lynn
Ctr)The PE30 . . . .**146** F5
Coll of W Anglia (Wisbech
Campus)The PE13 . . . .**152** E4
Coll of W Anglia (Wisech
Campus)The PE13 . . . .**152** E2
Coll of West Anglia
King's Lynn PE30 . . . .**43** F8
King's Lynn PE30 . . . .**146** F5
King's Lynn PE30 . . . .**147** A7
Colls Rd NR7 . . . .**159** D5
Colman Ave 1 NR34. . . . . .**89** F4
Colman Fst Sch NR4. . . . .**162** A3
Colman Hospl NR2 . . . . . .**162** A4
Colman Jun Sch
Norwich NR4 . . . .**161** F3
Norwich NR4 . . . .**162** A3
Colman Rd NR4. . . . .**161** F5
Colmans Cl NR19 . . . .**67** E4
Colmans Mustard Shop ★
NR1 . . . .**178** B2
Colman Way NR16 . . . . . .**118** D5
Colne Pl NR27 . . . .**139** B6
Colne Rd NR27 . . . .**139** B6
COLNEY NR4 . . . .**161** A4
Colney La Colney NR4 . . . .**160** F2
Colney NR4 . . . .**161** A3
Colney Rd PE30 . . . .**147** D5
Colomb Rd NR31. . . . .**170** D6
Colossus Way NR5. . . . . .**156** B1
COLTISHALL NR12 . . . .**54** C6
Coltishall La
Horsham St Faith & Newton St
Faith NR10. . . . .**53** D2
Tunstead NR12 . . . .**54** C5
Coltishall Prim Sch NR12 **54** D7
Coltishall Rd
Belaugh NR12 . . . .**164** A6

Coltishall Rd continued
Buxton with Lammas NR10.**53** F8
Frettenham NR10 . . . .**54** A7
Coltishall Sta NR12 . . . . . .**54** C7
COLTON NR9 . . . .**69** E4
Colton Rd Barford NR9 . . . .**69** E3
Easton NR9 . . . .**70** A7
Honingham NR9. . . . .**69** E6
Coltsfoot Rd NR10 . . . .**53** C2
Coltsfoot Way IP24 . . . . .**176** F5
Columbia Way PE30. . . . .**146** E6
Columbine Cl 4 IP24 . . . .**176** F5
Columbine Dr 12 NR26 . .**138** B6
Columbine Rd NR10. . . . . .**53** B2
Columbine The NR5 . . . . .**160** F8
Colvile Rd PE13 . . . .**152** E5
Colville Rd NR24 . . . .**142** B5
Comber Cl IP21. . . . .**130** C6
Comet Rd 7 NR25 . . . .**84** F3
Comfrey Way IP24 . . . . . .**116** C2
Commercial Rd NR19 . . . .**154** E5
Common Drift NR20 . . . . . .**49** C4
Common Dro
Flitcham with Appleton
PE31 . . . .**27** F5
Southery PE38 . . . .**97** B5
Common Drove
Northwold IP26 . . . .**99** C8
Stow Bridge PE34 . . . .**61** C2
Common End
Syderstone PE31 . . . .**15** A3
Weasenham All Saints
PE32 . . . .**47** C8
Common Hill IP22 . . . . . .**177** D2
Common La
Ashby St Mary NR14 . . . . . .**91** C4
Bawdeswell NR20 . . . .**50** F8
Beccles NR34. . . . .**110** C3
Beetley NR20 . . . .**49** E5
Binham NR21 . . . .**6** E2
Brancaster PE31 . . . . **3** D6
Brockdish IP21 . . . .**131** D6
Burgh & Tuttington NR11. . .**36** E6
East Walton PE32 . . . .**45** E3
Field Dalling NR25. . . . .**7** B1
Gayton PE32 . . . .**45** C4
Great Ryburgh NR21 . . . . . .**32** B6
Great Witchingham NR9 . . .**51** D4
King's Lynn PE30 . . . .**148** F2
Little Massingham PE32 . . .**29** E4
Morningthorpe & Fritton
NR15 . . . .**107** D3
North Runcton PE33 . . . . . .**43** F1
North Runcton PE33 . . . . . .**44** A2
North Tuddenham NR20. . . .**50** D1
Norwich NR7 . . . .**163** F5
Ranworth NR13 . . . .**56** A1
Sheringham NR26 . . . .**138** E6
8 Southery PE38 . . . .**97** B5
Thorpe Market NR11. . . . . .**22** A6
West Rudham NR21. . . . . . .**31** B3
Common La N 2 NR34 . .**110** C3
Common Loke
Chedgrave NR14 . . . .**92** A2
Crostwick NR12 . . . .**54** B2
Common Pl 3 NR22 . . . . . .**16** F7
Common Rd
Aldeby NR34 . . . .**111** B3
Ashwellthorpe NR16 . . . . .**105** A4
Barton Turf NR12. . . . .**38** F1
Botesdale IP22 . . . .**128** E1
Bressingham IP22 . . . .**119** F2
Bressingham IP22 . . . .**129** C8
Bressingham Common
IP22 . . . .**120** A1
Brumstead NR12 . . . .**24** A1
Burston & Shimpling IP22 **120** E2
Castle Acre PE32. . . . .**46** E1
East Tuddenham NR20. . . . .**69** B5
East Winch PE32 . . . .**44** F2
Forncett NR16 . . . .**105** E4
Foxley NR20 . . . .**33** D1
Gissing NR15 . . . .**120** F5
Great Yarmouth NR31 . . . .**170** C4
Hemsby NR29 . . . .**58** C3
Holkham NR23 . . . .**5** B3
Hopton IP22. . . . .**127** F6
Lessingham NR12 . . . .**24** E2
Martham NR29 . . . .**57** B4
Neatishead NR12. . . . .**55** E6
Pulham Market IP21 . . . . .**121** E7
Runcton Holme PE33. . . . . .**61** D4
Runhall NR20 . . . .**68** F4
Sandringham PE35 . . . .**27** E6
Scole IP21 . . . .**130** F8
Scole IP21 . . . .**131** A8
Shelfanger IP22. . . . .**119** F3
Shelton NR15 . . . .**107** B1
Skeyton NR10 . . . .**37** A6
Snettisham PE31 . . . .**12** C4
Somerton NR29 . . . .**57** E6
Surlingham NR14 . . . .**165** B1
Swafield NR28 . . . .**22** D4
Thurne NR29 . . . .**56** E3
Wacton NR15 . . . .**106** D2
Wells-next-the-Sea NR23 **136** A1
West Bilney PE32 . . . .**45** A1
West Walton PE14 . . . .**59** D7
Wickmere NR11 . . . .**20** F4
Wiggenhall St Germans
PE34 . . . .**60** F7
Commonside NR10 . . . . . .**35** A2
CommonThe
South Creake NR21 . . . .**16** A5
West Barsham NR21. . . . . . .**16** A4
Common The
All Saints South Elmham
IP19. . . . .**124** B1
Botesdale IP22 . . . .**128** F1

Common The continued
Bressingham IP22.......119 D3
Cockthorpe NR25.........6 E5
Dunston NR14..........89 E5
Freethorpe NR13..........92 E7
Guist NR20..........32 F4
Gunthorpe NR21..........18 A7
Hamrow NR20..........31 E2
Hanworth NR11..........21 B7
Hanworth NR11..........21 C6
Happisburgh Common
NR12..........39 B7
1 Harleston IP20..........122 D1
Harris' Green NR15..........107 C1
Herringfleet NR32..........111 D8
Honing NR28..........38 C6
Horningtoft NR20..........32 A2
Itteringham NR11..........20 C1
Itteringham NR11..........35 D8
Lyng NR9..........51 A4
Mellis IP23..........129 D1
Shelton and Hardwick
IP20..........122 C8
Shotesham NR15..........90 A2
South Creake NR21..........15 F6
Surlingham NR14..........165 A1
Tatterford NR21..........30 E6
Thornage NR25..........18 E6
Wolterton NR11..........20 E1
Commonwealth Way 12
NR7..........72 D4
Compass Ctr The NR31...94 A5
Compass Rd NR18..........173 F1
Compass Sch Lingwood The
NR13..........74 A3
Compit Hills NR27..........139 B3
Concorde Rd NR6..........158 C5
Conesford Dr NR1..........162 F3
CONEY WESTON IP31...127 B5
Coney Weston Rd
Barningham IP31..........127 C4
Sapiston IP31..........126 D2
Conference Way
Colkirk NR21..........31 E5
Wisbech PE13..........152 C8
Conge The NR30..........169 C4
CONGHAM PE32..........28 B2
Congham Rd PE32..........28 B1
Conifer Cl NR29..........167 A3
Coniston Cl
2 Hethersett NR9..........88 E8
King's Lynn PE30..........148 F1
2 Norwich NR5..........161 C6
Coniston Rd NR15..........90 E1
Coniston Sq 1 NR30...169 D4
Connaught Ave NR31...170 C3
Connaught Plain NR17..174 D5
Connaught Rd
Attleborough NR17..........174 D5
Cromer NR27..........139 D5
Norwich NR2..........162 B7
Conroy Cl NR7..........159 D5
Consort Rd PE30..........148 D2
Constable Cl
7 Attleborough NR17...174 B4
2 Diss IP22..........177 C4
Constable Ct 15 IP20...122 D2
Constable Dr 4 NR31...170 A7
Constable Pl
Downham Market PE38..172 E6
Methwold Hythe IP26...98 E5
Constable Rd NR4..........162 C1
Constitution Hill
Fakenham NR21..........141 B4
King's Lynn PE30..........147 A4
North Runcton PE33..........43 F4
North Runcton PE33..........44 A3
Norwich NR6..........158 E3
Constitution Opening
NR3..........158 E2
Convent Rd 4 NR2..........162 C5
Convy Priors NR30..........168 C6
Conway Rd
Great Yarmouth NR31...170 D6
Sheringham NR26..........138 F7
Conyers NR18..........173 C6
Cooke Cl 2 NR5..........160 E7
Cooke's Rd NR15..........91 B4
Cookley La IP23..........130 F1
Cook Rd IP25..........66 A3
Cook's La IP20..........122 F2
Cooks Terr NR18..........87 C6
Co-operative St NR26...138 D7
Cooper La NR30..........168 E5
Cooper La NR1..........89 F8
Cooper Rd
North Walsham NR28..151 D6
8 Sheringham NR26..138 C5
Swaffham PE37..........153 C1
Cooper Row NR13..........165 B5
Coopers Cl
Aslacton NR15..........106 B1
Taverham NR8..........155 E3
Cooper's Drift IP31..125 D1
Cooper's La NR11..........9 F1
Coot Dr NR7..........159 E5
Copeland Dr NR26..........138 D6
Copeman Rd
Aylsham NR11..........150 D5
Great & Little Plumstead
NR13..........73 A6
3 Roydon IP22..........129 D7
Copenhagen Way NR6...158 C2
Copince's La NR16..........119 C7
Copper Beech Cl
Fakenham NR21..........141 D6
Whissonsett NR20..........31 C2
Copperfield 4 PE30...147 C5
Copperfield Ave 1
NR30..........170 D8

Copperfield Ct IP21...121 E5
Copperfields 6 PE13..152 E3
Copper Hall PE37..........153 B3
Copper La 8 NR9..........86 C5
Copper Smith Way
NR18..........173 F5
Coppice Ave NR6..........157 E5
Coppice Dr NR8..........155 A1
Coppice The 6 NR17..174 C5
Coppins Ct PE14..........152 E2
Copse View NR27..........139 F4
Copsey Wlk NR19..........154 D3
Copyhold La NR15..........121 C7
Copys Gn NR22..........6 A2
COPY'S GREEN NR23..........6 A2
Corbet Ave NR7..........159 B2
Corbett Rd 2 NR28...151 C6
Corbyn Shaw Rd PE30...147 E4
Cordon St PE13..........152 C4
Cord Wainer Cl NR7..159 F4
CORDWELL NR16..........105 E4
Coriander Dr IP24..........176 F4
Coriander Rd PE38..........172 E6
Corie Rd NR4..........161 F4
Corkway Dro PE38..........97 E1
Cormorant Cl 5 IP22..177 F5
Cormorant Dr 6 NR7..159 E4
Cormorant Way 10 NR31..94 C8
Corncutters Cl NR3..........178 B3
Corner Comm Rd NR28..38 B7
Corner La NR10..........53 B3
Corner St 2 NR27..........139 B7
Cornfield Rd NR14..........89 B2
Cornfields IP21..........121 B1
Cornfield The NR25..........7 A3
Cornflower Way 8
NR17..........174 B5
Cornish Ave NR28..........22 E5
Cornish Way NR28..........151 C7
Cornwallis Cl 7 NR5...161 A4
Coronach Cl NR8..........156 A4
Coronation Ave
2 Marthan NR29..........57 D4
Nordelph PE38..........78 D3
1 Rollesby NR29..........57 D2
West Winch PE33..........43 F3
Coronation Cl NR6..........158 A4
Coronation Cotts PE32...47 F4
Coronation Cres NR15..107 D5
Coronation Gn NR31..........169 B3
Coronation Gr PE37..........153 B5
Coronation La
Blakeney NR25..........7 C6
Blakeney NR25..........7 D7
Somerton NR29..........57 F5
Coronation Pl IP27..........175 B2
Coronation Rd
Clenchwarton PE34..........146 A5
Great Yarmouth NR31..169 B3
Holt NR25..........137 C5
Norwich NR6..........158 A4
Whimpwell Green NR12 ...39 C8
Coronation Terr
Caston NR17..........102 F8
6 Great Yarmouth NR30..169 C4
Coronation Wlk NR31..151 A5
Coronilla Gn NR31..........170 B5
Corporation Rd PE13...152 D3
CORPUSTY NR11..........19 E1
Corpusty Prim Sch NR11..19 F1
Corpusty Rd
Thurning NR20..........19 C1
Thurning NR24..........19 B2
Wood Dalling NR11..........34 D7
Corpusty Mill NR11..........19 F1
Corton Rd NR1..........178 C1
Coslany Sq 7 NR3..........178 A3
Coslany St NR3..........178 A3
CossGr Cl NR3..........158 B3
COSTESSEY NR8..........156 F4
Costessey Inf Sch NR5..157 B1
Costessey La
Drayton NR8..........156 E6
Ringland NR8..........70 B8
Taverham NR8..........157 A7
COSTESSEY PARK NR5..156 D3
Costessey Prim Sch
NR5..........156 F1
Costessey Rd NR8..........156 B8
COSTON NR9..........69 A1
Coston La NR18..........87 A8
Coston Rd NR9..........69 B1
Cosy Cnr NR28..........151 B4
Cotman Cl IP22..........177 C4
Cotman Dr NR31..........170 A7
Cotman Fields NR1..178 C4
Cotman Rd NR1..........163 B5
Cotoneaster Ct 4 NR31..170 B6
Cottage Dr The NR7..163 E8
Cottage End NR11..........150 A6
Cottage Farm Abbey
PE32..........46 C2
Cottage Gdns IP27..........113 E1
Cottage Homes IP24..125 A6
Cottage Rd NR29..........57 E6
Cotterall Cl NR5..........161 A8
Cottinghams Dr NR10..157 E7
Cotton Rd NR9..........70 A4
Cotton's Cnr PE14..........77 D2
Cotton's Drove PE14..........77 D6
Cottons Head PE14..........77 E7
Cottons The PE14..........77 D7
Cotts La PE34..........144 F1
Coughtrey Cl NR7..........159 B5
Coulson La IP27..........175 C4
Coulton Cl PE30..........146 E7
Council Rd 4 IP23..152 E6
County Ct Rd 3 PE30..146 E4
Court Cl 4 NR29..........57 D2
Court Dr NR27..........139 B6

Courtenay Cl
4 East Dereham NR19 ..154 D5
2 Norwich NR5..........160 F8
Courtfields PE37..........153 B3
Court Gdns PE38..........172 C5
Court Green La
Great Snoring NR21..........17 B5
Rollesby NR29..........57 D2
Courtyard The 5 NR4..161 C5
Cousens Cl NR28..........151 B2
Covent Gdn Rd NR30 ...168 C7
Coventry St 2 NR21..........15 C2
Coventry Way IP24..........176 A4
Covert Sycamore IP24 ..176 A4
Covert The IP24..........176 E6
Covey The
Surlingham NR14..........91 C8
Taverham NR8..........155 D2
Covey Way IP27..........113 F1
Cow Croft La PE14..........59 F2
Cowdewell Mews 7
NR8..........155 D1
Cowfen La IP22..........128 D4
Cowgate NR3..........178 B4
Cow Hill NR2..........178 A3
Cow La Denver PE38..172 C1
Tharston & Hapton NR15 ..106 C7
Cow Lake Dro PE14..........59 D5
Cowle's Dro IP26..........113 D5
Cow Mdw Rd NR13..........92 C8
Cowper Cl NR11..........143 C5
Cowper Rd NR19..........154 E5
Cowslip Cl 14 NR14..........89 B3
Cowslip La NR26..........138 B6
Cowslip Wlk NR34..........61 B8
Cowtrott La NR29..........57 D3
Cow Twr ★ NR3..........178 C4
Cox Cl PE14..........152 A3
COXFORD NR31..........30 C8
Coxford Rd NR21..........30 D6
Coxhill Rd NR13..........74 C3
Cox's La PE13..........152 A3
Coxswain Read Way
NR30..........168 D4
Cozens-Hardy Rd NR7 ..159 B4
Cozens Rd NR1..........163 A4
Cozens-Wiley Rd NR5..165 A8
Crabapple Cl 7 NR18 ..173 E4
Crabapple La NR9..........68 D1
Crab Apple La NR4..110 E8
Crabbe Rd NR23..........5 E2
Crabbe's Cl 7 IP26..........98 E1
Crabbetts Marsh NR12 ..55 D4
Crabbe St NR34..........42 E1
Crabb's Abbey NR3..........61 B2
Crabbs La NR9..........52 A7
CRABGATE NR11..........34 C5
Crabgate La N NR11..........34 D6
Crabgate La S NR11..........34 D5
Crab La Boughton PE33 ...81 A5
Great Yarmouth NR31..170 B6
Crab Marsh PE13..........152 B8
Crabtree La NR34..........110 D1
Crabtree Rise IP21..........131 C6
CRACKTHORN CORNER
IP22..........128 D5
Cradle Wood Rd NR28..151 E3
Cradock Ave NR30..........169 D8
Craft La Eastgate NR10 ..35 C1
Northrepps NR27..........11 A1
Craft Rd NR11..........21 C7
Craft The
Raveningham NR14..........110 B8
Winterton-on-Sea NR29 ..58 B6
Cramp Cnr NR14..........91 F6
Cranage Rd NR1..........162 E1
Crane Cl NR19..........154 C3
Cranes Croft Rd NR7 ...159 C5
Crane's La NR10..........150 C1
Cranes Mdw IP24..........120 D2
Cranes Mdw Way NR18 ..87 D3
Cranes Meadow Way
NR18..........173 A2
Cranes Rd NR14..........88 F3
Cranleigh Rise NR4..........161 F1
Cranley Rd NR7..........72 E4
Cranmer Ave PE30..........148 C4
Cranmer Ct NR21..........141 C6
Cranmoor Drove PE15 ..95 A4
Cranny Field Chase PE14..41 E1
Cranwell Rd 10 IP20..........91 F6
CRANWICH IP26..........99 F6
Cranwich Rd
Cranwich IP26..........99 E5
Mundford IP26..........99 F5
Mundford IP26..........100 C3
CRANWORTH IP25..........85 E7
Cranworth Gdns NR1 ...178 A1
Craske Cl 3 NR26..........138 C5
Craske Dr NR13..........72 E7
Craske Fen NR34..........42 A7
Craske PE34..........140 A7
Craunching's Loke NR28 ..22 E4
Craven La PE33..........62 B6
Crawford Rd NR27..........139 D5
CRAYMERE BECK NR21 ..33 F8
Craymere Beck Rd
Briston NR24..........142 E1
Hindolveston NR24..........18 F1
Thurning NR24..........34 A8
Craymere Rd NR24..........142 E2
Creake Rd
Burnham Market PE31 ..135 D2

Creake Rd continued
Sculthorpe NR21..........141 A6
2 Norwich NR5..........160 F8
West Barsham NR21..........16 A4
Creammore Farm La
PE34..........61 A4
Creance Rd NR7..........159 C4
Crecen La PE36..........132 C4
Creek The PE31..........135 E7
Cremer Cl 14 PE31..........12 E4
Cremer's Drift NR26..........138 D7
Cremer St NR26..........138 D7
Cremorne La NR1..........163 B5
Crescent Pas PE13..........152 C5
Crescent Rd PE36..........132 C3
Crescent The
Ashwellthorpe NR16..........105 F8
Bacton/Walcott NR12..........24 A7
East Dereham NR19..........154 C1
East Harling NR16..........118 C4
Hemsby NR29..........167 D7
Hethersett NR9..........88 C7
4 Newton Flotman NR15..89 D1
Norwich NR2..........178 A2
Taverham NR8..........156 F8
Thurton NR14..........91 C4
Wisbech PE13..........152 C4
Cressener Cl NR6..........157 E5
Cressingham Rd
Ashill IP25..........83 F5
Ashill IP25..........83 F6
Saham Toney IP25..........84 B4
Cresswell Cl NR5..........161 B6
Cresswell St PE30..........146 E6
Crest Rd NR14..........140 C4
Cricket Cl NR8..........155 E3
Cricketers Cl NR21..........33 B6
Cricketers Way PE13..152 A6
Cricketer's Wlk NR13..........92 E7
Cricket Field View
NR13..........165 E2
Cricket Gd Rd NR1..........162 E3
Cricket Ground Rd IP24..117 A8
Cricket Pasture The
PE31..........3 E7
Crick's Wlk IP22..........177 A5
Crimp Cramp La NR34..111 B4
CRIMPLESHAM PE33..........80 B6
CRINGLEFORD NR4..........89 B8
Cringleford CE VA Prim Sch
NR4..........161 C1
Cringleford Chase NR4..161 C1
Cringles La NR16..........56 F6
Crinkle Hill NR29..........40 E1
Crinoline La NR20..........69 C5
Crisp Cl PE31..........140 C3
Crisp Rd NR35..........109 E3
Critoph Cl NR14..........90 D4
Critten's Rd NR11..........158 B4
Crockers La NR21..........15 E7
Crocus St NR18..........173 E6
Croft Cl Diss IP22..........177 C4
10 Harleston IP20..........122 D2
Crofters Cl PE30..........147 B8
Croft Gn NR17..........174 B3
Croft Hill NR9..........75 B5
Croftholme Way 2
NR7..........159 C6
Croft House Dr IP26 ...98 F2
Croft La Corpusty NR11 ...19 F2
Diss IP22..........177 C4
Marsham NR10..........150 C1
Croft Mdw PE37..........66 A4
Croft Rd
Caister-on-Sea NR30..168 E5
Norton Subcourse NR14..92 E1
Upwell PE14..........77 D3
Crofts Cl PE31..........135 C1
Crofts The 1 NR5..........160 F7
Croft The
Christchurch PE14..........95 A4
Costessey NR8..........156 F4
Cromer NR27..........139 B6
Little Snoring NR21..........17 C3
Swanton Novers NR24 ...18 B3
Croft Yd NR23..........136 D6
Cromarty Way NR30..168 D5
Cromber Rd NR11..........20 F5
Crome Cl IP22..........177 B4
Crome Dr NR12..........164 E6
Cromer Acad NR27..........139 C5
Crome Rd NR3..........162 F8
CROMER DISTRICT HOSP
NR27..........139 C7
Cromer Hospl NR27..........139 D6
Cromer Jun Sch NR27 ..139 C5
Cromer La PE31..........80 B6
Cromer Mus ★ NR27..........139 C7
Cromer Rd
Aylmerton NR11..........10 A1
Aylsham NR11..........150 C8
Blickling NR11..........36 B7
Erpingham NR11..........21 B1
Erpingham NR11..........21 A1
Felbrigg NR11..........10 C3
Felmingham NR28..........37 B8
Gresham NR11..........9 E5
Hevingham NR10..........36 B1
Holt NR25..........137 D7
Ingworth NR11..........36 C8
Ingworth NR11..........36 C8
Marsham NR10..........150 D1
Metton NR11..........21 B8
Mundesley NR11..........143 B7
Northrepps NR27..........139 F2
North Walsham NR28..151 A6
Norwich NR6..........158 A5

Cromer Rd continued
Ormesby St Margaret with
Scratby NR29..........167 A2
Overstrand NR27..........10 F3
Overstrand NR27..........139 F4
Runton NR27..........10 A5
Sheringham NR26..........138 E6
Sidestrand NR27..........11 B2
Southrepps NR11..........22 C8
Thorpe Market NR11..........22 A7
Thorpe Market NR27..........21 F7
Trimingham NR11..........11 C2
Cromer Sta NR27..........139 A7
Cromes Oak CT NR14..........90 C4
Cromes Pl NR10..........37 B2
Crompton Rd NR11..........150 C4
Cromwell Cl
6 Cromer NR27..........139 C6
3 Hethersett NR9..........88 D8
7 Marthan NR29..........57 D4
Swaffham PE37..........153 D3
Cromwell Rd
Cromer NR27..........139 C6
Great Yarmouth NR31..169 C1
Norwich NR7..........159 B3
Weeting-with-Broomhill
IP27..........114 E8
Wisbech PE13..........152 A2
Cromwell Retail Park
PE14..........152 A2
Cromwell Terr 6 PE30..146 E3
Crooks PE31..........178 A1
Crosby Row PE12..........41 A8
Cross Bank La IP26..........97 E1
Cross Bank Rd
King's Lynn PE30..........26 C6
King's Lynn PE30..........146 C6
Crossbill Cl NR8..........156 B6
Crossdale St NR27..........139 D1
CROSSDALE STREET
NR27..........139 D1
Cross Dro
Hilgay PE38..........96 D7
Southery PE38..........97 B3
Cross Drove PE14..........78 A2
Crossing Rd
Great Green IP21..........130 A5
Palgrave IP22..........177 D1
Cross Keys Cl 2 NR10...53 D2
Crosskeys Way 3 NR20..68 F6
Cross La
Brancaster PE31..........3 B7
Lessingham NR12..........24 E4
Northwold IP26..........99 C7
Norwich NR3..........178 A4
Runton NR27..........10 A4
Stanhoe PE31..........14 E7
Surlingham NR14..........91 A8
Cross Rd
Ashby with Oby NR29..........56 F1
Banham NR16..........119 E6
Cat's Corner NR10..........37 B7
Great Yarmouth NR31..170 D6
Starston IP20..........122 C2
Crossroad NR10..........37 C4
Crossroads The IP23..130 B3
Cross's Grave PE31..........29 E4
Cross St 6 Cromer NR27..139 B6
Harpley PE31..........29 C5
2 Holt NR25..........137 B6
Hoxne IP21..........131 A3
Salthouse NR25..........8 B6
Cross Stone Rd NR14..........92 B3
CROSS STREET IP21..131 A3
Crosstead NR30..........169 D8
Cross Way PE31..........133 C5
Crossways 4 NR31..........167 A2
CROSS WAYS NR31..........94 B4
Crossways La NR28..........23 D1
Crossway Terr
Acle NR13..........166 B4
5 Loddon NR14..........91 F1
Cross Wy 5 NR19..........154 E5
CROSTWICK NR12..........54 B3
Crostwick La NR14..........54 A2
CROSTWIGHT NR28..........38 D8
Croughton La PE31..........30 B8
Crowden Rd NR12..........24 D4
Crowes Loke NR13..........73 B7
Crowgate St NR12..........38 B1
CROWGATE STREET
NR12..........55 A8
Crow Green La NR15..........106 F1
Crow Hall Est PE38..........172 C3
Crow Hall Gn NR10..........170 C2
Crow Hall La NR10..........35 C1
Crow Hill NR11..........34 C7
Crow La Bircham PE31..........14 A2
Elsing NR20..........50 F4
Great Bircham PE31..........14 C1
Great Dunham PE32..........47 E1
Houghton PE31..........29 D8
West Rudham PE31..........29 E7
Crown Ave PE14..........95 A7
Crown Cres IP25..........84 E5
Crown Ctyd NR16..........119 A4
Crown Gdns
Dereham NR20..........154 F5
Wereham PE33..........80 E4
Crown Gn IP22..........120 E2
Crown House Cl 9
IP24..........176 D4
Crown La
Coney Weston IP31..........127 B4
Fransham NR19..........66 D6
Little Ellingham NR17..........85 F1
Crown Loke NR11..........22 B7
Crown Mdw NR10..........149 C5
Crown Pl 9 NR19..........154 D5

Crown Rd
Christchurch PE14..........95 A7
Colkirk NR21..........31 D5
East Dereham NR19..........154 F5
Great Yarmouth NR30..169 D3
Horsham St Faith NR10 ...53 D2
Lamas NR10..........36 F1
Mundford IP26..........100 B4
Norwich NR1..........178 B3
2 Old Buckenham NR17..104 D2
Crown Sq PE30..........147 A2
Crown St
Banham NR16..........119 D7
Brandon IP27..........175 A2
Methwold IP26..........99 A5
CROWNTHORPE NR18 ..87 C6
Crownthorpe Rd NR18 ..87 C6
Crown Way NR16..........119 D6
Crow Rd NR28..........151 C6
Crowshall La NR17..........174 B5
CROWSHILL IP25..........67 A1
Crow's La IP25..........84 C1
Crow St IP31..........127 B4
CROXTON
Croxton IP24..........116 C5
Fulmodeston NR21..........17 E2
Croxton Rd
Croxton IP24..........116 B7
East Wretham IP24..........102 A1
Fulmodeston NR21..........17 E2
Thetford IP24..........176 D4
Wretham IP24..........101 E1
Wretham IP24..........116 D8
Crudsole La NR28..........22 E4
Crummock Rd 3 NR5..161 C6
Cubitt Rd NR1..........163 C7
Cubitts Cl NR20..........33 B2
Cubitts Mdw NR10..........36 E1
Cuckoofield La NR14..........89 A3
Cuckoo Gn NR32..........94 D2
CUCKOO GREEN NR32..171 A4
Cuckoo Hill Rd PE31 ...14 B3
Cuckoo La
Brundall NR13..........73 E3
Carbrooke IP25..........85 B4
Redenhall with Harleston
IP20..........122 F2
Cuckoo Rd PE34..........79 A8
Cuck Stool La 5 PE32..46 F2
Cucumber La NR13..........165 B5
Cuffer La
New Buckenham NR17 ..104 F4
Old Buckenham NR16 ..104 F2
Culey CT PE30..........146 F7
CULFORDHEATH IP31 ..125 D1
Culford Heath IP31..........125 D1
Culley's Pit Rd NR12 ...38 A2
Culley's 1 NR31..........171 D4
Culling's Hill NR13..........72 F2
Culloden Ave NR5..........156 C1
Cullum Cl NR20..........50 B3
Cullyer Cres NR18..........173 A2
Culverin Cl 9 NR7..........72 D4
Culyers Cl NR14..........90 C6
Cumby Wy 4 NR31..........171 D4
Cummings Bvd NR21..........15 C2
Cunningham Ave 2
NR30..........169 D8
Cunningham Cl IP24..176 F6
Cunningham Rd 6
NR5..........161 C5
Cunningham Wlk 3
IP24..........176 F6
Curd's Hall NR19..........66 A7
Curie Dr NR31..........170 B1
Curlew Cl
Hunstanton PE36..........132 D1
7 Watton IP25..........84 C3
Curlew Cres NR18..........173 C1
Curlew Way NR31..........170 A6
Currie Cl NR28..........151 B2
Curson Cl 11 NR9..........88 C7
Curson Rd 8 NR15..106 F6
Cursons Mews NR18 ...173 B6
Curtis Dr 1 IP26..........98 D1
Curtis La NR26..........138 E7
Curtis Rd NR3..........158 B4
Cushing Cl 1 IP25..........67 B2
Cushing Dr 3 NR21..........17 B3
Custance Cn NR4..........161 E3
Customhouse St PE12..41 C8
Cuthbert Cl
4 King's Lynn PE30..148 C5
Norwich NR7..........159 B4
8 Thetford IP24..........176 F5
Cuthberts Maltings
IP22..........177 B3
Cutler Way
Bowthorpe NR5..........160 F6
Norwich NR5..........160 E8
Cut Lode NR14..........73 C1
Cutthroat La NR19..........68 A6
Cutting's Rd IP21..........121 E1
Cutting's Rd IP21..........131 C8
Cuttons Cnr NR31..........73 D6
Cydonia Gn 12 NR31..170 B6
Cygnet Cl NR17..........174 F6
Cygnet Ct NR15..........106 E4
Cygnet Rd NR10..........154 E1
Cygnet Wlk NR31..........153 C2
Cypress Cl NR8..........156 E8
Cypress Cres NR26..........138 D5
Cypress Pl PE36..........132 C4
Cypress Farm Loke
NR17..........174 C5
Cyprus Rd NR17..........174 C5
Cyprus St NR1..........162 E3
Cyril Rd NR7..........163 F7

D

Dacre Cl NR4 . . . . 161 E1
Dades La PE14 . . . . 60 B6
Dad's Army Mus★ IP24 .176 D4
Daffodil Cl NR18 . . . . 173 F7
Daffodil Way NR20 . . . . 68 E6
DAFFY GREEN NR19 . . . . . . 67 C4
Dagmar Mews 12 NR30 . .169 D2
Dairy Cres NR19 . . . . 154 D6
Dairy Drift PE32 . . . . 48 C2
Dairy Dro CB6 . . . . 95 F3
Dairy Farm Cl NR21 . . . . . 141 C6
Dairy Farm Ct NR17 . . . . .174 C5
Dairy La NR11 . . . . 9 E1
Dairy Wy PE30 . . . . 147 C7
Daisy Cl NR29 . . . . 57 E4
Daisy La PE38 . . . . 172 A5
Daisy St NR18 . . . . 173 F6
Daisy Way
  Damgate NR13 . . . . .166 B3
  Gillingham NR34 . . . . . . 110 B2
Dakenham Cl NR18 . . . . . . 72 F8
Dakin Rd NR3 . . . . 158 D1
Dakota Dr NR5 . . . . 158 D6
Dalbier Cl 2 NR13 . . . . 72 E4
Dale Cl IP25 . . . . 84 E3
Dale La NR29 . . . . 56 C8
Dale Rd
  East Dereham NR19 . . . .154 C6
  Scarning NR19 . . . . 67 A7
  Stanton IP31 . . . . 127 C1
Dales Ct 6 NR31 . . . . 94 C8
Dales Loke NR14 . . . . 163 D5
Dales The NR13 . . . . 165 D3
Dalrymple Way NR3 . . . . . 158 C4
Dam Brig NR16 . . . . 104 F1
DAMGATE
  Acle NR13 . . . . .166 C2
  Martham NR29 . . . . 57 E5
Damgate Back La NR29 . . 57 D6
Damgate Cl NR13 . . . . . . .166 C2
Damgate La Acle NR13 . .166 D2
  Martham NR29 . . . . 57 D6
Damgate St NR18 . . . . 173 B3
DAM GREEN NR16 . . . . . . 119 C4
Dam La IP22 . . . . 129 D3
Dams La IP22 . . . . 129 E3
Damson La NR23 . . . . 6 C6
Danacre Rd IP20 . . . . 123 C6
Danby Cl 6 NR4 . . . . 89 D8
Danby Rd NR31 . . . . 170 C6
Dane Cl IP24 . . . . 176 E5
DANEMOOR GREEN NR9 . 86 F8
Danemoor La NR9 . . . . 86 E8
Danemoor Rd NR9 . . . . . . 86 E7
Danesbower Cl NR13 . . . .165 F6
Danesbower La NR13 . . . .165 F6
Danesfort Dr 1 NR19 . . . .154 E6
Daniels Rd NR4 . . . . 162 B2
Danish House Gdns
  NR27 . . . . 11 A4
Daphne Cl NR19 . . . . .154 D4
Daphne Way 8 NR31 . . . .170 B5
Dark La
  Ashmanhaugh NR12 . . . .38 C1
  Dickleburgh & Rushall
    IP21 . . . . 130 B6
  Erpingham NR11 . . . . . . 21 A1
  Kimberley NR18 . . . . . . 87 B3
  Smallburgh NR12 . . . . . . 38 D3
  Somerton NR29 . . . . 57 F6
  Walton Highway PE14 . . 59 C7
  Wretham IP24 . . . . 101 F2
Darlington Mews NR3 . .158 A1
Darrell Pl NR5 . . . . 161 D7
Darrow Gn Rd IP20 . . . . . 122 F8
DARROW GREEN IP20 . . 122 E8
Darrow La IP22 . . . . 120 A1
Darrow Wood★ IP22 . . . . 122 F8
Darrow Wood La IP22 . . 120 A1
Darwin Cl 5 PE12 . . . . . . 41 B8
Darwin Wlk NR19 . . . . . . .154 D4
Daseley's Cl PE30 . . . . . . 148 A1
Dashwood Cl NR31 . . . . . . 93 F6
Dauber's La NR13 . . . . 74 C2
Davey Cl NR35 . . . . .124 C8
Davey Hill NR27 . . . . 10 C4
Davey Pl NR2 . . . . 178 B3
David Capp Rd NR15 . . . .165 C5
Davidson Cl NR7 . . . . 163 F7
Davidson Rd NR7 . . . . . . 163 F7
Davies Dr NR4 . . . . 161 B2
Da Volls Ct NR31 . . . . 170 D6
Davy Pl Heacham PE31 . .133 C5
  7 Loddon NR14 . . . . . . 92 A1
Dawber Cl PE30 . . . . 147 B4
Dawes La 2 PE31 . . . . 12 E4
Dawnay Ave PE30 . . . . . . 148 B1
Dawsons La NR20 . . . . 33 C3
Dawsons Way NR13 . . . . . 73 C6
Dawson Way NR18 . . . . . 105 A7
Day's La IP31 . . . . 127 E3
Day's Lode Rd PE14 . . . . . 95 A4
Deacon Cl NR13 . . . . 165 D4
Deacon Dr 14 NR9 . . . . . . 88 D8
Deas Rd PE30 . . . . 148 D1
Deben Dr 14 NR31 . . . . . . 94 A6
Debenne Rd NR28 . . . . . . 151 C6
Debnam Cl 10 NR31 . . . . . 94 A5
Deborah Rd NR31 . . . . . . 170 C2
De-Carle Smith Rd
  NR13 . . . . .166 C4
De Caux Rd NR3 . . . . 158 E1
Decoy Dr NR12 . . . . 164 E6

Decoy Rd
  Lakenheath IP27 . . . . . .112 F4
  Mautby NR29 . . . . 75 F5
  Mautby NR29 . . . . 76 A5
  Ormesby St Margaret with
    Scratby NR29 . . . . . . 167 A4
  Ormesby St Michael NR29. . 57 F2
  Potter Heigham NR29 . . . 56 F7
  Southery PE38 . . . . 97 E6
Deepdale NR13 . . . . 165 D3
Deepdale Ave 1 NR29 . . . 57 C4
Deep Rd NR18 . . . . 173 B8
Deer Row NR35 . . . . 109 D1
De Grey Cl NR5 . . . . 157 A1
De Grey Rd PE30 . . . . 147 B5
De Hague Rd NR4 . . . . . . 161 F4
De Havilland Rd
  Dereham NR19 . . . . . . .154 C6
  Wisbech PE13 . . . . .152 C6
Delane Rd NR8 . . . . 157 C1
Delft Way NR6 . . . . 158 A6
Delgate La PE31 . . . . 3 E7
Dell Cl NR15 . . . . 106 F8
Dell Cnr La NR13 . . . . 73 F5
Dell Cres NR5 . . . . 161 D7
Dell Loke NR14 . . . . 163 B2
Dell The Bodham NR25 . . . . 9 A3
  Elveden IP24 . . . . 125 A6
  Hingham NR9 . . . . 86 B5
  Mundesley NR11 . . . . . . 143 D5
  Trowse Newton NR14 . . .163 B2
Delph Rd IP27 . . . . 113 E2
Delta Cl NR5 . . . . 158 C4
De Lucy Cl IP22 . . . . 177 C5
De Morley Cl 4 IP22 . . . . 177 A5
De Morley Garth NR26 . . 138 D6
De-Narde Rd NR19 . . . . . 154 D7
Denbigh Rd NR2 . . . . 162 B5
Dene Ave NR29 . . . . 167 A3
Dene Side 1 NR30 . . . . . 169 D3
Denes The NR1 . . . . 163 C5
DENHAM IP21 . . . . 131 B1
Denham Low Rd IP21 . . . 131 A1
Denham Rd IP21 . . . . 131 B2
Denmark Ct IP22 . . . . 177 C2
Denmark Hill IP22 . . . . . . 177 C2
Denmark Opening NR3 . 158 E1
Denmark Rd
  Beccles NR34 . . . . 110 D1
  2 King's Lynn PE30 . . .147 B6
  Norwich NR3 . . . . 158 E1
Denmark Rise IP22 . . . . . 177 C4
Denmark St IP22 . . . . 177 C2
Denmead Cl 4 NR4 . . . . . . 89 D8
Dennis Rd NR6 . . . . 157 F7
Dennis Sneezum Ct
  NR28 . . . . .172 B4
Denny Rd PE30 . . . . 147 A4
Denny's Hill IP20 . . . . . . 123 A2
Denny's Wlk PE32 . . . . . . 63 E7
DENTON IP20 . . . . 123 A7
Denton Low Rd IP20 . . . . 123 B5
Denton Rd Alburgh IP20 . .123 A6
  Denton NR35 . . . . 108 C1
  Norwich NR3 . . . . 158 F3
  Topcroft NR35 . . . . 107 E2
  Topcroft NR35 . . . . 108 A2
DENVER IP20 . . . . 172 C2
Denver Hill PE38 . . . . 172 C3
Denver VC Prim Sch
  PE38 . . . . .172 D2
Denver Windmill★
  . . . . 172 B1
DEOPHAM NR18 . . . . 86 F3
DEOPHAM GREEN NR18 . . 86 E2
Deopham Rd
  Attleborough NR17 . . . .174 C7
  Deopham Green NR18. . . 86 E1
  Great Ellingham NR17 . . 103 F8
  Hingham NR9 . . . . 86 C4
  Morley NR18 . . . . 87 A2
DEOPHAM STALLAND
  NR9 . . . . 86 D2
Derby St NR2 . . . . 162 C7
DEREHAM NR20 . . . . 154 F4
Dereham 6th Form Coll
  NR20 . . . . .154 F5
Dereham CE Inf Sch
  NR19 . . . . .154 D5
Dereham CE Jun Acad
  NR19 . . . . .154 D4
Dereham Dr PE30 . . . . . . 147 A7
Dereham Hospl NR19 . . .154 E7
Dereham La NR19 . . . . 66 C8
Dereham Low Rd NR19 . . 49 A2
Dereham Neatherd High Sch
  NR20 . . . . .68 A8
Dereham Rd
  5 Bawdeswell NR20 . . . .50 E7
  Beeston PE32 . . . . 48 D4
  Beeston with Bittering
    PE32 . . . . .48 D2
  Bradenham IP25 . . . . . . 67 A4
  Briningham NR24 . . . . . . 18 D5
  Brinton NR24 . . . . .142 A8
  Bylaugh NR20 . . . . 50 C5
  Colkirk NR21 . . . . 31 E5
  Costessey NR5 . . . . 156 D1
  Dereham NR20 . . . . 68 A7
  East Dereham NR19 . . . .154 B5
  Easton NR9 . . . . 70 C5
  Garvestone NR9 . . . . . . .68 C1
  Gressenhall NR19 . . . . . .49 C2
  Hempton NR21 . . . . 141 B2
  Hockering NR20 . . . . .69 D7
  Honingham NR9 . . . . . . .69 D7
  Horningtoft NR20 . . . . . . 31 E1

Dereham Rd continued
  Kimberley NR18 . . . . . . .87 A7
  Litcham PE32 . . . . 48 A4
  Mattishall NR20 . . . . 68 D6
  North Elmham NR20 . . . .49 E6
  Ovington IP25 . . . . 84 E6
  Pudding Norton NR21 . . 141 B1
  Reepham NR10 . . . . 149 A4
  Scarning NR19 . . . . 154 A4
  Shipdham IP25 . . . . 67 A1
  Stanfield NR20 . . . . 48 E8
  Swanton Morley NR20. . . 50 B2
  25 Watton IP25 . . . . . . .84 D3
  Wendling NR19 . . . . .66 F7
  Whinburgh & Westfield
    NR19 . . . . 67 F5
  Whissonsett NR20 . . . . . 31 E2
  Yaxham NR19 . . . . 68 A5
DERSINGHAM PE31 . . . . . 140 D5
Dersingham Bog National
  Nature Reserve★ PE31 . 27 D7
Dersingham Bypass
  Dersingham PE31 . . . . . . 12 D2
  Dersingham PE31 . . . . . 140 D5
Dersingham Inf Sch
  PE31 . . . . .140 D4
Dersingham Prim Sch
  PE31 . . . . .140 F3
Dersley Ct 1 NR5 . . . . . . 160 E7
Derwent Ave PE30 . . . . . 148 F2
Desborough Way NR13. . 72 D4
Desmond Dr NR6 . . . . . . 158 F6
Devlin Dr 3 NR14. . . . . . . 90 C5
Devon Ave NR6 . . . . 157 E4
Devon Cres NR30 . . . . . . 148 D5
Devonshire Ct 1 PE30 . . .147 A7
Devonshire Rd NR30 . . . . 169 D2
Devonshire St 4 NR2. . . .162 C7
Devon Way NR14 . . . . . . 163 C1
De Warrenne Ct PE30 . . . 98 F5
De Warrenne Dr IP27 . . .175 B7
De Warrenne Pl PE32 . . . 47 A2
Dewdrop Cl NR13 . . . . . . 133 D6
Dewing Rd NR13 . . . . 72 E8
Dexter Rd PE34 . . . . 79 A7
Dial Cl PE38 . . . . 172 B5
Diamond Cl IP22 . . . . 120 B5
Diamond Rd NR6 . . . . . . 158 B5
Diamond St PE30 . . . . . . 146 D2
Diamond Terr PE30 . . . . . 146 D2
Diana Cl NR19 . . . . 154 C1
Dianas Dro PE36 . . . . . . 132 C2
Diana Way NR30 . . . . . . 168 C6
Dian Rd NR13 . . . . 165 E3
Dibden Rd NR3 . . . . 162 F8
Dickens Ave NR30 . . . . . . 169 D1
Dickens Ct 5 NR30 . . . . . 169 D1
Dickfool's La NR19 . . . . . . 66 F8
Dickleburgh Bypass
  IP21 . . . . 130 E8
Dickleburgh By Pass
  IP21 . . . . 121 B1
DICKLEBURGH MOOR
  IP21 . . . . 121 C2
Dickleburgh Rd
  Burston & Shimpling
    IP21 . . . . 121 A1
  Rushall IP21 . . . . 121 B1
Dickleburgh VA Prim Sch
  IP21 . . . . 121 B1
Dicks Mount NR34 . . . . . 111 D3
Dicky Hill IP20 . . . . 122 D3
Diddle's Dam PE34 . . . . . 42 F5
DIDLINGTON IP26 . . . . 99 E8
Didlington Drove IP26 . . 99 F7
Digby Dr NR21 . . . . 141 B6
Dilham NR28 . . . . 38 C4
Dilham Arts Ctr★ NR28. . 38 C4
Dilham Dr 1 NR12 . . . . . . 164 E7
Dilham Rd Honing NR28 . . . 38 C6
  Worstead NR28 . . . . 38 A4
Dilldash La IP21 . . . . 17 A5
Dinosaur Adventure Pk★
  NR9 . . . . 51 E4
Dirty La
  North Tuddenham NR20. . 50 L1
  Pulham St Mary IP21 . . 121 F3
Discovery Wlk PE13 . . . . 152 E2
DISS IP22 . . . . 177 D6
Diss Bsns Ctr IP21 . . . . . 130 B6
Diss CE Acad IP22 . . . . . 177 D4
Diss High Sch IP22 . . . . 177 E5
Diss Inf Sch IP22 . . . . . . 177 E4
Diss Mus★ IP22 . . . . .177 D4
Diss Rd Botesdale IP22 . . 128 F3
  Burston & Shimpling IP22 120 E1
  Garboldisham IP22 . . . . 128 A8
  Rickinghall Inferior IP22 128 D8
  Rickinghall Superior IP22 128 E1
  Scole IP21 . . . . 130 C5
  Scole IP21 . . . . 130 C5
  Shelfanger IP22 . . . . . . 120 B3
  South Lopham IP22 . . . . 128 F8
  Stradbroke IP21 . . . . . . 131 F1
  Tibenham NR16 . . . . . . 120 C8
  Wattisfield IP22 . . . . . . 128 B1
Diss Sta IP22 . . . . 177 F4
Diss Swimming & Fitness Ctr
  IP22 . . . . 177 E6
Distillery Sq 5 NR2. . . . . 162 C6
DITCHINGHAM CE Prim Acad
  NR35 . . . . .109 B2
Ditchingham Dam
  NR35 . . . . .109 A1
Dix Cl IP25 . . . . 133 E5
Dixon Rd Cromer NR27 . . .139 B5
  North Walsham NR28 . . . 151 D5
  Norwich NR7 . . . . 159 A4

Dixon's Dro PE14 . . . . 59 C8
Dixon's Fold NR6 . . . . . . 158 F4
Dobbs' La NR13 . . . . 54 D2
Dobby Dr PE30 . . . . 146 D6
Dobson Way 3 NR34 . . . . 110 D1
DOCKENEY NR34 . . . . . . 109 F2
DOCKING PE31 . . . . 134 C5
Docking CE Prim Sch
  PE31 . . . . .134 D4
Docking La PE31 . . . . 15 B1
Docking Rd
  Bircham Newton PE31. . . 14 A4
  Burnham Market PE31 . . . 3 E2
  Burnham Market PE31 . .135 A1
  Docking PE31 . . . . 2 F2
  Docking PE31 . . . . 134 B3
  Docking PE31 . . . . 134 B8
  Fring PE31 . . . . 13 E6
  Ringstead PE36 . . . . 2 B2
  Ringstead PE36 . . . . 2 D3
  Sedgeford PE36 . . . . . . 13 B7
  Stanhoe PE31 . . . . 14 D7
  Syderstone PE31 . . . . . . 15 A3
  Westgate PE31 . . . . . . 135 B2
Dock Tavern La NR31 . . . 170 D5
Doctors Hill NR10 . . . . . . 53 A8
Doctor's La IP21 . . . . 122 A2
Doctors Mdw 1 NR10. . . . 53 D2
Doctors Rd NR13 . . . . . . 165 E6
Dodd Cl NR30 . . . . 168 D7
Dodderman Way
  Norwich NR5 . . . . 160 F6
  Norwich NR5 . . . . 161 A6
Dodds Cl NR17 . . . . 174 B3
DODDSHILL PE31 . . . . . . 140 F3
Doddshill Rd PE31 . . . . . 140 F3
Dodds La PE32 . . . . 45 B2
Dodds Rd NR17 . . . . 174 B3
Dodd's La NR17 . . . . 174 B3
Dodgers La NR15 . . . . 91 A3
Dodmans Cl NR30 . . . . . 146 E5
Dodman's La NR20 . . . . . 31 F2
Dodmans The NR19 . . . . 154 D4
Dodma Rd NR13 . . . . 47 C8
Dodson Dr
  7 Beetley NR19 . . . . 49 C3
  7 Gressenhall NR20 . . . 49 C3
Doe La Banham NR16 . . . 119 E8
  Old Buckenham NR17 . . .104 E1
Dog Cnr NR11 . . . . 35 A5
Dogger La NR23 . . . . 136 C6
Doggetts La NR12 . . . . . . 24 D4
Dog La Easton NR9 . . . . . . 70 B6
  Horsford NR10 . . . . 155 F4
  Shelfanger IP22 . . . . . . 119 F4
  Shelfanger IP22 . . . . . . 120 A4
  Thorpe Marriot NR8 . . . . 155 F3
Dog's Hole NR14 . . . . 91 A8
Dogs La NR34 . . . . 110 C3
Dogwood Cl 6 NR18 . . . . 173 E4
Dogwood Rd NR6 . . . . . . 158 D4
Dohamero La 1 PE33 . . . 43 F2
Doit La IP22 . . . . 129 D7
Doit The IP22 . . . . 129 C6
Doles La NR31 . . . . 94 B7
Dolman Cl 13 NR31 . . . . 169 B4
Dolphin Gr NR2 . . . . 162 B8
Dolphin La NR11 . . . . 21 C3
Dolphin Rd NR5 . . . . 156 C1
Doman Rd NR1 . . . . 178 C1
Donchurch Cl 6 NR5 . . . 161 A7
Donkey Pond Hill PE35. . 27 E7
Doran Dr IP25 . . . . 84 C4
Doris Barnes Ct 1
  NR19 . . . . .154 E5
Doris Rd NR2 . . . . 162 B5
Dorking Rd NR1 . . . . 171 B4
Dormouse Way NR9 . . . . . 88 D8
Dorothea Dr 7 NR19 . . . .154 D3
Dorothy Ave NR31 . . . . . 94 C7
Dorrs Dr IP25 . . . . 84 D4
Dorset Cl
  4 Attleborough NR17 . .174 B3
  Great Yarmouth NR30 . .169 D3
Doubleday Cl IP22 . . . . . 177 C4
Double La PE32 . . . . 46 B8
Double Lodges Rd PE35. . 27 D6
Doughty's Hospl NR3 . . . 178 B4
Douglas Bader Cl NR28. .151 C7
Douglas Cl Croxton IP24. .116 C5
  Norwich NR5 . . . . 158 D7
Douglas Haig Rd NR5 . . .161 D6
Doune Way 9 IP20 . . . . . 122 D2
Douro Pl NR2 . . . . 162 C6
Dove Ave NR18 . . . . 173 F7
Dove Cl
  1 Great Yarmouth
    NR31 . . . . .170 A6
  9 Harleston IP20. . . . . 122 D1
Dovecote Cl NR15 . . . . . . 90 F2
Dovecote Rd PE14 . . . . . . 77 D3
Dovecot La PE14 . . . . 59 E8
Dovedale Rd NR16 . . . . . 105 F5
Dovedales Fold NR7 . . . .158 F4
Dove Gdns NR18 . . . . . . 150 E6
Dovehouse La NR11 . . . . 21 B4
Dove House La 4 NR29 . . 56 F6
Dovehouse Pightle
  NR18 . . . . .173 A1
Dove La NR15 . . . . 90 C3
Dover Cl NR30 . . . . 168 C5
Dover St NR2 . . . . 162 B5
Dove St 3 NR2 . . . . 178 A3
Dovetail Cl PE34 . . . . 79 D8
Dow Cl NR5 . . . . 160 F5
Dowding Rd
  Norwich NR6 . . . . 158 D6
  3 Watton IP25 . . . . 84 F3
DOWE HILL NR29 . . . . . . 167 C5
Dow La NR12 . . . . 54 C3
Downham Cres NR18 . . . 173 B6

Downham Dro PE32 . . . . . 63 F7
Downham-Eastern Bypass
  PE38 . . . . .172 E4
DOWNHAM MARKET
  PE38 . . . . .172 D4
Downham Market Acad
  PE38 . . . . .172 D5
Downham Mkt Sta
  PE38 . . . . .172 A5
Downham Prep Sch
  PE34 . . . . .79 E8
Downham Rd
  Crimplesham PE33 . . . . .80 B7
  Denver PE38 . . . . 172 C2
  Fincham PE33 . . . . 62 E1
  Nordelph PE38. . . . . 78 D3
  Outwell PE14 . . . . 77 F6
  Runcton Holme PE33. . . .61 D4
  Ryston PE38. . . . . 79 F4
  Stradsett PE33. . . . . 80 D8
  Swaffham PE37 . . . . 64 B4
  West Dereham PE33 . . . 80 A4
Downham Way IP27 . . . . 175 F4
Downing Ct NR31 . . . . . . 170 C4
Downing Mews NR5 . . . .160 D8
Downing Rd NR31 . . . . . . 170 C4
Down Mill Dr PE32 . . . . . 65 C6
Downs Cl PE36 . . . . 132 D4
Downs Rd PE36 . . . . 132 D4
Downs Farm La IP20 . . . 123 B3
Downs The NR25. . . . . 7 C6
Dowsing Ct 5 NR13 . . . . 72 D5
Dowson Rd NR3 . . . . 158 B1
DRABBLEGATE NR11. . . .150 D8
Drabblegate NR11 . . . . . 150 D8
Drabbs La NR12. . . . . 38 E6
Dragonfly La
  4 Cringleford NR4. . . . . .89 A8
  Cringleford NR4. . . . . . . 161 B1
Dragonfly Way
  4 King's Lynn PE30 . . .146 E2
  Swaffham PE37 . . . . . . 153 C2
Dragon Hall★ NR1. . . . . .178 C2
Dragoon Cl 27 NR7. . . . . . 72 D4
Dragway NR25. . . . . 7 E3
Drake Ave NR30 . . . . 169 D7
Drake Cl 24 NR9 . . . . 88 D8
Drake Gdns PE37 . . . . . . 153 C2
Drake Prim Sch NR30 . . .174 E6
Drake Rd IP24 . . . . 176 E5
Drakes Cl 5 NR16 . . . . . . 118 C5
Drakes Loke NR10 . . . . . . 36 F1
Dranes La NR14. . . . . 90 F5
Drapers La NR35. . . . . . . 109 A3
Draper Way
  Norwich NR5 . . . . 160 D8
  Taverham NR8 . . . . 155 A1
Draycote Cl PE30 . . . . . . 147 D8
Draycotts Rise IP22 . . . . 177 C1
DRAYTON NR8 . . . . 157 A8
Drayton CE Jun Sch
  NR8 . . . . 155 F1
  Norwich NR8 . . . . 156 F8
Drayton Com Inf Sch
  NR8 . . . . 155 F1
Drayton Gr NR8 . . . . 156 F8
Drayton Hall La NR19 . . 154 B3
Drayton Hall Pk Rd NR8 . 157 B8
Drayton High Rd NR8 . . .157 A8
Drayton Ind Pk NR8. . . . .156 F7
Drayton La Drayton NR10. . 53 A1
  Norwich NR8 . . . . 157 B8
Drayton Lodge Pk NR8 . .157 B7
Drayton Rd NR3 . . . . 158 B2
Drayton Wood Rd NR6 . .157 D6
Dreibholz Ct NR20 . . . . . 154 F5
Dreway Dr NR8 . . . . 155 E3
Dried Flower Ctr★ NR12 . 55 C7
Drifters Wy NR31 . . . . . . 169 C1
Drift Ind Est The NR21. . .141 D5
Drift La Gressenhall NR20. . 49 C2
  Guestwick Green NR20 . . 33 F5
Driftlands NR21 . . . . 141 D5
Drift Rd
  Caister-on-Sea NR30. . . 168 C2
  Lakenheath IP27 . . . . . 113 E2
Drift The
  Attleborough NR17 . . . . 174 D5
  Bawdeswell NR20 . . . . . 50 E6
  Beetley NR20 . . . . 49 A6
  Botesdale IP22 . . . . . . 128 E3
  Fakenham NR21 . . . . . . 141 D4
  Heacham PE31 . . . . 133 D6
  Ingoldisthorpe PE31. . . 140 C8
  Swardeston NR14 . . . . . 89 B5
Driftway PE30 . . . . 148 C1
Driftway The
  1 Holt NR25 . . . . 137 C5
  Sheringham NR26 . . . . . 138 D8
Drill St NR21. . . . . 15 F1
Drinkwater Cl 9 NR9 . . . . 86 C5
Drive The Acle NR13 . . . .166 D4
  East Winch PE32 . . . . . . 45 A2
  Hoveton NR12 . . . . 55 B4
  Kidd's Moor NR18 . . . . . 88 B6
  Norwich NR5 . . . . 161 B8
  Saham Hills IP25 . . . . . 84 C6
  Somerleyton, Ashby and
    Herringfleet NR32 . . . 94 B3
  Trowse with Newton
    NR14 . . . . 163 D1
Dross La IP21 . . . . 130 F4
Drout's La IP31 . . . . 127 C3
Drove La NR25. . . . . 6 C4
Drovers Rest NR15. . . . . 108 C8
Drove The Brandon IP27. . .114 D4
  Raynham NR21 . . . . 30 E4
  Taverham NR8 . . . . 155 C2
Dr Torrens Wy NR5 . . . . .156 D2

Drudge Rd NR31 . . . . 170 D4
Druids La Litcham PE32. . 48 A4
  Shelfanger IP22 . . . . . . 120 B2
Druids' La IP22 . . . . 120 A3
Drunken Dro PE32 . . . . . . 46 C8
Drury Cl 10 NR5 . . . . 161 B8
Drury La
  3 Castle Acre PE32 . . . .46 F2
  Litcham PE32 . . . . 48 A4
  6 Loddon NR14 . . . . . . 91 F1
  Mellis IP23. . . . . 129 D2
DRURYLANE IP25. . . . . . . 85 A4
Drury Sq PE32 . . . . 48 C1
Drusilla Wy NR19 . . . . . . 68 C6
Dryden Cl 1 IP24. . . . . . . 176 E6
Dryden Rd NR8 . . . . 156 D8
DRYMERE PE37. . . . . 64 C1
Duchy of Lancaster
  Methwold CE Prim Sch
    IP26 . . . . .99 A5
Duck Decoy PE31 . . . . . . 140 C3
Duck Dro CB7 . . . . 112 A2
Duck Drove CB7 . . . . 112 B3
Duckett Cl 2 NR1 . . . . . . 162 E1
Duck Row NR10 . . . . 52 C8
Duck's Foot Rd IP21 . . . . 121 F6
Dudley Cl IP25 . . . . 84 D3
Dudleys Cl IP22 . . . . 128 E5
Duffield Cres NR9 . . . . . . 51 A4
Duff Rd NR3 . . . . 158 D2
Duffys La NR10 . . . . 149 B3
Dugard Ave NR1 . . . . 163 B8
Duke of Lancaster Sch
  NR21 . . . . 99 A4
Duke Puddle Dr PE14 . . . 95 C6
Duke Rd NR31 . . . . 170 D6
Duke's La NR17 . . . . 102 E8
Duke's Rd NR35 . . . . 124 B7
Duke's Ride
  Barnham IP24 . . . . 125 A4
  Barnham IP24 . . . . 125 B4
  Barnham IP24 . . . . 125 E4
  Euston IP24 . . . . 126 A5
  Euston IP24 . . . . 126 D6
Duke St Norwich NR3. . . .178 A4
  Wisbech PE13 . . . . 152 D4
Dukesway 1 NR35. . . . . . 123 F8
Dulgate La PE32 . . . . 153 D2
Dulgate Rd NR35 . . . . . . 108 B3
Dull's Rd NR35 . . . . 109 C5
Dumbs La NR10. . . . . 53 E5
Dumplingbridge La
  IP27 . . . . 113 E1
Dumpling Gn
  Dereham NR19 . . . . .68 A6
  East Dereham NR19 . . . .154 F2
DUMPLING GREEN
  NR19 . . . . .154 F3
Dunburgh Rd NR34 . . . . 110 A2
Duncan Cl IP24 . . . . 176 F6
Duncan Rd NR30 . . . . . . 169 D2
Duncan Way NR28 . . . . . 151 B2
Dunces La PE14. . . . . 41 E3
Dun Cow Rd NR34. . . . . . 111 B4
Dunford La NR24. . . . . . . 102 A2
Dungar Rd NR7. . . . . 159 D5
Dunham Rd
  East Lexham PE32 . . . . . 47 E3
  Litcham PE32. . . . . 48 A4
  Necton PE37 . . . . 65 F6
  Sporle with Palgrave PE32 .65 C7
Dunhill La
  Thelnetham IP22 . . . . . . 127 F2
  Wattisfield IP22. . . . . . . 127 F1
Dunkerley Ct 16 NR12 . . 39 B4
DUNKIRK NR11 . . . . 150 E8
Dunkirk NR11 . . . . 150 E8
Dunlin Dr
  Cringleford NR4. . . . . . . 161 B1
  Wymondham NR18 . . . . 173 D2
Dunlop Cl NR19 . . . . 154 B6
Dunnett Cl NR17 . . . . . . 174 E5
Dunnetts Cl IP25 . . . . 84 A7
Dunning's La IP21 . . . . . 121 E6
Dunnock Dr NR8. . . . . . . 156 A5
Dunns La NR21 . . . . 4 D1
DUNSTON NR14 . . . . 89 E5
Dunston Dro PE31 . . . . . 133 B1
DUNTON NR21. . . . . 15 F1
Dunton Rd
  Shereford NR21. . . . . . . 31 A8
  Tatterford NR21 . . . . . . 30 F7
Dunwood Dr NR6 . . . . . . 158 F7
Durbidge's Hill IP22. . . . 120 E1
Durham Ave NR31 . . . . . 170 B2
Durham Rd NR30 . . . . . . 162 B4
Durham Way IP24. . . . . . 176 A5
Durrell Way 2 NR28 . . . .151 C4
Dussindale 3 NR18. . . . . 173 C6
Dussindale Dr 13 NR7. . . 72 E4
DUSSINDALE PARK NR13. 72 E4
Dussindale Prim Sch
  NR7 . . . . 72 D4
Duverlin Cl NR4. . . . . 162 A1
Duvernay Croft PE30 . . . 100 C5
Dyball's La NR12. . . . . . . 38 F8
Dyers Yd NR3. . . . . 178 A3
Dye's Rd NR13 . . . . 73 C7
Dyes The NR20 . . . . 33 E8
Dykebeck NR18. . . . . 87 D4

E

Eade Rd NR3 . . . . 162 D8
Eades Farm Rd NR33. . . 111 E1
Eagle Cl NR11 . . . . 21 B2
Eagle Rd NR11 . . . . 21 B2
Eagles Ct NR23 . . . . 136 E6
Eagles The 3 NR30 . . . . 169 D4

Eagle Wlk 2 NR2 162 C4
Earl Cl PE31 140 C3
Earles Gdns NR4 161 E6
EARLHAM NR4 161 D5
Earlham Gn La NR5 161 B7
Earlham Gr NR5 161 D6
Earlham Rd NR4 161 C5
Earlham W Ctr 5 NR5 161 C6
Earl of Brandon Ave PE31 30 B3
Earl Rd NR13 72 E8
Earlsford Rd IP23 129 D1
Earlsmead Gdns PE32 48 D6
Earls' St IP24 176 D4
Earl Warren IP24 116 C5
Earnshaw Ct NR1 163 D5
EARSHAM NR35 123 E8
Earsham CE VA Fst Sch NR35 123 F8
Earsham Dam NR35 123 F8
Earsham Dr PE30 147 D8
Earsham Rd NR35 108 E2
EARSHAM STREET IP21 131 F5
Earth La NR32 94 C1
East Anglian Way NR31 170 C6
East Anglia Transport Mus★ NR33 111 F1
East Ave NR13 165 E3
East Bank
Sutton Bridge PE12 41 B6
Sutton Bridge PE12 41 C8
EAST BARSHAM NR21 16 D4
EAST BILNEY NR20 49 A6
East Bilney Hall NR20 49 A6
East Bilney Rd NR20 49 A6
East Binley Rd NR20 49 A6
Eastbourne Pl NR1 178 C3
EAST CARLETON NR14 88 F4
East Carleton Rd NR14 89 A4
East Coast Coll NR31 169 C1
East Cres NR20 50 B5
East Croft Field La PE14 41 D4
East Dereham Sta NR20 154 E5
Eastells La NR14 89 F2
East End
Gooderstone PE33 82 B5
Hilgay PE38 79 E1
East End Cl NR30 168 E8
Easterley Way NR29 167 A7
Eastern Ave
Caister-on-Sea NR30 168 E6
Norwich NR7 72 D4
Eastern Cl
Caister-on-Sea NR30 168 E5
32 Norwich NR7 72 D4
Eastern Cres NR7 72 D4
Eastern Rd NR7 72 D4
Eastern Yd PE30 147 C7
East Farm La NR10 53 E3
Eastfen Dro IP26 114 B6
Eastfield NR8 156 D8
Eastfield Cl PE30 147 A6
Eastfield Rd
Hickling NR12 39 F2
Long Stratton NR15 106 F4
1 Wisbech PE13 152 E7
Eastfields
King's Lynn PE30 147 C4
Narborough PE32 63 F7
Eastfield Way PE13 152 C6
EASTGATE NR10 35 C2
Eastgate IP25 67 D3
Eastgate Com Prim Sch PE30 146 E5
Eastgate Dro
Congham PE31 28 D2
Grimston PE32 45 D8
Hillington PE31 28 C3
Eastgate Rd PE36 2 A6
Eastgate St
2 King's Lynn PE30 146 E5
North Elmham NR20 49 E7
Shouldham PE33 62 D4
East Gn NR9 68 F2
East Gr NR27 139 C5
East Harbour Way PE31 135 E7
EAST HARLING NR16 118 C5
East Harling Prim Sch NR16 118 C5
East Harling Rd NR16 118 F4
EASTHAUGH NR9 51 C4
Easthaugh Rd NR9 51 D4
Easthill La NR14 90 E8
East Hills Rd NR5 156 E1
East La PE31 134 E4
Eastland Cl NR17 174 E6
Eastlands Bank PE14 41 E5
Eastleigh Gdns 6 NR9 69 F2
EAST LEXHAM PE32 47 D3
Eastmans La PE32 28 C1
Eastmoor Cl PE33 81 E4
Eastmoor Rd PE33 81 C7
East Norfolk 6th Form Coll NR31 170 C5
EASTON NR9 70 B5
Easton & Otley Coll (Easton Campus) NR9 70 B4
Easton Rd NR9 70 B4
Easton Way NR10 35 C1
Easton Wy NR10 35 C2
EAST RAYNHAM NR21 31 A4
East Rd
Great Yarmouth NR30 169 D5
Watton IP25 84 D3
EAST RUDHAM PE31 30 A7
EAST RUNTON NR27 10 B5
EAST RUSTON NR12 38 E6
East Ruston Area Inf Sch NR12 38 F7
East Ruston Old Vicarage Gdn★ NR12 24 A3
East Ruston Rd
Honing NR28 38 D6
Lessingham NR12 39 C7
EAST SOMERTON NR29 58 A6
EAST TUDDENHAM NR20 69 C6
East View NR35 124 B1
East View Cres NR20 31 C2
EAST WALTON PE32 45 E3
East Walton Rd
Gayton PE32 45 D5
Gayton Thorpe PE32 45 E4
EAST WINCH PE32 44 F3
East Winchcommon (Nature Reserve)★ PE32 45 A2
East Winch Rd
East Walton PE32 45 D3
Leziate PE32 44 F5
Middleton PE32 44 C2
Eastwood PE31 134 F3
EAST WRETHAM IP24 102 A1
East Wretham Rd
Croxton IP24 116 A8
Lynford IP27 115 F8
EATON NR4 161 F2
Eaton Chase NR4 161 E2
Eaton Dro Sedgeford PE36 13 A7
Snettisham PE31 12 F5
Eaton Gate NR4 89 C7
Eaton Gdns NR19 154 E3
Eaton Hall Specialist Acad NR4 161 F3
Eaton Prim Sch NR4 162 A1
Eaton Rd NR4 162 B2
Eaton St Cringleford NR4 89 B8
Norwich NR4 161 E1
EAU BRINK PE34 43 A3
Eau Brink Rd PE34 43 A2
Ebbisham Dr NR4 161 F1
Ebble Cl PE30 148 C2
Ebenezer Pl NR3 178 A4
ECCLES ON SEA NR12 24 E4
Eccles Rd
East Harling NR16 118 D6
Holt NR25 137 C7
Eccles Rd Sta NR16 103 E1
ECCLES ROAD NR16 103 F1
Ecclestone Cl NR31 170 A4
Eccles Way NR25 137 E7
Eckersley Dr NR21 141 A6
Ecotech Ctr★ PE37 153 B6
Ecton Gr 6 PE14 59 A1
Ecton Wlk NR6 158 F5
Eddington Way NR9 70 B5
Eden Cl
Bacton/Walcott NR12 23 E4
Norwich NR7 163 C6
Edenhurst Cl NR4 161 F3
Eden La NR17 174 D5
Edenside Dr NR17 174 D5
Edgar Rd
Little Walsingham NR22 16 E8
Walsingham NR22 5 D1
Edge Bank PE14 77 F8
Edgebrook NR26 138 D6
EDGEFIELD NR24 19 D5
Edgefield Cl NR6 158 F7
Edgefield Rd
Briston NR24 142 E5
Hunworth NR24 19 B6
Little Barningham NR11 20 B4
EDGEFIELD STREET NR24 19 D4
EDGE GREEN NR16 119 B4
Edgehill 4 NR7 72 E4
Edges La 2 NR15 106 E3
Edge's La NR15 107 A3
Edgeworth Rd 6 NR5 161 C6
Edinburgh Ave
Great Yarmouth NR31 170 B2
King's Lynn PE30 147 C7
Edinburgh Cl
6 Barnham IP24 125 F6
Caister-on-Sea NR30 168 E5
13 Watton IP25 84 D3
Edinburgh Ct 7 PE30 146 E5
Edinburgh Dr
Fakenham NR21 141 C6
Wisbech PE13 152 C8
Edinburgh Pl
Great Yarmouth NR30 169 E3
1 Wiggenhall St Germans PE34 43 B1
Edinburgh Rd Holt NR25 137 C5
Norwich NR2 162 A6
Edinburgh Way
Dersingham PE31 140 D3
Thetford IP24 176 A5
EDINGTHORPE NR28 23 C3
EDINGTHORPE GREEN NR28 23 A2
Edison Way NR31 170 A8
Edith Cavell Cl
5 Thetford IP24 176 D7
Wymondham NR18 173 F6
Edma St PE30 146 E6
Edmondson Wlk NR21 141 D4
Edmund Bacon Ct 1 NR3 162 D8
Edmund De Moundeford VC Prim Sch IP26 98 E2
Edmund Moundford Rd 10 IP26 98 E1
Edmund Rd IP27 175 A2
Edrich Cl NR13 165 E6
Edrich Way NR5 160 E7
Edward Benefer Way
King's Lynn PE30 146 D6
North Wootton PE30 26 E1
Edward Gambling Ct 8 NR2 162 B8
Edward Rd NR29 58 B5
Edwards Cl NR20 50 B5
Edwards Ct
Attleborough NR17 174 D5
Norwich NR7 159 A5
Edward Seago Pl NR15 90 E2
Edwards Rd Norwich NR13 72 E4
Norwich NR7 159 A5
Edward St
10 King's Lynn PE30 146 E3
Norwich NR3 178 B4
Edward Ward Ct 14 PE32 45 C6
Edward Worlledge Com Prim Sch NR31 169 C2
Edwin Cl
Stratton Strawless NR10 53 B6
Wymondham NR18 173 B5
Edwin Way NR10 53 B6
Eelcatcher Cl NR14 91 C7
Eels Foot Rd NR29 57 E1
Eglington Mews NR3 158 C2
Egmere Medieval Village of★ NR22 16 B8
Egmere Rd
Little Walsingham NR22 16 E8
Walsingham NR22 16 F8
Egremont Rd IP22 177 B5
Egyptian Goose Rd NR7 159 E5
Eider Ct NR7 159 E5
Eighth Ave PE13 152 E4
El Alamein Way NR31 94 C8
Elan Cl NR18 173 D3
Elden's La IP26 98 F5
Elderberry Dr 5 NR20 68 A8
Elderberry Pl PE14 77 E6
Elderbush La NR29 56 C7
Elder Cl Hellesdon NR6 157 F3
New Costessey NR5 157 B2
Elderflower Mews NR5 160 F6
Elderflower Wy PE38 172 E6
Elder Gn NR31 170 B5
Elder La PE32 45 C8
Elders The IP27 113 F1
Elderton La NR28 22 B5
Elder Way NR18 173 D1
Eldon Ct NR17 174 F6
Eleanor Rd NR1 162 D3
Eleven Mile Rd NR18 87 C1
Elgars La PE31 29 F7
Elgin IP24 176 A5
Elgood's Brewery & Gdn★ PE13 152 A4
Eliot Cl IP24 176 E6
Elise Way NR18 173 D2
Elizabethan House Mus★ NR30 169 C3
Elizabeth Ave
Downham Market PE38 172 B5
Fakenham NR21 141 C6
Norwich NR7 163 F7
Elizabeth Cl
Attleborough NR17 174 C6
East Dereham NR19 154 D1
Hunstanton PE36 132 C3
Norwich NR7 159 A5
Reepham NR10 149 B4
Elizabeth Cres
Caister-on-Sea NR30 168 E6
4 Holt NR25 137 C5
Elizabeth Dr PE37 65 F3
Elizabeth Fry Cl 9 IP24 176 D7
Elizabeth Fry Rd NR2 161 F4
Elizabeth La
Frettenham NR10 53 F7
Frettenham NR10 54 A7
Elizabeth Rd
Brandon IP27 175 C3
Poringland NR14 90 C4
10 Poringland NR14 90 D5
Elizabeth Terr PE13 152 D4
Elizabeth Watling Cl 3 IP24 176 D7
Elizabeth Way
Aylsham NR11 150 E7
5 Eye IP23 130 C1
Elizabeth Wlk 27 IP20 122 D2
Elkins Rd NR18 173 B5
Ella Rd NR1 163 A6
Ellcar Rise 4 NR4 161 F1
Ellenhill NR27 139 D5
Ellerby Dr PE14 152 A3
Eller Dr PE33 43 E2
ELLINGHAM NR35 109 D3
Ellingham Mill Rd NR35 109 D2
Ellingham Rd
Attleborough NR17 174 B7
Scoulton NR9 85 E3
Ellingham VC Prim Sch NR35 109 D3
Ellington Rd
2 Barnham IP24 125 F6
Watton IP25 85 A3
Ellinor Rd NR28 151 D3
Elliott Cl NR25 137 C7
Ellis Cl 1 Sprowston NR7 159 E4
4 Stalham NR12 39 B4
Ellison Cl
Attleborough NR17 174 E4
Caister-On-Sea NR30 168 D5
Ellison Dr NR17 174 E4
ELM PE14 59 B1
Elm Ave NR31 170 C4
Elm CE Prim Sch PE14 59 B1
Elm Cl Acle NR13 166 C4
Brandon IP27 175 E3
Downham Market PE38 172 B6
King's Lynn PE30 148 D2
Lakenheath IP27 113 E2
5 Lingwood NR13 74 A3
Little Melton NR9 160 D2
7 Loddon NR14 91 F1
Elm Cl *continued*
Mulbarton NR14 89 B3
North Elmham NR20 49 E8
Norwich NR5 156 F2
Yaxham NR19 68 A5
Elmdon Ct 9 NR1 163 A6
Elmer's La NR15 107 A8
Elmfield Cl PE14 152 E1
Elmfield Dr PE14 152 E1
Elm Gr
Garboldisham IP22 128 A8
Sheringham NR26 138 E5
Elm Gr La NR3 158 D2
Elmgrove Rd NR31 170 C3
Elmham Rd Beetley NR20 49 D4
North Elmham NR20 50 A7
Elm High Rd PE14 152 E1
Elm Hill NR3 178 B3
Elmhurst Ave NR12 39 C2
Elmhurst Cl NR31 170 C3
Elmhurst Dr PE30 148 C2
Elm La PE31 30 D8
Elm Low Rd PE14 152 D2
Elm Pk NR19 154 E1
Elm Place PE33 82 A4
Elm Rd
Caister-on-Sea NR30 168 E4
Lingwood NR13 74 A3
Marham PE33 63 B4
Thetford IP24 176 B1
Wisbech PE13 152 D3
Elm Rd Prim Sch PE13 152 D4
Elms Cl 6 NR35 123 F8
Elmside PE14 59 D1
Elms Rd NR34 110 E5
Elmstead Rd PE30 147 C4
Elms The
Hindringham NR21 17 E6
Norwich NR6 158 E6
Elm Terr 2 NR18 173 C4
Elmtree Gr PE33 43 E1
Elsden Cl 2 NR25 137 C5
Elsie Rd NR31 169 B3
ELSING NR20 50 F3
Elsing Dr PE30 147 D8
Elsing La
Bawdeswell NR20 50 E6
Dereham NR20 50 C1
Etling Green NR20 68 B8
Elsing Rd Lyng NR9 51 A5
North Tuddenham NR20 50 E2
Swanton Morley NR20 50 C4
Elstead Cl 11 NR4 89 C8
Elswick Rd IP24 176 F7
ELVEDEN IP24 125 A7
Elveden Cl NR4 161 F1
Elveden Rd
Barnham IP24 125 D6
Wordwell IP31 125 C3
Elvers La PE34 42 B5
Elvina Rd 10 NR10 54 A2
Elvington PE30 147 D5
Elvin Rd NR19 154 D6
Elvin Way 3 NR3 157 F1
Elworthy Cl IP25 84 F3
Elwyn Rd 7 NR1 162 E2
Ely Pl 19 PE13 152 C5
Ely Rd Denver PE38 172 D2
Fordham PE38 79 D3
Hilgay PE38 97 B8
Ely Row PE14 42 B1
Ely St NR2 162 C7
Ely Way IP24 176 A5
Embry Cl NR6 158 D6
Embry Cres NR6 158 C6
Emelson Cl NR19 154 D6
Emerald Cl NR31 170 A2
Emery Cl 5 NR26 138 C5
Emerys Cl NR27 11 A2
Emery's La NR21 21 B6
Emmanuel Ave NR31 170 B2
Emmas Way NR13 73 B6
Emmerich Ct 6 PE30 146 E5
Emms's La NR21 17 E7
EMNETH PE14 59 D2
EMNETH HUNGATE PE14 59 F2
Emneth Prim Sch PE14 59 D2
EMORSGATE PE34 42 B7
Emorsgate PE34 42 B7
Empire Ave PE30 147 B8
Empress Rd NR31 169 B3
Empsons Loke NR29 58 B6
End Lodge PE31 133 C5
Enfield Rd NR5 161 C6
Enfield Row NR18 173 F6
Engine Rd Hilgay PE38 96 F7
Sculthorpe Airfield NR21 15 D2
England's La NR31 170 D4
Englands Rd NR13 166 B4
Englishes La NR35 124 C5
English Rd NR6 158 E4
Ennerdale Dr PE30 148 F2
Ensign Wy IP22 177 F3
Enterprise Gdns 9 NR5 156 C1
Enterprise Way
Easton NR9 70 A5
Fakenham NR21 141 E5
King's Lynn PE33 43 E4
Wisbech PE13 152 A2
Entrance La NR15 90 E2
Entry The IP22 177 D4
Enuo 12 PE33 63 D4
Eppingham Cl IP24 176 F6
Epsom Gdns NR19 154 E3
Erica Way NR31 170 B6
Erins The 1 NR6 158 E1
Eriswell Dr IP27 113 E1
Ernest Cl NR11 150 E7
Ernest Dr NR6 158 F7
Ernest Gage Ave NR5 156 B2
ERPINGHAM NR11 21 B2
Erpingham CE Prim Sch NR11 21 B2
Erpingham Ct PE36 132 E7
Esdelle St 9 NR3 162 D8
Esplanade NR27 139 B7
Esplanade The
Hemsby NR29 167 E5
Sheringham NR26 138 C7
Esprit Cl NR18 173 D2
Essex St NR2 162 C5
Estcourt Rd
2 Attleborough NR17 174 C5
Great Yarmouth NR30 169 D6
Estelle Way NR18 173 E6
Estuary Cl PE30 146 E7
Estuary Rd PE30 146 D7
Ethel Colman Way IP24 176 D7
Ethel Gooch Rd NR18 173 B5
Ethel Mann Rd NR35 124 B7
Ethel Rd NR1 163 A5
Ethel Terr 5 PE30 146 E3
Ethel Tipple Cl NR11 150 C4
Ethel Tipple Dr NR11 150 C4
Ethnie Gleaner Dr NR11 150 E7
ETLING GREEN NR20 68 B8
Eurocentre Ind Est NR30 169 B7
Europa Sq PE13 152 B2
Europa Way
Norwich NR1 163 A2
Wisbech PE13 152 B2
EUSTON IP24 126 B5
Euston Broad IP31 126 E4
Euston Broad Ride IP31 126 E4
Euston Hall★ IP24 126 B5
Euston Rd Barnham IP24 125 E6
Brettenham IP24 126 B7
Euston IP24 126 B6
Fakenham Magna IP24 126 C4
Great Yarmouth NR30 169 D4
Rushford IP24 126 E7
Thetford IP24 116 D1
Thetford IP24 176 F3
Euston Way PE30 148 D1
Euximoor Dro PE14 77 B1
Eva Cl 4 IP25 67 B2
Evans Gdns PE36 132 D3
Evans Lombe Cl NR29 57 A4
Evans Way NR6 158 D6
Eva Rd NR13 72 E7
Evelyn Cl IP21 131 A3
Evelyn Way 4 PE30 147 A8
Everett Cl NR7 159 D5
Eversley Rd NR6 158 B4
Everson Cl Norwich NR5 157 C1
11 Tasburgh NR15 106 F6
Evora Rd NR18 173 D2
Ewing Cl NR10 149 B4
Ewing Rd NR28 151 B3
Excalibur Dr PE37 153 D5
Excalibur Rd 2 NR31 170 B1
Exchange Ct NR8 155 D1
Exchange Rd 7 NR15 89 C1
Exchange Sq PE13 152 B5
Exchange St
Attleborough NR17 174 D5
32 Harleston IP20 122 D2
Norwich NR2 178 A3
Exeter Cres PE30 148 D5
Exeter Rd NR31 170 B4
Exeter St NR2 162 C7
Exeter Way 9 IP24 176 F5
Exige Wy NR18 173 D2
Exmouth Cl 23 NR9 88 D8
Exmouth Pl 11 NR30 169 D4
Exmouth Rd NR30 169 D1
Exton's Gdns PE30 146 F3
Exton's Pl PE30 147 A3
Exton's Rd PE30 146 F4
EYE IP23 130 C1
Eye Airfield Ind Est IP23 130 B2
Eye La PE31 30 B7
Eye Rd Brome IP23 130 B3
Hoxne IP21 130 F2
Yaxley IP23 130 A1

F

Factory La Diss IP22 177 B5
North Pickenham PE37 83 D8
Factory Rd NR30 169 D5
Faeroes Dr NR30 168 C6
Fair Cl Beccles NR34 110 D1
13 Feltwell IP26 98 E1
Fairfax Dr
6 Norwich NR7 72 D4
3 Weeting IP27 114 E1
Fairfax Gall★ PE31 135 C3
Fairfax Rd NR4 161 F4
Fairfield Cl
Great & Little Plumstead NR13 73 B7
Mundesley NR11 143 C6
Fairfield Dr NR17 174 C4
Fairfield La 10 PE33 61 D6
Fairfield Rd
Downham Market PE38 172 A5
5 Middleton PE32 44 B3
Norwich NR2 162 C3
4 Stoke Ferry PE33 81 A3
Fairfields Cawston NR10 35 B2
Thetford IP24 176 D5
Fairfields Ind Est NR29 57 E5
Fairfields Way NR11 36 D4
Fairfield Way 11 IP26 98 E1
Fair Gn IP22 177 C4
FAIR GREEN PE32 44 B4
Fairhaven CE VA Prim Sch NR13 74 B8
Fairhaven Ct NR2 162 A6
Fairhaven Woodland & Water Gdn★ NR13 74 A8
Fairhead Way IP25 84 D2
Fairhill Dro PE33 80 E2
Fairholme Cl IP25 84 A8
Fairholme Rd NR10 53 E4
Fairisle Dr NR30 168 C5
Fair La NR13 72 F2
Fairland St NR18 173 C3
Fairmile Cl NR2 162 B3
FAIRSTEAD PE30 147 D4
Fairstead Cl
North Walsham NR28 151 A3
Pulham Market IP21 121 E5
Fairstead Com Prim Sch PE30 147 D4
Fairstead Ct NR7 159 A3
Fairstead Dro PE33 62 D4
Fairstead La
Hempnall NR15 107 A5
Little Cressingham IP25 83 D3
Fairstead Rd NR7 159 A3
Fairstead The
Botesdale IP22 128 E3
2 Cley next the Sea NR25 7 E6
1 Holt NR25 137 B6
Scottow NR10 37 D2
Fairview Cl NR8 157 A7
Fairview Dr NR21 31 E5
Fairview Rd NR28 151 E4
Fairway
Caister-on-Sea NR30 168 E3
Costessey NR8 156 A5
5 Costessey Park NR8 70 C7
Fairway Dr IP25 84 C4
Fairways
Norwich NR6 157 D5
Stuston IP21 130 B5
Fairway The NR31 171 D8
FAKENHAM NR21 141 D6
Fakenham Acad NR21 141 B6
Fakenham Broad Ride IP31 126 E4
Fakenham Hill IP31 126 C2
Fakenham Ind Est NR21 141 E5
Fakenham Jun Sch NR21 141 C4
FAKENHAM MAGNA IP24 126 C3
Fakenham Mus★ NR21 141 B3
Fakenham Race Course NR21 141 D2
Fakenham Rd
Attlebridge NR9 52 C2
Barwick PE31 14 E5
Bawdeswell NR20 50 F7
Beetley NR20 49 C5
Brisley NR20 49 A8
Briston NR24 142 C5
Colkirk NR21 31 F6
Docking PE31 134 E4
East Rudham PE31 30 A7
Euston IP24 126 B5
Flitcham PE31 28 E4
Foxley NR20 33 C1
Great Snoring NR21 17 A5
Gunthorpe NR24 18 A6
Harpley PE31 29 C5
Helhoughton NR21 31 A6
Horningtoft NR20 32 A2
Houghton St Giles NR22 16 E6
Kettlestone NR21 32 B8
Letheringsett NR25 7 E1
Lexham PE32 47 B5
Morton NR9 51 F4
Oxwick NR21 31 C3
Ryburgh NR21 32 A6
Sculthorpe NR21 141 A5
Sharrington NR25 18 E8
South Creake NR21 15 E6
Sparham NR9 51 A6
Stibbard NR21 32 D7
Syderstone PE31 15 B2
Tattersett PE31 15 D1
Taverham NR8 155 B2
Thursford NR21 17 E4
Thursford NR21 17 F5
Tittleshall PE32 48 A7
Tittleshall PE32 48 B8
Twyford NR20 33 B3
Weasenham St Peter PE32 30 D1
Wells-next-the-Sea NR23 5 C4
Wells-next-the-Sea NR23 136 B3
Fakenham View NR21 31 E5
Fakes Rd NR29 167 D6
Falcon Ave IP22 177 F5
Falcon Cl NR31 171 D4
Falcon Ct 15 NR30 169 C4
Falcon Dr IP27 175 F3
Falconers Chase NR18 173 F5
Falcon Jun Sch NR7 159 C3
Falcon La Bungay NR35 109 A1
24 Wisbech PE13 152 C5
Falcon Mews NR7 159 C4
Falcon Rd
14 Feltwell IP26 98 E1
Norwich NR7 159 C3
Pulham Market IP21 121 E5
Snetterton NR16 103 D1
7 Wisbech PE13 152 C5
Falcon Rd E NR7 159 C2
Falcon Rd W NR7 159 C4
Falgate NR10 35 C2
Falkland Cl NR6 157 D5
Falklands Dr PE13 152 E3
Falklands Rd PE12 41 A8
Falkland Way 13 NR31 94 C6

Fallowfield
4 Hemsby NR29 . . . .**167** B7
8 Poringland NR14 . . . . . .**90** D5
Fallowfield CI NR1 . . . . . .**163** B8
Fallow Pipe Rd PE34 . . . . .**43** B2
Fallows The 3 NR8 . . . . . .**155** D2
Fallow Way NR17 . . . .**174** B3
Faraday PI IP24 . . . .**176** B2
Faraday Rd NR31 . . . .**170** A8
Fardell Rd 7 PE13 . . . . . .**152** C4
Farebrother Way 2
NR19 . . . .**154** C3
Farman Ave NR28 . . . .**151** D5
Farman CI 5 Belton NR31 .**94** A6
Lyng NR9 . . . .**51** A5
7 Salhouse NR13 . . . .**55** A1
Farman Way NR13 . . . . . .**165** F6
Farm CI Bungay NR35 . . . .**124** B8
Diss IP22 . . . .**177** C6
Lingwood NR13 . . . .**74** A2
11 Loddon NR14 . . . .**92** A2
Farm Ct St IP20 . . . .**123** A1
Farm Dr NR21 . . . .**141** C6
Farmers Ave NR1 . . . .**178** B2
Farm La Frost Row NR9 . . .**86** A5
Woodbastwick NR13 . . . . . .**56** A1
Farmland Rd NR5 . . . .**156** F1
Farm Rd
Heckingham NR14 . . . .**92** D1
Houghton St Giles NR22 . . .**16** E4
Worstead NR28 . . . .**38** A4
Farm View
Holme Hale IP25 . . . .**66** A2
North Walsham NR28 . . . . .**151** E5
Farmway 7 NR19 . . . .**154** D2
Farm Wlk Marham PE33 . . .**63** C5
6 Necton PE37 . . . .**65** F4
Farnborough Rd 9 IP25 . .**84** F3
Farrier CI NR18 . . . .**173** F5
Farrier Rd 18 IP25 . . . . . .**84** F3
Farrow CI
2 Great Moulton NR15 . .**106** B1
7 Mattishall NR20 . . . . . .**68** A6
4 Swanton Morley NR20 . .**50** B3
Farrow Rd NR5 . . . .**161** F6
Farthing CI Diss IP22 . . . .**177** D6
Loddon NR14 . . . .**109** D8
Farthing Dro
Beck Row, Holywell Row &
Kenny Hill IP27 . . . .**112** E2
Lakenheath IP27 . . . .**113** A2
Southery PE38 . . . .**97** A2
Farthing Rd PE38 . . . .**79** B5
Fastnet Way 1 NR30 . . . .**168** C6
Fastolf CI NR6 . . . .**157** E5
Fastolff Ave NR31 . . . . . .**170** B3
Fayers Terr PE30 . . . .**147** A4
Fayregreen NR21 . . . .**141** D4
Feale Abbey PE34 . . . . . .**144** A1
Fearns CI NR27 . . . .**139** D5
Fearn's CI NR27 . . . .**139** D5
Featherstone Ct 5
NR19 . . . .**154** D2
FELBRIGG NR11 . . . .**10** C2
Felbrigg CI PE30 . . . .**148** F1
Felbrigg Hall Garden &
Park★ NR11 . . . .**10** B2
Felbrigg Rd
Downham Market PE38 . . .**172** C6
Felbrigg NR11 . . . .**139** A1
Metton NR11 . . . .**21** C8
Roughton NR11 . . . .**21** D8
Felbrigg Wlk NR21 . . . . . .**30** C4
Fellowes Dr 2 NR31 . . . . .**94** C6
Fellowes Rd NR9 . . . .**69** E6
Fellows CI Norwich NR5 . .**161** D6
Scole IP21 . . . .**130** D5
Fell Way 3 NR31 . . . .**94** C8
FELMINGHAM NR28 . . . . . .**37** A8
Felmingham Rd
Antingham NR28 . . . .**22** B2
Banningham NR11 . . . .**36** F8
North Walsham NR28 . . . . .**37** C7
Skeyton NR10 . . . .**37** B5
Suffield NR11 . . . .**21** F1
Felsham Way NR8 . . . . . .**155** E2
Felsted Ave PE13 . . . .**152** E5
FELTHORPE NR10 . . . .**155** C8
Felthorpe Rd
Attlebridge NR9 . . . .**52** B3
Felthorpe NR10 . . . .**52** D4
Felthorpe NR10 . . . .**155** A7
FELTWELL IP26 . . . .**98** D1
Feltwell Rd
Hockwold cum Wilton
IP26 . . . .**113** F7
Methwold IP26 . . . .**98** E5
Southery PE38 . . . .**97** D5
Fence Bank
St John's Fen End PE14 . . . .**60** A7
Terrington St John PE14 . . .**42** A1
Fences Farm Rd PE34 . . . .**78** E8
Fen CI PE13 . . . .**152** E6
Fenditch La PE34 . . . .**42** B3
Fen Dro PE33 . . . .**81** F3
Fen Drove PE33 . . . .**62** D4
Fendyke Rd PE14 . . . .**59** E1
Fen Folgate 6 IP25 . . . . . .**67** F2
FENGATE PE10 . . . .**150** C1
Fengate
Heacham PE31 . . . .**133** C4
Marsham NR10 . . . .**150** D1
Fengate Dro IP27 . . . .**175** B6
Fengate Rd PE14 . . . .**59** C5
Fen La Banham NR16 . . . .**119** D4
Barton Turf NR12 . . . .**38** F2
Beccles NR34 . . . .**110** D2
Ditchingham NR35 . . . . . .**108** E3

Fen La continued
Garboldisham IP22 . . . . . .**127** E7
Garboldisham IP22 . . . . . .**128** A2
Grimston PE32 . . . .**45** A7
Harling NR16 . . . .**118** C6
Kenninghall NR16 . . . .**119** B6
Leziate PE32 . . . .**45** A6
Marham PE33 . . . .**63** A5
Rickinghall Inferior IP22 . .**128** E2
Roydon IP22 . . . .**129** C7
Smallburgh NR12 . . . .**38** F3
Thelnetham IP22 . . . .**128** B5
Fenland Rd
King's Lynn PE30 . . . .**147** C8
Wisbech PE13 . . . .**152** C6
Fenlands IP22 . . . .**177** B4
Fenland & W Norfolk
Aviation Mus★ PE14 . . . . .**59** C7
Fenmen PI 6 PE13 . . . . . .**152** E6
Fenn CI 3 NR28 . . . .**151** C4
Fenn Cres NR3 . . . .**158** B1
Fennel Cres PE38 . . . .**172** E6
Fennel Way IP24 . . . .**176** F4
Fenner Rd NR30 . . . .**170** E7
Fenn La PE38 . . . .**79** D2
Fenns CI PE31 . . . .**134** E4
Fen Rd Blo' Norton IP22 . .**128** C6
Carleton Rode NR16 . . . . .**105** C2
Hinderclay IP22 . . . .**128** C5
Marham PE33 . . . .**63** B4
Old Buckenham NR17 . . . .**104** C2
Scarning NR19 . . . .**154** B3
Watlington PE33 . . . .**61** D5
Wiggenhall St Mary Magdalen
PE34 . . . .**60** D5
Fen Rivers Acad The
PE30 . . . .**146** E8
FENSIDE NR29 . . . .**56** B8
Fenside PE31 . . . .**133** C4
Fen St Attleborough NR17 .**103** F3
Hopton IP22 . . . .**127** E6
Old Buckenham NR17 . . . .**104** C2
Redgrave IP22 . . . .**128** F6
Rocklands NR17 . . . .**103** B6
FEN STREET
Hopton IP22 . . . .**127** E6
Redgrave IP22 . . . .**128** F6
Fen The NR16 . . . .**119** B7
Fen View
Christchurch PE14 . . . .**95** A7
East Dereham NR19 . . . . .**154** C2
Fenway PE31 . . . .**133** B3
Fen Way 2 PE14 . . . .**59** A1
Ferguson Way NR17 . . . . .**174** F7
Fermoy Ave PE30 . . . .**146** E6
Fern Ct 3 NR18 . . . .**173** B4
Ferndale CI NR6 . . . .**157** E4
Fern Dr
1 Cringleford NR4 . . . .**89** A8
North Walsham NR28 . . . .**151** D5
Fern Farm La PE34 . . . .**25** C2
Fern Gdns NR31 . . . .**93** F5
Fern Hill
Dersingham PE31 . . . .**140** E4
Norwich NR1 . . . .**163** B5
Fernlea Rd PE30 . . . .**147** C4
Fern Rd PE30 . . . .**147** B8
Ferrers Gdns NR18 . . . . . .**173** A2
Ferrier CI 7 NR30 . . . . . .**169** D5
Ferrier Ct NR29 . . . .**167** B6
Ferrier Rd NR30 . . . .**169** C5
Ferry Bank PE38 . . . .**97** A4
Ferryboat La NR31 . . . . . .**170** D7
Ferry Ct NR29 . . . .**75** A5
Ferrygate La NR29 . . . .**57** D5
Ferry Hill NR31 . . . .**170** D7
Ferry La
Great Yarmouth NR31 . . . .**169** C2
17 King's Lynn PE30 . . . .**146** D5
Norwich NR1 . . . .**178** C3
Postwick with Witton NR13 .**73** A2
Stokesby with Herringby
NR29 . . . .**75** B5
Ferry Rd
Carleton St Peter NR14 . . . .**91** E5
Claxton NR14 . . . .**91** E6
Clenchwarton PE34 . . . . . .**145** F5
Horning NR12 . . . .**55** E3
King's Lynn PE34 . . . .**146** B6
Norton Subcourse NR14 . . .**92** D2
Oxborough PE33 . . . .**81** D3
Raveningham NR14 . . . . . .**110** A8
Reedham NR13 . . . .**92** E4
Surlingham NR14 . . . .**165** A1
Woodbastwick NR13 . . . . . .**55** D2
Ferry St PE34 . . . .**146** C5
Ferry View Rd NR12 . . . . . .**55** E3
FERSFIELD IP22 . . . .**119** D2
Fersfield Rd
Bressingham IP22 . . . .**119** E1
Bressingham IP22 . . . .**129** B8
South Lopham IP22 . . . . . .**128** F8
Festival CI PE30 . . . .**148** B1
Festival Rd NR30 . . . .**150** B7
Festival Way CB6 . . . .**96** E2
Ffolkes Dr
King's Lynn PE30 . . . .**148** C1
Terrington St Clement
PE34 . . . .**144** B5
Ffolkes PI 1 PE33 . . . .**61** D3
Fiddler's Alley NR10 . . . . . .**51** C8
FIDDLERS' GREEN NR17 . .**174** B8
Fiddler'S La NR20 . . . .**49** A8
Fiddlers Loke NR13 . . . . . .**54** B3
Fiddle Wood Rd NR6 . . . .**158** D4
Field Ave PE34 . . . .**144** B5
Field Barn Cotts PE32 . . . .**46** E3
Fieldbarn Dro PE33 . . . . . .**82** A4

Field Barn La
Bintree NR20 . . . .**33** A2
North Creake NR21 . . . .**4** D1
Runcton Holme PE33 . . . . . .**61** F3
Shernborne PE31 . . . .**13** D3
FIELD DALLING NR25 . . . . . .**7** B1
Field Dalling Rd
Field Dalling NR25 . . . .**7** A3
Gunthorpe NR21 . . . .**18** B8
Saxlingham NR25 . . . .**7** C2
Field End CI NR20 . . . .**147** B6
Fieldfare CI 6 NR12 . . . . . .**54** A1
Fieldfare Loke IP25 . . . . . .**67** C2
Fieldfare Way PE37 . . . . . .**153** C2
Field House Gdns IP22 . . .**177** B5
Fielding Dr NR19 . . . .**68** A5
Field La Beetley NR20 . . . . .**49** C5
10 Blofield NR13 . . . .**73** D6
Blofield NR13 . . . .**165** E8
Fakenham NR21 . . . .**141** B6
Forncett St Mary NR16 . . .**106** A5
Hempnall NR15 . . . .**107** C4
King's Lynn PE30 . . . .**147** B6
Marsham NR10 . . . .**36** B2
North Walsham NR28 . . . .**151** A4
Stanton IP22 . . . .**127** D1
Stibbard NR21 . . . .**32** D6
Stody NR24 . . . .**142** F8
Whinburgh & Westfield
NR19 . . . .**67** F4
Wretton PE33 . . . .**80** F3
Field Maple Rd IP25 . . . . . .**84** E3
Field Rd Brandon IP27 . . .**114** D4
Ringland NR8 . . . .**147** B5
South Walsham NR13 . . . . .**74** B8
Stalham NR12 . . . .**39** E3
Weston Longville NR9 . . . . .**51** F3
Fields Rd NR34 . . . .**110** E6
Fields The
Bradwell NR31 . . . .**170** B7
Forncett NR16 . . . .**105** C4
Hingham NR9 . . . .**86** C5
Fieldview NR5 . . . .**161** E6
Fiennes Rd 4 NR7 . . . .**72** D5
Fifers La NR6 . . . .**158** C6
Fifth Ave PE13 . . . .**152** E4
Fifty Dro CB6 . . . .**95** F3
Fifty Rd PE14 . . . .**95** A3
Filbert Rd NR14 . . . .**91** F1
Filberts PE30 . . . .**147** D5
FILBY NR29 . . . .**75** F8
Filby CI Earlham NR5 . . . .**161** E6
Filby NR29 . . . .**75** F8
Filby La NR29 . . . .**167** A1
FILBY HEATH NR29 . . . . . .**76** B8
Filby Prim Sch NR29 . . . . .**75** E8
Filby Rd Coltishall NR10 . . .**37** B2
Stokesby with Herringby
NR29 . . . .**75** C6
Swaffham PE37 . . . .**153** B2
FINCHAM PE33 . . . .**62** F1
Fincham Dro
South Acre PE32 . . . .**64** F8
Swaffham PE32 . . . .**64** B5
Fincham Drove PE32 . . . . .**46** F1
Fincham Rd
Barton Bendish PE33 . . . . .**81** A8
Crimplesham PE33 . . . .**80** A8
Fincham PE33 . . . .**63** A1
Shouldham Thorpe PE33 . . .**62** C2
Stow Bardolph PE34 . . . . . .**79** F8
Wereham PE33 . . . .**80** F6
Finch CI Cromer NR27 . . .**139** C4
Norwich NR7 . . . .**159** D2
Finchdale CI 5 PE30 . . . .**148** C4
Finchley CI 4 NR12 . . . . . .**62** B7
Finch Rd NR17 . . . .**174** A4
Finch Way NR13 . . . .**165** C3
Finishers Rd 8 NR6 . . . . .**158** C1
Finisterre Rise 2 NR30 . .**168** C6
Finkelgate NR1 . . . .**178** B1
Finningham Rd IP22 . . . . .**128** E1
Finsbury CI 1 PE38 . . . . .**172** B4
Fiona CI NR18 . . . .**173** E6
Fir CI Heacham PE31 . . . .**133** C6
Mundford IP26 . . . .**100** B4
Fir Covert Rd
Attlebridge NR10 . . . .**52** D3
Carleton Rode NR16 . . . . .**105** A1
Taverham NR8 . . . .**155** B4
Firecrest CI NR18 . . . .**173** D2
Firethorn CI NR8 . . . .**155** B2
Fir Gr NR26 . . . .**138** D4
Fir La NR10 . . . .**34** A1
Firman Ct NR7 . . . .**163** F8
Fir Pk IP25 . . . .**84** A7
Fir Rd IP24 . . . .**176** B1
Firs Ave PE30 . . . .**147** A4
Firside Jun Sch NR6 . . . . .**158** A6
Firs La NR12 . . . .**39** C2
Firs Rd
Hethersett NR9 . . . .**88** D7
Norwich NR6 . . . .**157** F6
First Ave PE13 . . . .**152** D5
First Dro IP27 . . . .**113** C3
Firs The
Downham Market PE38 . . .**172** D6
Lakenheath IP27 . . . .**113** F1
First Marsh Rd PE13 . . . . . .**59** A6
Firs Way IP27 . . . .**175** C2
Firtree CI NR13 . . . .**165** B4
Fir Tree CI NR29 . . . .**57** C1
Fir Tree Dr 7 PE33 . . . .**43** E2
Firtree Rd NR7 . . . .**159** E4
Firwood CI NR1 . . . .**163** C6
Fisher Ave NR30 . . . .**169** D8
Fishergate NR3 . . . .**178** B4

Fisherman's Her Ctr★
NR26 . . . .**138** D8
Fishermen's Ct NR17 . . . .**174** D6
Fisher Rd Diss IP22 . . . . . .**177** E4
Fakenham NR21 . . . .**141** B5
Fisher Row NR32 . . . .**111** F4
Fishers CI NR5 . . . .**156** E1
Fishers End CI 12 PE13 . . .**12** E5
Fishers La Beetley NR20 . . .**49** D6
Norwich NR2 . . . .**178** A3
Fisher's La IP21 . . . .**131** A4
Fishers' Quay 5 NR30 . . .**169** C4
Fisher Way IP24 . . . .**176** E5
FISHLEY NR13 . . . .**166** C6
Fishley View NR13 . . . . . .**166** B4
Fish Wharf 2 NR30 . . . . .**169** D1
Fiskes CI NR14 . . . .**89** F5
Fiske's Opening 6
NR31 . . . .**170** D4
Fison Way IP24 . . . .**176** C6
Fison Way Ind Est IP24 . .**176** C6
Fitton Rd PE34 . . . .**61** B8
Fitzalan CI 3 NR30 . . . . .**169** C4
Fitzgerald Rd
Norwich NR1 . . . .**162** E1
7 Poringland NR14 . . . . . .**90** D5
Fitzhenry Mews 8 NR5 . .**161** B8
Fitzwalter Rd IP22 . . . . . .**177** E4
Five Acre La NR35 . . . . . .**123** E7
Five Acres NR14 . . . .**89** F4
Five Alls Rd PE14 . . . .**41** F1
Five Crossways NR12 . . . .**164** D8
Five Elms 4 PE30 . . . . . .**147** C4
Five Mile Bank PE34 . . . . .**42** C4
Flag St NR12 . . . .**15** C2
Flax CI PE38 . . . .**172** B3
FLAXLANDS NR16 . . . . . .**105** C4
Flaxlands NR16 . . . .**105** B4
Flaxlands Rd NR16 . . . . . .**105** C3
Fleet La NR13 . . . .**56** B1
Fleet Rd Costessey NR8 . .**156** B6
Terrington St Clement PE34 .**42** B8
Fleetwood Dr 4 NR13 . . . .**72** D4
Fleggburgh CE VC Prim Sch
NR29 . . . .**75** C8
Fleggburgh Rd NR29 . . . . .**57** C2
Flegg Gn PE33 . . . .**80** D4
Flegg High Sch NR29 . . . . .**57** E6
Fleming CI NR31 . . . .**170** B1
Fleming Ct 8 IP25 . . . .**84** D3
Fletcher CI NR12 . . . .**55** A8
Fletcher Way Acle NR13 . .**166** D4
Cromer NR27 . . . .**139** B5
Norwich NR3 . . . .**158** C3
Flint Dr NR23 . . . .**136** D5
Flint Gate 17 PE12 . . . .**41** B8
Flint House CI NR9 . . . . . .**88** C7
Flint House Rd
Upwell PE14 . . . .**77** F1
Upwell PE14 . . . .**95** D8
Flint Way
5 Friday Bridge PE14 . . . .**77** A8
Lakenheath IP27 . . . .**113** E2
FLITCHAM PE31 . . . .**28** C5
Flitcham Abbey PE31 . . . . .**28** D5
Flitcham Barns Ind Units
PE31 . . . .**28** B5
Flitcham CE Prim Sch
PE31 . . . .**28** C5
FLIXTON NR35 . . . .**123** D5
Flixton Hall Est NR35 . . . .**123** D4
Flixton Marsh La NR32 . . .**111** F6
Flixton Rd Bungay NR35 . .**124** A7
Flixton NR35 . . . .**123** E6
Lound NR32 . . . .**94** C1
St Margaret, South Elmham
IP20 . . . .**123** E3
Somerleyton, Ashby &
Herringfleet NR32 . . . . . .**111** F8
Flood La NR20 . . . .**68** F4
Floral Loke NR32 . . . .**111** D8
FLORDON NR15 . . . .**106** D8
Flordon Rd
Bracon Ash NR14 . . . .**88** F1
Flordon NR15 . . . .**106** D1
Lower Tasburgh NR15 . . . .**106** E7
Florence Barclay CI
IP24 . . . .**176** D6
Florence Rd
18 King's Lynn PE30 . . . .**146** D4
Norwich NR1 . . . .**163** A6
Florence Wlk NR19 . . . . .**154** C2
Florence Wy NR35 . . . . . .**109** D3
Florida Bvd NR21 . . . .**15** C2
Florin CI NR35 . . . .**109** D8
Flowerday CI NR31 . . . . . .**171** D5
Flowerdew CI 12 NR9 . . . .**88** C7
Flowerdew Mdw 8
IP21 . . . .**130** D6
Flowerdew's La NR13 . . . .**74** B7
Flowerpot La NR15 . . . . . .**106** D3
Flowers La
Attleborough NR17 . . . . . .**174** B2
Attleborough NR17 . . . . . .**174** B3
Fludge's La NR20 . . . .**49** B6
Flycatcher Way 3 NR7 . . .**159** E4
Flymore La NR17 . . . .**103** A8
Foal La PE38 . . . .**172** B6
Focusbusiness Pk NR17 . .**174** F2
FODDERSTONE GAP
PE33 . . . .**62** C4
Foldgate La PE34 . . . .**61** A5
Folgate NR16 . . . .**88** D1
Folgate CI Costessey NR8 .**156** F5
Thornham PE36 . . . .**2** D6
Folgate La
Costessey NR8 . . . .**156** F4
Great Walsingham NR21 . . .**17** A8
Walpole PE14 . . . .**41** D3
Folgate Rd
Heacham PE31 . . . .**133** C4

Folgate Rd continued
North Walsham NR28 . . . .**151** B6
Folland CI NR20 . . . .**50** E7
Follens Rd PE14 . . . .**41** D5
Follies The PE37 . . . .**65** F4
Folly CI NR18 . . . .**173** C5
Folly Ct Fakenham NR21 .**141** D4
King's Lynn PE30 . . . .**147** B7
Folly Gdns NR18 . . . .**173** C5
Folly Gr PE30 . . . .**147** B7
Folly Hill PE35 . . . .**27** D7
Folly La Beetley NR20 . . . .**49** B6
Bressingham IP22 . . . .**119** F1
Bressingham IP22 . . . .**129** C8
Claxton NR14 . . . .**91** D5
Old Buckenham NR17 . . . .**104** F2
Folly Rd NR18 . . . .**173** C5
Folly View 5 PE37 . . . .**65** F4
Folly Yd PE32 . . . .**48** B7
Folwell Rd NR5 . . . .**156** E1
Footpath The 11 NR14 . . . .**90** C5
Ford Ave PE30 . . . .**148** D5
FORDHAM PE38 . . . .**79** D2
Fordham Bypass PE38 . . . .**79** E3
Ford Rd NR22 . . . .**16** E6
Ford St PE30 . . . .**176** D3
Foregate CI 2 NR8 . . . . . .**155** D2
Foreman CI PE31 . . . .**133** D3
Forest CI IP27 . . . .**175** C2
Forest Com Prim Sch
IP27 . . . .**175** C3
Forest Dr PE31 . . . .**133** C6
Forester CI 1 NR4 . . . . . .**162** C1
Forester Way NR11 . . . . . .**150** D6
Forester's Ave PE38 . . . . . .**97** A8
Forest Gr PE37 . . . .**153** C1
Forest Mount NR31 . . . . . .**93** E3
Forest Ret Pk IP24 . . . . . .**125** D8
Forest Rd Mattishall NR20 .**68** D6
Old Buckenham NR17 . . . .**104** D2
Poringland NR14 . . . .**90** D4
Forge Gr NR34 . . . .**110** C2
Forge La NR11 . . . .**20** F5
Forge Orchards 1 NR14 . .**89** B3
Forge Rd NR14 . . . .**91** F3
Forget-Me-Not Rd 3
PE31 . . . .**12** D4
Forge Way IP22 . . . .**128** A8
Forman CI 15 IP25 . . . .**84** E3
FORNCETT END NR16 . . .**105** E4
Forncett Ind Steam Mus★
NR16 . . . .**106** B5
Forncett Rd
Bunwell NR16 . . . .**105** F3
Tharston & Hapton NR15 .**106** D4
FORNCETT ST MARY
NR16 . . . .**106** B4
FORNCETT ST PETER
Forncett St Peter CE VA
Prim Sch NR16 . . . .**106** B3
Forster CI 2 NR11 . . . . . .**150** D6
Forster Way NR11 . . . . . .**150** D6
Forsythia Rd NR11 . . . . . .**170** B5
Forth CI NR30 . . . .**168** C5
Forties CI 5 NR30 . . . . . .**168** C6
Fortress Rd
Snetterton NR16 . . . .**103** D1
21 Watton IP25 . . . .**84** F3
Fortune Gn NR14 . . . .**90** E4
Forum The★ NR2 . . . .**178** A2
Forwater Rd NR10 . . . .**34** B3
Foster CI Brundall NR13 . .**165** B4
Ormesby St Margaret
NR29 . . . .**167** C2
Foster Harrison Memorial Dr
NR18 . . . .**173** B6
Foster Rd NR3 . . . .**158** D3
Foster's Drove IP26 . . . . . .**98** B2
FOUL ANCHOR PE13 . . . . .**41** A4
FOULDEN IP26 . . . .**82** A2
Foulden Rd
Didlington IP26 . . . .**99** E7
Foulden IP26 . . . .**82** C2
Ickburgh IP26 . . . .**100** B3
Foulgers Opening NR1 . . .**178** C1
Foulser CI NR6 . . . .**158** D7
Foulsham Prim Sch
NR20 . . . .**33** D3
Foulsham Rd
Bintree NR20 . . . .**33** C2
Guestwick NR20 . . . .**33** F4
Guist NR20 . . . .**33** D3
Hindolveston NR20 . . . .**33** D7
Wood Norton NR20 . . . . . .**33** B6
Foundry CI Bodham NR25 . . .**9** A3
Foulsham NR20 . . . .**33** D3
Northrepps NR27 . . . .**11** C2
Sculthorpe NR21 . . . .**16** C2
Foundry Cnr NR17 . . . . . .**174** F2
Foundry Cnr NR28 . . . . . .**151** B3
Foundry La PE36 . . . .**2** A3
Foundry PI PE31 . . . .**135** C3
Foundry Sq NR19 . . . .**154** D4
Fountaine Gr PE30 . . . . . .**148** C4
Fountains Rd NR4 . . . .**89** E8
Four Acres Est NR29 . . . .**167** C8
Fourth Ave PE13 . . . .**152** E4
Fowell CI NR5 . . . .**161** B6
Fowler's La NR17 . . . .**174** B2
Fox And Hounds La NR20 .**33** C2
Foxburrow Rd
Norwich NR7 . . . .**72** A7
Norwich NR7 . . . .**159** A5
Foxcotte CI NR6 . . . .**157** E7
Foxes CI NR14 . . . .**90** C6
Foxes Ct NR5 . . . .**157** B2

Foxes La IP20 . . . .**123** A1
Foxes Loke 12 NR14 . . . . .**92** A1
Foxes Mdw 2 PE32 . . . . . .**46** F2
Foxglove CI
Fakenham NR21 . . . .**141** F4
North Walsham NR28 . . . .**151** B5
Thurton NR14 . . . .**91** C4
Foxglove Ct 7 PE38 . . . . .**172** B4
Foxglove Dr 21 NR31 . . . . .**94** C6
Foxglove La NR26 . . . .**138** B6
Foxglove Rd
2 Attleborough NR17 . . . .**174** B5
Thetford IP24 . . . .**176** F4
Foxglove Wlk PE34 . . . . . .**61** B8
Fox Gr 7 NR16 . . . .**118** C5
Fox Hill East Ruston NR12 .**38** F4
St Cross, South Elmham
IP20 . . . .**123** C3
Foxhill Rd PE31 . . . .**28** F4
Fox Hill Rd NR12 . . . .**38** E7
FOXHOLE NR15 . . . .**107** A7
Foxhouse Rd 1 NR8 . . . . . .**70** C7
Fox La Anmer PE35 . . . . . .**28** D8
Brundall NR13 . . . .**165** F6
Framingham Pigot NR14 . . .**90** D7
North Tuddenham NR8 . . . .**68** F8
FOXLEY NR20 . . . .**50** D8
Foxley CI NR5 . . . .**161** D6
Foxley Rd
Bawdeswell NR20 . . . .**50** D8
Foulsham NR20 . . . .**33** C2
Foxley Wood National
Nature Reserve★ NR10 . . .**33** F1
Fox Rd Dereham NR19 . . . .**68** A7
Framingham Pigot NR14 . . .**90** D7
Fox's La King's Lynn PE34 .**146** C6
Thelnetham IP22 . . . .**128** B3
Foxs Loke NR11 . . . .**150** B6
Foxwood 9 NR10 . . . .**73** D6
Foxwood CI NR8 . . . .**155** E3
FRAMINGHAM EARL
NR14 . . . .**90** D4
Framingham Earl High Sch
NR14 . . . .**90** C6
Framingham Earl La
NR14 . . . .**90** E5
Framingham La NR14 . . . . .**90** F7
FRAMINGHAM PIGOT
NR14 . . . .**90** C6
Framingham Rd NR14 . . . . .**90** D7
Framlingham CI NR31 . . . .**169** C2
Francis CI NR27 . . . .**139** C5
Francis La NR13 . . . .**73** C6
Francis Rd NR15 . . . .**106** E3
Francis Stone Ct NR7 . . . .**72** D3
Francis Way NR5 . . . .**160** E8
FRANKFORT NR12 . . . .**38** A3
Frankfort NR12 . . . .**38** A3
Franklin CI PE34 . . . .**145** E6
Franklin Way NR17 . . . . . .**174** D2
Frank Stone Ct NR30 . . . .**169** E1
Frans Gn NR20 . . . .**69** D8
FRANS GREEN NR20 . . . . .**51** D1
Fransham Forge★ NR19 . . .**66** B8
Fransham Rd PE32 . . . .**48** B1
Frazer Cres NR11 . . . .**143** A4
Fred Ackland Dr PE30 . . . .**147** C3
Fred Edge Ct NR12 . . . . . .**54** A4
Frederick CI PE30 . . . .**148** D6
Frederick Rd NR30 . . . . . .**169** C2
Fred Nicholson Sch
NR19 . . . .**154** E2
Fredricks Ct 16 PE13 . . . .**146** E5
Fred Tuddenham Dr
NR10 . . . .**35** B3
Freebridge Haven PE33 . . .**43** F3
Freedom Bridge PE13 . . . .**152** B6
Free La NR35 . . . .**108** F2
Freeland CI NR8 . . . .**155** F2
Freeland Cnr NR10 . . . . . .**155** C6
Freeman CI
5 Hopton On Sea NR31 . .**171** D4
Loddon NR14 . . . .**109** D8
Freeman Sq NR2 . . . .**162** C8
Freeman St NR23 . . . .**136** C6
Free School Norwich The
NR1 . . . .**178** B2
Freestone Ct 7 PE30 . . . .**146** E4
FREETHORPE NR13 . . . . . .**92** F8
Freethorpe Com Prim Sch
NR13 . . . .**92** F7
Freethorpe Rd
Cantley NR13 . . . .**92** D6
Freethorpe NR13 . . . .**74** F1
Freezer CI NR19 . . . .**49** D4
Freiston 2 PE30 . . . .**147** C5
Fremantle Rd NR30 . . . . .**168** E1
Frenbury Ind Est NR6 . . . .**157** F3
French's Rd PE14 . . . .**41** C4
Frensham Rd NR3 . . . .**157** F2
FRENZE IP21 . . . .**130** B7
Frenze Hall La IP22 . . . . .**177** F5
Frenze Rd IP22 . . . .**177** E4
Frere Cnr 6 IP22 . . . .**129** D7
Frere Rd
30 Harleston IP20 . . . . . .**122** D2
Norwich NR7 . . . .**159** D1
Fresher Mews NR5 . . . . . .**160** F6
Freshfield CI NR5 . . . .**161** C7
Freshgap La NR20 . . . .**33** E6
Freshwater Way NR8 . . . .**155** F3
FRETTENHAM NR12 . . . . . .**54** A4
Frettenham Prim
Partnership Sch NR12 . . . .**54** A4
Frettenham Rd
Frettenham NR12 . . . .**54** A7
Hainford NR10 . . . .**53** F7
Horstead with Stanninghall
NR12 . . . .**54** B5
Freyden Way NR12 . . . . . .**54** A4
Friarscroft La NR18 . . . . .**173** B3

Friar's La PE31 . . . . 135 D4
Friars' La 3 NR30 . . . . 169 D2
Friars Quay NR3 . . . . 178 B3
Friars St PE30 . . . . 146 E3
Friars The 17 PE30 . . . . 146 D4
Friar Tuck Rd NR4 . . . . 162 C1
FRIDAY BRIDGE PE14 . . . . 77 A7
Friday Bridge Com Prim Sch
   PE14 . . . . 77 A7
Fridaybridge Rd
   Elm PE14 . . . . 77 A8
   Wisbech PE14 . . . . 59 A1
Friday Mkt 4 NR22 . . . . . . 16 F7
Friends Cl NR5 . . . . 161 D6
Friends Rd NR4 . . . . 161 C5
FRING PE31 . . . . 13 D5
Fring Rd Bircham PE31 . . . . 13 F4
   Bircham PE31 . . . . 14 A3
   Shernborne PE31 . . . . 13 C3
   Snettisham PE31 . . . . 13 A5
Frinton Way 4 PE13 . . . . . 152 E5
Frith Way NR15 . . . . 106 B1
Fritillary Dr NR18 . . . . . . 173 E4
FRITTON
   Fritton and St Olaves
      NR31 . . . . 93 E3
   Ludham NR29 . . . . 56 E5
   Morning Thorpe NR15 . . . 107 B3
Fritton St NR29 . . . . 167 B3
Fritton La NR29 . . . . 56 E6
Fritton Lake Ctry World ★
   NR31 . . . . 93 F2
Fritton Rd NR29 . . . . 56 E6
Frobisher Cl IP24 . . . . 176 F6
Frobisher Cres PE36 . . . . 132 D3
Frogge La Coltishall NR12 . . 54 C8
   Scottow NR12 . . . . 37 C1
Frog Hill Rd IP24 . . . . 116 B8
FROGSHALL NR27 . . . . 11 B1
Frogshall La NR18 . . . . . . 173 A5
Frogs Hall La 3 NR1 . . . . 163 B5
Frog's Hall La NR20 . . . . . 50 C2
Frogshall Rd NR27 . . . . . . 22 B8
Frogs Hole Blofield NR13 . 165 D6
   Somerleyton, Ashby &
      Herringfleet NR32 . . . . . 93 F1
Front Rd
   Tydd St Giles PE13 . . . . . . 41 A4
   West End NR30 . . . . 76 B6
   Wood Dalling NR11 . . . . . 34 D6
Front St Binham NR21 . . . . . 6 E2
   Burnham Market PE31 . . 135 C3
   Litcham PE32 . . . . 48 A4
   Trunch NR28 . . . . 22 E5
Front Way PE30 . . . . 147 A2
Frost Cl Norwich NR7 . . . . 163 F8
   20 Watton IP25 . . . . 84 D3
FROST ROW NR9 . . . . 86 B4
Frost's La NR15 . . . . 106 B1
Fry Frove NR13 . . . . 166 B3
Fugill Gn NR7 . . . . 159 D1
Fugill Rd NR7 . . . . 159 D1
Fulcher Ave NR27 . . . . . . 139 A2
Fulford Cl NR4 . . . . 162 A2
Fuller Cl
   2 Rackheath NR13 . . . . . 72 E7
   9 West Winch PE33 . . . . 43 F2
Fuller Mews 5 NR5 . . . . . 160 E8
Fuller Rd
   North Walsham NR28 . . . 151 B4
   Redenhall with Harleston
      IP20 . . . . 122 D1
Fuller's Cl NR34 . . . . 110 C5
Fuller's Hill 10 NR30 . . . . 169 C4
Fullers La 6 Trunch NR28 . 22 E5
   West Acre PE32 . . . . 46 C1
Fullers Loke NR8 . . . . 155 F2
Fulmar Cl 9 NR31 . . . . . . 94 C7
Fulmar Gdns PE36 . . . . . . 132 C1
Fulmar La PE32 . . . . 46 E2
Fulmerston Cl IP24 . . . . . 176 B2
Fulmerston Rd IP24 . . . . . 176 B2
FULMODESTON NR21 . . . . 17 F1
Fulmodeston Rd
   Croxton NR21 . . . . 17 D2
   Fulmodeston NR21 . . . . . . 18 B1
   Hindolveston NR20 . . . . . 33 C8
   Stibbard NR21 . . . . 32 E7
Fulton Cl NR4 . . . . 162 A1
FUNDENHALL NR16 . . . . . 106 A2
Fundenhall Rd NR16 . . . . 106 B7
Fundrey Rd PE13 . . . . 152 F6
Furlong Dro PE33 . . . . 81 A3
Furlong Rd 1 PE33 . . . . . . 81 A3
Furness Cl PE30 . . . . 148 F1
Further Fen La PE38 . . . . . 97 A6
Furthest Dro IP27 . . . . . . 113 C4
Furze Ave NR7 . . . . 163 E8
Furze Hill NR27 . . . . 139 C5
Furze Hill Dr NR28 . . . . . 151 E3
Furze La
   Great Witchingham NR9 . 149 C2
   Guist NR20 . . . . 33 A6
   Thorpe Marriott NR10 . . . 52 E3
Furze Rd NR7 . . . . 163 E8
Furze The NR12 . . . . 38 E7
Furze Way PE30 . . . . 129 B1
Fuschia Cl NR18 . . . . 173 E6
Fye Bridge St NR3 . . . . . . 178 B4
Fylands Rd NR15 . . . . 108 A7

G

Gablehurst Ct NR31 . . . . . 170 A4
Gables Ave NR11 . . . . 22 B7
Gage Rd NR7 . . . . 159 C4
Gagman's La NR19 . . . . . . 68 A5
Gainsborough Ave
   1 Diss IP22 . . . . 177 C4
   Great Yarmouth NR31 . . 170 A7

Gainsborough Cl 2
   PE38 . . . . 172 D6
Galahad Rd NR31 . . . . . . 171 B8
Gale Cl NR14 . . . . 109 F8
Gale Gdns NR11 . . . . 150 D7
Gales Ct NR23 . . . . 136 D6
Gales Rd NR23 . . . . 136 C6
Gallant's La NR16 . . . . . . 118 C5
Galley Cl 8 NR33 . . . . . . 111 F1
Galley Hill NR3 . . . . 158 A2
Gallops The 16 PE25 . . . . 84 F3
Galloway Cl 8 NR20 . . . . 68 A8
Gallow Dr PE38 . . . . 172 C7
Gallowhill La NR16 . . . . . 18 C3
Gallow Hill (Tumulus) ★
   NR25 . . . . 8 B5
Gallow La PE33 . . . . 62 D2
Gallows Hill IP22 . . . . . . 128 E5
Gallows La Elsing NR20 . . . 50 F7
   Quidenham NR16 . . . . . . 103 E1
Gallus Cl NR17 . . . . 11 A2
Galyon Rd PE30 . . . . 147 B8
Gambling Cl NR6 . . . . 158 A7
Gamecock Cl NR6 . . . . . . 158 C6
Gamewell Cl 6 NR1 . . . . 162 E2
Gangway The NR27 . . . . . 139 C7
Ganners Hill NR8 . . . . . . 155 E3
Gannet Rd NR29 . . . . 167 E4
Gant Cl 9 NR20 . . . . 68 F6
Gaol Hill NR2 . . . . 178 A3
Gaol St 13 PE13 . . . . 152 C4
Gapton Hall Ind Est
   NR31 . . . . 170 A8
Gapton Hall Rd NR31 . . . . 170 A8
Gapton Hall Ret Pk
   NR31 . . . . 169 A1
Garage La PE33 . . . . 61 E8
Garage Lane Ind Est
   PE33 . . . . 61 E8
GARBOLDISHAM IP22 . . . 128 A8
Garboldisham Church Prim
   Sch IP22 . . . . 128 A8
Garboldisham Rd
   Harling NR16 . . . . 118 C3
   Kenninghall NR16 . . . . . 118 F3
Garden Cl Briston NR24 . . 142 B4
   Bungay NR35 . . . . 124 B8
   North Walsham NR28 . . . 151 C6
   4 Watton IP25 . . . . 84 E3
Garden Ct
   King's Lynn PE30 . . . . . . 147 A8
   1 Loddon NR14 . . . . 92 A1
Garden Drove NR23 . . . . . . 6 A6
Gardeners Terr NR7 . . . . . 158 F4
Gardenhouse La IP22 . . . 128 E2
Garden La NR25 . . . . 8 A1
Garden Pl 2 NR3 . . . . 162 E8
Garden Rd Brundall NR13 . 165 E6
   Hemsby NR29 . . . . 167 D7
   Sheringham NR26 . . . . . 138 D6
   3 Wiggenhall St Germans
      PE34 . . . . 43 B1
Garden Row PE30 . . . . . . 146 E3
Garden St Cromer NR27 . . 139 B7
   Norwich NR1 . . . . 178 B2
Gardyn Croft 5 NR8 . . . . 155 D2
Garfield Rd NR30 . . . . . . 169 D7
Garfield Terr NR30 . . . . . 168 E4
Gargle Hill NR7 . . . . 163 F7
Gariannonum (Roman
   Fort) ★ NR31 . . . . 93 F7
Garlic St IP21 . . . . 122 A2
GARLIC STREET IP21 . . . . 122 A2
Garlondes 8 NR16 . . . . . 118 C5
Garners La PE14 . . . . 60 A5
Garner's La PE34 . . . . 41 D8
Garnham Rd NR31 . . . . . . 170 C7
Garrett Cl NR3 . . . . 158 F1
Garrick Gn NR6 . . . . 158 E5
Garrick Green Inf Sch
   NR6 . . . . 158 E5
Garrison Rd NR30 . . . . . . 169 C5
Garrood Dr NR21 . . . . . . 141 E5
GARVESTONE NR9 . . . . . . 68 C2
Garvestone Com Prim Sch
   NR9 . . . . 68 C2
Garvestone Rd NR20 . . . . 68 E4
Garwood Cl PE30 . . . . . . 147 E4
Gas Hill NR1 . . . . 163 A6
Gashouse Dro IP27 . . . . . 175 E4
Gashouse Hill NR11 . . . . . 150 D6
Gas House La PE12 . . . . . . 41 B8
Gaskell Way PE30 . . . . . . 148 C1
Gaskin Way NR17 . . . . . . 174 D3
Gassock Dr IP22 . . . . 177 D1
Gasthorpe Rd NR31 . . . . . 169 B3
Gatacre Rd NR31 . . . . . . 169 B3
Gate House Cl NR29 . . . . . 75 D8
Gatehouse La
   North Wootton PE30 . . . . 148 C6
   Themelthorpe NR20 . . . . 34 A3
Gatekeeper Cl NR18 . . . . 173 E4
GATELEY NR20 . . . . 32 C3
Gateley Gdns NR3 . . . . . . 158 B3
Gateley Rd
   Brisley NR20 . . . . 49 B8
   Broom Green NR20 . . . . . 32 E3
   Gateley NR20 . . . . 32 C3
Gaultree Sq PE14 . . . . . . 59 D2
Gavell St IP19 . . . . 124 D1
Gawain Rd NR31 . . . . 170 A1
Cowdy Cl 6 IP20 . . . . . . 122 D2
Gawdy Rd NR7 . . . . 159 D1
Gaye Cres 1 IP23 . . . . . . 130 C5
Gayford Rd NR10 . . . . . . 35 B2
Gaymer Cl NR14 . . . . 119 D7
Gaymer's Way NR28 . . . . 151 B6
Gaynor Cl NR18 . . . . 173 B5
GAYTON PE32 . . . . 45 C5
Gayton CE Prim Sch
   PE32 . . . . 45 C6

Gayton Rd
   Ashwicken PE32 . . . . 45 A6
   Bawsey PE32 . . . . 44 D6
   East Walton PE32 . . . . . . 45 B3
   East Winch PE32 . . . . 45 A4
   Gayton PE32 . . . . 46 B6
   Grimston PE32 . . . . 45 C8
   King's Lynn PE30 . . . . . . 147 C5
   Rougham PE32 . . . . 46 E6
GAYTON THORPE PE32 . . 45 E5
Gayton Wlk NR6 . . . . 158 F6
GAYWOOD PE30 . . . . 147 B6
Gaywood Cl NR30 . . . . . . 168 D5
Gaywood Com Prim Sch
   PE30 . . . . 147 C7
Gaywood Hall Dr PE30 . . 147 B5
Gaywood Rd PE30 . . . . . . 146 F5
Gdn Ct NR21 . . . . 141 F4
Geddes Way 5 NR20 . . . . 68 F1
Gedge Rd NR30 . . . . 168 E6
GELDESTON NR34 . . . . . . 109 F3
Geldeston Hill NR34 . . . . 109 F2
Geldeston Rd
   Ellingham NR35 . . . . 109 D2
   Geldeston NR34 . . . . 110 B2
Gelham Manor PE31 . . . . 140 C3
Generals Wlk 5 PE30 . . . 147 C5
Geneva Gdns NR1 . . . . . . 171 E4
Genista Gn 7 NR31 . . . . . 170 B6
Gentian Way 2 NR17 . . . . 174 B4
Gentle Ct IP27 . . . . 175 C4
Gentlemans Wlk NR14 . . . 92 A3
Gentleman's Wlk IP27 . . . 178 A3
Gentle Rise IP27 . . . . 113 E2
Gentry Pl NR5 . . . . 161 C8
Geoffrey Rd 4 NR1 . . . . . 162 F3
Geoffrey Watling Wy
   Norwich NR1 . . . . 163 A4
   Norwich NR1 . . . . 178 C1
George Baldry Wy NR35 . 124 B7
George Beck Rd 8 NR29 . 58 B6
George Borrow Rd
   2 East Dereham NR19 . . 154 F3
   Norwich NR4 . . . . 161 E5
George Cl NR8 . . . . 157 B8
George Cres 13 NR16 . . . 118 C5
George Dance Pl NR5 . . . 161 C7
George Dr NR8 . . . . 157 B7
George Edwards Rd
   NR21 . . . . 141 E5
George Eliot Way 6
   NR19 . . . . 154 D2
George Fox Way NR5 . . . 161 B5
George Hill Norwich NR6 . 158 E4
   Stanton IP31 . . . . 127 C1
George La Acle NR13 . . . . 166 B4
   2 Loddon NR14 . . . . 92 A1
   Stanton IP31 . . . . 127 C1
George Low Cl NR5 . . . . . 157 A1
George Morley Ct PE30 . 146 E2
George Pope Cl NR3 . . . . 158 C2
George Pope Rd NR3 . . . . 158 C2
George Raines Ct PE36 . . 132 C3
George Rd 2 PE14 . . . . . . 176 F5
Georges Rd NR19 . . . . . . 154 D5
George St Brandon IP27 . . 175 D3
   Great Yarmouth NR30 . . 169 C4
   6 King's Lynn PE30 . . . . 146 E6
   Sheringham NR26 . . . . . 138 D7
George Trollope Rd 15
   IP25 . . . . 84 D3
George Westwood Way
   NR34 . . . . 110 D2
George White Jun Sch
   NR3 . . . . 162 F8
George Winter Ct NR3 . . . 158 C2
Georgia Rd NR21 . . . . 15 C2
Gerald Cl NR1 . . . . 163 C8
Germander Ct 8 NR31 . . . 94 C6
German's La PE34 . . . . . . 42 A6
Gertrude Rd NR3 . . . . . . 158 F1
Ghost Hill Inf Sch NR8 . . 156 D8
Gibbet La
   East Beckham NR11 . . . . 138 D2
   Wereham PE33 . . . . 80 E5
Gibbs Cl NR9 . . . . 160 B2
Gibson Rd 5 IP25 . . . . . . 67 B2
Gidney Dr PE31 . . . . 133 C5
Gigli Cl NR28 . . . . 151 B3
Gilbard Rd NR5 . . . . 161 C7
Gilbert Cl NR14 . . . . 90 F4
Gilbert Rd NR30 . . . . 168 E6
Gilbert Way NR4 . . . . 161 D1
Gilchrist Cl 8 NR4 . . . . . . 89 E8
Gildencroft NR3 . . . . 178 A4
Gilderswood NR16 . . . . . 105 F3
Gilders Wy NR3 . . . . 178 C4
Giles Rd NR10 . . . . 54 A1
GILLINGHAM NR34 . . . . . 110 C1
Gillingham St Michaels CE
   Prim Acad NR34 . . . . . . 110 B2
Gillngham Dam NR34 . . . 110 C2
Gilman Rd NR13 . . . . 158 F1
Gilpin's Ride NR19 . . . . . 154 D4
Gilray Rd IP22 . . . . 177 F4
GIMINGHAM NR11 . . . . . 22 E7
Gimingham Rd
   Gimingham NR11 . . . . . . 22 E8
   Mundesley NR11 . . . . . . 143 A6
   Southrepps NR11 . . . . . . 22 C7
   Trimingham NR11 . . . . . . 11 E1
   Trunch NR28 . . . . 22 E6
Gipsies La NR29 . . . . 56 D6
Gipsies' La Banham NR16 . 119 B6
   Briston NR24 . . . . 9 A3
Gipsy Cl NR5 . . . . 161 D6
Gipsy La Norwich NR5 . . . 161 E6
   Southburgh IP25 . . . . . . 85 F7
   Thelnetham IP22 . . . . . . 128 A5
   Watlington PE33 . . . . 61 D5

Girling Rd NR19 . . . . 154 C6
Girlings La NR7 . . . . 163 E5
Girton Rd
   Great Yarmouth NR31 . . 170 A3
   Norwich NR2 . . . . 162 B4
GISSING IP22 . . . . 120 F4
Gissing Rd
   Burston & Shimpling
      IP22 . . . . 120 F2
   Tivetshall St Margaret
      NR15 . . . . 121 B4
Glade Com Prim Sch The
   IP27 . . . . 175 D3
Glade The Costessey NR8 . 156 F4
   Guist NR20 . . . . 32 F4
   Overstrand NR27 . . . . . . 11 A3
   Thetford IP24 . . . . 176 D6
Gladstone Rd
   Fakenham NR21 . . . . 141 B4
   4 King's Lynn PE30 . . . . 146 E3
Gladstone St NR2 . . . . . . 162 B6
Glamis Ct 26 IP20 . . . . . 122 D2
GLANDFORD NR25 . . . . . . 7 E4
Glandford Rd
   Cley next the Sea NR25 . . . 7 E5
   Glandford NR25 . . . . 7 D4
Glasbury Wlk PE13 . . . . . 153 C3
Glaven PE30 . . . . 147 C5
Glaven Cl NR28 . . . . 151 D5
Glaven Hale Cl NR25 . . . . 137 C6
Glaven Rd NR25 . . . . 137 D5
Glebe Ave
   Hunstanton PE36 . . . . . . 132 D5
   Watlington PE33 . . . . 61 E5
Glebe Cl
   Dersingham PE31 . . . . . . 140 C5
   Fransham NR19 . . . . 66 C7
   Hingham NR9 . . . . 86 B5
   19 Long Stratton NR15 . 106 E3
   Northwold IP26 . . . . 99 C8
   2 Potter Heigham NR29 . 56 F6
   Taverham NR8 . . . . 155 F1
   Thetford IP24 . . . . 176 D5
   Wreningham NR16 . . . . . 88 D1
Glebe Cres NR10 . . . . 35 B3
Glebe Ct NR28 . . . . 151 D6
Glebe Dr IP22 . . . . 177 B4
Glebe Est PE34 . . . . 144 F1
Glebe Farm Cl IP21 . . . . . 122 A4
Glebe House Sch PE36 . . 132 D5
Glebe La PE31 . . . . 135 F6
Glebeland Com Prim Sch
   NR34 . . . . 110 E7
Glebe Mdw NR17 . . . . . . 103 E7
Glebe Rd Acle NR13 . . . . . 166 C2
   Dersingham PE31 . . . . . . 140 C4
   Downham Market PE38 . . 172 D6
   Gissing IP21 . . . . 121 A4
   Halvergate NR13 . . . . . . 74 F1
   Norwich NR2 . . . . 162 A4
   7 Watton IP25 . . . . 84 E3
   Weeting IP27 . . . . 175 B7
Glebes The 13 NR31 . . . . 94 A5
Glebe The
   2 Harling NR16 . . . . 118 C5
   Hemsby NR29 . . . . 167 C8
   Honing NR28 . . . . 38 C6
   Postwick NR13 . . . . 72 F7
   Stibbard NR21 . . . . 32 E7
   Wells-next-the-Sea NR23 . 136 D6
Glebe Way 5 NR12 . . . . . 54 C6
Glenalmond NR4 . . . . . . 162 A1
Glenburn Ave NR1 . . . . . 159 A3
Glenburn Cl NR7 . . . . . . 159 A3
Glenda Cl NR5 . . . . 157 C1
Glenda Cres NR5 . . . . . . 157 B2
Glenda Rd NR5 . . . . 157 C1
Glendenning Rd 4 NR1 . . 163 B5
Glendon Gdns PE13 . . . . 152 A8
Glen Farm La NR11 . . . . . 21 B7
Glenfield Cl PE14 . . . . . . 78 A5
Glengarry Cl NR9 . . . . . . 88 C8
Glenham Ct PE31 . . . . . . 140 C4
Glenmore Ave NR30 . . . . 168 D7
Glenmore Gdns NR3 . . . . 158 B2
Glenn Rd NR14 . . . . 90 C4
Globe Ct NR13 . . . . 165 E6
Globe La NR13 . . . . 165 E6
Globe Pl NR2 . . . . 162 C5
Globe St IP26 . . . . 99 A5
Glosthorpe Manor PE32 . . 44 F5
Gloucester Ave NR31 . . . 170 C4
Gloucester Ct PE13 . . . . . 152 D7
Gloucester Pl NR24 . . . . 142 D4
Gloucester Rd PE30 . . . . 147 B6
Gloucester St
   Norwich NR1 . . . . 71 E2
   Norwich NR2 . . . . 162 C4
Gloucester Way IP24 . . . 176 A5
Glover Rd NR13 . . . . 166 B3
Goat Willow Cl IP25 . . . . 84 E3
Gobbett's Rd IP22 . . . . . 128 C4
Goddard Cres 1 PE13 . . . 152 D7
Goddards St 14 IP25 . . . . 84 D3
Godfrey Rd 5 NR10 . . . . . 54 A2
Godric Pl NR2 . . . . 161 F6
Godwick Medieval Village
   of ★ PE32 . . . . 31 C1
Godwin Rd PE13 . . . . . . 152 D7
Goffe Cl IP25 . . . . 84 D4
Gogg's Mill Rd NR21 . . . . 141 A3
Gogle Cl 8 NR20 . . . . . . 68 E6
Goldbrook IP21 . . . . 131 A3
Golden Ball St NR1 . . . . . 178 B2
Golden Corner NR9 . . . . . 85 E2
Golden Dog La NR3 . . . . 178 B4
Golden Gates NR23 . . . . . 136 B2
Golden Gates Dr NR23 . . 136 A2

Golden Gym
   Narborough PE32 . . . . . . 63 F7
   Pentney PE32 . . . . 63 C8
Golden Pightle 7 NR9 . . . 69 F2
Golden Sq 10 NR27 . . . . . 139 B7
Goldfinch Cl
   Downham Market PE38 . . 172 C7
   Wymondham NR18 . . . . . 173 D2
Goldfinch Dr
   Attleborough NR17 . . . . 174 B3
   Attleborough NR17 . . . . 174 B4
Goldfinch Way 13 IP25 . . 84 C3
Golding Pl Norwich NR2 . 162 C6
   16 Wisbech PE13 . . . . . 152 C4
Goldsmith St NR2 . . . . . . 162 C7
Goldsmith Way IP21 . . . . 121 F4
Golds Pightle PE36 . . . . . . 2 B3
Goldwell Rd NR1 . . . . . . 178 B1
Golf Cl King's Lynn PE30 . 148 D1
   Runton NR27 . . . . 10 A5
Golf Course Rd PE36 . . . . 132 E8
Golf La NR19 . . . . 154 D7
Golf Links Rd
   Brundall NR13 . . . . 165 D4
   Wymondham College
      NR18 . . . . 104 E8
Gong La PE31 . . . . 135 F6
Gonville Cl PE31 . . . . 133 C5
Gonville Hall La NR18 . . . 87 D3
Gonville Rd NR31 . . . . . . 170 A4
Gooch Cl Bacton NR12 . . . 23 E4
   North Walsham NR28 . . . 151 C6
GOODERSTONE PE33 . . . . 82 A4
Gooderstone CE Prim Sch
   PE33 . . . . 82 A5
Gooderstone Rd PE33 . . . 81 F5
Gooderstone Water Gdns ★
   PE33 . . . . 82 A5
Goodhale Rd 1 NR5 . . . . 161 B7
Gooding Cl PE34 . . . . 61 C2
Goodman Sq 2 NR2 . . . . 162 C7
Goodminns Estate PE36 . . 13 A7
Goodrick Pl PE13 . . . . . . 153 C4
Goodson Rd NR7 . . . . . . 159 D5
Goodwin Rd NR1 . . . . . . 143 C6
Goodwins Rd PE30 . . . . . 146 E3
Goodwood Cl NR7 . . . . . 159 E1
Goosander Cl 4 PE31 . . . 12 E5
Gooseacre La IP25 . . . . . . 67 D3
Gooseberry Hill NR20 . . . 50 B3
Gooseberry La
   Castle Rising PE30 . . . . . 148 E3
   South Wootton PE30 . . . . 27 C2
   Three Holes PE14 . . . . . . 77 E3
Goose Gn
   8 Sutton Bridge PE12 . . . 41 B8
   Winfarthing IP22 . . . . . . 120 C6
Goose Gn La IP22 . . . . . . 120 B6
Goose Gn Rd PE31 . . . . . . 12 E4
GOOSE GREEN IP22 . . . . 120 C6
Goose Green NR11 . . . . . 20 E3
Goose Green West 8
   NR34 . . . . 110 D1
Goose La
   Alby with Thwaite NR11 . 21 B3
   Harleston NR15 . . . . 39 C4
   Hemsby NR29 . . . . 167 C8
   Honing NR28 . . . . 38 C6
   Goose La North PE14 . . . 60 A5
   Goose La South PE14 . . . 59 F3
Goose's La PE14 . . . . 41 D5
Gordon Ave NR7 . . . . . . 163 C7
Gordon Ct PE13 . . . . 152 C3
Gordon Fuller Cl IP26 . . . 99 A7
Gordon Godfrey Way
   NR10 . . . . 53 A3
Gordon Rd Briston NR24 . 142 A5
   3 East Dereham NR20 . . 154 E5
   Great Yarmouth NR31 . . 169 C2
Gordon Sq NR1 . . . . 178 B1
Gordon Terr NR11 . . . . . . 143 B4
Gore La NR15 . . . . 121 C8
Gorgate Dr NR20 . . . . . . 49 D3
Gorgate Rd NR20 . . . . . . 49 E3
GORLESTON-ON-SEA
   NR31 . . . . 170 E4
Gormans La NR21 . . . . . . 31 D5
Gorse Ave NR6 . . . . 158 A5
Gorse Cl 4 Belton NR31 . . 94 A5
   2 East Dereham NR19 . . 154 C4
   Fakenham NR21 . . . . 141 B5
   Mundesley NR11 . . . . . . 143 B5
Gorse Ind Est IP24 . . . . . 125 C6
Gorse Rd NR7 . . . . 163 D8
Gorse View 4 NR20 . . . . 49 D4
Gorse Vw 4 NR20 . . . . . . 49 D4
Goshawk Dr NR31 . . . . . 171 D4
Goshawk Ri NR18 . . . . . . 173 D1
Goshawk Way 5 IP24 . . . 176 D2
Gosmoor La PE14 . . . . . . 59 B1
Gostling Cl IP22 . . . . 177 B4
Gothic Cl 2 IP20 . . . . . . 122 D1
Goulburn Rd NR7 . . . . . . 159 D1
Goulder Dr NR11 . . . . . . 150 B5
Goulders Farm La IP21 . . 131 E4
Goulders La
   Banningham NR11 . . . . . 36 F8
   Felmingham NR28 . . . . . . 37 A8
Gould Rd 1 NR2 . . . . 162 A4
Goulds Cl IP22 . . . . 177 D2
Gournay Rd NR31 . . . . . . 170 D2
Governors Ct NR1 . . . . . . 178 C1
Gower Cl PE36 . . . . 132 D4
Gowing Cl NR6 . . . . 157 F7
Gowing Ct NR3 . . . . 158 B3
Gowing Rd
   11 Mulbarton NR14 . . . . 89 B3
   Norwich NR6 . . . . 157 F6
Gowing Way NR15 . . . . . 107 B5
Gowthorpe La NR14 . . . . 89 C5
Grace Edwards Cl NR8 . . 155 F2
Grafton Cl PE30 . . . . 147 C8
Grafton Rd PE30 . . . . 147 C8

Graham Dr 2 PE32 . . . . . . 44 B3
Graham Sq NR7 . . . . 159 D1
Graham St PE30 . . . . 146 E3
Grammar Sch Rd NR28 . . 151 C4
Granary Cl Briston NR24 . 142 F3
   Earsham NR35 . . . . 123 F7
   Freethorpe NR13 . . . . . . 92 E7
   Hockering NR20 . . . . 69 B7
   9 Lingwood NR13 . . . . . 74 A3
Granary Ct PE30 . . . . 146 D4
Granary Fields IP25 . . . . . 84 A8
Granary La NR12 . . . . 54 F8
Granary Loke NR10 . . . . . 149 C4
Granary Rd NR17 . . . . . . 174 C4
Granary Way 4 NR9 . . . . 86 C4
Grand Cl NR19 . . . . 154 C4
Grange Ave NR27 . . . . . . 11 B3
Grange Cl Briston NR24 . . 142 E3
   Hoveton NR12 . . . . 164 E6
   Ludham NR29 . . . . 56 D5
   Norwich NR6 . . . . 158 E4
   10 Snettisham PE31 . . . . 12 E4
   Wroxham/Hoveton NR12 164 E6
Grange Cres PE33 . . . . . . 63 C5
Grange Ct NR28 . . . . 151 C4
Grange Farm La NR29 . . . 75 D8
Grange Farm La
   Coltishall NR12 . . . . 164 A8
   Shropham NR17 . . . . 103 A2
Grange La Honingham NR9 69 F5
   Little Massingham PE32 . . 29 F4
   West Rudham PE31 . . . . . 30 A5
Granger Cres NR18 . . . . . 88 B6
Grange Rd
   Caister-on-Sea NR30 . . . 168 D5
   Cantley NR13 . . . . 92 C6
   Flixton NR35 . . . . 123 E4
   Hainford NR10 . . . . 53 F5
   Ludham NR29 . . . . 56 D5
   Mundham NR14 . . . . 108 F4
   Mundham NR14 . . . . 108 F4
   9 New Buckenham NR17 104 F1
   Norwich NR2 . . . . 162 A4
   Scarning NR19 . . . . 154 A4
   Sutton Bridge PE34 . . . . . 41 E8
   Wendling NR19 . . . . 66 F8
   West Rudham PE31 . . . . . 29 F6
   West Rudham PE31 . . . . . 30 A5
   Wisbech PE13 . . . . 152 A7
GRANGE THE NR10 . . . . . 35 C1
Grange The PE37 . . . . 65 E3
Grange Wlk NR12 . . . . . . 164 C4
Granny Bard's La NR12 . . 54 C3
Granta Way 1 NR31 . . . . 170 B2
Grantly Cl PE30 . . . . 147 D5
Grant Rd NR10 . . . . 54 A2
Grant St NR2 . . . . 162 A7
Granville Cl 8 NR12 . . . . 39 B4
Granville Rd NR1 . . . . . . 169 B4
Granville Terr PE12 . . . . . 41 A8
Grapes Hill NR2 . . . . 162 C6
Grasmere 15 NR9 . . . . . . 88 D8
Grasmere Cl NR5 . . . . . . 161 C6
Grassgate La PE14 . . . . . 59 B7
Grassy La PE32 . . . . 28 B2
Gravel Bank PE14 . . . . . . 60 D8
Gravel Dam NR32 . . . . . . 111 E3
Gravelfield Cl NR1 . . . . . 163 B8
Gravel Hill NR14 . . . . 89 F4
Gravelhill La PE33 . . . . . . 43 F1
Gravel Pit Hill NR17 . . . . 102 F6
Gravel Pit Hill NR16 . . . . 106 A8
Gravelpit La
   Banham NR16 . . . . 119 C6
   Snetterton NR16 . . . . . . 103 C2
Gravel Pit La
   Bergh Apton NR15 . . . . . 91 B2
   Haddiscoe NR14 . . . . . . 110 F8
   Holt NR25 . . . . 137 C5
   Horningtoft NR20 . . . . . . 31 E2
   Lynford IP26 . . . . 100 F2
   Lynford IP26 . . . . 101 A1
Graves Ave NR6 . . . . 158 D7
Gray Dr NR20 . . . . 50 B4
Grayling Cl NR31 . . . . . . 170 A2
Grays Fair NR5 . . . . 156 F1
Grays Farm Cl IP25 . . . . . 84 C6
Grays La Aslacton NR16 . . 106 A2
   Emneth PE14 . . . . 59 C2
Gray's La Barsham NR22 . . 16 E6
   Pulham Market IP21 . . . 121 D5
Grays Rd NR34 . . . . 111 C3
Great Barn Rd NR23 . . . . . 5 A4
GREAT BARWICK PE31 . . 14 E6
Great Barwick Medieval
   Village of ★ PE31 . . . . . 14 E6
GREAT BIRCHAM PE31 . . 14 B3
Great Cl NR30 . . . . 168 D5
Great Comm La NR34 . . . 124 E5
GREAT COMMON NR34 . 124 D6
GREAT CRESSINGHAM
   IP25 . . . . 83 D4
Great Cressingham Rd
   Great Cressingham IP25 . 83 B5
   Little Cressingham IP25 . 83 D2
GREAT DUNHAM PE32 . . . 47 E1
Great Dunham Prim Sch
   PE32 . . . . 47 F1
Great Eastern Rd PE13 . . 152 E4
Great Eastern Way
   Fakenham NR21 . . . . 141 C5
   Wells-next-the-Sea NR23 136 E5
GREAT ELLINGHAM
   NR17 . . . . 103 E7
Great Ellingham Prim Sch
   Great Ellingham NR17 . . 103 E7
   Great Ellingham NR17 . . 103 E8
GREAT FRANSHAM NR19 . 66 B8

Great Gn IP21 . . . . .129 F3
GREAT GREEN
 Burgate IP22 . . . . .129 B3
 Thrandeston IP21 . . . . . . .130 A4
GREAT HAUTBOIS NR12 . . 54 C7
Great Hautbois Rd NR12 . . 54 C7
Greatheath Rd NR20 . . . . . 32 D1
GREAT HOCKHAM IP24 .102 E3
Great Hockham Prim Sch
 IP24 . . . . .102 E3
Great Hockham Rd
 IP24 . . . . .102 C3
Great Hospl NR1 . . . . . . .178 C4
Great Man's Way PE33 . . 81 A2
GREAT MASSINGHAM
 PE32 . . . . .29 D2
Great Massingham CE Prim
 Sch PE32 . . . . 29 E1
GREAT MELTON NR9 . . . . 70 B1
Great Melton Cl NR9 . . . . 88 D8
Great Melton Rd
 Hethersett NR9 . . . . 88 C8
 Little Melton NR9 . . . . . .160 A2
GREAT MOULTON NR15 .106 B1
Great Northern Cl NR30 .169 D6
Great Palgrave Medieval
 Village of ★ PE32 . . . . . . 65 B6
GREAT PLUMSTEAD
 NR13 . . . . .72 F5
GREAT RYBURGH NR21 . . 32 B6
Great Ryburgh Rd
 Fakenham NR21 . . . . 32 B8
 Kettlestone NR21 . . . . 17 A1
GREAT SNORING NR21 . . 17 A5
Great Snoring Rd
 Hindringham NR21 . . . . . .17 D6
 Little Snoring NR21 . . . . . 17 A4
GREAT WALSINGHAM
 NR22 . . . . .17 A8
Great Walsingham Rd
 NR21 . . . . 17 B8
GREAT WITCHINGHAM
 NR9 . . . . 51 E7
Great Witchingham CE Prim
 Sch NR9 . . . . 51 E5
GREAT YARMOUTH
 NR30 . . . . .169 A5
Great Yarmouth Charter
 Acad NR30 . . . . .169 E6
Great Yarmouth La
 NR31 . . . . .170 A5
Great Yarmouth Prim Acad
 NR30 . . . . .169 D1
Great Yarmouth Race
 Course NR30 . . . . 168 F2
Great Yarmouth Sea Life
 Ctr ★ NR30 . . . . .169 E2
Great Yarmouth Sta
 NR30 . . . . .169 B5
Grebe Cl
 Great Yarmouth NR31 . .170 A7
 7 Rollesby NR29 . . . . . .57 D2
Grebe Dr Chedgrave NR14 . 91 F2
 Sprowston NR7 . . . . .159 E5
Greenacre Cl
 Brundall NR13 . . . . .165 C4
 King's Lynn PE30 . . . . . . .148 B2
Green Acre Cl IP26 . . . . . .100 B5
Greenacre Rd NR9 . . . . . . 86 B5
Greenacres
 Bradwell NR31 . . . . .170 A3
 Little Melton NR9 . . . . . .160 C2
Greenacres Dr NR14 . . . . 90 C5
Green Bank
 Holme next the Sea PE36 . . 2 A5
 Walpole Highway PE14 . . 59 F7
Greenborough Cl NR7 . .159 E4
Greenborough Rd NR7 . .159 E2
Green Briar La PE31 . . . . . 13 E3
Green Cl Hempton NR21 . .141 A2
 Norwich NR5 . . . . .156 E1
Green Comm La PE31 . . . . 3 C6
Greencourts 10 NR29 . . . . 58 B6
Green Ct Fakenham NR21 141 E4
 Norwich NR7 . . . . .163 D7
Green Dr NR31 . . . . 94 A3
Green Dragon La NR23 .136 D5
Green Dro PE14 . . . . 77 D6
Green Drove
 Barton Bendish PE37 . . . . 63 D1
 Narborough PE33 . . . . 63 E4
Green Dyke PE14 . . . . 59 B7
Green End PE14 . . . . 77 E1
Greenfield NR5 . . . . .156 D1
Greenfield Cl NR27 . . . . . .139 C5
Greenfields NR16 . . . . . . .118 B5
Greenfields Rd NR20 . . . .154 F4
GREENGATE NR20 . . . . 50 B2
Greengate NR20 . . . . 50 B2
Greengate La
 Bircham PE31 . . . . 13 F4
 Great Massingham PE32 . . 29 C1
Greengates Way NR12 . .164 E6
Green Gr PE33 . . . . 81 D8
Greenhill Ave NR30 . . . .168 D8
Green Hill La
 Bagthorpe PE31 . . . . 14 C3
 Bircham PE31 . . . . 14 B3
Greenhill Rd PE32 . . . . . . 46 B2
Green Hills Cl NR8 . . . . . .156 F3
Green Hills Rd 6 NR3 . .162 D8
Greenhoe Pl PE37 . . . . . .153 E5
Green House La PE37 . . .153 E6
Greenhouse Rd 17 NR20 . 50 E7
Green La Alpington NR14 . . 90 F3
 Attleborough NR17 . . . . .174 C7
 Aylsham NR11 . . . . 35 F5

Green La continued
 Aylsham NR11 . . . . .150 A6
 Bawburgh NR9 . . . . .160 C4
 Bedingham NR35 . . . . . . .108 B1
 Beetley NR20 . . . . 49 D4
 Bessingham NR25 . . . . 20 C8
 Billingford NR20 . . . . 49 F8
 Brooke NR15 . . . . .108 A7
 Brooke NR15 . . . . .108 B8
 Burgh St Peter NR34 . . . .111 C4
 Burnham Thorpe PE31 . . . . 4 D3
 Burston IP22 . . . . .120 E2
 Caister-on-Sea NR30 . . . .168 E4
 Cawston NR10 . . . . 35 A1
 Cawston NR10 . . . . 35 A2
 Christchurch PE14 . . . . . . 95 A7
 Coltishall NR12 . . . . 54 C6
 Dereham NR19 . . . . 68 A7
 Dereham NR19 . . . . .154 B8
 Ditchingham NR35 . . . . . .109 B2
 Diss IP22 . . . . .177 A6
 5 Earsham NR35 . . . . .123 F8
 Edgefield NR24 . . . . 19 D4
 Erpingham NR11 . . . . 21 B2
 5 Feltwell IP26 . . . . . . 98 E1
 Filby NR29 . . . . 75 F8
 Foulsham NR20 . . . . 33 E3
 Great Ellingham NR17 . .103 E8
 Great & Little Plumstead
  NR13 . . . . 72 E5
 Great Moulton NR15 . . . .106 B1
 Great Yarmouth NR31 . . . 94 C6
 Guestwick Gn NR20 . . . . . 34 A4
 Guist NR20 . . . . 33 A5
 Hackford NR18 . . . . 87 A5
 Hales NR14 . . . . .109 E8
 Haveringland NR10 . . . . . 52 E7
 Hellington NR14 . . . . 91 B5
 Horsford NR10 . . . . 53 B4
 Kenninghall NR16 . . . . . .119 B5
 Kettlestone NR21 . . . . 17 A1
 King's Lynn PE30 . . . . . . .148 E2
 Little Ellingham NR17 . . . 86 A1
 Little Livermere IP31 . . . .125 F1
 Methwold IP26 . . . . 99 A7
 Mundford IP26 . . . . .100 B5
 North Creake NR21 . . . . . . 4 B1
 Norwich NR14 . . . . 72 D1
 Park's Wood NR35 . . . . . .108 B2
 Postwick with Witton NR7. . 72 E4
 Potter Heigham NR29 . . . 56 F6
 Pudding Norton NR21 . . .141 A1
 Redenhall with Harleston
  IP20 . . . . .122 E2
 Rocklands NR17 . . . . .103 C7
 Rockland St Mary NR14 . . 91 C7
 Saxlingham Nethergate
  NR15 . . . . .107 B7
 Shipdham IP25 . . . . 67 D4
 Somerleyton NR32 . . . . . .109 F1
 Somerleyton, Ashby &
  Herringfleet NR32 . . . .111 E8
 South Walsham NR13 . . . . 74 B6
 Stanhoe PE31 . . . . 14 E8
 Starston IP20 . . . . .122 D4
 Stow Bedon NR17 . . . . . .103 B8
 Swanton Morley NR20 . . . 50 A3
 Syleham IP21 . . . . .131 C4
 Terrington St Clement PE34 42 B7
 Thelnetham IP22 . . . . . . .128 A2
 Themelthorpe NR20 . . . . . 33 F3
 Thetford IP24 . . . . .176 E4
 Thornage NR25 . . . . 18 E8
 Thornham PE36 . . . . 2 D6
 Thrandeston IP21 . . . . . . .129 F2
 Tivetshall St Margaret
  NR15 . . . . .121 B5
 Toft Monks NR34 . . . . . . .110 C6
 Tottenhill PE33 . . . . 61 F5
 Troston IP31 . . . . .126 A1
 Tuttington NR11 . . . . 36 D7
 Upwell PE14 . . . . 95 B6
 Walpole St Peter PE14 . . . 41 F3
 Walsoken PE14 . . . . .152 F4
 Wicklewood NR18 . . . . . . 87 C5
 Winfarthing IP22 . . . . . . .120 A7
 Worstead NR28 . . . . 38 A5
 Wramplingham NR18 . . . . 87 F7
 Wymondham NR18 . . . . . .173 D1
 Yaxham NR19 . . . . 68 B6
Green La E NR13 . . . . 72 E7
Green La N NR13 . . . . 72 D5
Greenland Ave
 King's Lynn PE30 . . . . . . .146 E8
 Wymondham NR18 . . . . . .173 E6
Greenlands Way NR26 . .138 C6
Greenlands Way W 2
 NR26 . . . . .138 B6
Green La W
 Horsham St Faith NR13 . . . 53 D1
 Rackheath NR13 . . . . 72 D8
Green Man Cl IP21 . . . . . .130 E5
Green Man La NR15 . . . . .108 C8
Green Marsh Rd PE34 . . .144 C7
Green Oak Rd 2 IP25 . . . 84 D3
Greenpark Acad Prim Sch
 PE30 . . . . .146 F7
Greenpark Ave PE30 . . . .146 F6
Green Pk 42 IP20 . . . . . . .122 D2
Green Pk Rd NR10 . . . . . . 53 B3
Green Quay The ★ PE30 .146 D4
Green Rd Brandon IP27 . .175 E2
 Hales NR14 . . . . .109 E8
 Upwell PE14 . . . . 77 E4
GREENSGATE NR9 . . . . . . 51 E2
Greens La
 Terrington St Clement
  PE34 . . . . .42 D5
 Terrington St Clement
  PE34 . . . . .144 D2
Greens Rd
 East Dereham NR20 . . . .154 F3

Greens Rd continued
 North Walsham NR28 . . . .151 A5
Green's Road Ind Est
 NR20 . . . . .154 F4
Green St IP21 . . . . .131 A4
GREEN THE NR18 . . . . 87 B4
Green The
 Aldborough NR11 . . . . 21 A5
 Ashill IP25 . . . . 84 A7
 Banham NR16 . . . . .119 D7
 Beachamwell PE37 . . . . . . 81 F8
 Belton with Browston NR31 94 A5
 Binham NR21 . . . . 6 E2
 Boughton PE33 . . . . 80 F4
 Brisley NR20 . . . . 49 B8
 Burlingham Green NR13 . . 74 A5
 Burnham Market PE31 . . .135 C3
 Cockley Cley PE37 . . . . . . 82 D7
 Deopham NR18 . . . . 86 E2
 Dersingham PE31 . . . . . . .140 D4
 Edgefield NR24 . . . . 19 D5
 Edingthorpe Green NR28 . . 23 A3
 Fakenham NR21 . . . . .141 A3
 Felbrigg NR11 . . . . 10 C2
 Freethorpe NR13 . . . . 92 E8
 Gunthorpe NR24 . . . . 18 B5
 Haveringland NR10 . . . . . 52 E6
 Heydon NR11 . . . . 34 F6
 Hickling NR12 . . . . 39 E2
 Hickling NR12 . . . . 39 F2
 Hockham IP24 . . . . .102 E3
 Hunstanton PE36 . . . . . . .132 C4
 Kelling NR25 . . . . 8 D5
 Kimberley NR18 . . . . 87 B7
 Little Barningham NR11 . . 20 A4
 Little Barningham NR24 . . 19 F4
 Lound NR32 . . . . 94 C2
 Matlaske NR11 . . . . 20 D5
 Merton IP25 . . . . 84 C2
 Morningthorpe and Fritton
  NR15 . . . . .107 A2
 North Lopham IP22 . . . . .119 A2
 North Wootton PE30 . . . .148 C5
 Norwich NR3 . . . . .178 D2
 Ormesby St Margaret
  NR29 . . . . .167 A2
 Oxborough PE33 . . . . 81 E4
 Paston Green NR28 . . . . . 23 B4
 Paston Green NR28 . . . . .143 C1
 Plumstead Green NR11 . . . 20 A5
 Pulham Market IP21 . . . .121 E5
 Redgrave IP22 . . . . .128 E4
 Runhall NR9 . . . . 68 F2
 St Nicholas South Elmham
  IP20 . . . . .123 F2
 Saxlingham Nethergate
  NR15 . . . . .107 D7
 Sculthorpe NR21 . . . . 16 C2
 South Creake NR21 . . . . . . 15 E6
 South Wootton PE30 . . . .149 C2
 Stalham NR12 . . . . 39 C3
 Stanhoe PE31 . . . . 14 E8
 Surlingham NR14 . . . . 73 B1
 Thornham PE36 . . . . 2 D6
 Upper Sheringham NR26 .138 A4
 Upton with Fishley NR13. .166 B8
 Wicklewood NR18 . . . . . . 87 B4
 Witton NR13 . . . . 73 B4
 Witton NR13 . . . . .165 A6
 Witton NR28 . . . . 23 D2
 Woodbastwick NR13 . . . . . 55 C2
Green Way Barsham NR22 . 16 C6
 Stiffkey NR23 . . . . 6 C6
 Swaffham PE37 . . . . .153 B6

Gresham Rd
 Baconsthorpe NR25. . . . . . 20 B8
 Gresham NR11 . . . . 9 E2
 Norwich NR3 . . . . .158 B2
Gresham's Prep Sch
 NR25 . . . . .137 D7
Gresham's Sch NR25 . . . .137 C6
Gresham Village Sch
 NR11 . . . . 9 E1
Gresley Cl NR20 . . . . 49 C4
GRESSENHALL NR20 . . . . 49 B3
Gressenhall Farm &
 Workhouse ★ NR20 . . . . 49 D4
Gressenhall Rd
 Dereham NR19 . . . . .154 B8
 Gressenhall NR20 . . . . 49 D4
Greyfriars Cl NR6 . . . . . . .158 E5
Greyfriars Prim Sch
 PE30 . . . . .146 E4
Greyfriars Rd NR1 . . . . . .178 B3
Greyfriars Way NR30 . . . .169 C3
Greyhound La
 Banham NR16 . . . . .119 D7
 Hopton IP22 . . . . .127 E5
Greyhound Opening 7
 NR2 . . . . .162 C7
Greylag Cl
 11 Salhouse NR13 . . . . . 55 A1
 18 Sprowston NR7 . . . . .159 E4
Greyling Way PE37 . . . . . .153 D2
Grey Sedge PE30 . . . . . . .147 A7
Greys Manor NR16 . . . . . .119 D6
Grice Cl 4 NR26 . . . . . . .138 C5
Griffin Cl PE14 . . . . .152 F4
Griffin La
 Attleborough NR17 . . . . .174 D5
 Thorpe St Andrew NR7 . . . 72 D3
Grigg Cl IP22 . . . . .177 E5
Grigsons Wood 1
 NR16 . . . . .118 C5
Grime's Graves ★ IP27 . .115 C8
Grimmer La NR13 . . . . 92 B7
Grimmer's Rd 6 PE13 . .152 E7
Grimshoe Rd
 Downham Market PE38. . .172 B6
 Downham Market PE38. . .172 B7
GRIMSTON PE32 . . . . 28 B1
Grimstone La
 Harpley PE32 . . . . 29 A4
 Little Massingham PE32 . . 29 A2
Grimston La PE32 . . . . 28 F1
Grimston Pott Row Fst Sch
 PE32 . . . . 45 A8
Grimston Rd
 Congham PE32 . . . . 28 C2
 Gayton PE32 . . . . 45 C6
 King's Lynn PE30 . . . . . . .148 E1
Griston Ind Est IP25 . . . . 85 A1
Griston Rd Northacre IP25 . 85 B1
 Thompson IP24 . . . . .102 B8
 Watton IP25 . . . . 84 E3
Groomes Cl 4 NR31 . . . .171 D5
Grosvenor Rd
 Norwich NR2 . . . . .162 B5
 Wisbech PE13 . . . . .152 D7
Grouse Cl 10 NR7 . . . . . .159 E4
Grouts NR15 . . . . 8 B6
Grove Ave Norwich NR1 . .178 A1
 Norwich NR5 . . . . .157 A1
Grovebury Cl NR13 . . . . . .165 C4
Grove Cl
 8 East Dereham NR19 . .154 C4
 Holt NR25 . . . . .137 D6
 2 Newton Flotman NR15. . 89 C1
Grove Dale 3 NR15 . . . . . 89 C1
Grovedale Cl NR5 . . . . . . .157 A1
Grove End IP21 . . . . .131 F1
Grove Gdns 10 Elm PE14 . . 59 A1
 7 Gayton PE32 . . . . . . 45 C6
Grove House Inf Com Sch
 NR19 . . . . .154 D4
Grove La Booton NR10 . . . . 52 A8
 Fakenham NR21 . . . . .141 C6
 Forncett NR16 . . . . .106 A3
 Holt NR25 . . . . .137 D6
 Necton PE37 . . . . 66 A5
 Sparham NR9 . . . . 51 B6
 Stuston IP21 . . . . .130 B4
 Tasburgh NR15 . . . . .106 F7
 Thetford IP24 . . . . .176 D4
 Woodrising NR9 . . . . 85 F6
Grovelands PE31 . . . . .140 D8
Grove Rd Banham NR16 . .119 C6
 Barsham NR21 . . . . 16 C4
 Brockdish IP21 . . . . .131 C6
 Cantley NR13 . . . . 92 D8
 Cromer NR27 . . . . .139 D5
 Gissing IP21 . . . . .121 A4
 Hethersett NR9 . . . . 88 D8
 Ingham NR12 . . . . 24 C1
 4 Marthan NR29 . . . . . . 57 D5
 Melton Constable NR24. . .142 A4
 North Walsham NR28 . . . .151 D5
 Norwich NR1 . . . . .178 A1
 Ragmere NR17 . . . . .104 C1
 Repps with Bastwick NR29 57 A4
 Starston IP20 . . . . .122 C2
 Tivetshall St Margaret
  NR15 . . . . .121 B5
 Upper Street NR12 . . . . . . 55 F4
 Wells-next-the-Sea NR23 .136 E4
Groveside PE31 . . . . 30 A7
Grove The
 Brandiston NR10 . . . . 35 B1
 Clippesby NR29 . . . . 75 A8
 Coltishall NR12 . . . . 54 D6
 East Dereham NR19 . . . . .154 C4
 Fleggburgh NR29 . . . . 57 A1
 Little Witchingham NR10. .149 F1

Grove The continued
 2 Necton PE37 . . . . 65 F4
 Poringland NR14 . . . . 90 B4
 Roydon PE32 . . . . 28 A1
 Shotesham NR15 . . . . 90 B1
Grove Way NR15 . . . . 89 C1
Grove Wlk NR1 . . . . .178 A1
Growle Abbey NR24. . . . . . 19 B2
Grubb's La NR12 . . . . 24 C1
Grub La IP19 . . . . .124 E1
Grub St Happisburgh NR12 . 24 B4
 Shotesham NR15 . . . . 90 B2
Guanock Pl 12 PE30 . . . . .146 E3
Guanock Terr PE30 . . . . . .146 E3
Guardian Rd NR5 . . . . . . .161 F7
Guardian Road Ind Est
 NR5 . . . . .161 F7
Guelph Rd 2 NR1 . . . . . .163 A6
Guernsey Rd NR3 . . . . . . .162 E8
GUESTWICK NR20 . . . . . . 34 A6
GUESTWICK GREEN
 NR20 . . . . 33 F5
Guestwick Rd
 Foulsham NR20 . . . . 33 A6
 Hindolveston NR20 . . . . . 33 F7
 Tyby NR20 . . . . 34 C6
 Wood Norton NR20 . . . . . 33 C6
Guildford Way 2 NR2 . . .176 B5
Guildhall Hill 1 NR2 . . . .178 A3
Guildhall La IP21 . . . . .121 E5
Guildhall St IP24 . . . . .176 D3
Guild Rd PE13 . . . . .152 E6
Guild St NR22 . . . . 16 F8
Guiler's La NR18 . . . . .105 B8
Guilt Cross NR16 . . . . .118 E3
Guilt Cross Way PE38 . . .172 C6
Guinevere Rd NR31 . . . . . .171 B8
GUIST NR20 . . . . 32 F4
Guist Bottom NR20 . . . . . 32 E5
Guist Bottom Rd NR21 . . 32 E6
Guist La NR20 . . . . 33 A5
Guist Rd NR20 . . . . 33 C4
Gulagate La NR11 . . . . 21 A1
Gulgate La NR11 . . . . 21 A1
Gull La
 Framingham Earl NR14 . . . 90 E6
 Shipmeadow NR34 . . . . . .124 F8
Gullpit Dro PE34 . . . . 61 D1
Gunner Cl
 Cliftonville NR11 . . . . .143 C6
 8 Norwich NR7 . . . . . . 72 D5
Gunn Rd NR2 . . . . .159 D1
Gunns Cl NR13. . . . . .165 F6
Gunn's Cnr NR12 . . . . 38 D2
Gunn St NR20 . . . . 33 C3
Gun St 7 NR26 . . . . .138 C2
GUNTHORPE NR24 . . . . . . 18 B5
Gunthorpe La
 Swanton Novers NR24 . . . 18 B4
 Trunch NR28 . . . . 22 F5
Gunthorpe Rd
 Brinton NR24 . . . . 18 B6
 Gunthorpe NR21 . . . . 18 A7
 Sharrington NR21 . . . . 18 C7
 Sutton Bridge PE14 . . . . . 41 B5
 Thursford NR21 . . . . 17 F5
Gunton La NR5 . . . . .157 B2
Gunton Pk NR11 . . . . 21 E6
Gunton Rd Loddon NR14. .109 C8
 Norwich NR2 . . . . .161 F5
 Norwich NR18 . . . . .173 D4
Gunton Sta NR11 . . . . 22 B6
Gurney Cl
 9 Hopton On Sea NR31. .171 D4
 Norwich NR5 . . . . .161 B8
Gurney Ct NR5 . . . . .161 B8
Gurney Dr NR7 . . . . .159 D3
Gurney La NR4 . . . . .161 C2
Gurney Rd
 19 King's Lynn PE30 . . .146 D4
 Norwich NR1 . . . . .163 A6
 Norwich NR5 . . . . .157 A1
Gwyn Cres NR21 . . . . .141 F5
Gymkhana Way PE31. . . .133 B5
Gypsy La NR29 . . . . 69 B7

H

Habgood Cl NR13 . . . . . . .166 C4
HACKFORD NR18 . . . . 87 A5
Hackford Rd
 Hardingham NR9 . . . . 86 C6
 Wicklewood NR18 . . . . . . 87 A5
Haconsfield 8 NR9 . . . . . 88 D7
HADDISCOE NR14. . . . . . .110 F8
Haddiscoe Dam
 Haddiscoe NR14 . . . . .110 F8
 Haddiscoe NR31 . . . . .111 A8
Haddiscoe Rd NR34 . . . . .110 F6
Haddiscoe Sta NR31 . . . . 93 D1
Haddow Cl NR21. . . . . 33 C8
Hadfield Rd NR28 . . . . . . .151 B6
Hadley Cres PE31 . . . . . . .133 C5
Hadley Dr NR2 . . . . .161 F6
Hadley Rd NR26 . . . . .138 E6
Hagbech Hall Cl 2 PE14 .59 D2
Haggard's Cl IP25 . . . . 66 E3
Haggards Way NR19 . . . . 66 E6
Hagg Loke NR28 . . . . .151 E2
Haig Cl NR19 . . . . .154 D3
HAINFORD NR10. . . . . 53 E5
Hainford Prim Partnership
 Sch NR10 . . . . 53 E6
Hainford Rd NR10. . . . . 53 E7
Halcombe NR3 . . . . .158 E1
Haldane Dr
 Cringleford NR4. . . . . 71 A1
 Cringleford NR4. . . . . .161 B2
Halden Ave NR6 . . . . .157 B8
Hale Ct NR13 . . . . 73 A4

Hale Dro Littleport CB6 . . . . 96 B3
 Welney PE14 . . . . 95 E6
Hale Fen Rd CB6 . . . . 96 B1
Hale Rd Ashill IP25 . . . . . . 84 A7
 Bradenham PE33 . . . . 66 D3
 Holme Hale IP25 . . . . 66 A1
 Necton PE37 . . . . 65 F4
HALES NR14 . . . . .109 F8
Hales Cl NR30 . . . . .168 C5
Hales Cres NR15 . . . . .137 B6
HALES GREEN NR14. . . . .109 E7
Hales Hall & Gdns ★
 NR14 . . . . .109 D6
Hales St NR15 . . . . .121 A6
HALES STREET NR15 . . . .121 A6
Halesworth Rd NR34 . . . .124 E4
Haley Cl 4 PE13 . . . . .152 C8
Half Acre Cl NR27. . . . . 10 B4
Hallfield La NR18 . . . . 86 D2
Half Mile Cl NR3 . . . . .158 B2
Halfmile Drift PE25 . . . . . 66 D3
Half Mile Rd NR3 . . . . . . .158 B2
Half Moon NR3 . . . . .170 C1
Half Moon Cl IP22 . . . . . .127 E1
Halfmoon La IP27 . . . . . . .113 E2
Half Moon La IP22 . . . . . .128 E4
Half Moon Way 1 NR2. .162 B8
Halford Cl NR17 . . . . .174 D4
Halford La IP22 . . . . .129 A7
Halford Pl NR17 . . . . .174 D4
Halford Rd NR17 . . . . .174 D4
Halfpenny La
 Beetley NR20 . . . . 49 C5
 Elm PE14 . . . . 59 A2
 Wisbech PE14 . . . . .152 D1
Halfpenny Toll Rd PE14 . . 95 B8
Half Year Cl 7 NR27 . . . . 10 B5
Halifax Cres NR21. . . . . 15 C3
Haling Way IP24 . . . . .176 A4
Hallback La NR14 . . . . 90 A7
Hall Bridge Rd PE14 . . . . . 77 D5
Hall Cl Bodham NR25. . . . . . 9 A3
 Burgh St Margaret (Fleggburgh)
  NR29 . . . . 57 C1
 Fakenham NR21 . . . . .141 D4
 Heacham PE31 . . . . .133 D7
 4 Hemsby NR29 . . . . .167 A7
 5 Hethersett NR9 . . . . . 88 D7
 3 Hingham NR9 . . . . . . 86 C4
 3 Southery PE38 . . . . . . 97 B5
Hall Comm Rd NR29 . . . . . 56 C4
Hall Cres PE33 . . . . 63 C5
Hall Dike PE14 . . . . 77 F7
Hall Dr Costessey NR5 . . . .156 D2
 10 Feltwell IP26 . . . . . . 98 E1
 Honingham NR9 . . . . 69 E6
 Lakenheath IP27 . . . . .113 E2
 North Runcton PE33 . . . . . 44 A3
 Rollesby NR29 . . . . 57 C3
 Salhouse NR13 . . . . 55 A1
 Santon Downham IP27 . . .115 C6
 Stow Bardolph PE38 . . . . . 79 F8
Hall Farm Cl NR13 . . . . . . 74 F1
Hall Farm Dr IP26 . . . . 99 A6
Hall Farm Gdns PE32. . . . 44 F3
Hall Farm Pl NR9 . . . . . . .160 B6
Hall Farm Rd
 15 Gayton PE32 . . . . . . 45 C6
 Gunthorpe NR24 . . . . 18 A6
 Paston NR12 . . . . .143 F1
Hallfield Rd IP24 . . . . .102 A7
Hallfields
 Lakenheath IP27 . . . . .113 E2
 Shouldham PE33 . . . . 62 D4
Hallgate 2 NR13 . . . . 72 D6
Hall Green IP22 . . . . .121 A4
Hall Hills IP22 . . . . .177 C5
Hall La Baconsthorpe NR25. 19 F8
 Billockby NR29. . . . . 75 A8
 Binham NR21 . . . . 6 E2
 Blickling NR11 . . . . 35 F7
 Brampton NR10. . . . . 36 E3
 Bressingham IP22 . . . . . . .119 D1
 Burston & Shimpling IP21 121 A1
 Colkirk NR21 . . . . 31 E5
 Deopham NR18 . . . . 86 F4
 East Carleton NR14. . . . . . 88 E4
 East Dereham NR20 . . . . .154 F4
 East Rudham PE31 . . . . . . 30 C6
 East Ruston NR12 . . . . 24 A4
 East Tuddenham NR20. . . . 69 B6
 Felthorpe NR10 . . . . 52 E5
 Frettenham NR12 . . . . 54 B3
 Gasthorpe IP22 . . . . .127 D8
 Gunthorpe NR24 . . . . 18 A5
 Hingham NR9 . . . . 86 C5
 Horsford NR10. . . . . 53 B1
 King's Lynn PE30 . . . . . . .148 B1
 Long Stratton NR15. . . . . .106 F3
 Morley NR18 . . . . 87 B2
 Mulbarton NR14 . . . . 89 C2
 North Tuddenham NR20. . . 68 F8
 North Walsham NR28 . . . .151 D5
 Northwold IP26 . . . . 99 C7
 Postwick with Witton NR13. 72 F2
 Redgrave IP22 . . . . .128 E4
 Ringstead PE36 . . . . 2 A3
 Roydon IP22 . . . . .129 D7
 Roydon PE32 . . . . 27 F2
 Rushall IP21 . . . . .121 C1
 St Cross South Elmham
  IP20 . . . . .123 D7
 Saxlingham Nethergate
  NR15 . . . . .107 C7
 Scole IP21 . . . . .130 F8
 Shelfanger IP22 . . . . .120 B3
 Shelton NR15 . . . . .122 A8
 Suffield NR11. . . . . 21 D7
 Taverham NR8 . . . . .157 B8
 Tharston & Hapton NR15 106 F1

Hall La continued
Thompson IP24 . . . . **102** B7
Thornham PE36 . . . . **2** D6
Thursford NR21 . . . . **17** F5
Wacton NR15 . . . . **106** C1
West Winch PE33 . . . . **43** E2
Whissonsett NR20 . . . . **31** D2
Wiveton NR25 . . . . **7** C6
Wood Norton NR20 . . . . . . **33** B6
Wramplingham NR18 . . . . . **69** E1
Wramplingham NR18 . . . . . **87** E8
Hall Loke NR28 . . . . **38** C8
Hallmark Cl IP27 . . . . **113** C1
Hall Meadow NR11 . . . . . . **19** E8
Hall Moor Rd NR9 . . . . **86** C4
Hall Orchards PE32 . . . . . . **44** C3
Hallowing Cres 3 NR15 **106** B1
Hallowing La NR15 . . . . . **121** B8
Hall Plain NR30 . . . . **169** C3
Hall Rd
Aldborough NR11 . . . . **21** A4
Alderford NR9 . . . . **52** A5
Antingham NR28 . . . . **22** B2
Ashby St Mary NR14 . . . . . **91** C5
Barsham NR34 . . . . **124** F7
Barton Turf NR12 . . . . **55** E8
Bawdeswell NR20 . . . . . . **50** E7
Bedingham NR35 . . . . **108** C3
Beetley NR20 . . . . **49** D5
Blofield NR13 . . . . **165** C8
Bracon Ash NR14 . . . . **88** E4
Brockdish IP21 . . . . **131** D7
Bunwell NR16 . . . . **105** E2
Burnham Thorpe PE31 . . . . . . **4** D4
Burston & Shimpling IP22 **120** E3
Cantley NR13 . . . . **92** C8
Carleton Rode NR16 . . . . . **105** B4
Catfield NR29 . . . . **56** B8
Clenchwarton PE34 . . . . . . **26** B1
Clenchwarton PE34 . . . . . **145** D6
Cromer NR27 . . . . **139** B5
Earsham NR35 . . . . **108** D1
Earsham NR35 . . . . **123** E8
Easton NR9 . . . . **70** B5
Edingthorpe NR28 . . . . **23** B3
Ellingham NR35 . . . . **109** C3
Elsing NR20 . . . . **50** D2
Felbrigg NR27 . . . . **139** A4
Felmingham NR28 . . . . **37** A7
Fleggburgh NR29 . . . . **57** A1
Framingham Earl NR14 . . . **90** D5
Gimingham NR11 . . . . **22** D7
Great Melton NR9 . . . . **88** B8
Great Witchingham NR9 . . **51** F5
Hainford NR10 . . . . **53** E5
Hemsby NR29 . . . . **167** A7
Hoe NR20 . . . . **49** F3
Honing NR28 . . . . **38** C7
Hopton on Sea NR31 . . . **171** B6
King's Lynn PE30 . . . . **148** C1
Little Dunham PE32 . . . . . . **65** D8
Ludham NR29 . . . . **56** B4
Marthan NR29 . . . . **57** D4
Matlaske NR11 . . . . **20** E6
Mautby NR29 . . . . **76** A6
Mendham IP20 . . . . **123** B2
Northall Green NR19 . . . . . **49** F2
Northrepps NR27 . . . . **139** D2
Northrepps NR27 . . . . **139** D3
Norwich NR1 . . . . **178** B1
Norwich NR5 . . . . **157** A2
Oulton NR11 . . . . **35** B7
Outwell PE14 . . . . **77** F7
Postwick with Witton
  NR13 . . . . **165** A5
Pulham St Mary IP21 . . . **122** A4
Reedham NR13 . . . . **92** F6
Roudham NR16 . . . . **117** E6
Runhall NR20 . . . . **69** A4
Smallburgh NR12 . . . . **38** C2
Snettisham PE31 **9** **12** E5
Southrepps NR11 . . . . **22** A7
Spexhall IP19 . . . . **124** E1
Sustead NR11 . . . . **21** B7
Sutton NR12 . . . . **39** D3
Swafield NR28 . . . . **22** C5
Swanton Morley NR20 . . . . **50** A3
Tacolneston NR16 . . . . **105** E6
Tharston & Hapton NR15 **106** E5
Thurton NR14 . . . . **91** C5
Tivetshall St Margaret
  NR15 . . . . **121** B6
Toft Monks NR14 . . . . **110** D7
Trimingham NR11 . . . . **11** D1
Walpole Highway PE14 . . . **59** F8
Winfarthing IP22 . . . . **120** C5
Wingfield IP21 . . . . **131** F3
Wood Dalling NR11 . . . . . . **34** C6
Workhouse Common NR12 . **55** F7
Hall Sch NR6 . . . . **158** D5
Halls Cnr NR10 . . . . **53** B8
Halls Cnr Rd NR10 . . . . . **53** B8
Hall's Dr NR20 . . . . **49** C4
Hall's La IP25 . . . . **67** C3
Halls Meadow Cl IP26 . . . **99** A5
Hall St NR24 . . . . **142** E3
Hall Staithe NR21 . . . . . **141** B4
Hall View Rd PE30 . . . . . **147** B4
Hall Wlk NR9 . . . . **51** D5
Hallwong La IP20 . . . . . . **122** D3
Hall Wood Rd NR7 . . . . . **159** D5
Halstead Cl 2 PE13 . . . . **152** C5
Halton Rd 8 IP25 . . . . . . **84** F3
Halt Rd NR30 . . . . **168** D7
HALVERGATE NR13 . . . . . **74** F1
Halvergate Rd
Beighton NR13 . . . . **74** E1
Freethorpe NR13 . . . . **92** E8
Reedham NR13 . . . . **93** A6
Hambling's Piece NR16 **118** C4
Hamburg Way PE30 . . . . **147** A8

Hamilton Cl
North Walsham NR28 . . . **151** C5
South Walsham NR13 . . . . **74** A8
Hamilton Ct 1 NR21 . . . **141** B4
Hamilton Dr PE37 . . . . . . **153** D3
Hamilton Rd
  3 Cromer NR27 . . . . . . **139** B7
Great Yarmouth NR30 . . . **169** D7
Old Hunstanton PE36 . . . . **132** E7
Hamilton Rd W PE36 . . . . **132** E7
Hamilton Wlk 9 NR29 . . . **57** D4
Hamilton Wy NR35 . . . . . **109** B2
Hamlet Cl NR28 . . . . **151** D7
Hamlin Way PE30 . . . . . . **146** F1
Hammond Cl NR7 . . . . . . **159** E3
Hammond Rd 2 NR30 . . **169** D5
Hammond Way
Attleborough NR17 . . . . . . **174** D6
Norwich NR7 . . . . **159** E3
Hamon Cl PE36 . . . . **132** E7
Hamond Rd NR6 . . . . **157** D5
Hampden Dr 19 NR7 . . . . **72** D4
Hampden Rd 2 PE13 . . . **152** D5
Hampton Ave 3 NR14 . . . **91** E1
Hampton Cl Beeston PE32 . **48** D1
  Caister-on-Sea NR30 . . . **168** C5
HAMROW NR20 . . . . **31** D3
Hanbury Cl NR5 . . . . **161** D5
Hancock Cl 3 NR12 . . . . . **54** C7
Hancock Ct 5 NR5 . . . . . **160** E7
Handel Dr NR19 . . . . **154** F3
Handford Dr NR26 . . . . . . **138** E6
Hand La Barsham NR21 . . **16** C5
  Hoveton NR12 . . . . **164** C8
Hanging Dr IP26 . . . . **98** E6
Hanginghill NR13 . . . . **74** C6
Hankin Ct 3 NR4 . . . . . . **161** C5
Hankinson's Est PE34 . . . **42** A5
Hanly Cl NR7 . . . . **159** C2
Hanly Ct NR30 . . . . **168** D6
Hannah Cl NR26 . . . . **138** C6
Hannah Rd NR20 . . . . **50** B4
Hannant Rd NR28 . . . . . . **151** D6
Hanover Ct
Dersingham PE31 . . . . **140** E3
King's Lynn PE30 . . . . **147** D5
Hanover Gdns PE36 . . . . **132** D3
Hanover Rd NR2 . . . . **162** C4
Hanrae Ct NR26 . . . . **138** F6
Hansa Rd PE30 . . . . **146** F2
Hansard Cl NR3 . . . . **158** B1
Hansard La NR3 . . . . **178** A4
Hansard Rd NR3 . . . . **158** B1
Hansell Rd NR7 . . . . **163** F8
Hanson Cl NR7 . . . . **159** F4
Hans Pl 4 NR27 . . . . **139** B7
Hantons Loke NR13 . . . . . **74** B2
HANWORTH NR11 . . . . **21** B6
Hanworth Cross NR11 . . . **21** D5
HAPPISBURGH NR12 . . . . **24** C6
HAPPISBURGH COMMON
  NR12 . . . . **24** B4
Happisburgh Prim Sch
  NR12 . . . . **24** C5
Happisburgh Rd
East Ruston NR12 . . . . **24** A3
Lessingham NR12 . . . . **24** D4
North Walsham NR28 . . . **151** D4
Witton NR28 . . . . **23** E2
HAPTON NR15 . . . . **106** C7
Hapton CE VC Prim Sch
  NR15 . . . . **106** C7
Hapton Rd NR16 . . . . **106** B7
Harbord Cl 4 NR28 . . . . **151** C7
Harbord Cres NR30 . . . . **170** D8
Harbord Rd
Cromer NR27 . . . . **139** C5
Norwich NR4 . . . . **161** F5
Overstrand NR27 . . . . **11** A3
Harbour La IP22 . . . . **128** A7
Harbour Rd
  1 Frettenham NR12 . . . . **54** A4
Norwich NR1 . . . . **163** A5
Harbour Terr NR31 . . . . . **170** E4
Harbour Wy PE31 . . . . **3** D7
Harcourt Cl 3 NR3 . . . . **162** F8
Hardesty Cl 9 NR14 . . . . **90** D5
HARDINGHAM NR9 . . . . . . **86** E6
Hardingham Dr 6
  NR26 . . . . **138** C5
Hardingham Rd NR9 . . . . **86** D5
Hardings Wy PE30 . . . . . **146** D3
Hardlands Rd NR21 . . . . . **31** A4
Hardley Cross ★ NR14 . . . **92** E4
Hardley Hall La NR14 . . . **92** C3
Hardley Rd
Armingham NR14 . . . . **90** C5
Loddon NR14 . . . . **92** A4
Hardley St NR14 . . . . **92** B2
HARDLEY STREET NR14 . . **92** C4
HARDWICK
North Runcton PE30 . . . . . **147** B1
Shelton NR15 . . . . **122** B8
Hardwick Cl 1 NR4 . . . . **89** D8
Hardwick Ind Est PE30 . **147** A2
Hardwick Narrows NR3 . . **43** F4
Hardwick Narrows Ind Est
  PE30 . . . . **146** F1
Hardwick Rd
Bush Green IP21 . . . . **121** F6
King's Lynn PE30 . . . . **146** E2
King's Lynn PE30 . . . . **146** F2
Pulham Market IP21 . . . . . **121** F7
Shelton NR15 . . . . **122** C8
Hardy Cl
Downham Market PE38 . . . **172** B4
  1 North Walsham NR28 **151** C5
Thetford IP24 . . . . **176** D6
Hardy Dr NR14 . . . . **90** C4
Hardy Rd NR1 . . . . **163** A4

Hardy's La PE32 . . . . **46** C2
Hardys Loke NR15 . . . . . **107** D4
Harebell Rd
Attleborough NR17 . . . . . . **174** B3
Downham Market PE38 . . . **172** B3
Hare Cl 2 NR14 . . . . **89** B2
Hare Cres NR9 . . . . **88** D8
Harecroft Gdns PE30 . . . **146** E6
Harecroft Par 7 PE30 . . **146** E6
Harecroft Rd PE13 . . . . . **152** B5
Harecroft Terr PE30 . . . . **146** E6
Harefen La NR13 . . . . **74** B7
Harefens Loke NR13 . . . . . **74** B7
Harefield Rd PE34 . . . . . **116** C5
Harefields PE31 . . . . **134** D5
Hare Rd
Great & Little Plumstead
  NR13 . . . . **72** F5
West Lynn PE34 . . . . **146** C5
Hares Cl NR21 . . . . **17** C3
Harewood PE31 . . . . **134** F4
Harewood Dr
  9 King's Lynn PE30 . . . . **146** E6
  Taverham NR8 . . . . **155** E3
Harewood Par 8 NR13 . . **72** D8
Harfordbridge La NR35 . **109** A3
Harford Manor Cl NR2 . . **162** C2
Harford St NR1 . . . . **162** E3
Harfreys Ind Est
Gorleston-on-Sea NR31 . . **170** A8
Great Yarmouth NR31 . . . **169** B1
Harfrey's Rd NR31 . . . . . **170** B8
HARGATE NR16 . . . . **105** D2
Hargate La PE34 . . . . **42** B7
Hargham Cl 5 NR17 . . . **104** D2
Hargham Rd
Attleborough NR17 . . . . . . **104** A4
Attleborough NR17 . . . . . . **174** B3
Old Buckenham NR17 . . . **104** D2
Shropham NR17 . . . . **103** C3
Harkers La NR17 . . . . **50** B4
Harker Way 6 NR11 . . . . . **73** D6
HARLESTON IP20 . . . . . . **122** E2
Harleston Bypass IP20 . . **122** E1
Harleston CE VA Prim Sch
  IP20 . . . . **122** E2
Harleston Mus ★ IP20 . . **122** D2
Harleston Rd
Dickleburgh and Rushall
  IP21 . . . . **122** A1
  19 Harleston IP20 . . . . **122** D1
Pulham Market IP21 . . . . . **121** E4
Pulham St. Mary IP21 . . . **122** A3
Rushall IP21 . . . . **121** F1
Scole IP21 . . . . **121** D1
Wingfield IP21 . . . . **131** F5
Harley Rd NR30 . . . . **169** D6
Harling Dro IP27 . . . . . . **115** E7
Harling Rd
Garboldisham IP22 . . . . . . **118** C2
Hockham IP24 . . . . **102** E3
Kenninghall NR16 . . . . **118** F3
North Lopham IP22 . . . . . . **119** A2
Quidenham NR16 . . . . **118** E7
Snetterton NR16 . . . . **103** D1
Harling Rd Sta NR16 . . . **118** A6
HARLING ROAD NR16 . . . **118** A7
Harlington Ave NR6 . . . . **158** A4
Harlingwood La NR17 . . **104** E1
Harman Cl 12 NR9 . . . . . **88** D8
Harman's La IP20 . . . . . **122** C1
Harmer Cl NR28 . . . . **151** E5
Harmer Cres NR4 . . . . . . **161** C1
Harmer La NR4 . . . . **161** C1
Harmer Rd NR3 . . . . **158** D3
Harmer's La NR11 . . . . **21** B5
Harness Maker Way NR8 . **88** E8
Harnser's Reach NR13 . . **166** B8
Harp Cl NR21 . . . . **141** B5
HARPER'S GREEN NR20 . . **32** A1
Harpers La NR31 . . . . **94** C8
Harper's La NR20 . . . . **32** A1
Harp La NR11 . . . . **20** A6
HARPLEY PE31 . . . . **29** D4
Harpley CE VC Prim Sch
  PE31 . . . . **29** C4
Harpley Dams PE31 . . . . . **28** F5
Harpley Rd PE32 . . . . **30** C1
Harpsfield NR5 . . . . **160** E8
Harp's Hall Rd PE14 . . . . **59** E5
Harrier Cl 28 NR9 . . . . . **88** D8
Harrier Rd
Hopton on Sea NR31 . . . **171** D4
Old Catton NR12 . . . . **158** F7
Harrier Way 6 IP22 . . . . **177** F5
Harriet Cl PE12 . . . . **41** A8
Harriet Martineau Cl 10
  IP24 . . . . **176** D7
Harriott's Way NR11 . . . **150** B5
Harris Gn NR15 . . . . **107** C1
Harris Mews 2 NR5 . . . . **161** A7
Harrisons Dr NR7 . . . . . . **159** E3
Harrisons Yard IP22 . . . **177** D5
Harris Rd
  11 Swanton Morley NR20. . **50** B3
  12 Watton IP25 . . . . **84** F3
Harrold Cl
Heacham PE31 . . . . **133** E6
  1 South Walsham NR13 . . **74** B8
  Taverham NR8 . . . . **155** E2
Harrolds Cl PE13 . . . . **59** C3
Harrow Cl PE34 . . . . **146** C5
Harrow La
Garboldisham IP22 . . . . . . **118** C4
  8 Hethersett NR9 . . . . . . **88** C2
Hawthorne Ave
Grimston PE32 . . . . **28** B1
Hellesdon NR6 . . . . **158** A5
Sheringham NR26 . . . . **152** C8
Hawthorne Cl
  2 Loddon NR14 . . . . **91** F1
Wymondham NR18 . . . . . . **173** D6

Harry Perry Cl NR4 . . . . . **162** C2
Harry's La IP21 . . . . **121** E7
Harrys Way
Hunstanton PE36 . . . . **132** D1
Wisbech PE13 . . . . **152** D5
Harry Watson Ct NR6 . . **158** C3
Harsnett Cl NR5 . . . . **160** F8
Hartbee Rd NR6 . . . . **158** C6
Hart Ct NR7 . . . . **159** E5
Hartford Manor Sch
  NR4 . . . . **162** C2
Hartington Rd NR27 . . . . **139** D4
Hartismere High Sch
  IP23 . . . . **130** B1
Hart La NR25 . . . . **9** A2
Hartley Cl PE36 . . . . **132** D4
Hartmann Rd NR30 . . . . **170** E6
Harts Farm Rd NR18 . . . **173** E5
Harts La Cringleford NR4 . **161** C1
  Wortham IP22 . . . . **129** C4
Hart's La NR9 . . . . **160** A7
Hartwell Rd NR12 . . . . . . **164** C4
Harvard Rd 6 IP26 . . . . . **98** D1
Harvest La NR10 . . . . **53** E5
Harvest La NR21 . . . . **17** D6
Harvest Rd
Attleborough NR17 . . . . . . **174** B3
Watton IP25 . . . . **84** E3
Harvey Cl
  2 Hethersett NR9 . . . . . . **88** C7
Norwich NR7 . . . . **163** C7
Tasburgh NR15 . . . . **106** E7
Wymondham NR18 . . . . . . **173** F7
Harvey Dr NR28 . . . . **151** C7
Harvey Est NR11 . . . . **22** E7
Harvey Gn 10 NR14 . . . . . **91** F1
Harvey La
Caister-on-Sea NR30 . . . . **168** E4
Dickleburgh IP21 . . . . **121** C1
Norwich NR7 . . . . **163** C6
Harvey's La
Morningthorpe NR15 . . . . **107** A3
Seething NR15 . . . . **108** D6
Harvey St 21 IP25 . . . . . . **84** D3
Harwood Ave 4 IP24 . . . **176** E6
Harwood Rd NR1 . . . . . . **162** E1
Hase's La NR9 . . . . **51** C4
Haslips Cl 8 NR2 . . . . . . **162** C7
Haspalls Rd PE37 . . . . . . **153** B3
Hassett Cl 6 NR3 . . . . . . **162** F8
HASSINGHAM NR13 . . . . . **92** B8
Hassingham Rd
Hassingham NR13 . . . . **92** B8
Lingwood & Burlingham
  NR13 . . . . **74** A1
Hastings Ave NR6 . . . . . . **158** A4
Hastings Cl
Briston NR24 . . . . **142** A5
  6 Tasburgh NR15 . . . . . **106** F6
  12 Thetford IP24 . . . . . . **176** F5
Hastings Ct NR24 . . . . . . **142** E4
Hastings Dr PE36 . . . . . . **132** D6
Hastings La
  15 Sheringham NR26 . . . **138** D7
Wiggenhall St Germans
  PE34 . . . . **146** C5
Hastings Rd 6 IP25 . . . . . **84** F3
Hastings Way NR12 . . . . . **39** C3
Hatchett Way IP24 . . . . . **176** F7
Hatherley Gdns PE33 . . . . **81** B8
Hatton Rd NR1 . . . . **162** E3
Haugh Cnr NR16 . . . . **119** F7
Haugh Rd NR16 . . . . **119** F8
Haughs End Rd NR12 . . **164** F2
Hautbois Rd NR10 . . . . . . **37** B2
Hauteyn Ct NR6 . . . . **158** C2
Havaker The NR13 . . . . . . **92** F5
Havant Cl NR4 . . . . **161** E1
Havelock Pl 10 NR30 . . . **169** D2
Havelock Rd
Great Yarmouth NR30 . . . **169** D2
Norwich NR2 . . . . **162** B6
Sheringham NR26 . . . . **138** E5
Havergate 7 NR12 . . . . . . **54** C6
Haveringland Rd
Felthorpe NR10 . . . . **52** E6
Felthorpe NR10 . . . . **155** F8
Haverscroft Cl NR8 . . . . **155** D2
Haverscroft Ind Est
  NR17 . . . . **174** B2
Havers Rd NR3 . . . . **162** E8
HAWES' GREEN NR15 . . . **89** F2
Hawk Cl 28 NR9 . . . . **88** D8
Hawk Cres IP22 . . . . **177** F5
Hawkes La NR14 . . . . **89** B7
Hawkins Ave NR30 . . . . . **169** C8
Hawkins Cl NR30. . . . . . . **169** C8
Hawkins Dr
Dereham NR19 . . . . **154** E2
  1 Wisbech PE13 . . . . . . **152** E5
Hawk's Drove CB6 . . . . . . **95** F1
Hawthorn Ave 6 PE33 . . . **63** B4
Hawthorn Cl
Diss IP22 . . . . **177** F5
  3 Spixworth NR10 . . . . . **54** A1
  6 Watlington PE33 . . . . . **61** D5
Hawthorn Cotts PE31 . . . **140** D4
Hawthorn Cres NR31 . . . . **94** C6
Hawthorn Dr
Dersingham PE31 . . . . **140** D5
East Dereham NR19 . . . . . **154** B2
East Harling NR16 . . . . **118** D6
Ickburgh IP26 . . . . **100** B5
Sprowston NR7 . . . . **159** F3

Hawthorn Rd
  2 Downham Market
  PE38 . . . . **172** C6
Emneth PE14 . . . . **59** D1
  6 Gayton PE32 . . . . **45** C5
Great Yarmouth NR31 . . . **170** B6
Norwich NR5 . . . . **157** A2
Hawthorn Rise NR11 . . . **143** B5
Hawthorns PE30 . . . . **147** C4
Hawthorn Way
Fakenham NR21 . . . . **141** E6
Thetford IP24 . . . . **176** E6
Hawthorn Wlk 2 IP24 . . **176** F6
Haycroft 3 NR29 . . . . . . **167** B7
Hayes La NR21 . . . . **141** A5
Hayfield Rd PE30 . . . . . . **148** C4
Haygate 2 IP23 . . . . **130** C1
Hay Gn Rd PE34 . . . . **144** A1
Hay Gn Rd N PE34 . . . . . . **42** B6
Hay Gn Rd S PE34 . . . . . . **42** A5
HAY GREEN PE34 . . . . . . **144** A1
Haylett Cl NR30 . . . . **168** E5
Haylett Mws PE38. . . . . . **172** B5
Haylock Cl NR16 . . . . **105** D4
Haymarket NR2 . . . . **178** B2
Hay Mdw NR20 . . . . **49** F7
Haynton's Lane NR15 . . . **106** D2
Haystack La NR25 . . . . **6** D3
Hayhill La IP26 . . . . **98** D2
Hayward Cl 3 NR25 . . . . . **7** C6
Haywood End IP22 . . . . . **120** D6
Hazel Ave NR26 . . . . **138** D4
Hazel Cl Grimston PE32 . . **28** B1
  5 King's Lynn PE30 . . . . **148** C3
  Taverham NR8 . . . . **155** D1
  West Winch PE33 . . . . **43** E1
  Wymondham NR18 . . . . . . **173** D4
Hazel Covert IP24 . . . . . . **176** F5
Hazel Cres 4 PE33 . . . . . **63** B4
Hazel Dr 27 NR29 . . . . . . **57** D4
Hazel Gdns 1 PE13 . . . . **152** D4
Hazel Gr NR19 . . . . **154** F4
Hazel La
Great Witchingham NR10 . . **51** D7
Great Witchingham NR10 . **149** B1
Hazell Rd NR28 . . . . **151** C7
Hazel Rd
  4 Attleborough NR17 . . **174** B5
Norwich NR5 . . . . **156** F1
Hazel Way NR31 . . . . **170** B6
HEACHAM PE31 . . . . **133** E4
Heacham Hall Ind Est
  PE31 . . . . **133** E7
Heacham Inf Sch PE31 . **133** D5
Heacham Jun Sch PE31 **133** C4
Heacham Rd
Heacham PE31 . . . . **133** F5
Sedgeford PE36 . . . . **13** A7
Headington Cl NR31 . . . . **170** A5
Headland Dro IP26 . . . . . **113** A5
Headley Dr NR28. . . . . . . **151** C4
Hearne Ct 3 NR5 . . . . . . **160** E8
Heartsease La NR7. . . . . . **159** B1
Heartsease Prim Acad
  NR7 . . . . **159** C1
Heartsease Rd 3 IP24 . . **176** E5
Heartwell Rd NR27. . . . . . **139** C5
**Heartwood CE VC Prim &
  Nursery Sch** PE37 . . . . **153** C1
Heater La NR13 . . . . **73** F4
Heath Cl
  16 Horsford NR10. . . . . . **53** A3
  Lenwade NR9. . . . . **51** D5
Norwich NR6 . . . . **158** A6
Heath Cres NR6. . . . . **158** B5
Heath Dr Holt NR25. . . . . . . **8** C1
  Holt NR25. . . . . **137** D5
Heather Ave
Hemsby NR29 . . . . **167** D4
Norwich NR6 . . . . **158** A4
Heather Ave Inf Sch
  NR6 . . . . **158** B4
Heather Barrow Ct
  NR21 . . . . **141** D4
Heather Cl Hethersett NR9. **88** C8
North Walsham NR28 . . . **151** B6
North Wootton PE30 . . . . **148** D5
Heather Ct PE38 . . . . **172** A5
Heather Dr NR25. . . . . . . **137** B7
Heather Gdns NR31. . . . . . **93** F6
Heather Rd 12 NR31. . . . . **94** A6
Heather Way
Brandon IP27. . . . . **175** E3
Great Moulton NR15 . . . . **121** B8
Heatherwood Cl 7 NR13 . **72** D6
Heath Farm La NR11 . . . . **36** E6
Heath Farm Rd NR14 . . . . **90** B6
Heathfield Cl NR25. . . . . . . **8** E3
Heathfield Rd NR25 . . . . . **8** E3
Heathgate NR3 . . . . **163** A8
Heath Gn 1 NR31. . . . . . **170** B5
Heath House La PE31 . . . . **14** A1
Heath La Blofield NR13 . . **165** D8
Blundeston NR32 . . . . **93** D7
Fakenham NR21 . . . . **141** F4
Gimingham NR11 . . . . **22** D8
Great Massingham PE32 . . **46** D7
Great Witchingham NR9 . . **51** E6
Gunthorpe NR24 . . . . **18** B5
Lenwade NR9. . . . . **51** D5
Mundesley NR11 . . . . **143** B5
Quidenham NR16. . . . . . . **118** E8
Rougham PE32 . . . . **47** B6
Roughton NR11 . . . . **21** E8
Thursford NR21. . . . . **17** E4
Tittleshall PE32 . . . . **47** F7
Weasenham All Saints
  PE32 . . . . **47** D7
Heathlands
Swaffham PE37 . . . . **65** A2
Swaffham PE37 . . . . **153** D2

Heathlands Dr IP24 . . . . **176** D8
Heath Plantation La
  NR21 . . . . **17** F5
Heath Rd
Ashby with Oby NR29 . . . . **57** B2
Attleborough NR17 . . . . . . **104** A3
Banham NR16 . . . . **119** E7
Brandon IP27. . . . . **175** D3
Catfield NR29 . . . . **56** D8
Coney Weston IP31. . . . . . **127** A4
Corpusty NR11. . . . . **19** D1
Crostwight NR28 . . . . **38** C8
Dersingham PE31. . . . . **27** E8
Dersingham PE31. . . . . . . **140** D2
East Dereham NR19 . . . . . **154** C7
Felmingham NR28 . . . . **37** B8
Fritton & St Olaves NR31 . . **93** E1
Gateley NR20. . . . . **32** D2
Geldeston NR34. . . . . **110** A3
Gunthorpe NR24 . . . . **18** B5
Heydon NR11. . . . . **34** D8
Hickling NR12 . . . . **39** E1
Hockering NR20. . . . . **69** B8
Honing NR28 . . . . **23** E1
Honing NR28 . . . . **38** D7
Kenninghall NR16 . . . . **119** A3
Knettishall IP22 . . . . **127** C7
Lessingham NR12 . . . . **24** F2
Lyng NR9 . . . . **51** A4
North Walsham NR28 . . . **151** C5
Norwich NR3 . . . . **162** D8
Quidenham NR16. . . . . . . **118** D7
Quidenham NR16. . . . . . . **118** E8
Rollesby NR29 . . . . **57** B2
Sapiston IP31. . . . . **126** B3
Sheringham NR26 . . . . **138** D6
Shotesham NR15. . . . . . . **107** F8
  9 Thorpe End NR13 . . . . **72** D6
West Raynham PE32 . . . . . . **30** A3
Winfarthing IP22. . . . . . . **120** A7
Heath Rise
Fakenham NR21. . . . . **141** E4
Sculthorpe Airfield PE31 . **15** B3
Heathside Rd NR1 . . . . . **163** B5
HEATH THE
Fakenham NR21 . . . . **141** F4
Hevingham NR10. . . . . **53** A8
Stratton Strawless NR10. . **53** F8
Heath The
Hevingham NR10 . . . . **52** F8
Troston IP31 . . . . **126** B1
Heath Way
Blofield NR13 . . . . **73** C6
Fakenham NR21 . . . . **141** F4
Hebrides Way NR30. . . . . **168** C6
Hecham Rd NR29 . . . . . . **168** C8
HECKFIELD GREEN
  IP21 . . . . **131** B2
HECKINGHAM NR14. . . . . . **92** C1
Heckingham Holes NR14 . **92** B1
Heckingham Pk Dr
  NR14 . . . . **109** F8
HEDENHAM NR35. . . . . . . **108** E4
Hedgehog Wlk NR12 . . . . **24** E4
Hedgelands 1 PE13 . . . . **152** C8
Hedgemere 1 NR8 . . . . . **155** D2
Hedgerows The 8 NR5 . . **161** A7
Hedley La NR33. . . . . **111** F1
Heffer Cl NR19 . . . . **154** D3
Heggatt Rd NR12 . . . . **54** C5
Heggatt St NR12 . . . . **54** D5
Heidi Cl 7 NR19 . . . . **154** D3
Heigham Gr NR2. . . . . . . **162** C6
Heigham Rd NR2 . . . . . . **162** B6
Heighams La IP22 . . . . . . **128** B3
Heigham St NR2 . . . . **162** B6
Heigham Watering 5
  NR2 . . . . **162** B8
Heights The NR1. . . . . . . **163** B5
Heisker Gdns 9 NR1. . . . **177** A4
Helena Anderson Ct
  PE30. . . . . **147** A6
Helena Rd Norwich NR2 . **162** B6
Witton NR12 . . . . **23** F3
Helen Ave 7 NR29. . . . . . **57** C4
Helens Cl IP22. . . . . **128** E4
Helford St 6 NR2 . . . . . . **162** B8
HELHOUGHTON NR21. . . . . **30** E5
Helhoughton Rd
Hempton NR21 . . . . **31** C7
West Raynham NR21. . . . . . **30** E4
HELLESDON NR6. . . . . **157** F5
Hellesdon Cl NR5 . . . . . . **161** D6
Hellesdon Hall Ind Est
  NR6 . . . . **157** E3
Hellesdon Hall Rd NR6 . **157** E1
Hellesdon High Sch
  NR6 . . . . **157** E4
Hellesdon Hospl NR6. . . **157** D4
Hellesdon Mill La
Costessey NR6 . . . . **157** D2
Norwich NR6. . . . . **157** D1
Hellesdon Pk Rd NR6 . . . **157** E3
Hellesdon Rd NR6 . . . . . **161** D8
Hellgate La NR11 . . . . **20** F8
HELLINGTON NR14. . . . . . **91** B6
Hellington Cnr NR14. . . . . **91** B5
Hellington Hill NR14 . . . . **91** B6
Hellpit La NR24 . . . . **19** B2
Hell Pit La NR24 . . . . . . **142** F2
Helsinki Way NR19. . . . . **154** C2
Helska Leisure Ctr NR12 . **55** E3
HEMBLINGTON NR13 . . . . . **73** E6
HEMBLINGTON CORNER
  NR13 . . . . **73** D6
Hemblington Hall Rd
  NR13 . . . . **73** E6

Hemblington Prim Sch
NR13 . . . . .73 C6
Hemblington Rd NR13 . . .73 E4
Hemington Cl PE30 . . . .147 D8
Hemlin Cl NR5. . . . . . . .161 C6
Hemmant Way NR34 . . .110 B3
Hemmings Cl 4 NR5. . . .160 F7
Hemming Wy NR3 . . . . .158 B1
Hemnell Pl NR14. . . . . . .89 C5
Hempit La NR24 . . . . . . .18 C3
Hempland Cl PE31 . . . . . . .3 B6
HEMPNALL NR15 . . . . . .107 D5

HEMPNALL GREEN
NR15 . . . . .107 D4
Hempnall Prim Sch
NR15 . . . . .107 C5
Hempnall Rd
Hedenham NR35 . . . . . 108 D4
Woodton NR35 . . . . . . .108 A4

HEMPSTEAD
Hempstead NR25 . . . . . . .19 E8
Lessingham NR12 . . . . . .24 E3
Hempstead Rd
Edgefield NR11 . . . . .19 D6
Hempstead NR11 . . . . . .19 E8
Holt NR25 . . . . .137 D5
Lessingham NR12 . . . . . .24 D3
Plumstead NR11 . . . . . . .19 F6
Plumstead NR11 . . . . . . .20 A6
Hempsted Mews 4
NR5 . . . . .160 E7
HEMPTON NR21 . . . . . .141 A3
Hempton Green Rd
Hempton NR21 . . . . .31 D7
Hempton NR21 . . . . . . .141 A2
Hempton Rd
Fakenham NR21 . . . . . .141 E4
Toftrees NR21 . . . . .31 B6
HEMSBY NR29 . . . . . . .167 A4
Hemsby Prim Sch NR29 167 A7
Hemsby Rd
13 Marthan NR29 . . . . . .57 D4
Winterton-on-Sea NR29 . .58 B5
Henby Way NR3 . . . . . .163 D7
Henderson Green Prim Sch
NR5 . . . . .161 E7
Henderson Rd NR4 . . . .161 F5
Hendon Ave
13 Watton IP25 . . . . .84 F3
Watton IP25 . . . . .85 A3
Hendon Cl NR5 . . . . . . .157 B1
Hendrie Rd NR25 . . . . . .137 C7
Hendry Gdns NR18 . . . .173 F7
HENGRAVE NR9 . . . . . . .52 A6
Henley Rd NR2 . . . . . . .162 A4
Hennessey's Loke NR28 . .23 A3
Henry Bell Cl PE30 . . . .147 A5
Henry Cross Cl 1 IP25 . . .67 C2
Henry Page Rd NR11 . . .150 B5
Henry Preston Rd 1
NR15 . . . . .106 F6
Henry's St 1 IP25 . . . . . .84 F3
Henry St PE13 . . . . .152 C5
Henry Warby Ave 7
PE14 . . . . .59 A1
Henry Ward Rd 1 IP20 .122 D2
Henson Cl 3 PE13 . . . . .152 C8
Henstead Rd NR9 . . . . . .88 D8
HEPWORTH IP22 . . . . . .127 E1
Hepworth Rd IP31 . . . . .127 D3
Herbert Colman Cl NR13 .73 D7
Herbert Dr IP26 . . . . .98 F5
Herbert Nursery Cl NR8 .157 C7
Herbert Ward Way
PE34 . . . . .144 D6
Hercules Cl NR6 . . . . . .157 F4
Hercules Dr PE37 . . . . .153 D5
Hercules Rd NR6 . . . . . .157 F4
Hereford Way PE33 . . . . .43 E4
Hereward Rd 1 PE13 . . .152 D5
Hereward Way
5 Feltwell IP26 . . . . . . .98 D1
Weeting IP27 . . . . .175 A8
Weeting-with-Broomhill
IP27 . . . . .114 E8
Herman Mid Sch NR31 . .170 A3
Hermanus Leisure Ctr
NR29 . . . . .58 B6
Hermitage Cl
3 Acle NR13 . . . . .166 D4
9 Wisbech PE13 . . . . .152 E6
Herne Cotts NR19 . . . . . .67 D5
Herne Dro PE14 . . . . .95 D5
Herne La
Beeston with Bittering
PE32 . . . . .48 C1
Shipdham NR19 . . . . . . .67 D5
Herolf Way 11 IP20 . . . .122 D2
Heron Ave IP27 . . . . . . .175 E3
Heron Cl
Downham Market PE38 . .172 C7
6 Fakenham NR21 . . . .141 E4
Great Yarmouth NR31 . . .170 A7
10 Salhouse NR13 . . . . .55 A1
Salhouse NR13 . . . . .55 B1
Sprowston NR7 . . . . . . .159 E5
Heron Gdns NR12 . . . . . .39 B3
Heron La PE14 . . . . .146 E2
Heron Rd Costessey NR8 .156 B5
Wisbech PE13 . . . . .152 D2
Heron Rise NR18 . . . . . .173 D2
Heron Vale PE31 . . . . . . .10 B5
Heron Way Hickling NR12 . .39 E1
Necton PE37 . . . . .66 A3
12 Watton IP25 . . . . .84 C3
Herrick Rd NR8 . . . . . . .156 E8
Herries Cl 7 NR30 . . . . .169 C4

HERRINGFLEET NR32 . . .111 D8
Herringfleet Rd NR31 . . .93 E2
Herring La NR9 . . . . .69 A1
Herring's La PE31 . . . . . .135 C4
Hertford Way NR31 . . . .170 B4
HETHEL NR14 . . . . .88 F3
Hethel Old Thorn Nature
Reserve★ NR14 . . . . . . .88 E3
Hethel Rd NR16 . . . . . . .88 D2
HETHERSETT NR9 . . . . . .88 D8
Hethersett Acad NR9 . . .88 D8
Hethersett La NR4 . . . . .160 F3
Hethersett Rd
East Carleton NR14 . . . . .88 C5
Great Melton NR9 . . . . . .88 B8
Hethersett VC Prim Sch
NR9 . . . . .88 D7
Hethersett Woodside Prim
Sch NR9 . . . . .88 D8
Hettie Cl NR25 . . . . .7 C6
HEVINGHAM NR10 . . . . .53 B7
Hevingham Prim Sch
NR10 . . . . .53 B8
Hewett Acad The NR1 . .162 D2
Hewett Cl NR31 . . . . . . .170 D2
Hewett Rd NR31 . . . . . .170 A8
Hewitt Cl 18 NR14 . . . . . .90 C5
Hewitt Dr NR20 . . . . . . .68 D6
Hewitts Cl NR24 . . . . . .142 E4
Hewitts La NR18 . . . . . .173 C5
Hextable Rd PE30 . . . . .146 E6
HEYDON NR11 . . . . .34 F6
Heydon Hall★ NR11 . . . . .34 F6
Heydon La
Southgate NR11 . . . . . . .35 A4
Wood Dalling NR11 . . . . .34 E7
Heydon Rd
Aylsham NR11 . . . . .150 A7
Aylsham NR11 . . . . .150 C7
Cawston NR11 . . . . .35 A4
Corpusty NR11 . . . . .34 F8
Heydon NR11 . . . . .35 A5
Salle NR10 . . . . .149 E8
Salle NR11 . . . . .34 F4
Wood Dalling NR11 . . . . .34 D6
Wood Dalling NR11 . . . . .34 E6
Heyford Rd NR6 . . . . . . .158 C6
Heywood Ave IP22 . . . . .177 D6
Heywood Rd Diss IP22 . . .177 D6
Shelfanger IP22 . . . . . . .120 C2
Tibenham NR16 . . . . . . .120 D6
Winfarthing IP22 . . . . . .120 C4
Heywood The
Burston & Shimpling
IP22 . . . . .120 E5
Heywood IP22 . . . . .120 D3
Hickathrift Field PE14 . . .61 A4
HICKLING NR12 . . . . . . .39 F3
Hickling Broad National
Nature Reserve★ NR12 . .57 A8
Hickling Broad Visitor Ctr★
NR12 . . . . .40 A1
Hickling CE VC Inf Sch
NR12 . . . . .39 F2
Hickling Cl PE37 . . . . . .153 C2
HICKLING GREEN NR12. . .39 E1
HICKLING HEATH NR12. . .39 E1
Hickling La NR14 . . . . . . .89 D4
Hickling Rd
Sea Palling NR12 . . . . . . .24 F1
Sutton NR12 . . . . .39 C2
Hickling Way NR29 . . . .167 B3
Hickory Gdns 13 NR31 . . .94 C7
Hickory Rd NR25 . . . . . .147 C5
Higdon Cl IP22 . . . . . . .120 E2
Higham Cl NR7 . . . . . . .159 A3
Higham Gn 3 PE30 . . . .147 C4
High Ash IP26 . . . . .100 B7
High Ash La NR14 . . . . . .90 A6
High Ash Rd NR18 . . . . . .88 C5
High Banks NR18 . . . . . .173 C3
Highbridge Gravel Dro
IP27 . . . . .113 D2
Highbridge Rd PE34 . . . .78 F8
High Bridgham Rd
NR16 . . . . .117 C5
High Bungay Rd NR14. . .109 D8
Highbury Rd IP27 . . . . . .175 A2
High Comm NR18 . . . . . .87 D2
HIGH COMMON IP25 . . . .85 F8
High Common
Cranworth IP25 . . . . .67 F1
High Common IP25 . . . . .85 F8
High Common Rd IP22. . .118 F1
High Comm Rd IP22 . . . .128 C8
High Cross NR20 . . . . . . .33 A2
High Ct IP20 . . . . .122 E2
Higher Gn Cl 7 NR15 . . .89 D1
High Fen Dro IP27 . . . . . .98 D8
Highfield 3 Eye IP23 . . .130 C1
Field Dalling NR25 . . . . . .7 B2
Great & Little Plumstead
NR13 . . . . .73 B7
King's Lynn PE30 . . . . . .147 C5
Highfield Ave
Brundall NR13 . . . . .165 D3
Swaffham PE37 . . . . . . .153 A5
Highfield Cl
Foulsham NR20 . . . . .33 C4
North Lopham IP22 . . . .119 A2
1 Norwich NR7 . . . . . . .72 D3
Ryburgh NR21 . . . . .32 A6
Highfield La
Brooke NR15 . . . . .108 A8
Ryburgh NR21 . . . . .32 A6
Highfield Rd
East Dereham NR19 . . . .154 D8
Fakenham NR21 . . . . . .141 B5
Great Yarmouth NR31 . . .170 C7
Overstrand NR27 . . . . . . .11 B3
Taverham NR8 . . . . .155 F1

Highfields
Felmingham NR28 . . . . . .37 A8
Holly End PE14 . . . . .59 D1
Lakenheath IP27 . . . . . .113 F1
Norwich NR5 . . . . .156 D1
Tharston and Hapton
NR15 . . . . .106 D4
Woodton NR35 . . . . . . .108 C4
Highfields Mdw NR20 . . .49 B6
Highfield Way 4 NR12 . . .54 C7
Highgate PE30 . . . . .146 E5
Highgate Inf Sch PE30. . .146 F6
High Gn Brooke NR15 . . .90 D1
5 Great Moulton NR15 .106 B8
1 Great Moulton NR15 .106 B8
Great Moulton NR15 . . .121 B8
Norwich NR1 . . . . .163 B5
High Gn Gdns NR15 . . . .90 D1

HIGH GREEN
Bradenham IP25 . . . . . . .66 E2
Fransham NR19 . . . . .48 E1
Great Melton NR9 . . . . . .88 B8
Highgrove Ct NR14 . . . . .90 C6
High Hatter's Cl PE38 . . .172 C3
High Hill Rd NR12 . . . . . .38 F6
High House Ave 3
NR18 . . . . .173 D5
High House Cotts PE32 . . .47 E5
High House La 8 NR13 . . .73 D6
High House Rd NR20 . . . .49 C4
HIGH KELLING NR25 . . . . .8 E3
Highland NR14 . . . . .90 B6
Highland Ave NR2 . . . . .162 A4
Highland Cl NR13 . . . . . .92 C6
Highland Cres NR14 . . . .163 B2
Highland Rd
Norwich NR2 . . . . .162 A4
Taverham NR8 . . . . .155 D1
Highlands Costessey NR8 .156 F4
Thetford IP24 . . . . .176 D5
High Lodge Forest Ctr★
IP27 . . . . .115 C3
High London La IP22 . . .120 A4
Highlow Rd NR5 . . . . . . .157 A1
High Mill Rd NR31 . . . . .169 B3
Highmoor Dro
Foulden IP26 . . . . .81 F1
Foulden IP26 . . . . .82 A1
Foulden IP26 . . . . .99 D8
High Noon La
Hemblington NR13 . . . . . .73 E6
Hemblington NR13 . . . . . .73 F6
High Noon Rd
Erpingham NR11 . . . . . . .21 B2
Erpingham NR11 . . . . . . .21 D2
HIGHOAK NR18 . . . . .87 B4
High Oak La NR18 . . . . . .87 B4
High Oak Rd NR18 . . . . . .87 B3
High Rd Beighton NR13 . .74 B1
Bressingham IP22 . . . . . .129 C8
Briston NR24 . . . . .142 F3
Burgh Castle NR31 . . . . . .94 B8
Cantley NR13 . . . . .92 B8
Forncett NR16 . . . . .106 D6
Great Yarmouth NR31 . . .170 D7
Lessingham NR12 . . . . . .24 C2
Needham IP20 . . . . .131 E7
Repps with Bastwick NR29 .57 A4
Roydon IP22 . . . . .177 A5
Tilney St Lawrence PE34 . .60 F8
Toprow NR15 . . . . .106 B8
Wiggenhall St Germans
PE34 . . . . .42 F1
Wiggenhall St Germans
PE34 . . . . .60 F6
Wortwell IP20 . . . . .122 F3
Wortwell IP20 . . . . .123 A3
High St
Attleborough NR17 . . . .174 D5
Blakeney NR25 . . . . .7 C6
Brandon IP27 . . . . .175 C5
Caister-on-Sea NR30 . . .168 E5
Castle Acre PE32 . . . . . . .46 F2
Cawston NR10 . . . . .35 B3
Cley next the Sea NR25 . . .7 E6
Coltishall NR12 . . . . .54 C7
Cromer NR27 . . . . .139 B7
Docking PE31 . . . . .134 E4
Downham Market PE38 . .172 C5
East Dereham NR19 . . . .154 D5
Feltwell IP26 . . . . .98 E1
Fincham PE33 . . . . .62 E1
Foulsham NR20 . . . . .33 D3
Great Yarmouth NR31 . . .170 D6
Heacham PE31 . . . . .133 D5
Hilgay PE38 . . . . .79 E1
Holt NR25 . . . . .137 B6
Hopton IP22 . . . . .127 F6
Hunstanton PE36 . . . . . .132 C4
Ketteringham NR18 . . . . .88 D5
Ketteringham NR18 . . . . .88 E6
King's Lynn PE30 . . . . . .146 D5
Lakenheath IP27 . . . . . .113 E1
Little London NR10 . . . . .35 F2
Loddon NR14 . . . . .92 A1
Ludham NR29 . . . . .56 C5
Marsham NR10 . . . . . . .150 C1
Methwold IP26 . . . . .99 A5
Mundesley NR11 . . . . . .143 C5
Nordelph PE38 . . . . .78 E3
North Elmham NR20 . . . .49 E8
Northwold IP26 . . . . .99 C7
Overstrand NR27 . . . . . . .11 A3
Ringstead PE36 . . . . .2 A3
St Margaret, Ilketshall
NR35 . . . . .124 D3
5 Sheringham NR26 . . .138 D7
Shipdham IP25 . . . . .67 B2
Southrepps NR11 . . . . . . .22 B7
Stalham NR12 . . . . .39 B4
Stoke Ferry PE33 . . . . . . .81 A2

High St continued
Sutton Bridge PE12 . . . . .41 C8
Thelnetham IP22 . . . . . .128 B4
Thornham PE36 . . . . .2 D6
Thursford NR21 . . . . .17 D5
Tittleshall PE32 . . . . .48 B8
Upper Street NR12 . . . . . .38 A3
Walsingham NR22 . . . . . .16 F7
Watton IP25 . . . . .84 D3
Wells-next-the-Sea NR23 .136 D5
Whissonsett NR20 . . . . . .31 D2
Wicklewood NR18 . . . . . .87 B5
Wighton NR23 . . . . .5 F2
Wisbech PE13 . . . . .152 C5
High Starlings NR16 . . . .119 B6
HIGH STREET NR35 . . . .124 D3
High Terr NR21 . . . . . . .141 C6
High Tree Cl IP24 . . . . . .116 C5
Highview PE32 . . . . .65 D5
Highview Cl NR13 . . . . . .165 E6
High View Dr NR17 . . . . .174 B4
Highview Pk NR27 . . . . .139 C4
High Way 18 NR13 . . . . . .74 A3
High Wrong Cnr IP24 . . .115 C1
Hilary Ave NR1 . . . . . . .163 B8
Hilary Cl 6 NR13 . . . . . . .74 A3
HILBOROUGH IP26 . . . . .83 A3
Hilborough Rd
North Pickenham PE37 . . .65 D1
North Pickenham PE37 . . .83 D8
Hilda Brooks Wy NR5 . . .157 B2
Hilda Raker Cl IP24 . . . .117 B8
Hilda Rd NR11 . . . . .143 C6
HILGAY PE38 . . . . .79 E1
Hilgay Rd Ryston PE38 . . .79 F3
West Dereham PE33 . . . . .80 A4
Hilgay Village Prim Sch
PE38 . . . . .79 E1
Hillary Rd IP24 . . . . . . .176 C2
Hill Ave NR31 . . . . .170 D1
Hill Comm NR12 . . . . . . .39 F1
Rickinghall Inferior IP22 . .128 D3
Wattisfield IP22 . . . . . . .128 B1
Hindle The IP22 . . . . . . .127 F2
HINDOLVESTON NR20 . . .33 D8
Hindolveston Rd
Foulsham NR20 . . . . .33 D4
Fulmodeston NR21 . . . . . .17 F1
Guestwick NR20 . . . . . . .33 F6
Hindolveston NR21 . . . . .33 B8
Melton Constable NR24. . .18 D3
Melton Constable NR24. .142 A4
Thurning NR20 . . . . .34 A8
HINDRINGHAM NR21. . . .17 E7
Hindringham CE Prim Sch
NR21 . . . . .17 D7
Hindringham Rd
Binham NR21 . . . . .6 E2
Gunthorpe NR21 . . . . . . .18 A7
Thursford NR21 . . . . .17 E5
Walsingham NR22 . . . . . .17 A8
HINGHAM NR9 . . . . .86 C5
Hingham Prim Sch NR9. . .86 C5
Hingham Rd
Deopham NR18 . . . . .86 F5
Garvestone NR9 . . . . .86 C8
Great Ellingham NR17 . . .103 E8
Hardingham NR9 . . . . . . .86 E6
Little Ellingham NR17 . . . .86 A2
Hingley Cl NR31 . . . . . . .170 C8
Hinks Cl NR10 . . . . .155 C3
Hinshalwood Way NR8 . .156 E4
Hipkin Rd PE31 . . . . . . .140 C3
Hipperson Cl 2 NR28 . . .151 C7
Hippodrome★ NR30 . . .169 E3
Hobart Cl NR18 . . . . . . .173 C6
Hobart High Sch NR14. . .92 A1
Hobart La Aylsham NR11 .150 A5
Norwich NR1 . . . . .178 B1
Hobart 17 NR14 . . . . . . .91 F1
Hobart Sq NR1 . . . . . . .178 B1
Hobb's La
Cantley NR13 . . . . .92 D7
Woodton NR15 . . . . . . .108 D6
Hobbs's La NR15 . . . . . .108 D7
Hobby Dr NR18 . . . . . . .173 D1
Hobland Rd
Belton with Browston
NR31 . . . . .94 C4
Bradwell NR31 . . . . .171 A7
Hobrough La NR1 . . . . . .178 C2
HOCKERING NR20 . . . . . .69 B8
Hockering CE VC Prim Sch
NR20 . . . . .69 B8
HOCKERING HEATH
NR20 . . . . .51 C1
Hockering La NR9 . . . . . .160 B6
Hockering Rd NR9 . . . . . .51 D2
Hockham Rd
Croxton IP24 . . . . .116 D4
Great Hockham NR17 . . .102 F4
Stonebridge IP24 . . . . . .102 B3
Hockham St PE30 . . . . .146 D5
HOCKWOLD CUM WILTON
IP26 . . . . .114 A7
Hockwold & Methwold Com
Sch IP26 . . . . .99 A6
Hockwold Rd
Weeting IP27 . . . . .114 D7
Weeting IP27 . . . . .175 B7
Hodgson Rd NR4 . . . . . .161 F5
HOE NR20 . . . . .49 F3
Hoe Hall NR20 . . . . .49 E3
Hoe Rd Hoe NR20 . . . . . .49 F5
Hoe Rd E NR20 . . . . .50 A4
Hoe Rd N NR20 . . . . .50 A3
Hoe Rd S NR20 . . . . .50 A4

Hoe Rough Nature Reserve★
NR20 . . . . .49 E4
Hogarth Cl 18 NR13 . . . . .94 C8
Hogarth Rd PE38 . . . . . .172 E6
Hog Bog La NR10 . . . . . .53 F3
Hogg La NR35 . . . . .108 C1
Hogg's Dro PE33. . . . . . . .63 B5
Hogherd's La 9 PE13 . . .152 C5
Hog La NR34 . . . . .124 F2
Hogspond La
Denver PE38 . . . . .79 D3
Denver PE38 . . . . .172 B1
Hogsty La IP21 . . . . .122 A1
Holbrigg La NR21 . . . . . .17 C1
Holcombe Ave PE30 . . . .146 F3
Holders La IP26 . . . . .99 A7
Hole Farm Rd NR11 . . . . .19 D6
Holgate Hill NR25 . . . . . . .8 D4
Holgate La 5 NR27 . . . . .10 B5
Holgate Rd
North Walsham NR28 . . .151 F1
South Creake NR21 . . . . .15 C7
HOLKHAM NR23 . . . . .5 B6
Holkham Ave PE37 . . . . .153 B2
Holkham Cl 7 PE38 . . . .172 C6
Holkham Est Holkham NR23 .5 A4
New Holkham NR23 . . . . . .5 B6
Holkham Gn NR21 . . . . . .30 C4
Holkham Hall & Bygones
Mus★ NR23 . . . . .5 A5
Holkham National Nature
Reserve★ NR23 . . . . .5 B8
Holkham Rd NR23 . . . . .136 B6
Holland Ct 8 NR19 . . . . .154 D1
Holland's La NR35 . . . . .108 C3
Holley Wlk NR11 . . . . . .150 C4
Hollies The
Clenchwarton PE34 . . . .145 D5
5 North Walsham NR28 .151 C5
Hollingdale Ct NR12 . . . .39 C3
Holl La Billingford NR20. . .50 B7
Garvestone NR9 . . . . .68 B1
Holloway Rd NR14 . . . . . .91 B8
Hollow Hill Rd NR35 . . . .109 A4
Hollow La
Barningham IP31 . . . . . .127 D4
4 Langham NR25 . . . . . . .7 A4
Langmere IP21 . . . . .131 A8
Raynham NR21 . . . . .30 F3
Shotesham NR15 . . . . . . .89 F2
Stiffkey NR23 . . . . .6 D6
Hollow Tree Way NR24 . .142 E3
Hollow Way Hill NR34 . . .110 D4
Holl Rd NR11 . . . . .21 B4
Holls La NR15 . . . . .178 B1
Hollway La NR20 . . . . . . .33 A4
Holly Ave 12 Elm PE14 . . .59 A1
Great Yarmouth NR31 . . .94 C7
Holly Bank NR7 . . . . . . .159 A2
Holly Blue Mews NR8 . . .156 B6
Holly Blue Rd NR18 . . . .173 E4
Hollybush Rd NR28 . . . . .151 F5
Holly Cl Dereham NR19 . .172 B6
Holt NR25 . . . . .137 D7
King's Lynn PE30 . . . . . .148 D2
12 Loddon NR14 . . . . . . .91 F1
14 Marthan NR29 . . . . . .57 D4
Mattishall NR20 . . . . .68 E6
Rougham PE32 . . . . .47 B7
1 West Winch PE33 . . . . .43 E2
Holly Close NR32 . . . . . . .47 B7
Hollycroft Cl PE14 . . . . . .59 D1
Hollycroft Rd PE14 . . . . . .77 D8
Holly Ct
34 Harleston IP20 . . . . . .122 D2
Swaffham PE13 . . . . . . .153 C4
Wymondham NR18 . . . . .173 E6
Holly Dr NR2 . . . . .162 A7
HOLLY END PE14 . . . . . . .59 D1
Hollyend Ct PE14 . . . . . . .59 D1
Holly Farm Rd NR13 . . . . .93 A4
Holly Gr NR26 . . . . .138 C5
Holly Hill NR36 . . . . .13 A7
Holly La Blofield NR13 . . .165 D7
Horsford NR10 . . . . .157 D8
Kerdiston NR10 . . . . .34 C4
Reepham NR10 . . . . .149 A7
9 Tharston & Hapton
NR15 . . . . .106 D3
Wood Dalling NR11 . . . . .34 D5
Holly Meadows Sch PE32 .28 B1
Hollyoaks The NR18 . . . . .87 C1
Holly Rd NR17 . . . . .174 C4
Holly Tree La PE14 . . . . . .78 A5
Holly Way 13 NR31 . . . . .170 B6
Hollywell Gdns PE13 . . . .153 B4
Holman Cl NR11 . . . . . . .150 B7
Holman Rd NR11 . . . . . .150 B6
Holman's Chase PE38. . . .97 B6
Holme Ave NR4 . . . . .89 A8
Holme Cl Hopton IP22. . .127 C6
Runcton Holme PE33 . . . .61 D4
Holme Dunes National
Nature Reserve★ PE36. . . .2 A8
HOLME HALE IP25 . . . . . .66 B2
HOLME NEXT THE SEA
PE36. . . . . .2 A6
Holme Oak Gdns PE37 . .153 C3
Holme Rd Ringstead PE36. . .2 A4
Stow Bridge PE34 . . . . . .61 D2
Holmes Cl Acle NR13. . . .166 B4
Norwich NR7 . . . . .163 D8
Holmes Ct NR14 . . . . . . .90 C4
Holmesdale Rd NR11 . . .150 B7
Holmes Dr PE13 . . . . . . .152 E5
Holmes Rd
East Ruston NR12 . . . . . .38 F5

Holmes Rd continued
East Somerton NR29 . . . . . .58 A8
Somerton NR29 . . . . .57 F7
Holmes's La IP26 . . . . .99 A6
Holmwood Rise NR7 . . .163 C6
HOLT NR25 . . . . .137 D6
Holt Com Prim Sch
NR25 . . . . .137 B5
Holt Ct PE14 . . . . .41 E3
Holt Ctry Pk* NR25 . . . . .137 C4
Holt La NR25 . . . . .7 C3
Holt House La PE32 . . . . . .44 D5
Holt Rd Aylmerton NR11 . . . . 10 B3
Briningham NR24 . . . . .142 A8
Briston NR24 . . . . .142 E5
Cawston NR10 . . . . .35 D2
Cley next the Sea NR25 . . . . .7 E6
Cley Next the Sea NR25 . . . .8 A5
Corpusty & Saxthorpe NR24 34 F7
Cromer NR27 . . . . .139 A6
Edgefield NR25 . . . . .137 C2
Fakenham NR21 . . . . .141 C4
Felthorpe NR10 . . . . .52 F6
Field Dalling NR25 . . . . .7 B2
Gresham NR11 . . . . .9 E1
Guist NR20 . . . . .32 F4
Hempstead NR25 . . . . .137 F4
Hindolveston NR20 . . . . .18 B1
Hoe NR19 . . . . .154 C8
Horsford NR10 . . . . .53 B1
Hunworth NR24 . . . . .19 B6
Kelling NR25 . . . . .8 C4
Langham NR25 . . . . .7 A4
Letheringsett NR25 . . . . .7 E1
Letheringsett with Glandford
NR25 . . . . .8 A1
Little Snoring NR21 . . . . . . .17 C3
Melton Constable NR24 . .142 A5
Newgate NR25 . . . . .7 F5
North Elmham NR20 . . . . . .49 C7
Norwich NR10 . . . . .157 H8
Sheringham NR26 . . . . . . .138 B5
Stibbard NR20 . . . . .32 F6
Stody NR25 . . . . .137 A1
Thornage NR25 . . . . .18 F7
Thursford NR21 . . . . .17 F5
Upper Sheringham NR26. .138 C3
Walsingham NR22 . . . . .16 F7
Weybourne NR25 . . . . .8 E5
Holt's La PE38 . . . . .79 D1
Holt Sta NR25 . . . . .137 E8
Holway Cl NR27 . . . . .139 B3
Holway Rd NR26 . . . . .138 D5
Holway The NR29 . . . . .58 B6
Holworthy Rd NR5 . . . . . .161 B8
Holy Rd NR24 . . . . .18 D5
Holyrood Dr PE31 . . . . . . .140 D3
Homebred La [1] NR14 . . . 91 F1
Home Cl
Great Ellingham NR17 . . . .103 E8
Lyng NR9 . . . . .51 A4
[5] Sheringham NR27 . . . . .10 A5
Homecroft NR9 . . . . .160 B2
Home Farm Cl NR20 . . . . . .50 B2
Home Farm La NR18 . . . . .104 E8
Home Farm Rd NR35 . . . . .109 C3
Home Farm Rise NR25 . . . . .8 E6
Homefield Ave NR1 . . . . . . .94 C7
Homefield La NR24 . . . . . . .18 B5
Homefields La PE36. . . . . . .132 D4
Homefield VC Prim Sch
NR31 . . . . .94 C7
Home La Hilborough IP25 . . 83 B4
Hindringham NR21 . . . . .17 F7
Homeland Rd [10] PE30. . . .146 E6
Homelea Cres [13] NR13. . .74 A3
Home Piece IP22 . . . . .127 E4
Home Piece Rd
Claxton NR14. . . . . .91 D6
Wells-Next-The-Sea NR23 136 C5
HOMERSFIELD IP20 . . . . .123 B4
Homerton Ind Est NR18 . .103 E1
Home St NR2 . . . . .162 C8
Homestead Cl [7] NR13. . . .74 A3
Homestead Gdns NR29. . .167 B7
Honey Cl [2] NR1. . . . . .163 B7
Honeycombe Rd NR13 . . . .73 B8
Honey Dro PE33 . . . . .80 B1
Honey Hill PE34. . . . . .79 D8
Honey Hills PE31. . . . . .14 A5
Honeymoon Loke NR30 . .168 F4
Honeymoon Row NR23 . .136 C5
Honeypot Dro PE32 . . . . . .46 C5
Honeypot La
Kirby Cane NR35 . . . . .109 E5
Longham NR19. . . . . .48 F2
Seething NR15. . . . . .108 E3
West Somerton NR29 . . . . .57 F7
Honey Pot La NR15. . . . . .108 A8
Honeypot Mdw NR35. . . .124 A8
Honeysuckle Cl
Cringleford NR4. . . . . .161 B1
North Walsham NR28 . . . .151 C4
[5] Thetford IP24. . . . . . . .176 F4
Honeysuckle Dr NR20 . . .154 F4
Honeysuckle Sq NR18. . . .173 F6
Honeysuckle Way NR17 . .174 B5
HONING NR28 . . . . .38 C6
HONINGHAM NR9. . . . . .69 E7
Honingham La NR8 . . . . . . .70 A8
Honingham Rd
Barnham Broom NR9. . . . . .69 C3
Weston Green NR9 . . . . . . .51 E1
Honing Long La NR28 . . . .38 D7
Honing Rd
Dilham NR28 . . . . .38 D5
Worstead NR28. . . . . .38 A5
Honing Row NR28 . . . . .38 A5
HONINGTON IP31. . . . . . . .126 D1
Honington Airfield
IP31 . . . . .126 A2

Honington CE VC Prim Sch
IP31. . . . . .126 D1
Honington Rise IP31. . . . . .126 C1
Hood Way IP24 . . . . .176 E5
Hooker Rd NR7 . . . . .159 D1
Hooks Hill Rd NR26 . . . . . .138 C6
Hook's Wlk NR1 . . . . .178 C3
Hookwood La NR18 . . . . .104 C8
Hooper La NR3 . . . . .158 F2
Hooton's Row NR38 . . . . . .78 F6
Hope Ct PE30 . . . . .147 A8
Hope La PE14. . . . . .60 A4
Hopewell Gdns NR13. . . . .74 C2
HOPTON IP22 . . . . .127 F6
Hopton CE Prim Sch
NR31 . . . . .171 E4
Hopton CE VC Prim Sch
IP22 . . . . .127 F5
Hopton Cl [6] NR7 . . . . .72 D4
Hopton Cl [8] NR31. . . . . . .171 D5
Hopton Gdns NR31. . . . . . .171 D5
Hopton Rd
Barningham IP31. . . . . . . .127 D4
Coney Weston IP31 . . . . . .127 C5
Garboldisham IP22 . . . . . .128 A8
Thelnetham IP22. . . . . . . .128 A5
Horatio Ct [10] NR2. . . . . . .162 B8
Horizon Sch NR35 . . . . . . .124 B8
Horizon Views NR21 . . . . .24 A7
Hornbeam Cl
[5] Great Yarmouth
NR31. . . . . .170 B6
Norwich NR7 . . . . .159 D4
Hornbeam Dr
[9] Etling Green NR20 . . . . .68 A8
[15] Poringland NR14 . . . . . .90 C5
Hornbeam Rd NR28 . . . . . .151 C4
Horner Cl [3] IP22. . . . . . . .177 A5
HORNING NR12. . . . . .55 E4
Horning Cl NR5 . . . . .161 D7
Horning Com Prim Sch
NR12 . . . . .55 F3
Horning Rd
Hoveton NR12 . . . . .164 E5
Neatishead NR12. . . . . .55 D6
Woodbastwick NR13. . . . . .55 D2
Horning Rd W NR12. . . . . .164 C5
Horning Reach NR12. . . . . .55 D4
HORNINGTOFT NR20. . . . .31 F1
Horningtoft Rd
Whissonsett NR20. . . . . . . .31 E1
Whissonsett NR20. . . . . . . .31 E3
Hornington Rd NR20 . . . . .32 B3
Hornor Cl NR2. . . . . .162 C3
Horns La NR1. . . . . .178 B2
Horns Row NR21. . . . . .141 A3
Horsbeck Way NR10 . . . . . .53 A3
Horse Fair [2] PE13. . . . . . .152 C5
Horsefair Loke NR1 . . . . . .178 C3
Horsefen Rd NR29 . . . . .56 D4
Horsehead Dro PE14. . . . . .95 C8
Horseman Cl PE38 . . . . . . .172 B7
Horse Rescue Ctr*
NR16 . . . . .103 C2
Horses Head NR13 . . . . . . .166 B7
Horseshoe Cl NR5 . . . . . . .156 E1
Horse Shoe Cl [17] IP25 . . . 84 F3
Horse-Shoe Cnr PE13. . . . .152 B7
Horseshoe Hoele PE34. . . .25 D2
Horseshoe La
Briston NR24. . . . . .142 F4
Corpusty & Saxthorpe NR24 34 F8
Horse Shoe Rd NR20. . . . . .69 A4
Horseshoe Terr PE13. . . . .152 B7
Horseshoe The NR12. . . . . .39 C2
Horsesho La NR11 . . . . .19 E1
Horse Watering La
NR35 . . . . .109 A2
HORSEY NR29 . . . . .40 D2
HORSEY CORNER NR29 . . .40 D2
Horsey Gap NR29 . . . . .40 D2
Horsey Rd NR29 . . . . .57 E7
Horsey's La NR31. . . . . . . .170 D5
Horsey Windpump*
NR29 . . . . .40 D1
HORSFORD NR10 . . . . .53 B3
Horsford CE Jun Sch
NR10 . . . . .53 B3
Horsford CE Prim Sch
NR10 . . . . .53 B3
Horsford St [7] NR2 . . . . . .162 B8
HORSHAM ST FAITH
NR10 . . . . .53 D1
Horsley Dr
Great Yarmouth NR31 . . . .170 B1
Hopton on Sea NR31. . . . .171 D4
Horsley's Chase PE30 . . . .146 E2
Horsley's Ct [7] PE30 . . . .146 E2
Horsley's Field PE30 . . . . .146 E2
Horsley's Fields Ind Est
PE30. . . . . .146 E2
HORSTEAD NR12. . . . . .54 C6
Horstead La NR12. . . . . .54 A4
Horton Rd PE30. . . . . .147 D6
Hospital La
Hellesdon NR6. . . . . .157 D3
Norwich NR1 . . . . .162 E3
Salhouse NR13 . . . . .55 A2
Hospital Rd
Great & Little Plumstead
NR13. . . . . .73 A5
Sutton Bridge PE12. . . . . . .41 E8
Wicklewood NR18. . . . . . . .87 C4
Hospital Wlk PE30 . . . . . . .146 E4
Hotblack Rd NR2 . . . . .162 A8
Hotch La PE14. . . . . .60 B8
Hotson Cl [5] NR15 . . . . . .106 D3
Houghton Ave PE30. . . . . .148 D1

Houghton Cl [2] NR5 . . . . .161 B8
Houghton Hall* PE31. . . . .29 C7
Houghton La PE37 . . . . .65 E1
Houghton Rd PE31 . . . . . . .29 C5
HOUGHTON ST GILES
NR22 . . . . .16 E6
House Gdns NR10. . . . . .53 E5
Hovell's La IP26 . . . . .99 C7
HOVETON NR12. . . . . .164 D6
Hoveton Cl PE30. . . . . .147 D5
Hoveton Dr PE37. . . . . . . .153 C1
Hoveton Pl NR10. . . . . .37 B2
Hoveton & Wroxham Sta
NR12 . . . . .164 C5
Howard Cl
Harleston IP20 . . . . .122 E2
Norwich NR7 . . . . .163 D7
Swaffham PE37 . . . . .153 C6
[4] Swanton Morley NR20. . 50 B3
Terrington St Clement
PE34 . . . . .144 B4
Wortham IP22. . . . . .129 C3
Howard Cres NR19. . . . . . .154 D4
Howard Jun Sch The
PE30. . . . . .147 B4
Howard Mews NR3 . . . . . .158 E1
Howard St N [9] NR30 . . .169 C4
Howard St S NR30 . . . . . . .169 C4
Howards Cl PE36 . . . . .132 E7
Howard's Hill NR27 . . . . .139 A7
Howard's Hill Cl NR27 . . . 10 C5
Howard's Hill Rd NR28 . . .38 C7
Howards Hill W [1]
NR27. . . . . .139 A7
Howard's La NR15 . . . . . . .90 D3
Howard's Rd NR1 . . . . .178 A1
Howards The PE30. . . . . . .148 D4
Howards Way [12] PE32. . .45 C6
Howard's Way NR10 . . . . . .35 B2
Howard Way NR11 . . . . . . .150 C5
Howdale Rd PE38 . . . . .172 C5
Howdale Rise PE38 . . . . . .172 C5
HOWE NR15 . . . . .90 D3
Howe Gn NR15. . . . . .90 D2
Howe La Howe NR15. . . . . . .90 D3
Shotesham NR15. . . . . .90 C2
Shotesham NR15. . . . . . . .107 F8
Howell Rd NR8 . . . . .147 C4
Howe Rd NR30. . . . . .169 D7
Howes Cl [10] NR9. . . . . . . .88 D7
Howes La NR20 . . . . .68 D6
Howes Yd [1] NR25. . . . . . . .7 E6
Howfield Loke NR29 . . . . .56 B6
HOW HILL NR29. . . . . .56 B6
How Hill Nature Reserve*
NR29 . . . . .56 A6
How Hill Rd NR29 . . . . .56 B6
Howland Cl NR21 . . . . .141 B5
Howlett Cl
[4] East Dereham NR19 . .154 D3
North Walsham NR28 . . . .151 A5
Howlett Dr NR5. . . . . .161 A8
Howletts Hill PE13 . . . . . . .152 A7
Howletts Loke NR13 . . . . . .54 F1
Howletts Way [2] IP24. . . .176 D6
HOXNE IP21. . . . . .131 A4
Hoxne Rd Denham IP21 . . .131 B1
Eye IP23. . . . . .130 E1
Syleham IP21. . . . . .131 C4
Upper Weybread IP21. . . .131 A6
Hoy Dr IP24 . . . . .176 F6
Hubbard Cl
[11] Long Stratton NR15. . .106 E3
Wymondham NR18 . . . . . .173 A6
Hubbard's Dro PE38 . . . . . .79 F1
Hubbards La IP22. . . . . . . .128 B6
Hubbards Rd NR9 . . . . .51 D5
Hubbard's Loke [16] NR9 . .88 C7
Hudman's La NR16. . . . . . .105 F7
Hudson Ave NR14. . . . . . . .163 B3
Hudson Cl [1] IP24 . . . . . .116 A2
Hudson Leisure Ctr
PE13. . . . . .152 A5
Hudson Way NR5 . . . . .160 E7
Hugh Cl PE30 . . . . .148 C5
Hughenden Rd NR1 . . . . . .162 E3
Hughes Ct [8] NR9. . . . . . . .88 D8
Hulton Rd PE30. . . . . .147 A5
Hulver Rd NR13. . . . . .73 E8
Hulver St NR19 . . . . .66 F6
Humber Cl NR30. . . . . .168 C5
Humber Keel NR31. . . . . . .170 D1
Humberstone Rd [3]
NR31. . . . . .170 C7
HUMBLETOFT NR19 . . . . .154 C7
Humbletoft Rd NR19 . . . .154 C7
Humbleyard NR5 . . . . .161 A7
Hundred Acre La PE31 . . . 14 F5
Hundred Foot Bank
Downham CB6. . . . . .95 C1
Welney PE14. . . . . .95 F4
Welney PE14. . . . . .96 A6
Hundred La NR15 . . . . .121 C7
Hungate [1] NR34 . . . . . . .110 F1
Hungate Comm NR9 . . . . . .51 D2
Hungate La NR11 . . . . .150 C4
Hungate Rd PE14 . . . . .59 E2
Hungate St NR11 . . . . .150 D5
Hungry Hill NR27. . . . . .11 B2
Hun's Loke NR29. . . . . .56 C6
HUNSTANTON PE36. . . . . .132 E6
Hunstanton Commercial Pk
PE36. . . . . .132 D5
Hunstanton Inf Sch
Hunstanton PE36. . . . . .1 D1
Hunstanton PE36. . . . . . . .132 D4
Hunstanton Prim Sch
Erpingham PE36 . . . . .1 D2

Hunstanton Prim Sch
continued
Hunstanton PE36. . . . . . . .132 D2
Hunstanton Rd
Dersingham PE31 . . . . . . .140 D5
Heacham PE31. . . . . .132 D1
Old Hunstanton PE36 . . . . .1 F5
Hunstanton Sea Life
Sanctuary* PE36. . . . . . .132 B3
Hunt Cl Old Catton NR6 . . .158 E7
[5] Redenhall with Harleston
IP20. . . . . .122 D2
Hunter Ave NR20 . . . . .68 F5
Hunter Dr [4] NR31. . . . . . .94 C8
Hunter Rd Norwich NR3 . . . 71 E6
Norwich NR3 . . . . .158 C3
Norwich NR6 . . . . .72 A8
Spixworth NR12. . . . . .159 A7
Troston IP31 . . . . .126 B1
Hunters Cl Brundall NR13 .165 F5
Terrington St Clement PE34 42 E7
Terrington St Clement
PE34 . . . . .144 F6
Hunter's Dro PE14. . . . . . . .60 B6
Hunters Oak [2] IP25. . . . .84 E3
Hunters Ride NR17. . . . . . .102 E8
Hunters Rise PE33 . . . . . . .43 F4
Hunters Rowe PE14. . . . . .152 D2
Huntley Cres NR25. . . . . . .138 E6
HUNT'S CORNER NR16 . . .119 C7
Hunts Gn NR16 . . . . .105 B4
Hunts Mead NR16. . . . . . .106 C4
HUNWORTH NR24 . . . . . . .19 A6
Hunworth Rd Holt NR25. . . 19 B8
Holt NR25. . . . . .137 B3
Stody NR24 . . . . .19 E3
Stody NR24 . . . . .142 D8
Hurdle La
Cley Next the Sea NR25 . . . .8 A4
Letheringsett with Glandford
NR25. . . . . .7 E4
Hurd Rd NR4 . . . . .161 E3
Hurn Dr PE14. . . . . .95 D5
Hurn La NR16. . . . . .106 A6
Hurn Rd Dereham NR20 . . .68 A7
Hurrell Rd NR30 . . . . .168 D6
Hurricane Cl
Attleborough NR1 . . . . . . .174 A2
[22] Watton IP25. . . . . .84 F3
Hurricane Way NR6. . . . . . .158 C6
Hurst Rd [8] NR14 . . . . . . .92 A2
Hurth Way IP24. . . . . .176 E4
Husenbeth Ct NR8 . . . . . . .156 E4
Hutchinson Rd NR5. . . . . . .161 D6
Huxley Cl NR1 . . . . .162 F2
Huxley Rd NR1. . . . . .162 F2
Hyde Cl PE31 . . . . .14 D4
Hyde Ct NR13. . . . . .72 E5
Hyde Pk Rd PE31. . . . . .14 D4
Hyde Rd NR19. . . . . .154 D3
Hylands IP22. . . . . .177 C2
HYLTONS CROSSWAYS
NR28 . . . . .36 F8
Hyperion Row NR5. . . . . . .156 C1
Hypocrite La NR17. . . . . . .174 A2
Hyrn Cl NR29 . . . . .57 D4
Hythe Rd Feltwell IP26 . . . . .98 E3
Foulden IP26 . . . . .82 A1
Methwold IP26 . . . . .98 F5
Hythe Views Cl IP26 . . . . . .98 E5

I

Icarus Rise [8] NR5. . . . . . .156 C1
Ice House Ct [17] NR15 . . .106 E3
Ice House La NR15 . . . . . . .178 C1
Iceni Acad Hockwold
IP26 . . . . .114 A6
Iceni Dr [7] PE37 . . . . .153 D2
ICKBURGH IP26 . . . . .100 B6
Icklewood Rise NR18. . . . . .87 B4
Icknield Cl IP24 . . . . .176 B3
Icknield Way
Flitcham PE35 . . . . .28 B6
Shernborne PE31. . . . . . . .13 B2
Thetford IP24 . . . . .176 B3
Ickworth Cl PE30 . . . . .148 E1
Ilex Ct NR7 . . . . .159 D4
ILKETSHALL ST ANDREW
NR34 . . . . .124 E6
ILKETSHALL ST LAWRENCE
NR34 . . . . .124 F2
Ilketshall St Lawrence Sch
NR34 . . . . .124 F2
ILKETSHALL ST MARGARET
NR35 . . . . .124 B4
ILLINGTON IP24 . . . . .117 D8
Illington Rd
Illington IP24. . . . . .117 D8
Larling NR16 . . . . .118 A7
Wretham IP24. . . . . .117 C8
ILPH Hall Farm* NR16. . . .118 B7
Impala Cl PE14 . . . . .159 A6
Imperial Mews NR31. . . . .171 C4
Imperial Way NR10 . . . . . . .53 E1
Impson Way IP24 . . . . .100 A4
Incleborough Cl [2] NR27. 10 B5
Independent Way [14]
NR7. . . . . .72 D4
Indigo Rd PE33 . . . . .81 A3
Indigo Yd NR3 . . . . .178 A3
INGHAM NR12. . . . . .39 D4
Ingham Cnr NR12. . . . . .24 D1
Ingham Rd
Brumstead NR12. . . . . .24 B1
Brumstead NR12. . . . . .39 B6
Ingham NR12. . . . . .39 D4

Ingham Rd continued
Lessingham NR12 . . . . .24 D1
Stalham NR12 . . . . .39 B4
Inghams La IP26. . . . . .99 B8
INGLEBOROUGH PE14. . . .41 B1
Ingleby Cl Heacham PE31 .133 E6
King's Lynn PE30 . . . . .147 B4
Ingle Rd PE14. . . . . .59 B1
Ingloss La NR14. . . . . .109 B7
Ingoldale PE31 . . . . .140 D5
Ingoldisthorpe PE31 . . . . .140 D8
Ingoldisthorpe CE Prim Sch
PE31. . . . . .140 E8
Ingoldsby Ave PE31. . . . . .140 C6
Ingolside PE31 . . . . .12 D8
Ingram Ct NR1. . . . . .162 E3
Ingram's Rd IP21 . . . . .131 C7
INGWORTH NR11 . . . . .36 B8
Ingworth Rd NR11 . . . . .36 A7
Inman Rd NR7 . . . . .159 D4
Innes Pl NR4. . . . . .161 B2
Innovation Dr PE30 . . . . . .146 E1
INTWOOD NR4. . . . . .89 B7
Intwood La
East Carleton NR14. . . . . . .89 A5
Swardeston NR14 . . . . .89 C6
Intwood Rd NR4 . . . . .89 B8
Invaders Ct NR23 . . . . .136 D6
Ipswich Gr NR2. . . . . .178 A1
Ipswich Rd
Dickleburgh IP21. . . . . . . .121 B1
Norwich NR2 . . . . .178 A1
[2] Norwich NR4 . . . . .89 E8
Pulham Market NR15 . . . .121 C8
Saxlingham Nethergate
NR15. . . . . .107 A7
Scole IP21 . . . . .130 D5
Yaxley IP23. . . . . .130 A1
Yaxley IP23. . . . . .130 A2
Ireton Cl [25] NR7. . . . . . . .72 D4
Iris Cl NR17. . . . . .174 B5
Irmingland Rd NR11 . . . . . .34 F8
Ironside Way NR9. . . . . .86 D5
IRSTEAD NR12. . . . . .56 A7
Irstead Rd
Barton Turf NR12 . . . . .55 F7
Norwich NR5 . . . . .161 C6
IRSTEAD STREET NR12 . . . .55 F6
Irving Rd NR4 . . . . .162 C1
Irwin Cl NR10. . . . . .149 C5
Isaac's Rd NR31. . . . . .169 B4
Isabella Cl PE30. . . . . .147 D3
Isabella Sq NR30 . . . . .169 D3
Isbets Dale NR8. . . . . .155 D2
Isis Cl NR31. . . . . .170 B3
Isle Bridge Rd PE14 . . . . . .77 E6
Isle Rd PE14 . . . . .77 F7
Islington Rd PE34. . . . . .42 E3
Itteringham NR11 . . . . . . .20 C1
ITTERINGHAM COMMON
NR11. . . . . .35 D8
Itteringham Rd
Little Barningham NR11 . . .20 C4
Oulton NR11. . . . . .35 C8
Plumstead Green NR11. . . .20 B5
Iveagh Cl PE31 . . . . .140 E2
Ives Cl IP22. . . . . .177 E4
Ives Rd NR6 . . . . .158 D5
Ives Way NR11. . . . . .21 B2
Ivory Rd NR4 . . . . .161 E4
Ivy Cl Poringland NR14 . . . .90 D5
Setchey PE34. . . . . .61 F8
Ivy Gn NR31. . . . . .170 B5
Ivy Rd Earlham NR5 . . . . . .161 C2
Spixworth NR10. . . . . .54 A2
IVY TODD PE37. . . . . .66 B4
Ivy Todd Rd PE37 . . . . .66 B4
Ivy Way NR20 . . . . .68 E6
Ixworth Rd IP31 . . . . .126 D1

J

Jackdaw Cl NR18 . . . . .173 D1
Jack Plummer Way
NR30 . . . . .168 C7
Jack's La NR21 . . . . .15 A7
Jacob Dr NR20. . . . . .68 D6
Jaguar Dr NR10. . . . . .37 B1
Jaguar Rd [9] NR9. . . . . . . .88 D8
James Bradfield CE Comm
Prim Sch The PE33 . . . . .81 A2
James Cl PE30. . . . . .148 B1
James Gn NR10. . . . . .54 A7
James Green PE32. . . . . . . .46 F2
James Jackson Rd
PE31. . . . . .140 C3
James Paget Univ Hospl
NR31 . . . . .170 B1
James Rd [7] NR31 . . . . .169 D2
James Scott Cl [3] PE38 .172 A5
James St PE36 . . . . .132 D4
James Watt Cl NR31 . . . . .170 A8
Jamieson Pl NR5 . . . . .161 C8
Jamie Wright Cl NR26. . . .138 C7
Jane Austen Coll
Norwich NR3 . . . . .162 D6
Norwich NR3 . . . . .178 A3
Jane Forby Cl PE33 . . . . . . .80 E2
Jankin La PE34. . . . . .144 A1
Jannys Cl NR11. . . . . .150 B6
Jarrold Cl IP31. . . . . .127 D3
Jarrold Way NR5 . . . . .160 F8
Jarvie Cl PE36. . . . . .13 A7
Jarvis Dr NR21. . . . . .31 E5
Jarvis Rd PE30. . . . . .146 E8
Jasmine Cl PE13. . . . . .152 F7
Jasmine Cl Earlham NR4 . .161 C5
Thetford IP24. . . . . .176 F4
Jasmine Ct [1] NR17. . . . . .174 B5
Jasmine Gdns [7] NR31. . .94 C7

Jasmine Gn [7] NR31 . . . . .170 B5
Jasmine Wk [3] NR4. . . . . . .89 A8
Jasmine Wlk NR4. . . . . .50 B2
Javelin Rd NR6 . . . . .158 C7
Jay Cres NR18 . . . . .173 D1
Jay Gdns NR5. . . . . .160 E8
Jay La NR32 . . . . .171 C3
Jay's Gn IP20. . . . . .122 E2
Jeckyll Rd NR18 . . . . .173 F7
Jefferey Ave [4] PE13. . . . .152 E7
Jeffery Cl PE30 . . . . .146 E8
Jegon Cl NR11. . . . . .150 D5
Jellicoe Pl [6] IP24. . . . . . .176 E5
Jellicoe Rd NR30 . . . . .169 C8
Jema Cl NR31 . . . . .169 C7
Jenkinsons Pightle
NR35 . . . . .108 B4
Jenner Cl NR35. . . . . .124 B7
Jenner Rd [4] NR31. . . . . . .170 B1
Jennings Cl IP31 . . . . .133 C5
Jennings Way IP22 . . . . . .177 D5
NR4 . . . . .161 A2
Jenny Lind Cl NR11 . . . . . .150 E2
Jenny Rd [8] NR10. . . . . . . .54 A2
Jenson Cl IP26 . . . . .100 B4
Jentique Cl NR19 . . . . .154 E4
Jericho La NR11. . . . . .20 A4
Jermyn Rd PE30 . . . . .147 C6
Jermyn Way
Long Stratton NR15. . . . . .106 D4
[1] Tharston & Hapton
NR15. . . . . .106 D3
Jerningham Rd NR5 . . . . . .157 A1
Jervis Cl NR31. . . . . .169 C3
Jessopp Cl NR19. . . . . .67 B7
Jessopp Rd NR4 . . . . .161 F4
Jetty Cl NR27. . . . . .139 B7
Jetty Cliff NR27. . . . . .139 B7
Jetty St [2] NR27 . . . . .139 B7
Jewel Cl NR24 . . . . .142 B4
Jewel's La NR11. . . . . .150 B6
Jews' La [10] NR31 . . . . .94 C6
Jewson Rd NR3 . . . . .158 C2
Jex Ave NR5 . . . . .161 D8
Jex La NR5 . . . . .161 D8
Jex Rd NR5 . . . . .161 D8
Jex Wy [6] NR31 . . . . .171 D4
Jickling Yd NR23 . . . . .136 D6
Jimmy Brown Cl NR30 . . .168 C8
Joan Short's La PE31. . . . .135 D3
Jobie Wood Cl NR7 . . . . . .159 D5
Job's La IP22. . . . . .177 C1
Jocelyn Cl IP21 . . . . .121 E5
Joe Ellis Ct [6] NR5. . . . . .161 B8
John Bates Cl [2] NR19 . .154 E5
John Chapman Cl [5]
NR21. . . . . .141 E4
John Childs Way NR35 . . .124 B7
John Davis Way PE33 . . . . .61 D5
John Drewry Cl [2] NR14. .90 D5
John Evans Rd NR13 . . . . .165 E4
John F Kennedy Ct [2]
PE13. . . . . .152 D4
John Franklin Way NR11 . 21 B2
John Gale Ct NR8 . . . . .155 E3
John Goshawk Rd NR19 .154 E2
John Grant Sch NR30. . . .168 C7
John Hill Cl [6] NR15 . . . .106 E3
John Hyrne Wy NR5. . . . . .156 E1
John Jarrold Printing Mus*
NR1 . . . . .178 C4
John Kennedy Rd PE30. . .146 D4
John Morton Cres PE32 . . .29 D1
John of Gaunt Inf Sch
NR11. . . . . .150 C5
John O'Gaunt Cl NR11. . .150 B6
John Rd
Caister-on-Sea NR30. . . . .168 C7
Great Yarmouth NR31 . . . .170 D5
Johnson Cl
[7] East Dereham NR19 . .154 C3
New Costessey NR5 . . . . .156 E1
Johnson Cres NR31 . . . . . .133 C4
Johnson Ct NR31 . . . . .170 D5
Johnson Pl NR2 . . . . .162 C5
John Stephenson Ct [1]
NR6 . . . . .158 F1
John Thompson Rd [3]
PE13. . . . . .152 D4
John William Way NR25. . . 9 A3
John Wood Cl NR25. . . . . . .7 A1
John Woodhouse Dr
NR30 . . . . .168 C7
Jolly Gardeners Ct [13]
NR3 . . . . .162 D8
Jolly Sailor Yd NR23 . . . . .136 D6
Jolly's La NR13 . . . . .166 A2
Jones (GC) Way NR31. . . .169 B2
Jones's Dro PE14 . . . . .95 E8
Jordan Cl Norwich NR5 . . .161 B6
Taverham NR8 . . . . .155 E4
JORDAN GREEN NR10. . . . .51 A8
Jordan La NR10. . . . . .51 A8
Jordan Rd NR30 . . . . .168 E6
Jose Neville Cl [7] NR30 .168 D7
Joseph Clover Ct NR11. . .150 C6
Josephine Cl NR1. . . . . . . .162 D3
Joseph Lancaster Way [4]
NR3 . . . . .178 A4
Joshua Ct NR31. . . . . .171 D8
Josiah Dr IP24. . . . . .176 F7
Jotts La [8] NR20 . . . . .50 E2
Joy Ave [1] NR15 . . . . .107 A8
Joyce La Heacham PE31 . .133 D5
Walpole PE14. . . . . .41 F3

Joyce La continued
Walpole PE14 . . . . 42 A3
Joyce Rd NR35 . . . . 124 B8
Joyce Way 9 NR7 . . 72 D5
Joyland * NR30 . . . . . . 169 E4
Joy Pl NR9 . . . . 160 C1
Jubilee Ave
4 East Dereham NR20 . 154 E6
East Harling NR16 . . . . 118 C5
Fakenham NR21 . . . . . . 141 C4
Heacham PE31 . . . . 133 B5
Jubilee Bank Rd PE34 . . 146 A5
Jubilee Cl Cawston NR10 . . 35 B2
Downham Market PE38 . . 172 E6
Erpingham NR11 . . . . 21 B2
Hunstanton PE36 . . . . 132 C3
Repps with Bastwick NR29 57 A4
Thetford IP24 . . . . 176 B3
Weeting IP27 . . . . 175 B7
Jubilee Ct
7 King's Lynn PE30 . . . . 146 D4
Pentney PE32 . . . . 63 C8
Jubilee Dr
Dersingham PE31 . . . . . . 140 C5
Sheringham NR26 . . . . . 138 E6
Jubilee Gdns 7 PE31 . . 12 E4
Jubilee Hall La 2 PE32 . . 45 C6
Jubilee La Cromer NR27 . . 139 C4
Marshland St James PE14 . 60 A3
Jubilee Rd
5 Aylsham NR11 . . . . . . 150 A5
Heacham PE31 . . . . 133 A5
Holt NR25 . . . . 137 B6
Lackenheath IP27 . . . . . . 113 E2
Watton IP25 . . . . 84 D3
Jubilee Rise PE33 . . . . . . 61 D3
Jubilee Terr
Caister-on-Sea NR30 . . . 168 E4
Cromer NR27 . . . . 139 D4
Norwich NR1 . . . . 162 F3
Jubilee Way 11 PE37 . . 65 F4
Jubilee Wlk
30 Martham NR29 . . . . . . 57 D4
Wisbech PE13 . . . . 152 D8
Judas La IP23 . . . . 129 F1
Judges Dr NR4 . . . . 161 F2
Judges Gdns NR4 . . . . . 155 E2
Judges Wlk NR4 . . . . . . 161 F2
Juler Cl 4 NR28 . . . . . . 151 C6
Julian Dr NR14 . . . . 163 C2
Julian Hospl NR2 . . . . . . 161 F6
Julian Rd
King's Lynn PE30 . . . . . . 148 C5
6 Spixworth NR10 . . . . 54 A2
Julians Way IP21 . . . . . . 121 E5
Julian Way NR31 . . . . . 171 D5
Junction Rd Norwich NR3 . 71 E5
Norwich NR3 . . . . 158 C1
Juniper Cl
Cringleford NR4 . . . . 161 C1
2 Thetford IP24 . . . . . 176 F4
Juniper Dr 26 NR29 . . 57 D4
Juniper Gr NR26 . . . . . . 138 E5
Juniper Way NR8 . . . . . 155 B2
Jupiter Rd NR6 . . . . 158 C4
Jury St NR30 . . . . 169 D4
Jutland Rise NR18 . . . . . 173 F6

K

Kabin Rd NR5 . . . . 157 B2
Kalmia Gn 3 NR31 . . . 170 B6
Karen Cl
16 Hethersett NR9 . . . . . 88 C7
Scole IP21 . . . . 130 C5
Karoo Cl PE38 . . . . 79 F6
Kate's La NR21 . . . . 15 E8
Keable Cl 7 NR5 . . . . . 161 C6
Keats Cl
Downham Market PE38 . . 172 C6
East Dereham NR19 . . . . 154 C7
2 Thetford IP24 . . . . . 176 E6
Keats Rd NR8 . . . . 156 D8
Keble Cl PE30 . . . . 148 B4
Keble Rd NR31 . . . . 170 B3
Kedleston Dr 10 NR4 . . 89 B8
Keeble Ct PE30 . . . . 146 D6
Keelan Ct NR6 . . . . 158 B4
Keel Cl 12 NR8 . . . . 111 F1
Keeling Hall La NR20 . . . 33 E3
Keeling Way NR17 . . . . 174 B3
Keene Rd NR20 . . . . 146 D1
Keepers Cl NR20 . . . . . 154 F5
Keepers Corner IP24 . . . 102 A1
Keeper's La NR11 . . . . . . 20 B2
Keeper's Rd NR15 . . . . . . 89 F1
Keepham Rd NR20 . . . . . 33 F2
Keep Rise NR35 . . . . . . 124 A8
Keillers Cl PE13 . . . . . . 152 A7
Keith Rd 9 NR20 . . . . . 50 B3
Kellard Pl 1 PE30 . . . . 146 E2
KELLING 8 D5
Kelling Cl NR25 . . . . . . 137 C7
Kelling Heath Pk Sta NR25 8 E4
Kelling Hospl NR25 . . . . 137 F8
Kelling Prim Sch NR25 . . 8 D6
Kelling Rd
Hempstead NR11 . . . . 19 E8
Hempstead NR25 . . . . 8 E1
Holt NR25 . . . . 137 C7
Lower Bodham NR25 . . . . . 8 E5
Weybourne NR25 . . . . 8 E5
Kell's Acres NR34 . . . . . 109 F3
Kell's Way NR34 . . . . . . 109 F2
Kelsey Cl PE36 . . . . 132 D7
Kelvin Pl IP24 . . . . 176 A1

Kemp Ave NR13 . . . . . . 166 B3
Kemp Dr NR19 . . . . 154 C5
Kempe Cl NR7 . . . . 159 C1
Kempe Rd PE34 . . . . . . 146 C5
Kemp Rd NR8 . . . . 151 C4
Kemp's Cl PE38 . . . . 79 A4
Kemp's Rd IP21 . . . . . . 122 A5
Kenan Dr NR17 . . . . 174 F7
Kendal Cl 15 NR9 . . . . . 88 D8
Kendall Cl NR28 . . . . . . 151 B6
Kendle Rd PE37 . . . . . . 153 C1
Kendle Way PE30 . . . . . 147 E8
Kenhill Cl 2 PE31 . . . . . 12 E5
Kenlan Rd PE13 . . . . . . 152 D6
Kennel Loke NR31 . . . . 171 D8
Kenneth Mckee Plain
NR2 . . . . 178 A1
Kennett Cl NR4 . . . . 161 F4
KENNINGHALL 119 B5
Kenninghall Prim Sch
NR16 . . . . 119 A4
Kenninghall Rd
Banham NR16 . . . . 119 B6
Bressingham IP22 . . . . . 119 E2
Garboldisham IP22 . . . . 118 D2
Harling NR16 . . . . 118 E4
Kenninghall NR16 . . . . . 119 A3
Kenninghall NR16 . . . . . 119 A3
Kenninghall Cl NR14 . . . 89 B2
Kenninghall Hall La
NR14 . . . . 89 C2
Kenside Rd 1 PE31 . . . 12 E5
Kensington Cl NR15 . . . 107 C8
Kensington Pl NR1 . . . . 178 B1
Kensington Rd
Downham Market PE38 . . 172 B4
King's Lynn PE30 . . . . . . 147 B6
Kent Ave NR31 . . . . 170 C5
Kent Cl
Attleborough NR17 . . . . . 174 B3
2 Sutton Bridge PE12 . . 41 B8
Kent Dr PE33 . . . . 61 D5
Kentra Cl PE13 . . . . 152 A8
Kent Rd PE30 . . . . 147 B6
Kent Sq NR30 . . . . 169 D3
Kenwood Rd PE31 . . . . 133 D5
Kenwood Rd S PE31 . . . 133 D5
Kenwyn Cl NR25 . . . . . 137 C7
Kenyon Row NR34 . . . . 110 C2
Keppel Cl NR29 . . . . 48 A5
Keppel Rd 2 NR31 . . . 170 D4
Kerdgreen La NR20 . . . . 34 D4
Kerdy Green La NR20 . . 34 C4
Kered Cl NR6 . . . . 157 F6
Kered Rd NR6 . . . . 157 F6
Kerkham Cl PE34 . . . . . 144 B4
Kerrich Cl PE13 . . . . . . 140 C3
Kerridge Ct NR25 . . . . . 137 B6
Kerridges NR16 . . . . . . 118 C4
Kerridges The NR5 . . . . 156 F1
Kerridge Way
29 Harleston IP20 . . . . . 122 D2
Holt NR25 . . . . 137 B6
Kerrison Cl NR29 . . . . . 168 C8
Kerrison Rd
Bungay NR35 . . . . 124 B7
Norwich NR1 . . . . 163 A4
Kerville St 3 NR5 . . . . 161 A7
Kestrel Ave
Costessey NR8 . . . . 156 A5
Downham Market PE38 . . 172 C7
Kestrel Cl
Burnham Market PE31 . . 135 D1
Great Yarmouth NR31 . . 170 A7
Mulbarton NR14 . . . . 89 A3
Sutton Bridge PE12 . . . . . 41 A8
Swaffham PE37 . . . . . . 153 C2
Thetford IP24 . . . . 176 D1
Kestrel Dr Brandon IP27 . 175 F3
Holt NR25 . . . . 137 D6
2 Wisbech PE14 . . . . . 152 D2
Kestrel Rd NR7 . . . . . . 159 C4
KESWICK Bacton NR12 . . 23 F4
Keswick NR4 . . . . 89 C7
Keswick PE30 . . . . 147 D5
Keswick Cl NR4 . . . . 89 B8
Keswick Hall Rd NR4 . . . 89 C7
Keswick Rd Bacton NR12 . 23 F4
Cringleford NR4 . . . . 89 B8
KETTERINGHAM NR18 . . 88 E6
Ketteringham La NR9 . . . 88 D6
Ketteringham Pk NR18 . . 88 E6
Ketteringham Rd NR18 . 173 F3
Kettle La IP26 . . . . 98 C2
KETTLESTONE NR21 . . . 17 C2
Kettlestone Rd NR21 . . . 17 C2
Kettlewell La 1 PE30 . . 146 E5
Kett's Ave NR18 . . . . . . 173 C5
Kett's Cl
1 Hethersett NR9 . . . . . . 88 D7
Wymondham NR18 . . . . 173 C5
Ketts Ct NR28 . . . . 151 B4
Kett's Hill NR37 . . . . 66 A4
Kett's Hill NR1 . . . . 163 A7
Kett's La NR9 . . . . 52 A6
Kett's Lane NR35 . . . . . 108 B2
Kett's Oak NR9 . . . . 88 C6
Ketts Rd NR28 . . . . 151 B4
Kevill Davis Dr NR3 . . . . 73 A5
Kevin Wlk NR19 . . . . . . 154 D3
Kew Rd PE38 . . . . 172 B4
Key & Castle Yd NR3 . . . 178 A4

Keyes Ave NR30 . . . . . . 169 D7
Keyes Cl 5 NR1 . . . . . 162 E2
Keyes Rd NR1 . . . . 162 E2
Keymer Cl 4 NR11 . . . 150 A5
Keys Dr NR12 . . . . 164 B2
Keys Farm 4 NR20 . . . 68 F6
Keys The NR15 . . . . 90 F2
Kidas Way NR28 . . . . . . 151 D2
Kidds Cl 13 NR31 . . . . 171 D4
KIDD'S MOOR NR18 . . . 173 D8
Kilderkin Cl PE14 . . . . . . 77 A7
Kilderkin Wy NR1 . . . . . 178 B2
Kilham's Way
King's Lynn PE30 . . . . . 146 E7
North Wootton PE30 . . . . 26 E1
Kiln Cl Armingham NR14 . 90 C6
Norwich NR5 . . . . 158 C2
Kiln Farm La IP22 . . . . . 128 E1
Kiln La
Dickleburgh & Rushall
IP21 . . . . 130 F6
Needham IP20 . . . . 131 D8
Kiln Rd 5 NR11 . . . . . . 53 A3
Kiln Rise IP22 . . . . 128 E2
Kilverstone Rd
Brettenham IP24 . . . . . . 117 A2
Brettenham IP24 . . . . . . 117 C3
Kilverstone IP24 . . . . . . 116 F3
Thetford IP24 . . . . 116 D3
KIMBERLEY NR18 . . . . . 87 B6
Kimberley Pk Sta NR18 . 87 A6
Kimberley Rd NR28 . . . 151 D5
Kimberley St
1 Norwich NR2 . . . . . . 162 C5
Wymondham NR18 . . . . 173 C4
Kimberley Terr NR30 . . . 169 E2
Kimms Belt IP24 . . . . . . 176 B2
Kinderley Rd PE13 . . . . 152 C8
Kingcup PE30 . . . . 148 A1
King Edward VII Sch
PE30 . . . . 147 A5
Kingfisher Cl
6 Cringleford NR4 . . . . . 89 A8
8 Fakenham NR21 . . . . 141 E4
Great Yarmouth NR31 . . . 94 C7
Thetford IP24 . . . . 176 D1
Kingfisher Dr
Brandon IP27 . . . . 175 E3
Necton PE37 . . . . 66 A3
6 Wisbech PE14 . . . . . 152 D2
Kingfisher La
Hunstanton PE36 . . . . 1 D2
Hunstanton PE36 . . . . . . 1 D2
Kingfisher Mead NR18 . 173 D2
Kingfisher Rd
Attleborough NR17 . . . . . 174 F6
Downham Market PE38 . . 172 C7
Sprowston NR7 . . . . 159 E4
Kingfisher Way 11 IP25 . 84 C3
King George Cl 3 NR29 . 57 D2
King George Mews
IP22 . . . . 177 F5
King George Rd NR21 . . 31 C7
King George's Ave 2
NR29 . . . . 57 D2
King George V Ave
PE30 . . . . 146 F5
Kinghorn Rd NR2 . . . . . 161 F4
King John Ave PE30 . . . 146 D3
King John Bank PE14 . . . 41 C5
King's Arms St NR28 . . 151 C5
Kings Ave PE35 . . . . 27 F7
King's Ave Harleston PE31 28 C8
King's Lynn PE30 . . . . . 147 A3
Kings Cl IP21 . . . . 130 D6
King's Cl NR28 . . . . 151 C5
Kings Croft PE31 . . . . . 140 E4
Kings Ct NR29 . . . . 167 A8
Kingsdale 16 NR14 . . . . 74 A3
King's Dam NR34 . . . . . 110 B2
Kings Dr NR31 . . . . 94 C6
King's Gn 6 PE30 . . . . 147 C4
Kings Head La
Deopham NR18 . . . . 87 A5
North Lopham NR22 . . . . 119 A2
Kingshill IP24 . . . . 102 E3
Kingsleigh Cl NR28 . . . . 22 E5
Kingsley Ave PE13 . . . . 152 B4
Kingsley Rd NR1 . . . . . 178 A1
Kings Loke NR29 . . . . . 167 B8
Kings Loke Track NR29 . 167 B8
KING'S LYNN PE30 . . . . 147 A4
King's Lynn Acad PE30 . 147 A4
King's Lynn Arts Ctr
(Guildhall)** * PE30 . . 146 D5
King's Lynn Rd PE36 . . . 132 D4
King's Lynn Sports Ctr
PE30 . . . . 146 F5
King's Lynn Sta PE30 . . 146 E5
King's Oak Acad PE30 . 147 B4
King's Park Inf Sch
NR19 . . . . 154 E6
King's Pk NR19 . . . . . . 154 E6
Kings Rd Bungay NR35 . 124 B7
East Dereham NR19 . . . 154 E6
Fakenham NR21 . . . . . . 141 A5
Hunstanton PE36 . . . . . 132 D6
Wisbech PE13 . . . . 152 C5
King's Rd
Great Yarmouth NR30 . . 169 D2
Holt NR25 . . . . 137 C5
Topcroft NR35 . . . . 108 A4
Kings St NR20 . . . . 19 A6
King's Staithe La 2
PE30 . . . . 146 D4
King's Staithe Sq 1
PE30 . . . . 146 D4
King St East Harling NR16 . 118 C5
Great Yarmouth NR30 . . 169 C4
King's Lynn PE30 . . . . . 146 D5

King St continued
Neatishead NR12 . . . . 55 E7
Norwich NR1 . . . . 178 C1
13 Sutton Bridge PE12 . . 41 B8
Swaffham PE37 . . . . . . 153 B4
Thetford IP24 . . . . 176 C4
Winterton-on-Sea NR29 . . 58 B6
Wisbech PE13 . . . . 152 C5
Kingston Ave NR30 . . . . 168 E5
Kingston Dr 9 NR34 . . . 110 D1
Kingston Rd NR19 . . . . . 154 F3
Kingston Sq NR41 . . . . . 174 F3
Kingsway 7 Blakeney NR25 7 C6
4 Earsham NR35 . . . . . 123 F8
King's Lynn PE30 . . . . . 146 E8
Leverington PE13 . . . . . 152 F7
3 Newton Flotman NR15 107 A8
North Walsham NR28 . . 151 A6
Norwich NR5 . . . . 162 C8
Thetford IP24 . . . . 176 C2
Kings Way NR29 . . . . . . 167 B2
King's Wk 4 PE13 . . . . 152 C4
Kings Wlk
Downham Market PE38 . . 172 C5
9 Great Yarmouth NR31 170 B5
Kingswood Ave NR8 . . . 155 C2
Kingswood Cl
Brooke NR15 . . . . 90 E1
9 Norwich NR4 . . . . 89 C8
Kingswood Ct NR8 . . . . 155 D2
Kingswood Pk PE13 . . . 152 D3
King William Cl PE34 . . 144 C5
King William's Dr
Attlebridge NR9 . . . . 52 D3
Attlebridge NR9 . . . . . . 155 A6
Kinsale Ave NR6 . . . . . 157 E5
Kinsale Inf & Jun Sch
NR6 . . . . 157 E4
Kinver Cl NR4 . . . . 162 B3
Kipling Cl NR30 . . . . . . 168 D6
KIRBY BEDON NR14 . . . 90 E8
KIRBY CANE NR35 . . . . 109 E4
Kirby Cane Bypass
NR35 . . . . 109 D4
Kirby Cl 5 NR29 . . . . . 57 D5
KIRBY GREEN NR35 . . . 109 F5
Kirby Rd Bixley NR14 . . . 90 C8
Norwich NR14 . . . . 163 C2
KIRBY ROW NR35 . . . . 109 E3
Kirby St PE30 . . . . 146 E5
Kirkfield La PE14 . . . . . . 41 E4
Kirkgate La NR23 . . . . . . 6 A2
Kirkgate St
Holme next the Sea PE36 . 2 A6
Wisbech PE13 . . . . 152 E7
Kirkham's La PE14 . . . . . 77 C8
Kirkhams Mdw NR19 . . . 66 C7
Kirklands NR8 . . . . 156 E4
Kirklees 6 NR4 . . . . 89 E8
Kirkpatrick Rd NR3 . . . . 158 B2
Kirk Rd 2 PE14 . . . . . . 41 D4
Kirkstone Gr 2 PE30 . . 148 F1
Kirstead PE30 . . . . 147 D5
Kirstead Gn
Kirstead Green NR15 . . . 108 C8
Kirstead Green NR15 . . . 108 C7
KIRSTEAD GREEN NR15 108 C8
Kirstead Ling NR15 . . . . . 91 A1
Kirtons Cl 3 PE14 . . . . . 41 E4
Kitchener Cl
Lakenheath IP27 . . . . . . 113 E2
Wymondham NR18 . . . . 173 F6
Kitchener Rd
Great Yarmouth NR30 . . . 76 E3
Great Yarmouth NR30 . . 169 D5
Melton Constable NR24 . 142 B5
Kitchener St PE30 . . . . 146 D2
Kitlings Beck Rd
North Walsham NR28 . . . 38 A7
Witton NR28 . . . . 38 B8
Kittel Cl 24 IP25 . . . . . . 84 D3
Kittens La NR14 . . . . 91 F1
Kittiwake Cl 12 NR31 . . 94 C8
Kittiwake Cl 5 PE30 . . 146 E2
Kittles La Marsham NR10 . 36 A3
Marsham NR10 . . . . 150 A1
Kittles Rd NR10 . . . . 74 D1
Knappers Way IP27 . . . 175 D3
Knappers Wy 6 NR8 . . . 70 C7
KNAPTON 143 B1
KNAPTON GREEN NR28 . 22 F5
Knapton Rd Knapton NR28 . 22 F3
Mundesley NR11 . . . . . . 143 B4
Trunch NR28 . . . . 22 E5
Knaves La NR35 . . . . . . 108 C4
KNETTISHALL IP22 . . . . 127 C7
Knettishall Rd
Euston IP22 . . . . 126 F8
Rushford IP24 . . . . 126 F8
Knevet Cl NR17 . . . . . . 174 F6
Knights Gn NR26 . . . . . 138 C5
Knight's La NR15 . . . . . . 89 E2
Knights Rd NR3 . . . . . . 158 B2
Knight St NR22 . . . . 16 F7
Knipe Cl 2 NR16 . . . . . 105 F5
Knitting Needle La
NR23 . . . . 136 E6
Knoll Cl IP22 . . . . 128 E4
Knoll The
Hempstead NR11 . . . . . . 19 E8
Tunstall NR15 . . . . 74 F3
Knowland Gr NR5 . . . . . 161 C8
Knowle Cres NR26 . . . . 138 E5
Knowle Rd NR26 . . . . . 138 E6
Knowles' La NR12 . . . . . 38 C2
Knowsley Rd NR3 . . . . . 162 E8
Knox Ave NR1 . . . . 163 B8
Knox Cl NR1 . . . . 163 B8
Knox Rd NR1 . . . . 163 B7
Knudsen Cl 4 NR15 . . . 107 C5

Knyvett Gn NR16 . . . . . 105 F8
Koblenz Ave NR1 . . . . . 178 C1
Kooreman Ave PE13 . . . 152 D7
Kost Rd NR13 . . . . 157 A3
Krons The NR15 . . . . . . 107 C5
Kybird Cl NR8 . . . . 157 A7

L

Laburnham Rd NR28 . . . 151 B4
Laburnum Ave
2 Marham PE33 . . . . . . 63 B4
Taverham NR8 . . . . 155 B1
Laburnum Cl
8 Great Yarmouth NR31 . 94 C7
2 Horsford NR10 . . . . . 53 A3
1 Wisbech PE13 . . . . . 152 E7
Wymondham NR18 . . . . 173 F6
Laburnum Cres NR19 . . 154 E1
Laburnum Dr NR13 . . . 165 F6
Laburnum Gr
Reepham NR10 . . . . . . 149 C6
Sheringham NR26 . . . . . 138 D4
Thetford IP24 . . . . 176 B1
Laburnum Rd NR31 . . . 170 A5
Laburnum Wlk IP27 . . . 175 D2
Lacey Cl 6 PE33 . . . . . . 61 D6
Lacey Rd NR8 . . . . 155 C1
Lackford Cl IP13 . . . . . 165 C4
Lacon Rd NR30 . . . . . . 168 C5
Ladbroke Pl NR1 . . . . . 163 A7
Ladbrooke Cl 3 IP22 . . 177 C4
Ladbrooke Rd 4 NR31 . 169 B3
Laddus Bank PE14 . . . . . 77 A6
Laddus Dro PE14 . . . . . . 77 B6
Ladislaw Way 1 NR19 . 154 C3
Lady Ann's Rd NR23 . . . . 5 B7
Lady Betty Rd NR1 . . . . 162 D3
Ladybird La IP25 . . . . . . 84 C4
Ladybird Loke PE37 . . . 153 D2
Ladybroad La PE14 . . . . 57 D1
Lady Dro PE38 . . . . 79 A6
Lady Hamilton La NR29 . 167 C6
Lady Haven Mews 12
NR31 . . . . 169 C5
Lady Haven Rd 6 NR31 . 169 B4
Lady Jane Grey Rd
PE30 . . . . 146 F7
Lady La NR10 . . . . 53 E5
Lady Margaret's Ave
NR31 . . . . 170 B4
Lady Mary Rd NR1 . . . . 162 D3
Lady's Dro 1 PE14 . . . . 59 D2
Lady's La
Bressingham IP22 . . . . . 119 F1
Wymondham NR18 . . . . 173 A3
Ladysmock Way NR5 . . 161 B7
Ladywood Cl 9 PE33 . . . 63 B4
Ladywood Rd PE33 . . . . 63 B4
Laen Ct PE30 . . . . 146 E2
Lake Ave PE14 . . . . 95 C7
Lake Cl PE13 . . . . 61 D5
Lake Ct PE13 . . . . 152 D4
Lake Dro PE34 . . . . 61 C1
Lakeland 3 IP26 . . . . . 114 A7
Lakeland Rd NR13 . . . . 165 A8
Lakeland Way 1 NR9 . . 88 E8
Lakenfields NR1 . . . . . . 162 F2
LAKENHAM NR1 . . . . . 162 E2
Lakenham Prim Sch
NR1 . . . . 162 F3
Lakenham Rd NR4 . . . . 162 C2
Lakenham Way NR1 . . . 162 E3
LAKENHEATH IP27 . . . . 113 E2
Lakenheath Airfield
IP27 . . . . 114 B1
Lakenheath Com Prim Sch
IP27 . . . . 113 E5
Lakenheath Middle Sch
IP26 . . . . 98 D1
Lakenheath Sta IP27 . . . 113 F5
Lakes Ave NR14 . . . . 89 B3
Lakes End La PE14 . . . . . 95 C7
Lakesend La PE14 . . . . . 95 B7
Lakes Rd IP21 . . . . 121 D1
Lake View NR19 . . . . . . 51 D5
Lake View Dr NR13 . . . 165 B4
Lakeview Mdw IP22 . . . 128 F3
LAMAS NR10 . . . . 37 A2
Lamas La NR10 . . . . 37 C2
Lamas Rd
Badersfield NR10 . . . . . . 37 B2
Coltishall NR12 . . . . 54 C8
Lambert Cl 1 IP27 . . . . 114 E1
Lambert Rd NR7 . . . . . 159 A3
Lamberts Cl 20 IP26 . . . 98 E1
Lambert's La PE32 . . . . . 30 D1
Lamb La NR21 . . . . 31 C7
Lammas Rd 3 NR15 . . 106 F6
Lammas The IP26 . . . . . 100 A4
Lamport Ct 3 PE30 . . . 147 D6
Lamsey La PE31 . . . . . . 133 D3
Lancaster Ave NR21 . . . 141 C5
Lancaster Cl
Fakenham NR21 . . . . . . 141 C5
Methwold IP26 . . . . 99 A5
Norwich NR6 . . . . 158 B6
7 Stalham NR12 . . . . . . 39 B4
Lancaster Cres PE38 . . . 172 C6
Lancaster Estate NR11 . . 22 E7
Lancaster Gdns NR11 . . 150 D5
Lancaster Pl 11 PE31 . . . 12 E5
Lancaster Rd
Attleborough NR17 . . . . . 174 A3
4 Feltwell IP26 . . . . 98 E1
Great Yarmouth NR30 . . 169 D3
King's Lynn PE30 . . . . . 147 B4
Sculthorpe Airfield NR21 . . 15 C3
Swaffham PE37 . . . . . . 153 D5
Lancaster Rise NR11 . . . 22 F8

Lancaster Sq 13 NR30 . 169 D3
Lancaster Way PE32 . . . 44 F3
Lancelot Rd NR31 . . . . . 170 A1
Lanchester Ct 7 NR2 . . 162 B7
Landlow La NR9 . . . . 70 B1
Lane The Briston NR24 . . 142 D4
Little Barningham NR11 . . 20 C4
Salters Lode PE38 . . . . . 79 A4
Winterton-on-Sea NR29 . . 58 B6
Lane Gate Way NR25 . . . 7 B3
LANGHAM NR25 . . . . 7 B3
Langham Ct
Fakenham NR21 . . . . . . 141 D4
Sheringham NR26 . . . . . 138 C7
Langham Gn NR13 . . . . 165 E4
Langham La NR25 . . . . . . 7 C3
Langham Pl NR1 . . . . . 178 A1
Langham Rd Binham NR21 . 7 A2
Blakeney NR25 . . . . 7 C6
Field Dalling NR25 . . . . . . 7 A2
Morston NR25 . . . . 7 C3
Saxlingham NR25 . . . . 7 A3
Wiveton NR25 . . . . 7 D5
Langham St PE30 . . . . . 146 D2
Langhorn's La PE14 . . . . 78 A7
Langland PE30 . . . . 147 D6
Langley Abbey NR14 . . . 92 A6
Langley Cl 6 NR4 . . . . . 89 B8
Langley Gn NR14 . . . . . 91 F6
Langley Pk NR14 . . . . . . 91 D8
Langley Prep Sch NR7 . . 163 D6
Langley Rd Cantley NR13 . 92 C6
Chedgrave NR14 . . . . . . 91 F3
King's Lynn PE30 . . . . . 147 E8
Loddon NR14 . . . . 92 A2
Thurlton NR15 . . . . 91 D2
Langley Sch NR14 . . . . . 91 F3
Langley St NR14 . . . . . . 92 A4
LANGLEY STREET NR14 . 92 B4
Langley Wlk NR2 . . . . . 162 C7
Langmere Rd
Dickleburgh and Rushall
IP21 . . . . 121 D1
Scole IP21 . . . . 130 F8
1 Watton IP25 . . . . 84 C3
Langridge Cir PE33 . . . . 61 D5
Langton Cl 5 NR1 . . . . 161 B7
Langton Gn IP23 . . . . . 130 C1
LANGTON GREEN IP23 . . 130 C1
Lansdowne Cl 10 PE32 . . 45 C6
Lansdowne Rd NR6 . . . 158 B6
Lansdowne St 4 PE30 . 146 E6
Lantern La Binham NR21 . . 6 F1
Lanyard Way 7 NR31 . . 170 B3
Lapwing Cl 9 Diss IP22 . 177 F5
3 Great Yarmouth NR31 170 A6
Lapwing Ct NR18 . . . . . 173 D1
Lapwing Dr NR8 . . . . . 156 B5
Lapwing La PE36 . . . . . 132 D1
Larch Cl
Attleborough NR17 . . . . . 174 C4
Lakenheath IP27 . . . . . . 113 E2
Little Melton NR9 . . . . . 160 D2
Norwich NR7 . . . . 159 D4
Larch Cres NR25 . . . . . 137 C7
Larch Dr
18 Great Yarmouth NR31 . 94 C7
2 Lakenheath NR31 . . . 170 A5
Larch Gr NR20 . . . . 49 E7
Larch Rd PE34 . . . . 43 D4
Largate NR12 . . . . 54 A7
Lark Bank CB7 . . . . 112 A1
Lark Cl IP27 . . . . 175 F3
Lark Dr NR17 . . . . 174 E3
Larkey's La NR12 . . . . . . 38 F7
Larkins Cl NR16 . . . . . . 105 E4
Larkman La NR5 . . . . . . 161 D7
Larkman Prim Sch NR5 . 161 D7
Lark Rd 2 PE33 . . . . . . 61 D6
Lark Rise NR14 . . . . 89 A3
Larksfield PE13 . . . . . . 152 C3
Larks Pl NR20 . . . . 68 B8
Larkspur Cl
Downham Market PE38 . . 172 C3
King's Lynn PE30 . . . . . 147 B5
Larkspur Ct 8 NR19 . . . 154 D2
Lark Way NR31 . . . . 94 C7
LARLING NR16 . . . . 118 B8
Larner's Drift NR19 . . . . 154 C1
Larners Hill NR27 . . . . . 139 D1
Larners Rd NR19 . . . . . 154 C2
Larwood Cl 1 PE37 . . . . 66 A4
Larwood Dr NR20 . . . . . 68 D6
Larwood Way 6 IP25 . . 67 C2
Larwood Wy NR10 . . . . . 53 B4
Latchmoor La NR29 . . . . 56 D5
Latchmoor Pk NR29 . . . . 56 D5
Lathes The NR3 . . . . . . 178 A4
Latimer Rd NR1 . . . . . . 162 E1
Latimer Way PE37 . . . . . 65 E1
Laud Cl 24 NR7 . . . . . . 72 D4
Laughing Image Cnr 6
NR30 . . . . 169 C6
Launditch Cres PE38 . . 172 C6
Laundry Cl
3 Norwich NR7 . . . . . . 163 E7
Thorpe St Andrew NR7 . 163 E7
Laundry La
Attleborough NR17 . . . . . 104 A3
Blofield NR13 . . . . 73 B6
Norwich NR7 . . . . 163 F7
Sprowston NR7 . . . . . . 159 D4
Laundry Loke NR28 . . . 151 B6
Laurel Cl NR18 . . . . 87 A2
Laurel Dr Brundall NR13 . 165 B6
13 Elm PE14 . . . . 59 A1
Laurel Gr Brundall NR13 . 165 D3
Holt NR25 . . . . 137 D7
Laurel La
King's Lynn PE30 . . . . . 147 C5
Sculthorpe Airfield NR21 . . 15 C3
Swaffham PE37 . . . . . . 153 D5
3 West Winch PE33 . . . 43 E2

Laurel Rd NR7 . . . . 159 E1
Laurels Cres 1 NR29 . . . 56 C5
Laurels Rd NR29 . . . . . . 56 D7
Laurels The
  Bradwell NR31 . . . . . . 170 A7
  Hopton on Sea NR31 . . 171 D5
Lavare Ct NR6 . . . . 158 E6
Lavender Cl
  Attleborough NR17 . . . 174 B5
  Brandon IP27 . . . . 175 A2
  Heacham PE31 . . . . . . 133 E5
  Horsford NR10 . . . . 53 A4
Lavender Ct
  12 Hemsby NR29 . . . . . 58 B6
  5 King's Lynn PE30 . . . 147 B6
  1 Thetford IP24 . . . . . 176 F4
Lavender Dr
  Cringleford NR4 . . . . . . 161 B1
  Downham Market NR38 . . 172 D6
  9 Sheringham NR26 . . . 138 B6
Lavender Gdns NR31 . . . 170 B6
Lavender Gr NR19 . . . . . 154 D2
Lavender Rd
  King's Lynn PE30 . . . . . 147 B6
  Wymondham NR18 . . . . 173 E6
Lavender Way NR28 . . . . 151 B6
Lawn Ave NR30 . . . . 169 C6
Lawn Cl 11 Horsford NR10 . . 53 B3
  Knapton NR28 . . . . 143 B1
Lawn Cres 6 NR13 . . . . . 72 E6
Lawn's La
  Belton with Browston
  NR31 . . . . 94 A5
  Fleggburgh NR29 . . . . . . 57 B2
Lawns Loke
  Reepham NR10 . . . . 149 B3
  Stalham NR12 . . . . 39 A4
Lawns The
  Fakenham NR21 . . . . . . 141 C4
  Great Yarmouth NR30 . . 169 C7
  North Walsham NR28 . . . 151 C5
  Wisbech PE13 . . . . 152 B6
Lawnswood Dr NR30 . . . 168 D6
Lawrence Cl
  Fakenham NR21 . . . . . . 141 B5
  Harpley PE31 . . . . 29 D4
  Mundford IP26 . . . . 100 A4
Lawrence Pl NR20 . . . . . . 50 D8
Lawrence Rd
  King's Lynn PE30 . . . . . 146 E7
  7 Thetford IP24 . . . . . . 176 F5
Lawrence's La PE38 . . . . 79 E1
Lawrence Way
  Swaffham PE37 . . . . . . 153 A5
  Swanton Morley NR20 . . . 50 B4
Laws La NR14 . . . . 88 F2
Lawson Rd Croxton IP24 . 116 C5
  Norwich NR3 . . . . 158 E1
Lawson Way NR26 . . . . . 138 F7
Lawyer Corys NR31 . . . . 170 C1
Laxfield Rd Stalham NR12 . 39 C3
  Stradbroke IP21 . . . . . . 131 F1
Laxton Cl NR17 . . . . 174 E4
Layden La NR34 . . . . 109 F4
Layer Cl
  5 Aylsham NR11 . . . . . 150 D6
  Norwich NR5 . . . . 160 F7
Laylands Yd NR23 . . . . . 136 C6
Layson Dr NR3 . . . . 158 E2
Layton Cl NR18 . . . . 157 B7
Leach Cl
  Great Yarmouth NR31 . . 170 A4
  Wisbech PE13 . . . . 152 C2
Leach's Turn NR14 . . . . . 165 B1
Leafield Rd PE30 . . . . . . 147 C3
Leafyoak La NR4 . . . . 90 C3
Leamon Cl IP27 . . . . 175 D4
Lea Rd NR29 . . . . 56 C8
Leaside PE31 . . . . 133 B6
Lea The NR30 . . . . 169 C6
Leather Moor La PE14 . . . 41 F3
Leatherpool La NR25 . . . . . 7 E6
Leathway NR29 . . . . 167 B2
Lea Way PE30 . . . . 147 B8
Lebanon Dr PE13 . . . . . . 152 F7
Leeder Hill NR13 . . . . 72 F2
Leederspightle NR21 . . . . . 6 E2
Leeds Way 5 NR12 . . . . . 55 E4
Leete Way PE33 . . . . 43 E2
Lee Warner Ave NR21 . . 141 D6
Lee Warner Rd 10 PE13 . 153 C3
Leewood Cres NR5 . . . . 157 C1
Lefevre Way NR31 . . . . . 94 C8
Leffins La NR13 . . . . 166 B2
Lefroy Rd NR3 . . . . 158 A2
Legge-Bourke Ct PE13 . 152 F6
Legge Pl PE34 . . . . 43 B1
Legrice Cres NR28 . . . . . 151 C1
Leicester Ave PE30 . . . . 147 B5
Leicester Mdw NR21 . . . . 15 E5
Leicester Rd
  1 Great Yarmouth
  NR31 . . . . 170 D4
  Southgate NR21 . . . . . . 15 E5
Leicester St NR2 . . . . . . 162 C4
Leigh Cl NR17 . . . . 174 C5
Leman Cl 8 NR14 . . . . . . 92 A1
Leman Gr 9 NR14 . . . . . . 91 F1
Leman Rd NR31 . . . . 170 D2
Leming Cres PE36 . . . . . 132 E4
Le Neve Rd NR10 . . . . . 150 D1
Leng Cres NR4 . . . . 161 E2
Lenthall Cl 18 NR7 . . . . . 72 D4
LENWADE NR9 . . . . 51 D5
Leonard Cl 4 PE30 . . . . 147 B6
Leonard Medler Way
  NR10 . . . . 53 B8
Leonard's La IP26 . . . . . . 98 D1
Leonards St 10 NR3 . . . . 162 D8

Leopard Ct 3 NR3 . . . . . 178 B4
Leopold Cl 2 NR4 . . . . . 162 A3
Leopold Rd NR4 . . . . . . 162 A3
Lerowe Rd PE13 . . . . . . 152 E7
Les Baux Pl 5 PE13 . . . 152 E3
Lesley Wlk NR19 . . . . . . 154 D2
LESSINGHAM NR12 . . . . 24 D3
Lessingham Rd NR12 . . . . 39 C8
Le Strange Ave PE30 . . . 146 F7
Le Strange Cl NR2 . . . . . 161 F5
Lestrange PE36 . . . . 132 C4
LETHERINGSETT NR25 . . . 8 A1
Letheringsett Hill NR25 . 137 A6
Letheringsett Rd
  Thornage NR25 . . . . 18 F7
  Thornage NR25 . . . . 18 F8
Letherington's La NR12 . . 55 D5
Letton Cl IP25 . . . . 67 C2
Letton Gn IP25 . . . . 85 D8
LETTON GREEN IP25 . . . . 67 E1
Letton Rd IP25 . . . . 67 C2
Lettuce La NR29 . . . . 57 C4
Le Tunder Cl 2 NR7 . . . 163 E7
Leven Cl 8 NR7 . . . . 72 D5
Leveret Gdns PE38 . . . . 172 C6
Leveret Green PE37 . . . 153 D2
Leverington Rd PE13 . . . 152 A6
Levers Cl IP31 . . . . 127 D8
Leveson Rd NR7 . . . . . . 159 B3
Levine Cl NR13 . . . . 165 B4
Levishaw Cl NR10 . . . . . . 36 E1
Lewis Cl Ashill IP25 . . . . . 84 A7
  Hopton IP22 . . . . 127 F6
Lewis Dr Roydon IP22 . . 177 A5
  Wiggenhall St Germans
  PE34 . . . . 61 A8
Lexham Rd
  Great Dunham PE32 . . . . 47 E2
  King's Lynn PE30 . . . . . 147 E8
  Litcham PE32 . . . . 47 F4
  Rougham PE32 . . . . 47 B6
Lexington Cl NR29 . . . . . 167 A7
Leyland Cl IP24 . . . . 176 D6
Leys Cl NR31 . . . . 169 C1
Leys La
  Attleborough NR17 . . . . 174 D2
  Old Buckenham NR17 . . 104 B3
  Yaxley IP23 . . . . 129 F1
  Yaxley IP23 . . . . 130 A1
Ley's La NR20 . . . . 51 C1
LEZIATE PE32 . . . . 44 D6
Leziate Dro
  Grimston PE32 . . . . 45 A8
  Leziate PE32 . . . . 44 F6
Leziate Heath Nature
  Reserve* PE32 . . . . 44 E6
Liberator Cl
  Rackheath NR13 . . . . . . 72 E8
  23 Watton IP25 . . . . . . 84 F3
Liberator Cres 12 PE26 . . 98 D1
Liberator Rd NR6 . . . . . 158 B6
Libra Ct NR7 . . . . 159 C4
Library Cl NR13 . . . . 165 E6
Lichfield Rd NR31 . . . . . 169 B3
Lichfield St NR21 . . . . . . 141 B4
Licking's Dro PE13 . . . . 152 A2
Lifeboat Plain 18 NR26 . 138 D7
Lighthouse Cl
  Happisburgh NR12 . . . . 24 C5
  Hunstanton PE36 . . . . . 132 D7
Lighthouse La
  Happisburgh NR12 . . . . 24 C5
  Hunstanton PE36 . . . . . 132 D6
Light La PE14 . . . . 59 D6
Lilac Cl Brandon IP27 . . 114 D4
  9 East Dereham NR19 . 154 D2
  20 Great Yarmouth NR31 . 94 C7
  4 Great Yarmouth NR31 . 170 A5
  1 Horsford NR10 . . . . . . 53 A3
  Wisbech PE13 . . . . 152 F7
Lilac Dr
  Lackenheath IP27 . . . . 113 E1
  Lakenheath IP27 . . . . . 113 E1
Lilac Gr NR26 . . . . 138 D4
Lilac Wood PE30 . . . . . . 147 B8
Lilburne Ave NR3 . . . . . 158 D2
Lilian Cl NR6 . . . . 158 B4
Lilian Rd NR10 . . . . 54 A2
Lily Ave NR29 . . . . 69 B8
Lily La NR34 . . . . 111 A3
Lily Terr NR1 . . . . 178 B1
Limassol Rd NR1 . . . . . 154 C2
Lime Ave Stradsett PE33 . . 80 C8
  Wisbech PE13 . . . . 152 C7
Lime Cl
  7 Harleston IP20 . . . . . 122 D1
  Lakenheath IP27 . . . . . 113 F1
  Marham PE33 . . . . 63 A4
Lime Dr NR19 . . . . 154 D2
Lime Gr Gayton PE32 . . . 45 C6
  Sheringham NR26 . . . . . 138 D4
  7 Thetford IP24 . . . . . . 176 D4
Lime Kiln Cl
  5 Cley next the Sea NR25 . 7 E6
  6 Newton Flotman NR15 . 89 D1
Limekiln La
  Houghton PE31 . . . . 29 D6
  South End NR16 . . . . . . 106 C1
Lime Kiln La
  24 Feltwell IP26 . . . . . . 98 F1
  2 Stoke Ferry PE33 . . . . 81 A3
  Thetford IP24 . . . . 176 D4
Lime Kiln Mews
  9 New Catton NR6 . . . . 158 C1
  Norwich NR2 . . . . 162 C8
Lime Kiln Rd
  Bessingham NR11 . . . . . . 20 E7
  Gayton PE32 . . . . 45 C6
  Sparham NR9 . . . . 50 F5
  West Dereham PE33 . . . . 80 C5

Limekiln Wlk 1 NR30 . . . 169 C4
Limes Ave PE14 . . . . 59 A1
Limes Cl Little Melton NR9 . 70 D1
  Little Melton NR9 . . . . . 160 B2
Limes Rd 3 NR29 . . . . . . 56 C8
Lime St PE12 . . . . 41 C8
LIMES THE PE14 . . . . 59 C5
Limes The Ashill IP25 . . . . 84 A6
Lime Tree Ave
  Costessey NR8 . . . . 156 F4
  Long Stratton NR15 . . . 106 E2
  Norwich NR7 . . . . 163 C7
  Wymondham NR18 . . . . 173 D6
Lime Tree Cl 10 NR10 . . . . 53 B3
Lime Tree Rd
  Cromer NR27 . . . . 139 F4
  2 East Dereham NR19 . . 154 E6
  3 Mattishall NR20 . . . . . 68 E6
  Wymondham NR18 . . . . 173 D5
Lime Tree Cres NR19 . . . . 66 C7
Limetree Ct
  Great Yarmouth NR31 . . 169 C2
  Taverham NR8 . . . . 155 B2
Lime Tree Rd
  North Walsham NR28 . . . 151 D5
  Norwich NR2 . . . . 162 B3
Lime Tree Wlk IP25 . . . . . 84 D3
Lime Way NR31 . . . . 170 B5
Limmer Ave IP21 . . . . . . 121 C1
Limmer Rd NR31 . . . . . . 170 D4
LIMPENHOE NR13 . . . . . . 92 D6
Limpenhoe Rd
  Cantley NR13 . . . . 92 C7
  Reedham NR13 . . . . 92 E6
Linacre Ave NR7 . . . . . . 159 C4
Linacre Cl NR7 . . . . 159 C3
Linalls Dr NR8 . . . . 156 C4
Lincoln Ave
  Great Yarmouth NR31 . . 170 C3
  Hingham NR9 . . . . 86 D5
Lincoln Cl 12 NR20 . . . . . 50 B3
Lincoln Ralphs Sports Hall
  NR1 . . . . 178 C1
Lincoln Rd IP25 . . . . 84 F3
Lincolns Field NR9 . . . . . 69 C2
Lincoln Sq N PE36 . . . . 132 C5
Lincoln Sq S PE36 . . . . . 132 C5
Lincoln St
  Hunstanton PE36 . . . . . 132 D5
  Norwich NR2 . . . . 162 B5
Lincoln Way IP24 . . . . . 176 B5
Lincolnshire Way IP24 . . 176 B5
Linden Cl NR18 . . . . 86 E3
Linden Dr 5 NR9 . . . . 88 C7
Linden Gr Diss IP22 . . . . 177 C6
  Sheringham NR26 . . . . . 138 D4
Linden Rd
  Clenchwarton PE34 . . . 145 E5
  Norwich NR5 . . . . 157 C1
Linden Tree Gdns 15
  NR31 . . . . 94 C7
Lindford Dr NR4 . . . . 89 C8
Lindley Cl NR6 . . . . 158 E6
Lindley Rd 9 NR9 . . . . . . 88 C7
Lindley St NR1 . . . . 162 E3
Lindsay Rd NR1 . . . . . . 159 C4
Linen Post La NR31 . . . . 171 B4
Lineside NR19 . . . . 154 D3
Linford PE34 . . . . 145 D4
Linford Clapper La
  PE34 . . . . 145 E4
Linford Est PE34 . . . . . . 145 E5
Ling Cl 1 NR12 . . . . 54 C7
Ling Comm Rd PE30 . . . 148 D6
Lingheath Rd IP27 . . . . . 175 E3
Ling House Rd PE31 . . . . 13 B1
Ling Rd
  Garboldisham IP22 . . . . 118 F2
  Palgrave IP22 . . . . 177 B3
Lings Cl 5 NR10 . . . . 53 B3
Lings The NR9 . . . . 86 D8
LING THE NR15 . . . . 91 A1
Ling The IP22 . . . . 118 E1
Ling Way NR12 . . . . 54 C7
LINGWOOD NR13 . . . . . . 73 F3
Lingwood Cl IP31 . . . . . 127 D3
Lingwood Gdns 2 NR13 . . 74 A3
Lingwood La NR13 . . . . . 74 A4
Lingwood Long La NR13 . . 74 B3
Lingwood Prim Acad
  NR13 . . . . 73 F3
Lingwood Prim Sch
  NR13 . . . . 74 A3
Lingwood Rd
  Blofield NR13 . . . . 73 E4
  Brundall NR13 . . . . 165 F6
Lingwood Sta NR13 . . . . 74 A3
Link Rd
  Corpusty & Saxthorpe
  NR24 . . . . 34 F8
  Great Massingham PE32 . . 29 D1
  Horningtoft NR20 . . . . . . 31 E2
  Kerdiston NR20 . . . . 34 B4
  North Pickenham PE37 . . 83 D8
  North Walsham NR28 . . . 151 A6
  Surlingham NR14 . . . . . . 73 B1
  Weston Longville NR9 . . . 51 F2
  Weybread IP21 . . . . 131 F8
  Whittington PE33 . . . . . . 81 C1
Links Ave
  Brundall NR13 . . . . 165 C4
  Cromer NR27 . . . . 139 C4
  Norwich NR6 . . . . 157 F4
Links Cl
  Caister-on-Sea NR30 . . . 168 C4
  Norwich NR6 . . . . 157 F5
  6 Thurlton NR14 . . . . . . 92 F1
Links Cres NR26 . . . . . . 138 C7

Links Rd
  Great Yarmouth NR31 . . 171 D8
  Mundesley NR11 . . . . . 143 B6
  Sheringham NR26 . . . . . 138 C7
Links Way
  Sheringham NR27 . . . . . . 10 A5
  4 Thurlton NR14 . . . . . . 92 F1
Link The 2 IP24 . . . . 176 D4
Linmore Cres 3 IP25 . . . . 84 E3
Linmore Ct IP25 . . . . 84 E3
Linn Chilvers Dr PE31 . . 133 B5
Linnet Cl 6 NR31 . . . . . . 170 A6
Linnet Cres IP27 . . . . . . 175 E3
Linnet Rd Costessey NR8 . 156 A5
  Old Catton NR12 . . . . . 158 F7
Linnets The NR5 . . . . . . 156 F1
Linseed Wlk PE38 . . . . . 172 E6
Lintock Rd NR3 . . . . 158 D3
Linton Cl NR7 . . . . 159 B3
Linton Cres NR7 . . . . . . 159 B4
Lion & Castle Yd NR1 . . 178 B2
Lion Cl NR5 . . . . 156 C1
Lion La NR14 . . . . 91 C3
Lion Rd
  Buxton with Lammas
  NR10 . . . . 36 E1
  Palgrave IP22 . . . . 177 C1
Lion's Mouth NR11 . . . . . 20 F4
Lionwood Inf Sch NR1 . 163 B6
Lionwood Jun Sch NR1 . 163 B6
Lion Wood Rd NR1 . . . . 163 B7
Lisbon Rd NR19 . . . . . . 154 C2
Lishman Rd NR7 . . . . . . 159 E2
Lisle Rd NR5 . . . . 160 F7
Lister Cl NR31 . . . . 170 B1
Lister's Rd PE14 . . . . 77 E5
LITCHAM PE32 . . . . 48 A4
Litcham Close PE32 . . . . 47 F5
Litcham Hall PE32 . . . . . 48 A4
Litcham Rd
  Beeston with Bittering
  PE32 . . . . 48 D4
  Gayton Thorpe PE32 . . . 44 E6
  Great Dunham PE32 . . . . 47 F2
  Great Massingham PE32 . . 46 D8
  Gressenhall NR19 . . . . . 49 B3
  Gressenhall NR20 . . . . . 49 C3
  Litcham PE32 . . . . 48 A3
  Litcham PE32 . . . . 48 B4
  Little Dunham PE32 . . . . 65 F8
  Mileham PE32 . . . . 48 C5
  Tittleshall PE32 . . . . 48 A6
Litcham Sch Litcham PE32 . 48 A5
  Litcham PE32 . . . . 48 A5
Litchmere Rd NR14 . . . . 109 D6
Litester Cl NR28 . . . . . . 151 D4
Little Armes St NR2 . . . . 162 A8
Little Barney La 1 NR21 . . 17 F3
LITTLE BARNINGHAM
  NR11 . . . . 20 C4
Little Barningham La
  NR24 . . . . 19 F4
Little Barningham Rd
  NR11 . . . . 20 E5
LITTLE BARWICK PE31 . . 14 E6
Littlebeck La NR17 . . . . 105 B8
Little Bethel St NR2 . . . . 178 A2
Little Bittering Medieval
  Village of* NR19 . . . . . . 48 F4
Little Brigg La NR11 . . . . . 20 E7
Little Bull Cl NR3 . . . . . . 178 B4
Little Carr Rd PE30 . . . . 148 D5
Little Church St PE13 . . . 152 C5
LITTLE CRESSINGHAM
  IP25 . . . . 83 E2
Little Dowgate PE13 . . . 152 A7
Little Drift PE37 . . . . 66 B4
LITTLE DUNHAM PE32 . . . 65 E8
LITTLE ELLINGHAM
  NR17 . . . . 86 A2
Little Ellingham Rd NR9 . . 86 A3
Little Fendike La PE14 . . . 77 E8
Littlefields NR19 . . . . . . 154 D5
LITTLE FRANSHAM NR19 . 66 B7
Little Gn IP21 . . . . 129 F3
LITTLE GREEN IP22 . . . . 129 B1
LITTLE HALE IP25 . . . . . . 67 A1
Little Hale Rd NR25 . . . . . 66 F1
Little Hautbois Rd NR10 . . 37 A1
Little Heath IP20 . . . . . . 122 A5
Little Hockham La IP24 . 102 E2
Little Holme Rd PE34 . . . 41 F6
Little John Rd NR4 . . . . 162 C1
Little La Blakeney NR25 . . 7 C6
  1 Castle Acre PE32 . . . . 46 F2
  Docking PE31 . . . . 134 E4
  9 Horsford NR10 . . . . . . 53 B3
  Roydon PE32 . . . . 28 A1
  Stoke Ferry PE33 . . . . . . 80 F3
Little Lodge La NR20 . . . . 50 C5
LITTLE LONDON
  Corpusty NR11 . . . . 19 E1
  Marsham NR10 . . . . 36 A2
  North Walsham NR28 . . . 151 E7
  Northwold IP26 . . . . 99 D7
Little London Rd NR10 . . 150 A1
Little London St NR2 . . . 178 A3
Little Man's Way PE33 . . . 81 A3
Little Marsh NR25 . . . . 7 A1
Little Marsh La PE32 . . . . 7 A1
LITTLE MASSINGHAM
  PE32 . . . . 29 C3
LITTLE MELTON NR9 . . . 160 C2
Little Melton Prim Sch
  NR9 . . . . 160 C2

Little Melton Rd NR9 . . . 160 B1
Little Money Rd NR14 . . 109 C8
Little Oak La
  Didlington IP26 . . . . 82 B1
  Didlington IP26 . . . . 99 B8
Little Oulsham Dro IP26 . . 98 B2
LITTLE OUSE CB7 . . . . . 112 A8
Little Ouse Bank
  Feltwell PE38 . . . . 112 B7
  Littleport PE38 . . . . . . 112 C6
Littleouse Ct PE30 . . . . 146 F7
LITTLE PLUMSTEAD
  NR13 . . . . 73 B6
Little Plumstead CE Prim
  Sch NR13 . . . . 73 A5
Littleport Rd PE30 . . . . 146 E5
Littleport Terr 8 PE30 . . 146 E5
LITTLE RYBURGH NR21 . . 32 C7
Little Scratby Cres
  NR29 . . . . 167 E4
LITTLE SNORING NR21 . . . 17 B3
Little Snoring Com Prim
  Acad NR21 . . . . 17 B3
Little Snoring Rd
  Great Snoring NR21 . . . . 17 A5
  Kettlestone NR21 . . . . . . 17 C3
LITTLE THORNAGE NR25 . . 7 F1
Little Walsingham
  NR22 . . . . 16 F7
Little Walsingham Cl
  PE30 . . . . 148 C3
Littlewood NR8 . . . . 155 F1
Little Wood La NR24 . . . . 18 B3
Littlewoods La NR12 . . . 164 E5
Livermere Rd IP31 . . . . . 125 F1
Livingstone Rise NR11 . . . 22 F8
Livingstone St NR2 . . . . 162 A7
Lizard The NR14 . . . . 92 A5
Liz Jones Way 3 NR11 . . 150 A5
Lizzie's La IP22 . . . . 128 E3
Lloyd Ct PE30 . . . . 147 C6
Lloyd Rd Norwich NR1 . . 163 B7
  Taverham NR8 . . . . 155 B2
Loaning The NR1 . . . . . 162 F3
Lobelia Cl NR18 . . . . . . 173 F6
Lobelia La NR4 . . . . 89 B8
Lobster La NR2 . . . . 178 A3
Loch La IP25 . . . . 84 D4
Lockerbie Flats 13
  NR29 . . . . 138 D7
Lock Farm Rd NR11 . . . . 19 D2
Lockhart Rd NR35 . . . . . 109 D2
Lockheart Drive NR25 . . 137 E7
Lock Rd NR28 . . . . 38 D6
Locks La NR34 . . . . 124 F8
Lock's La Dockeney NR34 . 109 F2
  Shipmeadow NR34 . . . . 109 F1
Locksley Rd NR4 . . . . . . 89 E8
Locksley Sch The NR4 . . 89 E8
LODDON NR14 . . . . 92 A1
Loddon NR15 . . . . 108 C7
Loddon Bsns Ctr NR14 . . 92 A1
Loddon Ind Est NR14 . . . 92 A1
Loddon Inf Sch 15 NR14 . 92 A1
LODDON INGLOSS
  NR14 . . . . 109 B7
Lode Ave PE14 . . . . 77 F5
Lode St IP27 . . . . 175 C4
Lodge Breck NR8 . . . . . 157 A7
Lodge Cl NR25 . . . . 137 B5
Lodge Dr IP22 . . . . 120 B5
Lodge Farm Dr NR6 . . . 158 E6
Lodge Farm Mdws NR20 . 49 C4
Lodge Hill NR26 . . . . . . 138 A3
Lodge La
  Castle Rising PE31 . . . . . 27 C2
  Erpingham NR11 . . . . . . 21 B1
  Ingworth NR11 . . . . 36 C8
  Loddon NR14 . . . . 91 F1
  Norwich NR6 . . . . 158 E6
  Reepham NR10 . . . . 51 C8
  Riddlesworth IP22 . . . . 127 D7
  Shelfanger IP22 . . . . . . 120 C3
  Snettisham PE31 . . . . . . 12 E4
  Weasenham All Saints
  PE32 . . . . 47 D6
  Wretham IP24 . . . . 101 D1
Lodge Lane Inf Sch
  NR6 . . . . 158 E6
Lodge Pl NR7 . . . . 163 E6
Lodge Rd Catfield NR29 . . 56 B8
  Easton NR9 . . . . 70 C6
  Feltwell IP26 . . . . 98 F2
  Heacham PE31 . . . . 133 C5
  Lingwood & Burlingham
  NR13 . . . . 74 A3
  St John, Ilketshall NR34 . 124 C6
  Tivetshall St Margaret
  NR15 . . . . 121 C6
Lodge Way IP24 . . . . . . 176 C7
Lodore Ave NR6 . . . . . . 158 A6
Loe Rd NR35 . . . . 108 A3
Loke Rd PE30 . . . . 146 E6
Loke The Beighton NR13 . 74 B2

Loke The continued
  Belton with Browston NR31 . 93 F6
  Bessingham NR11 . . . . . 20 E7
  Briston NR24 . . . . 142 D4
  Brumstead NR12 . . . . . . 24 A2
  Calthorpe NR11 . . . . 21 A2
  Costessey NR5 . . . . 70 F6
  Costessey NR5 . . . . 156 E3
  Cringleford NR4 . . . . 89 C8
  Cromer NR27 . . . . 139 B6
  East Beckham NR11 . . . . 9 D2
  Felmingham NR28 . . . . . 37 B8
  Filby NR29 . . . . 75 E8
  Freethorpe NR13 . . . . . . 92 E7
  2 Gresham NR11 . . . . 9 E1
  Haddiscoe NR14 . . . . . 110 F8
  4 Hemsby NR29 . . . . . . 58 B6
  Ingham Corner NR12 . . . 39 D6
  Metton NR11 . . . . 21 B8
  Oulton NR11 . . . . 35 C8
  Salhouse NR13 . . . . 55 B2
  Strumpshaw NR13 . . . . . 73 F2
  Suffield NR11 . . . . 21 F3
  Thorpe Market NR11 . . . . 22 A7
Loke Wiffens 2 NR9 . . . . 88 D8
Lollards The
  1 Norwich NR1 . . . . . . 163 A6
  Norwich NR1 . . . . 178 C3
Lolly Moor Nature Reserve*
  NR19 . . . . 67 F5
Lombes La IP21 . . . . 121 F4
Lomond Rd NR17 . . . . . 174 F6
London La
  Mundford IP26 . . . . 100 A3
  South Creake NR21 . . . . 15 E5
London Rd
  Attleborough NR17 . . . . 174 B3
  Brandon IP27 . . . . 175 B3
  Downham Market PE38 . . 172 C4
  Downham Market PE38 . . 172 C5
  East Dereham NR19 . . . 154 E4
  Elveden IP24 . . . . 125 B7
  Harleston IP20 . . . . 122 D1
  King's Lynn PE30 . . . . . 146 E4
  Mundham NR14 . . . . . . 108 F8
  Snetterton NR16 . . . . . . 103 D1
  Suton NR18 . . . . 87 C1
  Thetford IP24 . . . . 176 B3
  Wymondham NR18 . . . . 173 A2
London Road Ind Est
  IP27 . . . . 175 B1
London St Brancaster PE31 . 3 D7
  Norwich NR2 . . . . 178 B3
  Swaffham PE37 . . . . . . 153 C4
  Whissonsett NR20 . . . . . 31 D2
Londs The NR27 . . . . 11 A3
Lone Barn Rd NR7 . . . . . 159 B2
Lonely Rd
  Pulham St Mary IP21 . . . 122 B6
  Scole IP21 . . . . 121 C2
Long Acre NR11 . . . . 10 A4
Long Barrow Dr NR28 . . 151 B3
Long Beach Est NR29 . . 167 C8
Longbow Cl 3 NR4 . . . . 162 C1
Long Bridle Rd IP25 . . . . 84 C3
Longbrooke Cl NR14 . . . . 89 D4
Long Church's La PE34 . . 79 D8
Long Comm La NR10 . . . . 37 D4
Long Common
  East Ruston NR12 . . . . . 24 A2
  East Ruston NR12 . . . . . 39 A6
Long Dale NR8 . . . . 155 E2
Longdell Hills NR5 . . . . . 156 E2
Long Dick's La NR10 . . . . 36 B2
Longdon Cl 4 PE12 . . . . 41 B8
Long Dro PE38 . . . . 97 D2
Long Drove PE32 . . . . . . 44 E3
Longe Rd NR6 . . . . 158 F6
Longfellow Rd NR10 . . . 168 D5
Longfield Cl 4 NR14 . . . . 91 F1
Longfield Gn 1 IP31 . . . 126 B1
Longfields IP37 . . . . 153 C5
Longfields Rd NR7 . . . . . 72 D5
Long Four Acres Ave
  NR4 . . . . 89 B2
Longfulans La NR31 . . . 171 D3
LONG GREEN IP22 . . . . . 129 B4
LONGHAM NR19 . . . . 49 A2
Longham La NR20 . . . . . . 49 B3
Longham Rd
  Gressenhall NR19 . . . . . 49 A3
  High Street NR19 . . . . . 48 F1
  Podmore NR19 . . . . 67 C8
  Wendling NR19 . . . . 66 F8
Longhead La PE14 . . . . . 59 A6
Long John Hill NR1 . . . . 162 E2
LONG JOHN'S HILL NR1 . 162 E2
Long La Aylsham NR11 . . 150 F3
  Baconsthorpe NR25 . . . . 20 A7
  Bawburgh NR9 . . . . 160 B8
  Besthorpe NR17 . . . . . . 104 D6
  Burston & Shimpling IP22 . 120 E4
  Catfield NR29 . . . . 56 D7
  Fakenham NR21 . . . . 16 C1
  Fakenham NR21 . . . . . . 141 C7
  Feltwell IP26 . . . . 98 D1
  Flordon NR15 . . . . 106 E8
  Great Yarmouth NR31 . . 170 A4
  Hoveton NR12 . . . . 164 F7
  Ingham NR12 . . . . 39 D5
  Marsham NR11 . . . . 36 A2
  Mulbarton NR14 . . . . 89 B2
  Saxlingham Nethergate
  NR15 . . . . 107 B8
  Southrepps NR11 . . . . . . 22 B7
  Stoke Holy Cross NR14 . . 89 F4
  Strumpshaw NR13 . . . . 165 F2
  Swaffham PE37 . . . . . . 153 E5

Long La continued
Tharston & Hapton NR15 ...106 D6
West Beckham NR25......9 B2
West Winch PE33 ...43 E2
Wighton NR22 ...6 C2
Winfarthing IP22......119 F7
Longland IP24......158 E6
Longlands Dr NR18 ...173 A6
Longlands La NR15 ...91 B3
Long Lots PE14 ...59 F3
Longmead 4 NR1 ...162 E2
Longmeadow NR13 ...165 B3
Longmeadow Cl
Great Bircham PE31 ...14 A3
Griston IP25......85 A1
Longmeadow Dr IP22...177 B5
Long Rd Barton Turf NR12..55 F7
Poringland NR14......90 C5
Saham Toney IP25...84 F8
Skeyton NR10 ...37 A4
Terrington St Clement
PE34......144 A8
Thurlton NR14......93 A1
Wymondham NR18 ...88 A1
Long Row Norwich NR3. .158 D1
Sneath Common NR15...121 A7
Tibenham NR16 ...120 D6
Longs Cl 4 NR15......89 C1
Long's Cres NR13 ...72 D7
Long's La NR21 ...31 E4
Long St NR17 ...103 E6
Long Straton Mill *
NR15......106 F3
LONG STRATTON NR15..106 E3
Long Stratton High Sch
NR15......106 E3
Long Stratton Ind Est
NR15......106 D3
Long Stratton Leisure Ctr
NR15......106 E4
Long Stratton Rd
Forncett NR16......106 A4
Tacolneston NR16 ...105 F4
Longview 1 NR9......88 D8
Longview 4 PE31......12 E4
Longwater La NR8 ...156 D3
Longwater Ret Pk NR5..156 A2
Lonsdale Cres NR9......86 B5
Lonsdale Rd NR13 ...72 E7
Lonsdale Terr PE13 ...152 C3
Loombe Cl 3 NR20 ...50 B3
Loop Rd NR11 ...11 D1
Lopham Rd
Bressingham IP22......128 F8
Harling NR16......118 D4
Kenninghall NR16 ...119 A4
Kenninghall NR16 ...119 C4
Redgrave IP22......128 D5
Lord Cres NR20......50 B5
Lord Montgomery Wy 26
NR31......94 C7
Lord Nelson Cl PE32 ...48 C2
Lord Nelson Dr NR5...156 C1
Lord Rd IP22......177 E4
LORDSBRIDGE PE34 ...60 E7
Lords Bridge PE34 ...60 F7
Lords Hill 7 NR8 ...70 C7
Lords La PE31......133 D5
Lord's La NR31......94 B7
Lord Walsingham Ct 1
IP24......176 E5
Lorraine Gdns NR33..158 E3
Losinga Cres NR3...158 B3
Losinga Rd PE30......146 E7
Lothian St NR2......162 C6
Louden Rd NR27......139 B7
Louie's La IP22......177 C6
Louis Cl NR6......158 D6
Louis Dahl Rd 3 NR31 ...94 A6
Louise 15 NR30......169 D2
LOUND NR32......94 C1
Lound Dam NR14......111 D2
Lound Rd
Belton with Browston
NR31......94 B4
Norwich NR4......161 F5
Somerleyton, Ashby &
Herringfleet NR32......111 F8
Lousybush La NR21......6 D2
Lovat IP20......122 E2
Love La Ellingham NR35...109 D2
Fransham NR19......66 D7
Morston NR25......5 F5
Morston NR25......7 A6
Outwell PE14......77 F8
Pulham Market IP21...121 F5
Sporle with Palgrave PE32..65 C6
Wisbech PE13......152 C4
Lovelace Rd NR4......161 E4
Lovell Gdns IP25......84 E3
Lovells The 6 PE14......59 D2
Lovell Way NR14......144 B4
Lovelstaithe NR1......178 C3
Lovers' La NR29......56 C4
Lovett Cl NR6......158 F6
Lovewell Rd NR31......170 D5
Low Bungay Rd NR14...92 A1
Low Comm
Aslacton NR16......106 A2
Bunwell NR16......105 E2
Deopham NR18......86 E4
Hellington NR14......91 B6
Reedham NR13......92 F5
South Lopham IP22......128 F7
Swardeston NR14......89 B6
Low Comm La NR34.....111 A5
LOW COMMON NR16...105 F3
Low Common Cl NR20...33 D3

Low Common La
Thompson IP25......84 E1
Thompson IP25......102 B8
Low Comm Rd
South Lopham IP22......128 E7
Thurton NR14......91 D3
Low Ditch Rd IP20 ...122 F4
LOWER BODHAM NR25...9 A2
Lower Clarence Rd NR1 178 C2
Lower Cliff Rd NR31......170 D4
Lower Drag Way IP22...128 D8
LOWER EAST CARLETON
NR14......89 B6
Lower Espl NR31......170 D3
Lower Farm Ct NR6 ...161 D8
Lower Farm Rd
Carleton St Peter NR14...91 E5
Great Snoring NR21......17 A5
Lower Globe La NR13...165 E7
Lower Gn NR13......92 E8
Lower Goat La 2 NR2...178 A3
Lower Hall La NR4 ...18 D7
Lower Hardley Rd NR14...92 A2
Lower Kiln La NR15 ...90 F3
Lower Lincoln St NR1...178 A3
Lower Lynn Rd PE31 ...29 C4
Lower Marine Par
NR31......170 D3
Lower Oakley PE21...130 D4
Lower Rd Holme Hale PE35..66 B3
Rockland St Mary NR14...91 C7
Lower Rose La IP21......177 E2
Lower Spink's La NR18...88 B4
Lower St Billingford IP21. .130 F5
Gissing IP22......120 F4
Happisburgh Common
NR12......39 B7
Horning NR12......55 E4
Hoveton NR12......55 C4
Matlaske NR11 ...20 E4
Salhouse NR13......55 A1
Southrepps NR11......22 C6
LOWER STOW BEDON
NR17......102 F5
LOWER STREET
Southrepps NR11......22 C6
Wickmere NR11......20 E5
LOWER TASBURGH
NR15......106 E7
LOWER THURLTON NR14...93 A2
Lower Wells Cl NR35...109 A2
Lower Wood Nature
Reserve * NR16......105 E8
Lowes Ave NR25......137 D5
Lowe's La PE31......4 D4
Lowestoft Coll (Lound
Campus) NR32......171 A3
Lowestoft Rd NR31......170 C1
Lowes View IP22......177 E3
Low Farm Rd
Halvergate NR13......75 A3
Reedham NR13......92 F5
Lowfield PE30......147 C4
Low Hatter's Cl PE38...172 B3
Lowick Cl 9 NR19 ...154 D3
Low La
Hevingham NR10 ...53 B8
Ingleborough PE14 ...41 B1
Rocklands NR17......103 B6
Scole IP21 ...130 E6
Sisland NR14......91 E1
Terrington St Clement
PE34......144 A5
Yaxham NR19......87 B6
Lowland Rd PE14......59 D8
Lowlands NR11......20 F1
Low Rd Alburgh IP20 ...122 F6
Bressingham IP22......129 B7
Bunwell NR16 ...105 E1
Denton IP20......123 B5
Dickleburgh & Rushall
IP21......130 E5
Easton NR9......70 B6
Forncett NR16......106 B5
Freethorpe NR13......92 F7
Great & Little Plumstead
NR13......72 E5
Grimston PE32......28 B1
Hackford NR18......86 F5
Haddiscoe NR14......110 F7
Hedenham NR35......108 D4
Hellesdon NR6......157 C5
Hingham NR9......86 B4
Illington IP24......102 D1
Illington IP24......117 D8
Keswick NR4......89 C7
Kimberley NR9......87 D8
King's Lynn PE30 ...148 C1
Lessingham NR12......39 D7
Mautby NR29......75 E5
Mettingham NR35......109 D1
North Tuddenham NR20...68 B4
Norton Subcourse NR14...92 E2
Repps with Bastwick NR29 57 A4
Rollesby NR29......57 D2
Roydon PE32......28 A1
St John, Ilketshall NR34 . .124 D6
St John's Fen End PE14...60 B6
Scole IP21......130 C5
Shelton NR15......107 B1
Shropham NR17......103 B3
Skeyton Corner NR10...37 B6
South Walsham NR13 ...74 B8
Starston IP20......122 C3
Stoke Ferry PE33......80 F2
Stow Bardolph PE34 ...61 C2
Stow Bedon NR17......102 E5
Strumpshaw NR13......165 F1
Swaffham PE37......153 A5
Tasburgh NR15......106 E7

Low Rd continued
Terrington St Clement
PE34......42 A7
1 Thurlton NR14......92 F1
Thurlton NR14......93 B2
Tibenham NR16......120 B8
Topcroft NR15......107 F3
Walpole Cross Keys PE34..42 A7
West Acre PE32......46 C2
West Acre PE32......46 C2
West Caister NR30......168 A3
Wicklewood NR18......87 C3
Wiggenhall St Germans
PE34......43 D3
Wimbotsham PE34......172 D8
Winterton-on-Sea NR29...58 B6
Wisbech PE14......152 E1
Woodbastwick NR13......55 C1
Wortham IP22......129 A6
Wortwell IP20......123 A3
Lowry Cl 3 NR1......170 A7
Lowry Cole Rd NR6 ...158 F5
Lowry Way PE38......172 E5
Low Side PE14......77 F6
Low's La IP22......177 D2
Low St Hardingham NR9...86 E8
Hoxne IP21 ...130 F4
Hoxne IP21......131 A4
Ketteringham NR18......88 D6
St Margaret, Ilketshall
NR35......124 B4
Sloley NR12......37 E3
Smallburgh NR12......38 E3
Weasenham St Peter PE32 30 D2
Wicklewood NR18......87 A5
Wicklewood NR18......87 B5
LOW STREET NR9......86 E8
LOW THARSTON NR15...106 D6
Lowther Rd NR4......162 B1
Low Wr La IP22......129 D5
Loxwood NR6......157 E6
Lubbock Cl NR2......161 F5
Lubeck Ct PE30......147 A8
Lucas Ct 2 NR1......72 D5
Lucas La PE31......135 E6
Lucas Rd 9 NR31......169 B4
Lucerne Cl NR6......158 F4
Lucerne Rd 3 NR31......94 C6
Lucky La PE14......41 D3
Lucombe Dr PE13......152 F7
Luddenham Rd NR20...50 B2
LUDHAM NR29......56 D5
Ludham Airstrip NR29 ...56 D6
Ludham Prim Sch NR29...56 C5
Ludham Rd Catfield NR29..56 C6
Potter Heigham NR29 ...56 F5
Ludkin Sq 8 NR30 ...169 C5
Lugger Yd IP22......136 D6
Lug's La NR35......109 B5
Luke Cl NR5......156 F2
Lupin Cl NR14......173 F6
Lurkins Cres NR7......159 D5
Luscombe Way 6 NR11...72 E7
Lusher Cl 1 NR26......138 C5
Lusher Rise NR5......161 D8
Lushers Cl NR14......158 A4
Lushers Mdw 3 NR17..174 C5
Lushers Meadow Wy 14
NR31......171 D4
Lushington Cl 9 NR5...161 B8
Luxembourg Way NR19 154 C2
Lydgate Cl NR19......154 D3
Lyhart Rd NR4......162 B1
Lynch Gn 6 NR9......88 D8
Lyndford Rd NR12 ...39 B4
Lyndhurst Cl NR31......170 B7
Lyndhurst Ct PE36......132 D3
Lynes Cl NR13......165 F6
Lynewood Cl NR27......139 D4
Lynewood Rd NR27......139 D4
Lynfield Rd NR28......151 C6
LYNFORD IP26 ...100 D2
Lynford Cross IP27 ...100 C1
Lynford Rd IP26......100 B5
LYNG NR9......51 A4
LYNGATE
North Walsham NR28 ...151 A8
Worstead NR28......38 A5
Lyngate Cl 8 NR9......88 C7
Lyngate Ind Est NR28..151 B6
Lyngate Rd NR28......151 B8
Lyng CE Prim Sch NR9...51 A4
Lyng Easthaugh Rd NR9..51 D4
Lyng Hall La NR20 ...33 A7
Lyng Hall Rd NR20 ...33 A7
Lyng La IP22......118 F1
Lyng Rd Easthaugh NR9...51 D4
Hockering NR20......69 A7
Hockering NR20......69 A8
Lyng NR9......51 A3
Primrose Green NR20...51 A1
Sparham NR9......51 B5
Lynn Cl 7 NR7......72 D5
Lynn Ct NR19......154 E4
Lynn Fields PE31......29 F6
Lynn Gr NR31......170 A6
Lynn Grove High Sch
NR31......170 A6
Lynn La PE32 ...29 D1
Lynn Mus * PE30......146 E5
Lynn Rd Anmer PE31 ...13 F1
Bawsey PE32......44 C6
Bawsey PE32......147 F5
Castle Rising PE30......148 F5
Castle Rising PE31......27 D1
Clenchwarton PE34......144 A5
Cranwich IP26......99 E5
Dersingham PE31......140 C2
Downham Market PE38...172 C6
East Rudham PE31......30 A7

Lynn Rd continued
East Walton PE32......45 F2
Gayton PE32......45 C6
Grimston PE32......28 B1
Heacham PE31......133 E3
Hillington PE31......28 A4
Hockwold cum Wilton IP26 99 C1
Ingoldisthorpe PE31 ...140 C7
King's Lynn PE30......147 A5
Littleport CB7......96 E1
Middleton PE32......44 D2
Narborough PE32......63 F7
Narborough PE32......64 B5
Rougham PE32......47 B6
Roydon PE32......27 E1
Roydon PE32......27 F3
Roydon PE32......28 A1
Runcton Holme PE33......61 F4
Sculthorpe NR21......16 B1
Setchey PE33......43 F1
Setchey PE34......61 F7
Shouldham PE33......62 D3
Shouldham Thorpe PE33 ...62 B2
Southery PE38......97 A6
Stow Bardolph PE34 ...79 E8
Stradsett PE33......80 C8
Swaffham PE37......153 A5
Terrington St Clement PE34 42 A2
Tilney St Lawrence PE34...42 C2
Tilney St Lawrence PE34...42 D2
Walpole Cross Keys PE34...41 F6
Walpole Highway PE14...42 A1
Walsoken PE14......59 B6
Watlington PE33......61 E6
Weeting IP27......114 D8
Weeting IP27......175 A8
Wereham PE33......80 D5
West Acre PE32......46 B2
West Newton PE31......27 F6
West Rudham PE31......29 F6
West Walton PE14......59 D8
West Winch PE33......61 F8
Wiggenhall St Mary Magdalen
PE34......61 B6
Wisbech PE13......152 C6
Wretton PE33......80 F3
Lynn Rd Layby PE14......59 F8
Lynn Rd Terr PE14......59 D8
Lynn Road PE32......45 A2
Lynn St PE37......153 B4
Lynton Rd NR12......24 A7
Lynwood Terr 13 PE30...146 E3
Lyons Gn NR19......66 E6
Lytton Rd NR14......156 D8

M

MacArthur Dr 3 NR19 ...154 C6
MacDonald Rd NR27 ...139 A7
Mace Dr PE32......48 D2
Mace Rd NR31......170 A3
MacKenzie Cl 1 NR31...170 B1
MacKenzie Rd NR2......176 A3
Mackintosh Cl NR13 ...165 F6
Mackintosh Rd NR13...72 E8
Mack's La NR31......156 D7
Macks Loke NR24......142 F2
Macmillan Way NR13...165 A8
Madam's La NR27 ...11 A3
Madden Ave NR30 ...169 D8
Maddermarket Theatre
NR2......178 A3
Mad Dog La PE32......29 C2
Maden Cl NR18......173 B5
Magazine Cl PE13......152 A4
Magazine La PE13......152 A4
Magdalen Cl 3 NR3 ...162 E8
Magdalen Gates Prim Sch
NR3......162 E8
Magdalen High Rd PE34..61 A6
Magdalen Rd
Norwich NR3......162 E8
Tilney St Lawrence PE34...60 D8
Wiggenhall St Germans
PE34......61 C7
Magdalen Sq NR31......170 A1
Magdalen St
Norwich NR3......178 A4
Thetford IP24 ...176 D4
Magdalen Village Sch
PE34......61 B5
Magdalen Way NR31...170 B4
Magic City Leisure Ctr
NR1......178 C3
Magnay Rd NR8......157 C7
Magnolia Cl
Fakenham NR21......141 D4
Horsford NR10......53 A4
Magnolia Dr IP27......113 E1
Magnolia Gn 8 NR3 ...170 B6
Magnolia Mws NR20 ...50 B2
Magnolia Wy NR8......156 A4
Magpie Cl
Costessey NR8......156 A5
Holt NR25......137 D6
Magpie Ct
Dereham NR19......154 D6
33 Harleston IP20......122 D4
Magpie Farm Rd NR32...45 D2
MAGPIE GREEN IP22 ...129 B5
Magpie Hill NR32......129 B5
Magpie La NR17......103 B7
Magpie Pl NR18......173 D1
Magpie Rd NR3......162 D8
Maida Vale NR2......162 B5
Maidens Cl 1 NR13......72 E4
Maiden's La PE32......29 D1
Maid Marian Rd NR4 ...162 C1
Maids Cross Hill
Lakenheath IP27......113 F1

Maids Cross Hill continued
Lakenheath IP27......114 A1
Maids Cross Way IP27 ...113 F2
Maidstone Rd NR1......178 B3
Main Cross Rd NR30 ...170 D8
Main Dereham Rd NR21...31 F4
Main Dr NR20......32 E4
Maine St
4 Thetford IP24......116 A1
Thetford IP24......176 A4
Main Rd Anmer PE35 ...28 E8
Bagthorpe PE31......14 D3
Bawdeswell NR20 ...50 F7
Burnham Norton PE31...135 B6
Christchurch PE14......95 C8
Clenchwarton PE34......145 B5
Crimplesham PE33......80 B6
Filby NR29......76 A8
Fincham PE33......62 F1
Fleggburgh NR13......166 F6
Fordham PE38......79 E2
Fransham NR19......66 D7
Holme next the Sea PE36...2 A5
Lingwood & Burlingham
NR13......74 A5
Methwold IP26......99 A7
Narborough PE32......63 E8
North Tuddenham NR20...50 D1
North Tuddenham NR20...68 D8
North Tuddenham NR20...68 F8
Ormesby St Margaret
NR29......167 A1
Rollesby NR29......57 D2
Sidestrand NR27 ...11 C2
Swardeston NR14......89 C5
Tilney All Saints PE34 ...42 E4
Upwell PE14......77 E3
Walpole Highway PE14...59 E8
Weeting IP27......66 E7
Wells-next-the-Sea NR23 .136 A6
Wendling NR19......66 E7
West Bilney PE32......45 D1
West Caister NR30......168 A6
West Winch PE33......61 F8
Wisbech PE14......77 A7
Mainsail Yd NR23 ...136 C6
Main St
Hockwold cum Wilton
IP26......113 F7
Welney PE14......95 D4
Malakoff Cl 9 NR30......169 D2
Malakoff Rd 4 NR30......169 D2
Malborough Gn Cres
NR29......57 D4
Malbrook Rd NR5......161 B7
Maldon Rd PE13......152 E5
Malin Cl 7 NR30......168 C6
Mallard Cl Brundall NR13 .165 E2
Chedgrave NR14 ...91 F2
7 Fakenham NR21......141 E4
9 Loddon NR14......92 A2
1 Salhouse NR13......55 A1
1 Snettisham PE31 ...12 E4
Mallard Ct 2 PE32......177 D4
Mallard End PE38......172 B6
Mallard Rd 10 IP25 ...84 C3
Mallard Way
Brandon IP27......175 E2
Great Yarmouth NR31 ...170 A6
Hickling NR12......39 F1
4 Mildenhall NR7......159 E5
Mallet Cl NR7......159 F4
Mallory Rd NR6......158 D6
Mallow Cl 1 NR17 ...174 B4
Mallow Rd 10 NR4 ...176 F5
Mallows Wlk The NR15...90 E1
Mallow Way NR18 ...173 D4
Malory Rd NR1......170 A1
Malsters Cl 1 IP26 ...100 B5
Malt Dr PE13......113 F8
Malthouse Cl
Heacham PE31......133 D5
9 Watton IP25......84 D2
Malthouse Cres PE31...133 D5
Malthouse Croft PE37...81 F8
Malthouse Ct
East Dereham NR20 ...154 E5
24 Redenhall with Harleston
IP20......122 D2
8 Snettisham PE31 ...12 E5
Thornham PE36 ...2 D6
Malthouse Dr NR12 ...164 E6
Malthouse La
Cantley NR13......92 B6
Gissing IP22......120 F4
Gissing IP22......121 A4
Great Yarmouth NR31 ...170 C8
Guist NR20......32 F4
Ludham NR29......56 D5
Malthouse Pl NR23 ...136 D6
Malthouse Rd
4 Hethersett NR9......88 C7
Norwich NR2......178 A2
Malthouse Yd NR10 ...149 C4
Malting Row IP31......126 D1
Maltings Cl IP22......177 F3
Maltings Dr 8 IP20......122 D2
Maltings La 4 PE38......172 A5
Maltings Way NR16 ...119 E6
Maltmas Dro PE14......77 A7
Malt's La PE14......113 F7
Malvern Cl PE30......148 D3
Malvern Rd 3 NR1......163 A6

Mangate St PE37......153 C5
Mangreen NR14......89 D6
Mangreen La
Keswick and Intwood
NR14......89 D6
Swardeston NR14......89 C5
Mann Cl NR18......173 F7
Manning's La IP22......128 B1
Mannington Hall * NR11...20 C3
Mannington Hall Rd
NR11......20 B3
Mannington Pl
King's Lynn PE30......148 E1
South Wootton PE30 ...27 B1
Mann's La NR20......50 B4
Manor Chase NR8......156 E6
Manor Cl
3 Aylsham NR11......150 D6
1 Great Yarmouth NR31 .170 C7
Hockering NR20......69 B8
Horsham St Faith & Newton St
Faith NR10......53 D2
Ingoldisthorpe PE31......140 D8
Lamas NR10......36 E1
4 Little Snoring NR21 ...17 F1
Tunstead NR12......37 F1
Manor Ct Aylsham NR11..150 C6
North Walsham NR28 ...151 E5
Manor Dr Litcham PE32...48 A4
Roydon IP22......177 A5
Swannington NR9 ...52 B6
St John, Ilketshall PE14...42 B1
Manor Drift
High Street NR19 ...48 E1
Wendling NR19......66 E8
Manor Farm Cl
Drayton NR8......53 A1
Taverham NR8......157 A8
Manor Farm Dr NR19 ...66 E8
Manor Farm La NR28...38 C4
Manor Farm Rd
Colby NR11......21 E2
Denton IP20......122 E2
St John, Ilketshall NR34 . .124 D7
Somerton NR29......58 A6
Manor Farn La IP20 ...49 E3
Manorfield Cl 1 NR29 ...167 A2
Manor Field Inf Sch
NR15......106 E3
Manor Gdns Diss IP22 ...177 D5
Hopton on Sea NR31...171 E4
3 Lingwood NR13 ...74 A3
Wisbech PE13......152 A4
MANOR HOUSE PE32......46 E2
Manor House Cl
Brandon IP27......175 B3
Mautby NR29......75 E5
Manor House Rd PE14 ...152 F4
Manor La Newton PE32......47 B2
North Green IP20......122 B9
Ryston PE38......79 F4
Ryston PE38......172 F1
Snettisham PE31......12 E5
Manor Pk Gdns 16
NR15......106 E3
Manor Rd
Bessingham NR11......20 F7
Bradenham PE35......66 D4
Brandon IP27......175 A3
Caister-on-Sea NR30......168 F5
Cantley NR13......92 B8
Dersingham PE31......140 D2
Docking PE31......134 D5
Garboldisham IP22......118 D1
Great Yarmouth NR31 ...170 C7
Griston IP25......85 A2
Heacham PE31......133 D8
Hilgay PE38......79 D1
Hindolveston NR21......33 F8
Hopton on Sea NR31...171 D4
Horsham St Faith & Newton St
Faith NR10......53 D3
Hunstanton PE36......132 C2
King's Lynn PE30......148 C5
Long Stratton NR15......106 E3
Mundesley NR11......143 C6
Nethergate NR24......34 A8
Newton St Faith NR10...53 D4
North Walsham NR28 ...151 C5
Roydon IP22......177 A5
Scarning NR19......154 A3
Stoke Ferry PE33......80 F2
Terrington St Clement
PE34......144 B5
Manor Ridge NR13......165 E6
Manorside PE31......140 D7
Manor Way
Ormesby St Margaret
NR29......167 A2
Swaffham PE37......153 C5
Manor Wlk NR25......137 B6
Manse Ct PE24......176 D4
Mansel Dr NR6......158 E3
Mansell Cl 2 IP22......177 A1
Mansell Rd PE13......152 D3
Mansfield La NR1......162 E1
MANSON GREEN NR9 ...86 C6
Manson Green NR9......86 B5
Manthorpe Cl 5 NR1 ...162 E1
Mantle Cl NR7......159 D4
Maple Ave PE13......152 C7
Maple Cl 10 Beetley NR20...49 D4
5 Gayton PE32......45 C6
20 Martham NR29......57 D4
Wymondham NR18......173 D6
Yaxley IP23......129 F1
Maple Dr
King's Lynn PE30......148 D3
Norwich NR2......161 F7
Sculthorpe Airfield NR21...15 C3
Taverham NR8......155 B1

Maple Gdns 17 NR31 . . . . . 94 C7
Maple Rd
 Downham Market PE38 . . 172 B6
 11 Elm PE14 . . . . 59 A1
 King's Lynn PE34 . . . . 43 D4
Mapletree Cl 1 NR4 . . . . . 161 C1
Maple Way 7 Eye IP23 . . 130 C1
 Great Yarmouth NR31 . . . 170 B6
 Norwich NR13 . . . . 72 E3
Maple Wy 10 NR34 . . . . . 110 D1
Mapplebeck Cl PE30 . . . . 147 E4
Marauder Rd
 Old Catton NR6 . . . . 158 D6
 24 Watton IP25 . . . . 84 F3
March Field Way NR17 . . 104 D1
March La
 Walpole Highway PE14 . . . 41 E1
 Walpole Highway PE14 . . . 59 E8
March Rd Elm PE14 . . . . . . 77 A7
 Welney PE14 . . . . 95 C5
March Riverside PE14 . . . . 77 B4
Mardle Cl PE37 . . . . 153 C1
Mardle Rd NR34 . . . . 110 D5
Mardle St NR5 . . . . 160 F5
Mardling Run NR13 . . . . . 166 D3
Marea Mdws PE31 . . . . . 133 D5
Margaret Cl
 3 East Dereham NR19 . 154 D1
 Norwich NR6 . . . . 157 D5
Margaret Cres NR7 . . . . . 163 F7
Margaret Dewing Cl
 NR10 . . . . 54 B2
Margaret English Cl
 NR26 . . . . 138 C5
Margaret Lilly Way 1
 NR11 . . . . 21 A5
Margaret Paston Ave
 NR3 . . . . 158 A2
Margaret Rd NR5 . . . . . . 157 B2
Margaret Reeve Cl 6
 NR18 . . . . 173 D5
Margaret Rose Cl PE30 . . 147 E4
Margarets Cl PE36 . . . . . 132 D2
Margaretta Cl PE34 . . . . 145 F5
Margetson Ave NR7 . . . . 163 C7
Marguerite Cl 11 NR31 . . . 94 C6
MARHAM PE33 . . . . 63 B4
Marham Airfield PE33 . . . 63 C3
Marham Cl PE34 . . . . 146 B5
Marham Rd Fincham PE33 . 62 E2
 Narborough PE32 . . . . 63 F7
 Narborough PE33 . . . . 63 E5
Marie Cl NR13 . . . . 92 B6
Marigold Cl 6 NR10 . . . . 53 A3
Marina Cl IP24 . . . . 176 F7
Marina Leisure Ctr
 NR30 . . . . 169 E3
Marina Rd NR11 . . . . 143 C6
Marine Cl NR31 . . . . 170 D1
Marine Cres
 Great Yarmouth NR30 . . . 169 E6
 5 Hemsby NR29 . . . . 58 B6
Marine Dr NR30 . . . . 168 E8
Marine Par NR31 . . . . . . 170 D2
Mariner's Cl NR31 . . . . . 171 D8
Mariner's Compass
 NR31 . . . . 171 C8
Mariners Hill NR25 . . . . . . 7 C7
Mariners La NR1 . . . . 178 B1
Mariners Pk Cl NR31 . . . 171 D5
Mariners' Rd NR30 . . . . . 169 D2
Mariners Way PE30 . . . . 146 F8
Marion Cl NR18 . . . . 173 C5
Marion Rd NR3 . . . . 158 E3
Marionville Rd NR3 . . . . 158 E3
Marion Wlk 1 NR19 . . . . 154 D2
Marjoram Cl NR31 . . . . . 151 E4
Marjoram Rd 24 NR31 . . . 94 C6
Market Ave NR1 . . . . 178 B3
Market Cl NR12 . . . . 54 F8
Marketfield La NR10 . . . . . 53 E2
Market Gates 8 NR30 . . . 169 D4
Market Hill
 Brandon IP27 . . . . 175 C3
 Colkirk NR21 . . . . 31 D5
 Diss IP22 . . . . 177 D4
 Foulsham NR20 . . . . 33 D4
Market La
 Baconsthorpe NR25 . . . . . 20 B8
 Blo' Norton IP22 . . . . . . 128 B7
 Blundeston NR32 . . . . . . 171 D1
 Brancaster PE31 . . . . 3 B6
 Burston & Shimpling IP22 120 E1
 Crimplesham PE33 . . . . . . 80 A6
 Filby NR29 . . . . 76 B7
 Great Melton NR9 . . . . . . 70 C1
 Great Moulton NR15 . . . 106 C1
 Herringfleet NR32 . . . . . 111 D8
 King's Lynn PE30 . . . . . . 146 D5
 Little Melton NR9 . . . . . . 160 A2
 Salthouse NR25 . . . . 8 B6
 Shotesham NR15 . . . . . . 107 E8
 Somerleyton, Ashby &
 Herringfleet NR32 . . . . . 94 A1
 Terrington St Clement PE34 42 B6
 Walpole Cross Keys PE14 . 41 F5
 Wells-next-the-Sea NR23 136 D4
Market Manor NR13 . . . . 166 C3
Market Mews PE13 . . . . . 152 C5
Market Pl Aylsham NR11 . 150 C6
 Diss IP22 . . . . 177 D4
 Downham Market PE38 . . 172 C5
 2 East Dereham NR19 . 154 D5
 Fakenham NR21 . . . . 141 B4
 22 Harleston IP20 . . . . . 122 D2
 Holt NR25 . . . . 137 B6
 4 Loddon NR14 . . . . 92 A1
 North Walsham NR28 . . . 151 C5
 Pulham Market IP21 . . . . 121 E5

Market Pl *continued*
 Reepham NR10 . . . . 149 B4
 Swaffham PE13 . . . . 153 C4
 1 Thetford IP24 . . . . . . 176 D4
 Westgate PE13 . . . . 135 C3
 14 Winterton-on-Sea NR39 58 B6
 Wisbech PE13 . . . . 152 C5
 1 Wymondham NR18 . . 173 C4
Market Rd
 Burgh Castle NR31 . . . . . 94 B8
 Potter Heigham NR29 . . . 56 E6
Market Rd Pl 27 NR30 . . 169 C4
Market Row 16 NR30 . . . 169 C4
Market St
 East Harling NR16 . . . . . 118 C5
 15 King's Lynn PE30 . . . 146 E5
 North Walsham NR28 . . . 151 C5
 Pulham Market IP21 . . . . 121 E5
 Shipdham IP25 . . . . 67 C2
 Tunstead NR12 . . . . 37 F1
 18 Wisbech PE13 . . . . . 152 C5
 Wymondham NR18 . . . . 173 C4
MARKET WESTON IP22 . 127 E4
Market Weston Rd
 Hepworth IP22 . . . . 127 E3
 Market Weston IP22 . . . . 127 F4
 Thelnetham IP22 . . . . . . 128 A3
Mark La IP27 . . . . 115 C6
Mark Lemmon Cl 2 NR4 . 89 F7
Mark's Cl La NR9 . . . . 52 A7
Marland Rd 4 NR8 . . . . 155 D2
Marlborough Ct PE13 . . . 152 A4
Marlborough Rd NR3 . . . 162 E8
Marlborough Sq NR30 . . 169 E4
Marlborough Terr NR30 . . 169 E4
Marle Ct NR31 . . . . 170 C4
Marle Pit Cl NR16 . . . . . 119 E7
Marl Hill Rd NR9 . . . . 51 F3
Marlinge Pl NR26 . . . . . 138 F5
MARLINGFORD NR9 . . . . . 70 A1
Marlingford Rd
 Easton NR9 . . . . 160 A7
 Marlingford NR9 . . . . 69 F4
Marlingford Sports Club
 NR9 . . . . 70 B4
Marlingford Way NR9 . . . 70 B5
Marlow Cl NR3 . . . . 158 E3
Marlpit La
 Long Stratton NR15 . . . . 106 F6
 Oulton NR11 . . . . 35 C7
Marl Pit La NR5 . . . . 161 C8
Marlpit Rd
 Hempstead NR25 . . . . 19 E7
 Thompson IP24 . . . . 102 A7
Marram Dr NR30 . . . . . . 168 E8
Marrams Ave NR27 . . . . 139 A7
Marrams The NR12 . . . . . 40 A6
Marrams Track The
 NR29 . . . . 167 E5
Marram Way PE31 . . . . . 133 B6
Marriot Cl NR2 . . . . 162 C7
Marriott Chase NR8 . . . . 155 E1
Marriotts Way 3 NR26 . 138 D7
Marriott Way NR24 . . . . 142 A5
Marryat Rd NR7 . . . . . . 159 C1
Marryats Lokc 3 NR25 . . . 7 A4
Marshall Cl Norwich NR5 161 B8
 13 Spixworth NR10 . . . . 54 A2
Marshall Howard Cl
 NR10 . . . . 35 B2
Marshall Rd NR3 . . . . . . 158 B3
Marshalls La IP20 . . . . . 123 B6
Marshall St 5 PE30 . . . . 146 E5
MARSHAM NR10 . . . . . . 150 D1
Marsham Prim Sch
 NR10 . . . . 150 C1
Marsh Cl 7 NR29 . . . . . . 57 D5
Marsh Farm Track PE34 145 E7
Marshgate NR28 . . . . . . 151 E6
Marsh La Aldeby NR34 . . 111 A6
 Bracon Ash NR14 . . . . . . 89 A2
 Burgh Castle NR31 . . . . . 93 F8
 Burgh Castle NR31 . . . . . 94 A8
 Burnham Norton PE31 . . . . 4 A7
 Burnham Norton PE31 . . 135 B2
 Burnham Overy Town PE31 . 4 B6
 Carlton Colville NR33 . . . 111 F2
 3 Earsham NR35 . . . . . 123 F8
 Fritton and St Olaves NR31 . 93 F4
 King's Lynn PE30 . . . . . . 148 A1
 5 New Buckenham NR16 104 F1
 North Cove NR34 . . . . . . 111 B1
 Somerleyton, Ashby &
 Herringfleet NR32 . . . . 111 C8
 South Wootton PE30 . . . 148 B2
 Tharston & Hapton NR15 106 E8
 Wells-next-the-Sea NR23 136 D5
 Wiveton NR25 . . . . 7 E6
 Worlingham NR34 . . . . . 110 F1
 Wortham IP22 . . . . 129 D4
Marshland Fen Rd PE14 . . 78 D8
Marshland High Sch
 PE14 . . . . 59 B8
MARSHLAND ST JAMES
 PE14 . . . . 60 A4
Marshland St James VC
 Prim Sch PE14 . . . . 60 A4
 Marshland Smeeth & Fen
 Mus * PE14 . . . . 60 C6
Marshland St NR34 . . . . 144 B5
Marsh Loke NR28 . . . . . . 23 D1
Marsh Rd Cantley NR13 . . 92 D6
 Fleggburgh NR29 . . . . . . 75 C8
 Fritton & St Olaves NR31 . 93 F3
 Great Yarmouth NR31 . . . 169 B3
 Halvergate NR13 . . . . 75 A1
 North Wootton PE30 . . . 148 A6
 Outwell PE14 . . . . 77 F8
 Potter Heigham NR29 . . . 57 A6
 Repps with Bastwick NR29 . 56 F4

Marsh Rd *continued*
 South Walsham NR13 . . . 74 B8
 Terrington St Clement
 PE34 . . . . 144 F6
 Thurne NR29 . . . . 56 E3
 Upton with Fishley NR13 . 166 B8
 Walpole PE14 . . . . 41 C4
 Wroxham/Hoveton NR12 164 D5
MARSH SIDE PE31 . . . . 3 C7
Marsh Side PE31 . . . . 3 B7
MARSH THE
 Thrandeston IP22 . . . . . . 129 F3
 Wortham IP22 . . . . 129 C4
Marsh The PE14 . . . . 41 C4
Marsh Wall NR29 . . . . . . 56 E4
Marsh Wlk PE13 . . . . . . 152 D5
Marston La 10 NR4 . . . . . 89 C8
Marston Moor 7 NR7 . . . 72 D4
MARTHAM NR29 . . . . 57 D5
 Martham Broad National
 Nature Resrve * NR29 . 57 D7
Martham Prim Sch NR29 57 D5
Martham Rd
 Martham NR29 . . . . 57 F4
 Rollesby NR29 . . . . 57 D3
 Somerton NR29 . . . . 57 E6
Martin Cl Brandon IP27 . . 175 E3
 3 Great Yarmouth NR31 . 94 C7
 Norwich NR7 . . . . 159 B4
 Wattlington NR34 . . . . . . 61 D6
 3 Weybourne NR25 . . . . . 8 F5
Martin De Rye Way
 NR30 . . . . 168 D4
Martineau La NR1 . . . . . 162 F1
Martin Rd Diss IP22 . . . . 177 E4
 3 Eccles on Sea NR12 . . . 39 B8
 Harleston IP20 . . . . 122 E2
Martins Cl IP25 . . . . 84 C4
Martin's La NR15 . . . . . . 108 C8
Martin Way NR13 . . . . . 166 B3
Martyn Cl IP22 . . . . 177 C1
Marvell Gn 10 NR7 . . . . . 72 D5
Marwood Cl NR18 . . . . . 173 B3
Mary Chapman Cl 31
 NR7 . . . . 72 D4
Mary Chapman Ct NR3 . . 178 A3
Maryland 3 NR23 . . . . . 136 D5
Mary Unwin Rd NR19 . . . 154 D4
Masefield Dr PE38 . . . . . 172 D5
Masefield Mews NR19 . 154 C7
Masefield Rd IP22 . . . . . 177 E4
Masefield Wlk 8 IP24 . . 176 E6
Mashs Row NR11 . . . . . 150 D8
Mason Gdns
 9 West Winch PE33 . . . . 43 E4
 11 West Winch PE33 . . . . 43 F2
Mason Rd Norwich NR6 . . 158 B3
 5 Swanton Morley NR20 . 50 B3
Mason Road Ind Est
 NR6 . . . . 158 C4
Masons Dr PE37 . . . . 65 F4
Masquers Cl NR31 . . . . . 170 C2
Massey Cl 2 NR21 . . . . . 141 C3
Massingham Rd
 Castle Acre PE32 . . . . 46 F2
 Gayton PE32 . . . . 45 F8
 Gayton PE32 . . . . 46 A8
 Grimston PE31 . . . . 28 C1
 Norwich NR3 . . . . 158 E1
 Weasenham All Saints
 PE32 . . . . 30 B1
 West Raynham PE32 . . . . 30 A3
Mast Cl 13 NR33 . . . . . . 111 F1
Masters Ct NR28 . . . . . . 151 D5
Mather La IP20 . . . . 122 B1
Mathwold Rd IP26 . . . . 100 A4
MATLASKE NR11 . . . . 20 D5
Matlaske Rd
 Little Barningham NR11 . . 20 B4
 Plumstead Green NR11 . . 20 B5
 Saxthorpe NR11 . . . . 19 F1
Matlock Rd 1 NR1 . . . . . 163 B5
Matsell Way NR19 . . . . 154 E5
Matthews Cl 14 NR15 . . 106 F6
MATTISHALL NR20 . . . . . . 68 E5
MATTISHALL BURGH
 NR20 . . . . 68 F7
Mattishall La
 Hockering NR20 . . . . 69 A7
 Mattishall NR20 . . . . 68 F7
Mattishall Prim Sch
 NR20 . . . . 68 F5
Mattishall Rd
 Dereham NR20 . . . . 68 B8
 East Tuddenham NR20 . . 69 B6
 Garvestone NR9 . . . . 68 D2
 Honingham NR9 . . . . 69 D6
 Runhall NR9 . . . . 69 A3
Maud St NR2 . . . . 162 B6
Maud Terr NR30 . . . . . . 169 D6
MaureCt Dr NR13 . . . . . 165 B5
Maurice Gaymer Rd
 NR17 . . . . 174 D4
Maurice Gaymer Road Ind
 Est NR17 . . . . 174 E4
Maurice Raes Cl 2
 NR3 . . . . 158 A1
MAUTBY NR29 . . . . 75 F7
Mautby La NR29 . . . . 75 F6
Mavish Cl NR5 . . . . 161 A6
Max Carter Cl NR28 . . . . 38 A4
Maynank NR28 . . . . 151 D7
May Cl NR18 . . . . 173 B5
Mayes Cl 7 NR5 . . . . . . 161 B8
Mayfair NR3 . . . . 67 B7
Mayfield Ave NR6 . . . . . 158 B4
Mayfield Dr NR27 . . . . . 139 B5
Mayfield Way NR28 . . . 151 D7
Mayflower Ave PE30 . . . 146 F7
Mayflower Rd 1 PE13 . . 152 E3
Mayflowers The NR11 . . 150 E6

Mayflower Way
 Bradwell NR31 . . . . 170 B7
 14 Harleston NR20 . . . . 122 D1
Mayfly Rd PE37 . . . . 153 C2
May Green NR21 . . . . 32 C7
Maygrove Rd 5 NR30 . . 169 D5
MAYPOLE GREEN NR34 110 C6
Maypole Mdw PE32 . . . 128 E2
Mayton Ave 2 NR12 . . . 54 A4
Maze Ave 8 NR8 . . . . 70 C7
Mckee Dr NR16 . . . . 105 F5
Mead Cl NR10 . . . . 36 E1
Meadon Way PE34 . . . . 146 B4
Meadowbrook Cl 5
 NR1 . . . . 162 F3
Meadow Brown Way 9
 NR18 . . . . 173 E4
Meadow Cl
 2 Beetley NR20 . . . . 49 D4
 Cromer NR27 . . . . 139 A6
 Felbrigg NR11 . . . . 10 C2
 3 Hemsby NR29 . . . . . . 167 A8
 Hethersett NR9 . . . . 88 C7
 Holt NR25 . . . . 137 D6
 King's Lynn PE30 . . . . . . 146 C8
 3 King's Lynn PE30 . . . . 148 C5
 Mundesley NR11 . . . . . . 143 C5
 Narborough PE32 . . . . . . 63 E7
 North Walsham NR28 . . . 151 C6
 North Walsham NR14 . . . 163 B2
 5 Thurlton NR14 . . . . . . 92 F1
Meadow Cotts PE32 . . . . 48 B6
Meadowcroft NR29 . . . . 168 C8
Meadow Ct
 Fakenham NR21 . . . . 141 E4
 Great Yarmouth NR31 . . . 171 C8
Meadow Dr
 1 Beetley NR19 . . . . 49 C3
 6 East Dereham NR19 . 154 C4
 1 Gressenhall NR20 . . . . 49 C3
 Lackenheath IP27 . . . . . . 113 E2
 Mundesley NR11 . . . . . . 143 C5
 Wroxham/Hoveton NR12 164 D5
Meadow Farm Dr NR4 . . . 89 B7
Meadow Farm La NR10 . . 53 E2
Meadowgate La PE14 . . 152 E2
Meadowgate Sch PE13 . 152 E3
Meadow Gdns NR6 . . . . 158 F4
Meadow Gr
 North Runcton PE33 . . . . 44 A2
 26 Watton IP25 . . . . 84 D3
Meadow La Briston NR24 142 C4
 Carbrooke PE25 . . . . 85 A5
 Kelling NR25 . . . . 8 D5
 North Lopham IP22 . . . . . 119 A2
 North Pickenham PE37 . . 65 E1
 Norwich NR7 . . . . 163 F6
 5 Rollesby NR29 . . . . . . 57 D2
 Southrepps NR11 . . . . . . 22 B7
Meadowland Dr 17 NR31 . 94 C6
Meadow Loke 2 NR10 . . . 50 E7
Meadow Patch NR28 . . . 151 C6
Meadow Rd
 Bungay NR35 . . . . 124 B8
 Cromer NR27 . . . . 139 B6
 Heacham PE31 . . . . 133 D5
 King's Lynn PE30 . . . . . . 148 C2
 Narborough PE32 . . . . . . 63 E7
 North Walsham NR5 . . . . 157 A2
Meadowrise NR21 . . . . . 15 E6
Meadow Rise
 Hemsby NR29 . . . . 167 A8
 South Creake NR21 . . . . 15 E6
Meadow Rise Ave NR2 . . 162 A4
Meadow Rise Cl NR2 . . . 162 A4
Meadow Rise Rd NR2 . . . 162 A4
Meadows Dr NR14 . . . . . 89 B2
Meadowside IP22 . . . . . 128 B6
Meadows The
 Aylsham NR11 . . . . 150 C7
 17 Hethersett NR9 . . . . . 88 C7
 3 Hingham NR9 . . . . 86 C4
 Shropham NR17 . . . . 103 B4
 2 Snettisham PE31 . . . . 12 D4
 South Wootton PE30 . . . 148 B2
 Thetford IP24 . . . . 176 E4
 Thurton NR14 . . . . 91 D4
Meadowsweet 13 NR10 . 53 A3
Meadowsweet Dr NR28 . 138 B6
Meadowsweet Loke
 NR17 . . . . 174 A3
Meadowsweet Rd
 Caister-On-Sea NR30 . . . 168 E4
 Swaffham PE37 . . . . 153 C2
 2 Wymondham NR18 . . 173 E4
Meadow Vale NR5 . . . . . 157 A3
Meadowvale Gdns PE30 147 B7
Meadow View
 Brundall NR13 . . . . 165 D4
 Great Melton NR9 . . . . . 70 A1
 Hockering NR20 . . . . 69 B7
Meadowview Cl PE32 . . . 48 B1
Meadow View Dr NR21 . . 31 E5
Meadow View Terr
 NR11 . . . . 150 B5
Meadow Way
 Attleborough NR17 . . . . 174 C3
 East Carleton NR14 . . . . 88 F5
 Horsford NR10 . . . . 53 B3
 Norwich NR6 . . . . 157 F5
 Poringland NR14 . . . . 90 C4
 Sheringham NR26 . . . . . 138 B6
Meadow Way Dr NR28 . . 22 E5
Meadway 18 NR4 . . . . . . 89 B8
Mear Gdns NR1 . . . . 163 B6
Mears Cnr NR16 . . . . . . 105 B5
Mede Ct NR29 . . . . 57 A4
Medeswell 2 NR29 . . . . 167 B7
Medeswell Cl NR13 . . . . 165 C5

Medway Cl PE13 . . . . . . 152 E4
Meer Dyke La PE14 . . . . . 59 D5
Meeting Hill Rd NR28 . . . 38 A7
MEETING HOUSE HILL
 NR28 . . . . 38 B7
Meeting House Hill Rd
 NR28 . . . . 38 B6
Melbourne Rd
 North Walsham NR28 . . . 151 D6
 4 Sheringham NR26 . . . 138 D7
Melford Bride Rd IP24 . . 176 D4
Melford Cl PE30 . . . . 148 E1
Melford Comm 4 IP24 . . 176 D4
Melford Ct 3 IP24 . . . . . 176 D4
MELLIS IP23 . . . . 129 C4
Mellis CE VC Prim Sch
 IP23 . . . . 129 E1
Mellisham Wlk PE30 . . . 147 C3
Mellis Rd
 Thrandeston IP21 . . . . . . 129 F2
 Wortham IP22 . . . . 129 D2
 Yaxley IP23 . . . . 130 A1
Melrose Dr NR10 . . . . . . 10 A2
Melrose Rd NR4 . . . . 162 A3
Melrose Terr 3 NR30 . . . 169 D2
Melton Cl Beetley NR20 . . 49 C5
 Wymondham NR18 . . . . 173 B6
MELTON CONSTABLE
 NR24 . . . . 142 B5
 Melton Constable Hall * . . 18 D2
Melton Constable Ind Est
 NR24 . . . . 142 A4
Melton Ct NR9 . . . . 88 C4
Melton Dr
 Hunstanton PE36 . . . . . . 132 C3
 Taverham NR8 . . . . 155 E1
Melton Gate NR18 . . . . . 173 B5
Melton Rd
 Briningham NR24 . . . . . . 142 A7
 Hindolveston NR20 . . . . . 33 D8
 Swanton Novers NR24 . . 18 B4
 Thursford NR21 . . . . 17 F4
 Wymondham NR18 . . . . 173 B5
 Melton St NR24 . . . . 142 A5
Melville Rd IP24 . . . . . . 116 C5
Memorial Rd NR10 . . . . . 53 B4
Memorial Way
 Thorpe St Andrew NR7 . . 72 E4
 Watton IP25 . . . . 84 D4
Memorial Wy 17 NR13 . . 74 A3
MENDHAM IP20 . . . . 123 A1
Mendham Cl
 38 Harleston IP20 . . . . . 122 D2
 Norwich NR1 . . . . 162 E2
Mendham La
 38 Harleston IP20 . . . . . 122 D2
 St Mary, South Elmham
 otherwise Homersfield
 IP20 . . . . 123 B3
Mendham Low Rd IP20 . . 122 F1
Mendham Prim Sch
 IP20 . . . . 123 A2
Mentmore Way NR14 . . . 90 C4
Mercedes Ave PE36 . . . . 132 D2
Merchants Ct NR27 . . . . 139 C7
Merchant Way NR6 . . . . 158 A4
Mere Cl PE25 . . . . 84 C4
Meredith Rd NR6 . . . . . . 157 E6
Mere Manor Ct IP22 . . . 177 D4
Mere Plot Dro PE33 . . . . 62 E5
Mere Rd Scoulton NR9 . . 85 F4
 Stow Bedon NR17 . . . . . 102 E7
Mereside NR15 . . . . 90 F2
Mere St IP22 . . . . 177 D4
Mergate La NR14 . . . . . . 89 A2
Meridian Way NR7 . . . . . 72 E3
Merlewood IP21 . . . . . . 121 C1
Merlin Ave NR7 . . . . 159 B4
Merlin Cl NR12 . . . . 164 D5
Merlin Mews NR7 . . . . . 159 C4
Merriman Rd 5 NR29 . . . 57 C4
Merrison'S La NR20 . . . . 34 E4
 Merrivale Model Village *
Merrow Gdns 7 NR4 . . . 89 C8
Merryweather Cl 3
 NR15 . . . . 106 C3
Merryweather Rd 9
 PE13 . . . . 153 C3
MERTON IP25 . . . . 84 C1
Merton Ave NR31 . . . . . 170 A3
Merton Rd Norwich NR2 . 162 A7
 Watton IP25 . . . . 84 D2
Mervyn King Cl NR21 . . . 141 C4
Messenger Cl NR3 . . . . . 158 A7
Metamec Dr NR19 . . . . . 154 E3
Metcalf Ave PE30 . . . . . 146 D2
Metcalf Cl 4 NR28 . . . . 157 F1
Metcalf Rd NR13 . . . . . . 72 D6
Methuen Ave NR30 . . . . 147 A6
METHWOLD IP26 . . . . . . 99 A5
METHWOLD HYTHE IP26 . 99 C6
Methwold Rd
 Brookville IP26 . . . . 99 A8
 Cranwich IP26 . . . . 99 F5
 Methwold IP26 . . . . 98 E5
 Northwold IP26 . . . . 99 B7
 Northwold IP26 . . . . 99 C7
METTINGHAM NR35 . . . . 124 F5
METTON NR11 . . . . 21 C8
Metton Rd Felbrigg NR11 139 A1
 Felbrigg NR11 . . . . 21 D8
 Roughton NR11 . . . . 21 A7
 Sustead NR11 . . . . 21 B8
Mews Ct 7 IP25 . . . . 67 C2
Mews The
 Great Yarmouth NR31 . . . 170 C1
 4 Norwich NR2 . . . . 162 C4
Micawber Ave 2 NR30 . . 170 D8

Michaels Ct NR19 . . . . . 154 C5
Midden Sta The NR23 . . 136 F4
Middlebrook Way
 Cromer NR27 . . . . 139 A6
 Runton NR27 . . . . 10 C4
Middle Dro Denver PE38 . 79 B4
 Marshland St James PE14 . 60 C2
Middlegate NR30 . . . . . . 169 D2
Middle Gates Dro
 Terrington St John PE14 . 42 B2
 Terrington St John PE14 . 60 B8
MIDDLE HARLING NR16 . 118 B4
Middle Hill
 Alby with Thwaite NR11 . 21 A5
 Reedham NR13 . . . . 92 F4
Middle La NR34 . . . . 111 D4
Middlemarch Rd 5
 NR19 . . . . 154 C5
Middle Mkt Rd NR30 . . . 169 D4
Middle Rd
 Blo' Norton IP22 . . . . . . 128 C6
 Docking PE31 . . . . 134 E4
 Earsham IP20 . . . . 123 C4
 Great & Little Plumstead
 NR13 . . . . 72 F5
 Hardingham NR9 . . . . . . 86 E8
 Morning Thorpe NR15 . . 107 B3
 Shouldham Thorpe PE33 . 62 C2
 Terrington St Clement PE34 42 B8
Middle Rd E 4 NR30 . . . 169 D1
Middle Rd W 3 NR30 . . . 169 D1
Middlesex La NR13 . . . . 166 C3
Middle St
 Trimingham NR11 . . . . . . 11 C1
 Trimingham NR11 . . . . . . 22 D8
Middlestone Cl NR31 . . . 170 C4
MIDDLETON PE32 . . . . . . 44 C3
Middleton Ave NR20 . . . . 50 B4
Middleton Cl
 Norwich NR3 . . . . 158 C3
 2 Sheringham NR26 . . . 138 C5
Middleton Cres NR18 . . . 156 E2
Middleton Ct 4 NR18 . . 173 B4
Middleton Gdns NR31 . . 170 C5
Middleton Rd NR31 . . . . 170 C4
Middleton's Ct NR6 . . . . 157 F4
Middleton's La NR6 . . . . 157 F5
Middleton St NR18 . . . . 173 B4
Middleton VC Prim Sch
 PE32 . . . . 44 C3
Middle Wall
 Potter Heigham NR29 . . . 56 F5
 Potter Heigham NR29 . . . 57 A6
Middlewood 2 NR30 . . . 147 C4
Midland Cl
 Caister-on-Sea NR30 . . . 168 F5
 1 Great Yarmouth NR30 169 D5
Midland Rd NR28 . . . . . 151 C4
Midland St NR2 . . . . 162 C7
Midland Wlk NR2 . . . . . 162 C7
Midmeadow 7 NR34 . . . 110 D1
 Mid Norfolk Rly * NR19 . 154 E5
 Mid Yare National Nature
 Reserve * NR13 . . . . . 165 D1
Mikanda Cl PE14 . . . . . . 152 C2
Mildenhall Rd CB7 . . . . 112 B3
MILE CROSS NR3 . . . . . 158 A2
Mile Cross La NR6 . . . . . 158 C4
Mile Cross Prim Sch
 NR3 . . . . 158 A2
Mile Cross Rd NR3 . . . . 162 B8
Mile End IP27 . . . . 175 A1
Mile End Cl NR4 . . . . . . 162 A3
Mile End Rd
 Littleport CB7 . . . . 112 A3
 Norwich NR4 . . . . 162 A3
MILEHAM PE32 . . . . 48 C6
Mileham Dr NR11 . . . . . 150 B6
Mileham Prim Sch PE32 . 48 C6
Mileham Rd
 Beeston with Bittering
 PE32 . . . . 48 C3
 Litcham PE32 . . . . 48 A4
Mile Rd
 Carleton Rode NR16 . . . 105 A5
 Cranworth IP25 . . . . 67 B1
 Garvestone NR9 . . . . 68 A1
 Winfarthing IP22 . . . . . . 120 A6
 Winfarthing NR16 . . . . . . 119 F7
Miles Lane NR29 . . . . . . 56 B7
Milestone Cl NR5 . . . . . 156 F2
Milestone La
 Earsham NR35 . . . . 123 F7
 Wicklewood NR18 . . . . . 87 A4
Milford Rd 5 NR2 . . . . . 162 B5
Millard Cl NR28 . . . . 151 A6
Mill Bank PE14 . . . . 59 F7
Millbrooks Cl NR18 . . . . 173 D2
Mill Cl
 2 Blofield Heath NR13 . . 73 D6
 Dickleburgh IP21 . . . . . . 121 B1
 Hempton NR21 . . . . 141 A3
 Hethersett NR9 . . . . 88 C7
 Hickling NR12 . . . . 39 F2
 Kirby Bedon NR14 . . . . . 90 E7
 Kirby Row NR35 . . . . 109 E3
 Mattishall NR20 . . . . 68 E5
 Norwich NR1 . . . . 162 E2
 Pulham Market IP21 . . . . 121 E5
 5 Salhouse NR13 . . . . . 55 A1
 Thurton NR14 . . . . 91 C4
 Wisbech PE13 . . . . 152 C6
 Wortham IP22 . . . . 129 C3
Mill Cnr NR9 . . . . 86 C4
Mill Comm NR14 . . . . . . 91 C4
MILL COMMON NR14 . . . 91 C4
Mill Common PE32 . . . . . 47 B3

200 Mil–Nec

Mill Common Track NR14 91 D4
Mill Comm Rd NR28 23 E2
Mill Comm Track NR14 91 D4
Mill Cotts PE31 27 D3
Mill Cres NR13 166 B4
Millcroft NR3 158 E1
Mill Croft Cl NR5 156 E1
Mill Ct Fakenham NR21 141 B3
Holt NR25 137 B6
Wells-next-the-Sea NR23 136 D5
Mill Dr NR20 33 D3
Mill Drift
Beeston with Bittering PE32 48 C3
Hockwold cum Wilton IP26 99 A1
Hockwold cum Wilton IP26 114 A7
Mill Dro Gooderstone PE33 81 F4
Middleton PE32 44 D2
Shouldham PE33 62 D4
Southery PE38 97 A5
Mill Drove Northwold IP26 99 A8
Upwell PE14 77 D5
Millennium Plain NR2 178 A2
Millennium Way
Clenchwarton PE34 146 A5
Sutton Bridge PE12 41 C7
Miller Cl 7 NR19 154 C4
Miller's Breck NR8 155 D1
Millers Cl NR35 124 B8
Millers Dr IP21 121 B1
Millers Gn 43 IP20 122 D2
Millers La Brandon IP27 175 B2
Harpley PE31 29 D4
Norwich NR3 158 D1
Scole IP21 130 C6
Skeyton Corner NR10 37 B6
Miller's La
2 Thetford IP24 176 C4
Wimbotsham PE34 79 E8
Millers Rise IP27 113 E2
Millers Sq NR17 174 C5
Millers Way 1 NR10 53 B3
Miller's Way IP22 128 B1
Millers Wlk NR21 141 C3
Mill Farm Nurseries PE37 153 B2
Millfield Ashill IP25 84 A8
Eye IP23 130 B1
Upwell PE14 77 E6
Millfield Cl 5 NR13 73 D6
Mill Field Cl PE14 42 C1
Mill Field Ct 5 NR12 54 A4
Millfield La PE33 43 F3
Millfield Prim Sch NR28 151 B3
Millfield Rd
Barningham IP31 127 D3
North Walsham NR28 151 B4
Millfields
Burgh Castle NR31 94 A6
2 Hempnall NR15 107 C5
Millfleet 4 PE30 146 E4
MILLGATE NR11 150 D7
Millgate NR11 150 D7
Millgate St IP26 99 A5
Mill Gdns
Bedingham NR35 108 B4
Horsford NR10 53 B3
Mill Gn
Burnham Market PE31 135 D3
Stoke Holy Cross NR14 89 F4
MILL GREEN IP22 120 E3
Mill Green IP22 120 E3
Mill Hill Bradenham IP25 66 E3
Bramerton NR14 90 F8
Brancaster PE31 3 B6
Brandon IP27 175 E3
2 Horning NR12 55 E4
Mettingham NR35 109 D1
Norwich NR3 158 E2
Salhouse NR13 55 B1
Strumpshaw NR13 73 F2
Millhill La NR18 86 F2
Mill Hill La PE32 28 A1
Mill Hill Rd Boughton PE33 80 F5
Norwich NR2 162 B5
Mill Houses PE30 146 F6
Millicent Oliver Cl 11 IP24 176 D7
Millie Ct PE30 147 A6
Millington Ct 6 IP24 176 D4
Millla PE31 29 F7
Mill La Acle NR13 166 C3
Aldborough NR11 21 A5
All Saints & St Nicholas, South Elmham IP20 123 E1
Aslacton NR15 106 A1
Attleborough NR17 174 F7
Aylmerton NR11 10 A1
Aylsham NR11 150 A6
Bacton/Walcott NR12 23 E4
Barnham IP24 125 E6
Bircham PE31 13 F3
Blackborough End PE32 44 C1
Brinningham NR24 18 D4
Briston NR24 142 F3
Brooke NR15 108 A8
Broom Green NR20 32 F2
Burnham Thorpe PE31 4 D4
Carbrooke IP25 85 B4
Catfield NR29 56 C7
Claxton NR14 91 E6
Clenchwarton PE34 145 F6
Crimplesham PE33 80 B7
Cromer NR27 10 B5
Dereham NR19 154 A8
Docking PE31 134 E4
Mill La *continued*
Downham Market PE38 172 D7
Ellingham NR35 109 E3
Felthorpe NR10 155 C8
Fleggburgh NR29 57 B1
Foulsham NR20 33 D4
Garboldisham IP22 128 A7
Great Ellingham NR17 103 D7
Great Massingham PE32 29 D2
Great Witchingham NR9 51 D8
Great Witchingham NR9 149 B1
Great Yarmouth NR31 94 C7
Haddiscoe NR14 110 D8
Happisburgh Common NR12 39 A8
Harpley PE31 29 D4
Hindringham NR21 17 E8
Hockering NR20 69 B7
Hockwold cum Wilton IP26 113 F7
Hockwold cum Wilton IP26 114 A7
Hoe NR20 49 D3
Honingham NR9 69 E6
Hopton IP22 127 F7
Horsford NR10 53 B3
Horsham St Faith & Newton St Faith NR10 53 E2
Itteringham NR11 35 D8
Kenninghall NR16 119 B5
Keswick NR4 89 D7
King's Lynn PE30 147 B8
Kirby Bedon NR14 90 F7
Long Stratton NR15 106 F3
Magpie Green IP22 129 B5
Marham PE33 63 A4
Marsham NR10 36 C2
Mill Common NR16 103 B1
Morley NR18 87 A3
Newton Flotman NR15 89 E2
Norwich NR3 162 E8
Ormesby St Margaret with Scratby NR29 58 A1
Ovington IP25 84 E5
Postwick with Witton NR13 73 A3
Pulham Market IP21 121 E5
Redgrave IP22 128 E5
Repps with Bastwick NR29 57 B3
Rickinghall Inferior IP22 128 D2
Rocklands NR17 103 C7
Saham Waite IP25 66 E1
Saham Waite IP25 84 E8
St John, Ilketshall NR34 124 E6
7 Scole IP21 130 D6
Seething NR15 91 C1
Shelton NR15 122 B8
Somerton NR29 57 F5
1 Southery PE38 97 B5
14 Sutton Bridge PE12 41 B8
Swaffham PE37 153 C3
Syderstone PE31 15 B3
Tattersett PE31 15 C1
Thetford IP24 176 D3
Tilney St Lawrence PE34 42 C2
Tunstead NR12 38 A3
Walpole Highway PE14 59 E7
Walpole Highway PE14 59 F7
Walsingham NR22 16 F8
West Acre PE32 46 D1
West Walton PE14 41 D1
West Walton PE14 59 C8
Whissonsett NR20 31 D2
Wighton NR22 6 A2
Woodton NR35 108 B4
Wreningham NR16 88 D1
Yaxham NR19 68 B5
Mill La IP24 125 E5
Mill Loke
Bergh Apton NR15 91 A4
4 Horning NR12 55 E4
Threehammer Common NR12 55 D6
Millmarsh Dro IP27 113 D2
Mill Orch IP21 121 E5
Mill Pightle NR11 150 B6
Mill Pool La NR35 109 D2
Mill Rd Alburgh IP20 122 E6
Aldborough NR11 21 A5
Aldborough NR11 21 A6
Ashby St Mary NR14 91 C4
Aylsham NR11 150 C6
Bacton NR28 23 A1
Banham NR16 119 D7
Barnham Broom NR9 69 B2
Barningham IP31 127 C3
Barton Turf NR12 38 E1
Bergh Apton NR14 91 A4
Bintree NR20 33 A2
Blofield Heath NR13 73 D6
Botesdale IP22 128 F2
Brancaster PE31 3 B6
Briston NR24 142 F3
Brockdish IP21 131 B7
Burgh Castle NR31 94 A7
Burgh St Peter NR34 111 B4
Burnham Market PE31 135 E4
Burston & Shimpling IP22 120 E2
Carleton Rode NR16 105 A4
Colby NR11 36 F7
Coltishall NR12 54 C6
Cromer NR27 139 C5
Dersingham PE31 140 F5
Dilham NR28 38 D4
Docking PE31 134 D5
East Ruston NR12 24 A4
Emneth PE14 59 D2
Forncett NR16 106 B3
Foxley NR20 50 D8
Freethorpe NR13 92 F8
Frettenham NR12 54 A4
Great Ryburgh NR21 32 C5
Mill Rd *continued*
Great Yarmouth NR31 169 B3
Gresham NR11 9 D1
Guist NR20 32 F3
Halvergate NR13 74 F1
Hardingham NR9 86 E8
Harpley PE31 29 D4
Hempnall NR15 107 C5
Hemsby NR29 58 A4
7 Hethersett NR9 88 C7
Honington IP31 126 D1
Hyltons Crossways NR11 38 F7
Kirby Row NR35 109 D3
Lakenheath IP27 113 E1
Little Melton NR9 160 B2
Loddon NR14 92 A1
Long Stratton NR15 107 A2
Marlingford NR9 70 A3
Marsham NR10 36 C2
Mattishall NR20 68 E6
Mautby NR29 75 E7
North Tuddenham NR20 50 D1
North Walsham NR28 151 D3
Old Buckenham NR17 104 C1
Potter Heigham NR29 56 F5
Reedham NR13 93 A5
Reepham NR10 149 B2
Repps with Bastwick NR29 57 A4
Ryburgh NR21 32 C6
Salhouse NR13 55 A1
Shelton NR15 122 B8
Shipdham IP25 67 B2
Shouldham Thorpe PE33 62 C3
Stalham NR12 39 A3
Stoke Holy Cross NR14 89 F4
Stokesby with Herringby NR29 75 A6
Strumpshaw NR13 73 F2
Surlingham NR14 91 B8
Sutton NR12 39 C3
Sutton NR12 39 D2
Terrington St John PE14 42 B1
Thelnetham IP22 128 B5
Thompson IP24 102 A7
Thurlton NR14 110 D8
Tibenham NR16 120 D8
Tivetshall St Mary NR15 121 B5
Topcroft NR35 107 F4
Upper Street NR12 38 B3
Walpole St Andrew PE14 41 E3
Watlington PE34 61 D8
Watton IP25 84 D3
Wells-next-the-Sea NR23 136 B5
West Newton PE31 27 F5
West Walton PE14 59 B8
Weybread IP21 131 F8
Whissonsett NR20 31 D2
Whissonsett PE32 31 C1
Wiggenhall St Germans PE34 43 C1
Wiggenhall St Mary Magdalen PE34 60 F4
Wiggenhall St Mary Magdalen PE34 61 B5
Winfarthing IP22 120 B4
Mill Rd S IP22 128 F2
Mill Rd Track NR29 75 B5
Mill Reach NR10 36 F1
Mill Row NR11 150 D7
Mills Cl NR8 155 C1
Millside Hales NR14 109 F8
Stalham NR12 39 B3
Mill St Bradenham IP25 66 E3
Elsing NR20 50 F4
Gimingham NR11 22 E7
Holt NR25 137 B6
Horsham St Faith NR10 53 E2
Lamas NR10 36 F1
Mattishall NR20 68 F5
3 Necton PE37 65 F4
Swanton Morley NR20 50 B4
MILL STREET NR20 50 E4
Millview NR29 167 A3
Mill View
Barnham Broom NR9 69 B2
Saham Toney IP25 84 C5
Sedgeford PE36 13 A7
Mill View Cl NR11 143 D5
Millview Way NR18 87 B5
Millway NR18 173 B6
Mill Way PE14 77 B8
Millway Ave IP22 177 E7
Millway La Diss IP22 130 A8
Diss IP22 177 F7
Palgrave IP22 177 B2
Wortham IP22 129 D5
Milner Rd PE13 152 C4
Milnes Way 3 NR33 111 F1
Milton Ave PE30 146 F5
Milton Cl
East Dereham NR19 154 C7
Norwich NR1 162 E3
3 Thetford IP24 176 E6
Milton Dr NR14 92 A1
Milton Rd
Great Yarmouth NR30 169 D8
8 Swanton Morley NR20 50 B3
Milton Way 1 PE38 172 D6
Milverton Rd 1 NR1 162 F3
Mindhams Yd NR23 136 C6
Mingay Rd IP24 176 B2
Minion Cl 8 NR7 72 D4
Minnow Ave 3 PE30 146 E2
Minnow Cl PE37 153 C2
Minnow Way NR14 89 B2
Minns Cres 17 NR14 90 C5
Minotaur Way 2 NR5 156 C1
Minsmere Rd 7 NR31 94 A6
Minster Ct PE30 147 C5
Minstergate IP24 176 C4
Mintlyn Wood Rd PE32 44 C6
Miriam Cl NR29 168 E8
Misburgh Way NR31 171 E4
MISERY CORNER IP20 122 F8
Mission Ct IP22 177 F3
Mission Hall Cl
1 Blofield NR13 165 D6
Brundall NR13 165 E6
Mission La Docking PE31 134 E4
Fakenham NR21 141 E4
Mission Pl NR30 169 D6
Mission Rd Diss IP22 177 F3
3 Great Yarmouth NR31 169 B4
Rackheath NR13 72 E8
Mission Way IP22 119 E3
Mitchell Cl
10 Feltwell IP26 98 D1
Watton IP25 84 D2
Mitchell Ct 4 NR5 160 F8
Mitchell Dr NR31 169 B2
Mitchell Gdns NR14 90 C5
Mitre Ct NR3 158 A3
Mitre Tavern Yd 4 NR28 151 C5
Mitre Yd 9 NR28 151 C5
Moat La 8 NR17 104 F1
Moat Rd
3 Great Yarmouth NR30 169 C5
Terrington St Clement PE34 144 B1
Model Farm Rd NR23 4 E6
Modney Bridge Rd
Hilgay PE38 96 F8
Hilgay PE38 97 A7
Modney Hall Rd PE38 97 A7
Moffett Rd NR20 50 B4
Mokyll Croft NR8 155 D2
Molehill Dr IP26 98 D3
Moles La NR34 124 D5
Molls Dro PE14 77 C7
Mona La PE37 66 B4
Monastery The NR3 178 B3
Money Bank PE13 152 E4
Moneyhill La NR9 86 C3
Moneypot La IP22 128 E5
Money Rd NR6 158 D7
Monkhams Dr 9 IP25 84 E3
Monks Cl PE31 14 D5
Monksgate IP24 176 B4
Monks La NR11 20 A1
Monkton Wy PE30 147 C3
Mons Ave NR1 163 A8
Montagu Cl PE37 153 C3
Montagu Dr 4 IP27 114 E1
Montague Rd NR26 138 C7
Montcalm Rd NR1 163 B6
Mont Cross 8 NR8 155 D2
Montgomery Cl 2 NR5 160 F7
Montgomery Way PE30 147 D4
Montpelier Dr 1 IP24 116 A1
Montrose Ct 1 NR7 72 D4
Monument Rd NR30 170 E7
Moorditch La PE34 42 E2
Moore Ave NR6 158 F5
Moorend La NR21 32 D7
Moorend Rd NR21 32 D7
Moorfield Rd 3 NR20 68 E6
MOORGATE NR19 154 D3
Moorgate Blickling NR11 20 F1
Ingworth NR11 36 A8
Moor Gate NR11 35 F8
Moorgate Rd
East Dereham NR19 154 D3
Hindringham NR21 17 E8
Moorhen Cl NR7 159 D5
Moorhouse Cl NR10 149 C5
Moorings The PE33 81 A2
Moor La Cranworth IP25 85 D7
Elsing NR20 50 F3
Fransham NR19 66 A7
Sculthorpe NR21 16 B2
Stalham NR12 39 C3
Moorland Cl NR7 159 A2
Moorlands CE Prim Acad NR31 94 A5
Moorland Way 3 NR31 94 A5
Moor Rd
Burston & Shimpling IP21 121 B2
Stalham NR12 39 C3
Moors The NR8 155 F2
Moor The Banham NR16 119 C7
Reepham NR10 149 E5
Morar Dr NR17 174 E6
Morello Cl NR4 161 E5
Morello Ct PE30 147 B8
Morgan's Field La PE31 29 B6
Morgans Way NR10 53 C8
Morgan Way NR5 160 F8
Morgrove La NR29 57 D6
Morley CE Prim Sch NR18 87 A2
Morleyfield La NR18 87 A3
Morley La NR18 87 C2
Morley Rd
Attleborough NR17 104 D8
Beighton NR13 74 D2
Deopham NR18 86 E1
Sheringham NR26 138 D6
Morley Rd N NR26 138 D6
MORLEY ST BOTOLPH NR18 87 B2
Morleys Leet PE30 146 D1
Morley St NR3 162 F8
Mormor La IP21 131 C8
MORNINGTHORPE NR15 107 A3
Mornington Rd NR2 162 A4
Morris Cl
3 Norwich NR5 161 B8
6 Stoke Holy Cross NR14 89 F4
Morris Dr NR13 165 A8
Morrison Cl NR28 151 B5
Morris Rd NR28 151 B4
Morris St NR26 138 D7
Morse Ave NR1 163 C7
Morse Cl Brundall NR13 165 D3
Great Witchingham NR9 51 D5
Morse Ct NR30 168 D6
Morse Rd
Horsham St Faith NR10 53 C1
Norwich NR1 163 C7
MORSTON NR25 7 B6
Morston Chase NR25 6 F6
Morston Rd Blakeney NR25 7 C6
Stiffkey NR23 6 D6
Mortice Hill NR20 49 A8
Mortimer Cl NR17 174 F6
MORTON NR9 52 A4
Morton Cl 1 NR11 150 D6
Morton Cres 22 NR31 94 C7
Morton Hall Est NR9 52 A2
Morton La NR9 51 F3
Morton Peto Cl NR32 111 D7
Morton Peto Rd NR31 170 B8
Morton Rd NR11 150 D6
Mosely Ct NR5 160 E8
Mosquito Cl 20 IP25 84 F3
Mossfield Cl NR1 163 B8
Mossymere NR11 20 B2
Mother Julian Cl 8 IP24 176 D7
Mother Quy's IP24 115 C1
Mottram Cl NR5 161 D6
Motum Rd NR5 161 C7
Moughton Ct 12 PE33 43 F2
Moulton Rd
Halvergate NR13 74 F1
Tivetshall St Margaret NR15 121 A7
MOULTON ST MARY NR13 74 D2
Mountain's Rd 2 NR11 19 F1
Mountbatten Cl 5 IP24 176 E6
Mountbatten Dr
2 East Dereham NR19 154 C6
Old Catton NR6 159 A6
Wisbech PE13 152 A7
Mountbatten Rd
Bungay NR35 124 A7
Dersingham PE31 140 C3
Mountbatten Way NR30 168 D6
Mount Cl Brandon IP27 175 D2
Swaffham PE37 153 A5
Mount Dr PE13 152 E4
Mounteney Cl NR7 159 A4
Mountergate NR1 178 B2
Mountfield Ave
Hellesdon NR6 157 F4
Norwich NR6 158 A4
Mount Pk Cl PE32 44 C3
MOUNT PLEASANT NR17 103 C5
Mount Pleasant
Diss IP22 177 D5
Little Walsingham NR22 16 F8
Norwich NR2 162 B4
Mount Pleasant Dr 12 NR16 118 C5
Mount Pleasant Rd PE13 152 C7
Mount Rd IP27 175 D2
Mounts Pit La IP27 175 D3
Mount St Cromer NR27 139 B7
Diss IP22 177 D5
King's Lynn PE30 146 F4
Mount Surrey 4 NR18 173 C6
Mount Tumbledown Cl 7 PE12 41 B8
Mousehold Ave NR3 163 A8
Mousehold Inf Sch NR3 162 F8
Mousehold La NR7 159 A3
Mousehold St NR3 178 C4
Mowles Rd NR20 68 C8
Moyse's Bank
Emneth Hungate PE14 59 F2
Marshland St James PE14 60 A2
Muck Heap Rd NR35 109 D1
Muck La NR13 72 F8
Muckleburgh Collection The★ NR25 8 E6
MUCKLETON PE31 3 F2
Muckleton La PE31 4 A2
Mudd's Dro PE14 77 F2
Mud Rd NR21 15 D2
Muir Dr NR9 86 B5
Muir La NR15 106 B2
MULBARTON NR14 89 B3
Mulbarton Prim Sch NR14 89 B3
Mulbarton Rd NR4 89 D7
Mulberry Cl
17 Feltwell IP26 98 E1
6 Norwich NR3 178 A3
Mulberry Ct 2 NR8 155 B2
Mulberry Gr 4 NR31 94 C6
Mulberry La NR15 107 A3
Mulberry Rd PE30 147 D4
Mulberry Tree Cl NR29 75 F8
Mullicourt Rd PE14 78 B6
Mull's Loke IP20 122 B5
Mumby's Dro PE14 77 E1
Munden Cl IP26 114 A7
MUNDESLEY NR11 143 B5
Mundesley Jun & Fst Sch NR11 143 B5
Mundesley Maritime Mus★ NR11 143 C6
Mundesley Rd
Gimingham NR11 22 E7
Gimingham NR11 22 F8
Knapton NR28 23 A5
Mundesley Rd *continued*
Knapton NR28 143 B1
Mundesley NR11 143 A4
North Walsham NR28 151 C6
Overstrand NR27 11 A3
Paston NR28 143 D3
Trimingham NR11 11 E1
Trunch NR28 22 F5
MUNDFORD IP26 100 B4
Mundford CE Prim Sch IP26 100 B4
Mundford Rd
Gooderstone IP26 82 C3
Methwold IP26 99 C3
Methwold IP26 99 D5
Thetford IP24 176 B8
Thetford IP24 176 C6
Thetford IP27 115 F6
Weeting-with-Broomhill IP27 175 D7
MUNDHAM NR14 91 C1
Mundham Comm Rd NR14 91 C1
Mundham La NR14 91 D2
Mundham Rd
Loddon NR14 91 E1
Mundham NR14 109 A8
Mundy's La IP20 123 A1
Munhaven Cl NR11 143 C5
Munnings Cl NR14 89 D4
Munnings Rd NR7 159 D1
Munns La NR12 38 F8
Munn's La NR12 23 F1
Munson's La IP26 98 E2
Munson's Pl IP26 98 E2
Murgot's La PE33 81 D7
Muriel Kenny Ct 10 NR9 88 C7
Muriel Rd NR2 162 A4
Muriel Way IP25 85 B4
Murrayfield Rd NR6 158 B5
Museum Sq PE13 152 C5
Music House La NR1 178 B2
Musketeer Way 29 NR7 72 D4
Muskett Way NR11 150 A5
Mus of the Broads The★ NR12 39 B3
Muspole St NR3 178 A4
MUSTARD HYRN NR29 57 C5
Musticott Pl PE13 152 F6
Mute Cres NR7 159 D5
Mutford Gn IP27 113 E2
Mws Ct NR13 165 E6
Myles Way PE13 152 C8
Myrtle Ave
Costessey NR8 156 F3
East Dereham NR19 154 E4
Myrtle Ct NR31 170 C6
Myrtle Rd NR9 88 C8

N

Naber Furlong 1 NR8 155 E2
Naidens La NR15 90 A2
Nan Hazles La IP22 129 A1
Napier Cl PE30 147 C5
Napier Ct 4 PE13 152 D4
Napier Pl Norwich NR2 162 C7
Thetford IP24 176 A1
Napier Wy NR19 154 F3
Naples Cl NR31 171 E4
Napoleon Pl 9 NR30 169 D3
Napthans La PE34 79 D8
NARBOROUGH PE32 63 E7
Narborough CE Prim Sch NR29 58 B6
Narborough CEVC Prim Sch PE32 63 E7
Narborough Hill PE33 63 E2
Narborough Rd
Narborough PE33 63 E5
Pentney PE32 63 D8
Nar Cl PE30 146 F7
Narford La
East Walton PE32 45 F2
Narford PE32 64 B7
Narford Rd
Narborough PE32 63 F7
Narford PE32 64 A8
West Acre PE32 46 C1
NARROWGATE CORNER NR29 57 C2
Narrowgate Way NR15 121 B8
Narrow La NR16 120 E8
Narrows Trading Est The PE30 147 A1
Naseby Way 23 NR7 72 D4
Nash Rd NR10 155 C8
Nash's La NR28 23 E1
Nasmith Rd NR4 161 E3
Nathaniel Cl NR8 155 A2
Natterers Rd NR9 88 C8
Naylor Rd 1 NR3 157 F1
Nazer Cl IP26 100 A4
Neale Ave NR14 90 C5
Neale Cl NR11 150 B6
Neatherd High Sch NR20 154 F5
Neatherd Moor
Dereham NR20 50 A1
Dereham NR20 154 F6
Neatherd Rd NR19 154 E5
NEATISHEAD NR12 55 E7
Neatishead Rd NR12 55 E5
Neatishead VC Primary Sch NR12 55 D7
NEATON IP25 84 E4
NECTON PE37 65 F4
Necton Rd IP25 66 A3

Necton VA Prim Sch
 PE37................66 A4
NEEDHAM IP20......131 D8
Needham Bank PE14...77 C8
Needham Rd
 Needham IP20......122 C1
 Weybread IP21.......131 F7
Neil Ave NR25.......137 B5
Neilsen Cl NR23......136 E6
Nelonde Dr 🟦 NR18..173 C5
Nelson Ave PE38......172 B5
Nelson Bsns Ctr PE30..146 E8
Nelson Cl
 🟦 Aylsham NR11......150 A5
 Bradenham IP25.......66 E3
 Harleston IP20......122 D3
 🟦 Hethersett NR9......88 E8
 🟦 Poringland NR14......90 C5
Nelson Cres
 Swaffham PE37.......153 D3
 Thetford IP24......176 C3
Nelson Ct IP25.......84 D4
Nelson Dr
 Hunstanton PE36.....132 D3
 Plumstead Green NR13..165 A8
Nelson Gdns PE13....152 D6
Nelson Hts NR2......139 A7
Nelson Inf Sch NR2...162 B7
Nelson Pl 🟦 NR19...154 D5
Nelson Rd
 Caister-on-Sea NR30...168 F4
 Diss IP22........177 F4
 Fakenham NR21......141 B4
 Great Yarmouth NR31..170 D4
 North Walsham NR28..151 D5
 Sheringham NR26...138 F7
Nelson Rd Central
 NR30............169 D3
Nelson Rd N NR30....169 D5
Nelson Rd S NR30....169 D2
Nelson's Loke NR17...103 D6
Nelson St
 King's Lynn PE30.....146 D4
 Norwich NR2.......162 B7
Nelson Way
 Hevingham NR10......53 B8
 Mundesley NR11.....143 A4
 🟦 North Walsham NR28.151 C5
Nenelands PE12.......41 C8
Nene Mdws PE12......41 C8
Nene Par PE13.......152 B6
Nene Quay PE13......152 C5
Nene & Ramnoth Sch
 PE13............152 D4
Nene Rd
 Hunstanton PE36.....132 C4
 🟦 Watlington PE33......61 D6
Neptune Cl 🟦 NR31...94 C7
Neptune Loke
 Costessey NR5......156 B1
 🟦 Costessey NR5......156 C1
Neptune Way PE37...153 D4
Netherby Dr PE14....152 F1
Nethergate NR21......33 F8
Nethergate St
 Ditchingham NR35....109 A1
 Ditchingham NR35....124 A8
 Harpley PE31.......29 C4
 Hopton IP22.......127 E6
Nether Row IP24......176 D3
Netherwood Gn NR1...162 F2
Nettle Hill E 🟦 NR30..169 D4
Nettle Hill W NR30...169 D4
Neve's Cl NR13.......73 F3
Neville Cl
 East Dereham NR19...154 E1
 Norwich NR7.......158 F3
 Saham Toney IP25.....84 B5
Neville La PE31......133 C6
Neville Rd
 Heacham PE31......133 C6
 Norwich NR7.......158 F3
 Stalham NR12.......39 C3
Newall Rd 🟦 IP24....125 F6
Newark La NR14......90 E7
Newark Cl 🟦 NR7....72 D4
Newarp Way NR30....168 D8
Newbegin Cl NR1....163 C7
Newbegin Rd NR1....163 B7
New Bridge PE14......77 D5
New Bridge La Elm PE14..59 A1
 Wisbech PE14......152 A1
New Bridge Rd PE14...77 D5
NEW BUCKENHAM
 NR16............104 F8
New Buckenham Rd
 Banham NR16......119 E8
 Old Buckenham NR17..104 D1
Newbuildings La NR13.165 D8
Newbury Way 🟦 NR7..72 D4
Newby Rd 🟦 PE30...147 D6
Newcastle Cl 🟦 NR7..72 D4
Newcastle Rd NR30...169 D1
NEW CATTON NR3....158 D1
New Cll NR13.......166 C3
New Coll Cl NR31....170 B5
Newcombe Cl PE14....42 B1
Newcombe Dr 🟦 IP26..98 E1
New Common Marsh
 PE34............25 A1
New Comm Rd IP22...127 F4
New Conduit St PE30..146 D5
NEW COSTESSEY NR5.157 A1
New Cut Bank Rd NR31.93 D2
New Dam NR14......92 F3
New Dro 🟦 PE13....152 D2
New Eccles Hall Sch The
 NR16............118 F7
Newell Cl NR25......137 E7

Newell Cresent NR27...10 A6
New England Way 🟦
 IP24............116 A1
Newey's Way 🟦 NR12.164 C5
New Fen Dro PE38.....97 A5
Newfen Gravel Dro
 IP27............113 D4
Newfields PE32.......65 C5
Newfound Dr NR4....161 C1
NEWGATE NR27......7 E5
Newgate
 🟦 Beccles NR34......110 D1
 Kirby Row NR35.....109 E3
NEWGATE CORNER
 NR29............75 C8
Newgate Gn NR25.....7 E6
Newgate La
 Kirby Cane NR35.....109 E3
 Wells-next-the-Sea PE37.153 C5
NEW HAINFORD NR10..53 D5
New Hampshire Way 🟦
 IP24............116 A1
Newhaven Cl NR27...139 B6
Newhaven Ct NR27...139 B6
NEW HOLKHAM NR23..5 A2
New Home La NR10....53 D1
NEW HOUGHTON PE31.29 D6
New Inn Hill NR14....91 C7
New Inn La NR19....154 B5
New La Banham NR16..119 B8
 Bradenham IP25......66 F4
 Kelling NR25.......8 C5
 Mattishall NR20......68 F5
 Woodbastwick NR13...55 C1
Newlands Ave PE30...146 E7
Newlands Cl 🟦 IP20..122 D2
Newlands Est NR12.....23 E4
Newlands La NR20....34 C4
Newman Dr NR21....141 C6
Newman Rd NR13.....72 D7
Newman's Drove IP27.113 B2
Newmarket Rd
 🟦 Cringleford NR4....89 B8
 Norwich NR2.......178 A1
Newmarket St NR2...162 C4
New Mills Yd NR3....178 A4
Newnham Gn NR31...170 A4
New N Rd NR17......174 D5
New Par NR27.......139 C7
Newport NR29.......167 D6
Newport Cotts Track
 NR29............167 D5
Newport Dr NR15....121 A8
Newport Rd
 Hemsby NR29......167 C6
 South Walsham NR13..74 A8
NEW RACKHEATH NR13.72 E7
New Rd Acle NR13....166 C3
 Attleborough NR17...174 B3
 Aylsham NR11......150 D7
 Baconsthorpe NR25....20 A8
 Badersfield NR10......37 B2
 Bawburgh NR9......160 B6
 Beccles NR34......110 D2
 Bessingham NR11.....20 E7
 Blakeney NR25.......7 C6
 Bodham NR25.......9 B1
 Brettenham IP24.....117 B2
 Brinton NR24.......18 D8
 Burnham Overy Staithe
  PE31............135 E7
 Carleton St Peter NR14.91 E5
 Catfield NR29.......56 C8
 Crimplesham PE33....80 A6
 Dickleburgh & Rushall
  IP21............130 D8
 Dunton NR21.......16 A2
 Fritton & St Olaves NR31.93 E3
 Gissing IP22.......120 F4
 Great Snoring NR21...16 F4
 Great Snoring NR21...17 A4
 Great Yarmouth NR30..169 A6
 Haddiscoe NR14.....110 F7
 Halvergate NR13.....75 B4
 Hethersett NR9......88 C7
 Hevingham NR10......53 B8
 Hingham NR9.......86 C3
 Itteringham NR11.....35 D8
 King's Lynn PE30....147 B6
 🟦 Lingwood NR13.....74 A3
 Longham NR19.......48 F2
 Methwold IP26.......98 E5
 Mettingham NR35....124 C7
 Morley NR18........87 A3
 Northrepps NR27......11 A2
 Northrepps NR27.....139 E1
 North Runcton PE33...44 A3
 North Walsham NR28..151 D5
 Norton Subcourse NR14.92 E1
 Oulton NR11........35 D7
 Outwell PE14.......77 E5
 Palgrave IP22.......129 F4
 Reedham NR13......92 F4
 Reepham NR10.....149 C5
 St Cross, South Elmham
  IP20............123 D1
 Saxlingham Nethergate
  NR15............107 B8
 Sculthorpe NR21.....16 A3
 Sheringham NR26....138 D7
 Shipdham IP25.......67 B2
 Shouldham PE33......62 D1
 Skeyton NR10.......37 A5
 South Creake NR21....15 D7
 Stanfield NR20.......48 F7
 Stokesby with Herringby
  NR29............75 A4
 Surlingham NR14......73 B1
 Sutton NR12........39 D2
 Sutton Bridge PE12....41 B8
 Tacolneston NR16....105 E5

New Rd continued
 Thelnetham IP22....127 F3
 Thetford IP24......176 C4
 Thrandeston IP21....130 A4
 Threehammer Common
  NR12............55 F6
 Tilney St Lawrence PE34.42 C1
 Tivetshall St Mary NR15.121 B4
 Toft Monks NR34....110 D6
 Trunch NR28........22 D5
 Welney PE14........95 D5
 Whissonsett NR20.....31 D2
 Wimbotsham PE34...172 E8
 Wiveton NR25........7 E6
 Wormegay PE33......62 C8
New Ride IP24......126 F5
New Roman Bank PE34.144 B7
New Row PE31.......133 D6
NEW SPROWSTON NR3.158 E3
New St Cawston NR10...35 B2
 Cromer NR27.......139 B7
 Holt NR25.........137 B6
 King's Lynn PE30....147 B7
 Sheringham NR26....138 D7
Newstead Gdns NR13..165 E5
Newstead's La NR27...10 C4
Newstead Wlk NR27..177 C6
NEWTON PE32........47 B2
Newton Cl
 Horsham St Faith & Newton St
  Faith NR10........53 D4
 🟦 Newton Flotman NR15.89 D1
 Norwich NR4.......162 B1
Newton Cross NR31...170 D1
NEWTON FLOTMAN
 NR15............89 C1
Newton Flotman CE VC Prim
 Sch NR15.........89 D1
Newton Gap Cl 🟦 NR31.171 D2
NEWTON GREENWAYS
 NR15............89 D2
Newton Pk NR10......53 E4
Newton Rd Hainford NR10.53 E5
 Newton by Castle Acre
  PE32............47 A2
 Sporle with Palgrave PE32.65 C7
NEWTON ST FAITH NR10.53 E4
Newton St NR10......53 D4
NEWTOWN NR30......169 D7
Newtown IP24.......176 C3
New Wellington Pl 🟦
 NR30............169 D2
Neylond Cres NR6....157 E6
Nicholas Ave PE34....145 E6
Nicholas Hamond Acad The
 PE37............153 C3
Nicholas Hamond Way 🟦
 PE37............153 C3
Nicholas Mews 🟦 NR2.162 B7
Nicholls Way IP22....177 A5
Nichols Gr NR13.....166 B3
Nickerson Cl NR29...168 C8
Nick's La IP23.......130 B2
Nicolson Ave NR20.....50 B5
Nidus Gdns NR19......67 E5
Nightingale Ave NR18.173 D1
Nightingale Cl
 Cromer NR27.......139 C4
 Denver PE38.......172 D2
 Fakenham NR21......141 F4
 Hemsby NR29......167 E4
 Mulbarton NR14......89 A3
 Taverham NR8......155 B1
Nightingale Dr NR8...155 B1
Nightingale Inf Sch
 NR8............155 B1
Nightingale La
 Denver PE38.......172 D3
 Downham Market PE38.172 D3
 🟦 Feltwell IP26......98 E1
 King's Lynn PE30....147 A7
 Norwich NR3.......162 B8
Nightingale Rd IP27...175 F3
Nightingale Way IP27.176 D1
Nightingale Wlk PE38.172 C2
Nightjar Cl 🟦 IP27...177 F5
Nightjar Way 🟦 NR7.159 E4
Nightmarsh La
 Castle Rising PE31.....27 C4
 North Wootton PE31...148 E8
Nile Rd
 Downham Market PE38.172 B4
 Great Yarmouth NR31..170 D4
Nile St 🟦 NR2......162 B7
Nimrod Cl 🟦 NR9.....88 D8
Nine Acre La NR24.....19 C4
Ninhams Ct NR2.....178 A3
Ninham St NR1......162 E3
Nobb's Corner NR35..108 A4
Nobb's Lane NR15....108 A6
Nobb's Loke NR12.....38 F4
Nobel Cres NR12.....164 B4
Noble Cl NR7.......159 D1
Noel Cl NR31.......171 C5
Noels Wlk 🟦 NR34..110 D1
NOGDAM END NR14...92 D3
Noot Alley 🟦 NR5....161 B7
NORDELPH PE38......78 D3
Nordelph Cnr NR9.....86 D6
NORDELPH CORNER
 NR14............86 C6
Nordle Corner IP22...119 E2
Norfolk Arena PE34..168 F2
Norfolk Barn Yard PE31.134 D6
Norfolk Dr NR17.....174 C6
Norfolk Lavender Visitor
 Ctr★ PE31........27 B6
Norfolkman Dr NR28..151 B5
Norfolk Motor Cycle Mus★
 NR28............151 C4

Norfolk Nelson Mus★
 NR30............169 C3
Norfolk & Norwich Univ
 Hospl NR4.........161 A3
Norfolk Rd
 🟦 Honington IP31...126 B1
 🟦 Marham PE33......63 B4
 Norwich NR4.......161 B3
 Sheringham NR26....138 D6
 Thetford IP24......176 C4
Norfolk Record Office
 NR1............162 F3
Norfolk Shire Horse Ctr★
 NR27............9 F5
Norfolk Sq
 Downham Market PE38.172 B5
 Great Yarmouth NR30..169 D5
Norfolk St
 🟦 King's Lynn PE30...146 E5
 Norwich NR2.......162 C5
 Wisbech PE13......152 C4
Norfolk & Suffolk Aviation
 Mus★ NR35.......123 D6
Norfolk Wildlife Ctr &
 Country Pk★ NR9....51 C6
Norfolk Wildlife Hospl
 (RSPCA)★ PE32.....44 F3
Norgate La IP21......130 E6
Norgate Rd NR4......161 B3
Norgate Way NR8....156 E8
Norman CE Prim Sch The
 IP26............99 C7
Norman Cl
 East Dereham NR19...154 C5
 Fakenham NR21......141 B6
Norman Dr
 Northwold PE33......81 B2
 Norwich NR6.......158 E7
Normandy Cl IP26....99 C7
Normandy Dr NR19...154 D7
Normandy Grove 🟦
 NR5............156 C1
Norman La 🟦 NR31..169 B4
Norman Rd Anmer PE35.28 F8
 Norwich NR3.......158 E1
Normans Bldgs NR1...178 B2
Normans La NR21......4 D1
🟦 Norman's Burrow Rd
 NR21............31 B3
Normans La NR21......4 D1
Norman Troller Ct 🟦
 NR27............139 B7
Norman Way NR1......15 B3
NORTHACRE NR17.....85 B1
Northall Gn NR19....154 E8
NORTHALL GREEN
 Dereham NR20......154 F8
 Hoe NR20..........49 F2
Northall Green NR20...50 A2
North Ave NR20......50 B5
North Barningham Rd
 NR25............20 D7
NORTH BARSHAM NR22..16 B6
North Beach PE36....132 B1
North Brink PE13....152 A4
NORTH BURLINGHAM
 NR13............74 A5
North Cambridgeshire Hospl
 PE13............152 D5
NORTH COMMON IP22.127 B5
North Common IP22..127 D2
North Common Rd
 IP22............127 D3
Northcote NR31......169 C5
Northcote Rd 🟦 NR3..162 E8
NORTH COURT IP27...114 C3
NORTH CREAKE NR21...4 D1
North Creake Rd NR23..5 D7
NORTH DENES NR30...168 F2
North Denes Airfield
 NR30............168 D2
North Denes Mid Sch
 NR30............169 D6
North Denes Prim Sch
 NR30............168 F1
North Denes Rd NR30.169 D6
North Dr Fakenham NR21.141 C5
 Great Yarmouth NR30..169 D4
NORTH ELMHAM NR20..49 E8
North Elmham Chapel★
 NR20............49 F8
North Elmham Prim Sch
 NR20............49 E8
NORTH END
 North End NR16......103 D3
 Snetterton NR16......103 C3
North End Haddiscoe NR14.93 B1
 Stoke Holy Cross NR14..89 E5
 Wisbech PE13......152 B6
North End La NR16...106 D3
Northern Cl NR30....168 F5
North Everard St PE30.146 E4
North Farm Loke NR14.110 B8
Northfield Ave NR23..136 D5
Northfield Cl NR18....173 B6
Northfield Cres NR18..136 E5
Northfield Gdns NR18.173 B5
Northfield La
 Plumstead NR11......20 B6
 Wells-next-the-Sea NR23.136 B6
Northfield Loke NR18.173 B6
Northfield Rd
 Bunwell NR16......106 A4
 Mundesley NR11.....143 C5
 North Walsham NR28..151 B6
 Swaffham PE37.....153 C6
Northfields NR4......161 B1
Northfields La NR19....67 E5
North Gage Cl NR7...159 C4
Northgate Beccles NR34..110 D1
 Dereham NR19......154 C7

Northgate continued
 🟦 Harleston IP20......122 D1
 Hunstanton PE36.....132 C5
 🟦 Thorpe End NR13....72 D6
Northgate High Sch
 NR19............154 D6
Northgate Hospl NR30.169 D6
Northgate Infants Sch
 NR30............169 C6
Northgate Prec PE36..132 C6
Northgate St NR30...169 C5
Northgate Way PE34..144 D7
North Gn NR9........68 B1
North Gn Rd IP21....122 A4
NORTH GREEN
 Garvestone NR9......68 C1
 Pulham St Mary IP21..122 A7
Northhall Gn NR19....49 F2
North La NR21.......17 E5
North Lawn PE38......97 B6
NORTH LOPHAM IP22..119 A2
North Lopham Rd NR16.119 A3
NORTH LYNN PE30...146 F7
North Lynn Bsns Village
 PE30............148 A1
North Lynn Ind Est
 PE30............147 A8
Northmead Dr NR28..151 C6
North Mkt Rd
 🟦 Great Yarmouth
  NR30............169 D4
 Winterton-on-Sea NR29.58 B6
North Norfolk Rly★ NR26..9 B5
Northolt Rd NR15......85 A3
NORTH PICKENHAM
 PE37............65 E1
North Pickenham Rd
 Necton PE37.......65 F3
 Sporle with Palgrave PE32.65 E3
 Swaffham PE37.....153 D4
North Pk NR21......141 B6
North Pk Ave NR4....161 E4
North Pk Dr NR4....161 F4
North Pole Rd PE31....14 F1
North Prom PE36.....132 C5
North Quay NR30....169 C4
North Rd Bunwell NR16..105 C4
 🟦 Great Yarmouth NR30.169 D5
 Great Yarmouth NR31..170 D4
 Hemsby NR29......167 A7
North St Brundall NR13.165 E6
 Burnham Market PE31..135 C3
 🟦 Castle Acre PE32....46 F2
 Great Dunham PE32....47 E2
 King's Lynn PE30....146 D6
 Langham NR25.......7 A4
 North Walsham NR28..151 C5
 Sheringham NR26....138 C7
 Wisbech PE13......152 C5
North Stow IP28.....125 A2
NORTH TUDDENHAM
 NR20............50 D1
Northumberland St
 NR2............162 B7
North View NR17......17 F3
North View Dr NR20...31 C2
Northview Rd NR5...157 C1
NORTH WALSHAM
 NR28............151 E6
North Walsham Bypass
 NR28............38 A6
North Walsham By-Pass
 North Walsham NR28...37 E2
 North Walsham NR28..151 C3
 North Walsham NR28..151 C5
North Walsham & District
 War Memorial Hospl
  NR28............151 C4
North Walsham High Sch
 NR28............151 D5
North Walsham Inf Sch
 NR28............151 D5
North Walsham Jun Sch
 NR28............151 D5
North Walsham Rd
 Antingham NR28......22 A3
 Bacton NR12........23 D4
 Coltishall NR12......54 D7
 Crostwick NR12......54 B2
 Felmingham NR28.....37 B8
 Honing NR28........38 C7
 Northrepps NR27......10 E1
 Norwich NR6.......159 A5
 Old Hall Street NR28...22 F4
 Paston NR28.......151 F7
 Scottow NR12.......37 E1
 Skeyton Corner NR10..37 B6
 Sprowston NR6......159 B6
 Suffield NR11........21 F3
 Swafield NR28.......22 E4
 Thorpe Market NR11...22 A7
 Witton NR28.........38 B8
North Walsham Sta
 NR28............151 C4
North Way PE30.....147 A8
Northwell Pool Rd
 PE37............153 C5
North-West Twr★
 NR30............169 C5

NORTHWOLD IP26.....99 C8
Northwold Rd IP26....99 A6
NORTH WOOTTON
 PE30............148 C5
North Wootton Com Sch
 PE30............148 D4
NORTON CORNER NR11..34 C7
Norton Corner NR11...34 D7
Norton Dr
 🟦 Norwich NR4......89 D8
 Norwich NR4.......162 A1
Norton Hill NR13......74 A8
Norton Rd NR14......92 B1
Nortonsfield Cl NR25..137 C7
Norton St
 Burnham Norton PE31...4 A6
 Burnham Norton PE31..135 B6
NORTON SUBCOURSE
 NR14............92 E1
Nortridge Rd NR5....161 A7
Norvic Dr NR4......161 B1
Norway Cl PE31......133 C6
NORWICH NR2......178 A3
Norwich NR4........71 A3
Norwich Arts Ctr★ NR2.178 A3
Norwich Bsns Pk NR4.162 D1
Norwich Castle Mus & Art
 Gall★ NR1........178 B3
Norwich Castle Mus & Art
 Gall★ NR1........178 B3
Norwich City FC NR1..163 A4
Norwich Cl 🟦 PE13...152 E6
Norwich Com Hospl
 NR2............161 F7
Norwich Comm NR18..173 F6
Norwich Dr NR20......32 E4
Norwich Gall★ NR1...178 B3
Norwich Gates PE35..140 E1
Norwich High Sch for Girls
 NR2............162 B3
Norwich Int Airport
 NR6............158 B7
Norwich Puppet Theatre
 NR1............178 B4
Norwich Rd Acle NR13.166 A3
 Ashmanhaugh NR12....55 C7
 Attleborough NR17...174 E6
 Aylsham NR11......150 C6
 Barnham Broom NR9...69 D2
 Bawdeswell NR20.....50 E7
 Booton NR10.......51 F8
 Bracon Ash NR14.....88 F2
 Brandiston NR10......52 C8
 Briston NR24.......142 E5
 Brome IP23.........130 B3
 Brooke NR15........90 E3
 Burgh & Tuttington NR11..36 E6
 Caister-on-Sea NR30...168 C5
 Cantley NR13.......92 D7
 Carbrooke IP25.......85 B3
 Cawston NR10.......35 B2
 Corpusty & Saxthorpe NR11.19 F1
 Corpusty & Saxthorpe NR24.34 F8
 Cromer NR27.......139 C5
 Denton IP20.......108 B1
 Denton IP20.......123 B7
 Denton IP20.......123 B8
 Dickleburgh & Rushall
  IP21............130 D6
 Ditchingham NR35....109 A1
 Earsham NR35......108 E1
 East Dereham NR20...154 F5
 East Tuddenham NR20..69 C6
 Edgefield NR24.......19 D6
 Fakenham NR21.....141 C4
 Flordon NR15........89 A1
 Foxley NR20........50 D8
 Gillingham NR34.....110 C2
 Great & Little Plumstead
  NR13............73 A7
 Great Snoring NR21...17 A4
 Guist NR20.........33 A4
 Hardingham NR9......86 B9
 🟦 Hethersett NR9......88 D7
 Hingham NR9.......86 B5
 Holt NR25.........137 B5
 Holverston NR14......91 A5
 Horning NR12.......55 E4
 Horsham St Faith NR10..53 D2
 Horstead with Stanninghall
  NR12............54 C4
 Kimberley NR18......87 B7
 Lingwood & Burlingham
  NR13............74 A2
 Little Ryburgh NR21...32 C7
 🟦 Loddon NR14......92 A2
 Long Stratton NR15...106 F5
 Ludham NR29........56 C5
 Marlingford NR9......69 F4
 Mattishall NR20......68 F6
 Mulbarton NR14......89 B4
 Neatishead NR12....164 F8
 Necton PE37.........66 A4
 New Buckenham NR16.105 C4
 North Walsham NR28..151 B3
 Norwich NR5.......157 B2
 Poringland NR14......90 B6
 Pulham St Mary IP21..121 F4
 Rackheath NR13......72 F8
 Reepham NR10.....149 C5
 Roughton NR11......21 D8
 Roughton NR27.......21 D5
 Salhouse NR13.......55 B1
 Saxlingham Nethergate
  NR15............107 B8
 Scole IP21........121 B1
 Shotesham NR15......89 F3
 Shouldham PE33......62 F3
 Skeyton Corner NR10..37 B6

Norwich Rd continued
Smallburgh NR12. . . . . .38 D2
Sporle with Palgrave PE32 .65 D4
Stibbard NR21. . . . . .32 E6
Stockton NR34. . . . . .109 F5
Strumpshaw NR13. . . . . . . .73 F2
Swaffham PE37. . . . . .153 D4
Swainsthorpe NR14. . . . . . .89 E4
Swanton Morley NR20. . . . . .50 B2
🖪 Tacolneston NR16 . . . . .105 F5
Tacolneston NR16 . . . . . . .106 A6
Tharston & Hapton NR15 .106 C7
Thetford IP24 . . . . .176 B3
Tivetshall St Mary NR15 . .121 D4
West Caister NR30 . . . . . .168 B6
Weston Longville NR9 . . . . .51 E5
Westwick NR10. . . . . .37 D5
Wisbech PE13 . . . . .152 E5
Woodton NR35. . . . . .108 C6
Wroxham/Hoveton NR12 .164 B3
Wymondham NR18 . . . . . .173 D5
Yaxham NR19 . . . . .68 B5
Norwich Rd Slip Rd NR20. 68 F8
Norwich Research Pk
NR4 . . . . .161 A4
Norwich Riverside NR1 .178 C2
Norwich Road Acad
IP24 . . . . .176 D4
Norwich Sch
Norwich NR1 . . . . .162 F6
Norwich NR1 . . . . .178 B3
Norwich NR1 . . . . .178 C3
Norwich St
East Dereham NR19 . . . .154 E5
Fakenham NR21. . . . . . .141 B4
Hingham NR9. . . . . .86 C5
Mundesley NR11 . . . . . .143 A7
Norwich Sta NR1 . . . . . .178 C2
Norwich Steiner Sch
Norwich NR1 . . . . .162 E3
Norwich NR7 . . . . .161 E6
Norwich Theatre Royal
NR2 . . . . .178 A2
Norwich Univ of the Arts
Norwich NR3 . . . . .162 D6
Norwich NR3 . . . . .178 A3
Norwood Rd IP27 . . . . . .175 A1
Notre Dame High Sch
NR1 . . . . .178 B1
Notre Dame Prep Sch
NR2 . . . . .162 B7
Nottingham Rd PE30. . . .146 E3
Nottingham Way NR30 .169 C3
Notykin St NR5 . . . . . . .161 A8
Nourse Dr PE31. . . . . . . .133 E5
Nouth Walsham Rd NR13. 73 E8
Novak Dr IP25. . . . . .84 E3
Nova Scotia Rd
Filby NR29 . . . . .168 A7
Ormesby St Margaret with
Scratby NR29 . . . . .167 B1
Novaturient Sch
Great Yarmouth NR30. . . .76 E2
Great Yarmouth NR30. . .169 E4
Nowhere La
Blackwater NR10. . . . . . . .51 C7
Wereham PE33 . . . . .80 D4
Nuffield Cl NR31. . . . . . .170 B4
Nuffield Cres NR31. . . . .170 B4
Nunnery Ct IP22 . . . . . . .177 C4
Nunnery Dr IP24. . . . . . .176 D1
Nunnery Pl IP27 . . . . . . .176 D2
Nunnery The★ IP24. . . . . .176 D2
Nunn's Way NR19. . . . . .154 D5
Nuns' Bridges Rd IP24 .176 D2
Nunsgate IP24. . . . . .176 D2
Nurseries Ave NR13. . . .165 E4
Nurserry La IP24. . . . . . .126 E8
Nursery Cl Acle NR13 . . .166 B4
🖪 Beetley NR19 . . . . . . .49 C3
🖪 Belton NR31. . . . . .94 A5
Bracon Ash NR14. . . . . . . .89 C4
🖪 Gressenhall NR20 . . . . .49 C3
King's Lynn PE30. . . . . . .148 C2
🖪 Marthan NR29. . . . . . . .57 D5
Norwich NR6 . . . . .157 E5
🖪 Roydon PE32 . . . . .28 A1
Terrington St Clement
PE34 . . . . .144 A5
Nursery Dr
Hunstanton PE36. . . . . . .132 D4
North Walsham NR28 . . .151 B3
Wisbech PE13 . . . . .152 E8
Nursery Gdns NR13 . . . .165 F6
Nursery La
Brancaster PE31 . . . . .3 E6
Costessey NR8. . . . . .156 F3
Felmingham NR10. . . . . . . .37 A7
Hockwold cum Wilton
IP26. . . . . .114 A4
King's Lynn PE30. . . . . . .148 C3
Pulham St Mary IP21 . . . .122 A4
Rushford IP24. . . . . .117 B1
Nursery Rd
Downham Market PE38. . .172 C6
Thurton NR14. . . . . .91 E2
Nursery Terr NR30. . . . .169 C6
Nursery Way PE32 . . . . . .28 A2
Nursey Cl NR35. . . . . . . .109 D3
Nutfield Cl NR14 . . . . . .161 F1
Nuthall Cres PE30. . . . . .147 A8
Nuthatch Rd 🖪 NR7 . . .159 E4
Nuthatch Way NR17. . . .174 B4
Nut La NR27. . . . . .139 F3
Nutmeg Wlk PE38. . . . . .172 C6
Nuttel Cl NR15. . . . . . . .107 C6
Nuttery Vale IP23. . . . . .130 F2
Nutwood Cl NR8. . . . . . .155 D2

O

Oakapple Dr NR19 . . . . .154 D8
Oak Ave
🖪 Great Yarmouth NR31. .94 C7
King's Lynn PE30 . . . . . .148 D2
🖪 Loddon NR14 . . . . . . .91 F1
Marham PE33 . . . . .63 B4
North Elmham NR20 . . . . .49 E7
Norwich NR7. . . . . .163 F8
🖪 Poringland NR14 . . . . .90 C5
West Winch PE33 . . . . . . .43 F2
Oak Cl 🖪 Hethersett NR9 . .88 D8
🖪 Tasburgh NR15. . . . . .106 F6
🖪 Thetford IP24 . . . . . . .176 A1
Oak Cres IP23 . . . . .130 C1
Oakcroft Dr NR14. . . . . . .90 C5
Oakdale Rd NR13 . . . . . .165 D3
Oakdene NR21. . . . . .15 C2
Oak Dr Outwell PE14. . . . .77 F7
Reepham NR10 . . . . .149 D6
Oakfield Cl PE38. . . . . . .172 C4
Oakfield Dr 🖪 NR13 . . . .74 B8
Oakfield Rd
Aylsham NR11. . . . . .150 C6
Long Stratton NR15. . . . .106 F3
Norwich NR14. . . . . .91 F2
Oakfields Cl 🖪 NR4. . . . . .89 C8
Oakfields Rd NR4. . . . . . .89 B8
Oak Gr 🖪 Horsford NR10 . .53 B3
Sheringham NR26 . . . . . .138 D5
Oakhill NR13 . . . . .165 D3
Oak La East Ruston NR12. . .38 E7
🖪 Hingham NR9. . . . . . . .86 C4
Norwich NR3 . . . . .158 D3
Oakland Dr 🖪 NR20. . . . . .49 D4
Oakland Mws NR13 . . . . . .73 F3
Oaklands
Little Snoring NR21 . . . . . .17 C3
🖪 Old Buckenham NR17 104 D2
Poringland NR14. . . . . . . .90 B5
🖪 Taverham NR8 . . . . . .155 B2
Oaklands Cl
Attleborough NR17 . . . . .174 C3
Halvergate NR13. . . . . . . .74 F2
Oaklands Dr 🖪 Belton NR31. .94 A6
Brandon IP27. . . . . .114 D4
Cringleford NR4. . . . . . . .161 C1
Walsoken PE13 . . . . .152 F7
Oaklands La 🖪 PE33 . . . . .61 D5
Oaklands Pk NR28. . . . . .151 B6
Oaklands The PE37. . . . . .153 C3
Oakleigh Cl NR28 . . . . . . .74 F7
Oakleigh Dr PE13. . . . . . .153 A5
OAKLEY IP21. . . . . .129 D4
Oakley Church La IP21. .130 D4
Oakley Cl PE13 . . . . .152 E4
Oak Lodge NR7. . . . . .163 C5
Oak Meadow IP25. . . . . . .67 B2
Oak Rd Dilham NR28 . . . . .38 D4
Great Yarmouth NR31. . .170 B6
North Walsham NR28 . . .151 B4
Stoke Ferry PE33. . . . . . . .81 A2
Oakroyd Cres PE13 . . . . .152 C5
Oaks Cl PE37 . . . . .153 C3
Oaks Dr Necton PE37. . . . .65 F4
Swaffham PE37. . . . . . . .153 C3
Oaks La NR34. . . . . .111 B5
Oak's La NR13 . . . . .72 F2
Oak St Fakenham NR21 . . .141 B4
Feltwell IP26. . . . . .98 E1
Norwich NR3 . . . . .178 A4
Oaks The Ashill IP25 . . . . .84 A7
🖪 Beetley NR19. . . . . . . .49 C3
Bradwell NR31. . . . . .170 A5
🖪 Elm PE14. . . . . .59 A1
🖪 Gressenhall NR20 . . . . .49 C3
Highoak NR18 . . . . .87 B3
Mattishall NR20. . . . . . . .68 F5
Oak Tree Bsns Pk NR13. . .72 E8
Oak Tree Cl 🖪 NR29 . . . . .57 D5
Oaktree Dr NR7. . . . . . . .159 B2
Oak Tree Way 🖪 IP20. . . .122 D1
Oak View Dr PE38. . . . . . .172 C6
Oak Wood NR13 . . . . .165 E5
Oakwood Cl NR19. . . . . . .154 D8
Oakwood Dr
Helleston NR6. . . . . .157 F3
Wymondham NR18 . . . . .173 E6
Oakwood Rd NR19 . . . . . .154 D8
Oasis Leisure Ctr PE36. .132 C4
Oasis Sport & Leisure Club
NR7 . . . . .72 D5
Oasis Way PE36. . . . . . . .132 C2
Oatfield Chase NR14. . . . .89 B2
Oatfield Rd PE13 . . . . . . .53 A3
Obelisk La NR28 . . . . .37 F5
Occupation Rd 🖪 NR20. . .68 F6
Octagon Dr 🖪 PE13. . . . .152 A6
Octavia Cl PE13. . . . . . . .152 F6
Octavia Hill Birthplace
Mus★ PE13. . . . . .152 C5
Oddfellows Field 🖪 NR25. 7 C6
Oddfellows Row PE31. . .134 E4
Oddon Rd
Chedgrave NR14. . . . . . . .91 F2
Langley with Hardley NR14. 91 F6
Thurton NR14. . . . . .91 F3
Offley Ct 🖪 NR5. . . . . . . .161 A8
Off Top Row NR16 . . . . . .106 B8
Ogden Cl NR18 . . . . .173 D5
Oil Mill La PE13. . . . . . . .152 B5
Old Allotment Ct 🖪
NR3. . . . . .162 E1
Old Bakery Cl The IP26. .99 A6
Old Bakery Ct PE31. . . . .133 C5
Old Barge Yd NR1. . . . . .178 C2

Old Barley Mkt The
NR2. . . . . .178 A3
Old Becclesgate NR19. . .154 D5
Old Bedford Row PE14. . . .95 D4
OLD BEETLEY NR20. . . . . .49 D5
Old Bell Way 🖪 PE13. . . .152 E6
Old Brandon Rd
Feltwell IP26. . . . . .98 F1
Feltwell IP26. . . . . .98 E2
Old Brewery Ct 🖪 PE30 .146 E3
Old Brewery La NR10. . .149 C4
Old Brewery La West
NR10 . . . . .149 B5
Old Bridge NR19. . . . . . . .49 C2
OLD BUCKENHAM
NR17 . . . . .104 D2
Old Buckenham Airfield★
NR17 . . . . .104 E4
Old Buckenham Com Prim
Sch NR17 . . . . .104 D2
Old Buckenham High Sch
NR17 . . . . .104 D2
Old Buckenham Rd
NR16 . . . . .105 A4
Old Bungay Rd NR35. . . .109 D4
Old Bury Rd
Palgrave IP22. . . . . .129 E4
Stuston IP21 . . . . .177 F1
Thetford IP24 . . . . .176 C4
Wortham IP22. . . . . .129 D4
Old Cantley Rd NR13. . . . .74 B1
Old Catton NR6. . . . . . . .158 E5
Old Catton CE Jun Sch
NR6 . . . . .158 E5
Old Chapel Cl PE33. . . . . .61 D5
Old Chapel Rd
Cantley NR13. . . . . .92 E7
🖪 Hemsby NR29 . . . . . . .58 B6
Old Chapel Way NR7 . . . .72 E3
Old Church Cl NR14. . . . . .89 F6
Old Church Rd
Hainford NR10. . . . . .53 E6
Hopton on Sea NR31. . . .171 D4
Horstead with Stanninghall
NR12. . . . . .54 A6
Snettisham PE31. . . . . . . .12 E5
Terrington St John PE14. . .42 B1
Tilney St Lawrence PE34. . .42 D1
Old Coach House Gdns The
NR10. . . . . .53 E6
Old Coaching Pl The
IP22. . . . . .177 E3
Old Coach Rd NR27 . . . . .139 C6
Old Coal Yd The PE31 . . . .12 E4
Old Coast Rd NR29. . . . . .167 E2
Old Comm Bank PE34. . . .42 A8
Old Common Bank PE34. .25 B1
Old Cromer Rd NR10 . . . . .53 F5
Old Fakenham Rd
Attlebridge NR9. . . . . .52 B3
Foxley NR20. . . . . .50 D8
Tattersett PE31 . . . . .30 D8
Old Fakenham St PE32. . . .29 A4
Old Farm La NR3. . . . . . .158 B1
Old Feltwell Rd IP26. . . . .99 A5
Oldfield Ave PE14. . . . . . .59 B1
Oldfield Cl 🖪 NR19 . . . . .154 E6
Oldfield Dr PE34. . . . . . . .144 B5
Oldfield La PE13. . . . . . . .152 B3
Old Field La PE36. . . . . .2 D6
Old Flixton Rd IP20 . . . . .123 B4
Old Forge Cl IP22. . . . . . .129 B4
Old Forge Ct Acle NR13 . .166 C4
Brockdish IP21 . . . . .131 D6
Old Forge Yard PE32. . . . .48 C2
Old Fountain NR21. . . . . .170 C1
Old Friendship La NR10 . .35 C2
Old Grammar La 🖪
NR35 . . . . .124 B8
Old Gr Ct NR3. . . . . .158 D2
Old Hall Cl
Ashwellthorpe NR16 . . . .105 F8
🖪 Norwich NR14 . . . . . .163 B2
Saham Toney IP25. . . . . . .84 B5
Old Hall Dr PE31. . . . . . . .140 E3
Old Hall Gdns
Brooke NR15. . . . . .90 F2
Buxton with Lammas NR10 .37 A2
Old Hall Gdns NR30. . . . .168 E5
Oldhall La NR16. . . . . . . .118 C5
Old Hall La
Beachamwell PE37 . . . . . .81 F8
Brinton NR25. . . . . .18 D7
North End NR10. . . . . . . .103 C2
Spixworth NR10. . . . . .53 F2
Themelthorpe NR20. . . . . .34 A3
Oldhall Rd NR4 . . . . .89 E8
Old Hall Rd
East Dereham NR19 . . . . .154 D2
Mattishall NR20. . . . . . . .68 D5
Witton NR28 . . . . .38 B8
Old Harleston Rd NR35. .123 E7
Old Hill The PE31. . . . . . .27 C3
Old High Rd IP22. . . . . . .177 A5
Old Hillington Rd IP22. . .27 D2
OLD HUNSTANTON
PE36. . . . . .132 E8
Old Hunstanton Rd
Castle Rising PE31. . . . . . .27 D4
Old Hunstanton PE36 . . .132 E7
Old Kiln PE13 . . . . .43 F2
Old La East Ruston NR12. . .24 A5
Happisburgh NR12. . . . . .23 F1
Reepham NR10. . . . . .35 B8
Thelnetham IP22. . . . . . .128 A2
Thurton NR14. . . . . .38 B2
Old Lakenham Hall Dr 🖪
NR1 . . . . .162 E1
Old Laundry Ct 🖪 NR2 .162 B8

Old Laundry Mews NR1 .163 A5
Old Liby Mews NR1 . . . .178 C2
Old Litcham NR32. . . . . . .48 C5
Old Lynn Rd PE13. . . . . . .152 E7
Old Maltings The PE13. .153 B4
Old Manor Cl PE30. . . . . .148 C1
Old Markshall Farm Rd
NR14 . . . . .89 E7
Old Methwold Rd
Feltwell IP26. . . . . .98 E2
Northwold PE33. . . . . . . .81 B2
Old Mill Dr IP21 . . . . .121 F4
Oldmill La NR29 . . . . .56 D5
Old Mill La NR11. . . . . . . .139 A1
Old Mill Rd
Caister-on-Sea NR30. . . .168 F5
🖪 Poringland NR14 . . . . .90 C5
Roughton NR11 . . . . .139 B1
Old Mill Terrace 🖪
NR34 . . . . .110 D1
Old Mkt PE13. . . . . .152 C5
Old Mkt Cl NR13. . . . . . . .166 C3
Old Mkt Gn 🖪 NR14. . . . .92 A1
Old Mkt Pl 🖪 IP20 . . . . .122 D2
Old Mkt St
🖪 King's Lynn PE30. . . .146 E5
Thetford IP24 . . . . .176 D3
Old Mkt Way NR15. . . . . .107 C5
Old Norwich Rd
Gayton Thorpe PE32 . . . . .45 F4
Horsham St Faith & Newton St
Faith NR10. . . . . .53 D1
Scottow NR10 . . . . .37 D2
Yaxley IP23. . . . . .130 A1
Old Oak Cl NR18. . . . . . . .173 F7
Old Orchard Cl 🖪 NR20 . .68 A8
Old Orch The NR17. . . . . .174 E6
Old Orwich Rd 🖪 NR20. . .50 E7
Old Pal Rd NR2. . . . . .162 B7
Old Pools Dro CB6 . . . . . . .95 F1
Old Post Office Ct PE31 . .29 C4
Old Post Office La NR35 .109 E3
Old Post Office St
🖪 Fakenham NR21. . . . .141 B4
🖪 Shipdham IP25. . . . . . .67 B2
Old Post Rd NR24 . . . . . .142 E4
Old Quarry NR19 . . . . . . .154 E6
Old Railway Rd NR35. . . .109 A1
Old Railway Yd PE31 . . . .135 C2
Old Rd Acle NR13. . . . . . .166 C5
🖪 Norwich NR15 . . . . . .106 B1
Old Rectory Cl
King's Lynn PE30 . . . . . .148 D5
🖪 Mulbarton NR14. . . . . .89 B3
Norwich NR7 . . . . .163 E6
🖪 Roydon IP22. . . . . . . .129 D7
South Wootton PE30 . . . .148 B1
Old Rectory La NR15. . . . . .7 D6
Old Rectory Rd NR12. . . . .24 A1
Old Reepham Rd 🖪
NR20. . . . . .50 E7
Old River Rd PE34. . . . . .145 C4
Old Roman Bank PE34 . .144 A7
Old Runway La NR14. . . . .86 D1
Old Sch Cl NR5. . . . . .161 E6
Old Sch Cl NR1. . . . . .178 C1
Old School Cl PE36. . . . . . . .2 D6
Old School Rd NR24. . . . .142 E3
Old Sch Rd
East Ruston NR12. . . . . . .38 F8
Guestwick NR20. . . . . . . .33 F5
Old Severalls Rd IP20 . . . .98 E6
Old South PE30. . . . . .147 C4
Old Southwood Rd NR13 . .74 B2
Old St 🖪 NR15. . . . . .107 A8
Old Stable Mws PE38. . . .172 C5
Old Sta La NR35. . . . . . . .109 D2
Old Station Yard NR10 . . .36 B3
Old Sta Way 🖪 NR25 . . . .137 C5
Oldsunway PE30. . . . . . . .146 D5
Old Town Way PE36. . . . .132 D6
Old Turnpike Rd NR11. . . .21 D7
Old Vicarage Pk PE32. . . .63 E7
Old Warren NR8 . . . . .155 D2
Oldwash La NR16. . . . . . .105 D3
Old Watton Rd NR4 . . . . .161 A5
Old Wellington Pl 🖪
NR30. . . . . .169 D3
Old Wells Rd
Fakenham NR21. . . . . . . .141 A6
Sculthorpe NR21. . . . . . . .16 A2
Sculthorpe NR21. . . . . . . .16 B1
Shereford NR21. . . . . .31 A8
Walsingham NR22. . . . . . .16 E8
Old Wicken NR32. . . . . . . .46 D3
Old Woman's La NR25. . . . .7 F6
Old Woman's La NR25. . . . .7 F6
Old Yarmouth Rd
Ellingham NR35. . . . . . . .109 C3
Gillingham NR34 . . . . . . .110 B3
Stalham NR12 . . . . .39 C2
Olive Ave NR15 . . . . .89 D1
Olive Cl NR5. . . . . .157 C1
Olive Cres NR10. . . . . .53 A4
Olive Fisher Ct NR21 . . . .141 B4
Oliver Ct
🖪 Cromer NR27. . . . . . .139 C6
🖪 Weeting IP27. . . . . . .114 E1
Olive Rd
Great Yarmouth NR31. . .169 B3
Norwich NR5. . . . . .157 C1
Oliver Mews 🖪 NR30. . . .169 D4
Olivet Way NR21. . . . . . .141 C4
Olivia Cl NR21. . . . . .141 A5
Ollands La NR11. . . . . .35 A5
Ollands Rd
Attleborough NR17 . . . . .174 C3
Reepham NR10 . . . . .149 C4
Ollard Ave PE13. . . . . . . .152 D7

Olley Rd 🖪 NR27. . . . . . . .10 A5
Olney Rd NR19. . . . . .154 D5
Olympian Cl PE13. . . . . . .152 C2
Onedin Cl PE31. . . . . .140 C5
Ongar Hill
Terrington St Clement PE34 25 D1
Terrington St Clement PE34 26 A3
Onley St NR2. . . . . .178 B3
Onslow Ave NR30. . . . . . .169 D7
Onyx Cl PE13 . . . . .152 C4
Open Acad NR7. . . . . .159 C1
Opie St NR2 . . . . .178 B3
Opportune Rd PE13. . . . .152 E6
Orange Gr 🖪 PE13. . . . . .152 C4
ORANGE ROW PE34. . . . .144 A6
Orange Row Rd PE34. . . .144 A6
Orange Row Rd PE34. . . .144 A6
Orchard Bank NR8. . . . . .156 E8
Orchard Cl Acle NR13. . . .166 B4
Ashill IP25 . . . . .84 A6
Attleborough NR17 . . . . .174 C5
Blofield Heath NR13 . . . . .73 C6
Brancaster Staithe PE31. . .3 D7
Briston NR24. . . . . .142 D4
Caister-on-Sea NR30. . . .168 E4
Dersingham PE31. . . . . . .140 D4
Downham Market PE38. . .172 D5
Fakenham NR21. . . . . . . .141 D4
Holt NR25. . . . . .137 E7
🖪 Ixworth NR9. . . . . .69 F2
Mundesley NR11 . . . . . . .143 B7
North Elmham NR20 . . . . .49 E7
North Walsham NR28 . . .151 C6
Norwich NR7 . . . . .163 C8
Roughton NR11 . . . . .21 D7
Sedgeford PE36. . . . . .13 B7
Sheringham NR26 . . . . . .138 C6
Tacolneston NR16 . . . . . .105 F4
Tilney St Lawrence PE34. . .60 C8
Watlington PE33 . . . . .61 E5
🖪 Wisbech PE14. . . . . . . .59 A1
Orchard Cres 🖪 NR15. . .106 B1
Orchard Ct
King's Lynn PE30 . . . . . .147 B6
Ormesby St Margaret
NR29 . . . . .167 A3
Orchard Dr
Helleston NR6. . . . . .157 D3
🖪 Potter Heigham NR29 . .56 F6
West Walton PE14. . . . . . .59 C8
Wisbech PE13 . . . . .152 E4
Orchard Gate IP22. . . . . .119 A2
Orchard Gdns
Emneth PE14 . . . . .59 D1
🖪 King's Lynn PE30 . . . .147 B6
Upwell PE14 . . . . .77 E5
Orchard Gr
Diss IP22 . . . . .177 C5
Kettlestone NR21. . . . . . . .17 C2
🖪 King's Lynn PE34 . . . .146 C3
Orchard La
Aylsham NR11. . . . . .150 D4
Castle Acre PE32. . . . . . . .46 F2
King's Lynn PE30. . . . . . .147 B5
Reepham NR10 . . . . .149 D5
Shouldham PE33 . . . . .62 D4
Orchard Loke NR11 . . . . . .22 B7
Orchard Pl
Swaffham PE37. . . . . . . .153 B4
Thompson IP24. . . . . . . .102 A7
Orchard Rd
🖪 Gayton PE32. . . . . . . .45 C6
Lingwood NR13 . . . . .73 F3
🖪 Mattishall NR20. . . . . .68 E6
🖪 Spixworth NR10. . . . . .54 A2
🖪 Wiggenhall St Germans
PE34 . . . . .43 B1
Orchards CE Prim Sch
NR13. . . . . .152 E8
Orchard St NR2. . . . . .162 C7
Orchard The
🖪 Belton NR31. . . . . . . .94 A6
Brandon IP27. . . . . .175 C3
Downham Market PE38. . .172 C5
Orchard Way
Banham NR16 . . . . .119 D7
🖪 Burgh St Margaret
(Fleggburgh) NR29 . . . . .57 C1
🖪 Hethersett NR9 . . . . . .88 D8
Southery PE38. . . . . .97 A5
🖪 Tasburgh NR15. . . . . .106 F6
Terrington St John PE14. . .42 B1
Thetford IP24 . . . . .176 D5
Wymondham NR18 . . . . .173 C4
Orch Cres PE30. . . . . .147 B8
Orchid Ave NR19. . . . . . .154 D1
Orchid Cl PE30. . . . . .138 B6
Orchids Cl NR35. . . . . . . .124 B7
Orde Ave NR31. . . . . .170 C2
Ordnance Rd NR30. . . . . .169 D1
Orford Cl 🖪 NR30. . . . . . .169 D3
Orford Hill NR1. . . . . .178 B2
Orford Pl
Norwich NR1 . . . . .178 B2
🖪 West Winch PE33. . . . .43 F2
Orford Rd PE37. . . . . .153 C6
Orford St NR2. . . . . .178 B2
Orhard Gr PE33 . . . . .43 E2
Oriel Ave NR31. . . . . .170 A3
Orion Dr 🖪 NR5. . . . . . . .156 C1
Origins™ NR2. . . . . .178 A2
Ormesby 🖪 PE30. . . . . . .147 D5
Ormesby Dr PE37. . . . . . .153 B1
Ormesby Glebe NR29 . . . .167 D6
Ormesby La NR29. . . . . . . .76 A8
Ormesby Rd
Caister-on-Sea NR30. . . .168 D7
Caister-on-Sea NR30. . . .168 D7
Caister-on-Sea NR30. . . .168 D8
Hemsby NR29. . . . . .167 A3

Ormesby Rd continued
Ormesby St Margaret with
Scratby NR29 . . . . .168 C8
Scottow NR10 . . . . .37 B2
ORMESBY ST MARGARET
NR29 . . . . .167 B3
ORMESBY ST MICHAEL
NR29 . . . . .58 A1
Ormesby Village Inf Sch
NR29 . . . . .167 A2
Ormesby Village Jun Sch
NR29 . . . . .167 A3
Ormiston Cliff Pk Prim Acad
NR31 . . . . .170 D2
Ormiston Herman Acad
NR31 . . . . .170 A3
Ormiston Venture Acad
NR31 . . . . .170 A3
Ormiston Victory Acad
NR5 . . . . .156 E2
Ormond Rd NR30. . . . . . .169 C5
Ormsby Cl 🖪 NR31. . . . . .171 C4
Orpley La NR28 . . . . .38 A7
Orville Pl 🖪 NR5. . . . . . . .156 C1
Orwell Cl
King's Lynn PE30. . . . . . .147 D4
🖪 Wymondham NR18. . .173 D5
Orwell Cres NR31. . . . . . . .94 A6
Osbert Cl NR21. . . . . .162 E1
Osborne Ave NR30. . . . . .169 C7
Osborne Cl 🖪 NR28. . . . .151 C7
Osborne Ct NR4. . . . . . . .162 B3
Osborne Pk PE13 . . . . . . .152 C5
Osborne Rd
Norwich NR4 . . . . .161 D2
Wisbech PE13 . . . . .152 B7
Osier Cl NR19. . . . . .154 B4
Osier La Mautby NR29 . . . .75 F7
Mautby NR29. . . . . .76 A6
West Beckham NR25. . . . . .9 C1
Osprey Cl NR12. . . . . . . .164 D5
Osprey Cres NR18. . . . . .173 D1
OSTEND NR12 . . . . .24 A7
Ostend Gap NR12. . . . . . .24 A7
Ostend Pl NR12 . . . . .24 A7
Ostend Rd NR12. . . . . .24 A6
Ostlers Rd PE38. . . . . . . .172 B7
Ostrich La NR19 . . . . .49 A3
Ottaway Cl NR5. . . . . . . .157 A3
Otter Cl
🖪 Downham Market
PE38. . . . . .172 A6
🖪 Salhouse NR13. . . . . . .55 A1
Otter Dr 🖪 NR14. . . . . . . .89 B3
Otter Rd Swaffham PE37. .153 C1
Swaffham PE37 . . . . .153 C2
Otters La NR11. . . . . .9 D2
Otter Trust The★ NR35 . .123 E7
OULTON NR11. . . . . .35 B7
Oulton Cl PE37. . . . . .153 C2
Oulton Rd
Itteringham NR11. . . . . . .20 C1
Norwich NR6. . . . . .158 C5
Oulton NR11. . . . . .35 C8
Oulton St NR11 . . . . .35 D6
OULTON STREET NR11. . . .35 D6
Ouse Ave PE30 . . . . .146 D2
Ouse Ave The IP24. . . . . .176 C3
Ouse La NR12. . . . . .39 F1
Outney Rd NR35. . . . . . . .124 D8
Out S Gates PE30 . . . . . .146 E3
OUTWELL PE14 . . . . .77 F8
Outwell Rd Emneth PE14 . .59 B2
Emneth PE14 . . . . .152 F1
Stow Bardolph PE34. . . . . .78 E8
Oval Ave NR5. . . . . .161 C8
Oval Cl NR5. . . . . .157 C1
Oval The IP25 . . . . .84 B5
Overbury Rd NR6 . . . . . . .158 A4
OVER CROSS NR16. . . . . .119 C8
Over Cross NR16. . . . . . . .119 C8
Overstone Ct NR6. . . . . . .158 F5
OVERSTRAND NR27. . . . . .11 A4
Overstrand Rd NR27 . . . .139 C6
Overstrand Sports Club
NR27 . . . . .11 A3
Overstrand Way NR7. . . .159 E4
Overton La PE30. . . . . . . .146 E3
Overtons Way 🖪 NR14. . .90 C5
Overton Wy NR10 . . . . . . .149 D6
Overwood La NR16. . . . . .106 A3
Overy Rd PE31. . . . . .135 D3
OVINGTON IP25 . . . . .84 E5
Ovington Rd IP25. . . . . . . .84 C4
Owencole Cl PE32. . . . . . . .29 D2
Owen Rd Diss IP22. . . . . .177 F4
Great Yarmouth NR31. . .169 B1
Owen's Cl 🖪 NR15. . . . . .106 E3
Owl Dr 🖪 NR14. . . . . .89 B3
OXBOROUGH PE33. . . . . . .81 D4
Oxborough Dr PE30. . . . .148 E2
Oxborough La NR21. . . . .141 C4
Oxborough Rd
Gooderstone IP26. . . . . . .82 A3
Gooderstone PE33. . . . . . .81 F3
Oxborough PE33 . . . . .81 D3
Stoke Ferry PE33. . . . . . . .81 A2
Oxborough Wlk 🖪
NR31. . . . . .169 D3
Oxburgh Cl 🖪 PE13 . . . . .152 A7
Oxburgh Hall Gdns &
Estate★ PE33 . . . . .81 E4
Oxburgh Sq NR21. . . . . . . .30 C4
Oxcroft NR13. . . . . .166 C4
Oxford Ave NR31. . . . . . . .170 B3
Oxford Pl
Terrington St Clement
PE34 . . . . .42 E7
Terrington St Clement
PE34 . . . . .144 F6

Oxford Rd
2 Feltwell IP26 . . . . .98 D1
7 Feltwell IP26 . . . . .98 E1
Oxford St NR2 . . . . .162 C5
Oxford Way **11** NR29 . . . .57 D4
OXNEAD NR10 . . . . .36 E2
Oxnead Dr NR30 . . . . . . .168 C7
Oxnead La Brampton NR10. 36 E3
  Hempnall NR35 . . . . .107 F4
Oxnead Rd NR3 . . . . .158 B2
OXWICK NR21 . . . . .31 D4
Oxwick La NR21 . . . . .31 C4
Oxwick Rd NR20 . . . . .31 E2
Oystercatcher Cl **5**
  NR7 . . . . .159 E4
Oyster Ct PE30 . . . . .146 E6

P

Pack La Alby Hill NR11 . . . .21 B4
  Briston NR24 . . . . .142 F3
  East Carleton NR14 . . . . . .89 A6
  Strumpshaw NR13 . . . . . . .73 F3
Packway The IP20 . . . . . .123 A3
Paddock Cl Belton NR31 . . .93 F6
  3 Fakenham NR21 . . . .141 E4
  Terrington St Clement
    PE34 . . . . .144 B5
  14 Watton IP25 . . . . . . .84 F3
Paddock Farm IP31 . . . . .127 B4
Paddock Farm Dr NR29 . . .75 F8
Paddock Gdns NR17 . . . . .174 E5
Paddock Rd **13** IP20 . . . .122 D2
Paddock St NR2 . . . . .162 C8
Paddocks The
  Aylsham NR11 . . . . .150 C6
  Bacton/Walcott NR12 . . . . .23 E4
  Beetley NR20 . . . . .49 D4
  Brandon IP27 . . . . .175 E4
  Bridgham NR16 . . . . .117 D3
  Downham Market PE38. . . .172 B5
  Griston IP25 . . . . .85 A1
  Lakenheath IP27 . . . . . . .113 E1
  Mileham PE32 . . . . .48 D6
  Norwich NR6 . . . . .158 F6
  Setchey PE33 . . . . .61 F8
  Stradbroke IP21 . . . . . . .131 E1
  Swaffham PE37 . . . . .153 B3
Paddocks Way NR14 . . . . .90 B6
Paddock The
  3 Cromer NR27 . . . . . . .10 B5
  Hemsby NR29 . . . . .167 A8
  Trowse with Newton
    NR14 . . . . .163 A2
Paddys La NR9 . . . . .69 E8
Paddy's La NR9 . . . . .51 E1
Paddys Loke NR30 . . . . . .169 A2
Padgate NR13 . . . . .72 D6
Padgett's Rd PE14 . . . . . . .95 A6
Page Cl
  3 North Walsham
    NR28 . . . . .151 C6
  Poringland NR14 . . . . .90 C5
Page Rd Brundall NR13 . . .165 C4
  Norwich NR3 . . . . .157 F1
Pages Cl **3** NR18 . . . . . .173 B3
Pages La IP25 . . . . .84 B5
Page Stair La PE30 . . . . . .146 D5
Paget Adams Dr **4** NR20 . 68 A8
Paget Cres NR31 . . . . . . .170 C1
Paget Rd NR30 . . . . .169 D4
Paige Cl **1** PE33 . . . . . . .61 D5
Paiges Cl PE31 . . . . .140 C4
Paine Cl IP22 . . . . .177 B5
Paine Rd NR7 . . . . .163 D8
Painter St IP24 . . . . .176 C4
Pakenham Dr PE31 . . . . . .140 C3
Palace St NR1 . . . . .178 B3
Pales Gn **4** PE32 . . . . . .46 F2
PALGRAVE IP22 . . . . .177 C2
Palgrave Cl NR8 . . . . .155 B1
Palgrave Prim Sch
  IP22 . . . . .177 D2
Palgrave Rd
  Great Dunham PE32 . . . . . .47 E1
  Great Yarmouth NR30 . . . .169 C5
  Little Dunham PE32 . . . . . .65 D8
  Sporle with Palgrave PE32 153 F8
Palling Rd Horsey NR29 . . .40 E2
  Ingham NR12 . . . . .24 D1
  Lessingham NR12 . . . . .39 D5
Palm Cl NR18 . . . . .173 B5
Palmer Cl NR3 . . . . .158 C2
Palmer Dr IP27 . . . . .113 E2
Palmer Rd
  Great Yarmouth NR31 . . . .170 D5
  8 New Rackheath NR13 . .72 E7
  Norwich NR3 . . . . .158 C3
Palmers La NR12 . . . . .55 C5
Palmer's La
  Aylsham NR11 . . . . .150 C6
  Freethorpe NR13 . . . . .92 F8
  Saxlingham Nethergate
    NR15 . . . . .107 C7
Palmerston Way NR11 . . . .150 E6
Palmer Way PE38 . . . . . . .172 C3
Palomino Dr PE38 . . . . . . .172 B6
Pandora **8** PE30 . . . . . . .147 C4
Pansey Dr PE31 . . . . .140 C4
Panton Cl PE30 . . . . .146 D2
Pantshorne La IP22 . . . . . .128 E4
PANXWORTH NR13 . . . . . .73 E7
Panxworth Church Rd
  NR13 . . . . .73 E8
Panxworth Rd NR13 . . . . . .73 F7
Paper Mill La NR8 . . . . . . .155 A1
Paper Mill Yard NR1 . . . . .178 C1
Paper St NR19 . . . . .68 C5
Papillon Rd NR18 . . . . . . .173 D4
Papplewick Cl **4** NR4 . . .162 C1

Paradise La
  6 Bawdeswell NR20 . . . .50 E7
  7 King's Lynn PE30 . . . .146 D5
Paradise Par **10** PE30 . . .146 D5
Paradise Pl NR1 . . . . .178 B2
Paradise Rd
  6 Bawdeswell NR20 . . . .50 E7
  Downham Market PE38. . . .172 B5
  6 King's Lynn PE30 . . . .146 D5
Paragon Pl **4** NR2 . . . . .162 C6
Parana Cl NR7 . . . . .159 C5
Parana Ct NR7 . . . . .159 C5
Parana Rd NR7 . . . . .159 C5
Parish Rd NR10 . . . . .53 D7
Park Ave **5** Barford NR9 . .69 F2
  King's Lynn PE30 . . . . . . .146 F4
  North Walsham NR28 . . . . .151 D5
  Scottow NR10 . . . . .37 D2
  Wisbech PE13 . . . . .152 C6
Park Cl Hethersett NR9 . . . .88 D7
  Holt NR25 . . . . .137 D5
  Norwich NR6 . . . . .158 E5
  Thurton NR14. . . . . .91 C4
  Wymondham NR18 . . . . . .173 D1
Park Cres PE34 . . . . .61 B5
Park Ct Harling NR16 . . . . .118 C5
  North Walsham NR28 . . . . .151 D5
Park Dr Beccles NR34 . . . .110 E1
  Hethersett NR9 . . . . .88 C7
  Homersfield NR35 . . . . . . .123 D4
Parker Cl NR13 . . . . .165 B4
Parker Dr NR21 . . . . .141 D4
Parker Rd NR2 . . . . .162 B5
Parker's CE Prim Sch
  IP25 . . . . .84 C5
Parkers Cl
  Saham Toney IP25 . . . . . . .84 C5
  Wymondham NR18 . . . . . .173 B6
Parker's Cl NR9 . . . . .70 C5
Parker's La
  Brumstead NR12 . . . . .39 B5
  Long Stratton NR15 . . . . . .106 F2
Parker's Rd **10** NR20 . . . .68 F6
Parkes La NR15 . . . . .106 D6
Park Est **3** IP25 . . . . . . .67 B2
Park Farm La
  Euston IP24 . . . . .126 C4
  Hoxne IP21 . . . . .131 C2
  Sparrow Green NR19 . . . . .49 B1
Park Gates NR11. . . . . .35 F7
Park Gn **12** NR29 . . . . . .75 F8
Park Highatt Dr **2** IP25 . . .67 C2
Parkhill **4** PE32 . . . . .44 B3
Park Hill PE31 . . . . .140 D5
Parkington Wy IP22 . . . . .128 B1
Park La Blofield NR13 . . . .165 B8
  Bressingham IP22 . . . . . . .128 F8
  Cromer NR27 . . . . .139 D4
  Deopham NR18 . . . . .87 A4
  Downham Market PE38. . . .172 B3
  Helhoughton NR21 . . . . . . .30 E5
  Heydon NR11 . . . . .35 A6
  Hockering NR20 . . . . .69 C8
  North Lopham IP22 . . . . . .119 B2
  North Walsham NR28 . . . . .151 C5
  Reepham NR10 . . . . .149 B4
  Scarning NR19 . . . . .67 B6
  Snettisham PE31 . . . . .12 E4
  Winfarthing IP22 . . . . .120 B5
  Wolterton NR11 . . . . .20 D3
  Wymondham NR18 . . . . . . .87 F2
  Wymondham NR18 . . . . . .173 C2
Parkland Cl **8** NR12 . . . . .55 E4
Parkland Cres
  9 Horning NR12 . . . . . .55 E4
  Norwich NR6 . . . . .158 F3
Parkland Dr NR31 . . . . . . .170 A5
Parkland Est NR29 . . . . . .167 A8
Parkland Rd NR6 . . . . . . .158 F3
Parklands NR8 . . . . .156 D4
Parklands Ave IP25 . . . . . .67 B2
Parklands Way **11** IP20 . .122 D2
Park Rd Bardwell IP31 . . . .127 A4
  Cromer NR27 . . . . .139 D5
  Diss IP22 . . . . .177 D4
  East Dereham NR19 . . . . . .154 E6
  Great Yarmouth NR31 . . . .170 D3
  Gressenhall NR20 . . . . .49 C3
  Hunstanton PE36. . . . . . . .132 C4
  St Cross, South Elmham
    IP20. . . . . .123 C3
  Spixworth NR10. . . . . .54 A1
  Upper Sheringham NR26 . .138 A4
  Warham NR23 . . . . .6 A4
  Wells-next-the-Sea NR23 . .136 C6
  Wisbech PE13 . . . . .152 D5
  Wroxham/Hoveton NR12 . .164 B3
Parkside PE34 . . . . .13 A7
Parkside Ct IP22. . . . . . . .177 C4
Parkside Dr NR6 . . . . .158 E5
Parkside Sch The NR2 . . . .162 A5
Park St **2** PE13 . . . . . . .152 D5
Park The
  East Harling NR16 . . . . . . .118 B5
  Euston IP24 . . . . .126 B5
Parkview IP24 . . . . .176 E4
Park View
  Botesdale IP22 . . . . .128 A3
  Brandon IP27 . . . . .175 B2
  Horsford NR10 . . . . .53 A2
  Rollesby NR29 . . . . .57 D3
  Weeting IP27. . . . . .175 A7
Park View Ave NR29 . . . . . .57 D3
Parkway NR7 . . . . .147 B4
Park Way NR6 . . . . .157 E5
Parliament Ct **5** NR7 . . . .72 D4
Parliament La IP24 . . . . . .102 E3
Parmenter Rd NR4 . . . . . .161 F3
Parmeter Rd NR11. . . . . . .150 D6

Parrow La NR11 . . . . .21 C6
Parr Rd NR3 . . . . .158 A1
Parsley Way PE38. . . . . . .172 E6
Parsons Cl IP27 . . . . .175 B2
Parsons La PE31 . . . . .14 D8
Parson's La IP22. . . . . . . .128 B8
Parsons Mead NR1 . . . . . .161 F1
Partridge Cl **12** NR7 . . . .159 E4
Partridge Dr
  Mulbarton NR14 . . . . .89 A3
  4 Thetford IP24 . . . . . .176 D2
Partridge Gr PE37 . . . . . . .153 D3
Partridge Rd NR11 . . . . . .150 B6
Partridge Rise **4** NR2 . . .177 F5
Partridge Way
  Holt NR25 . . . . .137 D6
  Norwich NR6 . . . . .71 E6
  Norwich NR6 . . . . .158 D4
Partridge Wlk IP27 . . . . . .175 F3
Parva IP27 NR11 . . . . .20 B4
Pascoe Dr NR29 . . . . .168 C8
Pascoe Pl IP27 . . . . .129 B8
Pashford Cl IP27 . . . . .113 F1
Pasteur Rd NR31. . . . . . . .169 B2
PASTON NR28 . . . . .143 D2
Paston Cl **4** NR11 . . . . . . .9 E1
Paston Coll NR28 . . . . . . .151 C5
Paston Dr NR30 . . . . .168 C8
Paston Great Barn ★
  NR28 . . . . .143 E2
PASTON GREEN NR28 . . . .143 E2
Paston Rd Bacton NR12 . . . .23 D5
  Edingthorpe NR28 . . . . . . .23 B4
  Great Yarmouth NR31 . . . .170 C5
  Mundesley NR11 . . . . .143 D5
  Paston NR28 . . . . .143 D1
  Paston Green NR28. . . . . .143 C1
  Witton NR28 . . . . .23 C1
Paston Way NR7 . . . . .159 E2
Pasture Cl PE31. . . . . .28 B4
Pastures The
  5 Blakeney NR25 . . . . . . .7 C6
  Great Yarmouth NR31 . . . .170 B7
  Hemsby NR29 . . . . .167 A8
  Little Snoring NR21 . . . . . .17 B3
Patch The NR21 . . . . .15 F1
Patricia Ave NR12 . . . . .54 C6
Patricia Rd NR1 . . . . .162 D3
Patrick Rd **4** NR15 . . . . .106 D3
Patten La NR15 . . . . .121 B3
Patternmakers Cl PE31. . . .135 C3
Patterson Cl **8** NR30. . . .169 C4
Patteson Cl **8** NR4 . . . . . .89 B8
Patteson Rd NR3. . . . . . . .162 D8
Pattinson's Rd NR30 . . . . .169 B6
Paul Dr PE32 . . . . .44 B3
Paul Engelhard Wy NR10 . .35 B3
Pauls La NR27 . . . . .11 A3
Pavilion Cl NR16 . . . . .119 D6
Pavilion Ct **5** IP22. . . . . .177 A5
Pavilion Rd NR31 . . . . . . .170 D4
Pavilion Theatre NR31 . . . .170 E4
Pavilion Wy NR20. . . . . . .154 F5
Paws La PE32. . . . . .45 B1
Paxfield Rd NR21 . . . . .30 C4
Paxman Rd PE30. . . . . . . .146 F2
Paxton Pl **3** NR2 . . . . . .162 C4
Paxton Terr PE30 . . . . . . .146 E5
Payne Ave PE13 . . . . .152 D7
Paynes Hill NR20 . . . . . . .122 F6
Payne's La IP26 . . . . .98 E1
Peabody Rd NR14 . . . . . . .150 A5
Peachaven Olde Cl
  NR29 . . . . .167 A6
Peachman Way **5** NR7. . . .72 E4
Peachtree St **6** NR11 . . . .15 C2
Peacock Chase NR18. . . . .173 D4
Peacock Cl Easton NR9 . . . .70 B5
  Hockwold cum Wilton
    IP26. . . . . .113 F6
  Holt NR25. . . . . .137 D6
Peacock Gr NR8 . . . . .156 A6
Peacock La Beetley NR20. . .49 F5
  Holt NR25. . . . . .137 D5
Peacock St NR3 . . . . .178 B4
Peacocks The NR25 . . . . . .137 C7
Peacock Way
  Attleborough NR17 . . . . . .174 B4
  Briston NR24 . . . . .142 A4
Peafowl Cl **7** IP22 . . . . . .177 F5
Peakhall Rd PE32 . . . . .48 B8
Peakwell Cl NR8. . . . . . . .155 C2
Pearce Rd IP22 . . . . .177 E4
Pearce's Cl **2** IP26 . . . . .114 A7
Pearmain Rd IP22 . . . . . . .177 D5
Pearsons Cl
  Freethorpe NR13 . . . . .92 E7
  Holt NR25 . . . . .137 C6
Pearson's Rd NR25 . . . . . .137 C6
Peartree Ave **2** NR29 . . . .57 C4
Pear Tree Cl NR29 . . . . . . .68 E6
Pear Tree Cnr NR11. . . . . . .15 B3
Peartree Way **9** PE14 . . . .59 A1
Peascod La NR14 . . . . .91 D6
PEASELAND GREEN
  NR20 . . . . .50 F3
Peaseland Green
  Elsing NR20 . . . . .50 F2
  Peaseland Green NR20. . . . .51 A2
Peatlings La PE13. . . . . . .152 A7
Pebble Cl **3** NR31 . . . . . .94 C6
Pebble View Wlk NR31. . . .171 E4
Peck Cl NR5 . . . . .160 E6
Peckover Dr PE13. . . . . . .152 E4
Peckover House ★ PE13 152 B5
Peckover Prim Sch
  PE13. . . . . .152 B6
Peckover Rd
  Fakenham NR21. . . . . . . .141 A6

Peckover Rd continued
  Norwich NR4 . . . . .161 E3
Peckover Way PE30. . . . . .147 B8
Pecks La NR24. . . . . .19 D5
Peddars Cl IP25 . . . . .84 C3
Peddars Ct **12** IP25 . . . . .84 C3
Peddars Dr PE36. . . . . . . .132 D6
Peddars' La NR34 . . . . . . .110 C6
Peddars Rise PE37 . . . . . .153 C4
Peddars Way Anmer PE35 . .28 F8
  Bridgham NR16 . . . . .117 C5
  Castle Acre PE32. . . . . . . .46 C5
  Little Massingham PE32 . . .29 B3
  Sedgeford PE31. . . . . .13 C6
  Sedgeford PE36. . . . . .13 C8
  Shadwell IP24 . . . . .117 D2
  Taverham NR8 . . . . .155 D2
Peddars Way N PE36 . . . . . .2 A4
Peddlars Turnpike NR20. . . .33 F3
PEDHAM NR13. . . . . .73 D7
Pedham Rd NR13 . . . . .73 E7
Pedlars Croft **2** NR29. . . .167 A8
Pedlar's Gr PE37 . . . . .153 C5
Pedlar's La IP27 . . . . .17 F1
Pedley La PE13 . . . . .152 A6
Peel Mews **5** NR5 . . . . . .178 A3
Peel St PE30 . . . . .146 F4
Pegasus Cl NR3 . . . . .168 D7
Pegg Cl NR9 . . . . .70 B5
Peggotty Rd NR30 . . . . . . .170 D8
Pegg Rd NR26 . . . . .138 C5
Pegg's La NR16 . . . . .105 E6
Pelargonium Dr NR18. . . . .173 F7
Peldon Dr PE13 . . . . .152 E5
Pelham Rd NR3 . . . . .158 D1
Pellew Pl
  Cringleford NR4. . . . . .161 B2
  North Walsham NR28 . . . . .151 C6
Pell Rd PE31. . . . . .140 D4
Pell Pl **2** PE31. . . . . .43 F2
Pembroke Rd **6** IP20 . . . .122 E7
Pembroke Ave NR31 . . . . .170 B4
Pembroke Rd NR2 . . . . . . .162 B5
Pendlesham Rise NR8. . . . .155 E2
Pendula Rd PE13 . . . . .152 E7
Penfold Dr NR18. . . . . . . .173 E5
Penfold St NR11 . . . . .150 C6
Penguin Rd NR29 . . . . . . .167 D4
Penhill La NR17. . . . . .103 D7
Penn Cl NR8 . . . . .156 D8
Penn Gr NR3 . . . . .158 C5
Pennington Way PE31. . . . .140 A1
Penn Rd NR8 . . . . .156 D8
Pennycress Dr
  6 Thetford IP24 . . . . . .176 F5
  Wymondham NR18 . . . . . .173 E4
Penny Gn NR16 . . . . .88 D2
Penny Croft **3** NR21 . . . . .15 C2
Pennyfields NR35. . . . . . . .124 A7
PENNYGATE NR12 . . . . . . .38 E2
Pennygate La NR12 . . . . . .38 F1
Penny Gn NR16 . . . . .88 D2
Pennyroyal **1** NR6. . . . . .158 D5
Penrice Rd NR13. . . . . .73 A5
Penrose Cl PE30 . . . . .147 B8
Penrose Gdns PE13 . . . . . .152 E4
Penryn Cl NR4 . . . . .161 E5
Penshurst Mews **5**
  NR4 . . . . .161 F1
Pensthorpe Nature Reserve
  & Gdns ★ NR21 . . . . .32 B8
Pensthorpe Rd
  Fakenham NR21. . . . . .32 A8
  Fakenham NR21. . . . . . . .141 F5
PENTNEY PE32 . . . . .63 C8
Pentney Abbey Leisure Ctr
  PE32. . . . . .63 A7
Pentney Dro PE33 . . . . . . .62 E6
Pentney La PE32 . . . . .63 D8
Pentney Rd PE32 . . . . .63 E8
Pepper La PE38 . . . . .97 C8
Peppers Cl IP27 . . . . .175 B7
Pepper's Gn PE30 . . . . . . .148 B1
Peppers High Hill
  Weeting IP27 . . . . .114 F7
  Weeting IP27. . . . . .175 C7
Percival Cl NR4 . . . . .161 E4
Percy Howes Cl **10** NR13 . 72 D6
Perebrown Ave NR30 . . . . .169 D7
Pereers Cl NR25 . . . . .137 A7
Peregrine Cl
  Cantley NR13. . . . . .92 C6
  Diss IP22 . . . . .177 F5
  Norwich NR7 . . . . .159 C5
Peregrine Gr NR18 . . . . . . .173 D1
Peregrine Mews
  8 Cringleford NR4. . . . . .89 A8
  Norwich NR7 . . . . .159 C4
Peregrine Rd
  Norwich NR7 . . . . .72 B6
  Norwich NR7 . . . . .159 C4
Perkin Field NR34 . . . . . . .144 B4
Perrings NR18 . . . . .173 B6
Perrys La NR10 . . . . .35 C2
Persimmon PE30 . . . . .147 C5
Peter Ave NR13 . . . . .166 B3
Peter Beales Roses ★
  NR17 . . . . .103 F3
Peter Cl
  Ormesby St Margaret with
    Scratby NR29 . . . . .168 D8
  4 Sprowston NR7 . . . . .159 C1
Peter Dr IP24. . . . . .176 F5
Peterhouse Ave NR31 . . . .170 C4
Peterhouse Prim Sch
  NR31 . . . . .170 B4
Peter Pulling Dr NR8. . . . . .155 D3
Peters Cl NR19 . . . . .154 C1
Peterscourt PE30 . . . . . . .147 D6
Peter's Dro PE34. . . . . .61 A7

Petersfield Cl NR15 . . . . . .106 F2
Petersfield Dr **11** NR12 . . .55 E4
Peterson Rd NR3 . . . . .158 A2
Peterson's La NR11 . . . . . .150 B7
Peters Point Rd PE12 . . . . .41 A7
Peters Wy NR19 . . . . .68 C6
Peto Ct NR5 . . . . .161 C7
Petre Cl **3** NR28 . . . . . . .151 C7
Petticoat Dro PE32. . . . . . .64 E8
Petticoat La PE33 . . . . .62 D6
Pettingales **3** NR14 . . . . .89 F4
Pettits La IP21. . . . . .130 C7
Petty Spurge Sq **8**
  NR18 . . . . .173 E4
PETTYWELL NR10 . . . . . . .34 C2
Petunia Cl NR18. . . . . . . .173 F6
Petunia Way IP25 . . . . . . .175 A2
Peverell Rd NR5 . . . . .161 B7
Phantom Cl PE37 . . . . . . .153 D5
Pheasant Cl Holt NR25 . . .137 D6
  Mulbarton NR14 . . . . .89 A3
Pheasant Dr IP22 . . . . . . .177 F5
Pheasant Loke **17** NR7 . . .159 E4
Pheasants Wlk NR35 . . . . .123 E8
Pheasant Way IP27 . . . . . .175 F4
Pheasant Wlk **2** NR13 . . . .74 B8
Phelps Rd NR7. . . . . .163 F7
Philadelphia La NR3 . . . . . .158 D2
Philip Ford Way NR18. . . . .173 C2
Philip Nurse Rd PE31. . . . .140 B3
Philip Pl NR19 . . . . .154 D2
Philip Rudd Ct PE32. . . . . . .45 A8
Philips' Chase PE36. . . . . .132 D2
Phillippo Cl **4** PE32. . . . . .28 A1
Phoenix Ave
  Norwich NR6 . . . . .72 A8
  Old Catton NR12 . . . . .158 F7
  Spixworth NR10 . . . . .159 A7
Phoenix Cl NR13 . . . . .166 C4
Phoenix Way
  Attleborough NR17 . . . . . .174 A3
  Costessey NR5. . . . . .156 C1
Piccamore Loke NR12. . . . .56 A7
Piccoli Cl NR3 . . . . .157 A4
Pickards Way PE13 . . . . . .152 A6
Pickford Cl NR28 . . . . .151 E6
Picton Cl NR14. . . . . .90 C4
Picton Rd NR15. . . . . .106 D4
Piebald Cl PE38. . . . . .172 B7
Pier Gdns NR31 . . . . .170 E4
Pier Pl NR30 . . . . .169 D2
Pier Plain NR31 . . . . .170 D5
Pier Rd NR31 . . . . .170 D4
Pier Wlk NR31 . . . . .170 D4
Pigeon St PE14 . . . . .41 D3
Pigg La NR3 . . . . .178 B4
Pightle Cl **21** NR14. . . . . .89 B3
Pightle The PE37 . . . . . . .153 C4
Pightle Way Lyng NR9 . . . . .51 A4
  Reepham NR10 . . . . .149 C5
Pigot La NR14 . . . . .90 C6
Pike La IP24. . . . . .176 D3
Pikeman Rd NR13 . . . . .72 E5
Pikes Nursery **4** NR29 . . . .56 C5
Pilgrims Way
  Little Cressingham IP25 . . .83 F3
  Weeting IP27. . . . . .175 A8
Pilgrim's Way **7** IP20. . . .122 D2
Pilling Pk Rd NR1 . . . . . . .163 B7
Pilling Rd NR1 . . . . .163 D7
Pilot St **2** PE30 . . . . . . .146 D5
PILSON GREEN NR13 . . . . .74 B8
Pimpernel Rd NR10 . . . . . . .53 B2
Pincents Drift IP25 . . . . . . .67 F1
Pincushion Dro PE14. . . . . .78 B5
Pinder Cl NR3 . . . . .158 A1
Pinder Rd NR13 . . . . .158 A1
Pine Ave
  Cockley Cley PE37 . . . . . . .82 D7
  Marham PE33 . . . . .63 B4
Pine Cl
  3 Downham Market
    PE38 . . . . .172 C6
  8 Eye IP23. . . . . .130 C1
  4 Harleston IP20. . . . . .122 D1
  17 Marthan NR29 . . . . . .57 D4
  Norwich NR4 . . . . .162 A3
  Ormesby St Margaret
    NR29 . . . . .167 A3
  3 Snettisham PE31 . . . .12 E4
  Thetford IP24 . . . . .176 B1
Pine Coombe **1** NR21 . . . .15 C2
Pinecot Ave **7** NR31 . . . . .94 C6
Pine Ct NR17 . . . . .174 D4
Pine Gn NR31 . . . . .170 B5
Pine Gr
  East Dereham NR19 . . . . . .154 D2
  Framingham Earl NR14 . . . .90 C6
  Sheringham NR26 . . . . . . .138 E6
Pineheath Rd NR25 . . . . . . .8 E3
Pinelodges The NR7 . . . . . .163 C6
Pine Loke NR14. . . . . .90 B5
Pine Mall PE31 . . . . .133 C6
Pine Rd King's Lynn PE30 . .148 D2
  Norwich NR7 . . . . .159 E1
Pines The NR4. . . . . .161 D1
Pine Tree Chase PE33. . . . .43 F1
Pine Tree Cl IP27 . . . . . . .127 F5
Pinetrees NR31 . . . . .93 E3
Pine Trees Bsns Pk
  NR7 . . . . .159 D3
Pinetrees Rd NR7 . . . . . . .159 D3
Pine View NR27. . . . . .139 F4
Pine Wlk **6** NR25 . . . . . . .8 F5
Pinewood Cl NR6 . . . . . . .157 F4

Oxf–Plu **203**

Pinewood Dr
  Brandon IP27. . . . . .175 C2
  6 Horning NR12. . . . . . .55 E4
Pinewood Leisure Ctr
  NR25 . . . . .9 B3
Pinfold La
  Hindolveston NR20 . . . . . .33 D8
  Northwold IP26 . . . . .99 B8
  Salthouse NR25. . . . . .8 B6
Pinfold Rd PE14 . . . . .77 E5
Pingle La PE34. . . . . .41 F6
Pingle Rd PE14 . . . . .78 A4
Pingles Rd PE30 . . . . .148 C4
Pingo Rd **17** IP25 . . . . . . .84 C3
Pinkney La NR24 . . . . .19 B5
Pintail Cl NR25 . . . . .8 B6
Pintail Dr
  2 Blakeney NR25 . . . . . . .7 C6
  Great Yarmouth NR31 . . . .170 A6
Pinto Cl PE38 . . . . .172 B6
Pioneer Rd NR6 . . . . .159 A6
Piper Rd King's Lynn PE30. 146 F1
  Norwich NR7 . . . . .159 E1
Piper's Gdns IP22 . . . . . . .177 C4
Pipit's Mdw NR11. . . . . . . .21 A5
Pippin Cl Dereham NR19. . .154 E3
  Ormesby St Margaret
    NR29 . . . . .167 A2
Pippin Gdns PE13. . . . . . .152 F7
Pippin Gn NR4. . . . . .161 E5
Pippin Pl PE13 . . . . .152 E2
Pirnhow St NR35. . . . . . . .109 B3
Pishmire Cl NR15 . . . . . . .160 F6
Pitchford Rd NR5 . . . . . . .161 C6
Pit Rd
  Aldeby, Wheatacre, Burgh St
    Peter NR34 . . . . .111 B4
  Hemsby NR29 . . . . .167 A7
  Northrepps NR27 . . . . .11 A1
  Woodbastwick NR13 . . . . . .55 D1
Pits La NR14. . . . . .92 A2
Pit St NR11 . . . . .22 C6
Pitt Farm Gn NR8 . . . . .70 B8
Pittocks La IP25 . . . . .86 A6
Pitt's Hill NR15 . . . . .107 B8
Pitts Hill Cl NR15. . . . . . . .107 B8
Pitt Sq NR9 . . . . .86 C4
Pitt St NR3 . . . . .178 A4
Pius Dro PE14 . . . . .77 E6
Plaford Rd Norwich NR7. . . .72 A5
  Norwich NR7 . . . . .159 A2
Plane Rd NR31 . . . . .170 B6
Plantation Cl NR7 . . . . . . .174 C3
Plantation Dr NR7 . . . . . . .159 D3
Plantation Gdn The ★
  NR2 . . . . .162 C5
Plantation La
  Ingworth NR11 . . . . .36 A7
  Swanton Novers NR24 . . . .18 B3
Plantation Rd
  Aslacton NR15 . . . . .121 A7
  Blofield NR13 . . . . .165 F7
  4 Fakenham NR21. . . . .141 E4
  Great Snoring NR21 . . . . . .17 A6
  Little Walsingham NR22 . . .16 F6
  North Walsham NR28 . . . . .151 E5
  Norwich NR6 . . . . .157 E6
  Rougham PE32. . . . . .47 A5
  West Barsham NR21 . . . . . .16 C3
Plantation The NR2 . . . . . .162 B4
Plantsman Cl NR2 . . . . . . .162 B3
Plasset Dr NR17 . . . . .174 F7
Platten's Cl **1** NR11 . . . . .19 F1
Plattens Ct NR12. . . . . . . .164 B3
Playbarn The ★ NR15. . . . .90 C3
Players Way NR6 . . . . .158 E6
Playingfield Rd NR20. . . . . .31 C2
Playing Field La **12** NR7 . .57 D4
Pleasance Cl PE30 . . . . . . .147 A5
Pleasant Cl NR5 . . . . .157 D5
Pleasant Ct **1** PE30. . . . .146 E4
Pleasant Pl PE31. . . . . . . .133 D6
Pleasant Row **1** PE37. . . .153 C4
Pleasure Beach ★ NR30 . . .169 E1
Plevna Terr NR1 . . . . .169 B3
Ploughboy La IP25. . . . . . .84 C6
Plough La
  Hardingham NR9 . . . . .86 D6
  Watlington PE33 . . . . .61 E5
Ploughman Rd PE30 . . . . .147 C4
Ploughman's Dro IP26 . . . .98 B1
Ploughman's La NR21. . . . .17 C6
Ploughman's Piece PE36. . . .2 E6
Plover Cl
  Great Yarmouth NR31 . . . .170 A4
  3 Thetford IP24. . . . . .176 D2
Plover Rd **18** IP25 . . . . . .84 C3
Plovers Ct IP27 . . . . .175 F3
Plovers Way IP26 . . . . . . .113 F7
Plowright Pl PE13 . . . . . . .153 B4
Plumbly Cl NR18 . . . . .151 D3
Plumb's Cl NR24 . . . . .142 E4
Plum La
  Great Hockham NR17 . . . .102 F4
  Gresham NR11. . . . . .20 C8
Plummers Hill NR23 . . . . . .136 D5
Plummer's La NR15. . . . . .107 C7
Plump Rd NR15 . . . . .106 D3
Plumsgate Rd NR12 . . . . . .39 C1
Plumstead Dr NR17 . . . . . .174 E6
PLUMSTEAD GREEN
  Great and Little Plumstead
    NR13 . . . . .73 B6
  Plumstead NR11 . . . . .20 B6
Plumstead Rd
  Baconsthorpe NR25 . . . . . .20 A7
  Edgefield NR24 . . . . .19 E5

Plumstead Rd *continued*
Great & Little Plumstead
  NR13 . . . . .72 E6
4 Norwich NR1 . . . . .163 C8
Plumstead Green NR11. . . .20 A5
Thorpe End NR13 . . . . . . .72 E6
Woodbastwick NR13 . . . . .73 D7
Plumstead Rd E NR7 . . .163 D8
Plymouth Cl **3** NR30 . .168 C6
Poachers Way PE34. . . . .144 A5
Pocahontas Way PE31 . .133 E5
Pochard St NR8. . . . . . . .156 B5
POCKTHORPE
Sparham NR9. . . . . .51 B5
Thompson IP24 . . . . . . .102 A7
West Rudham PE31. . . . . .29 F6
Pockthorpe NR13. . . . . . .75 A2
Pockthorpe Gate NR3. . .163 A7
Pockthorpe La IP24. . . . .102 A7
Pockthorpe Loke
Barnham Broom NR9. . . . .69 D2
Hickling NR12 . . . . .39 F2
Pockthorpe Rd NR9. . . . .88 A8
PODMORE NR19 . . . . . . .67 B7
Podmore La NR19. . . . . . .67 C8
Poethlyn Dr
Costessey NR8. . . . . . . .156 A5
Queen's Hills NR8 . . . . .156 B6
Point Dr **2** PE37. . . . .153 C3
Pokers Drift IP21 . . . . . .130 C7
Policemans Loke NR9. . . .86 E7
Police Rd PE14 . . . . .41 D4
Polka Rd NR23. . . . . . . .136 D5
Pollard Ct **7** IP22 . . . .177 F3
Pollard Rd NR10 . . . . . . .53 E6
POLLARD STREET NR12 . .23 D2
Poll Cl NR18. . . . . .173 F7
Pollywiggle Cl NR5 . . . . .161 A6
Pollywiggle Dr PE37 . . . .153 C1
Pollywiggle La NR21. . . . .31 A2
Pommer's La NR30. . . . . .170 D8
Pond Cl **10** NR9 . . . . . . .88 C7
Pond End NR3 . . . . .29 F5
Pond Hills Rd NR25 . . . . .19 E7
Pond La Brandon IP27. . .175 A2
Heckfield Green IP21 . . . .131 A2
Knapton NR28 . . . . .143 B2
Pedham NR13. . . . . .73 D7
Surlingham NR14. . . . . . .73 B1
Taverham NR8. . . . . . . .156 F8
Pond Loke IP25. . . . . .84 A6
Pond Rd Antingham NR28 . .22 B4
East Dereham NR19 . . . .154 C2
Great Massingham PE32 . .29 D1
Hempton NR21 . . . . . . .141 A3
3 Horsford NR10. . . . . . .53 A3
Paston NR28 . . . . .143 D2
Swafield NR28. . . . . .22 C3
Ponds End La IP22. . . . .127 E4
Pond Way NR7. . . . . . . .159 E5
Pond Wy NR18. . . . . . . .173 F7
Pooley's La IP25. . . . . . . .66 D2
Pooley St IP22. . . . . . . .128 F7
POOLEY STREET IP22. . .129 A8
Poorhouse La NR14 . . . . . .89 A2
Poor Land La PE14. . . . . .41 D5
Pope's La PE34 . . . . .144 A4
Poplar Ave
Great Yarmouth NR31 . . .170 C3
Heacham PE31. . . . . . . .133 C5
King's Lynn PE34 . . . . . . .43 D4
5 Marham PE33. . . . . . . .63 B4
Norwich NR4 . . . . .71 C1
Norwich NR4 . . . . .161 E1
Poplar Cl
Downham Market PE38. .172 B6
2 Honington IP31 . . . . .126 B1
12 Horsford NR10. . . . . . .53 A3
Long Stratton NR15. . . . .106 F4
Norwich NR5 . . . . .156 F2
Poplar Dr Filby NR29 . . . . .75 F8
Happisburgh NR12 . . . . . .23 F3
King's Lynn PE30 . . . . . . .148 D2
Poplar Fields Dr PE14. . . .59 D7
Poplar Gdns **13** NR14. . . .90 F5
Poplar Gr NR26 . . . . . . .138 E5
Poplar La NR17 . . . . . . .104 B2
Poplar Mws NR7. . . . . . .159 F3
Poplar Pl **11** NR20. . . . . .68 A8
Poplar Rd PE33 . . . . .43 F1
Poplar Row Dr PE14. . . . .78 B5
Poplars The Hilgay PE38 . .96 F8
Spexhall IP19. . . . . .124 F1
Swanton Abbott NR10 . . .37 C4
Tacolneston NR16 . . . . .105 F4
Poplar Way NR17 . . . . .174 C2
Pople St NR18 . . . . .173 B4
Poppy Cl Chedgrave NR14. .91 F2
Clenchwarton PE34. . . . .146 A6
2 Cringleford NR4. . . . . . .89 A8
18 Lingwood NR13 . . . . . . .74 A3
North Walsham NR28 . . .151 F5
4 Thetford IP24 . . . . .176 F4
Poppy Cres PE36. . . . . . . .1 E4
Poppy Dr **5** NR26. . . . . .138 B6
Poppyfields
14 Horsford NR10. . . . . . .53 A3
Norwich NR5 . . . . .161 B7
West Lynn PE34. . . . . . . .146 B4
Poppy Fields NR21. . . . .141 D4
Poppy Gr IP21. . . . . . . .121 C1
Poppy Mews **6** PE13. . . .152 E7
Poppy's La IP21. . . . . . . .121 F5
Poppy St NR18. . . . . . . .173 F6
Poppy Way
Damgate NR13. . . . . . . .166 B2
Norwich NR13 . . . . .72 E4
PORINGLAND NR14 . . . . . .90 C5

Poringland Prim Sch
  NR14 . . . . .90 D5
Poringland Rd NR14 . . . . .90 B5
Porson Rd NR7 . . . . .159 C1
Portal Ave IP25. . . . . .84 F3
Portal Cl
4 Barnham IP24 . . . . . . .125 F6
7 Feltwell IP26 . . . . .98 D1
Portalfield **10** NR12 . . . . .39 B4
Porterbush Rd **18** NR14 . . .89 B3
Porter Rd NR15 . . . . . . .106 E3
Portersfield Rd NR2 . . . .162 B5
Porter's La NR9. . . . . . . .51 E5
Porter's Loke
1 Belton NR31. . . . . .94 A6
Burgh Castle NR31 . . . . . .93 F6
Norwich NR7 . . . . .159 A3
Porter's Rd Beighton NR13. .74 E1
Freethorpe NR13 . . . . . . .92 E8
Porter St PE38. . . . . . . .172 A5
Porthole Cl **11** NR33. . . . .111 F1
Portland Cl NR31 . . . . . .169 C3
Portland Pl
Great Yarmouth NR30 . . .169 E3
King's Lynn PE30 . . . . . . .146 D2
3 Thetford IP24 . . . . .116 A1
Portland St
12 King's Lynn PE30 . . . .146 E5
Norwich NR2 . . . . .162 B5
Port Rd NR15 . . . . .122 B8
Port Row NR9 . . . . .51 B4
Portway Pl NR2 . . . . . . .162 C7
Portway Sq **10** NR2 . . . .162 C7
Portway The PE30 . . . . .146 D2
Postle Mews NR3. . . . . .158 A1
Postle's La NR28. . . . . . .22 E6
Post Mill PE30 . . . . .147 C5
Postmill Cl NR18. . . . . . .173 C4
Post Mill Cl
Newton St Faith NR10. . . .53 D3
Norwich NR7 . . . . .159 A3
Postmill Loke NR20. . . . . .50 B4
Post Office Cl **8** NR13. . . .74 A3
Post Office La
Corpusty NR11. . . . . .34 F8
Corpusty & Saxthorpe NR24 34 F8
Garvestone NR9 . . . . . . .86 B8
Weston Longville NR9 . . . .51 E2
12 Wisbech PE13 . . . . . . .152 C5
Post Office Rd
Frettenham NR12 . . . . . . .54 A4
Great & Little Plumstead
  NR13 . . . . .73 B7
Lingwood NR13 . . . . .74 A3
Lingwood & Burlingham
  NR13 . . . . .73 F3
Toft Monks NR34. . . . . .110 E5
POSTWICK NR13 . . . . . . .72 F2
Postwick La NR13. . . . . .165 A4
Postwick Sta NR7 . . . . . .72 E3
Potash Fen IP22 . . . . . . .177 F4
Potash La
Bracon Ash NR16. . . . . . .88 D2
Diss IP22. . . . . .177 B4
Eye IP23. . . . . .130 B2
Potato Dro PE14. . . . . . . .60 B4
Potspoon Hole
Coltishall NR12 . . . . .54 D8
Tunstead NR12. . . . . .37 D1
Pottergate NR2. . . . . . . .178 A3
Pottergate St NR15 . . . .106 A2
POTTERGATE STREET
  NR15 . . . . .106 B2
POTTER HEIGHAM NR29 . .56 F6
Potter Heigham Rd NR29 .56 D8
Potters Cres NR15 . . . . .121 C8
Potters Dr NR31 . . . . . . .171 D5
Potter's La
Rickinghall Superior
  IP22. . . . . .128 F1
Wymondham NR18 . . . . .105 B6
Potters Vale IP22. . . . . .128 C3
Potters Wy **2** NR14. . . . . .90 C5
Pottery Hill IP22. . . . . . .128 B1
POTTHORPE NR20. . . . . . .49 A8
Pottles Alley **4** NR9 . . . . .86 C5
Pottle's La NR13. . . . . . . .92 F5
Poulter's Dro PE14. . . . . .77 D1
Poultry Rd IP27. . . . . . . .113 A3
Pound Cl Banham NR16 . .119 D6
4 Harleston IP20 . . . . . .122 D2
Hevingham NR10. . . . . . .53 C8
Pound Corner IP21 . . . . .127 C4
Pound Gn La IP25. . . . . . .67 C2
Pound Hill IP25. . . . . .84 B5
Pound La Aylsham NR11. .150 B6
Brundall NR13 . . . . .165 F5
Burgh St Margaret (Fleggburgh)
  NR29 . . . . .75 C8
Ditchingham NR35. . . . .108 C2
Docking PE31. . . . . .134 D5
Filby NR29 . . . . .75 F8
Great Yarmouth NR31 . . .170 C3
Heacham PE31. . . . . . . .133 D6
Litcham PE32. . . . . .48 A4
Loddon NR14. . . . . .109 C8
Newton Flotman NR14 . . .89 D7
North Tuddenham NR20. . .50 D2
Norwich NR7 . . . . .72 D4
Runhall NR20. . . . . .69 A4
Sloley NR12 . . . . .37 F2
Toft Monks NR34. . . . . .110 F6
Woodton NR35. . . . . . . .108 C6
Pound Rd
11 Beccles NR34. . . . . . .110 D1
East Ruston NR12. . . . . . .38 F7
Hevingham NR10. . . . . . .53 C8
Ludham NR29. . . . . .56 C5
North Walsham NR28 . . .151 D5

Powell Ct **5** NR19 . . . . .154 C6
Powell's Yard NR31 . . . . . .3 B6
Power's Pl PE38 . . . . .79 D1
Poynt Cl NR18 . . . . .173 B5
Prangle La NR15 . . . . . . .121 C6
Pratts Hill NR14. . . . . .73 A1
Press La NR3 . . . . .158 C1
Preston Ave NR18. . . . . .173 A2
Preston CE VC Prim Sch
  NR15 . . . . .106 F7
Preston Cl
Freethorpe NR13. . . . . . . .92 E7
Wroxham/Hoveton NR12 .164 B2
Preston La NR14 . . . . . . .109 F8
Preston Rd NR28. . . . . . .151 D6
Pretoria Gr PE30. . . . . . .148 D3
Pretoria La PE32. . . . . . . .46 C4
Pretty Corner La NR26 . . . .9 D4
Pretty Dr IP21 . . . . .130 D6
Pride Way NR13 . . . . . . .72 E5
Primrose Ave
Downham Market PE38. .172 A5
5 Downham Market
  PE38 . . . . .172 B5
Primrose Cl
Attleborough NR17 . . . . .174 B5
Cringleford NR4. . . . . . . .161 B1
East Dereham NR19 . . . .154 B4
15 Mulbarton NR14. . . . . . .89 B3
Mundesley NR11 . . . . . .143 B5
Ormesby St Margaret
  NR29 . . . . .167 A2
Thetford IP24 . . . . .176 F4
Trunch NR28 . . . . .22 E5
PRIMROSE CORNER
  NR13 . . . . .55 C1
Primrose Corner NR13 . . .73 C8
Primrose Cres **2** NR7. . . .72 D3
Primrose Ct **3** NR7 . . . . .72 D3
Primrose Dr
Brandon IP27. . . . . .175 A2
Damgate NR13. . . . . . . .166 B2
PRIMROSE GREEN NR9. . .51 A3
Primrose Hill
Swanton Morley NR20. . . .50 B4
Tivetshall St Margaret
  NR15 . . . . .121 B4
Primrose La
Crostwick NR12. . . . . .54 C3
Kerdiston NR10 . . . . .34 B4
North Lopham IP22. . . . . .119 B1
Sheringham NR26 . . . . . .138 B5
Swanton Morley NR20. . . .50 B4
Primrose Pl NR2 . . . . . . .162 B5
Primrose Rd Hingham NR9. 86 B5
Norwich NR1 . . . . .163 A6
Primrose Sq NR20 . . . . . .50 B4
Primrose Way
East Tuddenham NR20. . . .69 C6
15 Great Yarmouth NR31. . .94 C6
10 Horsford NR10. . . . . . .53 A3
Primrose Wlk NR28 . . . .151 E4
Primula Dr NR4. . . . . . . .161 D5
Prince Andrew Dr PE31 .140 D3
Prince Andrew's Cl
2 Aldborough NR11. . . . . .21 A5
Norwich NR6 . . . . .158 B5
Prince Andrew's Rd
  NR6 . . . . .158 B5
Prince Charles Cl PE31. .140 D3
Prince Cl NR5 . . . . .156 B1
Prince Edward Cl NR7. . .163 F7
Prince Henry Pl PE38. . .172 D4
Prince of Wales Cl
  PE13. . . . . .152 D8
Prince Of Wales Dr
  NR11 . . . . .150 E7
Prince Of Wales Rd
Caister-on-Sea NR30. . . .76 D7
Caister-on-Sea NR30. . . .168 C6
Cromer NR27. . . . . .139 B7
Hargate NR16 . . . . .105 D2
Norwich NR1 . . . . .178 B3
Upton with Fishley NR13. .166 A8
Prince Regent Way
  IP22 . . . . .177 F3
Prince Rupert Way NR13 .72 D5
Princes Cl IP27 . . . . .175 A2
Princes Rd PE13 . . . . . . .152 C4
Prince's Rd Bungay NR35 .124 A7
Great Yarmouth NR30 . . .169 D4
Princess Beatrice Cl
Hellesdon NR6. . . . . .157 D2
Norwich NR6 . . . . .71 B5
Princess Cl **7** NR25. . . . . .84 D3
Princess Ct **5** NR25. . . . .137 C5
Princess Dr PE36 . . . . . .132 D2
Princess's Dr
Dersingham PE35 . . . . . .140 C1
Sandringham PE31 . . . . . .27 D6
Sandringham PE35 . . . . . .27 D6
Sandringham PE35 . . . . . .27 D7
Princes St
North Walsham NR28 . . .151 A5
Norwich NR3 . . . . .178 B3
Swaffham PE37. . . . . . . .153 B4
Prince's St PE12. . . . . . . .41 B8
Princess Theatre PE36 . .132 C4
Princess Way **5** NR35 . .123 F8
Prince St PE13. . . . . .152 C5
Princes Way PE30. . . . . .146 F5
Prince William Cl PE36. .132 C3
Prince William Wy IP27 .177 F5
Pringle Wy PE38 . . . . . . .97 B5
Prins Ave PE13. . . . . . . .152 D7
Prins Ct **3** PE13 . . . . . . .152 D7
Prior Bank Orch **3**
  NR27 . . . . .139 C6
Prior Cl **5** NR15 . . . . . . .106 F6
Prior Rd NR7 . . . . .72 D5

Priors Dr NR6. . . . . .158 E6
Priors Gro NR19 . . . . .68 A5
Priors La NR23. . . . . .62 A5
Prior Stephen Way
  IP24 . . . . .176 B3
Priorswood NR8. . . . . . .155 E3
Priory Chase
Downham Market PE38. .172 B5
Wormegay PE33 . . . . .61 F8
Priory Cl Acle NR13. . . . .166 C3
Alpington NR14. . . . . .90 F5
Caister-on-Sea NR30. . . .168 D4
2 Fritton & St Olaves
  NR31 . . . . .93 D2
7 Hethersett NR9 . . . . . . .88 D7
Palgrave IP22 . . . . .177 D1
Sheringham NR26 . . . . . .138 F5
Sporle with Palgrave PE32 .65 D6
Priory Cres NR21 . . . . .6 E2
Priory Ct Castle Acre PE32 . .46 F2
Thornham PE36 . . . . .2 D6
Priory Dro IP25. . . . . .83 D4
Priory Gdns
1 Fritton & St Olaves
  NR31 . . . . .93 D2
12 Great Yarmouth NR30 .169 C4
Priory La Ingworth NR11. .21 A1
12 King's Lynn PE30 . . . .146 D4
Shotesham NR15. . . . . . . .90 A2
Priory Maze & Gdns★
  NR26 . . . . .138 E6
Priory Pk IP24 . . . . .176 C5
Priory Pl PE32 . . . . .65 D6
Priory Plain **3** NR30. . . . .169 C4
Priory Rd Bacton NR12 . . .23 E4
Castle Acre PE32 . . . . . . .46 F1
Downham Market PE38. .172 B5
Fritton & St Olaves NR31 . .93 D2
Great Cressingham IP25. . .83 D5
Hethersett NR9 . . . . .88 D7
King's Lynn PE30 . . . . . . .148 C5
Palgrave IP22 . . . . .177 C1
Sheringham NR26 . . . . . .138 E2
Watton IP25 . . . . .84 E3
Woodbastwick NR13 . . . . .55 F1
Priory Row **11** NR9. . . . .169 C4
Priory St NR31. . . . . . . .170 D6
Priory Terr PE38 . . . . . . .172 B5
Priory Wood NR25 . . . . . . .8 E6
Priscilla Cl NR5. . . . . . . .161 D5
Priston Green La NR16 . .120 E8
Pristow Gn La NR15 . . . .120 E8
Private Rd
Earsham NR35. . . . . .123 D8
Ormesby St Margaret
  NR29 . . . . .167 A3
Procession La PE32. . . . .153 F8
Proctor Ave **3** NR14. . . . . .92 A2
Proctor Cl **4** NR14. . . . . . .92 A2
Proctor Rd
Chedgrave NR14. . . . . . . .91 F2
5 Loddon NR14. . . . . . . .92 A2
Norwich NR6 . . . . .158 F6
Proctors Cl PE30. . . . . . .146 C2
Progress Way IP23 . . . . .130 B1
Promenade
Overstrand NR27. . . . . . . .11 A4
Sheringham NR26 . . . . . .138 D7
Prom The NR29 . . . . .167 E4
Prophets Alley PE34 . . . . .61 B6
Prop St NR21 . . . . .15 D2
Prospect Dr NR13 . . . . . . .92 E7
Prospect Dr NR11. . . . . .150 E6
Prospect La NR11. . . . . . .34 D6
Prospect Pl PE13 . . . . . .152 C3
Proudfoot Way NR11. . . .150 B5
Provan Cres **8** NR31. . . . . .94 A5
Provence Pl **2** PE13 . . . .152 E3
Providence Dr NR19 . . . . .66 E7
Providence La NR16 . . . .105 A8
Providence Pl
Briston NR24. . . . . .142 E5
8 Thorpe Hamlet NR1 . . .163 A6
Providence St **5** PE30 . . .146 E4
Providence Terr PE13. . . .153 A5
Provision Mkt NR2. . . . .178 A3
Provost Rd IP26 . . . . .98 D1
Puddingmoor NR34. . . . .110 C1
PUDDING NORTON
  NR21 . . . . .141 B1
*Pudding Norton Medieval
Village of*★ NR21 . . . . . . .31 E6
PUDDLEDOCK NR17 . . . .104 C3
Pug St IP21 . . . . .121 B2
Pulham CE Prim Sch
  IP21. . . . . .121 E5
Pulham Rd Rushall IP21. .121 F2
Starston IP20 . . . . .122 C3
PULHAM ST MARY IP21 . .121 F4
Pullover Rd
King's Lynn PE34 . . . . . . .146 B1
Tilney All Saints PE34 . . . .146 A1
Pump House Cl NR8 . . . . .70 C6
Pumphrey Way NR11. . . .150 A5
Pump La NR30. . . . . .168 D3
Punsfer Way PE34 . . . . . .60 C8
Purbeck Cl PE33 . . . . . . .152 A4
Purdance Cl NR5 . . . . . .160 D8
Purdy St NR25. . . . . .8 B6
Purdy Way NR11. . . . . . .150 B6
Purfleet PE30. . . . . .146 D5
Purfleet St **11** PE30 . . . .146 D5
Purland Rd NR7 . . . . . . .159 D2
Purley Ct NR31 . . . . .169 A1
Pursehouse Way IP22. . .177 E4
Purslane St NR30. . . . . . .168 E4
Purtingay Cl NR4 . . . . . .162 A1
Putney Cl IP27. . . . . .175 A1
Putney Rd NR1 . . . . .178 C1
Pyebush La NR13. . . . . . .166 B5

Pyecroft Rd PE14. . . . . . .41 E3
Pyehurn La NR10 . . . . . . .53 A3
Pyehurn Mews NR8. . . . .155 E3
Pye La Cranworth IP25 . . .86 A6
Deopham NR18 . . . . .86 E2
Pyes Cl **1** NR25. . . . . .7 C5
Pye's La Castle Acre PE32. .46 F2
Redgrave IP22. . . . . .128 F4
Swanton Morley NR20. . . .50 C3
Pyes Mill Rd NR14 . . . . . .92 A1
Pyes Yd NR3. . . . . .178 B4
Pyghtle Cl **18** NR25. . . . . .22 E5
Pyghtle The **4** NR16. . . . .118 C5
Pyke Ct NR30. . . . . .168 D7
Pyman Cl **11** NR29 . . . . . .57 D5
Pymars La NR15. . . . . . .107 C6
Pymar's La **6** NR15. . . . .107 C5
Pym Cl NR13. . . . . .72 E5
Pynkney NR31 . . . . .30 D7
Pyrford Dr NR4 . . . . .161 F1

Q

Quail Gr NR18 . . . . .173 D1
Quaker Ct NR10. . . . . . . .52 E7
Quaker La
Fakenham NR21. . . . . . .141 B4
Norwich NR6 . . . . .53 E1
8 Spixworth NR12. . . . . . .54 A1
Tasburgh NR15 . . . . . . .106 F6
Wisbech PE13 . . . . .152 E3
Quarles NR23. . . . . .5 A1
Quarries Rd
New Holkham NR23. . . . . .5 A1
South Creake NR21. . . . . .15 E8
Quarry La NR9. . . . . .51 A5
Quarry Rd
Costessey NR8. . . . . . . .156 A5
Horstead with Stanninghall
  NR12 . . . . .54 C4
Quaves La NR35 . . . . . . .124 A8
Quay Angel NR31 . . . . . .170 D1
Quay La NR25. . . . . .7 A7
Quay Mill Wlk **3** NR30 . .169 C4
Quay Ostend NR31 . . . . .171 C8
Quay Rd NR31 . . . . .170 D4
Quay Side NR3 . . . . .178 B4
Quayside Ct IP27 . . . . . . .113 E2
Quay The Blakeney NR25. . .7 C6
Wells-next-the-Sea NR23 136 D6
Wiveton NR25 . . . . .7 E7
Quebec Cl **14** NR4. . . . . . .89 B8
Quebec Rd
Dereham NR19 . . . . .154 D7
Norwich NR1 . . . . .163 A6
Quebec St NR1 . . . . .154 D5
Queen Anne's Rd
Bush Green IP21. . . . . . . .122 A7
Great Yarmouth NR31 . . .170 C4
Queen Elizabeth Ave
  PE30. . . . . .147 B5
Queen Elizabeth Cl NR3 .178 C4
Queen Elizabeth Dr
Dersingham PE31 . . . . . .140 D3
Wisbech PE13 . . . . .152 D3
Queen Elizabeth Hospl
  PE30. . . . . .147 E5
Queen Elizabeth Way
Bawsey PE30. . . . . .147 F6
Castle Rising PE30. . . . . .27 C1
Dersingham PE31 . . . . . .140 C1
Queen Mary Rd PE30 . . .147 A4
Queen Mary's Ave IP28 .125 A3
Queens Ave PE30 . . . . . .146 D2
Queens Cl
6 Blakeney NR25. . . . . . . .7 C6
Norwich NR4 . . . . .162 A3
Queen's Cl PE33 . . . . .80 E4
Queen's Cres
Bircham PE31 . . . . .14 A3
Great Yarmouth NR31 . . .170 B3
Queens Ct **1** NR15. . . . . .106 E3
Queen's Ct NR17. . . . . . .174 D6
Queens Dr PE36 . . . . . . .132 C6
Queen's Dr PE14 . . . . . . .77 A7
Queens Gdns PE36. . . . .132 C6
Queens Head Cl **12** NR4 . .92 F1
Queen's Hill Prim Sch
  NR8 . . . . .156 A5
Queen's Pl **2** PE34 . . . . . .43 B1
Queens Rd
12 Beccles NR34. . . . . . .110 D1
Brandon IP27. . . . . .175 A2
Cromer NR27. . . . . .139 D4
Norwich NR1 . . . . .178 A1
Wisbech PE13 . . . . .152 C4
Queen's Rd
Attleborough NR17 . . . . .174 C6
Clenchwarton PE34. . . . .146 A5
Fakenham NR21. . . . . . .141 C4
Great Yarmouth NR30 . . .169 D2
Hethersett NR9 . . . . .88 D8
Holt NR25. . . . . .137 C5
Queen's Sq NR17 . . . . . .174 D5
Queen St
Great Yarmouth NR30 . . .169 C4
King's Lynn PE30 . . . . . . .146 D5
New Buckenham NR16 . . .104 F1
Norwich NR1 . . . . .178 B3
Stradbroke IP21 . . . . . . .131 E1
12 Sutton Bridge PE12 . . .41 B8
Swaffham PE37. . . . . . . .153 B4
Wisbech PE13 . . . . .152 C4
Wymondham NR18 . . . . .173 C3
Queensway
Caister-on-Sea NR30. . . .168 E4
7 Earsham NR35. . . . . . .123 F8
King's Lynn PE30 . . . . . . .147 C5
North Walsham NR28 . . .151 A5
Roydon IP22 . . . . .177 A5

Queensway *continued*
Thetford IP24 . . . . .176 C2
Watton IP25 . . . . .84 D3
Wymondham NR18 . . . . .173 B5
Queensway Com Jun Sch
  IP24 . . . . .176 C2
Queensway Inf Sch
  IP24 . . . . .176 C2
QUIDENHAM NR16 . . . . . .118 F6
Quidenham Rd
Banham NR16 . . . . .119 B7
Harling NR16 . . . . .118 D5
Kenninghall NR16 . . . . . .119 A5
Quidenham NR16. . . . . . .118 F8

R

Rabbit La
Downham Market PE38. .172 D6
Great Witchingham NR9 . . .51 E6
Raby Ave PE30. . . . . . . .146 E6
Racecourse Rd NR7. . . . .159 C1
Race Course Rd
Terrington St Clement
  PE34 . . . . .25 C2
Terrington St Clement
  PE34 . . . . .144 C8
Racecourse The
Fakenham NR21. . . . . . .141 C3
Hempton NR21 . . . . .31 D8
Raceway Rd NR16. . . . . .103 D1
Raceys Cl **4** PE14. . . . . . .59 D2
Rachel Cl **7** NR5. . . . . . . .161 C5
Rackham St IP22 . . . . . . .177 B4
Rackham Rd NR3 . . . . . .158 D2
RACKHEATH NR13 . . . . . . .72 E8
Rackheath La NR12 . . . . .54 B2
Rackheath Pk NR13. . . . . .72 D7
Radar Cl NR14. . . . . .90 B5
Radcliffe Rd NR8 . . . . . .155 E2
RAF Air Defence Radar
Mus★ NR12. . . . . .55 E5
Rafeman Cl **3** NR5 . . . . .160 E7
Raglan St NR1 **1**. 162 C6
RAGMERE NR17 . . . . .104 D1
Railway App **2** NR26. . . .138 D7
Railway Cl
Fakenham NR21. . . . . . .141 D4
Melton Constable NR24. .142 C4
Railway Hill IP20 . . . . . . .122 C2
Railway La PE12 . . . . .41 B7
Railway Mus★ NR18 . . . .173 D2
Railway Rd Briston NR24. .142 D3
Downham Market PE38. .172 A5
King's Lynn PE30 . . . . . . .146 E5
Wisbech PE13 . . . . .152 C3
Rainey Ct **37** IP20 . . . . . .122 D2
Rainsborough Rise NR13 72 D5
Rainsthorpe PE30. . . . . . .147 B8
Rainthorpe Hall★ NR15 .106 F8
Raleigh Ave NR30. . . . . .169 D7
Raleigh Inf Sch IP24 . . . .176 E6
Raleigh Rd PE30 . . . . . . .147 B4
Raleigh Way IP24. . . . . . .176 E6
Ramblers The NR14. . . . . .90 B6
Rambouillet Cl NR31 . . . .170 A4
Ramilles Cl **6** NR19 . . . . .154 E5
Ramirez Rd NR13 . . . . . . .72 E8
Ram La NR15 . . . . .121 C4
Ramms Ct NR23. . . . . . .136 D6
Ramm's La PE37. . . . . . . .66 A4
Ramnoth Rd PE13. . . . . .152 C4
Rampant Horse St NR2. .178 A2
Rampart Rd NR30. . . . . .169 C5
Rampart Way IP24. . . . . .176 D3
Ramsay Gdns PE36. . . . .132 D3
Ramsey Cl Norwich NR4 . .161 E3
Thetford IP24 . . . . .176 E3
Ramsgate St NR24 . . . . . .19 C4
Randall Cl **1** NR31. . . . . .171 D5
Randall Cres NR27. . . . . .139 B4
Randall Rd NR7. . . . . . . .159 F4
Randell Cl PE38 . . . . . . .151 D4
Randle Gn NR5. . . . . . . .161 C8
Randolf Rd NR1 . . . . . . .162 E2
Rands Drove
Emneth Hungate PE14. . . .59 F3
Marshland St James PE14 .60 A3
Rands Rd PE14 . . . . .60 C5
Rangoon Cl NR7. . . . . . .159 C4
Ransom Dr NR27. . . . . . .139 B4
Ransome Ave IP21. . . . . .130 D6
Ransome's Cl PE14 . . . . . .77 E5
Ranson Rd NR1. . . . . . . .163 B5
RANWORTH NR13. . . . . . . .55 F1
Ranworth Cl
8 Belton NR31. . . . . .94 A6
Swafield NR28. . . . . .22 C3
Ranworth Dr
Hoveton NR12 . . . . .164 B2
Ormesby St Margaret
  NR29 . . . . .167 B2
Ranworth Rd
Blofield NR13. . . . . .165 F8
Norwich NR5 . . . . .161 C1
South Walsham NR13 . . . .74 A8
Rapsy Tapsy La IP23 . . . .130 B1
Rash's Cres IP22. . . . . . .129 C6
Rash's Gn NR19. . . . . . . .154 F2
Rash's Green Ind Est
  NR19 . . . . .154 F2
Ratcliffe Rd NR21. . . . . .141 C4
RATTEN ROW NR14 . . . . . .59 F8
Ratten Row PE14 . . . . . . .41 F1
Rattle Row Mileham PE32. .48 C6
Wymondham NR18 . . . . .173 B4
Rattlerow Hill IP21 . . . . .131 F2
Rattler's Rd IP27 . . . . . . .175 C3

Raven Cl NR31 . . . . .170 A7
Raven Croft **7** NR4 . . . . . .89 A8
Ravenham Ctr The
  NR14 . . . . .110 B6
RAVENINGHAM NR14 . . . .110 A7
Raveningham Gdns★
  NR14 . . . . .110 A7
Raveningham Rd
  Gillingham NR34 . . . . .110 C4
  Stockton NR34 . . . . .110 A5
Ravens La PE31 . . . . .29 C5
Ravensmere Inf Sch
  NR34 . . . . .110 D1
Ravensway PE38 . . . . .172 C3
Ravine Rd NR31 . . . . .93 E1
Rawhall La NR20 . . . . .49 B5
Rawley Rd NR5 . . . . .161 B8
Rawlings Way **21** IP26 . . . .98 E1
Rawlinsons La NR11 . . . . . .150 C7
Raymond Cl NR6 . . . . .157 E7
Raymond Rd NR6 . . . . .157 F7
Raymond St
  Thetford IP24 . . . . .176 D3
  15 Wisbech PE13 . . . . . .152 C4
Rayna Loke NR28 . . . . .151 C4
Rayner's Cl **6** NR20 . . . . . .68 E6
Rayners Falgate NR17 . . . .102 D7
Rayner's La NR5 . . . . .109 D4
Rayner's Way NR20 . . . . . . .68 E6
Raynham Cl PE30 . . . . .147 B4
Raynham Rd Colkirk NR21 . .31 C4
  Dunton NR21 . . . . .31 C6
  Hempton NR21 . . . . .141 A2
  West Raynham NR21 . . . . . .30 C4
  Whissonsett NR20 . . . . . . .31 C2
Raynham Ride NR19 . . . . . .154 D7
Raynham St NR2 . . . . .162 B7
Rayns Cl NR6 . . . . .158 F5
Reaches Drove IP26 . . . . . . .99 A8
READING GREEN NR21 . . .131 C1
Read's Cross NR14 . . . . . . .109 E8
Readscross La NR14 . . . . . .109 E8
Recorder Rd NR1 . . . . .178 C3
Recreation Dr PE38 . . . . . . .97 A5
Recreation Gd Rd NR7 . . . .159 A4
Recreation Rd
  East Dereham NR19 . . . . . .154 C1
  Great Yarmouth NR31 . . . .170 C5
  Hethersett NR9 . . . . .88 C7
  North Walsham NR28 . . . . .151 B4
  Norwich NR2 . . . . .162 A5
  Stalham NR12 . . . . .39 A4
Recreation Road Inf Sch
  NR2 . . . . .162 A5
Rectory Cl
  Caister-on-Sea NR30 . . . . .168 E5
  Coltishall NR12 . . . . .54 D7
  21 Long Stratton NR15 . .106 E3
  5 Newton Flotman NR15 . .89 D1
  Rollesby NR29 . . . . .57 C2
  Roydon PE32 . . . . .27 F2
Rectory Ct NR3 . . . . .158 D2
Rectory Dr PE34 . . . . .145 E5
Rectory Gdns
  Hingham NR9 . . . . .86 B5
  Wisbech PE13 . . . . .152 E6
Rectory Green IP22 . . . . . . .128 E4
Rectory Hill IP22 . . . . .128 D2
Rectory La
  Bracon Ash NR14 . . . . .88 E3
  Bunwell NR16 . . . . .105 C4
  Burnham Thorpe PE31 . . . . . .4 D4
  Chedgrave NR14 . . . . .91 F2
  Great Ellingham NR17 . . . .103 E8
  Haddiscoe NR14 . . . . .110 F7
  Hedenham NR35 . . . . .108 D4
  Little Melton NR9 . . . . .160 A3
  Loddon NR14 . . . . .92 A2
  Mettingham NR35 . . . . . . .124 D8
  Mulbarton NR14 . . . . .89 B3
  North Runcton PE33 . . . . . .44 A3
  Poringland NR14 . . . . .90 D5
  Rockland St Mary NR14 . . . .91 B6
  Scole IP21 . . . . .121 C1
  Stuston IP21 . . . . .130 B4
  Watlington PE33 . . . . .61 D5
  Weeting IP27 . . . . .175 B7
  West Winch PE33 . . . . .43 F3
Rectory Mdw Diss IP22 . . . .177 E4
  Litcham PE32 . . . . .48 A4
Rectory Rd
  Aldeby, Wheatacre, Burgh St
    Peter NR34 . . . . .111 A4
  Bacton NR28 . . . . .23 C3
  Bodham NR25 . . . . .9 B1
  Brome & Oakley IP23 . . . .130 B3
  Broome NR35 . . . . .109 B3
  Burston & Shimpling IP22 .120 E2
  2 Coltishall NR12 . . . . . .54 C6
  Dickleburgh IP21. . . . . . . .121 B1
  East Carleton NR14 . . . . . .89 A4
  Edgefield NR24 . . . . .19 C5
  Elsing NR20 . . . . .50 F4
  Frogshall NR27 . . . . .22 B8
  Gillingham NR34 . . . . .110 B3
  Gissing IP22 . . . . .120 F4
  Haddiscoe NR14 . . . . .110 F7
  Hockering NR20. . . . . .69 B8
  Hoveton NR12 . . . . .55 A7
  Lyng NR9 . . . . .51 B4
  Matlask NR11 . . . . .20 C7
  Mellis IP23 . . . . .129 D1
  Northrepps NR27 . . . . .11 A1
  Outwell PE14 . . . . .77 F6
  Rocklands NR17 . . . . .103 B7
  Shelfanger IP22 . . . . .120 B2
  Suffield NR11 . . . . .21 F1
  Sutton NR12 . . . . .39 C3
  Swanton Morley NR20 . . . . .50 B4
  Tivetshall St Mary NR15 . .121 C4

Rectory Rd continued
  Topcroft NR35 . . . . .107 F4
  Weston Longville NR9 . . . . .51 D2
  Whissonsett NR20 . . . . . . .31 E2
  Wolferton PE31 . . . . .27 B7
  Wood Norton NR20 . . . . . . .33 A7
  Wortham IP22 . . . . .129 D6
Rectory Row NR21 . . . . .17 F3
Red Admiral Cl **1** NR18 . .173 E4
Red Admiral Way NR7. . . . .159 F4
Red Barn La
  East Beckham NR26 . . . . . .138 D1
  Easton NR9 . . . . .70 A5
  Gresham NR11 . . . . .9 D1
Redbrick Cotts IP27 . . . . . .175 D5
Redbricks Dr PE32 . . . . .48 C6
Red Bridge La NR5 . . . . . . .157 C2
Redcastle Family Sch
  IP24 . . . . .176 B3
Redcastle Rd IP24 . . . . .176 A4
Redcliffe Way NR11 . . . . . . .165 B4
Red Cottage Cl NR3 . . . . . .158 A2
Redell Cl **3** NR13 . . . . .55 A1
REDENHALL IP20 . . . . .122 F3
Redenhall Rd IP20 . . . . .122 D2
Redfern Cl
  East Dereham NR19 . . . . . .154 B4
  King's Lynn PE30 . . . . .147 E8
Redfern Rd NR7 . . . . .159 D1
Redgate IP24 . . . . .176 E4
Redgate Hill
  Heacham PE31 . . . . .133 E7
  Hunstanton PE36 . . . . .132 D2
Redgate Rd PE13 . . . . .41 A4
REDGRAVE IP22 . . . . .128 E4
Redgrave & Lopham Fen
  National Nature Reserve★
  IP22 . . . . .128 F6
Redgrave Rd
  South Lopham IP22 . . . . . .128 C2
  Wortham IP22 . . . . .129 A5
Red Hall La
  Southburgh IP25 . . . . .85 F8
  Southburgh IP25 . . . . .86 A8
Redhill Cl IP22 . . . . .177 E5
Redhill La IP25 . . . . .84 F5
Redland Rd PE37 . . . . .153 C1
Red Lion Cl
  Holme Hale IP25 . . . . .66 B2
  Hoxne IP21 . . . . .131 A3
Red Lion La NR16 . . . . .119 A4
Red Lion St
  3 Aylsham NR11 . . . . . . .150 C7
  Norwich NR1 . . . . .178 B2
Red Lion Yd NR23 . . . . .136 D6
Redman Rd NR28 . . . . .151 D3
Redmere Cl NR7 . . . . .112 D4
Redmere Cl **4** NR12 . . . . . .54 A4
Redmere Dro CB7 . . . . .112 D5
RED PITS NR11 . . . . .34 D7
Red Pits NR11 . . . . .34 D7
Red Pits La NR11 . . . . .34 D7
Redpoll Rd NR8. . . . . .156 B5
Red Robin Cl **9** NR15 . . . .106 D3
Redwell St NR2 . . . . .178 B3
Redwing Dr
  1 Great Yarmouth NR31 . .94 C7
  5 Wisbech PE14 . . . . . . .152 D2
Redwing Gdns **7** NR10. . . .54 A1
Redwings Horse Sanctuary
  (Caldecott)★ NR31 . . . . . .93 F4
Reeden Hand La NR20. . . . . .69 B5
Reeder Cl NR11 . . . . .154 D3
Reeder's La NR14 . . . . .90 E4
REEDHAM NR13 . . . . .92 E5
Reedham Dr NR12 . . . . .164 E7
Reedham Prim Sch NR13 . . .92 F5
Reedham Rd Acle NR13 . . . .166 B1
  Beighton NR13 . . . . .74 E1
  Cantley NR13. . . . . .92 D6
  Reedham NR13 . . . . .92 F5
Reed La NR19 . . . . .93 D2
Reeds La Marsham NR10 . . .150 C1
  St Olaves NR31 . . . . .93 D2
Reeds Wy **13** NR14 . . . . . . .92 A1
Reed Way **3** PE14 . . . . . . .77 A8
REEPHAM NR10 . . . . .149 B5
Reepham High Sch & Coll
  NR10 . . . . .149 B3
Reepham Prim Sch
  NR10 . . . . .149 B4
Reepham Rd
  Alderford NR9 . . . . .52 A6
  Bawdeswell NR20 . . . . .50 F8
  Briston NR24 . . . . .142 E2
  Cawston NR10 . . . . .35 B1
  Drayton NR10 . . . . .53 A1
  Felthorpe NR10 . . . . .155 D5
  Foulsham NR20 . . . . .33 D3
  Guestwick NR20 . . . . .34 A5
  Horsford NR10. . . . . .157 D7
  Little Witchingham NR9 . . . .51 F7
  Little Witchingham NR9 . . . .149 F1
  Norwich NR6 . . . . .157 E2
  Swannington NR9 . . . . .52 B5
  Thurning NR20. . . . . .34 B8
  Wood Dalling NR11 . . . . . . .34 D5
Reeve Cl IP21 . . . . .130 D6
Reeve Rd NR27 . . . . .139 D4
Reeve's **3** NR35 . . . . .124 B8
Reeves Ave PE30. . . . . .147 B8
Reeves Cl NR20 . . . . .50 E7
Reeves Corner NR13 . . . . . .72 E6
Reeves Ct NR25 . . . . .151 C5
Reeves La IP26 . . . . .114 A7
Reeve Way NR18. . . . . .173 F6
Reffley Acad PE30 . . . . .147 D8
Reffley La PE30 . . . . .147 D8
Regal Cl **28** IP25 . . . . .84 D3
Regal Rd PE13 . . . . .152 B2
Regency Ave PE30 . . . . . . .147 C5

Regency Ct NR1 . . . . .163 B7
Regent Bvd **10** NR30 . . . . .169 D4
Regent Cl Denver PE38. . . .172 C2
  East Dereham NR19 . . . . . .154 D1
Regent Pl **1** PE30 . . . . . . .146 E4
Regent Rd
  Downham Market PE38. . . .172 A4
  1 Great Yarmouth NR30 .169 D4
Regents Cl NR25 . . . . .137 B5
Regents Ct NR28 . . . . .151 B5
Regents Pk PE30 . . . . .147 C5
Regent St
  Great Yarmouth NR30 . . . .169 C3
  Wickmere NR11 . . . . .20 E4
Regent Way **6** PE30 . . . . . .146 D4
Reg Houchen Rd PE31 . . . .140 C3
Regina Rd NR1 . . . . .178 A1
Regis Ave **4** NR27 . . . . .9 F5
Regis Pl NR26 . . . . .138 E7
Reid Way PE30. . . . . .147 A8
Renowood Cl PE32. . . . . . . .48 B8
Renson Cl NR3 . . . . .158 C4
Renwick Pk E NR27 . . . . . . .10 A4
Renwick Pk W NR27. . . . . . .10 A4
REPPS NR29 . . . . .56 F4
Repps Rd
  Ashby with Oby NR29 . . . . .57 B3
  1 Martham NR29 . . . . . . .57 D4
  Thurne NR29 . . . . .56 E3
Repton Ave NR6 . . . . .158 D7
Repton Cl NR11. . . . . .150 D5
Reservoir Rd
  Buxton NR10 . . . . .36 D1
  Stratton Strawless NR10. . . .53 E8
Retreat Est PE38 . . . . .172 B6
Reve Cres **5** NR13 . . . . . . .73 C6
Revell Rd PE38 . . . . .172 B4
Reydon Cl **10** NR5. . . . . . .161 A7
REYMERSTON NR9 . . . . . . .68 C1
Reymerston Rd NR9 . . . . . . .68 B2
Reynolds Ave NR30 . . . . . . .168 C8
Reynolds La NR29. . . . . .56 E7
Reynolds Mews NR18 . . . . .173 B5
Reynolds Way PE31 . . . . . . .140 C3
Rhombus Bsns Pk NR6 . . . .158 B5
Rhond The NR12. . . . . .164 C5
Rhone Pl **3** PE13 . . . . .152 E3
Rhoon Rd PE34 . . . . .144 E8
Rice Way NR7 . . . . .159 C2
Richard Easter Rd PE34 . . .176 D6
Richard Haggard Cl **3**
  IP25 . . . . .67 C2
Richard Hicks Dr **9**
  NR19 . . . . .154 C4
Richard Oakes Rd NR11 . . .150 F8
Richardson Cres NR9 . . . . . .88 C8
Richards Rd NR21 . . . . .15 D2
Richard Young Cl **2**
  PE13. . . . . .152 C8
Richenda Cl **8** NR5. . . . . .161 C5
Riches Cl **2** NR15. . . . . . .106 F6
Richmond Cl
  Honingham NR9 . . . . .69 E6
  Lyng NR9 . . . . .51 A5
Richmond Ct PE13 . . . . . . .152 A4
Richmond Pk NR17 . . . . . . .174 F6
Richmond Pl NR9 . . . . .51 A4
Richmond Rd
  Brandon IP27 . . . . .175 A1
  Downham Market PE38. . . .172 B4
  4 Long Stratton NR15. . .106 E3
  Norwich NR5 . . . . .156 E1
  Saham Toney IP25 . . . . .84 C4
Richmond Rise NR10. . . . . .149 C5
RICKINGHALL IP22 . . . . . . .128 E2
Rickinghall Rd IP22 . . . . . . .128 C3
Rickwood Dr PE37 . . . . .153 C1
Riddlesworth Hall Sch
  IP22 . . . . .127 C8
Riddlings Ct NR3 . . . . .158 D2
Rider Haggard Rd NR7 . . . .159 D1
Ridgeway
  Caister-on-Sea NR30 . . . . .168 D8
  Cromer NR27. . . . . .139 C4
Ridgeway The NR1. . . . . . . .163 B8
Ridings The
  5 Cringleford NR4. . . . . .89 B8
  Fakenham NR21. . . . . .141 E4
  Poringland NR14 . . . . .90 C5
Riding The PE32 . . . . .65 D5
Ridland's Rd NR24 . . . . . . .142 C1
RIDLINGTON NR28 . . . . . . .23 E1
RIDLINGTON STREET
  NR28 . . . . .23 E1
Rigby Cl **1** NR14. . . . . .90 D5
Rigbys Ct NR3 . . . . .178 A3
Rigg Cl **2** PE13 . . . . .152 B3
Rightup Dro IP27 . . . . .113 E5
Rightup La NR18. . . . . .173 D2
Riley Cl NR7 . . . . .159 D1
Rill Cl PE30. . . . . .148 B4
Rimer Cl NR5 . . . . .160 F6
Ringbank La NR11 . . . . .21 A6
Ringers Cl **4** NR18. . . . . . .173 D5
Ringers La NR9 . . . . .86 C5
RINGLAND NR8 . . . . .70 B8
Ringland La
  Costessey NR8. . . . . .156 B6
  Easton NR9 . . . . .70 B5
  Morton on the Hill NR9 . . . .52 A2
  Weston Longville NR9 . . . . .51 F3
Ringland Rd NR8 . . . . .156 A1
Ringlet Rd PE37 . . . . .153 C2
Ringmere Cl **2** IP25 . . . . . .84 C3
Ringmere Rd **3** IP25 . . . . . .84 C3
Ringmore Rd PE38. . . . . . . .97 B6
Ring Rd NR7 . . . . .163 F7
Ringsfield Rd NR34 . . . . . . .124 F5
RINGSTEAD PE36 . . . . .2 A3
Ringstead Downs Nature
  Reserve★ PE36. . . . . .1 F2

Ringstead Rd
  Burnham Market PE31. . . . .135 A2
  Docking PE31. . . . . .134 A6
  Heacham PE31. . . . . .133 E6
  Ringstead PE36 . . . . .2 A2
  Sedgeford PE36. . . . . .13 B8
  Thornham PE36 . . . . .2 D6
Ringwood Cl NR9 . . . . .160 B2
Ripley Cl NR2 . . . . .161 F5
Ripon Way IP24 . . . . .176 B5
Rippingall Cl **6** NR11 . . . .150 D6
Rippingall Rd NR11 . . . . . . .150 D6
Rippinghall Yard NR25 . . . . .7 A4
Rise The **10** Loddon NR14 . .92 A2
  Sheringham NR26 . . . . . . .138 C4
Riseway Cl NR1. . . . . .163 B8
Rising Way **3** NR29. . . . . . .57 C4
Rising Wy **9** NR29 . . . . . . .57 C4
Risley Cl NR16 . . . . .117 E5
River Bank
  Brandon Creek CB6. . . . . . .96 F2
  Hilgay PE38. . . . . .96 F6
River Cl PE32 . . . . .63 E8
River Ct NR21. . . . . .141 A3
Riverdale Ct NR13 . . . . .165 D3
Riverdene Mews NR8 . . . . .155 E3
River Dro PE33 . . . . .80 F2
Rivergreen Ct NR3 . . . . . . .163 E6
  King's Lynn PE30 . . . . .147 A6
Rivermead NR12. . . . . .39 B3
River Rd Marham PE32 . . . . .62 F7
  Narford PE32 . . . . .64 C8
  West Acre PE32 . . . . .46 B1
  West Walton PE14 . . . . . . .59 A8
Riverside
  Cockley Cley PE37 . . . . . . .82 D7
  Diss IP22 . . . . .177 B3
  King's Lynn PE30 . . . . .147 B7
  Martham NR29 . . . . .57 B6
  Northwold IP26 . . . . .99 C7
  Norwich NR1 . . . . .178 C1
  Podmore NR19. . . . . .67 B8
  Reedham NR13 . . . . .92 F4
Riverside Cl NR6. . . . . .157 D2
Riverside Ctr NR12. . . . . . .164 C5
Riverside Est NR13. . . . . . .165 D1
Riverside Ind Ctr NR31. . . .170 D5
Riverside Ind Est PE30 . . . .146 D7
Riverside Maltings IP22. . . .177 B3
Riverside Pk Track NR31 . . .93 D2
Riverside Rd
  Great Yarmouth NR31. . . . .170 D6
  Holt NR25. . . . . .8 A1
  Norwich NR1 . . . . .178 C3
  Wroxham/Hoveton NR12 . .164 C4
Riverside Swimming Ctr
  NR1 . . . . .178 C1
Riverside Way
  Brandon IP27. . . . . .175 C5
  1 Wisbech PE13 . . . . . . .152 B3
Riverside Wlk IP24 . . . . . . .176 C4
Riversway PE30. . . . . .146 E7
River Terr PE13 . . . . .152 A8
River View Beccles NR34 . .110 C2
  7 Beetley NR20 . . . . .49 A8
River View Ct NR21. . . . . . .141 E4
Riverview Dr NR13 . . . . . . .166 B8
Riverview Wy PE30. . . . . . .147 C7
River Vw **7** NR20 . . . . .49 D4
River Way NR31. . . . . .93 F6
River Wlk
  Great Yarmouth NR30 . . . .169 C8
  King's Lynn PE34 . . . . .146 C6
Rix Pl PE37 . . . . .153 C1
RNLI Henry Blogg Mus★
  NR27 . . . . .139 B7
Roaches Ct NR3 . . . . .178 B3
ROAD GREEN NR15 . . . . . .107 E4
Roadhills NR21 . . . . .15 E8
Roadways The NR34 . . . . . .111 B3
Robberds Way NR5. . . . . . .160 E8
Robbs Chase PE14 . . . . . . .77 E7
Robbs La PE14 . . . . .77 E8
Robert Andrew Cl NR18 . . . .87 B2
Robert Balding Rd
  PE31. . . . . .140 C3
Robert Cl Trunch NR28 . . . . .22 E5
  5 Wymondham NR18. . . .173 C6
Robert Gybson Way
  NR2 . . . . .178 A3
Robert Herb Way **5**
  NR18 . . . . .173 E4
Robert Kett Prim Sch
  NR18 . . . . .173 C5
Robert Key Dr **2** NR20. . . .68 E6
Robert Linge Cres IP27 . . . .175 D3
Robert Norgate Cl NR12. . . .54 C6
Roberts Cl
  3 Hempnall NR15 . . . . . .107 C5
  Norwich NR5 . . . . .137 D6
Robertson Cl NR26. . . . . . .138 E6
Robert St **8** PE30 . . . . . . .146 E3
Robin Ave **16** IP20 . . . . . .122 D1
Robin Cl
  Costessey NR8. . . . . .156 A5
  Great Yarmouth NR31 . . . .170 A5
  Holt NR25. . . . . .137 D6
  Mulbarton NR14 . . . . .89 A3
Robin Gr NR18. . . . . .173 D1
Robin Hill PE31 . . . . .133 D8
Robin Hood Rd NR4. . . . . . .162 C1
Robin Kerkham Way
  PE34. . . . . .145 E6
Robin Mews **4** PE14. . . . . .152 D2
Robins La NR10. . . . . .149 B4
Robinson Rd IP21. . . . . . . .130 C5
Robinson's Loke NR28 . . . . .22 F5
Robin Wlk IP27 . . . . .175 F3
Robson Rd NR5 . . . . .161 B6

Robyns Rd
  3 Sheringham NR26 . . . . .9 F5
  Sheringham NR26 . . . . . . .138 F5
Rocelin Cl NR3 . . . . .158 E3
Rochford Rd **4** NR29 . . . . .57 C4
Rochford Wlk **5** PE13 . . . .152 E5
Rockall Way **6** NR30. . . . .168 C6
Rockingham Rd NR5. . . . . .161 C6
ROCKLAND ALL SAINTS
  NR17 . . . . .103 B7
Rockland Cl PE13 . . . . .153 B2
Rockland Dr NR7 . . . . .163 C6
Rockland La NR17 . . . . .85 F1
Rockland Rd
  Bramerton NR14 . . . . .90 F7
  Lower Stow Bedon NR17. . .102 F5
ROCKLAND ST MARY
  NR14 . . . . .91 B7
Rockland St Mary Prim Sch
  NR14 . . . . .91 B6
ROCKLAND ST PETER
  NR17 . . . . .103 B8
Rocklands Com Prim Sch
  NR17 . . . . .103 B7
Rocklands Rd NR17 . . . . . . .103 B4
Rode La NR16. . . . . .105 B3
Rodham Rd PE15 . . . . .77 A1
Rodney Rd NR30 . . . . .169 D3
Rodwell Cnr NR10 . . . . .35 C1
Roedich Dr NR8 . . . . .155 C1
Roe Dr NR5. . . . . .161 E6
Roger Ride **3** NR19. . . . . .154 D2
Rogers Cl **4** NR5 . . . . .161 B7
Roger's Cl NR31 . . . . .171 D5
Roger's La NR15 . . . . .89 F1
Rokery Cl NR11. . . . . .143 C5
Roland Dr NR15. . . . . .107 D5
Rolfe Cres PE31. . . . . .133 E5
ROLLESBY NR29 . . . . .57 D2
Rollesby Ave PE13 . . . . . . .153 B2
Rollesby Gdns **9** NR29. . . .57 D2
Rollesby Pl NR10. . . . . .37 B2
Rollesby Prim Sch NR29 . . .57 D3
Rollesby Rd
  Fleggburgh NR29. . . . . .57 C1
  King's Lynn PE30. . . . . . . .147 A3
  Martham NR29 . . . . .57 D4
  Swaffham PE37. . . . . .153 B2
Rollesby Way NR12 . . . . . . .39 D8
Rolleston Cl NR5. . . . . .161 B7
Rollingpin La NR19 . . . . . . .154 D4
Roman Cres PE37. . . . . . . .153 D2
Roman Dr NR13. . . . . .165 B3
Roman Pl **20** NR30 . . . . . .169 D4
Roman Rd
  Riddlesworth IP22 . . . . . . .127 E8
  South Creake NR21 . . . . . .15 F7
  South Creake NR21 . . . . . .16 A5
  West Harling IP22. . . . . . .118 B2
Roman Way
  6 Aylsham NR11 . . . . . . .150 A5
  Brancaster PE31 . . . . .3 B7
  Caister-on-Sea NR30. . . . .168 D5
  Thetford IP24 . . . . .176 C7
Romany Cl **8** NR29 . . . . . .57 D2
Romany Rd NR3 . . . . .158 F1
Romany Wlk **6** NR14 . . . . .90 C5
Romer Dro PE25 . . . . .81 B3
Romey Rd IP25 . . . . .84 F3
Romney Wlk NR19 . . . . . . .154 D4
Ronald Brown Dr **5**
  NR13 . . . . .73 A5
Ron Hill Rd NR8. . . . . .156 A5
Rook Dr NR8 . . . . .155 E2
Rookery Cl NR4 . . . . .145 E5
Rookery Farm Rd NR28. . . . .23 F2
Rookery Hill NR14 . . . . .91 B7
Rookery La
  Edgefield NR24 . . . . .19 C6
  Topcroft NR35 . . . . .107 F3
Rookery Rd PE34 . . . . .145 E4
Rookery The IP27 . . . . .114 D5
Rook's La **6** NR34 . . . . . . .110 D1
Room La NR15. . . . . .122 D8
Roosters Cl **13** PE31. . . . . .12 E5
Ropemakers Row **5**
  NR3 . . . . .158 C2
Roper Way NR28. . . . . .151 C3
Ropes Hill NR12 . . . . .55 D4
Ropes Hill Dyke NR12 . . . . .55 D4
Ropes Wk **3** NR13 . . . . . . .165 D6
Ropes Wlk NR13 . . . . .165 E6
Rope Wlk
  King's Lynn PE30 . . . . .146 E6
  5 Thetford IP24 . . . . . . .176 D4
Rosa Cl **1** PE30 . . . . .54 B1
Rosalie Cl NR6. . . . . .158 B4
Rosary Cl **8** NR14 . . . . . . .89 B3
Rosary Rd NR1. . . . . .163 A6
Rosa Vella Dr **3** NR20. . . . .68 A8
Roseacre Cl NR12. . . . . . . .162 C2
Roseacre Est NR25. . . . . . . .9 A2
Rose Ave Costessey NR8. . .156 A5
  Roydon IP22 . . . . .129 D7
Rosebay **1** PE30. . . . . . . .148 C3
Rosebay Cl **5** NR6. . . . . . .158 D5
Roseberry Rd PE14 . . . . . . .59 B1
Rosebery Ave
  King's Lynn PE30 . . . . .147 B6
  7 Poringland NR14 . . . . .90 D5
Rosebery Bsns Pk NR14. . . .90 C4
Rosebery Rd
  Cromer NR27 . . . . .139 C5
  Great & Little Plumstead
    NR13 . . . . .73 A4
  3 Sheringham NR27 . . . .10 A5
Rose Cl NR31. . . . . .170 B7
Rose Cottage's NR19. . . . . .66 D8

Rosecroft **4** NR17 . . . . . . .174 C5
Rosecroft Prim Sch
  NR17 . . . . .174 A3
Rosecroft Way IP24. . . . . . .176 F4
Rosedale Cres **5** NR11. . . .163 A6
Rosedale Gdns NR31. . . . . . .94 A5
Rose Dr Cringleford NR4 . . .161 B1
  8 Dereham NR20. . . . . . .68 A8
Rose Fair Cl PE13 . . . . .152 D3
Rosefields NR13 . . . . .165 E4
Rose Hall Gdns NR35. . . . . .124 A8
Rose La Bungay NR35 . . . . .124 A8
  Diss IP22 . . . . .177 F3
  3 Elm PE14 . . . . .59 A1
  Norwich NR1 . . . . .178 C3
  Palgrave IP22 . . . . .177 D1
Rose La Cl IP22 . . . . .177 D2
Rosemary La
  11 Gayton PE32 . . . . .45 C6
  2 New Buckenham NR16 .104 F1
  Norwich NR3 . . . . .178 A4
  Wingfield IP21. . . . . .131 F4
Rosemary Rd
  Blofield NR13 . . . . .73 C6
  Norwich NR7 . . . . .159 B4
Rosemary Terr NR21. . . . . .141 B5
Rosemary Way PE38 . . . . . .172 D6
Rosery The NR14 . . . . .89 C3
Roses Ct NR23 . . . . .136 D5
Rose Terrace IP22 . . . . .177 F3
Rosetta Rd NR10 . . . . .54 A2
Rose Valley **4** NR2 . . . . . .162 B5
Roseville Cl **2** NR1 . . . . . .163 B5
Rose Wlk Brundall NR13 . . .165 C3
  Sculthorpe Airfield NR21 . . .15 C2
  1 Wisbech PE13 . . . . . . .152 A6
Rosewood NR28 . . . . .151 E5
Rose Yd NR3 . . . . .178 A4
Roslyn Rd NR31. . . . . .170 C5
Rosslare NR2. . . . . .162 A1
Rossons Rd NR8 . . . . .155 C1
Rostwold Way NR3. . . . . . . .158 D2
Rothbury Cl NR18. . . . . . . .173 B4
Rothbury Rd NR18 . . . . . . .173 C4
Rotten Dr PE14 . . . . .95 B5
Rotten Marsh NR13 . . . . . . .166 C2
Rottenstone La NR29. . . . . .167 F3
Roudham Heath La
  IP24 . . . . .117 B6
Roudham Junction
  NR16 . . . . .117 B6
Roudham Park Ind Est
  NR16 . . . . .118 A6
Roudham Rd NR16 . . . . . . .117 F6
Rouen Rd NR1 . . . . .178 B2
ROUGHAM PE32 . . . . .47 B7
Rougham Cnr IP26 . . . . .99 F3
Rougham End PE32 . . . . . . .47 C8
Rougham Hall PE32. . . . . . .47 A7
Rougham Rd
  Castle Acre PE32 . . . . .47 A4
  Great Massingham PE32. . . .29 E1
  Rougham PE32. . . . . .47 A2
  Weasenham St Peter PE32 .30 B1
Roughlands IP27 . . . . .113 E1
Rougholme Cl
  6 Beetley NR19 . . . . .49 C3
  6 Gressenhall NR20 . . . . .49 C3
Rought Ave IP27 . . . . .175 D2
ROUGHTON NR11 . . . . .21 E8
Roughton Rd
  Felbrigg NR11 . . . . .10 C2
  Felbrigg NR11 . . . . .139 A1
  Roughton NR27 . . . . .139 B2
  Thorpe Market NR11. . . . . .21 F7
Roughton Rd Sta NR27. . . .139 A4
Roundabout La NR14. . . . . .109 B8
Roundham Medieval Village
  of★ NR16 . . . . .117 E6
Roundhead Cl **28** NR7 . . . .72 D4
Round House Hill IP20. . . . .123 B5
Round House Way
  Cringleford NR4. . . . . .89 D1
  Eaton NR4 . . . . .161 B1
Roundtree Cl NR7 . . . . .159 B2
Roundtree Way NR7 . . . . . .159 B2
Roundway Down **17** NR7 . .72 D4
Round Well Rd NR5 . . . . . . .156 D1
Rouse's La
  Downham Market PE38. . . .172 A4
  Starston IP20 . . . . .122 C3
Rowan Cl
  10 Great Yarmouth NR31 . .94 C7
  Helleston NR31 . . . . .157 F3
  Thetford IP24 . . . . .176 B1
  7 Watlington PE33. . . . . .61 D5
  Wisbech PE13 . . . . .152 F7
Rowan Ct NR5 . . . . .156 F1
Rowan Dr Brandon IP27 . . .175 C3
  Gayton PE32 . . . . .45 C6
Rowan Rd
  King's Lynn PE34 . . . . .43 D4
  Marthan NR29 . . . . .57 D4
Rowans The PE38 . . . . .172 C4
Rowan Way
  Fakenham NR21. . . . . .141 F4
  10 Great Yarmouth NR31 .170 B6
  Holt NR25. . . . . .137 B7
Rowden Way IP22 . . . . .177 B4
Rowe Pl PE37. . . . . .153 C1
Row Hill PE38 . . . . .43 F2
Rowington Rd NR1. . . . . . . .178 A1
Rowland Ct NR11 . . . . .178 B1
Rowley Cnr IP26. . . . . .83 A5
Row's Mdw **1** NR15 . . . . .107 C5
Row The Weeting IP27. . . . .175 A7
  Wereham PE33 . . . . .80 D3
  West Dereham PE33 . . . . . .80 B4

Rowton Heath 16 NR7 .... 72 D4
Roxley Cl NR7 .... 163 F5
Royal Albert Ct 5
NR31 .... 170 D4
Royal Arcade NR2 .... 178 B2
Royal Ave NR30 .... 169 D7
Royal Cl 11 PE12 .... 41 B8
Royal Estate The PE35 ... 27 F7
Royalist Dr 28 NR7 .... 72 D4
Royal Norfolk Regimental
Mus* NR1 .... 178 B3
Royal Pl 2 PE13 .... 152 C4
Royal Sovereign Ave 3
NR5 .... 156 C1
Royal Sovereign Cres 19
NR31 .... 94 C8
Royal Thames Rd NR30 .. 168 D7
Royden Way
3 Burgh St Margaret
(Fleggburgh) NR29 ...... 57 C1
Roydon IP22 .... 177 B4
ROYDON Roydon IP22 .... 129 D7
Roydon PE32 .... 28 A2
Roydon Common National
Nature Reserve* PE32 .. 27 F1
Roydon Fen IP22 .... 177 A4
Roydon Gdns IP22 ...... 177 A5
Roydon Prim Sch
IP22 .... 177 B5
Roydon Rd
Castle Rising PE31 ...... 27 D3
Diss IP22 .... 177 C5
Royston Gn NR28 .... 151 D6
Rubens Way 6 PE38 .... 172 D6
Ruckold'S La PE32 .... 47 B1
Rudd's Drift PE32 .... 48 E5
Rudds La NR10 .... 149 B3
Ruddy Duck La PE30 .... 146 E2
Rudham CE Prim Sch
PE31 .... 30 A6
Rudham Rd
Great Massingham PE32 ... 29 D2
Harpley PE31 .... 29 D5
Helhoughton NR21 .... 30 D5
Syderstone PE31 .... 15 A3
Tatterford NR21 .... 30 E7
West Rudham PE31 .... 29 E6
Rudham Stile La NR21 ... 141 B6
Rufus St NR8 .... 156 A5
Rugge Dr NR4 .... 161 E2
Ruggs La NR29 .... 75 C8
Rugg's La NR29 .... 75 C8
Ruin Rd NR28 .... 38 A5
Rumburgh La NR35 ..... 124 D2
Rumburgh Rd NR35 ..... 124 B1
Rump Cl 10 NR20 .... 50 B3
Runcton Cl NR5 .... 161 B7
RUNCTON HOLME PE33 .. 61 D3
Runcton Holme
CE Prim Sch PE33 ...... 61 E3
Runcton Rd PE33 .... 61 F2
RUNHALL NR9 .... 68 F2
Runhall Rd NR9 .... 69 A2
RUNHAM
Great Yarmouth NR30 .... 169 B5
Mautby NR29 .... 75 E6
Runham Rd
Great Yarmouth NR30 .... 169 B5
Stokesby NR29 .... 75 B5
Run La NR14 .... 91 B6
Runnel The NR5 .... 160 F6
Runton House Cl NR27 ... 10 A5
Runton Rd NR27 .... 139 A7
Rupert St NR2 .... 162 C4
RUSHALL IP21 .... 121 F1
Rushall Rd IP20 .... 122 B2
RUSHFORD IP24 .... 126 E8
Rushford Rd
Coney Weston IP31 ...... 126 F6
Coney Weston IP31 ...... 127 A5
Coney Weston IP31 ...... 127 B5
Euston IP24 .... 126 D7
Rushford IP24 .... 117 B1
Rushford IP24 .... 126 E8
RUSH GREEN NR9 .... 69 B1
Rush Green NR9 .... 87 B8
Rushmead Cl PE30 ...... 148 C3
Rushmeadow Cres
PE38 .... 172 A6
Rushmeadow Rd NR19 .. 154 A5
Rushmer Way NR26 ..... 138 C5
Rushmore Rd NR7 ...... 159 A4
Ruskin Ave NR31 .... 170 B2
Ruskin Cl PE31 .... 133 E5
Ruskin Pl 5 PE38 ...... 172 D6
Ruskin Rd NR4 .... 161 E4
Russell Ave
Caister-on-Sea NR30 ..... 168 E5
Great Yarmouth NR31 .... 170 C3
Norwich NR7 .... 159 B3
9 Spixworth NR10 .... 54 A2
Russell Cl
Downham Market PE38 ... 172 C4
Fairstead PE30 .... 147 C3
Wells-next-the-Sea NR23 . 136 C6
Russell Ct NR23 .... 136 D6
Russell Dr PE14 .... 77 E6
Russell Rd NR30 .... 169 D4
Russell Sq 24 NR30 .... 169 D4
Russell St
King's Lynn PE30 .... 146 F3
Norwich NR2 .... 162 C7
Wisbech PE13 .... 152 C6
Russell Terr
Mundesley NR11 .... 143 C6
Trowse Newton NR14 .... 163 B2
Russell Way NR18 ...... 173 C3
Russet Cl NR17 .... 174 E4
Russet Gr NR4 .... 161 E5
Russet Rd IP22 .... 177 C5
Russets The PE14 .... 77 E6
Russett Cl PE30 .... 147 C8
Russet Way NR19 ...... 154 E3
Rustens Manor Rd 2
NR18 .... 173 C5
Rustons Rd PE14 .... 59 F3
Ruthen Pl 1 NR19 ...... 154 D5
Rutherford Way IP24 ... 176 C6
Rutland St NR2 .... 162 C4
Ryalla Drift PE30 .... 148 B4
Ryburgh Dr NR20 .... 32 D5
Ryburgh Rd NR20 .... 32 D2
Rydal Cl NR5 .... 161 C6
Ryders Way IP22 .... 128 E2
Rye Ave NR3 .... 158 B3
Rye Cl
North Walsham NR28 .... 151 E6
Norwich NR3 .... 158 B2
Rye Gdns NR29 .... 75 C8
Rye La NR17 .... 174 C4
Ryeland Rd 2 PE30 .... 148 C4
Ryelands 5 NR29 ...... 167 B7
Ryelands Rd PE30 ..... 148 D4
Rye's Cl PE33 .... 62 D3
Ryley Cl PE30 .... 147 E8
Rymer Ct IP24 .... 125 F2
Rymer La IP24 .... 125 E2
Ryors La NR21 .... 33 A6
Ryrie Ct NR4 .... 161 E2
Ryston Cl PE38 .... 172 C4
Ryston End PE38 .... 172 C4
Ryston Pk PE38 .... 172 F1
Ryston Rd Denver PE38 ... 79 E4
Denver PE38 .... 172 D2
West Dereham PE33 ...... 80 B4

S

Sackville Cl 4 NR30 ... 169 C3
Sacred Heart Cath Sch
PE37 .... 153 C5
Saddlebow Ind Est PE34 . 43 C4
Saddlebow Rd
King's Lynn PE30 .... 146 D1
King's Lynn PE30 .... 146 E3
King's Lynn PE34 .... 43 D4
Saddler Cl NR17 .... 174 B3
Saddlers Dr 19 IP25 ..... 84 F3
Sadler Cl PE30 .... 146 F7
Sadler Rd NR6 .... 157 F7
Sadlers Ct 11 NR26 .... 138 D7
Sadlers La NR26 .... 138 C7
Sadlers Way NR28 ..... 151 E5
Saffron Ave NR18 .... 87 F2
Saffron Cl Brandon IP27 .. 175 B2
Downham Market PE38 .. 172 E6
15 Watton IP25 .... 84 C3
Saffron Sq NR6 .... 158 C3
Sage Rd PE38 .... 172 D7
SAHAM HILLS IP25 .... 84 C6
Saham Rd IP25 .... 84 C4
SAHAM TONEY IP25 ...... 84 C5
Sainsbury Ctr for the Visual
Arts* NR4 .... 161 C3
St Alban's Rd NR1 ..... 162 D3
St Albans Way IP24 ... 176 B5
St Andrew Cl 1 NR31 .. 171 E5
St Andrews Ave 5 NR7 .. 72 D3
St Andrew's & Blackfriars
Halls* NR1 .... 178 B3
St Andrew's CE Prim Sch
PE37 .... 65 E1
St Andrews CE VA Prim Sch
IP22 .... 119 A1
St Andrews Cl
Barningham IP31 .... 127 C3
Buxton with Lammas NR10 36 E1
Framingham Earl NR14 .... 90 D5
1 Hingham NR9 .... 86 C4
Long Stratton NR15 ...... 106 E4
Outwell PE14 .... 77 E7
Poringland NR14 .... 90 D5
West Dereham PE33 .... 80 C4
Worstead NR28 .... 38 A4
St Andrew's Cl
Blofield NR13 .... 165 E5
Caister-on-Sea NR30 .... 168 D7
Gorleston-on-Sea NR31 .. 170 C5
Holme Hale IP25 .... 66 A2
Holt NR25 .... 137 C6
Northwold IP26 .... 99 C8
3 Old Buckenham NR17 104 D2
St Andrews Dr
3 Norwich NR4 .... 89 C8
Quidenham NR16 .... 103 E1
St Andrews Drift 2 NR25 .. 7 A4
St Andrews Hill NR2 ... 178 B3
St Andrews La
Necton PE37 .... 65 F5
Rockland All Saints NR17 . 103 C7
Roydon PE32 .... 28 A2
South Runcton PE33 ...... 61 F4
Saint Andrews La PE32 ... 28 B2
St Andrews Rd
North Runcton PE30 ..... 147 B3
Norwich NR6 .... 157 D6
Scole IP21 .... 130 D5
St Andrew's Rd
Great Yarmouth NR31 .... 170 C6
Lingwood NR13 .... 73 F3
Sheringham NR26 .... 138 D6
St Andrews St NR2 .... 178 B3
St Andrews Way PE37 .... 65 F5
St Andrew's Way NR13 .. 165 E5
St Andrews Wlk PE33 .... 80 C5
St Anne's Cres
Clenchwarton PE34 ...... 145 D6
Great Yarmouth NR31 .... 170 B4
St Annes Rd 4 NR14 ..... 90 D5
St Ann La NR1 .... 178 C2
St Anns Fort PE30 ..... 146 D6
St Ann's St PE30 ...... 146 D5
St Anthony's Way IP27 .. 175 E4
St Antony's Ave NR31 .. 170 B2
St Audreys IP24 .... 176 D3
St Augustines Gate 12
NR3 .... 162 D8
St Augustine's RC Prim Sch
NR8 .... 156 E3
St Augustines Rd PE13 .. 152 C5
St Augustines St
Norwich NR3 .... 162 D8
Norwich NR3 .... 178 A4
St Augustines Way 3
PE30 .... 148 C4
St Austin's Gr NR26 .... 138 E7
St Barnabas Cl 2 IP24 .. 176 C1
St Bartholomews Cl 4
NR2 .... 162 B8
St Benedicts Cl NR34 .... 110 D5
St Benedicts Rd IP27 .. 175 E4
St Benedict's Rd 5
NR34 .... 110 D1
St Benedicts St NR2 ... 178 A3
St Benet's Abbey*
NR12 .... 56 C2
St Benets Ave NR28 .... 151 E4
St Benet's Cl 9 NR12 .... 39 B4
St Benets Gr PE30 ..... 148 D3
St Benets Rd NR29 .... 56 C3
St Benet's Rd
Great Yarmouth NR31 .... 170 B3
Stalham NR12 .... 39 B4
St Botolph's CE VC Prim Sch
IP22 .... 128 F3
St Botolph's Cl 3 PE30 .. 148 C3
St Catherine's Ave 5
NR29 .... 56 C8
St Catherines Rd NR7 ... 163 F8
St Catherine's Way
NR31 .... 170 B4
St Cecilia's Ct NR1 ... 178 C2
St Christopher Cl
16 Belton NR31 .... 94 A6
6 Caister-on-Sea NR30 . 168 D7
St Christophers Cl
NR15 .... 108 C7
St Clare Ct 6 NR31 .... 171 D5
St Clement Cl 2 PE14 .... 77 F6
St Clement Mews 7
NR31 .... 171 D5
St Clements Dr 4 PE38 . 172 C6
St Clement's High Sch
PE34 .... 144 C6
St Clements Hill NR3 ... 158 E2
St Clements Hill Prim Acad
NR3 .... 158 F2
St Clements Way NR13 . 165 C4
St Crispins Rd NR3 .... 178 A4
St Cross Rd IP20 ...... 123 B4
ST CROSS SOUTH ELMHAM
IP20 .... 123 D3
St Davids Cl
Brandon IP27 .... 175 D3
Long Stratton NR15 ...... 106 E4
St David's Cl 17 NR31 .... 94 A6
St Davids Dr 8 NR13 .... 72 D6
St David's Rd NR9 .... 88 C7
St Dominic Sq 8 PE30 .. 146 D5
St Domonic's Dr IP27 .. 175 E4
St Edmund Cl
Attleborough NR17 ...... 174 C5
Great Yarmouth NR31 .... 170 B3
Poringland NR14 .... 90 B6
St Edmund Rd IP27 ..... 114 E8
St Edmunds NR17 ...... 174 E5
St Edmund's Ave PE36 .. 132 D5
St Edmundsbury Rd
PE30 .... 146 E7
St Edmunds Cl
Costessey NR8 .... 156 F5
Norwich NR6 .... 157 E1
St Edmunds Ct 1 IP24 .. 176 C1
St Edmunds Dr PE14 .... 59 D1
St Edmunds Gate
Attleborough NR17 ...... 174 B4
5 Honington IP31 .... 126 B1
St Edmunds La PE31 ... 135 C3
St Edmund's Prim Sch
IP21 .... 131 A2
St Edmunds RC Prim Sch
NR35 .... 124 A8
St Edmunds Rd NR13 ... 166 B3
St Edmund's Rd
Downham Market PE38 .. 172 D5
Lingwood NR13 .... 73 F3
Taverham NR8 .... 155 C1
St Edmund's Rise 2
NR8 .... 155 C1
St Edmunds Sq 7 IP31 . 126 B1
St Edmunds Terr PE38 . 172 D5
St Edmund's Terr
Hunstanton PE36 .... 132 C4
King's Lynn PE30 .... 146 C7
St Edmunds Wharf NR3 . 178 B4
St Ethelberts Cl PE31 .. 135 C2
St Faith's CE Prim Sch
NR10 .... 53 E2
St Faith's Church* NR9 .. 51 F7
St Faith's Cl NR9 .... 51 E5
St Faith's Dr PE30 ..... 147 A6
St Faiths La NR1 ...... 178 C3
St Faith's Rd NR6 ..... 158 D6
St Felix Rise IP20 ..... 123 E5
St Francis Cl IP27 ..... 175 E4
St Francis Way NR30 .. 169 C4
St Furseys' Way 2 NR31 . 94 A6
St George Loke NR7 ... 158 F4
St Georges Cl NR12 ..... 23 E4
St George's Cl
Saham Toney IP25 .... 84 B5
Thurton NR14 .... 91 C4
St Georges Ct PE36 ...... 2 D6
St Georges Dr IP22 .... 128 E2
St George's Dr
Caister-on-Sea NR30 .... 168 D7
East Dereham NR19 ..... 154 D1
St Georges Inf Sch 17
NR30 .... 169 D3
St Georges Mid Sch
PE31 .... 13 A1
St Georges Rd NR31 ..... 94 A6
St George's Rd NR30 ... 169 D3
St Georges St NR3 .... 178 A4
St George's Theatre 18
NR30 .... 169 D3
St Germans Prim Sch
PE34 .... 43 B1
St Germans Rd PE34 ..... 61 E8
St Giles Gr PE14 .... 59 B1
St Giles' La IP24 ...... 176 D4
St Giles Rd NR24 .... 18 B2
St Giles St NR2 .... 178 A3
St Giles Terr NR2 ..... 178 A3
St Gregorys Alley NR2 .. 178 A3
St Guthlac Cl PE37 ..... 153 C6
St Helena Way NR10 .... 53 A3
St Helens Ct 1 IP24 ... 176 D6
St Helens Rd NR12 ...... 23 F3
St Helens Way IP24 ... 176 C7
St Hilary Park Rd PE30 .. 147 A1
St Hilda Cl NR19 ...... 154 C6
St Hilda Rd
Caister-on-Sea NR30 .... 168 D6
East Dereham NR19 ..... 154 C6
St Hilda's Cres NR31 .. 170 B5
St Hugh's Gn NR31 .... 170 B3
ST JAMES NR12 .... 54 E7
St James Cl NR3 ...... 178 C4
St James Cres 18 NR31 ... 94 A6
St James Ct NR3 ...... 178 B4
St James Dr PE38 ..... 172 B4
St James Mdw NR3 .... 178 C4
St James Rd IP19 ..... 124 A1
St James' Rd PE30 .... 146 E4
St James's Rd PE32 ..... 47 A2
St James St PE30 ..... 146 D4
St James Way NR15 ... 106 E4
St James Wlk 14 NR30 .. 169 D3
St John Maddermarket
NR2 .... 178 A3
St John's Ave NR31 ... 170 A4
St John's Bsns Est PE38 172 A4
St Johns Cl
2 Norwich NR1 .... 162 E2
Swaffham PE37 .... 153 C4
St John's Cl
Coltishall NR12 .... 54 D7
11 Hethersett NR9 .... 88 D7
Oxborough PE33 .... 81 E4
St John's Com Prim Sch
NR12 .... 164 D5
St Johns Ct PE13 ...... 153 C4
ST JOHN'S FEN END
PE14 .... 60 B6
ST JOHN'S HIGHWAY
PE14 .... 42 B1
St Johns La
Beachamwell PE37 .... 63 E1
Beachamwell PE37 .... 81 E8
Mundham NR14 .... 109 A8
St Johns Rd Belton NR31 .. 93 F6
Stalham NR12 .... 39 B4
St John's Rd
Bungay NR35 .... 124 A8
Terrington St John PE34 .. 60 C8
St John St NR1 .... 178 C2
St John's Terr
8 Great Yarmouth
NR30 .... 169 D3
King's Lynn PE30 .... 146 E4
St Johns Way
Downham Market PE38 .. 172 A4
Hoveton NR12 .... 55 A4
Hoveton NR12 .... 164 E5
St John's Way 12 IP26 ... 98 E1
Saint Johns Way PE38 ... 79 B4
St Johns West Gates
PE14 .... 42 A3
St John the Baptist Cath*
NR2 .... 162 C5
St Joseph's Rd NR26 .. 138 D6
St Julian Rd NR30 .... 168 E4
St Julians Alley NR1 .. 178 B2
St Laurence Ave NR13 . 165 C4
St Lawrence Dr NR4 ... 161 C1
St Lawrence La NR2 .. 178 A3
St Leger NR15 .... 106 E3
St Leonards Cl
Scole IP21 .... 130 D5
Wymondham NR18 .... 173 C6
St Leonards Rd NR1 ... 163 A6
St Leonards St IP26 ... 100 B4
St Leonards Terr 6
NR1 .... 163 A6
St Luke's Terr 4 NR31 .. 169 B4
St Magdalen Way PE13 . 153 C2
St Margarets Ave 8
PE33 .... 63 B4
St Margarets Cl NR10 .. 155 F3
St Margaret's Cl
3 Coltishall NR12 .... 54 C6
Upton with Fishley NR13 . 166 B8
St Margaret's Cres
IP24 .... 176 C3
St Margarets Dr NR7 .. 159 C5
St Margaret's Dr IP27 .. 175 A2
St Margarets Gdns
NR12 .... 164 D6
St Margarets La NR7 .. 159 B5
St Margaret's La
2 Cromer NR27 .... 139 C6
10 King's Lynn PE30 .... 146 D4
St Margarets Mdw
PE34 .... 145 E5
ST MARGARET SOUTH
ELMHAM IP20 .... 123 E2
St Margarets Pl NR12 ... 40 A5
St Margaret's Pl 11
PE30 .... 146 D4
St Margarets Rd
St Michael South Elmham
IP19 .... 124 A2
St Michael South Elmham
NR35 .... 124 C2
St Nicholas South Elmham
IP19 .... 123 F2
St Margaret's Rd
Bungay NR35 .... 124 A6
1 Cromer NR27 .... 139 C6
St Margarets St NR2 .. 178 A3
St Margarets Way NR14 .. 91 B6
St Margaret's Way
1 Burgh St Margaret
(Fleggburgh) NR29 ...... 57 C1
2 Hopton on Sea NR31 . 171 D5
St Marks Cl NR29 .... 57 A4
St Martha's RC Prim Sch
PE30 .... 147 C6
St Martin-at-Palace Plain
NR3 .... 178 B4
St Martins at Oak Wall La 7
NR3 .... 162 D8
St Martins Cl 4 NR3 ... 162 D8
St Martin's Cl NR27 ... 139 C5
St Martin's Gdns 1
NR16 .... 104 F1
St Martins La NR3 .... 178 A4
St Martin's Mdw IP24 .. 125 E6
St Martin's Rd
2 Norwich NR3 .... 162 D8
Wisbech PE13 .... 152 E7
St Martin's Way IP24 .. 176 B2
St Mary Cl NR17 ...... 174 C6
St Mary's 4 NR16 ...... 104 F1
St Mary's CE VA Prim Sch
NR11 .... 21 E8
St Marys Cl
Colkirk NR21 .... 31 D5
Great & Little Plumstead
NR13 .... 73 A5
Rockland St Mary NR14 ... 91 B6
Roughton NR27 .... 21 D8
St Mary's Cl
Alpington NR14 .... 90 F5
Flixton NR35 .... 123 E5
Harleston IP20 .... 122 E2
Heacham PE31 .... 133 E6
Hemsby NR29 .... 167 A7
Horsham St Faith &
Newton St Faith NR10 .... 53 E2
King's Lynn PE30 .... 148 C2
Newton Flotman NR15 ..... 89 C1
12 Snettisham PE31 ...... 12 E4
South Walsham NR13 ...... 74 A7
1 Watton IP25 .... 84 E3
Wroxham/Hoveton NR12 . 164 B4
St Mary's County Prim Sch
NR20 .... 49 D4
St Mary's Cres 5 IP24 .. 176 C3
St Marys Ct IP22 ...... 177 D5
St Mary's Ct 2 IP24 ... 176 C3
St Marys Dr NR16 ..... 103 E1
St Mary's Dr IP22 .... 177 E4
St Marys Gr NR7 ...... 159 C5
St Mary's Jun Acad
NR15 .... 106 E4
St Marys La 1 NR25 ...... 7 A4
St Mary's La NR31 .... 169 C3
St Marys Mdw PE32 ..... 63 C8
St Marys Mews IP27 ... 113 E1
St Marys Plain NR3 ... 178 A4
St Mary's RC Prim Sch
NR31 .... 170 C6
St Marys Rd
Ashby St Mary NR14 ...... 91 C4
Hemsby NR29 .... 167 D6
5 Norwich NR3 .... 162 D8
12 Stalham NR12 .... 39 B4
St Mary's Rd
Aldeby NR34 .... 111 A3
Cromer NR27 .... 139 B6
20 Long Stratton NR15 .. 106 E3
Poringland NR14 .... 90 D5
West Walton PE14 .... 59 B8
St Marys View PE32 ..... 65 D6
St Mary's Way 3 NR28 .. 151 C5
St Marys Wlk 1 NR15 .... 89 D1
St Matthew's Dr PE12 .... 41 B8
St Matthews Rd NR1 ... 178 C3
St Michael-at-Pleas
NR3 .... 178 B3
St Michaels NR12 .... 39 C2
St Michaels Ave NR11 .. 150 A6
St Michael's Ave PE13 .. 152 C7
St Michael's CE Prim Sch
PE30 .... 146 D1
St Michael's CE VA Prim Sch
NR11 .... 150 C7
St Michaels Cl NR20 .... 69 B7
St Michael's Cl
Aylsham NR11 .... 150 C7
Ormesby St Michael NR29 .. 58 A1
Thetford IP24 .... 176 C2
St Michael's Cres IP25 .. 83 D4
St Michaels Gn NR15 .. 106 B1
Saint Michaels La NR12 .. 54 E7
ST MICHAEL SOUTH
ELMHAM NR35 .... 124 A2
St Michaels Rd NR15 .. 106 E4
St Michael's Rd PE30 .. 146 D1
St Michael's VA Jun Sch
NR5 .... 160 F8
St Michaels Way NR13 .. 165 F2
St Mildreds Rd 3 NR5 .. 161 B7
St Nicholas Cl
Dersingham PE31 .... 140 E3
9 Gayton PE32 .... 45 C6
1 King's Lynn PE30 ...... 146 D5
St Nicholas Ct
1 Great Yarmouth NR31 ... 94 C6
10 North Walsham NR28 . 151 C5
St Nicholas Dr
Caister-on-Sea NR30 .... 168 D6
Feltwell IP26 .... 98 E2
St Nicholas Gdns 6
NR31 .... 94 C6
St Nicholas House Sch
NR28 .... 151 D4
St Nicholas Pl 1 NR26 .. 138 D7
St Nicholas Priory CE VC
Prim Sch NR30 .... 169 C4
St Nicholas Rd
Great Yarmouth NR30 .... 169 D4
North Walsham NR28 .... 151 D5
St Nicholas Retail Park
PE30 .... 146 D6
St Nicholas's NR14 ...... 88 F3
ST NICHOLAS SOUTH
ELMHAM IP20 .... 123 E2
St Nicholas St Diss IP22 . 177 D5
East Dereham NR19 ..... 154 D6
3 King's Lynn PE30 ..... 146 D5
Thetford IP24 .... 176 C4
St Nicholas Wlk IP27 .. 175 E4
ST OLAVES NR31 .... 93 D2
St Olaves Rd
Herringfleet NR32 .... 93 E1
Herringfleet NR32 .... 111 D8
Norwich NR3 .... 162 E8
St Omer Cl NR14 .... 89 B4
St Pauls Cl NR6 .... 158 A5
St Paul's Cl
Brockdish IP21 .... 131 C6
4 Horsford NR10 .... 53 B3
6 Wisbech PE13 .... 152 C4
St Paul's Rd N PE14 .... 59 D7
St Paul's Rd S PE14 .... 59 E7
St Pauls Sq 1 NR3 .... 178 B4
St Paul's Way NR30 ... 169 C7
St Peter & St Paul CE VC
Prim Sch IP25 .... 85 A5
St Peter's App IP27 ... 175 B3
St Peters Ave NR31 ... 170 B2
St Peter's CE (Aided) Jun
Sch PE13 .... 152 E6
St Peter's CE Prim Acad
NR9 .... 70 B5
St Peters Cl
3 Cringleford NR4 .... 89 B8
Knapton NR28 .... 143 B1
St Peter's Cl
Brockdish IP21 .... 131 C6
King's Lynn PE34 .... 146 B4
Rockland St Peter NR17 .. 103 B8
Strumpshaw NR13 .... 73 F2
Yaxham NR19 .... 68 A5
St Peters Dr NR9 .... 70 B5
St Peters Hill NR18 ..... 87 A2
St Peter's La NR12 ... 164 E8
ST PETER SOUTH ELMHAM
NR35 .... 124 A3
St Peter's Pl IP27 .... 175 B2
St Peters' Plain NR30 .. 169 D3
St Peters Rd Outwell PE14 . 77 E5
Watlington PE34 .... 61 C7
Wiggenhall St Germans
PE34 .... 61 B8
Wiggenhall St Peter PE34 .. 61 C8
St Peter's Rd
Brooke NR15 .... 90 F2
Fakenham NR21 .... 141 B6
Great Yarmouth NR30 .... 169 D3
King's Lynn PE34 .... 146 C5
Lingwood NR13 .... 73 F3
9 Sheringham NR26 ..... 138 D7
5 Wisbech PE13 .... 152 C4
St Peters St NR2 ..... 178 A2
St Peters Terr PE34 ... 146 C4
St Peter's Way 12 NR10 .. 54 A2
St Peter's Wlk IP26 ... 113 F7
St Philips Rd NR2 .... 162 B6
St Roberts Way 15 NR31 .. 94 A6
St Saviors La NR3 .... 178 B4
St Stephen's Cres IP27 .. 175 E4
St Stephens Rd NR1 ... 178 A1
St Stephens Sq NR1 ... 178 A1
St Stephens St NR1 ... 178 A2
St Swithins Rd NR2 ... 178 A3
St Thomas Cl IP27 .... 175 E4
St Thomas Dr NR18 ... 173 C2
St Thomas' La NR18 .... 88 C4
St Thomas More
RC Jun Sch NR2 ...... 162 A5
St Thomas Rd NR2 .... 162 A6
St Thomas's La
Ingoldisthorpe PE31 ..... 140 D8
Snettisham PE31 .... 12 F4
St Thomas's Rd NR29 .. 167 C7
St Valery La PE30 .... 146 D2
St Vedast St NR1 ..... 178 C3
St Vincent Wlk NR31 .. 171 E5
St Walstan Mdw NR9 ... 160 B5
St Walstan's Cl
Norwich NR5 .... 156 D1
Taverham NR8 .... 156 D8
St Walstan's Rd NR8 .. 156 D8
St Wandrille Cl NR14 ... 90 B6
St Williams Prim Sch
NR7 .... 163 D8
St Williams Way NR7 .. 163 C7
St Winnold Cl PE38 ... 172 B4

St Withburga La **8**
NR19 . . . . .154 D5
Saker Cl **11** NR7 . . . . . . .72 D4
Salamanca Rd **7** NR15. .106 D3
Salcott Dr PE13. . . . . . . .152 E5
Sale Ct **5** NR14. . . . . . . .92 A1
Sale Rd NR7 . . . . .159 D2
SALHOUSE NR13. . . . . . . .55 B1
Salhouse Bsns Pk NR7. .159 D3
Salhouse Dr PE37. . . . . .153 B2
Salhouse Rd
Dumpling Green NR19. . .154 F3
Great & Little Plumstead
NR13 . . . . .73 B6
Hoveton NR12 . . . . .164 E7
New Rackheath NR13 . . .72 E7
Norwich NR7 . . . . .159 C2
Sprowston NR13 . . . . . . .72 D6
Wroxham NR12. . . . . . . .164 B2
Salhouse Road Ind Est
NR7 . . . . .159 C2
Salhouse Sta NR13 . . . . .54 F1
Salhouse VC Prim Sch
NR13 . . . . .55 B1
Salisbury Rd
Cromer NR27. . . . . .139 D4
Great Yarmouth NR30 . . .169 D4
Norwich NR1 . . . . .163 B5
Sheringham NR26 . . . . . .138 E7
Salisbury Way IP24 . . . .176 B4
SALLE NR10 . . . . .149 E8
Sallow La
Framingham Pigot NR14. . .90 E7
Snetterton NR16 . . . . . . .118 B8
Wacton NR15. . . . . .106 C1
Salmond Dr **1** IP24. . . . .125 F6
Salmond Rd **11** IP25 . . . . .84 F3
Salmon Rd NR30. . . . . . .170 D8
Salmon's Way NR21. . . . .141 F5
Salter Ave 161 E5
Salter's La PE32 . . . . . . .48 E4
SALTERS LODE PE38. . . . .79 A4
Salter's Rd PE30 . . . . . . .146 E7
Salters Way PE13 . . . . . .152 A2
SALTHOUSE NR25 . . . . . . .8 B7
Salthouse Marshes Nature
Reserve★ NR25 . . . . .8 B7
Salthouse Rd NR25 . . . . . .8 D5
Saltings The PE34. . . . . .144 A5
Salt Lake Dereham NR19. . .68 A6
Dereham NR19 . . . . .154 F1
Saltpans Cl PE30. . . . . . .146 E6
Salts La Walpole PE14. . . .41 C2
Walton Highway PE14. . . .59 D8
West Walton PE14. . . . . .41 D1
Salts Rd PE14. . . . . .59 C8
Salvia Cl NR18 . . . . .173 F6
Samphire **5** PE30 . . . . . .147 B7
Samphire Cl **8** NR25. . . . .7 C6
Samphire Pl PE34. . . . . .146 C4
Sampson Rd NR28 . . . . . .151 C3
Samson Rd NR6 . . . . .157 F4
Samson's La IP22. . . . . . .129 C7
Samuel Rd **1** NR1 . . . . . .163 B7
Sancroft Way IP20. . . . . .123 A3
Sanctuary Mdw IP25. . . . .84 C4
Sandale Rd PE30. . . . . . .147 C4
Sandall Rd PE13 . . . . . . .152 C3
Sandfield La NR16 . . . . . .118 E8
Sandfield Rd **3** PE38 . . . .172 C6
Sandgalls Rd IP27 . . . . . .113 F1
Sandgalls The IP27 . . . . .175 B3
Sand Hills
Sea Palling NR12. . . . . . .39 F7
Sea Palling NR12. . . . . . .40 A6
Sandhole La NR13 . . . . . . .73 A7
Sandhole Rd NR13 . . . . . . .74 F1
Sandholme Cl NR1. . . . . .163 B8
Sandiacre La PE38. . . . . .172 D6
Sand La NR7. . . . . .11 B2
Sandover Cl **4** PE33. . . . .43 F2
Sandown Rd
Great Yarmouth NR30 . . .169 D5
Wisbech PE13. . . . . .152 A2
Sandpiper Cl **1** NR31. . . .170 A5
Sandpiper Ct **13** NR29. . . .58 B6
Sandpiper St PE36. . . . . .132 D1
Sandpiper Way **7** NR7. .159 E4
Sandpiper Wy PE30 . . . . .146 E2
Sandpit La Foulsham NR20. .33 C4
Gimingham NR11. . . . . . .22 E8
Saxlingham Nethergate
NR15 . . . . .107 A8
Thorpe Market NR11. . . . .21 F7
Sandringha Ave NR31 . . .134 D6
SANDRINGHAM PE35 . . . . .27 F7
Sandringham Ave
Great Yarmouth NR30 . . .169 D7
12 Marham PE33. . . . . . . .63 B4
Wisbech PE13 . . . . .152 D6
Sandringham Cres
King's Lynn PE30 . . . . . .148 D5
West Raynham NR21. . . . .30 C4
Sandringham Ct
Norwich NR2 . . . . .178 A1
6 Watton IP25. . . . . .84 D3
Sandringham Ctry Pk★
PE35. . . . . .27 E7
Sandringham Dr
Downham Market PE38. . .172 E5
Heacham PE31. . . . . . . .133 C4
Sandringham Gr NR36. . .132 C7
Sandringham House Mus &
Gdns★ PE35. . . . . .27 F7
Sandringham Rd
Dersingham PE31 . . . . . .140 E2
Hillington PE31 . . . . .28 A5
Hunstanton PE36. . . . . . .132 D4
King's Lynn PE30 . . . . . .147 C2
Norwich NR2 . . . . .162 B6
Sandringham Way PE37 .153 C2

Sandringham & West
Newton CE Prim Sch
PE31. . . . . .27 F6
Sands Cl NR31. . . . . .171 E4
Sand Stone Way IP22 . . .177 B4
Sandy Cl PE31 . . . . .140 C7
Sandy Cres PE31. . . . . . .140 C7
Sandygate La PE34. . . . .144 F5
Sandy Hill La NR25. . . . . . .8 A7
Sandy Hills
Worstead NR28 . . . . .38 A7
Worstead NR28 . . . . .151 C1
Sandy La Antingham NR28 . .22 B4
Ashby St Mary NR14 . . . .91 D5
Aylsham NR11 . . . . .150 B6
Bacton NR12 . . . . .23 D3
Barningham IP31. . . . . . .127 D4
Beighton NR13. . . . . .74 C3
Beighton NR13. . . . . .74 C3
Belton with Browston NR31 93 F5
Blackborough End PE32 . .44 C2
Bradwell NR31. . . . . .94 C8
Buxton with Lammas NR10. .53 F8
Canadas NR11. . . . . .10 A3
Cantley NR13. . . . . .92 E6
Castle Acre PE32. . . . . . .47 A2
Cromer NR27. . . . . .139 A6
Denver PE38 . . . . .172 C2
Dereham NR19 . . . . .154 C8
Diss IP22. . . . . .177 F4
Docking PE31. . . . . .134 D6
East Dereham NR19 . . . . .154 C6
East Tuddenham NR20. . . . .69 D8
Fakenham NR21 . . . . . . .141 A5
Felthorpe NR10 . . . . .52 D4
Felthorpe NR10 . . . . . . .155 A8
Fleggburgh NR29. . . . . . .75 B8
Great Ellingham NR16. . . .103 E7
Great Massingham PE32. . .46 E7
Great Massingham PE32. . .46 E8
Grimston PE32. . . . . .44 C8
Hardingham NR9 . . . . . . .86 D7
Hilgay PE38 . . . . .97 C8
Horsford NR10. . . . . .53 A4
Hoveton NR12. . . . . .55 C4
Ingoldisthorpe PE31 . . . .140 C7
King's Lynn PE30. . . . . . .148 F1
Little Walsingham NR22 . . .16 E7
Loddon NR14. . . . . .92 B1
Loddon NR14. . . . . .109 E8
Mundham NR14. . . . . . . .109 A7
Norwich NR4 . . . . .162 D1
Old Hunstanton PE36 . . . .132 E8
Oulton NR11. . . . . .35 B7
Outwell PE14 . . . . .78 A7
Raveningham NR14 . . . . .110 B8
Rocklands NR17. . . . . . .103 A6
Runton NR27 . . . . .10 C4
St Mary, South Elmham
otherwise Homersfield
IP20. . . . . .123 B3
St Olaves NR31 . . . . .93 E1
Sheringham NR27 . . . . . .10 A5
Somerton NR29 . . . . .57 E6
Southrepps NR11. . . . . . .22 B7
Southrepps NR11. . . . . . .22 C8
South Wootton PE30 . . . . .27 C1
Taverham NR8 . . . . .156 C8
Thurning NR20. . . . . .34 C8
West Acre PE32. . . . . . . .46 B2
Weston Green NR20 . . . . .51 D1
Weston Longville NR9 . . . .51 D4
Wisbech PE13 . . . . .152 F4
Wiveton NR25 . . . . .7 D6
Sandy La E NR19 . . . . . .154 C6
Sandyland PE13 . . . . . . .152 B5
Sandy Rd PE32. . . . . .63 E7
Sandy Way NR31. . . . . . .140 C7
Sankence La NR11. . . . . . .35 E5
Santolina Cl NR5. . . . . . .157 B1
Santon Cl IP24 . . . . .176 A3
SANTON DOWNHAM
IP27. . . . . .115 C6
Santon Downham Rd
IP27. . . . . .175 F4
Santon Rd IP27 . . . . .115 D7
SAPISTON IP31. . . . . . . .126 D2
Sapiston Rd IP31 . . . . . .126 D1
Sapphire Way NR6. . . . . .158 B5
Sapwell Cl NR11. . . . . . .150 A6
Saracen Rd NR6 . . . . . . .157 F6
Sarahs Rd PE36. . . . . . . .132 C2
Sarah W Cl NR2 . . . . . . .162 C4
Sarah Williman Cl **2**
NR4 . . . . .161 C5
Sardis Way NR19 . . . . . .154 D4
Sashmire La NR22 . . . . . .16 E8
Saturday Mkt Pl PE30. . .146 D4
Saunders Ct **1** NR1. . . . .163 A6
Savage Cl PE30 . . . . . . .147 D3
Savery Cl NR5. . . . . .161 B6
Savory Rd PE13 . . . . . . .152 B7
Sawmill Cl
Felthorpe NR10 . . . . .52 F5
Wymondham NR18 . . . . .173 B6
Saw Mill La
Brancaster PE31 . . . . .3 B6
7 Great Yarmouth NR31. .169 B4
Sawmill Loke PE32. . . . . .48 C6
Sawston **1** PE30 . . . . . .147 D6
Sawyers Cl NR5. . . . . . . .156 E1
Sawyer's La NR10. . . . . . .07 D2
Saxifrage Cl NR15. . . . . .106 D4
SAXLINGHAM NR15 . . . . . .7 C2
SAXLINGHAM GREEN
NR15 . . . . .107 D7
Saxlingham La NR15. . . .106 F7
SAXLINGHAM NETHERGATE
NR15 . . . . .107 C8
Saxlingham Nethergate CE
VC Prim Sch NR15. . . . .107 B7

Saxlingham Rd
Blakeney NR25 . . . . .7 C5
Saxlingham NR25. . . . . . . .7 D1
Saxlingham Nethergate
NR15. . . . . .107 C8
Shotesham NR15. . . . . . .89 F1
SAXLINGHAM THORPE
NR15 . . . . .107 A8
Saxon Bank IP24 . . . . . . .176 B3
Saxon Cl
29 Martham NR29. . . . . . .57 D4
Terrington St Clement
PE34 . . . . .144 B5
Saxoncote Ave
Norwich NR5. . . . . .71 A4
Norwich NR5 . . . . .161 A7
Saxon Cres **3** IP31 . . . . .126 B1
Saxon Ct PE37 . . . . .153 D2
Saxon Field PE31 . . . . .3 B6
Saxonfields NR14. . . . . . .90 C4
Saxon Gdns NR14. . . . . .168 D5
Saxonmdw IP22 . . . . . . .129 C4
Saxon Mdws **15** NR20 . . . .50 E7
Saxon Pl
Lakenheath IP27 . . . . . . .113 E1
3 Thetford IP24. . . . . . .176 C3
Weeting IP27. . . . . .175 A8
Saxon Rd NR30 . . . . .169 D4
Saxon Way
Dersingham PE31 . . . . . .140 D4
Wormegay PE33 . . . . . . .62 C6
Saxon Wlk IP26. . . . . . . .100 A4
SAXTHORPE NR11 . . . . . . .19 F1
Saxthorpe Rd
Saxthorpe NR11. . . . . . . .19 F1
Saxthorpe NR11. . . . . . . .20 A2
Sayer Cres NR27 . . . . . . .139 B5
Sayer Ct NR25 . . . . .9 A2
Sayers Gn **3** NR31. . . . . .171 D4
Sayers St **9** NR21. . . . . .162 C7
Scama La IP22. . . . . .129 A2
Scania Way NR30 . . . . . .147 A1
Scarborough Rd NR22 . . .17 A8
Scarfield La PE14 . . . . . . .59 C2
Scarlet Rd NR4 . . . . .162 D1
Scarnell Rd NR5 . . . . . . .161 C6
SCARNING NR19 . . . . .67 B7
Scarning Fen NR19 . . . . .154 C2
Scarning VC Prim Sch
NR19 . . . . .154 A4
Scarrow Beck NR11. . . . . .21 B2
Scarrow Beck La NR11. . . .21 A2
Sceptre Cl NR6 . . . . .72 F7
Scholars Way PE14 . . . . . .77 E5
Scholars Wlk IP22 . . . . . .177 C5
School Ave NR7 . . . . . . .163 F6
School Cl Blofield NR13. . .165 E6
Bracon Ash NR14. . . . . . .88 F3
Kenninghall NR16 . . . . . .119 A4
Knapton NR28 . . . . .143 A1
Lakenheath IP27 . . . . . . .113 E1
3 Ludham NR29. . . . . . . .56 C5
Northrepps NR27. . . . . . .11 A2
4 Rollesby NR29 . . . . . . .57 B4
School Comm Rd NR12. . .24 C3
Schoolfield NR10 . . . . . .155 C8
School Hill
Ranworth NR12. . . . . . . .55 F1
Ranworth NR13. . . . . . . .73 F8
Reedham NR13. . . . . . . .93 A4
Schoolhouse La 1
NR11 . . . . .150 C7
School La
Baconsthorpe NR11. . . . . .19 F7
Besthorpe NR17 . . . . . . .104 D6
Brandon IP27. . . . . .175 C3
Cantley NR13. . . . . .92 B7
Colney NR4 . . . . .160 E3
East Dereham NR19 . . . . .154 E1
East Harling NR16. . . . . .118 C5
Ellingham NR35. . . . . . . .109 D3
Hingham NR9. . . . . .22 E8
Great Yarmouth NR31 . . .170 D6
17 Harleston IP20. . . . . . .122 D2
Harpley PE31. . . . . .29 C4
Heckingham NR14 . . . . . .109 F8
Kenninghall NR16 . . . . . .119 A4
Little Dunham PE32. . . . . .65 E7
Little Melton NR9. . . . . . .160 C2
Neatishead NR12. . . . . . .55 D7
North Runcton PE33 . . . . .44 A2
Northwold IP26 . . . . .99 C7
Norwich NR7 . . . . .158 F3
Rockland St Mary NR14. . .91 B7
Runhall NR9. . . . . .68 F1
Skeyton NR10 . . . . .37 A5
Smallburgh NR12. . . . . . .38 D3
Stoke Ferry PE33. . . . . . .80 F2
Surlingham NR14. . . . . . .73 B1
Thelnetham IP22. . . . . . .128 B5
Thetford IP24 . . . . .176 D3
Walpole St Andrew PE14 . .41 E3
Wereham PE33 . . . . .80 E4
West Newton PE31 . . . . . .27 F6
Wiggenhall St Germans
PE34 . . . . .43 B1
1 Wisbech PE13 . . . . . . .152 C5
Wramplingham NR18 . . . .69 F1
Wymondham NR18 . . . . .167 A4
School Loke Bodham NR25. . .9 A2
Hemsby NR29 . . . . .57 F5
School Pastures PE31. . . . .3 E7
School Plain NR19 . . . . . .154 B5
School Rd Alburgh IP20 . .123 A5
Aldborough NR11. . . . . . .21 A5
Ashmanhaugh NR12 . . . . .55 B7
Rockland St Peter NR17 . .103 B8
Barton Turf NR12. . . . . . .38 E1
Bedingham NR35. . . . . . .108 A1
Beetley NR20. . . . . .49 C5

School Rd continued
Bergh Apton NR15. . . . . . .91 B2
Blofield NR13. . . . . .165 B8
Bracon Ash NR14. . . . . . .89 A3
Bradenham IP25. . . . . . . .66 D3
Bressingham IP22. . . . . .129 B8
Brisley NR20 . . . . .49 A8
Castle Rising NR31. . . . . .27 C3
Catfield NR29. . . . . .56 C8
Colkirk NR21 . . . . .31 D5
Earsham NR35. . . . . .123 F8
East Ruston NR12 . . . . . . .38 E7
Erpingham NR11 . . . . .21 B2
Foulden NR21 . . . . .82 A1
Freethorpe NR13. . . . . . .92 F7
Frettenham NR12 . . . . . . .54 A4
Great Massingham PE32. . .29 D1
Great Yarmouth NR30 . . .169 B5
Harpley PE31. . . . . .29 C4
Haveringland NR10 . . . . . .52 D7
Heacham PE31. . . . . . . .133 D5
Hinderclay IP22. . . . . . . .128 C3
Holme Hale IP25. . . . . . . .66 A2
Horning NR12 . . . . .55 F3
Kirby Cane NR35 . . . . . . .109 E4
Lessingham NR12 . . . . . . .24 D3
Lingwood NR13 . . . . .74 A3
Little Cressingham IP25. . .83 F2
Little Plumstead NR13. . . .73 B6
Ludham NR29. . . . . .56 B5
Marshland St James PE14 . .60 B4
Mautby NR29 . . . . .75 E5
Middleton PE32 . . . . .44 C2
Morning Thorpe NR15. . . .107 B3
Neatishead NR12. . . . . . .55 E7
Necton PE37. . . . . .65 F4
Newton Flotman NR15 . . . .89 D1
Outwell PE14 . . . . .77 D4
Potter Heigham NR29. . . . .56 F6
Reepham NR10 . . . . .149 B4
Runcton Holme PE33. . . . .61 E3
St Andrew, Ilketshall
NR34 . . . . .124 E6
Saxlingham NR15. . . . . . .107 B3
Sculthorpe Airfield NR21. . .15 C3
Seething NR15. . . . . . . .108 E8
Shernborne PE31. . . . . . .13 B3
Sloley NR10 . . . . .37 F3
1 Snettisham PE31 . . . . .12 E5
South Walsham NR13 . . . .74 A8
Strumpshaw NR13. . . . . . .73 F1
Swannington NR9. . . . . . .52 B5
Taverham NR8 . . . . .155 F1
Terrington St John PE14. . .60 B7
Thompson IP24 . . . . .102 B7
Tilney All Saints PE34. . . . .42 E4
Tilney St Lawrence PE34. . .60 C7
Tivetshall St Mary NR15 . .121 B5
Walpole Highway PE14. . . .59 F8
Walton Highway PE14 . . . .59 C8
Watlington PE33. . . . . . . .61 D6
Weasenham All Saints
PE32. . . . . .47 D8
Weasenham St Peter PE32 .30 D1
West Rudham PE31. . . . . .29 F6
West Walton PE14. . . . . . .37 D5
Westwick NR10 . . . . .37 D5
Whissonsett NR20. . . . . . .31 E2
Wiggenhall St Germans
PE34 . . . . .61 B8
Worstead NR28 . . . . .38 A5
School Rd Back 4
NR30 . . . . .169 C5
School Sq IP24 . . . . .102 E3
School Terr **3** NR14 . . . .163 B2
School View NR34. . . . . .124 F1
Scira La NR26. . . . . .138 B5
SCOLE IP21 . . . . .130 D6
Scole Comm IP21. . . . . . .130 C6
SCOLE COMMON IP21. . . .130 C7
Scole Comm Rd IP21. . . . .130 C6
Scole Dicklenburgh By Pass
IP21. . . . . .121 B2
Scole Prim Sch IP21. . . .130 D6
Scole Rd Brockdish IP21. .131 B5
Brockdish IP21. . . . . . . .131 C6
Scolt Head Island National
Nature Reserve★ PE31. . . .3 E8
Sconch Beck Rd IP20 . . .123 A2
SCO RUSTON NR12 . . . . . .54 E8
Scotch Belt
Sandringham PE35. . . . . .27 E7
Sandringham PE35 . . . . .140 E1
Scotch Hill Rd NR8. . . . .155 B1
Scotgate Cl IP24. . . . . . .102 E3
Scott Cl
2 Sprowston NR7. . . . . .159 E4
Thetford IP24. . . . . .176 D3
Scotter Rise **7** NR26. . . .138 C5
Scotgate Cl PE34. . . . . . .144 E4
SCOTTOW NR10 . . . . .37 D2
Scottow Rd
Buxton with Lammas
NR10. . . . . .37 B2
Scottow NR10 . . . . .37 C3
Scottow Row NR10. . . . . .37 C3
Scott Rd NR1 . . . . .163 B5
Scotts Corner NR13 . . . . .73 B8
Scott's Hill NR14. . . . . . . .89 A4
Scott's La IP22 . . . . .130 C6
SCOULTON NR9 . . . . .85 E3

SCULTHORPE NR21. . . . . .16 B2
Sculthorpe Airfield NR21 15 C3
Sculthorpe Ave NR21. . . . .146 B5
Sculthorpe Bvd **7** NR21. . .15 C2
Sculthorpe CE Prim Sch
NR21 . . . . .16 C2
Sculthorpe Eastgate
NR21 . . . . .141 A5
Sculthorpe Rd NR21 . . . .141 A5
Sea Bank La
Walpole St Andrew PE14. . .41 D4
Walpole St Peter PE14 . . .41 D3
Seabank Rd
Heacham PE31. . . . . . . .133 B6
Wisbech PE13 . . . . .152 F6
Seabank Way PE30. . . . .146 E2
Seabird Cl **4** NR30. . . . . .168 D7
Seabrook Cl **9** NR5. . . . .161 A7
Sea Cl PE31. . . . . .133 B6
Seacliff NR26. . . . . .138 E7
Seafield Cl **20** NR30 . . . . .169 D2
Seafield Rd N NR30. . . . .168 E6
Seafield Rd S NR30. . . . .168 D6
Seafields Dr NR31 . . . . . .171 D4
Seaforth Dr NR8 . . . . . . .156 E8
Seagate PE36. . . . . .132 C3
Seagate Rd PE36. . . . . . .132 B3
Seagull Rd NR29 . . . . . . .167 E5
Sea La PE36 . . . . .132 E7
Sea Lord Cl PE37. . . . . . .153 C6
Seaman Dr PE30 . . . . . . .147 C3
Seamere Rd NR9 . . . . . . .86 D4
SEA PALLING NR12 . . . . . .40 A6
Sea Palling Rd
Hickling NR12 . . . . .39 F3
Lessingham NR12 . . . . . . .39 F5
1 Necton PE37. . . . . .65 F4
Searle Cl NR21. . . . . . . .141 F5
Sears Cl NR11 . . . . .150 C6
Seaside La NR12 . . . . .24 E4
Seates The **6** NR8. . . . . .155 D7
Seathwaite Rd PE30. . . . .147 D8
Seaview Cres NR26 . . . . .138 D5
Sea View Rd
Hemsby NR29 . . . . .167 D7
Mundesley NR11. . . . . . .143 B7
Sea View Rise NR31. . . . .171 E4
Seawake Cl NR31. . . . . . .170 A4
Seaward Cres NR11. . . . .143 B6
Seaward Wlk NR30. . . . . .168 E8
Seckar Dr NR19. . . . . . . .154 C4
Second Ave
Caister-on-Sea NR30. . . . .168 D8
Wisbech PE13 . . . . .152 D4
Second Dro IP27 . . . . . . .113 C3
Second Marsh Rd PE14. . .59 A7
Sedge Cl NR21 . . . . .141 E4
Sedge Dro PE38 . . . . .96 C7
Sedgefen Dro PE38 . . . . .112 E7
Sedgefen Rd IP27 . . . . . .112 F3
Sedge Fen Rd
Lakenheath IP27 . . . . . . .113 E2
Southery PE38. . . . . .97 B3
SEDGEFORD PE36 . . . . . . .13 B7
Sedgeford La **5** PE36. . .146 D4
Sedgeford Prim Sch
PE36. . . . . .13 B7
Sedgeford Rd
Docking PE31. . . . . .134 B4
Ringstead PE36. . . . . .2 A2
Snettisham PE31 . . . . . . .12 F5
Sedgeford Road PE36. . . .13 A6
Sedge Rd
East Dereham NR19 . . . . .154 B4
Swaffham PE37. . . . . . . .153 C2
Seeche Abbey PE34. . . . . .43 D1
SEETHING NR14 . . . . . . .108 F8
Seething Fen NR15 . . . . . .91 C1
Seething Ling NR15 . . . . . .91 A1
Seething & Mumdham Prim
Sch NR15 . . . . .108 E8
Seething Old Hall Pk
NR15 . . . . .91 B1
Seething Rd NR35. . . . . .108 D5
Seething St NR15. . . . . . .108 E8
Seeview Cres NR12 . . . . . .24 A7
Sefton Ave PE13 . . . . . . .152 E6
Sefton La NR31. . . . . . . .169 C3
Sego Vale NR8. . . . . .156 E8
Segrave Rd **6** PE30. . . . . .147 A8
Selbrigg Rd NR25. . . . . . . .8 E2
Selby Pl **15** NR30. . . . . . .169 D2
Self's La IP22. . . . . .128 C7
Selwyn Ct IP21 . . . . .121 E5
Selwyn Dr **9** NR31. . . . . .94 A5
Selwyn Gdns IP21 . . . . . .121 E5
Selwyn Rd NR31. . . . . . . .170 A5
Semere Gn La IP21. . . . . .121 D2
Semere Green IP21 . . . . .121 D3
Semere La
Pulham Market IP21. . . . .121 D4
Pulham Market IP21. . . . .121 D4
Sendall Rd NR28 . . . . . . .151 B3
Senna Dr NR4 . . . . .161 E1
Sennowe Rd NR20 . . . . . .32 F4
Senters Rd NR31. . . . . . . .27 E8
Senter's Rd PE31 . . . . . .140 D2
Seppings Rd NR21 . . . . . .141 A6
Seppings Way NR13. . . . .72 E6
Serpentine La NR10. . . . . .53 C6
SETCHEY PE33. . . . . .61 E8
Setch Rd Middleton PE33 . .44 A1
West Winch PE33 . . . . . . .43 F1
Seton Rd NR8. . . . . .155 E1
Setons Halt Sta NR13. . . . .5 F2
Sevenacres La NR12 . . . . .54 C7
Seven Hills IP31 . . . . . . .125 E1
Seven Sisters Cl PE30. . . .146 D4
Seventh Ave PE13. . . . . .152 E4
Severalls Rd IP26. . . . . . .98 D5
Sewell Park Coll NR3. . . .158 E2
Sewell Rd Lamas NR10. . . .36 F1

Sewell Rd continued
Norwich NR3 . . . . .158 E1
Sewells Cl **5** NR15. . . . . . .89 C1
Sewell's La NR15. . . . . . .90 D3
Sexton NR35 . . . . .108 D2
Seymour Ave
Brandon NR27 . . . . .114 D4
Great Yarmouth NR30 . . .169 D8
Shack La NR13. . . . . .165 D6
Shadingfield Cl **16**
NR30 . . . . .169 D2
SHADWELL IP24. . . . . . . .117 C2
Shadwell Cl IP27 . . . . . . .175 B7
Shakers La
Little Cressingham IP25. . .101 C8
Pockthorpe IP24 . . . . . . .102 A7
Tottington IP24. . . . . . . .101 F7
Shakers Rd
Brandon IP27. . . . . .115 A1
Wangford IP27 . . . . .114 F1
Shakespeare Rd NR30. . .169 E8
Shakespeare Way
Taverham NR8 . . . . .156 E8
Thetford IP24 . . . . .176 E6
Shammer La
North Creake NR21. . . . . . .4 A1
Shammer NR21. . . . . .15 A8
Shannock Ct **14** NR26 . . . .138 D7
Shannon Dr **4** NR30. . . . .168 C6
Shannons Dr NR17 . . . . . .174 E4
Sharman Ave IP25. . . . . . .84 D4
Sharmans Loke NR31 . . . .93 F5
Sharon Cl
2 East Dereham NR19 . . .154 D1
Felmingham NR28. . . . . . .37 A8
Sharper's Cnr IP27 . . . . . .113 D2
Sharpes Corner IP27. . . . .113 E2
Sharpe Way NR29. . . . . . .167 B2
Sharp St NR29 . . . . .56 C7
SHARP STREET NR29. . . . .56 C7
SHARRINGTON NR24. . . . . .18 D7
Sharrington Rd
Brinton NR25. . . . . .18 D7
Gunthorpe NR24 . . . . . . .18 B5
Shawcross Rd NR27. . . . . .10 A4
Shaw's Yd PE31. . . . . .30 B7
Shearwater Dr
2 Great Yarmouth
NR31. . . . . .170 A7
8 Sprowston NR7. . . . . .159 E4
Sheckford La IP22. . . . . .121 C3
Sheddick Ct NR19. . . . . . .154 D6
Sheep La NR15. . . . . .90 D3
Sheep Mdw Cl NR15. . . . .156 E1
Sheffield Rd NR18 . . . . . .173 C5
Sheldonian Ct NR31. . . . .170 A4
Sheldrake Cl NR29. . . . . .141 F5
Sheldrick Pl NR19 . . . . . .154 E2
Shelduck Dr **7** PE31. . . . .12 E5
Shelduck Way **22** NR27. . .159 E4
SHELFANGER IP22. . . . . .120 C2
Shelfanger Ct IP22 . . . . . .177 C5
Shelfanger Rd IP22 . . . . .177 C7
Shelford Dr PE30 . . . . . . .147 B8
Shelley Cl NR30. . . . . . . .168 D6
Shelley Dr NR8. . . . . .156 D8
Shelley Way IP24 . . . . . .176 E6
Shell Mus The★ NR25 . . . .7 E4
Shelly Cl **3** PE38 . . . . . . .172 C6
Shelterhouse Cnr IP24. . .125 A4
SHELTON NR15 . . . . .107 A1
Shelton Spot NR15. . . . . .107 A2
Shelton with Hardwick Com
Sch NR15. . . . . .107 B2
Shepheard Ct **1** NR28 . . .151 C6
Shepheards Ct NR11 . . . .150 B4
Shepherd Cl
Norwich NR4 . . . . .161 D5
Sheringham NR26 . . . . . .138 B6
Shepherd Purse Way
NR5 . . . . .161 B7
Shepherds Cl
Cromer NR27. . . . . .10 B5
11 Horsford NR10. . . . . . .53 A3
Runton NR27 . . . . .10 B5
Shepherds Dr IP25 . . . . . .84 C4
Shepherd's Drove CB7. . .112 A6
Shepherd's Fold PE37. . . .153 D2
SHEPHERD'S GATE PE34 . .42 D4
Shepherdsgate Rd
PE34. . . . . .144 C1
Shepherds La
Burgate IP22. . . . . .129 B3
Oulton NR11. . . . . .35 B6
Shepherd's La NR10 . . . . .36 A2
Shepherds Pightle PE36. . . . .2 D6
SHEPHERD'S PORT PE31. . .12 B4
Shepherd Way NR8 . . . . .155 E2
Shepley Cres **2** PE30. . . .147 D5
Sheppard Dr NR19 . . . . . .88 B6
Sheppard Way NR17 . . . .174 C5
Sherbourne Pl NR11 . . . .178 C1
SHEREFORD NR21 . . . . . . .31 A8
Shereford Comm NR21. . . .31 A8
Shereford Rd
Fakenham NR21. . . . . . . .141 A3
Hempton NR21. . . . . .31 C8
Sheridan Cl NR8 . . . . . . .156 F8
Sheridan Sch IP26. . . . . . .99 A8
SHERINGHAM NR26. . . . .138 C7
Sheringham Com Prim Sch
NR26 . . . . .138 C5
Sheringham High Sch
NR26 . . . . .138 C5
Sheringham Little Theatre
NR26 . . . . .138 C6
Sheringham Mus★
NR26 . . . . .138 D7

Sheringham Pk★ NR26 ..... 9 B6
Sheringham Pk NR26 ....138 A5
Sheringham Pk Visitor Ctr★
NR26 .... 9 B4
Sheringham Rd
　East Beckham NR11 ...... 9 D2
　Upper Sheringham NR26..138 A4
　West Beckham NR25...... 9 B3
　Weybourne NR25........ 8 F5
Sheringham Sta NR26 ....138 C7
Sheringham Woodfields Sch
NR26 ....138 C5
SHERINGWOOD NR26 ....138 C6
Sheringwood NR26 ......138 E4
Sheringwood La PE31....15 C4
SHERNBORNE PE31.......13 B3
Shernborne Rd
　Anmer PE31.............13 D1
　Fring PE31..............13 D5
　Ingoldisthorpe PE31....140 E7
Sherndorne Rd PE35......28 D8
Sherwell Rd NR6........157 E6
Sherwood Ave PE13......152 D7
Sherwood Cl PE38 ......172 B5
Sherwood Rd NR4 ......162 C1
Sheval Cl NR15 ....121 A8
Shickle Pl IP22 ....127 F6
Shillgate Way NR8......155 B2
Shillito Rd NR13 ....165 F6
SHIMPLING IP21........121 A2
Shimpling Rd IP21.......121 B1
SHINGHAM PE37.........82 A8
Shingham PE37..........81 F8
Shipden Ave NR27 ......139 A7
Shipden Ct NR27........139 A7
SHIPDHAM IP25.........67 B2
Shipdham Airfield IP25...67 E2
Shipdham Airfield Ind Est
IP25 ....67 F2
Shipdham Rd
　Carbrooke IP25.........85 A5
　East Dereham NR19 ....154 D1
　Scarning NR19..........67 B6
　Shipdham NR19.........67 E5
　Westfield NR19.........67 E4
Shipfield NR3 ....158 F2
Shipgate Rd PE31.......29 B5
Ship La PE36............ 2 C6
SHIPMEADOW NR34.....124 F8
Shippea Hill Sta CB7....112 C3
Shipstone Rd NR13......162 D8
Shire Ave 5 NR31 ......94 C8
Shire Cl NR29...........167 A7
Shiregreen PE30........147 E4
Shire Horse Wy 16 IP25..84 F3
Shires The NR15 ....155 F2
Shirley Cl 3 NR12 ......54 A4
Shoals Rd NR12.........56 A7
Shoe Devil La NR35.....124 C4
Shoemakers La PE37.....64 E3
Shooters Cl NR8.........155 C1
Shop La Hethersett NR9 ...88 E8
　Tunstead NR12.........128 C5
　Wells-next-the-Sea NR23 136 D6
Shop St NR19............68 A3
Shorncliffe Ave NR3 ....158 C1
Shorncliffe Cl 1 NR3 ...158 C1
Short Beck 18 IP26 .....98 E1
Short Cl PE38...........172 C6
Short Dro
　Downham Market PE38..172 C6
　Downham Market PE38..172 C7
Short Fen Drove PE34....60 F6
Short Gn IP22...........120 B5
SHORT GREEN IP22.....120 A5
Short Green IP22........119 F5
Shortgrove La
　Hopton IP22...........127 F7
　Thelnetham IP22.......119 B5
Shortingate Rd IP24....176 F7
Short La Banham NR16 ..119 E8
　Billingford NR20........50 A8
　Feltwell IP26...........98 D1
　Happisburgh NR12 .....24 B3
　Harpley PE31...........29 D4
　Mautby NR29...........75 E6
　Swardeston NR14.......89 C5
Short Rd
　3 Attleborough NR17 ...174 C5
　Belton with Browston
　NR31..................94 A4
　Keswick NR4...........89 D7
Short St 8 NR15.........89 D1
Short-thorn Rd NR10 ...52 F5
Shotcroft La IP22.......120 A3
SHOTESHAM NR15.......90 A2
Shotesham La NR15.....107 C8
Shotesham Rd
　Howe NR15............90 C2
　Mulbarton NR14.......89 C3
　Poringland NR14.......90 B3
　Stoke Holy Cross NR15...89 F3
　Stoke Holy Cross NR15...90 A3
　Woodton NR35.........108 A6
Shotford Rd IP20........122 D1
SHOULDHAM PE33.......61 D8
Shouldham Cl PE31.....140 C3
Shouldham La
　Swaffham PE37.........64 E3
　Swaffham PE37........153 A4
Shouldham Rd
　Marham PE33...........63 A3
　Shouldham Thorpe PE33..62 C2
SHOULDHAM THORPE
PE33 ....62 C3
Shreeve Rd NR13.......165 F6
Shreeves Rd IP22.......177 E4
SHROPHAM NR17.......103 B4

Shropham Rd
　Harling Road NR16 .....118 B6
　Hockham IP24..........102 A3
Shrub Cl NR17..........174 D5
Shrub Hill Feltwell PE38 ..112 D6
　Feltwell PE38...........112 E6
　Feltwell PE38...........112 F7
　Feltwell PE38...........113 A7
Shrublands The
　Horsford NR10..........53 B4
　Norwich NR2..........162 B6
Shrublands Wy NR31 ...170 B5
Shuckford Cl 5 IP22 ...177 C4
Shurbbery Cl IP22.......95 A7
Shuttleworth Cl NR31 ...170 A8
Sidegate Rd
　Great Yarmouth NR30..169 C5
　Hopton on Sea NR31...171 B7
Sidell Cl 1 NR4.........89 B8
SIDESTRAND NR27.......11 C2
Sidestrand Hall Sch
NR27 ....11 B8
Sidestrand Rd NR11.....11 C1
Siding Rd NR34.........111 C1
Sidings The
　9 Earsham NR35.......123 F8
　Thetford IP24..........176 C5
　Thorpe Hamlet NR1....163 C5
Sidney Bunn Way NR8 ..157 A7
Sidney Cl
　2 Great Yarmouth
　NR30..................169 D2
　8 Martham NR29........57 C4
Sidney Rd Costessey NR8..156 F4
　Ingham NR12...........39 D4
Sidney St PE30..........146 F3
Sienna Mews 3 NR1.....163 B7
Sigismund Rd NR1......162 D3
Signal Cl
　Marshland St James PE14..59 F4
　Marshland St James PE14..60 A5
SILFIELD NR18...........88 A2
Silfield Ave NR18.......173 D1
Silfield Gdn PE36.......132 D4
Silfield Rd
　Ashwellthorpe NR16 ...105 D8
　Wymondham NR18 .....87 F2
　Wymondham NR18 ....173 C2
　Tibenham NR16........120 D7
Silfield St NR18.........88 A2
Silfield Terr PE30.......146 F4
Silkmill Rd 2 NR30......169 D4
Silt Rd Nordelph PE38.....78 B2
　Runcton Holme PE33.....62 B8
　Terrington St Clement PE34 25 F3
　Upwell PE14............77 F1
Silver Birch Cl NR27....139 E4
Silver Cour NR27........11 A2
Silver Dr NR8...........140 C4
Silver Drift
　Swaffham PE37.........64 C5
　Swaffham PE37.........64 E5
Silver End NR10 ....149 B5
SILVERGATE NR11.......35 F6
Silvergate La NR11......35 F6
Silver Gdns 5 NR31.....94 A5
SILVER GREEN NR15...107 E3
Silver Hill PE30.........147 D6
Silverlands Cl NR21....141 C6
Silver Rd NR3..........178 C4
Silver St
　Besthorpe NR17.......174 F6
　Besthorpe NR17.......104 D7
　Fleggburgh NR29.......75 C8
　Garvestone NR9........86 C8
　Norwich NR3..........162 E8
　South Lopham IP22....128 F7
　Wisbech PE13..........152 C6
Silvertree's Way PE33...43 E1
Silvo Rd NR8...........156 A5
Simon Scotland Rd
PE30 ....146 F2
Simons Cl NR31.........170 A6
Simpson Cl NR28.......151 B5
Simpson Wy NR18 .....173 F7
Sinclair Cl NR31........170 A8
Sir Alfred Munnings Rd
NR5 ....156 A3
Sir Archdale Rd PE37...153 C6
Sir Douglas Bader Espl
PE36 ....132 C4
Sir Edward Stracey Rd
NR13 ....72 D8
Sir Isaac Newton Sixth
Form
　Norwich NR1..........162 E3
　Norwich NR1..........178 A2
　Norwich NR2..........162 D5
　Norwich NR2..........178 A3
Sir Lewis St PE30.......146 E6
Sir Thomas Cl NR18....173 C5
Sir William's Cl NR11...150 D6
Sir William's La NR11...150 D7
Siskin Cl Costessey NR8..156 A5
　Great Yarmouth NR31...170 A6
SISLAND NR14...........91 E1
Sitka Cl PE31...........133 C6
Six Crossways NR14.....91 D3
Sixteen Foot Bank PE14..77 D1
Sixth Ave PE13.........152 E4
Skedge Way 6 NR13.....73 C6
Skelton Cl 1 IP22......177 E4
Skelton Rd Diss IP22...177 E4
　Norwich NR7..........163 C8
Skelton View NR28 ....116 F2
SKEYTON NR10..........37 A4
Skeyton Cnr NR10.......37 B6
SKEYTON CORNER NR10..37 B6
Skeyton New Rd NR28..151 B5
Skeyton Rd
　Coltishall NR10.........37 B2
　North Walsham NR28 ..151 A4

Skinners La
　Stradbroke IP21........131 E1
　Wroxham NR12..........54 E3
　Wroxham/Hoveton NR12 .164 B2
Skinner's La IP20........122 B4
Skinners Mdw IP20.....123 B8
Skipper Ct NR7.........159 F3
Skippers Piece Cl PE31...3 B6
Skipping Block Row
NR18 ....88 B6
Skippon Way NR13......72 D5
Skitfield Rd NR20.......33 E6
Skoner Rd NR5.........161 B8
Skoyles' La NR9.........88 A8
Skye Cl NR5............161 A8
Skye Gdns IP26..........98 F1
Sladden Rd NR8.........157 A8
Slade La Claxton NR14....91 D5
　Pleasant Pigot NR14....90 F6
　Old Buckenham NR17..104 B1
　Wortham IP22.........129 B6
　Yelverton NR14.........90 F6
Slade Rd NR21...........18 B7
Slad La Bylaugh NR20....50 C6
　Woodbastwick NR13....55 C1
Slaughter Rd NR11......22 E8
Sleaford Gn NR3........158 C2
Sleigh La IP25...........84 E2
Sleights Dr PE14........59 C5
Slessor Cl 2 IP25.......84 F3
Slip Rd NR14............93 A1
Slipshoe La NR15.......122 B7
Slip The PE36............ 2 C3
Sloane Way IP24........176 B2
Sloeberry La NR20......69 C7
Sloe La NR13............72 D8
SLOLEY NR28............37 F4
Sloley Rd Frankfort NR12 ..38 A2
　Scottow NR28..........37 E3
　Sloley NR10.............37 E3
　Worstead NR28.........38 A3
Slopers Rd NR18........87 F7
Slough La
　Attleborough NR17 ....174 E3
　Gissing IP22...........120 F5
　Gissing IP22...........121 A5
　North Tuddenham NR20...68 E8
　Tibenham NR16........120 E7
Slough Rd IP22.........129 A1
Slovenwood La
　Spooner Row NR18.....88 A1
　Wymondham NR18 .....87 F1
Slugs La NR32..........111 C8
Sluice Bank PE38........79 A3
Sluice Dro IP26.........113 E7
Sluice Rd
　Denver PE38...........172 B1
　Denver PE38...........172 C2
　Wiggenhall St Germans
　PE34...................61 A8
Slutshole La
　Besthorpe NR17.......104 D7
　Besthorpe NR17.......104 F7
　Wymondham NR17.....105 A7
SMALLBURGH NR12.....38 D3
Smallburgh Rd
　Barton Turf NR12.......55 E8
　Smallburgh NR12.......38 D3
Smallcroft Cres NR18...173 A2
Small Gate 15 NR34....110 D1
Smallholdings Rd PE34..145 D4
Small Lode PE14.........77 F5
SMALLWORTH IP22.....128 B7
Smallworth La IP22....128 B7
Smea The NR12..........39 E1
Smeat St 2 NR5.........161 B7
Smee Drift NR9..........68 E4
Smee La NR13...........72 E4
Smee Rd NR13..........72 F4
Smeeth Bank
　Emneth Hungate PE14....59 F4
　St John's Fen End PE14....60 A6
　Marshland St Emneth PE14..59 F2
　St John's Fen End PE14....60 A5
SMEETH THE PE14.......60 A5
Smith Ave PE30.........146 E6
Smith Cl NR13..........165 F6
Smithdale Rd NR5......157 B1
Smithdon High Sch
PE36 ....132 D4
Smithfield Rd NR12....162 E3
Smithson Dr IP21.......121 B1
Smith's Dro PE38.......112 C8
Smith Beach Rd
　Heacham PE31.........133 A4
　Hunstanton PE36......132 B3
South Brink PE13........152 A3
SOUTHBURGH IP25.....85 F7
Southburgh La NR9.....86 A5
Southburgh Rd
　Garvestone NR9........86 A7
　Garvestone, Reymerston &
　Thuxton IP25..........67 F1
　High Common IP25.....85 F8
　Southburgh IP25.......86 A8
SOUTH BURLINGHAM
NR13 ....74 B2
South Burlingham Rd
NR13 ....74 B3
South Cl NR29.......... 7 A6
South Cnr PE31......... 3 B7
SOUTH CREAKE NR21...15 D6
Southcreake Rd PE31...15 B7
South Creak Rd PE31...14 F7
South Croft NR7.........88 C7
SOUTH DENES NR30...170 E5
South Denes Rd NR30...170 D4
South Elmham Rd IP20..123 C4
Southend Bradenham IP25 66 D3

SNEATH COMMON
NR15 ....121 A8
Sneath Rd NR15........121 A8
SNETTERTON NR16.....103 C2
Snetterton Circuit
NR16 ....118 D8
SNETTISHAM PE31.......12 E5
Snettisham Beach PE31...12 A3
Snettisham Nature
　Reserve★ PE31.........12 A3
Snettisham Pk★ PE31...12 E4
Snettisham Prim Sch
PE31....................12 E5
Snettisham Rd Fring PE31 13 D4
　Great Bircham PE31.....14 A3
　Sedgeford PE36.........13 A6
Snoring Rd
　Great Snoring NR22.....16 F5
　Kettlestone NR21........17 B1
　Kettlestone NR21........32 B8
　Little Walsingham NR21 ..17 A6
Snowberry Cl 4 NR8 ..155 B2
Snowdrop Cl
　20 Bradwell NR31.......94 C6
　West Lynn PE34........146 B4
Snowdrop Dr
　Attleborough NR17 ....174 B4
　11 Dereham NR20.......128 B6
Snowdrop Gr 6 PE38...172 B4
Snowdrop St NR18......173 F6
Snowhill Drift NR19....154 D6
Snow's Hill 6 NR14.....92 A2
Snow's La NR14.........92 A2
Snow St IP22...........177 A6
SNOW STREET IP22....129 D8
Soame Cl NR11.........150 D5
Soames Pl NR19.........67 B7
Soanes Ct NR9..........51 A5
Softley Dr NR4.........161 C2
Soken Dr 5 Beetley NR19..49 C3
　Gressenhall NR19.......49 D4
　5 Gressenhall NR20....49 C3
Solace Cl NR35.........124 C8
Solario Rd NR8.........156 A5
Sole Cl 6 NR10.........53 B3
Soleme Rd NR3.........158 B1
Solent Cl NR30.........168 E5
Somerleyton Gdns NR2...163 A8
Somerleyton Hall & Gdns★
NR32 ....111 E8
Somerleyton Prim Sch
NR32 ....111 F8
Somerleyton Rd NR32...111 F8
Somerleyton St 2 NR2..162 C5
Somersby Cl 2 PE30....147 A8
Somerset Pl 22 NR30...169 D4
Somerset Way NR8 ....155 A1
Somers Rd PE13........152 B4
Somerton Rd
　Horsey NR29...........40 D1
　Horsey NR29...........57 D5
　Martham NR29.........57 D5
　Somerton NR29.........58 A6
Somerville Ave NR31...170 B3
Somerville Rd 1 PE30..146 E3
Sommerville Cres NR20...50 B4
Sorrel Ct PE30..........147 C8
Sorrel Dr
　Attleborough NR17 ....174 B4
　1 Thetford IP24........176 E4
Sorrel Gr NR4...........161 B1
Sorrel La NR20..........49 D5
Sorrel Rd 25 NR31......94 C6
Sorrel Way PE38........172 C3
Sotherton Rd NR4......161 F3
Soudan Cl 3 NR30......168 D7
Southacre NR17........174 E6
SOUTH ACRE PE32.......46 F1
Southacre Rd PE32......65 C7
South Acre Rd PE32.....46 F1
Southalls Wy NR3......158 F1
Southall Way NR7......159 F4
Southampton Pl 16
NR30 ....169 D4
South Ave Norwich NR7 ..163 E6
　Swanton Morley Airfield
　NR20..................50 B5
South Beach PE31......133 A3
South Beach Par NR30..170 E6
South Beach Rd NR30..169 E2

SOUTH END NR16......103 C1
Southend Rd PE36.....132 C3
Southern La 2 IP22....128 D5
Southern Reach 7 NR14. 89 B3
Southernwood NR6....158 D5
SOUTHERY PE38.........97 B5
Southery Bypass PE38...97 A6
Southery Prim Sch PE38. 97 A5
Southery Rd
　Brandon Creek PE38....97 A3
　Feltwell IP26...........98 B2
　Methwold IP26..........97 F3
South Everard St PE30..146 E3
South Fen NR12.........38 E6
Southfield PE32..........65 C5
Southfield Dr 8 PE31....43 F2
Southfield La NR11......55 C1
Southfields
　Downham Market PE38..172 B4
　1 King's Lynn PE30....147 B6
Southfields Cl PE13....152 E8
South Gage Cl NR7.....159 C4
SOUTHGATE
　Cawston NR10..........35 B3
　South Creake NR21.....15 E5
Southgate 12 IP20.....122 D1
Southgate Cl NR23.....136 C5
Southgate La
　Norwich NR1...........178 C1
　Snettisham PE31........12 E4
Southgates Dr NR21....141 B5
Southgates Rd NR30....169 D2
Southgate St PE30......146 E3
Southgate Wy NR24....142 E3
South Gdn NR31........170 C1
South Gn
　East Dereham NR19 ...154 E4
　Pulham St Mary IP21...122 A2
　Terrington St Clement
　PE34..................144 B5
South Gn Gdns NR19...154 E3
SOUTH GREEN
　East Dereham NR19 ...154 E3
　Hoxne IP23............130 F1
　Mattishall NR20........68 F5
　Pulham St Mary IP21...121 F2
　Terrington St Clement
　PE34...................42 B6
South Hill Cl NR7.......163 F8
South Hill Rd NR7......163 F8
South Icehouse Hill
NR31 ....170 D6
Southlands PE37.......153 B2
SOUTH LOPHAM IP22..128 D8
SOUTH LYNN PE30.....146 E2
South Lynn Plain PE30..146 E4
Southmill Rd
　Tatterford NR21.........30 F7
　Toftrees NR21...........31 A7
South Mkt Rd NR30....169 D4
South Moor Dr PE31...133 D4
South Pickenham
PE37 ....83 D6
South Pickenham Rd
　Great Cressingham IP25...83 C5
　North Pickenham PE37...65 D1
　North Pickenham PE37...83 D8
　Swaffham PE37.........65 B1
　Swaffham PE37........153 D1
South Pk IP27..........175 B7
South Pk Ave 2 NR4...162 A4
South Prom PE36.......132 B3
South Quay
　Great Yarmouth NR30..169 C3
　8 King's Lynn PE30....146 D4
South Quays La NR12...55 D4
SOUTH RAYNHAM NR21.. 30 F3
South Raynhamrd NR21..30 F3
South Rd
　Great Yarmouth NR30..169 C3
　Hemsby NR29..........167 D7
　Shouldham Thorpe PE33..62 C2
　Watton IP25............84 D3
South Rise NR28........151 B3
SOUTH RUNCTON PE33..61 F7
Southside PE34..........79 D8
South St
　Great Dunham PE32....47 F1
　Hockwold cum Wilton
　IP26...................113 F6
　2 King's Lynn PE30....146 E4
　Sheringham NR26......138 C7
SOUTHTOWN NR31.....169 B1
Southtown Prim Sch
NR31 ....169 B2
Southtown Rd NR31...169 C2
Southview Cl IP25.......84 D4
SOUTH WALSHAM
NR13 ....74 A7
South Walsham Rd
　Acle NR13.............166 A5
　South Walsham NR13...74 B5
Southwell Rd
　5 Horsham St Faith &
　Newton St Faith NR10...53 D2
　Norwich NR1..........178 A1
　Wisbech PE13.........152 C7
South Wlk NR13.........72 E5
SOUTHWOOD NR13.....92 D8
South Wood Dr NR14...90 B6
Southwood Rd
　Beighton NR13..........74 C1
　Cantley NR13...........92 C8
SOUTH WOOTTON
PE30 ....148 D2

South Wootton Jun Sch
　King's Lynn PE30......148 C2
South Wootton La PE30 .148 C1
Sovereign Cl 2 PE13 ...152 A6
Sovereign Way PE38...172 A4
Sowdlefield Wlk NR14...89 B2
Sow's Loke NR12........55 E6
SPA COMMON NR28....23 A1
Spa La Aylsham NR11.....35 F3
　Aylsham NR11.........150 B3
　Oulton NR11............35 B8
Spalding's Chair Hill
IP24 ....126 E8
SPARHAM NR9...........51 B6
SPARHAMHILL NR9.....51 C5
Sparhawk Ave NR7.....159 C4
Sparhawk Cl NR7......159 C4
Sparhawk Inf Sch NR7..159 C4
Spar Rd NR6............158 C5
Sparrow Cl
　Attleborough NR17 ....174 B3
　4 Great Yarmouth NR31..94 C7
Sparrowgate Rd PE14...59 C5
Sparrow Hawk Cl NR31..171 D4
Sparrow Hill
　Merton IP25............101 F7
　Thompson IP25........102 A8
Sparrows Hill
　Bawburgh NR9..........70 C3
　Bawburgh NR9.........160 A5
Spartan Cl PE13........152 E2
Speckled Wood Cl
NR17 ....174 B3
Speedway NR2.........162 A5
Speedwell Cl
　5 Attleborough NR17 ..174 B4
　3 Hopton On Sea NR31..171 D4
　2 Thetford IP24.......176 E4
Speedwell Rd NR18....173 D4
Speedwell Way
　Norwich NR5..........160 F5
　13 Redenhall with Harleston
　IP20..................122 D1
Speke St NR2...........162 A7
Spellow La PE34.........42 F7
Spelman Rd NR31......162 A4
Spencer Ave NR31.....170 C6
Spencer Cl
　Great & Little Plumstead
　NR13...................73 B7
　11 Lingwood NR13......74 A3
　West Walton PE14......59 B8
Spencer Cres IP22......177 B5
Spencer Ct 12 IP25.....84 D3
Spencer Rd NR6........158 C5
Spencers Ct NR20.......49 E7
Spencer St NR3.........162 E8
Spens Ave NR31........170 B3
Spenser Ave NR28.....151 D4
Spenser Rd PE30.......148 B1
Spice Chase PE34.......60 C7
Spicers Corner NR19....66 B6
Spicer's La NR16.......106 B5
Spiers Way IP22........177 B4
Spindle Cl NR18.......173 D4
Spindle Dr IP24........176 F5
Spindle Rd NR6.........158 D4
Spindrift Cl 11 NR29....58 B6
Spinks La Oulton NR11...35 A7
　Wymondham NR18 .....88 B4
Spinks' La NR35.......108 D2
Spink's La NR18........173 F6
Spinners Cl IP37.......153 B5
Spinners Ct NR12.......39 A4
Spinners La PE37......153 B5
Spinner's La IP31.......29 D5
Spinney Cl Beetley NR20..49 D4
　Brandon IP27..........175 C2
　King's Lynn PE30......148 B4
　9 Long Stratton NR15..106 B4
　Norwich NR7..........163 F8
Spinney Dr NR16.......118 C4
Spinney Rd NR7........163 E8
Spinney The NR14.....110 B7
Spire Norwich Hospl
NR5 ....161 A5
Spirkett's La IP20......122 D1
Spitalfields NR1........163 A7
Spitfire Cl NR17........174 A3
Spitfire Dr
　Swaffham PE37........153 D5
　28 Watton IP25........84 F3
Spitfire Rd NR6........158 C4
SPIXWORTH NR10.......54 A2
Spixworth Inf Sch NR10..54 A2
Spixworth Rd
　Hainford NR10.........53 F4
　Horsham St Faith & Newton St
　Faith NR10............158 E5
Splashes The PE37.....153 B7
Splash Leisure Complex
NR26 ....138 D2
Spong La
　Carleton St Peter NR14...91 D5
　East Carleton NR14.....88 F4
　Shropham NR17.......103 C4
SPOONER ROW 8 NR18 ..105 A8
Spooner Row Prim Sch
NR18 ....105 A8
Spooner Row Sta NR18 .105 A8
SPORLE PE32............65 C6
Sporle CE VC Prim Sch
PE32....................65 D6
Sporle Rd
　Little Dunham PE32.....65 D4
　Swaffham PE37........153 C5
Spot La Bawsey PE32....44 C7
　South Wootton PE30....27 C1
Spratts Green NR11......36 D3

Springbank NR1 . . . . .162 E2
Spring Cl PE30 . . . . .148 C1
Spring Ct PE33 . . . . .80 D4
Springdale Cres NR13 . . .165 B4
Springdale Rd NR13 . . . .165 B4
Springfield NR13 . . . . . . .166 C3
Spring Field NR24 . . . . .18 B5
Springfield Cl
  Crimplesham PE33 . . . . . . .80 B6
  Hemsby NR29 . . . . .58 A4
  4 Weybourne NR25 . . . . . . .8 F5
Springfield N NR29 . . . . . .58 A4
Springfield Rd
  Great Yarmouth NR31 . . . .170 D4
  Hemsby NR29 . . . . .58 A4
  Norwich NR7 . . . . .159 D2
  Taverham NR8 . . . . .155 C1
  Walpole St Andrew PE14 . . .41 D4
Springfields
  Attleborough NR17 . . . . . .174 B5
  12 Poringland NR14 . . . . .90 C5
Springfield Way NR9 . . . . .86 B5
Springfield Wlk IP21 . . . .121 E5
Spring Gate La NR14 . . . . .93 A1
Spring Gr PE34 . . . . .144 B4
Spring La Forncett NR16 . .106 B5
  Hempnall NR15 . . . . .107 E3
  King's Lynn PE30 . . . . .147 C7
  North Barsham NR22 . . . . . .16 A7
  North End NR16 . . . . .103 C3
  Shouldham PE33 . . . . .62 D4
  South Creake NR22 . . . . . . .16 A6
  Yaxham NR19 . . . . .68 B6
Springlane Drove PE32 . . .46 A1
Springles The **6** NR27 . . .10 B5
Spring Rd
  Bardwell IP31 . . . . .127 A1
  Honington IP31 . . . . .126 F1
Spring Sedge **4** PE30. . .147 A8
Springs La PE32 . . . . .46 A1
Springvale **3** PE32 . . . . .45 C6
Spring View **1** PE31 . . . .12 D4
Springwell La NR9 . . . . . . .51 F6
Springwell Rd NR20. . . . . .31 D2
Spring Wlk IP24 . . . . .176 B5
Springwood
  Taverham NR8 . . . . .155 E1
  Woodton NR35. . . . . .108 A6
Springwood High Sch
  PE30 . . . . .147 C6
SPROWSTON NR7 . . . . . .159 B3
Sprowston High Sch
  NR7 . . . . .159 B3
Sprowston Inf & Jun Sch
  NR7 . . . . .159 A4
Sprowston Rd NR3. . . . . .158 F2
Sprowston Ret Pk NR7. . .159 C2
Spruce Ave **2** NR29. . . . .167 A2
Spruce Cl PE31 . . . . .133 B6
Spruce Cres **4** NR14. . . . .90 C5
Spruce Dr IP27 . . . . .175 D2
Spruce Rd PE38. . . . . .172 B6
Spurdens Cres NR28 . . . . .151 D3
Spurge Sq **3** NR18 . . . . .173 E4
Spur Ind Est NR18 . . . . . .173 D4
Spur La NR14. . . . . .90 C6
Spynke Rd NR3 . . . . .158 B3
Squire's Dr PE14. . . . . .77 E3
Squires Hill NR13 . . . . .63 B4
Squires Oak La IP25 . . . . . .66 C4
Squire's Rd NR13 . . . . .75 A2
Stablefields IP26 . . . . .99 C7
Stable Field Wy NR29 . . . .167 A7
Stable La NR28 . . . . .23 B3
Stables The **18** IP25. . . . . .84 E3
STACKSFORD NR17 . . . . .104 C1
Stacy Rd NR3 . . . . .162 E8
Staden Pk NR11 . . . . .11 D1
Stafford Ave NR5 . . . . . . .156 F1
Stafford Rd NR31 . . . . . . .169 B2
Stafford St NR2. . . . . .162 B6
Stafford Way NR13. . . . . . .72 D6
Stag Pl PE30. . . . . .147 A7
Stainsby Cl PE31. . . . . .133 D4
Staithe Cl **3** NR12 . . . . . .55 E4
Staithe La Brundall NR13 .165 D3
  Dilham NR28 . . . . .38 D4
  Thornham PE36. . . . . .2 C6
  Thornham PE36. . . . . .2 C7
Staithe Rd
  Barton Turf NR12. . . . . .38 F1
  Burgh St Peter NR34. . . . . .111 C3
  Burnham Market PE31 . . . . . .3 D3
  Catfield NR29. . . . . .56 D8
  Halvergate NR13 . . . . .166 F1
  Heacham PE31. . . . . .133 C5
  Hickling NR12 . . . . .39 E1
  Langley with Hardley NR14. .91 F4
  Ludham NR29. . . . . .56 C5
  Marthan NR29 . . . . .57 D5
  Repps with Bastwick NR29 .56 F4
  Somerton NR29 . . . . .57 E6
  Stalham NR12 . . . . .39 B3
  Wisbech PE13 . . . . .152 E5
Staithe Stree NR23. . . . . .136 D6
Staithe The
  Dunkirk NR11. . . . . .150 D8
  Thurne NR29 . . . . .56 E2
Staitheway Rd NR12 . . . .164 C4
Staith Rd NR31 . . . . .93 E4
Stake Bridge Rd NR10. . . .37 B3
STALHAM NR12. . . . . .39 B4
Stalham Com Inf Sch
  NR12 . . . . .39 B4
Stalham Firehouse Mus *
  NR12 . . . . .39 B3
STALHAM GREEN NR12 . .39 C3
Stalham High Sch NR12 . .39 B4
Stalham Inf & Jun Sch
  NR12 . . . . .39 B3

Stalham Rd
  Ashmanhaugh NR12 . . . . . .55 C8
  Happisburgh Common
    NR12 . . . . .39 A7
  Hickling NR12 . . . . .39 E2
  Sea Palling NR12 . . . . .24 F1
  Wroxham/Hoveton NR12 . .164 D6
STALLAND COMMON
  NR17. . . . . .86 C1
Stalland La NR18 . . . . .86 D2
Stalland The NR18 . . . . . . .86 D2
Stallett Way PE34 . . . . . . .60 C8
Stammers Yard NR20 . . . .154 F5
Standard Pl **10** NR30 . . . .169 D3
Standard Rd
  Great Yarmouth NR30 . . . .169 E3
  Wells-next-the-Sea NR23 . .136 D6
Standley Ct NR18 . . . . . . .173 B4
STANFIELD NR20 . . . . . . .48 F7
Stanfield Rd Brisley NR20 .49 A7
  Mileham PE32 . . . . .48 E6
  Tittleshall PE32 . . . . .48 C7
  Wymondham NR18 . . . . . .173 F3
STANFORD IP24 . . . . .101 A5
Stanford Cres NR13. . . . . .73 B7
Stanford Ct NR5 . . . . .161 E6
Stanford Rd
  Lynford IP27 . . . . .100 C1
  Thetford IP24 . . . . .176 D6
  Weeting-with-Broomhill
    IP27. . . . . .115 A8
Stanford Tuck Rd NR28 . .153 F2
STANHOE PE31 . . . . .14 E8
Stanhoe Rd
  Burnham Market PE31 . . . .135 A1
  Docking PE31. . . . . .134 E4
  Great Bircham PE31 . . . . . .14 B3
  Muckleton PE31. . . . . .3 F2
  North Creake NR21. . . . . . . .4 B1
  Stanhoe PE31 . . . . .14 F8
Staniforth Rd IP24 . . . . . .176 B2
Stanley Ave
  Great Yarmouth NR31 . . . .170 C3
  Neatishead NR12 . . . . .55 E7
  Norwich NR7 . . . . .163 C5
Stanley Cl NR13 . . . . .92 B6
Stanley Dr
  11 East Harling NR16. . . . .118 C5
  Sutton Bridge PE12. . . . . . .41 A8
Stanley Rd
  Brundall NR13 . . . . .165 E4
  Diss IP22 . . . . .177 B4
  Great Yarmouth NR30 . . . .169 C5
  North Walsham NR28 . . .151 B4
Stanleys La NR18 . . . . . . .173 C2
Stanley St **10** PE30 . . . . .146 E5
Stanley Terr NR30 . . . . . . .169 D4
Stanley Trett Cl NR13 . . . .165 D8
Stanmore Rd NR7. . . . . . .163 E6
Stannard Cl **4** 177 C4
Stannard Rd NR4 . . . . . . .161 F5
Stanninghall Rd NR12. . . . .54 B4
Stan Petersen Cl NR1. . . .163 A6
STANTON CHARE IP31 . . .127 B1
Stanton Chare IP31. . . . . .127 B1
Stanton Rd
  Barningham IP31. . . . . . . .127 C4
  Dersingham PE31 . . . . . . .140 C3
  Stanton Chare IP31. . . . . .127 B1
Stantons Track NR22. . . . . .16 D7
Star Farm Cl IP31 NR31 . . .94 C6
Star Hill NR12 . . . . .24 C3
Stark Cl IP22 . . . . .177 C4
Star La
  Long Stratton NR15. . . . . .106 E3
  Rockland St Mary NR14. . . .91 B6
  1 Thetford IP24 . . . . . . .176 C3
  Tivetshall St Margaret
    NR15 . . . . .121 C5
Starling Ave **9** NR7 . . . .159 E4
Starling Cl NR11 . . . . .150 C5
Starling Rd NR3 . . . . .162 D8
Starling Rise NR27. . . . . . .11 B2
Starlings Wy NR9 . . . . . . .51 D5
Star Mdw NR13 . . . . .141 B4
Star Piece NR14 . . . . .91 B6
STARSTON IP20 . . . . .122 C3
Starston La IP20. . . . . .122 C1
Starston Rd IP20 . . . . .122 C8
Statham Cl NR4. . . . . .162 B2
Station App
  Norwich NR1. . . . . .178 C2
  12 Sheringham NR26 . . . .138 D7
  Wymondham NR18 . . . . . .173 C2
Station Cl
  East Dereham NR19 . . . . . .154 D6
  4 Lingwood NR13 . . . . . . .74 A3
  6 Marthan NR29 . . . . . . .57 D4
  Sheringham NR27 . . . . .10 A5
  Swainsthorpe NR14. . . . . . .89 D4
Station Dr Fransham NR19. .66 A8
  Reedham NR13 . . . . .92 F5
  Wisbech PE13 . . . . .152 C4
Station Drove CB7 . . . . . .112 B2
Station Gdns PE13 . . . . . .153 B5
Station Halt NR13. . . . . . .165 B3
Station Hill IP20 . . . . .122 D2
Station La
  Garvestone NR9 . . . . .68 D1
  Hethersett NR9 . . . . .88 E7
  Thetford IP24 . . . . .176 C5
  Thornham PE36. . . . . .2 C6
Station New Rd NR13 . . . .165 D3
Station Rd Acle NR13 . . . .166 B2
  Alburgh IP20 . . . . .123 A5
  Aldeby NR34 . . . . .110 F6
  Attleborough NR17 . . . . . .174 E5
  Attlebridge NR9 . . . . .52 A4
  Aylsham NR11 . . . . .150 D6
  Barnham IP24 . . . . .125 E6
  Beccles NR34. . . . . .110 D1

Station Rd continued
  Brundall NR13 . . . . .165 D2
  Burnham Market PE31 . . . .135 C3
  Burston & Shimpling IP21 .120 F2
  Cantley NR13 . . . . .92 C6
  Clenchwarton PE34 . . . . . .145 B4
  Coltishall NR12 . . . . .54 C7
  Congham PE32. . . . . .27 F3
  Corpusty NR11. . . . . .19 F1
  Cromer NR27. . . . . .139 D5
  Dersingham PE31 . . . . . . .140 B4
  Diss IP22 . . . . .177 F3
  Ditchingham NR35. . . . . . .109 B2
  Docking PE31. . . . . .134 D5
  Downham Market PE38. . . .172 A5
  2 Earsham NR35. . . . . . . .123 F8
  East Dereham NR19 . . . . . .154 E4
  East Rudham PE31 . . . . .30 B5
  East Winch PE32 . . . . .44 F3
  Ellingham NR35. . . . . .109 D3
  Flordon NR15. . . . . .106 E8
  Forncett NR16 . . . . .106 C4
  Foul Anchor PE13 . . . . .41 A4
  Foulsham NR20 . . . . .33 C3
  Fransham NR19 . . . . .66 B7
  Fulmodeston NR21 . . . . . . .17 F4
  Geldeston NR34. . . . . .109 F2
  Great Moulton NR15 . . . . .121 A4
  Great Ryburgh NR21 . . . . . .32 B6
  Great Yarmouth NR31 . . . .169 B3
  Guestwick NR20 . . . . .33 F5
  Haddiscoe NR31 . . . . .93 D1
  Hardingham NR9 . . . . .86 E8
  Harleston IP20 . . . . .122 D2
  Heacham PE31. . . . . .133 D6
  Hilgay PE38 . . . . .96 C6
  Hillington PE31 . . . . .28 C4
  Hindolveston NR20 . . . . . . .33 E8
  Holme Hale PE25 . . . . .65 F2
  Holt NR25. . . . . .137 C6
  Honing NR28 . . . . .38 C6
  Hopton on Sea NR31. . . . .171 D4
  Kimberley NR18. . . . . .87 A6
  King's Lynn PE30 . . . . .148 B5
  Lakenheath IP27 . . . . .112 E3
  Lenwade NR9. . . . . .51 E5
  Lingwood & Burlingham
    NR13. . . . . .74 A3
  Little Dunham PE32 . . . . . . .65 F3
  Middleton PE32 . . . . .44 C4
  Mundesley NR11 . . . . .143 B6
  North Elmham NR20 . . . . . .49 F7
  North Walsham NR28 . . .151 B4
  Ormesby St Margaret with
    Scratby NR29 . . . . .167 B2
  5 Potter Heigham NR29 . .56 F6
  Pulham Market IP21 . . . . . .121 E4
  Pulham St Mary IP21 . . . . .122 A4
  Quidenham NR16. . . . . . . .118 E8
  Rackheath/Salhouse NR13 .72 F8
  Reedham NR13 . . . . .92 F5
  Reepham NR10 . . . . .149 C5
  Roydon PE32 . . . . .28 A2
  Sheringham NR26 . . . . . . .138 D7
  6 Sheringham NR27 . . . . . .10 A5
  Snettisham PE31 . . . . .12 D4
  Somerleyton, Ashby &
    Herringfleet NR32 . . . . .111 C7
  South Wootton PE31 . . . . .149 C5
  Stanhoe PE31 . . . . .14 E8
  Strumpshaw NR13. . . . . . . .73 E1
  Strumpshaw NR13. . . . . . . .91 F8
  Taverham NR8 . . . . .156 F8
  Terrington St Clement
    PE34. . . . . .144 C2
  Thetford IP24 . . . . .176 C5
  Thorpe Market NR11. . . . . .22 A4
  Tilney All Saints PE34 . . . .144 F2
  Tivetshall St Margaret
    NR15 . . . . .121 B7
  Walpole Cross Keys PE14. . .41 F5
  Walsingham NR22. . . . . . . .16 F7
  Walsoken PE14 . . . . .59 E4
  Watlington PE33 . . . . .61 C6
  Wells-next-the-Sea NR23 . .136 D5
  Wendling NR19 . . . . .66 F7
  West Dereham PE33 . . . . . .80 B3
  Weybourne NR25. . . . . .8 F5
  Whinburgh & Westfield
    NR19 . . . . .67 F5
  Whinburgh & Westfield
    NR19 . . . . .68 A5
  Wolferton PE31 . . . . .27 C7
  Worstead NR28. . . . . .37 F3
  Wroxham/Hoveton NR12 .164 C5
  Wymondham NR18 . . . . . .173 C2
Station Rd Ind Est NR17 .174 E4
Station Rd N NR31 . . . . . . .93 F6
Station Rd S
  Belton NR31. . . . . .93 F5
  Walpole Cross Keys PE14. . .41 F5
Station Terr IP27 . . . . .175 C5
Station Way IP27 . . . . .175 C5
Station Yd PE13 . . . . .153 B5
Steading Mws IP25 . . . . . . .66 A1
Steam Mill La NR31 . . . . .169 B4
Stearn Cl NR9 . . . . .70 B5
Stearne Cl IP24. . . . . .176 B2
Stebbings Cl **3** PE32. . . . .28 A1
Steel's Dro PE38 . . . . .79 C1
Steepgreen Cl NR1 . . . . .163 C8
Steeple Chase NR8 . . . . . .155 F2
Steeple La NR15 . . . . .106 A2
Steeple View
  Swaffham PE13 . . . . .153 B4
  Wisbech PE13 . . . . .152 E7
Steeps The **6** NR30. . . . .169 D1
Steer Rd NR31 . . . . .27 B8
Steggles Dr IP22 . . . . .177 C5
Stegg's La NR19 . . . . .67 E4

Stephen Beaumont Way
  NR19 . . . . .154 F2
Stephen Cl
  3 Great Yarmouth
    NR30. . . . . .169 D5
  West Raynham Airfield
    PE31 . . . . .30 B3
Stephenson Way IP24. . . .176 A2
Stephenson Way Ind Est
  IP24. . . . . .176 A2
Stepping La NR1. . . . . . . .178 B2
Steppings La NR15. . . . . . .107 C3
Stepping Stone La12 . . . .39 A4
Stepshort NR31. . . . . .94 A6
Sterlet Gr NR14. . . . . .89 B3
Sterling Cl NR35 . . . . .109 D8
Stermyn St **22** PE13 . . . . .152 C5
Steven Cres PE38 . . . . .96 E7
Steven Drane Dr NR8 . . . .155 B3
Stevens Cl IP25. . . . . .84 D4
Steven's La
  Ashwellthorpe NR16 . . . . .106 B8
  Wreningham NR16 . . . . .88 E1
Stevenson Rd
  Norwich NR5 . . . . .161 B7
  Wroxham NR12 . . . . .164 B2
Stevens Rd Cromer NR27 .139 C4
  2 Little Snoring NR21 . . . .17 B3
Steward Cl
  Saxlingham Nethergate
    NR15 . . . . .107 B8
  1 Sheringham NR18. . . .173 D5
Stewards Cl NR10. . . . . . .149 C4
Steward St **4** NR3. . . . . .162 E8
Steward Way NR19. . . . . .154 C5
Stewart Cl NR16 . . . . .120 E8
Stewkis Hall Drift NR9 . . . .51 B6
STIBBARD NR21 . . . . .32 F7
Stibbard Rd
  Fulmodeston NR21 . . . . . . .17 F1
  Stibbard NR21. . . . . .32 E8
  Wood Norton NR20 . . . . . . .33 A6
Stickfast La PE14 . . . . .41 E4
Stickfer La NR16 . . . . .106 A6
Stickleback La **2** PE30. . .146 E2
STIFFKEY NR23. . . . . .5 F5
Stiffkey Cl **8** PE33. . . . . . .61 D6
Stiffkey Rd Warham NR23 . . .5 F5
  Wells-next-the-Sea NR23 .136 F5
  Westgate NR25 . . . . .4 E3
Stigand's Gate NR19 . . . . .154 D7
Stile Cl **12** NR14. . . . . .89 B3
Stile La NR18 . . . . .173 B5
Stileman Way **11** PE31 . . .12 E4
Stillington Cl NR7. . . . . . .159 B3
Stilwell Dr NR19 . . . . .154 B6
Stimpson Loke NR8 . . . . . .157 A3
Stirling Cl
  Downham Market PE38. . . .172 D6
  Taverham NR8 . . . . .155 F3
Stirling Rd
  Old Catton NR6 . . . . .158 C6
  Sculthorpe Airfield NR21. . .15 C3
Stirrups La NR32. . . . . . . .171 E1
Stitch The PE14. . . . . .77 B8
Stockdale Chase PE34 . . . .60 C7
Stockholm Way NR19 . . . .154 C2
Stock Lea Rd **1** PE30 . . . .148 C4
Stocks Cl PE31. . . . . .14 B3
Stocks Hill NR9 . . . . .160 B5
Stockshill Sq PE14. . . . . . . .59 F8
Stocks La NR13 . . . . .165 C5
Stocks Loke NR10 . . . . .35 B2
STOCKTON NR34 . . . . . . .109 F4
Stockton Rd NR34 . . . . . . .110 A3
Stockwell Rd NR8. . . . . . .156 A5
STODY NR24 . . . . .18 F6
Stody Dr PE30 . . . . .148 E1
Stody Rd Brinton NR24 . . . .18 D6
  Hunworth NR24. . . . . .19 A6
  Stody NR25 . . . . .18 E6
STOKE FERRY PE33 . . . . . .80 F3
Stokeferry Rd PE33 . . . . . .81 E4
Stoke Ferry Rd
  Barton Bendish PE33. . . . . .81 C5
  Boughton PE33 . . . . .81 A4
STOKE HOLY CROSS
  NR14 . . . . .89 F4
Stoke Holy Cross Prim Sch
  NR14 . . . . .89 F4
Stoke La NR14 . . . . .89 F5
Stoke Rd Bixley NR14 . . . .162 F1
  Boughton PE33 . . . . .81 A4
  Caistor St Edmund NR14. . . .89 F7
  Methwold IP26 . . . . .99 A6
  Poringland NR14 . . . . .90 B5
  Wereham PE33 . . . . .80 E4
  Wormegay PE33 . . . . .62 A5
Stokes Ave IP25. . . . . .84 C3
STOKESBY NR29. . . . . .75 A5
Stokesby New Rd NR13. . .166 F6
Stokesby Rd NR29 . . . . . . .75 B6
Stone Barn Ct PE32. . . . . . .46 F2
Stone Beck La NR24. . . . . .142 E3
Stone Breck NR5 . . . . .156 E2
STONEBRIDGE IP24. . . . . .102 B1
Stonebridge Rd NR28 . . . . .23 F2
Stone Brigg NR18. . . . . . . .87 A7
Stone Cl **2** PE33. . . . . .61 D5
Stone Corner NR13 . . . . . . .74 C3
Stone Cross La
  Denver PE38 . . . . .79 D5
  Downham Market PE38. . . .172 D6
Stonecross Rd
  Downham Market PE38. . . .172 D6
  Downham Market PE38. . . .172 D6
Stonecutters Way NR30 .169 C4
Stonecroft Rd
  Baconsthorpe NR25. . . . . . .20 A8
  Baconsthorpe NR25. . . . . . .20 B8
Stonegate Aylsham NR11 .150 A3

Stonegate continued
  Morley NR18 . . . . .87 A3
Stonegate St NR30. . . . . .146 D4
Stone Hill Rd NR30. . . . . .168 D6
Stonehill Way NR27. . . . . .10 C4
Stonehill Way Ind Est
  NR27 . . . . .10 C4
Stone House Rd
  Norwich NR7 . . . . .159 B4
  Salhouse NR13 . . . . .54 F7
  Upwell PE14. . . . . .77 E5
Stone La
  Ashmanhaugh NR12 . . . . . .38 B1
  Bintree NR20 . . . . .33 B3
  Blo' Norton IP22 . . . . .128 C6
  Bressingham IP22. . . . . . . .119 F2
  Hoveton NR12 . . . . .164 D6
  Langley with Hardley NR14. .91 F5
  Runhall NR9 . . . . .68 F3
Stonemasons Ct NR13 . . .166 C3
Stone Rd **6** Beetley NR20 . .49 D4
  Briston NR24. . . . . .142 E2
  East Dereham NR19 . . . . . .154 C2
  Great Yarmouth NR31 . . . .169 B4
  Halvergate NR13 . . . . .75 A1
  Hockering NR20 . . . . .51 B1
  Mattishall NR20. . . . . .68 C6
  Norwich NR3 . . . . .158 C1
  Strumpshaw NR13 . . . . . . .73 F1
  Yaxham NR19. . . . . .68 B4
Stone St
  St Lawrence, Ilketshall
    NR35. . . . . .124 D4
  Stone Street IP19 . . . . . . .124 D1
STONE STREET IP19 . . . . .124 F1
Stoney End **2** NR20. . . . . .68 F6
Stoney La Beetley NR20 . . . .49 B4
  Reepham NR10 . . . . .149 B6
Stoney Rd PE32 . . . . .27 F2
Stony Gr **2** NR8 . . . . .70 C7
Stony La
  Attleborough NR17 . . . . . .174 B6
  Raveningham NR14 . . . . . .110 B6
  Wortwell IP20 . . . . .122 F4
Stony Rd
  Pulham Market IP21 . . . . . .121 E7
  Tivetshall St Margaret
    NR15 . . . . .121 B5
Storbeck Rd **2** PE13. . . . .152 D7
Stores St IP27 . . . . .175 C3
Storey's Loke NR27 . . . . . .11 A2
Story's La NR16. . . . . .105 E5
STOW BARDOLPH PE34 . . .79 E8
Stow Barn Rd PE33 . . . . . .80 A7
STOW BEDON NR17. . . . . .102 E7
Stow Bedon Rd
  Caston NR17 . . . . .102 E8
  Thompson PE32 . . . . .102 C7
Stowborough La
  Gayton PE32 . . . . .46 A5
  Gayton Thorpe PE32 . . . . . .45 F4
STOW BRIDGE PE34. . . . . .61 B2
Stow Bridge Rd
  Stow Bardolph PE34 . . . . . .61 D1
  Wimbotsham PE34 . . . . . . .79 E8
Stowfields PE38 . . . . .172 C6
Stow Gdns PE13 . . . . .152 E4
Stowheath Rd NR28. . . . . .36 F6
Stow La PE13 . . . . .152 E4
Stowlay La NR17. . . . . . . .103 B6
Stow Rd Outwell PE14 . . . .78 A7
  Runcton Holme PE33. . . . . .62 B3
  Stow Bedon PE32 . . . . . . .102 E7
  Wiggenhall St Mary Magdalen
    PE34. . . . . .61 B3
  Wisbech PE13 . . . . .152 F5
Stow Windmill * NR28 . . .143 D4
Stracey Rd Lamas NR10 . . .36 F1
  Norwich NR1 . . . . .163 A5
Strachan Cl PE31 . . . . .133 E5
STRADBROKE IP21 . . . . . .131 E1
Stradbroke CE VC Prim Sch
  IP21. . . . . .131 E1
Stradbroke Prim Sch
  NR31 . . . . .170 D5
Stradbroke Rd
  Battlesea Green IP21 . . . . .131 E2
  Great Yarmouth NR31 . . . .170 C5
  Hoxne IP21 . . . . .131 B4
STRADSETT PE33 . . . . .80 D8
Stradsett Cl **4** PE38 . . . . .172 D6
Straight La **10** IP20 . . . . .122 D2
Strangers Hall * NR2 . . . .178 A3
Stranton Ave NR19. . . . . . .68 B3
Strasbourg Way NR14 . . . .154 B1
Stratford Cl
  Dersingham PE31 . . . . . . .140 E3
  Norwich NR1. . . . . .162 F2
Stratford Cres NR4 . . . . . .161 C1
Stratford Dr NR1. . . . . . . .162 E3
Stratton Cl **6** PE37 . . . . .153 C3
Stratton Rd Hainford NR10. .53 E6
  Stratton Strawless NR10. . . .53 F8
  Wacton NR15. . . . . .106 D2
STRATTON ST MICHAEL
  NR15 . . . . .106 F4
STRATTON STRAWLESS
  NR10. . . . . .53 E7
Strawberry Cl **3** NR13 . . .92 B6
Strawberry Fields NR12. . . .39 B3
Strawberry La NR11. . . . . . .20 A1
Straw Mus The * NR11 . . .21 D3
Strayground La NR18 . . . .173 B2
Street Farm Loke NR20. . . .49 E7
Street Hill NR26. . . . . .55 E7
Street The Acle NR13 . . . .166 C2
  Alburgh IP20 . . . . .122 F6
  Aldborough NR11. . . . . . . .20 F5
  Aldeby NR34 . . . . .110 F4

Street The continued
  Ashby St Mary NR14 . . . . . .91 C5
  Aylmerton NR11. . . . . .10 A2
  Baconsthorpe NR25. . . . . . .19 F8
  Bacton NR28 . . . . .23 B2
  Barnham IP24 . . . . .125 E6
  Barton Turf NR12 . . . . .38 F1
  Barton Turf NR12 . . . . .55 E8
  Bawdeswell NR20 . . . . .50 E7
  Beachamwell PE37 . . . . . . .81 E8
  Beeston with Bittering
    PE32 . . . . .48 C2
  Belaugh NR12 . . . . .164 A6
  Bergh Apton NR15. . . . . . . .91 A3
  Billingford NR20 . . . . .50 B7
  Bintree NR20 . . . . .33 B2
  Blo' Norton IP22 . . . . .128 B6
  Booton NR10 . . . . .149 E4
  Botesdale IP22 . . . . .128 C2
  Bracon Ash NR14. . . . . .89 A3
  Bramerton NR14 . . . . .90 F7
  Brampton NR10. . . . . .36 B3
  Brandon IP27. . . . . .175 A3
  Bressingham IP22. . . . . . . .119 D2
  Bridgham NR16 . . . . .117 E4
  Bridgham NR16 . . . . .118 A5
  Brinton NR24 . . . . .18 D6
  Brockdish IP21 . . . . .131 D6
  Brome & Oakley IP23 . . . .130 C3
  Brooke NR15. . . . . .90 E2
  Brundall NR13 . . . . .165 E5
  Burgh & Tuttington NR11. . .36 E4
  Caston NR17 . . . . .102 E8
  Catfield NR29. . . . . .56 C8
  Claxton NR14. . . . . .91 D6
  Cockthorpe NR25. . . . . .6 E5
  Coltishall NR12 . . . . .54 E7
  Coney Weston IP31 . . . . . .127 B4
  Corpusty NR11. . . . . .19 F1
  Costessey NR8. . . . . .156 E5
  Croxton IP24 . . . . .116 C6
  Dickleburgh IP21 . . . . .121 B1
  Dilham NR28 . . . . .38 D4
  Earsham NR35. . . . . .123 F8
  East Tuddenham NR20. . . . .69 C6
  Erpingham NR11 . . . . .21 A1
  Euston IP24 . . . . .126 B6
  Felthorpe NR10 . . . . .155 C8
  Flixton NR35 . . . . .123 E6
  Foxley NR20. . . . . .50 D8
  Framingham Pigot NR14 . . .90 C7
  Fulmodeston NR21 . . . . . . .17 F3
  Garvestone NR9 . . . . .68 B1
  Geldeston NR34. . . . . .109 F2
  Gooderstone PE33. . . . . . . .81 F5
  Great Cressingham IP25. . . .83 C4
  Great Snoring NR21 . . . . . .17 A5
  Great Yarmouth NR30 . . . . .76 F5
  Haddiscoe NR14 . . . . .110 F7
  Halvergate NR13 . . . . .74 F1
  Happisburgh NR12 . . . . . . .24 C5
  Hempnall NR15 . . . . .107 C5
  Hemsby NR29 . . . . .167 A7
  Hevingham NR10. . . . . .53 C8
  Heydon NR11 . . . . .34 F6
  Hickling NR12 . . . . .39 F2
  Hindercay IP22. . . . . .128 C3
  Hindolveston NR20 . . . . . . .33 D8
  Hindringham NR21 . . . . . . .17 E7
  Hockering NR20. . . . . .69 B8
  Honing NR28 . . . . .38 C6
  Honingham NR9 . . . . .69 E6
  Horsey NR29 . . . . .40 E1
  Houghton PE31 . . . . .29 D6
  Ingworth NR11 . . . . .36 B8
  Itteringham NR11 . . . . .20 C1
  Kelling NR25 . . . . .8 C5
  Ketteringham NR18. . . . . . .88 E6
  Kettlestone NR21. . . . . .17 C2
  Kirby Bedon NR14 . . . . .90 E8
  Knapton NR28 . . . . .143 B1
  Lamas NR10. . . . . .37 A1
  Lenwade NR9. . . . . .51 D5
  Lessingham NR12 . . . . .24 D3
  Little Barningham NR11 . . . .20 B4
  Little Dunham PE32. . . . . . .65 E7
  Little Snoring NR21 . . . . . . .17 B3
  Lound NR32 . . . . .94 C2
  Marham PE33 . . . . .63 B5
  Market Weston IP22 . . . . . .127 E4
  Marlingford NR9 . . . . .69 E4
  Mautby NR29 . . . . .75 E5
  Mileham PE32 . . . . .48 D6
  Morning Thorpe NR15 . . . .107 C4
  Morston NR25. . . . . .7 A6
  Morton on the Hill NR9 . . . .52 A3
  North Lopham IP22. . . . . . .119 A2
  North Pickenham PE37. . . . .65 E1
  Norwich NR14 . . . . .163 B2
  Oulton Street NR11. . . . . . .35 C5
  Ovington IP25 . . . . .84 C5
  Paston Green NR28. . . . . . .23 B5
  Poringland NR14 . . . . .90 C5
  Pulham St Mary IP21 . . . . .122 A4
  Pulham St Mary IP21 . . . . .121 F4
  Redenhall with Harleston
    IP20. . . . . .122 F1
  Redgrave IP22 . . . . .128 E5
  Reepham NR10 . . . . .149 C5
  Riddlesworth IP22. . . . . . . .127 D7
  Ringland NR8 . . . . .70 D8
  Rocklands NR17. . . . . .103 C7
  Rockland St Mary NR14. . . .91 B7
  Rougham PE32. . . . . .47 B7
  Rushall IP21 . . . . .122 C5
  Ryburgh NR21 . . . . .32 C7
  St Margaret, South Elmham
    IP20. . . . . .123 E2

Street The *continued*

Salle NR10 . . . . .149 D8
Saxlingham Nethergate
  NR15 . . . . .107 B8
Scoulton NR9 . . . . .85 D3
Sculthorpe NR21 . . . . .16 B1
Sculthorpe Airfield PE31 . . .15 B3
Sea Palling NR12 . . . . .40 A5
Shelton NR15 . . . . .122 B8
Shotesham NR15 . . . . .90 A2
Somerleyton, Ashby &
  Herringfleet NR32 . . . . .111 D8
Somerton NR29 . . . . .57 F6
South Lopham IP22 . . . . . . .65 C8
South Pickenham PE37 . . . .83 D7
South Walsham NR13 . . . . .74 A8
Sparham NR9 . . . . .51 B4
Sporle with Palgrave PE32 . .65 C7
Starston IP20 . . . . .122 C3
Suffield NR11 . . . . .21 F3
Surlingham NR14 . . . . . . .165 B1
Sustead NR11 . . . . .20 E7
Sustead NR11 . . . . .21 A8
Swafield NR28 . . . . .22 E3
Swafield NR28 . . . . .151 D8
Swanton Abbott NR10 . . . . .37 C4
Swanton Novers NR24 . . . . .18 C2
Tatterford NR21 . . . . .30 E7
Tattersett PE31 . . . . .30 C8
Taverham NR8 . . . . .156 B8
Themelthorpe NR20 . . . . . .33 F2
Themelthorpe NR20 . . . . . .33 F3
Thornage NR25 . . . . .18 E6
Thornage NR25 . . . . .18 E7
Thurlton NR14 . . . . .92 F1
Thurne NR29 . . . . .56 E2
Thurton NR14 . . . . .91 C3
Tibenham NR16 . . . . .120 E8
Tivetshall St Mary NR15 . .121 B5
Topcroft NR35 . . . . .107 F3
Upper Sheringham NR26 . . .9 C4
Warham NR23 . . . . .5 F4
Warham NR23 . . . . .6 A4
Waterloo IP21 . . . . .130 C5
Wattisfield IP22 . . . . .128 A1
Wellingham PE32 . . . . .47 F8
West Beckham NR25 . . . . . .9 B2
Weybourne NR25 . . . . .8 E5
Winfarthing IP22 . . . . . . .120 B4
Witton NR28 . . . . .23 E1
Wiveton NR25 . . . . .7 E6
Woodbastwick NR13 . . . . . .55 C2
Woodton NR35 . . . . .108 C5
Wramplingham NR18 . . . . .69 F1
Stretton Sch NR2 . . . . . . .162 C3
Strickland Ave **9** PE31 . . .12 E4
Strickland Cl **8** PE31 . . . .12 E4
Stringers La NR20 . . . . . . .33 C3
Stringside Dro PE33 . . . . . .81 B3
STRUMPSHAW NR13 . . . .73 F2
Strumpshaw Rd
  Brundall NR13 . . . . .165 E3
  Brundall NR13 . . . . .165 F2
  Lingwood & Burlingham
   NR13 . . . . .74 A2
  Strumpshaw NR13 . . . . . .74 A1
  Strumpshaw NR13 . . . . . .92 B8
Strumpshaw Steam Mus ★
  NR13 . . . . .73 E1
Stuart Cl Brandon IP27 . . .175 C2
  Great Yarmouth NR31 . . .170 B4
  7 Hethersett NR9 . . . . . .88 D8
Stuart Dr **2** IP24 . . . . . . .116 A2
Stuart Gdns NR1 . . . . .178 C3
Stuart Rd Aylsham NR11 . .150 C7
  Norwich NR1 . . . . .178 C1
STUBB NR12 . . . . .39 F1
STUBBING'S GREEN
  IP22 . . . . .129 A1
Stubb La NR35 . . . . .124 B2
Stubb Mill La NR29 . . . . . .57 B8
Stubb Rd NR12 . . . . .39 F2
Stubbs Cl
  Downham Market PE38 . .172 E5
  Wymondham NR18 . . . . .173 A2
Stubbs Gn La NR14 . . . . . .109 C8
STUBBS GREEN NR14 . . .109 C8
Stump Cross La NR11 . . . . .22 C7
Sturdee Ave NR30 . . . . . .169 D8
Sturdee Cl IP24 . . . . .176 F6
Sturmy Cl **15** NR15 . . . . . .106 E3
STUSTON IP21 . . . . .130 B5
Stuston Bypass IP22 . . . . .177 F1
Stuston La IP21 . . . . .130 B4
Stuston Rd IP21 . . . . .130 B5
Style Loke NR9 . . . . .69 F2
Styleman Rd PE36 . . . . . . .132 D4
Styles Cl NR31 . . . . .170 A4
Stylman Rd NR1 . . . . .161 A7
Suckling Ave NR3 . . . . . . .158 B3
Suckling Dro PE14 . . . . . . .78 C5
Suckling La
  Framingham Pigot NR14 . .90 D6
  Hethersett NR9 . . . . .88 E7
  Hickling NR12 . . . . .39 F1
Suckling Pl NR35 . . . . . . .108 C5
SUFFIELD NR11 . . . . .21 F3
Suffield Cl
  7 Cringleford NR4 . . . . . .89 B8
  3 Long Stratton NR15 . .106 D3
  North Walsham NR28 . . .151 A4
Suffield Ct NR6 . . . . .158 D2
Suffield Pk Inf Sch
  NR27 . . . . .139 C5
Suffield Rd
  Great Yarmouth NR31 . . .170 C4
  Suffield NR11 . . . . .21 F3
Suffield Way PE30 . . . . . .147 B8

Suffling Rd NR30 . . . . . . .170 D8
Suffolk Ave IP31 . . . . .126 B1
Suffolk Cl
  Great Yarmouth NR31 . . .170 C7
  11 Hopton On Sea NR31 . .171 D4
Suffolk Pl IP19 . . . . .154 C1
Suffolk Rd
  Great Yarmouth NR31 . . .170 C8
  King's Lynn PE30 . . . . . .147 C6
  Norwich NR4 . . . . .161 C3
  Sheringham NR26 . . . . . .138 D6
Suffolk Sq NR2 . . . . .162 C5
Suffolk Wlk NR4 . . . . .161 D3
Sugar La NR1 . . . . .140 E4
Sukey Way NR5 . . . . .160 F6
Sultan Rd NR31 . . . . .169 E3
Summer Cl
  13 Framingham Earl
   NR14 . . . . .90 D5
  4 Walpole St Andrew
   PE14 . . . . .41 E4
Summer Dr NR12 . . . . .164 D6
SUMMERFIELD PE31 . . . . . .2 E1
Summerfield Cl PE13 . . . . .152 A6
Summerfield Rd NR29 . . . . .58 A4
Summerhouse CI NR27 . . .139 A6
Summer La
  Candle Street IP22 . . . . .128 D1
  Carbrooke IP25 . . . . .85 A4
Summerwood Est PE32 . . . .29 D2
Sumpter Rd NR4 . . . . .161 E3
Sunart Cl NR17 . . . . .174 E6
Sun Barn Rd NR10 . . . . . .149 B4
Sun Barn Wlk NR10 . . . . .149 B4
Suncroft NR1 . . . . .162 F2
Sunderland Cl NR6 . . . . . .158 C6
Sundew Cl
  Caister-On-Sea NR30 . . .168 E4
  6 Thetford IP24 . . . . . .176 F4
Sunk Rd NR22 . . . . .16 F7
Sun La
  Great Yarmouth NR31 . . .94 C6
  Norwich NR3 . . . . .158 D1
Sunley Cl NR35 . . . . .109 C2
Sunningdale NR4 . . . . .162 A2
Sunninghill Cl
  18 Bradwell NR31 . . . . . .94 C8
  14 Great Yarmouth NR31 . .94 C8
Sunny Cl NR5 . . . . .157 B1
Sunny Cnr NR28 . . . . .151 B4
Sunny Gr NR5 . . . . .161 B8
Sunny Hill NR1 . . . . .162 E2
Sunnyside
  Bedingham NR35 . . . . . .108 C4
  Bergh Apton NR15 . . . . . .91 C2
  Diss IP22 . . . . .177 D5
  Heacham NR31 . . . . .133 D5
Sunnyside Ave **10** NR14 . . .90 C5
Sunnyside Cl NR35 . . . . . .133 D5
Sunnyside Rd PE32 . . . . . .29 D2
Sun Rd NR35 . . . . .109 B2
Sunsalve Ride NR19 . . . . .154 C1
Sunset Gdns PE13 . . . . . .152 E2
Sunset Wlk NR12 . . . . .24 E4
Supple Cl NR1 . . . . .163 C7
SURLINGHAM NR14 . . . . .73 B1
Surlingham Com Prim Sch
  NR14 . . . . .73 B1
Surlingham Dr PE37 . . . . .153 B1
Surlingham La
  Bramerton NR14 . . . . . . .90 F8
  Rockland St Mary NR14 . . .91 B8
Surrey Cl NR7 . . . . .159 C5
Surrey Gr NR1 . . . . .178 B1
Surrey St Cromer NR27 . . .139 C7
  6 King's Lynn PE30 . . . .146 D5
  Norwich NR1 . . . . .178 B2
Swan Terr **1** PE38 . . . . . .172 A6
  6 Wiggenhall St Germans
   PE34 . . . . .43 B1
Surrogate St NR17 . . . . . .174 D5
Sursham Ave NR6 . . . . . . .158 F4
Suspension Bridge PE14 . . .95 E3
Sussex Rd NR3 . . . . .170 D5
Sussex St NR3 . . . . .178 A4
SUSTEAD NR11 . . . . .21 A7
Sustead La NR11 . . . . .20 F8
Sustead Rd
  Aylmerton NR11 . . . . .10 A2
  Gresham NR11 . . . . .9 F1
  Sustead NR25 . . . . .20 F8
Susted Rd NR11 . . . . .21 A6
Suters Dr NR8 . . . . .155 E2
Sutherland Ave NR6 . . . . .158 A4
Sutherland Ct Gdns
  NR27 . . . . .139 C6
SUTON NR18 . . . . .87 D2
Suton La NR18 . . . . .173 A1
Suton St NR18 . . . . .87 D1
SUTTON NR12 . . . . .39 C3
SUTTON BRIDGE PE12 . . . .41 B7
Sutton Bridge Westmere
  Comm Prim Sch PE12 . . .41 B8
Sutton Cres NR13 . . . . .92 F8
Sutton Est PE31 . . . . .135 C2
Sutton Fst Sch NR12 . . . . .39 C2
Sutton Lea PE31 . . . . .135 C2
Sutton Mdws PE13 . . . . . .152 A8
Sutton Rd Catfield NR29 . . .39 C1
  Great Yarmouth NR30 . . .169 D1
  Hickling NR12 . . . . .39 D1
  Swaffham PE37 . . . . . . .153 B1
  Terrington St Clement
   PE34 . . . . .144 A4
  Walpole Cross Keys PE34 . .42 A7
  Wisbech PE13 . . . . .152 A7
Suttons Cl **1** PE14 . . . . . . .77 F6
Sutton Way NR12 . . . . .39 D8
Sutton Windmill & Broads
  Mus ★ NR12 . . . . .39 D2

SWAFFHAM PE37 . . . . . . .153 D4
Swaffham CE Prim Acad
  PE37 . . . . .153 C2
Swaffham Com Hospl
  PE37 . . . . .153 C5
Swaffham Gap PE26 . . . . . .82 C1
Swaffham Leisure Ctr
  PE37 . . . . .153 C2
Swaffham Mus ★ PE37 . . .153 B4
Swaffham Raceway PE37 . . .64 C4
Swaffham Rd Ashill IP25 . . .84 A7
  Ashill PE37 . . . . .83 E7
  Barton Bendish PE33 . . . .63 C2
  Cockley Cley PE37 . . . . . .82 C6
  Cockley Cley PE37 . . . . . .82 D7
  East Dereham NR19 . . . .154 D6
  East Raynham NR21 . . . . .31 B5
  Hilborough IP26 . . . . .82 F1
  Ickburgh IP26 . . . . .100 B5
  Mundford IP26 . . . . . . .100 B4
  Narborough PE32 . . . . . .63 F7
  Narborough PE32 . . . . . .64 A6
  North Pickenham PE25 . . .65 F2
  North Pickenham PE37 . . .65 D1
  Oxborough PE33 . . . . . . .81 E4
  Raynham NR21 . . . . .30 F2
  South Pickenham PE37 . . .83 D7
  Swaffham PE37 . . . . .64 A4
  Watton IP25 . . . . .84 C4
  Wendling NR19 . . . . .66 F7
SWAFIELD NR28 . . . . .22 E3
Swafield La NR28 . . . . .22 F3
Swafield Rise NR28 . . . . . .151 D7
Swafield St NR5 . . . . .160 F7
SWAINSTHORPE NR14 . . . .89 D3
Swale The NR5 . . . . .160 F6
Swale View IP24 . . . . .176 F6
Swallow Cl **6** NR31 . . . . .170 A7
Swallow Dr
  Brandon IP27 . . . . .175 E3
  Wymondham NR18 . . . . . .87 F2
  Wymondham NR18 . . . . .173 D1
Swallowtail Rd PE30 . . . . .147 C4
Swallowtail Cl
  Besthorpe NR17 . . . . . . .174 F6
  Bowthorpe NR5 . . . . . . .160 F5
Swallowtail Gr NR7 . . . . . .159 F3
Swamp La
  Great Ellingham NR17 . . .103 F7
  Roydon IP22 . . . . .177 A6
Swan Cl Aylsham NR11 . . .150 C6
  Swannington NR9 . . . . . .52 B5
Swan Cotts PE32 . . . . .47 D5
Swan Dr NR20 . . . . .49 C3
Swan Entry IP22 . . . . .16 F7
Swan Flower Way PE37 . . .153 C2
Swangey La NR17 . . . . . . .103 D4
Swan La
  Coney Weston IP31 . . . . .127 B4
  Fincham PE33 . . . . .62 E1
  King's Lynn PE30 . . . . . .147 A6
  Redenhall with Harleston
   IP20 . . . . .122 D2
  Shipdham IP25 . . . . .67 C3
  Sprowston NR7 . . . . . . .159 D5
  Tharston & Hapton NR15 . .106 E4
Swann Gr NR25 . . . . .137 C6
SWANNINGTON NR9 . . . . . .52 B6
Swanns Yd NR28 . . . . .38 A4
Swan Rd NR25 . . . . .7 B3
Swans Croft La NR25 . . . . .18 C7
Swansea Rd NR2 . . . . .162 B5
Swansgate NR6 . . . . .158 E6
Swan St Fakenham NR21 . .141 B3
  Horsham St Faith NR10 . . .53 D2
Swanston's Rd NR30 . . . . .170 D8
Swanton Abbot Rd NR10 . . .37 A5
SWANTON ABBOTT
  NR10 . . . . .37 C4
Swanton Abbott Com Prim
  Sch NR10 . . . . .37 B5
Swanton Abbott Rd
  NR10 . . . . .37 C4
Swanton Ave NR19 . . . . . .154 E7
Swanton Cl NR19 . . . . . . .154 E7
Swanton Dr NR20 . . . . . . .154 E6
Swanton Gr NR19 . . . . . . .154 E6
SWANTON HILL NR10 . . . . .37 C5
SWANTON MORLEY
  NR20 . . . . .50 B3
Swanton Morley Prim Sch
  NR20 . . . . .50 B4
  Hoe NR20 . . . . .50 A6
  North Elmham NR20 . . . . .49 F6
SWANTON NOVERS
  NR24 . . . . .18 B3
Swanton Rd
  Dereham NR20 . . . . .50 A1
  East Dereham NR19 . . . .154 E7
  Elsing NR20 . . . . .50 E3
  Gunthorpe NR20 . . . . . . .18 B5
  Norwich NR3 . . . . .162 B8
  Swanton Novers NR24 . . . .18 B4
SWARDESTON NR14 . . . . . .89 C5
Swardeston Comm NR14 . . .89 B5
Swardeston La
  East Carleton NR14 . . . . .89 B6
  Lower East Carleton NR14 . .89 B6
  Mulbarton NR14 . . . . . . .89 C4
Swargate La NR15 . . . . . .108 E8
Swash La NR13 . . . . .54 D2
Swatman Gr NR18 . . . . . . .173 F7
Sweden Pl IP27 . . . . .175 B2
Sweetacres PE29 . . . . . . .167 B6
Sweetbriar Gdns NR29 . . . .49 C4
Sweetbriar La
  Edgefield NR24 . . . . .19 D5

Sweetbriar La *continued*
  Sheringham NR26 . . . . . .138 C7
Sweet Briar Rd
  7 Long Stratton NR15 . .106 E3
  Norwich NR6 . . . . .161 F8
Sweet Briar Rd Ind Est
  NR3 . . . . .157 F1
Sweetbrier La NR11 . . . . . .21 C5
Sweyn Cl IP24 . . . . .176 B2
Swiffers La NR10 . . . . .52 D5
Swift Rd NR18 . . . . .173 D1
Swim Rd NR29 . . . . .75 F6
Swinbourne Cl NR6 . . . . . .158 E3
Swindells Cl NR5 . . . . . . .157 A2
Swingy La NR18 . . . . .87 A3
Swirle's Pl **8** NR30 . . . . .169 D4
Swiss Terr PE30 . . . . .146 F5
Sybil Rd PE13 . . . . .152 C6
Sybil Wheeler Cl **5**
  IP24 . . . . .176 D6
Sycamore Ave
  16 Great Yarmouth
   NR31 . . . . .94 C7
  23 Martham NR29 . . . . . .57 D4
  Sprowston NR7 . . . . . . .159 F3
  Wymondham NR18 . . . . .173 C6
Sycamore Cl
  Attleborough NR17 . . . . .174 C4
  King's Lynn PE30 . . . . . .148 D2
  8 Loddon NR14 . . . . . . .91 F1
  North Walsham NR28 . . .151 D6
  Palgrave IP22 . . . . .177 C1
  Thompson IP24 . . . . . . .102 A7
Sycamore Covert
  Thetford IP24 . . . . .116 D2
  11 Thetford IP24 . . . . . .176 F5
Sycamore Cres NR1 . . . . . .161 F7
Sycamore Ct **2** NR4 . . . . .161 C1
Sycamore Dr **1** IP25 . . . . .85 A2
Sycamore Gn **2** NR31 . . .170 B6
Sycamore Gr NR26 . . . . . .138 D5
Sycamores The NR19 . . . .154 E5
Sycamore View IP22 . . . . .129 C2
Sycamore Way IP22 . . . . .177 F5
Sydenham Cl NR13 . . . . . .166 B4
SYDERSTONE PE31 . . . . . . .15 B3
Syderstone Common
  Nature Reserve ★ PE31 . .15 A3
Syderstone Rd
  Bagthorpe PE31 . . . . . . .14 D3
  East Rudham PE31 . . . . .14 E1
  Sculthorpe Airfield NR21 . .15 B3
  Tattersett PE31 . . . . .15 C1
  West Rudham PE31 . . . . .29 E8
Sydney Dye Ct PE32 . . . . . .65 C5
Sydney Rd **11** NR10 . . . . . .54 A2
Sydney Terr **2** PE30 . . . . .146 D1
Syers La PE32 . . . . .48 D2
SYLEHAM IP21 . . . . .131 D5
Syleham Hall La IP21 . . . .131 F5
Syleham Rd IP21 . . . . . . .131 B4
Sylvan Cl NR6 . . . . .157 E6
Sylvan Way
  2 Blofield Heath NR13 . . .73 C6
  Taverham NR8 . . . . .156 E8
Sylvden Dr IP23 . . . . .152 F6
Symonds Ave NR29 . . . . . .167 C2
Symonds Cl NR13 . . . . . . .165 F6
Symphony Gdns **11**
  NR17 . . . . .174 B4
Syon Cl IP38 . . . . .172 B4
Sywell Cl NR6 . . . . .158 F6
Sywell Gr **5** NR4 . . . . . . .59 A1

T

TACOLNESTON NR16 . . . .105 F5
Tacolneston CE Prim Sch
  NR16 . . . . .105 F6
Tagg's Lane PE14 . . . . .77 E8
Tagg Way **3** NR13 . . . . . . .72 E7
Talante La NR35 . . . . .109 E1
Talbot Cl IP18 . . . . .173 C5
Talbots Mdw IP21 . . . . . . .130 E5
Talbot Sq NR3 . . . . .178 A4
*Tales of the Old Gaol
  House* ★ PE30 . . . . .146 D4
Taleworth Cl **11** NR5 . . . . .161 A7
Tallon End IP26 . . . . .82 A3
Tallon St IP26 . . . . .82 A2
Tamarind Mews NR4 . . . . .161 C1
Tamarisk PE30 . . . . .148 B1
Tamarisk Dr NR30 . . . . . .168 E4
Tamworth La NR31 . . . . . .169 B2
Tanager Cl NR3 . . . . .158 D3
Tan La NR30 . . . . .168 E4
Tanners Gn NR9 . . . . .69 C3
Tanner St **4** IP24 . . . . . . .176 C4
Tanning La **7** NR16 . . . . .104 F1
Tanns La IP22 . . . . .119 A2
Tansy Cl NR3 . . . . .158 D4
Tansy La NR25 . . . . .7 D2
Tantallon Dr NR17 . . . . . .174 F6
Tanyard La
  Great Ellingham NR17 . . .103 F8
  Great Ellingham NR17 . . .104 A8
Target Hill IP20 . . . . .123 B2
Tarragon Cl **16** NR31 . . . . .94 C6
Tarragon Rd PE38 . . . . . . .172 D7
Tar Works Rd NR30 . . . . . .169 C6
TASBURGH NR15 . . . . . . .106 F7
Tasburgh Cl PE30 . . . . . . .147 D3
Tasburgh Hill NR15 . . . . .106 E8
Tasburgh Rd NR15 . . . . . .106 F8
Tasman La NR14 . . . . .22 F8
Tas Valley Vineyard ★
  NR16 . . . . .106 A3
Tate Loke NR12 . . . . .39 F1
TATTERFORD NR21 . . . . . . .30 E7
Tatterford Dr NR31 . . . . . . .30 E7

Tatterford Longrow
  Dunton NR21 . . . . .15 E1
  Tatterford NR21 . . . . .30 E8
Tatterford Rd
  Broomsthorpe PE31 . . . . .30 D7
  Dunton PE31 . . . . .15 F1
  Dunton NR21 . . . . .30 E8
TATTERSETT PE31 . . . . . . .15 C1
Tattersett Pk Bsns Ctr
  NR21 . . . . .15 C1
Tattersett Rd
  Dunton NR21 . . . . .15 C1
  Sculthorpe NR21 . . . . . . .16 A1
  Syderstone PE31 . . . . . . .15 C4
  Tattersett PE31 . . . . .15 B2
Tattlepot Rd IP21 . . . . . . .121 E5
TAVERHAM NR8 . . . . .155 C1
Taverham Chase NR8 . . . .156 D8
Taverham Hall Sch NR8 . . .156 A4
Taverham High Sch
  NR8 . . . . .155 B2
Taverham Jun Sch NR8 . . .156 C8
Taverham La NR8 . . . . . . .156 C6
Taverham Rd
  Felthorpe NR10 . . . . . . .155 C7
  Honingham NR9 . . . . . . .69 F6
  Taverham NR8 . . . . .156 D8
Tavern Cl NR20 . . . . .49 D4
Tavern La Diss IP22 . . . . . .177 F3
  East Dereham NR19 . . . .154 E3
Tavistock Rd PE13 . . . . . .152 D5
Tawny Owl Way NR5 . . . . .137 D6
Tawny Sedge **3** PE30 . . . .147 A8
Taylor Ave **9** NR4 . . . . . . .89 B8
Taylor Drift NR16 . . . . . . .118 D4
Taylor Rd Diss IP22 . . . . . .177 B4
  Norwich NR6 . . . . .161 C6
Taylor's La
  Gressenhall NR20 . . . . . .49 C3
  Norwich NR6 . . . . .158 D6
  Trimingham NR11 . . . . . .11 E1
Taylors Loke
  3 Cley next the Sea NR25 . .7 E6
  11 Hemsby NR29 . . . . . .167 A8
Taylors Rd NR34 . . . . .111 B3
Taylor Wy NR15 . . . . .165 A8
Taymor Pl PE14 . . . . .95 D4
Teal Cl **3** PE31 . . . . .12 E5
Teal Dr NR8 . . . . .156 B5
Teal Wlk
  Brandon IP27 . . . . .175 E4
  16 Great Yarmouth NR31 . .94 C8
Teasel Cl IP24 . . . . .68 A8
Teasel Dr IP24 . . . . .176 E5
Teasel Rd NR17 . . . . .174 B4
Teasel Rise **4** NR26 . . . . .138 B6
Tebbutt Ave **6** NR19 . . . .154 C3
Tedder Cl
  5 Barnham IP24 . . . . . .125 F6
  18 Watton IP25 . . . . . . .84 E3
Ted Ellis Nature Reserve ★
  NR14 . . . . .91 D8
Tee Cl **1** NR14 . . . . .89 B2
Telegraph Hill
  Easton NR9 . . . . .70 A7
  Honingham NR9 . . . . . . .69 F8
Telegraph La E NR1 . . . . .163 B6
Telegraph La W NR1 . . . . .163 A6
Telford Cl
  King's Lynn PE30 . . . . . .147 D4
  2 Norwich NR3 . . . . . . .157 F1
Telford Way
  Thetford IP24 . . . . .116 B3
  Thetford IP24 . . . . .176 B6
Temple Cl NR25 . . . . .8 F6
Temple Dr NR25 . . . . .8 F6
Templemere NR3 . . . . . . .159 A2
Temple Rd
  Great Yarmouth NR30 . . .169 D4
  King's Lynn PE30 . . . . . .148 D1
  Norwich NR3 . . . . .158 D1
Templewood La NR25 . . . .137 F8
Ten Acre La NR11 . . . . .34 D7
Ten Bell Ct NR2 . . . . .178 A3
Ten Bell La NR2 . . . . .178 A3
Tench Cl NR14 . . . . .89 B2
TEN MILE BANK PE38 . . . . .96 E7
Ten Mile Bank
  Hilgay PE38 . . . . .96 F6
  Littleport CB6 . . . . .96 E1
Ten Mile Bank Prim Sch
  PE38 . . . . .96 F7
Tennyson Ave PE30 . . . . . .146 F4
Tennyson Rd
  3 Diss IP22 . . . . .177 E4
  3 Great Yarmouth NR30 .169 D8
  King's Lynn PE30 . . . . . .146 F4
Tennyson Way IP24 . . . . . .176 E6
Tensing St NR35 . . . . .108 C5
Tenwinters Pightle NR15 . .91 A3
Terence Airey Ct **25**
  IP20 . . . . .122 D2
Terence Ave NR7 . . . . . . .159 A4
Teresa Rd IP21 . . . . .39 B4
Tern Cl **9** IP25 . . . . .84 C3
Tern Gdns NR31 . . . . .170 A6
Tern Rd NR29 . . . . .167 C5
Terrace Wlk NR1 . . . . .178 B1
Terrington Cl **3** PE14 . . . . .59 D2
TERRINGTON ST CLEMENT
  PE34 . . . . .144 B4
Terrington St Clement
  Bypass
  Terrington St Clement
   PE34 . . . . .42 B5
Terrington St Clement Com
  Sch PE34 . . . . .144 C6
TERRINGTON ST JOHN
  PE34 . . . . .42 C2

Terrington St John Cty Prim
  Sch PE14 . . . . .60 B8
Terr The
  North Pickenham PE37 . . .65 E1
  12 North Walsham NR28 . .151 C5
Tesmonde Cl NR5 . . . . . . .160 E7
Testerton Cotts NR21 . . . . .32 A6
Teulon Cl NR31 . . . . .171 C5
Texas Ave NR11 . . . . .15 C2
Texel Way NR11 . . . . .143 A7
Thacker Way NR5 . . . . . . .160 F6
Thain's La NR27 . . . . .10 B5
Thamesfield Way NR31 . . .169 B2
Thams Way **8** NR30 . . . . .168 E5
THARSTON NR15 . . . . . . .106 E5
Thatche Cl NR29 . . . . .167 A6
Thatched Cottage Rd
  NR28 . . . . .23 C2
Thatchwood Ave PE14 . . . .59 C2
Theatre Plain NR30 . . . . . .169 C4
Theatre Rd NR23 . . . . . . .136 C6
Theatre St
  East Dereham NR19 . . . .154 D6
  Norwich NR2 . . . . .178 A2
  Swaffham PE37 . . . . . . .153 B4
THELNETHAM IP22 . . . . . .128 B5
Thelnetham Rd
  Blo' Norton IP22 . . . . . . .128 B6
  Hopton IP22 . . . . .127 F5
THELVETON IP21 . . . . .130 D8
THEMELTHORPE NR20 . . . .33 F2
Themelthorpe Rd
  Foxley NR20 . . . . .33 E1
  Foxley NR20 . . . . .50 E8
Theobald Rd NR1 . . . . .89 E8
THETFORD IP24 . . . . .176 B4
Thetford Acad The IP24 . . .176 E7
*Thetford Ancient House
  Mus* ★ IP24 . . . . .176 C4
Thetford Gram Sch
  IP24 . . . . .176 C4
Thetford L Ctr & Waterworld
  IP24 . . . . .176 D5
Thetford Priory ★ IP24 . . .176 C4
Thetford Rd
  Barnham IP24 . . . . .125 E6
  Brandon IP27 . . . . .175 E3
  Brettenham IP24 . . . . . .116 C1
  Coney Weston IP31 . . . . .127 B4
  Euston IP24 . . . . .126 B6
  Garboldisham IP22 . . . . .127 F8
  Kilverstone IP24 . . . . . . .116 F5
  Northwold IP26 . . . . .99 B8
  Santon Downham IP27 . . .115 B5
  Watton IP25 . . . . .84 D3
  Wretham IP24 . . . . .117 A7
Thetford Sta IP24 . . . . . . .176 C5
Thetford Warren Lodge ★
  IP24 . . . . .115 E3
Thetford Way PE30 . . . . . .148 C3
Thicket The **6** NR8 . . . . .155 E2
Thiefgate La PE34 . . . . . . .43 D2
Thieves' Bridge Rd PE33 . .63 F4
Thieves La NR13 . . . . .55 A1
Thieves' La
  Attleborough NR17 . . . . .174 E5
  Burgh & Tuttington NR11 . .36 E6
  Little Ellingham NR17 . . .103 C8
Third Ave PE13 . . . . .152 E5
Third Marsh Rd PE14 . . . . .59 A7
Thirlby Rd NR28 . . . . .151 D3
Thirlmere **18** NR9 . . . . . . .88 D8
Thirty Acre La PE31 . . . . . .13 E7
Thistle Cl Norwich NR5 . . .160 F5
  3 Thetford IP24 . . . . . .176 F5
Thistledown Rd NR10 . . . . .53 B2
Thistle Hill Rd PE38 . . . . . .79 F1
Thistleton Cl NR25 . . . . . . .7 C6
Thomas Bardwell Dr
  NR35 . . . . .124 B7
Thomas Bole Ct IP22 . . . .128 A8
Thomas Bullock Prim Sch
  IP25 . . . . .67 C2
Thomas Cl **4** PE31 . . . . . .61 D5
Thomas Clarkson Acad
  PE13 . . . . .152 D3
Thomas Dix Ct NR28 . . . . .151 D5
Thomas Drew Cl PE31 . . . .140 C3
Thomas Glover Ct NR6 . . .158 C2
Thomas Manning Rd
  IP22 . . . . .177 E4
Thomas Paine Ave **3**
  IP24 . . . . .176 C4
Thomas St PE30 . . . . .146 E3
Thomas Vere Rd NR7 . . . .163 F7
Thomas Way NR30 . . . . . .168 C6
Thomas Wyatt Cl NR2 . . . .178 A1
THOMPSON IP24 . . . . .102 A8
Thompson Ave **7** NR25 . . .137 C5
Thompson Cl NR30 . . . . . . .50 B4
Thompson Prim Sch
  IP24 . . . . .102 B7
Thompson Rd
  Griston IP25 . . . . .85 A1
  Merton IP25 . . . . .84 D1
  Norwich NR7 . . . . .163 F8
  Thompson IP25 . . . . . . .102 A8
Thompson's La IP25 . . . . . .85 A1
Thompsons Yd NR3 . . . . . .178 B4
Thor Cl NR7 . . . . .163 F7
Thoresby Ave PE30 . . . . . .147 B4
Thoresby Coll PE30 . . . . . .146 D4
Thor Loke NR7 . . . . .163 E7
THORNAGE NR25 . . . . .18 F7
Thornagerd NR25 . . . . .7 F1
Thornage Rd Holt NR25 . . .137 A5
  Thornage NR25 . . . . .18 E8
  Thornage NR25 . . . . .18 F8
Thorndike La 41 C1

THORNHAM PE36 . . . . .2 D6
Thornham Cl NR7. . . . . . .159 B2
Thornham Cnr PE36 . . . . . . .2 E2
Thornham Rd Docking PE31 2 E1
 Docking PE31. . . . . .13 E8
 Methwold IP26 . . . . .99 A6
 Norwich NR7 . . . . .159 B2
 Ringstead PE36 . . . . .2 C4
 Yaxley IP23 . . . . .129 E1
Thorn La NR1. . . . . .178 B2
Thorn Rd Catfield NR29. . . .56 C8
 Fakenham NR21. . . . . . . .141 D4
Thornton Cl NR24. . . . . . .142 E4
Thornycroft Gdns ❶ 111 F1
Thoroughfare La NR7. . . . .167 B4
Thoroughfare The IP20. .122 D2
Thorp Ct NR19. . . . . .154 D4
THORPE NR14 . . . . .93 B1
THORPE ABBOTTS IP21 131 B6
Thorpe Ave NR7 . . . . .163 E8
Thorpe Cl NR7. . . . . .163 F7
Thorpe Dr NR17 . . . . .174 D4
Thorpe END NR13 . . . . . . .72 D6
Thorpe End Dr NR13 . . . . .72 E6
Thorpe Hall Cl NR7 . . . . .163 C5
THORPE HAMLET NR1. .163 B6
Thorpeland Cl ❹ PE33. . .61 D3
Thorpeland La ❸ PE33. .61 D3
THORPE MARKET NR11 . .22 A6
Thorpe Market Rd NR11. .22 A8
THORPE MARRIOTT
 NR8. . . . . .155 F2
Thorpe Mews NR7 . . . . . .163 F6
Thorpe Mkt Rd NR11 . . . .21 E7
Thorpe Rd
 Haddiscoe NR14 . . . . .110 F8
 Norwich NR1 . . . . .178 C2
 Southrepps NR11. . . . . . . .22 A7
THORPE ROW IP25 . . . . . .67 C4
THORPE ST ANDREW
 NR7 . . . . .163 F8
Thorpe St Andrew Sch
 NR7 . . . . .72 D4
Thorpe St IP22 . . . . .128 B4
THORPLAND PE33 . . . . . . .61 D3
Thorpland Fakenham NR21 16 F3
 Fakenham NR21. . . . . . . .141 F8
 Great Snoring NR21 . . . . . .17 A4
Thorpland Rd NR21 . . . . .141 E6
Thor Rd NR7. . . . . .163 E7
THRANDESTON IP21. . . .129 F3
Thrandeston Rd
 Brome IP23 . . . . .130 B3
 Mellis IP21. . . . . .129 E2
Threadneedle St NR15 . .91 A4
Three Acre Cl NR12 . . . . .164 C6
Three Acre Row IP20 . . . .122 F6
Three Cnr Dr NR6. . . . . . .158 F6
THREE COCKED HAT
 NR34 . . . . .110 D7
THREEHAMMER COMMON
 NR12 . . . . .55 E6
THREE HOLES PE14 . . . . .77 E3
Three King La NR2. . . . . .178 A3
Three Mile La NR5 . . . . . .156 F1
Three Oaks ❻ PE30. . . . .147 C5
Three Post Rd ❺ IP25 . .84 C3
Three Score Rd
 Colney NR5 . . . . .161 A5
 Norwich NR5 . . . . .160 F5
Threxton Rd
 Saham Toney IP25. . . . . . . .84 A4
 Watton IP25 . . . . .84 C3
Threxton Road Ind Est
 IP25. . . . . .84 C3
THRIGBY NR29 . . . . .75 D7
Thrigby Hall Wildlife Gdns★
 NR29 . . . . .75 E7
Thrigby Rd PE30. . . . . . . .75 E6
Throckmorton Yd ❺
 NR3 . . . . .162 E8
Thrush Cl ❷ NR14. . . . . .89 B3
Thumb La NR20. . . . . .31 F2
Thunder La NR7. . . . . . . .163 E7
THURGARTON NR11 . . . . .20 F5
Thurgarton Hall Rd NR11. 20 F7
Thurgarton Rd
 Aldborough NR11. . . . . . . .21 A5
 Sustead NR11. . . . . .21 A7
Thurland's Dro PE14 . . . . .77 D5
Thurlby Rd NR5. . . . . . . .160 E8
Thurling Loke NR7. . . . . .159 E1
Thurling Plain NR7 . . . . .159 E1
Thurlin Rd PE30 . . . . . . .147 B4
Thurloe Cl PE13 . . . . . . .152 C2
THURLTON NR14 . . . . .92 F1
Thurlton Prim Sch NR14 . 92 F1
Thurlton Rd NR14. . . . . . .110 B7
THURNE NR29 . . . . .56 E3
Thurne Rd NR29 . . . . .57 A2
Thurne Rise ❷ NR29 . . . .57 D5
Thurne Way NR29. . . . . . .167 B3
THURNING NR11. . . . . . . .34 C7
Thurning Mill La
 Briston NR24 . . . . .142 F1
 Craymere Beck NR20 . . . . .19 A1
Thurning Rd
 Briston NR24 . . . . .142 F1
 Hindolveston NR20 . . . . . .33 E8
THURSFORD NR21. . . . . . .17 E1
Thursford Collection★
 NR21 . . . . .17 D5
THURSFORD GREEN
 NR21. . . . . .17 D5
Thursford Rd
 Great Snoring NR21 . . . . . .17 A5
 Hindringham NR21 . . . . . . .17 E6
 ❶ Little Snoring NR21 . . . .17 B3
 Little Snoring NR21. . . . . .17 C4

Thursford Rd continued
 Thursford Green NR21. . . .17 C6
Thursford Wood Nature
 Reserve★ NR21. . . . . . . .17 D4
Thurston Cl
 Caister-on-Sea NR29. . . . .168 C4
 ❸ Norwich NR5 . . . . . . .160 F8
Thurst Rd NR27 . . . . .11 A3
Thurtles La NR29 . . . . . . .167 D6
THURTON NR14. . . . . .91 D4
Thurton Prim Sch NR14. .91 D4
THUXTON NR9 . . . . .68 D2
Thuxton Sta NR9 . . . . .68 C2
Thwaite Common NR11 . .21 B3
Thwaite Hill NR11. . . . . . .21 A4
Thwaite Rd
 Aldborough NR11. . . . . . . .21 A4
 Ditchingham NR35. . . . . . .109 A2
 Erpingham NR11 . . . . .21 A3
 Mundham NR14. . . . . . . .109 A8
THWAITE ST MARY
 NR35. . . . . .109 A5
Thwaites Oak Cl NR15. . .121 B5
Thyme Cl
 Attleborough NR17 . . . . . .174 B4
 Thetford IP24 . . . . .176 F5
Thynne's La NR20. . . . . . .68 E5
TIBENHAM NR16. . . . . . . .120 E8
Tibenham Rd
 Aslacton NR15 . . . . .121 A8
 Tibenham NR15. . . . . . . .120 F8
Tiercel Ave NR7 . . . . .159 C4
Tillett La NR29 . . . . .167 C2
Tillett Rd NR3 . . . . .158 E2
Tillett Way NR13 . . . . .72 E4
Tills Cl NR6. . . . . .158 F4
Tills Rd NR6. . . . . .159 A5
TILNEY ALL SAINTS
 PE34. . . . . .144 F1
Tilney All Saints CE VC Prim
 Sch PE34. . . . . .42 E4
TILNEY CUM ISLINGTON
 PE34. . . . . .60 F8
TILNEY FEN END PE34. . .60 C6
TILNEY HIGH END PE34 . .42 D4
Tilney Rd NR20 . . . . .69 C6
TILNEY ST LAWRENCE
 PE34. . . . . .60 D8
Tilney St Lawrence Com
 Prim Sch PE34 . . . . .60 C8
Timberhill NR1. . . . . .178 B2
Timber Hill NR16 . . . . . . .117 E4
Timber Rd NR16 . . . . .118 C5
Timbers The IP31. . . . . . .126 D1
Timber Yard Gdns NR12 .152 B8
Time & Tide Mus of Great
 Yarmouth★ NR30. . . . . .169 D2
Timothy Cl NR1. . . . . . . .163 B8
Timperley Est NR21 . . . . . .31 D5
Tindall Cl PE13 . . . . .152 C8
Tinker's Cl NR11 . . . . .21 A5
Tinker's Dro PE13. . . . . . .152 D7
Tinkers La NR13 . . . . .165 F1
Tinkers' La
 Garvestone NR9 . . . . .68 C1
 Strumpshaw NR13. . . . . . . .73 D1
Tinker's La NR15. . . . . . . .121 C4
Tinkers Wy PE38. . . . . . . .172 B6
Tinkler's Drove PE31. . . . .29 C4
Tintern Gr ❹ PE30. . . . . .148 C4
Tipperary Ave NR18. . . . .173 F6
Tippett Cl NR5. . . . . .160 F6
Tipples' La NR21. . . . . . . .33 C8
TIPPS END PE14 . . . . .95 C6
Tipton Cl NR19 . . . . .154 D2
TITCHWELL PE31 . . . . .2 F7
Titchwell Marsh Nature
 Reserve★ PE31. . . . . .2 F3
Titchwell Rd PE31 . . . . . . .2 F3
Tithe Barn Cl IP26 . . . . . .100 C5
Tithebarn La
 Marham PE33 . . . . .63 D6
 ❷ Thurlton NR14. . . . . . .92 F1
Tithe Barn La NR24 . . . . .142 F3
Tithing Cl ❷ IP24. . . . . .176 E5
Titlow Rd ❷ IP20 . . . . . .122 D2
TITTLESHALL PE32. . . . . . .48 B8
Tittleshall Rd
 Litcham PE32. . . . . .48 A5
 Mileham PE20 . . . . .48 A8
 Tittleshall PE32 . . . . .48 C6
Tivetshall Prim Sch
 NR15. . . . . .121 B5
Tivetshall Rd IP21 . . . . . .121 D5
TIVETSHALL ST MARGARET
 NR15. . . . . .121 B5
TIVETSHALL ST MARY
 NR15. . . . . .121 B5
Toad Hole Cottage Mus★
 NR29 . . . . .56 A6
Toad La
 Ditchingham NR35. . . . . . .108 F5
 Great & Little Plumstead
  NR13 . . . . .72 F5
 Thwaite NR35. . . . . .109 A5
Todd La NR2. . . . . .162 C3
Todhunter Ave NR34 . . . .110 C2
Todkill's La ❷ IP24. . . . . .176 F3
Toftes Cl NR5. . . . . .161 B8
Toftmead Cl NR19 . . . . . .154 E3
TOFT MONKS NR34 . . . . .110 D5
TOFTREES NR21. . . . . . . .31 D6
Toftrees Rd NR21 . . . . . . .31 B7
TOFTWOOD NR19. . . . . . .154 E2
Toftwood Inf Sch NR19. .154 E1
Toftwood Jun Sch
 NR19 . . . . .154 E1
Tointons Rd PE14 . . . . .77 F4
Tolhouse Mus★ NR30. . . .169 C3
Tolhouse St NR30. . . . . . .169 C3
Toll Bar NR21. . . . . .141 A6

Tollgate Rd NR31 . . . . . . .169 C1
Tollgate Way NR5. . . . . . .161 A5
Tollhouse Rd NR5. . . . . . .161 E7
Toll's Hill Rd NR27 . . . . . .11 A2
Tolls View NR27 . . . . .11 A3
Tolwin Wlk ❸ NR6. . . . . .158 F1
Tolye Rd NR5 . . . . .160 F7
Tombland NR1 . . . . .178 B3
Tom Milford Pl IP25 . . . . .84 D3
Tooks Comm La NR34 . . . .124 F5
Topcliffe Ave ❷ NR13. . . .55 A1
Top Common NR27 . . . . . .10 C4
TOPCROFT NR35. . . . . . . .107 F3
Top Croft NR35. . . . . .108 B1
TOPCROFT STREET
 NR35. . . . . .107 F2
Top Drag Way IP22 . . . . . .128 C8
Top Driftway IP24 . . . . . . .117 C8
Topps Hill Rd NR11 . . . . . .22 A6
Top Rd Belaugh NR12 . . . .164 A6
 Ashmanhaugh, Ilketshall
  NR34 . . . . .124 C5
 Sidestrand NR11 . . . . .11 C1
 Southrepps NR11. . . . . . . .22 C8
 Wicklewood NR18 . . . . . . .87 B4
 Wingfield IP21. . . . . .131 E3
TOPROW NR16 . . . . .88 E1
Top Row NR16 . . . . .106 B8
Topshill Rd NR11 . . . . .21 E6
Torrey Cl PE31. . . . . .133 E5
Tortoiseshell Dr ❿
 NR17 . . . . .174 B4
Tortoishell Way NR18. . . .173 E4
Tottenham St ❸ NR30 . . .169 D5
TOTTENHILL PE33 . . . . . . .62 A5
TOTTENHILL ROW PE33 . .61 E7
Tottenhill Row PE33 . . . . .61 F6
Totters Hill
 Antingham NR28 . . . . .22 A3
 Suffield NR11. . . . . .21 F3
TOTTINGTON IP24. . . . . . .101 C6
Tottington Cl
 ❻ Norwich NR5 . . . . . . .160 F8
 Thetford IP24 . . . . .176 D6
Tottington La IP22. . . . . . .177 B4
Tottington Rd IP24 . . . . . .102 A7
Tower Cl Brandon IP27 . . .175 B3
 Costessey NR8. . . . . .156 C4
Tower Ct NR21. . . . . .141 D5
TOWER END PE32. . . . . . . .44 C4
Tower Gdns PE13 . . . . . . .152 B4
Tower Hill
 Costessey NR8. . . . . .156 C4
 Norwich NR7 . . . . .163 D6
Tower La Middleton PE32 . .44 D4
 Sidestrand NR27 . . . . .11 B3
Tower Mdws PE37 . . . . . . .153 C5
Tower Mill Rd NR5. . . . . .160 F8
Tower Pl ⓭ PE30 . . . . . .146 D4
Tower Rd Anmer PE35 . . . .28 C7
 Burgh St Margaret (Fleggburgh)
  NR29. . . . . .57 C1
 Burnham Overy PE31 . . . .135 E2
 Canadas NR11. . . . . .10 A4
 Elm PE14 . . . . .77 A7
 Fleggburgh NR29. . . . . . . .75 D8
 Hilgay PE38 . . . . .79 A4
 Repps with Bastwick NR29 57 A5
 Terrington St Clement
  PE34 . . . . .144 C7
Tower St PE30 . . . . .146 D4
Towler Dr ⓫ NR7. . . . . . .159 E4
Towlers Ct IP27 . . . . .175 C3
Town Bridge ㉕ PE13 . . .152 C5
Town Cl Corpusty NR11. . . .19 E1
 East Winch PE32. . . . . . . .44 F3
 Holt NR25. . . . . .137 B6
 Saxthorpe NR11. . . . . .19 E1
Town Cl House Prep Sch
 NR2 . . . . .162 C3
Town Cl La NR11. . . . . . . .19 E1
Town Cl Rd Norwich NR2 .162 C3
 Saxthorpe NR11. . . . . .19 D2
Town Cnr NR10. . . . . .53 C8
Town Drove PE14 . . . . .78 B7
Town End NR11. . . . . . . .143 C6
Town Est PE38. . . . . .172 B5
Town Gn Alby Hill NR11. . . .21 A4
 Wymondham NR18 . . . . . .173 B4
Town Gn Rd IP25 . . . . .84 E3
TOWN GREEN
 Alby with Thwaite NR11. . . .21 C4
 South Walsham NR13 . . . . .74 A7
Town House Drift PE32. . .48 B2
Town House La IP22 . . . . .128 B2
Town House Mus★
 PE30. . . . . .146 D4
Town House Rd NR8 . . . . .156 F4
Town La Aylsham NR11 . . .150 C7
 Brancaster Staithe PE31. . . .3 D7
 Castle Acre PE32. . . . . . . .46 F2
 Garvestone NR9 . . . . .68 C2
Townland La NR15. . . . . . .107 C3
Townlands NR31. . . . . . . .170 B7
Town Lands Trading Est
 NR81. . . . . .170 B7
Townley Cl PE14 . . . . .77 E5
Townley Prim Sch PE14 . .95 A7
Town Rd
 Burgh St Margaret (Fleggburgh)
  NR29. . . . . .57 C1
 Ingham NR12. . . . . .39 C4
Townsend NR10 . . . . .53 F8
Townsend Gn N NR21 . . .141 F5
Townsend Rd
 Norwich NR4 . . . . .162 C1
 Upwell PE14 . . . . .77 F3
Townsend Cl ❸ NR30. . .169 D3
Townsend Gn E NR21 . . .141 F5
Townsend Gn W NR21 . . .141 F5

Townshend Pl ❹ IP25 . . .67 C2
Townshend Rd
 Dereham NR19 . . . . .154 D7
 Wisbech PE13 . . . . .152 D6
Townshend Terr ❷
 PE30. . . . . .146 E6
Town St Hickling NR12. . . .39 F3
 Outwell PE14 . . . . .77 D5
 Swanton Morley NR20. . . . .50 B4
Town Wall Mews ❾
 NR30. . . . . .169 C5
Town Wall Rd NR30 . . . . .169 C5
Town Yd NR25 . . . . .7 E6
Tracey Rd NR7. . . . . .159 E1
Trafalgar Ct
 Cliftonville NR11 . . . . .143 B7
 Great Yarmouth NR30. . . . .169 E3
 Wisbech PE13 . . . . .152 D6
Trafalgar Ind Est PE14 . .172 A4
Trafalgar Rd
 Downham Market PE38. . . .172 B4
 ❷ Great Yarmouth NR30 169 D3
Trafalgar Rd E NR31 . . . . .170 D6
Trafalgar Rd W NR31 . . . .170 C6
Trafalgar Sq
 Great Yarmouth NR30 . . . .169 E3
 Poringland NR14 . . . . .90 C4
Trafalgar St NR1. . . . . . . .178 B1
Trafalgar Wy Diss IP22 . . .177 F3
 Thetford IP24 . . . . .176 F5
Trafalgar Yd NR1. . . . . . . .150 C6
Trafford Est PE14. . . . . . .59 C8
Trafford Pk ❶ PE13. . . . .152 E6
Trafford Rd
 Norwich NR1 . . . . .178 A1
 Wisbech PE13 . . . . .152 D5
Trafford Wlk NR12. . . . . .164 B2
Trafford Wy NR10. . . . . . . .54 B2
Traice Rd NR16. . . . . .105 D7
Tramway The PE14. . . . . . .77 F6
Transport La NR14 . . . . . .109 D7
Trap La NR21. . . . . .141 B6
Trap's La NR20 . . . . .69 C7
Trelawny Rd ❺ NR29 . . . .57 D4
Tremaine Cl NR6. . . . . . . .157 E1
Trenchard Cres ❹ IP25 . .84 F3
Trenchard Sq IP26. . . . . . .98 D1
Trendall Rd NR7 . . . . .159 C4
Tren Dr ⓴ NR7 . . . . . . .159 E4
Trenowaths Pl ⓭ PE30 .146 D5
Trent V C C IP26 . . . . .99 A5
Tretts Loke NR29 . . . . .57 C1
Trident Dr NR1. . . . . .163 A7
Trilithon Cl NR6. . . . . . . .157 E1
TRIMINGHAM NR11 . . . . . .11 D2
Trimming Wlk NR8 . . . . . .156 E8
Trinity Ave NR31. . . . . . . .170 B4
Trinity Cl
 East Dereham NR19 . . . . . .154 D6
 Norwich NR3 . . . . .72 D8
Trinity Gdns NR35 . . . . . .124 A8
Trinity Hospl
 (Bede House)★ PE31 . . . .27 C3
Trinity Pl ㉕ NR30. . . . . . .169 D1
Trinity Rd
 Fakenham NR21. . . . . . . .141 E6
 Walpole Highway PE14. . . . .59 F8
 Wisbech PE13 . . . . .152 C2
Trinity Sch PE13 . . . . . . .152 C2
Trinity St NR2 . . . . .162 C5
Trinity Sq ❶ NR30. . . . . .169 D1
Triple Plea La NR35. . . . . .108 B4
Triple Plea Rd NR35. . . . . .108 B4
Trix Rd NR2 . . . . .162 C4
Tropical Butterfly World★
 NR17. . . . . .103 F5
Trory St NR2. . . . . .162 C5
Troston Rd IP31 . . . . .126 C1
Trotwood Mws PE13. . . . .152 D3
Troutbeck ㉑ NR9 . . . . . .88 D8
TROWSE NEWTON
 NR14 . . . . .163 B2
Trowse Prim Sch NR14. . .163 B2
True's Yd Fishing Heritage
 Mus★ PE30. . . . . .146 D4
Truman Cl
 ❶ Norwich NR4 . . . . . . .161 C5
 Rackheath/Salhouse NR13 .72 F8
Trumpery La NR14 . . . . . . .90 C8
TRUNCH NR28. . . . . .22 E5
Trunch Hill IP20 . . . . .123 A7
Trunch Rd Denton IP20 . . .123 B6
 Mundesley NR11 . . . . .143 B4
 Mundesley NR11 . . . . .143 B5
 Swafield NR28 . . . . .22 E4
 Trunch NR11. . . . . .22 D6
Trust Cl NR29. . . . . .57 C1
Tubby Dr NR14 . . . . .90 C5
Tucker St NR27 . . . . .139 B7
Tucks Rd NR28 . . . . .38 A5
Tuckswood Com Prim Sch
 NR4 . . . . .162 D1
Tuckswood Ctr ❷ NR4 . .162 C1
Tuckswood La NR4 . . . . . .162 D1
Tuddenham Rd NR11. . . . .150 B6
Tud La NR9 . . . . .69 E6
Tudor Ave IP22 . . . . .177 A5
Tudor Cl Hoxne IP21. . . . .131 A3
 Thetford IP24 . . . . .176 C2
Tudor Cres PE36. . . . . . . .132 D2
Tudor Rose Wy ㊺ IP20 .122 D2
Tudor Way
 Dersingham PE31 . . . . . . .140 D4
 ❻ Mulbarton NR14. . . . . .89 B3
Tudor Wlk
 Great Yarmouth NR31. . . . .170 C1
 ❻ Honington IP31. . . . . .126 B1
Tuesday Mkt Pl ❺
 PE30. . . . . .146 D5
Tuffen La IP22. . . . . .128 B4

Tulip Cl
 Attleborough NR17 . . . . . .174 C5
 Gillingham NR34 . . . . .110 B2
Tulip Gdns NR4 . . . . .89 B8
Tulip Tree Dr ❺ NR14. . . .90 C5
Tumbler Hill PE37 . . . . . .153 C6
Tumbleyhill Rd PE32. . . . .46 C3
Tumbril La IP21 . . . . .131 D7
Tummel Way NR17. . . . . .174 E6
Tunbeck Cl IP20 . . . . .123 A3
Tunbeck Rd IP20 . . . . . . .123 A4
TUNGATE NR28. . . . . .37 C8
Tungate Cres NR4 . . . . . . .89 B8
Tungate Rd NR28 . . . . . . .151 A5
Tungate Way ❻ NR12. . . .54 C6
Tunneys La NR35 . . . . . . .109 B2
Tunn St ❹ NR21. . . . . . .141 B4
Tunns Yd NR23 . . . . .136 D6
Tuns Rd PE37. . . . . .65 F4
TUNSTALL NR13 . . . . .74 F3
Tunstall Cl ❺ NR5 . . . . .161 A7
Tunstall Rd NR13 . . . . .74 F2
TUNSTEAD NR12 . . . . .37 F1
Tunstead Prim Sch NR12. 37 F1
Tunstead Rd
 Badersfield NR10. . . . . . . .37 B2
 Coltishall NR12 . . . . .54 E7
 Frankfort NR12 . . . . .38 A2
 Hoveton NR12 . . . . .55 A6
 Tunstead NR12. . . . . .37 E1
 Tunstead NR12. . . . . .37 F2
 ❶ Wroxham/Hoveton
  NR12. . . . . .164 C5
Tuppenny Grove NR25 . . .20 B8
Turbine Way PE37 . . . . . .153 B6
Turbo Rd NR21 . . . . .15 D2
Turbus Rd PE30. . . . . . . .146 E7
Turf Fen La Ludham NR29. .56 A5
 Ludham NR29 . . . . .56 B5
Turf Lot Dro PE14 . . . . . . .95 B5
Turf Moor Rd NR21 . . . . . .16 C1
Turin Way NR31 . . . . .171 E4
Turkey La NR14. . . . . .19 D6
Turnberry NR4 . . . . .162 A1
Turner Cl
 Ditchingham NR35. . . . . . .109 B2
 ❺ Great Yarmouth NR31 .170 A7
 Wymondham NR18 . . . . . .173 E5
Turner Rd NR2. . . . . .162 A7
Turner's Cl PE34. . . . . . . .79 E8
Turner Way PE38 . . . . . . .172 E5
Turnham Gn ❿ NR7 . . . .72 D4
Turning The NR26. . . . . . .138 C6
Turnpike Cl Foxley NR20 . .50 D8
 Hellesdon NR6. . . . . .157 F2
 ❷ Hellesdon NR6 . . . . . .152 E6
Turnpike The
 Ashwellthorpe NR16 . . . . .106 A7
 Bracon Ash NR14. . . . . . . .88 F2
 Carleton Rode NR16 . . . . .105 D2
Turn The NR10. . . . . .53 A8
Tusser Rd NR8. . . . . .156 E8
Tusting Cl NR7 . . . . .158 F4
TUTTINGTON NR11 . . . . . .36 E6
Tuttington Rd
 Aylsham NR11. . . . . .150 F8
 Banningham NR11. . . . . . . .36 E7
 Tuttington NR10. . . . . .36 F5
 Tuttington NR10. . . . . .37 A5
Tuttles La E NR18 . . . . . . .173 D6
Tuttles La W NR18 . . . . . .173 B6
Tuxhill Chase PE34. . . . . .42 B4
Tuxhill Rd PE34. . . . . . . .42 B5
Twelveacre NR4 . . . . .161 F4
Twickenham Ave IP27 . . .175 B1
Twickenham Rd NR6. . . . .158 B5
Twiss Cl ❺ IP22 . . . . . . .129 D7
Two Acres ❻ PE32. . . . . .44 B3
Two Fields Way ❶ NR20 . .50 E7
Two Furlong Hill NR23 . . .136 C5
Two Saints Cl NR12. . . . . .164 D7
Two Sisters Cl ❻ PE12. . .41 B8
Twrs The PE38. . . . . .172 C5
TWYFORD NR20. . . . . .33 B3
Twyford La NR20. . . . . . . .33 C3
Twyford Rd NR20 . . . . .33 A6
TYBY NR11. . . . . .34 B6
Tydd Bank PE14. . . . . . . .41 C7
Tydd Rd PE13. . . . . .41 B6
Tyndale PE30 . . . . .148 C5
Tyne Mews NR30 . . . . . . .168 C5
Tyrell Cres PE30. . . . . . . .148 D1
Tyrolean Sq NR31. . . . . . .169 B4
Tyrrell's Rd ❷ NR31 . . . .169 B4

U

UEA Sportspark NR4. . . . .161 C4
Ulfkell Rd IP24 . . . . .176 B2
Ullswater Ave
 Castle Rising PE30. . . . . . .27 C1
 King's Lynn PE30 . . . . . . .148 F1
Ullswater Dr ⓴ NR9 . . . .88 D8
Ulph Pl PE31. . . . . .135 D3
Uncle's La IP19 . . . . .124 B2
Undley Rd IP27 . . . . .113 E1
Unicorn Yd
 ❷ Aylsham NR11 . . . . . .150 C6
 Norwich NR3 . . . . .178 A4
Union Drift NR20. . . . . . . .68 A8
Union La
 ❹ King's Lynn PE30 . . . .146 D4
 Wortham IP22 . . . . .129 D5
Union Pl ⓱ PE13. . . . . . .152 C5
Union Rd Aylsham NR11 . .150 E7
 ❼ Great Yarmouth NR30 169 D4
 Smallburgh NR12. . . . . . . .38 C3
Union St Norwich NR2. . . .178 A2
 ❹ Wisbech PE13 . . . . . .152 C5

University Cres NR31. . . .170 B4
University Dr NR4 . . . . . . .161 C5
University of E Anglia
 Norwich NR4 . . . . .161 C3
 Norwich NR6 . . . . .157 D4
Univ Tech Coll Norfolk
 NR4 . . . . .89 E8
Unthank Rd NR4 . . . . . . .161 F2
Upcher Cl ㉓ IP26 . . . . . .98 E1
UPGATE NR9 . . . . .52 C5
Upgate NR14. . . . . .90 D5
Upgate Rd NR15 . . . . . . .108 E7
Upgate St
 Carleton Rode NR16 . . . . .105 A4
 Southery PF38. . . . . .97 B5
UPGATE STREET
 Bedingham NR35. . . . . . . .108 B2
 Old Buckenham NR16 . . . .105 A3
Uphalle NR8. . . . . .155 D1
Uplands Ave NR30 . . . . . .168 D5
Uplands Pk NR26 . . . . . . .138 C6
Uplands Way IP22 . . . . . .177 D5
Upland Terr IP20 . . . . . . .123 A8
UPPER BRANDON PARVA
 NR9 . . . . .68 E3
Upper Breckland Rd
 NR5 . . . . .156 F1
Upper Brook La IP20. . . . .131 E8
Upper Burnthouse La
 IP20. . . . . .131 E8
Upper Cliff Rd NR31. . . . .170 D4
Upper Goat La NR2 . . . . .178 A3
Upper Grange Cres
 NR30 . . . . .168 D5
Upper Green La NR3 . . . . .178 A4
UPPER GUIST NR20. . . . . .33 A5
Upper Hall La NR24 . . . . . .18 D8
Upper Harmans La IP20 122 B1
UPPER HELLESDON
 NR3 . . . . .158 C3
Upper Kiln La NR15 . . . . . .90 F4
Upper King St NR2 . . . . . .178 B3
Upper Mkt ❸ NR21 . . . . .141 B4
Upper Olland St NR35. . . .124 A8
Upper Rose La IP22 . . . . .177 E2
Upper St Giles St NR2 . . .178 A3
Upper St La IP22. . . . . . . .128 A1
UPPER SHERINGHAM
 NR26 . . . . .138 A5
Upper St
 Brome & Oakley IP21 . . . .130 E4
 Gissing IP22 . . . . .120 F4
 Salhouse NR13 . . . . .55 B2
Upper Stafford Ave NR5. 156 F1
Upper Staithe Rd ⓯
 NR12 . . . . .38 B4
UPPER STOKE NR14. . . . . .90 B5
UPPER STREET
 Dickleburgh and Rushall
  IP21. . . . . .130 F6
 Horning NR12 . . . . .55 F4
 Hoveton NR12 . . . . .55 C5
 Southrepps NR11. . . . . . . .22 B7
 Tunstead NR12. . . . . .38 A3
Upper Tumbril La
 Brockdish IP21 . . . . .131 D8
 Needham IP20. . . . . .122 A1
 Scole IP20 . . . . .131 D8
UPPER WEYBREAD
 IP21. . . . . .131 E6
UPTON NR13 . . . . .166 A8
Upton Broad Nature
 Reserve★ NR13. . . . . . . .74 C8
Upton Cl NR4 . . . . .162 A3
Upton Dr PE37. . . . . .153 B2
UPTON GREEN NR13 . . . .166 B8
Upton Rd Norwich NR4 . . .162 A3
 South Walsham NR13 . . . . .74 B8
Uptons Way IP26 . . . . .82 A2
Upton Way
 Happisburgh NR12 . . . . . . .24 C5
 Whimpwell Green NR12 . . .39 C8
UPWELL PE14 . . . . .77 F5
Upwell Com Prim Sch
 PE14. . . . . .77 D4
Upwell Rd PE14 . . . . .95 A7
Utopia Way NR12 . . . . . . .39 B3
Utting Cl ⓳ NR14 . . . . . . .90 C5

V

Vale Cl ❽ NR10. . . . . . . .53 B3
Vale Ct ❺ IP27 . . . . .114 E1
Vale Gn NR6. . . . . .158 B1
Valentine Ct PE36. . . . . . .132 D5
Valentine Rd PE36 . . . . . .132 D4
Valentine St ❸ NR2. . . . .162 C6
Vale Rd High Kelling NR25. . .8 E2
 Mundesley NR11 . . . . .143 A8
 Thurton NR14. . . . . .91 C3
Valerian Rise PE14 . . . . . .116 D2
Valinger's Pl ❻ PE30 . . . .146 E4
Valingers Rd PE30 . . . . . .146 E3
Valley Cl ❶ NR35 . . . . . .123 F7
Valley Dr The NR1 . . . . . .163 B8
Valley Gdns ❽ NR28 . . . .151 E5
Valley Farm La NR14 . . . . .90 A6
Valley La Aylsham NR11 . . .150 E4
 Burston IP22 . . . . .120 F1
 Holt NR25. . . . . .137 B5
 Shimpling IP21 . . . . .121 A2
Valley Prim Sch NR5. . . . .161 C8
Valley Rd
 Corpusty & Saxthorpe
  NR24 . . . . .34 F8
 Norwich NR5 . . . . .157 C1
 ❾ Tasburgh NR15. . . . . .106 F6

Valley Rise PE31 . . . . .140 C4
Valleyside NR18 . . . . .173 C3
Valley Side Rd **1** NR1 . .163 C8
Valley View NR19 . . . . . .154 C6
Valley View Cres NR5 . . .157 A1
Valley Way NR21 . . . . . . .141 E4
Valpy Ave NR3 . . . . .158 A1
Vancouver Ave PE30 . . . .146 E3
Vancouver Ct
 15 King's Lynn PE30 . .146 D5
 North Lynn PE30 . . . . . .147 C7
Vancouver Rd **3** NR7 . .163 C8
Vane Cl NR7 . . . . .72 D4
Vanguard Chase NR5 . . .156 C1
Vanguard Rd
 2 Great Yarmouth NR31 . .94 C8
 Great Yarmouth NR31 . .170 A8
Varsity Rd IP25 . . . . .84 F3
Varvel Ave NR7 . . . . .159 C4
Varvel Cl NR7 . . . . .159 C3
Vassar Ct **6** NR20 . . . . .68 F6
Vaughan Cl NR27 . . . . . .139 B4
Vaunces La Rushall IP21 .121 E1
 Scole IP21 . . . . .131 B8
Vaunce's La IP21 . . . . . . .131 B8
Vauxhall St NR2 . . . . .162 C5
Vauxhall Terr NR30 . . . . .169 C6
Vawdrey Rd NR8 . . . . . . .155 F1
Veltshaw Cl PE31 . . . . . .133 B4
Velvet Cl NR18 . . . . .87 F2
Venables Cl NR1 . . . . . . .163 B7
Venta Icenorum (Roman
 Town)★ NR14 . . . . .89 E6
Ventura Cl IP26 . . . . .98 F5
Vera Cl **10** NR13 . . . . . .72 E7
Vera Rd
 New Rackheath NR13 . . .72 E7
 Norwich NR6 . . . . .158 B4
Verbena Dr NR18 . . . . . .173 E6
Verbena Cl NR4 . . . . .161 B1
Verdon's La NR18 . . . . . . .87 F2
Verdun Rd PE13 . . . . . . .152 D5
Veronica Gn **9** NR31 . . .170 B6
Vervain Cl **23** NR31 . . . .94 C6
Vesta Cl PE37 . . . . .153 D4
Vetch Cl NR18 . . . . .173 D4
Viburnum Way **6** NR31 .170 B6
Vicarage Cl
 Costessey NR8 . . . . .156 F5
 Foulden IP26 . . . . .82 A1
 1 Potter Heigham NR29 . .56 F6
 Terrington St Clement
 PE34 . . . . .144 A5
Vicarage La
 Anchor St NR12 . . . . .38 B2
 Bungay NR35 . . . . .124 C8
 13 Gayton PE32 . . . . . . .45 C6
 Hoveton NR12 . . . . .55 B5
 Hoveton NR12 . . . . .164 E5
 Marham PE33 . . . . .63 A4
 Shernborne PE31 . . . . . .113 B8
Vicarage Mdws NR19 . . .154 D4
Vicarage Rd
 Cromer NR27 . . . . .139 B6
 Deopham NR18 . . . . .86 D3
 Dilham NR28 . . . . .38 C5
 East Ruston NR12 . . . . . .24 A3
 Foulden IP26 . . . . .82 A2
 Hockham IP24 . . . . .102 D3
 Norwich NR13 . . . . .158 C1
 Paston NR28 . . . . .143 D2
 Salhouse NR13 . . . . .55 A2
 Sheringham NR26 . . . . .138 C6
 Thetford IP24 . . . . .176 D5
 Wingfield IP21 . . . . .131 E3
Vicarage St NR28 . . . . . .151 C5
Vicarage Wlk **11** IP25 . . .84 E3
Vicar St NR18 . . . . .173 B4
Viceroy Cl PE31 . . . . . . .140 C4
Victor Charles Cl PE27 . .175 B7
Victoria Arc NR30 . . . . . .169 C3
Victoria Ave
 Brandon IP27 . . . . .175 C3
 Hunstanton PE36 . . . . . .132 D5
Victoria Cl Diss IP22 . . . .177 E3
 Heacham PE31 . . . . .133 E6
 King's Lynn PE30 . . . . . .147 A8
 Taverham NR8 . . . . .156 C8
Victoria Cotts PE31 . . . .133 D6
Victoria Ct
 Sheringham NR26 . . . . .138 E7
 22 Watton IP25 . . . . . . .84 D3
Victoria Gdns
 7 Great Yarmouth
 NR30 . . . . .169 D2
 Wattisfield IP22 . . . . . . .128 A1
Victoria Hill IP23 . . . . . . .130 E1
Victoria La Deopham NR18 .86 F3
 Fakenham NR21 . . . . . . .141 E4
Victoria Pl **17** PE13 . . . .152 C4
Victoria Rd Diss IP22 . . . .177 D4
 5 Great Yarmouth NR30 .169 D2
 Great Yarmouth NR31 . .170 D3
 Mundesley NR11 . . . . . .143 C6
 3 Taverham NR8 . . . . . .155 C1
 Taverham NR8 . . . . .156 C8
 Terrington St John PE34 . .42 C4
 Wisbech PE13 . . . . .152 C4
Victoria St
 Caister-on-Sea NR30 . . .168 F4
 2 Downham Market
 PE38 . . . . .172 A5
 Great Yarmouth NR30 . .169 D6
 Great Yarmouth NR30 . .169 D6
 Norwich NR1 . . . . .178 A1
 Sheringham NR26 . . . . .138 D7
Victoria Terr PE34 . . . . . .146 C4
Victoria Way NR5 . . . . . .157 B2

Victory Ct
 3 Bradenham IP25 . . . . .66 E3
 Diss IP22 . . . . .177 F3
Victory Gr NR5 . . . . .156 C1
Victory La PE34 . . . . .60 C8
Victory Rd
 Downham Market PE38 . .172 B4
 Wisbech PE13 . . . . .152 B3
Victory Way IP24 . . . . . . .176 F7
Vienna Wlk NR19 . . . . . .154 C1
Viewpoint Mws NR34 . . .124 E8
Viking Cl
 Great Yarmouth NR31 . .170 D2
 Swaffham PE37 . . . . . . .153 D2
Viking Rd **1** NR31 . . . . . .94 C8
Vikings Cl IP22 . . . . .177 D5
Village Cl **4** NR4 . . . . . .161 C5
Villarome NR30 . . . . .168 C5
Villavon Way **4** NR13 . . .73 D6
Villebois Rd PE33 . . . . . . .63 B4
Vimy Rd NR18 . . . . .173 D4
Vimy Ridge NR18 . . . . . .173 D4
Vincent Cl IP26 . . . . .98 E1
Vincent Pl **18** IP25 . . . . .84 D3
Vincent Rd Norwich NR1 . .163 A7
 Sheringham NR26 . . . . .138 E7
Vincents Rd NR9 . . . . .69 A4
Vince's Rd IP22 . . . . .177 F4
Vine Cl
 Coney Weston IP31 . . . .127 B5
 Hemsby NR29 . . . . .167 B8
Vine Ct NR21 . . . . .141 B4
Vinegar La IP20 . . . . .122 F6
Vine Hill PE34 . . . . .61 C2
Vinery Cl **1** PE34 . . . . . .146 C5
Viola Cl NR1 . . . . .89 B8
Violet Cl
 Attleborough NR17 . . . . .174 C5
 18 Great Yarmouth NR31 . .94 C6
Violet Dr NR26 . . . . .138 B6
Violet Elvin Ct NR5 . . . . .161 F5
Violet Rd NR3 . . . . .158 F1
Violet Way NR19 . . . . . . .154 C4
Virginia Cl NR7 . . . . .159 C4
Viscount Cl IP22 . . . . . . .177 E4
Vole Ct PE30 . . . . .147 C7
Vong La Grimston PE32 . . .28 B1
 Roydon PE32 . . . . .45 A8
Vulcan Cl **1** 89 B8
Vulcan Rd N NR6 . . . . . . .158 C5
Vulcan Rd S NR6 . . . . . . .158 C5
Vulcan Way PE37 . . . . . . .153 D5

W

WACTON NR15 . . . . .106 C2
Wacton Rd NR16 . . . . . . .106 C4
Waddington Ct **6** NR2 . .162 B7
Waddington St NR2 . . . . .162 B7
Waddling La NR32 . . . . . .111 F7
Wade Cl NR11 . . . . .150 C5
Wadehall La NR34 . . . . . .111 A1
Wades Way NR28 . . . . . . .22 E5
Wadham Cl NR31 . . . . . .170 B3
Wadham Rd NR31 . . . . . .170 B3
Waggon & Horses La
 NR3 . . . . .178 B3
Wagtail Cl **2** NR31 . . . . .170 A6
Wagtail Way IP24 . . . . . .176 D1
WAINFORD NR35 . . . . . .109 B1
Wainford Mills Rd NR35 .124 C8
Wainford Rd
 Bungay NR35 . . . . .124 C8
 Wainford NR35 . . . . . . .109 C1
Wainscot Dr NR31 . . . . .170 A2
Wakefield Rd NR5 . . . . . .161 C5
Wakehurst Cl **6** NR4 . . .161 F1
Wakes La NR19 . . . . .154 D5
Walcot Cl NR5 . . . . .161 A7
WALCOT GREEN IP22 . . .177 F6
Walcot Rd IP22 . . . . .177 E6
Walcot Rise IP22 . . . . . . .177 E6
WALCOTT NR12 . . . . .24 A7
Walcott Gn NR12 . . . . . . .24 A5
Walcott Road N12 . . . . . .23 E4
Walcup's La PE32 . . . . . . .29 D2
Waldeck Rd NR4 . . . . . . .162 A3
Waldemar Ave NR6 . . . . .158 B5
Waldemar Pk NR6 . . . . . .158 B5
Wales Bank PE14 . . . . . . .59 A1
Wales Ct PE38 . . . . .172 C5
Walkers Cl PE31 . . . . . . .155 D2
Walker St **1** PE30 . . . . .146 E6
Walkers Wy NR35 . . . . . .124 A8
Walks The NR34 . . . . . . .111 A4
Walk The
 Great Yarmouth NR31 . .170 B6
 Hickling NR12 . . . . .39 F3
 Oulton NR11 . . . . .35 A8
Walkway The NR12 . . . . . .24 A7
Wallace Cl
 Dereham NR19 . . . . .154 B6
 King's Lynn PE30 . . . . . .147 D4
Wallace Twite Way
 PE31 . . . . .140 C3
Waller Cl NR13 . . . . .72 D5
Waller Dr NR17 . . . . .174 C5
Wallers La NR31 . . . . .33 C3
Wallflower Cl NR31 . . . . .170 B6
Wallflower La PE34 . . . . .146 B4
Wallgate La NR21 . . . . . . .17 D5
Wall Rd Erpingham NR11 . .20 F3
 Norwich NR3 . . . . .158 E2
Wall's La NR25 . . . . .7 F3
Walnut Ave **5** PE33 . . . .43 E2
Walnut Ave N **2** PE33 . . .43 E2
Walnut Cl Brandon IP27 . .175 C2
 Foulden IP26 . . . . .82 A2
 Hopton IP22 . . . . .127 F5
 Taverham NR8 . . . . .155 D2

Walnut Dr IP26 . . . . .83 A3
Walnut Gr
 1 Fakenham NR21 . . . . .141 E4
 Watton IP25 . . . . .84 D4
Walnut Hill NR21 . . . . . .141 E4
Walnut La NR7 . . . . .159 F3
Walnut Pl PE33 . . . . .82 A5
Walnut Rd PE14 . . . . .41 E3
Walnuts The
 Grimston PE32 . . . . .28 B1
 Norwich NR4 . . . . .162 A2
Walnut Tree Ave **24**
 NR29 . . . . .57 D4
Walnut Tree Dr
 Framingham Earl NR14 . . .90 C6
 Newton St Faith NR10 . . .53 E4
Walnut Wlk PE33 . . . . . . .63 B4
Walnut Wy NR19 . . . . . . .154 E4
Walpole Bank PE14 . . . . . .41 E3
Walpole Cl NR35 . . . . . . .109 B2
WALPOLE CROSS KEYS
 PE34 . . . . .41 F7
Walpole Cross Keys Bypass
 PE34 . . . . .41 F6
Walpole Cross Keys Com
 Prim Sch PE34 . . . . .42 A6
WALPOLE HIGHWAY
 PE14 . . . . .59 F8
Walpole Highway Prim Sch
 PE14 . . . . .59 F8
WALPOLE MARSH PE14 . .41 C4
Walpole Rd
 Great Yarmouth NR30 . .169 D7
 King's Lynn PE30 . . . . . .146 E7
WALPOLE ST ANDREW
 PE14 . . . . .41 D4
WALPOLE ST PETER
 PE14 . . . . .41 E3
Walpole St NR2 . . . . .178 A2
Walpole Way **3** PE33 . . .43 E2
 St Peter, South Elmham
 NR35 . . . . .123 F3
 Saxlingham Nethergate
 NR15 . . . . .107 D8
 Shelfanger IP22 . . . . . . .120 B2
 Sneath Common NR15 . .121 A8
 South End NR16 . . . . . . .103 B1
 Topcroft NR35 . . . . .108 A4
 Whissonsett NR20 . . . . . .31 E2
 Woodton NR35 . . . . . . .108 D5
Wash National Nature
 Reserve The★ PE30 . . . .26 B5
Washpit PE36 . . . . .13 A7
Washpit Dro
 South Acre PE32 . . . . . . .64 D8
 Swaffham PE37 . . . . . . .153 C8
 West Rudham PE31 . . . . .29 F6
Washpit Drove PE32 . . . . .46 C1
Wash Rd Littleport CB6 . . .95 D2
 Welney PE14 . . . . .95 E4
WALSOKEN PE13 . . . . . .152 F6
Walsoken Rd PE14 . . . . . .59 D3
Walter Howes Cres PE32 . .44 C3
Walter Rd NR4 . . . . .154 F3
Walters Cl NR31 . . . . . . .171 D5
Walters Rd NR8 . . . . .156 C8
Walton Cl NR9 . . . . .148 C4
WALTON HIGHWAY PE14 .59 D8
Walton Low Bank PE14. . .59 E6
Walton Rd
 Castle Acre PE32 . . . . . . .46 F5
 East Walton PE32 . . . . . .45 F3
 East Winch PE32 . . . . . . .45 B3
 Norwich NR1 . . . . .162 E3
 Rougham PE32 . . . . .47 A5
 St John's Fen End PE14. . .60 A5
 West Walton PE14 . . . . . .59 F5
 Wisbech PE13 . . . . .152 E7
Waltons Way IP27 . . . . . .175 D2
WALTON WARREN PE32 . .45 E2
WANGFORD IP27 . . . . . .114 C2
Wangford Rd IP27 . . . . . .113 F3
Wansbrough Rd **10**
 NR15 . . . . .106 E3
Wanton La PE14 . . . . . . .144 A5
Waples Way NR19 . . . . . .154 D3
Wapping NR29 . . . . .167 A2
Warbler Cl
 6 Great Yarmouth NR31 . .94 C7
 16 Sprowston NR7 . . . .159 E4
Wardley Hill Rd NR35 . . .109 D4
Ward Rd NR13 . . . . .55 B1
Ward's Chase PE34 . . . . . .79 B8
WARHAM NR23 . . . . .6 A4
Warham Rd Binham NR21 . .6 E2
 Wells-next-the-Sea NR23 .136 E4
 Wighton NR22 . . . . .6 A3
Warham St Mary's Halt Sta
 NR23 . . . . .6 A4
Waring Rd NR5 . . . . .161 B6
Warman's Cl NR9 . . . . . . .160 B6
Warman Way NR16 . . . . .105 E8
Warner Ave NR19 . . . . . .154 E7
Warners End NR9 . . . . . . .85 E3
Warnes Cl **4** NR27 . . . . .139 C6
Warnett Rd NR7 . . . . . . .159 D1
Warren Ave
 Fakenham NR21 . . . . . . .141 E4
 Norwich NR6 . . . . .158 A5
Warren Cl Brandon IP27 . .175 D3
 High Kelling NR25 . . . . . . .8 E3
 16 Horsford NR10 . . . . .53 A3
 Thetford IP24 . . . . .176 A3
 Watlington PE33 . . . . . . .61 D5
Warren Ct **7** NR27 . . . . .139 C6
Warren Dr NR11 . . . . . . .143 B5
Warren Gn NR13 . . . . . . .72 F8

Warren La The NR14 . . . .89 C4
Warren Loke NR31 . . . . . .93 E3
Warren Pl **4** NR19 . . . . .154 D1
Warren Rd
 Great Yarmouth NR31 . .171 D8
 High Kelling NR25 . . . . . . .8 E3
 Hopton on Sea NR31 . . .171 D5
 Methwold IP26 . . . . .99 A3
 Shouldham PE33 . . . . . . .62 D4
 Southrepps NR11 . . . . . . .22 C6
Warrens La IP22 . . . . . . .128 E2
Warren's La NR7 . . . . . . .174 C6
Warren's Rd PE34 . . . . . .145 D6
Warren's Way **5** NR16 . .105 F5
Warrens Yd NR23 . . . . . .136 C6
Warren The
 Bawburgh NR9 . . . . .160 B6
 Beachamwell PE37 . . . . .63 E1
 Claxton NR14 . . . . .91 E6
 Cromer NR27 . . . . .139 C6
 Horsham St Faith & Newton St
 Faith NR10 . . . . .53 D2
 Little Snoring NR21 . . . . .17 C3
 Norwich NR6 . . . . .158 E4
Warren View NR14 . . . . .109 D8
Warstade Way PE37 . . . . .153 B4
Warwick Dr NR18 . . . . . .173 C5
Warwick St NR2 . . . . . . .162 B5
Washbridge **10** NR19 . . .154 D5
Washingford Bridge La
 NR15 . . . . .91 D2
Wash La Alburgh IP20 . . .122 E7
 Aslacton NR15 . . . . .106 A1
 Banham NR16 . . . . .119 D6
 Burgh St Peter NR34 . . .111 C4
 Caistor St Edmund NR14 . .89 F6
 Clenchwarton PE34 . . . .145 E6
 Gissing IP22 . . . . .120 E5
 Hales NR14 . . . . .109 E6
 Hinderclay IP22 . . . . . . .128 C4
 Howe NR15 . . . . .90 C2
 Poringland NR14 . . . . . . .90 D4
 Redgrave IP22 . . . . .129 A5

Waterfield La NR21 . . . . .141 D5
Waterfield Cl **2** NR21 . . .141 C5
Waterfield Mdws NR28 . .151 E5
Water Gdns IP27 . . . . . . .177 C4
Water Gdns The PE13 . . .152 A5
WATERHEATH NR34 . . . .110 E5
Waterheath Rd NR34. . . .110 E5
Waterhouse NR21. . . . . . .16 D3
Watering La PE33. . . . . . . .43 E2
Watering Piece La NR29. . .56 C7
Wateringpit La NR17. . . . .55 A8
Watering Rd IP21 . . . . . . .131 B1
Watering The **3** NR13 . .162 D8
Water La Barnham NR24 . .125 E6
 Barnham IP24. . . . . .125 F6
 Barsham NR21. . . . . .16 F4
 Croxton IP24. . . . . .116 B8
 Great Cressingham IP25. . .83 D4
 Great Ellingham NR17. . .103 D8
 Great Melton NR9. . . . . . .70 B2
 Griston IP25. . . . . .85 A2
 Hingham NR9. . . . . .86 B5
 Hockham NR16. . . . . . . .102 E4
 Larling NR16. . . . . .118 A8
 Little Cressingham IP25. . .83 F2
 Little Melton NR9. . . . . . .160 B4
 Lower Stow Bedon NR17. .102 F5
 Merton IP25. . . . . .84 C2
 North Pickenham PE37. . .83 C8
 Shipdham IP25. . . . . .84 F8
 Shipdham NR16. . . . . . . .103 A1
 Shropham NR17. . . . . . . .103 A4
 South Pickenham PE37. . .83 D7
 Stow Bedon NR17. . . . . .102 D7
 Swaffham PE37. . . . . . . .153 D2
 Thompson IP25. . . . . . . .102 A8
 Wretham IP24. . . . . .102 A1
Waunci Cres NR19. . . . . .170 D2
Wavell Rd NR19. . . . . . . .154 C7
Waveney Ave **4** IP22. . .129 D7

Waterloo Cl
 3 Horsham St Faith
 NR10 . . . . .53 D2
 7 Thetford IP24 . . . . . .176 F4
Waterloo La NR21 . . . . . .130 C6
Waterloo Pk Ave NR3 . . .158 C1
Waterloo Pk Cl **6** NR3 . .158 C1
Waterloo Rd
 Great Yarmouth NR30 . .169 E2
 Hainford NR10 . . . . .53 E4
 Horsham St Faith NR10 . .53 E2
 Norwich NR3 . . . . .162 D8
Waterloo St **13** PE30 . . .146 E5
Waterlow Rd
 Hay Green PE34 . . . . . . .144 B1
 Terrington St Clement PE34 .42 C4
Waterman Rd **2** NR7 . . .161 F7
Waterman's La PE38 . . . . .79 D1
Waterman's Way PE38 . . .79 A4
Water Mdw Cl NR29 . . . .167 A3
Water Mdw La NR14 . . . .110 B8
Water Mdw Way **2**
 PE38 . . . . .172 A6
Watermeadow Cl **3**
 NR14 . . . . .91 F1
Watermill Cl NR11 . . . . . . .9 F1
Watermill Gn IP24 . . . . . .176 C3
Watermill La
 Oxborough PE37 . . . . . . .82 A6
 Weybread IP21 . . . . .131 F8
Watermill Rise NR15 . . . .106 F7
Water Moor La NR14 . . . .141 C6
Watersfield Way NR19 . . .154 D2
Waterside PE30 . . . . .146 F7
Waterside Dr NR35 . . . . .109 B1
Waterside The NR6 . . . . .157 D3
Waters La NR29 . . . . .167 A7
Water Sports Ctr PE34 . . .43 C3
Water Tower La IP22 . . . .119 A1
Water Twr Rd NR14 . . . . .88 E4
Waterway Loke NR11 . . . .150 D8
Water Works La NR12 . . . .55 F3
Waterworks Rd
 Norwich NR2 . . . . .161 F7
 Norwich NR2 . . . . .162 A7
 Old Hunstanton PE36 . . .132 F7
 Ormesby St Michael NR29. .57 C2
Watery La
 Beeston with Bittering
 PE32 . . . . .48 B3
 Grimston PE32 . . . . .45 B8
 Guist NR20 . . . . .33 A4
 Little Barningham NR11 . .20 C4
 Matlask NR11 . . . . .20 D5
 Necton PE37 . . . . .66 B4
 Scarning NR19 . . . . .154 A1
 Shipdham IP25 . . . . .67 C2
Wathen Way NR10 . . . . . .150 C1
Watkin Rd NR4 . . . . .89 E8
Watling Cl NR30 . . . . . . .168 E6
Watling Rd
 Attleborough NR17 . . . . .174 F6
 Norwich NR7 . . . . .159 D1
Watlings Ct **8** NR2 . . . .162 C6
Watlings La NR19 . . . . . . .67 A6
Watlings The NR19 . . . . . .67 B6
WATLINGTON PE33 . . . . .42 C4
Watlington Com Prim Sch
 PE33 . . . . .61 D5
Watlington Rd
 Tottenhill PE33 . . . . .61 F6
 Wiggenhall St Germans
 PE34 . . . . .61 D8
Watlington Sta PE33 . . . . .61 D5
Watson Gr **3** NR2 . . . . .162 B8
Watsons Cl NR31 . . . . . . .171 E4
Watson-Watt Gdns
 NR11 . . . . .143 A7
WATTISFIELD IP22 . . . . .128 B1
Wattisfield Rd
 Hinderclay IP22. . . . . . . .128 B3
 Thelnetham IP22. . . . . . .128 A2
WATTLEFIELD NR18 . . . .105 C7
Wattlefield Rd
 Tacolneston NR16. . . . . .105 C6
 Wymondham NR18. . . . . .88 A1
WATTON IP25. . . . . .84 E3
WATTON GREEN IP25. . . .84 F3
Watton Jun Sch IP25. . . . .84 D3
Watton Rd Ashill IP25. . . .84 F8
 Barford NR9. . . . . .69 E2
 Colney NR4. . . . . .160 F4
 Great Cressingham IP25. . .83 D4
 Great Ellingham NR17. . .103 D8
 Hingham NR9. . . . . .86 B5
 Hockham IP24. . . . . .102 E4
 Larling NR16. . . . . .118 A8
 Little Cressingham IP25. . .83 F2
 Little Melton NR9. . . . . . .160 B4
 Lower Stow Bedon NR17. .102 F5
 Merton IP25. . . . . .84 C2
 North Pickenham PE37. . .83 C8
 Shipdham IP25. . . . . .84 F8
 Shropham NR16. . . . . . . .103 A1
 Shropham NR17. . . . . . . .103 A4
 South Pickenham PE37. . .83 D7
 Stow Bedon NR17. . . . . .102 D7
 Swaffham PE37. . . . . . . .153 D2
 Thompson IP25. . . . . . . .102 A8
 Wretham IP24. . . . . .102 A1

Waveney Cres **2** NR35. .123 F7
Waveney Dr
 5 Belton NR31. . . . . . . .94 A6
 Wroxham/Hoveton NR12 .164 D5
Waveney Hill NR32. . . . . .111 F3
Waveney Hts IP21. . . . . . .131 C6
Waveney Rd
 Bungay NR35. . . . . .124 B8
 Diss IP22. . . . . .177 E3
 Ditchingham NR35. . . . . .109 B2
 Great Yarmouth NR31. . .169 C1
 Hunstanton PE36. . . . . .132 C3
 King's Lynn PE30. . . . . . .147 D5
Waveney Valley Swimming
 Pool NR35. . . . . .124 B7
Waverley Rd NR4. . . . . . .162 A2
WAXHAM NR12. . . . . .40 C5
Waxham Ct NR12. . . . . . . .40 A5
Waxham Rd NR12. . . . . . .40 A5
Waxwing Way **13** NR7. .159 E4
Waxworks **28** NR30. . . .169 D4
Wayford Rd NR12. . . . . . .38 F4
Wayland Ave **4** IP25. . . .84 C3
Wayland Cl NR17. . . . . . .174 D5
Wayland Com High Sch
 IP25. . . . . .84 D3
Wayland Hospl NR17. . . .174 A7
Wayland Rd NR17. . . . . . .103 C8
Wayland Way NR16. . . . .119 D7
Wayland Wlk PE38. . . . . .172 B7
Wayside Estate NR14. . . . .95 A7
WEASENHAM ALL SAINTS
 PE32. . . . . .47 C8
Weasenham CE Prim Sch
 PE32. . . . . .47 D8
Weasenham La **1** PE13 .152 D2
Weasenham Rd
 Great Massingham PE32. .29 E1
 Litcham PE32. . . . . .47 E7
 Little Massingham PE32. .29 E3
 Weasenham St Peter PE32 .30 A1
 Weasenham St Peter PE32 .30 A3
WEASENHAM ST PETER
 PE32. . . . . .30 D1
Weatherby Rd NR5. . . . . .160 D8
Weavers Cl
 4 Horsham St Faith
 NR10. . . . . .53 D2
 North Walsham NR28. . .151 B4
Weavers Croft **8** IP20. .122 D2
Weavers Ct IP22. . . . . . . .177 D5
Weavers View NR12. . . . . .37 F1
Webb Dr **4** NR13. . . . . . .72 E7
Webbs Cl **2** NR28. . . . . .151 E5
Webdell St **3** NR1. . . . . .162 E1
Webster Cl
 5 Norwich NR5. . . . . . .156 E1
 8 Stoke Holy Cross NR14 .89 F4
Webster Way NR30. . . . . .168 E6
Wedge Wood NR11. . . . . .22 C7
Wedge Wood Rd NR11. . . .22 C7
Wedgwood Dr PE13. . . . .152 D5
Weedon Way PE30. . . . . .147 D4
WEETING IP27. . . . . .175 B8
Weeting Castle★ IP27. . .114 E4
Weeting Heath National
 Nature Reserve★ IP27 114 C2
Weeting VC Prim Sch
 IP27. . . . . .175 B8
Welbeck Ave **8** NR29. . . .57 D4
Welbeck Rd PE13. . . . . . .152 E4
WELBORNE NR20. . . . . . .69 A4
Welborne Rd NR20. . . . . .68 F5
WELBOURNE COMMON
 NR20. . . . . .68 F4
Welden Rd Dereham NR19 .67 D7
 East Dereham NR19. . . . .154 B4
Welgate Cl **11** NR20. . . .68 E6
Welgate Rd NR20. . . . . . . .68 E6
Welholme's Cl **13** NR15 .106 E3
Wellbeck NR5. . . . . .90 F2
Wellbeck Rd NR15. . . . . . .91 A2
Well Cl NR9. . . . . .51 A6
Well Creek Rd
 Outwell PE14. . . . . .77 F6
 Outwell PE14. . . . . .78 A6
Welldon La NR13. . . . . . . .54 F2
Well End PE14. . . . . .77 A7
Wellesley Ave NR1. . . . . .163 B7
Wellesley Ave N **4** NR1 .163 B7
Wellesley Ave S NR1. . . .163 B6
Wellesley Cl NR14. . . . . . .90 C4
Wellesley Rd
 Great Yarmouth NR30. . .169 D5
 8 Long Stratton NR15. .106 D3
Wellesley St **11** PE30. . .146 E5
Well Hall La PE32. . . . . . . .45 A6
Well Hill NR19. . . . . .68 C5
WELLINGHAM PE32. . . . . .30 F1
Wellingham Rd
 Litcham PE32. . . . . .47 F6
 Tittleshall PE32. . . . . . . .48 A8
 Wellingham PE32. . . . . . .47 F8
Wellington Cl
 Brandon IP27. . . . . .175 D3
 Gimingham NR11. . . . . . .22 F8
Wellington Cres NR21. . . .15 C3
Wellington Gn **7** NR2. . .162 C6
Wellington Pl **12** NR30 .169 D4
Wellington Rd
 Attleborough NR17. . . . .174 A2
 Briston NR24. . . . . .142 B4
 East Dereham NR19. . . .154 D5
 3 Feltwell IP26. . . . . . . .98 E1
 6 Great Yarmouth NR30 .169 D2
 6 Long Stratton NR15. .106 D3
 Norwich NR2. . . . . .162 B6

Wellington Terr 1
  PE13. . . . . .152 C4
Well La NR9 . . . . .51 A6
Well Loke NR3. . . . . .158 B3
Well Medieval Village of *
  PE32. . . . . .45 B7
Well Opening 24 NR30 . .169 D2
Well Rd Cantley NR13 . . . .92 D6
  Great Yarmouth NR30 . . 169 D2
Wells Ave NR28. . . . . . . .151 A3
Wells Cl 2 NR10. . . . . . . .53 E5
Wells Comm Hosp
  NR23. . . . . .136 B5
Wells Community Hospital
  NR23 . . . . .5 C6
Wellsdry Rd NR21. . . . . . .16 D2
Wells Green La
  Little Dunham PE32. . . . . .65 C8
  Newton by Castle Acre
    PE32. . . . . .47 C1
Wells' La IP20 . . . . .122 D1
Wells Loke NR12. . . . . . . .38 E7
Wells Maritime Mus *
  NR23 . . . . .136 B6
WELLS-NEXT-THE-SEA
  NR23 . . . . .136 C5
Wells-next-the-Sea Prim
  Sch NR23 . . . . .136 E5
Wells-next-the-Sea Sta
  NR23 . . . . .136 F4
Wellspring Rd NR11. . . . . .22 C8
Wells Rd Barsham NR21 . .141 A8
  Burnham Overy PE31 . . . .135 F4
  Burnham Overy Staithe
    PE31 . . . . .135 E7
  Fakenham NR21. . . . . . .141 B4
  Hindringham NR21 . . . . . .17 D6
  Needham IP20. . . . . . . .122 C1
  North Creake NR21 . . . . . .4 D1
  Stiffkey NR23. . . . . .6 C6
  Walsingham NR22. . . . . . .5 F1
  Walsingham NR22. . . . . . .16 C8
  Walsingham NR22. . . . . . .16 F8
  Warham NR23. . . . . . . .136 F4
  Wighton NR22. . . . . .6 A2
  Wighton NR23 . . . . .5 F3
  Wighton NR23. . . . . .5 F4
Well St Docking PE31. . . .134 C5
  Great Yarmouth NR30 . . 169 D4
  Thetford IP24 . . . . .176 D3
  Witton NR28 . . . . .23 D3
Wells Wondy La PE32 . . . .45 D6
WELNEY PE14. . . . . .95 D4
Welney Rd PE14 . . . . .95 C6
Welney Wildfowl Refuge *
  PE14. . . . . .95 F6
Welsford Rd
  5 Norwich NR4 . . . . .89 D8
  Norwich NR4 . . . . .162 B1
Weltons Loke NR9 . . . . . . .52 A6
Wendals Cl PE14. . . . . . . .41 E4
Wendene NR5. . . . . .160 F7
WENDLING NR19 . . . . .66 F8
Wendling Rd NR19. . . . . . .48 F2
Wendover Rd NR13 . . . . . .72 D8
Wenman Ct 5 NR5 . . . . .160 F8
Wensom Cl 3 PE33. . . . . .61 D6
Wensum Cres NR6. . . . . .157 D3
Wensum Ct NR21 . . . . . . .32 C6
Wensum Dr NR20 . . . . . . .49 F7
Wensum Gdns 1 NR20. . .50 B3
Wensum Jun Sch NR2 . . .162 A7
Wensum La PE31 . . . . .30 A6
Wensum Meadows Rd
  NR6. . . . . .71 B6
Wensum Rd NR9. . . . . . . .51 A4
Wensum St NR3 . . . . . . .178 B3
Wensum Valley Cl
  Hellesdon NR6. . . . . . . .157 D4
  Norwich NR6 . . . . .71 B6
Wensum Way
  1 Belton NR31 . . . . .94 A6
  2 Fakenham NR21. . . . .141 E4
  King's Lynn PE30. . . . . .146 F6
Wensum Wlk NR8. . . . . . .155 F3
Wentworth Cl 6 IP27. . . .114 E1
Wentworth Gn NR4 . . . . .161 F2
WEREHAM PE33 . . . . .80 E4
Wereham Bypass PE33. . .80 D4
Wereham Row PE33 . . . . .80 D3
Wesgate St NR25 . . . . .7 C6
Wesley Ave PE34. . . . . . .144 B5
Wesley Cl
  Downham Market PE38. .172 B5
  4 Mattishall NR20 . . . . .68 C6
  Mundesley NR11. . . . . .143 D5
  Terrington St Clement
    PE34. . . . . .144 B5
Wesley Rd
  King's Lynn PE30. . . . . .148 C5
  Terrington St Clement
    PE34 . . . . .144 B5
Wessex St NR2 . . . . .178 A1
WEST ACRE PE32 . . . . . . .46 D4
Westacre Dr NR6 . . . . . . .158 E7
West Acre Gdns * PE32. . .46 D4
West Acre Rd
  Castle Acre PE32. . . . . . .46 E2
  Swaffham PE37 . . . . . . .153 A6
West Ave
  Great Yarmouth NR31 . . .170 C3
  Ormesby St Margaret
    NR29 . . . . .167 A3
West Bank PE12 . . . . .41 C8
West Bank La PE31. . . . . .131 B5
WEST BARSHAM NR21. . . .16 C4
West Barsham Rd NR21 . . .16 D4
WEST BECKHAM NR25 . . . .9 C2
WEST BILNEY PE32 . . . . . .45 B2
Westbourne Ct 4 NR31 170 C7
Westbourne Rd NR12 . . . .54 D7

Westbriggs Dro PE33 . . . .62 B5
Westbrook Ave 1 NR31 170 B6
WESTBROOK GREEN
  IP22. . . . . .177 C7
WEST CAISTER NR30. . . .168 C4
West Carr Rd
  Attleborough NR17 . . . . .174 A4
  Attleborough NR17 . . . . .174 B4
West Church St NR16 . . . .119 A5
West Cl NR5. . . . . .157 A2
West Cliff Cromer NR27 . . .139 B7
  Sheringham NR26. . . . . .138 D7
Westcliff Ave NR27 . . . . .139 A7
West Cres NR20 . . . . .50 A5
West Croft NR9. . . . . .88 C7
WEST DEREHAM PE33 . . . .80 B4
West Dereham Rd PE33. . .80 D3
West Dr Brandon IP27 . . .175 A2
  1 Friday Bridge PE14 . . . .77 A8
West Dro N PE14. . . . . . . .59 D8
West Dro S PE14 . . . . .59 D5
West Drove Link Rd PE14. .59 E8
West Earlham Inf & Jun Sch
  NR5. . . . . .161 D6
WEST END Necton IP25 . . . .66 A4
  West Caister NR30 . . . . . .76 B6
West End Briston NR24. . .142 F5
  Costessey NR8. . . . . . . .156 C4
  Erpingham NR11. . . . . . .21 A1
  Hilgay PE38 . . . . .79 D1
  Northwold IP26. . . . . . . .99 B8
  Saxlingham Thorpe NR15 .107 A8
  Whissonsett NR21. . . . . . .31 C2
  Wickmere NR11. . . . . . . .20 F3
West End Ave
  Brundall NR13 . . . . .165 A4
  Costessey NR8. . . . . . . .156 C5
West End Ct 6 IP25 . . . . .84 C3
West End St NR2. . . . . . .162 B7
Westerley Cl NR30 . . . . . .168 D4
Westerley Way NR30 . . . . .168 D4
Western Ave NR7 . . . . . . .163 E6
Western Bypass
  Aylsham NR11. . . . . . . .150 B5
  Bradwell NR31. . . . . . . .170 C4
  Downham Market PE38. .172 A5
  Great Yarmouth NR30 . . .169 B3
Western Cl
  4 Feltwell IP26 . . . . .98 D1
  Upper Stoke NR14. . . . . .90 B5
Western Rd NR11. . . . . . .170 C4
WESTFIELD NR19 . . . . . . .67 F4
Westfield NR13 . . . . .74 D7
Westfield Ave NR23. . . . .136 C6
Westfield Cl 2 NR29 . . . . .57 C1
Westfield Inf Sch IP25 . . .84 D3
Westfield La
  Dereham NR19 . . . . .154 F1
  Terrington St Clement PE34 25 B1
Westfield Rd
  Brundall NR13 . . . . .165 D4
  East Dereham NR19 . . . .154 E2
  Swaffham PE37 . . . . . . .153 B4
  Wisbech PE13 . . . . .152 E7
Westfields
  Attleborough NR17 . . . . .174 B4
  King's Lynn PE30. . . . . .147 C4
  Narborough PE32 . . . . . .63 E7
  Tilney St Lawrence PE34. .60 C8
Westfields Cl
  Terrington St John PE14. . .60 C8
  Tilney St Lawrence PE34. .42 C1
Westfield View NR4. . . . .161 E1
WESTGATE Binham NR21. . . .6 D3
  Burnham PE31 . . . . .135 B3
Westgate Hevingham NR10 53 B8
  Hunstanton PE36. . . . . .132 C4
  Norwich NR6 . . . . .157 F5
  Shropham NR17. . . . . . .103 B4
  Walsingham NR22. . . . . . .16 F8
West Gate NR18 . . . . . . .173 B4
Westgate Cl NR22. . . . . .162 A4
Westgate Ct NR18 . . . . . .173 B4
Westgate Gdns NR18. . . .173 A2
Westgate Gn NR10. . . . . .53 B8
Westgate Rd PE36. . . . . . .1 F6
Westgate St
  Hevingham NR10. . . . . . .52 B8
  Hilborough PE33 . . . . . . .83 A3
  Holme next the Sea PE36. . .2 A6
  Shouldham PE33 . . . . . . .62 D4
  Southery PE38. . . . . .97 A5
WESTGATE STREET
  NR10 . . . . .53 B8
Westhall IP21 . . . . .131 F1
West Hall Rd
  Dersingham PE31 . . . . . .140 D3
  Mundford IP26 . . . . .100 B4
WEST HARLING NR16 . . .118 A3
West Harling Rd
  Harling NR16. . . . . .117 F2
  Harling NR16. . . . . .118 A4
WEST HEAD PE34. . . . . . .78 F8
West Head Rd PE14 . . . . . .78 F8
West Herne La IP22. . . . .128 D5
Westhorpe Cl 3 PE30. . . .147 A8
West La Brundall NR13 . . . .73 A3
  Horsham St Faith NR10. . .53 D1
  Horsham St Faith & Newton St
    Faith NR10. . . . . .53 D1
Westland Chase PE33. . . .43 F1
Westlegate NR1 . . . . .178 B2
WEST LEXHAM PE32 . . . . .47 C4
West Lexham Hall PE32 . . .47 C4
WEST LYNN PE34. . . . . . .146 C5
West Lynn Prim Sch
  PE34. . . . . .146 C5
Westmark PE30. . . . . . . .147 C4
Westmead Dro PE13. . . . .152 E2
Westmead Rd NR21. . . . .141 C4
Westminster Cl 7 PE13 152 E6

Westmoor Dro CB6 . . . . . .95 E1
WEST NEWTON PE31 . . . . .27 F6
West Newton Rd PE31 . . . .27 F4
Weston Bury La IP22. . . .127 C3
Weston Cl 1 NR13. . . . . . .73 C6
Weston Ct NR6 . . . . .158 F6
WESTON GREEN NR9 . . . . .51 E1
Weston Green Rd NR20 . . .51 D1
Weston Hall NR9 . . . . .51 D3
Weston La IP22. . . . . . . .127 C3
WESTON LONGVILLE
  NR9 . . . . .51 E3
Weston Miller Dr PE13 . .152 C7
Weston Rd
  Hinderclay IP22. . . . . . .128 B4
  Norwich NR3 . . . . .158 C3
  Ringland NR8. . . . . .52 A1
  Weston Longville NR9 . . . .51 F2
  17 Wisbech PE13. . . . . .152 C4
Weston Rise NR30 . . . . . .168 D5
Weston Sq 3 NR31 . . . . .137 B6
Weston Terr NR26 . . . . . .138 E7
Weston Wood Cl NR7. . . .163 D7
Weston Wood Rd NR7. . . .163 D7
West Parade
  Norwich NR2. . . . . .162 B6
  Wisbech PE13 . . . . .152 B7
West Paynham Rd PE31 . .29 F6
West Pk Farm Cl PE26. . .100 C5
WEST PORINGLAND
  NR14 . . . . .90 B4
West Pottergate NR2 . . . .162 B5
WEST RAYNHAM NR21. . . .30 E4
West Raynham CE Prim Sch
  NR21 . . . . .30 F4
West Raynham Rd
  Little Massingham PE32 . . .29 F3
  Little Massingham PE32 . . .30 A3
  Raynham NR21 . . . . .30 F4
  South Raynham NR21. . . .30 F3
  West Raynham NR21. . . . .30 C4
West Rd
  Caister-on-Sea NR30 . . .168 D4
  Dersingham PE31 . . . . . .140 D3
  Great Yarmouth NR30 . . .168 F1
  Norwich NR2. . . . . .157 A2
  Ormesby St Margaret
    NR29. . . . . .167 A2
  Shouldham Thorpe PE33 . .62 C2
  Tacolneston NR16 . . . . . .105 F4
  Watton IP25 . . . . .84 D3
  West Caister NR30 . . . . . .76 D6
  West Caister NR30 . . . . .168 B4
WEST RUDHAM PE31 . . . .29 F7
WEST RUNTON NR27. . . . .10 A5
West Runton Sta NR27. . . .10 A5
Westry Cl PE13 . . . . .59 C5
WEST SOMERTON NR29. . .57 E6
West St North Creake NR21. . .4 D1
  Rickinghall Inferior IP22. .128 C1
  Wisbech PE13 . . . . .152 C4
West Stree 18 NR30. . . . .169 D2
West Suffolk Coll IP24. . .176 C1
WEST TOFTS IP26 . . . . . .100 F4
West Tofts Rd IP26 . . . . .100 D3
West View
  Dereham NR19 . . . . .154 C1
  Poringland NR14 . . . . . . .90 C4
  South Pickenham PE37 . . .83 D7
West View Dr NR13 . . . . . .74 A2
West View Rd NR13 . . . . .165 E6
WEST WALTON PE14. . . . .59 B8
West Walton Com Prim Sch
  PE14. . . . . .59 C8
West Way
  Downham Market PE38. . .172 B4
  Stow Bardolph PE34. . . . .61 D1
  Tacolneston NR16 . . . . . .105 E5
  Wimbotsham PE34. . . . . .79 D8
WESTWICK NR10. . . . . . . .37 D6
Westwick Dr NR28 . . . . . .151 A4
Westwick Rd
  Worstead NR28. . . . . . . .37 F5
  Worstead NR28. . . . . . . .38 A5
Westwick St NR2 . . . . . . .178 A3
WEST WINCH PE33 . . . . . .43 E3
West Winch Prim Sch
  PE33. . . . . .43 E2
West Winch Rd PE33. . . . .43 F4
West Wood Cotts NR31. . . .32 B5
Westwood Dr NR6 . . . . . .157 D6
Westwood Gdns NR18. . . .173 A6
Westwood La NR21 . . . . . .32 B5
WEYBOURNE NR25 . . . . . . .8 F5
Weybourne Rd
  Bodham NR25 . . . . .9 A3
  Kelling NR25 . . . . .8 D5
  Sheringham NR26. . . . . .138 B7
  Upper Sheringham NR26. .138 A6
Weybourne Sta NR25 . . . . .8 F5
Weybread Rd IP21. . . . . .131 D5
Weynor Gdns NR25 . . . . . .8 E5
Whalers Farrow PE30 . . .146 E2
Wharf St PE12. . . . . .41 B8
Wharton Dr NR28. . . . . . .151 E7
Whartons La 6 NR18 . . . .173 B3
WHEATACRE NR34. . . . . .111 B5
Wheatacre Cl 9 NR10 . . . .53 A3
Wheatacres IP24 . . . . . . .176 D5
Wheatcroft Way NR20. . . .68 A8
Wheatfield Rd 34 NR4. . . .89 D7
Wheatfields
  Hillington PE31 . . . . .28 B4
  Rickinghall Superior IP22 .128 E2
Wheat Fields NR8. . . . . . .155 F2
Wheatfield Way NR15. . . .106 F4
Wheatley Bank PE14 . . . . .59 C5
Wheatley Dr PE30. . . . . . .148 A4
Wheatley Rd NR2 . . . . . . .161 F7
Wheelbarrow La IP20. . . .123 F4

Wheeler Cres NR9 . . . . . . .70 B5
Wheeler Rd NR3 . . . . . . .158 A1
Wheelers La NR15 . . . . . .108 E8
Wheel Rd NR14. . . . . .90 E4
Wheelwright Rd NR3. . . . .147 C5
Wheelwrights Cl NR13 . . .92 E8
Wherry Cl
  Chedgrave NR14 . . . . . . .92 A2
  North Walsham NR28 . . .151 E7
Wherry Loke NR1 . . . . . . .178 C1
Wherry Rd Bungay NR35. .124 C8
  Norwich NR1 . . . . .162 C3
Wherry Reach 2 NR13. . .166 D4
Wherry Sch The NR1. . . . .162 D2
Wherry Way NR30 . . . . . .169 C7
Whetstone Wy PE14 . . . . .77 E6
Whey Curd Rd
  Great Walsingham NR21. . .17 A8
  Walsingham NR22. . . . . . . .6 A1
Whiffler Rd NR3 . . . . .157 F2
Whiffler Road Trad Est
  NR3. . . . . .158 A2
Whiley La 17 NR12 . . . . . .39 B4
Whimbrel Dr
  8 Great Yarmouth NR31 . .94 C8
  1 Great Yarmouth NR31 .170 A7
WHIMPWELL GREEN
  NR12 . . . . .24 C4
Whimpwell St NR12. . . . . .24 C4
WHINBURGH NR19. . . . . . .68 A3
Whinburgh Rd NR19 . . . . .67 F3
Whinchat Way 3 NR31. . . .94 C7
Whin Common Rd PE33 . . .61 F6
Whin Comm Rd
  Denver PE38. . . . . .172 D1
  Tottenhill PE33. . . . . .61 F6
Wincraft La NR12. . . . . . . .39 B6
Whinmere Rd NR12 . . . . . .39 E3
Whipp's La NR16. . . . . . .105 F7
Whisson Cl 1 NR30 . . . . .147 A8
WHISSONSETT NR20. . . . . .31 D2
Whissonsett Rd
  Horningtoft NR20. . . . . . .31 F2
  Oxwick NR21 . . . . .31 D4
  Stanfield NR20. . . . . .48 E8
Whistle Dro IP28 . . . . . . .112 D1
Whistlefish Ct NR5. . . . . .161 E7
Whitby Rd NR29 . . . . .168 C8
Whitby St 3 PE13. . . . . . .152 C5
Whitbeam Cres IP25. . . . .84 E3
White City Rd PE14 . . . . . .78 D6
White Clover Rd 26 NR31. .94 C6
White Clover Wy 12
  NR31. . . . . .171 D4
White Cross
  Burgh & Tuttington NR11. . .36 E4
  Hardingham NR9 . . . . . . .86 E8
Whitecross La PE34. . . . .144 E4
White Cross Rd PE37. . . . .153 C4
Whitedike Dro IP26. . . . . .113 B8
White Farm La NR7 . . . . .163 C6
Whitefriars NR3 . . . . .178 B4
Whitefriars CE Sch
  PE30. . . . . .146 D3
Whitefriars Rd PE30 . . . .146 D3
Whitefriars Terr PE30. . . .146 D3
White Gate La NR11. . . . . .11 D2
White Gates NR5 . . . . .56 B5
White Gates NR5 . . . . . . .156 E1
Whitegates Cl 6 NR9 . . . .88 D7
Whitegates Rd NR11. . . . .22 B7
White Hall NR21 . . . . .15 C3
White Hall Dr NR34. . . . .144 C4
White Hall La IP25. . . . . . .84 C4
Whitehall Rd NR2 . . . . . .162 B5
Whitehall Yd 8 NR26. . . .138 D7
Whitehart La Filby NR29 . .67 F1
  Filby NR29 . . . . .75 F8
Whitehart St 6 IP24. . . . .176 C4
White Hart St
  2 Aylsham NR11. . . . . . .150 C7
  East Harling NR16. . . . . .118 C5
  Foulden IP26. . . . . .82 A2
White Heath Rd NR15 . . . .91 B3
White Horse Dr PE31. . . . .140 C4
White Horse Gdns NR28. . .38 A8
White Horse La NR17 . . . .174 C5
White Horse La
  Bixley NR14. . . . . .89 F8
  Trowse with Newton
    NR14. . . . . .163 A1
  Worstead NR28. . . . . . . .38 B6
Whitehorse Plain 7
  NR30 . . . . .169 C5
Whitehorse St
  1 Fakenham NR21. . . . . .141 C3
  Wymondham NR18 . . . . .173 B3
White Horse St IP27 . . . . .175 A2
White House Ct NR3. . . . .158 B3
White House Dr 29
  NR15 . . . . .106 E3
White House East NR27 . .139 D4
White House Farm La
  IP21. . . . . .122 B2
White House Farm Prim Sch
  NR7 . . . . .159 E5
White House Gdns 12
  NR14 . . . . .90 D5
Whitehouse La
  Earsham NR35. . . . . . . .108 C1
  Wicklewood NR18. . . . . . .87 C4
White House La
  Attleborough NR17 . . . . .174 F5
  Syleham IP21. . . . . .131 C5
Wilbey Rd Norwich NR1. .162 E1
  Quidenham NR16. . . . . .118 F8
Wild Apple Cl NR5. . . . . .161 A7
Wildbriar Cl PE34. . . . . . .145 A5
Wild Cherry Cl IP25 . . . . .84 E3
Wilde Rd NR14. . . . . .159 C4
Wilderness Cl 3 IP20. . . .122 D1
Wilderness La IP20 . . . . .122 D2
Wilderness Rd
  Banham NR16 . . . . .119 A4
  Costessey NR8. . . . . . . .156 A5
Wilderness The NR13 . . . .72 F2
Wildfields Cl PE34. . . . . .145 D5
Wildfields Rd PE34. . . . . .145 C6
Wild Flower Ctr * NR25 . . .7 E3
White Lion Ct 14 PE30. . .146 D5
White Lion Rd
  Coltishall NR12. . . . . .54 D6

White Lion Rd continued
  Wheatacre NR34. . . . . . .111 B4
White Lion St Holt NR25. .137 B6
  Norwich NR2. . . . . .178 A2
White Lodge Bsns Est
  NR4 . . . . .89 E8
White Oaks PE30. . . . . . . .65 E2
Whiteplot Rd IP26 . . . . . . .98 D5
Whitepost La IP21 . . . . . .131 C8
White Post Rd
  Hanworth NR11. . . . . . . .21 D4
  Hanworth NR11. . . . . . . .21 D5
White Rd
  Barton Bendish PE33. . . . .63 D1
  Methwold IP26 . . . . .99 A5
White Rose Cl NR5. . . . . .161 D8
White Sedge PE30 . . . . . .147 A8
White St NR29 . . . . .57 D5
Whitethorn Cl 6 NR6. . . .158 D5
Whitetop La NR11. . . . . . .35 F7
Whiteway Rd
  Burnham Deepdale PE31. . .3 F6
  Burnham Market PE31 . . .135 B3
White Woman La NR6. . . .159 A6
White Woman La Sch
  NR6. . . . . .158 F6
Whiting Rd NR4 . . . . .162 D1
Whiting's La NR7 . . . . . . .103 A6
Whitley Cl
  11 Feltwell IP26 . . . . . . .98 D1
  Old Catton NR6 . . . . . . .158 C6
Whitley Cl
  Dersingham PE31 . . . . . . .140 D3
Whitlingham Ctry Pk *
  NR7 . . . . .163 E4
Whitlingham La NR14. . . .163 C4
Whitsands Rd PE37 . . . . .153 A5
WHITTINGTON PE33 . . . . .81 B2
Whittington Hill PE33 . . . .81 B2
Whittome Mill PE38. . . . . .79 D1
Whitwell Comm
  Blackwater NR10. . . . . . .51 C7
  Whitwell NR10. . . . . . . .149 A1
Whitwell Rd
  Hornington NR20. . . . . . .31 F2
  Reepham NR10 . . . . .149 A2
  Sparham NR9. . . . . .51 B6
Whitwell St NR10 . . . . . . .149 C3
WHITWELL STREET
  NR10 . . . . .149 C3
Whitworth Ave 1 NR17 .174 C5
Whymark's Wlk NR15 . . .106 D3
Whytehead Gdns IP22 . . .177 D4
WICKEN GREEN VILLAGE
  NR21 . . . . .15 D2
Wick Farm Cl 3 IP25 . . . .84 D3
Wickfield Ct PE13. . . . . . .152 D4
WICKHAMPTON NR13. . . . .93 A8
Wickhampton Rd NR13. . .93 A8
Wick La NR29 . . . . .57 D2
WICKLEWOOD NR18. . . . . .87 B5
Wicklewood County Prim
  Sch NR18 . . . . .87 B5
Wicklewood La NR18 . . . .87 B6
Wicklewood Rd NR18 . . . .87 B6
WICKMERE NR11 . . . . .20 F4
Wickmere Rd NR11. . . . . .20 C5
Wicks Yd 5 NR19. . . . . . .154 D5
Wiclewood Way PE31. . . .140 C3
Widgeon Cl NR31 . . . . . . .170 A6
Wier Ave NR20. . . . . .68 F6
WIGGENHALL ST GERMANS
  PE34. . . . . .43 C1
WIGGENHALL ST MARY
  MAGDALEN PE34. . . . . . .61 B6
WIGGENHALL ST MARY THE
  VIRGIN PE34 . . . . .61 A8
WIGGENHALL ST PETER
  PE34. . . . . .61 C8
Wiggets La NR11. . . . . . . .34 D7
Wigg Rd NR21 . . . . .141 B6
Wiggs Rd NR14 . . . . .110 F7
Wight Dr NR30. . . . . .168 C6
Wightmans La NR31 . . . . .170 D5
WIGHTON NR23. . . . . .6 A2
Wighton Hall Sta NR23. . . .5 F3
Wighton Rd
  New Holkham NR25. . . . . . .5 A2
  Warham NR25 . . . . .6 A4
  Wighton NR23 . . . . .5 E3
  Wighton NR23 . . . . .136 D1
Wigwam Hill IP22 . . . . . .129 C5
Wilberforce Rd
  Norwich NR5 . . . . .161 B6
  Wisbech PE13 . . . . .152 D5
WILBY NR16. . . . . .119 A8

Wilkins Rd PE14 . . . . .59 D3
Wilks Farm Dr NR7. . . . . .159 A5
Willbye Ave IP22 . . . . . . .177 E5
William Booth Rd PE30. .147 D5
William Booth St NR1. . . .72 A5
William Brown Dr 4
  NR13 . . . . .165 D6
William Brown Way 1
  IP22. . . . . .177 A5
William Bush Cl NR10. . . .35 B2
William Childerhouse Way
  6 NR5. . . . . .160 E7
William Cl
  5 Watton IP25. . . . . .84 D3
  6 Wymondham NR18. . .173 C6
William Cowper Cl
  NR19 . . . . .154 E1
William Frost Wy NR5. . .156 B3
William George Way
  PE32. . . . . .44 D1
William Green Way 5
  NR13 . . . . .165 D6
William Kett Cl NR11. . . .163 A6
William Lant Cl NR16. . . .105 F4
William Marriot Mus *
  NR25 . . . . .137 E8
William Marshall VC Sch The
  PE14. . . . . .95 D4
William Mear Gdns NR1. .163 B6
William O'Callaghan Pl 11
  NR19 . . . . .154 D5
William Paston Rd
  NR28 . . . . .151 D6
William Peck Rd 7
  NR10 . . . . .54 A2
William Rd
  Fakenham NR21. . . . . . .141 F5
  Wisbech PE13 . . . . .152 C5
Williams Loke NR7. . . . . .163 D8
Williamson Cl Diss IP22 .177 D6
  Norwich NR7 . . . . .159 C2
Williamson Cres 4
  IP24. . . . . .176 C2
William St 9 PE30. . . . . .146 E3
Williams Way
  3 Holt NR25. . . . . .137 C5
  5 North Walsham NR28. .151 C6
William Way NR19 . . . . . .154 C1
Williman Cl PE31 . . . . . . .133 D6
Willis St NR3 . . . . .178 A4
Willoughby Way 5 NR18. .72 E7
Willow Ave NR31 . . . . .94 C7
Willowbrook Cl 4
  NR33. . . . . .111 F1
Willow Cl Brandon IP27 . . .175 D2
  Brundall NR13 . . . . .165 E2
  Lingwood NR13 . . . . .74 A2
  18 Loddon NR14. . . . . . .91 F1
  Long Stratton NR15. . . . .106 E2
  10 Mattishall NR20. . . . .68 E6
  Middleton PE32 . . . . .44 B4
  North Walsham NR28 . . .151 D7
  Stradbroke IP21 . . . . . . .131 F1
  Watlington PE33 . . . . . . .61 D5
  Wortwell IP20 . . . . .123 A4
  Wymondham NR18 . . . . .173 D5
Willow Corner
  Carbrooke IP25 . . . . .85 A5
  Wortham IP22. . . . . .129 C4
Willow Cres 3 NR15 . . . . .63 B4
Willowcroft Wy NR4 . . . . .89 B8
Willow Ct
  3 Attleborough NR17 . . . .174 B5
  Beetley NR20. . . . . .49 D4
Willow Dr
  Black Carr NR18 . . . . . . .105 A7
  Clenchwarton PE34. . . . .145 E5
  Dersingham PE31 . . . . . .140 D3
  Hempnall NR15 . . . . . . .107 D5
  King's Lynn PE33 . . . . . . .43 F4
  West Winch PE33 . . . . . . .43 F1
Willow Gdns NR7 . . . . . . .159 F3
Willow Gn IP31. . . . . .126 D1
Willow Gr
  East Dereham NR19 . . . .154 D2
  Sheringham NR26. . . . . .138 E5
Willow Heath Rd NR31. . . .80 B7
Willow Herb Dr PE37. . . .153 C1
Willow Herb Wlk 4
  NR18 . . . . .173 E4
Willow La Banham NR16. .119 D6
  Bedingham NR35. . . . . .108 B3
  Broome NR35. . . . . .109 C3
  Carbrooke IP25 . . . . .85 B5
  Heywood IP22 . . . . .120 D4
  Norwich NR2 . . . . .178 A3
Willow Pk PE30. . . . . . . .147 C8
Willow Pl PE33 . . . . .62 A5
Willow Rd
  Downham Market PE38. .172 B6
  East Dereham NR19 . . . .154 B4
  Hunstanton PE36. . . . . .132 C3
  King's Lynn PE30. . . . . .148 D2
  King's Lynn PE34. . . . . . .43 C4
Willows Cl 16 NR29 . . . . .57 C4
Willows The
  Bradwell NR31. . . . . . . .170 A3
  Norwich NR2 . . . . .161 F7
Willow Tree Cl PE34 . . . .146 B5
Willow Way
  2 Ludham NR29. . . . . . .56 C5
  18 Marthan NR29 . . . . . .57 D4
  Wisbech PE13 . . . . .152 D3
WILNEY GREEN IP22. . . . .129 A8
Wilshere Ct 11 NR30. . . .169 D3
Wilson Dr PE32 . . . . .44 F3

Wilson Mws NR26 . . . . 138 D5
Wilson Rd **5** NR1 . . . . . . 163 B5
Wilson's Dro PE32 . . . . 45 E3
Wilson's Way NR25 . . . . 7 D6
Wilton Cres **2** PE30 . . . . . 148 C5
Wilton Rd Feltwell IP26 . . . . 98 E1
 Feltwell IP26 . . . . 113 E8
 Heacham PE31 . . . . 133 C6
Wilton View NR28 . . . . 151 D5
Wiltshire Dr NR31 . . . . 170 A2
Wimbledon Ave IP27 . . . . 175 A1
Wimbledon Way **2**
 PE38 . . . . 172 B4
WIMBOTSHAM PE34 . . . . . . 79 D8
Wimbotsham Rd PE38 . . . 172 C6
Wimbotsham & Stow Com
 Sch PE34 . . . . 79 D8
Wimpole Dr PE30 . . . . 148 E1
Winalls Yard NR1 . . . . 178 B1
Winceby Cl
 15 Norwich NR7 . . . . 72 D4
 Wisbech PE14 . . . . 152 A3
Winchcomb Rd NR2 . . . . . 161 F7
Winchester Twr NR2 . . . . . 162 C5
Winchester Way IP24 . . . 176 B5
Winch Rd PE32 . . . . 45 C5
Wincliff Dr NR25 . . . . 8 E3
Windermere Cl NR15 . . . . . 90 E2
Windermere Rd PE30 . . . . 148 F2
Windhover Cl NR19 . . . . 67 E5
Windle La NR13 . . . . 74 B6
Windle The NR13 . . . . 74 C5
Windmill Ave NR20 . . . . . . 68 A8
Windmill Cl
 Poringland NR14 . . . . 90 C4
 Thetford IP24 . . . . 176 D5
Windmill Ct **7** PE30 . . . . 147 C5
Windmill Gdns PE14 . . . . 152 E8
Windmill Green NR11 . . . . 143 C5
Windmill Hill PE31 . . . . 14 A3
Windmill La
 Costessey NR8 . . . . 157 A4
 Syleham IP21 . . . . 131 D4
 Wretham IP24 . . . . 102 B1
Windmill Loke **1** NR28 . . 151 C4
Windmill Rd
 Gimingham NR11 . . . . 22 F8
 1 Marham PE33 . . . . . . 63 B4
 Norwich NR3 . . . . 158 F2
 Worstead NR28 . . . . 38 A6
 Wortwell IP20 . . . . 123 A3
Windsor Ave NR30 . . . . . . 169 D7
Windsor Chase NR8 . . . . . 155 D1
Windsor Cl **7** PE30 . . . . 125 F6
Windsor Cres PE31 . . . . . . 133 C5
Windsor Ct Diss IP22 . . . . 177 F5
 4 Watton IP25 . . . . 84 D3
Windsor Dr
 Dersingham PE31 . . . . . . 140 D3
 Wisbech PE13 . . . . 152 D8
Windsor Pk
 East Dereham NR19 . . . . 154 D8
 2 King's Lynn PE30 . . . 146 E8
Windsor Pk Gdns NR6 . . . 159 A6
Windsor Rd
 Caister-on-Sea NR30 . . . 168 E6
 Cantley NR13 . . . . 92 C6
 King's Lynn PE30 . . . . . . 146 E3
 Norwich NR6 . . . . 158 A5
Windsor Rise PE36 . . . . . . 132 C2
Windsor St **1** PE38 . . . . 172 A6
Windsor Terr PE30 . . . . . . 146 E3
Windsor Way NR30 . . . . . . 170 B4
Windy Cres PE33 . . . . 63 B3
Windy La
 Foxhole NR15 . . . . 107 B7
 Saxlingham Nethergate
  NR15 . . . . 107 B8
Windy Ridge PE33 . . . . 63 B3
WINFARTHING IP22 . . . . . 120 B4
Winfarthing Ave PE30 . . . 146 D3
Winfarthing Rd
 Banham NR16 . . . . 119 D6
 Shelfanger IP22 . . . . 120 B2
Wingate Way NR2 . . . . . . 162 C7
WINGFIELD IP21 . . . . 131 E4
Wingfield Ave IP27 . . . . . 113 E2
WINGFIELD GREEN
 IP21 . . . . 131 D4
Wingfield Rd
 Lakenheath IP27 . . . . . . 113 E2
 Norwich NR3 . . . . 162 D8
 Syleham IP21 . . . . 131 D5
 Weybread IP21 . . . . 131 F6
Wingfields PE38 . . . . 172 C3
Wing's La NR20 . . . . 33 B7
Wings Rd IP27 . . . . 113 E1
Winifred Ct NR26 . . . . 138 E7
Winifred Rd NR31 . . . . 169 B3
Winifred Way NR30 . . . . . 168 D8
Winmer Ave **6** NR29 . . . . 58 B6
Winners Wlk NR8 . . . . 155 E3
Winnold St PE38 . . . . 172 A6
Winn's Cl NR25 . . . . 137 A7
Winsford Way NR5 . . . . . . 157 C1
Winstanley Rd **21** NR7 . . 72 D4
Winston Churchill Dr
 PE30 . . . . 147 C4
Winston Dr NR21 . . . . 15 E6
Winter Gdns★ NR30 . . . 169 E2
Wintergreen Way NR4 . . . 89 A8

Winter Nelis Way PE30 . . 147 A8
Winter Rd NR2 . . . . 162 A6
Winterton Dunes National
 Nature Reserve★ NR29 . 58 B7
WINTERTON-ON-SEA
 NR29 . . . . 58 C6
Winterton Rd
 Hemsby NR29 . . . . 167 B8
 Somerton NR29 . . . . 57 F6
WISBECH PE13 . . . . 152 A6
Wisbech Bypass
 Walsoken PE14 . . . . 59 C4
 Wisbech PE13 . . . . 152 C1
Wisbech Castle★ PE13 . . 152 C4
Wisbech & Fenland Mus★
 PE13 . . . . 152 C4
Wisbech Gram Sch
 PE13 . . . . 152 B5
Wishing Well Cl IP27 . . . . 175 D4
Wissey Cl PE30 . . . . 146 F6
Wissey Gr IP25 . . . . 84 C3
Wissey View IP26 . . . . 100 B4
Wistaria Rd PE13 . . . . 152 F7
Wisteria Cl NR20 . . . . 154 F4
Wisteria Dr NR18 . . . . 173 F7
Witard Cl NR7 . . . . 159 D1
Witard Rd NR7 . . . . 163 D8
Witchcraft Wy NR13 . . . . . 72 E8
WITHERGATE NR28 . . . . . . 38 A6
Withergate Rd
 Withergate NR28 . . . . 37 F6
 Worstead NR28 . . . . 38 A5
Withersdale Rd IP20 . . . . 123 A1
Withington St **1** PE12 . . 41 B8
Withy Way NR8 . . . . 155 E1
WITTON NR13 . . . . 165 A6
WITTON BRIDGE NR28 . . . 23 E2
Witton Cl Heacham PE31 . 133 C5
 Reedham NR13 . . . . 92 F5
Witton Gn NR13 . . . . 92 F5
Witton Heath NR28 . . . . . 23 C1
Witton La NR13 . . . . 165 A8
Wittons La IP21 . . . . 131 A3
Witton Woods NR28 . . . . . 23 C2
WIVETON NR25 . . . . 7 E6
Wiveton Rd Blakeney NR25 . 7 D6
 Langham NR25 . . . . 7 C4
Wlk The
 16 Beccles NR34 . . . . . 110 D1
 Ludham NR29 . . . . 56 C4
 Thurton NR14 . . . . 91 C4
Woburn St NR2 . . . . 162 C5
Wodehouse Ct **1** NR12 . 39 B4
Wodehouse Ct **11** IP25 . 84 D3
Wodehouse Rd
 Bacton NR12 . . . . 23 D4
 Old Hunstanton PE36 . . 132 E7
Wodehouse St NR3 . . . . . 162 E8
Wolfe Rd NR1 . . . . 163 B4
WOLFERD GREEN NR15 . . . 90 B2
WOLFERTON PE31 . . . . 27 B7
Wolferton Dr PE37 . . . . . . 153 B2
Wollaston Ave NR19 . . . . 154 D7
Wolseley Rd NR31 . . . . . . 169 B2
WOLTERTON NR11 . . . . 20 E2
Wolterton Pk★ NR11 . . . . 20 E2
Wolterton Pk NR11 . . . . . . 20 E2
Wolterton Rd NR11 . . . . . . 20 C2
Womersley Cl **5** NR1 . . 163 B7
Womersley Rd NR1 . . . . . 163 B5
Wood Avens Way
 Wymondham NR18 . . . . 88 A4
 Wymondham NR18 . . . . 173 E4
WOODBASTWICK NR13 . . 55 D2
Woodbastwick Rd
 Blofield NR13 . . . . 165 E7
 Blofield Heath NR13 . . . . 73 C6
 Woodbastwick NR13 . . . . 55 E1
Woodbine Cl
 North Walsham NR28 . . . 151 F5
 Potter Heigham NR29 . . . 56 F7
Woodbridge Rd NR29 . . . 167 D4
Wood Cl Brandon IP27 . . 175 D2
 Kenninghall NR16 . . . . . 119 A4
Woodcock Cl NR3 . . . . . . 158 D3
Woodcock Hill **4** NR8 . . 70 C7
Woodcock La
 Wiggenhall St Germans
  PE34 . . . . 61 B7
 Wiggenhall St Mary Magdalen
  PE34 . . . . 61 B6
Woodcock Mews **4**
 NR31 . . . . 170 A6
Woodcock Rd
 Cromer NR27 . . . . 139 B5
 Norwich NR3 . . . . 158 C4
 Stonebridge IP24 . . . . . . 102 B2
Woodcock Rise IP27 . . . . 175 F4
Woodcote Pk PE13 . . . . . 152 A4
Woodcroft Cl NR7 . . . . . . 159 E2
Woodcutters The NR17 . . 86 B1
Woodcutters Wy IP27 . . . 113 E2
WOOD DALLING NR11 . . . . 34 D6
Wood Dalling Rd
 Briston NR24 . . . . 142 F1

Wood Dalling Rd continued
 Corpusty & Saxthorpe NR24 34 E8
 Guestwick NR20 . . . . 34 A6
 Reepham NR10 . . . . 149 C6
 Saxthorpe NR11 . . . . 19 E1
 Thurning NR20 . . . . 19 B1
 Thurning NR24 . . . . 34 B8
Wood-Dene Sch NR11 . . . . . 9 F3
Wood Dr **11** NR20 . . . . . . 49 D4
Wood End Cl NR14 . . . . . 109 F8
Woodend Rd PE31 . . . . . . 133 E5
Woodfarm La NR31 . . . . . 170 A2
Woodfarm Rd NR9 . . . . 68 F2
Woodfield Briston NR24 . 142 C4
 1 East Dereham NR19 . 154 D1
Woodfield Rd PE31 . . . . . 133 E5
Woodforde Cl NR9 . . . . 51 F2
Woodforde Rd NR7 . . . . . 159 D2
Woodfordes Brewery &
 Visitors Ctr★ NR13 . . . . 55 C2
WOODGATE NR20 . . . . 50 C3
Woodgate
 Blickling NR11 . . . . 35 E8
 12 Cringleford NR4 . . . . 89 B8
 Itteringham NR11 . . . . . . 21 E1
Woodgate La NR20 . . . . . . 50 B3
Woodgate Rd
 Dereham NR20 . . . . 50 A2
 Swanton Morley NR20 . . 50 C3
Woodgate Way PE31 . . . . 134 F4
Woodgate Wy NR11 . . . . 150 A5
Wood Gdns NR14 . . . . 89 C5
Wood Gn NR13 . . . . 72 F8
WOOD GREEN NR15 . . . . . 106 F2
Woodgrove Parade NR6 158 D3
Woodhall Rd PE38 . . . . 97 B8
Woodham Leas NR6 . . . . 158 E6
Wood Hill NR8 . . . . 156 D8
Woodhill Rise NR5 . . . . . . 161 C8
Woodhouse Cl **1** NR26 . 138 B6
Wood La Aldeby NR34 . . . 110 E5
 Banham NR16 . . . . 119 C5
 Bardwell IP31 . . . . 126 F4
 Bedingham NR35 . . . . . . 108 C2
 Bradenham IP25 . . . . 66 D4
 Bressingham IP22 . . . . . 119 E2
 Bunwell NR16 . . . . 105 D3
 Burgh & Tuttington NR11 . 36 D5
 Dickleburgh & Rushall
  IP21 . . . . 130 F6
 Garveston, Reymerston &
  Thuxton NR9 . . . . 68 E2
 Great Ellingham NR17 . . 103 D8
 Hardwick IP21 . . . . 122 A8
 Hempnall NR16 . . . . 107 D5
 Hepworth IP22 . . . . 127 E2
 Holme Hale IP25 . . . . 66 B1
 Honingham NR9 . . . . 69 E8
 Kelling NR25 . . . . 8 C5
 Little Dunham PE32 . . . . 65 E7
 Little Ellingham IP17 . . . . 86 A1
 Long Stratton NR15 . . . . 107 A2
 Morley NR18 . . . . 87 A1
 Pulham Market IP21 . . . 121 E8
 Scole IP21 . . . . 130 F8
 Shotesham NR15 . . . . 89 F1
 Shotesham NR15 . . . . . . 107 D8
 Starston IP20 . . . . 122 C5
 Strumpshaw NR13 . . . . . . 73 F2
 Swardeston NR14 . . . . . . 89 C5
 Tharston NR15 . . . . 106 D5
 Thelnetham IP22 . . . . . . 128 A2
 Watton IP25 . . . . 84 E3
 Wicklewood NR18 . . . . . . 87 B4
Woodland Dr
 Bungay NR35 . . . . 124 A7
 Ellingham NR35 . . . . 109 E3
 Norwich NR6 . . . . 158 E6
 Taverham NR8 . . . . 155 E1
 Thorpe End NR13 . . . . . . 72 D5
Woodland Farm Ind Units
 NR10 . . . . 53 A6
Woodland Gdns PE30 . . . 148 D5
Woodland La NR24 . . . . . 142 F2
Woodland Rd NR6 . . . . . . 157 E6
Woodland Rise
 Cromer NR27 . . . . 139 E4
 Sheringham NR26 . . . . . 138 E5
 12 Tasburgh NR15 . . . . 106 F6
Woodland Rise W NR26 . 138 D4
Woodlands
 35 Harleston IP20 . . . . 122 D2
 Lakenheath IP27 . . . . . . 113 E2
 7 Thorpe Marriott NR8 . 155 B2
Woodlands Cl Holt NR25 137 D7
 Scratby NR29 . . . . 167 D3
 4 Thetford IP24 . . . . . 176 E6
Woodlands Cres **1** NR7 . 72 D5
Woodlands Ct PE13 . . . . . 152 F7
Woodlands Dr IP24 . . . . . 176 D6
Woodlands Mid Sch
 NR31 . . . . 94 C6
Woodlands Pk NR10 . . . . . 52 D8
Woodlands Rd NR5 . . . . . 157 A2
Woodlands Rise IP27 . . . 175 A2
Woodlands The
 Ashill IP25 . . . . 84 A7
 Dereham NR19 . . . . 154 E3
 Sneath Common NR15 . . 121 A7
Woodland View Jun Sch
 NR10 . . . . 54 A2
Woodland View Mobile
 Home Pk NR10 . . . . 53 D6
Woodlark Cl **2** IP24 . . . 176 D7
WOOD NORTON NR20 . . . . 33 A7

Wood Norton Rd
 Foulsham NR20 . . . . 33 C5
 Stibbard NR21 . . . . 32 E7
Woodpecker Ave NR25 . . 137 D6
Woodpecker Dr **8** NR25 . 84 C3
Woodpecker La NR4 . . . . 161 B1
Woodpecker Mews **5**
 NR31 . . . . 170 A6
Woodpecker Way PE37 . . 153 D2
Woodpecker Wy NR8 . . . 156 B5
Wood Rd NR11 . . . . 20 C5
WOODRISING NR9 . . . . 85 E6
Woodrow Ave NR25 . . . . . 137 B5
Woodrow La NR15 . . . . . . 121 A8
Woodrow Pl NR1 . . . . 163 B6
Woodruff Cl **3** NR6 . . . 158 D5
Wood St NR29 . . . . 56 B8
Woods Cl
 Ditchingham NR35 . . . . . 109 A2
 3 Hethersett NR9 . . . . . 88 C7
Woods End
 Attleborough NR17 . . . . 174 C4
 Hellesdon NR6 . . . . 157 D6
 Postwick NR13 . . . . 72 F1
Woodside
 Burnham Market PE31 . . 135 A2
 5 King's Lynn PE30 . . . 147 C4
 North Walsham NR28 . . 151 E4
Woodside Ave
 Dersingham PE31 . . . . . 140 C5
 Heacham PE31 . . . . 133 D4
Woodside Cl
 Attleborough NR17 . . . . 174 C3
 Dersingham PE31 . . . . . 140 C5
Woodside Ct NR17 . . . . . 174 C3
Woodside Pk NR17 . . . . . 174 C3
Woodside Rd NR7 . . . . . . 159 E1
Wood's La NR20 . . . . 49 B8
Woods Pl NR21 . . . . 17 C3
Wood St Norwich NR1 . . 178 A1
 Wisbech PE13 . . . . 152 B6
Woodstock La
 Aslacton NR15 . . . . 120 F8
 Tibenham NR15 . . . . 120 F8
Woodstock Way **3** NR29 52 D4
WOODTON NR35 . . . . 108 C4
Woodton Prim Sch
 NR35 . . . . 108 C5
Woodton Rd
 Brooke NR15 . . . . 108 A4
 Shotesham NR35 . . . . . . 108 A7
Woodview NR28 . . . . 38 A4
Woodview Cl IP25 . . . . 84 C4
Woodview Rd NR7 . . . . 70 B5
Wood View Ct NR5 . . . . . 157 A2
Wood View Rd NR6 . . . . . 157 E5
Woodward Ave
 12 Necton PE37 . . . . . . 65 F4
 5 Necton PE37 . . . . 66 A4
Woodward Cl PE33 . . . . . . 62 D4
Woodward Rd NR3 . . . . . 158 B2
Woodwark Ave **3** PE30 . 146 E6
Woodyard **14** NR16 . . . 118 C5
Woodyard Cl NR35 . . . . . 109 A2
Woodyard Sq The NR35 . 108 C5
Woolhouse Way NR4 . . . 161 B2
Wooll Dr NR28 . . . . 151 D7
Woolner's La NR14 . . . . . . 90 E7
Woolstencroft Ave PE30 146 F7
Wootton Rd PE30 . . . . . . 147 B7
Worcester Cl **3** NR29 . . 167 A2
Worcester Way
 New Costessey NR5 . . . 156 C1
 Wisbech PE13 . . . . 152 C7
Wordsworth Dr NR28 . . . 172 D5
Wordsworth Gn IP24 . . . 176 F7
Wordsworth Rd
 2 Diss IP22 . . . . 177 A4
 Norwich NR5 . . . . 161 C6
Workhouse Corner NR10 . 37 C3
Workhouse La
 Foulsham NR20 . . . . 33 D4
 Lundy Green NR15 . . . . 107 D3
 Thurning NR20 . . . . 20 A1
 Tilney St Lawrence PE34 . 42 C1
 Upwell PE14 . . . . 77 D4
Workhouse Rd NR12 . . . . 38 C3
Worlds End NR13 . . . . 74 C1
Worlds End La NR16 . . . . 106 A2
World's End La NR12 . . . . 38 B1
WORMEGAY PE33 . . . . 62 C7
Wormegay CE Prim Sch
 PE33 . . . . 62 A6
Wormegay Rd
 Blackborough End PE32 . 44 C1
 Wormegay PE32 . . . . 62 D8
WORSTEAD NR28 . . . . 38 A5
Worstead CE VA Sch
 NR28 . . . . 38 A5
Worstead Rd NR28 . . . . . . 38 B3
Worstead Rd
 Dilham NR28 . . . . 38 B4
 Sloley NR10 . . . . 37 F4
 Worstead NR28 . . . . 37 F4
WORTHAM IP22 . . . . 129 B4
Wortham Cl **3** NR5 . . . 161 B4

Wortham Prim Sch
 IP22 . . . . 129 C4
WORTHING NR20 . . . . 49 F6
Worthing Rd
 Hoe & Worthing NR20 . . 49 F4
 North Elmham NR20 . . . . 49 F4
 Swanton Morley NR20 . . 50 B6
WORTWELL IP20 . . . . 123 B4
WRAMPLINGHAM NR9 . . . . 69 E1
Wramplingham Rd
 NR18 . . . . 173 D8
Wrench Cl NR11 . . . . 150 D6
Wrench Rd NR5 . . . . 161 D6
Wren Cl Brandon IP27 . . . 175 E3
 Necton PE33 . . . . 66 A3
 Norwich NR4 . . . . 161 E2
Wren Dr
 2 Great Yarmouth NR31 . 94 C7
 Great Yarmouth NR31 . . 170 A6
 Holt NR25 . . . . 137 D6
WRENINGHAM NR16 . . . . . 88 D1
Wreningham VC Prim Sch
 NR16 . . . . 88 D1
Wreningham Rd NR6 . . . 158 E6
Wrens Cl IP22 . . . . 177 C4
Wrens The **1** IP24 . . . . 176 D2
Wretham Rd
 Croxton IP24 . . . . 116 C7
 Great Hockham IP24 . . . 102 E3
 Stonebridge IP24 . . . . . 102 C2
WRETTON PE33 . . . . 80 E3
Wretton Fen Dro PE33 . . . 80 F1
Wretton Rd PE33 . . . . 80 F2
Wretton Row PE33 . . . . . . 80 E3
Wright Ave NR19 . . . . 154 D1
Wright Cl NR30 . . . . 168 E7
Wright Dr NR19 . . . . 154 C4
Wrights Cl NR11 . . . . 150 C7
 1 Taverham NR8 . . . . . 155 C1
Wright's Cl Holt NR25 . . . 137 C7
 North Walsham NR28 . . 151 B4
Wright's La PE12 . . . . 41 B8
Wright's Loke NR28 . . . . . 22 E5
Wright's Wlk IP19 . . . . . . 154 D5
Wrights Yard NR25 . . . . 7 E6
Wroe The PE14 . . . . 59 C1
Wrong La NR15 . . . . 91 B3
Wroo Rd NR17 . . . . 103 F5
Wroughton Infant Sch
 NR31 . . . . 170 B6
Wroughton Jun Sch
 NR31 . . . . 170 B7
WROXHAM NR12 . . . . 164 D3
Wroxham Ave PE37 . . . . . 153 C2
Wroxham Rd
 Coltishall NR12 . . . . 54 E6
 Rackheath NR13 . . . . 72 D8
 Salhouse NR13 . . . . 54 E2
 Sprowston NR7 . . . . 159 C5
Wroxham Sta NR12 . . . . . 164 C6
Wroxham Way NR12 . . . . . 24 C5
Wyatt St PE30 . . . . 146 E5
Wyatt Way NR24 . . . . 176 B7
Wycliffe Rd NR4 . . . . 161 D3
Wylde Croft NR8 . . . . 155 D2
Wymans Way NR21 . . . . . 141 E5
Wymbur Dr NR17 . . . . 174 E4
Wymer Dr NR11 . . . . 150 C4
Wymerhill La NR25 . . . . 7 F5
Wymers La NR13 . . . . 74 B8
Wymer St NR2 . . . . 162 B6
WYMONDHAM NR18 . . . . 173 E5
Wymondham Abbey
 (rems)★ NR18 . . . . 173 B3
Wymondham Abbey Sta
 NR18 . . . . 173 A3
Wymondham Bsns Pk
 NR18 . . . . 173 B2
Wymondham Bypass
 Besthorpe NR17 . . . . . . 104 E8
 Wymondham NR18 . . . . . 87 E2
Wymondhamby Pass
 NR19 . . . . 88 A3
Wymondham By Pass
 Wymondham NR18 . . . . 173 F4
 Wymondham NR18 . . . . 173 E6
Wymondham Coll NR18 . . 87 B1
Wymondham Coll Prep Sch
 NR18 . . . . 87 B1
Wymondham Heritage Mus★
 NR18 . . . . 173 C4
Wymondham High Acad
 NR18 . . . . 173 C5
Wymondham Hist Rly Sta★
 NR18 . . . . 173 D2
Wymondham Leisure Ctr
 NR18 . . . . 173 C4
Wymondham Rd
 Ashwellthorpe NR16 . . . 105 E8
 Ashwellthorpe NR16 . . . 106 A8
 Aslacton NR15 . . . . 106 A1
 Barnham Broom NR9 . . . 69 C1
 Bracon Ash NR14 . . . . . . 88 E2
 Bunwell NR16 . . . . 105 B5
 East Carleton NR14 . . . . 88 F4
 Flordon NR15 . . . . 106 C8
 Flordon NR15 . . . . 106 D8
 Kimberley NR18 . . . . 87 B6
 Long Stratton NR15 . . . . 106 E3
 Morley NR18 . . . . 87 A4
 New Buckenham NR16 . . 105 A2
 Tharston & Hapton NR15 106 C7
 Wramplingham NR18 . . . 69 F1
 Wramplingham NR18 . . . 87 F8
 Wreningham NR16 . . . . . 88 D3
 Wymondham NR18 . . . . 105 A8

Wymondham Sta NR18 . 173 C2
Wyndfields **10** PE37 . . . . 65 F4
Wyndham Pk NR27 . . . . . . 10 C5
Wyndham St NR26 . . . . . 138 D7
Wyngates NR13 . . . . 165 F6
Wynne's La PE34 . . . . 145 C4

Y

Yallop Ave NR31 . . . . 171 D8
Yare Cl
 Caister-on-Sea NR30 . . . 168 D6
 Great Yarmouth NR30 . . 169 C6
Yare Cres PE30 . . . . 146 F6
Yare Rd NR31 . . . . 94 A6
Yare Valley Dr
 Cringleford NR4 . . . . 71 B1
 Cringleford NR4 . . . . . . 161 C2
Yare Valley Rise NR25 . . 165 C3
Yare View NR13 . . . . 92 F4
Yarmouth Bsns Pk
 NR31 . . . . 169 B2
Yarmouth Rd
 Blofield NR13 . . . . 165 F6
 Broome NR35 . . . . 110 C2
 Brundall NR13 . . . . 165 C5
 Caister-on-Sea NR30 . . . 168 D3
 Corton NR32 . . . . 171 D1
 Dilham NR28 . . . . 38 C4
 Geldeston NR34 . . . . . . 110 A3
 Hales NR14 . . . . 109 E8
 Hales NR14 . . . . 109 F8
 Hemsby NR29 . . . . 167 A6
 Kirby Cane NR35 . . . . . . 109 E3
 Lound NR32 . . . . 94 B3
 Ludham NR29 . . . . 56 C5
 North Walsham NR28 . . 151 C4
 Ormesby St Margaret
  NR29 . . . . 167 C1
 Postwick with Witton
  NR13 . . . . 165 A5
 Potter Heigham NR29 . . . 56 E6
 Raveningham NR14 . . . . 110 B8
 Stalham NR12 . . . . 39 A4
 Stalham NR12 . . . . 39 B3
 Stockton NR34 . . . . 110 A4
 Thurlton NR14 . . . . 93 A1
 Toft Monks NR34 . . . . . . 110 C5
 Worstead NR28 . . . . 38 A6
Yarmouth Stadium
 NR30 . . . . 168 E2
Yarmouth Way NR30 . . . 169 C3
Yarn Mews **2** NR3 . . . . 178 B4
Yarrington Way NR5 . . . . 160 E8
Yarrow Cl IP24 . . . . 176 F5
Yarrow Rd Bintree NR20 . . 33 B2
 2 Dereham NR20 . . . . . 68 A8
YAXHAM NR19 . . . . 68 A5
Yaxham Prim Sch NR19 . 68 C6
Yaxham Rd
 East Dereham NR19 . . . 154 C4
 Mattishall NR20 . . . . 68 C6
Yaxham Sta NR19 . . . . 68 A4
YAXLEY IP23 . . . . 130 A1
Yaxley Loke NR27 . . . . . . 139 B4
Yaxley's La NR11 . . . . 150 C6
Yaxley's Rd NR30 . . . . . . 169 B6
Yaxley Way NR5 . . . . 161 A8
Yeats Way NR19 . . . . 154 B6
YELVERTON NR14 . . . . 90 E5
Yelverton Cl NR6 . . . . 157 D5
Yelverton Rd NR14 . . . . . . 90 E5
Yeoman's Cl **2** NR35 . . 124 B8
Yesmere **16** NR14 . . . . . . 89 B3
Yew Ct NR7 . . . . 159 D4
Yew Dr IP27 . . . . 175 D2
Yew Tree Cl **24** NR31 . . 94 C7
Yew Tree Ct NR20 . . . . 69 B7
Yew Tree Hollow **25**
 NR15 . . . . 106 E3
Yew Tree Rd NR17 . . . . . . 174 C5
Yew Tree Wy **12** NR20 . . 68 A8
York Ave PE36 . . . . 132 D5
York Gdns PE13 . . . . 152 D6
York La **13** NR12 . . . . 39 B4
York Rd **4** Cromer NR27 . 139 D5
 Great Yarmouth NR30 . . 169 D3
 King's Lynn PE30 . . . . . . 146 E3
 Wisbech PE13 . . . . 152 D6
York Row PE13 . . . . 152 C5
York St NR2 . . . . 162 B4
York Terr Cromer NR27 . . 139 D5
 Wisbech PE13 . . . . 152 C6
York Villa Cl NR29 . . . . . . 75 E8
York Way IP24 . . . . 176 B5
Youell Ave NR31 . . . . 170 D1
Younger Dr NR26 . . . . . . 138 D5
Youngmans Cl NR28 . . . . 151 D3
Youngmans La NR12 . . . . 38 E6
Youngman's La NR12 . . . . 38 E6
Youngmans Rd NR18 . . . 173 C8
Young's Cres NR13 . . . . . . 92 F2
Young's La NR28 . . . . 22 D5
Young's Row PE12 . . . . . . 41 A8

Z

Zara Way NR19 . . . . 154 C1
Zephyr Cl NR30 . . . . 168 D7
Zig-Zag La NR15 . . . . 108 C8
Zobel Cl NR3 . . . . 157 F2
Zurich Cl NR31 . . . . 171 E4